THE COMPLETE PUBLIC ENEMY ALMANAC

THE COMPLETE PUBLIC ENEMY ALMANAC
PUBLISHED BY CUMBERLAND HOUSE PUBLISHING, INC.
431 Harding Industrial Drive
Nashville, TN 37211-3160

Cover design: Gore Studio, Inc.
Text design: John Mitchell and Mary Sanford

Library of Congress Cataloging-in-Publication Data

Helmer, William J.
The complete public enemy almanac : new facts and features on the people, places, and events of the gangster and outlaw era: 1920–1940 / William J. Helmer and Rick Mattix.
p. cm.
Includes bibliographical references and index.
ISBN-13: 978-1-58182-524-4 (alk. paper)
ISBN-10: 1-58182-524-2 (alk. paper)
ISBN-13: 978-1-58182-506-0 (pbk. : alk. paper)
ISBN-10: 1-58182-506-4 (pbk. : alk. paper)
1. Gangsters—United States—History—20th century. 2. Outlaws—United States—History—20th century. I. Mattix, Rick. II. Title.
HV6446.H37 2006
364.1092'273—dc22
2006008396

Printed in the United States of America

1 2 3 4 5 6 7—13 12 11 10 09 08 07

THE COMPLETE PUBLIC ENEMY ALMANAC

NEW FACTS AND FEATURES ON THE PEOPLE, PLACES, AND EVENTS OF THE GANGSTER AND OUTLAW ERA: 1920–1940

WILLIAM J. HELMER and RICK MATTIX

CUMBERLAND HOUSE
NASHVILLE, TENNESSEE

For Marjorie Eker McDougall . . .

. . . Who as an attractive young student at the Worsham College of Embalming Science helped make one of her professors make a death mask of the notorious outlaw John Dillinger, only to have it confiscated by an officious Chicago cop, Sergeant Mulvaney, who probably was in league with another mask-maker intending to sell copies at the Chicago World's Fair. In the crowded, carnival atmosphere of the Cook County Morgue, Marjorie flirted with Mulvaney, keeping him distracted and out of the "cool room" while her colleagues made a second mold of Dillinger's face and slipped it out undetected—as she revealed for the first time while being interviewed at a Peoria, Illinois, retirement home, where she died of natural causes in February 1999. The original mask ultimately ended up with Calvin Goddard's Scientific Crime Laboratory in Chicago and the other disappeared.

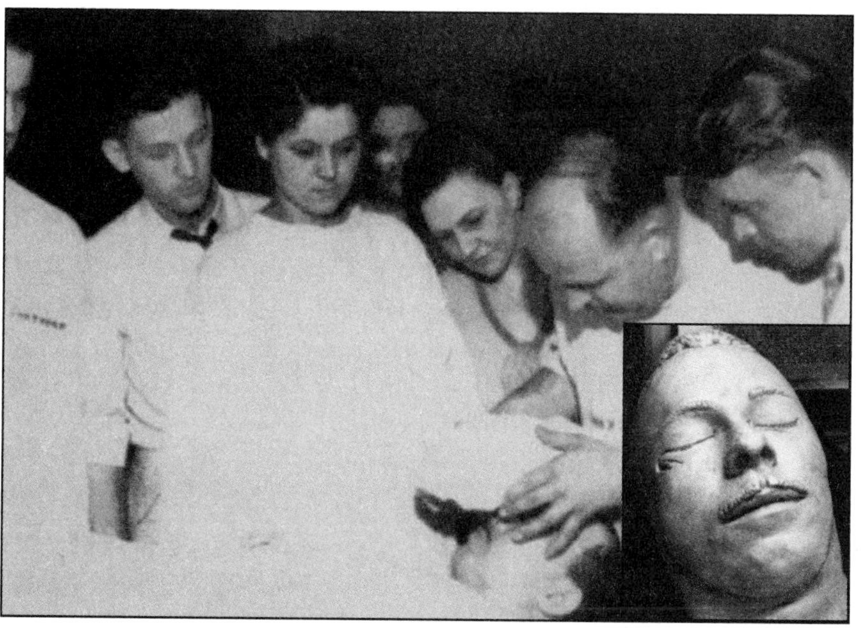

Marjorie Eker McDougall (second from left)

CONTENTS

FOREWORD

The criminal is as old as civilization itself, and those who rose to the top of their profession incurred equal measures of public wrath and fascination. The Golden Age of Shipping had the feared and revered Edward Teach (Blackbeard) and Captain William Kidd. As the American West was being won, many a gunslinger from Jesse James to Black Bart rode the range or robbed the stage. Their Gilded Age counterpart was Herman Mudgett, who killed dozens in his Chicago "murder castle" and attracted an equal number of female admirers. During the Roaring Twenties, "Scarface" Al Capone and George "Bugs" Moran made millions proving to the reformers that Americans loved booze as much as jazz. When the market crashed in October 1929 and ushered in the Great Depression, "people's bandits" like John Dillinger and his fellow outlaws robbed banks and often were cheered by resentful citizens who had lost businesses and farms to the same institutions.

Before Prohibition, crime was a localized phenomenon, with such small-scale activities as burglary, extortion, armed robbery, and petty thievery being the disorder of the day. Some gang leaders, like New York's "Monk" Eastman, acquired limited notoriety, but only in rare instances did they become known outside the neighborhoods where they were born, made their money, and usually ended up murdered. They were local menaces and, during elections, were attack dogs for the warring politicians.

Then came the Liquor Gold Rush—a new kind of crime supported by the public. Prohibition invited the first middle-class rebellion, and buying forbidden booze brought gangster and respectable citizen together as smirking and winking conspirators to defy a law that an acetic rural populace had imposed on the cities, already known for their "depravity." But it was in the cities that yesterday's thugs turned into public benefactors, because they made sure the booze got through. During the Roaring Twenties and into the Great Depression, the paths first paved by bootleggers became the roads traveled by racketeers, who organized locally and then nationally, and threaded their way into the American economic and social fabric.

When the Jazz Age gave way to breadlines, it was the country's unemployment and bleak economic conditions that distracted the public with more excitement than dread over the "Machine Gun" Kellys and "Pretty Boy" Floyds, who were all-American outlaws, thumbing their noses at danger while making the cops look foolish. Their legends were enhanced by a press in need of thrilling headlines and by such lawmen as J. Edgar Hoover and Melvin Purvis, who played them up as criminal masterminds to explain why they could not be captured by the cops. Only after the U.S. Constitution's interstate-commerce clause had been stretched enough to declare a federal "War on Crime" could the colorfully nicknamed bandits of the thirties be tracked down and often killed, usually by "G-men"—and in less than three years.

Besides educating newcomers about America's criminal past, *The Complete Public Enemy Almanac* offers historians original insights on the Roaring Twenties and the Depression Thirties, presenting both with an indispensable research tool. It is more than a grand collection of gangster biographies and chronologies of crime; it includes a wealth of rare photographs, editorial cartoons, and newspaper headlines of the period, as well as sections and sidebars on the beer wars, bombings, and political corruption. It also reveals new information on the St. Valentine's Day Massacre, "Pretty Boy" Floyd, and "Baby Face" Nelson; as well as the inside story of Dillinger's "wooden pistol" escape. William J. Helmer and Rick Mattix even describe the development of police radio, the forensic sciences, and police professionalism, and they look at the influence crime has had on politics and popular culture.

To understand the gangster and the outlaw requires a fresh examination of the society in which they flourished, and the *Almanac* explores their lives and their times in equal detail. And it concludes with a true-crime bibliography that must be the largest ever assembled.

The Complete Public Enemy Almanac escorts the reader on a fascinating tour through the dark side of America's consciousness between 1920 and 1940—from Prohibition through the Depression—and the authors discover that if crime does not pay, it sometimes can be a shortcut to immortality.

— *Rose Keefe*

Author of *Guns and Roses: The Untold Story of Dean O'Banion, Chicago's Big Shot Before Al Capone*; and *The Man Who Got Away: The Bugs Moran Story.*

ACKNOWLEDGMENTS

Mario Gomes, Rose Keefe, Pat Downey, and Michael Webb deserve special thanks for their contributions to this project.

For sharing their information, recollections, and valuable suggestions, our lasting gratitude goes to Mari Abba, Jim Adams, David Albert, Frank Ballinger, William Balsamo, Bob Bates, Brian Beerman, Tony Brucia, Bryan Burrough, Ed Butts, Marian Caporusso, Victoria Cerenich, Dan Churney, Don Costello, Estella Cox, Jonathan Davis, Dennis DeMark, Anne Diestel, Geoff Fein, Bob Fischer, Glenn Ferguson, Verla Geller, Jimmy Gillman, Bruce Hamilton, Chris Hegle, Gordon Herigstad, Tracie Hill, Prof. Dennis Hoffman, Tom Hunt, Lori Hyde, David Jones, Sandy Jones, Paul Kavieff, Jeff King, Jim Knight, Jack Koblas, Harry Lawrence, Mark Levell, Richard Lindberg, Robert Livesey, Paul Maccabee, Allan May, Jared McDade, Dale Meyer, Howard Meyer, Shelley Mitchell, R. D. and Naomi Morgan, Debborah Moss, Dr. Horace Naismith, Taylor Pensoneau, Pat Penrod, Jim Perkins, Tony Perrin, John Neal Phillips, the late Joe Pinkston, Rick Porrello, Ellen Poulsen, Tom Prior, Lawrence Raeder, Tim Rives, Davis Rorer, Ron Rosner, Gus Russo, Joe Sanchez, Jim Sanseverino, Tamara Shaffer, Chuck Schauer, Richard Shaw, Brad Smith, Patterson Smith, Walter Smith, Tom Smusyn, Norm Stringer, Patty Terry, Pam Tippet, Neal Trickel, Sid Underwood, Robert Unger, Ron Van Raalte, Larry Wack, Dan Waugh, Terry Whitehead, and Robert Winter, many of whom belong to an expanding network of researchers, writers, and collectors known on the Web as Partners in Crime, some with Web sites devoted to one or more notorious lawbreakers; to the Oklahombres; and to a more recent newsgroup called Gangsterologists.

Thanks also to Editor John Mitchell, whose patience, perseverance, and skill quelled a riot of facts into an orderly mob of research material; with our condolences to Linda Mattix, Jan Rekemeyer, and Sharon DiRago, who patiently endured; and apologies to anybody we missed.

Vaughn Pruess kept the computers running.

All photos in this book are from the authors' collections, unless otherwise noted.

INTRODUCTION

If American crime enjoyed a golden age, it would have been from 1920 to 1940—two decades bracketed by great wars—the roller-coaster years when a rural nation became urbanized, and when the nineteenth century finally gave way to the twentieth. The automobile came of age. So did the airplane, the telephone, radio, and motion pictures. After a period of fragile prosperity, economic disaster crippled state and municipal agencies and gave rise to a more centralized national government. It was a time when technological, political, and cultural changes occurred so rapidly that many American institutions, including the criminal justice system, were slow to understand and adapt to their significance.

Law enforcement was only beginning to emerge from a tradition of regional independence. In the West public safety generally had been a do-it-yourself proposition; crime control was the job of local sheriffs, marshals, rangers, posses, vigilance committees, and private agencies who divided their efforts between breaking strikes and catching bank and train robbers.

In cities, police departments were replacing watchmen and guards by the 1850s, but these often amounted to little more than untrained, non-uniformed, and sometimes competing teams of muscular mercenaries paid and more or less controlled by the ruling political organization. They maintained the peace with as much brutality as public opinion would tolerate. Full-time uniformed policemen serving under a captain of a district or precinct, and a separate "detective" force under a central chief or superintendent, represented the first steps toward police professionalism that took place near the end of the century and slowly developed into a unified and organized city service.

The same forces that reshaped society also changed the face of crime. With the settlement of the West, the industrial revolution combined with waves of immigration to create an urban version of the frontier in rapidly growing and poorly managed cities. Slums, violence, disease, vice, and corruption spawned a Progressive Movement that began battling urban decay, the most conspicuous signs of which were labor unrest, street crime, and public drunkenness.

An unprecedented reform effort called Prohibition seemed imperative to the survival of the traditional American value system, but like other panaceas it demonstrated the doctrine of unintended consequences. Outlawing intoxicants gave America not the era of "clear thinking and clean living" that idealists promised. Instead, it vastly increased political and police corruption, transformed drunkenness from a working-class vice into a form of middle-class rebellion, and laid the foundation for nationally organized crime. Compared with modern racketeers, the bootleggers of the 1920s seem as grand and gaudy as the cars they drove. Both were primitive by later standards, but they had novelty and a style that evoked as much excitement as fear. They were symbols of their era.

The Roaring Twenties and Prohibition gave way, one after the other, to the Great Depression, a period no less memorable for conditions of a different and frightening kind. After 1930, people who had pitied the "poor working stiff" considered themselves lucky to have jobs, and men in breadlines could no longer identify with swaggering gangland toughs. It was easier to condone the exploits of a Robin Hood, or any reasonable facsimile. Americans in the Depression found something to admire in the bold and desperate men who only "stole from the banks what the banks stole from the people."

The big-city gangsters who corrupted government and turned city streets into battlegrounds often were foreign-born with foreign sounding names. But the Depression desperadoes were red-blooded, all-American outlaws in the Jesse James tradition who "came from good homes" and were "driven to crime" by circumstances. They were underdogs in a nation of underdogs, "people's bandits" who shook their fists in the face of corrupt authority and attacked the symbols of wealth. Daring, colorful, sometimes gallant, they led the cops a merry chase and died with their boots on.

At least so go their legends, created partly by the press and partly by badly outclassed lawmen to explain their inability to bring them down. These criminals worked as teams instead of in syndicates, used force instead of bribes, lived as fugitives instead of businessmen, and soon fell victim to the technological and legal changes they helped bring about.

Sanitized by the passage of time, the urban mobsters of the 1920s like Al Capone can now be glamorized as classic criminals, the first of a new breed that came in with Prohibition, while a Depression-era bandit like John Dillinger represents the last of an old one that now substituted automobiles for horses. In both categories, those best remembered had an outrageous style that mocked authority and enthralled a largely apathetic public whose main source of entertainment was a shamelessly sensational press.

A striking caricature of Chicago crime czar "Scarface" Al Capone

To combat the increasing gangster chic, the Chicago Crime Commission ingeniously countered by declaring them "public enemies," which newspapers seized on just as eagerly as a major gangland killing and the need for reforms, but the public's continued fascination with crime, its perception of criminals, and its remarkably flexible value system remained a fairly good index to the average citizen's priorities and sense of right and wrong. Celebrity criminals of the "public enemy" era taught Americans that while crime does not pay, it can be a shortcut to immortality.

That simplistic summary implies that the crime problem of the past was a manageable one compared with the mindless murder and mayhem that confronted the country later. With a greatly expanded population, the problem has predictably worsened in many respects, but not to the degree suggested by all-news television networks, assumed by the fans of true-crime "cop" programs, the opponents of drugs, the critics of "gangsta rap" music, and by lawmakers whose apprehensions are shaped more by journalists and entertainers than by historians. This phenomenon is not uniquely American, but it now combines with a political process that is averse to historical comparisons. As a result, crime and violence still are proclaimed a national peril instead of being viewed as a national norm.

The dynamics of this are simple enough: Crime, violence, and corruption are the legitimate concerns of a free press in a democratic society, whose citizens need an awareness of these problems to make informed decisions and shape public policies. As it happens, crime, violence, and corruption also sell newspapers and TV shows, which by their nature report on them as novel and newsworthy events rather than as simply the latest manifestation of social problems that have plagued this country since it was settled. Among readers whose memories are as short as a cub reporter's, the impression created by the daily press and reinforced by television news is that conditions are bad and getting worse, and that the end is near.

At the opposite end of the information spectrum, textbook historians describe great movements, great leaders, and great wars that have altered the course of world events. Even social historians, with the clarity of hindsight, record the perils of the past without hysteria, as storms that either never materialized or were successfully weathered, once the problem was confronted sensibly. It's not their job (or the desire of their publishers, for that matter) to reassure the reader that, for instance, modern-day murder is proportionately less than that of the 1970s or the 1930s, and even less than in some earlier times and places; that our streets are safer now than a hundred years ago; or that the murder rate for handguns, say, is about the same as the fatality rate for birth control pills—an otherwise meaningless comparison that only illustrates the importance of viewing perils in perspective.

Some countries, from the vantage point of experience, have long observed this nation's continual reform efforts with interest and sometimes amusement, marveling at three traits that seem to be uniquely American: a penchant for equating sin with crime, a greater ability to perceive problems than to correct them, and a limited sense of history affirming the adage that people who do not learn from their mistakes tend to repeat them.

Foreign intellectuals in particular note a fundamental conflict between two of our most cherished principles: that America has "a government of laws, and not of men," with its goals of equal opportunity and equal justice; and a passion for personal freedom embodied in the expression, "that government is best which governs least." Attracted to whichever proposition serves their purpose, Americans demand action and the quick fix and have never subscribed to the more realistic view of theologian-philosopher Reinhold Niebuhr that "Democracy is finding proximate solutions to insoluble problems."

So while representative government is expected to protect individual freedom, it also is expected to solve the nation's problems. This makes reform possible, but sometimes impossibly slow. Totalitarian governments need not submit controversial issues to public debate. But the democratic process compels the office seeker and office holder to either exaggerate or minimize the problems of the day and, like a physician with a good bedside manner, prescribe new laws that either topically treat the symptoms or promise a cure for a condition that, in fact, is chronic.

The country's political leadership thus includes many faith healers whose nostrums sometimes actually work, through a placebo effect or because a given problem resolves itself naturally. But it remains a standard campaign practice to depict any recurring evil as an imminent peril, blame it on the wrongheaded policies of the incumbent, and call on voters to throw the rascal out.

Many historical, demographic, and political factors have combined to create a U.S. population that is at once the most lawmaking and lawbreaking in the world—a country whose citizens still believe in the magic powers of legislation to foster a safe and just society, but readily exempt themselves from any rules they consider inapplicable to themselves or an infringement on their rights. Many laws that are eminently ignorable or patently unenforceable are enacted chiefly for their symbolic value, as a statement of lofty moral principles or to "send a message," though their usual effect is only to create more statutory criminals and to complicate police work. During Prohibition, the prisons filled up with bootleggers; today the majority of inmates are drug users, not even convicted of dealing.

An increasing number of social scientists are looking at the national record of more than 200 years and concluding that many of the country's problems are simply intractable; that some traits are too ingrained in the national character even for police-state remedies; that with our continuing enthusiasm for laws goes an almost moral obligation to break them. These are scholars and intellectuals whose admonitions largely will be ignored, if American politics runs true to form. But occasionally they may persuade an "honest politician" that if sin cannot be abolished by making it a crime, and if crime cannot be abolished by even draconian punishment, the next best thing is to separate the two. Take the profit out of vice through regulation, and otherwise craft enforceable statutes aimed only at reducing to tolerable levels the crime and violence that history suggests can never be totally eliminated.

So the "golden age" is not a measure of actual crime and violence, which fluctuate wildly depending on many factors, but of public excitement over the celebrity criminal spawned by Prohibition and by the revival of banditry made possible by motor cars. The new-style 1920s "gangster" was essentially a businessman who mocked the law through bribery and could flaunt his wealth in public, while the successful outlaw committed crimes of violence and exploited primitive police methods to avoid identification and capture. It took lawmakers more than a decade to acknowledge the failure of Prohibition, by which time the organized urban gangs were learning what happens to "public enemy" racketeers. The armed robbers, who had thrived on interstate anonymity, were netted almost as soon as new police technology could combine names and faces and apply the "public enemy" treatment to them.

Supreme Court Justice Charles Evans Hughes once described this country as "the greatest law-making factory the world has ever known." He might have added that some laws are more enforceable than others, and that recognition of a problem does not always mean that it has a solution.

THE COMPLETE PUBLIC ENEMY ALMANAC

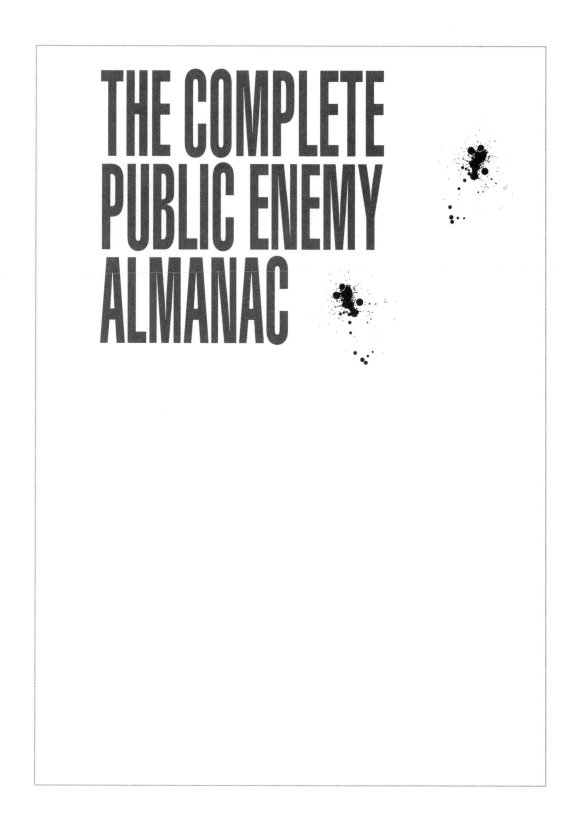

1

MOBSTERS vs. OUTLAWS

Using the terms *gangster* and *public enemy* to describe both Al Capone the racketeer and John Dillinger the outlaw reflects a popular misconception of criminals, which also bedevils the U.S. legal system. The confusion lies in the failure to distinguish between consensual crime and violent crime, and to recognize that the strategies for combating one are ineffective against the other.

Capone was in the business of supplying illegal goods and services to willing consumers. This is consensual crime—too often called "victimless"—which involves violence only to the extent that the business itself is unlawful and any territorial or personal disputes require settlement "out of court." Laws against gambling, prostitution, drunkenness, drugs, private sexual acts, and even illegal firearm ownership are hard to enforce because the only complainants are the law enforcers themselves; so long as the crime goes undetected, there is no "victim" in the legal sense of the word, only customers. As Capone once complained, "When I sell liquor, they call it bootlegging; when my patrons serve it on silver trays on Lake Shore Drive, they call it hospitality."

Robbery, on the other hand, is by definition a crime of violence from which an unconsenting victim seeks the protection of the law. Dillinger was a professional criminal whom the police and the press could declare a "public enemy" (a term wrongly ascribed to the FBI), but he was not a gangster in the style of Al Capone. More precisely, he was an outlaw—indeed, among the last of the outlaws in the Jesse James tradition: a fugitive whose survival depended on avoiding recognition and capture. Outlaw (or bandit) gangs were not "racketeers" but raiding parties.

It's true that the criminal community in the 1920s and early thirties had not yet been clearly divided into separate populations. The neighborhood bootlegger might be more an adventurer than a career criminal, but he did business with professionals, including gunmen, and some who normally were robbers also did their share of bootlegging. So whether they worked together or not, the gangsters and outlaws often knew each other socially from frequenting the same taverns and roadhouses, and from patronizing the same doctors, lawyers, bail bondsmen, mechanics, and fences who constituted an underworld support group. Professional courtesies and services were readily exchanged (unless the bandits generated too much "heat"), and some criminals divided their time between armed robbery, kidnapping, and working for a crime "syndicate" trying to control a specific territory or a labor union.

Al Capone (left), America's most notorious gangster, and John Dillinger, America's most notorious outlaw, represented the opposite poles of lawlessness in the 1920s and '30s.

The following short biographies include gangsters and outlaws who achieved notoriety in one type of crime instead of (or more than) the other. But their notoriety, like the crimes listed in the chronology, commonly reflected the public's perception of the problem rather than actual crime conditions. Some bandits robbed between fifty and one hundred banks during Prohibition, when the country was preoccupied with bootleggers and beer wars, and the police had not yet developed an effective criminal-identification system. With repeal and the increasing police professionalism promoted by the newly formed FBI, national excitement shifted to outlaws whom the bureau could readily name, widely publicize, and then track down, partly to demonstrate the inability of local cops to deal with interstate crime.

Ironically, it was Prohibition that hampered local crime control by closing the saloons where criminals routinely congregated, and where police and their informants could easily keep tabs on thieves, burglars, and robbers. Following repeal, it was the FBI's preoccupation with interstate banditry and new law enforcement technology that enabled local racketeering to expand into nationally organized crime.

The country's first "public enemies" were locally organized criminals spawned chiefly by Prohibition and so-named by the Chicago Crime Commission. After repeal and the arrival of federalized crime control, they became the handful of newsworthy kidnappers and bank robbers whose careers were as short as they were colorful, thanks to the New Deal Justice Department's J. Edgar Hoover. So the criminal celebrities who earned a place in the history books as "Pretty Boy" or "Machine Gun" or "Baby Face" did not necessarily represent the type or extent of lawlessness occurring at the time they were making news. Virtually forgotten are the early "motorized bandits" and outlaw gangs who made only local news as the unidentified gunmen who held up the town bank and made good their escape.

MIDWEST GANGSTERS AND OUTLAWS
1920–1940

Accardo, Anthony Joseph "Joe Batters" (true name: Antonino Leonardo Accardo) [1906–1992] Born in Chicago, April 28, 1906, the son of Francesco and Maria Accardo. Capone gunman and bodyguard-chauffeur of "Machine Gun" Jack McGurn and alleged to have participated, probably as a police-pursuit blocker, in the St. Valentine's Day Massacre. This point is a matter of some controversy among crime historians, though seemingly confirmed by FBI-bugged conversations in the 1950s. Named as a "public enemy" by the Chicago Crime Commission in 1931 and listed as a suspect in the murders of Joe Aiello, Jack Zuta, and Mike "de Pike" Heitler. Rose to prominence in the Chicago mob in the thirties and forties, succeeding to leadership about 1945 after the suicide of Frank Nitti and imprisonment of Paul "The Waiter" Ricca. Resided for years at a palatial estate at 1407 Ashland Avenue in suburban River Forest. Retired as boss in 1956 and named Sam Giancana as his successor until the latter fled to Mexico a decade later, but many consider Accardo to have reigned as "Chairman of the Board" and the real power behind the Chicago mob until his death by natural causes on May 27, 1992. Perhaps the most untouchable of Chicago mobsters, Accardo's criminal record dated to 1922 and listed more than two dozen arrests for murder, extortion, kidnapping, gambling, and other violations. Often but wrongly reported to have never spent a night in jail. His one conviction, for income tax evasion, was reversed on appeal in 1960, and he was acquitted in a second trial. Many consider Accardo, Joey Aiuppa, and a few lesser mobsters to have been the Chicago underworld's last links to the Capone era.

Adams, Edward J. (Eddie) (true name reportedly W. J. Wallace) [1887–1921] Probably born near Hutchinson, Kansas. Prison escapee from Missouri and Kansas; convicted murderer and bank robber. Led gang that terrorized Kansas, Missouri, and Iowa with bank, store, and train robberies, committing seven murders in 1921. Killed by police at Wichita, Kansas, November 22, 1921.

Aiello, Joseph [1890–1930] Born in Bagheria, Palermo, Sicily. Chicago bootlegger, alky cooker, and de facto leader of local Sicilian community whose small "kitchen" stills produced most of the raw alcohol used in the manufacture of illegal liquor, the cutting of smuggled liquor and the "needling" of legal "near beer" to bring it back to full strength. Resented Capone's efforts to control the Unione Siciliana in Chicago's Little

Joe Aiello (center) and members of his Sicilian gang Mike Bizarro (left) and Joe Rubinelli await booking in Chicago after an arrest in 1927.

Sicily west of the Near North Side, and so ultimately allied himself with the North Side O'Banions then controlled by "Bugs" Moran. Battled Capone for control of Chicago's Unione Siciliana in what became known as the "War of the Sicilian Succession," one of several factors that led to the St. Valentine's Day Massacre in 1929. The Massacre left Aiello without North Side associates, and he was murdered by Capone machine-gunners at 205 Kolmar Avenue, Chicago, on October 23, 1930.

Aiuppa, Joseph John (alias Joey O'Brien, "Doves") [1907–1997] Born December 1, 1907, in Chicago. Arrest record dates to 1935 but had several previous arrests which probably were expunged. Was one of several men arrested in Bellwood, Illinois, January 6, 1934, in vicinity of the house where "Handsome Jack" Klutas (of the College Kidnappers) was killed. Minor Capone lieutenant involved in suburban gambling and nightclubs who avoided publicity in the thirties, although FBI records indicate that he had an "untouchable" record as a henchman of Claude Maddox (aka Johnny Moore) and a reputation as an expert bank robber. He also was suspected of harboring the Dillinger and Barker-Karpis Gangs at his Hy-Ho Club (sometimes called the Hi-Ho in FBI documents) in Cicero and Moulin Rouge Club in Maywood, and of furnishing them with guns, ammunition, and bulletproof vests. Aiuppa's partners in the Hy-Ho Club included "Baby Face" Nelson's friends Jack Perkins (tried but acquitted of the South Bend bank robbery) and "Tough Tony" Capezio. Aiuppa also was one of the select few who attended Al Capone's funeral in 1947. He acquired the nickname "Doves" when convicted in the 1960s of the unlikely crime of illegally shooting some 500 mourning doves in Kansas and transporting them to Chicago. Soon rose to prominence in the Chicago Outfit, emerging as its leader (though possibly deferring to former boss Tony "Joe Batters" Accardo) in the 1970s. Convicted in old age of racketeering, Aiuppa was paroled in poor health to die shortly afterward of cancer in Chicago on February 22, 1997.

Alterie, Louis "Two-Gun," or "Diamond Jack" (true name: Leland DeVaraign, shortened to Leland Varain) [1888–1935] Leading member of Chicago's North Side mob in twenties and close to Dean O'Banion but often at odds with other gang members. Notorious gunman, bootlegger and labor racketeer. Also a part-time cowboy who owned a ranch (the Sweetwater) in Jarre Canyon near Sedalia, Colorado, to which he would retire when Chicago got too hot. Well-known in the Denver area, where he dressed in cowboy clothes and diamond-studded cufflinks and belt buckles and drove a car decorated with huge bull horns. O'Banion bought Chicago gangland's first known Tommyguns in Denver in 1924, though they didn't see service until a year later when the Saltis-McErlane gang used one in an unsuccessful attempt to kill "Spike" O'Donnell. When O'Banion was killed, Alterie offered to "shoot it out with Deanie's killers" at the corner of State and Madison streets, inciting newspaper and police indignation and bringing down the ire of "Bugs" Moran, who ordered him out of town. Leaving Chicago, Alterie reportedly acted as an agent of Al Capone in an unsuccessful bid to buy the 101 Ranch in Oklahoma. His fortune plummeted in the Depression, and he lost his Colorado ranch in 1932. Arrested on suspicion of kidnapping a Chicago bookmaker, he indignantly protested that kidnappers didn't live in his kind of poverty and was later acquitted. Convicted of shooting two men in a Denver hotel brawl, Alterie received only a fine and probation on condition that he leave Colorado for five years. Returned to Chicago and involved himself again in labor racketeering, taking over a janitors union. He also stored machine guns at the union for "Machine Gun" Kelly, according to testimony at the Urschel kidnapping trial. Shot to death by unknown killers (probably from the Nitti-led Outfit then monopolizing Chicago union activities) outside his apartment at 926 Eastwood Terrace, July 18, 1935.

Annenberg, Moses Louis "Moe" [1878–1942] Born in Kalwichen, East Prussia, February 11, 1878, the son of Tobias and Sarah Annenberg.

Moved to U.S. with mother and siblings in 1885 and joined father in Chicago. With brother Max, was employed by the Hearst papers in the newspaper circulation wars with the *Chicago Tribune* in early 1900s (though sympathetic biographers note that Moe was less violence-prone than Max). Hearst appointed Moe circulation manager for the *Chicago Examiner.* Moved to Milwaukee in 1907, worked in a similar capacity for Hearst, and bought his own newspaper. Later expanded into racing news with the *Daily Racing Form* and the Chicago-based Nationwide News Service, a wire service for bookies that allegedly enjoyed a million-dollar-per-year protection service from Al Capone. Used gangland associations and muscle to expand his business and invested the profits into a publishing empire which included the *Philadelphia Inquirer,* earning himself an estimated income of $6 million per year at the height of the Depression. Pleaded guilty, in exchange for dismissal of charges against his son Walter in the same case, in 1940 to evading payment of $8 million in income tax and sentenced to three years in federal prison. Released from Lewisburg Prison on June 11, 1942, suffering from a terminal brain tumor which was later complicated with pneumonia. Died at St. Mary's Hospital in Rochester, Minnesota, July 20, 1942. By taking the rap himself in the biggest income tax case in U.S. history, Moe allowed his son Walter a clear public record and a chance to salvage the Annenberg name as a legitimate publishing magnate whose holdings eventually would include *TV Guide.* In 1969, President Nixon appointed Walter Annenberg ambassador to the Court of St. James's, ironically the same post given by President Roosevelt years earlier to ex-bootlegger Joe Kennedy.

Anselmi, Albert, and Scalise, John Both born in Sicily Known as the "Homicide Squad" or the "Mutt and Jeff of murderers," who worked first for the Gennas and then for Capone. Suspected of the murders of Dean O'Banion and "Hymie" Weiss. On June 13, 1925, with Mike Genna, killed policemen Harold Olson and Charles Walsh and wounded detective Michael Conway in a gun battle at Western Avenue and Fifty-ninth Street in Chicago. Genna was mortally wounded in the same battle. Anselmi and Scalise were captured and ultimately acquitted in 1927 after three trials on grounds of self-defense. Prominent West Side Italian businessmen, including Henry Spingola, Augustino and Antonio Morici, and Vito Bascone, allegedly were murdered for refusing to contribute to the Anselmi-Scalise defense fund. Later suspected (with many others) in the St. Valentine's Day Massacre. Scalise was indicted but never tried. Both were found murdered, with associate Joseph "Hop Toad" Guinta, at Lake Wolfe near Hammond, Indiana, May 8, 1929. First presumed to be victims of Moran revenge; however, the story has since been widely accepted that they were killed by Al Capone personally during a formal gang dinner at a roadhouse after he discovered their part in a plot to depose him as head of the Chicago mob.

Bailey, Harvey John (later called himself John Harvey Bailey) [1887–1979] Born at Jane Lew, West Virginia, August 23, 1887, son of John and Amanda Bailey. Probably America's leading bank robber in the twenties. Participated in some two dozen large bank robberies across the U.S., 1922–33, with various partners, including "Killer" Burke, Gus Winkeler, Verne Miller, Frank Nash, "Machine Gun" Kelly, Alvin Karpis, Fred Barker, and Wilbur Underhill. Prime suspect in the so-called Denver Mint robbery of December 18, 1922 (actually the robbery of a Federal Reserve Bank truck parked outside the mint), and the $2 million robbery of the Lincoln National Bank & Trust Co. at Lincoln, Nebraska, September 17, 1930 (Bailey always denied involvement in either crime). Captured by FBI agents and police at Kansas City, Missouri, July 7, 1932. Convicted of Fort Scott, Kansas, bank robbery and sentenced to ten to fifty years. With Wilbur Underhill, led mass breakout of eleven convicts from state prison at Lansing, Kansas, May 30, 1933. Wrongly suspected of involvement in the Kansas City Massacre of June 17, 1933. Captured at Shannon ranch, near Paradise, Texas, August 12, 1933, during FBI roundup of the Urschel kidnapping gang. Escaped from Dallas County Jail, Dallas, Texas, September 4, 1933; recaptured same day at Ardmore, Oklahoma. Convicted, probably erroneously, of involvement in Urschel kidnapping and sentenced to life in federal prison. Served time in Leavenworth, Alcatraz, and the Federal Correctional Institution at Seagoville, Texas, before being paroled on July 24, 1961. Rearrested by Kansas authorities who still wanted him for his 1933 prison escape. Paroled, March 31, 1965. Died at Joplin, Missouri, March 1, 1979.

Banghart, Basil Hugh "The Owl" **[1900–1982]** Born in Berlin Township, Michigan, September 11, 1900, the son of Frank and Ellen Banghart. Extremely skilled outlaw, master of disguise, pilot (sometimes known as "Larry the Aviator"), an escape artist noted for his often desperately zany jailbreaks. Once called "the most crime-wise man in the nation," Banghart began his criminal career in Detroit in the twenties when he was suspected of more than one hundred car thefts. Convicted in 1926 of violating the National Motor Vehicle Theft Act and sentenced to two years at the federal penitentiary in Atlanta, Banghart took advantage of a window-washing detail to jump twenty feet from the window and outrun bloodhounds through an open field to freedom on January 25, 1927. After organizing a New Jersey car theft ring, he was recaptured in Philadelphia and returned to Atlanta, serving out the remainder of his sentence only to be again arrested on the same charge, pleading guilty and receiving another two-year term. Discharged on November 2, 1931, Banghart was arrested in South Bend, Indiana, January 20, 1932, for armed robbery and automobile banditry. On March 27 he threw pepper in a guard's face, seized a machine gun, and shot his way out of the South Bend jail.

IDENTIFICATION ORDER No. 900
May 31, 1927

WANTED
BASIL HUGH BANGHART, alias BASIL LAWRENCE MARKEY

DEPARTMENT OF JUSTICE
BUREAU OF INVESTIGATION
WASHINGTON, D. C.
APPREHENDED 2804
ESCAPED FEDERAL PRISONER

Fingerprint Classification
18 1 Ur 20
1 U 19

$60
REWARD

Age, 22 years
Height, 5 feet 8½ inches
Weight, 137 lbs.
Build, medium
Hair, blond
Eyes, blue
Complexion, fair
Wrinkles across forehead
Small mouth

22683

Wife, Mrs. Mary Banghart, Smith Creek, Mich.
Mother, Mrs. N. Banghart, 6026 Penn. Ave., Detroit, Mich.

Basil Banghart

Basil Hugh Banghart was sentenced May 7, 1926, at Dayton, Ohio, to serve two years at the U. S. Penitentiary, Atlanta, Ga., for violation of the National Motor Vehicle Theft Act, and escaped therefrom on January 25, 1927. The warden states that the above reward will be paid for his apprehension.

Law enforcement agencies kindly transmit any additional criminal record or other information to nearest office, Bureau of Investigation.

If apprehended, notify Special Agent in Charge, Bureau of Investigation, Federal Building, Columbus, Ohio.

Issued by J. Edgar Hoover, *Director.*

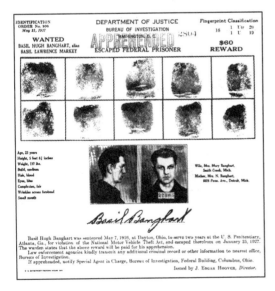

Federal wanted poster for escape artist Basil "The Owl" Banghart.

Soon aligning himself with Chicago's Touhy gang, Banghart took part in a $100,000 mail truck robbery at Charlotte, North Carolina, as well as probably other mail robberies around the country with "Terrible Tommy" Touhy. Captured in Baltimore on February 10, 1934, Basil was brought to Chicago to testify for the defense of Tommy's brother Roger Touhy, then for trial for kidnapping Jake "The Barber" Factor. Banghart claimed he and Ike Costner had been hired by Factor to fake the kidnapping, thus helping Factor avoid extradition to England where he was wanted for a gigantic stock swindle (and also aiding the Capone Syndicate in removing a competitor by framing Roger). Banghart made a less-than-impressive defense witness, and the jury chose to believe Costner, who claimed he and Banghart had been hired by Roger Touhy to kidnap Factor. Banghart was convicted of mail robbery and sentenced to thirty-six years but was turned over to Illinois where, like Roger Touhy before him, he received a ninety-nine-year sentence for the Factor kidnapping. On October 2, 1935, Banghart and other convicts commandeered a truck and crashed through prison gates at Menard, Illinois, only to be soon recaptured. Transferred to Joliet, he escaped again with Roger Touhy and others on October 9, 1942. The FBI was soon on their trail, under the somewhat novel jurisdictional premise that the escapees had violated the

Selective Service Act by changing addresses without notifying the draft board.

Tracked to Chicago, Banghart and Touhy were captured at 5116 Kenmore Avenue on December 29, 1942, by FBI agents led by J. Edgar Hoover. After his arrest Banghart joked and chattered incessantly, complimenting Hoover on the bureau's efficiency and commenting on the wrong timing of the break, about being "hindered by too many wartime restrictions" and adding, "If I had broken out two years ago, I could have gotten out of the country, maybe gone to South America and gotten a job flying." The government kept Banghart this time, sending him to Alcatraz on his mail robbery conviction. Returned afterward to Illinois to complete time for the Factor kidnapping, Banghart's sentence was commuted to forty-five years by Governor William Stratton in 1961, owing to popular and credible belief the conviction was a frame-up and to his poor health, and he was paroled on June 29. Banghart was suffering from a heart condition and showed symptoms of Parkinson's disease but managed to live, uneventfully, long afterward, marrying his old girlfriend Mae Blalock and working as a hotel custodian in Los Angeles, where he died on April 5, 1982.

Barker, Arizona Donnie Clark (alias Arrie or Kate "Ma" Barker) [1873–1935] Born Arizona Donnie Clark, daughter of John and Emmeline Clark, near Ash Grove, Missouri, October 8, 1873 (though her death certificate gives date of October 8, 1879, and other birthdates have been published, most commonly 1872). Married George Elias Barker, September 14, 1892, at Ash Grove. Mother of the notorious Barker brothers. In her later years traveled with her sons and was used by them as a cover. Killed by the FBI in a four-hour gun battle with son Fred in a house in Ocklawaha, Florida, January 16, 1935. A Thompson submachine gun was found next to her body (not in her hands, as newspapers reported), but whether she participated in the fight is doubtful. Sensitive to the implications of killing somebody's mother, who was so far unknown to the general public, J. Edgar Hoover instantly publicized her as the evil genius and mastermind of the of the murderous Barker-Karpis Gang, and her offspring the vicious criminal product of parental overindulgence. Karpis would later claim that while she knew her sons were criminals, she was too slow-witted to participate in their crimes, much less plan them.

Barker, Arthur Robert "Doc" or "Dock" (alias Bob Barker) [1899–1939] Born in Missouri, June 4, 1899, the son of George and Arizona "Ma" Barker. Convicted of murder in 1922 and sentenced to life in state prison at McAlester, Oklahoma. Paroled in 1932, allegedly through bribery of state officials by gang associates. With brother Fred, Alvin Karpis and others committed bank robberies, several murders, and the ransom kidnappings of William A. Hamm Jr., and Edward Bremer, 1932–34. Arrested by FBI at 432 Surf Street, Chicago, January 8, 1935, the same day G-men killed one member of the gang and captured others in an apartment building gun battle at 3920 North Pine Grove. Convicted of Bremer kidnapping and sentenced to life. Killed while attempting to escape from Alcatraz, January 13, 1939.

Barker, Frederick "Freddie" or "Shorty" [1903–1935] Born in Missouri, December 12, 1903, son of George and "Ma" Barker. Co-leader, with Alvin Karpis, of the Barker-Karpis Gang. Paroled in 1931 from state prison at Lansing, Kansas, where he had met Alvin Karpis while serving time for burglary. Became a notorious bank and payroll robber, killer, and a kidnapper of wealthy St. Paul businessmen William A. Hamm and Edward G. Bremer. Died with his mother during prolonged gun battle with FBI, Ocklawaha, Florida, January 16, 1935.

Barker, Herman "Bert" or "Slim" (alias Bert Lavender, J. H. Hamilton) [1893–1927] Born in Missouri, October 30, 1893, to George and "Ma" Barker. Leading member of Terrill-Barker-Inman Gang of southwestern bank burglars in late 1920s (sometimes called the "Kimes-Terrill Gang," though their affiliation with the Kimes brothers may owe more to newspaper speculation than fact). Known to have murdered two law officers: Deputy Sheriff Arthur E. Osborn, near Pine Bluffs, Wyoming, August 1, 1927, and Patrolman Joseph E. Marshall, at Wichita, Kansas, August 29, 1927. Wounded by police and committed suicide at Wichita, Kansas, August 29, 1927.

Barker, Lloyd William (Bill) "Red" [1897–1949] Born in Missouri, March 16, 1897, the son of George and "Ma" Barker. Served in U.S. Army during World War I and honorably discharged. Reportedly arrested in Tulsa for vagrancy in 1921, Lloyd's only major crime appears to have been a mail robbery at Baxter Springs, Kansas, on June 17, 1921. Convicted of mail robbery and sentenced to twenty-five years. Received at Leavenworth Federal Penitentiary, January 16, 1922. His imprisonment kept him from participating in the crime wave carried on by his brothers in the twenties and thirties, and his brothers' crimes, in turn, may have prevented Lloyd's early parole in 1934. Finally paroled on October 29, 1938 (though various published accounts erroneously state that he served his full sentence). Worked as a cook at a P.O.W. camp at Ft. Custer, Michigan, during World War II; again honorably discharged from the Army with a good conduct medal. Later assistant manager of a bar and grill in Denver. Murdered by his wife, Jennie Barker, outside their home at Westminster, Colorado, near Denver, March 18, 1949.

Barrow, Clyde Champion (true name: Clyde Chestnut Barrow but adopted new middle name) [1910?–1934] Born at Teleco, Texas, March 24, 1910 (according to family records, though gravestone reads 1909), the son of Henry and Cumie Barrow. Paroled from the state prison at Huntsville, Texas, in 1932 after serving a sentence for burglary and car theft. With girlfriend Bonnie Parker, led the Barrow Gang, often called the "Bloody Barrows," a motley collection of small-time thieves who robbed grocery stores, gas stations, and small banks throughout the Southwest and Midwest, murdering at least a dozen men, between 1932 and 1934. Betrayed by a relative of an accomplice and killed May 23, 1934, with Bonnie Parker, when they drove into an elaborate ambush set up by former Texas Ranger Frank Hamer on a country road between Sailes and Gibsland, Louisiana.

Barrow, Marvin Ivan "Buck" or "Ivy" [1903?–1933] Born near Jones Prairie, Texas, probably on March 14, 1903 (though his gravestone reads 1905). Older brother of Clyde Barrow and member of Barrow Gang. Mortally wounded by police near Platte City, Missouri, July 19, 1933, and captured with wife, Blanche, near Dexter, Iowa, July 24. Died at Perry, Iowa, July 29, 1933.

Bentz, Edward Wilhelm (Eddie), "Doc" [1894–1979] Born in Pipestone, Minnesota, June 21, 1894, the son of German immigrants. Father killed by a runaway horse about 1906. Moved with his mother and siblings to Tacoma, Washington. Despite superior intelligence and cultural interests, Bentz spent time in a Washington reformatory for burglary while still in his teens, then graduated to safecracking and eventually took up bank robbery in the early twenties (he committed more than a hundred, by his own estimation, around the country without being identified). His increasingly notorious colleagues enjoyed high-profile post-robbery sprees, so he changed crime partners frequently and lived in quiet luxury, amassing a small fortune in rare books and coins and even dabbling in legitimate business. He cased jobs thoroughly and prepared detailed getaway charts that made him a legend in the criminal community, especially as the reputed leader of

Eddie Bentz

Nebraska's million-dollar Lincoln National Bank robbery in 1930, the largest then on record.

By the time he moved to Long Beach, Indiana, in 1933, he had semi-retired and acted mostly as a consultant, but he was dragged into the nearly bungled holdup of the bank in Grand Haven, Michigan, by "Baby Face" Nelson, who also had moved to Long Beach, knew Bentz by reputation, and at his suggestion drove to San Antonio to buy submachine guns and specially modified machine pistols from gunsmith H. S. Lebman. Nelson was believed to have later killed the gang's getaway driver, who had fled at the sight of a police car, causing Earl Doyle to be captured and leaving Nelson and Bentz to escape from Grand Haven in a stolen car. Bentz's brother Theodore was wrongly identified and sentenced to prison for the robbery, but was eventually exonerated. After passage of the new federal anti-crime laws in 1934, Bentz made the mistake of robbing a bank at Caledonia, Vermont—the FBI's first federal bank case—and some clever sleuthing led to his arrest on March 13, 1936. Agents found him hiding in a dumbwaiter at 1492 Bushwick Avenue in Brooklyn. Supposedly, he surprised them by saying he wanted to be sent to Alcatraz, "because all my friends are there." Bentz got his wish but never identified his partner in the Caledonia holdup except as a "Smitty" from Chicago. Eventually, a tip sent Chicago police looking for the elusive "Smitty," better known as Clyde Nimerick, allegedly the killer of local mob-connected sportsman and government informant Edward J. O'Hare, for whose Naval aviator son, an early World War II hero, the city's O'Hare Airport is named. Paroled in the fifties, Bentz was arrested for a store holdup in 1954 and served a term in the state prison at Waupun, Wisconsin. Died in Tacoma, Washington on October 31, 1979.

Birger, Charles (Charlie) (true name: Shachna Itzik Birger) [1880?–1928] Born at Gambany (or Guainbainy), Russia, either January 1 or 11, in either 1880 or 1883, according to different records, although he claimed a New York City birth. Raised in Illinois but ran away from home as a teenager, working on a Montana ranch where he later claimed to have met Harvey "Kid Curry" Logan and Harry "The Sundance Kid" Longabaugh. Enlisted in U.S. Cavalry in 1901 and served in Philippines before returning home and opening a saloon. Colorful twenties gang leader who fought the Shelton Brothers for control of bootlegging and rackets in southern Illinois, in a bloody gang war noted for its extensive military-style use of machine guns, homemade "tanks," and even efforts (not very successful) at aerial bombing. Arrested with several members of his gang for murder in 1927. Convicted of killing Mayor Joe Adams of West City, Illinois, and sentenced to death. Publicly hanged at Marion, Illinois, April 19, 1928, cracking jokes on the scaffold.

Blumenfeld, Isadore "Kid Cann" [1900–1981] Born in Romania in 1900 and arrived in U.S. as a child. With brothers Harry and "Yiddy," who changed their names to Bloom, organized the Minneapolis Combination, an all-Jewish mob that dominated bootlegging, gambling, and

Isadore "Kid Cann" Blumenfeld (center), following his 1936 acquittal in the murder of Walter Liggett.

In "Bloody Williamson" County in southern Illinois, warfare between the gangs of Charlie Birger (above, in bulletproof vest atop car) and the Shelton Brothers approached military proportions with the use of machine guns, "tanks," and airplanes. The homemade tanks were heavily armored trucks with gun ports, and Birger's fortress-like roadhouse, "Shady Rest," was "bombed" by a crop-duster using dynamite charges that either missed their target or failed to explode. Sentenced to death for murder, Birger went to the gallows (right) cracking jokes with his executioners.

Photos from Mike Webb Collection

rackets operations in that city, often collaborating with St. Paul gangsters to make the Twin Cities a haven for such fugitive criminals as the Dillinger and Barker-Karpis Gangs. Indicted with Verne Miller for the shooting of two policemen in a Minneapolis nightclub, but charges were dropped. Arrested by the FBI in 1933 for passing ransom money from the Urschel kidnapping, but charges again were dropped, though two of Blumenfeld's lieutenants, Edward "Barney" Berman and Clifford Skelly, were tried and convicted. Suspected of involvement with Barker-Karpis Gang in the Hamm kidnapping. Tried and acquitted of the 1935 machine-gun murder of *Mid-West American* publisher Walter Liggett, whose muckraking journal exposed Blumenfeld's ties to politicians. Also suspected in the killings of journalists Howard Guilford and Arthur Kasherman and arrested over the years for numerous other crimes. Involved with "Bugsy" Siegel in the El Cortez Hotel in Las Vegas in 1940s. Avoided serious legal consequences until 1960s, when he served four years in federal prison on white-slavery and jury-tampering charges. Made millions in later years from Miami hotel investments with Meyer Lansky. Died of heart disease at Mt. Sinai Hospital in Minneapolis on June 21, 1981.

Bradshaw, Ford **[1906–1934]** Born near Vian, Indian Territory (later Oklahoma), 1906. Notorious bank robber and killer, based in Oklahoma's Cookson Hills, whose brutal style is said to have appalled "Pretty Boy" Floyd. Wanted for several murders, including the 1932 carjack slaying of forty-eight-year-old mother and grandmother Susie Sharp. Later worked regularly with Wilbur Underhill, another infamous murderer known as the "Tri-State Terror." Bradshaw's end was as despicable and cowardly as his own misdeeds. He was shot to death by Deputy William Harper while disarmed and fleeing in handcuffs outside the deputy's roadhouse in Arkoma, Oklahoma, on March 3, 1934. Bradshaw's killing outshined John Dillinger's Crown Point, Indiana, jailbreak in the headlines of some southwestern newspapers.

Brady, Alfred James (Al) **[1910–1937]** Born at Kentland, Indiana, October 25, 1910, and orphaned in his youth. Reportedly boasted he would "make John Dillinger look like a piker." With Rhuel James Dalhover and Clarence Lee Shaffer Jr., comprised the Brady Gang, which terrorized Indiana, Ohio, and Wisconsin during 1935–37 with numerous bank and store robberies and several murders. Along the way they acquired an impressive arsenal, including three .30–06 Marlin "tank guns," two of which were American Legion monuments stolen from Ohio parks. Their quest for a Tommygun led them to a sporting goods store at Bangor, Maine, where Brady and Shaffer were killed by FBI agents and police on October 12, 1937. Dalhover was captured at the same time and later convicted of murder. He was executed at Indiana's state prison on November 18, 1938. The Brady case also brought Captain Matt Leach's dismissal as head of the Indiana State Police following complaints from the FBI, whom Leach had criticized since the Dillinger investigation.

Burke, Fred "Killer" **(true name: Thomas Camp) [1893–1940]** Born in Mapleton, Kansas, May 28, 1893. Notorious criminal noted for his police impersonations and early use of the Thompson submachine gun in bank robberies in the 1920s. A graduate of the Egan's Rats gang of St. Louis and a professional killer in the employ of Al Capone during the late twenties. Wanted across the United States for numerous bank and payroll robberies and murders, including the St. Valentine's Day Massacre of the "Bugs" Moran gang in 1929 (one bank-robbing associate, Harvey Bailey, claimed with annoyance that the two actually were drinking beer in Calumet City at the time of the mass murder, which made Burke too "hot" to work with thereafter). The two machine guns used in the Massacre were found in his house in St. Joseph, Michigan, when it was raided by local police looking for a motorist who had just killed Patrolman Charles Skelly during a traffic altercation in December 1929. Arrested near Green City, Missouri, March 26, 1931, on a farm rented from relatives of Harvey Bailey.

Extradited to Michigan, convicted of the Skelly murder, and sentenced to life imprisonment, Burke never was tried for his alleged role in the Massacre. He reportedly had enough money to live in relative luxury at the Marquette state prison, where he became fat and diabetic and died on July 10, 1940.

Callahan, John [1866–1936] Wichita, Kansas, bootlegger and drug trafficker. For years probably the largest receiver of stolen goods in the Southwest, whose "treaty" with Wichita police made the city a safe haven for visiting outlaws. A former bank robber from horseback days, Callahan reportedly served as a "Fagin" figure to young apprentice criminals of later notoriety, including twenties bank and train robber Eddie Adams and "Pretty Boy" Floyd, who began his career hauling booze for Callahan. Convicted of smuggling narcotics in the late twenties, he served seven years of a twenty-five-year sentence and died at his home in Wichita, June 8, 1936.

Campagna, Louis "Little New York" or "Lefty Louie" [1900–1955] Born in Brooklyn but left New York in his teens and settled in Chicago by the time of Prohibition. Convicted of a 1918 bank robbery in Argo, Illinois, and sentenced to one to fourteen years in the state reformatory at Pontiac. Joined the Capone organization about 1925 and rose through the ranks as a gunman despite occasional setbacks. Arrested in November 1927, when he led a Capone contingent in surrounding the detective bureau at 625 South Clark Street, apparently waiting to ambush arrested gang leader Joe Aiello. Placed in a cell with Aiello, Campagna's death threats were overheard by an Italian-speaking policeman in an adjoining cell. Under police escort, Aiello left Chicago for several months before returning to ally himself with "Bugs" Moran against Capone. Campagna was part of the hit team, along with Fred "Killer" Burke and Gus Winkeler, dispatched to Brooklyn in 1928 to kill Frankie Yale and nearly blew their cover by making long-distance phone calls, later traced, to a girlfriend in Chicago. This incited Capone's ire, but Winkeler was able to talk him out of killing Campagna, who eventually found his way back into the boss's good graces and became a major figure in the new setup under Capone's successor, Frank Nitti. Convicted in the movie-extortion plot in the forties but scandalously paroled early, along with Ricca, D'Andrea, Charles "Cherry Nose" Gioe, and John Rosselli. Remained active in the Chicago Syndicate until May 30, 1955, when he died of a heart attack while on a Florida fishing trip.

Capezio, Anthony "Tough Tony" [1901–1955] A graduate of Chicago's juvenile "42" Gang and a boyhood friend of Lester ("Baby Face" Nelson) Gillis and Alvin Karpis, Tony Capezio joined the Capone-allied Circus Gang under the leadership of Claude Maddox. A partner of Maddox in the Circus Café on North Avenue, whose close proximity to Moran territory, and Maddox's own ties to former St. Louis colleagues from the Egan's Rats gang, proved vital to the planning of the St. Valentine's Day Massacre. Dismantling the killers' getaway Cadillac with an acetylene torch in a garage at 1723 North Wood Street, Capezio supposedly earned his nickname by surviving the resulting gasoline explosion and fire. Capone rewarded Capezio by making him manager of a Stickney brothel, and he continued to prosper under Frank Nitti and Tony Accardo, despite FBI scrutiny as a Dillinger-Nelson contact and as a principal in the Syndicate wire service takeover in the forties. Died of a massive heart attack (not struck by lightning as some accounts have it) while playing golf at White Pines Country Club in suburban Bensenville on July 7, 1955.

"Tough Tony" Capezio

Capone, Alphonse (Al), "The Big Fellow," "Scarface," or "Snorky"* **(aka Al Brown and other names when traveling) [1899–1947]** Born January 17, 1899, the son of Gabriel and Theresa Capone, in Brooklyn (not Naples or Castelamara, Italy, as often reported). History's most notorious mobster. Graduate of New York street gangs who worked as a waiter-bouncer for Frankie Yale's Harvard Inn at Coney Island in the summer of 1917, where his face was badly scarred in a knife attack by one Frank Galluccio, avenging what he regarded as a flirtatious insult to his sister. Sought by police for attempted murder, Capone moved to Chicago about 1919 or 1920 to work for former Brooklynite and Yale associate Johnny Torrio, now managing the interests of local vice lord "Big Jim" Colosimo. After the murder of Colosimo (probably by Yale), he rose from the lowly positions of pimp and saloon bouncer to an ostensible used-furniture dealer with a business card, and eventually become the most powerful and prominent underworld leader of the Prohibition era—the "Babe Ruth of American Gangsters." (By coincidence, he turned twenty-one the day Prohibition went into effect.)

As understudy to Torrio, he forged or forced alliances with other gangs to form the Chicago Syndicate. The "Outfit," as he began to call it, soon dominated bootlegging, gambling, vice, and business and labor racketeering, first on Chicago's South Side and in the town of Cicero, and eventually throughout the city and several of its suburbs. Presumably arranged the "handshake" murder of North Side Gang leader Dean O'Banion in November 1924, which set off five years of gangland killings known as the Chicago Beer Wars. Inherited leadership of the mob after Torrio was shot in retaliation in January 1925 and "retired" to the relative safety of New York. Two of O'Banion's successors were subsequently killed: "Hymie" Weiss by the Capone gang, and Vincent "The Schemer" Drucci by a Chicago policeman. The warfare culminated in the St. Valentine's Day Massacre of February 14, 1929, in which six North Side Gang members and one visiting optometrist "groupie" were lined up against a garage wall at 2122 North Clark Street and machine-gunned by Capone gangsters, some wearing police uniforms. Gang leader "Bugs" Moran, the intended target, was not present, but the Massacre finished him as an underworld power. His chief ally, Joe Aiello, was machine-gunned by Capone's men the next year.

Al Capone and his son, Albert Francis

The Massacre generated public outrage and pressure against the underworld, particularly Capone, who found himself declared Public

* "Snorky" was the then-current term meaning snazzy or spiffy.

Al Capone (seated at right) at Jimmy Emery's backyard picnic in Chicago Heights. In one or more early photographs, Frankie LaPorte (seated at left, next to Vera Emery) is misidentified as Jack McGurn. Standing (from left) are Rocco DeGrazia, Louis Campagna, and Claude Maddox.

Enemy No. 1 in a stunt thought up by the Chicago Crime Commission to turn public sentiment against Capone, who had been acquiring celebrity status with his colorful style and antics. The Massacre created such political turmoil, locally and nationally, that the country's top mobsters met in convention in Atlantic City in May 1929, holding what amounted to a peace conference to reestablish a degree of underworld harmony. This meeting led to new alliances and procedures for the peaceful settlement of disputes, and the beginning of nationally organized crime. Upon leaving the conference, Capone and his bodyguard were arrested, probably through prearrangement, in Philadelphia, probably as a reprimand for the mass murder and for protection from vengeful remnants of the North Sider mob. Within twenty-four hours, Capone was serving his first jail sentence—one year on a gun-possession charge—and by the time he returned to Chicago he was facing the might of a federal government determined to destroy him as a symbol of underworld power.

Convicted of income tax evasion on October 17, 1931, he was sentenced to eleven years in the Atlanta Federal Penitentiary and fined $50,000, plus $30,000 in court costs. The FBI also made a successful case against Capone for contempt of federal court, as a result of his failure to appear and give testimony in a bootlegging case. Other leaders of the original Capone Outfit were convicted of tax violations until the familiar names were no longer in the news. Partly for that reason, partly because of repeal, and partly because the Depression would usher in a new political philosophy and preoccupation with the crimes of outlaws instead of racketeers, the Capone organization would not only endure but prosper under the leadership of Frank Nitti. Only Capone the individual was destroyed. From Atlanta he was transferred to Alcatraz, the new federal prison "for the worst of the worst," on August 22, 1934, and finally paroled on November 16, 1939, with mental problems resulting from untreated syphilis. He died at his palatial estate at Palm Island, Florida, January 25, 1947, eight days after his forty-eighth birthday.

Capone, Ralph "Bottles" [1893–1974] Born in Naples, Italy. Older brother and chief lieutenant of Al Capone. Served a short sentence for tax evasion in early thirties. Remained active in the Outfit for years but was never of importance after Al's imprisonment. He eventually retired to Mercer, Wisconsin, where he owned a bar and enjoyed local popularity. Died in Hurley, Wisconsin, November 22, 1974.

THE MAN WHO CARVED CAPONE

It would have taken an unusually gutsy reporter to ask Al Capone how he earned the nickname "Scarface." Rumored explanations included a childhood fight in a Brooklyn schoolyard, a dispute with a New York barber (Capone's father had operated a barbershop), and the one Capone himself preferred—shrapnel wounds while fighting with the "Lost Battalion" in France.

This last explanation was accepted by his original biographer, Fred Pasley, possibly as a courtesy, and newsmen researching Capone's early years did, in fact, discover that an Al Capone had enlisted in the Army at Atlantic City during World War I. This turned out to be another and unrelated Al Capone, though the coincidence of names would one day inspire a series of detective magazine articles whose author became convinced that the "real" Capone had been killed sometime in the twenties and that an obscure look-alike relative had been recruited to masquerade as the world's most notorious mobster. That idea gained enough currency that the FBI was called upon to check it out and resolved the mystery to its satisfaction.

Knife scars are deliberately exaggerated in this picture of Al Capone, who tried to avoid photographs of the left side of his face. He was called "Scarface" in local newspapers until he complained and the papers complied.

Variations on the knife-fight story remained in circulation, but the details of the incident were revealed for the first time by William Balsamo, a retired longshoreman turned crime researcher who had relatives in the Brooklyn Mafia and managed to arrange a personal, though long unreported, interview with an aging member of the Genovese crime family named Frank Galluccio who actually had wielded the blade. His youthful scrap with Capone left the future Chicago mob boss with deep scars on the left side of his face that probably enhanced his image as a ruthless gangster but also embarrassed him the rest of his days. How Capone's attacker lived to tell the tale is a significant part of the story.

Balsamo met with Galluccio at Lento's Bar & Grill in Brooklyn in the fall of 1965. He agreed not to divulge the details of their conversation (published here with his permission) until after Galluccio's death, which occurred from natural causes several years ago.

FRANK GALLUCCIO: One thing I want you to do for me, Bill. Whatever I tell you now, I don't want you to say anything about it till I'm long gone.

WILLIAM BALSAMO: Mr. Galluccio, I will respect your wishes.

GALLUCCIO: I heard from Esposito and several dockworkers that you wanted to talk to me about Al Capone.

BALSAMO: Yes, I do.

GALLUCCIO: The first thing I want to ask you, what was Battista Balsamo's son's name?

BALSAMO: Vito. He was my mother's first cousin.

GALLUCCIO: Yes, that's right. That makes you the great nephew of Battista Balsamo from Columbia and Union Street. I hope you don't mind me asking about your family, Bill, but it's for my own satisfaction.

BALSAMO: I understand. . . . I've heard that you are the man who cut Al Capone's face. Is that right?

GALLUCCIO: Well, I would never admit that to the detectives or anyone connected with newspapers, but the answer is yes, I did it. I had every right to do it. Nobody insults my sister like that. Especially in public at a dance hall, when I was with my date.

BALSAMO: When did this happen and where?

GALLUCCIO: It happened in the summer of 1917 at a dance hall that was owned by Frankie Yale. You ever heard of him?

BALSAMO: Of course. What was the name of the dance hall?

GALLUCCIO: The Harvard Inn, on the Bowery in Coney Island. Al was just a bartender/bouncer in those days. He was a disappointed gangster.

William Balsamo

Frank Galluccio, a young hoodlum whose sister was "complimented" by waiter Al Capone, attacked Capone with a knife at the Harvard Inn, owned by Brooklyn's Frankie Yale.

BALSAMO: He was a nobody then. Why did you cut his face? What did he do to your sister? By the way, what was her name?

GALLUCCIO: Lena. I was with Maria Tanzio. I took both of them out that evening to dine and dance at the Harvard for a good time. Capone was trying to put the make on Lena, and Lena ignored him every time, and every time he would pass our table he would try to talk to her. It seemed to me she didn't want to be bothered with him, she was getting mad. Whenever he passed the table, he would try to say something. I thought she knew him, so I asked her; you know that guy? Or something like that. My sister told me she never saw him before, and he had a lot of nerve. She said:

"He won't give up, Frank. He can't take a hint. But I don't like him, he is embarrassing me. Maybe you could ask him to please stop in a nice way." Capone was passing by the table again, and I was about to ask him to leave my kid sister alone, in a nice way, of course. And he leans over and tells her that she had a nice ass.

BALSAMO: Did you hear that or did she tell you what he said?

GALLUCCIO: You kidding? He said it loud enough that people sitting at a table next to ours overheard the insult, too. "You got a nice ass, honey, and I mean it as a compliment. Believe me." When I heard that, I jumped up from the table and said to him, "I won't take that shit from nobody. Apologize to my sister now, you hear?" He smiled and came toward me with his hands out and his palms open as if to say, "Come on, buddy, I'm only joking." I shouted back that that is no fucking joke, mister. Capone wasn't smiling anymore after that. He still came toward me. I called for the owner. He just kept coming toward me. So I whipped out a pocketknife and went for the son of a bitch's neck.

BALSAMO: How come you got his face instead?

GALLUCCIO: Well, I was drinking that night, and I was a little drunk. I think maybe my aim was not good because of the booze, you know. But I think I sliced him two or three times. I don't remember. It was a long time ago. But fuck him, he deserved it. I'm sure if it was the other way around, he would do the same thing I did. I mean, that was my kid sister, you know. Nobody likes to be insulted. Especially at a dance.

BALSAMO: Then what did you do after that?

GALLUCCIO: I grabbed my sister and Maria and ran out of the joint right away. Later I find out from some neighborhood guys that this big guy is looking for me.

BALSAMO: How big was he then?

GALLUCCIO: To me, he looked like at least five feet eleven or six feet. But you got to remember, I was a little under the booze. So to me he looked big and stocky, and I'm only five feet six. I must have been about 148 pounds then. This guy looked like he was 200 pounds. Hey, this guy could hurt me bad if I let him get me. I better strike first and quick, and I knew that a punch was not enough to stop him, so fuck that. I had to use what I learned in the streets. A few days later I still keep hearing that this guy is looking for me. He's telling people that he is with Frankie Yale.

BALSAMO: What did he mean, he was with Frankie Yale?

GALLUCCIO: It means he belongs to Yale's crew. Then about a week later I went to see my friend from the East Side, Albert Alterio. He was related to Two Knife Willie in some way. I told Albert about this problem, so he takes me to see Giuseppe Masseria—"Joe the Boss"—and Charley Luciano. Albert pleaded my case, and Joe the Boss and Charley agreed nobody should insult another man in front of his own family and get away with it.

What happened then was a sit-down at the Harvard Inn between me, Charley, Frankie, and Capone. You know, I was really sorry what I did to his face. But I was a little drunk, and he insulted Lena. So I did what I thought was right at the time. The decision at the sit-down was Al Capone was ordered by Luciano and Yale not to look for revenge, and I was ordered to apologize. As a matter of fact, the look of the cuts I put on his face kind of shook me up, because I was really sorry for what I had done to him. Jesus, Bill, Capone had to go through life with those scars.

BALSAMO: Did you ask him how many stitches he got that day?

GALLUCCIO: No, not personally. But Charley later told me it was close to thirty. Luciano said they took him to Coney Island Hospital to get patched up.

BALSAMO: How were things after that?

GALLUCCIO: The few times we saw each other face to face, he would smile like he was trying to be nice to me. He did say to me that he was wrong when he insulted my sister in public. We never associated together while he was still living in Brooklyn.

BALSAMO: Would you say Luciano and Yale made Capone understand that if he went looking for you, it would be his funeral?

GALLUCCIO: You could put it that way. I guess that was the understanding. Now remember, Bill. Don't tell anyone about this till I am long gone. Capice?

BALSAMO: No problem. I swear on my mother, not a word.

Galluccio never attained prominence in the Genovese crime family, but Balsamo heard that on Capone's trips to Brooklyn in the 1920s he would request the services of Galluccio as chauffeur and bodyguard.

Capone, Salvatore (Frank) [1895–1924] Born in Brooklyn. Brother of Alphonse and Ralph, Frank Capone's budding career was cut short when killed by police while terrorizing poll workers and voters during the Cicero municipal elections on April 1, 1924. [Al's younger brothers, Albert, John (called "Mimi"), and Matt, joined the mob in later years but never amounted to much.]

Chapman, Irving Charles (Charley) [1898–1942] Born in Philadelphia, Mississippi, December 29, 1898. Once a successful highway contractor in Arkansas whose business fell on hard times, Chapman changed professions and became a criminal in about 1931. After minor arrests in Florida and New Jersey, he embarked on a decade-long career, earning a reputation as a prolific and elusive bank robber and expert jailbreaker. Sentenced in 1932 to nine to fourteen years for a Minden, Louisiana, bank robbery, Chapman escaped with two others from the Caddo Parish Jail in Shreveport, December 5, 1932, lowering themselves from their eighth-story cell with a rope improvised from mattress covers. Convicted of a Mississippi bank robbery in 1934, Chapman was sentenced to fifteen years but was turned over to Arkansas, where he received another fifteen-year sentence for another bank robbery, escaping from Tucker Prison on August 25, 1936.

Chapman twice robbed the First National Bank of Atlanta, Texas. Captured and convicted the second time and sentenced to sixty years, he joined nine others in a bloody mass breakout from Eastham Prison Farm. The others were soon captured or killed, but Chapman continued to elude police and FBI agents in a series of robberies, car chases, and gun-blazing escapades, for a time accompanied by notorious Oklahoma outlaw Roy (Pete) Traxler. This was to the dismay of two other Texas convicts who'd been wrongly convicted of the first Atlanta robbery and were counting on Chapman's confession to set them free. Once was shot by Mississippi police and presumed killed, but no body was found and Chapman was reportedly named by the FBI as Public Enemy No. 1 in 1939 (according to the press; in fact, the FBI actually had no numbered fugitives until the "Ten Most Wanted" list in 1950). He remained a fugitive another three years, shooting a Meridian, Mississippi, policeman in January 1942. Trapped by an FBI roadblock only a few miles from his birthplace on February 22, 1942, Chapman elected to shoot it out and was killed in the proverbial hail of bullets. His last words were, "Go ahead and shoot, you bastards!"

Chase, Vivian (alias Gracie Chase, Gracie Adams) [1905?–1935] Born Vivian Davis in Nebraska, Missouri, or Oklahoma, by varying accounts. Married in 1922 to bank robber George Chase, with whom she was arrested on suspicion by police in Kansas City, Missouri, on December 23, 1923. George Chase reportedly was killed while committing a robbery about 1924. Vivian later was implicated with robbers Lee Flournoy, Lyman Ford, and Charles Mayes, and bankers G. C. Robertson and Clarence R. Howard, in the prearranged robbery of the Montgomery County National Bank in Cherryvale, Kansas, May 26, 1926. She was arrested but soon released for insufficient evidence. With boyfriend Luther Jordan, she robbed two banks in the Kansas City area and was suspected of several gas station holdups during April and May of 1932. Captured with Jordan at North Kansas City, June 7, 1932, where they were charged with robbing the National Bank & Trust Co. on April 9, 1932. Jordan was tried, convicted, and sentenced to twenty-five years; Vivian escaped in October 1932 from the Clay County Jail at Liberty, Missouri, and linked up with remnants of the Egan's Rats gang of St. Louis and the gang of "Irish" O'Malley.

With O'Malley, she allegedly masterminded the kidnapping of August Luer, a seventy-eight-year-old retired Alton, Illinois, banker and meatpacker, in July 1933. Luer was released unharmed and without payment of ransom when the kidnappers became concerned for his health. Most of the gang was soon apprehended. O'Malley was captured in Kansas City, May 27, 1935, pleaded guilty later to kidnapping and was sentenced to life. Vivian returned to Kansas City about June 1935 and was suspected of seven robberies in the area in the ensuing months, but she and a male accomplice were never apprehended. She was found shot to death in a parked car outside St. Luke's Hospital in Kansas City, November 3, 1935, a pistol in her hand.

Cleaver, Charles "Limpy" [1872–1968] Born October 16, 1872. Left home at an early age to train as a boy jockey and went on to become a tramp, lumberjack, miner, steamfitter, and bootlegger before finding his true calling in middle age as a bandit once called "Chicago's most dangerous criminal," about whom one police official reportedly said, "Cleaver makes Jesse James look like a piker." Arrested for killing a policeman and a former policeman at a South Side saloon in 1921, Cleaver was acquitted in 1924. A year later he was tried for a bank messenger robbery in which another policeman was shot. In both cases Cleaver was defended by Charles S. Wharton, formerly a U.S. Congressman and assistant prosecutor under Robert E. Crowe.

With William Donovan, he led five other men in a $133,000 mail-train robbery at the Santa Maria station in suburban Evergreen Park on February 25, 1928 (same location as an earlier train robbery by Thomas Holden and Francis Keating). Trapped by wiretaps and doomed by the testimony of their own wives, Cleaver and Donovan were apprehended within forty-eight hours. Found in a secret room of Cleaver's house at 10235 South Elizabeth Street were two Tommyguns, seven shotguns, assorted ammunition, bombs, nitroglycerine, burglary tools, and $9,000 in cash. The machine guns were believed to have been bought from gang leader Joe Saltis, a friend of Cleaver, but originally had been purchased from the Auto-Ordnance company through a bogus "Mex-America Corporation" Also caught in the dragnet was attorney Wharton, in whose basement the loot was divided (Wharton subsequently was convicted of two counts of conspiracy and imprisoned for two years; after his release he wrote a book on the case titled *The House of Whispering Hate*). On June 10, 1928, Cleaver and four others escaped from the DuPage County Jail at Wheaton, beating Deputy William Edgeton with a crude "blackjack" improvised by concealing a can of condensed milk in a sock, and stealing his keys. They then robbed the jail arsenal of three shotguns and a machine gun, though forgetting to pick up any .45-caliber ammunition. Fleeing in the deputy's car, the group soon split up, but Cleaver and Joe Farina were trapped in a field near Melrose Park on June 14. Surrounded by forty police armed with rifles and machine guns, the pair took cover behind an embankment and elected to shoot it out. Riddled with bullets, they finally surrendered, and Cleaver survived to face a twenty-five-year sentence for mail robbery, eventually winding up on Alcatraz. Paroled June 16, 1944, at age seventy-two, Cleaver worked as a night watchman in Blue Island, Illinois, for seventeen years before retiring. Died in Oak Forest, Illinois, in April 1968 at age ninety-five.

Colbeck, William P. "Dint" or "Dinty" [1891–1943] Born in St. Louis. Early twenties boss of Egan's Rats, a notorious St. Louis bootlegging and robbery gang, graduates of which included St. Valentine's Day Massacre suspects Fred "Killer" Burke, Gus Winkeler, Bob Carey, Ray Nugent, and Claude Maddox. Convicted of Staunton, Illinois, mail robbery, November 1924, and sentenced to twenty-five years in federal prison. Convicted of St. Louis mail robbery, January 1925, and sentenced to fifteen years. Paroled in 1941. Victim of a machine-gun murder—by then a rare occurrence—in St. Louis on February 17, 1943, supposedly for muscling in on gambling operations in southern Illinois.

Colosimo, James "Big Jim" or "Diamond Jim" [1878–1920] Born in Cosenza, Calabria, Italy. Came to America in 1895 with his father Luigi, settling in the Levee District on Chicago's Near South Side where criminal opportunities abounded. As bagman for notoriously corrupt Aldermen "Bathhouse" John Coughlin and "Hinky Dink" Kenna, young James made the acquaintance of a homely but prosperous madam who liked his style and decided the two had a future together. Soon James was

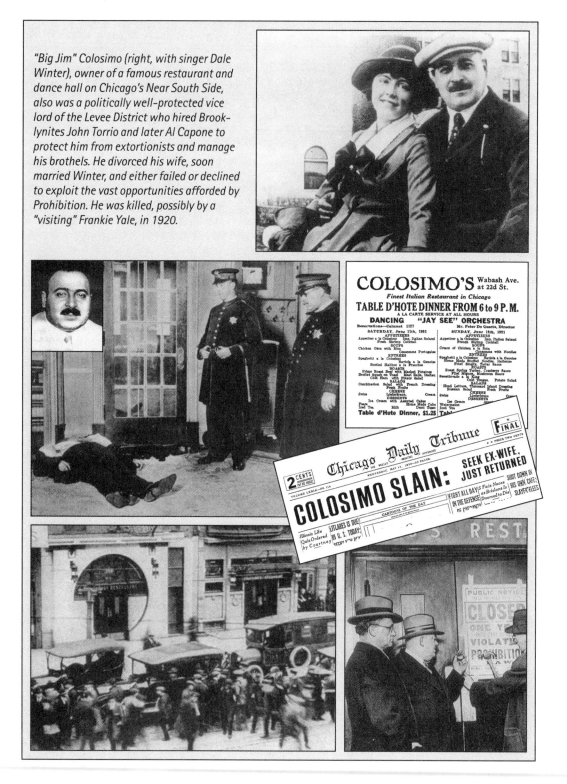

"Big Jim" Colosimo (right, with singer Dale Winter), owner of a famous restaurant and dance hall on Chicago's Near South Side, also was a politically well-protected vice lord of the Levee District who hired Brooklynites John Torrio and later Al Capone to protect him from extortionists and manage his brothels. He divorced his wife, soon married Winter, and either failed or declined to exploit the vast opportunities afforded by Prohibition. He was killed, possibly by a "visiting" Frankie Yale, in 1920.

COLOSIMO'S Wabash Ave. at 22d St.

Finest Italian Restaurant in Chicago

TABLE D'HOTE DINNER FROM 6 to 9 P. M.

A LA CARTE SERVICE AT ALL HOURS

DANCING "JAY SEE" ORCHESTRA

Reservations—Calumet 1127

Mr. Peter De Quarto, Director

SATURDAY, June 11th, 1921

APPETIZERS
Appetizer a la Colosimo Imp. Italian Salami
Fresh Shrimp Cocktail
SOUPS
Chicken Okra with Rice
Consomme Portugaise
ENTREES
Spaghetti a la Colosimo
Raviola a la Genoise
Broiled Halibut a la Franchee
ROASTS
Prime Roast Beef with Mashed Potatoes
Broiled Squab on Toast Meat Balls, Italian
Cold Ham with Potato Salad
SALADS
Combination Salad with French Dressing
Fresh Fruits
CHEESE
Swiss Liederkrans, Cream
DESSERTS
Ice Cream with Assorted Cakes
Pears Home Made Cake
Iced Tea Milk Demi Tasse

Table d'Hote Dinner, $1.25

SUNDAY, June 12th, 1921

APPETIZERS
Appetizer a la Colosimo Imp. Italian Salami
French Shrimp Cocktail
SOUPS
Cream of Chicken a la Rein
Consomme with Noodles
ENTREES
Spaghetti a la Colosimo Raviola a la Genoise
Home Made Stuffed Noodles, Italienne
Fried Smelts, Tartar Sauce
ROASTS
Roast Spring Turkey, Cranberry Sauce
Filet Mignon, Mushroom Sauce
Sweetbreads a la King
Cold Tongue. Potato Salad
SALADS
Head Lettuce, Thousand Island Dressing
Russian Salad Fresh Fruits
CHEESE
Swiss Liederkrans
DESSERTS
Ice Cream
Watermelon
Iced Tea

Chicago Daily Tribune

THE WORLD'S GREATEST NEWSPAPER

FINAL

PRICE TWO CENTS

2 CENTS PAY NO MORE!

VOLUME LXXIX.—NO. 114

WEDNESDAY, MAY 12, 1920—32 PAGES.

COLOSIMO SLAIN: SEEK EX-WIFE, JUST RETURNED

SHOT DOWN IN HIS OWN CAFE; SLAYER FLEES

FIGHT ALL DAY IN THE DEFENSE

5 Face Noose as Brislane Is Doomed to Die

CARTOONS OF THE DAY

LITLARES IS DUE IN U. S. TODAY;

Illinois Life Quiz Ordered by Courtney

"Big Jim" Colosimo, vice lord of the Levee, whose riches from prostitution and gambling permitted him to refine his tastes. In 1910 he opened Chicago's most opulent nightclub, Colosimo's Café, at 2126 South Wabash, which featured the best entertainment and the best clientele, who enjoyed the adventure of rubbing shoulders with some of the worst criminal elements in the city. When harassed by Black Hand extortionists, "Big Jim" sent to Brooklyn for John Torrio (his wife's cousin, by some accounts, or his own nephew), whose suave manners belied his efficiency at simply killing Colosimo's tormentors. Torrio was promoted to manager of Colosimo's vice empire and was shopping for an assistant when he learned that a young scar-faced hoodlum from back home needed a new start in life.

Meanwhile, "Big Jim" had outgrown the frumpy wife who had sponsored his early enterprises and dumped her for a beautiful young songbird named Dale Winter who was performing at his café. In recapturing his lost youth, "Big Jim" not only left Torrio in charge of his vice empire but displayed no interest in capitalizing on the vast opportunities presented by Prohibition. Love-smitten and neglecting his vice business, he married Dale, and barely two weeks later, on May 11, 1920, was found shot to death in the vestibule of his café. Police initially suspected the brothers of the wife who had been scorned, divorced, and generally humiliated, but their discovery that Frankie Yale happened to be in town persuaded most that he had been summoned by Torrio to kill his former boss. Torrio and the Brooklyn-born Al Capone expanded Colosimo's lucrative but local operations into a bootlegging and racketeering empire such as the country had never imagined possible.

Crapo, Alton **[1902–1949]** Born in Kansas, June 8, 1902, the son of George and Hannah Crapo. Notorious bank robber often linked to the Barker Gang, though any close association is doubtful. First arrested for vagrancy at Wichita, Kansas, January 3, 1922. Convicted of bank robbery in Colorado in 1927 and sentenced to nine to fourteen years in state prison at Canon City; paroled August 18, 1931. More than twenty arrests for bank robbery and other serious crimes and numerous misdemeanors around Wichita, Kansas, such as drunkenness, fighting, speeding, and disorderly conduct. Suspected of involvement in numerous bank robberies in Kansas, Nebraska, Missouri, Oklahoma, and Colorado. Convicted in 1937 of violation of the National Firearms Act of 1934 for possession of a sawed-off shotgun and sentenced to five years in Leavenworth. Paroled in 1941, but a subsequent arrest led to revocation, and Crapo was returned to Leavenworth the next year and transferred to Alcatraz in 1943, later receiving an additional term for violation of the National Motor Vehicle Theft Act. Released in 1946, Crapo resumed his career of crime and with frequent partner Albert Gladson, another veteran bank robber whose record dated to the 1920s, robbed two Lincoln salesmen of $75,000 in jewelry near Lyons, Nebraska, on June 17, 1949. Less than three hours later they were trapped by a police roadblock near Howells, Nebraska, elected to fight it out, and were killed.

Dalitz, Morris Barney "Moe" **(alias Moe Davis) [1899–1989]** Born in Boston, December 24, 1899, and moved at an early age to Michigan. By some accounts was an early member of the Detroit Purple Gang before moving to Cleveland, where he joined forces with Morris Kleinman, Louis Rothkopf, and Sam Tucker to form the Cleveland Syndicate—a powerful, largely Jewish bootlegging combine that, in turn, allied with Frank Milano's Italian Mayfield Road Mob. Allegedly harbored "Pretty Boy" Floyd and Adam Richetti in Cleveland after the Kansas City Massacre. After Prohibition, became heavily involved in operating illegal casinos throughout Ohio and in Newport and Covington, Kentucky. The Harvard Club, in the Cleveland suburb of Newburgh Heights, was a frequent haunt of the Barker-Karpis Gang. Dalitz and his partners also were involved with Meyer Lansky and others in the Molaska Corp., which fronted for the operation of huge illegal distilleries from Ohio to New Jersey after Prohibition. Dalitz and company invested their profits in numerous legitimate businesses, and in the 1950s they migrated to Las Vegas to operate legal casinos, among them the Desert Inn and Stardust. A multimillionaire in his later years, Dalitz built hospitals, golf courses, and shopping malls, as well as casinos, and was a largely respected philanthropist, though he never entirely overcame the stigma of his racket associations. The American Cancer Research Center and Hospital named Dalitz its Humanitarian of the Year in 1976, and in 1982 the Anti-Defamation League of B'nai B'rith gave him the Torch of Liberty Award. The "Godfather of Las Vegas" set up the Moe Dalitz Charitable Remainder Unitrust in 1979, a million-dollar trust that was inherited after his death by fourteen nonprofit organizations. Died in Las Vegas of natural causes on September 6, 1989, though some writers have been misled by Bill Roemer's novel *War of the Godfathers* into believing that he was killed in a gang war.

D'Andrea, Philip Louis (Phil) **[1891–1952]** Born in Buffalo, New York, but moved with family to Chicago at an early age. Reportedly graduated high school and attended law school before World War I, then entered the trucking business, hauling booze after Prohibition began. Became a gunman and bodyguard for Al Capone, who got him an appointment as a deputy court bailiff despite an impressive record of arrests for such offenses as receiving stolen property, assault, and carrying weapons. Partnered with gambler Billy Skidmore in the bail bond business. With Capone's help, D'Andrea expanded his trucking business, landing lucrative garbage-hauling contracts with the city until 1941. Arrested on October 10, 1931, for carrying a revolver into Federal Court during Capone's tax trial, resulting in a six-month jail sentence for contempt of court. A power in the First Ward Democratic organization, D'Andrea continued to rise under Capone's successor, Frank Nitti. Served as president of Chicago's Italo-American National Union (the former Unione Siciliana) from 1934 to 1941, bringing mobsters Tony Accardo, Paul "The Waiter" Ricca, Charlie Fischetti, John Capone, and Nick Circella into the organization. Convicted with Ricca, Louis Campagna, and others in the Hollywood movie-extortion case in the forties and sentenced to ten years, but paroled after serving the bare minimum. In failing health, D'Andrea gave grudging and sparse testimony before the Kefauver Committee in 1951. Died in Riverside, California, September 18, 1952.

Daugherty, Roy **(alias "Arkansas Tom" Jones)** **[1870–1924]** Last survivor of the 1890s Bill Doolin Gang of Oklahoma train and bank robbers. Paroled from a life sentence for murder on November 29, 1910, Daugherty worked briefly at a succession of honest jobs, including playing himself in a 1915 silent film entitled *The Passing of the Oklahoma Outlaws*, then resumed his criminal career, serving a sentence for bank burglary after which he robbed a bank in Asbury, Missouri, in 1923. Killed by police at 1420 West Ninth Street in Joplin, Missouri, August 18, 1924.

DeGrazia, Rocco "Rocky" or "Mr. Big" **(aka DeGrazio; in his later years called "Gramps")** **[1897–1978]** Born in Italy December 8, 1897, although he claimed to be twenty-three when he entered the U.S., and most newspapers accepted 1900 as his birth date. Associated with Al Capone's Outfit as a driver and gunman before rising to prominence as a gambling and loan-sharking figure. Also affiliated with Claude Maddox's Circus Gang operating out of his Circus Café on North Avenue, considered a Capone beachhead in Moran-Aiello territory. According to Mrs. Gus Winkeler (who, in her book-length manuscript and statements to the FBI, for some reason called him DeGroce), DeGrazia harbored St. Valentine's Day Massacre shooters at his apartment until they were called that morning by lookouts. In July 1932, he suffered serious spinal injuries in a wreck two miles west of Bloomingdale, Illinois, and was hospitalized in Elgin, where he refused to discuss the machine gun in the back seat of his car or the police star he was wearing at the time. (With him was gangster Anthony "Tony the Mouth" Bagniola, and they had crashed into a farmer's vehicle while driving at high speed to a roadhouse, partly owned by DeGrazia, that had just been raided.) Arrested in November 1932 with Tony Accardo and Sam "Golf Bag" Hunt in a barbershop at 954 Harrison Street and charged with disorderly conduct. Later named by Chicago Crime Commission informant as one of the killers, along with Louis Campagna and Willie Heeney, of Sheet Metal Workers Union boss "Wild Bill" Rooney, shot to death at 1517 North Austin Boulevard on March 19, 1931.

In 1934 Rocco, living at 1040 North Elmwood in Oak Park, threatened to kill IRS agents until he learned who they were. He and his brother Nick, residing in Maywood, were indicted on July 27, 1934, for failure to pay income taxes during 1929 and 1930 on some eighteen handbooks in Melrose Park, for which he paid $1,200 a month protection. On February 5, 1935, he pleaded guilty and was sentenced to eighteen months in Leavenworth, plus a fine of $1,000. In 1946 Rocco and his brother Andrew, partners in a tavern called the Lumber Gardens, were picked up and questioned for allegedly threatening a Melrose Park pharmacist over opium and morphine, which they were demanding to settle the druggist's gambling debts. Rocco surrendered to authorities on March 19,1946, and the disposition of that case is unknown. (Rocco had insisted that the drugs were for doping horses, although his brother was believed to be addicted. Andrew's wife later committed suicide with a gun, and Andrew himself ended up, in May of 1958, falling asleep at the table and choking to death on, ironically, an Italian sausage). Another of Rocco's brothers, Anthony, served as a Chicago police lieutenant until a 1959 vacation trip to Europe with Tony Accardo led to his suspension. This scandal also brought unwanted publicity to Rocco, whose undertaking license was revoked on the basis of "poor moral character" and "hoodlum connections."

In his later years DeGrazia dropped in stature, becoming a minor henchman of Sam Battaglia. His sole remaining holding was his lavish gambling club, the Casa Madrid at 171 North Twenty-fifth Street in Melrose Park, which doubled as his residence. On September 23, 1961, Rocco was arrested at the Casa Madrid, and safes were seized, but the disposition of the case is unknown. The club was later closed, but Syndicate bosses continued to meet in the basement as late as 1969. DeGrazia's wife Margaret died in 1975 and he faded into obscurity afterward, dying largely unnoticed of natural causes in Melrose Park on December 17, 1978.

Denning, Maurice "Blondie" or "Bubbles" [1907–?) Born near Houghton, Iowa, March 21, 1907. Co-leader, with Tom Limerick, of the Limerick-Denning Gang. One of the last of the major Depression bank robbers and the only one completely unaccounted for. Minor criminal record (two arrests for possessing stolen license plates and bootlegging) until May 23, 1934, when Denning and two other men committed the robbery and torture-murder of elderly farmer George Church at his home near Tabor, Iowa; Denning torched Church's feet, and the old man died from the burns. Denning later participated, with Limerick and others, in the robbery of a National Guard armory in Windom, Minnesota, escaped a police raid on the gang's hideout in a Nebraska ghost town, and was suspected of involvement in thirteen Midwest bank robberies before disappearing forever with his beautiful mistress, Evelyn Bert. The other gang members were captured in time, and Limerick eventually was killed in an attempted escape from Alcatraz. Denning and Bert were never heard from again. Despite rumors that he successfully fled the country, the most common and perhaps most likely theory is that Denning and Evelyn Bert were murdered by their underworld associates. Denning would be largely forgotten today, however, if not for the book *Rap Sheet*, a mostly fictional autobiography by a small-time criminal named "Blackie" Audett, who claimed to have witnessed the Kansas City Massacre and named Denning and "Solly" Weissman as two of the actual gunmen. Unfortunately for the story, Audett was in prison at the time, Weissman had been dead for more than two years, and Denning had nothing to do with it.

WANTED

JOHN HERBERT DILLINGER

On June 25, 1934, HOMER S. CUMMINGS, Attorney General of the United States, under the authority vested in him by an Act of Congress approved June 6, 1934, offered a reward of

$10,000.00

for the capture of John Herbert Dillinger or a reward of

$5,000.00

for information leading to the arrest of John Herbert Dillinger.

Age, 32 years; Height, 5 feet 7-1/8 inches; Weight, 153 pounds; Build, medium; Hair, medium chestnut; Eyes, grey; Complexion, medium; Occupation, machinist; Marks and scars, 1/2 inch scar back left hand, scar middle upper lip, brown mole between eyebrows.

All claims to any of the aforesaid rewards and all questions and disputes that may arise as among claimants to the foregoing rewards shall be passed upon by the Attorney General and his decisions shall be final and conclusive. The right is reserved to divide and allocate portions of any of said rewards as between several claimants. No part of the aforesaid rewards shall be paid to any official or employee of the Department of Justice.

If you are in possession of any information concerning the whereabouts of John Herbert Dillinger, communicate immediately by telephone or telegraph collect to the nearest office of the Division of Investigation, United States Department of Justice, the local addresses of which are set forth on the reverse side of this notice.

JOHN EDGAR HOOVER, DIRECTOR,
DIVISION OF INVESTIGATION,
UNITED STATES DEPARTMENT OF JUSTICE,
WASHINGTON, D. C.

June 25, 1934

WILLIAM BALSAMO

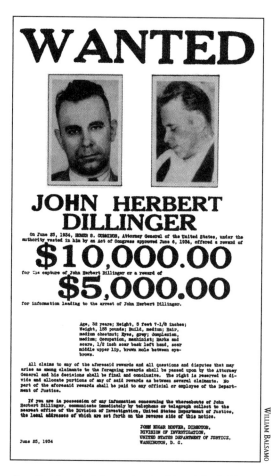

Despite his notoriety as a bank robber, John Dillinger did not become a federal fugitive—with a $10,000 price on his head—until he drove a stolen car across state lines after his "wooden pistol" escape from the Lake County Jail in Crown Point, Indiana.

Dillinger, John Herbert [1903–1934] Born in Indianapolis, Indiana, June 22, 1903, the son of John Wilson and Mollie Dillinger. Most notorious, as well as glamorous, of all the Depression outlaws and the only one, besides "Pretty Boy" Floyd, to acquire some of the folk hero status enjoyed by Jesse James. Released from the state prison at Michigan City, Indiana, in May 1933, Dillinger's criminal career lasted only fourteen months but captured the public's imagination, and his exploits did much to popularize, and embarrass, the FBI. He robbed at least a dozen banks, was blamed for dozens more, raided police stations for guns, shot his way out of police and FBI traps, was twice captured and escaped. His use of a wooden pistol to bluff his way out of the supposedly escape-proof jail in Crown Point, Indiana, stealing the female sheriff's car in the process, guaranteed him a permanent place in American criminal history—even if the escape was facilitated with bribes, according to later revelations. He was set up by a former Indiana madam named Anna Sage, "the woman in red" (actually dark orange, she later complained), who expected to collect the reward money and avoid deportation on morals charges. New evidence indicates that Dillinger and Sage (nee Ana Cumpanas) had mutual acquaintances in the Northern Indiana criminal community and that her friends in the East Chicago Police Department, who contacted the FBI, insisted on participating in the ambush to make sure Dillinger was killed so he wouldn't learn of his betrayal and expose their corruption. He was shot from behind on the night of July 22, 1934, as he left Chicago's Biograph Theatre on Lincoln Avenue in the company of Sage and his then-girlfriend Polly Hamilton, after watching the Clark Gable gangster movie *Manhattan Melodrama*.

Doll, Edward (aka Eddie LaRue, Ed Foley, "Burlington Eddie") [1902–1967] Born in Chicago, January 20, 1902, the son of Edward and Emma Doll, orphaned by age fifteen. Served brief term in Illinois reformatory and later enlisted in Marines where he was convicted of sodomy in 1920 and escaped while en route from Parris Island to a Naval prison in New Hampshire. Despite the somewhat shoddy beginning, Doll, or LaRue as he also was commonly known, became associated with Chicago bootleg gangs, committed bank robberies and burglaries with the likes of Eddie Bentz and Avery Simons, and, according to J. Edgar Hoover, developed an impressive criminal resume as "bank robber, holdup man, member of an automobile theft ring, and a reputed 'spot killer' for some of Chicago's most desperate gangsters of the period." For a time he was a

"How Al Capone Would Run This Country"

After the St. Valentine's Day Massacre and the Atlantic City mob conference that prescribed his Pennsylvania prison sabbatical, Al Capone found himself declared Public Enemy No. 1, pictured on the cover of *Time*, vilified by the country's editorial cartoonists, and facing prosecution on federal tax charges.

Capone finally was a household name, and *Liberty* magazine found itself so titillated by "the Master Gangster of America" that it assigned an equally prominent writer of the day, Cornelius Vanderbilt Jr., to interview Capone in his fourth-floor office at Chicago's Lexington Hotel. The article concluded with Vanderbilt's picture and a deposition affirming that America's master gangster had indeed been interviewed, as though he was in hiding. Readers could ignore the magazine's and Vanderbilt's obligation to disparage "The Big Fellow" for his "impudence" in presuming "How Al Capone Would Run This Country."

Once he became Public Enemy No. 1, Al Capone was personally interviewed for Liberty *magazine by Cornelius Vanderbilt Jr., a nationally prominent writer of the day who found himself awed by Capone's manner and personality.*

In the prologue to the interview, Vanderbilt noted that police had appealed to Capone, an adamant opponent of the "snatch racket," to resolve a kidnapping, which he did, with no ransom paid. Later, Vanderbilt lapsed into momentary candor when observing that Capone "did nothing for effect; and I am sure he wasn't trying to show off for my benefit."

The following dispenses with the post-interview moralizing and gives Capone his opportunity to philosophize:

"This is going to be a terrible winter. Us fellas has gotta open our pocketbooks, and keep on keeping them open, if we want any of us to survive. We can't wait for Congress or [President] Hoover or anyone else. We must help keep tummies filled and bodies warm. If we don't, it's all up with the way we've learned to live. Why, do you know, sir, America is on the verge of its greatest social upheaval? Bolshevism is knocking at our gates. We can't afford to let it in. We've got to organize ourselves against it, and put our shoulders together, and hold fast. We need funds to fight famine.

"We must keep America whole, and safe, and unspoiled. If machines are going to take jobs away from the worker, then he will need to find something else to do. Perhaps he'll get back to the soil. But we must care for him during the period of change. We must keep him away from Red literature, Red ruses; we must see that his mind remains healthy. For, regardless of where he was born, he is now an American.

"I guess I'm like you, Mr. Vanderbilt, I get more blame from the crowd for things I never do than praise for the good I do.

"The news gang are forever riding me. Seems as if I'm responsible for every crime that takes place in this country. You'd think I had unlimited power and a swell pocketbook. Well, I guess I got the power all right; but the bank book suffers from these hard times as much as anyone else's.

"My payroll is about as big as it ever was, but the profits have done their share of dwindling. Say, you'd be surprised if you knew some of the fellas I've got to take care of.

"People respect nothing nowadays. Once we put virtue, honor, truth, and the law on a pedestal. Our children were brought up to respect things. The war ended. We have had nearly twelve years to straighten ourselves out, and look what a mess we've made of life!

"War legislators passed the Eighteenth Amendment. Today more people drink alcohol from speakeasies than passed through all the doors of all the saloons in America in five years before 1917. That's their answer to law respect. Yet most of those people are not bad. You don't classify them as criminals, though technically they are.

"The mass feeling that Prohibition is responsible for a lot of our ills is growing. But the number of law-breakers is increasing, too. Sixteen years ago I came to Chicago with forty dollars in my pocket. Three years afterward I was married. My son is now twelve. I am still married and love my wife dearly. We had to make a living. I was younger then than I am now, and I thought I needed more. I didn't believe in prohibiting people from getting the things they wanted. I thought prohibition an unjust law, and I still do.

"Somehow I just naturally drifted into the racket. And I guess I'm here to stay until the law is repealed. . . . And when it is, I'd be out of luck if I hadn't arranged to do business elsewhere. You see, Mr. Vanderbilt, prohibition forms less than 35 percent of my income.

"I believe Mr. Hoover may make the text of his December message to Congress a suggestion that the nation's legislators raise the percentage of the alcoholic content of liquor. That will be his best card for renomination.. Besides, you know he has always called the Volstead Act a 'noble experiment.'

"In time, though, people won't tolerate even that. They'll demand a return to normal drinking; and if they exercise enough pressure they'll beat the Anti-Saloon League and the industrialists who have waxed fat and wealthy at the expense of thirst.

"The law will be repealed. There will be no further need of secrecy. I will be spared an enormous payroll. But as long as the act remains in effect, and there are people left who will continue to break the law, then there must be positions for persons such as I, who find it devolves upon us to keep the channel open.

"People who respect nothing dread fear. It is upon fear, therefore, that I have built up my organization. But understand me correctly, please. Those who work with me are afraid of nothing. Those who work for me are kept faithful, not so much because of their pay as because they know what might be done with them if they broke faith.

"The United States government shakes a very wobbly stick at the lawbreaker and tells him he'll go to prison if he beats the law. Lawbreakers laugh and get good lawyers. A few of the less well-to-do take the rap. But the public generally isn't any more afraid of a government prison sentence than I am of [State's Attorney] Pat Roche.

As the "Babe Ruth of American Gangsters," Al Capone made the cover of Time *magazine, which was immediately denounced for glorifying a criminal.*

"Things people know about amuse them. They like to laugh over them and make jokes. When a speakeasy is raided, there are a few hysterical people, but the general mass are lighthearted. On the other hand, do you know of any of your friends who'd go into fits of merriment if they feared being taken for a ride?

"The Democrats will be swept in on a record vote. The masses will think they'll get relief from the Depression that way. I know very little about world finance; but I don't think the end of the Depression is going to come like that. I think it will take longer. A series of circumstances will bring about a relief, if we don't let the Reds try to bring it about before. Roosevelt's a good fellow, but I'm afraid his health is pretty shaky, and a leader needs health.

"The world has been capitalized on paper. Every time a fellow had a new idea, they'd increase the capital stock—give themselves so much cash and their stockholders so much paper. The rich got richer; the stockholders speculated with the paper. Someone found out it paid to keep a rumor factory going. Someone else interested women in gambling on the big board. The world was wild. Amalgamations took place. The more clever a fellow was with turning paper recapitalizations into cash, the greater became his vice-presidential titles. Young men who ought, many of them, to be resting behind the bars of penitentiaries for stealing paper rose overnight in the world of prosperity. Our entire prospectus of living turned topsy-turvy.

"Crooked bankers who take people's hard-earned cash for stock they know is worthless would be far better clients at penal institutions than the poor little man who robs so that his wife and babies may live. Why, down in Florida, the year I lived there, a shady newspaper publisher's friend was running a bank. He had unloaded a lot of worthless securities upon unsuspecting people. One day his bank went Hooey. I was just thanking the powers that be that he'd got what was coming to him when I learned of another business trick that would make safe-cracking look like miniature golf. The crooked publisher and the banker were urging bankrupt depositors who were being paid thirty cents on the dollar to put their money in another friend's bank. Many did so; and just about sixty days later that bank collapsed like a house of cards, too.

"Do you think those bankers went to jail? No, sir. They're among Florida's most representative citizens. They're just as bad as the crooked politicians. I ought to know about them. I've been feeding and clothing them long enough. I never knew until I got into this racket how many crooks there were dressed in expensive clothes and talking with affected accents.

"Why, when I was held the other day for evasion of federal taxes I nearly got myself into a fine pickle. Certain officials wished to make a bargain with me. If I'd plead guilty and go to jail for two and a half years they'd dismiss the charges they had against me. A pretty penny had to be paid, but I thought that that was better than the strain of a long-winded trial. A day or so before the bargain was to be struck, though, I learned that someone was going to go to the Appellate Court, and that there'd be a fly in the ointment, and they'd have me in Leavenworth for ten and a half years. So I decided I could be just as foxy, and we entered a plea of not guilty, and when the case comes up we'll see what we will see.

"A little while ago in one of the Chicago newspapers it said that a local millionaire manufacturer had been found to be some fifty-five thousand dollars in arrears with his personal-property tax. A day later it was printed that this had been printed in error, and that the situation had been satisfactorily cleaned up.

"If Mr. Hoover's government wants me to explain my federal taxes I shall be very glad to do so. I think I could enlighten him and several other officials a considerable bit, and any time they need any sensational matters to talk about I shall have them ready to give out.

"Graft is a byword in American life today. It is law where no other law is obeyed. It is undermining this country. The honest lawmakers of any city can be counted on your fingers. I could count Chicago's on one hand.

"Virtue, honor, truth, and the law have all vanished from our life. We are smart-alecky. We like to be able to get away with things. And if we can't make a living at some honest profession, we're going to make one anyway.

"The home is our most important ally. The stronger we can keep our home lives, the stronger we can keep our nation.

"When enemies approach our shores we defend them. When enemies come into our homes we beat them off. Homebreakers [home invaders] should be undressed and tarred and feathered, as examples to the rest of their kind. . . .

"Last winter I fed about three hundred and fifty thousand persons a day here in Chicago. This winter it's going to be worse. I think we both speak the same language; and I think we're both patriots. We don't want to see them tear down the foundations of this great land. We've got to battle to keep free. Good luck. I'm glad I met you."

A recent Supreme Court ruling had held that even illegal income was taxable; the government refused Capone's offer to plead guilty and pay up with penalties; and he was sentenced to eleven years instead of the one-to-three usually handed down. During a mock trial in Chicago arranged by the American Bar Association in 1990, Capone was posthumously acquitted.

member of the College Kidnappers, headed by "Handsome Jack" Klutas, with whom he was wanted for the 1931 kidnapping of Blue Island gambler James Hackett; and he was associated with other Chicago mobsters, including Gus Winkeler and the Touhy gang. Rarely arrested, his surplus of aliases left some confusion as to his identity. He was most commonly identified as either Doll or LaRue. Known to have participated in the million-dollar bank robbery at Lincoln, Nebraska, in 1930 with Eddie Bentz and others, but also joined George "Machine Gun" Kelly in 1932 in a Mississippi bank robbery and the flaky kidnapping of South Bend businessman Howard Woolverton, who had to be released when unable to pay the ransom.

Doll's talent as a con man shined when he married a respectable girl named Doris Crane, telling her he was a wealthy cattleman from Texas. They lived together in domestic bliss for a couple of years, moving around the country under different names as Doll explained to his wife that he wasn't really a rancher at all but a "private investigator" on the trail of criminals, later modifying this to say he'd been hired by the government as a federal narcotics agent. Doll apparently had a genuine love for Doris, and the strain of his double life prompted him to eventually "retire" to a Florida chicken farm. The lies came tumbling down when Doll and his still-naive wife were arrested by federal agents in St. Petersburg, Florida, on February 14, 1934. Suddenly conscience-stricken, Doll gave a long confession to the FBI exonerating his wife. Sentenced to ten years for violation of the National Motor Vehicle Theft Act, he wound up on Alcatraz and, upon release, faced detainers from Massachusetts and Nebraska on bank robbery and other charges. Faded into obscurity after final release and died in Las Vegas in February 1967.

Drucci, Vincent "The Schemer" (true name: Ludovico di Ambrosia) [1901–1927] Born in Chicago, April 28, 1901, the son of John and Rose di Ambrosia. Succeeded Dean O'Banion and "Hymie" Weiss as leader of Chicago's North Side Gang. World War I Navy veteran who began his crime career robbing pay telephone boxes. Known as "The Schemer" allegedly for his wild and bizarre plots for robbing banks and kidnapping millionaires but supposedly also entertained grandiose schemes of assassinating those in power and eventually becoming president. Appeared in a porno film, *Bob's Hot Story*, filmed in Chicago in the early twenties. Shot during a police raid on his office, but recovered and refused to press charges. Killed April 4, 1927, in the back seat of a police car en route to headquarters for questioning, by another policeman who claimed Drucci had tried to disarm him.

Druggan, Terence J. (Terry) [d. 1954], and Lake, Frank (Frankie) [d. 1947] Graduates of the West Side Valley Gang who began their partnership as juvenile thieves stealing packages from delivery trucks but emerged as Chicago's first millionaire beer barons, thanks to an early partnership with brewing magnate Joseph Stenson, from whom they acquired five breweries. Druggan and Lake also had the good sense to later cut Johnny Torrio and Al Capone in as partners. Seemingly inseparable, they dressed in near-matching suits and fedoras. Both wore horn-rimmed glasses and were sometimes called the Damon and Pythias or Mutt and Jeff of the underworld, an image heightened by their bizarre antics, such as getting arrested for petty crimes long after attaining wealth. One legend has it that Druggan, while hijacking a beer truck near a church, ordered two Jewish gangsters to remove their hats while passing "the house of God" or he'd shoot them off. Despite the scope of their operation, Druggan and Lake seem never to have expanded beyond their home territory in "the Valley," with the exception of acquiring the original Little Bohemia Restaurant from Emil Wanatka (who years later would host the Dillinger Gang at his northern Wisconsin resort, also called Little Bohemia).

Though considerably less violent than their competitors, Druggan and Lake are sometimes accused of the 1921 slaying of "Big Steve" Wisniewski, often erroneously reported as the first "one-way ride" victim (a crime also attributed in various accounts to either "Hymie" Weiss or Frank McErlane). In 1924, they were convicted of contempt of court for continuing to operate a brewery despite a federal injunction and sentenced to a year in jail. Scandal arose when a *Chicago American* reporter telephoned the jail to interview the pair and was informed that both were "out." While ostensibly serving their sentences, Druggan and Lake were actually coming and going as they pleased, leaving the jail in chauffeur-driven limousines to meet their wives, dine out, shop, golf, and whatever. Cook County Sheriff Peter Hoffman and Warden Wesley Westbrook were fined and sentenced to short jail terms of their own for these cozy infractions. Indicted for income tax evasion in 1928, Druggan and Lake pled guilty the following year but managed to delay imprisonment until 1932, when they were sentenced to two and a half years and eighteen months, respectively. Apparently out of touch with Capone's successors, the once brotherly pair were never able to regain their prominence after their release and reportedly split up after quarreling at a party. Lake moved to Detroit and invested his wealth in a coal and ice company, gaining respectability before dying of natural causes in his fifties on January 11, 1947. Druggan, plagued with health problems, died in poverty on May 4, 1954.

Duree, Jefferson Davis (Jeff) [1893–1961] Born in Bartlesville, Oklahoma, July 22, 1893, the son of Miles and Margaret Duree. A prolific robber and burglar whose career spanned the 1920s to 1950s and who claimed kinship to the James boys, Duree was known as the "Ghost Bandit" or "Phantom Bandit." Convicted of horse theft in 1913, he served a short sentence in the state reformatory at Granite, Oklahoma. Later bought a pool hall in Daugherty, Oklahoma, which served as headquarters for a burglary gang. Convicted of an Edmond, Oklahoma, train robbery in 1921, Duree appealed and was freed on $10,000 bond a year later. With a gang including brother Charlie (killed in 1924), Ray Terrill, Roland Williams, and Harry Campbell, committed a series of bank heists in Oklahoma and Kansas. The usual technique involved breaking into a bank at night, winching out the safe onto a truck, and driving away to crack it at the gang's leisure. This was Duree's innovation though credited to Terrill. Disappearing after his brother's death, Duree was captured in May 1925 at his chicken ranch near Phoenix, Arizona. He was returned to Leavenworth to complete his twenty-five-year sentence for mail robbery while his gang continued robbing with other partners, including the Barker brothers. Transferred to the federal prison at Atlanta in 1930 and paroled in 1939, Duree found work with the Oklahoma highway department but it didn't last long and he was convicted of robbing a post office at Copan, Oklahoma, in 1940, which earned him a five-year sentence in Leavenworth. Released in 1944, he again returned to crime. Duree was wounded and captured by Tulsa police in July 1958 after breaking into a supermarket. Released on bond, he robbed a bank in Peru, Kansas, and became a federal fugitive. Captured by the FBI weeks later at a ski resort near Denver, Duree was subsequently convicted of bank robbery and sentenced to life in the state prison at Lansing, Kansas, where he died on June 27, 1961.

Durkin, Martin James (Marty) [1901–1981] Born in Chicago, April 29, 1901. Marty Durkin committed many minor crimes before going into car theft in a big way. He burglarized car dealerships, stole expensive autos (usually Pierce-Arrows, Cadillacs, or Packards), and sold them in other states. Durkin shot it out with police when necessary, wounding three officers in Chicago and one in California. On October 11, 1925, in a garage at 6237 Princeton Avenue, he shot and killed federal agent Edwin C. Shanahan, then escaped after another shootout in Chicago and was finally captured on January 20, 1926, by federal agents and local detectives on a train coming into St. Louis. Convicted in two Chicago trials of killing Shanahan and of interstate car theft, he received sentences totaling fifty years but avoided the death penalty partly because Shanahan, the first agent of the future FBI to die

Martin Durkin was little more than a prospering car thief until 1925 when he shot and killed Edwin C. Shanahan, the first Department of Justice agent to die in the line of duty.

in the line of duty, had not identified himself. Durkin served the murder sentence at the Statesville prison in Joliet, Illinois, and was transferred to Leavenworth in 1946 on the car theft charge. Released on July 28, 1954. Died in Port Charlotte, Florida, on January 5, 1981.

Esposito, Giuseppi Giachino "Diamond Joe" **[1872–1928]** Born in Acerra, Italy, April 28, 1872, the son of Giachino and Theresa Esposito. Arrived in the U.S. in 1895 and worked as a laborer in Boston and Brooklyn before moving on to Chicago, where he opened a bakery in 1905. Indicted in October 1908 for killing bartender Mac Geaquenta in an argument over a woman, but charges were dropped. Opened a saloon at 1048 West Taylor Street where one Cuomo Coletta was killed in a 1917 shootout with customers. Dabbled in union activities, organizing the International Hod Carriers Building and Construction Laborers Union and becoming their business agent and treasurer. Entered politics in 1920 for Charles Deneen's faction, defeating Thompson candidate Chris Mamer as Republican ward committeeman of the Nineteenth Ward. By then a flamboyant figure adorned with diamond rings, stickpins, and belt buckles, Esposito opened the Bella Napoli Café at 850 South Halsted, celebrated for its cuisine and clientele of politicians and celebrity gangsters. The manager was Anthony "Mops" Volpe, and one of Esposito's waiters was a young murder fugitive from Italy named Felice DeLucia, later known as Paul "The Waiter" Ricca. As political, social, and business leader of Little Italy, Esposito avoided direct involvement in bootlegging but furnished political protection to the Genna gang and also sold much of the sugar used for alky cooking. Killed by shotgun blasts outside his home at 800 South Oakley Boulevard, March 21, 1928, possibly for refusing to step down from a race against Capone-backed Thompson politician Joseph P. Savage. The killing was witnessed by Esposito's eleven-year-old daughter, Jeanette.

Fernekes, Henry J. "Midget" **[1897–1935]** Born in Illinois (according to the FBI), the son of Mr. and Mrs. J. C. Fernekes, on July 27, 1897 and raised in Valparaiso, Indiana. Standing only five feet four, "Midget" Fernekes, a former welder, chemist, and electrician, apparently began his crime career by robbing the First National Bank in Valparaiso on September 19, 1914, seeking funds to marry his sweetheart. Caught in a robbery on the tenth floor of the First National Bank building in Chicago, he was soon identified in a half-dozen other holdups and sent to the state reformatory at Pontiac. His wife divorced him in 1915. Released in 1918, he pulled a $105,000 robbery of the Argo State Bank and was suspected of many others in the following years as he blossomed into one of Chicago's most fearsome bandits. Suspected in 1921 of killing two bank messengers in Pearl River, New York, and two Pennsylvania state policemen. With Dan McGeoghegan and John Flannery, allegedly robbed the Inland Trust & Savings Bank in 1924, killing building and loan treasurer Michael Swiontowski. Captured, Fernekes made at least four escape attempts, once blasting a fifteen-inch hole in a Cook County Jail wall using smuggled explosives. Convicted of murder in 1926 and sentenced to hang, but conviction was later reversed on appeal.

On learning of the machine-gun murder of Assistant State's Attorney William McSwiggin, who had obtained the murder conviction, Fernekes mailed his written condolences to head prosecutor Robert E. Crowe on losing "a brilliant and conscientious member" of his staff and later sent Christmas greetings to the judge who'd sentenced him to death. Sentenced to ten years to life for robbery, "Midget" escaped from prison at Joliet on August 3, 1935, simply walking out in civilian clothes he'd somehow obtained, and returned to Chicago where he was believed to have $60,000 or more hidden away. Trailed from a rented apartment at 2233 West Erie, where he had been posing as a Western Electric employee, Fernekes was arrested on October 28, 1935. The following day Fernekes, who'd boasted he'd never return to Joliet and would rather be handed over to New York to face outstanding murder charges, committed suicide in the Cook County Jail by swallowing cyanide from a vial which he had sewn into his trousers.

Fitzgerald, Charles Joseph (Chuck) "Big Fitz," or "Chi Slim"; with numerous aliases [1877–1945] Born in St. Louis, March 16, 1877. Old-time "yegg" with extremely long arrest record dating to 1898 and extensive Chicago Syndicate connections. By his own admission was involved in at least fifty robberies and burglaries. Robbed banks throughout twenties with Harvey Bailey, Gus Winkeler, Fred "Killer" Burke, "Shotgun" George Ziegler (the alias of Fred Goetz), Eddie Bentz, "Big Homer" Wilson, and others. Participated in $200,000 American Express robbery in Toledo in 1928. Reputed planner of the million-dollar robbery of the Lincoln National Bank & Trust Co. on September 17, 1930. Joined the Barker-Karpis Gang and participated in the kidnapping of William Hamm on June 15, 1933 (Fitzgerald was the middle-aged "businessman type" who shook hands with Hamm and held him off guard for the others to seize). Wounded and partially crippled in a South St. Paul payroll robbery in 1933, Fitzgerald dropped out of sight and retired until captured by the FBI in Los Angeles in April 1936. Pleaded guilty to the Hamm kidnapping and was sentenced to life on Alcatraz. Transferred back to Leavenworth in 1942 and died there on January 9, 1945.

Fleagle, Jacob Henry "Little Jake" (alias William Harrison Holden) [1890–1930] Born near Garden City, Kansas, January 1, 1890, the son of Jacob and Ann Margaret Fleagle, formerly of Iowa. Leader of the notorious Fleagle Gang of bank robbers who committed several large holdups in Midwest and West, but were not identified until the spectacular $200,000 robbery of the First National Bank at Lamar, Colorado, May 23, 1928, which resulted in the murders of four men. Fleagle's brother Ralph and gang members Herbert Royston and George Abshier soon were apprehended for this crime and hanged in Colorado, but Jake evaded capture until shot and mortally wounded by police and postal inspectors while boarding a train at Branson, Missouri, October 14, 1930. He died the next day at Springfield, Missouri. [The FBI later claimed that Fleagle was the first criminal to be identified by means of a single fingerprint; he apparently also inspired Al Capp to create an "Evil Eye Fleegle" in his *Li'l Abner* comic strip.]

Floyd, Charles Arthur "Pretty Boy" [1904–1934] Born Adairsville, Georgia, February 3, 1904, the son of Walter and Mamie Floyd but moved as a child to a farm near Sallisaw on the outskirts of Oklahoma's Cookson Hills. Colorful outlaw regarded as something of a Robin Hood figure in Oklahoma, but elsewhere considered a dangerous career criminal. Accused of ten murders and at least twice as many bank robberies. Convicted of highway robbery in Missouri in 1925 and sentenced to five years in the state prison at Jefferson City. Convicted of bank robbery in Ohio but escaped December 10, 1930, from a train taking him to prison. Accused by the FBI of participating in the Kansas City Massacre of June 17, 1933, also known as the Union Station Massacre. This was an unsuccessful attempt to free captured bank and train robber Frank Nash from police custody at the railroad station in Kansas City. Killed in the shooting were federal agent Raymond Caffrey, an Oklahoma police chief, two Kansas City police detectives and Nash himself. The other attackers were alleged to be Adam Richetti, Floyd's chief crime partner at the time, and Verne Miller, a Kansas City gunman and bank robber associated with Nash. According to bank robber Harvey Bailey, who knew several of the criminals involved, "Pretty Boy" was, in fact, one of the gunmen (a matter still debated by some researchers), along with Verne Miller, but Ricchetti, although captured and executed for the crime, may have been innocent—for the simple reason that a night of excessive drinking had left him too hung over to participate.

While the death of Nash is usually ascribed to bad shooting, or a shot fired accidentally by a federal agent, an unlikely theory persists that he was killed deliberately to prevent him from talking. Floyd was killed by federal agents on a farm near East Liverpool, Ohio, October 22, 1934, while fleeing across a field, according to the official version. Another version, told by former East Liverpool, Ohio, police officer Chester Smith in 1974 was that the wounded and disabled Floyd was simply "executed" by a federal agent on orders from Melvin Purvis when he refused to talk. The last surviving FBI agent in the party declared the story false, as might be expected.

Fresina, Carmelo [1890–1931] Born in Abruzzi, Italy. Leader of an Italian bootlegging and extortion mob in St. Louis and a rival of the Egan's Rats, Hogans, Cuckoos and Green Dagoes. Fresina was shot in the buttocks in 1928 and afterward carried a pillow to sit on. His gang became known as the Pillow Gang. Fresina was found shot to death in Edwardsville, Illinois, on May 7, 1931 and the remnants of his gang were eventually absorbed into what became the Giordano crime family.

Genna Brothers Six brothers from Marsala, Sicily, known as the "Terrible Gennas," whose South Side gang first operated a virtual warehouse in Little Italy with booze going out the back doors while police lined up at another to receive payoffs. They later controlled a large community of alky cookers operating small stills in their homes and apartments. Originally allies of Torrio and Capone, the Gennas became a liability when their territorial disputes with the North Side O'Banion gang led to the murder of O'Banion and open conflict between the North Siders and the Torrio-Capone Syndicate. "Bloody Angelo" Genna was murdered by O'Banion's successors, the Weiss-Drucci-Moran gang, May 25, 1925. Mike "The Devil" Genna was fatally shot by police, who interrupted another gang battle, June 13, 1925. Tony "The Gentleman" Genna was murdered, allegedly by a disgruntled gang member named Giuseppe Nerone, July 8, 1925. The remaining Gennas (Sam, Pete and Jim) all fled Chicago and went into hiding. They eventually returned and attempted a comeback, but Jim died of natural causes November 8, 1931, and the others retired from the rackets. Capone inherited the services of John Scalise and Albert Anselmi, two murderous torpedoes allegedly imported from Sicily by the Gennas. Pete Genna died on May 13, 1948, after a month's illness, and Sam Genna died of a heart attack on December 20, 1951, in Blue Island, Illinois.

Tony Genna

Goetz, Fred (alias "Shotgun George" Ziegler, or Zeigler; also George Goetz, George Siebert) [1897–1934] Born in Chicago, February 14, 1897. Became an army pilot during the World War and attended the University of Illinois.

While working as a lifeguard at Clarendon Beach in 1925 he was arrested for "attempted rape" of a young girl, Jean Lambert, but skipped on the bond posted by his parents. Suspected of robberies and murder, he joined Capone as a hit man and took part in the St. Valentine's Day Massacre, according to both Georgette Winkeler and Byron "Monty" Bolton, who had been one of the Massacre lookouts. (Bolton had carelessly left behind a letter addressed to himself in one of the lookout rooms and years later correctly recalled the false name he had used to buy one of the cars used by the killers.) Later Ziegler (as Goetz) joined the Barker-Karpis Gang and participated in robberies and the Hamm and Bremer kidnappings.

Shot to death in front of 4811 West Twenty-second Street, Cicero, Illinois, on March 21, 1934, probably on orders of Nitti, fearful that he would be arrested and talk. Pocket change included a one-thousand dollar bill, supposedly given him by Reno gamblers as consolation for their refusing to "launder" kidnapping money, and police found no less than six hacksaw blades concealed in his belt. At the time of his death he was moonlighting as a landscape gardener under the alias of George Siebert, had several bank accounts under different names and investments in distillery stocks, and held a membership in a Bensenville country club. (On October 5, 1925, Goetz and one "Hymie" were implicated by accomplice Roger Bessner in the attempted robbery of Dr. Henry R. Gross and murder of the doctor's chauffeur, Barney Hernandez. Goetz also was accused on October 18, 1925, of robbing Mr. and Mrs. Paul Izenstark of 587 Hawthorne Place of $12,000 in money and jewelry and stealing their car. A year later, when "Hymie" Weiss was killed, newspapers were reporting an unlikely speculation that Weiss was Goetz's robbery partner.)

Goodman, John "Kaiser Bill" **(aka White, Hale, Smith, O'Dell, and other aliases) (?–1934]** True name unknown but claimed to have been born in Pennsylvania in the 1850s and known to have served several prison sentences under Goodman and other names. Known as the "Fagin of the Hills," Goodman began his career of crime in the horseback age of banditry, reputedly robbing a train in Kansas in the 1880s and later (by his claim) riding with the Dalton Gang. Operating out of the Cookson Hills of eastern Oklahoma, Goodman, known as "Kaiser Bill" for his handlebar mustache, became a legend to area lawmen and outlaws alike in the World War I era and afterward, an aging phantom who robbed banks by horseback or auto with the likes of Mount Cookson and Ed Lockhart. Last imprisoned for bank robbery in 1924, Goodman was paroled in May 1933 and relaunched his career as an auto bandit working with such Depression outlaws as Wilbur Underhill and Ford Bradshaw. Killed with his partner and a hostage banker in a bloody shootout near Grove, Oklahoma, July 12, 1934, after a bank robbery at Ketchum, Oklahoma.

Guzik, Jake (Jack) "Greasy Thumb" **(sometimes spelled Cusick) [1887–1956]** Born in Russia, the son of Max and Mamie Guzik, and emigrated to U.S. in 1892. Former Colosimo

THE CHICAGO DAILY NEWS

FINAL MARKETS

REVEALS FLOW OF GOLD TO GUZIK

Son Gives Blood to Save Premier Shot by Assassin

TODAY'S RACE RESULTS

AT LATONIA, KY.

AT PIMLICO, MD.

U. S. TAKES HAND IN PLANNING FOR '33 WORLD FAIR

LAMONT SEES FORWARD MARCH RESUMED SOON

PREMIER IS TARGET OF ASSASSIN

WOUNDED AS HE WAITS IN STATION

AIR MAIL LINE OVER ATLANTIC

GAMBLING PROFIT IN CICERO PUT AT $38,000 A MONTH

NEVER SHOWED A LOSS

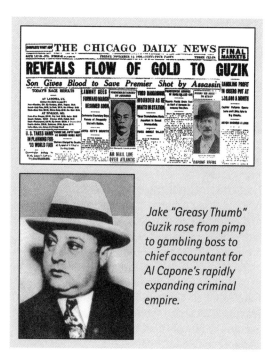

Jake "Greasy Thumb" Guzik rose from pimp to gambling boss to chief accountant for Al Capone's rapidly expanding criminal empire.

pimp (with brothers Harry and Sam) who became gambling boss and chief accountant and treasurer for the Capone Syndicate. Served short sentence for income tax evasion in the early thirties. Reportedly kidnapped by rival mobsters in 1944. Died of natural causes, February 21, 1956. His son Charles was then in prison in Arizona on a morals charge.

Hamilton, Raymond Elzie (Ray) **[1913–1935]** Born near Schulter, Oklahoma, May 21, 1913, the son of John H. and Alice Hamilton. Sometime partner of Clyde Barrow, but also pursued his own career as a noted bank robber and jail-breaker. Captured at Bay City, Michigan, December 5, 1932; convicted of murder and several robberies, and sentenced to 263 years at Eastham Prison Farm near Weldon, Texas. Using guns planted by Bonnie and Clyde, killed a prison guard and escaped from a road gang with Joe Palmer and others on January 16, 1934. Recaptured near Howe, Texas, April 25, 1934. Convicted of murder and sentenced to death along with Joe Palmer, the two again obtained smuggled pistols and managed to escape from the Texas state prison's Death House on July 22, 1934, the same date John Dillinger was killed by federal agents in Chicago. Recaptured at Grapevine, Texas, April 6, 1935, and, with Palmer, executed on May 10.

Hogan, Daniel "Dapper Dan" **[1880–1928]** "Irish Godfather" who ruled St. Paul's underworld in the twenties from his headquarters at the Green Lantern Saloon at 545½ Wabasha. Besides his profitable bootlegging and gambling operations, Hogan, in partnership with the police department, made St. Paul a safe haven for fugitives from around the country, so long as they made regular protection payments and committed no crimes within the city limits. This unique form of crime control, which paradoxically transformed St. Paul into a city largely devoid of street crime while playing host to many of the nation's most infamous criminals, had been devised at the turn of the century by former Police Chief John O'Connor. Hogan extended the welcome mat further by offering his services as a buyer of hot money and securities, handling, among other things, loot from the Denver Mint robbery. Hogan was killed by a car bomb outside his home at 1607 West Seventh Street on December 4, 1928, probably engineered by his successor, Harry "Dutch" Sawyer. Under Sawyer's leadership, visiting criminals remained welcome in St. Paul and the police department was as corrupt and blind to the situation as ever, but the city's "crime-free" existence was soon shattered by robberies, kidnappings, and murders plotted by visiting criminals and sometimes instigated by Sawyer himself.

Hogan, Edward "Jelly Roll" **[1886–1963]** Son of a St. Louis policeman and leader of the Hogan gang who fought Egan's Rats for control of bootlegging in St. Louis in the twenties but led a double life as a Democratic politician. Suspected of ordering the 1921 murder of William Egan. Shot at several times, once supposedly telling police, "I'll identify them, all right. I'll identify them with a shotgun." Outlasting the Rats, Hogan survived Prohibition and prospered as a political leader. First elected to the state legislature in 1916, he served five terms in the state house and four in the state senate, retiring in 1960 after his defeat by Theodore McNeal, the first black man elected as a Missouri state senator. Hogan also worked as a business agent for a bottlers union. Died August 11, 1963, after a long illness.

Holden, Thomas James (Tommy) "Red" **[1895–1953]** Born in Chicago, April 22, 1895. With partner Francis Keating, robbed a U.S. Mail train of $135,000 at Evergreen Park, Illinois, on September 10, 1926. Both were convicted of mail robbery and sentenced to twenty-five years. Received at Leavenworth in 1928, both escaped on February 28, 1930. Over the next two years they committed a series of major bank robberies in the Midwest, usually in partnership with Harvey Bailey, Frank Nash, "Machine Gun" Kelly, Verne Miller, Fred Barker, and Alvin Karpis. Captured with Keating and Bailey at Old Mission Golf Course, Kansas City, Missouri, July 7, 1932.

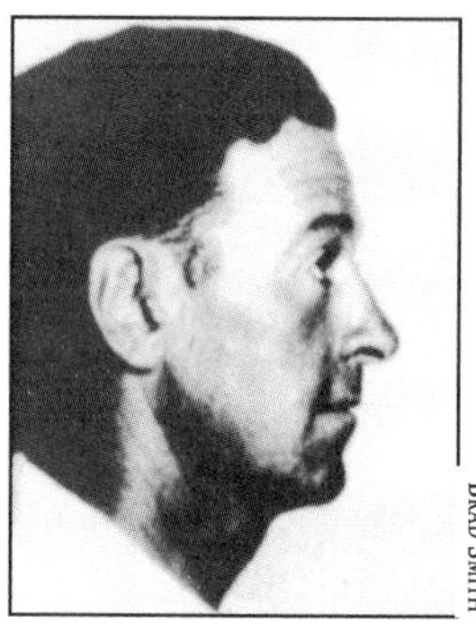
BRAD SMITH

Tommy Holden

Returned to Leavenworth; later transferred to Alcatraz. Paroled, November 28, 1947. Murdered his wife, Lillian, and her two brothers in a drunken quarrel at their Chicago apartment, June 5, 1949, and again became a fugitive. First man named to FBI's "Ten Most Wanted List," March 14, 1950. Captured by FBI at Beaverton, Oregon, June 23, 1951. Convicted of murder and sentenced to life in the Illinois state prison at Joliet, where he died on December 18, 1953.

Humphreys, Murray "The Camel," or "Curley" (true name: Llewelyn Morris Humphreys, sometimes spelled Humpries) [1899–1965] Robber and kidnapper who became a prominent labor racketeer and political fixer for the Capone Syndicate. For years he remained a top-ranking member of the Chicago mob and was sometimes regarded as Capone's successor by police or reporters still unaware of Frank Nitti. Named Chicago's Public Enemy No. 1 in January 1933 and soon after received a brief prison term for income tax evasion. Died of natural causes in Chicago on November 23, 1965.

Hunt, Samuel McPherson "Golf Bag" [1901–1956] Born in Birmingham, Alabama, where he was first arrested for grand larceny in 1919. After several other arrests migrated to Detroit, then Chicago, where he found employment as a gunman for Al Capone. Noted for carrying shotguns in golf bags but once also arrested with guns concealed in a toolbox. Served brief jail terms in the early thirties for gun violations and vagrancy and arrested many times over the years for murder. He avoided serious legal difficulties until July 4, 1942, when he allegedly shot and killed one Michael Wade in a dispute over an auto accident. Hunt was acquitted after four trials. Prospered in bookmaking and numbers after Prohibition and spent much of his time in Florida. Suffered from heart disease in later years and contracted pneumonia in August 1956 while visiting relatives in Schenectady, New York, dying in a hospital there on August 19.

Jawarski, Paul (true name: Paul Poluszynski) [1900–1929] Born in Poland and immigrated to U.S. with parents in 1905, settling first in Butler, Pennsylvania, and later in Hamtramck, Michigan. Ruthless killer and leader of the Detroit-based Flatheads Gang, which committed numerous bank, store, and payroll robberies from Michigan to Pennsylvania in the 1920s. Boasted at the time of his capture of having killed twenty-six men, though his actual total probably was less than a dozen. Jawarski and his gang committed many spectacular and violent robberies but are best remembered for dynamiting an armored car at Coverdale, Pennsylvania, and escaping with a $104,000 payroll of the Pittsburgh Terminal Coal Co. on March 11, 1927. This was probably the nation's first robbery of a professionally armored car. Captured soon afterward, Jawarski was convicted of murder and sentenced to death but, with another inmate, shot his way out of the Allegheny County Jail in Pittsburgh and escaped, fatally wounding a guard. Recaptured in Cleveland, September 13, 1928, after a gun battle in which he killed another policeman. Died in the electric chair at the Rockview state prison at Bellefonte, Pennsylvania, January 21, 1929.

Jones, Ezra Milford [1896–1932] Milford Jones, despite his frail looks and schoolboy face, was a graduate of the Egan's Rats and Cuckoo gangs of St. Louis and was so well connected with politicians and powerful gambling interests that he exceeded the notorious Fred "Killer" Burke in his murdering and other lawbreaking but avoided Burke's notoriety. He worked "snatching" other gangsters for ransom and killing for hire, and between 1913 and 1927 he was arrested some 130 times by St. Louis police for everything from bank robbery to rape, but spent only a few months in prison for a holdup. He had a special animosity for Italian mobsters, murdering many and kidnapping many others in Detroit, where he and Burke moved their "snatch racket." He continued feuding with the Italians until they shot him to death in a Detroit speakeasy on June 15, 1932.

Karpis, Alvin "Old Creepy" or "Ray" (Alcatraz listing, Albin Francis Karpaviecz; Francis Albin, according to FBI; simplified to Karpowicz in his autobiography) [1908–1979] Born Montreal, Canada, August 10, 1908, the son of John and Anna Karpaviecz. Co-leader, with Fred Barker, of the Barker-Karpis Gang. Burglar, bank, mail and train robber. Obtained a total of $300,000 in ransom money from the kidnappings of two wealthy St. Paul businessmen—William A. Hamm Jr. on June 15, 1933, and Edward G. Bremer on January 17, 1934. From 1931 to 1936, Karpis and his partners stole more than a million dollars and killed approximately ten men. Reportedly captured by FBI Director J. Edgar Hoover in New Orleans, May 1, 1936 (Karpis was unarmed and later claimed he was held at gunpoint by many federal agents so Hoover could arrest him personally). Pleaded guilty to Hamm kidnapping and sentenced to life in a federal penitentiary. Spent thirty-three years in prison, mostly on Alcatraz. Paroled, January 14, 1969, and deported to Canada. Moved to Spain in 1973 and died in the town of Torremolinos on August 26, 1979, of an apparently accidental overdose of sleeping pills (to which he may have been addicted) combined with alcohol. Collaborated on two books, *The Alvin Karpis Story* (1971), also published under the title *Public Enemy No. 1*, and *On the Rock* (1980). In the 1960s, his son Raymond attracted newspaper attention when arrested for a string of burglaries. He was gratuitously called "Creepy," son of the "notorious 'Old Creepy.'"

Kaufman, Julian "Potatoes" or "Spuds" [1898–1939] Chicago gambler closely allied with the North Side Gang and at times the West Side Hirschie Miller mob. The son of a millionaire broker, Kaufman owed his underworld nickname to investments in potato stocks. His mother was murdered in a holdup in December 1911 and relatives blame the light sentence received by her youthful killer for Julian's disgust with the justice system, according to crime historian Rose Keefe. Kaufman was questioned with Dean O'Banion in 1924 for the killing of former Philadelphia gangster John Duffy. He was a partner of "Bugs" Moran in the posh Sheridan Wave gambling club at 621 Waveland Avenue, which was closed by police after the St. Valentine's Day Massacre. The North Siders' attempt to reopen the club the following year may have resulted in the murder of *Chicago Tribune* crime reporter Alfred "Jake" Lingle, who demanded 50 percent of the club's take in exchange for interceding with the police. Following Lingle's murder on June 9, 1930, Kaufman fled Chicago and was active in gambling with Meyer Lansky and Vincent "Jimmy Blue Eyes" Alo in New York and in Hallandale, Florida, where they refurbished a tomato packing shed into the Plantation casino. Died of a heart attack on May 31, 1939.

Keating, Francis "Jimmy" [1899–1978] Chicago train and bank robber in 1920s and longtime partner of Thomas Holden. Sent to Leavenworth in 1928 for an Evergreen Park, Illinois, train robbery but escaped with Holden on February 28, 1930, using trusty passes allegedly forged by bootlegger George Kelly (later known as "Machine Gun" Kelly), who worked in the prison's photocopy shop. Robbed banks with Harvey Bailey, Frank Nash, Verne Miller, Alvin Karpis, Fred Barker, and others in early 1930s, in a loose combine usually known as the Holden-Keating Gang, though Bailey was probably the actual leader (this group later evolved into the Barker-Karpis Gang). Basically freelance, Keating and Holden worked with no gang on a permanent basis but were inseparable partners. They also were a study in contrast, with Keating regarded as rarely violent and Holden as somewhat unstable. Captured with Bailey while playing golf in Kansas City in July 1932, Keating and Holden were returned to Leavenworth to complete their twenty-five-year sentences for mail robbery and later transferred to Alcatraz. After his parole, Keating reformed and lived peacefully in the Twin Cities, dying of natural causes in a St. Louis Park, Minnesota, nursing home on July 25, 1978.

Kelly, George "Machine Gun" **(true name: George F. Barnes Jr.) [1900–1954]** Born in Chicago, July 17, 1900 (not July 18, 1895, as often reported), the son of George and Elizabeth Kelly Barnes. Moved at an early age to Memphis, Tennessee, and later attended the University of Mississippi. Despite a good family background, Kelly dabbled in bootlegging and was arrested for Prohibition violations and smuggling liquor onto an Indian reservation. He later committed several bank robberies without attracting much attention and might have remained an obscure, small-time criminal but for a weakness for "wilder" kinds of women. A particularly attractive one named Kathryn Thorne became his wife and introduced him to friends with criminal records and inclinations. With them he participated in a sensational $200,000 kidnapping of Oklahoma City oilman Charles F. Urschel on July 22, 1933. The FBI quickly captured all the gang members but the Kellys, whose reputations grew—or were deliberately exaggerated by the Justice Department—far out of proportion to their dangerousness or criminal histories.

Newspapers had not given Kelly his memorable nickname "Machine Gun" until such a weapon was captured at the ranch where Urschel was held and traced to a pawnshop whose owner identified the purchaser as Kathryn Kelly. The two were captured without incident by police and FBI agents in Memphis, Tennessee, September 26, 1933 (the same day ten inmates escaped from the Indiana's state prison at Michigan City using guns supplied by John Dillinger), and it became official FBI legend that Kelly coined the bureau's enduring nickname when, confronted by federal agents, he cried, "Don't shoot, G-men!" Though the line doesn't appear in contemporary news accounts and apparently went unnoticed by the Memphis policemen present, the story may be partly true. William A. Rorer, the leading FBI agent interviewed by telephone immediately after the capture, reported that Kathryn used the term "G-men" and later told his son Davis that Kelly did indeed utter the immortal words. "G-men" actually had been a popular slang term for all federal agents since at least the 1920s. Convicted on October 12, 1933, the Kellys received a life sentence. Kathryn went to the federal women's prison at Milan, Michigan, and George was transferred from Leavenworth to Alcatraz in September 1934. He was returned to Leavenworth in 1951 and died there of a heart attack on July 18, 1954. Kathryn Kelly was freed on bond, pending appeal, in 1958. She was never retried because the FBI refused to release records on the case, which included a 1933 handwriting expert's report disputing Kathryn's alleged authorship of ransom notes. She died under another name in Oklahoma in 1984.

Kimes, Matthew (Matt) **[1905–1945]** Born February 12, 1905. With brother George led one of the major southwestern outlaw gangs of the late twenties, often linked publicly with bank burglar Ray Terrill, though little evidence exists of any such association. After robbing two banks at Covington, Oklahoma, and murdering Deputy Perry Chuculate at Sallisaw, Oklahoma, Matt and George Kimes were captured near Rudy, Arkansas, on August 28, 1926. Convicted of murder at Sallisaw and sentenced to thirty-five years. George went to prison, but Matt appealed and stayed in the Sallisaw jail long enough to be rescued, November 21, 1926 (probably by relatives, though Ray Terrill and others were suspected). After another series of crimes, including another double bank robbery and the murder of Marshal J. N. McAnally, he was recaptured while marveling at the Grand Canyon in Arizona, June 24, 1927. Retried for the Chuculate slaying and received a sentence of death that later was reduced to life imprisonment. Received another life sentence for the McAnally murder at Beggs, Oklahoma. Granted a leave of absence in 1945, he allegedly robbed a bank at Morton, Texas, only to be run over by a truck at North Little Rock, Arkansas, on December 1, 1945. Died two weeks later in a Little Rock hospital. George Kimes, serving a fifty-year sentence for bank robbery, escaped from the Oklahoma state prison at McAlester on July 2, 1948, but was recaptured at Burns, Oregon, on June 6, 1949. George was paroled on May 25, 1958, and lived respectably until his death at Carmichael, California, on January 3, 1970.]

Klutas, John "Handsome Jack" (true name often wrongly given as Theodore; known to friends as "Ted") [1900–1934] Born in Lyndon, Illinois, November 28, 1900, the son of William and Ida Klutas. Former University of Illinois student and onetime Capone gangster. In 1930s led the College Kidnappers, a Chicago-area gang that specialized in kidnapping underworld figures for ransom. Betrayed by a member of his gang and killed by police at Bellwood, Illinois, January 6, 1934.

Lake, Frank See **Druggan, Terence.**

Lamm, Hermann K. "Baron" (true name: probably Thomas Bell; aka Herman Madsden) [1890?–1930] More commonly known in his day as Tom Bell who, as "Baron" Lamm, supposedly was a former Prussian army officer who had emigrated to the U.S., where he improved on the craft of bank robbery through precise military-style planning. Much of this background, reported but undocumented by John Toland in *The Dillinger Days* and copied by subsequent writers, remains unverified. The Utah state prison, where Lamm supposedly served a short term for bank robbery, has no record of him by either Lamm or any of his known aliases. He did successfully rob banks across the country in the twenties, but the strategic tactics he employed did not differ greatly from the methods of Harvey Bailey, Eddie Bentz, or many contemporary big-time bandits. Killed by a posse near Sidell, Illinois, December 16, 1930, after a robbery at Clinton, Indiana. Two survivors of Lamm's gang, Walter Detrich and James "Oklahoma Jack" Clark, were later associated with John Dillinger, who adopted Lamm's system of carefully casing banks well in advance of a robbery and planning escape routes using detailed notes and practice runs.

Lazia, John [1897–1934] Born John Lazzio. Boss of North Side Italian mob in Kansas City and politically affiliated with Tom Pendergast's Democratic machine. The city assumed jurisdiction over the police department, previously controlled by the state, in 1932, and Pendergast virtually handed the department to Lazia, who hired seventy ex-convicts as officers. Probably furnished the machine guns used in the Kansas City Massacre. Killed outside the Park Central Hotel at 300 East Boulevard on July 10, 1934, by a machine gun that ballistics tests indicated had been used in the Kansas City bloodbath.

Levin, Hyman "Hymie" or "Loud Mouth" (aka "Hymie" Levine) [1896–1951] Loop bookmaker, bootlegger, and Capone's collector of protection payments from independent operators. Like many gangsters, Levin enlisted in the Army during World War I. Had a minor criminal record during Prohibition but did serve a year in Chicago's Bridewell [as the city jail was called,

NOBODY'S PERFECT

By the middle of 1928 Al Capone virtually ruled the city of Chicago, and the mistakes he made could be counted on one hand, or maybe two or three, if one includes his early bust for slots and brothels, the (alleged) shooting of Joe Howard, his downtown car accident that led to an arrest, the unintentional killing of Assistant State's Attorney McSwiggin, and the future St. Valentine's Day Massacre.

Two lesser blunders also were self-inflicted, and they made only short human-interest stories at the time.

One was the Saturday in September 1928 when he accidentally shot himself while playing golf. After a pleasant outing with Johnny Patton, "the Boy Mayor of Burnham," Capone was squeezing his sizeable self into a car with other golfing partners when an automatic pistol in his back pocket went off. The bullet streaked down one leg and lodged in the other. Much commotion ensued, and Capone was rushed to St. Margaret's Hospital in Hammond, Indiana. He was admitted under the assumed name of Geary, and his entourage occupied five rooms, with no weapons showing.

The wounds were not too serious, and after a few days he was released, the gunshot conveniently unreported. It made almost half a column on the front page of the *Chicago Tribune*, which did not get wind of the story for almost a week. Many years later it was the subject of an article by his caddy in *Sports Illustrated.*

On another occasion Capone learned that taverns in Oklahoma were entertaining their patrons with turtle racing. He thought that such a "sport" might be introduced in Chicago, with the crowd betting on and rooting for their particular turtle, its shell painted a garish color and numbered like a race horse without a jockey. He dispatched his men to Ponca City where they purchased some 5,000 turtles from a local breeder without bothering to learn the secret of racing turtles—that the area under the starting gate and the "turf" had to be uncomfortably warm to inspire the creatures to compete. In Chicago, tracks were built but the turtles refused to perform. They either holed up in their shells and remained motionless, or wandered along their assigned tracks aimlessly.

A sorely disappointed Capone, stuck with 5,000 turtles, ordered them released into Chicagoland's many ponds and lagoons. Given the life span of turtles, it's possible that some of the older ones harvested by any dedicated turtle-collectors might well be "Capone originals."

after a notorious old prison in London] for liquor violations. Arrested in 1931 on a vagrancy warrant from Judge John H. Lyle, but granted a change of venue. Of Levin's nickname, District Attorney Frank Mast said, "I think they call him 'Loud Mouth' because he squawks so loudly when arrested." Named in a Chicago police gang list turned over to the FBI in 1930s as "acting leader" of the Capone mob while Capone and Frank Nitti served their sentences for income tax evasion (if true, this alone would negate the FBI's description of the Outfit as a "Cosa Nostra" family, which couldn't be led by a Jew). Charged with income tax evasion in 1934, Levin pleaded guilty and was sentenced to eighteen months in Leavenworth. With Jake Guzik, Tony Accardo, Murray Humphreys, and others, led the Outfit's takeover of the race-wire business in the mid-forties, resulting in the murder of their major competitor, James M. Ragen. Paralyzed by a stroke, Levin spent his final years confined to his apartment at 215

East Chestnut Street but continued to operate his wire service, the R&H Publishing Co. at 177 North State Street, issuing his orders in writing after he lost control of his voice. Levin died at St. Luke's Hospital on June 19, 1951, a week after checking in under the alias of Charles Morton. He reportedly hated lavish gangland funerals and left instructions that his remains be cremated.

Licavoli Brothers Accompanied by various cousins and in-laws, St. Louis-born Peter Joseph Licavoli and his younger brother Thomas "Yonnie" Licavoli moved to Detroit in the mid-twenties and established the River Gang, which grew into a major rumrunning combine while other Italian factions fought each other and the Jewish Purple Gang fell apart from the competition, legal pressure, and internal dissent. As the Purples self-destructed, thinned by murders and imprisonments, the Licavolis fled town when suspected of the murder of crusading radio reporter Gerald Buckley in 1930, prospering in Ohio and forging an alliance with Moe Dalitz's powerful Cleveland syndicate. Peter returned when the heat died down and merged with other Italian factions, notably the intermarried Zerilli-Tocco clan, to form the modern Detroit crime family, which they ruled into the 1960s.

"Yonnie" Licavoli's attempted takeover of the Toledo underworld was thwarted by his conviction for the 1933 murder of bootlegger Jackie Kennedy, resulting in a life sentence. Despite the best efforts of his relatives, who claimed they had raised a $250,000 fund to free him and donated $5,000 to Drew Pearson's J. Edgar Hoover Foundation to fight juvenile delinquency, "Yonnie" remained behind bars until paroled in 1972. He died of a heart attack in Gahanna, Ohio, on September 9, 1973. Peter Licavoli eventually "retired" to Tucson, Arizona, where he served a short jail sentence in the early 1980s for receiving stolen artwork, dying not long afterward on January 11, 1984. ["Yonnie" and Peter Licavoli sometimes are confused with their St. Louis cousins who also moved north: Peter "Horseface" Licavoli who died in the Marquette, Michigan, state prison in 1953 after serving thirty-three years for the murder of a rival Detroit bootlegger, and James "Blackie" Licavoli who in later years became boss of the Cleveland crime family.]

Limerick, Thomas Robert (Tom) [1902–1938] Born in Council Bluffs, Iowa, January 7, 1902. Justified his criminal career by claiming that police had murdered his father so he needed to "even the score." Served early prison sentences in Iowa and Nebraska for grand larceny, car theft, and parole violation. In 1934 joined the Midwest bank robbery gang led by Billy Pabst. When Pabst was captured, Limerick and Maurice Denning reportedly took over leadership of the gang and after a succession of robberies—and the deaths of Dillinger, "Pretty Boy" Floyd and "Baby Face" Nelson—typically were declared "public enemies" by newspapers, reading that into Justice Department "most wanted" press releases. Other members of the gang were captured in a police raid on their "ghost town" hideout of Kinney, Nebraska, on November 30, 1934, but Limerick and Denning escaped, found new allies and robbed more banks.

Limerick later worked with Walter "Irish" O'Malley's gang until captured after a nightclub altercation in St. Joseph, Missouri, on May 25, 1935. He confessed to five bank robberies but refused to inform on associates, including Denning, whose avoidance of prosecution may have owed much to Limerick's loyalty: "If Maurice was in here and I was outside, I wouldn't want him telling where I was." Limerick later pleaded guilty to a Dell Rapids, South Dakota, bank robbery, was sentenced to life, and ended up at Alcatraz. On May 23, 1938, Limerick was shot to death in a failed escape attempt in which he and two accomplices fatally bludgeoned Alcatraz guard Royal C. Cline with a hammer. His accomplices, Jimmy "Tex" Lucas (who had once stabbed Al Capone with a pair of scissors) and Rufus "Whitey" Franklin were wounded and recaptured and given additional life terms. Franklin, who had wielded the hammer, spent fourteen years in solitary and most of his remaining life in prison.

Lockhart, David Edward (Ed) [1890–1924] Decorated veteran of World War I who joined Henry Starr on his last bank robbery at Harrison, Arkansas, in 1921, escaped and embarked on an outlaw career of his own, operating out of Oklahoma's Cookson Hills. Robbing a succession of banks and making his getaways by horseback and by automobile, Lockhart became a regional legend and rivaled the more-remembered Al Spencer in newspaper headlines proclaiming him as Henry Starr's successor—the new "Bandit King" of the Southwest. Killed by police near Sperry, Oklahoma, March 26, 1924, just after breakfast at a friend's farm.

Looney, John Patrick [1865–1947] Born Patrick John Looney in Ottawa, Illinois, October 5, 1865, the son of Irish immigrants Patrick and Margaret Looney. Lawyer, unsuccessful political candidate, and publisher of a scandal sheet called the *Rock Island News*. For two decades he controlled an empire of gambling, prostitution, extortion, narcotics, bootlegging, and political corruption that eventually extended from Illinois and Iowa into Missouri and Wisconsin, tainting Rock Island for years as a "gangster city." Looney ruthlessly killed underworld rivals, and his newspaper libeled reformers and its more respectable rival, the *Rock Island Argus*, which crusaded against him. In 1922 Looney ordered the murder of William Gabel, a saloon owner and former policeman who had informed on him to federal agents. This touched off a gang war resulting in twelve murders that included Looney's son Connor. Looney's Rock Island saloons and brothels were soon closed, and he fled to New Mexico where he was captured a year later by Pinkerton detectives. Convicted of the Gabel murder mainly on the testimony of former henchmen who were promised leniency, Looney was sentenced to fourteen years. Paroled in 1934, he faded from public view, dying of tuberculosis in El Paso, Texas, in 1947. Looney commonly is thought to be the basis for Paul Newman's character in the movie *Road to Perdition*.

Maddox, Claude "Screwy" (true name: John Edward Moore; aka Johnny Moore, John Manning) [d. 1958] Former St. Louis gangster, a graduate of the Egan's Rats gang, who moved to Chicago and headed the Capone-allied Circus Gang, headquartered at the Circus Café, 1857 West North Avenue, just inside Moran's territory. He helped plot the St. Valentine's Day Massacre, the likely perpetrators of which included such former St. Louis colleagues as Fred "Killer" Burke, Gus Winkeler, Raymond "Crane-Neck" Nugent, who divided his time between Chicago and Toledo, and Chicago's Fred Goetz (Capone's "American boys"). Though also suspected of participation in the Massacre, Maddox turned out to have an ironclad alibi—he was in court on the morning of February 14, 1929. He did arrange for the garage at 1723 North Wood Street, near his Circus Café, which caught fire while "Tough Tony" Capezio was dismantling the killers' Cadillac. Later a notorious labor racketeer, controlling Local 450 of the Bartenders, Waiters, Waitresses, and Miscellaneous Workers Union from 1935 until his death. Died of natural causes at his suburban Riverside home, June 21, 1958.

McErlane, Frank [1894–1932] Co-leader, with "Polack Joe" Saltis, of the Saltis-McErlane gang, bootleggers who initially were allied with Al Capone. Once shot a lawyer in a Crown Point, Indiana, bar solely to display his marksmanship, but the murder charge was dropped after the key witness was found clubbed to death. Apparently murdered his own mistress, Elfrieda Rigus (usually spelled Elfreda or Elfrida), along with her two dogs, in his car at 8129 Phillips Avenue, on October 8, 1931. Case was dismissed for lack of evidence. The alcoholic gangster had health and mental problems (he also had been arrested for wildly firing a shotgun at imaginary enemies), was considered dangerously demented even by underworld standards, and died of pneumonia in a Beardstown, Illinois, hospital, October 8, 1932. McErlane evidently was the first to discover and introduce the Thompson submachine gun into gangland warfare in an unsuccessful effort to kill bootlegging rival Edward "Spike" O'Donnell, who had invaded Saltis-McErlane territory on Chicago's South Side. In a classic "drive-by" shooting at the busy corner of Western Avenue and Sixty-third Street on September 25, 1925, a machine-gunner aiming at O'Donnell missed him but thoroughly riddled the windows of a drug store. That attack and two others in quick succession caused both the Capone gang and the North Siders to acquire this new armament, which was legal to possess because it did not violate the city's concealable-weapon law. The use of machine guns helped make Chicago the "gangster capital of the world."

McGeoghegan, Daniel (Dan or Danny) [1895–1982] An inveterate, violent, and, by some accounts deranged, criminal who probably survived into old age only through long years of imprisonment. Sentenced to death with Henry "Midget" Fernekes for killing Michael Swiontowski in the 1924 robbery of the Inland Trust & Savings Bank but beat the rap on appeal. Between robberies, he formed a bootlegging gang on Chicago's South Side that included George "Yorkie," or "Yama," Downes, brother-in-law of Martin Durkin (the first criminal to kill an FBI agent). Later involved in a four-way gang war with the forces of "Spike" O'Donnell, Frank McErlane, and Danny Stanton and eventually formed an alliance with Michael "Bubs" Quinlan. Suspected in the 1932 machine-gun murder of Charles O'Donnell and a machine-gun attack on "Spike" O'Donnell's house. With Lenny Patrick (later a notorious Outfit enforcer), John Patrick, Jack Gray, and others, robbed the Culver Exchange Bank at Culver, Indiana, on May 29, 1933, only to be captured by police and vigilantes after a wild car chase and shootout. Sentenced to thirty-five years in the Indiana state prison at Michigan City, McGeoghegan became acquainted with John Dillinger's friends there and may have joined the planned breakout then being organized. An early batch of guns thrown over the prison wall by Dillinger was retrieved by guards, and McGeoghegan and Culver accomplices Jack Gray and Eddie Murphy were the suspected recipients and were thrown into solitary, thus missing the historic crashout of September 26. (Ironically, the Culver bank also had been robbed in 1920 by Joseph Burns, one of the Michigan City escapees).

Imprisoned for years and reported to have gone insane, McGeoghegan was freed in the late forties and resumed his old ways, being named in the ransom kidnapping of black "policy king" Edward Jones, the murder of a retired engraving executive in Wilmette, a $13,000 armored car holdup on the South Side, and a rooming house robbery in which a dozen residents were herded into the basement and bound while the landlord's safes were looted of $11,000 in cash and jewelry. On February 1, 1947, "the McGeoghegan gang" attempted to rob a South Side Chicago Realtor's office. Two of his accomplices were killed and three policemen wounded in the resulting gun battle, and McGeoghegan again returned to prison on a long stretch. Reportedly free and back in Chicago by the 1960s, he faded into obscurity, apparently broken only by old age and years in the penitentiary. Died on July 22, 1982.

McGurn, "Machine Gun" Jack (true name: Vincenzo or Vincent Gibaldi, which he changed to Gebardi, but also used DeMora, the name of his stepfather, and James Vincent) [1905–1936] [See p. 198] Born in Licata, Sicily, and immigrated to U.S. with his mother, his father, Tommaso, arriving separately and later murdered in New York. Adopted the name Gebardi (possibly to avoid disgracing his family) and sometimes DeMory or DeMora (after his stepfather). Former boxer (under the name Jack McGurn because of Irish domination of that sport) who reputedly turned killer to avenge the 1923 murder of his stepfather. Only one early news report has him working as a North Side gunman before joining Al Capone, whom he actually may have met through Frankie Yale in New York. (Supposedly he had killed the men responsible for the death of his real father before moving to Chicago.) Became Capone's chief lieutenant, bodyguard, and torpedo, and therefore a suspect in the St.

THE TALE OF MORTON'S HORSE

Gangster "Nails" Morton died on May 13, 1923, after a fall from a horse that he rode for pleasure on the bridle paths of Chicago's Lincoln Park. That any gangster would be an equestrian, or be killed accidentally, had enough news value to receive substantial coverage in the local press. The thing that earned Morton a permanent place in Prohibition-era history is what supposedly happened next. Legend has it that Morton's grieving friends, occasionally led by Dean O'Banion but usually by Louis "Two-Gun" Alterie, later took the same horse from the Parkway Riding Academy at 2153 North Clark (in the same block as the garage where the St. Valentine's Day Massacre took place) and executed it, either in Lincoln Park or outside of town, and then told the stable owner where he could retrieve the saddle.

Samuel "Nails" Morton

There's no disputing how Morton died, but the murder of the horse appears to be mythical, possibly based on a passing comment by Charles Gregston implying a horse-murder in the *Chicago Daily News* for November 19, 1924, in a short feature on Torrio when O'Banion's death was still in the news. Killing a horse that someone needed in his business already was a practice of extortionists. Even after the automobile was commonplace, the city's horse population was large enough for some to die of natural causes. So dead horses were not exactly rare, and this may have inspired the Morton horse story, especially if it started out as a joke that turned into a rumor and seemed entirely plausible, given the North Siders' penchant for pranks. Nobody has been able to verify that it happened, and in those glory days of the "Chicago school of journalism," newspapers were not shy about printing higher truths that transcended mere facts.

Valentine's Day Massacre. Indicted but never tried due to lack of evidence. [Frustrated authorities later convicted him and his girlfriend, Louise Rolfe—his "Blond Alibi" for the Massacre—of conspiring to violate the Mann Act by transporting themselves across state lines for "immoral purposes." The convictions eventually were reversed by the U.S. Supreme Court, which found that the law did not anticipate a woman conspiring to "debauch" herself. Thus McGurn's conspiracy conviction also had to be voided for lack of a co-conspirator.]

McGurn fell on hard times after Capone went to prison—too hot to employ as a gunman and out of touch with Capone's successors. Police spoiled his attempt to supplement his income as a professional golfer, and McGurn's fortunes plummeted. He was shot to death in a Chicago bowling alley at 805 Milwaukee a few minutes into February 15, 1936, probably on orders of Frank Nitti, who earlier had killed several other Capone loyalists. Where McGurn picked up the nickname "Machine Gun" isn't known, for all his presumed killings were committed with a pistol, and he once claimed in print, with annoyance, that he didn't own a machine gun and (less convincingly) had never fired one. That he left nickels in the hands of his victims may be another part of the McGurn legend. [John Armando was named by the Cook County Coroner as a suspect, along with McGurn, in three 1926 murders, plus three more in 1928. He supposedly worked for Morris Eller and was a precinct captain in the "Bloody Twentieth" Ward. Involved in election fraud, kidnapping, terrorism, and suspected in several shootings. Stood trial for the killing of black lawyer Octavius Granady, challenging Eller for Ward committeeman, but was acquitted when a female witness refused to testify after her brother was kidnapped and she was threatened with death.]

Merlo, Michele (Mike) [1880–1924] Born in Sicily, January 4, 1880. Business and political leader in Chicago's Sicilian community, friend of the O'Banion and Torrio-Capone mobs who long kept the peace between them. Became president of the local chapter of the Unione Siciliana after the murder of its previous leader, Anthony D'Andrea, on May 11, 1921. Founded in Chicago in 1895, the Unione was a fraternal organization for the betterment of Sicilian immigrants but was taken over in some cities by mobsters who found irresistible possibilities in the monthly dues paid by thousands of members and the kitchen stills kept by many Italian and Sicilian households. Both Merlo and D'Andrea are commonly regarded as early Chicago Mafia bosses, though whether a "Mafia family" as such has ever existed in Chicago is debatable. When Dean O'Banion set up Torrio on the Sieben Brewery sale in 1924, bringing about his second bootlegging arrest and a short jail term, Merlo urged diplomacy and kept the peace for a few months. His death by cancer on November 8 was followed two days later by O'Banion's murder in his own flower shop.

Miller, Vernon Clate (Verne) [1896–1933] Born near Grinnell, Iowa, August 25, 1896, the son of Charles and Emma Miller. World War I Army veteran, former South Dakota sheriff, and convicted embezzler turned gangster, bootlegger, bank robber, and professional killer. Hired to rescue (or, by unlikely accounts, silence) Frank Nash in what became the Kansas City Massacre, and regarded as a trigger-happy psychopath. According to a statement given the FBI by "Machine Gun" Kelly, it was Miller, on a mission of personal revenge, rather than Capone or other gangsters, who shoved a machine gun through the back window of Manning's resort hotel at 14 North Pistakee Lake Road, Fox Lake, in northern Illinois, and killed or wounded several bootleggers in the so-called Fox Lake Massacre of 1930. After the Kansas City killings he was harbored for a time in the East by mobsters Louis "Lepke" Buchalter and Abner "Longy" Zwillman, but intense federal pressure forced them to drop him like a hot potato. Miller was found murdered in a ditch at the corner of Harlow Avenue and Cambridge Road in Detroit, November 29, 1933.

Moran, George "Bugs" (true name: Adelard Cunin; alias George Gage, George Miller, and George Morrissey) Cunin [1891–1957] Born in St. Paul, Minnesota, August 21, 1891, the son of Jules and Diana Cunin. Of French-Canadian ancestry, though often erroneously described as Irish (because of his adopted names) or Polish. Last of Chicago's North Siders to oppose Al Capone. The St. Valentine's Day Massacre and the murder of ally Joseph Aiello drove Moran out of town in the early thirties, and the remnants of his gang were taken over by Ted Newberry, who made peace with the Outfit and became essen-

George "Bugs" Moran

tially a satellite of Capone gangster Gus Winkeler. Briefly relaunched his bootlegging and racketeering in Waukegan and Wisconsin, with occasional forays into the St. Paul and St. Louis underworlds, but never regained his former glory, and his post-Prohibition criminal career quickly spiraled downward. Convicted in 1939 with former airplane bootlegger Frank Parker of conspiring to counterfeit and pass $62,000 worth of American Express checks in 1939 and sentenced to one year. Appealed and remained free on bond until 1943 when he was arrested in Chicago after a drunken scuffle with a Coast Guardsman. After his release gained a small measure of revenge by connecting with Chicago's "Bookie Gang" who specialized in robbing Syndicate bookmakers, and also robbed a series of banks in Indiana, Ohio, and Kentucky with Virgil Summers and Albert Fouts. All three were convicted of a $10,000 Dayton payroll robbery in 1946 and sentenced to ten to twenty years in Ohio's state prison at Columbus. Paroled in November 1956, all three were again tried and convicted of a 1945 bank robbery at Ansonia, Ohio, and received another five-year sentence. Already dying of lung cancer, Moran arrived at Leavenworth on January 14, 1957 and expired on February 25.

Morton, Samuel "Nails" (true name: Samuel J. Marcovitz) [1893–1923] Born in Chicago, July 3, 1893. Chicago Jewish gangster who gained respect as a defender of his people against gangs of "Jew baiters," and by his frequent acts of charity and excellent war record. Enlisted in the Army during World War I and earned both a battlefield commission as lieutenant and the French Croix de Guerre by leading a charge despite shrapnel wounds (many gangsters were World War vets, but few became officers). Afterward engaged in strong-arm work and stole cars, which he sold to contacts in Detroit's Little Jewish Navy gang, and became a close ally of North Side mobster Dean O'Banion and the West Side Miller brothers' gang. When O'Banion hijacked a truckload of whiskey outside the Bismarck Hotel in December 1919, Morton helped peddle it to local saloon owners and sold the truck to a Peoria brewery. Prospering in bootlegging, Morton and O'Banion later bought shares in William Schofield's flower shop at 738 North State Street, which became headquarters for the North Side Gang, as well as the major supplier of flowers for gangland funerals. Morton made headlines on August 23, 1920, when he and Hirschie Miller killed two policemen in the Beaux Arts Café at 2700 South State Street in an argument over the proceeds from a liquor deal. Both ultimately were acquitted, probably by jurors more sympathetic to bootleggers than crooked cops. Morton's promising gangland career was cut short by an unusual end on May 13, 1923. A devotee of horseback riding, "Nails" was thrown from his horse and fatally kicked in the head on his way to the Lincoln Park riding trails. Popular legend has it that the horse was later abducted from the Brown Riding Academy at 3008 North Halsted and "bumped off" in retaliation by Louis Alterie (or O'Banion, by some accounts). The unverified horse killing became a staple of gangster lore, and Morton even made it into the 1930 Cagney movie *The Public Enemy* as a character called "Nails Nathan." His funeral was attended by hundreds, and his nobler deeds were extolled, leaving only newspapermen and police to comment on "the other side of his career."

Murphy, Timothy "Big Tim" [1886–1928] Onetime Illinois legislator turned big-time labor racketeer. Allegedly masterminded $385,000 mail robbery at Chicago's Polk Street station on April 6, 1921. Convicted and sentenced to six years in Leavenworth, Murphy claimed he was framed by William Fahy, the "ace" postal inspector who sometimes solved cases in just that manner and was himself later convicted of being the inside man on the $2 million Rondout train robbery in 1924 [see p. 150]. "Big Tim" became a major figure in Chicago gambling and bootlegging and attempted to take over the Cleaners and Dyers Union. Machine-gunned, probably by Capone gangsters, outside his home at 2525 West Morse on June 26, 1928.

Murray, James (Jimmy) [1889–1963] Born in Chicago, March 31, 1889 [although some records have his birth date 1887]. Acquired clout early on as a Cook County court clerk and bail bondsman. Went into politics with connections that made him virtually indispensable to much of Chicago's underworld. At onset of Prohibition became a bootlegger, operating several breweries in Chicago and Wisconsin, fronting for Joseph Stenson, which made him a millionaire. Also set up a network of "safe houses" in Illinois, Wisconsin, and Michigan for friends on the run. Often erroneously described as the brother of "Hymie" Weiss bodyguard Patrick Murray (they actually were cousins with same last names who married sisters, becoming also brothers-in-law). Masterminded the famous $2 million train robbery committed by the Newton boys and others at Rondout, Illinois, June 12, 1924 [see p. 150]. Sentenced to twenty-five years, Murray exchanged $385,000 in bonds from the Rondout job for an early parole in 1931—thoroughly unrepentant, thanks in part to a loyal but equally lawless wife.

From his new front, the Rainbo Barbecue at 7190 West North Avenue in Chicago, Murray bought and sold hot cars, guns, and stolen bank bonds, and provided refuge and contacts for many criminals, including John Dillinger and "Baby Face" Nelson (even planning a repeat of the Rondout robbery with them at the time of Dillinger's death), but somehow avoided prosecution on harboring charges despite the confessions of Dillinger-Nelson Gang associates implicating him. "Baby Face" Nelson died at a Wilmette house owned by Murray, and he supposedly helped Helen Gillis move Nelson's body the night he died. He may have been turned into a double agent for the FBI, for he had hoped to sell out Dillinger to beat a stolen bond charge while later feeding bureau information to Nelson. Murray's immunity ended in 1938 when he was convicted of a $115,000 Clintonville, Pennsylvania, bank robbery and sent to Alcatraz on a twenty-five-year sentence. Paroled in 1954, Murray returned to his longtime home at 109 South Parkside in Chicago and died on January 20, 1963.

Nash, Frank "Jelly" **[1887–1933]** Oklahoma bandit convicted of murdering an accomplice in 1912 and sentenced to life in Oklahoma's state prison. Sentence was commuted in 1918 so Nash could join the Army. Fought in France (despite many popular accounts stating he never enlisted) and afterward received another life sentence for robbing a Corn, Oklahoma, bank in 1919. Paroled in 1922, he joined the Al Spencer Gang and took part in Oklahoma's last train robbery. Convicted of mail robbery in 1924 and sentenced to twenty-five years in Leavenworth. Escaped in 1930 and worked with the Barker-Karpis Gang and others. Recaptured at Hot Springs, Arkansas, June 16, 1933; killed the next day in the Kansas City Massacre.

Nelson, George "Baby Face" **(aka Jimmy Williams; true name: Lester Joseph Gillis, although FBI "wanted" posters listed his middle initial as "M") [1908–1934]** Born in Chicago December 6, 1908, living first at 942 North California before moving next door to 944, where his father committed suicide in 1924. A car thief, bootlegger, bank robber, and escapee from a taxi en route to the state prison at Joliet, Illinois, he later was associated with John Dillinger. Close to several Chicago mobsters and occasionally may have worked as a Syndicate gunman. Killed three FBI agents during his brief and bloody career. He was never shot during his many robberies but was mortally wounded in a battle with federal agents at Barrington, Illinois, November 27, 1934. Escaped with his wife, Helen, in the FBI's car, with accomplice John Paul Chase driving, to a house owned by Jimmy Murray in Wilmette, where he died a few hours later from his many wounds.

Newberry, Edward (Ted) Bodyguard of "Bugs" Moran, whose delay by a barbershop appointment saved them both from the St. Valentine's Day Massacre. Newberry took control of the North Side when Moran left town and made peace with Capone, who turned the territory over to Gus Winkeler. Murdered and dumped near Bailey Town, Indiana, on January 7, 1933, probably on orders of Frank Nitti.

Newton Brothers Originally cowboys and ranchers from Uvalde, Texas, Willis, Jess, William "Dock," and Joe Newton became experts at robbing trains and looting as many as eighty banks from Texas to Canada, usually without violence, between 1914 and 1924. On June 12, 1924, they joined some hoodlums from Chicago and St. Louis in committing one of the last and largest train robberies in U.S. history when they commandeered the Chicago, Milwaukee & St. Paul mail train at Rondout, Illinois, making off with more than $2 million. The almost perfectly executed crime failed when one of the brothers accidentally was shot by a fellow robber, and Chicago police, responding to reports of a wounded man, bagged him and one of the ringleaders, a politician-bootlegger named James Murray, whose "inside man" on the job was none other than "ace" postal inspector and bandit-catcher William F. Fahy. The wounded Newton survived and, with Murray, traded much of the hidden loot for shortened sentences. Willis and Joe Newton robbed a bank in Medford, Oklahoma, in April 1932, two weeks before receiving a pardon from President Hoover, and were subsequently sentenced to twenty years. Surviving injuries and their prison terms, the brothers thereafter went straight, although "Dock" Newton came out of retirement at age seventy-seven and robbed the bank at Rowena, Texas (incidentally the home town of Bonnie Parker), in 1968. He was shot (an accomplice, suspected to be a brother, escaped) and spent a few months in a prison hospital before admission to a nursing home, where he died in 1974. Jess Newton had already died of lung cancer in 1960, and Willis and Joe Newton lived without further excitement until 1979 and 1989, respectively.

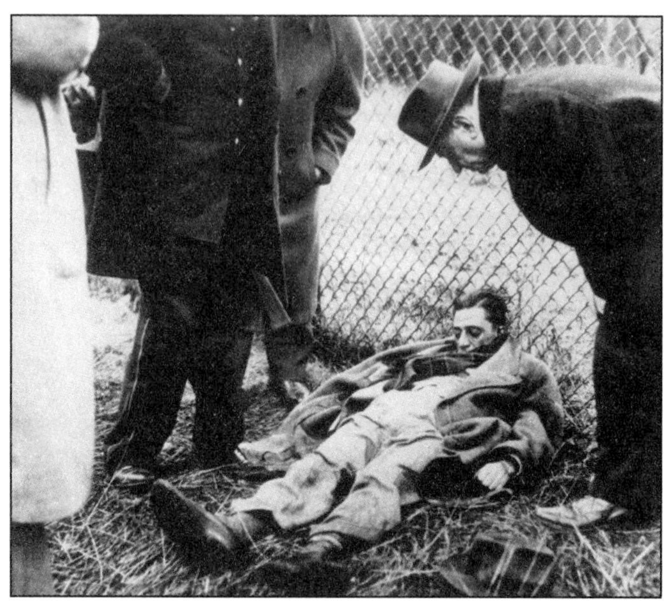

With Al Capone in prison, Frank Nitti assumed control of the Chicago Outfit and, after seeing to the murder of several Capone loyalists, managed to get it back on the more businesslike track originally envisioned by John Torrio. In 1943, facing a likely conviction for extortion and possibly suffering from cancer, he apparently became drunk, staggered from his house to some nearby railroad tracks, and killed himself with two shots, the first of which only blew off his hat.

Nitti, Frank "The Enforcer" (true name: Francesco Raffele Nitto; possibly nicknamed "The Enforcer" by a local journalist) [1886–1943] Born in Angri, Italy, January 27, 1886, the son of Luigi and Rosina Nitto. Released from his own term for tax evasion soon after Capone's imprisonment, Nitti conspired with friends to kill potential rivals and emerged as head of the Chicago Syndicate in the middle 1930s. Involved in post-Prohibition racketeering, he was indicted in a movie-extortion case that probably would have sent him to prison. Facing that prospect and reportedly suffering from cancer, he committed suicide on March 19, 1943.

O'Banion, Dean Charles "Deanie" (Dion O'Banion was his baptismal name frequently used by writers) [1892–1924] Born at Maroa, Illinois (often wrongly reported as Aurora), July 8, 1892,

Chicago Daily Tribune

KILL O'BANION, GANG LEADER

CONGRESS MAY PROMPTLY STOP TAX PUBLICITY

NEWS SUMMARY

BEGIN BILL SUIT TO LEARN WHAT IS INTOXICATING

Shot 4 Up in Bank Vault in $15,000 Raid

3-GUN FLORIST SLAIN IN SHOP NEAR CHURCH

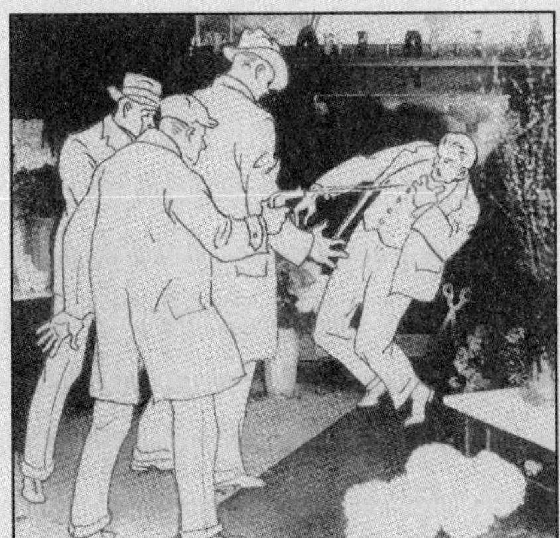

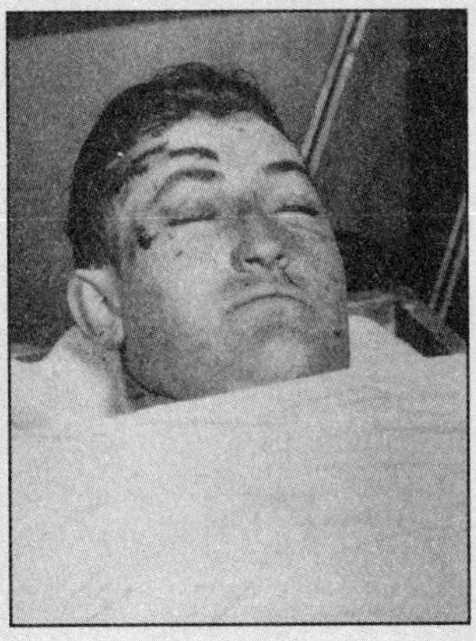

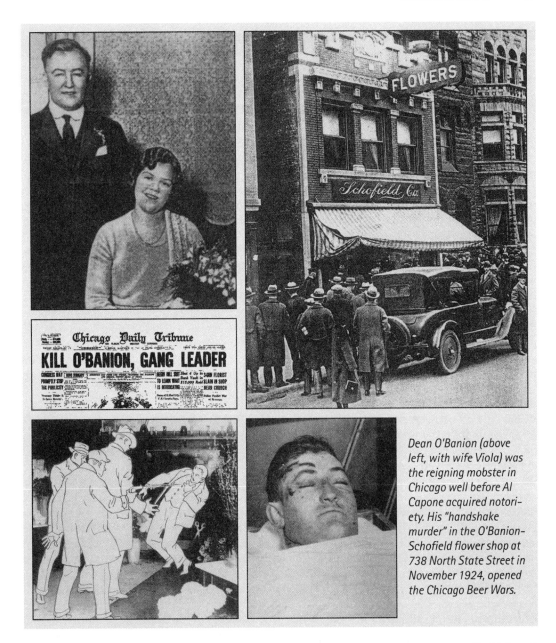

Dean O'Banion (above left, with wife Viola) was the reigning mobster in Chicago well before Al Capone acquired notoriety. His "handshake murder" in the O'Banion-Schofield flower shop at 738 North State Street in November 1924, opened the Chicago Beer Wars.

the son of Charles and Emma O'Banion. Split with Torrio and Capone in the early twenties to become independent leader of Chicago's North Side mob. Safecracker, bootlegger, and hijacker alleged to have killed a dozen or more. Operated out of Schofield's Flower Shop at 738 North State Street, directly across from the Holy Name Cathedral, controlling the wealthy "Gold Coast" and northern Lakefront neighborhoods. Personal contempt for the South Side Italians led him to swindle Torrio in a brewery deal, which led to Torrio's arrest and imprisonment as a second-time violator of the Volstead law. In retaliation, O'Banion was killed in his flower shop on

November 10, 1924, in the famous "handshake murder," probably by New York gangster Frankie Yale, who likely had killed "Big Jim" Colosimo four years earlier, also as a favor to Torrio and Capone. This was the first killing of a major gang chieftain and set off five years of Chicago Beer Wars between bootlegging factions, represented mainly by the Capone interests and O'Banion's successors, until the North Siders were routed in the St. Valentine's Day Massacre of 1929.

Oberta, John "Dingbat" [1903–1930] Bootlegger and gunman for Saltis-McErlane gang, sometimes spelling his name O'Berta when it suited him to sound Irish. Married Florence Diggs, widow of "Big Tim" Murphy. Murdered with bodyguard Sam Malaga, Chicago, March 6, 1930, probably in retaliation for a hospital attack on Frank McErlane with whom Oberta had recently split. [Oberta, Tim Murphy, and their wife, Florence, called "The Black Widow" in newspapers, are buried next to one another in Chicago.]

O'Connor, Thomas "Terrible Tommy" [1886–?] Notorious Chicago robber and murderer. Surrounded by police at his brother-in-law's house at 6415 South Washtenaw Avenue on March 23, 1921, O'Connor shot his way out, killing Detective Sergeant Patrick O'Neill. Captured in Minneapolis while trying to rob a train porter, he was returned to Chicago, convicted of murder on September 7, 1921, and sentenced to hang. Escaped from Cook County Jail on December 11, four days before his scheduled execution, and was never recaptured. Presumed to have fled to his native Ireland.

O'Donnell, James Edward "Spike" [1889–1962] Leader of Chicago's South Side O'Donnells gang, which also included his nine brothers (though most accounts mention only "Spike," Steve, Walter, and Tommy). Serving a sentence for bank robbery at the onset of Prohibition, "Spike" O'Donnell's political clout gained him an early parole in 1923 and led to the first of Chicago's celebrated Beer Wars as he challenged the South Side reign of the Torrio-Capone gang. Several members of his gang, including brother Walter, were killed, and "Spike" himself survived at least ten attempts on his life, one of which was the first recorded Tommygun attack at Sixty-third and Western on September 25, 1925, by the Saltis-McErlane gang. Another brother, Charles, was killed in a machine-gun attack on April 4, 1932. "Spike" eventually made peace with Capone, or at least called off hostilities, and continued to prosper as an independent bootlegging and gambling power, dabbling after Prohibition in real estate, coal, and road paving. In January 1943, "Spike" beat street superintendent James Butler in his office for failing to pay for a paving contract. Two months later, on March 15, O'Donnell was shot by Syndicate gunmen and nearly died, probably for embarrassing the city administration by boasting of his close ties to the mayor. "Spike" O'Donnell seemingly reformed after this, became deeply religious, and joined the Knights of Columbus, living respectably until his death by a heart attack on August 26, 1962.

O'Donnell, William "Klondike" [1886?–1976] With brother Myles, led Chicago's West Side O'Donnell gang, whose territory extended into Cicero. A third brother, Bernard, was of lesser prominence. No relation to the South Side O'Donnells. Fought the Torrio-Capone invasion of Cicero, which later included a machine-gun attack in April 1926 that wounded O'Donnell gunman James "Fur" Sammons at girlfriend Pearl Hruby's beauty shop. Then, in Chicago's first "mini-massacre"(because a public official died), Capone machine-gunners opened fire on a group of celebrants that included "Klondike" and Myles outside Harry Madigan's Pony Inn in Cicero, killing two of their friends, as well as Assistant State's Attorney William McSwiggin—a major blunder that sent Capone into hiding for three months. McSwiggin's night of carousing with bootleggers was never satisfactorily explained, but the public's agitation eventually blew over, as did Klondike's wrath, and he ended up affiliating with Capone's Outfit. Myles O'Donnell died of pneumonia in 1932, but "Klondike" remained active in Cicero gambling into the 1950s before dying of natural causes in December 1976. Bernard O'Donnell died in 1974.

O'Malley, Walter "Irish" (true name: Walter Holland; aka Leo O'Malley) [1898–1944] Born in St. Louis, orphaned and raised in a foster home. Joined the U.S. Army in 1915 and deserted, but then enlisted in the Canadian Army in 1917 under the name Daniel O'Hare and fought in France. Returned to St. Louis under the name O'Malley, worked as a hotel clerk before becoming involved in bootlegging, burglary, and robbery with members of the Egan's Rats gang. Convicted of a 1921 Panama, Illinois, bank robbery, O'Malley was sentenced to one to twenty years in prison but was found so unbalanced he soon was transferred to the Chester State Hospital for the Criminally Insane. Escaped with forty others in 1923, but all were soon caught. Released in 1929 and reunited with underworld friends in St. Louis. With Vivian Chase and others kidnapped elderly Alton, Illinois, banker August Luer in July 1933 but collected no ransom, releasing the old man when they became concerned for his health. Most of the gang were soon captured, but O'Malley fled to Kansas City, where he became involved with John Langan, Clarence Sparger, "Dapper Dan" Heady, former Barker-Karpis Gang members Volney Davis and Jess Doyle, and others in robberies, burglaries, hijackings, and counterfeiting.

O'Malley and Heady later joined Leonard Short's Ozark Gang in a series of large bank and jewelry store robberies in Oklahoma, Missouri, and Arkansas, including a double robbery in Okemah, Oklahoma, on December 22, 1934. O'Malley and Heady were captured in Kansas City in May 1935. O'Malley was sent to Illinois, and Heady was returned to Oklahoma, where he escaped with other gang members from the Muskogee jail in December 1935, killing Chief of Detectives Ben Bolton. They were tracked to a mountain hideout where Heady was killed and the others recaptured. In Illinois, O'Malley was tried on state kidnapping charges and received a life sentence, followed by a twenty-five-year federal sentence for bank robbery. Complaining of head pains from an old war wound, O'Malley again was declared insane and sent to a mental institution, where he died on May 1, 1944.

Parker, Bonnie Elizabeth [1910–1934] Born in Rowena, Texas, October 1, 1910, the daughter of Charles and Emma Parker. Married at age sixteen to burglar Roy Thornton who deserted her and was in prison at the time of her death (Bonnie had Roy's name tattooed on her thigh, never divorced him, and was wearing her wedding ring when killed). Girlfriend and accomplice of Clyde Barrow, given to writing maudlin poetry and having snapshots taken of herself and Clyde clowning with guns. Despite her "petite" size (barely 100 pounds, according to the FBI; 80–90 pounds say relatives and friends; and Clyde's weight was only 130), the two typically relied on Browning Automatic Rifles (BARs) stolen from National Guard armories instead of the Thompson, and were regarded by other outlaws of the day as two-bit killers and robbers of gas stations and grocery stores. Died with Barrow in a roadside ambush by Texas and Louisiana peace officers between Sailes and Gibsland, Louisiana, May 23, 1934.

Pierpont, Harry "Pete" [1902–1934] Born at Muncie, Indiana, October 13, 1902, the son of Gilbert and Lena Pierpont. A bank-robbing prison mentor of John Dillinger and regarded by many as the true "brains" of the so-called "first Dillinger Gang," formed in Indiana's state prison at Michigan City. Pierpont and nine others escaped from Michigan City on September 26, 1933 (the same day "Machine Gun" Kelly was captured), using guns smuggled into the prison by John Dillinger. They then returned the favor by busting Dillinger out of the Allen County Jail at Lima, Ohio, on October 12, 1933, killing Sheriff Jesse Sarber. After a series of raids on police stations and banks, Pierpont was captured, along with Dillinger, Charles Makley, and Russell Clark in Tucson, Arizona, in January 1934. Dillinger was transferred to Crown Point, Indiana, where he soon made his legendary wooden-gun escape, but Pierpont and the others were shipped back to

Ohio, tried, and convicted of the Sarber murder. Pierpont and Makley were sentenced to death and Clark to life imprisonment. Makley was killed and Pierpont wounded in an attempted escape from the Death House of the state prison in Columbus on September 22, 1934. They had tried to emulate Dillinger by using fake guns carved from soapstone (not soap as commonly reported). Pierpont died in the electric chair on October 17, 1934.

Reid, John (Johnny) [1891–1926] Born in Kansas City, Missouri. World War I veteran and later a member of the Egan's Rats gang of St. Louis before moving on to Detroit. Indicted for murder in 1919 after killing a man over a woman, and fled to New York where he became involved in another romantic dispute and was shot in the head by con man "Dapper Don" Collins. Reid survived but lost his left eye and returned to Detroit where he joined the Purple Gang in bootlegging, fighting a gang war with an Italian mob led by Mike DiPisa. Reid was joined in the conflict by former St. Louis colleagues Gus Winkeler, Fred "Killer" Burke, Milford Jones, Bob Carey, and Joseph "Red" O'Riordan. The St. Louis crew committed several Detroit murders and organized a successful kidnapping gang. John Reid was killed in a shotgun ambush while parking his car outside his apartment at 3025 East Grand Boulevard on December 25, 1926. Winkeler, Burke and Carey later shifted to Chicago, joining Capone to execute the St. Valentine's Day Massacre.

Remus, George [1876–1952] Born in Germany and settled in Chicago, where he obtained a license to practice law before moving to Cincinnati in 1920. There he organized drug companies to obtain huge supplies of "medicinal spirits" from U.S. warehouses, dispensed graft to hundreds of officials, and became known as "King of the Bootleggers" because of the size of his operations. Served a short prison term during 1926–27 for violation of the Volstead Act. On October 6, 1927, shot and killed his estranged wife, Imogene, who had left him for Franklin Dodge, a federal agent instrumental in Remus' conviction. Tried for murder and acquitted by reason of insanity. Briefly institutionalized. Died at Covington, Kentucky, January 20, 1952.

Ricca, Paul "The Waiter" (true name: Felice DeLucia; aka Paul Maglio and numerous other aliases) [1897–1972] Born in Naples, Italy, November 14, 1897. Convicted of murder in his homeland (the result of a family feud), Felice DeLucia served only two years in an Italian prison and after his release murdered a witness who had testified against him. Stealing the passport of one Paolo Maglio, DeLucia fled to the U.S. while an Italian court convicted him, in absentia, of the second murder and sentenced him to life imprisonment. Settling in Chicago as Paul Ricca, he joined the Capone mob after a brief stint as a waiter at "Diamond Joe" Esposito's Bella Napoli Café, where he picked up his famous nickname. Ricca rose swiftly in the Outfit and became a lifelong friend of another up-and-coming Capone bodyguard named Tony "Joe Batters" Accardo. By some accounts Ricca, not Frank Nitti, was the true successor of Al Capone and regarded as such by out-of-town mobsters. Whatever the truth of the matter, Ricca was evidently high in the Chicago mob by April 1932 when he was arrested at the Congress Hotel with Capone's cousin Rocco Fischetti and New York gangsters "Lucky" Luciano and Meyer Lansky.

Ricca was seen definitely as boss of the Outfit after Frank Nitti's suicide in 1943 but only for a short time before being convicted in the Bioff-Browne movie-extortion case. Along with other ranking Capone mobsters, Ricca was paroled in 1947 by a unanimous vote of the U.S. Parole Board after serving less than a third of his ten-year sentence, causing grief to the Truman administration and especially Attorney General Tom Clark. Increasing legal difficulties, including income tax investigations and discovery of his fraudulent immigration, forced Ricca into semi-retirement and escalated Accardo to the top position. Denaturalized in the 1950s, Ricca avoided deportation, supposedly by mailing newspaper clippings of his underworld career to the embassies of Italy and other nations. His Italian murder conviction was somehow voided, but after being turned down by forty-seven countries Ricca stayed in Chicago until his death from natural causes on October 11, 1972. At the time FBI and newspaper speculation had it that Accardo and Ricca had both come out of retirement to jointly run the Outfit in the absence of Sam Giancana, who had fled to Mexico, and other would-be bosses who were then in prison.

Richetti, Adam "Eddie" **(true name: Ricchetti, pronounced "Ri-KET-tee") [1909–1938]** Born in Strom, Texas, August 5, 1909. Oklahoma bank robber and partner of "Pretty Boy" Floyd. Only man convicted for the Kansas City Massacre, on highly circumstantial evidence. Wounded and captured by police near Wellsville, Ohio, October 21, 1934, and sentenced to death for the killing of Kansas City Police Detective Frank Hermanson, one of the massacre victims. Died in the gas chamber at Missouri's state prison, October 7, 1938, protesting that this was the one crime of which he was innocent.

Rio, Frank **(alias "Slippery Frank," Frank Cline) [1895?–1935]** Born in Luvito, Italy, June 30, 1895, the son of Antonio and Rosa Rio, according to his death certificate (though no records have been found to substantiate this, and police and press reports give other varying and contradictory versions of his age and background). Known as a petty thief and burglar in 1918, Rio progressed to jewel and fur thefts and bank robberies and was arrested in 1921 with $40,000 in bonds taken in a Union Station mail robbery, but seemed always to beat the rap. Attracted the attention of the Torrio-Capone mob by the mid-twenties and soon was recognized as Capone's most loyal and trusted bodyguard. Legend has it that Rio saved Capone's life by throwing him to the floor and holding him down during "Hymie" Weiss's motorcade assault on the Hawthorne Hotel in 1926 and that Rio later tipped Capone to the plot by Albert Anselmi, John Scalise, and Joseph "Hop Toad" Guinta to depose him, but there is little to substantiate this. Rio surrendered with Capone to Philadelphia detectives on gun-carrying charges in May 1929, in a probably prearranged arrest, and served a year in prison with his boss. Sent to New Jersey in 1932 as Capone's emissary to Charles Lindbergh, offering Capone's help to locate the aviator's kidnapped baby in exchange for release from jail. The offer was turned down. Though reported as a possible contender to succeed Capone, Rio, suffering from heart disease, became less active under the Nitti regime and died of natural causes at his home in suburban Oak Park on February 23, 1935.

Saltis, Joseph "Polack Joe" **(sometimes spelled Soltis) [1894–1947]** Co-leader, with Frank McErlane, of a Southwest Side Chicago bootlegging gang sometimes allied with Al Capone, but gravitated to the North Siders. Considered a violent thug who supposedly once had clubbed a woman to death for refusing to sell his beer in her ice cream parlor. Amassed a considerable fortune and retired to a resort estate at Barker Lake, Wisconsin, but died a pauper at the county hospital in Chicago in August 1947.

Sammon, James **(alias James "Fur" Sammons) [1884?–1960]** Convicted as a minor of raping a twelve-year-old girl. Bootlegger and gunman for Chicago's West Side "Klondike" O'Donnell gang, also a fur and jewel thief and suspect in Chicago's $80,000 International Harvester Co. payroll robbery on March 6, 1926. Wounded in an early machine-gun attack on girlfriend Pearl Hruby's beauty shop at 2208 South Austin on April 23, 1926. Proficient with a Tommygun but somewhat unstable, legend has it that extra gunmen always were assigned to accompany "Fur" on gangland hits to prevent him from getting carried away and shooting innocent bystanders. With other former O'Donnell gangsters such as William "Three-Fingered Jack" White and George "Red" Barker, Sammon later worked for Al Capone as a killer and labor racketeer but continued to moonlight as a robber. Suspect in the July 1932 machine-gun murder of North Side gangster Willie Marks and Teamsters official Patrick Berrell at Shawano, Wisconsin, possibly in retaliation for the murder of "Red" Barker. Fought a running machine-gun battle with Tommy Touhy at Harlem and North avenues, near Jimmy Murray's Rainbo Barbecue, on February 2, 1933. Touhy was crippled in the attack, but Sammon and two accomplices escaped unharmed in their armored car. Sammon reportedly was wearing a woman's hat and fur coat at the time. Sammon was arrested in Kansas City in July 1933 and later successfully prosecuted in Indiana by Robert Estill (of Dillinger case fame) as a habitual criminal and sentenced to life imprisonment. Paroled on March 8, 1943, and nearly blind, Sammon was returned to Illinois to complete an old fifty-year sentence for murder and robbery but finally released on December 17, 1952. Died of a heart attack in his bed at Chicago's Englewood Arms Hotel on May 20, 1960.

Sankey, Verne [1890–1934] Former Canadian Pacific Railroad employee and South Dakota rancher who became one of the country's most wanted criminals in 1933–34. With partner Gordon Alcorn, reportedly robbed several banks in U.S. and Canada before kidnapping Haskell Bohn, son of a St. Paul refrigerator manufacturer on June 30, 1932. Demanded only $35,000 in ransom and released Bohn unharmed after payment of $12,000. Kidnapped Denver millionaire Charles Boettcher II, February 12, 1933, transporting him to Sankey's turkey ranch near Chamberlain, South Dakota, and releasing him unharmed upon payment of $60,000 ransom. Wrongly suspected of Hamm and Bremer kidnappings, which were carried out by the Barker-Karpis Gang. Arrested by police and FBI agents at a Chicago barber shop on January 31, 1934. Removed to South Dakota for trial in the Boettcher kidnapping and held in the state prison at Great Falls, where he hanged himself with his necktie on the night of February 8, 1934. Sankey's partner, Alcorn, was captured in Chicago on February 2, 1934, and received a life sentence.

Sawyer, Harry "Dutch" (true name: Harry Sandlovich) [1890–1955] Born in Lithuania and came to America as an infant with his parents. Arrested in January 1920 for a $115,000 bank robbery in an Omaha, Nebraska, suburb, Sawyer jumped bond and fled to the Twin Cities where he became a bootlegger and partner of St. Paul crime boss "Dapper Dan" Hogan, whom he succeeded after the latter's murder in December 1928. It was later reported that the Omaha robbery was instigated by political boss Tom Dennison to discredit a reform mayor, and Sawyer reportedly later initiated crime waves of his own to cast doubts on similar would-be reformers in St. Paul. Used his police connections to shelter fugitives in St. Paul, most notably the Barker-Karpis and Dillinger Gangs, sometimes planning crimes and hiring gangs to commit them. The kidnapping of Edward Bremer was Sawyer's brainchild and downfall, as federal investigations brought to light the sorry municipal conditions in the city. Sawyer became a fugitive in 1934 and was apprehended by the FBI in Pass Christian, Mississippi. He refused to "rat" on his connections in St. Paul, despite the tearful pleadings of his wife, Gladys, and wound up with a life sentence for kidnapping. Paroled in February 1955, he died of cancer in Chicago on June 23 of that year.

Harry "Dutch" Sawyer

Scalise, John **See Anselmi, Albert.**

Seadlund, John Henry (alias Peter Anders) [1910–1938] Born in Ironton, Minnesota, and spent his youth drinking, hunting, fishing, and stealing until he had a chance encounter with Tommy Carroll of the Dillinger Gang in March 1934. Briefly harbored Carroll in a fisherman's cabin near Ironton and afterward aspired to become a major criminal. Committed several small holdups of stores, gas stations, and taverns in St. Paul and Brainerd, Minnesota, and was captured near Brainerd in July 1934. Escaped from Crow Wing County Jail in Brainerd on July 25, 1934. Led the life of a hobo, petty thief, drug addict, and occasional lumberjack, but managed to rob banks in Milltown and Eagle River, Wisconsin, and in Shakopee, Minnesota. Briefly owned a lumber camp near Spokane, Washington, but remained dedicated to crime, sensible and otherwise. With partner James Atwood Gray, plotted to kidnap major league baseball players for ransom. When this proved unfeasible, they instead kidnapped Olive Borca, wife of a Chicago nightclub owner, near Lake Geneva, Wisconsin, on September 2, 1937. Unable to collect the ransom, they released Mrs. Borca on her promise that her husband would later pay $2,000.

On September 25, 1937, Seadlund and Gray kidnapped retired businessman Charles S. Ross on Wolf Road near Chicago, demanding a ransom of $50,000. Seadlund collected the money but then murdered his accomplice and Ross, concealing their bodies at the place of Ross's captivity, an underground pit in a wooded area near Spooner, Wisconsin. Seadlund buried $30,000 of the cash and exchanged some of the rest for clean bills at the betting windows of racetracks. Arrested by FBI agents at the Santa Anita racetrack near Los Angeles on January 14, 1938, Seadlund received a death sentence in Illinois and was electrocuted at the Cook County Jail in Chicago on July 14, 1938.

Sheldon, Ralph [1902–1944] South Side Chicago bootlegger and member of a huge street gang called Ragen's Colts. A largely Irish gang that figured in Chicago's 1919 race riots, the Colts were founded as a juvenile athletic club by politician Frank Ragen at the turn of the century. Acquitted of highway robbery at age sixteen and arrested several more times by 1920, Sheldon organized a bootlegging faction of the Colts and sensibly aligned himself with the Torrio-Capone Syndicate. Charles Kelly and mortally wounded Thomas Hart became gangland's first recorded Tommygun fatalities in the Saltis-McErlane gang's drive-by strafing of Sheldon's headquarters, the Ragen Athletic Club at 5142 South Halsted, on October 3, 1925. Barely a month later, Sheldon's cigar store at Sixty-third Street and Ashland Avenue was bombed by the South Side O'Donnells. Sheldon survived the gang wars but, afflicted with tuberculosis, moved to California about 1929, where his career plummeted.

This rare photograph shows Al Capone at a downtown Chicago hotel, probably the Sherman, where he met with local politicians and civic leaders in an unsuccessful effort to restore peace among the city's warring gangs.

Captured in a gun battle with police after the abortive kidnapping of a Los Angeles gambler in December 1930, Sheldon was acquitted of shooting a policeman but ultimately convicted of kidnapping and sentenced to ten years to life. Died in San Quentin in 1944.

Shelton Brothers Bootlegging partners of Charlie Birger in the early twenties who later became his chief rivals. On November 12, 1926, they hired an Iowa cropduster to drop dynamite bombs on Charlie Birger's heavily fortified Shady Rest headquarters near Harrisburg, Illinois, which probably qualifies as the first aerial bombing in the U.S. (The only bomb to explode was far off its target.) The Birger and Shelton gangs also employed machine guns and specially made armored cars in their numerous battles in and around "Bloody Williamson" County in southern Illinois until 1927, when Birger had Carl, Earl, and Bernie Shelton framed for mail robbery and sentenced to twenty-five years in Leavenworth. Sheltons later were freed when a Birger gang member confessed to perjury. The Sheltons moved back to East St. Louis, Illinois, and operated rackets there until the late 1940s, when their former henchman, Frank "Buster" Wortman, took control, allegedly with the backing of the Chicago Syndicate. Carl Shelton was murdered on his farm near Fairfield, Illinois, October 23, 1947. Bernie Shelton was killed outside his tavern near Peoria, July 26, 1948. Roy Shelton was shot to death on his farm in Wayne County, June 7, 1950. Earl Shelton survived a murder attempt and fled the state, living to old age and dying in Jacksonville, Florida on October 8, 1986.

Simons, Avery Lee (aka Avery Simmons, Jim Ripley, Dan Ripley, "Young Dannie," "South American Fat," and other aliases) [1902–1987] Born at Corvallis, Oregon, September 21, 1902, the son of Louis and Cora Simons. Longtime "yegg" regularly teamed with Eddie Doll, alias Eddie LaRue. They were known as the "Gold Dust Twins" and eventually switched from bank burglaries to daylight robberies, working often with Eddie Bentz, "Baron" Lamm, Charles Fitzgerald, Homer Wilson, Clyde Nimerick, and other members of the bank-robbing elite. Like Doll/LaRue, his surplus of aliases served to downplay notoriety for Simons, and his arrests were generally few and far between. Convicted of robbery in Indiana, Simons was sent to the state reformatory at Pendleton on July 6, 1924, under a ten-year sentence but escaped on September 21, 1925. Recaptured at Winston-Salem, North Carolina, on February 27, 1927, he again escaped on March 6, jumping a train at Vulcan, West Virginia, while being returned to Indiana. With Bentz, Doll, Fitzgerald, and others robbed the Lincoln National Bank & Trust Co. in Lincoln, Nebraska, of more than $2 million on September 17, 1930, at that time the world's largest bank robbery (which eventually forced the bank's closing, despite the recovery of stolen bonds by Capone gangster Gus Winkeler, who had been wrongly accused of participating). This was the culmination of a string of successful bank jobs that allowed Simons to amass a fortune, and he fled to Bolivia, marrying a wealthy landowner's daughter and prospering in the cattle business until political turmoil forced his return to the U.S. and resumption of his criminal career.

He rejoined Eddie Bentz for a string of eastern bank robberies in 1934, but they soon found themselves federal fugitives thanks to the newly passed anti-crime bills lobbied through Congress by Attorney General Homer Cummings and J. Edgar Hoover. Captured by the FBI in Los Angeles on May 14, 1936, while attempting to flee the country, Simons eventually pleaded guilty to bank robberies in Danville and Brandon, Vermont, and was sentenced to twenty-five years, winding up on Alcatraz. He was wanted for other bank robberies in Indiana, North Carolina, and Canada. Changing political regimes brought a huge monetary settlement from loss of his Bolivian property, and Simons found himself released from prison with sufficient funds to forestall further legal difficulties and acquire a new young bride. Died in Van Nuys, California, October 1, 1987.

Slaughter, Tom "Curly" [1893–1921] Born in Virginia and moved at an early age to Texas. A southwestern badman who progressed from horse theft to "motorized banditry," Slaughter lived up to his name as a ruthless killer, keeping score of his victims by carving notches on his .351 Winchester. Often captured but always escaping during his bank-robbing career, Slaughter finally was sent to Tucker Prison Farm in Arkansas on a life sentence for the murder of a Hot Springs policeman in 1920. He later killed two armed trusty guards in a failed escape attempt and was sentenced to die in the electric chair at Little Rock. On December 8, 1921, having somehow acquired an automatic pistol, Slaughter virtually took over the prison, locking up the warden and his family and several guards, freeing six other prisoners, and escaping in a stolen car. Slaughter's body was found not long after a gun battle with Benton, Arkansas, police, and one of the escapees, Jack Howard, soon surrendered, claiming he had been forced against his will to join the break and had killed Slaughter. Some authorities doubted Howard's story, but he received a reward and parole.

Spencer, Ethan Allen (Al) "Junkey" [1887–1923] Born near Lenapah, Oklahoma, December 26, 1887. Outlaw based in the Osage Hills of Oklahoma and reputedly a onetime member of Henry Starr's gang. Former horse and cattle thief who gained notoriety in early 1920s as a "motorized" bank robber. Linked by many writers with the Barkers during their Tulsa days, though no evidence of this association appears in contemporary records. With Frank Nash and others, was credited with robbing forty-two banks during 1922–23, though this certainly is exaggerated. Robbed *Katy Limited* mail train of $20,000 near Okesa, Oklahoma, on August 21, 1923 (the last train holdup committed in Oklahoma). Killed by police and federal officers on the Osage Indian Reservation near Bartlesville, Oklahoma, on September 15, 1923 (though some accounts have him killed elsewhere, possibly on a farm near Coffeeville, Kansas, belonging to a turncoat associate, with the body moved to protect the informer and possibly actual killer).

Starr, Henry "Buck" or "The Bearcat" [1873–1921] Born near Fort Gibson, Indian Territory, December 2, 1873, the son of George "Hop" Starr and Mary Scott Starr, and nephew of Sam and Belle Starr. "Halfbreed Cherokee outlaw" and a transitional figure between the outlaws of the Old West and the "motorized bandits" of the twenties. Often but wrongly credited as the first American bank robber to switch from horse to automobile (nor did he ever drive a Stutz Bearcat, as at least one writer claimed). After a long criminal career that included several prison terms interspersed with brief periods of legitimate work, Starr was wounded and captured at Stroud, Oklahoma, after his gang had successfully robbed two banks there on March 27, 1915. Sentenced to twenty-five years, Starr was paroled in 1919 and embarked on a brief but unprofitable career as the star of silent Western films, even playing himself in the movie version of the Stroud robberies, entitled *A Debtor to the Law.* An earlier attempt at self-promotion was a 1914 autobiography, written in the Colorado's state prison, entitled *Thrilling Events.* It was later suspected, and probably true, that Starr continued robbing banks even during his movie-making days. Starr was mortally wounded while robbing a bank at Harrison, Arkansas, on February 18, 1921, and died four days later, after boasting that he had "robbed more banks than any man in America." It was apparently the only career at which he enjoyed any success.

Terrill, George Raymond (Ray) [1898–1980] Born in Oklahoma, November 15, 1898. 1920s bank burglar noted for his frequent escapes from jails and prisons and his alleged association with Al Spencer and the Kimes brothers. Often went by the alias of Patton, his stepfather's name. Considerable doubt exists as to whether there ever was a "Kimes-Terrill Gang," but their names often were linked in newspaper headlines. Terrill and his actual partners, including Jeff Duree, Herman Barker, and Elmer Inman, devised the technique of backing a truck up to a bank door at night, then winching out the safe and cracking it elsewhere, unlike the Kimes boys, who preferred daylight stickups. Apprehended for the last time at Hot Springs, Arkansas, November 26, 1927, Terrill was returned to Oklahoma's state prison at McAlester to complete a twenty-year sentence for bank burglary. Paroled in 1936, apparently reformed, after having reportedly invented a "burglar-proof" locking mechanism for safes. Operated a nightclub in Oklahoma City for several years, later moved to California, then Arizona. Died in Oatman, Arizona, October 16, 1980.

Thompson, Irvin "Blackie" [1893–1934] Notorious southwestern bank robber, murderer, and prison escapee, linked in the 1920s to such outlaws as Al Spencer and Ray Terrill. Sentenced in 1920 to five years in the McAlester, Oklahoma, state prison for auto larceny. Paroled but was returned in 1923 on a bank-robbery conviction. Again paroled in 1924 on his promise to act as an undercover informant in a series of murders of oil-rich Osage Indians, but broke parole by robbing a bank in Avery, Oklahoma, with Joe Clayton and Bill Donald (real name Phenix Donald, alias "Lapland Willie" Weaver, later a member of the Barker-Karpis Gang), and killing two law officers in Drumright, Oklahoma. Returned to McAlester on a life sentence, Thompson escaped with William "Whitey" Walker and Roy Johnson on August 30, 1933, failing to return from a fishing excursion on a prison farm pond. The "Fishing Hole Gang" then committed a series of bank robberies in Texas in the fall of 1933, some of which were blamed on the Barrow Gang, before being recaptured in Florida in January 1934. Convicted of robbery with firearms, a capital offense in Texas, Walker and Johnson were sentenced to life imprisonment, Thompson to death. Escaped from the Death House at the state prison in Huntsville with former Barrow Gang members Raymond Hamilton and Joe Palmer on July 22, 1934 (the day John Dillinger was killed in Chicago). Two other would-be escapees, Charlie Frazier and "Whitey" Walker, were shot, the latter fatally. Thompson was killed by police at Amarillo, Texas, December 6, 1934.

Torrio, John (Johnny) [1882–1957] Born in Orsara di Puglia, Italy, near Naples, January 20, 1882, the son of Thomas and Maria Torrio. Entered the U.S. with his widowed mother in 1884 and was "discovered" a few years later by Brooklyn gangster Frankie Yale. Possibly related to Chicago vice lord "Big Jim" Colosimo (by varying accounts, Torrio was either Colosimo's nephew or the cousin of his wife, Victoria), he

BILL BALSAMO

John Torrio (left), in a photo taken before he was shot outside his South Side apartment in retaliation for ordering the murder of Dean O'Banion. At right is probably the earliest photograph of Al Capone, who inherited Torrio's bootlegging empire.

was commissioned to deal with local Black Hand extortionists threatening Colosimo. He did so simply by killing them in a South Side railroad underpass and became Colosimo's second-in-command. About 1919 or 1920, Torrio provided employment for young Brooklyn fugitive Alphonse Capone, who had become a murder suspect in New York while working for Yale. And about that time Torrio conspired to kill Colosimo, who had left his wife to marry singer Dale Winter and, mainly, was neglecting his brothels and ignoring the bootlegging opportunities afforded by Prohibition. Brooklyn mobster Frankie Yale was suspected of the murder. In any case, Torrio and Capone took over Colosimo's organization, expanded into large-scale bootlegging and racketeering, and then used persuasion and violence to forge a citywide crime cartel known as the Chicago Syndicate, or the Outfit. After the Sieben

Brewery swindle that led to Torrio's arrest and O'Banion's murder in 1924, Torrio himself was nearly killed by O'Banion's successors on January 24, 1925, outside his apartment at 7011 Clyde Avenue. He recovered, turned the organization over to Capone, served a brief jail sentence stemming from the Sieben Brewery raid, and fled to Italy. He later returned to the U.S. as a "gangster emeritus," remaining active in New York rackets but also working to shape the future of U.S. organized crime. In 1939 he pleaded guilty to income tax evasion, was sentenced to two and a half years in Leavenworth, and then evidently retired, though FBI reports note his presence as an "arbitrator" for a Chicago mob as late as July 1954. Died of a heart attack in Brooklyn, April 16, 1957.

Touhy, Roger "The Terrible" [1898–1959] Best-known of five gangster brothers (collectively called the "Terrible Touhys") whose father was a Chicago policeman who changed the family name from Toohey to Towey. Roger became a major bootlegger and labor racketeer who controlled the Northwest suburbs in defiance of the Capone Syndicate. The Touhy mob also included several men, including brother Tommy, who were wanted for a number of mail and bank robberies and who allegedly worked with the Chicago kidnapping gang of "Handsome Jack" Klutas. Arrested by the FBI near Elkhorn, Wisconsin, on July 19, 1933, Roger was charged, tried, and acquitted of kidnapping William Hamm, who actually was abducted by the Barker-Karpis Gang. The next year Touhy was convicted of kidnapping Jake "The Barber" Factor, a Capone associate and international confidence man, and sentenced to ninety-nine years in Joliet. Touhy always maintained that he had been framed by the Capone mob and Factor to put him out of business. Convinced his case was hopeless, he joined Basil "The Owl" Banghart, Eddie Darlak, and others in a successful prison break on October 9, 1942. He was recaptured at 5116 Kenmore Avenue in Chicago on December 29, 1942, by FBI agents led by J. Edgar Hoover (performing his last "personal" arrest). Two other escapees, James O'Connor and St. Clair McInerney, were killed by FBI agents the same day, at 1254 Leland. The escape cost Touhy an additional 199 years. In 1954, federal Judge John P. Barnes reviewed the case, concluded that the Factor kidnapping was bogus and set Touhy free, but state authorities soon returned him to prison on his escape conviction. His sentence finally was commuted and he was paroled in November 1959, but was shot to death on December 16 outside his sister's Chicago home at 125 North Lotus. Author of *The Stolen Years* (1959) and buried under the family name Towey. [Touhy's only surviving brother, "Terrible Tommy," died in Chicago a few months later of a liver ailment on May 16, 1960, under the name Thomas Toohey.]

Trainor, Nicholas "Chaw Jimmie" (alias J. S. Sloane) [1887–1922] Reportedly born in Ireland and rumored to have been an IRA gunman before emigrating to the U.S. Midwest. Bank robber and sometime partner of Harvey Bailey, and the only man ever positively identified as a participant in the Denver Mint robbery of December 18, 1922. Mortally wounded in battle with Mint guards, one of whom was killed. Carried off by his accomplices, Trainor's body was found in the abandoned getaway car in a garage at 1631 Gilpin Street in Denver, January 14, 1923. Notorious bank robber Thomas Bell, now better known as "Baron" Lamm, reportedly helped Trainor's widow, Florence, acquire his share of the Mint loot and became her new companion until his own demise after a Clinton, Indiana, bank robbery in 1930.

Underhill, Wilbur "Mad Dog" (true name: Henry Wilbur Underhill Jr.) [1901–1934] Born in Newtonia, Missouri, March 16, 1901, the son of Henry Wilbur and Nancy Almira Underhill. Violent mugger and holdup man turned bank robber and reputed drug addict known as the "Tri-State Terror." Supposedly kicked out of the "Kimes-Terrill Gang" (itself probably a newspaper fiction) in 1920s for his homicidal ways. Twice convicted of murder but escaped from state prisons in Oklahoma and Kansas. Robbed banks with Harvey

HOME

Chicago Daily Tribune

THE WORLD'S GREATEST NEWSPAPER

TOUHY GANG SECRETS BARED

MONETARY BILL ON LAST LAP IN SENATE TODAY

Committee Limits It to 3 Years

NEWS SUMMARY

MYRTLE AND HER COP'S WIFE TAKE TURNS ON STAND

Each Gives Her Side of Love War.

U.S. Notifies Cuban Regime of Recognition

STATE REVEALS BASIS OF FACTOR KIDNAPING CASE

Trial Jury Complete in Surprise Move

2 CENTS

Chicago Daily Tribune

FINAL

FACTOR TELLS TORTURE TALE

ROOSEVELT MEN WIN IN SENATE TEST ON MONEY

NEWS SUMMARY

VICTIM POINTS OUT KIDNAPERS IN COURT DRAMA

Touhy Identified as Gang Leader.

CENTURIES APART

Entire State Relief Board Resigns CWA

DILLINGER GANG FACING DEATH AS STATES ACT

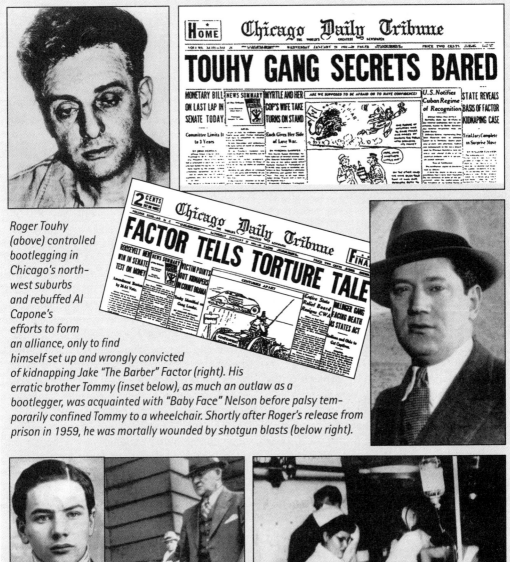

Roger Touhy (above) controlled bootlegging in Chicago's northwest suburbs and rebuffed Al Capone's efforts to form an alliance, only to find himself set up and wrongly convicted of kidnapping Jake "The Barber" Factor (right). His erratic brother Tommy (inset below), as much an outlaw as a bootlegger, was acquainted with "Baby Face" Nelson before palsy temporarily confined Tommy to a wheelchair. Shortly after Roger's release from prison in 1959, he was mortally wounded by shotgun blasts (below right).

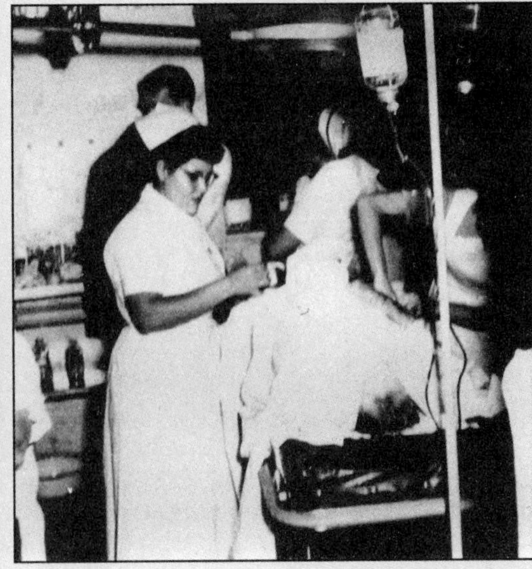

Bailey and others in Oklahoma and Kansas during 1933. Suspected, with many others, in the Kansas City Massacre. Mortally wounded by police and FBI agents in Shawnee, Oklahoma, on December 30, 1933. Died at the prison hospital, McAlester, Oklahoma, January 6, 1934. While largely forgotten today, Underhill was a nationally headlined criminal in 1933 and the first fugitive killed by the FBI.

Walker, William Jennings Bryan "Whitey" [1897–1934] Longtime Texas and Oklahoma outlaw suspected of involvement in many southwestern bank robberies with such bandits as Matt Kimes, Ray Terrill, and "Blackie" Thompson. Arrested in 1929 as a suspect in the infamous Lamar, Colorado, bank robbery actually committed by the Fleagle Gang, which resulted in the murders of four men. Convicted of bank robbery in Oklahoma in 1929 and sentenced to ninety-nine years, Walker escaped from Oklahoma's state prison with "Blackie" Thompson and Roy Johnson, August 30, 1933, and embarked on a series of bold Texas robberies. Recaptured in Florida in January 1934, Walker was convicted again of armed robbery and sentenced to life in the Texas state prison at Huntsville. Killed by guards while attempting to escape, July 22, 1934, though his partner Thompson successfully made it over the wall with Raymond Hamilton and Joe Palmer.

Weiss, Earl "Hymie" (true name: Henry Earl Wojiechowski, sometimes spelled Wajiechowski) [1898–1926] Born in Chicago in 1898. Succeeded Dean O'Banion as leader of Chicago's North Siders. Often and erroneously credited with inventing the "one-way ride," although he may have coined the phrase. Spurned Capone's peace offers and made several attempts on his life, prompting Capone to buy his famous armored Cadillac sedan and retaliate in self-defense. On October 11, 1926, three weeks after Weiss had sent several carloads of gunmen to attack Capone's Cicero headquarters in the Hawthorne hotel, he and bodyguard Patrick Murray were killed and two others wounded by a Capone shotgun and machine-gun firing from the upstairs window of an apartment next to Schofield's flower shop, where O'Banion had been killed but which had remained headquarters for the North Side Gang. [The machine gun jammed after thirty-five rounds and was tossed onto the roof of a doghouse by the escaping shooters.]

Weissman, Saul Snider "Big Solly" or "Cutcher-Head-Off" A St. Louis native and supposed former member of Egan's Rats, 300-pound "Solly" Weissman arrived in Kansas City at the beginning of Prohibition and made a name for himself in gambling, bootlegging, jewelry heists, and as a slugger for Tom Pendergast's Democratic political machine. Partner with John Lazia in a dog track until 1929 when he moved to Minneapolis, possibly crowded out by Lazia or others, although Weissman told newspapers that he feared no living man. He said he was leaving only because of seasonal "asama" and hay fever, and would return as soon as the first frost hit the ground. Three Weissman associates were killed at White Bear Lake in August 1930, by varying accounts either for hijacking liquor from Twin Cities allies of "Bugs" Moran or by Verne Miller for cheating his friends of robbery proceeds. Weissman returned to Kansas City on October 28, 1930, to face Prohibition charges—which were quickly dismissed—but he was shot dead only a few hours later in a downtown bookie joint by wire service manager Charlie Haughton, who was never charged with the crime. [Solly also is often confused with William Weissman, an unrelated ex-St. Louis and Kansas City mobster who joined the Zwillman mob and was murdered in Irvington, New Jersey, in 1941.]

Winkeler, August Henry (Gus) (alias "Big Mike," James Ray, Rand; spelled Winkler by police and the press) [1900–1933] Born in St. Louis, Missouri, March 28, 1900. Graduate of St. Louis' Egan's Rats gang and longtime partner of Fred "Killer" Burke in bank and payroll robberies. With Burke, joined the Capone Syndicate as a special-assignment gunman who helped kill defector

Frankie Yale, which supposedly qualified him and his murder squad to perform the big one: the St. Valentine's Day Massacre. Wrongly suspected in the $2 million bank robbery at Lincoln, Nebraska, in 1930, but knew the perpetrators and avoided prosecution by arranging the return of a large part of the loot. Rose in the ranks of Capone's organization as one of his "American boys" and was rewarded with control of much of Chicago's prosperous North Side, once Moran's hold was broken and Joe Aiello killed. Opened several popular night spots, including the 225 Club, whose manager, Edgar Lebensberger, died in a supposed suicide that may have been murder. Part owner of Twenty-second Street garage in Cicero, with Joe Bergl, who supplied cars specially equipped with armor plating, sirens, and smokescreen devices to major mobsters and outlaws, including "Machine Gun" Kelly and the Barker-Karpis Gang. Lived in luxury at 3300 North Lake Shore Drive and increasingly sought respectability as his holdings expanded, including his interest in the beer distributing company of Charles H. Weber, whose trucks reportedly rushed the first legal brew to the Chicago World's Fair when the Volstead Act was amended in 1933 to permit 3.2 beer.

Winkeler was murdered on October 9, 1933, by shotgun blasts from a panel truck parked outside the Weber Distributing Co. at 1414 Roscoe Street on Chicago's Mid-North Side. The killers probably were sent by Frank Nitti in his campaign to take over the Capone organization by eliminating his potential competition, especially the "American boys." However, Winkeler also was talking with federal agents, much to Nitti's alarm. After Winkeler's murder, his loyal and long-suffering wife, Georgette, who had urged Gus to get out of the rackets, attempted suicide in their swank Lake Shore Drive apartment, but she tipped her hand by telephoning the wife of Fred "Killer" Burke, who had moved into the neighborhood after her husband had gone to prison. Mrs. Burke perceived Georgette's depressed state of mind and reached the Winkeler apartment in time to call the fire department's rescue squad.

Zerilli, Joseph [1897–1977] Born in Terrasina, Sicily, December 30, 1897. With bootlegging partner William "Black Bill" Tocco (another Terrasina native who was Zerilli's cousin and brother-in-law), survived the wars of various rival Italian bootlegging factions in Detroit and allied with Angelo Meli, John "Papa John" Priziola, the Licavoli brothers' River Gang, and others to form the city's modern crime family. With the decline of the Jewish Purple Gang, Zerilli emerged in the mid-thirties as Detroit's major organized crime leader and prospered over the years in gambling, narcotics, labor racketeering, and a multitude of sometimes-legitimate businesses, including grocery stores, bakeries, restaurants, linen services, motels, construction companies, and the Hazel Park Racing Association and Racetrack. He remained largely anonymous until publicly identified by Joe Valachi in 1963. Zerilli, whose only convictions resulted in small fines (for gun carrying and speeding in the 1920s), remained largely untouchable to the end, though his family's power gradually eroded from intense federal pressure and the encroachments of black narcotics gangs. Near the end, Zerilli himself was named by federal investigators as the most likely instigator of Jimmy Hoffa's disappearance. He died after a long illness on October 31, 1977. Membership in the Zerilli crime family, which had sixty-three identified members, dwindled to twenty-three by the mid-nineties, and most are now in prison.

Zuta, Jack (true name: Jacob U. Zoota; "Jake," but preferred "John") [1888–1930] Born in Poland, February 15, 1880, but often wrongly described as Russian. Prominent North Side gangster involved in bootlegging, gambling, and prostitution, and allied with "Bugs" Moran and Joe Aiello against the Capone Syndicate. A suspect in the Jake Lingle murder, of which Leo Brothers, represented by Dillinger's future lawyer Louis Piquett, was convicted on flimsy evidence and given only fourteen years. Machine-gunned in spectacular fashion on the dance floor of the Lake View Hotel near Delafield, Wisconsin, on August 1, 1930, presumably on orders of Al Capone.

EAST COAST GANGSTERS AND OUTLAWS
1920–1940

Adonis, Joe (true name: Giuseppe Dato, Americanized to Joseph Doto) [1902–1971] Born in Montemarano, Italy, November 22, 1902, son of Michele and Maria Dato (birth record falsified in 1933 to Passaic, New Jersey, November 5, 1901). Headed the Broadway Mob of rumrunners during Prohibition. Lieutenant of "Lucky" Luciano and suspect in 1931 murder of "Joe the Boss" Masseria. Brooklyn waterfront racketeer, loan shark, suspected narcotics trafficker, and partner of Frank Costello and Meyer Lansky in illegal gambling casinos in New York, New Jersey, and Florida, 1930s to the fifties. Convicted in 1951 of gambling conspiracy and sentenced to two to three years in New Jersey state prison. Deported to Italy, January 3, 1956. Arrested in Milan, June 1971, in anti-Mafia drive by Italian police. Exiled to Serra de Conti, Italy. Died at Ancona, Italy, November 26, 1971.

Amberg Brothers Small-time Brooklyn gangsters. Herman (or Hyman) "Hymie the Rat" Amberg, was arrested in 1926 for the murder of a Bronx jeweler. He committed suicide along with another accused murderer, Mike "Red" McKenna, and jewel thief Robert Berg, after an unsuccessful escape attempt from Manhattan's Tombs prison on November 3, 1926, in which the warden and a guard were slain. Joe and Louis Amberg later gained notoriety in loan-sharking—in competition with "Dutch" Schultz—and narcotics. Joe Amberg, at age forty-three, was executed with his chauffeur, Morris Kessler, by an underworld firing squad at a Brooklyn warehouse on September 30, 1935. His thirty-six-year-old brother, Louis "Pretty" Amberg, reportedly so named because of his ugliness, was suspected of instigating the Newark murders of the Schultz mob, but was killed on the same day, October 23, 1935. He was hacked up with an axe and left in a burning car near Brooklyn's Navy Yard. Another brother, Oscar, worked with Joe and "Pretty" in the 1930s.

Anastasia, Albert (true name: Umberto Anastasio) [1902–1957] Born in Tropea, Italy, September 26, 1902. Entered U.S. in 1919, becoming a Brooklyn waterfront racketeer closely allied with Louis "Lepke" Buchalter. Called by the press the "Lord-High Executioner of Murder, Inc." and known in the underworld as "The Executioner" and "The Mad Hatter." Convicted with Joe Florina, alias Speranza, of the 1920 murder of George Terillo (or Tirello) and sentenced May 25, 1921, to be executed. Both ordered retried on December 6, 1921. Charges dropped, reportedly after four witnesses were shot to death and a fifth placed in a mental institution. Convicted in 1923 of gun possession and sentenced to two years. A suspect in numerous murders over the years, including the 1931 killing of "Joe the Boss" Masseria. Anastasia allegedly headed the New York Syndicate's execution squad, known in the press as "Murder, Inc." For years controlled Local 1814 of the International Longshoremen's Association through his brother, Anthony "Tough Tony" Anastasio.

Anastasia was identified by informers Abe Reles and Albert Tannenbaum as instigator of the 1939 slayings of Teamsters official Morris Diamond and longshoreman Peter Panto. Charged with the Diamond slaying and became a fugitive, joining the Army under an assumed name. Charge dropped when witness Abe Reles died under suspicious circumstances, falling or getting pushed from the window of a hotel room where he was in protective custody of New York police. Said by mob informer Joe Valachi to have ordered the 1952 murder of Arnold Schuster, who had turned in bank robber Willie Sutton. Underboss of

THE "GOOD KILLERS" GANG

Deaths attributed to the "Good Killers" made front-page copy for New York newspapers in the early 1920s and briefly attracted police attention in other cities, but the gang was long forgotten by the time Murder, Inc. was discovered in 1940. Nearly twenty years after that, the "Killers" were rediscovered by an FBI team, headed by Assistant Director William Sullivan, who was trying to persuade a still-reluctant J. Edgar Hoover that interstate organized crime did exist. The following, based on early published accounts and somewhat overstated, is reprinted from a book-length document that the bureau called "The Mafia Monograph," dated July 9, 1958:

> [I]n 1921, police in several big cities uncovered an early version of Murder, Inc., in the form of a Mafia gang which had been given the name "Good Killers." This group of assassins was suspected of some 125 unsolved murders of Italians in New York City, Pittsburgh, Detroit, and Chicago. Persons in this Mafia operation had immigrated to the United States about 12 years before from the Castellammare area of Sicily. They became so noted for their talents that their services were widely sought and highly paid for. They specialized in the murder of individuals for any reason, but their activities also included the robbery of successful Italian merchants and the control of the Italian policy game. One method utilized by the "Good Killers" was to force or hire other Italian gangsters to do the actual killings and then murder them as a coverup. The "Good Killers" gang was reported to have accumulated a "war chest" of $200,000. Several leaders of that murder band established themselves in business in the Italian communities of cities in order to conceal the criminal manner in which they acquired their wealth. . . .

As in the case of Murder, Inc., the "Good Killers" came to the attention of the authorities when one of their recruited murderers learned that he himself was now "on the spot" and spilled what he knew about the assassination gang. Newspapers of the day inflated the scope and wealth of the gunmen, thanks to the fearful witness or to the police, or both.

On August 9, 1921, some crab fishermen netted a bag from the Shark River in New Jersey containing the remains of an Italian bootlegger named Camillo Caizzo. Police typically were stumped until a few days later when Bartolo Fontano ran into their arms with a strange tale of a "murder gang" that had forced him to kill his best friend. He had learned from another friend that the gang now planned to "burn him," and he was terrified. Fontano was speaking literally, as the Bonventre Gang (named for an early leader who'd been cremated in the oven of his own Brooklyn bakery) had even adopted a battle cry: "We will burn you." It was typical of the gang, Fontano said, to hire or forcibly recruit outside assassins to commit murders, then kill them to cover their tracks.

Fontano named six men as leaders of the gang: Stefano Magaddino, Barcolomero Di Gregorio, Vito Bonventre, Giuseppi Lombardi, Mariano Galliade, and Francesco Puma. He and Caizzo were members of the gang, all of whom came from the Castellammare del Golfo region of Sicily. The gang had been formed in the early 1900s and had moved to Detroit after their founder's death, then had returned to Brooklyn about 1913. Fontano connected the gang to nine killings in Detroit and seven in New York.

Evidently they were early racketeers in that they controlled the Italian policy game (a numbers racket) and resorted to robbery or black-hand tactics in dealing with successful Italian merchants. Possibly they were linked with, or at least well-known to, the Unione Siciliana, the immigrant benevolent society that was taken over by "civic-minded" gangsters who earned a measure of respect in Italian and Sicilian neighborhoods even as they promoted "home distilling," which produced much of the alcohol used to cut and counterfeit foreign liquor. They usually killed for "business" reasons, but several of the murders were a continuation an old family vendetta in Sicily.

Magaddino was living undercover as an illegal alien, but police set a trap for him, using Fontano as bait. Fontano called Magaddino, saying the police were after him and he needed money to get out of town. Magaddino met Fontano at Grand Central Station, gave him $30, and ordered him to go to Buffalo. Detectives immediately grabbed Magaddino and soon afterward rounded up the other gang leaders in their homes. At police headquarters, Magaddino grabbed Fontano by the throat and screamed, "I'll burn you for this!" He was quickly subdued with a blackjack.

The story was a sensation, and when Fontano casually remarked that the gang was "good at killing," they instantly were headlined as the "Good Killers." New York police, especially Detective Michael Fiaschetti, who had succeeded Joe Petrosino as head of the Italian Squad, made greatly exaggerated statements to the press about "Mafia" and "Camorra" murder squads, and detectives from other cities were eager to link the crew with their own unsolved slayings. Within a few days, the *New York Times* was reporting the gang to be responsible for 125 murders in four cities.

Fiaschetti, in his overblown memoirs nine years later, wrote of the Bonventre crew:

> [T]he gang, as it turned out, was one of the worst Camorrist organizations on record. It had ramifications throughout the United States and was responsible for a score of murders. The killing of Camillo Caiozzo [sic] had been one of its characteristic acts, a barbarous episode fit for another and utterly barbarous era. . . .

By Fiaschetti's account, the case "marked one of the important stages in the breaking up of the Black Hand in New York," with Fontano getting a long prison sentence and several others going to the chair. Actually, though, only Fontano went to prison, and the gang leaders went free. One, Francesco Puma, was murdered a few years later. The "Good Killers" soon were forgotten by the press and public.

In his commendable book *Gangster City: The History of the New York Underworld, 1900–1935,* Pat Downey re-examined the "Good Killers" and made some interesting connections the FBI somehow missed. One was that the gang was the same Castellammarese faction later led by Salvatore Maranzano in his war against "Joe the Boss" Masseria [see p. 102]. Magaddino's cousin Joe Bonanno entered the U.S. illegally about 1924 and joined this group, working as a bootlegger and in his uncle Vito Bonventre's bakery, according to his own recollections later. In 1930, Joe Valachi joined the family, probably with the sponsorship of Bonanno, reciting an oath along the lines of, "This is how I will burn, if I betray the secret of Cosa Nostra."

Downey speculates that the burnings of the "Good Killers'" victims possibly inspired that part of the oath, but other Mafia informers in Sicily and America have recalled similar initiations. The burning might have referred to the fires of hell, unless the Castellammarese preferred to roast their victims first in case one of them was heaven-bound.

Avoiding prosecution in the New York murders, Magaddino moved to Buffalo. "Old Joe" DiCarlo, who headed the Sicilian family there, died in 1922, and his son Joe Jr. went to prison soon after. Magaddino shortly emerged as the new Buffalo boss, quietly consolidating his control while police dismantled the noisier Polish bootlegging and robbery gang headed by John "Big Korney" Kwatowski. Magaddino came to dominate upstate New York for the next fifty years and even expanded into Toronto to seize remnants of Rocco Perri's bootlegging empire [see p. 206]. With his brother he opened an undertaking parlor, which may have provided a subtler method for disposing of murder victims.

In 1961, a suspected heroin trafficker named Albert Agueci was found murdered in a field near Rochester, a hit attributed to the Magaddino Family. Agueci was bound and tortured—with pounds of flesh sliced from his body—before being doused with gasoline and set afire. The murder and burning were ordered by one of the last survivors of the "Good Killers," maybe out of respect for tradition.

Stefano Magaddino died of natural causes in 1974 after a lifetime of avoiding prosecution for a multitude of crimes.

Vincent Mangano crime family from 1931 to 1951, when Mangano disappeared, presumably murdered, and Anastasia assumed leadership. Shot to death October 25, 1957, in barbershop of Park Sheraton Hotel (formerly the Park Central, where Arnold Rothstein had been slain in 1928). His murder was attributed to Vito Genovese's takeover of the Costello crime family, inasmuch as Anastasia was an ally of Costello, but also to Meyer Lansky, as Anastasia allegedly was attempting to muscle in on pre-Castro Cuban gambling operations.

Anderson, George "Dutch" (true name: Ivan Dahl Von Teller) [1879–1925] Born in Denmark, son of a noble family. Supposedly a graduate of the universities of Upsala and Heidelberg. Well educated, fond of music and literature, and multilingual. Came to U.S. 1899 or 1900. Attended University of Wisconsin but did not graduate. Began a life of petty crime about 1907 and served prison sentences in Ohio, Wisconsin, and Illinois. Arrested in Rochester, New York, in 1917 for a 1913 burglary, convicted, and sentenced to five years in Auburn Prison, where he met Gerald Chapman. Both paroled in 1919. After working briefly as bootleggers in Detroit, Toledo, and New York, Anderson and Chapman, with another Auburn parolee named Charles Loerber, robbed a U.S. Mail truck on Leonard Street in New York City, October 24, 1921, taking $2,400,000 in cash, bonds, and jewelry. All three captured in New York July 3, 1922. Anderson and Chapman each sentenced to twenty-five years in Atlanta Federal Penitentiary. Chapman escaped on April 5, 1923, and Anderson on December 30. Both later suspected of numerous bank robberies and other crimes. Though Chapman was the more notorious, Anderson was regarded as the leader. When Chapman was recaptured, Anderson murdered the informer, Ben Hance, and his wife near Muncie, Indiana, August 11, 1925. On October 31, 1925, in Muskegon, Michigan Detective Charles DeWitt Hammond attempted to arrest Anderson for passing counterfeit money and was shot. Though mortally wounded, Hammond wrested away Anderson's gun and killed him with it.

Antinori, Ignacio [d. 1940] Reputed Mafia leader in Tampa, Florida, allegedly active in gambling and narcotics. Murdered October 22, 1940.

Ashley, John [1895–1924] Everglades-based bank robber, bootlegger, hijacker, and pirate whose gang terrorized Florida for a decade, becoming folk heroes in the process. His criminal career apparently began with the murder of a Seminole Indian in 1911, and he became one of the first "motorized bandits," using cars rather than horses in his robberies. In addition to bank jobs, the Ashley Gang is reputed to have disrupted rumrunning between the Bahamas and Florida in the early twenties with their frequent hijackings, and reportedly raided liquor warehouses at Bimini. Ashley and three of his gang were ambushed and killed by police at Sebastian, Florida, November 1, 1924.

Avena, John "Big Nose" (alias John Nazzone) [d. 1936] Reputed boss of Italian crime family in Philadelphia. Murdered on August 17, 1936.

Bazzano, John [1890–1932] Apparently succeeded Joseph Siragusa as boss of Pittsburgh Mafia family. Found strangled and stabbed to death and sewn into a burlap bag on a street in Brooklyn, August 8, 1932.

Bitz, Irving [1904–1981], and Spitale, Salvatore "Salvy" [b. 1897] New York bootleggers and drug dealers who gained brief notoriety in the early thirties as suspects in the killings of "Legs" Diamond and "Vannie" Higgins and as underworld intermediaries in the Lindbergh kidnapping. Spitale was convicted of burglary in 1914 at age seventeen. Bitz was convicted of selling narcotics in 1926 and served a two-year sentence in Atlanta Federal Penitentiary. When "Legs" Diamond was shot at the Hotel Monticello in October 1930, he admitted to a reporter that Bitz and Spitale had done it in revenge for a botched drug deal, adding, "You can print it after I'm dead." New York police, in time, named Bitz and Spitale as prime suspects in another attempt and Diamond's eventual murder. Later named by

Abe Reles as liaisons between the Syndicate and New York's independent gangs. Forgotten after Prohibition, Bitz and Spitale remained lifelong criminals. Bitz was sentenced to three to six years in Sing Sing on gun-carrying and bail-jumping charges in 1934. Spitale was arrested several times on similar charges, convicted in 1939 of grand larceny, and returned to prison in 1948 for parole violation. He worked as a "special employee" for the Federal Bureau of Narcotics in the 1950s, probably dealing in narcotics, as well, and afterward faded into obscurity. Bitz largely avoided the limelight but prospered in racketeering with a New York Newspaper and Mail Deliverers Union, gaining a monopoly on newspaper and magazine distribution. He pleaded guilty in 1959 to antitrust and labor racketeering violations and was sentenced to five years in federal prison. Bitz was kidnapped on September 2, 1981, and a $150,000 ransom reportedly was paid. But he was murdered by his abductors. His body washed ashore on Oakwood Beach in Staten Island three weeks later. Bitz had been strangled.

Boiardo, Ruggiero "Richie the Boot" [1890–1984] Born in Naples, Italy, on either November 8 or December 8, 1890, according to varying records. Led North Ward Italian mob in Newark that fought Abner "Longy" Zwillman during Prohibition and was seriously wounded in a shooting on November 26, 1930. Later made peace with Zwillman in a treaty allegedly mediated by Al Capone (a 1930 photo of Boiardo shows him wearing a diamond belt buckle, a gift often bestowed to friends of Capone). Zwillman and Boiardo became close allies. Allegedly head of the Newark faction of the Vito Genovese family, Boiardo remained active in the rackets for decades. He later was assisted by his son Anthony ("Tony Boy"), who once described to associates and a hidden FBI microphone how he and "The Boot" once beat a man to death with a hammer and crowbar. "The Boot" lived in a huge stone mansion in Livingston, New Jersey, surrounded by garish statues of himself and his family, but he avoided the limelight until 1969 when his control of City Hall was exposed and Mayor Hugh Addonizio was convicted on racketeering charges. Ruggiero Boiardo was convicted of gambling conspiracy and entered the state prison at Leesburg on a two-to three-year sentence on November 18, 1970. He outlived his son by six years, dying on October 29, 1984.

Bonanno, Joseph "Joe Bananas" [1905–2002] Born in Castellammare del Golfo, Sicily, January 18, 1905. Son of a Sicilian Mafia boss and heir to the family tradition who fled to the U.S. in early twenties to avoid Mussolini's anti-Mafia crusade. Participated in New York's so-called Castellammarese War in 1930–31 on the side of Salvatore Maranzano. Gained brief notoriety under the alias of "Joseph Bonventre" in January 1931 when arrested in Brooklyn and erroneously accused of smuggling machine guns to Al Capone in Chicago. Succeeded Maranzano in September 1931 as boss of Brooklyn's Castellammarese crime family, since known simply as the Bonanno Family. Last survivor of the original Commission set up by "Lucky" Luciano in 1931 as ruling board of the Italian crime families (the members of which probably included the other four New York bosses, plus Capone, briefly, and Cleveland boss Frank Milano). Bonanno's long reign in Brooklyn ended in the 1960s after a gang war and his forced retirement for allegedly plotting against fellow Commission members, though the actual cause may have had more to do with the dissatisfaction of some of his own followers for promoting his son Bill as his intended successor. Bonanno relocated to his winter home in Tucson, Arizona, and surprisingly outlived his former enemies, despite authoring an autobiography that gang-busting prosecutor (later Mayor) Rudolph Giuliani used to bolster his successful "Mafia Commission" trial in the 1980s. Bonanno's refusal to testify in the case resulted in his first, brief, jail sentence. Died of heart failure in Tucson, May 11, 2002.

Bruno, Joseph (true name: Joseph Dovi) [1889–1946] Succeeded John "Big Nose" Avena as boss of the Philadelphia Mafia in 1936. Died of natural causes in New York on October 22, 1946.

The Philadelphia family reportedly was founded in the early 1900s by Salvatore Sabella, who was acquitted of a double murder in 1927 but deported to Italy. The city's dominant organized crime figures in the period were mainly Jewish gangsters such as Max "Boo Boo" Hoff, Irving "Waxey Gordon" Wexler, and Harry "Nig Rosen" Stromberg.

Buchalter, Louis "Lepke" [1897–1944] Born in New York City, February 12, 1897, the son of Barnet and Rose Buchalter. Infamous New York labor racketeer and narcotics trafficker, reputed to have ordered the murders of dozens of enemies and potential witnesses against him. Suspect in 1927 murder of Jacob "Little Augie" Orgen and wounding of bodyguard "Legs" Diamond. Some FBI informants named Buchalter as the principal New York contact of the Barker-Karpis Gang, and he harbored Verne Miller after the Kansas City Massacre, at least until things got too hot, and may have ordered Miller's death. Probably planned the 1935 murder of "Dutch" Schultz. Arranged through radio personality Walter Winchell to surrender in person to J. Edgar Hoover in New York City on August 24, 1939. Convicted of narcotics conspiracy in 1939 and sentenced to fourteen years in Leavenworth.

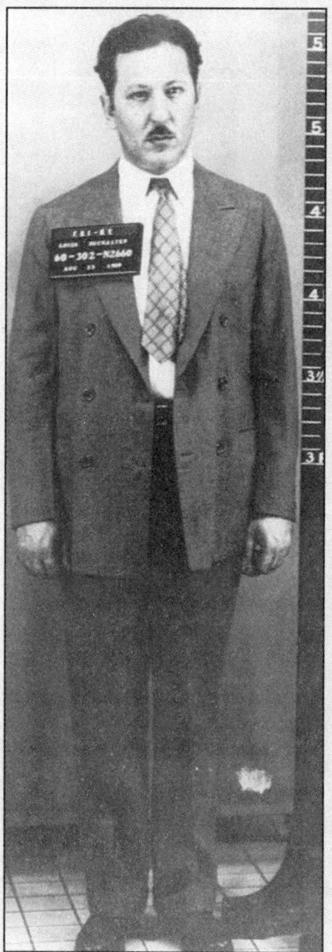

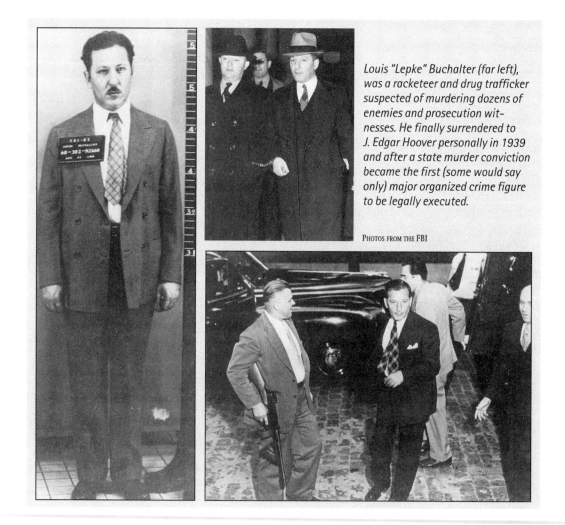

Louis "Lepke" Buchalter (far left), was a racketeer and drug trafficker suspected of murdering dozens of enemies and prosecution witnesses. He finally surrendered to J. Edgar Hoover personally in 1939 and after a state murder conviction became the first (some would say only) major organized crime figure to be legally executed.

PHOTOS FROM THE FBI

Convicted of murder in New York, 1941, and sentenced to death. Died in the electric chair at Sing Sing Prison, Ossining, New York, March 4, 1944, the first Syndicate boss to ever be executed legally.

"Buster from Chicago" (true name unknown) Supposed gunman for Salvatore Maranzano in the Castellammarese War, credited by Joe Valachi with several murders. Never identified but claimed by Valachi to have been murdered during a crap game on the Lower East Side in 1931. Valachi described "Buster" as a former Chicago gangster who "looked like a college boy" and carried a machine gun in a violin case (contrary to legend and gangster cartoons, a Thompson does not fit in a violin case). Joseph Bonanno recalled a colleague named Bastiano "Buster" Domingo but said he did not resemble Valachi's "Buster." Author Patrick Downey in *Gangster City* found a more likely candidate named Frank Marco, a former Aiello gangster who fled Chicago as a suspect in the murders of Tony Lombardo and Jake Lingle and was killed on the Lower East Side in 1931. Other researchers have suggested that "Buster" is a fictional character concocted by Valachi (but possibly the FBI) to conceal his own killings, for which he might have been extradited back to New York on old murder charges.

Chapman, Gerald [1888?–1926] Convicted of grand larceny in 1907 and served one year of a ten-year sentence. Convicted of burglary in 1908 and served three years. Convicted of armed robbery in 1911 and sent to Auburn Prison, where he met George "Dutch" Anderson, his future partner in crime. Both paroled in 1919. Chapman and Anderson achieved national notoriety as the decade's first "super-bandits" when they robbed a U.S. Mail truck of $2,400,000 on Leonard Street in New York City on October 24, 1921. Both captured July 3, 1922. Sentenced to twenty-five years in the federal penitentiary at Atlanta. Shot in escape attempt March 27, 1923. Escaped on April 5, 1923. Anderson escaped on December 30, 1923. With Anderson, suspected of bank and mail robberies and various major crimes in 1924. With Walter Shean, attempted to burglarize a store in New Britain, Connecticut, October 12, 1924, killing policeman James Skelly. Shean later was captured and named Chapman as his accomplice. Chapman and Anderson were harbored at Muncie, Indiana, by Ben Hance, who later turned informer, causing Chapman's capture at Muncie on January 18, 1925 (Hance then was murdered by Anderson). Convicted of the Skelly murder and sentenced to death. Chapman's attorneys appealed, questioning the state's right to execute Chapman when he still owed the federal government twenty-four years on his mail-robbery conviction. President Coolidge mooted that issue by commuting the federal sentence, and Chapman was hanged at Wethersfield, Connecticut, April 26, 1926.

Coll, Vincent "Mad Dog" [1908–1932] Born in Ireland, July 20, 1908. Former gunman for New York's "Dutch" Schultz mob who broke away in 1930 to form his own gang and wage war on Schultz. Later teamed with the Diamond mob against Schultz. Hijacked liquor and kidnapped other mobsters for ransom, including George "Big Frenchy" DeMange, partner of "Owney" Madden. Allegedly contracted by Mafia boss Salvatore Maranzano to murder "Lucky" Luciano and Vito Genovese in 1931, though this never came off. Accused of the Harlem "Baby Massacre," the shooting of five children, one fatally, during an unsuccessful attempt to kill gangster Joe Rao in front of the Helmar Social Club at 208 East 107th Street, July 28, 1931. Acquitted when attorney Samuel Liebowitz established that witness George Brecht gave perjured testimony. Machine-gunned, probably on orders of Madden, though it was popularly attributed to Schultz, in a telephone booth in the London Chemist drugstore, 314 West Twenty-third Street, February 9, 1932.

Coppola, Michael "Trigger Mike" [1900–1966] Born near Salerno, Italy, July 29, 1900, son of Giuseppe and Angelina Coppola. Moved at an early age to New York, where he became notorious as a gunman reputedly associated at various times with Vincent "Mad Dog" Coll, Louis "Lepke"

They only kill each other—and any innocent man or woman or child who gets in the way

New York mobster Vincent Coll (above) earned his nickname "Mad Dog" when his attack at the Helmar Social Club missed an intended victim but hit several children, killing one. He was later fatally machine-gunned in a drugstore telephone booth and given something less than an elaborate burial (bottom).

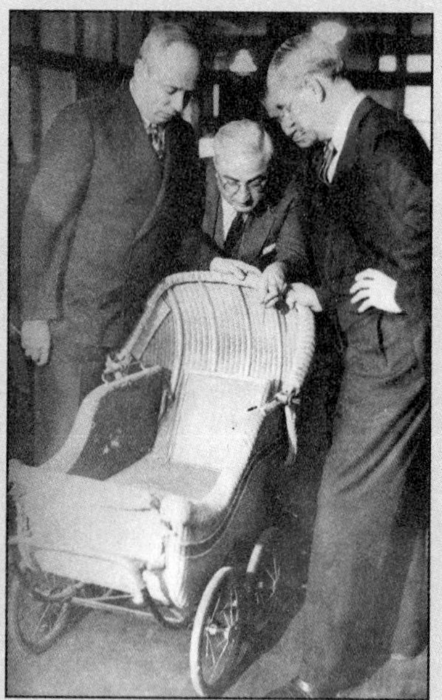

Buchalter, and Jack "Legs" Diamond. Suspected of masterminding the robbery of guests (mostly politicians and gangsters) at a Democratic Club's supper honoring Judge Albert Vitale at the Roman Gardens Restaurant in the Bronx, December 7, 1929. The supper had been organized by Ciro Terranova, Harlem crime boss and lieutenant of "Joe the Boss" Masseria. Coppola sided with Salvatore Maranzano against Masseria in the Castellammarese War of 1930–31. Later became a lieutenant of "Lucky" Luciano, replacing Ciro Terranova in mid-thirties as boss of the Harlem numbers racket. Prime suspect in the beating death of East Harlem Republican leader Joseph R. Scottoriggio on election day, November 5, 1946. In later years involved in Brooklyn waterfront racketeering and Florida gambling. Pleaded guilty to income tax evasion in 1962 and served a short prison sentence. His former wife, Ann Drahmann Coppola, who suspected Coppola of murdering his first wife and who had cooperated with the IRS investigation, apparently committed suicide six months later in Rome, Italy. "Trigger Mike" Coppola died in a Boston hospital on October 1, 1966.

Costello, Frank (true name: Francesco Castiglia) [1891–1973] Born in Lauropoli, Calabria, Italy, January 26, 1891, the son of Luigi and Maria Castiglia. With partner William Vincent "Big Bill" Dwyer, ran largest rumrunning operation in New York in 1920s. Expanded into slot machines in 1928, becoming known as the "Slot Machine King." Apparently inherited control of Tammany Hall political machine after the murder of Arnold Rothstein in 1928. Succeeded "Lucky" Luciano as boss of New York's largest Mafia family in 1937, after Luciano was convicted of controlling prostitution and his underboss, Vito Genovese, fled to Italy to avoid prosecution for murder. Involved for years in illegal and legal casino operations with Meyer Lansky, Joe Adonis, and others in New York, New Jersey, Florida, Kentucky, Louisiana, and Nevada. Apparently retired from the rackets after May 2, 1957, when he survived a murder attempt by Vincent "The Chin" Gigante, a soldier of Vito Genovese, who then assumed control of the family. Costello served a term for income tax evasion and was denaturalized for lying on his citizenship application, but avoided deportation. Died of a heart attack in a New York hospital, February 18, 1973.

Crowley, Francis "Two-Gun" [1912–1932] Born in New York City, October 31, 1912, the illegitimate son of Dora Dietz; father reputed to have been a New York City policeman. Foster brother, John Crowley, was killed by New York police while resisting arrest for disorderly conduct in 1925. Francis became a juvenile gunman and cop killer who terrorized New York City in the spring of 1931. Involved in numerous holdups and several shootings. Suspected participant in robbery of Huguenot Trust Co., New Rochelle, New York, March 15, 1931. Shot and killed Patrolman Frederick Hirsch at North Merrick, Long Island, May 6, 1931. Captured by New York police after a spectacular gun battle at an apartment building at 303 West Ninetieth Street, where an extra gun holstered to his leg earned him the nickname "Two-Gun." Convicted of murder and executed at Sing Sing, January 21, 1932. Crowley's partner, Rudolph "Fats" Duringer, also known as "Tough Red," was captured at the same time, convicted of murdering dance hall hostess Virginia Brannen, and executed at Sing Sing on December 10, 1931.

Cugino, Anthony "The Stinger" Philadelphia's Public Enemy No. 1 in 1934. Gang leader, bandit, and murderer, allegedly affiliated with the Tri-State Gang. Most noted for the extreme treachery he displayed by murdering some of his own crime partners to avoid sharing the loot. Betrayed by an accomplice and captured in New York City, September 8, 1935. Confessed to eight murders, then committed suicide by hanging himself in his cell.

D'Aquila, Salvatore "Toto" [1878–1928] Born in Sicily. Police record dated to 1906. Supposed "boss of bosses" of Italian crime families in 1920s though, as is inevitably the case, even his authority in New York was debatable. Bootlegger and olive oil and cheese importer who headed the future Mangano-Anastasia-Gambino Family. Shot to death after parking his car at 211 Avenue A near Thirteenth Street in Brooklyn on October 10, 1928. His murder is attributed to the family of "Joe the Boss" Masseria.

DeMange, George Jean "Big Frenchy" (aka George Fox) [1896–1939] Well-known Manhattan bootlegger, close friend of "Owney" Madden and variously described as Madden's lieutenant or partner. They had been enemies before Prohibition as members of the rival Hudson Dusters and Gophers gangs but joined forces in the early twenties when both worked for bootlegger Larry Fay. "Big Frenchy" was kidnapped by Vincent "Mad Dog" Coll in 1931, and Madden paid $35,000 ransom for his release. Interviewed afterward, DeMange commented only that it was "a little business deal with friends." He prospered in nightclubs (Club Argonaut, Park Avenue, Silver Slipper) before dying of a heart attack on September 18, 1939. DeMange's *Time* obituary described him as a "cagey onetime hoodlum, highjacker [sic] and bootlegger, latterly a millionaire Broadway restaurateur."

Diamond, John Thomas (Jack) "Legs" (alias John T. Noland, often erroneously given as his birth name) [1898–1931] Irish heritage, but born at 2350 East Albert Street in Philadelphia, July 11, 1898. Bodyguard and gunman for Arnold Rothstein and Jacob "Little Augie" Orgen. Bootlegger, narcotics trafficker, hijacker, bank robber, suspected of numerous murders. Reputedly a onetime rumrunning partner of Al Capone. Later allied with Vincent "Mad Dog" Coll's mob in an unsuccessful gang war against "Dutch" Schultz. Arrested more than two dozen times and survived at least four assassination attempts, which earned him the newspaper nickname of "Clay Pigeon of the Underworld." Once supposed to have bragged that "they haven't invented the bullet" that could kill him, he was murdered in a rooming house at 67 Dove Street, Albany, New York, December 17, 1931.

DiCarlo, Joseph Peter Sr. "Old Joe" [1873–1922] Born in Vallelunga, Sicily. Boss of Buffalo Mafia family in early twenties. Died of natural causes on July 9, 1922, and (after the murders of Philip Mazzeri, Joseph Benedetto, and several other "Mafiosi") was succeeded by Stefano Magaddino, who continued smuggling liquor and narcotics from Canada. DiCarlo's son, Joseph Jr., went to federal prison in Atlanta in 1924 on a six-year sentence for intimidating a government witness. [This Joseph is probably the Joseph "Jerry the Wolf" DiCarlo who later was prominent in the Magaddino Family and supposedly once was named Buffalo's Public Enemy No. 1.]

Duffy, Mickey (true name: Michael Joseph Cusick) [1889–1931] A Pole with an Irish alias, Mickey Duffy opened a brewery in Camden in the early twenties and soon emerged as the "Beer Baron of South Jersey." Expansion into Philadelphia brought him into conflict with bootleg king Max "Boo Boo" Hoff and led to that city's first machine-gun shooting on February 25, 1927, outside Duffy's Club Cadix at Twenty-third and Chestnut streets. Bodyguard John Bricker was killed, but Duffy survived, only to be shot dead in his sleep at his Ambassador Hotel suite in Atlantic City on August 29, 1931.

Dwyer, William Vincent "Big Bill" [1883–1946] Ex-stevedore who became a bootlegger during Prohibition, then established the largest rumrunning syndicate on the East Coast with help of boyhood friends from the Gophers and Hudson Dusters street gangs. First to engage in wholesale bribery of U.S. Coast Guard crews and employ some as rumrunners. Partner in Phenix Brewery [not "Phoenix"] with "Owney" Madden and "Waxey" Gordon. Also worked with Frank Costello, Frankie Yale, Larry Fay, and Charles "Vannie" Higgins. Convicted of bootlegging in 1926 and sentenced to two years in the Atlanta Federal Penitentiary. Succeeded by Frank Costello, who was acquitted in the same case. Dwyer traded liquor interests to his associates for racetrack interests, gaining a reputation as a millionaire sportsman. Once owner of the

After being shot on several occasions, New York mobster Jack "Legs" Diamond became known as the "Clay Pigeon of the Underworld." He finally was killed by rivals in an Albany, New York, rooming house after his 1931 acquittal in a kidnapping case.

Brooklyn Dodgers football team. Brought professional hockey to New York. Acquitted of income tax evasion in 1934 but convicted on another tax charge in 1939. Reportedly died penniless in 1946.

Eastman, Edward "Monk" [1876–1920] Notorious early 1900s New York gang leader. Sent to prison in 1904 for shooting a Pinkerton detective in a holdup. Enlisted in the Army during World War I and served with distinction in France. Later a bodyguard and collector for Arnold Rothstein. Shot to death in New York, December 26, 1920. A Prohibition agent later pleaded guilty to manslaughter in this case, claiming to have shot Eastman in an argument over tipping a waiter.

Fay, Larry [1888–1933] New York cab driver who smuggled enough whiskey in from Canada to eventually become a prominent mobster, rumrunner, nightclub operator, and owner of a large fleet of taxis. Chiefly remembered as the promoter and financial backer of "Texas" Guinan, the "Hello, Sucker!" girl who served as hostess of Fay's El Fey Club. In addition to his other interests, Fay took over the New York Chain Milk Association and monopolized the milk industry in New York. He was shot to death at his Club Casa Blanca on January 1, 1933, by Edward Maloney, the club's drunken doorman, whose wages had been cut. The Fay-Guinan story inspired the Bogart-Cagney gangster film *The Roaring Twenties.*

Fein, Benjamin "Dopey Benny"(true name: Feinschneider) [1887–1962) Former pickpocket who succeeded "Big Jack" Zelig as leader of a Lower East Side gang and became New York's pioneer union slugger in the years before World War I. Sold his services exclusively to labor and fought rival gangsters employed as strikebreakers. He eventually organized the business, forming treaties with other gangs and dividing the city's labor rackets by geographic territories. Convicted of assaulting a policeman in 1914, Fein was sentenced to five years in Sing Sing but after four months was freed on appeal. Jailed a few months later for threatening a butchers union officer, Benny turned informer when his previous employers refused to put up bail. Twenty-three labor leaders and eleven gangsters were indicted on charges, including murder, assault, extortion, and rioting.

Fein was released in May 1915 but arrested again on January 1, 1916, for assaulting a strikebreaker. Charged later in the year with Irving "Waxey Gordon" Wexler and others for the 1913 murder of Frederick Strauss, an innocent bystander killed in a gang battle. All were acquitted, but Benny's career as a gang leader ended. Popular accounts have Fein reforming and prospering as a legitimate businessman, but he was suspected of narcotics involvement in the twenties and in 1931 was arrested for throwing acid on a shopkeeper. Convicted in 1941 with "Nigger Abe" Cohen of leading an interstate burglary ring, Fein received a mandatory life sentence as a four-time offender. The sentence was reduced to ten to twenty years after a judge's ruling that one of Fein's prior convictions was for a misdemeanor. Fein and Cohen were freed on appeal in 1944, retried and acquitted, and faded from public view. Fein had a long and prosperous career in the clothing business and proved more than capable of using his gangster instincts to throw the racketeers out when they came after him. Fein died July 23, 1962.

Gagliano, Tommaso (Tom) [1884–1951] Leader of the dissident Reina crime family of New York, who switched sides from Masseria to Maranzano in the 1930–31 Castellammarese War after the murder of boss Tom Reina. After the murders of Masseria and Maranzano, Gagliano continued as family boss and Commission member until his death from natural causes on February 16, 1951. Reina was succeeded by the more publicized Thomas "Three Finger Brown" Lucchese.

Genovese, Vito "Don Vitone" [1897–1969] Born in Naples, Italy, November 21, 1897. Entered U.S. in 1913. Murderous New York gangster, chief lieutenant and heir-apparent to "Lucky" Luciano. Prominent figure in the Castellammarese War of 1930–31 and allegedly one of the killers of "Joe the Boss" Masseria. The Genovese faction also is credited in FBI records (which seem to tie everything from the period to the testimony of Joe Valachi) with the murder of "Legs" Diamond. Allegedly ordered the New York murder of Gerard Vernotico, March 16, 1932, marrying Vernotico's widow twelve days later. Eventually Anna Genovese would divorce Vito, testifying he was a millionaire gambling and narcotics boss. Genovese fled to Italy before World War II to avoid prosecution for the murder of Ferdinand "The Shadow" Boccia. Became an intimate of Mussolini and allegedly ordered the 1943 murder of Carlo Tresca, publisher of an anti-Fascist Italian-language newspaper in New York. Organized extensive black market operations in cooperation with the Sicilian Mafia and the Neapolitan Camorra during the war, but also may have spied on Mussolini for the American OSS. Later an official in Allied Military Government. Arrested in 1944 by

U.S. Army CID investigator Orange C. Dickey, who brought Genovese, over protests of his superiors, back to the U.S. to face trial for murder. Murder charge dropped in 1946 after key witness Peter LaTempa was poisoned in a Brooklyn jail. Assumed leadership of former Luciano-Costello crime family in 1957 after the attempted murder of Frank Costello. Convicted of narcotics conspiracy in 1959 and sentenced to fifteen years. Died in prison February 14, 1969.

Gordon, "Waxey" (true name: Irving Wexler) [1886–1952] One of New York's most powerful Prohibition era mobsters, whose influence also extended to Philadelphia. Former pickpocket and member of pre-World War I "Dopey Benny" Fein mob of labor racketeers, a major cocaine dealer before Prohibition. Credited with organizing the first large-scale rumrunning operation in early 1920s, financed by Arnold Rothstein. Established huge brewery operations in New Jersey, supplying beer to that state, New York, and Pennsylvania. Fought gang wars with "Dutch" Schultz and the Bugs & Meyer Mob, headed by "Bugsy" Siegel and Meyer Lansky. Convicted of income tax evasion in 1933, sentenced to ten years in Leavenworth, and fined $20,000; paroled in 1940. Convicted of selling narcotics, December 13, 1951, and sentenced to 25 years to life in Sing Sing. Soon transferred to Attica, then indicted on federal narcotics conspiracy charge and temporarily detained on Alcatraz for one month until he died on June 24, 1952.

"Waxey" Gordon

Higgins, Charles "Vannie" [1897–1932] Notorious New York bootlegger and murderer. Onetime lieutenant of "Big Bill" Dwyer. Briefly allied with "Legs" Diamond, "Mad Dog" Coll, and "Little Augie" Pisano against "Dutch" Schultz, but later an enemy of Diamond. Suspect in the murders of gangsters Samuel Orlando and Robert Benson and in the October 1930 shooting of Diamond at New York's Hotel Monticello. Once knifed in Baltimore. Wounded in a gun battle at Blossom Heath Inn speakeasy in New York, 1931. Amateur aviator who once angered Governor Franklin Roosevelt by flying to the state prison to dine with the warden. Fatally shot by rival gangsters outside the Knights of Columbus clubhouse in Prospect Park, June 18, 1932.

Hoff, Max "Boo Boo" [1893–1941] Born in Philadelphia, the son of Russian-Jewish immigrants. Gambling and boxing promoter who became Philadelphia's "King of the Bootleggers" during Prohibition. Sometimes compared to Al Capone and probably introduced the Tommygun to Philadelphia's gang-war scene in 1927. A grand jury investigation in 1928 revealed that more than eighty police officers were on Hoff's payroll, and he additionally distributed thousands of dollars to city officials as Christmas bonuses. Hoff's underworld star waned after Prohibition as he invested his fortune in nightclubs and jukebox joints that went broke, and the IRS sued him for $21,000 in back taxes. Lansky associate Harry "Nig Rosen" Stromberg replaced him as Philadelphia's new mob leader, and Hoff died penniless at his West Philadelphia home on April 27, 1941, supposedly of natural causes, though a nearly empty bottle of sleeping pills found at the scene led to some early suspicion of suicide.

Johnson, Enoch "Nucky" [1884–1969] Republican political boss and numbers racketeer in Atlantic City who controlled the police department and "taxed" the bootlegging, gambling, and vice operators of that wide-open town. Entered politics in 1904 and served various terms as undersheriff, sheriff, and city treasurer. Hosted the May 1929 mobster convention at Atlantic City's President Hotel (often cited as the beginning of a national crime syndicate) and was photographed walking with Al Capone. Johnson's organization largely was broken up by an IRS

THE MACHINE-GUN MURDER OF FRANKIE YALE

The daylight shooting of Brooklyn's Frankie Yale on July 1, 1928, was the first time a machine gun had been used in New York, and this caused a major uproar. Because of the Tommygun, police attributed the killing to Chicagoans, who already had made the Thompson notorious as a "gangster" weapon, and the press viewed it ominously as the spread of Chicago-style violence to New York. Both were right. Ballistics tests later established that one of the two submachine guns used on Yale also was used in Chicago's St. Valentine's Day Massacre a few months later by Fred Burke and others working for Al Capone's organization.

TRADE EXPANSION
—Enright in the New York *World*.

Capone had learned that Yale, his onetime boss and mentor who usually was described as the leader of New York's Unione Siciliana, was sabotaging his booze shipments from the East, lusting after a piece of Capone's dog tracks, and supporting his rivals for leadership of the Chicago Unione. Contrary to most reports, he was not killed by "Machine Gun" Jack McGurn, who had grown up in New York, but by Fred Burke, Gus Winkeler, Bob Carey (Capone's "American boys"), and Louis "Little New York" Campagna, whose mother's house was in the same vicinity and who incurred Capone's wrath by violating orders not to make calls to his wife in Chicago.

The murder of Frankie Yale persuaded Gotham's gangsters that they were lagging behind in the arms race, and soon the warring forces of "Dutch" Schultz, Vincent Coll, and other mobsters adopted the Thompson as standard gangland issue.

investigation in the late thirties, and he was convicted of income tax evasion in 1941. Just before his sentence of ten years, Johnson married girlfriend Flossie Osbeck, and his lawyer announced, "Nucky is marrying her so she can visit him in jail." Died at Atlantic Convalescent Home on December 12, 1969.

Kaplan, Nathan "Kid Dropper" or "Jack the Dropper" (true name Caplin by some accounts) [1895–1923] Notorious pre-Prohibition New York mobster. Member of Five Points Gang, headed by Paolo Antonini Vaccarelli, alias Paul Kelly. Fought celebrated gun duel in 1911 with rival gangster Joseph Weyler, alias Johnny Spanish. Convicted of robbery same year and sentenced to seven years in Sing Sing. Paroled in 1917 and formed his own gang, the Rough Riders of Jack the Dropper. Suspected in the murder of Johnny Spanish, July 29, 1919. Later fought Jacob "Little Augie" Orgen's gang in laundry workers union dispute. Participated in August 1923 gun battle in which Orgen gang member Jacob "Gurrah" Shapiro was wounded and two bystanders killed. Soon arrested on weapons charge. Shot to death while leaving Essex Market Courthouse under supposed police guard, August 19, 1923, by Louis Cohen, alias Kushner, an Orgen gangster subsequently convicted of manslaughter (Cohen would be murdered by Louis "Lepke" Buchalter's mob on January 24, 1939).

Kastel, Philip "Dandy Phil" [1894–1962] Bucket shop operator and henchman of Arnold Rothstein in 1920s. Later Frank Costello's partner in slot machine operations in New York and New Orleans. Brought slot machines to New Orleans in 1930s at the invitation of Huey Long, after Mayor Fiorello LaGuardia's anti-gambling crusade in New York. Headed Costello's gambling operations in Louisiana and later founded Beverly Club casino near New Orleans in partnership with Costello, Meyer Lansky, and others. Going blind and suffering from abdominal cancer, committed suicide by shooting himself at his Claiborne Towers apartment in New Orleans, August 16, 1962.

Kelly, Paul (true name: Paolo Antonini Vaccarelli) [1876–1936] Early 1900s New York fighting gang leader, slugger for Tammany Hall politicians, and a mentor of Frankie Yale and Johnny Torrio. Like Yale and many others, Vaccarelli adopted an Irish alias in the years before Italian gangsters acquired underworld dominance. Later active in waterfront labor racketeering, Kelly eventually achieved a small measure of respectability as vice president of the International Longshoremen's Association and reverted to his original name before his death by natural causes on April 3, 1936.

Lansky, Meyer (true name: Maier Suchowljansky) [1902?–1983] Born in Grodno, Russia, the son of Max and Yetta L. Suchowljansky, on either July 4 or August 28, 1902, or August 28, 1900, depending on various accounts. (A July 4 birthday is claimed in Lansky's 1921 Declaration of Intention to become a U.S. citizen.) With "Bugsy" Siegel, he headed the Bugs & Meyer Mob in New York in 1920s, allegedly committing murders, hijackings, and strong-arm activities for other gangs.

Meyer Lansky

Closely associated with "Lucky" Luciano, Frank Costello, and Joe Adonis in bootlegging and gambling. Allegedly a Bahamian rumrunning partner of Al Capone in the late twenties. Attended 1929 gangster convention in Atlantic City. Named by New York press in 1935 (along with Siegel, Luciano, Buchalter, Shapiro, Costello, Adonis, Johnny Torrio, and Abner "Longy" Zwillman) as one of the leaders of a New York Syndicate that ordered the murder of "Dutch" Schultz and took over his gang. Moved to Miami in the thirties and became a major gambling figure in Florida and Cuba. In later years was credited with pioneering international casino operations and the practice

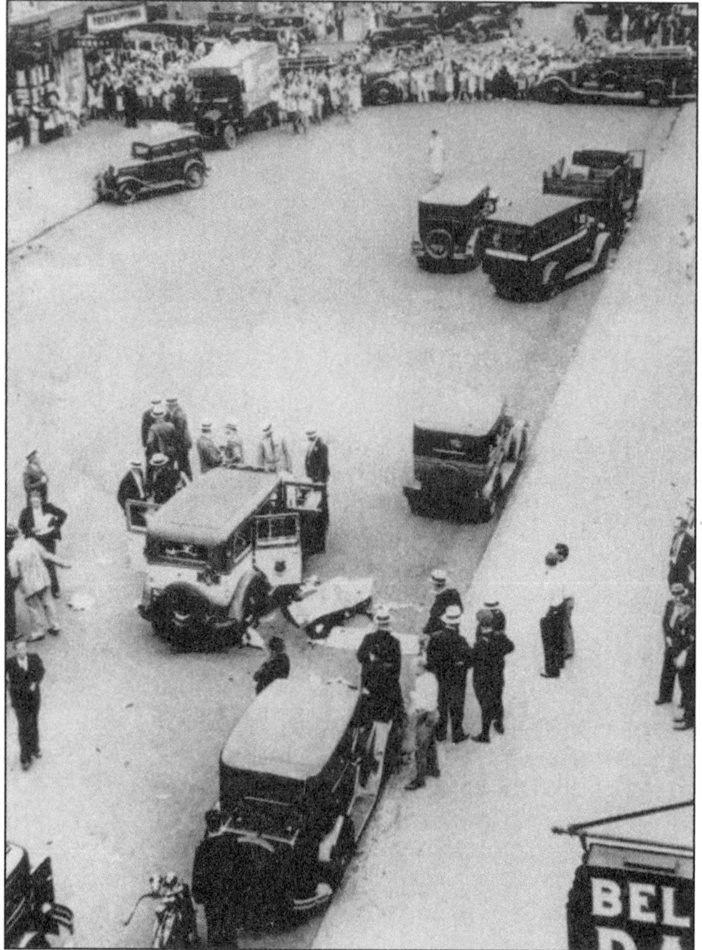

Crowds gather in the aftermath of a bloody running gun battle between payroll robbers and New York police on August 21, 1931 [see "Chronology"].

of laundering mob money through foreign banks. Successfully resisted all efforts to jail him over the years (though he briefly fled to Israel in the early 1970s) and died of natural causes at Miami Beach, Florida, January 15, 1983.

Lanza, Joseph "Socks" [1904–1968] Born in New York. Luciano lieutenant, loan shark, and numbers racketeer who dominated New York's Fulton Fish Market in the twenties and thirties through his control of Local 594 of the United Seafood Workers Union, taxing the unloading of ships and selling protection to market wholesalers. Arrested several times for murder, burglary, gun-carrying, and other crimes but served no time in prison until 1934 when convicted of antitrust violations. Released in 1939, he was convicted in 1943 of extorting money from a Teamsters local and sentenced to seven to fifteen years. Contacted by Naval Intelligence during World War II, Lanza cooperated in protecting the waterfront from Axis sabotage and put them in touch with the imprisoned Luciano, the one man Lanza insisted could guarantee full underworld protection of the docks. Paroled in 1950, Lanza was arrested in 1957 for parole violations (gambling, living beyond his means, and consorting with criminals, including one Dorothy "Madame Ladyfingers" Stirrat, a paroled jewel thief and suspected narcotics trafficker who was photographed with "Socks" at the Copacabana). Parole Commissioner James R. Stone dismissed charges against Lanza and ordered his parole restored, but public furor resulted, Stone resigned, and Lanza ended up returning to prison for a few years. He resumed control of the Fish Market until his death on October 11, 1968.

Legurenza, Walter "Polack Joe" (alias Legenza or William Davis) [1894–1935] **and Mais, Robert Howard "Little Jew"** [1906–1935] Led the so-called Tri-State Gang, which actually operated in several eastern states in the early thirties, committing bank and payroll robberies, hijackings, and murders. Captured by Baltimore police, Legenza and Mais were extradited to Virginia, tried and convicted of murdering a bank messenger, and sentenced to death. Using a smuggled pistol, they escaped from the Richmond jail on September 29, 1934, killing a policeman. Reorganizing their gang, Legenza and Mais staged other robberies and the ransom kidnapping of Philadelphia racketeer William Weiss, whom they murdered. Captured by FBI agents in New York City in January 1935, Mais and Legenza were returned to Richmond, Virginia, and died in the electric chair there on February 2, 1935.

Lonergan, Richard "Peg Leg" Last leader of Brooklyn's Irish White Hand gang. Shot to death with henchmen Cornelius "Needles" Ferry and Aaron Harms in an altercation with Italian gangsters at one of their hangouts, the Adonis Social Club, 152 Twentieth Street, on December 26, 1925. Several Italian gangsters present, including Chicago's Al Capone, were arrested and released.

Lovett, William "Wild Bill" [1894–1923] Brooklyn White Hand gang leader who was a decorated World War veteran, married the sister of "Peg Leg" Lonergan. Arrested several times for robbery, assault, disorderly conduct, and murder. After a heavy night's drinking, he wandered into a building at 25 Bridge Street to sleep it off and was bludgeoned to death by unknown killers on October 31, 1923.

Luciano, Charles "Lucky" (true name: Salvatore Lucania) [1897–1962] Born in Lercarra Friddi, Palermo province, Sicily, November 24, 1897, son of Antonio and Rosalia Lucania. Entered U.S. in 1907. Arranged murders of "Joe the Boss" Masseria and Salvatore Maranzano in 1931 and succeeded them as New York's most powerful Mafia boss. Onetime member of "Legs" Diamond gang in 1920s. Ran gambling, bootlegging, and narcotics operations. Closely associated with Frank Costello, "Bugsy" Siegel, Meyer Lansky, "Dutch" Schultz, and others. As a "white slaver," he was convicted on state charges of compulsory prostitution and sentenced to thirty to fifty years at Dannamora Prison, Clinton, New York. Luciano's conviction greatly advanced the political career of the prosecutor Thomas E. Dewey, who, as governor, pardoned the mobster in 1946 for his supposed contributions to national defense during World War II. Deported to Sicily, February 9, 1946. Moved to Cuba in 1946 but ousted under pressure from the U.S. government. Resettled in Naples, Italy, where he died, January 26, 1962. In his later years, Luciano was under constant surveillance by Italian police and the U.S. Federal Bureau of Narcotics, who claimed he was running an international heroin-smuggling network. Despite his known associations with American and Italian underworld figures, no hard evidence of this was ever presented.

"Lucky" Luciano

Lupo, Ignazio or Ignatius "Lupo the Wolf" (alias Ignazio Saietta) [1877–1947] Born in Corleone, Sicily, March 19, 1877. Fled to New York to escape murder charge in 1899. True name was Lupo but also was commonly known by his mother's maiden name of Saietta. Brother-in-law of Giuseppe Morello and Ciro Terranova, most infamous of the early Italian gang leaders in New York. Underboss of Morello crime family in early 1900s. Suspect in 1903 "barrel murders." Active in Black Hand extortion, counterfeiting, and narcotics. Suspected kidnapper. Proprietor of so-called "Murder Stable" at 323 107th Street in Harlem, where twenty-three men allegedly were killed between 1900 and 1917. Victims supposedly were hung on meat hooks or burned alive in the stable's furnace. Convicted of counterfeiting in 1910 and sentenced to thirty years in Atlanta. Paroled in 1921 with full pardon from President Warren G. Harding. Pardon revoked by President Roosevelt in

1936 after New York State authorities discovered Lupo was running a lottery and extorting the bakery and grape industries. Paroled in 1944. Died of natural causes, January 13, 1947.

Madden, Owen Vincent "Owney the Killer" [1891–1965] Born in Leeds, England, December 18, 1891 [other dates and years are incorrect], son of Francis and Mary Madden. Emigrated to U.S. at early age and became leader of the Gophers street gang. Arrested forty-four times before Prohibition. Convicted in 1914 of murdering "Little Patsy" Doyle, a member of the rival Hudson Dusters, and sentenced to ten to twenty years in Sing Sing. Paroled in 1923. Became a major bootlegging power in New York in the twenties, known as the "Duke of the West Side," with partnerships in the Cotton Club, the Stork Club, the Silver Slipper, and other nightclubs. Closely associated with other old-time mob leaders such as "Waxey" Gordon and Larry Fay, who were left out when New York mobs syndicated in the early thirties.

Madden's close friend and lieutenant "Big Frenchy" DeMange once was held for ransom by the Coll mob, and Madden supposedly placed a $50,000 bounty on Coll's head. Along with "Dutch" Schultz, was suspected of instigating Coll's murder in 1932. Returned to prison for parole violation on July 7, 1932. Released on July 1, 1933, and "retired" to Hot Springs, Arkansas, then a notoriously corrupt city and favorite hiding place for big-time criminals. Allegedly ran illegal gambling operations in Hot Springs until the 1960s. Died of natural causes, April 24, 1965. [In 1933, a Madden henchman named "Tough Tommy" Protheroe had been arrested for another murder, and a machine gun in his possession was ballistically determined to have killed Coll. He was nevertheless released and murdered a short time later.]

Magaddino, Stefano (Steve) [1891–1974] Born in Castellammare del Golfo, Sicily, October 10, 1891. Emigrated to U.S. with brother Antonio, first settling in Brooklyn. Survived a shooting attempt and beat the rap for several murders in 1921, the result of a family feud carried over from Sicily [see "The 'Good Killers' Gang," p. 84]. The Magaddinos moved on to Buffalo and prospered in bootlegging and legitimate businesses (including a funeral parlor), later expanding across the border to grab remnants of Rocco Perri's crime empire. Magaddino's sister, Mrs. Nicholas Longo, who lived next door, was killed by a bomb blast probably intended for him on May 19, 1936. A cousin of Brooklyn mobster Joseph "Joe Bananas" Bonanno and sometimes called the Mafia's "Grand Old Man," Magaddino became boss of the Buffalo crime family in the early twenties and reigned until his death from natural causes on July 10, 1974.

Mais, Robert **See Legurenza, Walter.**

Mangano, Vincenzo (Vincente or Vincent) [1887–1951?) Born in Villabati, Palermo province, Sicily. Reportedly entered U.S. in 1922 with father, Gaetano, and friend Joseph Profaci. One of twenty-three Sicilian gangsters arrested in a conference at a Cleveland hotel in December 1928. Maranzano ally in Castellammarese War. Became boss of a Brooklyn crime family in 1931, assisted by brother Philip and underboss Albert Anastasia. Said to have served for years as chairman of the "national commission" of Italian-American crime families and also as a liaison to representatives of the Sicilian Mafia. Disappeared in 1951, supposedly murdered by or on orders of Anastasia, who took over the family. Mangano's body was never found. His brother Philip was shot to death in Brooklyn on April 19, 1951.

Maranzano, Salvatore [1886–1931] Born in Castellammare del Golfo, Sicily. Battled Giuseppe "Joe the Boss" Masseria for control of the Italian underworld in New York in the Castellammarese War of 1930–31. After Masseria's murder, Maranzano set himself up as the "boss of bosses" of the Italian crime families and reportedly plotted to murder any organized crime figures

THE CASTELLAMMARESE WAR

While Chicago's mobsters volleyed and thundered at one another, New York had managed to keep a lid on open gang warfare during most of the 1920s. Not that New York was less corrupt than Chicago, but its corruption was less extravagant thanks to Tammany Hall, which had evolved into a political machine so centralized and powerful that "Jazz Age" Mayor Jimmy Walker could use the city's police department to discourage Chicago-style violence.

Many of New York's gangland murders occurred outside Manhattan and among rival Italian and Sicilian communities that were difficult for police (who were predominantly Irish) and reporters to penetrate. The killings that did take place in New York City usually happened in Little Italy, where they didn't count if bodies turned up in the Hudson or East rivers. Toward the end of the decade, however, a mounting number of murders could be attributed to a feud between one Giuseppe Masseria, self-proclaimed boss of bosses, and Salvatore Maranzano, a contender from Castellammare del Golfo, Sicily.

Masseria's camp included "Lucky" Luciano, Frank Costello, Albert Anastasia, Joe Adonis, and possibly Carlo Gambino, among others. In Maranzano's organization the rising stars were Joe Bonanno, Joe Profaci, and Tommy Lucchese, who had been with Masseria before switching his allegiance. These "underbosses" grew to regard Masseria and Maranzano as old-country "Mustache Petes," whose personal vendetta had them battling one another instead of collaborating in matters of bootlegging, loan-sharking, and similar rackets. Luciano, already in league with Meyer Lansky, "Bugsy" Siegel, and other non-Italian mobsters, secretly conferred with Lucchese and then engineered the murders of Masseria and Maranzano in 1931. This ended the so-called Castellammarese War, and the bosses were replaced by a five-family Commission whose leaders agreed to respect one another's territories or rackets or both.

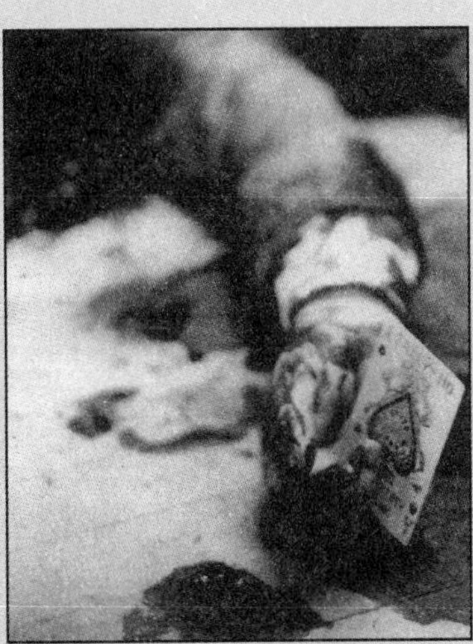

An enterprising New York news photographer enhanced his picture by placing the ace of spades in the blood-soaked hand of murdered gangster "Joe the Boss" Masseria.

The War did not culminate in a great gangland bloodbath of some forty men, as later legend would have it. "The Night of the Sicilian Vespers" seems to have been first described in a series of newspaper articles by mob attorney Dixie Davis, who may have picked it up from "Bo" Weinberg. It alluded to a Sicilian revolt in the thirteenth century, and it had become a part of Mafia lore that was widely accepted by crime writers of the day, as well as by the FBI. But in recent times a number of respected researchers, including Humbert Nelli and Virgil W. Peterson, examined newspapers from around the country and found that the only evidence of a "nationwide purge" was two or three killings in the New York-New Jersey area.

The murders that did follow the Castellammarese War were the hits on Vincent "Mad Dog" Coll, "Dutch" Schultz, "Legs" Diamond and lesser known independents, mostly by a Brooklyn gang of hired killers that later would become notorious as Murder, Inc.

unwilling to submit to his rule. These included "Lucky" Luciano, Vito Genovese, Frank Costello, their non-Italian ally "Dutch" Schultz, and Chicago mob boss Al Capone. Any such plot was ended when gunmen of the Bugs & Meyer Mob, allies of Luciano, shot and stabbed Maranzano to death at his office in New York's Eagle Building, 230 Park Avenue, on September 10, 1931. The group may have included Schultz gunman Abe "Bo" Weinberg, who became separated from the others during their escape, found himself in a crowded Grand Central Station, and ditched his hot gun by slipping it into the coat pocket of an unsuspecting commuter, to his own great amusement.

According to an enduring legend that may have started with Weinberg, that killing signaled the start of a concerted nationwide slaughter of forty or more of Maranzano's contemporaries in what popular crime historians still call the "Night of the Sicilian Vespers," which supposedly purged the Sicilian-dominated Mafia of the old "Mustache Petes." Thus emerged a modernized "American" Mafia ruled by a new generation of Italian-American organized crime figures led by Luciano but closely associated with Jewish and other prominent underworld figures. The Mafia did acquire new leadership in the early thirties, but several scholars since have debunked the colorful "bloodbath" story, discovering only four other killings around this time that might be linked to that of Maranzano.

Marlow, Frankie (true name reportedly Gandalfo Civito or Curto) Important New York bootlegger, reputedly chief lieutenant of Frankie Yale. Owned Silver Slipper nightclub at Broadway and Forty-eighth Street in partnership with "Owney" Madden and Bill Duffy. Also a partner, with gangster Larry Fay and comedian Jimmy Durante, in Les Ambassadeurs club. Owned racehorses and managed several boxers, including Jack Gannon, Ricardo Bertalazzo, and middleweight world champion Johnny Wilson. Shot to death by unknown gunmen at 166th Street and Queens Avenue, Flushing, June 24, 1929. Suspects included Ciro Terranova, "Joe the Boss" Masseria, and Boston gang leader Charles "King" Solomon.

Masseria, Giuseppe "Joe the Boss" [1879?–1931] Defeated Umberto Valente in the early twenties to emerge as boss of the largest Italian crime family in New York during Prohibition. By 1930 was being challenged by the crime family of Maranzano, composed largely of recent immigrants from the area around Castellammare del Golfo, which inspired the term "Castellammarese War." This rivalry appears to have centered mainly in the New York-New Jersey area, though Nicola Gentile, Joe Valachi, Joe Bonanno, and others have linked it to the struggles of the Italian underworld in other parts of the country, claiming that Al Capone's archenemy in Chicago, Joseph Aiello, who sought control of the Unione Siciliana, supported Maranzano while Capone backed Masseria. The "war" ended on April 15, 1931, when Masseria was betrayed by his underboss, Charles "Lucky" Luciano, and murdered at Gerardo Scarpato's Coney Island restaurant, allegedly by Benjamin "Bugsy" Siegel, Joe Adonis, Albert Anastasia, and Vito Genovese.

Mineo, Manfredi (alias Mineo Manfredi—his name simply reversed—and Alfred Mineo) [1894–1930] Bootlegger and numbers racketeer, ally of "Joe the Boss" Masseria, and boss of the future Mangano Family. Killed with associate Stephen Ferrigno in a shotgun ambush outside an apartment complex at 750–760 Pelham Parkway in the Bronx on November 5, 1930.

Mock Duck (true name: Sai Wing Mock) [1879–1941] Most notorious of Chinese gang leaders. Gambler, opium addict, and allegedly chief hatchetman for the Hip Sing Tong. Principal figure in Chinatown wars in San Francisco and New York between rival tongs, or associations, the Hip Sing and the On Leong, for control of gambling, prostitution, and opium trafficking from about 1900 to 1930. Arrested many times and survived many attacks, eventually died of natural causes in Brooklyn, July 24, 1941.

Morello, Giuseppe (alias Joe or Peter Morello; sometimes used his half-brother's name, Terranova) [1867–1930] Born in Corleone, Sicily. Often referred to as "The Clutching Hand" though contemporary records indicate this nickname actually belonged to another New York gangster, Giuseppe Piraino. Emigrated to U.S. in 1892 after being charged with murder and counterfeiting. Reputedly first boss of the New York Mafia, assisted by brothers Antonio, Vincent, and Nicholas, half-brother Ciro Terranova, and brother-in-law Ignazio "Lupo the Wolf" Saietta. Engaged in Black Hand extortion in the Italian community, counterfeiting, and warfare against Brooklyn branch of the Camorra, a Neapolitan criminal society whose members began immigrating to this country around the 1890s. Prime suspect in "barrel murders" of Joseph Catania, July 23, 1902, and Benedetto Madonia, April 14, 1903. Convicted of counterfeiting in 1910 and sentenced to twenty-five years in the Atlanta Federal Penitentiary. Paroled in 1921 and eventually became a lieutenant of "Joe the Boss" Masseria, who named him puppet "boss of bosses" of the Italian crime families. Shot to death with Giuseppe Pariano by members of the Maranzano crime family in his office at 362 East 116th Street, August 15, 1930.

Moretti, Guarano "Willie" **(alias Willie Moore) [1894–1951]** Born in New York City, June 4, 1894. Operated from New Jersey with "Longy" Zwillman, "Waxey" Gordon, "Lucky" Luciano, Joe Adonis, and Frank Costello. Named as murderer in 1931 deathbed statement by victim William Brady, a Hackensack, New Jersey, cab driver who had informed police about a still. Charge dropped when Brady's statement disappeared. Sided with Masseria faction in Castellammarese War. After Prohibition, Moretti became a prominent gambling figure in New Jersey. Admitted to Kefauver Committee his acquaintance with many notorious gangsters, including Al Capone, whom he described as "well charactered" like himself. By that time, Moretti was reportedly syphilitic, losing his faculties and talking too much for the comfort of his associates, who shot him to death at Joe's Elbow Room, 793 Palisades Avenue, in Cliffside Park, New Jersey, October 4, 1951.

Orgen, Jacob "Little Augie" **(true name: Orgenstein) [1901–1927]** Member of the old "Dopey Benny" Fein mob of pre-World War I labor racketeers in New York, and Fein's apparent successor after the 1923 murder of rival gang leader Nathan "Kid Dropper" Kaplan. Early lieutenants included Louis "Lepke" Buchalter, Jacob "Gurrah" Shapiro, Jack "Legs" Diamond, and Irving "Waxey Gordon" Wexler. Murdered at Delancey and Norfolk streets, New York, October 15, 1927, allegedly by Buchalter and Shapiro, who had formed their own gang on opposite sides in a painters union dispute. Bodyguard "Legs" Diamond was wounded at the same time.

Pinzolo, Joseph **(true name: Pinzolo Bonaventura) [1887–1930]** Born in Sicily, criminal record dated to 1908 when he was caught by legendary New York police lieutenant Joseph Petrosino in the act of bombing a building. Puppet boss appointed by "Joe the Boss" Masseria after the murder of Tom Reina. Reina's followers rejected their new leader, and Pinzolo was shot to death in a Broadway office building on September 5, 1930.

Piraino, Giuseppe "The Clutching Hand" **[d. 1930]** His bizarre alias, the result of a paralyzed right hand, is often wrongly given to Giuseppe Morello. Reportedly arrived in U.S. about 1911 after escaping from a Palermo prison. Shot while resisting arrest in 1920 when caught stealing liquor on a Brooklyn pier and ended up serving two years in Sing Sing. Was arrested three times for murder, although police speculated he may have been responsible for as many as twenty killings. By the late twenties was a major Bay Ridge liquor supplier and possibly boss of what became the Joseph Profaci crime family. An ally of Salvatore Maranzano, Piraino was an early victim of the Castellammarese War, gunned down at 151 Sackett Street in Brooklyn on March 27, 1930. His son Carmine was murdered in Brooklyn on October 6, 1930.

Pisano, "Little Augie" **(true name: Anthony Carfano) [1898–1959]** With Joe Adonis, succeeded Frankie Yale as principal Italian gang

"MURDER, INC."

It was uncovered in 1940, and the public was enthralled, but "Murder, Incorporated" has turned out to be less than met the eye. The widely-accepted story goes like this:

When local organized crime became nationally organized in the 1930s, and a Commission was formed to regulate racketeering, its leadership wanted to insulate itself from the kinds of murder that police often could attribute to a particular criminal "family." The solution conjured up by "Bugsy" Siegel and Meyer Lansky (and continued by Louis Buchalter and Albert Anastasia) was to hire the members of Brooklyn neighborhood gangs to serve as the crime syndicate's special enforcers. They worked for a salary, eliminating persons they did not know and for reasons they also might not know, in New York and other cities, earning an extra $1,000 or more for every Commission-ordered killing. Many of their victims were witnesses, mob informants, and embezzlers of gang-family funds. During the 1930s, their toll reached into the hundreds, according to several writers.

Prosecutors at the time—Thomas E. Dewey and William O'Dwyer—were, in fact, harassing mobsters in New York but had been largely unaware of this gang of professional killers before a Riker's Island inmate, framed for a murder and written off by the Commission, dropped his dime on Abe "Kid Twist" Reles, among others. Reles, himself now targeted, turned state's evidence in 1940 in exchange for immunity and testified in numerous trials that crippled what the press had been headlining as "Murder, Inc."

Part of this is true. Reles was able to provide Brooklyn Assistant District Attorney Burton Turkus with information that led to many convictions, including that of "Lepke" Buchalter, the only top mob leader to be executed, in 1944, in the electric chair at Sing Sing. But much of this thrill-packed chronicle of murder by shooting, ice pick, burning, strangling, drowning, and burying alive came from testimony that was partly hearsay and often enhanced by reporters.

The so-called Murder, Inc. crew actually was assembled after the merger of two Brooklyn neighborhood gangs headed by Abe Reles and Harry "Happy" Maione, who had overcome their own animosities and had taken out the Shapiro Brothers so they could control a small rackets empire in the early thirties. The direct cause of the war appears to have been the Reles-Maione combine's move on the Brownsville pinball racket, with the approval of the Bugs & Meyer Mob headed by Ben Siegel and Meyer Lansky. Siegel and Lansky were close allies of Luciano, Buchalter and others in the emerging New York Syndicate (popularly known as the "Big Six"), and their own crews sometimes had supplied killers for Luciano and Buchalter. Despite their encouragement, Siegel and Lansky stayed away from the gang war, awaiting its outcome.

Supposedly, Reles and Maione dispatched the Shapiro gang with such efficiency that they impressed the reigning Syndicate bosses, some of whom enlisted them as enforcers. And they did receive traveling expenses and money to lay low after a killing, which might have carried a bonus; but their regular income came from their own gambling, shylocking, and narcotics operations. They couldn't count on any formal support from the Syndicate for themselves or their families, and they evidently took their orders mainly from Buchalter, Joe Adonis, and Albert Anastasia. As Joe Valachi would explain years later, the Cosa Nostra, as he called it, typically used its own "soldiers" rather than rely on the boys from Murder, Inc.

When this arrangement was formalized is hard to say. As early as 1928, Reles had done occasional "favors," including a shooting and burglaries and strong-arm work, for Louis Capone, a henchman of Anastasia. Anastasia is alleged to have ordered or participated in at least eight murders between 1930 and 1935, only two of which can be traced to the Reles-Maione gang. During this same period, the Murder, Inc. boys committed four killings for reasons of their own. The "Big Six"-authorized murder of "Dutch" Schultz in October 1935, usually credited to

The six-floor plunge of Abe Reles from his heavily guarded "Canary Suite" at Coney Island's Half Moon Hotel.

Murder, Inc., was done by Buchalter's own gunmen. Buchalter seems not to have called on the Brooklynites until 1936, when he began using them extensively to deal with potential witnesses against him.

The first identifiable "contract" killings by the Brownsville crew appear to be the murders of Abraham Meer and Irving Amron on September 15, 1935, committed by Harry "Pittsburgh Phil" Strauss and Martin "Buggsy" Goldstein on behalf of Vincent "Jimmy Blue Eyes" Alo in retaliation for the kidnapping of an associate. Fifteen days later Maione and Strauss took part in the murders of Joe Amberg and Morris Kessler on the orders of Albert Anastasia.

Mob historians who ultimately sorted this out were Ralph Salerno, former NYPD organized crime expert; Virgil Peterson, former federal agent who became director of the Chicago Crime Commission; and Alan Block, who made an extensive study of police records and William O'Dwyer's papers in the New York's municipal archives. Salerno commented on the public's fascination at hearing about "an exotic group of professional killers for hire who had turned murder into a business." Peterson counted "about eighty-five killings committed in Brooklyn." It was doubted that Reles knew many of the Syndicate's top men other than by name, or its leaders outside of New York.

As for Abe Reles, his testimony against Murder, Inc. killers was cut short when he went out a sixth- floor window of the Half Moon Hotel in Coney Island on November 12, 1941. The room was guarded by police, there was a sheet hanging from the window, and the death was ruled accidental; but many believe he was murdered, and he still is remembered as the "canary who could sing but couldn't fly."

In the 1950s the Kefauver Committee decided that Brooklyn District Attorney O'Dwyer (by then New York's mayor) had done little to prosecute higher-ups in the organization—other than Buchalter—and believed he had deliberately dragged his feet in going after the likes of Adonis and Anastasia. In his defense, O'Dwyer claimed a perfect murder case against Anastasia "went out the window with Reles," and he was supported by his deputy police commissioner, Frank Bals, who had earlier commanded the detail guarding Reles. They claimed Reles could have provided the corroborative evidence needed to indict Anastasia for the killing of union official Morris Diamond. A Brooklyn grand jury investigating police corruption disagreed: "Our investigation has disclosed that Abe Reles was not a corroborating witness in that killing. On the contrary, as a matter of law, he was only one of several accomplices. In view of the availability of the other accomplices, it follows that Reles was not even an essential witness. The prosecution of Anastasia required corroboration and Reles could not have supplied it."

Mayor O'Dwyer avoided further embarrassment by resigning his post and accepting a hasty appointment as ambassador to Mexico. Anastasia was shot to death in 1957. After Joe Valachi himself turned canary, he commented, "I never met anyone who thought Abe went out that window because he wanted to."

leader in Brooklyn and rumrunning partner of Al Capone. Sometime associate of "Legs" Diamond, whom he briefly joined in a gang war against "Dutch" Schultz. Later a lieutenant of "Joe the Boss" Masseria, "Lucky" Luciano, and Frank Costello. Under increasing legal pressure, moved to Miami in 1933, where he invested in hotels and illegal gambling. Shot to death in Queens, New York City, with friend Janice Drake, September 25, 1959, apparently as a victim of Vito Genovese's takeover of the former Luciano-Costello crime family. [Janice Drake was a former Miss New Jersey.]

Profaci, Joseph [1897–1962] Born in Villabati, Palermo, Sicily, October 2, 1897. Reportedly entered U.S. in 1922 with Vincent Mangano. Boss of a Brooklyn crime family from early1930s until his death. Arrested at Hotel Statler in Cleveland, December 5, 1928, along with twenty-two other Sicilian gang leaders. Ally of Salvatore Maranzano in Castellammarese War. Long suspected of bootlegging, narcotics trafficking, and other major crimes but never convicted. In later years a multimillionaire and the country's largest importer of olive oil and tomato paste, Profaci allegedly collected $25 in monthly dues from each member of his crime family. Attended Apalachin, New York, mob conference in 1957. Died of cancer at the South Side Hospital, Long Island, New York, June 7, 1962, as his family was torn by internal strife from the dissident Gallo brothers' faction.

Reginelli, Marco "The Little Guy" [1897–1956] Born in Neppazzano, Italy, January 2, 1897, and entered U.S. in 1914. Emerged in 1930s as a south New Jersey gambling power and reputedly served from his base in Camden as underboss of the Philadelphia Mafia family under Joseph Bruno, although more publicized and often considered the real leader. A 1942 Mann Act conviction stripped Reginelli of his citizenship, but he avoided deportation through the efforts of Richard Nixon's attorney friend, Murray Chotiner, and died of natural causes in Baltimore on May 26, 1956.

Reina, Gaetano (Tom) [1890–1930] Boss of an Italian crime family allied to "Joe the Boss" Masseria. Allegedly held a near monopoly on ice distribution in New York City. Shotgunned to death on Masseria's orders, February 26, 1930, causing many members of the family to secretly defect to Salvatore Maranzano. Reina's daughter later married Joe Valachi.

Reles, Abe "Kid Twist" [1907–1941] Chief executioner for "Murder, Inc.," as newspapers called the Brooklyn gang that handled enforcement duties for the Syndicate. Alleged to have personally participated in at least thirty murders. Turned informant in 1940, providing insights into the organization of the national crime cartel and solutions to dozens of gang killings. Reles's testimony encouraged other mob informers to come forth and doomed Louis "Lepke" Buchalter, to date the only top Syndicate boss ever legally executed. State's witness Reles mysteriously fell to his death from his well-guarded room on a high floor of the Half Moon Hotel in Coney Island, November 12, 1941, becoming a posthumous celebrity as "the canary who could sing but couldn't fly."

Rothstein, Arnold "The Brain" [1882–1928] Born in New York City, son of Abraham and Esther Rothstein. Big-time gambler, controller of Democratic political machine at Tammany Hall, suspected narcotics trafficker, and underworld financier known as "The Big Bankroll." Allegedly masterminded the 1919 World Series fix (the "Black Sox" scandal) by bribing eight members of the Chicago White Sox to throw the games to the Cincinnati Reds. Rothstein's guilt in this has never been proven and is doubted by some historians, though he certainly knew the games were rigged and made money from it. Alleged to have financed "Waxey" Gordon and "Big Maxey" Greenberg in the first rumrunning operations from Europe in early 1920s. Suspected of masterminding the theft of $5 million in bonds in Wall Street robberies, for which his lieutenant Nicky Arnstein went to prison. Fatally shot at the Park Central Hotel in Manhattan, November 4, 1928,

Arnold "The Brain" Rothstein

possibly during a high-stakes card game or, more likely, because of the ambitions of his former bodyguard, Jack "Legs" Diamond. [The card-game shooting was considered because it included such unsavory characters as "Nigger Nate" Raymond, Alvin "Titanic" Thomas (a supposed survivor of the *Titanic* sinking), and George "Hump" McManus, the last of whom was tried for the murder and acquitted.]

Schultz, "Dutch" (true name: Arthur Flegenheimer) [1902–1935] Born at 1690 Second Avenue, New York City, August 6, 1902, the son of Herman and Emma Flegenheimer. Onetime gunman for "Legs" Diamond who became a speakeasy owner in the late twenties, expanded his operation to become beer baron of the Bronx, then branched out into labor racketeering and gambling. Muscled black operators and seized control of the Harlem numbers racket. Gained much notoriety in 1930–32 during a violent gang war with his former henchman, Vincent "Mad Dog" Coll. Indicted for income tax evasion in 1933 and went into hiding, becoming a federal fugitive. Surrendered at Albany, New York, November 28, 1934. Acquitted after two trials in 1935. Fatally shot, with three gang members, at the Palace Chop House, Newark, New Jersey, October 23, 1935, by Charles "The Bug" Workman and others. The Schultz murder likely was ordered by "Lucky" Luciano and "Lepke" Buchalter, who feared that the pressure to clean up local corruption would only become more intense if the hot-headed Schultz carried out his plan to assassinate Special Prosecutor Thomas E. Dewey.

Shapiro Brothers Meyer, Irving, and Willie Shapiro (no relation to "Gurrah" Shapiro) controlled a mob in the Brownsville section of Brooklyn. Active in bootlegging, bookmaking, slot machines, loan sharking, labor racketeering, and prostitution. Abe "Kid Twist" Reles and others, disenchanted with their meager share, broke away from the Shapiros in 1930 and set themselves up as competing bookmakers. The Shapiros supposedly retaliated by raping Reles' girlfriend, and a yearlong gang war resulted. Reles put personal differences aside in an ultimately successful alliance with the rival Ocean Hill mob headed by Harry "Happy" Maione. Irving Shapiro was ambushed and shot dead in his home at 691 Blakeman Avenue on July 11, 1931. Meyer was gunned down a month later on September 17, driven to Manhattan, and dumped in a tenement hall. Willie Shapiro fled, leaving Brownsville to the opposition, but returned in July 1934, only to be beaten, tortured, and buried alive in a Canarsie sand dune. New York Syndicate bosses known as the "Big Six" were suitably impressed by the killing efficiency of the Reles-Maione "Combination" and soon hired them as the enforcement squad called "Murder, Inc." by newspapers.

Shapiro, Jacob "Gurrah" [1897?–1947] Born in Minsk, Russia, May 5, 1897, or May 5, 1900, by differing accounts. New York labor racketeer and longtime partner of "Lepke" Buchalter. Suspect in the 1927 murder of "Little Augie" Orgen and wounding of his bodyguard, "Legs" Diamond. Convicted in October 1936 of violating federal antitrust laws by conspiring to restrain trade in rabbit skins and sentenced to two years. Freed on $10,000 bond, he jumped bail and became a fugitive. Later indicted by New York County on numerous counts of extortion in the garment and baking industries. Surrendered to authorities on April 14, 1938. Convicted in 1943 on thirty-two counts of extortion and sentenced to fifteen years to life. Died in Sing Sing in Ossining, New York, June 9, 1947.

Siegel, Benjamin "Bugsy" [1906–1947] Born in Brooklyn, February 28, 1906, son of Max and Jennie Siegel. With Meyer Lansky, led the Bugs & Meyer Mob in New York in 1920s. Later closely associated with "Lucky" Luciano. Prime suspect in several murders who reportedly boasted of having personally killed twelve men. Moved to Los Angeles in the thirties and allegedly organized and ran West Coast branch of the national crime syndicate. Best known as the underworld founder of Las Vegas, along with Moe Dalitz. With financial backing from eastern mobsters, built the Flamingo, first of the luxury hotel-casinos on the "Strip," but it failed to pay off while he was living. Suspected of skimming the funds, Siegel was murdered June 20, 1947, at the mansion of his mistress, Virginia Hill, at 810 North Linden Drive in Beverly Hills.

Solomon, Charles "King" [1886–1933] Born in Russia, August 6, 1886. Former New Yorker who became New England's premier bootlegger during Prohibition, but also dabbled in morphine and cocaine smuggling, receiving of stolen goods, prostitution, and bail bonds. Shot to death by Irish gangsters at his Cotton Club in Boston, January 24, 1933.

Stacher, Joseph "Doc" (aka Joseph "Doc" Rosen and numerous aliases) [1902–1977] Born in Poland or Russia, by varying accounts, and came to U.S. at age ten, growing up in Newark but never becoming a U.S. citizen. After youthful employment as a shoeshine boy, newsboy, and pushcart fruit vendor, Stacher joined Abner "Longy" Zwillman in bootlegging and bookmaking. Under the alias of Joseph Rosen, Stacher was arrested ten times by Newark police between 1924 and 1930 on charges including burglary, larceny, assault and battery, robbery, and interfering with a federal officer guarding a still. Nine of these charges were dismissed, the only disposition being a $50 fine. Stacher was one of nine men arrested while in conference at New York's Franconia Hotel on November 11, 1931. Others present included Louis "Lepke" Buchalter, Jacob "Gurrah" Shapiro, and Benjamin "Bugsy" Siegel. Long associated with Meyer Lansky, Stacher was considered a principal figure in the so-called "Jewish Mafia." He built the Sands and Fremont Hotels in Las Vegas in the fifties with loans from the Teamsters Union and also was active in Cuban gambling before the Castro takeover. After settling income tax difficulties in 1963, Stacher was ordered deported but could not be returned to a Communist nation. Under the "Law of Return" he moved to Israel in 1965, settling in a luxury hotel in Tel Aviv with a twenty-three-year-old girlfriend, and spent the remainder of his days enjoying the celebrity status of a "famous American gangster." Died in March 1977.

Strauss, Harry "Pittsburgh Phil" [1909–1941] Born in Brooklyn, July 28, 1909. One of the most prolific killers of Brooklyn's Murder, Inc. crew, "Pittsburgh Phil" had a record of thirty arrests and has been credited with a hundred or more murders, often committed by strangulation or ice pick. Convicted with a partner, Martin "Buggsy" Goldstein, of killing a minor hood named Irving "Puggy" Feinstein in 1940. Both sentenced to death. Strauss and Goldstein died in Sing Sing's electric chair on June 12, 1941, shortly after a visit from Evelyn Mittleman, a

"THE NIGHT OF THE SICILIAN VESPERS"

Among the most enduring myths associated with organized crime is "The Night of the Sicilian Vespers"—a nationwide purge of old-guard mafiosi, or "Mustache Petes," and some of their loyalists after the Castellammarese War [see p. 101].

Apparently the story first saw print in a series of articles written in the late thirties by Dixie Davis, a New York mob lawyer relating what he had been told by hoodlum "Bo" Weinberg. It must have been an item of mobster lore already, for it was repeated by Abe Reles before his fatal "defenestration" in 1940, during Thomas Dewey's investigation of Murder, Inc. Joe Valachi told of it again during the Senate hearings in the 1960s, though when asked to elaborate he could think of only three or four victims whose deaths occurred around that time.

A number of researchers over the past twenty years have found no evidence of any sudden surge of bloodletting. Two of the most prominent, Humbert Nelli in *The Business of Crime* and Virgil Peterson in *The Mob*, scanned newspapers around the country and found no remarkable increase in gangland murders or missing persons, concluded that any "purge" was confined to New York and New Jersey, and that the victims could be counted on one hand. Even such Maranzano supporters as Joe Bonanno and Joe Profaci, active at the time, were left untouched.

When the murderous "Night" came into gangland vogue is a matter of conjecture, but the name itself almost certainly derives from the historical "Sicilian Vespers," a late-thirteenth-century insurrection in which the people of Sicily rose up to slaughter their French Angevin rulers. In modern times, "The Night of the Sicilian Vespers" was featured in the Kirk Douglas movie *The Brotherhood*, most recently in *The Godfather*, and it has yet to be discarded by the Federal Bureau of Investigation's "Chronological History of La Cosa Nostra."

girlfriend of "Pittsburgh Phil" and one of a number of "gang molls" who was christened by the press the "Kiss of Death Girl."

Sutton, William Francis "Willie the Actor" [1901–1980] Noted for using trickery instead of violence, Sutton supposedly stole more than $2 million during his long criminal career. His elaborate disguises included makeup and uniforms (police, fire, messenger, etc.), which also helped him escape. Convicted of bank burglary in New York, 1926, and sentenced to five to ten years (Sing Sing and Dannamora). Paroled in 1929. Worked briefly for "Dutch" Schultz. Convicted of bank robbery in 1931 and sentenced to thirty years in Sing Sing. Escaped in December 1932. Recaptured in Philadelphia in 1934, convicted of another bank robbery there, and sentenced to twenty-five to fifty years at Eastern State Penitentiary in Philadelphia. Transferred to Holmesburg prison after another escape attempt. With several others, escaped from Holmesburg on February 10, 1947. Suspected in Boston's Brink's robbery in 1950 and named to FBI's "Ten Most Wanted List." Robbed his last bank in New York in March 1950. Finally captured in Brooklyn, February 18, 1952, on a tip from Brooklyn clothing salesman Arnold Schuster, who was murdered on March 9. Given a long sentence for two counts of gun possession and for bank robbery, added to previous a thirty-year sentence. Released from Attica Prison on December 24, 1969. Died at his sister's home in Spring Hill, Florida, November 2, 1980.

Terranova, Ciro "The Artichoke King" (alias Ciro Morello) [1889–1938] Sicilian gang boss in Harlem and member of the large Morello-Terranova clan. Half-brother of Joe Morello, supposedly the founder of the first New York Mafia family. Notorious produce racketeer who monopolized the artichoke market in New York before Prohibition. Indicted in 1918 for ordering the murders of Charles Lombardi and Joe DiMarco; the indictment dismissed. Italian lottery boss and narcotics trafficker, later a bootlegger. Allied with "Dutch" Schultz in the late twenties and became a partner with Schultz in the Harlem numbers racket formerly controlled by black operators. Hosted a banquet for Judge Albert Vitale at Roman Gardens Restaurant in the Bronx, December 7, 1929, where guests were held up and robbed by gunmen. New York police later claimed, almost comically, that Terranova masterminded the robbery in order to recover a "written murder contract" from a Chicago mobster for the killings of Frankie Yale and Frankie Marlow. By other accounts, the robbery was committed by underworld rivals, possibly working for Salvatore Maranzano, to embarrass Terranova. Terranova's notoriety supposedly forced him to turn over his artichoke business to a lieutenant, Joseph Castaldo. The artichoke racket ended in 1936 when Mayor Fiorello LaGuardia actually banned the sale of artichokes. Terranova's power already had declined, however, and he was forced into retirement by Luciano. The murder of Schultz removed Terranova's most important ally, and he was replaced as Harlem gang boss by "Trigger Mike" Coppola. He died penniless on February 20, 1938, after suffering a paralyzing stroke.

Trafficante, Santo Sr. [1886–1954] Born in Allesandria Della Rocca, Sicily, May 28, 1886. Immigrated to the U.S. in 1904, naturalized in 1925, and took up residence in Tampa, Florida, where he gained control of gambling, narcotics, and other criminal enterprises in a series of gang wars, ruling until the 1950s. Died of natural causes on August 11, 1954, and was succeeded by his son, Santo Jr.

Uffner, George (alias George Hoffman) During the twenties, specialized in narcotics with Arnold Rothstein, "Legs" Diamond, and "Lucky" Luciano. Arrested with Luciano and Thomas "Fats" Walsh in November 1928 as a suspect in the Rothstein murder. Convicted of forgery and grand larceny in 1933 and sentenced to prison for four to eight years. After release became a partner of Frank Costello in Texas and Oklahoma oil deals. Killed in plane fire and explosion over Texas on September 29, 1959, with thirty-three other passengers. Wreckage yielded more than $200,000 in diamonds believed to have been Uffner's.

Wall, Charles "Dean of the Underworld" [1888–1955] Longtime gambling boss of Tampa, Florida, who survived three murder attempts between 1930 and 1944. Eventually forced into retirement by his rival, Santo Trafficante Sr. Testified before Kefauver Committee in 1950 and managed to survive until April 18, 1955, when he was found with his throat cut in his Tampa home.

Walsh, Daniel (Danny) Major Providence, Rhode Island, rumrunner and target of a 1928 income tax evasion charge, but was allowed to settle for less than the $350,000 the government claimed he owed. Disappeared on February 2, 1933. Walsh's brother later received a ransom demand and delivered $40,000 in Boston, but Danny was never seen again, and no body was ever found.

Weinberg, Abe "Bo" [1897–1935] Chief gunner for "Dutch" Schultz and also a close partner who often acted as Schultz's goodwill ambassador to smooth things over after the temperamental "Dutchman" had managed to insult or upset his erstwhile underworld friends. Allegedly was a member of the group whose phony badges gained them entrance to the office of Salvatore Maranzano, who was then shot and stabbed to death. Joined Luciano when the government appeared to have Schultz on the ropes for income tax evasion, and was killed for his apparent disloyalty when Schultz beat the rap. Disappeared about September 9, 1935. Body never found. [Weinberg's brother George, also a Schultz lieutenant, committed suicide on January 29, 1939.]

Whittemore, Richard Reese [1903–1926] Youthful gang leader who escaped from Maryland state prison, February 20, 1925, after fatally beating guard Robert H. Holtman with an iron pipe. Four days later led his gang in a violent, $16,000 dairy-payroll robbery in Baltimore, the first of a series of spectacular crimes, including hijackings, jewel robberies, and murders there and in New York, which brought the Whittemore Gang to headline infamy in their brief but deadly career. Captured with gang members (including wife Margaret "Tiger Lil" Whittemore) by New York police, Whittemore was returned to Maryland, convicted of the Holtman murder, and hanged on August 12, 1926. [Similar to but more prominent than New York's "Cowboy Tessler Gang" in the 1920s and the "Arsenal Gang" in the 1930s.]

Yale, Frankie (true name: Francesco Ioele; also called Uale) [1893–1928] Born in Calabria, Italy. Leader of Brooklyn gang whose most famous graduates were Johnny Torrio and Al Capone. Continued his association with Torrio and Capone after their move to Chicago, in bootlegging and probably as a killer. Yale was the principal suspect in the murder of Chicago crime figures "Big Jim" Colosimo in 1920 and Dean O'Banion in 1924, presumably at the request of Torrio and Capone. Yale became New York's first Tommygun victim on July 1, 1928. Use of submachine guns led police to believe the killers were from Chicago. Yale had allowed the hijacking of Chicago liquor shipments and supposedly further antagonized Capone by opposing his candidate for president of the Chicago branch of Unione Siciliana (a largely Midwest organization in which Yale probably had little or no influence in, despite being commonly identified as its "national head"). Murdered by Fred "Killer" Burke, Gus Winkeler, and Louis "Little New York" Campagna, not by Jack McGurn, John Scalise, and Albert Anselmi as generally believed. A Thompson submachine gun later seized at Burke's Michigan hideout would be linked ballistically to the murder of Yale and to Chicago's St. Valentine's Day Massacre the next year.

Zwillman, Abner "Longy" [1904–1959] Born in Newark, New Jersey, July 27, 1904, the son of Avraham and Anna Zwillman. Bootlegging and gambling boss of northern New Jersey during Prohibition, founding member of the national crime syndicate, and a major organized crime figure in the East until his death. Fought 1930 gang war with Ruggiero "Richie the Boot" Boiardo, who was seriously wounded in a murder attempt in Newark on November 26, 1930. Either Al or Ralph Capone reportedly went to Newark to help settle differences between Zwillman and Boiardo, who eventually became close allies. Zwillman harbored outlaw Verne Miller after the Kansas City Massacre of June 17, 1933, until things got too hot or, by a less likely version, Miller supposedly killed a member of Zwillman's mob. Miller was found murdered in Detroit on November 29 of that year, possibly on Zwillman's orders (later FBI reports speculate that the Kansas City mob returned the favor for Miller's death by providing the gunmen who killed "Dutch" Schultz, although Charles "The Bug" Workman, a "Lepke" Buchalter gunman, was convicted of the Schultz hit). Zwillman is thought to have ended his own remarkably long crime career on February 26, 1959, by hanging himself in the basement of his mansion at West Orange, New Jersey, but many believe he was murdered. [In the 1930s, Zwillman had been romantically involved with film star Jean Harlow.]

2

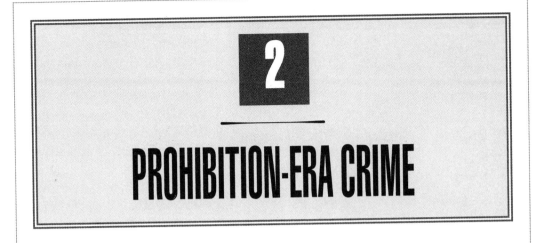

PROHIBITION-ERA CRIME

Crime reporting at any given time is less likely to reflect the seriousness of the problem than the public's awareness of it; and awareness often is shaped by press coverage based less on statistics than on the pronouncements of elected and appointed officials.

In the several decades that led to and included the First World War, crime and violence had become serious problems in urban areas but still were localized, consisting mainly of thievery, burglary, shopkeeper extortion, one-man stickups, and interpersonal violence of the bedroom and barroom variety. Compared to present times, even fewer people ventured out at night alone or without arms, especially in neighborhoods that were understood to be free-fire zones. *Gem of the Prairie* author Herbert Asbury described conditions in Chicago during the crime wave of 1905–06:

> [T]he average citizen, and especially the average woman, was probably in greater danger of being robbed and murdered than at any other time in the history of Chicago. . . . With nothing to stop them, bands of thugs and hoodlums prowled the streets from dusk to dawn. They robbed every pedestrian they encountered, and many of these holdups were remarkable for brutality; sometimes the footpads stripped their victims, tied them to lamp posts, and cut shallow slits in their flesh with razors and knives. They broke into stores and residences, held sex orgies and drinking parties on the lawns and porches of private homes, and pursued every woman they saw.

Still, such crime presented no challenges that were new to urban life at the turn of the century or could not be controlled, or

Unlike the small five- or ten-gallon stills given to (or forced upon) families in Chicago's Little Italy and Little Sicily, where tight quarters often put them inside the house or apartment, "American" stills usually were much larger, installed in a shed or outbuilding, and tended by alky-cookers with at least a rudimentary knowledge of the process.

at least confined, by municipal police or county sheriffs. Even gang crime could be suppressed, when political considerations demanded, by conventional police methods, however primitive they were.

By 1920, however, the automobile had revolutionized crime. It revived the kind of hit-and-run robbery that had greatly declined with better neighborhood policing, improved security measures, telephone communications, and travel by railroad instead of stagecoach.

The cities were the first to experience a dramatic rise in daylight holdups of banks, jewelry stores, and payroll messengers by gangs of "strangers" who might have been the James Brothers or the Daltons except for their use of cars. The police and the press, for want of new terminology, first labeled these raiding parties "highwaymen," a relic of the nineteenth century. Their use of automobiles soon popularized the term "motorized bandits," but that lacked formality for law enforcement purposes, and as the use of getaway cars became standard procedure, the term "armed robbery" was widely adopted by law-enforcement agencies.

It quickly became apparent that traditional police methods were all but useless against criminals in cars. Even when city governments conceded the need to equip their departments with cars and motorcycles, they were so parsimonious that a district or precinct might rate only one or two vehicles, usually Model T Fords that made a police force look like Keystone Kops compared with their adversaries in Lincolns, Packards, and Cadillacs. The central detective force enjoyed the prestige of patrolling the city in high-powered machines, but these served little purpose other than getting them to the scene of the crime rapidly and in style.

While inventors and visionaries came up with some truly goofy ideas to achieve parity with the crooks, such as armored chase cars with ramming features and motorcycles equipped with sidecar-mounted machine guns, the more typical situation was that which prevailed in Chicago on the morning of February 14, 1929. The neighborhood police station's two Model A Fords already were out on patrol, and the one officer on enforcement duty had to hitch a ride with a civilian to the scene of the St. Valentine's Day Massacre. (Coincidentally, several Chicago police officials had just arrived in Detroit to inspect the country's first successful police radio system.)

Even with improved equipment, poor criminal-identification methods limited police effectiveness throughout the twenties. This helped the anonymous "motorized bandits" of that decade enjoy relatively long careers and far greater profits than the celebrated "public enemies" of the 1930s, who by then could be identified quickly and pursued doggedly and barely made expenses before becoming colorfully nicknamed legends in the annals of American crime.

Police were slow to appreciate how well the earlier gangs were organized or how professionally they worked until some were tripped up through the fencing industry. Much loot in the form of jewelry, furs, and securities had to be transformed into cash; and by infiltrating the fencing business, police "detectives" were able to stamp out several major criminal operations. For example, New Yorkers were impressed to learn that their own Whittemore and "Cowboy" Tessler Gangs (unheralded until their capture) had maintained staffs of jewelers and garages to store and service their automobiles, used guns with silencers, and otherwise represented state-of-the-art criminality. A number of gangs plundered the Midwest throughout the 1920s, robbing banks in one state and harboring in another, until they were taken by local authorities for perhaps a single job that satisfied their captors but hardly did "justice" to the quantity or quality of their long criminal careers.

Consequently, the press focused its attention on the criminal phenomenon that was most conspicuous, easily understood and had the virtue of novelty—the bootlegging gangs, whose leaders did not need anonymity to avoid prosecution, but only money to enrich politicians and pay off police. The corruption fueled by Prohibition made them nearly invulnerable, except to the gunfire of rivals.

Paradoxically, then, the news fodder of the twenties was not the major and often deadly robberies by unidentified gunmen (though these were reported with great excitement locally), but crimes associated with Prohibition's gang wars, political and police corruption, and Prohibition itself. In truth, the celebrity bootleggers of the twenties were merely the vanguard of the nationally organized crime that would begin to flourish (again with anonymity) only after the Depression, the fall of Capone, and the passage of Repeal ended the so-called Roaring Twenties.

PROHIBITION-ERA CRIME CHRONOLOGY
1920–1929

Including 1919 as a prologue

1919

January 1—After a nationally publicized robbery in 1917 that included two murders and a long siege by police, the Chicago Association of Commerce establishes the Chicago Crime Commission.

January 3—Detroit gang leader Tony Giannola is killed by a gunman while attending the wake of a murdered friend.

January 16—Thirty-six states ratify the Eighteenth Amendment to the Constitution that will ban the manufacture, transportation, and sale of alcoholic beverages beginning one year after this date.

January 19—Two New York policemen are wounded while raiding Arnold Rothstein's crap game in a fourth-floor apartment at 301 West Fifty-seventh Street. Rothstein will be indicted for felonious assault, but the charges are later dismissed.

— "Auto bandits" rob a Philadelphia jewelry store of $10,000 in gems. L. J. Gale is arrested in New York City. This and several other large robberies begin attracting national attention to the new problem of "gas bandits" or "motorized bandits" who have little difficulty eluding the police—who still rely on electrical call boxes, the telephone, and neighborhood foot patrols.

January 21—Policeman foils robbery of the Water-Tower Bank in St. Louis. One bandit is slain.

February 4—"Auto bandits" rob Frank Sternberger's saloon in the Bronx.

February 11—After many delays, Chicago gangster Edward "Spike" O'Donnell finally is incarcerated in the state prison at Joliet on a bank robbery conviction.

March 3—Robbers dynamite the First National Bank safe in Ansted, West Virginia.

March 7—Milton Strohm, messenger for L. M. Prince, is attacked in a New York office building and robbed of $65,800 in securities and Liberty Bonds. Six men are soon arrested, and the loot is recovered.

March 8—New York bandits rob Sinclair Valentine Co. messengers of a $3,800 payroll.

March 9—Four bandits rob the Southside Bank in Kansas City, Missouri, killing cashier G. M. Shockley.

April 1—Republican William Hale "Big Bill" Thompson is elected, with underworld support, to a second term as mayor of Chicago.

May 19—A Lehigh & Hudson freight train is robbed near Maybrook, New York.

June 21—South Side Chicago gang leader Edward "Spike" O'Donnell is freed on bond, pending appeal of his bank robbery conviction.

July 26—Longshoremen stevedore and allegedly reformed gang leader Thomas "Tanner" Smith is fatally shot by three gunmen while playing poker at his Marginal Club in Manhattan.

July 28—Gangsters Louis Valenti and James Grazino are killed while leaving a lower Manhattan café in an ambush of forty or more shots. Brooklyn gangster Joseph Magnefecco is caught red-handed by a policeman while still firing into Valenti's corpse, but the other killers flee. Magnefecco's brother Richard is arrested later, along with Sam Giordano and Michael Cantelo.

— Race riots occur in Chicago, lasting three days and killing thirty-six. The Ragen's Colts, a South Side Irish gang, figures prominently. Similar riots take place the same summer in Washington, D.C., St. Louis, and Arkansas.

July 29—East Side gang leader Joseph Weyler, alias Johnny Spanish, is shot to death by rival gangsters outside a restaurant at 19 Second Avenue in New York.

July 31—Irish gangsters Robert "Rubber" Shaw and George "Chicky" Lewis are ambushed by gunmen in Hoboken, New Jersey, apparently in retribution for the murder of "Tanner" Smith. Shaw is killed. Lewis is seriously wounded and recovers, eventually pleading guilty to manslaughter in the Smith killing and receiving a three-year sentence at Sing Sing.

"Big Bill" Thompson, here introducing famed aviator and national hero Charles Lindbergh to ballpark patrons, stood behind his promise to make Chicago "wetter than the middle of the Atlantic Ocean" by ordering police (whatever they smelled from the street) not to invade places without a search warrant, which local judges might put low on their lists of "Things to Do."

August 20—Railway Express truck stolen in New York City; driver and helper kidnapped.

September 4—Michael Stenson, a reputed member of "Tanner" Smith's "Marginal Gang," drops dead on a New York streetcar track while chasing the man who shot him. One witness reports that a policeman was watching but did nothing.

October 1–9—Eight members of the Chicago White Sox, bribed by gamblers, throw the World Series to the Cincinnati Reds. No one is convicted. New York gambler and underworld financier Arnold Rothstein will be accused of organizing the World Series fix, though his involvement may have been marginal.

October 2—Gang leader Sam Giannola is shot and killed by gunmen of the rival Vitale gang in a parked car at Russell and Monroe avenues in Detroit.

October 4—Near Baxter Springs, Kansas, four gunmen rob a Treece State Bank cashier of $3,500.

October 16—"Motor bandits" rob the First National Bank at Roselle, New Jersey, of $25,482, shooting police Sergeant F. Keenan.

November 11—New York police find Ederiage "Louis the Barber" Guiliano, an alleged gang war participant, stabbed to death in a Greenwich Village alley. Guiliano had been shot several days earlier but refused to identify his attackers.

November 21—Gunmen lock New York Central West Shore pier watchmen in an ice box and steal two truckloads of whiskey.

November 25—Chicago records 250 robberies in one week.

December 8—Morris Klein's jewelry shop in Chicago is robbed of $100,000.

Egan's Rats and the Purple Gang

The one island of law and order is St. Louis, whose police are notably well equipped and whose police chief, Colonel Joseph A. Gerk, is outstandingly able and honest.

— Fortune, *August 1934*

Chicago dominated the true-crime books of the late twenties and early thirties until the national "War on Crime" captured the attention of writers suddenly fascinated by bank robbers and kidnappers and their pursuit by the newly empowered FBI. Probably for this reason, New York's mob killings—Frankie Yale, "Mad Dog" Coll, "Dutch" Schultz, "Legs" Diamond—yielded more headlines than manuscripts. And nearly ignored, except by their local newspapers, were the bootlegging gangs and racketeers of other cities whose politicians and police were similarly corrupt.

Chief among these were St. Louis, Detroit, St. Paul, Minneapolis, Kansas City, Philadelphia, Cleveland, Reno, and Hot Springs, the last of which afforded mobsters and outlaws a welcome respite from their respective battlefields. Most crime books ignore these other cities except for the occasional mention of the Purple Gang. It even has become a common hook for writers to suggest that "all" the big gangsters originated in New York or Chicago, usually citing as examples Capone and Torrio, who moved from Brooklyn to Chicago, or Lansky and Siegel, New Yorkers who transplanted themselves in Florida and California, or the Chicago Outfit branching out to Miami and Las Vegas.

All of this overlooks the basic reality that all cities foster underworlds, and that gangsters, by the very nature of their business, are a migratory lot anyway. St. Louis, for example, supplied more than its share of manpower to the underworlds of other cities.

Many prominent gunmen were from St. Louis, chiefly veterans of Egan's Rats, who began migrating northward in the middle twenties, mainly to Detroit and then Chicago, where their talents always were in demand.

♔ ♔ ♔

The gang called Egan's Rats can be traced to the beginning of the twentieth century when they provided political muscle for Missouri State Senator Tom Kinney of St. Louis in what was then the Fourth Ward. Thomas Egan, a saloon owner, supported Kinney for his clout and corruption and rallied many of the local underworld to assist. Ballot boxes were stuffed, and many a citizen was induced to vote more than once under different names at different polling places.

Tom Egan soon diversified the gang, with little prodding required, into the fields of robbery, burglary, and theft from railroad boxcars. Egan's saloon was the primary meeting place and hangout for the group. Several times its license was suspended or revoked, but any stolen property either vanished or was conveniently overlooked.

The name of the gang, Egan's Rats, found its way into the newspapers around 1909, but how the gang acquired that name has several versions. One has it bestowed upon them by the police because of their furtive ways and seeming fondness for darkness and alleys. Another contends that in about 1907 a number of young men found themselves picked up for voting violations (then referred to as "repeating"), and when a police lieutenant called headquarters to advise of the arrests, he was asked who they were. He replied, "Oh, a bunch of rats." Asked where they were from, he said, "They hang out at Egan's saloon." Legend has it that they were known thereafter as Egan's Rats.

Due to political boundary changes, the old Fourth Ward became the part of the Fifth Ward, and Egan continued his political, as well as personal, allegiance to Kinney. Kinney, in fact, married Egan's sister. Egan's domination of the group, as well as his political influence, continued until his death at home in 1919 after a long illness.

In addition to other criminal activity, at least twenty gang murders were attributed to Egan's Rats during his reign. Tom Egan himself had been charged with two of them but was acquitted on both.

After Tom Egan's death, his brother William was the natural choice to continue the gang's legacy. By this time almost any criminal activity in St. Louis had to meet the approval of the gang's leader, and failure to do so had dire consequences. Over the years, the gang would acquire a group of cruel and proficient killers.

Prohibition provided the Rats with yet another money-making opportunity—bootlegging. However, along with Prohibition came competition—mainly in the form of the Hogan gang, led by Edward J. "Jelly Roll" Hogan and his brother James. Allied with the Rats were the Cuckoo gang, headed by the Tipton brothers, Herman, Roy, and Ray. These gangs, too, became known for their ruthless tactics and brutal gunmen.

In March 1920, William Egan was able to obtain a presidential commutation of sentence for gang member Max Greenberg, who was serving federal time for interstate theft. A few months later Greenberg swindled Egan for $2,000 on a liquor deal and joined sides with the Hogan forces. An attempt was made on Greenberg's life in March of 1921, but he survived.

The next October 31, William Egan was

mortally wounded outside his tavern, and he, likewise, refused to identify his attackers. Greenberg and the Hogans were suspected, but Greenberg provided an airtight alibi: He had caught a train for New York four hours before the shooting and had been observed boarding it by a city police inspector. Greenberg soon joined "Waxey" Gordon in organizing some of the earliest rumrunning operations, financed by Arnold Rothstein. Greenberg and Max Hassell were shot down at Gordon's Carteret Hotel headquarters in Elizabeth, New Jersey, on April 12, 1933, probably by the Bugs & Meyer Mob; although the hits often are attributed to "Dutch" Schultz. Gordon escaped out a window but soon was captured by police and convicted of income tax evasion.

The reins of the Rats gang were handed down to William P. "Dinty" Colbeck, a plumber by profession and a loyal lieutenant of Egan's. Retaliation was quick, and twenty-three bodies fell in the two-year war that followed.

In March 1923, after a car-to-car shootout along St. Louis' "Automobile Row" of car dealerships, an outraged public demanded action by the police. In what practically amounted to a press conference, Colbeck, like a local Al Capone, complained to reporters: "We are not insensitive to the fact that the public is aroused over what the newspapers have consistently characterized as the violence attending the fights between the Hogan and Egan factions. Our men are not trying to disturb peaceful citizens, and it is unfair every time violence occurs in St. Louis to attribute it to myself, my men, or the rival gang." The next month, the Rats and Hogan went so far as to sign a truce that was published in a St. Louis newspaper, but the shooting didn't stop.

Despite the truce, the Egan and Cuckoo gangs immediately committed a crime that would become their downfall—the $2.4 million mail truck robbery in downtown St. Louis on April 2, 1923. The loot soon was recovered at the home of gang member William "Whitey" Doering. Tried and convicted of the robbery, Doering appealed and was free on bond when killed in November 1923 by Charlie Birger at his Halfway resort near Marion, Illinois (Birger claimed self-defense and beat this rap, just as he'd done a few days earlier after killing his own bartender).

Another gang member, Raymond Renard, a participant in the robbery but facing other charges, felt betrayed when the Rats made no effort to help him on an interstate freight theft conviction. He decided to make a deal with postal inspectors to testify against the gang for the mail robbery, as well as a $55,000 postmaster robbery that had since occurred in Staunton, Illinois.

The first trial, in November 1924, ended in a hung jury. A second trial in 1925 resulted in the convictions of twelve principal gang members (nine Rats and three Cuckoos) with sentences ranging up to twenty-five years. And so ended the reign of Egan's Rats, which inspired the migration of the gang's professional killers to several northern cities, where the action was.

Slightly more intact, the Cuckoos continued through the twenties, first battling the rising Italian factions, the Green Dagoes and the Russo brothers' gang. Anthony

"Shorty" Russo and Vincent Spicuzza were murdered in Chicago in 1927, allegedly after responding to Joe Aiello's $50,000 bounty on Al Capone. The Cuckoo-Russo war raged for a couple of years and racked up a dozen or more killings before July 29, 1928, when police escorted the three surviving Russo brothers out of town. The Shelton Brothers, formerly of East St. Louis, returned to their home territory in the aftermath of their feud with Charlie Birger and turned their attentions to the Cuckoos, urging recently paroled gang member Tommy Hayes to rebel against Herman Tipton.

Tipton finally threw in the towel, and Hayes emerged as leader of the dominant Cuckoo faction. He later turned against the Sheltons, machine-gunning three of their associates in an East St. Louis roadhouse in February 1931. Hayes and two gang members were murdered near Madison, Illinois, in April 1932. The gang was largely broken up by this time, though some ex-Cuckoos remained active in St. Louis crime for decades afterward. One of the last survivors, Jimmy Michaels, was killed by a car bomb in 1980.

The Sheltons eventually shifted their base north to Peoria, leaving East St. Louis in the hands of an ambitious henchman named Frank "Buster" Wortman. Carl and Bernie Shelton were murdered in the late forties, and Earl Shelton fled the state after being seriously wounded. He died in Florida in 1986. Another brother, Roy, was killed in 1950, and a sister and her husband were wounded in a machine-gun attack. The remnants of the Shelton empire were picked up by the Chicago Syndicate and Wortman, essentially their satellite, died of cancer in 1968.

The Hogan gang broke up more slowly as "Jelly Roll" Hogan expanded his political ambitions. He eventually was elected a state representative and then became a state senator. He finally died a natural death in 1963. Colbeck, meanwhile, served sixteen years in federal prison. He attempted to move into the gambling rackets after his release but likewise came up against the Wortman syndicate. He was machine-gunned to death on February 17, 1943.

♔ ♔ ♔

The turmoil in St. Louis produced an exodus of St. Louis gangsters to other cities. Johnny Moore (later known as Claude Maddox) and Willie Heeney, two former Egan's Rats, migrated early to Chicago and found employment with Capone. They were joined in 1927 by Gus Winkeler, whose pals Fred Burke, Milford Jones, Bob Carey, and Isadore Londe had moved on to Detroit where another ex-Rat, Johnny Reid, had established himself as a liquor distributor for the Purple Gang. Reid enlisted them in a war with an Italian gang led by Mike DiPisa and also organized the ransom kidnappings of various local bootleggers and gamblers.

Another member of the kidnapping gang was Carey's brother-in-law, Joseph "Red" O'Riordan, who had moved to Detroit before Prohibition. Reid was shotgunned to death in the parking lot of his apartment building on Christmas Day of 1926, which, in turn, may have led to a machine-gun triple killing.

Reid's killer supposedly was a former Chicago or St. Louis gangster named Frank Wright, who was cut down with friends

Joseph Bloom and Reuben Cohen in Room 308 of Detroit's Milaflores Apartment Building on March 28, 1927. Wright survived just long enough to tell police a curious story about being summoned to the room on the pretext of negotiating the release of a kidnapped gambler. Fred Burke and Purple Gang member Abe Axler were arrested but soon released, and the "Milaflores Apartment Massacre" remained officially unsolved.

Burke and Carey worked for the Purples awhile, then branched out with others into bank robberies across the Midwest, being among the first bandits to employ Tommy-guns. They eventually landed in Chicago where they made the mistake of kidnapping a friend of Al Capone.

Gus Winkeler convinced Carey and Ray "Crane-Neck" Nugent to meet with Capone, who turned out to be the forgiving sort and offered them employment on the condition they give up their extracurricular activities. They joined forces with Fred Goetz, then known as "Shotgun" George Ziegler (or Zeigler) and Byron "Monty" Bolton, gaining favor as Capone's "American boys" and proving their worth with New York's first machine-gun killing, of Frankie Yale, in 1928 and Chicago's St. Valentine's Day Massacre the following February 14.

♔ ♔ ♔

Where the Purple Gang got its "colorful" name no one knows. The name hit the headlines suddenly in 1927, but the group had been in business for years, originating as a juvenile gang on Hastings Street in Detroit's Jewish ghetto. The most popular account has it that they began their careers robbing and extorting neighborhood pushcart peddlers who called the boys "purple"—tainted or off-color—because they preyed on their own people.

By other accounts, an early gang member or leader was one Norman Purple, whose name may have been shortened from something else. One gang member, Sam Cohen, also was called "Sammy Purple," supposedly for his preference for purple sweaters. Another story, attributed to a Detroit detective who knew the gang from their younger days, was that the boys once had a baseball team, the "Hastings Street Purples" who wore purple jerseys, again a fashion statement attributed to "Sammy Purple."

In the mid-twenties, the gang branched out from bootlegging to labor racketeering, extorting hundreds of thousands of dollars from the cleaning and dyeing industry, and a *Detroit Times* article from 1933 suggested this as the origin of the name:

> So-called "purple gangs" were known long ago, some historians claim. Dyers, they say, have been associated always with the purple dye because it was the first discovered by the Phoenicians, who originated the art of dyeing. Purple, therefore, has become the symbol of the dyer. Thus, according to this explanation, the "purple" gang becomes the "dyers" gang.

Gang members themselves denied ever using the name. "This Purple Gang stuff makes me sick," Joe "Honeyboy" Miller said in a 1929 interview. "Who got up that name? Everybody's a Purple. I talk to a guy a minute—the police spot him as a Purple. I have friends—they're Purples." Miller's real name was Salvatore Mirogliotta. Wanted for murder in Ohio, he was the only Italian member of the otherwise all-Jewish gang.

Obviously much of the Purple Gang story is pure legend. It is often written that Moe Dalitz was an early member of the Purples, abandoning Detroit for Cleveland in 1923, where he entered into his own successful rumrunning partnership with Morris Kleinman, Lou Rothkopf, and Sam Tucker, which became the powerful Cleveland syndicate. Purple Gang historian Paul Kavieff has found no evidence to support this. Dalitz once lived near Detroit, and his father owned a laundry in Ann Arbor, which seems to be as close as he ever got to the Purples. By the time these stories saw print any criminal from the Detroit area was automatically labeled a member of the Purple Gang. As late as the 1960s the name was still in popular use, and Mafiosi such as Joe Zerilli were routinely described as leaders of the Purple Gang.

His early years were spent as a robber and killer from St. Louis, but by the time he was captured, Fred "Killer" Burke had acquired Chicago "citizenship" thanks to his role as one of Capone's "American boys" in the St. Valentine's Day Massacre.

The Hastings Street crew, led by the Bernstein and Fleisher brothers, emerged in the mid-twenties as enforcers for the Oakland Sugar House Gang, led by Henry Shorr and Charles Leiter, and were soon promoted to full partners in the bootlegging business. It was a gang within a gang, but it was the Purples who gained immortality as the parent organization faded into obscurity.

Thoroughly undisciplined and mercenary, the Purples were the most disorganized of organized-crime groups. They preferred hijacking to rumrunning, and their Little Jewish Navy faction—yet another gang within a gang—specialized in running stolen liquor from Canada. Supposedly, they organized a defense group for local gamblers victimized by Fred Burke's interloping kidnap gang, then decided it was more profitable to form an alliance with Burke in the "snatch racket." They sold protection to gamblers, bootleggers, and narcotics traffickers, and their violence soon rivaled that of Chicago's gang wars. No one was immune from harm, and policemen and innocent citizens numbered among the gang's victims. By the end of the decade, the Purple Gang was the most recognizable gang outside Chicago, but they already were falling apart and shooting at one another. As an entity they would not survive Prohibition, though many former gang members remained active criminals for years to come.

The cleaners and dyers protection racket was broken up in 1928 with the arrest of a dozen Purples, including reputed leader Abe Bernstein and his brother Ray. All were acquitted, but the gang already was disintegrating. The next year, Harry and Phil Key-

St. Louis-area Gangsters Who Moved to Other Cities

Egan's Rats and Cuckoos

Leo Brothers—Convicted in the killing of *Chicago Tribune* reporter Jake Lingle but received only a fourteen-year sentence (probably thanks to his lawyer, future Dillinger attorney Louis Piquett). Sometimes claimed to have taken the rap for the Lingle slaying to avoid prosecution for another in St. Louis.

Fred "Killer" Burke—Moved to Detroit and headed a kidnapping gang. Also a professional killer and bank robber. Suspected of machine-gunning three men in the "Milaflores Apartment Massacre" in 1927. Burke later became one of Capone's "American boys" and took part in the Brooklyn murder of Frankie Yale and the St. Valentine's Day Massacre.

Bob Carey (alias Conroy, Newberry, Sanborn, etc.)—Member of Burke's kidnapping and robbery gang and another of the "American boys" who participated in the St. Valentine's Day Massacre. Turned up in New York as small-time counterfeiter and worked with his girlfriend in blackmailing wealthy marks; briefly sought by the law and the Capone mob as a suspect in the Lindbergh kidnapping. Found dead with his girlfriend in 1932 in what New York police called a murder-suicide, but there is reason to believe he was tracked down and killed by "Bugs" Moran in revenge for the Massacre.

Max "Big Maxey" Greenberg—Moved to New York in early twenties and partnered with "Waxey" Gordon in some of the earliest trans-Atlantic rumrunning, financed by Arnold Rothstein. Became a prominent Gordon lieutenant but was killed in April 1933 with Max Hassell by gunmen from the Bugs & Meyer Mob at the Carteret Hotel in Elizabeth, New Jersey. Gordon escaped out a window and fled to upstate New York but soon was captured and convicted of income tax evasion.

William J. (Willie) Harrison—Friend of Gus Winkeler. St. Louis bootlegger and professional golfer. Later operated speakeasies in Cleveland, Toledo, and Calumet, Illinois, where he allegedly worked for Al Capone. Eventually joined the Barker-Karpis Gang, only to be murdered by "Doc" Barker and thrown into well and Ed Fletcher were wrongly named as suspects in the St. Valentine's Day Massacre, and Fletcher and Abe Axler were convicted of Prohibition violations and sent to Leavenworth. In November 1929, Morris Raider was sentenced to twelve to fifteen years for shooting a young boy. At some point the Little Jewish Navy splintered off into a rival faction, and war erupted. Further complicating matters were the encroaching Italian mobs, including some new St. Louis refugees.

At the onset of Prohibition, also in Detroit, the Sicilian underworld was rocked by a savage gang war between the rival Giannola and

a burning barn near Ontarioville, Illinois, in January 1935.

Tommy "Mad Dog" Hayes—Leader of dissident faction of the Cuckoos gang of East St. Louis. Aided Shelton Brothers in wars against Charlie Birger and Cuckoo leader Herman Tipton, but later fought the Sheltons, as well. Killed in Illinois in 1932.

Willie Heeney—Former Egan's Rat who became a prominent member of the Capone Syndicate.

Milford Jones—Former St. Louis partner of Gus Winkeler and Fred Burke with a hatred for Italian gangsters, against whom he feuded in St. Louis and Detroit. Murdered in a Detroit speakeasy in 1932.

John Moore (alias Claude Maddox)—Former Egan's Rat who moved to Chicago in early twenties and headed Capone-allied Circus Gang at the Circus Café on North Avenue, bordering Moran territory. Maddox and Heeney probably were instrumental in bringing the Burke-Winkeler crowd into the Capone organization and in organizing the St. Valentine's Day Massacre.

Walter "Irish" O'Malley—St. Louis-born bank robber and kidnapper with early bootlegging affiliation to Egan's Rats. Involved with Vivian Chase in the Luer kidnapping.

John Reid—Former St. Louis and Kansas City gangster involved with Purple Gang. Murdered in Detroit, December 25, 1926.

Solly "Cutcher-Head-Off" Weissman—Former Egan's Rat later prominent in Kansas City and St. Paul rackets. Murdered in Kansas City, October 28, 1930.

William "Two Gun" Weissman—Former St. Louis gangster later associated with "Waxey" Gordon and "Longy" Zwillman mobs. Often claimed to be a brother of Solly, but a detective who knew both disputed this. Murdered in New Jersey in 1941.

August (Gus) Winkeler (spelled Winkler by the police and press)—Fred Burke's partner and one of Capone's "American boys" who participated in the St. Valentine's Day Massacre. Murdered in Chicago, probably on orders of Frank Nitti, October 9, 1933.

Green Dagoes (Egan's Rats Rivals)

- Joseph "Scarface Joe" Bommarito
- Francesco (Frank) Cammarata
- James "Blackie" Licavoli
- Peter Licavoli
- Peter "Horseface" Licavoli (cousin)
- Thomas "Yonnie" Licavoli
- Giovanni (John) Mirabella
- Anthony "Shorty" Russo
- Anthony Spicuzza

Vitale families that reportedly claimed more than a hundred lives. A truce eventually was mediated among the survivors, and an alliance known as the Pascuzzi Combine developed. The group was presided over by local Unione Siciliana head Sam "Sings in the Night" Catalonotte, who managed to keep the peace until his death by pneumonia on February 14, 1930, one day short of his thirty-sixth birthday. War broke out again and various Sicilian gang leaders were killed, among them Gaspare Scibilia, alias Milazzo, Sam "Sasha" Parina, and Cesare (Chester) LaMare.

Peter and Thomas "Yonnie" Licavoli had arrived in Detroit from St. Louis in the late twenties, along with a large contingent of relatives and friends. By some accounts they were "imported" by the Purples as hired guns but soon emerged as rivals. Peter married the sister of an established hood named "Scarface Joe" Bommarito, and Joe married Peter's sister. Joining forces with Leo "Lips" Moceri, Licavoli formed the River Gang, a powerful rumrunning combine whose fleets brought tons of Canadian booze across Lake Erie and Lake St. Clair, bribed Customs agents and local officials, and exterminated competitors.

Charles Bowles was elected mayor in 1929. Bowles had campaigned as a "dry," but Detroit soon was a wide-open town. His police commissioner, Harold Emmons, avoided making any gambling raids until the mayor left town to attend the 1930 Kentucky Derby. Emmons then allowed police to accompany reporters to betting parlors and make arrests. He was fired when Mayor Bowles returned. The mayor's apathy extended to the gang killings, as well. "It is just as well to let these gangsters kill each other off, if they are so minded," he told reporters. "You have the scientists employ one set of parasites to destroy another. May not that be the plan of Providence in these killings among the bandits?"

The violence peaked in July 1930 with ten unsolved gang murders in nineteen days. Two Chicago gangsters, George Collins and William Cannon, were shot down outside the La Salle Hotel, an event witnessed by radio newscaster Gerald Buckley, whose studio was on the hotel mezzanine. Buckley laid the blame for the killings on the laxity of Mayor Bowles and led a successful on-the-air crusade for a recall election. On July 22, the voters responded by ousting Bowles. Buckley broadcast the election results from City Hall, then returned to the hotel lobby at 1:30 a.m. to meet a mystery woman who'd promised him a story. He was met instead by three gunmen who killed him.

The result was an uproar comparable to that following the murder of *Chicago Tribune* reporter Jake Lingle a month earlier. Many gangsters, including Harry Fleisher of the Purple Gang and the Licavoli brothers, fled the city. The home of "Cockeyed Joe" Catalonotte was raided and one of the murder weapons found. Warrants were issued for Pete Licavoli, Joseph Massei, and Frank Cammarata.

The Licavolis fled to Toledo with many of their followers and soon reestablished themselves there and in Youngstown, Ohio. Peter Licavoli was arrested in October 1931 and returned to Detroit, but charges were soon dropped. "Yonnie" Licavoli was convicted in 1934 of ordering the murder of a Toledo bootlegger named Jackie Kennedy, sentenced to life, and spent most of his remaining years in an Ohio prison. Warrants were issued for the actual killers, John Mirabella, Joe "The Wop" English, and Russell Syracuse, but they simply vanished. The FBI would eventually learn that Mirabella settled in Youngstown under the alias of Paul Mangine, protected by the local underworld until his death by natural causes in April 1955. These three also were accused of the Buckley slaying.

Two members of the Licavoli mob, George Sargent and Anthony Labrizzetta, were wrongly convicted of a 1935 train robbery at Garrettsville, Ohio. It actually was committed by the Alvin Karpis Gang. Both were pardoned in 1937 in a remarkably rare instance of federal leniency toward falsely imprisoned gangsters.

Pete Licavoli eventually would combine with the intermarried Zerilli-Tocco clan, headed by Joseph Zerilli and "Black Bill" Tocco, to form the modern crime family that would dominate Detroit's underworld from Repeal until the 1970s.

♔ ♔ ♔

The backbone of the Purple Gang was broken with the "Collingwood Massacre" on September 16, 1931. Three members of the Little Jewish Navy, Isadore Sutker, Joseph "Nigger" Lebovitz, and Herman "Hymie" Paul, were shot down in Apartment 211 of the Collingwood Manor Apartments on Collingwood Avenue. The gang made the mistake of sparing a witness, an old friend named Solly Levine. Ray Bernstein, Harry Keywell, and Irving Milberg were convicted of the killings and sentenced to life, joining Fred "Killer" Burke and other old friends in Michigan's state prison at Marquette. The once-powerful mob now was shattered, most of its members in prison, in hiding, or dead.

The Purples' notoriety as supposed inventors of the "snatch racket" was renewed in 1932 as they were wrongly named as serious suspects in the Lindbergh kidnapping. Milford Jones, one of their former Egan's Rats colleagues, was shot to death in June 1932 at the bar of Detroit's Stork Club after a long career of murdering Italian gangsters. Abe and Joe Bernstein gradually withdrew from the rackets and spent most of their remaining years seeking a pardon for their brother. The Fleisher brothers went to prison.

Henry Shorr of the old Oakland Sugar House Gang disappeared in 1934 and is believed to have been murdered. Abe Axler and Ed Fletcher had risen to Detroit's Public Enemies No. 1 and No. 2 by the time they were found shot to death in a car on an Oakland County road on November 26, 1933. Headlines proclaimed that their deaths left the Purples leaderless. Similar headlines appeared when Harry Millman was murdered in 1937.

Over the years some of the former gang members continued to operate on the fringe of the underworld, but the gang was long dead. Detroit's version of the Mafia replaced them.

December 24—Four bandits fire on a payroll truck of the L. Q. White Shoe Co. in an attempted robbery at Bridgewater, Massachusetts.

December 30—Dean O'Banion hijacks a truckload of Grommes and Ullrich whiskey outside the Bismarck Hotel in Chicago.

December 31—Four bandits steal $115,000 in a holdup of the Farmers & Merchants Bank in the Omaha suburb of Benson. Headlines call it "The Greatest Haul Ever Made in Nebraska." Bootlegger Harry Sawyer is later arrested as a suspect.

1920

January 16—In Chicago, on the day the Eighteenth Amendment (national Prohibition) officially becomes law, six masked gunmen seize watchmen and railroad employees and loot two freight cars of $100,000 worth of whiskey. The heist is attributed to the West Side "Herschie" Miller gang. Other Chicago gunmen hold a Coca-Cola Co. watchman at bay with revolvers and steal four barrels of alcohol from a warehouse.

January 17—At 12:01 a.m., the Volstead Act goes into effect, providing for the enforcement of the National Prohibition Act.

February 3—Maurice "Mossy" Enright, Chicago labor racketeer, is shot to death in front of his home at 1110 West Garfield Boulevard. Attributed to a fight over control of the Street Cleaners Union. "Big Tim" Murphy is suspected.

February 5—The *New York Times* notes revival of "highway robbery" through use of automobiles.

March 31—Dennis "Dinny" Meehan, leader of a Brooklyn Irish waterfront gang, is shot to death in his home on Warren Street. Later attributed to Frankie Yale's Italian mob but probably the work of rival Irish gangsters headed by "Wild Bill" Lovett.

April 6—Tom Slaughter and Fulton "Kid" Green rob a bank in Cave City, Kentucky.

April 15—Bandits, later believed to be acknowledged anarchists Nicola Sacco and Bartolomeo Vanzetti, kill paymaster Frederick Parmenter and guard Allessandro Berardelli in a $15,776 payroll robbery of the Slater & Morrill Shoe Co. at South Braintree, Massachusetts.

April 17—New York police uncover a huge drug-smuggling ring after Salvatore Messina is killed at the home of father-and-son drug traffickers Giovanni and Louis Mauro in what police describe as "a fight over cocaine." Some $75,000 worth of cocaine is found in the Mauro home and another $150,000 worth in the home of relative Giuseppe Gangarossa, who is arrested for shooting Messina.

April 22—Eddie Coleman, head of the Chicago Teamsters Union, is fatally shot by an unidentified gunman hiding in his office at 184 West Washington Street.

April 26—Seven bandits rob the First National Bank at Sandy Springs, Maryland.

May 5—Sacco and Vanzetti, both carrying guns, are arrested in a police trap set to catch the South Braintree payroll robbers. Vanzetti is soon suspected of the attempted robbery of a payroll truck in Bridgewater, Massachusetts, the previous December 14.

May 7—The Drovers National Bank in East St. Louis, Illinois, is robbed. One bandit is killed and another captured.

May 11—James "Big Jim" Colosimo, South Side Chicago vice lord and restaurateur, is shot to death in the vestibule of his famous café at 2126 South Wabash Avenue by a gunman hiding in the coat-check room. Police suspect the killer was Brooklyn gangster Francesco Ioele, alias Frankie Yale, former associate and employer of both Johnny Torrio and Al Capone, who supposedly could not interest Colosimo in exploiting the opportunities afforded by Prohibition.

– Brothers Joseph and Batiste Vultaggio are found shot to death in their apartment above their Brooklyn grocery store. Investigation reveals they were members of a gang counterfeiting fifty-cent pieces. Vito Grillo is later arrested and confesses to killing the Vultaggios in an argument over profits.

May 13—Chicago gangsters Edward "Spike" O'Donnell and Danny McFall are acquitted of

HOT SPRINGS, ARKANSAS—UNDERWORLD RESORT

New York and Chicago have drawn the most attention from historians of the gangster era, with occasional nods to Detroit's Purple Gang, Max "Boo Boo" Hoff in Philadelphia, Egan's Rats in St. Louis, Pendergast's Kansas City, Moe Dalitz and the Cleveland syndicate, and the Kid Cann mob in Minneapolis, but little explored are other cities such as Hot Springs, Arkansas, whose flagrant corruption also served as a magnet for the nation's "public enemies."

Criminals of the twenties and thirties sometimes categorized cities as either "NJ towns" (for No Justice), where gangsters were apt to be arrested on sight, or "Safe towns," where fugitives with money or political connections were welcome and virtually immune from arrest, so long as they behaved themselves. Changing city administrations sometimes would alter the situation, as in 1923 when the election of reform Mayor William E. Dever in Chicago forced the Torrio-Capone mob to temporarily move to suburban Cicero. Likewise, Twin Cities gangsters could conveniently set up shop in either St. Paul (usually their favorite) or Minneapolis, depending on which had the more agreeable municipal administration at the time.

Some cities lay in between these extremes. Joplin, Missouri, was hometown to the Barkers and Wilbur Underhill and also to a bootlegging center of the Southwest, but it seems to have had a reasonably efficient and honest police department. Joplin attracted criminals from throughout the region, apparently for its close proximity to the Kansas, Oklahoma, and Arkansas borders, which made quick getaways a cinch. Until the early twenties, Wichita, Kansas, had an arrangement similar to St. Paul's, courtesy of John Callahan. He fronted as a junk dealer but actually was a bootlegger, narcotic trafficker, and head of a large-scale fencing operation. Callahan enjoyed a long-standing "treaty" with Wichita police, who agreed not to bother any of "the boys" who came to visit him so long as they committed no crimes within the city. An honest chief of detectives, S. W. Zickefoose, eventually nullified the treaty, although this likely would have brought him a demotion somewhere else.

Denis Tilden Lynch, in his 1932 book *Criminals and Politicians*, classed Buffalo as one of the "NJ towns" after the breakup of the DiCarlo and "Big Korney" mobs in the early twenties, failing to note that Stefano Magaddino would replace them as ruler of that city's underworld. After the Kansas City Massacre, "Pretty Boy" Floyd and Adam Richetti hid out for more than a year in Buffalo, emerging to meet their comeuppance in Ohio.

East St. Louis, Rock Island, Moline, and Davenport were classic "safe towns" on the Mississippi, noted for their graft, vice, and violence, and similar conditions existed in such mini-Gomorrahs as Newport and Covington, Kentucky; Phenix City, Alabama; and Reno, Nevada. Best known of the criminal resorts was St. Paul, whose criminal history is covered elsewhere in this volume and detailed exquisitely in Paul Maccabee's *John Dillinger Slept Here*. "If you were looking for a guy you hadn't seen for a few months," Alvin Karpis recalled in his memoirs, "you usually thought of two places—prison or St. Paul. If he wasn't locked up in one, he was probably hanging out in the other."

St. Paul served for years as headquarters of the Barker-Karpis Gang, but Karpis would eventually become well acquainted with the hospitality of Hot Springs, Arkansas, a gaudy resort town with perhaps the most wildly corrupt police department in America.

♔ ♔ ♔

Settled in the 1820s as Thermopolis in a valley of the Ouchita Mountains, Hot Springs was long noted for the curative powers attributed to its natural springs. President Andrew Jackson signed a bill in 1832 to protect the springs, and in 1851 the settlement was officially incorporated as the town of Hot Springs.

John C. Hale arrived in 1838 and built the first bathhouse. Nearly deserted during the Civil War, it revived in a postwar boom as more settlers were attracted by the springs. Among those seeking the baths was a wealthy former New Yorker named "Diamond Joe" Reynolds, who came in 1874 seeking a cure for his rheumatism and brought the railroad to town. A bumpy stagecoach ride is said to have convinced him of this need, as well as the stagecoach robberies that were common at the time.

Two such robberies occurred near Hot Springs that year—one popularly attributed to the James Gang—that may have been an ominous portent of crime to come. At any rate, "Diamond Joe" and his railroad soon put Hot Springs on the map as the country's friendliest health spa, and its population grew from 201 in 1860 to 8,096 in 1890.

Some vacationers wanted more than the legendary waters, and Hot Springs was happy to oblige. Gambling, though illegal, had been on hand for years but mushroomed in the 1870s, controlled by the rival factions of Frank Flynn and Major S. A. Doran. Police took their cut and looked the other way. Horse racing was popular in the late 1800s, and the Essex Park Racetrack opened in 1904, followed the next year by the Oaklawn Race Track. Brothels and saloons sprang up to provide further amusement.

A gunfight in 1884 between the Flynn and Doran factions brought the hasty convening of a vigilante group who rounded up many of the gamblers and herded them to the train station, but the gambling bubble did not burst and the situation soon reverted to normal. A political dispute in 1899 resulted in another gun battle, this time between the county sheriff and his supporters and members of the police department. Five men were killed, including Police Chief Thomas Toler, and Sheriff Bob Williams and others were indicted for murder in trials that ended with hung juries or acquittals. It was reminiscent of the gunfight at the O.K. Corral in more ways than one. Earlier in the year, Toler had run Wyatt Earp out of Hot Springs when the legendary gunman caused a drunken disturbance after a losing streak at the tables.

Such a wide-open playground was bound to attract outside criminals, and as the corruption became more systematic in the twenties nearly every underworld figure of note found the city to their liking. Some relatively small-time outlaws like Tom Slaughter, Ray Terrill, and Elmer Inman ran afoul of local police, but those with money remained untouched. Some developed unusual business ties with ranking police officers.

Joseph Wakelin was appointed chief of police of Hot Springs in April 1927. Born there in 1876, he had "engaged in law enforcement work practically all his adult life with experience in private detective work . . . as well as being connected with the Sheriff's Office and Police Department," according to an FBI report. He was married and had an adult married son. He also had a mistress, Grace Goldstein, true name Jewell LaVerne Grayson, formerly of New Orleans, and may have been a business partner in the several brothels she ran in Hot Springs. Best known of these were a house at 123 Palm Street and the Hatterie Hotel at 233½ Central Avenue.

Grace, whom the FBI described as "a vicious type of criminal who had no fear of law or any punishment which might be meted out to her," later admitted to nightly "business meetings" with Wakelin at her business addresses and various other places, including parked-car sessions in wilderness areas. Another of Grace's business partners—and also a regular client—was Herbert "Dutch" Akers, Wakelin's chief of detectives, who kept the girls furnished with hot diamonds and may have helped in the recruitment process, as well. Three young prostitutes later testified that they had been first seduced in the city jail by Akers and that police officers often would arrest girls and persuade them to engage in sex to gain their release. (By one account, every month the

Hot Springs brothels would empty, the women would march in procession to city hall, plead guilty to prostitution, and pay a small fine, which would be split among the mayor, police chief, and others as their protection fee.)

Akers was a master of the shakedown and made a killing during the racing season by arresting visiting gangsters, gunmen, bookies, and con men, impounding their money and then calling a lawyer friend to represent them. The lawyer would charge whatever amount of cash had been taken from the man, get him released, then split the fee with Akers. Wakelin and Akers developed the business further by selling criminals immunity from arrest and even guns and cars belonging to the police department. Both men had the reputation of hiding any fugitive for the right price.

Al Capone sometimes visited Hot Springs and is said to have had a reserved suite at the Arlington Hotel. Popular legend has it that North Side Gang leader Vincent "The Schemer" Drucci once trailed Capone south and violated the local neutrality by firing on his car with a shotgun. Serious Capone researchers in recent years have failed to turn up any evidence of this supposed attack, or of an even more dubious report that has Drucci attempting to strangle Capone in a bathhouse.

Other gangland luminaries who regularly vacationed in Hot Springs included New York mobsters Owney Madden, Charles "Lucky" Luciano, Louis "Lepke" Buchalter, and Benjamin "Bugsy" Siegel. Federal agents would later uncover phone calls from Buchalter's Arlington Hotel suite to the residence of Verne Miller at 6612 Edgevale Road in Kansas City. An avid golfer, bank robber, freelance hit man, and former South Dakota sheriff, Miller was a frequent visitor to Hot Springs and New York, where he and Frank Nash and their ladies were Thanksgiving guests of the Buchalters in 1932. There was later speculation that Miller was involved in several New York killings during a gang war between the Luciano-Buchalter group and "Waxey" Gordon's mob that same year.

Moonshine stills abounded in the timbered hills around Hot Springs. One was found on the property of former Garland County Sheriff Hubert Houpt in 1922. Charges against Houpt were dismissed when he stated he'd ordered the moonshiners to move the still. He hadn't bothered reporting it, he said, out of fear for his safety. More booze was produced in Hot Springs itself, in a Park Avenue warehouse bottling plant, and in huge underground chambers under buildings. Liquor was supposedly shipped to Capone in Chicago from Hot Springs in railroad tanker cars painted with the words "Mountain Valley Water."

Another Hot Springs regular was Frank "Jelly" Nash, a train robber who escaped from Leavenworth in 1930. Nash robbed banks with the Holden-Keating and Barker-Karpis Gangs in the early thirties, involved himself in bootlegging and gambling in St. Paul and Chicago, and became a close friend of Verne Miller. At the O. P. Inn, a hangout run by Capone gangster Louis "Doc" Stacci in the Chicago suburb of Melrose Park, he met a young divorcee named Frances Luce, telling her he was a "businessman," which (to her, anyway) explained his out-of-town trips and frequent changes of name and address. Frances was swept off her feet, though she suspected he was a bootlegger.

On March 26, 1933, they were married in Hot Springs (polygamously, as Nash already had wives in Oklahoma and Mexico). Nash took her north, joined the Barker-Karpis Gang for a Fairbury, Nebraska, bank robbery, and they stayed awhile at Fred Barker's house at 204 Vernon Avenue in St. Paul, returning to Hot Springs in early June and taking up residence at a tourist camp as Mr. and Mrs. George Miller.

The Justice Department's Bureau of Investigation was hot on Nash's trail as an escaped federal prisoner, and their Oklahoma City office received a tip he was in Hot Springs. On June 16, Special Agents Frank Smith and F. J. Lackey, accompanied by McAlester, Oklahoma, Police Chief Orrin "Otto" Reed, took Nash at gunpoint from the White Front Cigar Store and Pool Hall at 310 Central Avenue, run by Dick Galatas, a bookie and former con man. The capture was more a kidnapping than a capture, for federal agents had no arrest power at that time. But they knew they couldn't count on any help from local police, who would only warn Nash away. Chief Reed was asked to assist, partly because he knew Nash but probably also to give the capture the color of state authority, even if it was outside his jurisdiction. The agents and Reed spirited Nash into a car and headed north.

Dick Galatas watched the abduction, then raced to City Hall and called on Chief of Detectives Akers for help. In the meantime, a policeman named Joe Scott telephoned Akers to report the "kidnapping" at the White Front. Akers answered, "For Christ's sake, get off this line and stay off!" Akers and Chief Wakelin then telephoned the police departments in Benton and Little Rock to alert them to the "kidnapping." A cabdriver named Porter Anstell later saw Galatas drive by in his red Ford with his wife and Frances Nash, followed by Akers in Galatas's Cadillac and Chief Wakelin in another car. Anstell would report this to G-man Harold Anderson and then die soon afterward in a suspicious auto accident.

Police at Benton and Little Rock stopped the federal car on the false kidnapping tip, and the agents were forced to show their identification. At Fort Smith, "through official orders from the Attorney General of the United States, issued through the Director of the United States Bureau of Investigation," the agents and Chief Reed boarded a train for Kansas City with their prisoner.

In the meantime, Galatas flew with Frances Nash to Joplin, Missouri, in a plane piloted by John Stover, operator of the Hot Springs Municipal Airport. Galatas and Mrs. Nash then took a taxi to Joplin's Midway Drug Store, 1512 Main Street, run by a former St. Louis gangster named Jack Richards and actually a front for a bootlegging and dope operation. They were picked up there by a friend of Nash named Herb Farmer, who took them to his chicken farm south of town and telephoned others in Chicago and Kansas City, finally reaching Verne Miller. The Hot Springs police and John Stover had helped set the stage for the Kansas City Massacre [see p. 352].

In early June 1935, a young man calling himself Ed King rented a cottage at Lake Catherine near Hot Springs and moved in with his "brother" Harold. Ed actually was Alvin Karpis, whose usual haunts in Cleveland and Toledo were now too hot, and Harold was Fred Hunter, a gambler-turned-robber from Warren, Ohio. Soon after their arrival, they visited Grace Goldstein's whorehouse at 123 Palm Street. Grace was so taken with Karpis that she became, as she later put it, his "common-law wife," and Fred Hunter also found a companion in one of Grace's girls, Connie Morris, whose real name was Ruth Hamm Robison.

If Police Chief Wakelin was annoyed by any of this, he gave no indication. Wakelin even loaned Grace a set of his own license plates for a trip she made to Texas with Karpis. The plates were delivered by Lieutenant Cecil Brock, the department's identification officer, who afterward returned them to Wakelin. Perhaps Grace divided her time between the two men. At any rate, the Hot Springs police didn't bother Karpis or Hunter. In fact, an old wanted poster of Karpis ("yellow with age," according to the FBI) hung by the department's mailbox.

For all three, it was business as well as pleasure. Karpis flew around the country, conferring with associates and scouting out future robberies, often piloted by John Stover, the airport operator who had flown Dick Galatas and Mrs. Frances Nash to Joplin before the Kansas City Massacre. Stover also kept Karpis advised whenever the FBI was in town. Wakelin collected his protection money, and Karpis remained invisible to local police.

In the fall of 1935, Grace Goldstein brought her own niece, Margaret Thompson, from Blossom, Texas, to Hot Springs to work as a prostitute. On November 7, the Karpis Gang robbed a train in Garrettsville, Ohio, and a former rumrunning pilot named John Zetzer flew the gang members to various points around the country afterward, with Karpis and Hunter returning to Hot Springs. According to an FBI report, Grace Goldstein "openly bragged of the fact that she was closely connected with the Hot Springs Police Department and advised that she would be notified of any investigation conducted by the FBI or any other outside law enforcement agency, stating that she could obtain this information from officers of that police department. Investigation also established that Grace Goldstein was proud of her association with outstanding criminals and gloated over any newspaper publicity which concerned her connection with Alvin Karpis."

Karpis and Hunter moved to another rented cottage at Dyer's Landing on Lake Hamilton and soon drew the suspicion of neighbors. They packed up and left, and Chief of Detectives "Dutch" Akers covered his tracks afterward by notifying the FBI that he suspected Alvin Karpis was living at Dyer's Landing. Akers himself had earlier visited Karpis. An ice delivery man spotted him and asked the owner's wife, Mrs. Al Dyer, what "the law" was doing there, and she replied that they were just down to see "the boys."

On March 31, 1936, FBI agents, following a lead developed by postal inspectors, raided and shot up a house on Malvern Road, south of Hot Springs. Karpis had been there but was gone already. A little over a month later he and Hunter were finally captured in New Orleans in what would long be celebrated as "J. Edgar Hoover's first personal arrest" [see "The Rise and Fall of the Last Great Outlaw Gang," p. 449].

Charles "Lucky" Luciano also was in Hot Springs in the spring of 1936, dodging a New York State indictment for compulsory prostitution, and he once met Karpis on the street there. Luciano had nothing to fear from Hot Springs police, and the FBI had little or no interest in him. Thomas E. Dewey, Manhattan's gangbusting prosecutor, pressured Hot Springs police into arresting Luciano, but he was released immediately on $5,000 bail.

Realizing the futility of dealing with local authorities, Dewey leaned on the governor and attorney general of Arkansas. Governor Marion Futtrell ordered Chief Wakelin to rearrest Luciano, but extradition proceedings were stalled until Attorney General Carl Bailey sent five carloads of Arkansas Rangers to the city jail and forced Wakelin and Akers to hand over Luciano for transfer to Little Rock. The extradition hearings took place in the state capital, with courthouse entrances guarded by machine-gun-toting Rangers. Luciano soon returned to New York where he received a thirty- to fifty-year sentence as head of a vice ring.

After their capture of Karpis, the FBI launched a massive investigation of the Hot Springs Police Department. Chief of Police Wakelin, Chief of Detectives Akers, and Lieutenant Brock were convicted of harboring Karpis in October 1938. Each was sentenced, along with with Goldstein, to two years in prison. Two months later Goldstein received an additional five-year sentence for violation of the Mann Act, and Akers received another two years for harboring Thomas Nathan Norris.

Norris's gang had robbed the Palmetto State Bank at Ieke City, South Carolina, of $114,000 on September 4, 1934, and also was responsible for burglaries, robberies, and at least one murder in Texas. Ruth Hamm Robison, alias Connie Morris, who had been arrested in New Orleans with Karpis and Hunter, had already been sentenced, in June 1936, to a year and a day for harboring. John Stover, the Hot Springs airport operator, and Mr. and Mrs. Al Dyer and their caretaker, Morris Loftis, also were charged with harboring Karpis. They were acquitted.

The FBI investigation also disclosed the shakedowns of visiting criminals for money. Brock and two other officers were accused of beating to death a prisoner named John Dickson, who was killed in the city jail on December 24, 1936.

The FBI cleanup didn't extend beyond the police department, and Wakelin, Akers, and Brock may be seen as the fall guys in Hot Springs' long-accepted corruption, or simply as overextending grafters who went too far out of bounds. Leo McLaughlin was still the mayor, and under his "Little Combination" gambling and prostitution continued to flourish in Hot Springs for years to come, sometimes fading out but then returning, according to the dictates of changing political administrations.

Former New York gangster "Owney" Madden settled in Hot Springs in 1935, allying himself with the mayor, marrying the postmaster's daughter, and bringing in a slot-machine franchise from Frank Costello, who then was feeling the blows of Mayor LaGuardia's anti-gambling crusade. By the early sixties, Hot Springs reportedly housed the largest illegal casino network in the United States, and many believed Madden, often visited by the likes of Costello, Meyer Lansky, Mickey Cohen, and Carlos Marcello, to be the national crime syndicate's representative there. Madden claimed to be simply "retired," and law enforcement agencies, including the FBI, were never able to prove otherwise.

Before his televised testimony on what he called "Cosa Nostra," Joe Valachi was approached in private by Arkansas Senator John L. McClellan. The committee chairman, sensitive to voter reaction back home, asked Valachi to say nothing about Hot Springs. Valachi naturally obliged, being a low-level hood who knew little about anything outside New York. (During the hearings, other Midwest senators asked Valachi about organized crime conditions in Des Moines and Omaha, both cities he'd never heard of before.)

Justice Department pressure ultimately forced Arkansas Governor Orval Faubus, who previously had left enforcement to local authorities, to order the Hot Springs casinos closed, and the Arkansas House of Representatives followed with a resolution that banned gambling. Police Chief John Erney personally delivered the message to all Hot Springs operators that March 28, 1964, would be their last night of business. Dane Harris closed his Vapors Club in the final hour with the words, "All this has been a way of life here so long, it's more like a grocery store."

burglarizing the Merry Gardens nightclub at 6040 South Cottage Grove.

June 6—New York jeweler Samuel Schonfeld is attacked and robbed of $100,000 in gems.

June 16—Bandits rob the Dressel Commercial & Savings Bank in Chicago, killing a bank customer and wounding a policeman.

June 17—Patrick "Paddy the Bear" Ryan, leader of Chicago's Valley Gang, is shot at Fourteenth and Halsted, probably by Walter Quinlan.

July 3—Gunmen impersonating Prohibition agents rob three trucks of $100,000 worth of whiskey in Kearney, New Jersey.

August 3—The Commercial Savings Bank at Moline, Illinois, is robbed of $20,000.

August 10—Two gunmen rob Sol Bergman's jewelry store at 1969 East Ninth Street in Cleveland of $35,000 in diamonds, severely beating two clerks.

August 16—Gangster Alfred Graziano, alias Mike McCarthy, is fatally wounded outside a New York cabaret in a shotgun attack. The killers drop their guns, and the guitar case used for carrying them, before fleeing. Jerry "The Wolf" Ruberto is arrested as a suspect.

August 21—New Jersey hijacker Frederick Eckert is found shot to death in a parked car on Staten Island, an early victim of the "one-way ride"—a phrase coined later in Chicago, probably by "Hymie" Weiss.

— The Chicago Field Office of the U.S. Department of Justice's Bureau of Investigation (later FBI) is established, with James P. Rooney as special agent in charge.

August 28—Federal Prohibition Agent Stanton Weiss, Oklahoma County Deputy Homer Adrean, and black bootlegger Charles Chandler are killed in a gun battle resulting from a liquor raid on Chandler's home near Arcadia, Oklahoma. The bootlegger's son, Claude Chandler, who shot Adrean, is captured. He is taken that night by vigilantes out of the county jail in Oklahoma City and lynched.

September 5—Eddie Adams and Ray and Walter Majors, notorious Wichita, Kansas, criminals, attempt to rob Harry Trusdell's gambling house at 1209 Grand Avenue in Kansas City, Missouri. In the resulting gun battle, gambler Frank Gardner is slain, and Adams and the Majors brothers are captured. Adams will be convicted of murder and sentenced to life in the state prison at Jefferson

City, Missouri. The Majors brothers will receive five-year sentences for robbery.

September 7—James "Sunny Mack" Mackin is killed and Sylvester Agoglia wounded in a brawl between Italian and Irish gangsters in front of Mackin's Brooklyn home.

September 9—New York Judge McIntyre announces he will sentence all holdup men to twenty years.

September 11—Sacco and Vanzetti are indicted for the two murders and the payroll robbery in South Braintree, Massachusetts.

September 16—"Wall Street Bomb" explodes in horse-drawn wagon at the corner of Wall and Broad streets in New York City, kills thirty-eight, injures hundreds, and shatters windows for several blocks; never explained or solved, but presumed to be the work of anarchists.

September 28—Grand jury in Chicago indicts eight members of the White Sox baseball team for allegedly throwing the 1919 World Series to the Cincinnati Reds.

October 1—In New York, a paymaster and guard for the American Cigar Co. are beaten and robbed of $10,000.

October 10—Outlaws Tom Slaughter and Fulton "Kid" Green kill Deputy Roy Brown and wound two other officers in a gun battle near Hot Springs, Arkansas.

October 15—Tom Slaughter robs the Alluwee, Oklahoma, bank of $5,000 in cash and Liberty Bonds. Pursuing officers accidentally run over and kill six-year-old Frank Miles near Nowata, Oklahoma. Slaughter is pursued through four Oklahoma counties and into Kansas, but escapes.

October 29—Tom Slaughter is captured by deputies at Sedan, Kansas. Fulton Green and Frank McGivens are arrested at nearby Cedarvale, Kansas. Lawmen believe the trio planned to rob banks in both towns. Slaughter admits to participating in two Oklahoma bank robberies and others in Texas, Louisiana, Arkansas, Tennessee, and Kentucky.

November 2—Warren G. Harding elected president of the United States.

November 4—Detroit bank messengers are robbed of $20,000.

November 5—Gunmen rob a messenger of the Hyde Park State Bank in Chicago, escaping with $41,000 in Liberty Bonds and $27,000 in checks after shooting and beating the messenger and a bystander.

November 9—Private detective John E. Jones and Benjamin Stern, former bailiff for Federal Judge Kenesaw Mountain Landis, are indicted in Chicago with eight others for conspiracy to possess and sell forged prescriptions.

— U.S. Secret Service agents announce discovery of a Minneapolis "clearing house" that has handled more than $400,000 in bonds stolen in Midwest bank robberies.

November 10—Federal indictments charge Chicago gangsters Mike "de Pike" Heitler and Robert Perlman with violations of the Volstead Act, including selling $200,000 worth of whiskey to saloon keepers, then sending men to steal it back. Federal authorities predict at least thirty more indictments of bootleggers, saloon keepers, and policemen for Prohibition violations.

— Ottawa, Illinois, police call the state prison at Joliet looking for safecrackers who can rescue a teller believed to be locked in the National City Bank's vault.

November 11—In response to the "Black Sox" scandal, the alleged throwing of the 1919 World Series by eight members of the Chicago White Sox, Federal Judge Kenesaw Mountain Landis accepts a new position as commissioner of Major League Baseball.

— Federal Prohibition agents stage night raids on five saloons and a still claimed to be the source of Chicago's moonshine supply. One saloon customer reportedly tells the raiders, "Judge Landis will soon be in the baseball business, and we won't have to think about him."

November 13—Four young men rob Chicago, Burlington & Quincy mail train No. 7, near Council Bluffs, Iowa, stealing mail sacks containing an estimated $3.5 million in bonds and cash. By November 18, three Council Bluffs youths, Orville and Merl Phillips and Fred Poffenberger, have been arrested and have confessed to the crime. Most of the loot is never recovered, and Poffenberger claims to have burned $800,000 in bonds he was unable to sell.

November 16—Indianapolis police announce discovery of a plot to steal 200 cases of whiskey from a Cleveland dealer.

November 17—New York City home invaders rob Mrs. C. K. Palmer of jewelry worth $400,999.

November 19—Prohibition Agent Kirby Frans is fatally shot by bootlegger George Wills during a raid on Wills's home in Perry, Oklahoma. Wills escapes.

November 21—300 tourists disembarking from car caravans witness an apparent tong killing in New York's Chinatown. A young Chinese man is pursued by one of his countrymen through the crowd and into a pool hall at 12 Pell Street and shot. The gunman escapes, and about forty other Chinese flee the building, which immediately fills with sightseers and police. The victim's white wife identifies him as Leong Yung, recently expelled from the Hip Sing Tong as a police informer.

November 28—Keith Collins, last of the Council Bluffs train robbers, is captured at Westville, Oklahoma. He admits his involvement, claiming $25,000 as his cash share, and states that he threw a suitcase containing $500,000 in bonds into the Missouri River.

December 4—A Thompson-Starrett Construction Co. paymaster is robbed of $12,000 in Detroit.

December 12—Buffalo jeweler reports being kidnapped and robbed of $70,000 in gems.

December 16—New York jeweler murdered by bandits who escape with $50,000 in gems.

December 17—Baltimore reports 100 holdups and burglaries in two months.

— Robbers victimize passengers of a trolley car in Elizabeth, New Jersey.

December 22—New Jersey legislature will vote on bill providing for life terms for armed thieves.

December 24—Prohibition agent J. F. McGuiness is found murdered in Bayonne, New Jersey.

— In Chicago, thirty-one indictments are returned against policemen, a railroad official and two officers of a Louisville distillery for violations of the Volstead Act. Illinois Attorney General Brundage files suit to restrict the operations of more than seventy Chicago saloons.

December 26—"Monk" Eastman, bodyguard and collector for gambler Arnold Rothstein, is found shot to death outside the Blue Bird Café at 62 East Fourteenth Street in New York. Eastman previously had led a powerful East Side street gang. Prohibition agent Jerry Bohan will receive a three- to ten-year prison sentence after pleading guilty to manslaughter, saying he shot Eastman in the course of an argument.

December 29—Cheese merchant Salvatore Mauro is shot to death at 222 Chrystie Street in New York. Mauro, possibly involved in bootlegging, was armed with a pistol at the time. Giuseppe "Joe the Boss" Masseria, is arrested and released for lack of evidence.

— Five bandits hold up the State Exchange Bank in Culver, Indiana, mortally wounding citizen J. Russell Saine in a gun battle. Two escape in a Marmon automobile, but three, John R. Burns, Joe Beyers, and Art Silbert, are captured by local citizens. All will be convicted in May and sentenced to life in the state prison at Michigan City, Indiana, despite a defense by Clarence Darrow. (Robber John R. Burns is, in fact, Joseph Burns, one of ten men who will escape from Michigan City in 1933 with the help of John Dillinger. The true name of John or Joseph Burns was John C. Heaps.)

1921

January 4—New York transit officials confer with police after a series of robberies of subway stations and passengers.

January 9—Pennsylvania Railroad towerman held up in Kearney, New Jersey; police commandeer engine to pursue robber.

January 15—Ray Terrill, Arthur "Doc" Barker, Harry Campbell, and Roland "Shorty" Williams are arrested at Coweta, Oklahoma, and a quantity of rifles, shotguns, pistols, ammunition, and nitroglycerin is found in their possession. They are charged with attempted bank burglary and transported on January 30 to the Oklahoma state prison at McAlester to await trial.

January 24—Five bandits hold up two trolley cars in Summit, New Jersey.

January 27—As Al Brown, Al Capone is indicted in the Criminal Court of Cook County, Illinois, for keeping a disorderly house and slot machines.

February 5—$10,000 bank robbery in Hamilton, Indiana.

February 8—New York City police will begin guarding United Cigar Store chain as these businesses become a favorite target of armed robbers.

February 11—Eddie Adams and Julius Finney rob a bank and store in Cullison, Kansas.

February 17—Eddie Adams, having escaped from a train on his way to prison, and Julius Finney are captured by possemen near Garden Plains, Kansas. Adams will be convicted of bank robbery and sentenced to ten to thirty years in the state prison at Lansing, Kansas.

February 18—Notorious bank robber Henry Starr is fatally shot while robbing the Peoples National Bank at Harrison, Arkansas. Accomplices Ed Lockhart, Charlie Brackett, and Rufus Rollen escape by automobile and leave it burning outside of town. They will later be named by Starr in a deathbed confession.

February 26—One trolley bandit is shot and two others captured in Townley, New Jersey. They confess to twenty-one holdups and burglaries since December 12.

March 8—Paul Labriola, Municipal Court bailiff for fifteen years, is shot down near his home at 843 West Congress Street in Chicago. The same day Harry Raimondi is shot and killed at his cigar store at 910 Garibaldi Place. Both had supported Nineteenth Ward alderman John "Johnny de Pow" Powers in his successful re-election campaign and probably were killed by the Genna gang working for Powers's opponent, Anthony D'Andrea.

April 6—A U.S. Mail truck is robbed of $385,000 in cash and bonds after leaving the Dearborn Street railroad station in Chicago. In a clever ruse, the robbers, including Peter Gusenberg, pretended to be playing baseball in an adjoining lot before the robbery. "Big Tim" Murphy, labor racketeer and former state legislator, will be convicted of organizing the robbery.

April 8—The State Bank at Malden, Illinois, is robbed by men hired to install a burglar alarm.

April 14—Al Capone (as Al Brown) pleads guilty to keeping a disorderly house and slot machines, and is fined $150 plus $110 costs.

April 15—One bandit is killed and two are wounded in holdup of the Cicero State Bank in Cicero, Illinois.

— Two Chicago bank messengers robbed of $638,000—in canceled checks.

May 11—Anthony D'Andrea, who lost to Alderman "Johnny de Pow" Powers in Chicago's Nineteenth Ward, is shot to death while entering his home at 902 South Ashland.

May 21—The Hunterstown Bank in Hunterstown, Indiana, is robbed of $21,500.

May 24—The Union National Bank in Newcastle, Pennsylvania, is robbed of $40,000. Police use a machine-gun-equipped automobile in futile pursuit of the bandits.

June 3—In Minneapolis, Millers & Traders Bank messengers are robbed of $16,000.

June 7—Bandits use occasion of local police parade to hold up Merchants' Ice & Coal Co. in St. Louis.

June 10—One bandit captured after $40,000 messenger robbery in Pittsburgh.

June 17—Lloyd "Red" Barker, William Green, and Gregory O'Connell rob a U.S. Mail truck in Baxter Springs, Kansas.

June 22—Roy Sherrill escapes from the U.S. penitentiary at Leavenworth, Kansas, with Joe Davis. Sherrill, serving a twenty-five-year sentence for mail robbery, was a member of the Lewis-Jones Gang, an early band of automotive bank and train robbers operating in the Midwest after the world war.

July 14—Sacco and Vanzetti are convicted of murder and sentenced to death.

July 18—Bootlegger "Big Steve" Wisniewski is kidnapped and murdered by rival Chicago gangsters, probably the Druggan-Lake mob, and dumped near Libertyville, Illinois. Later legend will credit Wisniewski as first victim of the "one-way ride," though similar gang murders in automobiles were reported in New York as early as 1917, and even those were likely not the first.

July 20—Illinois Governor Len Small is indicted by the Sangamon County Grand Jury on embezzlement charges stemming from his term as state treasurer.

August 3—Judge Kenesaw Mountain Landis bans the eight players involved in the "Black Sox" scandal from further participation in Major League Baseball.

August 8—In Chicago, a Jefferies State Bank messenger is robbed of $10,000.

August 12—Three policemen are killed and four are wounded in the robbery of a Ford Motor Co. paymaster in Memphis, Tennessee.

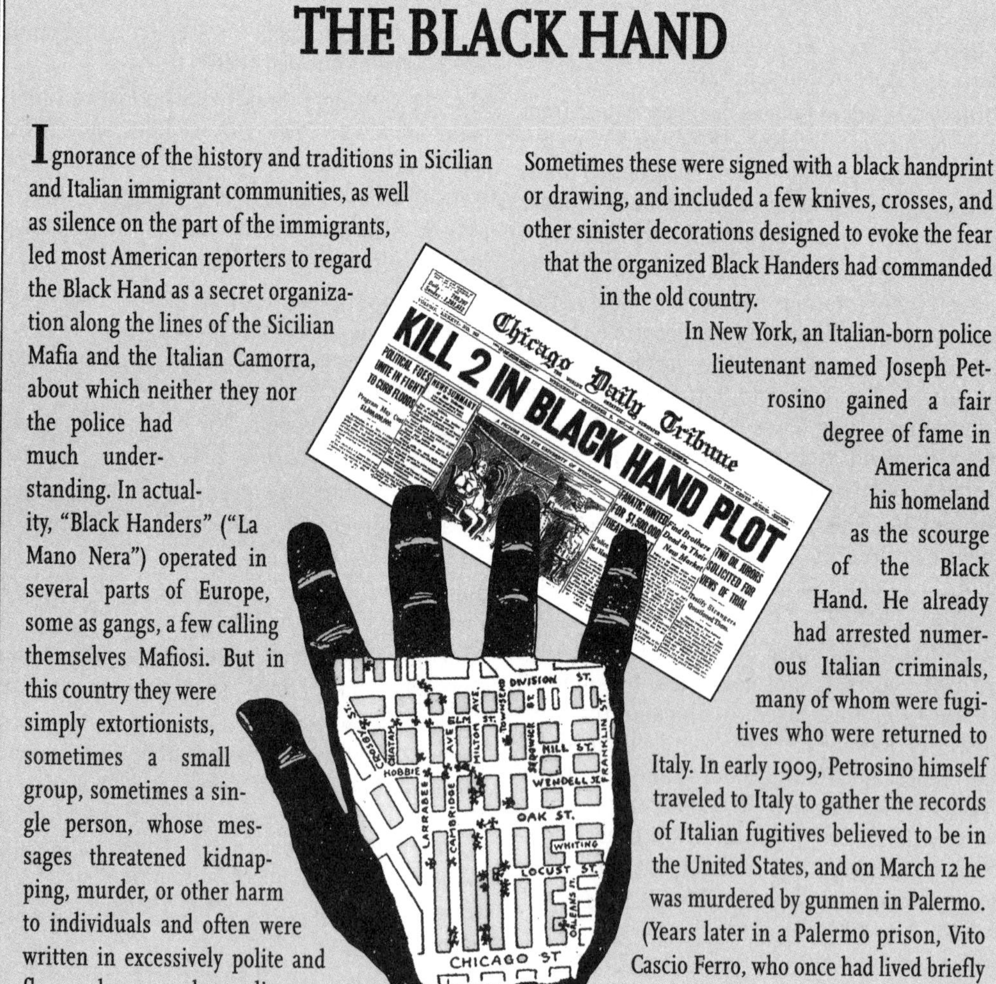

THE BLACK HAND

Ignorance of the history and traditions in Sicilian and Italian immigrant communities, as well as silence on the part of the immigrants, led most American reporters to regard the Black Hand as a secret organization along the lines of the Sicilian Mafia and the Italian Camorra, about which neither they nor the police had much understanding. In actuality, "Black Handers" ("La Mano Nera") operated in several parts of Europe, some as gangs, a few calling themselves Mafiosi. But in this country they were simply extortionists, sometimes a small group, sometimes a single person, whose messages threatened kidnapping, murder, or other harm to individuals and often were written in excessively polite and flowery language demanding money. Sometimes these were signed with a black handprint or drawing, and included a few knives, crosses, and other sinister decorations designed to evoke the fear that the organized Black Handers had commanded in the old country.

In New York, an Italian-born police lieutenant named Joseph Petrosino gained a fair degree of fame in America and his homeland as the scourge of the Black Hand. He already had arrested numerous Italian criminals, many of whom were fugitives who were returned to Italy. In early 1909, Petrosino himself traveled to Italy to gather the records of Italian fugitives believed to be in the United States, and on March 12 he was murdered by gunmen in Palermo. (Years later in a Palermo prison, Vito Cascio Ferro, who once had lived briefly in New York and was considered the domi-

August 13—After sabotaging the prison's electric plant, Eddie Adams and fellow convicts Frank Foster, George Weisberger, and D. C. Brown scale walls of the Lansing, Kansas, state prison and escape. Brown is soon recaptured, but the others, with Billy Fintelman, form the new Adams Gang.

– The Kincaid Loan & Trust Co. at Kincaid, Illinois, is robbed of $114,000.

August 21—The eight White Sox players accused of "fixing" the 1919 World Series are acquitted in federal court in Chicago when legal records are discovered missing, but their careers are ruined.

August 25—Night watchman Thomas J. Sherrill is shot to death at the partially constructed St. John's Hospital in Tulsa by burglars attempting to rob the safe of the Fuller Construction Co. Members of the gang, including Arthur "Doc" Barker, are soon apprehended. Barker is a son of the later notorious Kate "Ma" Barker.

nant Sicilian Mafia boss, reportedly confessed to the murder of Petrosino.)

A 1911 trial of Camorra leaders in Viterbo, Italy, including former Harlem resident Enrico Alfano, revived the name briefly in the American press, and in the years before World War I, Sicilian and Neapolitan crime families battled one another for control of gambling and rackets in New York's Little Italy in what has been called a "Mafia-Camorra war." Several of the Neapolitan gang members were convicted of murder in 1917 and went to prison or the electric chair, and the remnants of Brooklyn's "Camorra" were integrated with the Sicilians in what could be seen as the first "Americanized Mafia." The families would be further Americanized by the Castellammarese War in 1930–31.

Meanwhile, back in Chicago, a Black-Hand target usually was a prosperous businessman who didn't always know how to treat such threats, since the would-be extortionists operated on the hope that they sounded like an organization and would be taken seriously. This could backfire. When Chicago's "Big Jim" Colosimo was threatened, he sent for a Brooklyn relative, Johnny Torrio, who met with three so-called Black Handers in a South Side railroad underpass, ostensibly to pay them off, and instead simply killed them. That message was clear enough in the local Italian community that Colosimo, with his already-famous restaurant and major vice operations in the old Levee district, was left in peace.

Confusing the issue among the general public were groups calling themselves "White Handers." In New York these were Irish toughs who emulated the Italian and Sicilian extortionists, while Chicago's Italians, often lacking much police protection, formed a White Hand group that for a time tried to deal with Black Handers vigilante-style. In any case, the racket faded with the coming of Prohibition, when Black Handers and White Handers alike found gainful employment in bootlegging gangs.

* In the *Chicago Tribune* for November 24, 1918, reporter Jack Lait— the same one who "identified" the shooters of John Dillinger by sniffing gun barrels—wrote of the hijinks he and other fledgling newsmen had pulled during the "golden age" of Chicago's yellow journalism some years earlier. He described how one aging reporter had been forced to come out of retirement, was assigned to the police beat in Little Italy, and had earned the nickname "Walrus" because of his large mustache. When not playing pranks on him, the other reporters took pity, helping him turn grudges into "vendettas" and converting knives into "stilettos" so that his bare-bones stories would at least see print. With his job always in peril, "Walrus" suddenly stunned his colleagues with a thrilling front-page account of an Italian banker receiving an extortion letter signed "The Black Hand." Frantic at being scooped, a crowd of reporters rousted the banker, who claimed he had shown the letter to absolutely no one, although it was printed word-for-word in Walrus's story. They then descended on Walrus, who smiled and conceded that while he couldn't write properly embellished news, he could make news; that he had written the letter himself; and that another letter already was in the mail revealing the first to be a hoax. The afternoon papers duly (if barely) reported the receipt of the second letter, and the Black Hand became the new source of any extortion letter, as quickly popularized by reporters and fiction writers alike. Just as quickly, genuine Italian extortionists adopted the ominous name and added the threatening symbols, creating the impression they were the American reincarnation of that Old World society. When the elderly Walrus died a few months later, said Lait, he and his fellow scribes sent the departed reporter a floral piece in the shape of a black hand.

August 26—The Huntington Park branch of the Los Angeles Trust Co. is robbed of $20,000.

August 28—In Chicago, vaults of the Security Trust & Deposit Co. are looted of $250,000. Two guards are suspected.

August 30—An armed robber is arrested during a holdup of United Cigar Store on Lexington Avenue. Thirty-one of these stores have been robbed in New York City since the first of the year.

September 29—Robbers take $25,000 payroll of the Western Coal & Mining Co. at Herrin, Illinois.

October 8—The Eddie Adams Gang battles officers near Anoly, Kansas, wounding Deputy Benjamin Fisher.

— Sheriff W. S. McPherson is killed by bootleggers in Monarch, Wyoming.

October 10—A Grand Avenue Bank messenger is robbed of $17,650 in St. Louis.

— Five men are captured after robbing the Spring City National Bank in Spring City, Pennsylvania, of $17,500.

October 13—Manhattan bootlegger "Diamond Joe" Viserte is killed by a gunman in a coffeehouse at 237 Broome Street.

— Chinese shopkeeper Chong Sing is shot to death outside his shop at 222 South Wyoming Street in Butte, Montana, in what is later alleged to be the opening salvo of a war between the Hip Sing and Bing Kung Tongs.

October 18—The Adams Gang burglarizes stores in Attica and Columbia, Iowa, in the culmination of a burglary and robbery spree across Missouri and Iowa.

October 19—The Adams Gang battles a posse near Murray, Iowa, killing Charles W. Jones before making their escape in a car stolen from Sheriff Ed West.

October 20—En route to Wichita, stealing and abandoning cars, the Adams Gang robs eleven stores at Muscotah, Kansas. Near Wichita, they abduct and rob two motorcycle patrolmen, setting fire to their motorcycles.

October 24—Gerald Chapman, George "Dutch" Anderson, and Charles Loerber rob a U.S. Mail truck of $2.4 million in cash, bonds, and jewelry on Leonard Street in New York.

October 29—President Warren G. Harding pardons New York Mafia figure Ignazio "Lupo the Wolf" Saietta from a thirty-year sentence for counterfeiting.

October 31—John "Red" Brennan, Patrick "Gospel Pat" Toca, and "Shotgun Larry" Hirsch rob the Niagara Falls Trust Co. of $5,000, shooting a policeman and four others.

November 1—Willie Egan, leader of the Egan's Rats, is shot to death in St. Louis, probably by gunmen of rival Edward "Jelly Roll" Hogan's gang.

November 2—Chicago jewelry salesmen robbed of $100,000 in uncut diamonds.

November 5—The Eddie Adams Gang robs a Santa Fe express train of $35,000 near Ottawa, Kansas.

— Policeman A. L. Young is murdered in Wichita, Kansas. Later attributed to Eddie Adams.

November 9—Detroit bandit leaps from one moving car to another and escapes with $4,000 payroll.

November 10—The Adams Gang burglarizes a bank in Rose Hill, Kansas.

November 20—Joyriding with prostitutes in Wichita, the Adams Gang are stopped by police. Gang member Frank Foster murders Patrolman Robert Fitzpatrick, and the gang escapes. Later that night, they attempt to steal a car from Cowley County farmer George Oldham, who is shot to death by Adams.

November 22—Eddie Adams is slain by police in a gunfight at a Wichita, Kansas, garage. Detective Charles Hoffman is mortally wounded by Adams in the same battle.

November 26—St. Louis gangster James "Pappie" Fleming is found shot to death near Edwardsville, Illinois.

December 4—Robbery victim who kills his assailant is charged with homicide and violation of New York's Sullivan gun law; murder charge later dropped, but he is held for illegal possession of handgun.

December 7—Two policemen are slain by bandits during the robbery of the Grand Rapids Savings

Bank at Grand Rapids, Michigan. Robert Leon Knapp, alias Walker, and Frank "The Memphis Kid" McFarland are wanted as suspects. Both will later be accused of the Denver Mint robbery.

December 8—Notorious outlaw Tom Slaughter, awaiting electrocution for the murders of two armed trusty guards at Arkansas's Tucker Prison Farm, uses a smuggled pistol to escape from the Death House of the state prison at Little Rock. He releases another white convict, forger Jack Howard, and five black inmates; captures and imprisons several guards and the warden and his family; and virtually takes over the prison, stealing food from the commissary and escaping in a prison car. Slaughter is later seriously wounded in a gun battle with police at Benton, Arkansas. Saline County Sheriff J. J. Crow later discovers the dead bodies of Slaughter and one of the black escapees. Jack Howard surrenders, claiming he joined in the

DEATH CORNER

An area a half-mile or so square just across the river to the west of Chicago's Near North Side originally had been settled as a drunken, violent shantytown for Irish immigrants who called themselves "Kilgubbins." Around the turn of the century, large numbers of Italians and Sicilians were making their way west from Ellis Island, settling in the run-down sections of cities, and turning the formerly Irish shantytown into an upscale slum of flats and small apartment buildings known as "Little Hell," thanks to the Chicago River's gas-house fires that gave the nighttime sky an ominous red cast. "Little Hell" also was called Little Sicily and adjoined Little Italy, a mile or so to the south, although some Italians and Sicilians lived in both places. What made Little Sicily special was its central intersection of Oak Street and Milton Avenue (now Cleveland), known as Death Corner.

From about 1910 until the early twenties, nearly forty persons were shot or dumped there, initially by Black Hand extortionists or on their orders (early on they employed the so-called "Shotgun Man," killer of some fifteen victims, confident that no one would dare identify him to police, who might later receive an anonymous phone call if the body was blocking a doorway). Appalled by the continuous slaughter, Father Louis Giambastiani, pastor of a Catholic church named for St. San Fillipo Benizi, draped an Italian and an American flag around the front doors and above that hung a large banner that read:

> BROTHERS!
>
> For the honor you owe God, for the respect of your American country and humanity—pray that this ferocious manslaughter, which disgraces the Italian name before the civilized world, may come to an end.

The slaughter diminished only after the onset of Prohibition, when the Unione Siciliana began turning Little Sicily, house by house, into an industrial complex for the cooking of homemade alcohol used by various bootlegging gangs to "needle" near-beer back up to proof and to cut the whiskey that was flooding in, mainly from Canada and England. In the late twenties, when war broke out between the Aiellos and the Lombardos for control of the Sicilian Union, residents working with one faction or the other began moving in or out of the district, almost within hours, in what newspapers called a panic. Only when Tony Lombardo and his successor "Patsy" Lolordo (both supported by Capone) were killed, the St. Valentine's Day Massacre had wiped out the Moran mob that depended on Little Sicily's "alky cookers," and Aiello went into deep hiding (only to be killed in 1930), did Al Capone's Outfit bring a measure of peace to the neighborhood.

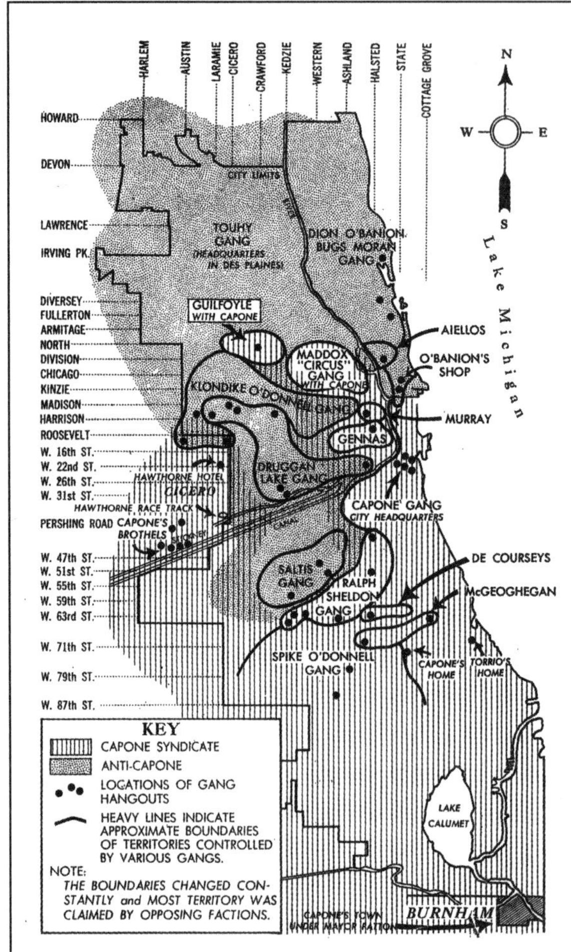

In 1926, a Chicago newspaper published an elaborate gangland map that acknowledged the constant shifting of mob territories.

escape only to bring Slaughter and the others back and that he killed Slaughter to prevent him from murdering the Negroes. Authorities doubt much of Howard's story, but he is paroled soon afterward.

December 11—Four days before his scheduled hanging, Chicago cop killer "Terrible Tommy" O'Connor escapes from the Cook County Jail. He is never recaptured.

December 20—Three masked men rob the Bank of North Arkansas in Everton, Arkansas, of $4,000 and escape on horseback. A few hours later two men on horseback rob the Farmers Bank in Gore, Oklahoma, of $1,600. Outlaw Ed Lockhart, a former member of Henry Starr's gang, is suspected in both holdups.

December 28—$30,000 worth of whiskey is stolen from La Montagne's Sons' warehouse in Lexington, Kentucky.

1922

January 14—Arthur "Doc" Barker is convicted in Tulsa of the murder of Thomas J. Sherrill and sentenced to life at the state prison in McAlester. Barker is a son of Kate "Ma" Barker.

January 16—Lloyd Barker, Will Green, and Gregory O'Connell are received at the federal prison in Leavenworth under a twenty-five-year sentence for mail robbery. Lloyd is another of "Ma" Barker's sons.

January 17—Robbers bind clerks and steal $25,000 in diamonds from the Star Loan Bank in Chicago; two bank messengers are shot and robbed of $9,600.

January 20—Three men rob the First National Bank in Hulbert, Oklahoma, and escape on horseback with $2,300.

January 25—John "Red" Brennan, "Gospel Pat" Toca, and "Shotgun Larry" Hirsch are captured in Pittsburgh. They will be returned to New York State and receive twenty-year sentences for robbing the Niagara Falls Trust Co.

January 26—United Cigar Store at Ninety-second Street and Second Avenue, New York, is held up for the third time in one month.

January 27—Cattle rustler Al Spencer escapes from the state prison at McAlester, Oklahoma. In coming months Spencer will gain notoriety as a horseback and "motorized" bank robber.

— Cashier H. T. Moss is killed in the $32,000 robbery of the First National Bank at Grafton, Pennsylvania.

January 28—A Hoboken police lieutenant is fatally shot during the $21,000 robbery of a First National Bank messenger.

February 12—Prohibition agent W. Meade is ambushed and killed in Wayne County, West Virginia.

February 13—Al Spencer and Silas Meigs rob the American National Bank at Pawhuska, Oklahoma.

– Hum Mon Sen, a reputed member of the Bing Kung Tong, is killed outside his China Alley herb shop in Butte, Montana, by a Chinese gunman in a beaver cowboy hat.

February 21—Al Spencer and Silas Meigs rob the McCurtain County Bank at Broken Bow, Oklahoma, of more than $7,000.

February 23—Jerry "The Wolf" Ruberto is killed and three others are wounded in a gun battle in a New York City café. Attributed to feuding bootleggers.

February 25—Bank robber Silas Meigs and posseman Claude Collins are slain in a gun battle near Bigheart, Oklahoma.

February 26—Joseph Marone is killed in a drive-by shooting in New York's Little Italy. The killing is witnessed by a busload of tourists on their way to Chinatown. Police attribute the killing to Marone double-crossing fellow gang members in the division of burglary loot.

March 1—A Palmolive Co. paymaster is robbed of $19,000 in Milwaukee.

March 11—Detroit gangster Paul Jawarski robs the Bernard-Gloekner Co. paymaster of $15,000 on Penn Avenue in Pittsburgh. On the same day, Jawarski's gang robs the paymaster of the W. J. Rainey Coal Co., en route to the company's Allison, Pennsylvania, plant, wounding guard Elmer Hill and stealing $27,000.

March 14—$500,000 in checks saved by New York bank messenger despite bullet through his coat.

March 20—The Nierman jewelry store in Chicago is robbed of $100,000 in gems.

March 24—Near Lenapah, Oklahoma, five masked gunmen rob the express car and passengers of a Missouri Pacific mail train and escape on horseback.

March 26—Samuel Licht, Arami Duonifaci, and Henry Stern are all shot on the same day in apparently unrelated New York City gang killings.

March 28—The Commonwealth State Bank in Detroit is robbed of $75,000.

April 4—Pennsylvania Railroad cashier is robbed of $75,000 in Chicago; robbers drop the loot.

May 8—Vincent Terranova, brother of Harlem crime boss Ciro "The Artichoke King" Terranova, is shot to death on East 116th Street in New York. Later in the day, Terranova's bootlegging partner, Joseph Peppo, is murdered on Broome Street near police headquarters.

– Four innocent bystanders are shot in a gun battle at 194 Grand Street between Italian gangsters. Umberto Valenti escapes unharmed, but Silva Tagliagamba is fatally wounded. Giuseppe "Joe the Boss" Masseria is captured nearby after a detective spots him throwing away a pistol (for which he has a permit). Masseria will be charged with the Tagliagamba slaying but never tried.

May 15—Joseph Behan, member of Brooklyn's White Hand gang, is murdered.

May 16—George Remus, Cincinnati's biggest bootlegger, is convicted of conspiracy to violate the Volstead Act, sentenced to two years in a federal prison, and fined $10,000.

May 22—A Sinclair Oil Refining Co. cashier is robbed of $11,463 in Chicago.

May 24—One bandit is killed and three captured in Bridgeport, Connecticut, during attempted robbery of $19,000 payroll.

June 15—Chicago police are baffled by the "noiseless bullet" that wounds café owner James Costello near East Forty-Second and State streets. One "Albert Capona" takes Costello to Wesley Hospital. Neither the victim nor persons nearby heard any shots. Probably an early gangland use of the silencer.

– Jake Fleagle Gang robs the McPherson-Citizens State Bank at McPherson, Kansas, of $3,060.

June 16—Al Spencer and Dick Gregg rob the Elgin State Bank at Elgin, Kansas, taking about $2,000 in cash and $20,000 in bonds.

June 24—Illinois Governor Len Small is acquitted of embezzlement charges in Waukegan.

June 25—150 cases of whiskey are stolen from the American Distillery in Pekin, Illinois.

June 30—Philadelphia policeman prevents bank messenger robbery in a shootout that leaves six wounded.

July 3—Million-dollar mail robbers Gerald Chapman, George "Dutch" Anderson, and Charles Loerber are captured by New York police at 102nd Street and Broadway.

July 5—St. Louis bank messenger is robbed of $99,200.

July 31—William Gabel, bootlegger and ex-policeman, is shot dead outside his tavern at 2319 Fourth Avenue in Rock Island, Illinois, after informing on gangster John Patrick Looney.

August 7—Ko Low, national president of the Hip Sing Tong, a Chinese criminal society, is shot to death outside the Delmonico Restaurant on Pell Street in New York's Chinatown. The Hip Sing Tong has carried on periodic warfare for years with the rival On Leong Tong for control of gambling, opium dens, and brothels in the nation's Chinatowns.

August 9—Gunmen fire on "Joe the Boss" Masseria in Fritz Heiney's Millinery Shop at 82 Second Avenue in New York, but miss. This may have started the legend that Masseria could "duck bullets."

August 11—Lured to a "peace conference" by his enemy "Joe the Boss" Masseria, New York gang leader Umberto Valenti is killed by Masseria gunmen while leaving a restaurant on East Twelfth Street near Second Avenue. A twelve-year-old bystander, Agnes Esslinger, is wounded.

August 30—After colliding with a taxi at Randolph and Wabash and threatening the driver with a gun, Al Capone is arrested by Chicago police and charged with drunken driving, assault with an automobile, and carrying a concealed weapon. The charges are dropped and expunged from the record.

September 8—Al Spencer and others rob the First State Bank at Centralia, Oklahoma, of more than $3,000 in cash and bonds.

September 26—Five bandits are wounded, three fatally, and captured in a street battle with police and vigilantes at Eureka Springs, Arkansas, after robbing the First National Bank of $70,000 in cash and Liberty Bonds.

September 28—Harvey Bailey, Nicholas "Chaw Jimmie" Trainor, and others rob the Hamilton County Bank in the Cincinnati suburb of Walnut Hills of $265,000 in bonds and cash.

September 30—Joseph Simboli, Black Hand leader, is stabbed to death in Boston.

— I. LaBarbera is killed in a bootleggers' feud on Second Avenue in New York City.

October 6—Gunmen fire on the parked car of gang leader John Patrick Looney outside the Sherman Hotel in Rock Island, Illinois. Looney's son and bodyguard, John Connor Looney, is killed.

October 13—A gang of five robs the First State Bank at Osage, Oklahoma, of $1,188. Two of the robbers reportedly are men dressed as women.

October 18—Three men rob the Security National Bank at Dewey, Oklahoma, of $2,453 and escape in a Hudson driven by a female accomplice.

October 24—Al Spencer and others rob the state bank at Talala, Oklahoma, of $1,200.

November 9—Three men rob the state bank at Valeda, Kansas. Al Spencer is suspected.

November 30—Thomas "Turk" Flanagan, one of a gang of bandit brothers known as the "Four Fierce Flanagans," is shot by unknown parties at "Yumpsy" Cunningham's New York saloon. Taken to Bellevue Hospital, Flanagan defiantly curses police on his deathbed and refuses to name his attackers.

December 2—Four gunmen rob the state bank at Towanda, Kansas, of $22,000 in cash and bonds. The Spencer gang is suspected.

December 8—Giuseppe Maggio, "King of the Black Hand," is murdered by unknown persons in Chicago.

December 12—In Kansas City, Missouri, police stake out the wrong bank after a false anonymous tip as five gunmen rob messengers of the

Drovers National Bank of $97,000, shooting Thomas Henry.

December 18—Five bandits rob a Federal Reserve Bank truck of $200,000, killing guard Charles Linton outside the U.S. Mint in Denver. One of the gang is wounded and carried away by his partners. Although the attack is on a delivery truck, this becomes known as the "Denver Mint robbery."

December 19—Rowland K. Goddard, chief of the local U.S. Secret Service office, and Denver Captain of Detectives Washington Rinker predict that the Mint robbers will be arrested within forty-eight hours. Escaped Chicago cop killer "Terrible Tommy" O'Connor and Roy Sherrill, of the old Lewis-Jones Gang of bank and train robbers, are named as probable leaders of the robbery. Other speculation points to the gang that recently robbed Drovers National Bank messengers in Kansas City.

– A rumrunning vessel carrying 4,000 cases of "holiday whisky," valued at an estimated $500,000, is seized by the Coast Guard in New York.

– The Spencer gang robs M. L. Truby's jewelry store at Independence, Kansas.

December 20—Three men rob the First National Bank at Dyer, Indiana, and flee in an automobile with $5,000, though one of the escaping bandits, "dressed as a woman," is reportedly shot by a grocer.

December 21—Sheriffs' posses, police, and state Rangers swarm over northern Colorado in futile pursuit of "suspicious men" spotted at an abandoned house near Greeley. The phantom fugitives, described as "eastern gunmen" and suspected to be the Denver Mint robbers, reportedly escape the dragnet in two cars, one headed east toward Kansas or Nebraska and the other reportedly fleeing to the old bandit stronghold of Jackson's Hole in Wyoming. The "fugitives" later turn out to be harmless coyote hunters from Denver.

December 22—Six bandits armed with sawed-off shotguns rob a Stix, Baer & Fuller Co. money truck in St. Louis of $5,000.

– The *Denver Post* reports that the mint robbery investigation has disrupted the holiday supply lines of bootleg booze.

December 23—Ross Dennis, Pittsburgh Terminal Coal Co. paymaster, is ambushed on his motorcycle near Beadling, Pennsylvania, and shot to death by Paul Jawarski's Flatheads Gang, who escape with the $28,000 payroll Dennis was carrying.

December 28—Eugenio Orgento, a "shopkeeper" with numerous arrests for liquor violations, is found stabbed to death in his East Village shop. New York police attribute the killing to a bootleggers' quarrel.

December 30—Paymasters of the Buick Automobile Co. and the Ferry Cap & Screw Co. are robbed in Cleveland.

– Stephen Piraino is shot to death in a New York City bootleggers feud.

1923

January 8—Angelo DeMora is shot to death in front of his grocery store at 936 Vernon Park Place in Chicago. DeMora is the stepfather of Vincent Gebardi (originally Gibaldi, later notorious as "Machine Gun" Jack McGurn).

January 14—The frozen corpse of Mint robber Nicholas "Chaw Jimmie" Trainor is found in a bullet-riddled car in a garage at 1631 Gilpin Street in Denver.

January 15—Dan Culhane, described as a member of a "million-dollar gambling syndicate," is arrested in Chicago as a suspect in the Denver Mint robbery. Ted Hollywood also is sought as a suspect.

January 16—Al Spencer and his gang rob the State Bank at Cambridge, Kansas, taking $17,500 in cash, coins, and bonds. Gang member Ralph Clopton is wounded and captured.

January 23—In New York, four bandits hijack a Municipal Bank car carrying $50,000, throw the guards out, and escape. The car is later found abandoned, still containing $3,700.

January 27—The bullet-riddled body of S. Santaniello is found in Red Bank, New Jersey. Suspected bootlegging connection.

February 1—Owney "The Killer" Madden, New York gang leader, is released from Sing Sing in Ossining, New York, after serving nearly eight years of a ten- to twenty-year sentence for the murder of rival gangster "Little Patsy" Doyle.

February 7—Bank and train robber Frank Holloway is found murdered in Tulsa, apparently slain by his own gang.

February 17—$80,000 from the Denver Mint robbery, and $73,000 worth of bonds stolen from the Hamilton County Bank in Walnut Hills, Ohio, are recovered by authorities in Minneapolis. The Mint robbers evade capture.

February 24—Former Egan's Rats gangster Clarence "Little Red" Powers is murdered by gunmen while sleeping at his Country Club roadhouse on Olive Street in St. Louis.

– Chicago jeweler robbed in elevator of diamonds worth $100,000.

February 28—Japanese gangster Iyekatsu "Baldy" Yamamoto is found stabbed to death on the roof of a New York barber shop.

March 26—The Al Spencer Gang robs the Mannford State Bank at Mannford, Oklahoma. In a running fight with possemen, Spencer is wounded, and gang member Bud Maxfield and Mannford resident J. B. Ringer are slain. Spencer and the others manage to escape into the Osage Hills.

March 27—Gerald Chapman is shot and wounded in an attempted escape from the federal penitentiary in Atlanta.

– Bandits rob the Farmers State Bank at Westmoreland, Kansas, and shoot and wound Sheriff Albert E. Mayer.

March 31—The Spencer Gang robs the First National Bank at Gentry, Arkansas, of $2,000 and escapes into Oklahoma after battling a posse.

April 2—The Egan's Rats gang robs a U.S. Mail truck in St. Louis of $2.4 million in bonds.

April 3—Circuit Court Judge William E. Dever is elected mayor of Chicago. The election of an honest mayor will force Johnny Torrio and Al Capone to move their headquarters outside the city limits to Cicero.

April 4—A Minneapolis grand jury indicts some twenty people as part of nationwide ring dealing in stolen bonds.

April 5—Gerald Chapman escapes from Atlanta Federal Penitentiary.

– Bill Rush, a member of the St. Louis Cuckoos gang, is slain by gunmen in a back room of his newly opened dance hall at Granite City, Illinois.

April 6—A New England Telephone & Telegraph Co. paymaster is robbed of $23,000 in Boston.

April 17—Howard McLaren is slain in a Philadelphia bootleggers' feud.

April 20—St. Louis police raid the home of Egan's Rats gangster William "Whitey" Doering and recover loot from the multimillion-dollar mail robbery.

May 20—The Philadelphia murder of James Harrington is attributed to a "professional gunman."

May 21—A "Black Hand gang" is sought in the fatal shooting of Mrs. Rosa Chicarelli in Alpha, New Jersey.

May 24—Roy Sherrill, Lewis-Jones Gang member and Leavenworth escapee, is recaptured near Scipio, Oklahoma, along with Jack Lacey and Bart Clark, alias Leo Crucе. Sherrill also has been named as a suspect in the Denver Mint robbery.

May 26—The St. Louis Egan's Rats gang commits a $54,130 mail robbery at Staunton, Illinois.

June 16—A Pullman Co. paymaster is robbed of $50,000 on Long Island.

July 2—Seven gunmen rob the United Railways Co. at Thirty-ninth Street and Park Avenue in St. Louis of $38,306. Fred "Killer" Burke later will be tried and acquitted.

July 24—Six bandits, including the four Newton Brothers from Texas, rob fourteen bank messengers in Toronto of $130,000, shooting four people. Toronto police express suspicion that the same gang committed the Denver Mint robbery.

July 30—One is killed and three wounded as seven bandits hold up a Moosic, Pennsylvania, trolley car to get a $70,000 payroll.

August 1—The Baltimore Trust Co. in Baltimore is robbed of $16,000.

THE UNIONE SICILIANA

How many "chapters" it had in other cities and what names they went by are difficult to determine, but in Chicago the Unione Siciliana was first chartered in 1895 as the Siciliana de Mutuo Soccorso negli Stati Uniti, and by the middle 1920s it had enough political power to control several city wards. Originally its purpose was to help Sicilian immigrants with death benefits, reduced insurance premiums and legal paperwork. When its influential president, Mike Merlo, died of natural causes in 1924, the bootlegging gangs that had restrained themselves out of deference to his counsel let slip the dogs of war.

10 CENTS
Chicago Sunday Tribune
FINAL EDITION
PANIC GRIPS 'LITTLE SICILY'
CAN WIN THE MOST VOTES BUT STILL LOSE
NEWS SUMMARY
THE MASTER OF THE WORLD
$12 MILLION LOAN ASKED TO MEET CITY PAY ROLLS
47 Planes in Race and Not One Casualty
HUNDREDS FLEE WAR OF AIELLOS AND LOMBARDO

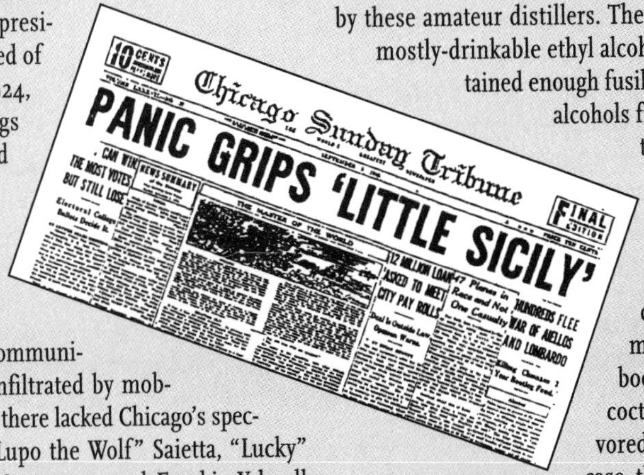

In New York, the Italian and Sicilian communities also had been infiltrated by mobsters. The bloodshed there lacked Chicago's spectacle, but Ignazio "Lupo the Wolf" Saietta, "Lucky" Luciano, Salvatore Maranzano, and Frankie Yale all achieved enough prominence in the Little Italys of Manhattan and Brooklyn for the police to regard them as leaders of something, and thus grew a "national" Unione Siciliana—at least among cops and reporters who wanted to attach that increasingly notorious name to their homegrown organizations. (In many newspaper articles and most subsequent books, each gangster is described as the president or head of a national Unione, with various spellings of Siciliana, and it may in fact have had small chapters in Indiana, Michigan, and Ohio. Researcher Mario Gomes speculates that because of its link with Sicily, New Yorkers may have used it as an alternative name for "mafia.")

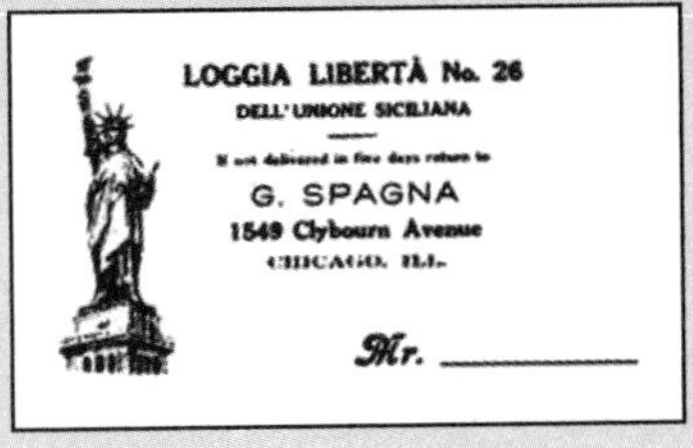

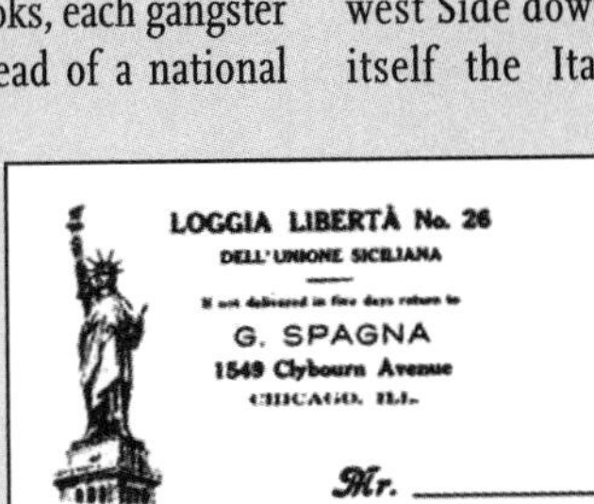

LOGGIA LIBERTÀ No. 26
DELL' UNIONE SICILIANA
If not delivered in five days return to
G. SPAGNA
1549 Clybourn Avenue
CHICAGO, ILL.
Mr. ____________

Before Prohibition, many residents of Chicago's Little Sicily and their Italian counterparts were adept at making wine. After Prohibition they began "alky cooking" in copper stills and selling it to those who supplied the equipment, although they sometimes had to abandon their homes and businesses practically overnight, depending on which warring faction they had been doing business with.

Poor fermentation techniques too often were used by these amateur distillers. Their product might be mostly-drinkable ethyl alcohol, but it often contained enough fusil oils (amyl and butyl alcohols from incomplete rectification) to make it dangerous, if not poisonous, especially if consumed straight instead of cut several times, mixed with smuggled booze, and then concocted into heavily flavored "highballs." In any case, the neighborhoods of Little Sicily and much of Little Italy (neither of which was disturbed by Chicago's largely Irish police) could easily be recognized by the pervasive odor of fermenting mash.

In the mid-twenties the Unione moved its offices from the Little Sicily area on Chicago's Near Northwest Side down to a building in the Loop, renamed itself the Italo-American National Union, and claimed to be freeing itself from criminal influence. However, its president in the years after 1934 was former Capone henchman Phil D'Andrea, who brought in Chicago's future mob leaders Paul Ricca and Tony Accardo.

August 2—President Warren G. Harding dies in office, avoiding any future implication in the corruption scandals surrounding his administration.

August 19—Seven gunmen rob 150 guests of $25,000 at the Allendale Inn in Detroit, killing a policeman and wounding six customers.

August 20—Al Spencer, Frank "Jelly" Nash and others rob the *Katy Limited* mail train near Okesa, Oklahoma, of $20,000 in bonds and cash. It is Oklahoma's last train robbery.

August 21—Ed Lockhart, serving a twenty-year sentence for bank robbery, is granted a six-month leave of absence from the Oklahoma state prison at McAlester.

August 22—Two men rob the Southern State Bank at Maize, Oklahoma, of $1,644 and escape police in an automobile chase. Ed Lockhart is suspected.

August 28—New York labor racketeer Nathan "Kid Dropper" Kaplan, while leaving Essex Market Courthouse under police guard, is shot to death by Louis Cohen, a member of the rival gang headed by Jacob "Little Augie" Orgen.

September 5—Chicago police arrest Al Capone for carrying a concealed weapon. Discharged by Judge O'Connell of the Municipal Court.

September 7—Jerry O'Connor, one of Edward "Spike" O'Donnell's bootleggers, is shot to death in Joseph Klepka's saloon at 5358 South Lincoln (later Wolcott) in Chicago by attacking gunmen of the Saltis-McErlane and Ralph Sheldon gangs. Frank McErlane is suspected of being the actual killer. O'Connor's death marks the beginning of increasingly violent disputes between Chicago's bootlegging gangs.

September 13—The Indiana National Bank in Indianapolis is robbed of $40,000 in securities.

September 15—Train robber Al Spencer is slain by a posse led by U.S. Marshal Alva McDonald and Deputy Luther Bishop on the Osage Indian reservation near Bartlesville, Oklahoma.

September 17—The Saltis-McErlane mob kills George Meegan and George "Spot" Bucher, affiliated with the O'Donnells, who have been trying to expand their operations on Chicago's South Side.

September 27—Forty men raid a Philadelphia distillery, making off with $30,000 worth of liquor.

October 10—Burglars steal a safe containing $12,000 from the Mechanics State Bank in Cedar Springs, Michigan.

October 11—Gang loots New York City warehouse of $125,000 in furs during a four-hour robbery.

— Roy, Ray, and Hugh DeAutremont attempt to rob a Southern Pacific mail train near Siskiyou, Oregon. They dynamite the mail car, setting it afire and killing a mail clerk; shoot three railroad employees to death; and flee without any loot. The U.S. Postal Department will offer a reward of $15,900 in gold for the apprehension of the DeAutremont brothers.

$15,900 REWARD IN GOLD!

ROY A. A. DE AUTREMONT.
(Picture taken early in 1923.)

Roy A. A. DeAutremont, alias R. A. Harris, alias R. A. Burton, age 23 in 1923; weight 135-140 pounds; height 5 feet 6 inches. Complexion medium light. Hair medium light brown. Eyes peculiar looking, narrow and squinty, light brown. Wears glasses in reading. Face broad at the cheek bones. Nervous, and a "dreamer." Likes to argue against the Bible. Long, turned up nose and prominent nostrils. Tonsils have been removed. Head round. Wears No. 6 shoe. Boastful and egotistical. Clips his words. Forward and presuming with women. First upper right molar tooth has amalgam filling, as have both first right and left lower molars.

RAY CHARLES DE AUTREMONT.
(Picture taken in 1920. He now resembles closely his twin brother Roy.)

Ray DeAutremont, alias R. C. Burton, alias William Elliott, alias Chas. R. Joseph, age 23 in 1923. Height 5 feet 6 inches. Weight 135-140 pounds. Complexion medium light. Hair medium light brown. Broad face. Prominent nostrils. Short cut neck. Eyes, peculiar looking, light brown, small and squinty. Wears glasses when reading. Big toe nail on left foot turned up. Cut scar at tip of left forefinger inner, and at back of second joint right middle finger, also round cut scar back of head. Gold foil in upper left cuspid, mesial surface. Amalgam filling, upper left first molar, occlusal surface. Gold inlay, upper right cuspid, mesial and incisive angle.

HUGH DE AUTREMONT.
(Picture taken in 1923.)

Hugh DeAutremont, alias E. E. James, alias Hugh DeKay, alias Hugh DeLerious, alias Hugh DeCoy. Age 19 in 1923, looks older. Height 5 feet 7 inches. Weight about 135 pounds. Complexion fair, eyes blue. Nose slightly pug. Hair medium light, slightly sandy and curly. Amalgam filling right and left molars, and same in first right upper molar. Likes to argue and is good debater. Fond of sports, particularly boxing and running. Expressed desire for traveling, and has boasted of trips he has made by riding freight trains. He is bright and alert and has a high school education. Little fingers turn outward at first joint.

Postal Department reward poster for the DeAutremont brothers, who killed four men during an attempted train robbery in 1923.

October 20—In Oakland, Illinois, burglars shoot the watchman, blow the safe of the First National Bank, and escape with $15,000.

October 28—Fifth robbery of United Cigar Store on Second Avenue in New York.

October 31—Brooklyn gang leader William "Wild Bill" Lovett is bludgeoned and shot to death by unknown killers at the Lotus Club speakeasy at 25 Bridge Street.

November 2—The Jake Fleagle Gang robs the First National Bank at Ottawa, Kansas, of $150,000.

November 6—Two banks are robbed in Spencer, Indiana.

November 9—In Detroit, a Ford Motor Co. messenger saves $25,000 from bandits by throwing the payroll onto a passing locomotive.

– Frank "Jelly" Nash, last of the Okesa train robbers, is arrested by U.S. Marshal Alva McDonald near Sierra Blanca, Texas, after returning from Mexico.

November 15—At his Halfway resort, between Marion and Johnston City, Illinois, bootlegger Charlie Birger kills his bartender, Cecil Knighton, in a gun fight. Birger will be acquitted on a plea of self-defense.

November 18—Charlie Birger kills St. Louis gangster William "Whitey" Doering in another shooting at his Halfway resort. A member of Egan's Rats, Doering was free on appeal after a mail robbery conviction. Birger again will successfully plead self-defense.

November 22—New York police capture four in a burglary attempt but also file assault charges against two shopkeepers who shot at them.

November 26—Aging outlaw Roy "Arkansas Tom" Daugherty and three accomplices rob the Bank of Asbury in Asbury, Missouri, of $1,000 and escape police and vigilantes after a gun battle and fifteen-mile car chase.

November 28—New York City gangster J. Teich is slain by an unknown assailant.

December 1—Maurice "Morrie" Keane and William Egan, beer runners of the "Spike" O'Donnell gang, are shot in a booze hijacking near Lemont, Illinois. Keane is killed, but Egan survives. Frank McErlane is suspected.

December 3—Owney Madden and two others are charged with the theft of 200 cases of whiskey from the Liberty Storage Warehouse in New York City.

December 4—The Vandergrift Distillery warehouse near Frederickstown, Pennsylvania, is looted for the fifth time.

December 5—Torrio-Capone gangster Dominic Armato is found murdered on the Dixie Highway in suburban Homewood. O'Donnell gang truck driver Martin Brandl identifies Armato as one of the hijackers who killed Maurice Keane on December 1.

December 16—New York City robbery victim rings fire bell for help and is arrested for turning in false alarm.

December 17—Chicago gang boss Johnny Torrio pleads guilty to Prohibition law violation and is fined $2,500.

December 22—Prohibitionist vigilantes of the Ku Klux Klan, led by former federal agent S. Glenn Young, stage massive liquor raids in southern Illinois. Other raids follow on January 5 and 7, 1924.

December 26—The New York City murder of J. Tomasullo is attributed to a "gamblers' feud."

December 30—George "Dutch" Anderson, serving 25 years for mail robbery, escapes from the federal penitentiary in Atlanta.

1924

January 2—Two gunmen rob the First National Bank at Shidler, Oklahoma, of $8,000.

January 17—New York City gunmen rob three Thom McAn shoe stores in one day.

February—New York police assign 500 detectives to catch female bandit known as "Bob-Haired Girl."

February 2—New York police capture "Broadway Navy" gang of dishonorably discharged sailors.

February 8—At Nevada's state prison, Chinese criminal Gee John becomes the first murderer in the United States to die in the gas chamber. A

Jimmy Murray and the Great Rondout Train Robbery

It was the one of the last and probably the largest mail-train robbery in U.S. history, the loot supposedly ranging from $1.5 million to $3 million before authorities agreed that it probably came to some $2 million in cash, bonds, and jewelry—about $22 million today.

And the mastermind was one James Murray, whose lifelong dedication to criminal enterprise should have established him as one of this country's most ambitious, energetic, all-purpose felons. His lack of notoriety probably derives from his involvement in so many kinds of lawbreaking that he fit no criminal category that would have branded him as either a gangster or an outlaw; and he probably didn't kill anyone.

Jimmy Murray, a lifelong lawbreaker who began as a corrupt politician and fixer involved in bootlegging, masterminded the Rondout train robbery.

Murray was born in Chicago on March 31, 1889, and completed only eight grades before entering the workplace and local politics, where he rose to prominence under Alderman John "Johnny de Pow" Powers in the "Bloody Nineteenth" Ward. This helped land him a job as a clerk in the Cook County Superior Court from 1912 to 1916, where he took evening classes in law and also acted as a bail bondsman.

After that, he entered the "real estate business," which meant that he joined brewery magnate Joseph Stenson in purchasing a dozen or so breweries in Illinois and Wisconsin from nervous owners anticipating wartime Prohibition, and in the "trucking business," which after 1920 translated as bootlegging.

At some point he worked as a slugger for a Chicago cab company, but his greater prosperity came from supplying beer to Chicago's gangs, especially John Torrio on the South Side and North Sider Dean O'Banion, who were in cahoots until the Sieben Brewery swindle by O'Banion led to his murder in 1924. Gang warfare had started the previous year, putting a strain on mob relationships, and that was when Murray fell back on the criminal expertise he had acquired as a court clerk and bail bondsman.

He presumably had gotten to know William F. Fahy, "ace postal inspector" who had an excellent record of convicting mail robbers, including "Big Tim" Murphy (the Polk Street robbery) and many others, which led his superiors to tolerate his "lone wolf" approach that ultimately suggested Fahy was fingering the jobs himself. It didn't hurt that Murray's earlier employment had included work as a driver for the Adams Express Co. and as a "conductor" for the Pullman Palace Car Co. With Fahy, they decided to rob a train.

And not just any train. On June 12, 1924, the Chicago,

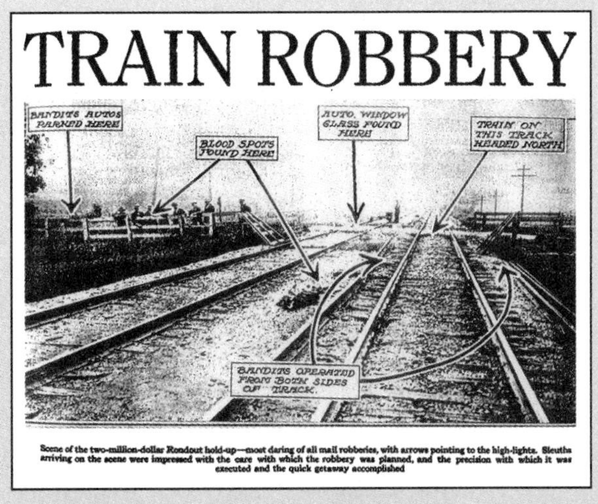

Newspaper coverage of the historic Rondout train robbery, thirty miles north of Chicago, placed the value of the stolen loot somewhere between $1 million and $3 million before authorities settled on $2 million in cash, bonds, and jewelry.

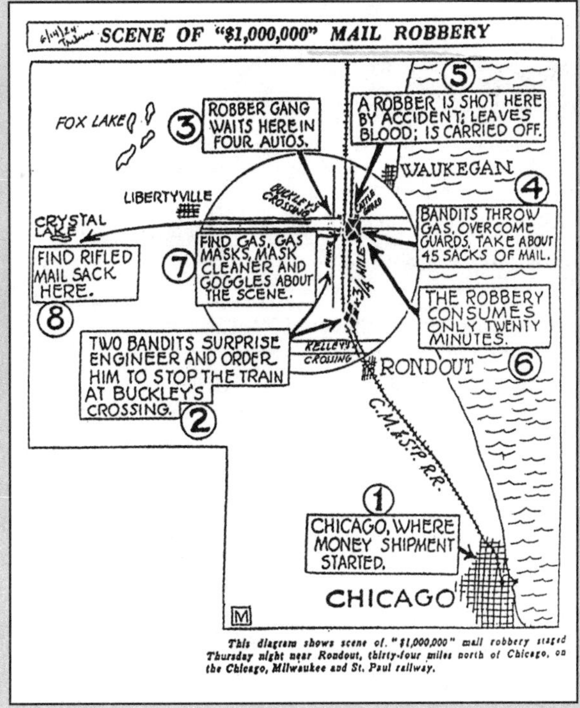

Milwaukee, St. Paul & Pacific Railroad's No. 57 would be a special—pulling eleven cars of cash, registered mail (including jewelry), and bonds. Its first scheduled stop: Milwaukee. Hiding on board were two men who ordered the engineer to stop at a grade crossing just north of Rondout, Illinois, a hamlet some thirty miles north of Chicago. Waiting there were several men with rifles, revolvers, and sawed-off shotguns, plus formaldehyde bombs and gas masks, as well as dynamite and nitroglycerine, if needed. The formaldehyde did the trick, and the bandits escaped in two automobiles. They might have pulled off a perfect crime except for the vengeful wife of a man wrongly convicted by Fahy in a recent postal robbery, and because in the dark one bandit had mistakenly shot another (one of the notorious Newton Brothers, whose bank jobs had ranged from Texas to Canada).

William Fahy, "ace postal sleuth," the tip-off man for the Rondout train robbery (and probably one or two others) who did not exactly "confess" and whose continued insistence on his innocence earned him more prison time than that meted out to the actual bandits.

41,783 AKRON BEACON JOURNAL FINAL EDITION

POSTAL SLEUTH CONFESSES TO ROBBERY

Start Work On Drafting N. O. T. Franchise

CITY RECEIVES AUDIT ON VALUE OF N. O. T. LINES

Akron Diving Girl Gives Up Career For Family

G. O. P. LEADERS COMPLETE PLANS FOR OHIO DRIVE

HELD AS LEADER OF MUCH SOUGHT GANG OF BANDITS

STATE ATTORNEY

PRESIDENT NAMES

Police already had rounded up many of Chicago's star criminals, including Dean O'Banion, who had been approached by Murray searching for a doctor. To spare himself and his men the grief of suspicion and interrogation, he (presumably) tipped police that they could find a guy "full of bullet holes" in an apartment at 53 North Washtenaw, a house owned by Murray and his wife, Jennie. There they found a badly shot-up Newton, whom they took to a hospital, and a short time later they arrested one James Mahoney, who already had secured emergency medical treatment, driven the doctor back home, and then returned to the flat with blood on him. Mahoney turned out to be Jimmy Murray, well enough known to the cops for both bonding out and hiding crooks.

A few days later, Fahy's superiors were approached by the wife of a man claiming he'd been framed by Fahy, and she told them that she had made a point of getting herself picked up by the philandering Fahy at a bar he frequented. Although married, he had regularly wined and dined her and had gotten drunk enough to spill some inside details of the Rondout robbery. When postal officials planted a phony telegram where Fahy alone would see it, he immediately called Murray on a phone whose line was tapped. Now they had the goods on Murray as well as Fahy, who had been diligently "investigating" the case. Both were sentenced to twenty-five years in Atlanta, with the other robbers receiving that much or less, depending on how well they cooperated and how much loot they coughed up.

Fahy served most of his time, but Murray had enough friends in high places to get his sentence commuted and make early parole in 1931. His parole application was brimming with a tone of sincerity that did not reflect the literacy that might have been expected of a court clerk taking classes in law; or, for that matter, his intentions to reform:

> During my incarceration here I have gained much "WISDOM" and I feel that never again will temptation receive any consideration from ME.
>
> There is no material gain in THIS WORLD that could REPAY MY WIFE, My CHILDREN and MYSELF, for My separation from them.
>
> My plans in the future are to LIVE a quiet peaceful LIFE of a GOOD AMERICAN CITIZEN.
>
> My reasons for wanting PAROLE are to get back with My FAMILY and children that have suffered this confinement as well as MYSELF. They need My Personal Help and assistance, WHO are dependent and need My support.
>
> If granted Parole I will take pride in obeying every rule, laid down By THE PAROLE BOARD.
>
> I will prove this by LIVING THE LIFE of a UPRIGHT CITIZEN, I promise that if GRANTED PAROLE, THIS PAROLE [Board] WILL NEVER HARBOR REGRET for doing So.
>
> My LIBERTY will CERTAINLY BE APPRECIATED BY MY FAMILY as well as MYSELF WHO has been away for this long period.
>
> I sincerely Hope My Prayers will be answered and that I will be granted PAROLE.
>
> /s/ James Murray
> Register No. 19950

Murray's wife, Jennie, not only had stuck by him during his seven years in stir, but was practically his "partner in crime," or at least a continuing inspiration. Their post-prison plans included opening a lavish barbecue restaurant at 4190 West North Avenue—the Rainbo, on a northeast corner, a few feet outside Chicago's jurisdiction, which soon became a hangout for the better class of fugitives. It had bunk beds in a small room upstairs and (supposedly) a cupola affording them a 360-degree view for watching or shooting. His home still was at 109 South Parkside, across the street from gang leader "Klondike" O'Donnell; he knew Father Phillip Coughlan, a "whiskey priest" at the nearby St. Catherine of Sienna parish, who would become spiritual adviser to "Baby Face" Nelson; and the Dillinger Gang had rented apartments on the same street.

By some accounts, Murray was picked up for questioning regarding the sale of hot bank bonds, which he may have tried to beat by promising information; and supposedly his wife, Jennie, had to fork over $10,000 when he was kidnapped by the Touhy mob, whose territory had to be crossed by trucks making beer deliveries from his Wisconsin brewery.

Before Repeal in 1933, Murray had peddled beer to Emil Wanatka, whose Little Bohemia Lodge in Northern Wisconsin was another "safe place" and became, the next year, a battle scene from which the Dillinger Gang escaped the FBI. After Repeal, Dillinger himself was harbored upstairs at the restaurant but insisted on fraternizing with customers and employees until Murray packed him off to a house on Crawford Avenue, thinking good riddance. Dillinger was so hot at the time that Murray would have sold him out to get stolen-bond charges dropped, and one newspaper edition mistakenly described the "former mail bandit" and his wife as the betrayers until the FBI revealed their tipster to be Anna Sage.

It was four months later, November 27, that "Baby Face" Nelson killed two federal agents in the "Battle of Barrington" [see p. 430], showed up mortally wounded on Father Coughlan's doorstep in Wilmette, and died a mile or so away at 1627 Walnut, one of several "safe houses" used by Jimmy Murray.

With Al Capone in prison and the North Siders in shambles, Murray seemed to long for more action than he could find in simply harboring crooks. He sold the Rainbo in the mid-1930s (under new management it became the Pickininny, specializing in fried chicken) and turned to robbing banks. This would end up costing him more than one jail sentence, and by the time he was released most of his cronies were dead or too old to sprint out of banks. (Except for the Newtons. Two of them had settled down near Uvalde, Texas, a rifle near each window, making do on their savings and Social Security. In their seventies and low on cash, they came out of "retirement" and robbed the bank in Rowena—coincidentally the birthplace of Bonnie Parker. One was shot and captured, and the one who escaped was assumed to be his brother.)

Dale Meyer, a great-nephew of Murray, remembers "Uncle Jimmy" (actually a great-uncle) from his childhood and set up an interview in Chicago with his own uncle, Charles Wallace, the nephew of Murray who had known him during and after his Rainbo days. As a youngster in his late teens, Wallace had bootlegged beer from Murray's brewery in New Glarus, Wisconsin, to Chicago, where Capone's men picked it up at a location regarded as Roger Touhy's territory. It was a time, from about 1930 to 1934, when every bootlegger, gangster, and outlaw seemed to know one another. According to Wallace:

> The Rainbo Barbecue was on the northeast corner of North Avenue and Harlem, across from Hays' Skyline Club. Aunt Jennie had been in partnership with Hays, who was screwing around with his secretary, cheating on his wife. They screwed Aunt Jennie out of everything. I think that's when she opened the Rainbo. Me and my brother [Edward, or "Buddy"] worked there, taking food orders, sometimes till five in the morning.
>
> On the east side and the west side we

had a porch where people could sit, and upstairs we had an office. One night the Touhys and the Capones shot it out at that corner. A Touhy guy I knew named Slim came in and made a phone call to find out where Capone was at, because he was supposed to be coming down Harlem Avenue. Touhy's cars were parked on the southeast corner, and Slim went back out and was leaning over the right front fender with a shotgun. When Capone hit the intersection, they shot the hell out of the car. Capone's car was bulletproof, but they shot the radiator all up and the car stopped in the middle of the intersection. So they jumped out and commandeered a car from a woman coming from the east. It was a Cadillac, and just when they were taking her car the River Forest police pulled up. As the police were getting out of their squad car, the Capone men pointed their guns and the coppers put their hands up. Then the Capone men went south on Harlem for a block and turned west. The coppers jumped back in their car and started chasing them, but they were never able to catch them.

My Uncle Tom was sitting out in his car in front of the Barbecue watching things. He pulled his car over by Capone's car and took the guns out and took off before the police could get back. Then Tommy Touhy's daughter Marie Touhy came running up to the corner, and I ran across the street and told her everything was all right and to get the hell out of there.

We had the bar at the west end of the building, and everybody hung out there—"Golf Bag" Hunt and every gangster you could think of. He was called that because he carried a gun in his golf bag. My brother and I sometimes caddied for him. One time when we were leaving he saw some sprinklers he thought would go good with his place at Lake Zurich. We said we'd get them for him and he said no, but we got them anyway and he gave us each twenty-five dollars.

Uncle Jimmy also had a house in Wauconda, on Wilson Street, with porches and cots set up where seven or eight people could sleep. Us kids slept in the back. Every gangster and his brother would come out, all hours of the night. There were a couple of big fights out there. . . .

Aunt Jennie was the greatest aunt I ever had. She gave us everything. When I was sixteen or seventeen I was wearing $150 suits. They were stolen by another aunt of mine. I'd go in the bedroom at the Wauconda place and there'd be suits and overcoats laying all over the bed, and she'd say take whatever you want. . . .

We knew Louie Cernocky at Fox River Grove, and he had his hand in everything. Same thing at Lake Como. Everybody hung out there, Hermansen's place.

When Baby Face died in the house in Wilmette, Jimmy called my grandmother and told her where he was, and he wanted my mother to come over, and my old man said, "If you go over there, I'll kill him and you both."

Howard Meyer, two years younger than his brother Dale, is a retired fireman who now operates a successful fishing-guide service in Northern Wisconsin. He also knew "Uncle Jimmy" from his own childhood and learned some of the family's history—including their rowdy lifestyles:

> Jimmy Murray was my great uncle. After his release from Alcatraz in the mid-fifties he moved back to his old home at 109 South Parkside, and I sometimes visited him there. If we walked together up to Madison Street, where there was a drug store and other businesses, he sized up everybody we saw. He was always on the lookout for cops. If we went into a hardware store, he'd come out with a wrench or something that wasn't paid for.
>
> The grandfather on my mother's side was Eddy Wallace, who I heard had been a debt collector for Capone. My grandmother, Elizabeth, or Liz, had two sisters, Jennie and Mary. Jennie married Jimmy Murray, who had been in politics and I believe also was a jail guard and a court bailiff. I imagine that's how he met Fahy, and through somebody else hooked up with the Newton Brothers and the others who robbed the mail train in 1924. During that job one of the Newtons was accidentally shot, which eventually led to Jimmy's conviction and the years he spent at Atlanta.
>
> My grandmother's sister, Mary, married Patrick Murray, a cousin of Jimmy. Paddy, as he was called, was killed with "Hymie" Weiss in 1926.
>
> When Jimmy was later released, he and Jennie opened a full-service barbecue restaurant called the Rainbo at Harlem and North avenues, and which served as a message center for the "boys" when they needed to contact someone. Cars would park in a certain spot under a grove of trees in the back and could only be approached by my mother's brother, Uncle Bud [Edward Wallace], who was one of the toughest, craziest, and strangest individuals one could hope or hope not to meet. He used to box at the open-air fights on North Western Avenue in the Rogers Park neighborhood, and the local newspaper describing the previous night's bouts reported that Bud's opponent had refused to come out of the corner because of the crazy look in Bud Wallace's eyes. That was before my time, but I believe it, because I used to meet him at a local bar when he was in his seventies, and the bartender would laugh and kid him that nobody would sit directly across at the U-shaped bar because they couldn't stand to have those cobalt blue eyes looking at them while they sipped their beer.
>
> My Aunt Jennie was a beautiful woman and tough as nails. Once, when the police came to arrest her on suspicion of burning down a rival's restaurant and bar, I was told that she answered the door wearing only a $10,000 mink coat and a diamond necklace. She was extremely colorful. On the day of Uncle Jimmy's funeral in 1962, my mother and I and some others were riding with her in her Cadillac when we were stopped for going the wrong way on a one-way street. After a brief argument, she went into her purse for a gun, which my cousin wrestled away before she could unload it at the officer. She died in 1973.
>
> My Aunt Mary, the widow of Paddy, was as colorful as Aunt Jennie. She looked and

talked like Mae West, and once on her way home from work a guy tried to rob her. She took his gun away, shot him in the leg, and just went home. She died in the late 1960s.

It was no coincidence that Dillinger and his friends chose to stay at Little Bohemia because Uncle Jimmy supplied beer to Emil Wanatka when he had his place in Chicago, and it came from Jimmy's brewery in New Glarus when Emil moved up to Wisconsin. I think I learned about this from Emil's daughter, who's a good friend of ours.

Ralph Capone lived in Mercer in his later years, near "Li'l Bo," and not very far from my home. He owned a tavern called Billy's Bar, and I talked to him several times about Jimmy, whom he knew well from Prohibition days. Jimmy had close ties to the North Side Gang, but his ties to the Capone gang were just as strong, because his liquor, political and criminal justice connections made him indispensable to both sides. He could play both sides of that street, and I got the feeling that Ralph had great respect for him. Ralph said he had the city and the system "wired" like no one else.

He never surrendered all of his take from the big train robbery. He turned in part of it for an early parole, but family legend has it that the sisters supplemented their incomes with it. Sometimes I would get a very old twenty-dollar bill in a birthday card. . . .

James Murray is buried at Chicago's Queen of Heaven Cemetery, along with other members of one of the city's most criminally industrious families, whose grandchildren have become firemen, policemen or otherwise successful and respectable citizens.

member of the San Francisco based Hop Sing Tong, Gee was convicted of the 1921 murder of Tom Quong Kee in Mina, Nevada, during a Western tong war.

February 24—Bookie Joseph "Big Mac" Mahoney is fatally shot in a New York restaurant during a scuffle with former partner John Quigley. Quigley claims self-defense, saying he wrestled the gun away from Mahoney by "jiu jitsu" and it went off accidentally.

March 3—Train robber Frank "Jelly" Nash is received at Leavenworth under a 2twenty-five-year sentence for mail robbery.

March 26—Bank robber Ed Lockhart is killed by police near Sperry, Oklahoma.

March 31—Four gunmen in a taxi kill bookmaker Louis Greenberg and fight manager Max Kanowitz, alias Max Belmont, outside Kanowitz's East Village poolroom in New York.

March-April—More than 200 alleged liquor violators, including gang leader Charlie Birger, are tried in federal court at Danville, Illinois. Convicted of bootlegging and possession of liquor and counterfeit tax stamps, Birger receives concurrent sentences of one year and ten months in jail and fines of $2,800, plus costs.

April 1—During the municipal election at Cicero, Illinois, Salvatore (Frank) Capone, Al's brother, is killed by police while terrorizing voters. Dave Hedlin and Charlie Fischetti escape. The North Side O'Banion gang, the West Side "Klondike" O'Donnell gang, and the Ralph Sheldon gang aid the Torrio-Capone mob in Election Day intimidation.

April 25—Charles F. Murphy, longtime boss of the New York Democratic political machine at Tammany Hall, dies, leaving an estate of nearly $2 million.

April 28—The bullet-riddled corpse of Detroit gangster Isidor Kantrowitz is dragged from New York City's East River.

May 5—In a Crown Point, Indiana, bar Chicago gangster Frank McErlane settles a drunken bet on his marksmanship by shooting lawyer Thaddeus Fancher. McErlane becomes a fugitive until the murder of a witness leads to dismissal of charges.

May 8—Bootlegger Joe Howard is shot to death at Heinie Jacobs's saloon, at 2300 South Wabash Avenue, Chicago, allegedly by Al Capone, for having slapped around Jake "Greasy Thumb" Guzik, Capone's colleague and bookkeeper. Capone briefly becomes a fugitive until witnesses lose their memories.

May 9—William J. Burns, director of the U.S. Justice Department's Bureau of Investigation, resigns in the aftermath of government corruption scandals.

May 10—New U.S. Attorney General Harlan Fiske Stone appoints J. Edgar Hoover as acting director of the Bureau of Investigation.

May 13—Thirteen convicts, including bank robber Edward Delano, escape through a tunnel under the wall after short-circuiting the prison lights at the McAlester, Oklahoma, state prison.

May 17—Paul Jawarski and his Flatheads Gang rob the Detroit Bank branch at West Fort Street and West End in Detroit of $40,000.

May 19—Johnny Torrio is arrested in a raid on the Sieben Brewery at 1470 North Larrabee in Chicago after being set up by North Side mob boss Dean O'Banion, who said he was quitting the booze business and had sold him the plant.

May 21—Outlaw Dick Gregg, a former member of the Al Spencer Gang, robs the Farmers State Bank at Burbank, Oklahoma.

May 22—Dick Gregg is captured after a gun battle at Lyman, Oklahoma.

May 23—Driving to East St. Louis from a Ku Klux Klan rally in Harrisburg, Illinois, Prohibition vigilante S. Glenn Young is ambushed by gunmen in a passing car. Young is wounded in the leg and his wife, Maude, is permanently blinded by bullets.

May 24—Jack Skelcher, of the Shelton Brothers gang, is killed by Ku Klux Klansmen near Herrin, Illinois, in retribution for the ambush of S. Glenn Young.

— Drug addict William "Yellow Charleston" Miller shoots John Parker in a Harlem card game, then flees to the nearby Exclusive Club cabaret owned by popular black sporting figure Barron D. Wilkins where he demands money to leave town. Wilkins refuses, is shot, and he and Parker both die. Waving a gun, "Yellow Charleston" commandeers a taxi and flees to Jersey City but, fearful of a lynching, returns the following day and surrenders to police.

May 31—The Argentine State Bank in Kansas City, Kansas, is robbed of $20,000.

June 11—Gunmen steal a $100,000 gem shipment in a truck robbery at Eighth Avenue and Twelfth Street in New York. Jack "Legs" Diamond's mob is suspected.

June 12—Well-organized bandits commandeer the Chicago, Milwaukee & St. Paul mail train, force it to stop where their cars are waiting near the Rondout, Illinois, crossing some thirty-two miles north of Chicago and steal more than $2 million in what is one of the last and largest train robberies in U.S. history. The well-executed crime unravels when one of the robbers mistakenly shoots an accomplice in the dark, and Chicago police later respond to reports of a wounded man in an apartment at 53 North Washtenaw. Postal Inspector William J. Fahy will receive a twenty-five-year prison sentence for providing inside information to the gang led by Chicago politician-bootlegger James Murray, who also is sentenced to twenty-five years. The actual robbers, including the outlaw Newton Brothers from Texas, and Murray will exchange a large portion of the loot for early release. Murray will resume his life of crime, harboring fugitives and later robbing a bank.

— Jack "Legs" Diamond, Eddie Diamond, John Montforte, and Eddie Doyle are arrested by New

York police for the June 11 $100,000 jewel robbery. They will be discharged, June 14.

June 14—"Babe" Pioli, a member of "Legs" Diamond's mob, murders prize fighter Bill Brennan at his Tia Juana Club on Manhattan's West Side. Pioli will plead guilty to manslaughter.

June 19—Ray Terrill, serving a ten-year sentence for burglary, escapes from the state prison farm at Tucker, Arkansas. Terrill was associated with the Barker Gang in Tulsa and also an alleged member of Al Spencer's Gang.

June 27—Guard killed during $9,500 robbery of Brink's Express Co. in New York City.

July 2—Irvin "Blackie" Thompson, Joe Clayton, and Phenix Donald, alias William Weaver, rob the Avery State Bank at Avery, Oklahoma, then kill Police Chief Jack Ary and Officer U. S. Lenox in a gun battle near Drumright, Oklahoma. Thompson is on parole at the time in the custody of federal agents employing him as an undercover informant in the frequent murders of oil-rich Osage Indians.

July 19—"Blackie" Thompson's parole from Oklahoma's state prison is revoked.

July 24—Mazer Co. of Detroit robbed of $125,000 in jewels.

July 25—Bootlegger Louis Munda is murdered by a gunman in front of hundreds of witnesses during a religious festival while making a donation at the shrine of Our Lady of Mount Carmel in Brooklyn. The killer escapes.

August 18—Bank robber Roy "Arkansas Tom" Daugherty is killed by police at the home of associate "Red" Snow at 1420 West Ninth Street in Joplin, Missouri. Police Chief Verna P. Hine, who hid in a nearby weed patch during the gun battle, will later be forced to resign after his officers accuse him of cowardice.

— Coney Island "freak show" robbed of $13,500.

August 27—North Side gangster John Phillips is killed in a shootout with police outside the Northern Lights Café at 6342 Broadway in Chicago.

August 28—While standing in front of an open window at his intended bride's Brooklyn home, grape dealer Anthony Panno is killed by five shots in the back from a silenced pistol.

August 29—North Ward National Bank messengers in Newark are robbed of $112,000 in checks.

September 12—John Ashley and his gang kidnap a cab driver in West Palm Beach, steal his taxi, and use it to rob the Bank of Pompano at Pompano, Florida, of $23,000 in securities and cash.

September 20—"Dutch Louie" Cassaza is shot to death in New York.

September 21—At 7:45 p.m. gunmen in a passing taxi fire at gangster Harry "Kid Portchester" Marks outside a barbershop on New York's Lower East Side. Marks, out on bail on a murder charge and a reputed member of the "Little Augie" mob, tells police, "Don't know anything about it. Somebody out to do some shooting, I guess." Marks is killed two hours later at the same spot by gunmen in a taxi. One Benjamin Siegel (not the later notorious "Bugsy") is arrested.

September 25—A bank messenger for the Union Trust Co. of Springfield, Massachusetts, disappears with a $100,000 shipment of currency.

September 27—Gunmen rob the Kincaid Trust & Savings Bank in Kincaid, Illinois, and escape with $7,785 after a battle with townspeople.

October 1—North Side Chicago gangsters Vincent "The Schemer" Drucci and Frank Gusenberg are arrested as suspects in a $200,000 jewel robbery in the Loop.

October 3—The "flashily dressed" corpse of a man, shot and stabbed, is found on Review Avenue in Long Island City, New York. A loaded .38 revolver, $33 in cash and a quantity of diamond-studded jewelry are found on the body, and police attribute the murder to a "bootleggers' feud." The victim eventually is identified as Jack Miller, described as a gangster and "the best safecracker in New York." Miller was sentenced to life in Sing Sing in 1920 as a habitual criminal, and the Parole Board has no record of his release.

October 11—Giro "Jerry the Wolf" Sciotti, recently acquitted of murdering a policeman, is shot twelve times by four men while emerging from a car on a Queens, New York, street. Typically described as the result of a "bootleggers' feud," Sciotti's killing is the fifth Queens murder in three weeks.

– The Chicago murder of Sal Him is attributed to Chinatown tong war.

October 12—Gerald Chapman murders policeman James Skelly in an attempted store burglary in New Britain, Connecticut.

October 13—Federal agents and Pittsburgh police raid the local Hip Sing Tong headquarters at 521 Third Avenue, arresting three Chinese gunmen and seizing 1,000 empty "toys" presumed to be opium containers. Yyalock Yunck, said to be manager of the building, escapes through a window.

October 21—Jer Bong is hacked to death by other Chinese men wielding hatchets in a Queens tea room. Police fear a new outbreak of tong war.

October 28—Police arrest twenty-seven Chinese in a raid in Yonkers, New York, naming one Lou Chow as one of the Queens "hatchetmen."

October 30—Pittsburgh police called to six holdups in fifteen minutes.

November 1—Bank robber and bootlegger John Ashley, known as "King of the Everglades," is killed, along with gang members Hanford Mobley, Ray Lynn, and Bob Middleton, in a police ambush at Sebastian, Florida.

– Bill Tilghman, famous deputy U.S. marshal of the territorial days but still an active lawman at age seventy, is shot to death in Cromwell, Oklahoma, by Wylie Lynn, a drunken and corrupt Prohibition agent.

November 3—In another bout of Chicago election violence, John Mackey is killed and Claude "Screwy" Maddox and Anthony "Red" Kissane seriously wounded when their car is ambushed by rival gangsters outside a polling place at 405 South Hoyne. Martin O'Leary, "Terrible Tommy" Touhy, Joseph Stone, and David Stark are arrested, and the shootings are linked to strife over the Teamsters Union.

November 2—Calvin Coolidge elected president of the United States.

November 8—Mike Merlo, head of the Chicago branch of the Unione Siciliana, dies of cancer. A much-respected Sicilian civic leader with gangland ties, Merlo had tried to serve as peacemaker between the Torrio-Capone Syndicate, the Genna brothers, and the O'Banion mob.

November 10—Dean O'Banion, leader of Chicago's North Side Gang, is shot to death by three gunmen who commit the "handshake murder" in his flower shop at 738 North State Street, opposite the Holy Name Cathedral. Police suspect Brooklyn gangster Frankie Yale, friend of Torrio and Capone, who once again is discovered to be in the city, ostensibly for the funeral of Mike Merlo. Earl "Hymie" Weiss succeeds to the leadership of the North Side mob.

November 23—Eddie Tancl and Leo Klimas are shot and killed in a pistol duel with gangsters in Tancl's cabaret, the Hawthorne Park Café in Cicero, Illinois. Myles O'Donnell and James Doherty will be tried and acquitted.

November 24—At a "racket," or banquet, thrown by gangster Vito Genovese at the Fortino Gardens in New York's Greenwich Village, one Alfredo Bocci fatally shoots Giuseppi Barracono. Police pursue and capture Bocci and recover his .38-caliber revolver.

December 2—Bank robber Ray Terrill escapes from the Lincoln County Jail at Chandler, Oklahoma.

December 6—Two are killed and five wounded in a bandit raid on a saloon in South Bend, Indiana.

December 8—Six gunmen rob Milwaukee's Northwestern National Bank of $296,200. Later attributed to Hermann "Baron" Lamm, aka Tom Bell.

December 10—Four men rob the Federal National Bank at Shawnee, Oklahoma. Ray Terrill and Irvin "Blackie" Thompson, alleged former members of the Al Spencer Gang, are suspected but later exonerated.

December 19—Bandits set fire to Valley View, Texas, after robbing two banks.

December 24—Bandits take over Paradise, Texas, and rob the bank and every store.

December 25—Joseph Cascio, Patsy Rosseta, Gaetano Sabatiano, Rocco Mascetti, and Joseph Scogni are shot down by rival gangsters while

Gangland's "Black Widow"

Margaret Collins, sometimes known as Mary, was not what she seemed to be. On the surface she was a stunning, if brassy, blonde, an alluring example of the flaring flapper. It was a time when ballsiness in women was all the rage, but Margaret took it a step further by becoming the darling of the Chicago underworld and wielding her own gun. The fearless and violent qualities she sought in her men were ones she also nourished in herself.

When Margaret first arrived in Chicago about 1922, she was grieving as well as rebellious. Back in her native New York, she had been the sweetheart of a prominent hoodlum identified only by the last name of Thomas. She would say later that he was murdered in 1920 or 1921. It did not take her long to catch the lusting eye of rough-hewn North Sider Johnny Sheehy, who saw no need to become refined with the onset of bootlegging wealth.

"Kiss of Death Girl" Margaret Collins

On the night of December 8, 1923, Sheehy and Margaret went to the Rendezvous Club at Diversey Parkway and Broadway to celebrate her birthday with a small group of friends. A drunken Margaret demanded a bowl of ice so that she could throw cubes at the jazz band onstage. When the waiter refused and the burly café steward intervened in the resulting argument, Sheehy drew a gun and killed them both.

Detective Sergeant John O'Malley put a bullet into the rampaging gangster's side, resulting in a fatal wound. Sheehy's dying words were, "Just tell 'em I was full of hooch and didn't know what I was doing." Margaret was questioned as a witness, then released. She genuinely mourned John Sheehy, buying an impressive monument for his grave in Mount Carmel. There's no record of what, if anything, the gangster's long-suffering wife, Julia, had to say about it.

Dean O'Banion took a platonic concern in Margaret's welfare and offered her moral and financial support. His actions would lead to later speculation that the two were romantically involved, although Margaret was a personal friend of Viola O'Banion, as well. The two never were lovers; the assertive blonde took up with tough-guy Johnny Phillips. Phillips was a gun-happy loudmouth who saw nothing wrong in pushing women around, but he never tried it with Margaret, who was as handy with her pistol as he was. Instead, he slapped around singer Dorothy Kessner on the night of August 27, 1924, when she was trying to entertain the crowd at the Northern Lights Café. Louis Alterie, his brother Bert Varain, and a companion added to the spectacle by menacing café patrons who tried to interfere. The police arrived and shot Phillips dead when he tried to take one of their number hostage. Margaret soon was attending her third gangster-lover funeral.

She found solace and sexual companionship with David "Jew Bates" Jerus, another North Sider. Unlike the Torrio-Capone Syndicate in the South Side, who saw women as good wives or better whores, the North Side Gang admired and encouraged spirit and strength in their consorts. Viola O'Banion was no one's doormat, nor was Vincent Drucci's wife, Cecelia, who once beat up a dress shop owner who accused her husband of robbing the store's safe. Jerus, who looked like silent-movie star Harold Lloyd with his owlish specs, saw no reason to shield Margaret Collins from the seamier side of his lifestyle. One night in late October 1924, Margaret, O'Banion, Jerus, Louis Alterie, labor leader "Dago Mike" Carrozzo, and Carrozzo's wife were having dinner and an informal business discussion at the Friar's Inn. The two ladies quarreled, but Margaret took it to the next level by smacking Mrs. Carrozzo across the face. Dago Mike tried to give her a taste of her own medicine, but her chivalrous companions stepped in and kicked him all over the barroom. The "battle of the ladies" was remembered in November, when O'Banion was murdered. Margaret was questioned but never held as a witness.

She and Jerus ended their relationship after O'Banion's funeral, with Jew Bates fleeing to New York to hide out. Once the heat died down, he quietly headed south and ended up in Covington, Kentucky, where he operated as a bootlegger for six years. In January 1930 he and cohort Lawrence Coates tried to take one Charles J. Stubbs for a one-way ride but neglected to search the intended victim before shoving him in the car. Stubbs drew a pistol when the vehicle started, killing Bates and wounding Coates.

By December 1924, her new paramour was Irving Schlig, of whom she would later remember, "He was a swell friend and a great provider, but he had a terrible temper." He kept Margaret in diamonds—literally. In January 1925, the lovers were questioned about the theft of $200,000 worth of diamonds from the Parkway Hotel. They were inseparable for months until he took up with a stunning brunette named Paula Livingstone. On August 28, he and fellow bootlegger Harry Berman were found dead on the line between Chicago and Stickney township, bullets embedded in their skulls. Joining Miss Livingstone at the grave site, face ashen and tears streaking her mascara, was Margaret. Those who remembered the pathetic sight gaped in shock when Eugene "Red" McLaughlin was formally charged with the double murder in March 1926. At McLaughlin's side, looking defiant and cool, was Margaret.

By this time, Margaret Collins had acquired an unflattering sobriquet of "The Jinx Girl of Gangland," which later was dramatized to "The Kiss of Death Girl." She was a karmic black widow whose lovers died violently. That didn't stop them from coming to her, though. When "Red" McLaughlin's body, wrapped in chains and seventy-five pounds of weights, was brought to the surface of the Chicago Sanitary Canal at Summit on June 8, 1930, Sam Katz became companion number six. Katz was an extortionist and gunman whose gang was well known to the Chicago police. In early June, Lt. Edward Birmingham had warned him, "You fellows will wind up in the county morgue pretty soon if you don't quit your rackets." Katz sneered and maintained the reckless bravado that Margaret worshipped until July 16, when officers from the state's attorney's squad caught him and two others robbing a gambler a mere block from City Hall. They shot and killed the three desperados when Katz turned his weapon on them.

Chicago finally was too much for Margaret, who had lost five lovers by then to its savage streets. She left the city after Katz was buried and turned up in Cincinnati. Grief did nothing to inspire her to abandon her own criminal instincts. In June 1931, Cincinnati police caught her and a friend, May Howard, in the act of stealing dresses from a downtown shop and sentenced both women to sixty days in the workhouse plus a $400 fine. Upon her release, she returned to Chicago, where she met boyfriend number seven, Sol Feldman, in November 1932.

When Feldman survived a shooting attack that same month, newspapers and underworld onlookers wondered if "The Jinx" had finally been broken. Feldman and his partner were in the act of smashing a window at Leschin's Fur Shop at 318 South Michigan Avenue on the night of November 29 when policeman Ted J. O'Barr came upon them. When they refused to surrender, O'Barr fired, wounding Feldman. Margaret was observed visiting him every day at Mother Cabrini Hospital, but she also may have been carrying on "the business" while he recovered.

In December, fur shop owner Ethel Gittler initially accused her of stealing a $600 coat but recanted her story before Judge Frank M. Padden of the Felony Court. (Reporters raised their brows when Margaret and Miss Gittler were observed embracing outside the courtroom afterward.)

The couple separated in early 1933, and Feldman announced his intention to marry another woman. But the two could not remain apart for long, and they reconciled despite Feldman's engagement. On April 5, 1933, Feldman was standing outside Judge John Prystalski's courtroom, where he was scheduled to be tried on a burglary charge. Suddenly the hoodlum cried out and collapsed to the floor. The bullet wound from O'Barr's gun, thought to have long since healed, had mysteriously re-opened.

The truth later came to light: Three days before, Feldman and Margaret had attended the wedding party of his youngest sister, where Margaret danced too closely with another man for Feldman's liking. Drunk and raging, he snatched up a beer bottle and broke it over her head. Three husky male guests tackled him in response, breaking several ribs and nearly causing the loss of an eye. The reopened wound became infected, leading to fever and collapse. Feldman survived, and Margaret evidently forgave him for the bottling. On the night of August 21, 1933, the pair were arrested and taken to the Warren Avenue Station "for investigation" after they were caught driving a car with no plates. When a photographer tried to snap her picture, Margaret told him, in very unladylike terms, what she thought of him. But when Feldman blasted another photographer with a flurry of curses, she scolded, "Why, Sol, you mustn't use that kind of language in front of me."

The next September 7, Margaret achieved the unenviable distinction of being the first woman named in a vagrancy warrant under the new "reputation law" that sought to jail wealthy lawbreakers with no visible means of support. "This is outrageous," she protested to Judge Irwin J. Hasten as she was led off to jail. She was soon bailed out and appeared again before Hasten on October 13, which happened to be a Friday. When the judge asked her if she was nervous that it was Friday the thirteenth, she retorted, "I'm not a bit superstitious."

Margaret's whereabouts in the ensuing years continued to crop up in news stories. On February 7, 1935, Milwaukee police arrested her and two female companions for stealing fur coats. She told the arresting officers that her name was Fay Sullivan, but photos and fingerprints sent to Chicago confirmed her identity. In November, Mrs. Rose Choromokis identified her as the woman who fostered her friendship strictly for the purpose of setting her up for robbery. Chicago police cast out a net for one of the suspected robbers, Thomas De Santo, whom the press dubbed Margaret's new boyfriend.

This relationship was troubled by neither "The Jinx" nor waning passion. On August 24, 1940, they were arrested together, along with Margaret's sister Anne Martin, in a "dope raid" at 500 Fullerton Parkway. They may even have been married: When Margaret was acquitted two days later (Judge Bonelli being convinced that the $4,000 worth of heroin found on the premises had belonged to a woman now dead), the press referred to her as De Santo's wife. One of her final press mentions was in June 1942, when she was observed visiting friend James Quirk minutes after the police arrived to search his room at the Maryland Hotel. She was not arrested.

Margaret Collins disappeared from the public eye soon after that. The age of the flapper was long since over, and after twenty years of living fast and hard Margaret evidently settled down, or otherwise found peace, of one kind or another.

—Rose Keefe

ANOTHER "BLACK WIDOW"

Florence Diggs may not equal Margaret Collins in her number of Chicago gangland lovers, but the two she met and married were mobsters of greater prominence.

After leaving the Blue Ridge country of Virginia at age 18, Florence went to work for a politician in Washington. While there she fell in love with another congressman's secretary named Timothy Murphy, a lanky fellow from the Stockyards section of Chicago. They soon were married. He and she moved back to Chicago, where he managed to serve two terms in the Illinois state legislature before an old school friend, Mossy Enright, introduced him to the lucrative labor union racket. Extortion, bombings, and killings were part of the business, and after their bitter falling out Enright himself was taken out by shotgun blasts on February 3, 1920.

Florence Diggs

After walking away from several arrests and trials unscathed, "Big Tim" was fast becoming a legendary gangster when his seeming immunity from the law led him to sponsor a truly imaginative postal robbery. Several men ostensibly playing baseball behind a downtown railway station pounced on the postal employees loading a truck and made off with bags of registered mail containing some $385,000 in cash and securities.

This was clearly a case for a fast-rising postal inspector, William F. Fahy [see p. 152]. He squeezed a couple of postal employs into admitting they had supplied mail-delivery information to "Big Tim" Murphy, whose men pulled the job. That robbery had taken place on April 6, 1921, and part of the loot was found in the home of Florence's father. During his six years in Leavenworth the local Gas Workers' Union continued to elect him president, paying his salary to Florence, and he returned home in 1926 to a gala reception.

In the meantime, bootlegging gangs had been taking over labor racketeering, and Murphy tried to open a nightclub and gambling operation on Chicago's Upper North Side. Despite financing by Nicky Arnstein, husband of Ziegfeld Follies comedienne Fanny Brice, "Big Tim" could not pay off enough police to prevent disastrous raids.

He tried to muscle his way back into the labor rackets and found himself at even greater odds with Al Capone. He was living at the time in a classy Rogers Park neighborhood, 2525 West Morse, when the doorbell rang on the evening of June 26, 1928. "Big Tim"

Chicago Daily Tribune

FINAL EDITION

2 CENTS

GANG'S GUNS KILL BIG TIM

Silver Tongued Keynoter Dazzles Convention

DEMOCRATS GO WILD WHEN HE SOUNDS WAR CRY

Enforcement Plank to Suit Smith Planned

MURPHY, DEAN OF RACKETEERS, SLAIN AT HOME

SMITH'S EX-FOES FIGHT FOR SEATS ON BANDWAGON

NEWS SUMMARY

HARMONY

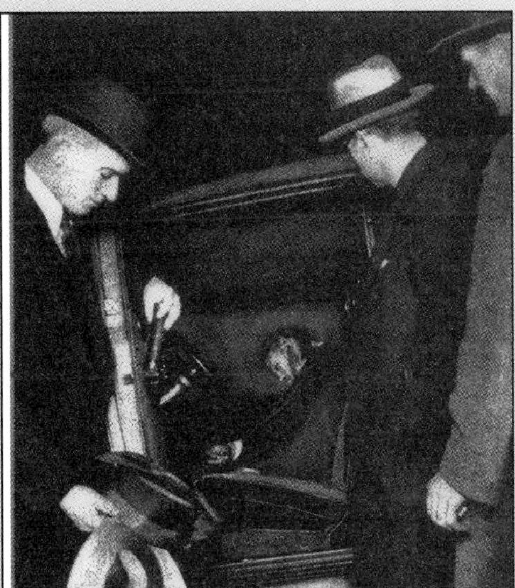

Victims of Frank McErlane's homicidal fury: "Dingbat" Oberta, dead in his car (above), and girlfriend Elfrieda Rigus, murdered with her two dogs (below right).

found no one on his porch, but as he walked down the steps to look around, a Thompson gun opened up, spraying "Big Tim" and the front of his house with bullets whose marks can still be seen.

Widow Murphy was comforted in her grief by Tim's friend and pallbearer John "Dingbat" Oberta, who married her ten months later. Oberta had gained major-mobster status by running booze with the Saltis-McErlane gang [see p. 62] and, with Frank McErlane, had been acquitted of murdering rival bootlegger John "Mitters" Foley in 1926. McErlane and Oberta later had a falling out, and in late 1929 his girlfriend, Elfrieda Rigus (who went by the name Marion Miller), put a bullet in his leg, probably in self-defense. While he was recovering at the German Deaconess Hospital, his leg in traction, two men entered the room on February 25, 1930, and put more bullets in him, but McErlane fought back with a gun he kept under his pillow. He wouldn't tell police who had attacked him—"Just look for those fellows in a ditch" – but the police traced a dropped pistol to Sam Malaga, driver for Oberta. On March 6, nine days after the "battle of the hospital," Oberta's car was found nose down in a rain-filled ditch on the Far South Side with Oberta dead at the wheel and Malaga floating outside in the ice-covered water. (McErlane had his hospital alibi and was never charged.)

When Florence recovered enough to speak to reporters, she said: "Talk about raw deals. Here I've been going around working for the church and doing good to everybody all my life and look at the breaks I get. Married to two of the swellest guys that ever lived, and both get bumped off. . . . But I've had more love and better husbands than most women."

Which was better luck than befell the girlfriend of Frank McErlane. A full-blown alcoholic, McErlane already had been arrested for shooting a bar patron for sport (a witness was killed later and friends provided an alibi), suspected of the murder of John Foley, and later for publicly firing a shotgun at the ghosts of his ten or so victims, not counting Oberta and Malaga. In October of 1931, police found Elfrieda Rigus shot to death in the back seat of McErlane's car, parked on Chicago's South Side. Also killed were her two dogs, which appalled the most hard-boiled of Chicagoans.

McErlane again skated for lack of evidence, but one year after the death of Elfreda, on October 8, 1932, he lost a battle with pneumonia aggravated by drinking and died in a hospital with four men trying to hold him down.

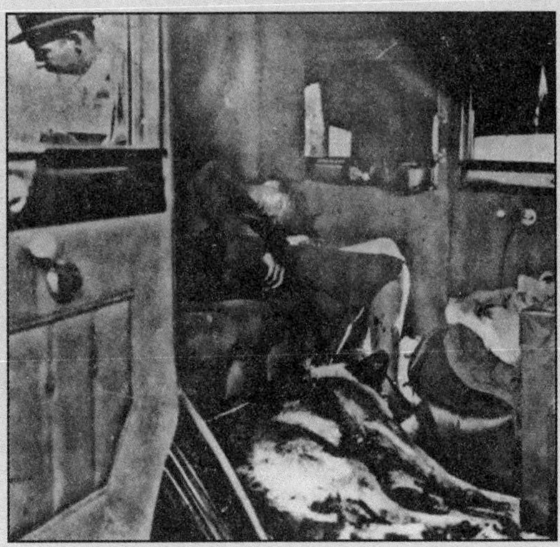

playing cards in the rear of Samuel Cardello's New York pool hall.

– A posse led by U.S. Marshal Alva McDonald captures bank robber Irvin "Blackie" Thompson in Bartlesville, Oklahoma.

– Milford, Indiana, bank cashier J. T. Shepherd reported missing with $200,000.

– United Cigar Store at Forty-second Street and Second Avenue, New York, reports sixth holdup.

1924–25—Tong wars being a major topic of the day, papers report "over eighty murders" in the Chinatowns of New York, Boston and Chicago between the Hip Sing and On Leong Tongs.

1925

January 2—Bandit captured during $18,000 robbery of American Express Co. payroll in Chicago.

January 5—Robbers hold up Kearney, New Jersey, cab driver, escape in locomotive.

January 12—Al Capone's car is riddled with shotgun and pistol fire by North Side gangsters at State and Fifty-fifth streets in Chicago. Capone is not in the car at the time, but chauffeur Sylvester Barton is wounded. Capone orders a $20,000 armored Cadillac with bulletproof glass.

January 17—Federal agents in St. Paul seize three carloads of alcohol valued at $500,000 and reputedly stolen from a Philadelphia distillery.

January 18—Gerald Chapman is captured at Muncie, Indiana.

– Johnny Torrio is sentenced in Chicago Federal Court to nine months in DuPage County Jail and fined $5,000 on his second conviction for violation of the Volstead Act.

January 24—Free on bond from his bootlegging conviction, Johnny Torrio is seriously wounded in an attack by members of the North Side mob outside his apartment at 7011 Clyde Avenue in Chicago. The suspected attackers are "Hymie" Weiss, Vincent "The Schemer" Drucci, and George "Bugs" Moran. Torrio will survive, serve his short jail term resulting from the Sieben Brewery arrest, and then leave Chicago, turning the organization over to Al Capone.

– Bootlegger and Deputy Sheriff Ora Thomas, Ku Klux Klan vigilante S. Glenn Young, and two of his henchmen are killed in a gun battle in Herrin, Illinois.

January 27—Mail messenger at Collinsville, Illinois, is robbed of a $21,000 mine payroll.

February 5—Atlanta grocery chain, after twenty-one robberies in a month, designates three stores for robbers to visit.

February 20—Robber Richard Reese Whittemore escapes from the Maryland state prison, killing guard Robert H. Holtman.

February 22—U.S. Marshal Alva McDonald captures bank robbers Ray Terrill and Roland Williams in Sapulpa, Oklahoma.

February 24—Richard Reese Whittemore and his gang rob a Western Maryland Dairy Co. car in Baltimore of $16,304, shooting the driver and guard.

March 16—In Baltimore, the Whittemore Gang robs J. Wahl Holtzman, American Banking Co. messenger, beating him and stealing $8,792 in cash, plus securities.

March 20—Local posse, tipped off to robbery of Farmers Bank of Steeleville, Missouri, kills two bandits and captures two others.

March 26—Posters hung on Mott and Doyer streets in New York's Chinatown announce peace between the Hip Sing and On Leong tongs.

March 27—Harry Pierpont, Thaddeus Skeers, and others rob the South Side Bank in Kokomo, Indiana, of $10,000.

March 30—Thom McAn shoe store chain in New York City reports fifty-fifth robbery in six months.

April 2—Harry Pierpont and Thaddeus Skeers are captured in Detroit

April 5—The Whittemore Gang robs the Metro Sacks jewelry store at 43 West 125th Street in New York of $16,000.

– Suspected bank robbers Ray Terrill and Roland Williams escape from jail in Pawnee, Oklahoma.

April 6—Chicago police raid a Torrio-Capone mob headquarters at 2146 South Michigan Avenue, arresting Frank Nitti, John Patton, Bob

McCullough, Joe Fusco, and others, and seizing financial records indicating millions of dollars of bootlegging profits for the mob's leaders.

April 10—As Al Brown, Al Capone is arrested for carrying a concealed weapon in Chicago. He will be discharged the next day.

April 14—Paul Jawarski and the Flatheads Gang rob the American State Bank branch at Oregon Avenue and Epworth Boulevard in Detroit of $7,000, fatally shooting employee Charles J. Taggert Jr.

April 19—Murderer "Midget" Fernekes is captured in Chicago.

April 26—Five bandits rob seventy-five patrons of the Café de l'Europe in New York City.

April 29—Chicago police find $50,000 loot in a boys' club that made stealing an initiation test.

April 30—Gus Winkeler and Fred "Killer" Burke are suspected of robbing the Portland Bank at Louisville, Kentucky.

May 9—Richard Reese Whittemore and his gang rob jeweler Jacques Ross, at 290 Grand Street in New York, of $25,000 in diamonds.

May 11—Henry "Doggy" Ginsburg and Hyman Jacobson are killed by gunmen armed with silenced pistols at a crowded "smoker" at the Durant Social Club on New York's East Side. Attributed by police to a war between rival Brownsville gangs for control of the laundry racket.

May 22—United Cigar Store at 1357 First Avenue, New York, reports eleventh robbery.

May 26—Gang leader Angelo Genna, who has succeeded Mike Merlo as Chicago president of the Unione Siciliana, is killed by four men with sawed-off shotguns after a car chase that ends in a crash at Ogden and Hudson avenues. Police attribute the murder to the North Side Gang, in retaliation for the slaying of Dean O'Banion.

June 1—The Whittemore Gang robs the Levy Jewelry Co. at 483 Main Street in Buffalo of $50,000 in gems.

June 6—A cashier with a pistol thwarts Paul Jawarski's Flatheads Gang in their attempted robbery of the Peninsular State Bank at Chene Street and Fourth Avenue in Detroit.

June 7—Walter O'Donnell, brother of "Spike" O'Donnell, and Harry Hassmiller are mortally wounded in a gang shooting in an Evergreen Park, Illinois, roadhouse. Hassmiller dies the same day. O'Donnell lingers until June 9. Attributed to the Ralph Sheldon mob.

June 13—Gangster Mike Genna and Chicago police detectives Charles Walsh and Harold Olsen die after a gun battle at South Western Avenue and Fifty-ninth Street, and detective Michael Conway is badly wounded. Genna's associates, John Scalise and Albert Anselmi, are captured and charged with murder.

– Agents Luther Bishop and Lee Pollock of the Oklahoma Crime Bureau apprehend bank robber and prison escapee Edward Delano near Ellsworth, Kansas. Under the alias of Leon Gentry, Delano had been working for a Kansas sheriff as a Bertillon expert.

– Paul Jawarski and the Flatheads Gang rob the Central Savings Bank in Detroit of $27,000, killing a policeman.

June 24—Drug dealer Erisano Grambino is found stabbed to death outside a drugstore in New York's Little Italy.

July 1—While driving along Fifth Avenue, New York gangster Jack "Legs" Diamond is slightly wounded by shotgun pellets from a passing car. Diamond drives himself to Mount Sinai Hospital.

July 8—Chicago gangster Tony Genna is lured to a meeting with three men at the corner of Curtis (later Aberdeen) and Grand avenues and fatally shot in another "handshake murder." The remaining Genna brothers, Sam, Pete, and James, go into hiding.

July 16—The Whittemore Gang robs Stanley's jewelry store at 269 West 125th Street in New York of $50,000 in gems.

July 18—Chicago gangsters James Vinci and Joe Granata kill one another in a gun duel in the saloon of John Genaro at 2900 South Wells.

August 6—Attempted holdup of 125th Street crap game in New York results in gun battle with police who shoot three robbers, killing one and fatally wounding another.

The Gun That Made the Twenties Roar

The Thompson Submachine Gun

The timing could not have been worse—or better, as the case may be. In 1920, the same year that Prohibition became the law of the land, the Auto-Ordnance Corp. of New York contracted with the Colt's Patent Firearms Manufacturing Co. of Hartford, Connecticut, to produce 15,000 Thompson submachine guns. At the time no one knew what a "submachine" gun was, but five years later it would become a world-recognized symbol of American gangland violence—the criminal equivalent of the cowboy's six-shooter.

Intended for the Army, the Tommy-gun was the brainchild of Brigadier General John Taliaferro Thompson, a retired Ordnance Department officer with an inventive streak who believed that Allied infantrymen needed more individual firepower in the European war. After a false start on an automatic rifle in 1916, he produced the first "submachine" gun—a term he coined to describe a small, fully automatic weapon that used pistol instead of rifle ammunition and could be fired from the hip by a soldier on the run. It was an odd-looking weapon, weighing only ten pounds, with pistol grips front and rear, and it fired the army's standard .45-caliber Automatic Colt Pistol cartridge at a rate of 800 per

General John T. Thompson, who conceived and developed the Thompson submachine gun.

minute from twenty-shot straight magazines or circular drums holding fifty or 100 rounds. Thompson called it his "trench broom" and had completed a working prototype just as the war ended. That was only the start of the Auto-Ordnance Corp.'s long run of bad luck.

With a small fortune already invested in the project, Auto-Ordnance tried to market the gun commercially. At demonstrations in 1920, weapons experts acclaimed its revolutionary design, reliability and enormous firepower, and one dazzled police official predicted it would either kill or cure the country's gunmen, rioters and "motorized bandits." But that early enthusiasm never translated into sales, and the gun slipped back into obscurity until 1926, when a *Collier's* writer described it less approvingly:

> . . . This Thompson submachine gun is nothing less than a diabolical engine of death . . . the paramount example of peacetime barbarism [and] the diabolical acme of human ingenuity in man's effort to devise a mechanical contrivance with which to murder his neighbor.

The reason for that outburst was the machine-gun murder of an assistant state's attorney in Cicero and the otherwise increasing use of Thompsons by Chicago's bootleggers, for whom subtlety and public image were never major considerations. In 1929, the St. Valentine's Day Massacre sealed Chicago's reputation as gangster capital of the world, and the gun's reputation as a gangster weapon. Called in to work on the Massacre, ballistics expert Major Calvin Goddard wrote that the Thompson was being used in eleven percent of gangland killings, meaning that "the usefulness of such weapons in gang warfare has been grasped by the lower element, which has put them to extremely practical use during the past few years."

The Beer Wars that broke out after the "handshake" murder of North Side mob leader Dean O'Banion in November 1924 already were attracting national attention

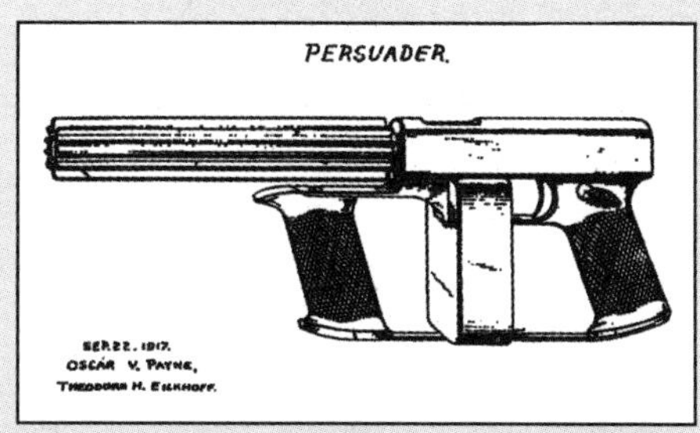

The first prototype submachine gun, dubbed "The Persuader" by the engineering staff, refused to feed reliably from a belt-fed magazine.

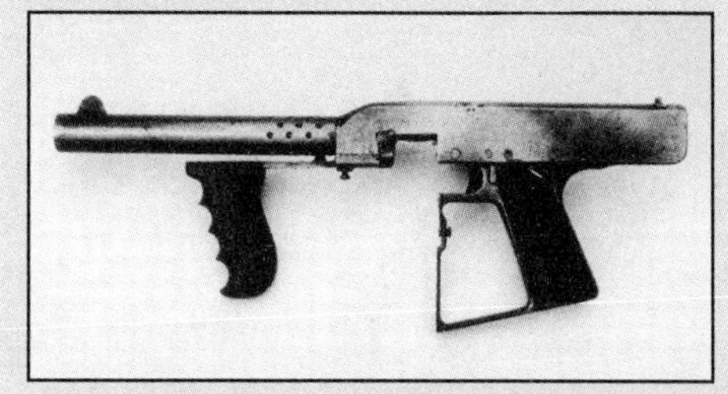

because many of the killings and gun battles were taking place in broad daylight on the city's busiest streets. But what secured Chicago's notoriety was the introduction of the Thompson submachine gun, which signaled a major escalation in the fighting.

Ironically, the gun had been discovered by Dean O'Banion himself on his last vacation trip to Colorado, where he and his men regularly amused themselves with rodeos and

The Thompson Submachine Gun

The Most Effective Portable Fire Arm In Existence

THE ideal weapon for the protection of large estates, ranches, plantations, etc. A combination machine gun and semi-automatic shoulder rifle in the form of a pistol. A compact, tremendously powerful, yet simply operated machine gun weighing only *seven* pounds and having only *thirty* parts. Full automatic, fired from the hip, 1,500 shots per minute. Semi-automatic, fitted with a stock and fired from the shoulder, 50 shots per minute. Magazines hold 50 and 100 cartridges.

THE Thompson Submachine Gun incorporates the simplicity and infallibility of a hand loaded weapon with the effectiveness of a machine gun. It is simple, safe, sturdy, and sure in action. In addition to its increasingly wide use for protection purposes by banks, industrial plants, railroads, mines, ranches, plantations, etc., it has been adopted by leading Police and Constabulary Forces, throughout the world and is unsurpassed for military purposes.

Information and prices promptly supplied on request

AUTO-ORDNANCE CORPORATION

302 Broadway *Cable address: Autordco* New York City

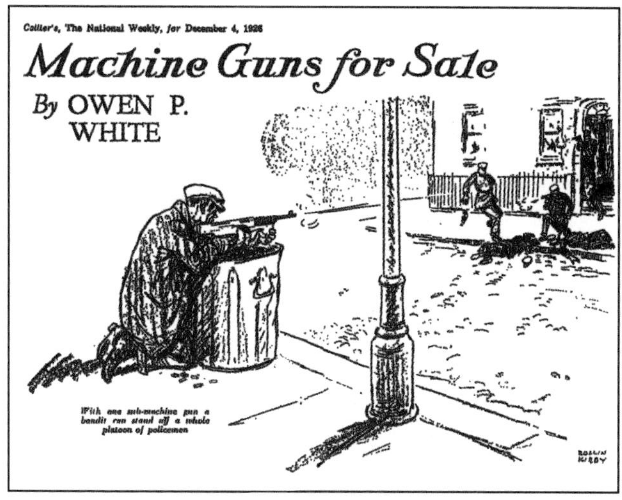

The killing of Assistant State's Attorney William McSwiggin in 1926 inspired Collier's and other publications to denounce the unrestricted sale of submachine guns.

other horseplay at the "Diamond D" Ranch of fellow mobster Louie "Two-Gun" Alterie. While a handheld machine gun seemed mainly a novelty to both the police and the peacetime military when first demonstrated, it had found a market among private security guards and agencies hired by certain large industries, including Colorado mining companies, to deal with labor violence. On his return to Chicago, O'Banion and his entourage stopped in Denver to stock up on weapons which, a local paper reported, included three "baby" machine guns.

A few days later the city's then-most-colorful gangster was murdered in his flower shop on North State Street. In reporting on his lavish funeral, Chicago papers published rumors that the South Side gang of Joe Saltis and Frank McErlane had drifted away from the Torrio-Capone Outfit to form a secret alliance with O'Banion, and a few months later they would be the first to thrill and chill America with a revolutionary weapon that would soon become known as the "Chicago Typewriter."

Saltis and McErlane probably obtained their Thompson from the North Siders to use on "Spike" O'Donnell, a dapper but particularly pesky poacher whose fainthearted brothers had allowed themselves to be gerrymandered out of their rightful South Side territory while "Spike" was cooling his heels in prison. Unintimidated by McErlane's threats, O'Donnell was standing at the busy northwest comer of 63rd Street and Western Avenue on the evening of September 25 when a barrage of bullets from a passing car missed him and took out the plate-glass windows of a large drugstore (now a currency exchange). With typical savoir faire, "Spike" went inside to the soda fountain and asked for a drink of water, and had nothing to say to the police. Newspapers duly recorded another skirmish in the South Side beer war and ascribed the unusually large number of bullet holes to "shotguns and repeating rifles."

The Thompson advertisement at left, designed in 1920, seems less ridiculous in light of Pancho Villa's attack on Columbus, New Mexico, just four years earlier.

His second time out, McErlane at least managed to score with his new gun and get it mentioned in the papers. On the Saturday night of October 4 the headquarters of the Ralph Sheldon gang was strafed with .45 bullets that killed one Charles Kelly (presumably the Thompson's first gangland victim) and

Chicago Police Captain John Stege demonstrates that a Thompson gun will not quite fit in a violin case—evidently a cartoon staple as far back as the 1920s.

wounded a Thomas Hart. This time the police figured out what all the bullet holes meant, as reported in the *Chicago Daily News*:

> . . . A machine gun, a new note of efficiency in gangland assassinations, was used to fire the volley from the black touring car, killing one man and wounding another in front of the Ragen Athletic club . . . at 5142 South Halsted St. last Saturday night. Captain John Enright of the stockyards police said today his investigation satisfied him that a machine gun had been used, and that the same gun had been used in an attack on Spike O'Donnell at 63rd St. and South Western Ave.

Despite the machine gun, the story was buried on an inside page. The wire services picked it up as a short human-interest item—the latest wrinkle in Chicago gangland warfare, but that was all. Finally, Chicago's Tommygun pioneer made the front page. Despite the usual poor marksmanship, it rated a banner headline in the *Chicago Tribune* for February 10, 1926:

Daily . . . 815,635
Sunday . . 1,248,707

Chicago Daily Tribune
THE WORLD'S GREATEST NEWSPAPER

FINAL

WEDNESDAY, FEBRUARY 10, 1926—40 PAGES.

PRICE TWO CENTS

MACHINE GUN GANG SHOOTS 2

Italy Seizes Tyrol Arms Cache; 50 Held

NEWS SUMMARY

TEMPTED

RAKE SALOON IN BEER WAR; ONE MAY DIE

Find Bessner Guilty; Given 20 Year Term

SMALL'S FINAL PLEA REJECTED; TALK OF OUSTER

The story reported an attack on Martin "Buff" Costello's speakeasy, 4127 South Halsted, which had left two men wounded. This caused Chicago Police Captain John Stege to grump, "McErlane and Saltis have one of these guns," and therefore, "It is imperative that [the police] be armed accordingly."

Not to lag behind in the underworld arms race, the South Siders (now led by Al Capone) quickly obtained Thompsons of their own, as did other gangs, and they started using them against one another in spectacular shootouts. Their open warfare culminated in the grandest bloodfest of all—the St. Valentine's Day Massacre of 1929, which took out seven men in a garage at 2122 North Clark Street.

By this time, the Thompson's worldwide notoriety had inspired rumors that the Auto-Ordnance Corp. was giving them free to gangsters for promotional purposes. In fact, the company was nearly bankrupt, with most of its guns still stacked in a Colt's warehouse.

Repeal ended the Chicago Beer Wars, but not the gun's evil reputation. By 1933, "Machine Gun" Kelly, John Dillinger, "Baby Face" Nelson, and other Depression outlaws were either buying submachine guns on the black market or stealing them from police stations, and using them to drive the last few nails in the Auto-Ordnance coffin. In 1939, the nearly defunct company was forced to sell to a shady Connecticut industrialist named Russell Maguire for only $529,000—about the wholesale value of the 4,700 guns still in inventory, with manufacturing equipment thrown in. Before he died in 1940 at the age of 79, General Thompson wrote a last melancholy note to one of the young engineers who had helped design the submachine gun in the closing days of the Great War. It said, in part,

> I have given my valedictory to arms, as I want to pay more attention now to saving human life than destroying it. May the deadly T.S.M.G. always "speak for" God and Country. It has worried me that the gun has been so stolen by evil men and used for purposes outside our motto, "On the side of law and order."

That note was received on August 1, 1939, after Thompson had lost the company to Maguire. Exactly a month later, the German Wehrmacht invaded Poland behind their version of the submachine gun, the 9mm MP-38, popularly but mistakenly called the "Schmeisser." Suddenly, every Allied army was clamoring for submachine guns, and the only one ready for mass production was the Thompson. Maguire sold over two million in both commercial and military models before the end of World War II, becoming wealthy and famous as America's "Tommygun Tycoon."

Adapted from *The Gun That Made the Twenties Roar.*

Although the first submachine guns were brought to Chicago by Dean O'Banion shortly before his death, their initial use, by the Saltis-McErlane gang, led by 'Polack Joe" Saltis (above left) and Frank McErlane (above center), missed rival mobster "Spike" O'Donnell (left) but riddled a drugstore.

THE TOMMYGUN IN CRIME

In October of 1924 Chicago North Side mob leader Dean O'Banion purchases three Thompson submachine guns in Denver and brings them to Chicago, but he is murdered before he can put them to use.

September 25, 1925—First known submachine gun attack. Saltis-McErlane gang, possibly using a Thompson acquired from the late Dean O'Banion, suspected in a drive-by shooting that misses South Side gang leader James Edward "Spike" O'Donnell.

October 3, 1925—Attack on Ralph Sheldon gang headquarters at 5142 South Halsted, again attributed to Saltis-McErlane gang. First Thompson fatalities are Charles Kelly killed outright and Thomas Hart mortally wounded.

October 16, 1925—Spectacular gun battle at railroad crossing at Ninety-first and Rockwell in suburban Evergreen Park when car carrying "Spike" O'Donnell, his brother Tom, brother-in-law William Barcal, and possibly others are ambushed by suspected members of Saltis-McErlane gang. Approximately forty rounds of pistol (possibly from Tommygun), rifle, and shotgun ammo fired at O'Donnell's car. O'Donnell group returns fire and flees. "Spike" and Tom O'Donnell (who has a slight head wound) and Barcal are later arrested. No other confirmed casualties, but O'Donnell car's backseat is saturated with blood.

February 9, 1926—Martin "Buff" Costello's saloon at 4127 South Halsted is raked with Tommygun fire. William Wilson and John "Mitters" Foley are wounded.

February 10, 1926—*Chicago Tribune* banner headline reads MACHINE GUN GANG SHOOTS 2, and the Capone gang, suitably impressed, orders three such guns from South Side sporting goods dealer Alex Koracek.

April 23, 1926—Pearl Hruby's beauty shop at 2208 South Austin Blvd. is strafed in drive-by shooting, and Pearl's boyfriend, James "Fur" Sammons, is wounded. Sammons (birth name Sammon) is a gunman for the West Side O'Donnell brothers' gang, headed by William "Klondike" O'Donnell (no relation to the South Side O'Donnells led by "Spike").

April 27, 1926—Assistant State's Attorney William McSwiggin and bootleggers James Doherty and Thomas Duffy (both of West Side O'Donnell gang) are machine-gunned outside Harry Madigan's Pony Inn at 5613 West Roosevelt Road in Cicero. Capone gang is blamed for what immediately becomes a media sensation, with Al himself going into hiding and the state's attorney trying to explain what McSwiggin was doing at a speakeasy in the company of several gangsters.

September 20, 1926—"Hymie" Weiss leads North Side Tommygunners in a motorcade (anywhere from five to eleven cars by various accounts) that shoots up Capone's Hawthorne Hotel headquarters in Cicero but fails to kill anyone.

October 11, 1926—Capone's men kill "Hymie" Weiss and bodyguard Patrick Murray outside Holy Name Cathedral on North State Street in a Tommygun and shotgun ambush from a rented apartment next door to Dean O'Banion's flower shop.

(Soon after this, Capone calls a peace treaty at the Hotel Sherman, attended by all the major gangs in Chicago, but the truce lasts only a few months. By this time the underworld arms race has escalated in Chicago to the point where every major gang has Thompson submachine guns.)

October 14, 1926—Tommygunning bandits kill driver and wound postal employee and policeman in Elizabeth, New Jersey mail robbery. This was the first known Tommygun crime in the east and also resulted in the U.S. Marines acquiring their first Thompsons and using them to guard mail shipments.

February 25, 1927—Gang leader Mickey Duffy is wounded and associate John Bricker killed outside their Club Cadix in Philadelphia's first machine-gun attack, attributed to Duffy's rival, Max "Boo Boo" Hoff.

March 16, 1927—Three gangsters are killed in Detroit's "Milaflores Apartment Massacre." The machine-gunner is suspected to be former St. Louis gangster Fred Burke on contract for the Purple Gang, before joining with Capone to participate in the St. Valentine's Day Massacre.

December 19, 1927—Bank messenger John Hopson is the first person to be slain by Tommygun fire in St. Louis. Nine days later, on December 28, gang leader Vito Giannola becomes the second when he is is killed by machine-gunners at his girlfriend's house.

July 1, 1928—Brooklyn's top mobster Frankie Yale is killed in New York's first machine-gun murder. Capone is blamed when an abandoned Thompson is traced to Chicago gun dealer Peter Von Frantzius, and New York fears that Chicago-style violence is spreading to the East Coast.

February 14, 1929—The St. Valentine's Day Massacre follows the continuing efforts of North Siders to kill Capone, the murder of two Capone-supported mobsters over control of the Unione Siciliana, and "Bugs" Moran's alliance with Joe Aiello, who had been supported by New York's Frankie Yale.

June 1, 1930—Two are killed and three wounded in the Fox Lake Massacre in Illinois, initially headlined as a resumption of Capone-Moran warfare but more likely committed by professional killer Verne Miller in retaliation for the murder of a bootlegger friend.

October 23, 1930—Joe Aiello, intending to escape to Texas by train, is spectacularly killed while leaving the apartment of a henchman and walking into bullets from two Tommyguns firing from windows in nearby apartments.

By this time the use of Thompsons has spread to southern Illinois and figures prominently in the war between Charlie Birger and the Shelton Brothers. Elsewhere their use by mobsters remains sporadic:

Machine guns are used occasionally in New York's Castellammarese War of 1930-31, but they attract the most attention after the "Baby Massacre" of July 28, 1931, by "Mad Dog" Coll and his subsequent murder in a Manhattan drug store telephone booth on February 9, 1932.

After that, national attention begins to focus on kidnappers and bank robbers such as "Machine Gun" Kelly, "Pretty Boy" Floyd, John Dillinger, "Baby Face" Nelson, and the Barker-Karpis Gang.

August 8—Paul Jawarski and the Flatheads Gang rob Detroit scrap metal dealer Henry Velick of $1,500.

August 11—Ben Hance and his wife are murdered near Muncie, Indiana, apparently for informing on mail bandit Gerald Chapman. The slayings are attributed to Chapman's partner, "Dutch" Anderson.

August 21—Gunmen rob bookies and customers at a race book owned by Jack Lynch and Mont Tennes at 120 South Clark Street in Chicago, fleeing with an estimated $15,000 to $25,000.

– Robbers shoot bank messenger J. E. Gallagher to death and flee with a $14,000 payroll in Perth Amboy, New Jersey.

August 22—Leo Lanzetti, one of five brothers heading a bootlegging mob, is killed by masked gunmen with shotguns in a drive-by shooting outside his pool hall at Seventh and Bainbridge streets in Philadelphia. His brother Lucien escapes unharmed.

September 6—Gangster Benny Tesmer and his girlfriend, Dorothy Taylor, alias "Toots" or "Trixie" Clark, are murdered by a gunman at the Valley Park clubhouse near St. Louis.

September 7—Frankie "Eleven Fingers" Guiffreda, suspected opium dealer, burglar, and bootlegger—born with an extra finger on his left hand—is shot and killed by an unknown gunman in Harlem. His "eleventh finger" recently had been removed surgically, but the scar and fingerprints left no doubt as to his identity.

September 8—Mrs. C. B. Cook, president of the Benton County Christian Temperance Union, is shot through her window in Vinton, Iowa. A bootlegging gang is suspected because of her activity against them.

September 11—Charles Arthur Floyd, Fred Hilderbrand and Joe Hlavaty rob the Kroger Grocery & Baking Co. in St. Louis of $11,934. Police confuse Floyd with another criminal named "Pretty Boy" Smith, and the nickname sticks.

September 13—Charles "Pretty Boy" Floyd and Fred Hilderbrand are arrested in Sallisaw, Oklahoma. They will be returned to St. Louis on September 17, where Hilderbrand will confess to the Kroger Grocery robbery, implicating Floyd and Hlavaty.

September 14—The Whittemore Gang robs David Bick's store at 360 Third Avenue in New York of $50,000 in jewelry.

September 25—The Saltis-McErlane mob attempts to kill gang leader Edward "Spike" O'Donnell at Sixty-third Street and Western Avenue in Chicago, using a Thompson submachine gun (probably one of the three purchased in Denver by Dean O'Banion shortly before his death). O'Donnell escapes unharmed from the first known Tommygun attack in gangland warfare.

October 3—The Saltis-McErlane mob sprays the Chicago headquarters of the Ralph Sheldon gang at 5142 South Halsted with machine-gun fire that kills Charles Kelly and mortally wounds Thomas Hart, who dies a few days later, making them presumably the Tommygun's first gangland fatalities. The suspected machine-gunner is Frank McErlane.

— "Yeggs" blow three safes at Jewelers' Exchange on New York's Bowery.

October 5—The Whittemore Gang robs Mrs. J. Linherr's store at 193 Sixth Avenue in New York of $30,000 in jewelry.

October 10—Two gunmen are sentenced to death for a murder committed during the robbery of Chicago's Drake Hotel.

October 11—Special Agent Edwin C. Shanahan of the U.S. Justice Department's Bureau of Investigation is killed in a garage at 6237 Princeton Avenue in Chicago by car thief Martin James Durkin, who claimed that Shanahan failed to identify himself. He is the first agent of what will be later called the FBI to die in the line of duty.

October 16—A spectacular gun battle erupts at the Grand Trunk railroad crossing at Ninety-first and Rockwell between the Evergreen Country Club and Beverly Country Club golf courses. En route to their Evergreen Park brewery, South Side Chicago gang leader "Spike" O'Donnell, his brother Tom, and their brother-in-law, William Barcal, are ambushed on the tracks by suspected members of the Saltis-McErlane mob, who fire an estimated forty rounds at the O'Donnells' car. The O'Donnells return fire, flee, and are later arrested. Tom O'Donnell suffers a slight head wound, but there are no confirmed kills on either side. The O'Donnells' car is found later, the back seat saturated with blood, which leads police to suspect other casualties, but no bodies are found.

October 17—The New York police department's experienced fence squad charges eleven male and one female member of the notorious "Cowboy" Tessler Gang with eighty holdups and one murder.

October 18—Arrest of the Rothenberg Gang, suspected of one-quarter of New York's burglaries during the preceding six months, is considered another triumph of the police department's "older," more experienced detectives after their capture of the Tessler gangsters.

October 20—The Whittemore Gang robs John Sandford, salesman for Larter & Sons, of $25,000 worth of watches and jewelry at Eighty-fourth Street and Broadway in New York.

October 24—Michael Orzo, Vincenzo Siannameo and Samuel Di Stuvio, all known criminals, are killed in a gunfight with unidentified men after an argument at John Maglioretti's midtown New York basement café.

October 29—Six bandits rob a Federal Reserve Bank car in Buffalo of $93,000, killing the driver and a guard. The crime is variously attributed to "Dutch" Anderson, the Whittemore Gang, and others.

October 31—Bootlegger Edwin "Spike" Kenny is shot in a Baltimore roadhouse and names Richard Reese Whittemore as his attacker. The shooting apparently was motivated by Kenny's romantic involvement with his assailant's wife, Margaret "Tiger Lil" Whittemore.

– Mail robber "Dutch" Anderson mortally wounds police detective Charles DeWitt Hammond in Muskegon, Michigan. The dying officer wrests away Anderson's gun and kills him.

November 1—Speakeasy owner, and former deputy U.S. marshal and politician, Joseph V. Sheridan is killed by a gunman while playing solitaire in the Lone Owl Club speakeasy at 518 West Forty-seventh Street in New York. Police suspect the motive to be revenge for Sheridan's beating up two gangsters the previous week.

November 13—Bootlegger Salvatore "Samoots" Amatuna (with various spellings of his first name, and head of the Unione Siciliana after Mike Merlo) is fatally shot in a barber shop at 804 Roosevelt Road in Chicago.

November 16—Chicago bootlegger Eddie Zine (also called Zion) is killed by gunmen in his back yard at Willow Springs, Illinois, after attending the funeral of "Samoots" Amatuna.

– Gang leader Ralph Sheldon's cigar store near West Sixty-third Street and South Ashland Avenue in Chicago is bombed, probably by "Spike" O'Donnell's South Side mob.

November 20—Paul Jawarski and the Flatheads Gang rob a Brink's car in Detroit, stealing $19,500. Guard Ross Loney is killed, and guard Walter Radcliffe is seriously wounded.

– Chicago gangster Abraham "Bummy" Goldstein is shot to death by two gunmen in a drugstore at 1400 Blue Island Avenue, allegedly in retaliation for the murder of "Samoots" Amatuna. Tom "Hump" Kane and James Gibbons of the "Klondike" O'Donnell gang, are suspected.

November 24—Six bandits hold up Drovers National Bank money car for $57,760 in Chicago. Two gunmen and one policeman are shot.

– Jimmy Wright, a member of Paul Jawarski's gang, is found shot to death near Farmington, Michigan.

November 27—While on stakeout for fugitive Martin Durkin, Chicago policemen James Carroll and James Henry are fatally shot by a raiding party of gunmen at Thomas McKeone's saloon at 5253 South Halsted. Taxi driver Marshall Custer also is mortally wounded. Attributed to an ongoing war between the Ralph Sheldon and Saltis-McErlane mobs.

December 1925—Charlie Birger and the Shelton Brothers, later enemies, form a slot machine partnership in southern Illinois.

December 2—The Whittemore Gang robs M. G. Ernest's jewelry store at 566 Columbus Avenue in New York of $75,000 in diamonds.

– Jimmy Stone, Missouri robbery fugitive, is found shot to death on a country road west of Halfway, Illinois. A note in the dead man's hand blames the killing on the "K.K.K.," but informers later will attribute the murder to Charlie Birger and his gang.

December 4—Federal agents proclaim smashing the country's largest liquor smuggling ring with arrests in New York of "Big Bill" Dwyer, Frank Costello, and fifty others.

December 8—"Pretty Boy" Floyd pleads guilty to first-degree robbery and is sentenced to five years in the state prison at Jefferson City, Missouri, where he will be received on December 18.

December 12–24—John Burns, John Whalen, Robert "Red" Hill, and Thomas McCarthy are killed in separate shooting incidents within blocks of one another in what New York police call an East Side gang war.

December 19—Four "yeggs" dynamite a bank safe in Washington, Arkansas, shoot it out with police, and flee with $7,000.

December 21—Simon Gilden, a member of the Whittemore Gang, is found shot to death in New York.

December 22—Gangster "Dynamite Joe" Brooks and Cook County highway patrolman Edwin Harmening are found shot to death in Marquette Park in Chicago. The Saltis-McErlane mob is suspected.

December 23—The Whittemore Gang robs Folmer Prip, jeweler at 90 Nassau Street in New York, of $10,000.

December 24—Paul Jawarski and the Flatheads

Gang murder Pittsburgh Terminal Coal Co. guard Isaiah Gump in a $48,000 payroll robbery at Mollenaur, Pennsylvania.

December 26—At the Adonis Social Club, an Italian mob hangout in Brooklyn, Richard "Peg Leg" Lonergan, head of the Irish White Hand gang, is shot to death, along with gang members Cornelius "Needles" Ferry and Aaron Harms. Several Italian gangsters, including visiting Chicago mob boss Al Capone, are arrested and questioned.

– Joseph Ross, a member of the Whittemore Gang, is found shot to death near Elizabeth, New Jersey.

1926

January 10—Chicago lawyer Henry Spingola, brother-in-law of Angelo Genna, is shot to death while leaving Amato's Restaurant on South Halsted, allegedly for refusing to contribute to a gangland defense fund of cop killers Albert Anselmi and John Scalise.

January 11—At 22 West Forty-eighth Street in New York, the Whittemore Gang robs Belgian diamond merchants Albert Goudvis and Emanuel Veerman of $175,000 in gems.

January 24—Tammany Hall politicians Pasquale "Patsy Griffin" Cuoco and Vincenzo "Red Russo" Montalvo are fatally shot by a man known only as "The Kibitzer" after a card game at New York's Second Assembly District Democratic Club.

January 26—Brothers Agostino and Antonio Morici are ambushed and slain on Ogden Avenue in Chicago. Wealthy wholesale grocers in competition with Capone mobster Antonio Lombardo, the Moricis also may have refused to contribute to the Scalise and Anselmi defense fund.

– At Webster Grove, Missouri, near St. Louis, police and Bureau of Investigation agents board the *Katy Texas Special* train from San Antonio and arrest Martin James Durkin, killer of federal agent Shanahan. Durkin later is convicted and sentenced to fifty years.

February 2—Chicago gang leader Ralph Sheldon's car is demolished by a dynamite bomb.

February 9—Martin "Buff" Costello's saloon, at 4127 South Halsted Street in Chicago, is raked by machine-gun fire from the Saltis-McErlane mob. William Wilson and John "Mitters" Foley are wounded.

February 10—Al Capone's gang orders three Thompson submachine guns from South Side hardware and sporting-goods dealer Alex Korecek.

February 13—Two bandits who robbed Chicago's Drake Hotel are hanged for murder.

February 15—Orazio "The Scourge" Tropea, collector for the Anselmi-Scalise defense fund, is shotgunned to death on Chicago's Halsted Street.

February 23—Ecola "The Eagle" Baldelli, a Tropea henchman and collector, is found shot to death in an alley at 407 North Curtis in Chicago.

February 24—Vito Bascone, another Tropea collector for the defense fund, is found dead in a ditch near Stickney, Illinois, shot between the eyes. (By some accounts, the murders of Tropea, Baldelli, and Bascone were committed by "Machine Gun" Jack McGurn, in revenge for the slaying of his stepfather.)

February 26—Rumrunner Duncan "Red" Shannon is killed by Coast Guardsmen near Miami's Flamingo Hotel.

March 2—Salvatore Vista, sixty-year-old Staten Island bootlegger posing as a perfume salesman, is fatally shot on an East Village street, and police find twenty gallons of alcohol in his car. Murder attributed to a "price war" between rival bootleg factions on the Lower East Side, Staten Island and New Jersey.

March 6—Gunmen steal $80,000 in a payroll robbery of the International Harvester Co. plant at 2600 West Thirty-first Street in Chicago. Fifteen suspects are arrested, including Tony Capezio, William "Three-Fingered Jack" White, Frank and Peter Gusenberg, and Tommy Schupe.

March 19—Richard Reese Whittemore and gang members Bernard Mortillaro, Pasquale Chicarelli, Morris "Shuffles" Goldberg, Jake and Leon Kramer, Anthony Paladino, and Margaret "Tiger Lil" Whittemore are captured by New York police, suspected of murdering a holdup witness.

March 29—"James Gebhardt," former boxer known as Jack McGurn, is unharmed but receives bullet holes in his hat when shot at by four gunmen outside his mother-in-law's home at 1230 Oregon Avenue in Chicago. Possibly the earliest significant newspaper report on the later notorious "Machine Gun" Jack McGurn.

March 30—Four gunmen rob the National Bank in San Antonio of $19,000 and make their getaway in a touring car driven by a woman.

April 3—Chicago hoodlum Walter Quinlan is gunned down, allegedly by John "Paddy the Cub" Ryan, in Joe Sindelar's Yankee Saloon at 1700 South Loomis, probably in belated revenge for the 1920 murder of Ryan's father, "Paddy the Bear." It is reported as the city's twenty-seventh unsolved gang murder of the year.

April 4—New York police capture and blackjack six members of the "English Harry" Wallon Gang after a card game holdup.

April 10—John Tuccello and Frank DeLaurentis, ex-Genna gangsters working for Ralph Sheldon, are abducted by the Saltis-McErlane mob while attempting to deliver liquor to Roman Duchovitz's saloon at 1310 West Fifty-first Street in Chicago. Tuccello and DeLaurentis later are found murdered in their car in front of Sheldon's home at 6553 South Rockwell, apparently parked there as a warning to Sheldon to keep out of Saltis-McErlane territory.

April 13—Election Day gunfire erupts outside the Masonic Temple polling place in Herrin, Illinois, between Prohibitionist Ku Klux Klansmen and members of the Birger and Shelton gangs. Six men are killed, and the power of the Klan in "Bloody Williamson" County is broken.

April 23—Capone machine-gunners riddle Pearl Hruby's beauty shop at 2208 South Austin Boulevard in Cicero with ninety-two bullets, wounding Pearl's boyfriend, James "Fur" Sammons.

April 26—Gerald Chapman is hanged for murder at Wethersfield, Connecticut.

April 27—Assistant State's Attorney William H. McSwiggin, and gangsters James Doherty and Thomas Duffy of the "Klondike" O'Donnell gang, are killed by machine-gun bullets in front of Harry Madigan's saloon at 5613 West Roosevelt Road in Cicero. The killings are attributed to the Capone gang, and some claim Capone himself wielded the Tommygun.

— A Buffalo jury is discharged after failing to reach a verdict in the murder and bank-car robbery trial of Richard Reese Whittemore. He will not be retried.

April 30—Whittemore is turned over to Baltimore authorities to be tried for the murder of a prison guard.

May 8—The Baraseck Gang (William and Kasimir Baraseck and John Maxwell), wanted in Brooklyn for murder and numerous holdups of United Cigar shops and A&P stores, are captured by a lone policeman in Darien, Connecticut. All will be returned to New York, convicted of murder, and sentenced to death.

May 18—New York labor racketeer William Mack is found shot to death near the Fulton Fish Market.

May 21—Richard Reese Whittemore is convicted of murder in Baltimore. He is sentenced to death on June 10.

May 27–29—William Dorsch, Daniel Ahearn, Harry Bender, and Frank "Rags" Loonie are killed in separate New York shootings attributed to a "bootleggers' feud."

June 2—Chicago Heights bootlegger Geralanes (James) Lamberto and girlfriend, Crystal Barrier, are murdered by three gunmen with pistols and shotguns at the Derby Inn roadhouse at 175th and Halsted streets in Thornton, Illinois.

— Four bandits rob the Jefferson Bank & Trust Co. at Oak Cliff, Texas, of $17,000, locking eleven people in the vault.

June 7—Captured driving a stolen car in Fort Scott, Kansas, Herman Barker and Elmer Inman are extradited to Oklahoma to face robbery charges. Both soon are free on bond. Barker is the oldest son of Kate "Ma" Barker.

June 9—Chicago Heights mobster Frank Camera is murdered in a "one-way ride" shooting, allegedly for providing police with information on the Lamberto slaying that occurred June 2.

June 17—Matt Kimes is arrested for car theft in Bristow, Oklahoma.

June 18—Ex-convict Charles Caffrey is found shot to death in a parked Chrysler in Harlem. Attributed by police to a "thieves' feud."

June 19—A "one-way ride" is witnessed by several people as union official Zito Blandi is shot and thrown from a passing Ford sedan on a Brooklyn street.

— Gangster George Smolen, wounded by gunfire on a Manhattan street corner, refuses to identify his attacker, saying, "He's a brave guy with a gun, but I'll handle this matter myself."

June 22—Matt Kimes saws through the bars of his cell and escapes.

June 30—Matt and George Kimes rob the Depew State Bank, at Depew, Oklahoma, of $7,000.

July 2—Al Capone is indicted in Chicago for conspiring to swear falsely to qualify voters. The indictment will be quashed in December.

July 7–27—"Big Bill" Dwyer is tried and convicted of liquor smuggling and sentenced to two years in the federal penitentiary in Atlanta.

July 8—Striking garment worker Samuel Landman is fatally shot on a picket line at 22 West Twenty-second Street in New York and names gangster Jacob "Little Augie" Orgen as his assailant. Orgen is later tried and acquitted.

July 12—Boyd "Oklahoma Curly" Hartin is killed in a gunfight in a Herrin, Illinois, roadhouse—probably an early casualty of the Birger-Shelton gang war.

July 22—Gangster Philip Piazza is shot to death by two gunmen outside his Milano Café at the corner of Sixteenth and Lowe in Chicago Heights, Illinois.

July 23—Chicago gangster John Conlon is shot to death in a saloon at 6154 South Ashland. John "Mitters" Foley and Hilary Clements of the Sheldon mob are suspected and may have been actually gunning for Vincent McErlane, who escaped unharmed.

July 25—Mike Santarelli is killed in a drive-by shooting outside a restaurant in New York's Little Italy. Though he has no local police record, cops suspect that Santarelli was a hired killer "imported" from Buffalo to work in a bootleg war.

July 29—In Chicago, a criminal complaint against Al Capone (as "Alphonse Caponi," alias "Scarface Brown") for the murder of Assistant State's Attorney William McSwiggin is dismissed by Judge Thomas J. Lynch.

August 3—Anthony Cuiringione, alias Tommy Ross, Al Capone's chauffeur, is found tortured and shot to death in a cistern in southwest Chicago.

August 5—Matt and George Kimes rob the Farmers National Bank at Beggs, Oklahoma, of $4,630.

August 6—John "Mitters" Foley is killed by gunmen near the corner of Sixty-fifth and Richmond in Chicago. "Polack Joe" Saltis, John "Dingbat" Oberta, Frank "Lefty" Koncil, and Ed "Big Herb" Herbert are arrested by police, but charges eventually will be dropped.

August 10—Four Capone gangsters attack Earl "Hymie" Weiss and Vincent "The Schemer" Drucci with pistols in front of the Standard Oil Building at 910 South Michigan Avenue. No one is hit, but Chicago police arrest and question Drucci and Capone gunman Louis Barko.

— Chicago gangster Louis "Big" Smith is shot to death by unknown killers, believed to be a revenge slaying for the murder of Abraham "Bummy" Goldstein.

August 12—Richard Reese Whittemore is hanged.

August 15—"Hymie" Weiss and "Schemer" Drucci are reportedly again attacked and missed by Capone gunmen outside the Standard Oil Building (this report appeared in only one Chicago newspaper, which didn't report the earlier attack, and so may be erroneous).

August 20—Joseph "The Cavalier" Nerone, alias Antonio Spano, suspect in the murder of Tony Genna, is shot to death by unknown killers at 435 West Division Street in Chicago.

August 22—Harry Walker and Everett Smith, of the Shelton Brothers gang, are shot to death in a roadhouse near Marion, Illinois.

August 26—Matt and George Kimes and their gang rob the American State Bank and the Covington National Bank at Covington, Oklahoma.

August 27—The Kimes brothers kill Deputy Perry Chuculate in a gun battle at Sallisaw, Oklahoma, take Chief of Police J. C. Woll and farmer Wesley Ross hostage, and flee into Arkansas. The hostages are released unharmed.

August 28—Matt and George Kimes are wounded and captured at the home of their cousin, Ben Pixley, near Rudy, Arkansas. George Kimes will be convicted of bank robbery and sentenced to twenty-five years in the state prison at McAlester, Oklahoma. Matt will be convicted of murder and sentenced to thirty-five years, pending an appeal.

By the late 1920s, the flamboyant Al Capone had virtually replaced Mayor "Big Bill" Thompson as the lightning rod for everything that was "wrong" with Chicago—its political and police corruption, bootlegging, racketeering, gambling houses, and prostitution—to the dismay of "The Big Fellow," who had to acknowledge that gangland violence was frightening off tourists and therefore "bad for business."

August 30—"Girls" lead bandit raid on Chicago "car barn" cashier; seven people shot, two fatally.

September 9—"Big Benny" Befanti, gangster and barbers union official, is killed in a Bronx basement card game by gunman Frank Mazzola who leaps out a window and escapes down an alley.

September 10—Thomas Holden and Francis (Jimmy) Keating rob a U.S. Mail train of $135,000 at the Chicago suburb of Evergreen Park, Illinois.

— Bud Whitman and A. L. Slaton rob the Red River National Bank at Clarkesville, Texas, of $33,125, but they are ambushed and killed outside the bank by a posse led by Texas Ranger Tom Hickman.

September 12—While leaving a roadhouse between Herrin and Johnston City, Illinois, Shelton gangster "Wild Bill" Holland is machine-gunned to death and two others are wounded by the Charlie Birger gang.

— Gambler John Brocco is shot to death at a shoeshine stand across the road from his Catherine Street restaurant in New York. Attributed to a gamblers' quarrel.

September 14—Two men rob the Alma, Arkansas, bank of $4,975 and escape in a Chevrolet touring car.

September 17—Lyle "Shag" Worsham is machine-gunned to death by members of the Birger gang for defecting to the Sheltons, then he is cremated in an abandoned house near Pulley's Mill, Illinois.

September 18—The shotgunned corpse of an unidentified man is found in a hog lot near Shawneetown, Illinois. Attributed to the Birger-Shelton gang war.

September 19—Vito Salvi is killed in a Lower East Side apartment building, and the gunman escapes on foot despite shots fired by a pursuing policeman. Attributed to a gamblers' feud.

September 20—A motorcade of "Hymie" Weiss gangsters riddles the Hawthorne Hotel in Cicero with machine-gun and shotgun fire in an unsuccessful attempt to kill Al Capone. Neighboring Anton (later renamed Alton) Hotel and many parked cars are hit; Capone pays for all damage and for injuries sustained by a female passerby.

– Four unidentified boy bandits rob the First National Bank of Columbus, Wisconsin, of more than $1 million.

– Samuel Sanders, alias Sol Leitner, is shot in a "ride" killing in the Bronx.

September 24—Bootlegger Gaetano Neapolitano is found murdered in a Boonton, New Jersey, ditch.

September 27—Arrested for burglary, Ray Terrill and Elmer Inman overpower a jailer and escape from the Carter County Jail at Ardmore, Oklahoma.

October 1—A Federal Grand Jury in Chicago indicts Al Capone for conspiracy to violate the National Prohibition Act.

October 4—Shelton gangsters open fire on Birger gangster Art Newman's car from a specially armored truck near Harrisburg, Illinois. Mrs. Newman is wounded.

– The *New York Times* reports a crime-free day in the city, at least for reported crimes.

October 11—"Hymie" Weiss and bodyguard Patrick Murray are killed in front of the Holy Name Cathedral by Capone machine-gunners firing from an upstairs window in the building next to the late Dean O'Banion's State Street flower shop, which has remained headquarters for the North Siders. Gangsters Sam Peller and Benny Jacobs and mob attorney W. W. O'Brien are wounded. Another machine-gun nest, covering the flower shop's alley, is found later in a building diagonally across from the church. Vincent "The Schemer" Drucci succeeds Weiss as boss of the North Side mob.

October 14—Seven bandits, armed with Tommyguns, rob a U.S. Mail truck in Elizabeth, New Jersey, of $161,000, killing the driver and wounding his assistant and a policeman. Because of the machine guns, the killers are assumed to be Chicago gangsters, but soon will be identified as a New York gang headed by James "Killer" Cunniffe.

October 16—President Coolidge discusses the New Jersey mail robbery with his Cabinet. The next day, 2,500 Marines will be assigned to guard mail shipments.

– Tommyguns are stolen from the Rosiclare Spar Mining Co. at Rosiclare, Illinois. The Charlie Birger gang is suspected.

– The Jake Fleagle Gang robs the Exchange Bank of Schmidt and Koester at Marysville, Kansas, missing a large cash shipment and obtaining only $741.

October 21—A peace conference, called by Al Capone and attended by thirty Chicago gang leaders, results in a temporary truce.

October 23—New York police arrest Moe Salanta, considered the city's "best safecracker," and four members of his gang for burglary but release them for insufficient evidence. Salanta is killed twelve hours later at a Brooklyn candy store by members of his own gang. Shot outside, he manages to walk into the store and enter a phone booth before dying.

October 26—Burnett "High Pockets" McQuay is found machine-gunned in a car near Herrin, Illinois, and the bullet-riddled body of Ward "Casey" Jones is found in the Saline River, near Equality, Illinois. Both were members of the Birger gang. The Shelton gang is blamed.

October 27—In Chicago, the trial of Albert Anselmi and John Scalise in the slaying of Detective Harold Olson begins.

October 31—William "Ice Wagon" Crowley, one of the New Jersey mail robbers, kills James "Killer" Cunniffe and his girlfriend in an argument at the Highland Court Apartments, 257 Highland Avenue, in Detroit. Police arrive to investigate, and in the resulting gun battle, Crowley and Patrolman Ernest Jones also are slain.

November 3—Accused murderers Mike "Red" McKenna and Hyman "Hymie the Rat" Amberg (brother of Louis "Pretty" Amberg) and jewel thief Robert Berg try to shoot their way out of Manhattan's Tombs prison, killing Warden Peter Mallon and keeper Jeremiah Murphy. Trapped at the prison wall, the would-be escapees shoot themselves to avoid recapture.

November 6—Jeff Stone, mayor of Colp, Illinois, and John "Apie" Milroy are shot to death in the Birger-Shelton gang war. A tripod-mounted machine gun reportedly is used. Each gang attributes the killings to the other.

November 10—A bomb thrown from an automobile misses "Shady Rest," Charlie Birger's fortified log-cabin headquarters near Marion, Illinois.

November 12—First "aerial bombing" in the United States. A cropduster pilot is hired by the Shelton gang to drop three dynamite bombs on rival Charlie Birger's "Shady Rest." One bomb misses the target; the others fail to explode.

— Carl and Bernie Shelton are arrested by postal inspectors in Benton, Illinois, and charged, with brother Earl, with committing a January 1925 mail robbery in Collinsville, Illinois, in a frame-up engineered by Charlie Birger.

— In Chicago, Albert Anselmi and John Scalise are convicted of manslaughter in the killing of Detective Harold Olson. They are sentenced to fourteen years in the state prison at Joliet, Illinois.

— Harvey Bailey and others rob the Peoples Trust & Savings Bank at La Porte, Indiana, of $140,000 in cash and bonds.

November 13—George Nelson and John Such are captured in Fox Lake, Illinois, half an hour after robbing the Spring Grove State Bank at Spring Grove of $4,500. Contrary to later legend, the robber Nelson was not "Baby Face" Nelson.

November 21—A gang of gunmen, later alleged to include notorious bank burglar Ray Terrill, force their way into the Sallisaw, Oklahoma, jail and free convicted murderer Matt Kimes (later accounts by members of the Kimes family indicate that he actually was freed by relatives).

November 23—Harlem policy operator James Connors is stabbed to death at the Negro Golden Democratic Club allegedly by one Ralph Brown for failing to pay off winnings to Brown.

November 25—Bootlegger Virgil Hunsaker's house in Harrisburg, Illinois, is wrecked by a bomb blast. Hours later, Hunsaker and friends Louis Robinson and Millard Vinson are wounded in a machine-gun attack on their car west of Harrisburg.

November 28—Theodore "The Greek" Anton, owner of the Anton Hotel (eventually renamed the Alton) in Cicero, Illinois, and manager of Capone's Hawthorne Hotel headquarters next door to it, is kidnapped and tortured to death. Usually attributed to the North Side Gang, though some accounts indicate Capone had Anton killed after an argument.

November 30—The Charlie Birger gang robs the Bond County State Bank at Pocahontas, Illinois, of $5,000.

December 4—The Harvey Bailey Gang robs the Olmsted County Bank & Trust Co. at Rochester, Minnesota, of $30,000.

— Luther Bishop, ace investigator for the Oklahoma State Crime Bureau, is assassinated in his home at 1515 Northwest Twenty-eighth Street in Oklahoma City. His wife will be tried and acquitted of the crime, and Bishop probably was killed by one of the many outlaws he pursued. Ex-convict Burt Meredith will testify at Mrs. Bishop's trial that Ray Terrill admitted killing Bishop.

December 12—Mayor Joe Adams, a Shelton ally, is murdered by the Birger gang at West City, Illinois.

— Wilbur Underhill and Ike "Skeet" Akins shoot Fred Smythe in a holdup in Picher, Oklahoma.

December 20—Outlaw Earl Jarrett scales the wall of the Oklahoma's state prison and escapes with another convicted killer, J. L. Haynes. A third would-be escapee, Ace Yarber, is shot down by guards.

— The Terrill Gang burglarizes the bank of Buffalo, Kansas, stealing its safe, which contained more than $6,000 in cash and $2,000 in travelers checks.

December 23—The Illinois Supreme Court grants Albert Anselmi and John Scalise a retrial in the killing of Chicago policeman Harold Olson.

December 25—Wilbur Underhill and Ike "Skeet" Akins attempt to rob the Purity Drug Store in Okmulgee, Oklahoma, and murder a nineteen-year-old customer, George Fee.

December 26—Former St. Louis and Kansas City gangster John Reid is killed by a shotgun assassin outside his apartment at 3025 East Grand Boulevard in Detroit.

December 27—Terrill Gang member Elmer Inman is captured while burglarizing a store in Oklahoma City.

December 28—Charlie Birger is charged with the murder of Joe Adams.

December 31—Hilary Clements of the Ralph Sheldon gang, who disappeared on December 16, is found murdered in a deserted house at 336 West Sixtieth Street in Chicago, shattering the multigang October peace treaty engineered by Al Capone. The Saltis-McErlane mob is suspected.

1927

January 1—Burglars steal a safe containing $2,000 in cash and bonds from the West Fork, Arkansas, bank. Herman Barker and Ray Terrill are suspected.

January 3—John Hamilton (later Dillinger Gang member) and ex-policeman Raymond Lawrence rob a Kent State Savings Bank branch at Grand Rapids, Michigan, of $22,500.

January 7—$80 million worth of legally stored whiskey is stolen from a New York Chemical Co. warehouse.

— Wilbur Underhill and Ike "Skeet" Akins, wanted for murder and robbery, are captured in Tulsa.

January 8—"Shady Rest," headquarters of the southern Illinois Birger gang, is destroyed by fire. Four bodies are found in the ruins.

January 10—Matt Kimes and others rob the bank at Sapulpa, Oklahoma, of $40,000. Ray Terrill, rightly or not, also is identified as a participant.

January 16—The safe is stolen from a Rogerville, Missouri, bank, probably by the Terrill Gang.

January 17—The Terrill Gang (also known as the Terrill-Barker-Inman Gang) attempts to burglarize the bank in Jasper, Missouri, but flee in two cars when a posse arrives. One car escapes to Kansas. Two gang members, Ray Terrill and Herman Barker, are trailed to a house at 602 East Main in Carterville, near Joplin, and captured after a gun battle in which Barker is wounded.

January 19—Ray Terrill escapes from a car while being returned to the state prison at McAlester, Oklahoma, from which he has previously broken out.

— Illinois Highway Patrolman Lory Price and his wife, Ethel, disappear. Price allegedly was a partner of Charlie Birger in a stolen car racket.

January 21—Herman Barker is transferred from Joplin, Missouri, to Fayetteville, Arkansas, to face charges of robbing a West Fork bank.

January 25—Warrants are issued in Miami, Oklahoma, for the arrests of former County Judge Quil P. McGhee, attorney Frank Burns, Justice of the Peace Jeff Sexton, and former Deputy Sheriff Frank Warner on charges of aiding and abetting fugitives Herman Barker and Elmer Inman.

January 25-27—Albert Anselmi and John Scalise are freed on $25,000 bond pending their new trial for the killing of Chicago policeman Harold Olson.

January 30—Wilbur Underhill, Ike "Skeet" Akins, "Duff" Kennedy, and "Red" Gann escape from the Okmulgee County Jail in Okmulgee, Oklahoma.

— Gangster Benedetto Mariano is killed in a drive-by shooting at an intersection in Brooklyn's Williamsburg section.

January 31-February 5—Carl, Earl, and Bernie Shelton are tried and convicted of the 1925 Collinsville, Illinois, mail robbery, largely on the perjured testimony of Birger gang members. The Sheltons are sentenced to twenty-five years in a federal penitentiary.

February 1—George Kimes is wounded in an attempted escape from the state prison at McAlester, Oklahoma. Another convicted murderer, Leonard Mayfield, makes it over the wall but is recaptured two hours later.

February 5—The body of Highway Patrolman Lory Price, shot to death by the Birger gang, is found in a field near Dubois, Illinois. His wife's body will be recovered from an abandoned mine on June 13.

February 7—The Shelton Brothers begin serving their sentence for mail robbery at Leavenworth.

— Helen Holbrook, Illinois socialite, is found dead of chloroform poisoning in St. Petersburg, Florida.

A former mistress of Charlie Birger and of Carl Shelton, Helen is rumored to be the cause of the Birger-Shelton gang war. A coroner's jury will rule her death a suicide.

– In New York an unknown man is found strangled with sash cord in a burlap bag on an East Village street. He is wearing clothes from a Detroit tailor, and police deduce the victim to be a Detroit gangster.

February 9—Elmer Inman is convicted of burglary in Oklahoma City and sentenced to seven years in the state prison at McAlester.

– Oklahoma murderer Ike "Skeet" Akins is captured in Lamar, Missouri.

February 10—Albert Anselmi and John Scalise go to trial in Chicago in the murder of Detective Charles Walsh.

– St. Louis police arrest Florida resident Arthur McDonald for questioning in the death of Helen Holbrook. McDonald will be released and marries a sister of the Shelton Brothers in East St. Louis on February 18.

February 11—Following a tip from a soldier, Postal Inspector Fred Smith travels to the Philippines and arrests U.S. Army Private James C. Price, who admits his true identity as Hugh DeAutremont, long sought for the bloody attempted robbery of a Southern Pacific mail train in Siskiyou, Oregon.

February 12—While being returned to Okmulgee County, Oklahoma, Ike "Skeet" Akins attempts to escape and is killed by Sheriff John Russell.

February 13—Wilbur Underhill robs a Picher, Oklahoma, theater of $52 but is caught by Constable George Fuller. Underhill seizes Fuller's gun, kills deputized citizen Earl O'Neal, and escapes.

February 22—Bootlegger Edward Fallon is killed in a drive-by shooting in New York.

February 25—Philadelphia gang leader Michael "Mickey" Duffy is wounded and his associate John Bricker killed outside the Club Cadix on Chestnut Street by machine-gunners in a drive-by shooting. Philadelphia's first Tommygun murder is attributed to Duffy's rival, Max "Boo Boo" Hoff.

March 5—Members of the West Side O'Donnell gang are captured using a hose to siphon whiskey from a government warehouse at 824–902 South May in Chicago. William "Klondike" O'Donnell, James "Fur" Sammons, James Barry, and John Toohig are arrested.

March 7—Samuel Raplansky, member of New York's Madison Street Boys gang, is killed by gunmen in the hallway of the gang's clubhouse.

March 11—An armored truck carrying a $104,250 payroll of the Pittsburgh Terminal Coal Co. is dynamited and robbed by the Flatheads Gang near Coverdale, Pennsylvania. Five guards are seriously injured in what probably is the first robbery of an armored car.

– Saltis-McErlane gangsters Frank "Lefty" Koncil, and Charles "Big Hayes" Hubacek (or Hrubec) are shot to death at Thirty-ninth and Ashland in Chicago, and real estate dealer Benjamin J. Schneider is killed in a separate shooting. Attributed to the Ralph Sheldon gang, but the South Side O'Donnells also are suspected.

– Hugh DeAutremont, in the custody of Postal Inspector Fred Smith, leaves Manila for the United States aboard the U.S. transport *Thomas.*

March 12—Paul Jawarski, leader of the Flatheads Gang, is captured at a farmhouse near Bentleyville, Pennsylvania.

– Boston police, acting in cooperation with the district attorney's office and the Boston Booksellers' Committee, suppress sales of nine "modern books," including some bestsellers, deemed to be "indecent and obscene or as tending to corrupt morals."

March 15—John Hamilton and Raymond Lawrence are captured by South Bend, Indiana, police after attempting to rob the South Bend State Bank.

March 16—St. Louis gamblers Frank Wright, Joseph Bloom, and Reuben Cohen are machine-gunned to death in the "Milaflores Apartment Massacre" in Detroit. Attributed to former St. Louis gangster Fred "Killer" Burke on assignment from Detroit's Purple Gang.

March 17—Elmer Inman and Alvin Sherwood escape from a train near Bolton, Oklahoma, while en route to the state prison at McAlester.

The St. Valentine's Day Massacre

The crime most closely associated with Prohibition was the firing-squad execution of six Chicago bootleggers and one optometrist "groupie" on February 14, 1929, by rival gangsters masquerading as police. The St. Valentine's Day Massacre was so cold-blooded that it made the front page of virtually every daily newspaper in the country, and it probably did more than any other single event to tip public opinion in favor of Repeal. The mass murder confirmed what most Americans already believed—that Prohibition not only had failed to solve the country's chronic alcohol problem, it actually had aggravated it, corrupted government at every level, and was bringing gangland violence to intolerable proportions.

The Massacre caused total turmoil as Chicago police, in a rare spasm of law enforcement, clamped down on thousands of speakeasies and issued almost daily declarations that the case was all but solved. However, this amounted to rounding up the usual suspects against whom they had no evidence, declaring the murders a Capone-sponsored bloodbath intended to complete the conquest of Chicago (although Capone himself was in Miami), and coming up with the wrong shooters largely on the basis of their presumed grievances against the "Bugs" Moran gang. Moran had inherited leadership of the North Siders after the deaths of Dean O'Banion, "Hymie" Weiss and Vincent Drucci during four years of Beer Wars, which had included hundreds of gangland murders and introduced Americans to the previously unknown Thompson submachine gun (soon dubbed the "Chicago typewriter"). And now Moran was hooked up with Joe Aiello, who had put a $50,000 bounty on Capone's head.

The Massacre remains officially unsolved, but the usual account has it engineered by Capone's right-hand man, "Machine Gun" Jack McGurn, who supposedly tricked the Moran gang into assembling at 2122 North Clark Street, their Near North Side booze depot, to take delivery of a

The machine-gun murder of seven men in a North Clark Street garage shocked the entire country and probably did more than anything else to convince the public that Prohibition was a costly failure that had not ushered in an era of "clean living and clear thinking" but had thoroughly corrupted local and state governments.

load of Old Log Cabin whiskey hijacked from Capone. This turns out to have been a bad guess based on McGurn's notoriety and the statement of a federal Prohibition official who had learned of a recent hijacking. (The victims, except for a mechanic and the optometrist, were gang royalty, dressed in their best; and a relative of Moran's later dismissed the hijacked-liquor story altogether, saying "Bugs" called the meeting to plan retaliation for an assassination attempt.) The same Prohibition official also thought the killers might well be crooked Chicago cops on a personal mission—an accusation he later denied making but which still caused his banishment to another city.

In any case, about 10:30 a.m. on February 14, 1929, most of the Moran lieutenants had arrived at the garage (innocuously identified as the S.M.C. Cartage Co.) when they were interrupted by two men in police uniforms who slipped in through the back door when it was opened to admit a truck. Annoyed but not particularly worried at what they assumed would be a shakedown, they surrendered their weapons and were ordered to line up facing the north wall, about the only place not cluttered with cars and trucks used in their particular line of "cartage." Instead of demanding a payoff, one of the phony cops let in two or three well-dressed gunmen who raked the Moran men

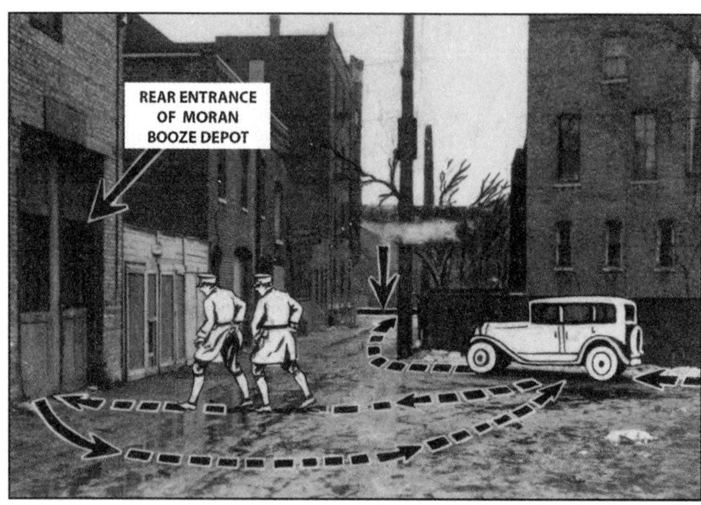

In the uproar following the St. Valentine's Day Massacre, only a handful of newspapers reported (and then only in passing) that not one but two cars had been used, and that the phony cops entered the garage from the rear, disarmed the occupants, and let the machine-gunners in through the front. The real police immediately sought Jack McGurn, but his "Blond Alibi" insisted he was with her that morning at the Stevens Hotel.

with seventy bullets from two Thompsons, plus a couple of shotgun blasts. The killers then were marched, as if arrested, out the front door to another phony police car, which sped off.

"Bugs" Moran, the intended target, survived only because he arrived a few minutes late, saw the bogus police car, and retreated. (Two other North Siders also were running late, and it now appears that one of them, or another gang member, had secretly defected to the Capone Outfit.)

A female neighbor heard what sounded like gunfire and the howling of a dog, and she asked her roomer to investigate. In the back of the garage, still reeking with gunsmoke, he found six dead men and one who would die a short time later.

This much was reported by the newspapers, and the mass murder horrified Chicago as well as the rest of the country. Police arrested McGurn in a room at the luxurious Stevens Hotel on Michigan Avenue (now the Hilton Towers), but his girlfriend, Louise Rolfe, whom he later married, would always stick to her story that Jack had been in the sack with her all morning. McGurn used his interest in the Guyon Hotel at 3000 West Washington to post bond and eventually was set free for lack of evidence.

In the months after the Massacre, a coroner's jury of prominent Chicagoans met many times without developing enough evidence to prosecute anyone, though police work established that the killers had headquartered at Claude Maddox's Circus Café, 1857 West North Avenue,

2 CENTS

Chicago Daily Tribune

FINAL

SEIZE M'GURN FOR MASSACRE

Lindbergh Hurt; Anne Morrow Safe

while awaiting the word from lookouts in rented rooms across from the S.M.C. Cartage Co. garage. Further evidence that the killers were not the "usual suspects" came from a woman in nearby Lincoln Park whose horseback-riding companion had noticed them earlier and described them as "West Side gangsters," as opposed to Moran's North Siders.

A major blunder on the part of Fred Burke later confirmed his involvement in the Massacre. The following December, while lying low as "Frederick Dane" near the lakeside town of St. Joseph, Michigan, Burke panicked after a minor traffic accident and killed a policeman named Charles Skelly. He escaped, but sheriff's officers ransacking his lavishly furnished house uncovered a cache of weapons that included two Thompson submachine guns. These were sent to Chicago for ballistic testing by firearms-identification expert Calvin Goddard, a pioneer in that field who had been hired by two civic-minded businessmen. Using comparison microscopes and other new techniques, Goddard convinced the coroner's jury that the seventy .45-caliber bullets used on the Moran gang could have been fired only by Burke's Thompsons, one fitted with a fifty-round drum and the other a straight twenty-round box magazine (possibly used because drum magazines had a greater tendency to misfeed). Goddard discovered, moreover, that one of the Valentine's Day guns previously had been used to kill New York gangster Frankie Yale in 1928.

When Burke was captured in 1931, Michigan authorities refused to send him to Illinois even for questioning, and he was

O'Banion Remnants Assassinated by One Volley at Garage; Moran Feared Kidnaped; Slayers Wear Police Uniforms; Sirens Clear Path for Flight

Chicago gangsters graduated yesterday from murder to massacre.

They killed seven men in a group. There was just a few seconds of machine gun and shotgun fire. They

In describing the mass murder, the Chicago American*'s front-page story used a lead sentence (above) that made journalistic history, and* True Detective Mysteries *provided what must be the Massacre's most literate and lurid account, as quoted below.*

THREE CENTS THE CHICAGO DAILY NEWS BLUE STREAK

MASSACRE 7 OF MORAN GANG

KAFFA CHANGES HIS MIND; WILL FIGHT PRISON

"KILLING SCENE" TOO GRUESOME FOR ONLOOKERS

VICTIMS ARE LINED AGAINST WALL; ONE VOLLEY KILLS ALL

THE agonizing shrieks of the wounded, the throaty coughs of the dying and the barking guns drowned out the panting and cursing of the hard-working executioners, repeating that left-to-right right-to-left sweep of destruction as they glutted their murderous appetites upon the feast of blood. Bullets ripped into soft, yielding flesh, some tearing off bits and burying themselves with the ribbons of flesh in the wall ahead. Others tore into the fresh wounds and made gaping holes. A shotgun roared above the din, its charge obliterating a man's face, stenching the air with the acrid smell of powder fumes and loosing the steam of warm flesh and blood. The withering blast kept up until the last man was down. Satisfied with the havoc wrought, the leader ordered a halt. The four right-faced and marched out, two in front with their hands up, the two in uniform behind them, prodding them with their smoking guns.

The St. Valentine Day Massacre was finished!

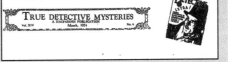

TRUE DETECTIVE MYSTERIES
A MACFADDEN PUBLICATION
Vol. XIV March, 1931 No. 6

Fred Burke, who soon became the Massacre's prime suspect, foolishly (and perhaps drunkenly) killed a cop in Michigan, and at his house police found an arsenal of weapons that included the two submachine guns used in the Chicago murders. Arrested six years later for a kidnapping, Byron Bolton admitted that he had been a Massacre lookout and that the actual shooters were Capone's hit squad of "American boys," who had moved to Chicago from St. Louis.

sentenced to life in the Michigan state prison for the murder of Officer Skelly. Burke never broke his silence on the Massacre, then or ever, but six years after the Chicago bloodbath, Byron Bolton did.

In January, 1935, several members of the Barker-Karpis Gang were captured in an FBI raid on a Chicago apartment building at 3920 North Pine Grove Avenue and charged with kidnapping. A few days later Bolton (possibly through some friend and probably because he believed the mob, then controlled by Frank Nitti, had tipped off the FBI to their hideout) somehow managed to give a new version of the Massacre to the *Chicago American*—to the amazement and surprise of J. Edgar Hoover. The FBI director declared that his kidnapping suspect had no connection whatsoever with the Massacre, that the story was totally false, and he then ordered his usually thorough agents to squeeze Bolton for details. The last thing Hoover wanted was for his kidnapping suspect to drag the bureau into what he considered a purely local crime.

Bolton denied having leaked the story but revealed that he, not the Keywell Brothers from the Detroit Purple Gang, had been one of the Clark Street lookouts. He added that the original planning had taken place at a resort in Wisconsin operated by Fred Goetz, with two state legislators present. He had been the errand boy, he said, who not only catered the meeting but also purchased one of the two cars used by the principal gunmen; and those included Fred

Goetz, Fred Burke, Ray Nugent, Bob Carey and Gus Winkeler (spelled Winkler in newspapers).

These were not the suspects originally named by Chicago police and reported by the press. What Bolton would not have known is that Gus Winkeler's widow had contacted Melvin Purvis a month before his arrest, and that she had given the FBI a book-length manuscript describing her murdered husband's criminal activities—including his participation in the Massacre. Her account independently confirmed the five names Bolton had given the bureau during his further interrogation.

In her manuscript Georgette Winkeler called the group the "American boys" and described how most of them had been imported from St. Louis to serve as Capone's special-assignment squad. She discussed the killing of Yale and the Massacre, mentioning that Goetz had brought the police uniforms to her and Gus's residence; and how the two had amused themselves by wearing them to upset visiting hoodlums. She added that Bolton, as a lookout, not only had mistaken another North Sider for "Bugs" Moran but also had left behind a bottle of prescription medicine with his name on it; and that after the murders Gus, Carey and Goetz sat around discussing mistakes that had been made.

"Bugs" Moran, the main target of the killers, had called the meeting of his top lieutenants but was delayed by a haircut that saved his life.

♔ ♔ ♔

The widely-accepted story—and the one that persists in crime-history books and television documentaries—describes one bogus detective car arriving at the S.M.C. Cartage Co., but an elderly woman in the building next door was looking out her bay window, had seen two such cars (one of which stopped), and wondered what was going on. Police likewise ignored the statement of a neighborhood youngster who said that he had seen a second car in the alley behind the garage; and that two men dressed as police had first gone in the back double doors when they were opened for a

Massacre Myths Dispelled

What we now know about the St. Valentine's Day Massacre comes not from the countless books, articles, and television specials that simply repeat the standard newspaper accounts, or from the documentary-style Jason Robards movie. Those correctly identified the gangs, the victims, the address of the garage, and the date of the murders, but not much else.

- The February 14 meeting had been set up two weeks earlier by Moran, not Capone, because of an attempt on his life outside a North Side nightclub. (Why else have lookouts watching the S.M.C. Cartage Co. garage for a month?)
- The hijacked-whiskey story was based entirely on the widely published guess of one federal Prohibition official, later fired, who had heard of an unrelated hijacking, who initially blamed the Chicago police, and who failed to note that Moran's group included his top lieutenants rather than his workmen (which also would have obviated the need for the monthlong surveillance).
- Jack McGurn knew of plans to kill Moran, but by 1929 he was too notorious to "mastermind" the Massacre (which was handed off by Capone to Nitti, who assigned it to Heeney, who assigned it to Goetz) and had taken the precaution of holing up at the Stevens Hotel with Louise Rolfe.
- The lookouts were not Detroit's Keywell Brothers, as "partially identified" by a witness (who later changed her mind).

And on and on . . .

truck. Sensing that some excitement would soon occur, he had then hurried around to the front, probably about the time of the shooting, and there witnessed the scene described by others: Two armed men in uniform marching other men in civilian clothes to the Clark Street detective car, which then sped away.

Many random facts went unnoticed or unreported, but some came together on February 21 when a car fitted out to resemble a detective Cadillac exploded in an alley garage on Wood Street, about a block from Maddox's Circus Café and maybe a ten-minute drive from Clark Street. Arriving firemen found a siren, a police gong and a Luger pistol in the wreckage, and police learned that the garage had been rented by Maddox himself, using a phony name and an address next door to his Circus Café (which had suddenly gone out of business). Both buildings were empty, but the one next to the café obviously had served as a meeting place for Maddox's Circus Gang, which included his St. Louis friends and amounted to a Capone beachhead on Chicago's Near North Side.

Someone had seen a burned man run from the garage toward a nearby hospital, but he left minutes later without waiting for treatment and possible questioning by police. That minor mystery was cleared up some forty years later when outlaw Alvin Karpis published his biography. The burn victim was "Tough Tony" Capezio, ally of Capone and a friend of Karpis (whose family lived in Chicago), who had been tediously dismantling a 1927 Cadillac. He evidently was unaware that the fuel system included a canister of gasoline attached to the firewall

Chicago researcher Chuck Schauer carefully reconstructed the Massacre and assembled photographs (above) of those who planned, participated in, or were otherwise involved, some only as police "suspects." This and other scenes were part of his display at the 2006 convention of The American Thompson Association, which included the two submachine guns recovered at Fred "Killer" Burke's house. The known shooters are (second row, from left) Burke, Fred Goetz, Gus Winkeler, Ray Nugent, and Bob Carey. Lookout Byron Bolton is sixth from left.

and had gotten into it with a cutting torch.

The blast ended that project, and the leads it provided were not diligently pursued. Nor did the police pay close attention when a second murder car, a 1926 Peerless, was blasted with dynamite in the suburb of Maywood on February 27. There cops found another police gong and gun rack, as well as a pocket notebook belonging to Albert Weinshank, one of the Massacre victims. Maddox lived in Maywood, but nothing came of that lead, either, possibly because the town was a stronghold of Capone.

The FBI remained silent on the names it learned from Bolton and from Georgette Winkeler, but in later years most of them came up in newspaper articles written by reporters and retired detectives who had stayed on the case. One of the cops calculated that eleven or more men participated in the Massacre—probably five inside the garage, those driving the getaway cars, at least two lookouts, and some who would have been parked on Clark Street to block any pursuit by district police. Two of these probably were Tony Capezio, part owner of the Circus Café, and Rocco DeGrazia, at whose apartment some of the gunmen were

Shall Chicago Stand for This?

NO WORDS can add to the force of this cartoon. Chicago stands ashamed before the civilized world. Lawbreaking in this city has reached its climax in a mass murder that makes law-abiding people everywhere gasp with horror. Chicagoans who feel themselves dishonored in the dishonor of their city will rally to its defense and, if necessary, appoint a committee to take the municipal government out of the hands of public servants who have betrayed their fellow citizens.

This editorial cartoon appeared on the front page of the Chicago Herald and Examiner *a few days after the Massacre.*

staying at the time. According to Georgette Winkeler, DeGrazia was part of the Massacre crew, probably as a lookout, and a name added to the group in more recent times was that of Tony Accardo, then a rookie who drove for Jack McGurn but who would one day boss all organized crime in Chicago.

♔ ♔ ♔

The role of Al Capone remains a mystery—whether he personally ordered the Massacre out of a murderous megalomania (as popular history would have it); ordered the killing of Moran, partly in self-defense (a month earlier his men had tried to kill Moran outside the Club Chez Pierre); or if he truly was exasperated with the continuing gangland violence (as he always claimed) and had left the matter to Frank Nitti, who delegated it to Willie Heeney, who put Fred Goetz in charge of the "American boys," expecting them to use good judgment. And there were other likely motives.

The North Siders had teamed up with gangster Joe Aiello in his war with Capone for control of the Unione Siciliana. Originally an immigrants' benevolent society, the Unione had turned small-scale distilling into a major cottage industry in Little Sicily, a neighborhood that bordered Moran's territory on Chicago's Near North Side. Two of the men Capone supported to head the Unione recently had been murdered by Moran and Aiello.

Also, Moran had discovered the enormous profit potential in both racketeering and gambling, which pitted him against Capone allies (including the "American boys") who were invading his own North Side. Moran's unruly gang had never ceased sniping at Capone since the murder of Dean O'Banion in his flower shop in 1924; and Capone had lately deeded North Side gambling operations to Gus Winkeler and his friends, if they could muscle Moran out of the picture.

According to Bolton, the shooters did not know Moran by sight and (perhaps when nobody raised his hand) decided they should kill everyone. One can only imagine Capone in Miami thinking to himself, *If you want anything done right, you got to do it yourself.*

For the St. Valentine's Day Massacre was a public-relations disaster that cost the Chicago Syndicate millions of dollars after the police department's crackdown on speakeasies (which numbered 8,000 to 10,000) and countless gambling joints, ranging from handbooks to betting parlors to casino-size clubs. It caused economic turmoil in the business community that had thrived on out-of-town visitors, and left the city with a scar as conspicuous as those on Capone's left cheek. It also blackened the name of Capone, who had rather enjoyed his improving image as the "Babe Ruth of American Gangsters." And it inspired two wealthy businessmen to fund the establishment of the country's first full-service crime lab, to be operated by Northwestern University's Law School because Chicago's police were so notoriously corrupt.

As for "Bugs" Moran: After the Massacre, with his North Side mob in shambles, Moran's own criminal career spiraled downward. He hid out for many months before venturing back to the Chicago area, where he tried to place slot machines in the northern suburbs. He had suspected a traitor in his ranks, and it might have been Ted Newberry, who too soon was welcomed into the Capone mob.

That Moran eventually learned the identity of the shooters (or some of them) is suggested by a conversation he had in 1932 with an old friend and former booze-truck driver he encountered in a suburban bar. He offhandedly remarked that he had just returned from "the coast," where he had "taken care of" a Bob Carey. Neither the now-elderly trucker nor his recent interviewer, Rose Keefe, knew that name, but Carey, according to both Bolton and Georgette Winkeler, was one of the Valentine's Day shooters.

Adapted from *The St. Valentine's Day Massacre: The Untold Story of the Gangland Bloodbath That Brought Down Al Capone*, based largely on the unpublished manuscript of Georgette Winkeler (spelled Winkler in the press), FBI documents, three newspaper features in later years, and an Alvin Karpis footnote in John Kobler's *Capone*.

– Hugh DeAutremont arrives in San Francisco and is confined in the U.S. Military Disciplinary Barracks on Alcatraz Island.

March 18—Anselmi and Scalise are acquitted of the Walsh slaying.

– Policeman Coke Buchanan is murdered by gunmen in Borger, Texas. Matt Kimes and Ray Terrill are named as suspects.

March 20—Murderer Wilbur Underhill is captured in Panama, Oklahoma.

March 24—Moy Sing and Moy Yuk Hong, members of the On Leong Tong, are murdered in Chicago.

March 26—Two gunmen rob the First State Bank at Ovalo, Texas, of $16,000 in cash and bonds.

March 30—Herman Barker and forger Claude Cooper saw through the bars of their cell and escape from the Washington County Jail at Fayetteville, Arkansas.

March 31—The First National Bank at Pampa, Texas, is robbed of $32,542, allegedly by the "Kimes-Terrill Gang." Suspects named include Matt Kimes, Ray Terrill, Asa "Ace" Pendleton, William "Whitey" Walker, and Owen Edwards.

April 1—The bodies of Deputies Pat Kenyon and A. L. "Chick" Terry are found near Pampa, Texas, presumably having been gunned down by the Pampa bank robbers.

April 4—Vincent "The Schemer" Drucci is arrested, then killed, in a scuffle with Detective Daniel Healy in a squad car at Clark Street and Wacker Drive in Chicago. George "Bugs" Moran succeeds to leadership of the North Siders.

– Capone favorite "Big Bill" Thompson is elected to a third term as mayor of Chicago, defeating incumbent Democratic reformer William E. Dever. Overloaded with 1,500 partying celebrants, Thompson's schooner slowly sinks to the bottom of Belmont Harbor. No one is hurt.

April 8—A lone bandit, posing as a Treasury agent looking for counterfeit bills, robs the First National Bank at Bells, Texas, of $700. He wrecks his car outside town but catches a bus and escapes.

April 11—Paul Jawarski, leader of the Flatheads Gang, is convicted of armed robbery in Pittsburgh and sentenced to thirty to sixty years.

April 26—Five men rob the First National Bank at Cushing, Oklahoma, of $10,000. Ray Terrill is suspected.

– Burglars steal $6,000 from the First State Bank of Tehuacana, Texas.

May 2–11—Hugh DeAutremont is tried for murder in Jacksonville, Oregon. Judge C. M. Thomas declares a mistrial after juror S. W. Dunham turns ill and dies. A new trial is scheduled for June 25.

May 4—After former Birger gang member Harvey Dungey repudiates his perjured testimony, the Shelton Brothers are granted a new trial for the Collinsville mail robbery and freed on $25,000 bond.

May 9—Ray Terrill is suspected in a $4,000 jewelry store robbery in Miami, Oklahoma.

May 12—Bandits haul away a safe containing $207,000 in cash and securities from the McCune State Bank at McCune, Kansas. Ray Terrill is suspected.

May 18—Matt Kimes and eight accomplices stage simultaneous raids on the Farmers National Bank and the First National Bank in Beggs, Oklahoma, stealing about $18,000 and killing Marshal W. J. McAnally. Robberies are attributed to the "Kimes-Terrill Gang," though no real evidence exists of an alliance between Kimes, a daylight bank robber, and Ray Terrill, whose crew specializes in nighttime bank burglaries.

– Paul Jawarski is convicted of murder in Pittsburgh and sentenced to death.

May 22—Birger gangster Art Newman, wanted in Illinois for the Joe Adams murder, is arrested in Long Beach, California.

May 25—New York gangster Tony Torchio is machine-gunned to death in Chicago after responding to Joe Aiello's offer of a $50,000 bounty on Al Capone. Aiello and Capone war over control of the Unione Siciliana, whose members supply much of the city's home-distilled alcohol.

– The Oregon murder trial of Hugh DeAutremont is moved to June 6.

May 27—Roy "Blackie" Wilson and Owen Edwards, members of the Kimes Gang, are captured by Texas Rangers at Borger, Texas, and extradited to Oklahoma for the murder of Marshal W. J. McAnally. Three other men and a woman are in custody for the same crime.

June 1—Aiello gangster Lawrence LaPresta is killed by the Capone mob.

June 3—Wilbur Underhill is convicted of murder at Okmulgee, Oklahoma, and sentenced to life imprisonment.

June 8—Twins Roy and Ray DeAutremont are captured in Steubenville, Ohio, where, as the "Goodwin brothers," they have been working for a steel company.

June 9—In Chicago, Albert Anselmi and John Scalise are again tried for the killing of Detective Harold Olson. They will be acquitted on June 23, by reason of self-defense.

June 11—Bootlegger Michael McNamara is found shot to death in a Queens cemetery.

June 12—Five men rob the Oilton State Bank in Oilton, Oklahoma, of $1,000 and escape in a car with twin machine guns mounted on the hood, according to witnesses. They fire on an oncoming motorist, puncturing the radiator.

June 13—Acting on information from gangster Art Newman, the body of Ethel Price is found in a mine near Johnston City, Illinois. Ethel and her husband were murdered by the Birger gang.

June 21—Hugh DeAutremont is convicted of murder and sentenced to life in the Oregon state prison. Roy and Ray DeAutremont arrive in Jacksonville, Oregon, the same day and plead guilty in exchange for life sentences.

June 24—Matt Kimes and associate Raymond Doolin are captured while marveling at the Grand Canyon in Arizona. Kimes will be sent to the Oklahoma's state prison on two life sentences for murder.

June 24-July 7—Birger gangsters Rado Millich and Eural Gowan are tried at Marion, Illinois, for the murder of Ward "Casey" Jones. Both are convicted. Millich is sentenced to death, Gowan to life imprisonment.

June 27—The Fleagle Gang robs the National Bank at Kinsley, Kansas, of $20,000.

June 29–30—Diego Attlomionte, Numio Jamericco, and Lorenzo Alagna—Aiello gangsters—are gunned down by the Capone mob.

July 1—In Brooklyn, gangster Anthony "Tony the Shoemaker" Paretti is convicted and sentenced to death for the ten-year-old slayings of Harlem gangsters Nicholas Morello and Charles Ubriaca.

July 6–24—Charlie Birger, Art Newman, and Ray "Izzy" Hyland are tried and convicted at Benton, Illinois, of the murder of Mayor Joe Adams of West City. Birger is sentenced to death, Newman and Hyland to life imprisonment.

July 7—James D'Amato is killed in a drive-by shooting in Brooklyn. (According to later popular accounts, D'Amato worked for Al Capone, was spying on Frankie Yale, and his death supposedly sealed Yale's doom. This seems unlikely, however, as Yale would not be killed until the following July. Other sources indicate that Capone instead was acting on new information from another spy only a month before Yale's death.)

July 8—Adolph Ramono is killed in a Harlem drive-by shooting. Attributed by police to a bootleggers' feud.

July 9—Police and federal agents arrest "Legs" Diamond on a narcotics smuggling charge in Mount Vernon, New York.

July 11—Giovanni Blandini (Blaudini, Baludin), an Aiello gangster, is shot to death in Chicago.

July 17—Dominic Cinderello, an Aiello gangster, is found murdered in the Calumet Sag Channel near Eighty-sixth Avenue in Palos Township, near Chicago. "Machine Gun" Jack McGurn is suspected.

July 21—Frank Badgley, Russell Clark, and Charles Hovious rob a Paragon, Indiana, bank of $2,000.

July 27—Gangster Frank Hitchcock, who switched sides from Capone to Aiello, is found shot to death at 135th Street and Hoxie Avenue in Chicago.

August 1—Herman Barker kills Deputy Arthur Osborn near Pine Bluffs, Wyoming. The crime first

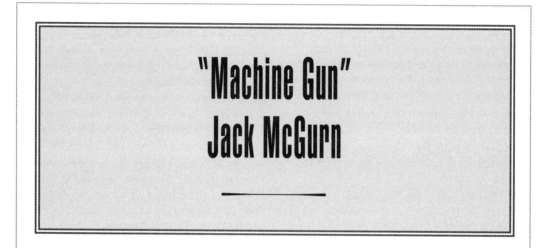

"Machine Gun" Jack McGurn

Jack McGurn, aka Vincenzo Gebardi, or Gibaldi, or DeMora, or Demore, or DeMory, lost his stepfather, Angelo DeMora, to gunmen on January 8, 1923, before the outbreak of Chicago's Beer Wars. McGurn stalked and killed two or three of them in the early twenties and eventually signed on with the Capone "Outfit," where he became the right-hand triggerman for the "Big Fellow" himself. He had adopted the name McGurn as a young prizefighter in a sport dominated by the Irish. How he picked up the nickname "Machine Gun" isn't clear since most of

BLOND BEAUTY -:- BACKS ALIBI OF -:- MASSACRE SUSPECT
McGURN'S BLOND ALIBI

Suspected of masterminding the St. Valentine's Day Massacre—largely on the basis of his notoriety—Jack McGurn alibied his way out when his girlfriend, Louise Rolfe, insisted that the two were together at the Stevens Hotel on the morning of the murders. The inset photo at right shows Rolfe about 1990.

the killings attributed to him were carried out with a pistol, and most of the victims were local or imported bounty hunters gunning for his boss. Supposedly his trademark was a nickel put in the hand of the deceased to proclaim him a "cheap hood."

In public, however, McGurn exemplified the Roaring Twenties "sheik," a spiffy dresser in the style of actor George Raft, favoring light-blue outfits, strumming the ukulele, having his pick of showgirls (despite a wife and children), and surviving more than one shooting. He supposedly ordered the almost-fatal knifing of popular comedian Joe E. Lewis at the North Sider-owned Commonwealth Hotel when Lewis and his act jumped ship at the Green Mill Gardens nightclub (in which McGurn held an interest) for the Rendezvous, a Moran-sponsored club at the intersection of Clark, Diversey, and Broadway. He was Capone's chief torpedo until Capone received an eleven-year prison sentence, and he fell on hard times.

Although indicted for the St. Valentine's Day Massacre, the charge had to be dropped for lack of evidence, especially when his "Blond Alibi," Louise Rolfe, insisted they had spent the entire morning in his suite at the Stevens Hotel making St. Valentine's Day love.

In frustration, local authorities prevailed on the Justice Department to charge McGurn and Rolfe with conspiring to violate the Mann Act—transporting a woman across state lines for "immoral purposes" when visiting Capone in Florida. Both were convicted and sentenced under a law from 1910 originally intended to suppress organized prostitution rather than hassle consenting adults. Angry at the misuse of the statute, McGurn and Rolfe took their appeals all the way to the U.S. Supreme Court, where justice of a sort prevailed. The Court concluded that the law, as worded, did not contemplate a woman "debauching" herself and reversed the conviction of Louise, whom Jack had since married. This left McGurn with no one to have conspired with, and thus his conviction also had to be vacated. So, thanks to McGurn and his "Blond Alibi," federal prosecutors have since found it harder to convict an unmarried couple of engaging in "white slavery" when they travel together, or when the motel they find happens to be a few miles down the road in a neighboring state.

When popular entertainer Joe E. Lewis decided to jump ship at the Green Mill in which "Machine Gun" Jack held an interest, McGurn or his criminal colleagues attacked Lewis in his hotel room, badly cutting his throat.

After Capone's income-tax conviction, Frank Nitti maneuvered for control of the Chicago Outfit, which included purging those who had been especially close to "The Big Fellow" or were rapidly expanding their North Side operations in the vacuum left by the vanquished Moran gang. Possibly seen as a threat to the new order, McGurn was gunned down in a bowling alley at 805 Milwaukee Avenue in 1936, a few minutes after midnight of the seventh anniversary of the St. Valentine's Day Massacre. The killing initially was blamed on patient remnants of the Moran gang, then on Nitti's men in the course of housekeeping. Evidently the comic card, alluding to his economic distress, was waiting for him when he arrived, not dropped on his body by the shooters, as most accounts state.

Years later, on telephone-surveillance tapes made by the FBI, Murray "The Camel" Humphreys ("Curley" to his friends) talked about the killing of McGurn. He remarked that one of the shooters was McGurn's longtime colleague in crime, Claude Maddox, whose Circus Café on North Avenue had been a meeting place for the "American boys" involved in the Massacre. Maddox, originally from St. Louis and therefore an "American" himself, was one of the few to survive and prosper when Nitti became the de facto leader of the Chicago mob and presumably ordered McGurn's killing.

To make sure McGurn's young half-brother did not exact revenge, he was killed at another pool room a few days later.

After McGurn's death, "Blond Alibi" Louis Rolfe remarried several more times and made her last appearance in Chicago when a gangster museum opened. After that, she returned to California, where she died February 21, 1995, at the age of eighty-eight.

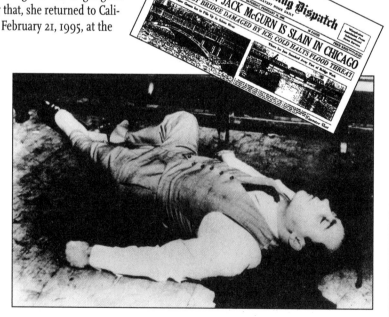

McGurn was killed by gunmen at a bowling alley in 1936, on the seventh anniversary of the Massacre, probably for trying to rejoin the Outfit now controlled by Frank Nitti. Police found a Valentine card (top right) poking fun at his relative poverty.

is attributed erroneously to Elmer Inman, another member of the Terrill Gang.

August 7—Two Coast Guardsmen and a Secret Service agent are killed by rumrunner James Alderman at Government Cut, Florida.

August 8—Frank Badgley, Russell Clark, and Charles Hovious rob the New Castle State Bank in Indianapolis of $3,000.

August 10—Anthony K. Russo and Vincent Spicuzza, St. Louis gangsters attracted by Joe Aiello's $50,000 bounty on Capone, are machine-gunned near the intersection of North and Mannheim in Chicago.

August 18—Using smuggled pistols, Paul Jawarski and John Vassbinder, convicted murderers under sentence of death, escape from the Allegheny County Jail in Pittsburgh, fatally wounding a guard.

August 19—Harvey Bailey and gang rob the Farmers National Bank at Vinton, Iowa, of $15,000.

August 22—Three gunmen rob the University Bank in Austin of $6,600 in cash and Liberty Bonds. The National Guard is mobilized to search for the robbers.

August 23—Sacco and Vanzetti are executed in Massachusetts.

August 29—Fleeing from a Newton, Kansas, robbery, Herman Barker kills Patrolman J. E. Marshall at Wichita. Wounded by other officers, Barker commits suicide. One accomplice, Charles Stalcup, is captured. Another, Porter Meeks, will be slain by Wichita police the next day.

– Carl, Earl, and Bernie Shelton, along with four other men, are indicted for the 1924 Kincaid, Illinois, bank robbery.

September 6—Paul Jawarski and the Flatheads Gang rob the General Baking Co. in Detroit of $4,900.

September 9—In St. Louis, Alphonse Palizzola, leader of the Green Dagoes, is shot to death by four gunmen at the intersection of Tenth and Wash streets. (The Green Dagoes was an Italian gang then competing with the Hogans and the Cuckoos.)

September 13—First theft of seaplane in Boston raises legal issue of whether it is aircraft or vessel.

September 15—Three or four masked men rob the Plano National Bank at Plano, Texas, of $1,091, scattering roofing nails behind their car to discourage pursuit.

September 24—Sam Valente, Cleveland gangster hired by Joe Aiello to kill Capone, is machine-gunned in Chicago.

September 28—Safecracker A. A. (Danny) Daniels is captured by police in Colorado Springs, Colorado, after an abortive burglary and gunfight. Three other gang members escape, but two, Ralph Scott and F. C. Kasiah, are arrested the next day in Pueblo. The fourth member of the gang is identified as Ray Terrill.

October 5—While a large crowd throngs nearby listening to World Series results being broadcast from inning-by-inning radio reports, two bandits hold up the Liberty National Bank at Pawhuska, Oklahoma, for $2,000. Ray Terrill is suspected.

October 6—Cincinnati bootlegger George Remus murders his estranged wife, Imogene. Remus will be acquitted by reason of insanity and briefly institutionalized.

October 8—Philadelphia criminals Ernest Yorkell and Jack Brownstein are found shot to death on the outskirts of Cleveland after their alleged "shakedown" attempts on local bootleggers and gamblers.

October 13—Mobster "Big Joe" Lonardo is shot to death with his brother John in the Porrello brothers' barber shop at Woodland Avenue and East 110th Street in Cleveland.

October 15—Labor racketeer Jacob "Little Augie" Orgen is shot to death and bodyguard Jack "Legs" Diamond wounded at 103 Norfolk Street in New York, allegedly because of a painters' union dispute with rival mobsters Louis "Lepke" Buchalter and Jacob "Gurrah" Shapiro.

October 21—Birger gangster Rado Millich is hanged for the murder of Ward "Casey" Jones at the Williamson County Jail in Marion, Illinois.

November 1—Bandits kill police Captain Charles Arman while robbing the Tippecanoe Loan &

Trust Co. at Lafayette, Indiana. Later attributed to the "Baron" Lamm Gang.

– Two men rob the First National Bank at Texas City, Texas, while most of the employees are out to lunch.

November 3—The First State Bank of Tehuacana, Texas, burglarized only months earlier, is robbed of $2,500 by four gunmen.

November 9—Gangsters cut the throat of singer-comedian Joe E. Lewis, narrowly missing his jugular vein, in his room at the Commonwealth Hotel, 2757 Pine Grove. Lewis manages to alert a bellboy and is rushed to Columbus Memorial Hospital, where his life is saved in a seven-hour operation. Lewis, an entertainer at the McGurn-sponsored Green Mill Gardens, intended to take his act to the Rendezvous, a club owned by the rival "Bugs" Moran gang.

– Four bandits rob the First State Bank at Bangs, Texas, of $7,000, locking seven witnesses in the vault.

November 10—Robert and Frank Aiello, rivals of Al Capone, are shot to death at Springfield, Illinois.

November 20—Bombs damage a restaurant owned by gangster Jack Zuta at 323 North Ashland and the real estate office of John P. Remus at 5315 Fullerton Avenue in Chicago.

November 21—Two gunmen rob the First State Bank at Stonewall, Oklahoma, of $3,000, locking a cashier and a customer in the vault.

November 22—Al Capone is arraigned in Chicago on charges of vagrancy and disorderly conduct. Discharged by Judge William E. Helander.

– Two gunmen rob the Citizens State Bank at Hedrick, Oklahoma, of $1,500, locking bank employees and customers in the vault.

November 23—A bomb damages the headquarters of the Jack Zuta-Billy Skidmore-Barney Bertsche vice combine at 823 West Adams in Chicago.

– Chicago police engage in a running gun battle with gangsters surprised in front of Tony Lombardo's home at 4442 West Washington. Lombardo is the Capone-backed head of the Unione Siciliana. A machine-gun nest is discovered opposite Lombardo's home.

November 25—The apartment of Angelo Genna's widow at 5501 Gladys Avenue in Chicago is bombed.

– Bank robber Dick Gregg escapes from the county jail at Pawhuska, Oklahoma.

November 26—Ray Terrill and Elmer Inman are captured by police in Hot Springs, Arkansas.

November 27—Former judge Quil P. McGhee is convicted in Oklahoma of using a bogus warrant to gain the release of Herman Barker after an arrest in Memphis. McGhee is sentenced to seven years.

November 29—Carmen Ferro, wire wholesaler and alleged bootlegger, is shot to death and his body thrown into a ditch near Bensenville, Illinois.

December 4—John Touhy, brother of Roger and Tommy, is shot to death in a "ride" killing in Chicago.

December 9—The Fleagle Gang robs the First National Bank at Larnard, Kansas, of $23,344.

December 17—The Haymarket Hotel, at 734 West Madison, is damaged in Chicago's 108th bombing of the year.

– Al Capone arrives in Chicago in his armored Cadillac, delayed by his arrest in Joliet where he had gotten off a train from California the previous day.

December 22—The Carney State Bank in Carney, Oklahoma, is robbed for the fourth time in ten years.

December 23—Four bandits, one wearing a Santa Claus suit, rob the First National Bank at Cisco, Texas. In the resulting gun battle, Police Chief G. E. "Bit" Bedford and Officer George Carmichael are slain, along with gang member Louis Davis, and six citizens and two bandits are wounded. Marshall "Santa Claus" Ratliff, Henry Helms, and Robert Hill are captured the next day. The incident is headlined as the "Santa Claus Bank Robbery."

December 28—Vito Giannola, another leader of the Green Dagoes, is machine-gunned to death by rivals at his girlfriend's house in St. Louis.

1928

January 1—Burglars raid thirty-two stores in town of Galesburg, Illinois.

January 3—Bombs damage the Forest Club, an alleged gambling resort at 7214 Circle Avenue, Forest Park, Illinois, and the Newport Hotel, a Zuta-Bertsche-Skidmore gang hangout, at 2351 West Madison in Chicago.

January 5—Capone gangsters shoot up the Aiello Bros. Bakery at 473 West Division in the Capone-Aiello war. "Dago Lawrence" Mangano and Phil D'Andrea, Capone lieutenants, are sought by the police.

January 5–7—Carl, Earl, and Bernie Shelton are tried and convicted at Taylorville, Illinois, of a 1924 Kincaid bank robbery and sentenced to ten years to life. One of the prosecution witnesses is Birger gangster Art Newman. The Sheltons are released on $15,000 bond pending appeal.

January 21—Speakeasy owner Tim Sullivan is fatally shot at his A-1 Club in west Harlem.

January 23—Marshall Ratliff, leader of the "Santa Claus Bank Robbery," is tried for armed robbery at Eastland, Texas. He will be convicted on January 27 and sentenced to ninety-nine years.

— Painters union worker Alexander Berkowitz is killed in a New York restaurant by a gunman outside firing through a window. Attributed to strikebreakers of the "Little Augie gang," now led by the largely unknown Louis "Lepke" Buchalter and Jacob "Gurrah" Shapiro.

January 26—Chicago homes of Dr. William H. Reid, 1257 West Garfield Boulevard, and Charles C. Fitzmorris, 5533 Hyde Park Boulevard, two leaders of the Mayor Thompson cabinet, are bombed by gangsters.

January 31—Watchman H. Bermish is shot to death by a gang attempting to burglarize the Herman Gabbe Fur Co. on West Twenty-second Street in New York.

— Detroit policeman Vivian Welch is murdered by gunmen at St. Aubin and Faber streets in Hamtramck, Michigan, allegedly for "shaking down" speakeasies owned by the Purple Gang.

February 2—New York police raid the Paramount Building at Broadway and Forty-second Street, recover $20,000 worth of stolen furs and arrest "Legs" and Eddie Diamond and fourteen others. "Legs" Diamond is charged with murder but discharged the next day.

February 3—Policemen James Trepanier and Bernard Wynne are shot and wounded while attempting to quell a disturbance at the Cotton Club in Minneapolis. Bootleggers Isadore "Kid Cann" Blumenfeld, Verne Miller, and Bob Kennedy will be indicted for the shooting, but the charges are dropped.

February 5—Al and Ralph Capone are arrested in New Orleans on "suspicion" and then discharged.

February 6—The Harvey Bailey Gang robs the Peoples & Drovers Bank at Washington Court House, Ohio, of $225,000 in cash and bonds.

— Verne Miller suspected of robbing with two other men the Farmers State Bank in Good Thunder, Minnesota, of $5,000.

February 10—Joe Galas, alias John Romano, is found shot to death on a New York street. Attributed to a "bootleggers feud."

February 16—Brooklyn gangster Anthony "Tony the Shoemaker" Paretti dies in the electric chair at Sing Sing.

— Louis "The Wop" Fabrizio is killed by a gunman while changing a tire in New York's East Village.

February 20—Henry Helms, of the "Santa Claus Bank Robbery" gang, is tried for murder at Eastland, Texas. He will be convicted and sentenced to death.

— New York murder of William Doll leads to discovery of an international ring of safecrackers and diamond smugglers.

February 21—A bomb damages the home of Lawrence A. Cuneo, brother-in-law and secretary to State's Attorney Robert E. Crowe, at 2917 Pine Grove in Chicago.

February 25—Armed with Tommyguns, Charles "Limpy" Cleaver and his gang rob a U.S. Mail train of $135,000 at Evergreen Park, Illinois. The machine guns were purchased from the Auto-Ordnance Corp. in New York by a bogus

"Mex-America Corporation." A train was robbed at the same location, for the same amount, by Thomas Holden and Francis Keating in 1926.

March 4—Residence of Melvin Purvis, at 5335 South Mozart in Chicago, is bombed (this was not "G-man" Purvis, of later Dillinger case fame).

– Well-known gambler John Henry "Scarface" Spencer is found dying on a Brooklyn street, bludgeoned with a tire iron after winning $75,000 in a crap game.

March 7—"Machine Gun" Jack McGurn is shot and wounded by the Moran gang's Gusenberg brothers, Pete and Frank, in the cigar store of Chicago's McCormick Hotel at 616 North Rush Street.

March 19—Robert Hill, of the "Santa Claus" gang, is tried at Eastland, Texas, for armed robbery. He will be sentenced to life.

March 21—"Diamond Joe" Esposito, prominent Chicago politician with many underworld connections, is killed by shotgun blasts near his home at 800 South Oakley Boulevard.

March 26—Bombs damage the Chicago home of Senator Charles S. Deneen and that of Circuit Judge John A. Swanson, running against incumbent Robert E. Crowe for the office of state's attorney.

– Marshall Ratliff, leader of the "Santa Claus Bank Robbery," is tried at Abilene, Texas, for the murder of Police Chief "Bit" Bedford. He will be convicted on March 30 and sentenced to death. After being denied a sanity hearing, Ratliff will be returned to Eastland County Jail at Eastland, to be tried on another charge of robbery with firearms (punishable by death in Texas).

April 10—Octavius C. Granady, a black attorney running against Capone ally Morris Eller for boss of Chicago's Twentieth Ward, is machine-gunned to death at Thirteenth Street and Hoyne Avenue.

April 16—Gus Winkeler; Fred Goetz, alias "Shotgun" George Ziegler; Ray "Crane-Neck" Nugent; Bob Carey, alias "Gimpy" Newberry; and Charles J. Fitzgerald kill a policeman in Toledo after robbing an American Express Co. truck of $200,000.

April 17—"Machine Gun" Jack McGurn escapes unharmed when his car is riddled with bullets in a gangland shooting near his mother's home at Morgan and Harrison in Chicago.

April 19—Charlie Birger, cracking jokes on the gallows, is publicly hanged for murder at Benton, Illinois.

April 22—Ben Newmark, former chief investigator for State's Attorney Robert E. Crowe, is killed by a shot through a bedroom window of his bungalow at 7316 Merrill Avenue in Chicago.

May 14—Paul Jawarski and the Flatheads Gang rob a Kresge's variety store in Highland Park, Michigan, of $1,410.

May 20—Patrick "The Link" Mitchell, bootlegger who boasted of being "the last of the Hudson Dusters," is shot dead in a Greenwich Village speakeasy by James "Jimmy the Gin" Russell, who quickly is caught by a policeman in a commandeered taxi. Largely unknown in life, Mitchell receives much posthumous publicity, and his death is theorized as revenge for a liquor hijacking.

May 23—The Jake Fleagle Gang robs the First National Bank at Lamar, Colorado, of $200,000, killing bank president A. N. Parrish and his son John, a cashier. Teller Everett Kessinger is taken hostage and later murdered in Kansas. Dr. William Winneger at Dighton, Kansas, is forced to treat wounded gang member Herbert Royston, then also is murdered.

June 6—Paul Jawarski and the Flatheads Gang rob the *Detroit News* business offices of $15,000, killing one policeman and wounding another.

June 14—During the Republican National Convention, gunmen stage a $19,000 holdup of the Home Trust Co. in Kansas City, Missouri, killing policeman James "Happy" Smith and wounding five others.

June 17—Lower East Side gangster Edward Jerge is shot to death while waiting on a traffic light at a Broadway intersection. Police say Jerge had posed as a federal narcotics agent to shake down a drug dealer for $1,500.

June 21—Cornelius "Neely" Kimes, father of the notorious Kimes brothers, is killed by deputies at

Bowlegs, Oklahoma, allegedly while resisting arrest for bootlegging.

June 26—Gangster and racketeer "Big Tim" Murphy is machine-gunned to death at the front door of his home at 2525 Morse on Chicago's Northwest Side.

July 1—Brooklyn crime boss Frankie Yale is killed in New York's first Tommygun murder. The slaying is attributed to the Capone mob because of disputes over control of the Chicago Unione Siciliana, hijackings of Capone liquor shipments, and the fact that Chicago has become notorious as the world's "machine-gun capital."

– Gunmen wearing handkerchief masks with eyeholes kill gangster Frank Ducallo and wound Vincent Diambolo in a Brooklyn barbershop soon after Yale's murder.

– Benjamin Kanowitz, who claimed to be a businessman and "former bootlegger," is killed by a car bomb in New York.

July 3—James "Hickey" Santore is found shot to death in a Brooklyn gravel pit. Though wearing a silk suit and silk underwear and reported to have been carrying more than $1,000, Santore is described by the police as a small-time bookie.

July 18—A robbery by men on horseback is committed in Parkerford, Pennsylvania.

July 19—Dominick Aiello, uncle of Joe Aiello, is murdered in front of his store at 928 Milton Street in Chicago.

July 24—Anthony Iannello is killed in a drive-by shooting near his Brooklyn home. Iannello reportedly had killed a man in New York nine years earlier, fled to Italy, and only recently had returned to the United States illegally.

September 7—Tony Lombardo, Capone-backed head of the Unione Siciliana, and Joseph Ferraro, his bodyguard, are shot to death at the corner of Madison and Dearborn streets in Chicago.

– "Dago Lawrence" Mangano, a Capone gangster, is charged with bombing the home of Chicago Police Captain Luke Garrick at 1473 Summerdale Avenue.

September 13—Paul Jawarski is wounded and captured after killing one policeman and wounding another in a Cleveland gun battle.

September 14—Paul Jawarski is indicted in Cleveland for the murder of policeman Anthony Wieczorek. Jawarski will not be prosecuted for this murder, however, but later extradited to Pennsylvania, where he is already under a sentence of death.

September 17—Men disguised as armored car guards rob a New York company of $18,000.

September 18—Political boss and slot machine czar Joseph "Mose" Flannery is fatally shot outside a Camden, New Jersey, speakeasy.

September 24—John McDonald discovers the decomposed body of a woman on his farm near Waukegan, Illinois. The woman will be identified later as Ella Blake, formerly the consort of Chicago gangsters, who was last seen leaving a party with Joseph "Hop Toad" Guinta at the Derby Inn at 175th and Halsted outside Chicago on the morning of July 13, 1928.

October 5—Gangster Tony Marlow is fatally shot outside New York's Harding Hotel. "Legs" Diamond is suspected.

October 6—Michael "Mikey Shatz" Abbatemarco, a former lieutenant of Frankie Yale, is found shot to death in his parked car in Brooklyn, supposedly killed for hijacking his own gang's beer trucks to cover his gambling losses.

October 10—Brooklyn Mafia boss Salvatore "Toto" D'Aquila is killed by three gunmen after parking his car at 211 Avenue A, near Thirteenth Street.

October 15—Joey Noe, bootlegging partner of Arthur "Dutch Schultz" Flegenheimer, is mortally wounded outside the Chateau Madrid on West Fifty-fourth Street in New York. Noe will survive for more than a month, dying in the Bellevue Hospital prison ward on November 21. The shooting is attributed to the "Legs" Diamond mob.

– The Illinois Supreme Court sets aside the Shelton Brothers' bank robbery conviction and orders a new trial.

October 18—The Special Intelligence Unit of the Internal Revenue Service opens a file on Al

Rocco Perri: Canada's Al Capone

In history and lore, Prohibition has been considered an exclusively American phenomenon. Few people are aware that the sale of liquor was at one time illegal in some Canadian provinces, and that the struggle for control of the traffic in illicit alcohol was just as treacherous for Canadian criminals as it was for their American counterparts. The province of Ontario, in particular, witnessed high rates of lawlessness and violence during its Prohibition. It was the established home base of a criminal who came to be known as "Canada's Little Caesar." His name was Rocco Perri, and at the height of their influence he and his partner, Bessie Starkman Perri, were grossing more than a million dollars a year from their illegal businesses.

Rocco Perri

At 7 p.m., on Saturday, September 16, 1916, the Ontario Temperance Act became provincial law. Introduced as a wartime measure, the OTA made it illegal to buy or sell liquor and consume it outside one's own home. Personal "cellar supplies" were permitted, but bars and taverns were closed. Alcohol could be sold only for sacramental, industrial, or medicinal uses. No beverages could be sold if their alcoholic content was more than 2.2 percent.

Initially, bootleggers eluded the OTA by skillful manipulation of the Royal Mail. It was legal for any resident of a province covered by Prohibition to order alcohol from a Wet province, so bootleggers served their Ontario customers with stock ordered from Quebec. The following year, however, on December 23, 1917, nationwide Prohibition was declared through the War Measures Act, on the grounds that the use of liquor adversely affected "the vigorous prosecution of the war." The mail-order system was outlawed by the federal government. But on constitutional grounds, any individual city that wished to remain Wet could do so by a majority vote.

The manufacturing of liquor for export to the United States and foreign countries was never outlawed, and bootleggers made up for the loss of the mail-order system by "reimporting." Boatloads of alcohol, cleared by customs officers for export to the States or overseas, would leave the shores of Toronto or Hamilton, turn around somewhere in the middle of Lake Ontario, and return to an isolated inlet on the Ontario shoreline. The liquor then would be unloaded and sold to Canadian customers.

Before the advent of the OTA, the name Rocco Perri was unknown beyond his home city of Hamilton. A native of Calabria, Italy, he had come to New York in 1904 and entered Canada four years later. He and his common-law wife, Bessie Starkman, had first come to the attention of the police in early 1917 when their home at 157 Caroline Street North in Hamilton was reported as a disorderly house. An investigation confirmed the report, and Bessie, the legal owner of the house, was fined $50. They abandoned the business and bought a grocery store at 105 Hess Street South, where Rocco began selling whiskey to customers at fifty cents a glass. Behind the scenes he must have been cultivating special friendships; when he and Bessie were charged again in March 1918 with keeping a bawdyhouse, the case was dismissed.

On New Year's Eve 1919, the alley beside Perri's home was the scene of a murder. Two constables who were patrolling Hess Street heard three shots and saw someone run out of the alley into the night. Investigating, they found a man lying in the snow. Rocco allowed them to carry him into the house, the scene of a noisy party, and the man was identified as Tony Martino. The guests all were questioned, but they volunteered nothing. After Martino died in the hospital the next morning, the police acted on suspicion and raided the house/grocery store. They discovered a vast quantity of liquor and bottling equipment, including counterfeit labels, on the premises and confiscated everything. Rocco was convicted by Magistrate F. Jelfs of breach of the OTA and fined $1,000. Bessie, who held the purse strings in the business, paid the fine.

Retaining the services of attorney Michael J. O'Reilly, Rocco appealed the conviction. A license inspector examined the house, decided the confiscated liquor had been legal "cellar stock," and recommended that the alcohol be returned. Not only did the court accept this opinion, but it ruled also that $700 of the $1,000 fine be returned to Bessie. At the same time, the judge presiding over the inquiry into Tony Martino's death absolved the Perris of any blame in the matter. Their first serious brush with the law saw them emerge relatively unscathed.

In January 1920 the War Measures Act expired, and it became legal again to manufacture liquor for consumption in Wet provinces. At the same time, when total Prohibition became law south of the border in the U.S., Rocco and other Canadian bootleggers saw a brand new source of riches in supplying Americans with Canadian liquor. Prohibition enforcement officials in the States also were aware of this potential, and a request was made to the RCMP to keep Canadian alcohol at home. In July 1920 RCMP officials stated to the *New York Times*, "It is really for the American authorities to see that liquor does not cross the border."

By now Rocco and Bessie Perri had become influential names in Canadian rum-running, and their gang was a force to be reckoned with. Bessie handled the cash, paying for shipments of alcohol intended for resale at a greater price and managing the profits that came in daily. Rocco made the deals with American buyers and established contacts among the other high-level bootleg mobs. Among these contacts were the Scaroni mob in Brantford, led by Domenic Scaroni, who in police reports has been named Ontario's first Godfather, and the Serianni family in Niagara Falls, New York

In November 1921 Rocco made an official application for Canadian citizenship. He appeared before Judge C. G. Snider for naturalization, and when asked if he had ever been charged with any offense, answered that on a few occasions he had been fined for speeding. The application was approved, but when mention of it appeared in the *Hamilton Herald*, two protest letters were mailed to the secretary of state in Ottawa. One was sent by Mrs. T. D. McIlroy, governor of the Citizenship Committee of the Local Council of Women, who reported Rocco's 1919 conviction under the OTA. The other letter came from Lieutenant Colonel Charles McCullough, honorary president of the Association of Canadian Clubs. He advised Thomas Mulvey, undersecretary of state, to reject Rocco's application and contact Hamilton Police Chief William Whatley for details about his criminal undertakings.

Under Whatley's approval, four Hamilton detectives who were familiar with Rocco all sent letters to Mulvey recommending that he be barred from citizenship. As a result, the undersecretary wrote to him on April 12, 1922, "I regret to inform you that the Secretary of State in his discretion has decided not to grant your application."

The following May, Rocco, through his lawyer Charles Bell, appealed the rejection. Bell wrote a letter to Thomas J. Stewart, onetime mayor of Hamilton and at the time a member of parliament for Hamilton West, asking him to intercede in the matter. He outlined Rocco's versions of the disorderly house charge of 1917 and the OTA conviction of 1919, including affidavits that Rocco himself had written, and noted, "In connection with the disorderly house charge and the OTA charge, Perry might well have been given the benefit of the doubt. . . . I feel that if this is all that has come up about Rocco Perri in 15 years' residence in this country, he is better than the average foreign resident and may fairly be granted naturalization."

At the bottom of the letter, Bell added one phrase whose true meaning can only be guessed at: "If his naturalization application is granted, I am sure that we can count on him in times to come."

Perhaps they were hoping that Perri's influence over the Italian colonies in the towns of southern Ontario could be used to help the cause of the Conservative Party (of which Bell and Stewart were members) in future elections. At any rate, Mulvey rejected the appeal, and Rocco's citizenship plans had to be shelved.

When Prohibition became law in the United States in 1920, Ontario bootleggers who had previously tolerated each other suddenly decided to eliminate competitors. Supremacy in the alcohol trade with the U.S. became their No. 1 objective, and what police historians call "The Niagara Bootleg War" erupted. The first victim was a farmer, Thomas Matthews, who had business dealings with rumrunners. His body washed up on a beach near Stoney Creek, Ontario, in September 1920. The cause of death was a knife thrust under the left arm, and the circumstances of his murder were a good indication of the nature of future casualties. All the later victims would die in a manner at least as violent.

Blows at Rocco Perri and his allies, the Scaroni family in Brantford, were struck by the Stefano Magaddino mob from Buffalo, New York. They already dominated the bootleg trade in the Niagara region, and police were certain that Magaddino intended to seize control of the Ontario network. One of the more important casualties was James Saunder, whose body was found outside Welland in June 1921. He had formerly worked for Rocco as a chauffeur and was serving Domenic Scaroni in a similar capacity at the time of his murder.

On May 10, 1922, Rocco and Domenic Scaroni attended a mob banquet at a saloon in Niagara Falls, New York. At 11:30 p.m. the same evening, a bus driver found Scaroni's body on nearby Lewiston Hill. He had been shot three times in the head and evidently tossed from a car. His murder granted the title of Calabrian mob boss to Rocco, who previously had been only second to him in terms of wealth and underworld influence.

Two more Scaroni men, Jimmy Loria and Tony Leale, were shot to death during the next four weeks. On June 15, Sam Scaroni, brother-in-law to Domenic, and a business partner were shot at from a passing car but escaped injury. A witness noted the license plate number of the vehicle. Its ownership was traced to Charlie Bordonaro, a Perri henchman, but there is no record of any subsequent police action.

The fall of the Scaroni family was complete when, on September 5, the body of Joe Scaroni, the gang enforcer, was found at the bottom of the Weiland Canal. Only the day before, he had met with Rocco and two Perri associates, Charlie Bordonaro and John Trott, and informed them of his intention to avenge Domenic's death.

Suspicion fell on Rocco. With the exception of the Magaddino mob, his gang would have benefited the most from the removal of the Scaroni. He had been seen with both Domenic and Joe only hours before their murders, and Charlie Bordonaro, who apparently had been involved in the shooting attempt on Sam Scaroni, had been present during the meeting with Joe. But concrete proof was lacking, and Rocco proceeded to absorb the Scaroni territories and businesses as his own. He continued to struggle intermittently with Magaddino, only now with the Seriannis as his sale allies.

It was through a conflict with the Perri gang that next autumn that the police were made aware of the technical difficulties of enforcing the OTA. On the evening of October 5, 1922, the Pape Avenue police station was informed by a phone call that something was "going on" at the foot of Leslie Street, which ended by the waterfront. Patrol Sgt. William Kerr and Constables William Mitchell, James Rooney, and George Fraser recognized the spot as a favorite unloading site for bootleggers and drove to the scene in a police vehicle. At the sight of the flashing lights, several of the rumrunners ducked into the bushes while a boat, the *Hattie C*, slid back into the water. The police officers seized the men who had been hiding, and Kerr shouted to those on board the boat, "Stop your engines or I will sink you!"

He drew his pistol, fired one shot in the air and three at the boat. When his warning appeared to have been unheeded, he called out the order to sink the vessel. The other officers opened fire. Rocco, who was one of the prisoners taken, yelled something in Italian toward the boat and shouted to the police, "Don't shoot—there are people on that boat!" The *Hattie C* drifted to shore, and Constable Mitchell boarded her. In the cabin he found two men crouched over a third with a bullet wound in the right side of the chest. Mitchell shouted for an ambulance, but by the time it arrived, it was too late. John Gogo, age twenty-four, had died.

The arrested rumrunners, including Rocco, appeared in police court the next morning on charges of bootlegging. They pleaded not guilty, and bail was set at $3,000 each. Bessie arrived at once to bail out Rocco. Chief Coroner George Graham and Chief Crown Attorney Eric Armour soon decided that an inquest into Gogo's death was necessary, as they wondered whether the police were justified in using firearms to enforce the OTA. At the inquest, Armour put Sgt. Kerr through a relentless series of questions, reminding him that revolvers were "provided for police on night duty and were not to be used unless in defence of life or some other emergency." Kerr replied that he had felt justified in drawing his weapon to prevent an escape.

The jury came back with the verdict that Gogo died from a bullet wound as a result of police use of firearms in enforcing the OTA. They stated, "The OTA being a provincial law and its breach not a criminal offence, the jury find that the police officers . . . made use of them (revolvers) without justification."

On November 2, the grand jury, after listening to the evidence, came back with a true bill charging Sgt. Kerr and Constables Mitchell, Rooney, and Fraser with manslaughter. Bail was set at $3,000 each and was put up by a former mayor of Toronto, Robert Fleming, who firmly supported the OTA and was appalled at the charges against the police.

The bootleggers themselves came to trial on November 14, and the outcome was stunning, in view of the judgments made earlier against the four policemen. Sidney Gogo, owner of the *Hattie C*, and Frank DiPietro, a gang member whose truck had been used to load liquor from the boat, were found guilty of breaching the OTA and fined $1,000 each. The case against Rocco and the others was dismissed. The police officers also had the charges against them dropped in February 1924, after two trials had ended in deadlocked juries. Attorney General William Nickle stated that at least the point had been made: firearms were not permitted as tools of enforcement of the OTA.

The name of the Perri gang was to blacken the police reputation once more, this time shortly after the death of Hamilton Police Chief William Whatley in April 1924. The police department already was being investigated for corruption. Few records of the investigation still exist, so it is impossible to determine many of the specific reasons for the suspicion. One report, filed by a Pinkerton detective in the employ of the Ontario Provincial Police, has managed to survive and sheds some light on the matter. The report was based on a conversation with Mildred Sterling, an independent Hamilton bootlegger.

"Why, it was not anything to see Chief Whatley and his wife in Rocco Perri's car. I remember very well one occasion when Perri stopped at a gas station with his car and Perri made an effort to pay for the gas and Chief Whatley interfered and said to the man at the station, 'Never mind, just charge that to me.' That expense was put on the books and paid by the people of Hamilton instead of Whatley. . . . If the big fellows wanted to ruin Perri, they could do it very easily, but they are afraid to open up because Perri has too much on them. . . ."

In November 1924 Rocco gave an interview to the *Toronto Star* in which he freely admitted to being a bootlegger, one who operated on an extremely high level. Predictably, his brashness angered the temperance and religious communities in Ontario, and there were angry mutterings that he should be deported immediately. The *Hamilton Herald* contacted Bessie, who confirmed that Rocco had been denied citizenship. She explained that police officials, including Whatley, had reported to the secretary of state that Rocco's application should be denied.

This raises an important question: the information sent to Ottawa had been classified "confidential." So how had Bessie acquired knowledge of it? Clearly, there was leak within the Hamilton police department.

In November 1926, after the police scandal had died down, the Royal Commission on Customs and Excise began hearings in Ottawa. Its purpose was to investigate corruption among customs officials and charges that liquor was being shipped into Canada from St. Pierre et Miquelon without the payment of proper taxes, and to determine whether liquor had been sold for consumption in Ontario in violation of the OTA. Representatives of major breweries and distilleries, such as Gooderham & Worts, were questioned about their export practices and whether they had ever had dealings with Ontario bootleggers such as Rocco and Bessie Perri. Any knowledge of the Perris was denied by every representative who took the stand.

On November 18 Bessie Perri, who had been subpoenaed before to the hearings, took the stand. She said that Rocco had gone to Ottawa ten days before, and at present she did not know where he could be found. R. L. Calder, K.C., questioned her extensively about telephone calls that had been made daily from the Perri mansion at 166 Bay Street South to the Gooderham &

Worts distillery in Toronto. She denied making them herself and suggested that Rocco's friends, some of whom were American, could have used her telephone to order shipments of liquor to be sent to their home addresses. No satisfaction could be gotten from her as a witness, and at one point in the questioning, Calder declared in frustration, "Mrs. Perri . . . you are the most incurious woman I have ever met."

On April 1, Rocco was cornered behind his house by two Hamilton cops and served a subpoena to appear at the hearings on April 4. He proved to be even more difficult as a witness than Bessie. He claimed that the interview he had given to the *Toronto Star* had been a pack of lies—"A little story to get them away from my door," that he sold macaroni for a living, and that his friends, such as Joe Penn from Wilson, New York (a name given to a number of distilleries when orders were made by telephone from the Perri mansion), were in the alcohol business. These men, he explained, were frequent guests at his home. The prosecutors did not accept his explanations and tried to catch him in a lie, but he was frustratingly evasive. Below is a sample exchange from the hearings transcript:

ROWELL, R. C.: "How much did you get a case?"

PERRI: "A case for what?"

ROWELL: "For the goods ordered over the phone."

PERRI: "I never ordered no stuff over the phone."

ROWELL: "How much were you paid?"

PERRI: "All I pay or they pay me?"

ROWELL (uncertainly): "They pay you?"

PERRI: "Who?"

ROWELL: "Penn."

PERRI: "Penn pay me?"

ROWELL: "Yes."

PERRI: "What for?"

It had been determined earlier that any money made by the Perris, legitimate or otherwise, had been deposited in banks under Bessie's name. An auditor uncovered eight of her accounts and testified that as of March 1927 there was an amount of $265,000 in her Hamilton accounts alone, a far cry from the $800 that she had earlier estimated herself to be worth.

At the conclusion of the hearings in Hamilton in May 1927, the chairman, Chief Justice Brown, issued warrants for the arrest of Rocco and Bessie Perri on charges of perjury. But they were nowhere to be found; they had fled Hamilton after Rocco had finished testifying. They eventually were located in the U.S. and persuaded to return to Canada to testify in court against Gooderham & Worts distillery, which had failed to pay taxes on unexported liquor. In exchange for their testimony at the December 1927 trial, which would prove that large amounts of liquor had been sold for Canadian consumption and not exported as the company claimed, the Crown promised the Perris that the perjury charges would be reduced or possibly dropped. Rocco and Bessie cooperated fully, admitting to their roles as bootleggers. Bessie explained that she had placed the orders for liquor with the company and overseen all financial transactions. The government won its case, and the Crown kept its promise to the star witnesses; Rocco was sentenced to six months at the Ontario Reformatory at Guelph on one count of perjury instead of the original seven, and the charges against Bessie were dropped. She served no time.

The RCMP had long suspected that the Perris were behind the epidemic of drug use that had reached immense proportions in Ontario by the late twenties. In a memo dated March 23, 1926, Corporal Webster of the Hamilton RCMP wrote, "This man [Rocco Perri] is the biggest liquor smuggler in this district and at the same time is believed to be concerned in the smuggling of narcotic drugs, although there is no direct evidence of this."

The RCMP was determined to gather evidence. Sergeant Frank Zaneth, a legend among the Mounties for his successes in undercover work and sharp eye for incriminating details, was assigned the job of gathering proof that could link the Perri mob with drug activities in Hamilton and Toronto. His first raid was on the home of Toronto dealer Nick Italiano on Dundas Street on June 21, 1929. The police discovered and seized on the premises a quantity of drugs with a street value of $3,500. Suddenly, while the raiders were in the process of questioning Italiano and searching the house, Bessie Perri walked in. She insisted that she was only making a social call, but a search of her handbag revealed hundreds of dollars. The police had no evidence to charge her, but Zaneth was positive that she had come to collect a fresh supply of drugs for her Hamilton contacts. Nick's brother Ned later testified that Bessie had come to give him a loan on some building property. Nick was sentenced to six months in jail and fined $300 for drug possession.

The attempt by the police to link the Perri gang with drug trafficking proved futile. In July 1929 Sergeant Zaneth assumed the alias of Arthur Anderson, henchman of Chicago gangster George "Bugs" Moran, and spread the word around the Ontario underworld that he was a drug dealer seeking a Canadian source of morphine. He was repeatedly tested by cautious Perri dealers, and it was not until September that he was granted an audience with a noncommittal Bessie at a roadhouse on the outskirts of Toronto.

Unfortunately, the trial of Ned Italiano began on September 23, and as the officer who had engineered the raid on the Dundas Street house, Zaneth was required to testify on behalf of the Crown. His cover was exposed, and the infiltration effort had to be abandoned. In his last report to his supervisor, Superintendent Jennings of the RCMP "O" Division, Zaneth made the following conclusions about those who directed the flow of narcotics in Ontario: "There is no doubt this is the cleverest gang of drug runners in the country. Every one of these men used to be employed by Rocco Perri in rum-running, and when the liquor racket was exhausted they turned to narcotic drugs. I may also say that Mrs. Perri is the brains of the whole gang and nothing is being done without her consent."

The drug business provided Rocco and Bessie Perri with no shortage of wealth; they maintained a nineteen-room mansion at 166 Bay Street South in Hamilton, owned three expensive cars, and paid the salaries of numerous gang members. All attempts by the RCMP to shake them from their perch had failed. It appeared as if their lives were charmed.

Then, in August 1930, tragedy struck. Rocco and Bessie left their home early on the morning of August 13, 1930, and did not return until close to 11:30 p.m. They drove into their backyard garage, which led to the kitchen of the house by way of a small door. Rocco parked their Marmon coupe next to their sixteen-foot-long Marmon limousine, and went to close the garage doors while Bessie walked to the kitchen door. Suddenly, gunfire erupted from behind the limousine, and Rocco fled the garage. He ran out of the alley behind the mansion and bumped into a neighbor, David Robbins, who was walking his dog along Duke Street. Robbins, who later described Perri to be in "a state of hysterics," accompanied him to the mansion, where they entered the garage through the kitchen door. They found Bessie's body lying a few feet from the kitchen steps, covered with blood. She had been hit at close range by two shotgun blasts. Robbins had to call the police; Rocco already had started to lapse into shock.

The murder made the front page of the August 14 editions of the *Globe and Mail, Toronto Star, Hamilton Herald,* and other major newspapers across Canada. The press hinted that the Perris, because of their wealth, might have been the target of extortionists and that Bessie, the keeper of the purse, had been shot when she refused to pay them. Eight months later, on March 25, 1931, Sgt. Zaneth offered a possible explanation for the murder in a memo to Jennings. He contended that he had received this information from a longtime acquaintance of the Perris:

> Some time previous to Mrs. Perri being killed, she had purchased a large amount of narcotic drugs from a gang operating from Rochester N.Y., U.S.A., with the understanding that she would pay immediately after delivery was made.
>
> According to my informant, Mrs. Perri refused to pay this debt and challenged the trafficker to go to the law if he wanted his money. On the night before the tragedy took place, three men called on Mr. and Mrs. Perri at 166 Bay Street South, Hamilton, and demanded payment for the drugs. There a heated argument took place. Rocco Perri insisted that Bessie pay for the drugs but Mrs. Perri refused to do so and ordered the men out of the house. The next evening Mrs. Rocco Perri was shot to death while leaving her garage. . . .

That is conceivable, as Bessie was notorious for her arrogance and inclination to cancel financial deals on a moment's notice, with little concern for anyone who might be left in the lurch. In the past she had frequently refused financial aid to family members of her own hoods who had been jailed or fined and left destitute. If she was in any way dissatisfied with the stock sent by the Rochester mob mentioned in Zaneth's memo, she would have thought little of withholding payment.

Rocco appeared to be badly shaken by the close brush with death and catatonic with grief over Bessie's loss. Everyone interviewed by the police had to agree that he had

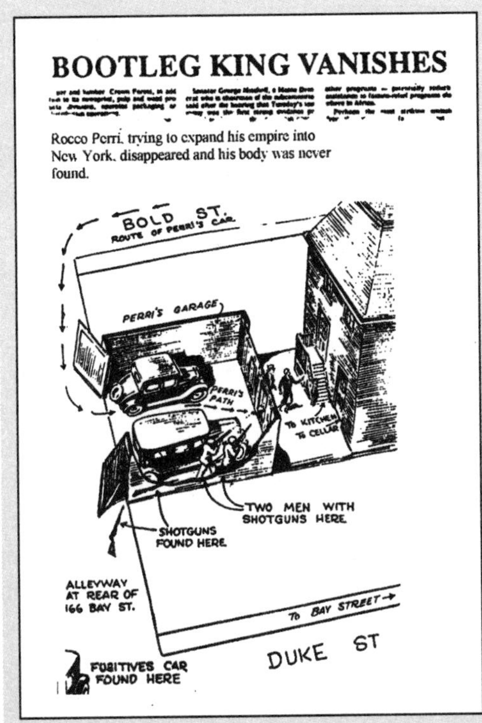

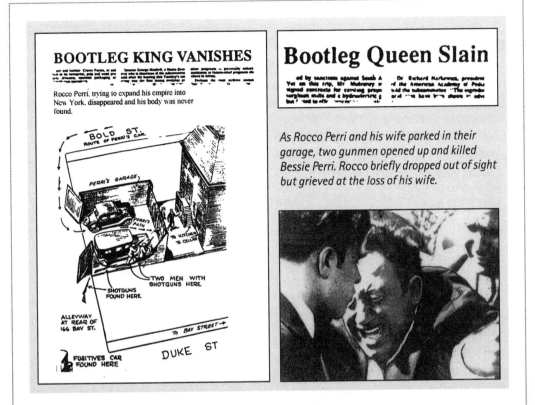

Rocco Perri, trying to expand his empire into New York, disappeared and his body was never found.

Bootleg Queen Slain

As Rocco Perri and his wife parked in their garage, two gunmen opened up and killed Bessie Perri. Rocco briefly dropped out of sight but grieved at the loss of his wife.

depended heavily on her, and it was predicted that without her the Perri mob would collapse. Rocco shook off his depression long enough to offer a $5,000 reward for information leading to the apprehension of the killers, but for the most part he remained subdued and silent. Some people interpreted his lethargy as a refusal to assist the police in the murder investigation, and the widow of one Perri lieutenant even went so far as to send a letter to the RCMP stating, "Rocco Perri murdered his wife for her money and did a good job."

The murder of Bessie Perri ultimately was marked unsolved. But she had posthumously drawn public attention to the fact that gangsterism and organized crime were not confined to the United States. Canada had her own share of these social evils, and the flood of newspaper editorials that followed Bessie's funeral sought to educate the public about the reality of such myth-like figures as the millionaire bootlegger and the rings of dope smugglers.

The history of the old Perri mob ends with the slaying of Bessie. Without her financial talents, Rocco sank deeper into criminal oblivion and actually was sued by two former henchmen for a total of $10,000. He was on the verge of being written off as a failure by enemies who were waiting to seize his businesses when his lucky streak found him again in the person of Annie Newman.

Like Bessie, she was a Polish Jew who had immigrated to Canada while young and had a talent for bookkeeping and organizing. How and where she and Rocco Perri met is not known, but they first appeared together as "business partners" in 1933. One of their first criminal ventures was to establish contacts among crooked customs officials who, for a price, would allow carloads of Perri liquor to go from Canada to the U.S., and vice versa, without paying the appropriate tax.

By 1933 Prohibition had been repealed in the U.S., and Canadians were having their liquor rationed to them by government liquor stores. Rocco and Annie did a profitable business supplying the Canadian people with as much alcohol as they were willing to pay for. The RCMP, after a period of surveillance over the activities of Rocco and Annie, arrested them in 1939 on charges of bribery and conspiracy to breach the Customs Act. The chief Crown witness was David Armaly, one of the dishonest customs officials in Annie's employ, who had agreed to turn King's Evidence in exchange for freedom from prosecution. It appeared to be an airtight case, but the mob attorneys, Joseph Bullen and Paul Martin, completely demolished Armaly on the witness stand. By the end of the eight-day trial, the Crown's case had collapsed, and Rocco and Annie were acquitted by the jury. David Armaly was tried later for fraud based on testimony during the trial.

It was to be Rocco Perri's last victory over the law. On June 10, 1940, Mussolini declared war on England and the RCMP was authorized to arrest any Italians in Canada who might harbor pro-Fascist sympathies and place them in internment camps. Rocco was at the top of the list of suspects and was taken into custody that same day. Almost immediately he was imprisoned at Camp Petawawa under the War Measures Act. Annie Newman turned to every political connection that she had at her disposal, but she was powerless against the federal government.

After realizing that freeing Rocco was beyond her capability, she channeled her energy into a money-making scheme. In partnership with Sidney Faibish, a Toronto optometrist, she organized a gold-smuggling ring that funneled gold bullion from the mines of Timmins, Ontario, to jewelers in New York City. The American and Canadian police worked together to trap the smugglers. In October 1941 police investigators seized a shipment of gold nuggets that was being smuggled across the Peace Bridge. The raid led to charges being laid against Annie Newman, Sidney Faibish, and a group of conspirators. At the end of a monthlong trial, a guilty verdict was rendered against the entire gang. Annie was sentenced to three years in Kingston Penitentiary and ordered to pay a $5,000 fine.

She was still in prison when Rocco was released from the internment camp on October 10, 1943. The Magaddino mob, his longstanding foes, had almost succeeded in absorbing his territory during his absence, and he was determined to regain his former power. He moved into the home of his cousin, Joe Serge, at 49 Murray Street East in Hamilton, and began to formulate plans to move against the Buffalo syndicate. At 10:30 a.m. on April 23, 1944, he told Serge that he was going out for a stroll, which was his habit whenever he needed to think.

Rocco never returned. Two days later, his cousin contacted Hamilton police and reported him missing, but it clearly was too late. A body was never found to prove conclusively that he had been murdered, but within the next eighteen months several ranking members of the Perri gang were gunned down, paving the way for Stefano Magaddino to seize control of the illicit businesses in southern Ontario. This chain of events makes it a moral certainty that Rocco Perri had been picked up by Buffalo gunmen during his walk that fateful morning, and Canadians today are more apt to recognize the names of Al Capone or "Lucky" Luciano than those of Rocco Perri, Bessie Starkman-Perri, or Annie Newman. They should be considered secondary to Capone only in personal notoriety, for they were the pioneers of modern Canadian law-breaking and established guidelines and practices that are imitated by organized crime to this day.

—*Rose Keefe*

Capone for possible violations of the income tax laws.

October 25—The Bailey gang robs the Whitney Loan & Trust Co. in Atlantic, Iowa, of $49,000.

– Three men rob the Security Savings Bank at Albert City, Iowa, of $4,500.

November 4—Gambler Arnold Rothstein is fatally shot in Manhattan's Park Central Hotel. Gambler George "Hump" McManus is sought as a suspect.

November 5—Eddie Diamond, brother of Jack "Legs" Diamond, escapes unharmed when his car is riddled by machine-gun fire on a Denver street. Denver police arrest Eugene Moran and James Piteo, former bodyguards of Arnold Rothstein, and charge them with assault. Moran and Piteo are released on $15,000 bond and skip town. Frank "Blubber" Devlin also is a fugitive on this charge.

November 7—Herbert Hoover is elected president of the United States.

November 16—John G. Clay, secretary of the Laundry and Dyehouse Chauffeurs Union, is shot dead in his office at 29 South Ashland Avenue in Chicago. Attributed to Capone-Moran labor rackets war.

– Poultry racketeer Charlie Herbert is wounded and his bodyguard, Isadore "Fatty" Walker, is killed by an unknown gunman at Berger's Restaurant, 20 Avenue C in New York.

November 17—Charles "Lucky" Luciano, George Uffner and Thomas "Fats" Walsh are charged with robbery by New York police, questioned about the Rothstein murder, and released.

November 27—George McManus surrenders to New York police.

December 1—State of Texas reports only three bank robberies for the year and all robbers captured.

December 4—George McManus is indicted for the Rothstein murder. McManus will be acquitted, and the slaying will be attributed to either Rothstein's lieutenant, "Legs" Diamond, or to "Dutch" Schultz, in retribution for the murder of Joey Noe.

– St. Paul crime boss "Dapper Dan" Hogan is killed by a car bomb outside his home at 1607 West Seventh Street.

December 5—Twenty-three Sicilian gangsters, from New York, Chicago, Buffalo, Tampa, Detroit, St. Louis, and Newark are arrested while meeting at the Statler Hotel in Cleveland. Newspapers describe the event as a meeting of the "Grand Council" of the Mafia.

December 6—On the eve of testifying before a

federal grand jury investigating local bootlegging, South Chicago Heights Police Chief Leroy Gilbert is assassinated by shotgun blasts fired through the window of his home. The Chicago Heights mob is suspected.

December 8—Federal agents seize millions of dollars worth of narcotics in three raids in New York City, Buffalo, and Chicago, based on information contained in the records of the late Arnold Rothstein, whom U.S. Attorney Charles H. Tuttle considers to have been the country's major source for illegal drugs.

December 17—The Harvey Bailey Gang robs the Sturgis National Bank at Sturgis, Michigan, of $80,000.

December 18—Federal agents seize a ton of narcotics on a Jersey City pier.

December 20—The Bailey Gang robs the First National Bank at Clinton, Indiana, of $40,000 in cash and bonds.

December 31—Hugh "Stubby" McGovern and William "Gunner" McPadden, of the Danny Stanton mob, are shot to death at the Granada Café at 6800 Cottage Grove Avenue, Chicago gangland's last murder victims of the year.

— George Maloney of the "Bubs" Quinlan mob, in a rare conviction, is sentenced to fourteen years.

1929

January 6—Chicago and Cook County officers stage raids in Chicago Heights, arresting twenty-four people and uncovering ledgers detailing bootlegging and gambling operations involving Al Capone.

January 8—Pasqualino Lolordo, successor to Tony Lombardo as Chicago head of the Unione Siciliana, is shot to death in his home at 1921 West North Avenue. Attributed to the combined Moran-Aiello gangs.

January 17—Casimo Paladino is blasted with a shotgun in his apartment in New York's Little Italy, then stumbles outside to die in the street. Police find the murder weapon in the tenement's backyard, along with eighteen barrels of wine, and list the crime as a bootlegging murder.

January 21—A Bronx garage is held up twice in a half hour. The first robbers get $300, leaving none for the second robbers.

— Paul Jawarski dies in the electric chair in Rockview state penitentiary at Bellefonte, Pennsylvania.

February 14—The St. Valentine's Day Massacre. Six members of the "Bugs" Moran gang and a visiting optometrist are mowed down by Capone machine-gunners, some disguised as policemen, in the S.M.C. Cartage Co. garage at 2122 North Clark Street in Chicago. The victims are Frank and Peter Gusenberg, James Clark, Adam Heyer, John May, Albert Weinshank, and Dr. Reinhart Schwimmer (born Reinhardt but who later dropped the "d").

February 15—Major Frederick D. Silloway, chief Prohibition agent in Chicago, publicly accuses Chicago police of committing the St. Valentine's Day killings.

— Cook County State's Attorney John A. Swanson announces a $25,000 reward for information leading to the capture of those responsible for the Massacre.

February 17—The Fleagle Gang robs a Haines, Oregon, bank of $2,060.

February 18—The Cook County Board of Commissioners votes not to approve Swanson's $25,000 reward offer.

February 22—Called to a burning garage at 1723 North Wood Street, Chicago firemen discover the burned and partially dismantled remains of a 1927 Cadillac touring car, along with a police siren and other evidence suggesting this was a car used by the St. Valentine's Day killers of the Moran gang.

— Six suspects are arrested and warrants are issued for seventeen more, including Capone gangsters Claude "Screwy" Maddox and Anthony "Tough Tony" Capezio.

— Two safes in Camillus, New York, are cracked by a "yegg" who phones police to brag of his feat.

February 27—The dynamited remains of another car, a 1926 Peerless, are discovered in the Chicago suburb of Maywood, along with another police siren, police-style license plates, two spent shotgun shells and a notebook belonging to

St. Valentine's Day Massacre victim Albert Weinshank, indicating the killers used two cars.

– Al Capone attends the heavyweight championship fight between Jack Sharkey and "Young" Stribling at Flamingo Park in Miami Beach as the guest of Jack Dempsey.

March 5—Frank "Blubber" Devlin, wanted for the Denver machine-gun attack on Eddie Diamond, is found shot to death on a farm near Somerville, New Jersey. "Legs" Diamond is suspected.

March 6—Thomas "Fats" Walsh, former henchman of Arnold Rothstein, is shot to death at the Biltmore Hotel in Miami.

March 7—"Pretty Boy" Floyd is released from the state prison at Jefferson City, Missouri.

March 9—"Pretty Boy" Floyd is arrested by police of Kansas City, Missouri, for "investigation."

March 20—Dick Gregg robs the Wynona National Bank in Wynona, Oklahoma.

October 24, 1931 Liberty

The Twilight of the GANGSTER

How Much Longer Are We Going to Put Up with Him?

By EDWARD DOHERTY

Picture by W. D. Stevens

(Reading time: 19 minutes 25 seconds.)

PART ONE - "THEY ONLY KILL EACH OTHER"

WE, the people of the United States, are a queer lot—perhaps the queerest in the world. We're a sluggish, blind, and lazy lot. We're as paradoxical as an Irish bull. But we have our moments! We call America the Cradle of Liberty, and vote it dry. We boast of our courage, and let criminals run us and rob us and kill us. We boast of our democracy. We high-hat such kingdoms as Italy, and most of us think Benito Mussolini is a despot. Italy has Fascism. But we have feudalism.

We've created a host of robber barons in the last [illegible] years. We've let them amass enormous riches. We've let them pillage and slay. We've pampered and petted them. We've made them idols. We've cheered Alphonse "Scarface" Capone every time he was acquitted. We've cried "Persecution!" every time he went on trial. We've cheered Jack "Legs" Diamond when he was acquitted of burning the feet of a man he was charged with kidnaping.

We were glad to see these piratical figures get away with it. But we were well fed then. America, a full-stomached America, could laugh at the gunmen and their quaint and picturesque murders, could be

[CONTINUED ON NEXT PAGE]

When police announced a crackdown on bootleggers and racketeers, Liberty *magazine, a little prematurely, published articles in 1931 predicting the end of the gangster era.*

April 12—Five robbers hold up the Irvington, New Jersey, Smelting & Refining Co. for $18,000 in bar gold.

– Bootleggers George Clifford and Michael Reilly are found shot to death at the rear of Al Capone's Hawthorne Hotel in Cicero, Illinois.

April 17—Five men carrying machine guns make off with the payroll of New York's Bell Telephone Laboratories.

April 24—Dr. Frank L. Brady, a dentist said to be friendly with gangsters, is murdered by two gunmen in his office at 2059 West Madison Street in Chicago. Narcotics connection suspected.

April 26—Drug dealer Harry Gordon is found shot to death on the East Chester Bay shore in the Bronx. With an arrest record dating to 1903, Gordon occasionally has been confused with Irving "Waxey Gordon" Wexler. Shot four times, but a fifth bullet, estimated by police to be at least five years old, is found in Gordon's hip.

May 1—After a nine-month trial, 150 alleged Mafia members are convicted and imprisoned in Sicily. Many Italian fugitives have fled to the United States since the beginning of Mussolini's anti-Mafia drive in 1922.

— The *New York Times* reports a week free of homicides as of April 27, something rarely if ever seen by New Yorkers.

May 6—Police in Kansas City, Kansas, arrest "Pretty Boy" Floyd for vagrancy and suspicion of highway robbery. He is released the next day.

May 9—John Scalise, Albert Anselmi, and Joseph "Hop Toad" Guinta are found murdered near Hammond, Indiana. Police first attribute the slayings to the Moran-Aiello gang, in revenge for the St. Valentine's Day killings, but informants report that the three were beaten and shot to death at a gang dinner party, supposedly by Al Capone himself, after he learned they were plotting to betray him.

— Police in Pueblo, Colorado, arrest "Pretty Boy" Floyd for vagrancy. He is fined $50 and sentenced to sixty days in jail.

May 13–15—Midwestern and East Coast mobsters meet at the President Hotel in Atlantic City to adopt a system for peacefully arbitrating their disputes. This is considered by some as the official beginning of a national crime syndicate. Delegates include Al Capone, Frank Nitti, Jake "Greasy Thumb" Guzik, Frank McErlane, and "Polack Joe" Saltis of Chicago; Johnny Torrio, Charles "Lucky" Luciano, Frank Costello, "Dutch" Schultz, Meyer Lansky, Joe Adonis, Owney "The Killer" Madden, Larry Fay, and Frank Erickson of New York; Joe Bernstein from the Detroit Purple Gang; John Lazia and Solly "Cutcher-Head-Off" Weissman of Kansas City; Max "Boo Boo" Hoff and Harry "Nig Rosen" Stromberg of Philadelphia; Abner "Longy" Zwillman of Newark; Moe Dalitz, Louis Rothkopf, and Chuck Polizzi of Cleveland; and Atlantic City political boss Enoch "Nucky" Johnson.

May 15—Detective Raymond Martin of the Chicago Police Department is killed by gangsters on Laramie Avenue while acting as a decoy in a $50,000 kidnapping plot. He was impersonating Moses L. Blumenthal, who was to pay a $10,000 ransom for his brother Philip, a former bootlegger.

May 16—Returning from the Atlantic City meeting, Al Capone and bodyguard Frank Rio are arrested in Philadelphia on gun-carrying charges. The arrest probably is prearranged with detective friends of Capone, but they are sentenced the next day to a year in prison, and Chicago applauds such "swift justice."

May 18—Members of Detroit's Purple Gang are arrested on charges of protecting narcotics dealers.

May 22—Chicago police detective Joseph Sullivan, looking for the killers of Detective Raymond Martin, is shot to death in "Red" Bolton's saloon at 1610 Polk Street.

May 24—Messenger car for American First National Bank of Oklahoma City held up for $75,000 by Russell "Slim Gray" Gibson, James "Cowboy" Hayes, and Neal Merritt. Gibson will be arrested but escapes from the county jail in Oklahoma City.

June 11—Salvatore "Black Sam" Todaro, successor to "Big Joe" Lonardo, is shot to death at Woodland Avenue and East 110th Street in Cleveland. Joe Porrello succeeds to leadership of the local Italian crime family.

June 13—Jack "Legs" Diamond and bodyguard Charles Entratta kill William "Red" Cassidy, Peter Cassidy, and Simon Walker in a gun battle in Diamond's Hotsy Totsy Club, 1721 Broadway, New York. Diamond and Entratta become fugitives.

— Two gunmen rob First State Bank courier Herman Flack of $18,000 on a public bus in San Antonio, Texas. They order the bus driver to stop at Laredo and Herff streets and flee in a coupe parked nearby.

June 20—A Bridgeport, Connecticut, burglar gives up after hiding six hours under a bed occupied by talking girls.

June 22—Using a .30-caliber Browning machine gun, Frank Smith, alias Frank Ellis, Charles Berta, and James Sargert rob a Southern Pacific mail train of $16,000 near McAvoy, California. Jake Fleagle is suspected.

June 24—Gandalfo Civito, alias Frankie Marlow, a

follower of the late Frankie Yale, is shot to death by unknown gangsters at 166th Street and Queens Avenue in New York.

June 25—U.S. Department of Justice agents arrest "Machine Gun" Jack McGurn and girlfriend Louise Rolfe for conspiracy to violate the Mann Act by traveling from Illinois to Florida for "immoral purposes."

June 29—New York speakeasy owner Thomas Kearns is found murdered in his Montrose Pleasure Club, the apparent victim of a robbery.

July 2—Salvatore Sileo is killed by two gunmen at Joseph "Peppy Ross" Centerelli's Old Timers Café in New York's Little Italy. Attributed to a dispute over narcotics.

July 19—Hotsy Totsy Club waiter Walter Wolgast is found murdered at Bordentown, New Jersey. Some ten other witnesses to the Hotsy Totsy Club murders disappear.

July 27—Purple Gang member Irving "Little Irvy" Shapiro is murdered by unknown gunmen at 2469 Taylor Avenue in Detroit.

July 31—James "Bozo" Shupe, an ex-convict and machine-gun supplier, and Thomas McNichols, a former court bailiff, kill one another in a pistol duel at the corner of Madison and Aberdeen in Chicago.

August 4—Yee Sun, a member of the Hip Sing Tong, is murdered in Chicago after an attack in Boston on another Hip Sing member. War briefly erupts in Chinatowns of the East and Midwest between the Hip Sings and On Leongs.

August 6—Mafia boss Steve Monastero is murdered by gunmen outside the Allegheny General Hospital in Pittsburgh.

August 10—A man is found shot and burned in a car in a Newark city dump. The body eventually will be identified as that of Eugene Moran, jewel thief and former bodyguard of Arnold Rothstein. "Legs" Diamond mob suspected.

August 12—Special Agent Paul E. Reynolds, of the U.S. Bureau of Investigation's El Paso Field Office, is found shot to death in a canal near Phoenix, Arizona. The murder is never solved.

August 17—Rumrunner James Alderman is hanged at Ft. Lauderdale, Florida, for the 1927 murders of two Coast Guardsmen and a Secret Service agent.

August 29—The Harvey Bailey Gang robs the Emmet County State Bank at Estherville, Iowa, of $5,350.

— Tulsa County Highway Patrolmen Abraham Bowline and Ross Darrow are killed in a gun battle with bank robber Dick Gregg, who also dies, between Sand Springs and Tulsa, Oklahoma.

September 2—Gangster Henry "Hoop-a-Daisy" Connors is shot to death by unknown killers at the C & O Restaurant, 509 North Clark Street, in Chicago.

— Under the alias of Joe Scott, Charles "Pretty Boy" Floyd is arrested in Kansas City, Missouri, for investigation.

September 6—Henry Helms, of the "Santa Claus" gang, is executed in the electric chair at Huntsville, Texas, state prison.

September 11—Boys retrieving a baseball find murdered gangster James Batto in a parked car at 2 East 107th Street in Harlem.

September 13—Crusading District Attorney John A. Holmes is assassinated by a gunman in the vice- and crime-infested oil town of Borger, Texas.

September 26—Frank Smith, alias Ellis, and his gang rob a state bank in Rodeo, California, of $28,000, killing Constable Arthur McDonald.

September 27—Members of the Fleagle Gang are in custody on suspicion of the Lamar, Colorado, bank holdup that resulted in four murders. Ralph Fleagle was arrested in Peoria, Illinois, Herbert Royston in San Andreas, California, and George Abshier in Grand Junction, Colorado. Still at large is the gang's leader, Jake Fleagle. Before the gang's identification, several criminals, including notorious Oklahoma outlaws William "Whitey" Walker and Floyd Jarrett, were wrongly charged with the crime.

October 6—The Palm Gardens Road House near Lansing, New York, is held up for the fifth time in three months. Robbers dance with guests.

October 17—New York gangster Charles "Lucky"

Luciano is abducted, beaten, and dumped from a car on Staten Island by plainclothes detectives searching for fugitive murderer "Legs" Diamond (according to Luciano's own later account). Luciano is hospitalized, and the legend begins that he has survived a "one-way ride" at the hands of gangland rivals.

— A Brink's Express Co. armored truck carrying ten payrolls is stolen in New York City.

October 18—Fred "Killer" Burke and Gus Winkeler are suspected in the $93,000 robbery of the First National Bank at Peru, Indiana.

October 28—Purple Gang member Zigmund "Ziggie" Selbin is murdered in Detroit.

October 29—"Black Friday." The stock market crash plunges the United States into its worst economic depression.

November 7—The Farmers & Merchants Bank at Jefferson, Wisconsin, is robbed of $352,000 in cash and bonds. Most of the loot will be recovered later from the Michigan hideout of Fred "Killer" Burke, but Mrs. Gus Winkeler later will attribute the robbery to Harvey Bailey's gang.

November 14—Walter Floyd, "Pretty Boy" Floyd's father, is shot dead in an altercation with a neighbor, Jim Mills, in Sallisaw, Oklahoma. Mills will disappear after his acquittal on grounds of self-defense, either leaving Oklahoma or being murdered by a vengeful "Pretty Boy," according to various rumors.

— The mutilated corpse of gangster Mortimer "Monkey" Shubert is found in a parked car near the corner of Broadway and La Salle in Lower Manhattan.

November 18—"Santa Claus" bank robber Marshall Ratliff shoots and mortally wounds popular jailer "Uncle Tom" Jones in an attempted escape from Eastland, Texas, county jail. A lynch mob drags Ratliff from the jail and hangs him.

— Kansas City, Missouri, police arrest "Pretty Boy" Floyd for investigation in a holdup. Floyd is released the next day.

November 25—A blanket warrant is issued charging Gus Winkeler, Robert Carey (alias Bob Newberry), Fred Goetz, John Carl Conley (alias John Anderson), Raymond Nugent (alias Herman Roy Anderson), and Herman Tipton with the Jefferson, Wisconsin, bank robbery.

December 2—After several trial delays, the indictment against "Machine Gun" Jack McGurn for the St. Valentine's Day Massacre is dismissed.

— Two gunmen in a passing car fire at police detective Burt Haycock with shotguns on South Sixty-First Street in Kansas City, Missouri, missing him. Haycock identifies one of the gunmen as "Pretty Boy" Floyd.

December 7—Guests at a Democratic Club banquet for Judge Albert Vitale, hosted by Harlem racketeer Ciro Terranova, are robbed by gunmen at the Roman Gardens Restaurant in the Bronx.

December 11—Prohibition Agent O. P. Butler is fatally shot and his partner George S. Danhour wounded during a liquor raid on John and Latosca Young's barber shop in Cushing, Oklahoma. Deputies arrest the Youngs.

December 14—Patrolman Charles Skelly is shot to death while investigating an auto accident in St. Joseph, Michigan. The killer, going by the name of Frederick Dane, escapes, but his home is raided by Berrien County deputies who discover an arsenal that includes two Thompson guns. Dane soon is identified as Fred "Killer" Burke, wanted for the St. Valentine's Day Massacre and numerous other crimes. Ballistics tests by Major Calvin Goddard, director of the country's first full-service Scientific Crime Detection Laboratory (privately established at the Northwestern University Law School in Chicago), will discover that Burke's machine guns were used in the Massacre and that one also was used in the New York slaying of Frankie Yale.

3

THE NOBLE EXPERIMENT

In Colonial America alcohol was considered nutritious, an aid to digestion, and a convenient substitute for water, which not only lacked "food value" but also was often contaminated. It was essential to farm animals (which further diminished its appeal), but otherwise was useful mainly for cooking, washing, and navigation. Liquor also reflected the increasing abundance of grain whose most manageable and marketable form was whiskey, preferred over sour wines and bitter brews. Sometimes it was a victual necessity for washing down salty, greasy, or rancid food. Getting a little drunk in the process was the cross one had to bear.

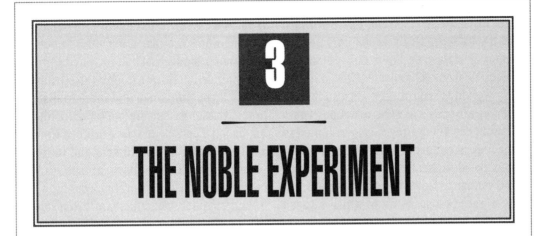

With the development of new grain products and markets, the upheaval of the Civil War, and then an Industrial Revolution with its opportunities for progress and economic prosperity, the feeble and religious-oriented "temperance" movement in the United States began finding more and more allies. The social cost of widespread drunkenness was conspicuous on city streets that looked like battlefields littered with dead and wounded, and in the destruction of families dependent on meager wages to pay for food and rent instead of the transient solace provided by the saloon. "Drink is the curse of the working class," declared the captains of industry plagued by absenteeism and reeling workmen, and if they were supported first by extremists like Carrie Nation, whose flailing hatchet destroyed saloons (often to the merriment of spectators), the new Progressive Movement worked hard to remedy every urban ill from alcoholism to poverty to ignorance to disease, all of which ravaged the urban slums.

By the turn of the century, many states, especially in the South and West, had enacted their own Prohibition laws, following the lead of a spreading Temperance Movement that now could win state and local elections and even nominate presidential candidates. This campaign might have failed in the major cities, whose large immigrant populations considered beer and wine a birthright and also depended on the neighborhood tavern or saloon for many personal and community services not yet provided by the city. Besides being the only source of recreation for the working poor, the saloon functioned as a post office, message center, first-aid station, counseling clinic, soup kitchen, and campaign headquarters for ward bosses and aldermen.

The Temperance Movement had its firmest roots in Kansas as a poorly organized women's campaign that could get away with destroying saloons because they technically were illegal under state law. But even as this campaign evolved into a movement supported by less violent but more influential organizations, such as the Women's Christian Temperance Union, it remained a moral crusade. An Anti-Saloon League, which originated in Ohio as a nonsectarian organization and included some high-minded politicians, found itself supported by businessmen and industrialists beset by absenteeism and workers drinking on the job. Soon the League expanded from a state to a national movement and in the process found itself (with changes in leadership and policies) absorbing local Prohibitionist groups, which transformed it into the country's most powerful lobby for banning the sale of booze wherever and whenever possible.

A complete standoff was averted by the First World War and appeals to patriotism. The idea that supposedly scarce grain and other foodstuffs were being denied starving orphans in Europe inspired image-conscious politicians to enact a special and presumably temporary wartime Prohibition law that gave the president authority over agricultural production.

With so many drinking-age citizens in the military, and the remainder either accommodating wartime Prohibition or ignoring it, the last few states ratified the Eighteenth Amendment in January 1919, barely two months after the Armistice, without giving much thought to its enforcement. It was sincerely believed that a decree enshrined in so hallowed a document as the U.S. Constitution would be observed by nearly everyone as a matter of principle, and it gave distillers, brewers, and taverns a transitional period of exactly one year before the amendment took effect. To deal with those few who might think they could ignore such a powerful mandate, Congress

"WETS" VS. "DRYS"

Prohibition's memorable cartoon character—"a man with threadbare black clothes, a prim-faced, red-nosed man with a long thin countenance"—originated in print with the British novelist Charles Dickens, who had taken a strong dislike to the "English Nonconformist" ministers of the late nineteenth century and so-caricatured them in his *Pickwick Papers*.

British beverage interests, under attack from the Nonconformists, dressed the fellow up in a frock suit and stovepipe hat, carrying the Englishman's customary umbrella, to symbolize their opposition to the ministers' ideas of reform. The *New York World* liked his looks and imported him to symbolize the American Prohibitionist.

In the hands of such popular editorial cartoonists as Rollin Kirby and the Hearst newspapers' Winsor McCay, this unsavory chap soon found almost universal acceptance among "Wets" to represent "Drys." One classic instance was McCay's adaptation of Pierre Fritel's "The Conqueror" in which he replaced Alexander, Caesar, and Napoleon on horseback with dour, top-hatted, rifle-bearing, bespectacled fanatics approaching on a nighttime path lined on either side with corpses—presumably the "1,360" innocent victims of Prohibition forces—as the public considered the prospect of Repeal.

"John Barleycorn," the unkempt, beer-bellied fellow sometimes tipsy and sometimes pathetic, was used by both sides to represent the boozer. He was inspired by Jack London's book by the same name published in 1913. London had been a heavy drinker in his early years and later lamented, "A cocktail or several, before dinner, enabled me to laugh wholeheartedly at things which had long since ceased being laughable. The cocktail was a prod, a spur, a kick, to my jaded mind and bored spirits."

Although borrowed from the British press, the prim and proper "Dry" was turned into America's Prohibitionist, while "Wets" were similarly caricatured as "John Barleycorn," inspired by a Jack London novel.

then passed a criminal law commonly called the Volstead Act (over a presidential veto) that provided basic penalties of a fine up to $1,000 and up to six months in jail for a first offense—at a time when the average city worker made less than $1,500 per year. Congress also allocated only a modest sum to establish a federal enforcement agency, partly because many politicians and businessmen privately held interests in the liquor and beer industries and partly because the law also required the states to pass their own versions of the Volstead Act.

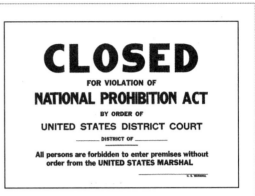

The flush of victory did not last long. The opportunities afforded by Prohibition provided the urban poor with what historian Daniel Bell one day would call a "queer ladder of upward social mobility" that accomplished precisely the opposite of what the Prohibitionists intended. Beer and liquor Prohibition, like drug criminalization later, transformed many relatively harmless neighborhood gangs into wealthy underworld organizations that corrupted government from top to bottom, including the police, who ranged from a few genuinely dedicated public servants to thinly disguised goon squads controlled by the ruling ward boss.

CLOSED

FOR VIOLATION OF

NATIONAL PROHIBITION ACT

BY ORDER OF

UNITED STATES DISTRICT COURT

______ DISTRICT OF ______

All persons are forbidden to enter premises without order from the UNITED STATES MARSHAL

__________ U. S. MARSHAL

The Eighteenth Amendment banned the manufacture, transportation, and sale—everything but the actual drinking—of any beverage containing more than 0.5 percent of alcohol. At last awakening to what this meant, several states belatedly rebelled, only to have their efforts to circumvent or modify the law quickly knocked in the head by the U.S. Supreme Court.

The metropolitan press commonly blamed Prohibition on rural worries over crime and vice of the "big city."

Amateur Distiller—Good Lord! When are they going to stop this sort of thing? I've voted against it often enough!

Home stills exploded with enough regularity to attract the attention of cartoonists, who contended that Chicagoans needed them to wake up.

So the Amendment took effect on January 16, 1920—a day remembered for the desperate efforts of countless Americans using everything from wagons to baby carriages to stock their cellars—and one minute after that midnight the Volstead Act officially created a dry America. Each time it was challenged, the Supreme Court only tightened its provisions.

Promoted as an unprecedented national reform that would introduce an "era of clear thinking and clean living," Prohibition was much more than that. It was a major victory for an ascetic rural and Protestant value system over the vice and depravity of the city—one that was somehow expected to magically change the life-

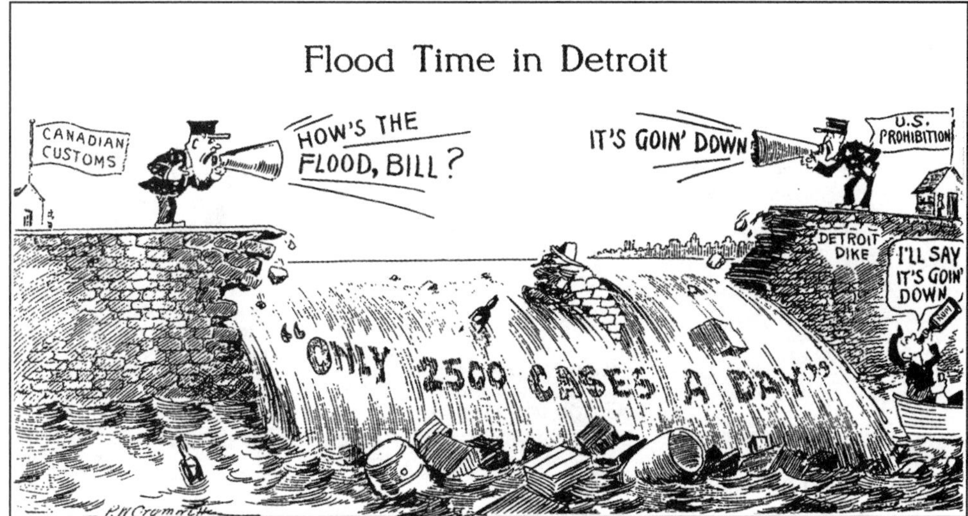

Prohibition also was adopted by Canada, but its distillers could export booze and joined Caribbean rumrunners who parked their vessels just outside U.S. waters.

long social habits of tidal waves of immigrants, at that time mainly Catholics from Italy and Ireland (who had only their religion in common), but also Germans, Poles, and Jews, all of whom were seen as rejecting traditional American values in favor of hedonistic, criminal, or mercenary ones of their own.

Prohibition reduced per capita drinking for a time, but turned it from a working-class vice into a form of safe, middle-class rebellion against stodginess and

The Brand-name Dilemma

When court cases failed and the reality of national Prohibition sank in, the beer and liquor industries scrambled to preserve their trade names by marketing other products. The beer people figured out quickly enough that they could peddle malt syrup called Budweiser, Schlitz, and (Pabst) Blue Ribbon, and perish the thought that it might be used for home-brewing.

The ads showed, for instance, a smiling, middle-aged, slightly overweight, housewife-looking, obviously Germanic lady delighted by her discovery of a "full 3-pound" can of Blue Ribbon Malt Extract. (You could, if you wished, write for "Lena's Free Recipe Book of delicious foods and candies." And if you looked elsewhere, you could find another ad for a do-it-yourself home capping machine, featuring a container that looked remarkably like a beer bottle.)

Liquor companies had more difficulty. They could produce and lavishly decorate their "medicinal spirits" whiskey, but they couldn't advertise it; a few tried to market non-alcoholic "liquors" that flopped. ("Rumo . . . Non-intoxicating . . . Tastes like rum.") Johnny Walker cigarettes helped preserve that brand name but haven't stood the test of time.

respectability. Worse, it made drunkenness fashionable among the middle class and almost obligatory among the wealthy few. Intoxication was even humorous (figurines of drunks hanging on lamp posts, songs like "How Dry I Am"), and that, combined with the proliferation of automobiles and drunken driving, created an even greater national problem. With Repeal thirteen years later, the local gangs that had prospered from bootlegging lost their source of wealth and concentrated on racketeering, traveling the intercity routes established in the twenties for the distribution of liquor. What began as a collaboration with their criminal counterparts around the country evolved into a powerful and profitable nationwide confederation that started organizing in the 1930s and by the 1950s represented modern organized crime.

In 1920, before the "noble experiment" blew up in the country's face, the *Literary Digest* sampled opinion from newspapers of the day expressing varying degrees of hope, righteousness, apprehension, disgust and fatalistic acceptance of a legal reality:

New Haven Courier-Journal: "We are about to enter upon the greatest social experiment any civilized nation ever undertook [and] of all the civilized nations on the earth this nation is best calculated to make it a success—if a success can be made."

New York Evening Post: "No one who assists in violating the prohibition law can be called a good citizen; the buyer of a drink is no better than the seller."

Providence Journal: "No law-abiding citizen will think of attempting to evade the Volstead Act, which, strictly construed, is a criminal statute."

Washington Post: "Involved in the problem of making people both temperate and happy is the fact that a large proportion of the industrial population is made up of aliens or new naturalized citizens whose lifelong habits differ from those of native Americans."

New York Evening World: "The people of the United States are in the grip of a law which a majority of them do not approve and which large numbers of them do not respect. A law can be constitutional without being the will of the people—if misrepresentatives turn their backs on the people.

"The enforcement of nationwide prohibition can only continue to be what it already is—a costly and unsuccessful effort productive of evasion, subterfuge, and hypocrisy."

Boston Herald: "The Prohibition Amendment may have been unwise; it may or may not express actually the majority sentiment of the people, but the act was passed and ratified—and there you are."

THE PRICE OF PROHIBITION

The cost of the noble experiment in money, lives, and permanent disabilities was impossible to calculate because "Wets" and "Drys" were equally willing to distort any data available. Prohibitionists were well aware that many politicians owned stock in distilleries, would vote dry but drink wet, and were loath to spend money on anything resembling strict or even intelligent enforcement. The Hearst newspapers, meanwhile, reveled in Prohibition's failure and routinely published feature articles listing the names of every Prohibition fatality, without always describing the circumstances. Its count in 1929 was 1,360 dead, illustrated by a Winsor McCay cartoon of Prohibitionists with guns riding gaunt horses past endless rows of corpses.

While one cartoonist parodied a famous painting to illustrate the death toll of poisonous booze (above), others denounced the government's efforts to chemically "denature" alcohol (below).

Prisons overflowed with small-time bootleggers, including a few who received "life for a pint" under a drastic state law passed in Michigan. Wet and Dry leaders would continually dispute how many thousands were permanently maimed, blinded, or killed by industrial alcohols "poisoned" by the previous administration in its search for denaturing methods that would defy rectification by "alky-cookers" (not many of whom had degrees in chemistry or, for that matter, lost much sleep over the purity of their product).

The safest source of good booze was the local pharmacist who could issue cold-sufferers (or anyone else) a pint a week of

NEW YORK VS. CHICAGO

What Chicago lacked in class and understatement it made up for in a quirky combination of Midwest cornpone and ostentation. The simple business card was New York's key to a speakeasy, which served drinks and might have some entertainment but outwardly looked like a respectable brownstone—sometimes compelling neighbors to post signs on their doors or sidewalk gates to the effect that "This is NOT a speakeasy." (Later came the "nightclub," such as the Hotsy Totsy and the Cotton Club, with bands, dancing, and floor shows.)

Chicago, on the other hand, might stop short of putting a large beer sign out front, but otherwise blatantly advertised its places of booze, dancing, and floor shows in entertainment guides, complete with goofy typography, dancing cooks, singing waiters, and euphemisms like "Bottle Goods and Special Drinks not listed." It saw nothing inconsistent in combining a barnyard theme with a "Monsieur Francois" to add what Midwesterners might think was a touch of class.

The *New Yorker*'s trademark character Eustace Tilly, the foppish dandy who makes his appearance on the magazine's cover once a year, would never have visited Chicago voluntarily and could not have been forced into Bert Kelly's Stables except at gunpoint. If wearing his spiffy *New Yorker* outfit, he might have passed for one of the entertainers. But as a prospective customer he would be the butt of jokes, beaten up, thrown out, or all three, and would have rushed back to Gotham happy that the only souvenir of his Chicago visit was a bullet hole fired in sport through his top hat.

By the same token, few Chicagoans would have had a clue to how to find, gain entrance to, or comport themselves in a New York "speak"; they probably would have gawked like tourists, or otherwise embarrassed the regulars until politely asked to leave. If New York gave rise to the "nightclub," Chicago had the "roadhouse," as the automobile proliferated. It also had restaurants with bands, "soft drink" parlors, "joints" with stylish jazz bands, wicked South Side black-and-tan clubs given to "race mixing," and grubby "beer flats" and taverns where many carried pistols unless the management insisted that they be checked at the door.

For reasons not entirely clear, New York took less heed of its Prohibition-era gangsters than did Chicago, where not a sparrow fell uncounted. Several factors might account for this. The most obvious was the relative flamboyance of Chicago's hoods who received credit (mistakenly, as it turns out) for inventing the "one-way ride," pioneered the drive-by shooting, introduced machine guns and the smoke-screen getaway car to gang warfare, held downtown gunfights, challenged each other in print, shot rivals in hospital beds, devised the "handshake" murder, battled with bombs, ambushed enemies from apartment windows, riddled a state prosecutor, and generally comported themselves like cowboys. "Lucky" Luciano supposedly returned from a business trip to Chicago and declared the city "A goddam crazy place. Nobody's safe on the streets!"

Also, the Chicago Crime Commission was the first organization of its kind, recorded every "gangland-style" killing beginning in 1919, labored to keep track of the various gangs, and eventually conceived the idea of "public enemies," to the delight of local newspapers, whose crime coverage was distinctive enough to become notorious as the "Chicago school of journalism."

New York's five-borough system probably provided natural boundaries for criminal activities, and while Tammany Hall corruption functioned as smoothly and quietly as a well-oiled machine, Chicagoans had to contend with the recurring reform movements that kept city politics in a constant uproar, as well as clown Mayor "Big Bill" Thompson who went in and out of office on promises to keep Chicago "wetter than the middle of the Atlantic ocean" and threats to punch England's King George in the nose. Reform-minded Alderman Robert Merriam might lament that "Chicago is unique. It is the only totally corrupt city in America." And if someone remarked that other cities were just as corrupt, he would huffily respond, "But they aren't nearly so big!"

While Chicagoans railed against the Second City's crime conditions, many followed the local gang wars like an underworld series and took a perverse pride at being the First City in that respect, of which they were constantly reminded by an effete New York press. The Chicago newspapers had to keep their sense of humor in the face of New York sarcasm. A story filed by the *New York Sun*'s Chicago bureau reported that "Big Bill's" pre-election "street parade, augmented by last-hour recruiting of additional tumbling clowns, bucking horses and yipping cowboys, was well up to the average of such demonstrations when undertaken by any of the big traveling circuses." Thompson virtually commandeered the Loop, the reporter explained, and "Inside the theaters his singing policemen trilled a note of victory when they chanted time and again the following ditty:

The gang is feeling swell again,
Big Bill is coming back again,
He was out for a while,
But he's back with a smile,
and he'll shove the others all about,
Just like they took his appendix out.

It's not clear from the article whether the returning mayor's singing policemen were on or off duty, but the paper quoted him in his habitual third-person style: "Those steamboat whistles from New Orleans ought to be heard in Chicago inside of six months. But unless Bill Thompson goes up there to prod them into action it will take two years."

By 1930 Chicago-style violence had reached New York, to that city's embarrassment, as its own criminals took up the Tommygun. This was quickly (and, for that matter, correctly) blamed on Chicago. In fact, New York's first machine-gun victim was Brooklyn's Frankie Yale, whose car was riddled by Chicago gunmen on orders of Yale's onetime employee, Al Capone. By this time New York had a few celebrity gangsters, but most were mavericks not intimately part of the evolving system of crime families whose names would not make headlines for several years. The several independents were killed in spectacular fashion between 1928 and 1935 by each other or by the new breed of racketeers who would become household names in the 1950s, but who for the most part eluded the spotlight during nationally organized crime's important formative years.

Meanwhile, Chicago had learned the disadvantages of spectacle and publicity, and when Capone and Prohibition became history, along with the Roaring Twenties, most people perceived the "gangster era" as over. That and other other national developments shifted the spotlight of publicity from the urban mobsters, whom the public identified with bootlegging, to the Depression-era bank robbers, who suddenly would acquire fascinating nicknames like Pretty Boy and Baby Face and become the focus of national attention in a new era of "federalized" crime control.

With the Chicago's underworld series over, the public found plenty of excitement and distraction in a new national game of cops-and-robbers that featured J. Edgar Hoover's G-men in Washington battling the "midwestern crime wave" mainly out of their Chicago office in the Bankers' Building. During the twenties New York had fielded a couple of impressive robbers like the Whittemores and the Cowboy Tessler gang, but these were colorless stickup artists—smokeshop, jewel, and fur thieves to be pursued by city cops—who did not make national news. Because of its Wild West geography, political corruption, existing reputation for lawlessness, gangster-happy newspapers, FBI presence, and the spectacular killing of John Dillinger, Chicago retained its worldwide reputation as the nation's crime capital, whether it was or not.

Chicago's fascination with colorful criminality was reflected in the carnival of good-natured tastelessness that accompanied the killing of Dillinger. At least three groups talked or bribed their way past cops to make death masks, and the Cook County Morgue felt obliged to keep the corpse on display an extra day so that thousands of citizens could ignore the worst heat wave in decades, the reek of formaldehyde, and the buzz of houseflies to marvel at the remains.

Half a century later, when New Yorkers were smiling at novelty items reading "I ♥ New York," Chicagoans amused themselves with T-shirts that pictured Al Capone's face, rising like the sun over the city's skyline, with the caption, "Chicago—Where the Weak are Killed and Eaten."

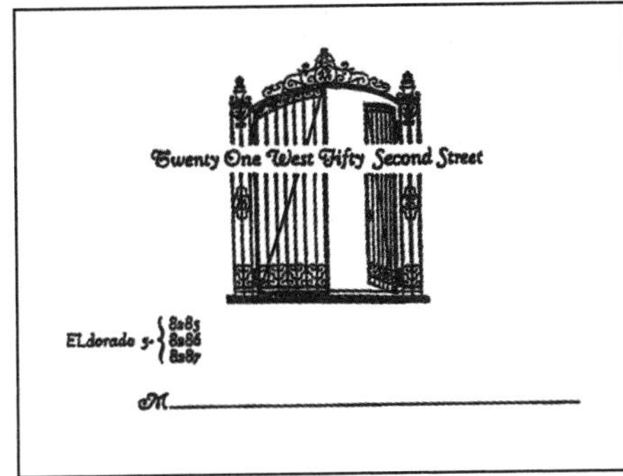

New Yorkers promoted their speakeasies with business cards (above), but Chicagoans had no qualms about outlandish advertising on flyers and in newspapers (below).

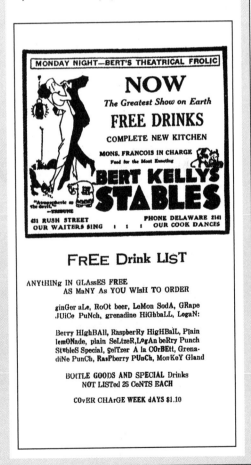

FrEE Drink LIST

ANYtHINg IN GLAssES FREE
AS MaNY As YOU WIsH TO ORDER

ginGer aLe, RoOt beer, LeMon SodA, GRape JUiCe PuNch, grenadine HiGhbaLL, LogaN:

Berry HIghBAll, RaspberRy HigHBalL, Plain lemONade, plain SeLtzeR, LogAn beRry Punch StebleS Special, SelTzer A la COrBEtt, GrenadiNe PunCh, RasPberry PUnCh, MonKeY Gland

BOttLE GOODS AND SPECIAL Drinks
NOT LISTed 25 CeNTS EACH

COvER CHArGE WEEK dAYS $1.10

"medicinal spirits" on a doctor's prescription—which often was issued for treating a head cold whose symptoms could not yet be detected, or even as a sensible precaution against colds that were "going around." This led to a few hundred thousand doctors and pharmacists obtaining licenses to dispense "medicinal spirits," and to the prosecution of many for turning this loophole into their major source of income. It also sustained several large distilleries, some of which did little more than add "for medicinal purposes only" to the label on their booze bottles.

An abbreviated table (below) taken from the November 1933 "Gala Repeal Issue" of the liquor industry's magazine *Mida's Criterion* (whose cover featured a smiling woman in a flowing gown with her shackles broken) offered their statistics on the cost of Prohibition.

Mida's added those and other government and private costs and estimated that the thirteen-year price of Prohibition exceeded by some $10 billion the cost of America's participation in the World War. In a second table, *Mida's* used federal records and press accounts to calculate the loss of life at 512 agents and 1,170 civilians.

One of the magazine's writers offered this dubious claim: "Some historians are agreed that, had a regiment of Kentucky Colonels visited Boston in 1860 and introduced the Mint Julep to the Abolitionists, there would have been no War between the States."

Cost of the "Noble Experiment" for 13 Years

FEDERAL LIQUOR REVENUE LOST	**$11,988,000,000**
State and municipal liquor revenue lost	**6,540,620,000**
Congressional enforcement appropriations	**132,958,530**
State appropriations (8 years only)	**5,585,850**
Assessed value of property seized	**186,867,322**
Coast guard appropriations for enforcement	**152,503,464**
Customs service enforcement	**93,232,230**

Source: *Mida's Criterion*

PROHIBITION CHRONOLOGY
1920–1933

Liquor regulation and prohibition, experimented with for decades, and often including beer, got off to a shaky legal start when Maine enacted a statutory Dry law in 1851. The next significant event did not occur for another twenty-nine years, when Kansas adopted constitutional prohibition. That was challenged but upheld in 1887 by the U.S. Supreme Court, which ruled in *Mugler vs. Kansas*: "A state law, enacted as a police regulation looking to the preservation of public morals, prohibiting the manufacture and sale of intoxicating liquors, is not repugnant to any clause of the Constitution of the United States."

Over the next thirty years, an increasing number of states adopted prohibition by statute or amendment, and some states modified or repealed it or retained it as "local option." But by December 18, 1917, the Eighteenth Amendment had been adopted by Congress and sent to the states, and in slightly over two years, on January 16, 1919, it was ratified by the necessary thirty-six states, to take effect in exactly one year.

1920

January 16—National Prohibition (the Eighteenth Amendment), following a period of "wartime prohibition" forbidding the use of certain food materials for brewing or distilling, becomes the law of the land.

January 17—The Volstead Act (the National Prohibition Enforcement Act, vetoed earlier by President Woodrow Wilson but overridden by Congress) goes into effect at one minute after midnight, providing penalties for violations of the Prohibition law.

January 30—Bureau of Internal Revenue issues regulations of the medicinal use of wine and liquor but limited prescriptions to one pint a week.

January 31—Congress informed by the U.S. Customs Service director that the wholesale smuggling of liquor was in progress, that an "infinitesimal quantity" was being seized, and asked for the immediate appropriation of an additional $2 million.

March 2—Governor of New Jersey defiantly signs bill permitting manufacture and sale of 3.5 percent beer.

June 1 & 7—Supreme Court rules the Eighteenth Amendment valid, upholds the Volstead Act's limit of 0.5 percent, and declares it binding on all legislative bodies, courts, and public officials.

August 18—Nineteenth Amendment granting voting rights to women, traditionally in the forefront of the Prohibition movement, adopted after ratification by Tennessee.

1921

March 3—U.S. Attorney General A. Mitchell Palmer acts to remove limits on permits for medicinal liquor.

March 8—Attorney general authorizes sale of beer for medicinal purposes.

May—Mrs. Mabel Willebrandt becomes assistant U.S. attorney general in charge of Prohibition enforcement.

June 10—Roy A. Haynes appointed national Prohibition commissioner.

July 11—Ships forbidden to bring even secured liquor within three miles (territorial limits) of the U.S.

July—Federal Prohibition Supervising Agents are abolished; enforcement is put under 48 state directors.

August 30—The appearance of mysterious ships off New Jersey coast causes rumors of pirates and even "Bolshevists"; U. S. Coast Guard seizure of several vessels reveals them to be loaded with contraband liquor, the first of a growing smuggling fleet that will become known as "Rum Row."

November 23—Willis-Campbell Supplemental Act prohibits medicinal beer and creates the U.S. Bureau of Prohibition.

1922

February 17—Congress empowers the commissioner of Internal Revenue to seize and store distilled spirits in government-bonded warehouses.

May 21—Chicago City Council votes to oppose expenditures of any city funds for the enforcement of the Volstead Act.

October 6—U. S. attorney general holds that Prohibition law extends to all American ships, government or privately owned, anywhere in the world.

December 11—Supreme Court decision in *U.S. vs. Lanza* holds that state prosecution does not bar prosecution in federal court.

1923

April 30—Supreme Court decision in *Cunnard S.S. Co. vs. Mellon* holds that Eighteenth Amendment does not apply to U.S. and foreign shipping beyond the three-mile limit, but ships may not bring intoxicating liquors into port.

May 4—New York state legislature exhibits displeasure with the Volstead law by repealing its own Prohibition Enforcement Act.

November—Both houses of the state legislature repeal Nevada's prohibition enforcement law.

1924

April 17—Harlan F. Stone appointed U.S. attorney general after Attorney General Daugherty has resigned at the request of President Calvin Coolidge.

April 21—Congress extends three-mile limit to twelve miles.

May 19-June 30—Liquor smuggling treaties signed with Germany, Sweden, Norway, Denmark, Italy, Canada, and France; treaty with Great Britain formalized on May 22.

June 9—Supreme Court upholds 1921 law forbidding sale of beer as medicine.

November-December—Congressional investigations of Internal Revenue Department and the Bureau of Prohibition; Senator Reed attacks "legal poisoning of industrial alcohol."

1925

March 2—Supreme Court upholds right to search automobiles without a federal warrant on basis of "probable cause."

March 3—Congress authorizes confiscation of vessels and vehicles used in violation of national Prohibition law.

April 1—General L. C. Andrews named assistant secretary of the Treasury to reorganize federal Prohibition enforcement.

May 3—First major mobilization of Coast Guard to combat rumrunning off Long Island.

1926

February 2—House Committee hearings on Civil Service and Prohibition.

April 5—Hearings before the Subcommittee of the Judiciary on National Prohibition.

April 27—U.S. House passes bill to separate Prohibition Unit from the Bureau of Internal Revenue and place enforcement under Treasury Department.

May 8—President Coolidge issues executive order making state, county, and municipal officers federal officials for purposes of Prohibition enforcement.

November 26—Supreme Court upholds limitation on prescriptions for medicinal whiskey.

"UPWARD MOBILITY"

Why should [the Italian gangsters] be outcasts in the opinions of the ignorant, humble, needy, hard-working people around them? They are the successes of the neighborhood. The struggling, foreign-born peasant woman sees them in their expensive cars and their fur-trimmed overcoats. She hears they are sending their children to private schools. She hears them called "beer barons," and if she can read the headlines in the English-language newspapers, she sees them described as "beer barons" and "booze kings" in print . . . the words "king" and "baron" have a most lofty significance. About all she knows is that these richly dressed young men are making or selling something that the Americans want to buy.

Incidentally, she hears in gossip with another toil-worn neighbor that Johnny Torrio, "king" of them all, gave his mother back home in Italia a villa with fifteen servants to run it.

If the robber, labor thug, and racketeer Tim Murphy, who was the co-criminal of the gangsters spoke at a Thirteenth Ward meeting in behalf of one of gangdom's political henchmen, that did the candidate no harm. For was not a priest sitting next to Murphy on the platform? If some tactless soul asked, "Is he the Tim Murphy that they said robbed the mails?" the response was deeply resentful. The attitude of the ignorant foreign-born who judged gangdom in the terms of its success would be, first, that it was doubtful whether Murphy did rob the mails and, second, "What harm did that do us?"

Thus, and in a hundred other ways, the whole issue between good and bad government and good and bad men is befuddled, and the sole conviction of the ignorant is that these "successes of the neighborhood" seem to take vastly more interest in neighborhood matters than men not in the racket do.

— *Illinois Association for Criminal Justice*

1927

March 3—The Federal government's Prohibition Unit is officially established as the Bureau of Prohibition under the Treasury Department, and the Civil Service Act is extended to field agents.

May 16—In *U.S. vs. Sullivan*, Supreme Court holds that profits derived from illicit liquor traffic are not exempt from federal income tax (a decision that will be used in the prosecution of Al Capone).

May 21—Hon. Seymour Lowman replaces Gen. L. C. Andrews as Assistant Secretary of the Treasury in charge of Prohibition; Dr. James M. Doran appointed commissioner of Prohibition.

September 5—Death of ardent prohibitionist Wayne B. Wheeler, general counsel for the Anti-Saloon League.

November 21—In *Marron vs. U.S.*, Supreme Court upholds law permitting seizure of books and papers even if not described in a search warrant.

1928

January 13—More than 1,500 out of 2,000 Prohibition agents fail to pass civil service examination.

June 4—In *Olmstead vs. U.S.*, Supreme Court holds that evidence of conspiracy obtained by telephone wiretaps is admissible in criminal trials.

August 11—In accepting the Republican nomination for president, Herbert Hoover calls Prohibition "a great social and economic experiment, noble in motive, and far-reaching in purpose."

August 22—In accepting the Democratic nomination, New York Governor Al Smith calls for a referendum on national Prohibition and state determination in the matter.

December 25—The Durant Prize of $25,000 for proposing the best methods of Prohibition enforcement is awarded to Major Chester P. Mills.

The Volstead Market Day

The "three-mile limit" was soon extended to twelve miles, which mainly required the "go-through guys" to be more cautious of the Coast Guard or get bigger or faster boats.

1929

March 2—President Coolidge signs Increased Penalties Act (Jones-Stalker Bill) providing up to five years imprisonment and fines up to $10,000 for violation of the Volstead Act.

May 20—Wickersham Commission appointed; establishes National Commission on Law Observance and Enforcement to investigate crime conditions in major cities, especially those associated with bootlegging gangs.

WHO WILL PROHIBIT THIS?
PROHIBITION

May 26—Mrs. Mabel Willebrandt resigns as U.S. assistant attorney general in charge of Prohibition enforcement; she will endorse a "grape brick" product for making wine at home.

June 1—Publisher William Randolph Hearst awards $25,000 prize to Franklin C. Hoyt for best essay on Prohibition and Temperance.

October 1—President Hoover appoints John McNab to draft a project for better enforcement of Prohibition.

December 3—In a message to Congress, President Hoover recommends transfer of investigation functions from Treasury to Department of Justice.

December 5—Alabama court declares purchaser of liquor guilty under state law.

1930

January 20—Secretary of War extends Prohibition to U.S. military forces throughout the world.

January 23—Attorney General Mitchell announces his intention to appoint as U.S. attorneys and marshals only abstainers and those who personally support Prohibition.

February 10—Senator Burton Wheeler introduces resolution to investigate Bureau of Prohibition.

March 31—The *New York World*'s bootlegger poll reveals widespread violation of Volstead Act.

May 5—In *Danovitz vs. U.S.*, Supreme Court rules that barrels and containers are forfeitable when offered for sale for use in the unlawful manufacture of alcoholic beverages.

May 26—In *U.S. vs. James E. Farrar*, Supreme Court holds that the purchaser of intoxicating liquor is not guilty of violating the Volstead Act.

July 1—Prohibition Reorganization Act of 1930 transfers enforcement of the Volstead Act to the Justice Department; the Bureau of Industrial Alcohol is organized and remains under the Treasury Department.

November 18—American Bar Association votes for Repeal, 13,779 to 6,340.

1931

January 15—President Herbert Hoover signs the Stobbs Act mitigating the Increased Penalties Act.

January 20—Report of the Wickersham Commission: Two of the eleven commissioners vote for immediate repeal of the Eighteenth Amendment, seven for revision, and two for retention without change.

March 13—Massachusetts legislature requests that Congress call a Repeal convention. Legislatures of New York, Rhode Island, Connecticut, Wyoming, and New Jersey pass similar resolutions.

September 24—American Legion votes 1,008 to 394 in favor of holding a referendum on national Prohibition.

October 17—Al Capone convicted of tax evasion and failure to file returns or report profits from unlawful acts, i.e., bootlegging.

1932

January 8—Hearings before a Senate committee on the Amendment of Prohibition Act.

March 14—House of Representatives defeats the Beck-Linthicum resolution to restore to the states the right to abolish or continue the Eighteenth Amendment.

April 19—Hearings before a senate committee on modification or repeal of national Prohibition.

May 14—Beer Parade in New York City calling for its legalization.

July 2—New York Governor Franklin D. Roosevelt tells the Democratic National Convention in Chicago that national Prohibition is "doomed."

August 11—President

MAKING IT A THOROFARE

WE CAN'T GO ON DRIVING RIGHT THRU THE FENCE

AND NOT EXPECT THE CATTLE TO GET OUT OF THE PASTURE

Hoover, in his renomination acceptance speech, abandons national Prohibition.

November—Franklin Roosevelt is elected president, and by now twelve states have voted in favor of Repeal.

December 21—U.S. House adopts the Collier Bill modifying the Volstead Act to legalize 3.2 percent beer.

DAILY MIRROR

FINAL

MUrray Hill 2-1000

WEATHER

NRA

VOL. X. No. 142

New York, Wednesday, December 6, 1933

2 cents

PROHIBITION ENDS AT LAST!

New York got the breaks from Utah. . . . The lid is off! . . . The 36th and most necessary State to ratify repeal of the Prohibition Amendment had dillied and dallied yesterday while New York fumed and then "out of consideration for the rest of the nation" . . . New York in particular . . . the long-dry Mormons opened their hearts and cast their ballots for repeal hours ahead of the time expected. . . . Then the fun began!

Utah can't have a drink until Jan. 1, anyway—be-

1933

February 20—Congress submits Twenty-first (Repeal) Amendment to the states.

March 13—President Roosevelt proposes immediate modification of the Volstead Act to allow the sale of beer.

April 7—The manufacture and sale of 3.2 percent beer is legalized by Congress.

April 10—Michigan holds first convention to vote on ratification of the Twenty-first Amendment.

November 7—Thirty-six states, the number required, vote to end Prohibition in the United States.

– Mayor John Catlin of Carmel, California, organizes the National Association for the Advancement of the Fine Art of Drinking, whose motto is "No more gin-guzzling and whiskey-swigging."

December 5—Utah approves the Twenty-first Amendment by convention, officially repealing national Prohibition.

NO MORE SALOONS

When national Prohibition was repealed in 1933, most cities wanted to prevent the return of the old swinging-door, belly-up-to-the-bar saloon, which not only fostered indoor fights that often spilled into the street but also might include gambling and prostitution.

Chicago's solution to the problem (besides the obvious ones of forbidding sales after closing time and to patrons obviously drunk) was to mandate stools along the bar, increase the indoor illumination, require that women be "escorted," and to put in windows that afforded a view from the street. Tavern operators shrugged and complied on the matter of stools and bigger light bulbs, took their chances on "unescorted women," and soon discovered that the city had not specified the size of the window. To this day, places where only drinks are served comply with the window requirement by installing one so small, perhaps one foot by two feet, and often so high that short people have to stand on tiptoes to see inside.

The Wrecking of the Eighteenth Amendment

Declaring that the Eighteenth Amendment had been passed by Congress and ratified by forty-six out of forty-eight states, Prohibitionists argued that it should be "recognized as having expressed the considered will of the American people." In truth, the people may not have been carefully polled by Congress or their state legislatures, who knew a righteous movement when they saw one. In *The Wrecking of the 18th Amendment,* Ernest Gordon blamed Prohibition's failure squarely on the government, Wall Street, and the press, and not without careful documentation:

> [T]he will of the nation was quietly defied and the Amendment itself nullified by the very man charged with its enforcement. That man was Andrew W. Mellon, Secretary of the Treasury during three administrations. Mellon, himself, had large whisky investments. Dry law enforcement was properly the task of the Department of Justice. It almost seems as if it had been left largely in Mellon's control that he might weaken and ultimately break down this law. . . . In the period 1921–25 Secretary of the Treasury Mellon refunded taxes on his Gulf Oil Co. to the tune of $3,996,000 and taxes on bootleggers to the amount of $2,097,371.
>
> In the very year in which Mr. John D. Rockefeller abjured Prohibition as the source and cause of bootlegging, his major company, Standard Oil of New Jersey, was organizing jointly with National Distillers [to form] the Standard Alcohol Company. . . . Mrs. C. H. Sabin, leader of the Women's Association for Prohibition Reform, was wife of a director of the largest beer and whisky bottle manufacturing concern in the U.S. . . . The wife of the President of the United States succeeded her son as director of a large and lucrative whisky insurance business. . . .

The government itself had been putting out various Farmers Bulletins and Department of Agriculture directions on the simplicity of manufacturing alcohol from a dozen or more crops ranging from apples and oats to sugar beets and watermelon. (A wicked but potable version of ethyl alcohol required nothing more than a tea kettle, a quart of corn meal, and a bath towel, said Charles Merz in *The Dry Decade.*) And having put General Walker took charge of Volstead Act enforcement, Treasury Secretary Mellon beefed up the Coast Guard to make war on Rum Row that brought in "the Real McCoy" (so-named for an early and reputable rumrunner), but otherwise busied himself minting money and collecting taxes.

Besides the rapid increase in smuggling and home brewing, an equally vexing problem involved plants licensed to make industrial alcohol. Instead of being "industrialized" at the time of its distillation, it was shipped to thirty or so separate "denaturing" plants that General Lincoln Andrews, in charge of Prohibition enforcement as of 1925, described as "nothing more or less than bootlegging organizations." Industrial alcohol production increased from 28 million gallons in 1920 to 81 million in 1925, much of it diverted to secret bottling plants where it could be watered down, flavored up, and concocted into something like 150 million to 180 million quarts of illegal booze with counterfeit labels.

By 1923 this was becoming an increasingly risky business, as government chemists had developed more than seventy-five different denaturing formulas that might be present in the distillate, depending on when the diversion took place. Some were relatively harmless infusions of oil of peppermint or menthol crystals (later, one that smelled like rotten eggs), while others were iodine, benzene, and sulfuric acid.

By 1926 the government was under pressure from Prohibitionists to start using or increase the use of wood (or methyl) alcohol because it had a boiling point so close to ethyl (drinkable) alcohol it would be nearly impossible to cook out. Andrews declared that "Under the new formula there will be less chance of poisoning than heretofore. A strong trace of wood alcohol is so offensive that it will warn the most reckless drinker." Andrews' chief chemist thought otherwise: "It is impossible to detect wood alcohol except by a thorough chemical analysis performed by a skilled chemist in a well-equipped laboratory."

With some reluctance, government chemists bumped the amount of wood alcohol up from 2 percent to 4 percent, which did not deter the "aftermarket" bootleggers from watering it far down, spiking it back up with a little smuggled booze, and then promoting multi-ingredient "cocktails" and "highballs" to mask the taste. Hangovers

BOOTLEGGER SPECIAL

Powerful, speedy 8-cylinder road car, in perfect shape. Fine tires. Just traded by prominent business man. One trip will pay for it. $435. Trial allowed.

NASH SALES CO. OF SYRACUSE
713 W. GENESEE ST.

A Nash dealer in Syracuse, New York, clearly enjoyed thumbing his nose at Prohibition enforcers in this newspaper advertisement.

from such drinks were ferocious and occasionally fatal.

From 1920 to 1925 the Prohibition Unit (as it was then called) struggled along with a staff averaging 3,000 agents, including their clerical assistants. By the end of 1925, New York City alone had 5,100 doctors writing a million prescriptions a year to be filled by 1,200 drugstores, and a grand total of seventeen federal inspectors to police this bedlam. Most of the agents were riff-raff unable to pass civil service exams, when those came along.

Nevertheless, by 1924, Prohibition arrests had clogged the federal courts with some 68,000 cases, a third to a half unprosecuted or "unfinished." And by now one state after another was either repealing its own "Little Volstead" law or otherwise saying the hell with it. Even in Chicago, where Mayor William Dever took office in 1924 vowing to end police corruption and to enforce the law, he found himself lamenting to a Congressional committee in 1926:

> I presume I am like the mayor of every other large city in this country, hoping for a day to come when our efforts may be given to something else than Prohibition. I want to be relieved, if I can; I have a human longing either to pass the burden of this great subject on to somebody else, or else from the aid of constructive legislation to be relieved of its annoyance. It is an everyday—yes, an hourly—difficulty with us in Chicago. The mayor of that city has great powers. He is responsible for everything that occurs there. The school board, the library board, the great hospitals, the police, fire, everything is brought to the door of the chief executive; and yet, notwithstanding the growing need for attention to these highly important matters, our attention is engrossed with this particular subject. It is almost impossible to give anything approaching good government along general lines, this one subject presses so closely upon our attention. Even I, who have tried to divest myself personally and as chief executive of the subject, and not to allow myself to be embroiled in it, find myself immersed in it, to the very great damage of the city, from morning until night.

Two years later "Big Bill" Thompson would be reelected mayor of Chicago, declare himself "wetter than the middle of the Atlantic Ocean," and Prohibition law enforcement would all but end, leaving only federal agent Eliot Ness to pester Al Capone without any help from the locals—many of whom were spending their off-duty hours guarding booze shipments against attacks by rival gangs when traversing enemy territory.

RHYMES OF THE TIMES

I REMEMBER, I REMEMBER

I remember, I remember
The house where I was born;
The cellar's been rigged out complete
For making "brew" and "corn";
You'd hardly know the old place now.
It's dazzling to the eye,
For father's made a fortune
Since the Country voted Dry.

He don't get up at three A.M.
To do the farm work now;
He discharged all the hired hands,
And gave away the plow;
But he has hired a chauffeur,
A butler and two cooks,
A French maid, three stenographers
And a man to keep his books.

The wheat field's been converted
Into a golf course grand;
There's a swimming pool of marble
Where the horse trough used to stand;
And the house has been remodeled,
Till there is scarce a trace
Of anything left to remind
Me of the dear old place.

The walls have secret panels;
There are "plants" beneath the floors
And we have electric buzzers,
On the windows and the doors,
And the little window where the sun
Peeped in on me a morn,
Is bricked in now to hide the mash
From which pa makes the "corn."

Oh, I tell you Prohibition
Is doing lots of good,
And by most folks who voted "Dry,"
This fact's well understood;
It's creating jobs for thousands,
Jobs free of worldly cares,
And making both the "Prohibits"
And "Bootleggers," millionaires.

— J. Flanagan
in the *Ohio Penitentiary News*

If I was to work, and save all I earn,
I could buy me a bar and have money to burn.

I passed by a saloon, and heard someone snore,
And I found the bartender asleep on the floor.

I stayed there and drank till a copper came in,
And he put me to sleep with a slap on the chin.

Next morning in court I was still in a haze,
When the judge looked at me, he said,
"Thirty days."

— Street song

GREETINGS TO YOU FOR THE END OF OUR PERF (HIC) DAY

When we come to the end of our Perf (hic) Day
The end of the rickey and high,
And we say goodbye to the cool frappe
And the rollicking rock and rye,
We will have to revel in buttermilk
And sarsaparilla gay,
And, Oh, the pain of drinking rain
At the end of our Perf (hic) Day.

The rockets' red glare,
The bombs bursting in air,
Gave proof through the night
That Chicago's still there.

— Newspaper columnist

Play it across the table.
What if we steal this city blind?
If they want any thing let 'em nail it down
Harness bulls, dicks, front office men,
And the high goats up on the bench,
Ain't they all in cahoots?
Ain't it fifty-fifty all down the line,
Petemen, dips, boosters, stick-ups, and guns—
what's to hinder?
Go fifty-fifty.
If they nail you, call in a mouthpiece.
Fix it, you gazump, you slant-head, fix it. . . .

— Carl Sandburg, in "Cahoots"

(A harness bull is a uniformed cop wearing a Sam Browne belt; dicks are detectives; dips are pickpockets; boosters are thieves; and petemen are safe-crackers.)

The squad cars, death cars, gangsters' hacks
Across the town make smoking tracks.
While motorcycle coppers ride
Along the edges of the tide.
Patrolmen flivver through the night
And alky truckmen rise and fight.
And that's Chicago as we've seen
Presented on the stage and screen.
But ah! 'Twas just the other day
We read of one lad gone away
Reflecting credit on the town:
A milkman's horse had run him down.

— *Chicago Daily News* columnist Robert J. Casey

(commenting on abandoned second-hand "death cars" being too plentiful to bother buying new ones)

4

CHICAGO'S BEER WARS

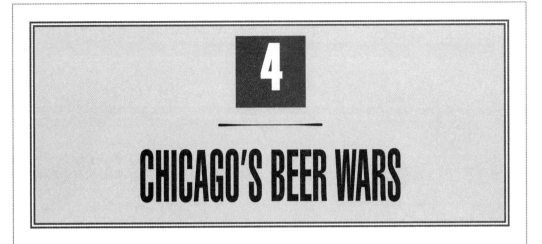

When national Prohibition became the law of the land, the city's most prominent saloons seemed to join the public and the press in grudgingly accepting the idea of a dry America. Wartime Prohibition already was in place, pushed through as a patriotic measure to keep farm products in the food chain for eating instead of drinking; and while this already had disrupted public hooch habits, most of the political quarreling concerned exemptions, exceptions, local option matters, special closing laws, and the amount of alcohol permissible in beer.

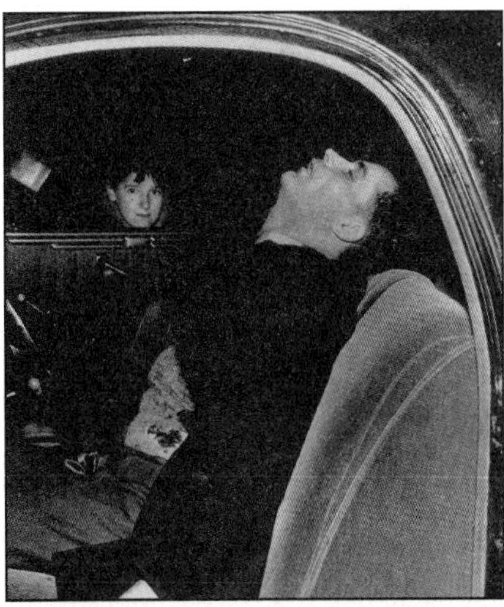

In the days before "crime scenes" and the ubiquitous yellow tape, police generally didn't care who "ogled a stiff"—this one unidentified.

But on January 16, 1920, a day widely celebrated (or mourned) in the press and major drinking establishments, the Eighteenth Amendment became enforceable under the Volstead Act, which took effect at one minute after midnight on January 17. This legally created a dry America and inspired Chicago's colorfully corrupt Alderman Michael "Hinky Dink" Kenna to ceremoniously donate his giant personal beer stein to the Chicago Historical Society.

The general assumption was that the Volstead Act, which created a National Prohibition Bureau with federal police

ARTIST'S CONCEPTION OF GANG WAR AS A SPECTACLE, INSPIRED BY NEBRASKA FARMER'S OPINION OF CHICAGO

powers, and which obligated state authorities to cooperate, could be enforced. No one doubted it could and would be violated, but buttressed by the moral authority of a Constitutional Amendment, Chicago's existing criminal and quasi-criminal gangs, thinking small, regarded bootlegging merely as a new and welcome source of illegal revenue, without appreciating Prohibition's incredible potential.

The murder of "Big Jim" Colosimo in 1920 freed John Torrio to expand into bootlegging, and his first efforts were to bring to it some semblance of order. With hundreds of breweries closing or converting to tepid "near beer," he masterminded the purchase of dozens of these plants, usually in collusion with their former owners and usually in partnership with other gang leaders, which created a pax Torrio of interlocking financial interests as everyone worked like a beaver to develop his allocated territory.

Ironically, this reduced the city's crime rate. The enormous profits in illicit beer and liquor provided a new and less-risky occupation for safecrackers, burglars, and thieves, as well as for gunmen who became bodyguards and the underworld's police force. Now they provided security against independent hijackers too lazy or contrary to become team players, sometimes working with off-duty cops who could earn a month's police pay just for shepherding a truckload of booze through hostile neighborhoods, or from an illegal distillery to a distribution point. They could defend their cargo against rival gangs, but more often they would negotiate a reasonable toll expected by brother officers working the streets.

By 1923 the low-key, unheralded Torrio had emerged as head of a loosely knit liquor syndicate that included formerly law-abiding brewers, Prohibition agents and many police. He also was the recognized leader of the local criminal community that included Dean O'Banion, "Hymie" Weiss, George Moran, Terry Druggan, Frankie Lake, Joe Saltis, Frank McErlane, "Dapper Dan" McCarthy, Walter Stevens, Danny McFall, Louis "Two-Gun" Alterie, the West Side O'Donnells, and even the notorious Genna brothers—a veritable equal-opportunity Godfather who had taken the city's safecrackers, Black Handers, burglars, and teenage gang members and put them gainfully to work. Even young Al Capone, on the lam from murder charges in New York, was acquiring business skills, despite occasional slipups.

With a few exceptions, this harmony prevailed during the first three years of Prohibition, then unraveled because of forces beyond Torrio's control.

The kind of young men inclined to crack safes and crack heads for politicians, newspapers, and cab companies could not always resist the temptation to hijack a load of booze, challenge the sovereignty of another gang, or get into personal disputes that led to shootings. An outbreak of such violence in 1923, combined with election violence, led to the defeat of "Big Bill" Thompson by William E. Dever, a reform candidate (though not a dedicated "dry") who pledged to strictly enforce the largely ignored Prohibition law and purge the city of its flamboyant corruption.

Among Dever's unprecedented actions was a well-orchestrated raid on the Sieben Brewery, which O'Banion, tipped off in advance, had just sold to Torrio for a reported half-million dollars in cash. That O'Banion regarded this as a grand prank meant that Torrio was losing not only control of his affiliates but also the political protection his operations had enjoyed under the Thompson administration. Battles already had broken out in several parts of the city, and with O'Banion's declaration of independence inspiring even more revolts, Torrio felt obliged to roll out his own forces, captained by Al Capone.

A series of killings failed to restore order, leading newspapers to start counting casualties among rival gangs, which came to a head when the primary elections of 1924 turned into a bloodbath. Harassed by Dever, the South Siders had moved their operations a short distance west along Twenty-second Street to the adjoining town of Cicero. Capone's brother Frank was killed near a polling place by Chicago police sent in by Dever to restore order, making O'Banion's treachery in the Sieben raid all the more intolerable, especially when the North Sider would scornfully refer to his Italian colleagues as "greaseballs."

Two days after the natural death of the city's underworld peacekeeper, Mike Merlo, a level-headed leader of the Sicilian Union respected by O'Banion and Torrio alike, three men walked into Schofield's flower

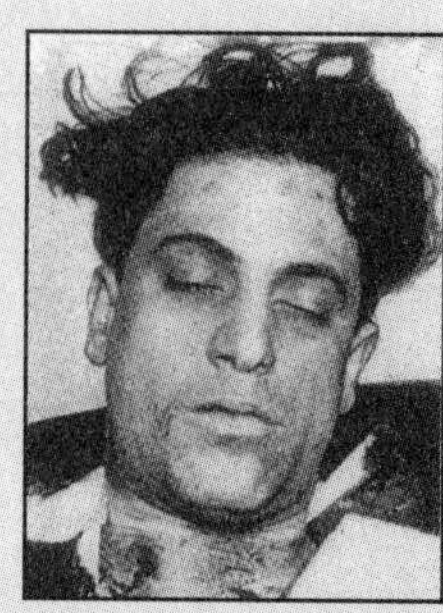

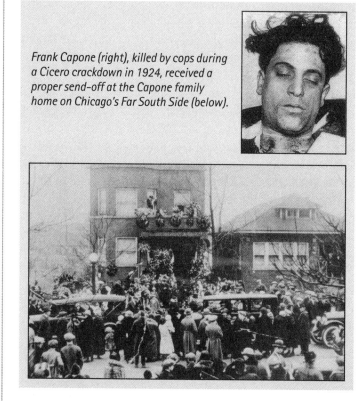

Frank Capone (right), killed by cops during a Cicero crackdown in 1924, received a proper send-off at the Capone family home on Chicago's Far South Side (below).

shop and blew O'Banion away. The *Chicago Tribune*'s banner headline read:

Chicago Daily Tribune

KILL O'BANION, GANG LEADER

CONGRESS MAY PROMPTLY STOP TAX PUBLICITY

NEWS SUMMARY

BEGIN HILL SUIT TO LEARN WHAT IS INTOXICATING

Shot 4 Up in Bank Vault in $15,000 Raid

3-GUN FLORIST SLAIN IN SHOP NEAR CHURCH

This was the first assassination of a Chicago gang "chieftain," a man who had left the Torrio fold to take personal control of the city's wealthy Gold Coast neighborhood and most of the North Side. It was correctly viewed as the opening shot in what would become known as the Chicago Beer Wars, which would rage for nearly five years. A few killings had been taking place since about 1923, but the press and the public (who had previously regarded bootleggers as perhaps a civic problem but an interesting one, and important providers of a public service) found themselves witnessing spectacular inter-gang gun battles that amounted to an underworld series whose spectators rarely were injured by foul balls.

The murder of O'Banion in such a conspicuous manner and place—at noontime in a State Street flower shop across from the Holy Name Cathedral, seat of the local archdiocese, after the unprecedented Sieben Brewery raid staged by the city's new reform administration, and the takeover of Cicero by Torrio and Capone—awakened the city's newspapers. Bootlegger killings were no longer viewed as border skirmishes or personal retaliations but evidence that the gangs were far better organized than previously supposed and now had gone to war.

One indication of this was the swift response of the North Siders to the death of their leader. Within the next few weeks they shot up the car of Capone, hitting his chauffeur, and then badly wounded Torrio, who passed the torch to young "Scarface" and retreated to New York as gangster emeritus. Their attacks on what were now Capone-affiliated gangs had the paradoxical effect of enhancing Capone's reputation as a ruthless killer. The North Siders were rowdy Irish in temperament if not in fact, and their repeated efforts to get at him usually involved more fireworks than careful planning. One attempt—which probably still holds the record for drive-by shootings—involved a midday motorcade of several cars filled with gunmen who riddled Capone's Hawthorne Hotel headquarters on the main street of Cicero. Capone emerged unscathed but not unimpressed and even paid the medical bills of a bystander injured in the action.

Three weeks later Dean O'Banion's successor, "Hymie" Weiss, and four others were mowed down by machine-gun and shotgun fire from an upstairs window in the flat next to O'Banion's flower shop. Weiss and a bootlegger/bodyguard died in front of the cathedral, whose bullet-scarred cornerstone became a minor tourist attraction. The killers and their presumed backups in parked cars departed quickly, and investigating officers later discovered a second machine-gun nest in another apartment covering the flower shop's alley. Capone left nothing to chance—unless one counts the killing of Assistant State's Attorney William McSwiggin. For reasons never satisfactorily explained, McSwiggin had accompanied two bootlegger buddies to a speakeasy in Capone's home territory of Cicero and was in the group when it was sprayed with machine-gun bullets fired from a passing

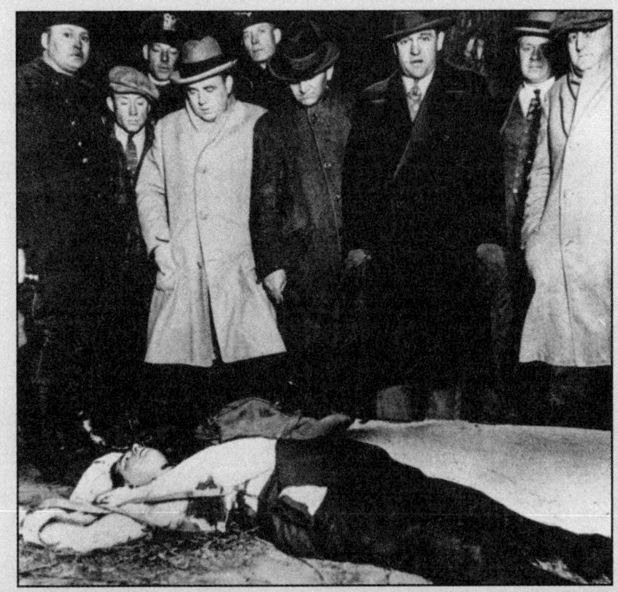

In the first major "assassination" by Capone gunmen in 1926, Assistant State's Attorney William McSwiggin (above) was machine-gunned—probably by accident—outside an illegal Cicero tavern and then rushed to the home of rival gang leader "Klondike" O'Donnell (left), who told the driver to get far away and dump the body. Two other gang members died in the shooting, but no one could satisfactorily explain McSwiggin patronizing a speakeasy.

car. At first McSwiggin's murder was considered a flagrant disregard of the tacit understanding, shared by police and citizens alike, that gangsters shooting gangsters was only good for the gene pool, with public officials a protected species. Several grand juries investigated the case and eventually concluded that McSwiggin was not the intended target. McSwiggin's choice of friends did raise eyebrows, however, especially when one of his fellow victims turned out to have been a defendant acquitted in a murder case that he had tried. Nevertheless, McSwiggin's death was regarded as a rare case of poor planning by Capone, who went into hiding at the home of Dominic Roberto and his wife, featured dance-band singer Rio Burke, until the furor subsided.

Another indication that gangs were acquiring political control over their former masters was the enormous wealth they were reaping from Prohibition. Street punks who once had depended on trolley transportation now dressed like the nouveau riche they were and employed chauffeurs to drive them around in expensive automobiles. They also thumbed their noses at the criminal justice system, paying generous bribes to police and judges or intimidating potential jurors and witnesses. Many public officials found it hard to reject a payoff that might represent an entire year's salary, especially knowing that such gratuities could come on a regular basis.

SUMMER SHACK OF A STRUGGLING YOUNG BOOTLEGGER

The enormous profits in bootlegging provided many Italian, Irish, and other immigrants, who had the stomach for the risks, their quickest escape from poverty, usually through the corruption of local government officials.

Indeed, a poorly paid policeman sometimes had the wisdom to hoard his wealth, using it later to move to a better neighborhood and give his children a college education. Many a Chicagoan owes his current prosperity to a father who saw the folly of Prohibition first-hand and considered bootlegger bribes to be his family's only means of social and economic advancement. Likewise, at least some bootleggers contented themselves simply to flee the slums, invest in honest enterprises and put their kids through school. Daniel Bell was among the first to recognize such crime as a ladder of upward social mobility, without going into much detail. Perhaps it

MACHINE-GUN NESTS

The press and the police attributed dozens of murders to Al Capone, and he may well have committed several. But only one—the face-to-face shooting of Joe Howard in Heinie Jacobs's saloon in the old Levee district—can be attributed to him personally with any degree of certainty. To the extent he ordered others, he could have claimed that the devils made him do it.

Most of the devils were the North Siders, a thoroughly rowdy bunch who were Irish in temperament if not in nationality. They spent five years sniping at Capone to avenge the slaying of their leader, Dean O'Banion, after he broke ranks with Capone's boss, John Torrio, swindling him in a brewery deal that also sent him to jail. The difference was that they (and others) continually missed their target, and Capone, in carefully planned retaliation, did not. That "Bugs" Moran survived the St. Valentine's Day Massacre was pure luck, and the result of Capone leaving the job to others.

More typical was the 1926 killing of O'Banion's successor, "Hymie" Weiss, after he used a small caravan of cars loaded with gunmen to lay siege to Capone's headquarters, then in the Hawthorne Hotel on the main street of Cicero. Three weeks later, Weiss and four others went down in a hail of bullets from a machine-gun nest in the upstairs window of a building next to O'Banion's flower shop, across from

"Hymie" Weiss (top left), Dean O'Banion's successor on Chicago's North Side, died at O'Banion's flower shop with his bodyguard Patrick "Paddy" Murray (top right, a relative of Jimmy Murray, often misidentified as Weiss), in Al Capone's first machine-gun ambush. Police later found a second but unused ambush site in the apartment window marked with a circle (above).

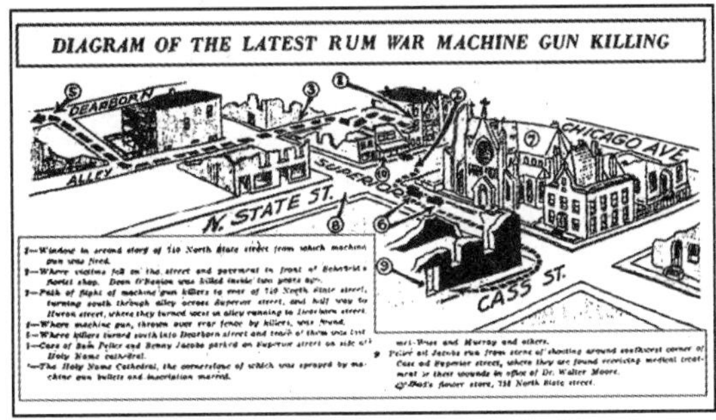

the Holy Name Cathedral; and police later found a second, backup nest covering the flower shop from the south, as well as the alley behind it. The main shooter's Thompson had jammed after thirty-five rounds because the bullet from a faulty cartridge failed to clear the barrel, but those slugs—plus several loads of buckshot from the same window—were fatal to Weiss and bootlegger/bodyguard Patrick Murray (see also James Murray).

In 1930 an even more sophisticated trap took out Capone's main adversary, Joe Aiello, who had teamed up with the North Siders before the Massacre and also coveted leadership of the Unione Siciliana, a major source of Chicago's home-distilled alcohol. Leaving an apartment building at 205 Kolmar, Aiello walked into a blaze of machine-gun fire from a nest across the street and ran for a place of shelter that was directly under a second nest in the building next door. Police found he had taken fifty-nine slugs, setting what was then a record.

The nests that rival mobsters had set up for Capone or his associates were somehow discovered by police.

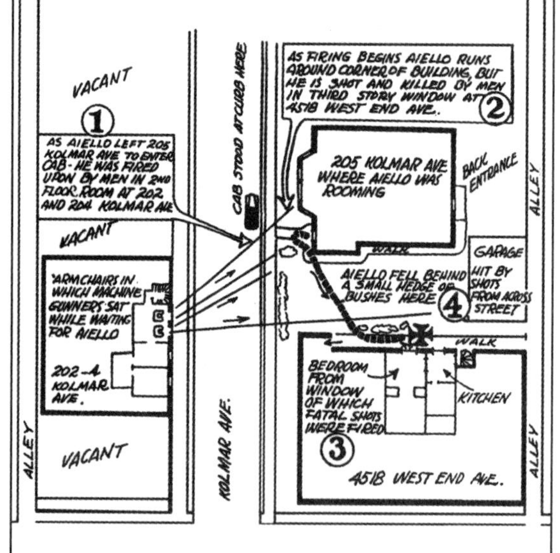

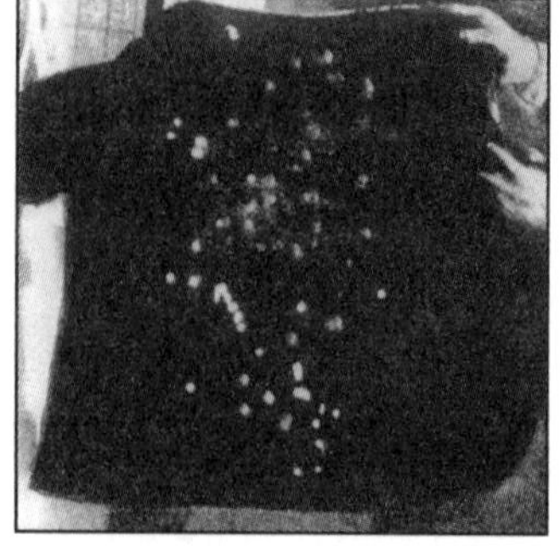

Capone's most elaborate machine-gun nest took out rival Joe Aiello (right) in 1930 as he ran from one blast of gunfire into another from the apartment building next door (above). His riddled overcoat (far right) is testament to the effectiveness of the plan.

was sufficiently obvious that a cop could lose his job, a bootlegger his life, and either could go to prison if he lacked good judgment or good luck. Ironically, national Prohibition filled the country's prisons with mostly harmless lawbreakers, while providing others with opportunities rarely encountered in the course of honest labor. A special talent for risk management probably made the difference.

This situation prevailed nationwide. Where Chicago and New York differed greatly was in their toleration of the violence that accompanied Prohibition. By the 1920s New York regarded itself as cultured and cosmopolitan; and to the extent that crime increased, a worried local Establishment closed down its vice district, vanquished its "fighting gangs," and promoted the city as America's undisputed leader in the fine arts and civilized living. Its handsome and colorful mayor, Jimmy Walker, was forced to resign, but his stylishness had compensated for his corruption; and until Arnold Rothstein's murder in 1928, he had been a gentleman gangster who bankrolled criminal enterprises while discouraging public gun battles.

By contrast, Chicago's mayor was "Big Bill" Thompson, a slobbish onetime cowboy elected mainly because his political incompetence and toleration of gang wars made up for his embarrassing public pronouncements. He had less couth than Capone in a city that attracted so much attention with the Thompson submachine gun that it became known as the "Chicago Typewriter."

With the city's magnificent lakefront, creative post-fire architecture, world-class museums, and commercial importance, the average Chicagoan regarded New Yorkers as pansies. Rather than enter a cultural competition they would have lost, they agreed with Carl Sandburg to be the city of broad shoulders and hog butcher to the world; to the annoyance of civic leaders they took a certain perverse pride in the outrageousness of their gangsters. Most agreed with the wisecrack of Capone: "When I sell liquor, they call it bootlegging; when my patrons serve it on silver trays on Lake Shore Drive, they call it hospitality."

Unlike New York, Chicago enjoyed its tough reputation, as reflected in a local newspaper's amazingly casual coverage of one election day's action:

> GUNMEN FIGHT ELECTION WAR;
> OTHER VIOLENCE
>
> One man was killed and two were wounded, one probably fatally, during election disturbances yesterday.
>
> Voters and precinct workers in some sections of the city were slugged, intimidated and even kidnapped. There were narrow escapes from death as rival gunmen in fast automobiles fired volleys while near polling places.
>
> A gun battle between two groups of gangsters in automobiles ended almost in front of a polling place at 405 South Hoyne Street, when John Mackey, 1224 West Madison Street, a well known police character, was shot and killed. Eleven bullets were found in Mackey's head and body.
>
> Two Others Wounded
>
> One of his companions, Claude Maddox, was shot in the back and a second, Anthony Kissane, another notorious character, was found huddled in an alley

nearby a few minutes later, splattered with the blood of his dead friend and nursing a sprained ankle which he suffered in the leap from Mackey's car. Mackey and Kissane were arrested ten days ago as the bandits who robbed a Northwest Side bank, but were freed when they established alibis. . . .

Even the *Chicago Tribune*, smarting from the disparaging remarks that New York and other cities enjoyed heaping on the "Gem of the Prairie," found a poetic way to shrug off critics. Referring to the publicity generated when the governor of Illinois decided National Guard troops might be needed to keep the peace, the "*Trib*," tongue firmly in cheek, found the silver lining in an April 1927 editorial:

THE TERRIFYING CHICAGOAN

Our officialdom, local and state, did something to help [Chicago's reputation] along. The National Guard touch, a few days before the voting, indicated that each voter might go to the polls under the protection of bayonets. The police machine-gun squads and the riot details helped out the picture. . . .

Thus far the most inspired picture of political life in Chicago has been given in London by the *London Daily News*: "Three thousand hooligan gangs are carrying on a campaign of brigandage and murder," etc. Machine guns, bullet swept streets, death lists and the casualties all over the place.

It may be for the best. A Chicagoan soon will be regarded as a person who is alive because of particular individual hardihood, courage and marksmanship. He will be known as the hard boiled egg of the world. He has survived. That is sufficient. He may have a quiet, even chastened, appearance, but no one, particularly no one abroad, will rely on that. The man probably can shoot from six pockets at once and will if annoyed. . . .

Under the eccentric leadership of publisher "Colonel" Robert R. McCormick (who modestly billed the *Chicago Tribune* as "The World's Greatest Newspaper" beneath its front-page logo and required it to "Americanize" the spelling of many English words), the "*Trib*" battled Mayor "Big Bill the Builder" Thompson, trumpeted against his corruption, championed reform as a matter of principle, but above all defended Chicago against its detractors, especially those in New York. And in a city whose newspapers had fought circulation wars with the same sluggers and gunmen used by its politicians, and condoned nearly any trick or scam a reporter might use to scoop the opposition (giving rise to the "Chicago school of journalism"), the *Chicago Tribune*'s staunch opposition to Prohibition mitigated its view of bootlegging as a crime. This forced the paper to agree on some issues with Chicago's clown mayor, who named pet rats after his political enemies, threatened (for the benefit of Irish and German voters) to burn history books uncritical of the British, and to "punch King George in the snoot."

The middle ground that most Chicago papers took was to condemn crime in general but blame it largely on a foolishly conceived and badly enforced law, and beyond that simply to report every gangland killing for the benefit of its readers.

RIO BURKE AND AL CAPONE

She was born in Richmond, Kentucky, in 1903, learned to play the piano and violin as a teenager, and moved to Chicago in 1919 where a cousin who was in the "follies" helped her land a singing job at "Big Jim" Colosimo's lavish restaurant on South Wabash, in Chicago's New Levee vice district. Under her given name, Ray Rucker, she also sang at a nightclub in Chicago Heights, where she met and married a handsome devil named Dominic Roberto, aka Ray Roberts, on April 14, 1924. He was spiffy, debonair, worked for Al Capone, and kept her in diamonds and fur coats, which was an exciting change from her old Kentucky home. That he was one of Capone's lieutenants was immaterial, though at one point her maid found a gunny sack full of pistols and sawed-off shotguns stashed in a closet. "When I asked Dominic about them, he said, 'Oh, a bunch of the boys are going hunting.'"

Rio Burke was a featured singer with prominent bands of the day, among them, the Enrique Madriguera Orchestra (above), which employed Fidel Castro (fourth from right) as a visiting musician. She earlier had performed at Colosimo's, married South Side gangster Dominic Roberto, and once played host to Al Capone when he was "on the lam." She enjoyed talking about her young and exciting flapper days before her death in 1994.

It was a few months later that she became the hostess of Al Capone himself. After the machine-gunning of several of "Klondike" O'Donnell's friends outside the Pony Inn in 1926—inadvertently including Assistant State's Attorney William McSwiggin, who happened to be palling around with the bootleggers—the resulting uproar sent Capone into hiding at the home of Rio and Dominic Roberto. During the eight days he was at their abode in Chicago Heights, Capone was a perfect gentleman—undemanding, eating what he was served—and pleasant company, Rio remembers. When the immediate heat was off, he and Dominic drove to Indiana, north to Michigan, then to Wisconsin.

Dominic contacted others who would keep Capone out of sight, and after three months, Capone arranged to have authorities meet him at the Illinois-Indiana state line. Facing no indictments or warrants for his arrest, he returned to Cicero, where he headquartered at the Hawthorne Hotel while maintaining rooms at the Metropole Hotel in Chicago.

A few years later Rio and Roberto divorced but remained friends. He was later deported to Italy and the two lost contact. Rio continued her singing career, at one point joining Cuban bandleader Enrique Madriguera, whose orchestra at one time employed a young Fidel Castro, who briefly toured the U.S. with Madriguera before returning to Cuba, where he eventually decided to go into politics.

Once the Chicago Beer Wars were going full-blast, the Cook County Morgue found itself hard-pressed to keep up with the number of gangland murder victims killed in cars, bars, and on the street.

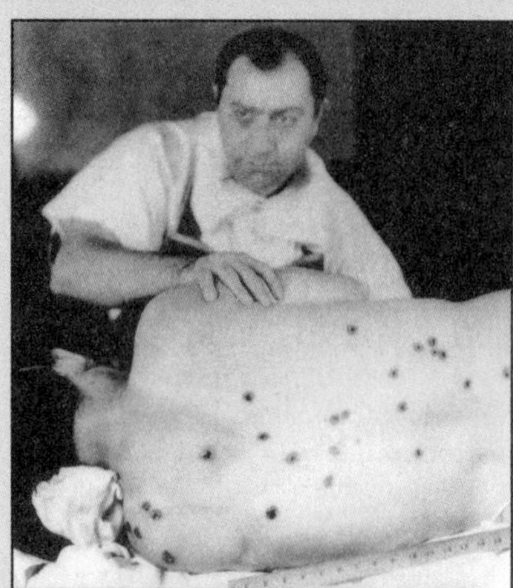

The Chicago Crime Commission

The period of lawlessness that typically follows major wars began in the U.S. even before the armistice was signed in 1918 and was aggravated by several factors. Besides inflation and unemployment for returning veterans, the country had to deal with race riots and increasing labor unrest. The best new career opportunity was created by Prohibition. Technically, bootlegging was a consensual crime, but the automobile had put crime on wheels instead of horses, and soon enough the neighborhood bootlegger would find himself drawn into the established criminal community. And not long after that he would start carrying a gun, just in case.

Meanwhile, most urban political leadership remained a monument to bad government. New York had long been ruled by the Tammany Hall politicians who carried on the corruption of Boss Tweed even after the Tweed Ring's flagrant lawbreaking landed him in jail. They remained impervious to reform during the city's adolescence in the nineteenth century, controlling street crime with gang muscle during elections; they granted or denied immunity from the law

In Chicago, an "honest politician" was defined as one who, "When you bought him, he stayed bought."

by way of their own goon squads and those credentialed as police.

Even New York's professional cops did not venture into certain neighborhoods, such as the notorious "Five Points" intersection in lower Manhattan, where vice and violence could flourish without civic interference. Bodies were dumped in the East River or carted to neutral territory where they could be collected without a lot of aggravating paperwork. Official police did not trespass there except when a respectable or prominent citizen had been mistaken for an ordinary drunk, survived and protested a beating and robbery, or when influential family members identified a body that made waves at City Hall. If a "copper" investigated, he would take along several colleagues and, in some cases, a small army of New York's "finest."

The era of New York's fighting gangs predated the revolution in transportation, communications, and journalism that took place around the turn of the century, by which time the Tammany political machine had become powerful enough to impose controls and polish the city's image.

Meanwhile, Chicago still was a growing trade center, starting to clean house after the days of wide-open prostitution and gambling in its Levee vice districts that bordered what would become the "Loop" (so-called for the rectangle of elevated tracks around the central business district). But it remained controlled by ward politicians who were more responsive to their ethnic constituents than to City Hall, and who maintained order mainly by subsidizing the larger gangs in their social activities by way of "athletic clubs," whose members engaged about equally in baseball and burglary. Except for occasional brawling, they also functioned as a kind of underworld police, providing neighborhood businessmen with affordably priced protection against outsiders, or themselves.

Chicago politicians and police, many of them on gangland payrolls, seemed indifferent to "organized crime," and some cops even moonlighted as guards on bootleggers' trucks.

For years the hardcore vice district even had its own newspapers, which thrived on gossip, criticized "unethical" conduct by named prostitutes, and warned citizens about brothels that were hazardous to patronize. Such peer pressure usually was more effective than any half-hearted law enforcement. When dogooders tried to close down the increasingly notorious Levee district, lavish and well-regulated whorehouses like one operated by the Everleigh sisters simply instructed their inmates to don their Sunday best and either march in protest or go door to door in respectable neighborhoods, asking to rent rooms.

These stunts often were inspired by such prominent Chicago aldermen as "Hinky Dink" Kenna and "Bathhouse" John Coughlin, who rivaled or exceeded New York officials in their unabashed venality and who controlled local politics for decades. Their boldness prompted the reform-minded Alderman Robert Merriam to remark, with a sense of perverse pride, that "Chicago is unique; it is the only totally corrupt city in America." (If someone pointed out that other cities were equally corrupt, he would add, "But they aren't nearly as big.")

Because of primitive communications and parochial journalism, New York had weathered its own worst years in the middle and late nineteenth century without attracting national publicity. Chicago acquired its reputation as the country's capital of crime and corruption only after it, too, became a major metropolis, which coincided with such other early twentieth-century developments as newspaper chains connected by telegraphic wire services and the novel forms of crime and violence that accompanied Prohibition.

Despite a fledgling movement to professionalize, most police departments remained relics of the past in their organization, administration, enforcement practices, and allegiance to ward bosses who easily circumvented civil-service rules. But the corruption and incompetence that people were helpless to correct at the polls could at least be mitigated by commercial interests, the traditional source of a city's prosperity. Crime, especially murder and other violence, was bad for business, and Chicago still was in an uproar over a bloody daylight robbery on the western outskirts of the city.

"Ammunition Eddie" Wheed

On August 18, 1917, one "Ammunition Eddie" Wheed and two accomplices held up the Winslow Brothers iron plant at 4500 West Harrison, killing two Brink's Express guards and standing off 250 police in a spectacular two-hour gun battle that attracted national attention. Wheed was captured and later hung, but this was considered the most outrageous crime in anyone's memory, and newspaper publisher Col. Henry Barrett Chamberlin appealed to the Chicago Association of Commerce to sponsor an anti-crime committee. Chamberlin and other prominent Chicago businessmen had enough leverage to demand such reforms, and the device created to accomplish this was an independently organized, privately funded crime commission formed in 1919—the first such organization in the country.

The Chicago Crime Commission became a watchdog group formed to investigate and report "upon the prevalence and prevention

THE "PUBLIC ENEMY" CAMPAIGN

The expression that would translate into English as "public enemy" appears as early as Roman times and over the centuries has cropped up occasionally in other lands and languages. In this country, according to author Rose Keefe, "public enemy" dates back at least to May 1757 when the *American Magazine and Monthly Chronicle for the British Colonies* published a paper vilifying the North American Indian. Although the writer made use of the term only once in the fifteen-page essay, his gruesome description of the tortures that "savages" inflicted on their foes seemed calculated more to alarm than inform his readers about the perils of being captured—a journalistic practice that the Chicago Crime Commission would have found instructive when it released its first "public enemy" list on April 24, 1930.

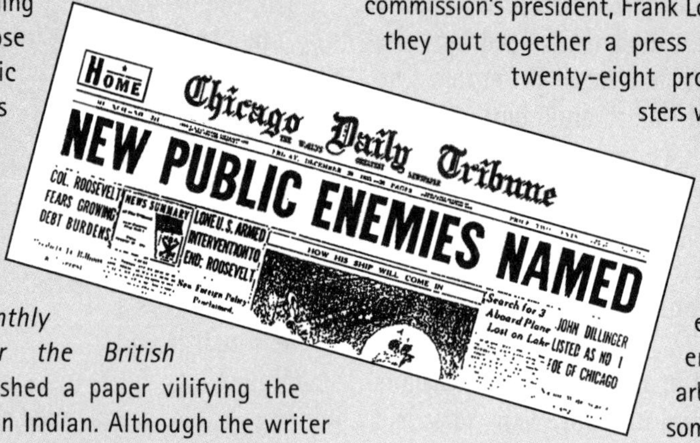
HOME
Chicago Daily Tribune
NEW PUBLIC ENEMIES NAMED
COL. ROOSEVELT FEARS GROWING DEBT BURDENS
NEWS SUMMARY
LONE U.S. ARMED INTERVENTION TO END: ROOSEVELT
New Foreign Policy Proclaimed.
HOW HIS SHIP WILL COME IN
Search for 3 Aboard Plane Lost on Lake
JOHN DILLINGER LISTED AS NO 1 FOE OF CHICAGO

Likely no one at the CCC had encountered the 1757 essay or any rare historical reference, so the credit for conceiving the commission's famous "public enemy" campaign goes to its finance chairman George Paddock. He had been reading Arthur Train's "Mister Tutt" stories, in one of which a wealthy New York murderer had been nailed for a violation of the municipal code. He wondered if the same approach might be used against Chicago's seemingly invulnerable gangsters and took the idea to the CCC's operating director, Henry Barrett Chamberlin, who shared it with the commission's president, Frank Loesch. Together they put together a press release listing twenty-eight prominent mobsters who had eluded justice, not to mention the Chicago police force. The twenty-eight apparently was an arbitrary number, some truly notorious, some virtually "retired," and some missing.

The first list was alphabetical, starting with Joe Aiello followed by Capone in fourth place. In an elaborating phone call with *Chicago Tribune* reporter James Doherty, Chamberlin had used the term "public enemies," which so charmed Doherty that Chamberlin used it in subsequent interviews with other reporters. One way or another, the alphabetical list was rearranged to put Al Capone at the top, and immediately Big Al was being declared Public Enemy No. 1. In concurrent interviews, Frank Loesch echoed Chamberlain's sentiments, and as the commission's president he often was credited with coining the expression.

Thus, Capone became universally declared

"No. 1," and the "public enemies" campaign was soon adopted by other states and cities. Loesch generously proposed that the U.S. Justice Department create a similar list, only to have the idea rejected by J. Edgar Hoover on the disingenuous grounds that other hoodlums would start aspiring to reach the top. But the phrase became so popular with journalists that they were declaring any notorious criminal a "public enemy," and Hoover did not go so far as to send out press releases "correcting" the newspapers. He obviously benefited from the publicity, although he and the FBI never officially used the term. To thoroughly confuse the issue, the comic strip *Dick Tracy* (a G-man-type cop, with grotesque villains inspired by such outlaws like "Pretty Boy" Floyd and "Baby Face" Nelson) and the James Cagney movie *The Public Enemy* both appeared in 1931, followed by radio shows celebrating the FBI.

By the middle 1930s Hoover had capitulated to the extent of naming his "Most Wanted" criminals, which sometimes numbered ten, with Hoover (when asked) trying to explain to an obstinate press that their ranking was entirely arbitrary. The result was that newspapers continued declaring FBI's top fugitives to be "public enemies," sometimes contradicting themselves over which of the criminals—"Baby Face Nelson" or "Pretty Boy" Floyd, say—was currently "No. 1."

Finally surrendering to journalistic insistence on calling a "Most Wanted" criminal a "public enemy," Hoover created an official "Ten Most Wanted" list on March 14, 1950. But as far as writers and editors are concerned, the credit for creating the "public enemy" campaign always goes to the FBI, which, in its glory days of the 1930s, was tolerating the confusion as a useful adjunct to its "War on Crime."

THE PUBLIC ENEMY LIST

(Spellings by the Chicago Crime Commission)

1. ALPHONSE CAPONE "Scarface"
2. ANTHONY VOLPE "Mops"
3. RALPH CAPONE
4. FRANK RIO "Frank Kline," "Frank Cline," and "James Costa"
5. JACK McGURN "Machine Gun," "Jack DeMore"
6. JAMES BELCASTRO
7. ROCCO FANELLI
8. LAWRENCE MANGANO
9. JACK ZUTA
10. JACK GUSICK
11. FRANK DIAMOND "Frank Permaratta"
12. GEORGE "Bugs" MORAN
13. JOE AIELLO
14. EDWARD "Spike" O'DONNELL
15. JOE SALTIS "Polack Joe"
16. FRANK McERLANE
17. VINCENT McERLANE
18. WILLIAM NEIMOTH
19. DANNY STANTON
20. MYLES O'DONNELL
21. FRANK LAKE
22. TERRY DRUGGAN
23. WILLIAM O'DONNELL "Klondike"
24. GEORGE BARKER "Red"
25. WILLIAM WHITE "Three Finger Jack"
26. JOSEPH GENERO "Peppy"
27. LEO MONGOVEN
28. JAMES "Fur" SAMMONS

of crime," monitor police performance, and work to improve police services through better administration. It had no law-enforcement authority and, in fact, was barred by its charter from engaging directly in crime fighting. But through its sponsoring association it could initiate and influence legislation, and it could make life uncomfortable for city politicians and their personally appointed police officials, who had little if any aptitude, experience, training, or administrative ability. The Commission aimed to coax and/or threaten city government into professionalizing the police department, the way stockholders might force changes in a badly run corporation. Because the same conditions prevailed in nearly every city, the Chicago Crime Commission became the prototype for dozens of similar organizations at municipal and state levels throughout the country, all sponsored by associations of businessmen.

By 1925 the idea was so popular, and the crime problem so pressing, that a National Crime Commission was formed in New York City at the behest of Elbert H. Gary, chief of the United States Steel Corp., who then pressured such prominent men as Chief Justice Charles Evans Hughes, future president Franklin Roosevelt, former Illinois governor Newton Baker and a former U.S. secretary of war to serve as its executive committee. American police agencies everywhere found themselves operating in a spotlight of publicity and being pressed to organize more efficiently, modernize their procedures, set up centralized fingerprint files and criminal identification bureaus, adopt radio and other new technology, and network with each other to exchange information.

The Chicago Crime Commission not only pioneered the movement but formalized the concept of "public enemies." Its first such list, issued in 1930, named Al Capone as "Public Enemy No. 1," much to Capone's annoyance. "The Big Fellow" had emerged as the city's leading bootlegger but had gone to some pains to portray himself as a businessman and public benefactor whose troops fought only to make sure the booze got through. When the Depression struck, he opened soup kitchens, to which merchants donated cheerfully when visited by young men whose suits were specially tailored to accommodate shoulder holsters. Most Chicagoans had no beef with Big Al, and some considered him a true Horatio Alger character to have done so much with so little.

Declaring Capone the city's top "public enemy" was a public-relations triumph for the commission, just as the recent St. Valentine's Day Massacre had been a public-relations disaster for Capone. Newspapers everywhere bannered this new publicity gimmick, and the "public enemy" concept captured the nation's imagination. It helped transform him from the Babe Ruth of American gangsters, as someone put it, back into "Scarface" and confirmed Chicago as the gangster capital of the world.

A few years earlier, the Chicago Crime Commission, its novelty diminishing, had saved itself from extinction by subordinating its police advisory function to full-time gangster-bashing. The machine-gun murder of State's Attorney William McSwiggin in 1926 appeared to violate the understand-

Several prominent Chicago businessmen, members of the Chicago Crime Commission, banded together as the "Secret Six" and collaborated with Eliot Ness's "Untouchables" in certain extralegal (and sometimes illegal) crime-fighting schemes. Eventually they themselves were disbanded because of staff corruption.

ing that gangsters only killed each other, and though McSwiggin's death was probably a fluke (a case of his visiting a speakeasy in the company of bootleggers, for reasons never satisfactorily explained), the crime commission launched a major investigation that revived public alarm over gangland violence. It also worked with a special squad of anonymous crime fighters nicknamed the "Secret Six." Limited by its own charter to improving police administration, it supported the Chicago Association of Commerce's plan to grow an "action arm" of unidentified prominent citizens who organized a private, extralegal police force, composed mainly of off-duty cops and possibly some federal prohibition agents. (Eliot Ness's famed Untouchables had some connection with the "Secret Six," at least according to Ness's coauthor Oscar Fraley.)

The Association of Commerce eventually had to disband the "Secret Six" for using vigilante tactics, but the crime commission survived by becoming professional mob-watchers—pestering the gangs with publicity and creating voluminous files on every hoodlum in town.

A most remarkable project of the Chicago Crime Commission was to start and keep a running body count of every "gangland-style" (to use its own terminology) slaying since 1919, which provided statistics of a sort and always made good newspaper copy, by documenting the shortage of suspects and the nearly total absence of prosecutions, much less convictions, in Chicago's gangland murders. For the victims, it served no worthwhile purpose except to give each at least some small measure of immortality.

THE ONE-WAY RIDE

It would have required no great leap of imagination to conceive the idea of killing someone in a car instead of on the street, but in the early twenties the automobile itself was enough of a novelty that taking someone for a "ride" seemed like a significant advance in murder technology. Accordingly, writers of the day declared a number of different gangsters, all Chicagoans, to be the "inventor" of the "one-way ride."

Modern writers, all cribbing from the same few books, whose authors had cribbed from even fewer sources, usually attribute the first "ride" murder to "Hymie" Weiss, as if this were gospel. (Different newspaper writers of the day named Frank McErlane, "Nails" Morton, Dean O'Banion, and others.) In fact, a survey of killings finds instances of bodies dumped from cars in New York rather than Chicago as early as 1918 and in Connecticut as far back as 1912. While there had to be a first time that someone was murdered in a car, it would be historically interesting to discover which writer launched the legend that credits Weiss with originating the "one-way ride." Weiss possibly was the first to coin the expression and was credited with that. Just as likely, some Chicago reporter used the phrase to describe yet another murder v\ictim whose body was discarded on a country road sometime in the twenties, and it became instant shorthand for such killings.

Another gangland practice was the disposal of murder victims in lakes and rivers, giving rise to another item of gangster lore—the "concrete overshoes" (or overcoat, or kimono), a technique that involved planting someone's feet in a washtub (or its equivalent) of fresh cement to be later pushed off a pier or the back of a boat. If this was a common practice, New York's East River, Chicago's Lake Michigan, and many other waterways should be cluttered with hundreds of rusty washtubs with leg bones sticking up like potted plants. A fairly thorough search of books on gangster history, as well as the *New York Times* Index, reports the occasional corpse in a sunken car, but no divers engaging in their popular sport or searching for shipwrecks or artifacts have found the remains of a gangster scuttled in the classic movie manner.

The fact is, bodies are hard to dispose of in water. They tend to bloat and float to the surface, as in the case of one mobster, suspected of skimming, who was stabbed with ice picks,

Cop—Oh! Pardon me! I thought maybe it was a dead gangster!

weighted with heavy slot machines, and dumped in a lake in the Catskills. The wounds sealed with swelling, and he eventually came bobbing to the surface, slot machines and all. Similarly, crewmen on a ship in Boston Harbor were surprised to discover a female murder victim, still secured in a full-size bathtub where her homicidal husband had left her, when she surfaced in her porcelain vessel and was deemed an obstruction to shipping.

A practice that originated with the press was "X Marks the Spot," in one form or another. Usually this occurred when a reporter reached the scene after the body had been removed, or if an editor, aware of reader sensibilities, deliberately used a post-corpse photograph because the original was too gruesome. In the St. Valentine's Day Massacre, some papers declined to use pictures of the bodies or "grayed" them out, while the more sensational press splashed the scene across the entire front page.

An "X" often was used in newspapers when a photographer arrived after removal of the body. Along with that went "X Marks the Spot" and the gangland expression of being "Put on the Spot."

Teacher: NOW WHICH OF YOU KNOWS WHAT THAT SIGN MEANS?
Small Bobby: I KNOW, TEACHER! IT MARKS THE SPOT WHERE THE BODY WAS FOUND.

Bombs and Bombast

Chicago's "Pineapple Primary"

Chicago became the American underworld's bombing capital before the turn of the century. By the late 1920s the practice had evolved into a cross between an art and a science, thanks to the greater precision demanded by a new breed of criminal known as the racketeer.

In the city's Italian neighborhoods, Black Hand extortionists had long used bombs against shopkeepers, just as they used kidnappings against those whose wealth was not in the form of business property. In other neighborhoods, particularly the Irish, extortionists also used bombs but refined their threats from simple ultimatums to offers of "protection" (mainly against the protectors).

During Chicago's "Pineapple Primary" of 1928, citizens were said to jokingly complain that without a bomb to wake them up in the morning, many would be late getting to work.

But the bomb also was a popular means of exposing a small-scale brothel or gambling parlor that was demonstrating too much independence. With painted ladies running around in housecoats, or clouds of smoke and betting slips billowing out of a gutted storefront, the arriving police had no choice but to announce the discovery of an illegal establishment. During the Chicago gambling war of 1907, pool halls and whist clubs, the usual fronts for gambling operations, were popping like champagne corks.

The bombs used to expose rival vice or gambling operations usually were little more than large, homemade firecrackers—a sizable cardboard container filled with homemade flash powder or black gunpowder. Such "cannon crackers," as they were called, produced much noise and smoke but usually did only superficial damage and rarely hurt anyone. However, a few serious Black Hand bombers might add bolts, nails, glass, and other shrapnel to their cannon crackers to make them genuine antipersonnel devices. (In the commercial fireworks trade, any unusually large firecracker still is known as a "Dago bomb.")

252 IT'S A RACKET

Sept. 30—Jackson Park, Parked Automobile. Revenge or racket.

Sept. 30—5425 Broadway. Taxi Cab Garage. Revenge.

Sept. 30—3300 N. Halsted St. Taxi Cab Garage. Revenge.

OCTOBER

Oct. 3—5345 Cottage Grove Av. Garage. Max Finkel. Racket.

Oct. 12—101 Wacker Drive (lower level). Soft Drink Parlor. Joseph Ryan. Prohibition.

Oct. 13—8041 St. Lawrence Av. M. E. Daily. Private garage. Unknown.

Oct. 14—4154 W. 16th. Kazimir Lipkin. Chicken store. Racket.

Oct. 14—5620 Stony Island Av. W. T. Woodley. Garage Racket.

Oct. 16—2050 W. Roosevelt Rd. Kenard Shoe Store. Racket.

Oct. 16—4032 W. Roosevelt Road. Irving Wittenberg. Bakery Shop. Racket.

Oct. 17—5507 So. Michigan Av. Speedway Tire Service. Racket.

Oct. 17—2354 So. Crawford Av. Kostka Bros. Auto Accessory & Battery Shop. Racket.

Oct. 18—4032 W. Roosevelt Road. Irving Wittenberg. Bakery Shop. Racket.

Oct. 20—4065 Sheridan Road. Apt. House. Earl Leatherman. Racket.

Oct. 24—220 No. Clark. Wacker Grill—Steffeo & Kaplin. Prohibition.

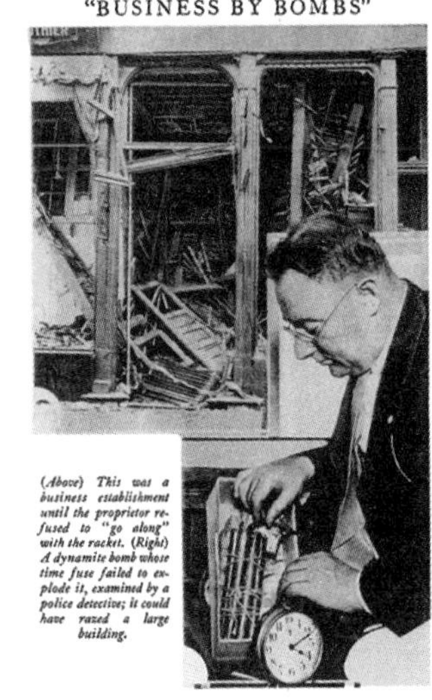

"BUSINESS BY BOMBS"

(Above) This was a business establishment until the proprietor refused to "go along" with the racket. (Right) A dynamite bomb whose time fuse failed to explode it, examined by a police detective; it could have razed a large building.

This two-page spread from It's a Racket! *(Hostetter and Beesley, 1929) discusses Chicago's bombing war that reached all-time heights during the "Pineapple Primary" of 1928 when Mayor Dever's crackdown on bootlegging had failed and gangsters were developing more sophisticated "time" bombs for "racketeering."*

Crime had been "organized" at the local level long before the twenties, but the arrival of Prohibition in 1920 led to the proliferation of rival bootlegging gangs and labor racketeers whose bombs became more sophisticated and more lethal. Cannon crackers gave way to dynamite, the longtime favorite of labor radicals, and to the homemade pipe bomb, a three- or four-inch length of pipe threaded and capped at both ends, drilled for a fuse, and packed with ordinary black powder available from any gun shop.

The typical dynamite bomb consisted of two to five sticks taped together and detonated by a commercial fuse leading to a blasting cap, or by an electric blasting cap wired to a car's ignition system or attached to a battery and timing device. The more powerful bombs could dismantle an automobile or brick building.

The pipe bomb had only a fraction of the power of dynamite, but its size and weight would carry it through a plate-glass window when thrown from a passing car, and the metal casing fragmented into sharp projectiles, especially if serrated with a file or hacksaw. The professional version of the pipe bomb was the Army's Mark I Mills hand grenade—the traditional "pineapple" which was regularly stolen from Army and National Guard armories.

The more exotic types of military and industrial explosives—TNT, nitroglycerin, and the like—were never widely used by gangsters, for the simple reason that they were harder to come by, more dangerous to handle, and dynamite or black powder would usually do the job. (Safecrackers often used nitro because of its shearing power, and the fact that it could be poured into a safe door through seams or a drilled hole, but the usual means of obtaining it—literally by cooking it out of dynamite sticks over a stove, made safe-blowing a fairly hazardous business.

Chicago bombing reached its all-time high in the late twenties, when rival gangs were not only competing for territorial control, extorting businesses, and seizing labor locals, but also terrorizing political-reform candidates on behalf of the mob-controlled machine. The local election of April 1928 made history of sorts as the "Pineapple Primary," for political power, as well as civic policy, city jobs, and police priorities, were determined by the winning faction, for whom the general election in November was little more than a formality. This particularly violent period inspired one journalist to write:

The rockets' red glare,
The bombs bursting in air,
Gave proof through the night
That Chicago's still there

By the end of the twenties, Chicago bombers were taking professional pride in their work. In one rare instance of prosecution, a defendant indignantly explained to a judge that the absence of injuries to upstairs residents of a blasted building was no accident: "It was technical skill. I build a bomb to do its work and quit."

In the thirties, with the rise of the Syndicate and its more subtle and businesslike forms of crime, Chicago-style terror bombing declined; but for certain hard cases who could not be moved by friendly persuasion, or who were too wily and well-guarded to be removed by bullets, the bomb in the car remained a popular tactic.

Because dynamite was powerful, yet relatively easy to obtain and handle, and because it could be detonated by an electrical blasting cap, it always has been the explosive of choice for car bombers. Besides the ignition-system trigger, some bombers hooked charges to car horns, headlights or even homemade switches installed in the suspension system to conceal the connections from prospective victims who might check under the hood for any strange wires.

Weather Forecast
Fair, slightly warmer tonight; Wednesday warmer, probably showers Wednesday night.

ONLY AFTERNOON PAPER IN COLUMBUS RECEIVING ASSOCIATED PRESS DISPATCHES

Columbus Evening Dispatch.

VOL. LVII, NO. 285.

TUESDAY, APRIL 10, 1928.

Phone Number of OHIO'S Greatest Home DAILY ADams 6161

PRICE TWO CENTS.

CHICAGO VOTES IN TERROR

SINCLAIR HIT, DEFENDED AS TEAPOT TRIAL OPENS

DEFENSE QUICK TO USE FALL'S DEPOSITION

Wright's Opening Argument Obviously Takes in Evidence of Document.

STORIES AT VARIANCE

"Corruption" and "Patriotism" Versions of Leasing Given by Lawyers.

Connect Poor Ventilation and Congressional Deaths

WITNESS SAYS KLAN CAUSED RIOT IN NILES

Story of "Night Riders" and Proposed "Reign of Terror" Told in Court.

DETECTIVE TESTIFIES

Trial in Federal Court to Oust Klansmen from Pennsylvania Is Now On.

NEW PRESIDENT OF KENT NORMAL

CHICAGO, APRIL 10.—(INS.)—In the first four hours of Chicago's voting in the primary election today the following disorders were reported to police:

One alderman was released after he was said to have been kidnaped.

One political worker was shot.

Four election workers were kidnaped.

Three election workers were badly beaten.

Seven reports were received of ballot box stuffing.

Eleven poling places reported invaded by hoodlums.

The entire election board, officials and clerks of a precinct polling place on the West side was reported kidnaped by gangsters today and the ballot boxes wrecked.

ONE SHOT, FOUR KIDNAPED AND THREE BEATEN

Polls Open Amid Charges of Ballot Box Stuffing and Wild Disorder.

ALDERMAN IS RELEASED

Hoodlums Reported Wrecking Election Places While Police Roam City.

THE WEATHER

CHICAGO AMERICAN

Closing N.Y. STOCKS

BOMBINGS LAID TO RACKET WAR

Turf Fans Flock to 2 Tracks as Racing Opens Here

THIS IS GOOD NEWS

GANGS' BATTLE FOR TEAMING LINKED TO BLASTS

Flight of Sailor From Hibbard Building Told by Witness

BASEBALL

SPORTSMAN'S AND AURORA MECCAS

Warm Afternoon Makes Conditions Ideal for Bangtails

Morgan to Face Bank Quiz

SENATE VOTES $500,000,000 STATE AID

Bill Now Returns to House for Action on Amendments

In his review of Prohibition-era bombings, University of Chicago sociologist John Landesco came up with the following figures:

1920	51	1925	113
1921	60	1926	89
1922	69	1927	108
1923	55	1928	116
1924	92		

While bombings were a communal Chicago tradition—one reporter quipped that without a pre-dawn explosion to wake them up, many citizens would be late getting to work, and another observed that the main service performed by the police bomb squad was to record the dimensions of the window glass that would need replacement—the election of reform Mayor William Dever in 1924 upset the city's acceptable level of corruption and doubled the workload of Chicago's "bomb trust," as reporters called it, which included one James Belcastro, "King of the Bombers."

The Dever victory and his crackdown on speakeasies, combined with the death of peacekeeper Mike Merlo and Dean O'Banion's decision to branch out on his own, ended nearly four years of relative harmony known as the pax Torrio, after John Torrio, who had persuaded rival gangs to respect one another's territories. O'Banion's murder triggered nearly five years of "beer wars" as the city's booze cartel fragmented, and bootleggers sought to expand their respective territories.

First swindled by O'Banion in the Sieben Brewery bust and then badly wounded by his former North Side colleagues, Torrio (who had been blamed for O'Banion's murder), took the jail term mandated by a second Volstead Act conviction and turned his own expanding beer, vice, and gambling empire over to Capone, a young understudy who had come a long way since Brooklyn. Mostly for show, he shrugged off Dever's closing of his cramped offices in the Four Deuces club at 2222 South Wabash and rented several floors of the Metropole Hotel at Michigan Avenue and Twenty-third Street. However, he moved his main headquarters a few miles west to the Chicago suburb of Cicero, residing first at the Anton (later Alton) until its neighboring hotel, the Hawthorne, was rehabbed to his specifications.

"Big Bill" Thompson's defeat by Dever's reformers did not diminish Thompson's news value, however. He amused the press by ordering construction of a large yawl for a South Seas expedition to capture an elusive "tree-climbing fish" he'd heard about somewhere and believed might be anthropology's missing link. That vessel and venture made it only as far as New Orleans before it foundered on a reef of cash-flow problems, but by then Capone was making up for any shortage of headlines with spectacular gun battles, including a mini-massacre whose victims included—probably by an unlucky coincidence—Assistant State's Attorney William McSwiggin. New York's "Lucky" Luciano supposedly returned from a business trip to

Chicago declaring the city "a goddam crazy place. Nobody's safe on the streets."

Actually, the streets were safe enough for the average citizen, because one thing Capone demanded of his troops was that they abandon the predatory crime on which many had subsisted and enjoy the prosperity that came with working for Big Al, who paid well for obedience. Capone had to continually remind businessmen and short-sighted officials that any truly determined effort to close down his booze operations would lead to a serious revival of street crime by unemployed bootleggers.

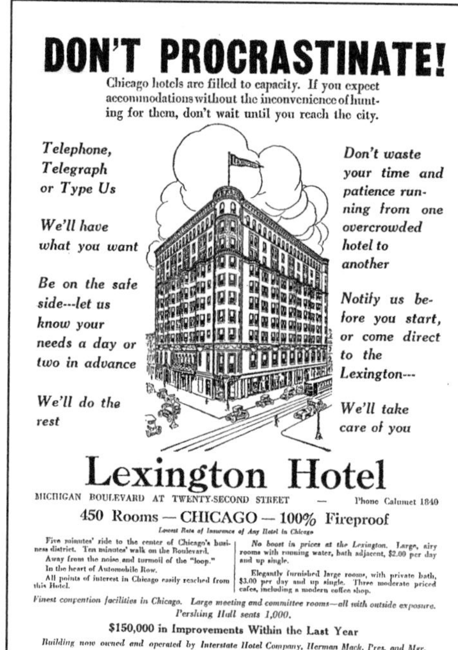

DON'T PROCRASTINATE!
Chicago hotels are filled to capacity. If you expect accommodations without the inconvenience of hunting for them, don't wait until you reach the city.
Telephone, Telegraph or Type Us
We'll have what you want
Be on the safe side---let us know your needs a day or two in advance
We'll do the rest
Don't waste your time and patience running from one overcrowded hotel to another
Notify us before you start, or come direct to the Lexington---
We'll take care of you
Lexington Hotel
MICHIGAN BOULEVARD AT TWENTY-SECOND STREET — Phone Calumet 1840
450 Rooms — CHICAGO — 100% Fireproof
Lowest Rate of Insurance of Any Hotel in Chicago
Five minutes' ride to the center of Chicago's business district. Ten minutes' walk on the Boulevard.
Away from the noise and turmoil of the "loop."
In the heart of Automobile Row.
All points of interest in Chicago easily reached from this Hotel.
No boost in prices at the Lexington. Large, airy rooms with running water, bath adjacent, $2.00 per day and up single.
Elegantly furnished large rooms, with private bath, $3.00 per day and up single. Three moderate priced cafes, including a modern coffee shop.
Finest convention facilities in Chicago. Large meeting and committee rooms—all with outside exposure. Pershing Hall seats 1,000.
$150,000 in Improvements Within the Last Year
Building now owned and operated by Interstate Hotel Company, Herman Mack, Pres. and Mgr.

When Al Capone moved back to Chicago after "Big Bill" Thompson's mayoral victory in 1927, he left offices at the Metropole Hotel but moved his headquarters one block north to the more elegant Lexington.

The daytime and downtown gun battles that Dever could not control had made Chicago the gangster capital of the country, even the world, and with the introduction of the Tommygun, the killing of McSwiggin, and the "Pineapple Primary," the peaceful majority of citizens decided they'd had enough of the well-intentioned Dever. In 1927 they reelected "Big Bill" Thompson—who was thoroughly, but at least predictably, corrupt—and could therefore revive systematic graft as a means of restoring order.

Thompson reassured his supporters (much to the delight of the city's gambling, drinking, and entertainment interests) that he was "wetter than the middle of the Atlantic Ocean," and Capone decided it was once more safe to relocate his main headquarters from the Hawthorne Hotel in Cicero to the luxurious Lexington at Michigan and Twenty-second Street, a block north of the Metropole. One disgruntled reformer already had conceded the situation hopeless. "Chicago is unique," he declared. "It is the only totally corrupt city in America."

The bombing war subsided on orders of Capone, to whom city leaders and officials had been forced more than once to go hat in hand with their special requests. After the wild "Pineapple Primary," Frank J. Loesch, president of the Chicago Crime Commission and an ardent foe of Capone, decided he had no choice but to arrange a secret meeting at the Lexington where he all but begged "The Big Fellow" to rein in his hoodlums for the sake of a peaceful national election. No doubt flattered, but also mellowing with age, power, and fatherhood, Capone conceded that the city needed to spruce up its image for a presidential-election year, as well as for the Century of Progress World's Fair that Chicago businessmen were beginning to fear might suffer from the city's gangster reputation. He reportedly said, in a display of magnanimity, that he could control the "dagoes" by simple edict; and as for his competitors and independents, "I'll have the cops send over squad cars the night before the election and jug all the hoodlums and keep them in the cooler until the polls close."

Thus, Chicago enjoyed not only a peaceful election, but a jolly one. A story filed by the *New York Sun*'s Chicago bureau reported that Big Bill's pre-election "street parade, augmented by last-hour recruiting of additional tumbling clowns, bucking horses, and yipping cowboys, was well up to the average of such demonstrations when undertaken by any of the big traveling circuses." Thompson forces virtually commandeered the Loop, one reporter said, and inside the theaters the Chicago Police Quartet regularly interspersed Big Bill's patriotic favorites with the following ditty:

Fearful that the city's gangster reputation would keep voters away from the national elections in November 1928 and the 1933 World's Fair, Chicago Crime Commission Director Frank Loesch met secretly with Al Capone, who made good on his election promise to "control the Dagoes and have the cops jug the other hoods" but was convicted of tax evasion by 1933, after shootings had resumed and inspired an editorial cartoonist to compliment the city on building a replica of Chicago's original Fort Dearborn.

Happy days are here again,
The gang is feeling swell again,
The mayor's coming back again . . .
He was out for while,
But he's back with a smile,
And he'll shove the others all about,
Just like they took his appendix out!

The paper also quoted "Big Bill" in his customary third-person style: "Those steamboat whistles from New Orleans ought to be heard in Chicago inside of six months. But unless Bill Thompson goes up there to prod them into action, it will take two years."

Meanwhile, New York, its own machine working smoothly, had taken the ingenuous position that the worst of its criminal element had been nightsticked into leaving town and was causing a ruckus in places like

Philadelphia, Buffalo, Cleveland, Toledo, and especially Chicago. But that same year Manhattan's gentleman gangster, Arnold Rothstein, had been fatally shot in a downtown hotel room by someone who pitched his pistol out the window; and its less gentlemanly gangster, Frankie Yale, had been blown away Chicago-style as he motored to his home in Brooklyn. His was New York's first machine-gun murder, and New Yorkers had to assume that the last few years of comparative tranquility were coming to an end as Chicago's "Big Bill the Builder," himself on the verge of a breakdown, was making Capone his unofficial chief of police.

Chicago could not be fathomed by the rest of the country, as illustrated in a full-page *Chicago Tribune* ad paid for by supporters of Thompson rival Anton J. Cermak, who portrayed himself as more of a reformer than he was. The ad quoted other papers in the country:

> If [Thompson] wins in April, decent Chicagoans might as well take to the trees.
>
> — *Tiffin (Ohio) Daily Advertiser*

> Mayor Thompson has served three terms and during these years lawlessness has become one of the most highly specialized and profitable industries in the Windy City.
>
> — *Augusta (Ga.) Chronicle*

> No city in the atlas has earned itself as much ridicule in Bill's time as our strident sister on the lake.
>
> — *Detroit News*

> The present mayor of Chicago is the master ballyhooer, showman and four flusher in the politics of America today—bar none. He knows his Chicago better, perhaps, than he knows his ABC's. He has earned from long experience to place his reliance in the rabble, the underworld, the self-seeking, office-holding and office hungry politicians, and they have yet to fail him in the pinches.
>
> — *Springfield (Mo.) News*

> [The prospective World's Fair visitor] is a class that is disposed to think of Thompson and Capone as representatives of the spirit of Chicago, to regard Chicago as a place so wicked, vile and abominable that it should be avoided by decent people. If Chicago expects to retain Thompsonism and Caponeism and yet attract this host with a glittering exposition, it has one more guess coming.
>
> — *State Tribune Leader,*
> Cheyenne, Wyoming

> Big Bill Thompson, the blustering, bellicose, boisterous, belligerent Chicago bull-slinger.
>
> — *Springfield (Mass.) Evening Union*

> Chicago will hardly fail to have both Mayor Thompson and Al Capone on exhibition at its World's Fair in 1933. It would be almost impossible to overestimate their advertising value.
>
> — *Springfield (Mo.) News*

Of the more than 200 names sponsoring the ad, only one was obviously Italian. And only one newspaper seemed to grasp the fundamental craziness of Chicago politics that the average resident took for granted and probably enjoyed for the notoriety that made him the object of conversation and curiosity wherever he went. The *Nebraska City News Press* wrote: "Outsiders, apparently, do more worrying about the plight of Chicago than the residents themselves."

Unfortunately for Capone, the Internal Revenue Service was being pressured by the press, the business community, and even President Hoover to get him, his brother Ralph, and other top mobsters, one way or another, for violating U.S. income tax laws. This, plus the "public enemy" label hatched by the Chicago Crime Commission in 1930, distracted Capone from his civic duties. By the time the Depression set in, he had been sent to prison and his chosen candidate in the 1932 mayoral election, Anton J. Cermak (Capone had suffered embarrassment because of his link to Thompson) had been killed the following year in Miami by a bullet intended for President-elect Franklin Roosevelt.

With Capone and Prohibition out of the headlines, Chicago arbitrarily declared its gangster era over and was smiling at the gang wars brewing in New York. In 1935, Cermak's successor. Edward Kelly, and his Irish crony Patrick Nash rode the national Democratic landslide to victory in the race for mayor. They created Chicago's first truly functional political machine, which would survive until recent times.

Without Capone to make news, his successors, particularly Frank Nitti, consolidated the crime syndicate without fanfare or excessive gunfire, and they turned the avenues originally used for the inter-city distribution of beer and booze into turnpikes of nationwide racketeering. From Capone, everyone had learned the hazards of notoriety; from Tammany Hall, the Kelly-Nash machine had learned how to make Chicago "the city that worked"—one way or another, using the same anonymous community of sluggers against rebellious unions that the city's newspapers and cab companies once had used against each other.

Gangland bombings largely ceased in favor of discreet shootings that didn't wake up a residential neighborhood, and bodies were deposited in the trunks of cars stolen for that specific purpose and parked in the suburbs. Instead of employing mad bombers like Belcastro, the mob turned to its friends, many of whom were cops with basement workshops and inventive streaks, interested in the design and modification of firearms. After World War II, Chicago became the country's principal source of homemade silencers, more properly called suppressors. Some of these were substantial improvements on the commercial versions, which still could be purchased from properly licensed dealers but qualified as Class Three ordnance strictly controlled under federal and state laws.

By the time New York's crime families had revived Chicago-style warfare in the 1950s and '60s, Chicago had learned to maintain the outward appearance of tranquility, quietly (with a few major exceptions) dispatching hard cases with professionally fabricated silencers threaded onto the barrel of the common .22 Long Rifle target pistol, then stashing the corpse in the trunk of a car left in the long-term parking lot at O'Hare airport or on some remote side street to ripen until somebody called the cops.

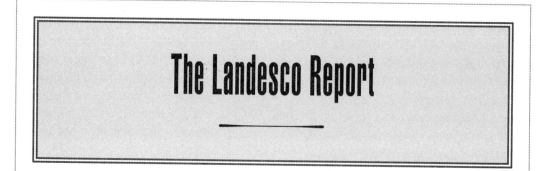

The Landesco Report

After the middle 1920s, the Chicago gang wars (as well as the Birger-Shelton feud in southern Illinois) were attracting so much national attention that several business and civic organizations joined forces to sponsor the most comprehensive study of the problem yet attempted. Experts were called in from around the country, and over a period of about three years they delivered themselves of a massive, 1,100-page *Illinois Crime Survey* that state and local politicians all but ignored. The only part to catch the eye of scholars and criminologists was a section by John Landesco, a University of Chicago sociologist who went beyond the study's simplistic theme of blaming crime on criminals and a faulty criminal justice system and sought to explore the social roots of criminal behavior.

What became known as the Chicago school of sociology already had attracted much attention and some disapproval by abandoning the "outhouse counting" which had characterized that discipline nationally; instead, it examined urban problems

A family gathering of the "Terrible Gennas" who stubbornly maintained their independence in Little Italy until enough were shot or fled the city.

(including criminality) from the new perspective of "cultural relativism" pioneered by progressive anthropologists of the period. As adapted by the Chicagoans, this was the notion that cultures or subcultures, in urban as in primitive societies, should be examined on their own terms rather than judged by an outsider's value system. Contrary to conventional thinking, the adult criminal was not necessarily abnormal or maladjusted but was, in fact, a conformist. In his world, only the maladjusted might aspire to become, say, a doctor.

Of equal importance, Landesco virtually coined the term "organized crime" to describe the kind of institutionalized or systematic lawbreaking that was so common in Chicago and elsewhere as to have escaped recognition, except as targets for specific reforms. The crime Landesco referred to was organized locally, and had been for decades, enduring through the simple practice of bribing police, politicians, or both. And if Landesco could see that bootleggers were fostering this corruption to an unprecedented degree, it was still too soon to appreciate that Prohibition would result in the networking of gangs throughout the country. After Repeal, the avenues created for distributing booze would be traveled less obviously by racketeers who used the next few years of armed-robber hysteria to evolve nearly unmolested into nationally organized crime.

But in mapping the rise of the Syndicate that eventually would control Chicago, Landesco himself became caught up in the gangland battles and sometimes studied them less like a scholar than a war correspondent. He presented a detailed report on the machine-gun murder of Assistant State's Attorney William McSwiggin and his bootlegger friends as a case study in political corruption and police incompetence, whose solution defied a coroner's jury and six grand juries, one after the other, because of conflicting agencies, investigations, and agendas. His hope was that this example would awaken citizens to the need for reform and professionalism. He then proceeded to cover the fighting in a manner that he thought reflected the existing gangs and rivalries and alliances.

Landesco became entangled in his civic geography and oft-changing gang affiliations, sometimes putting a murder in the wrong "casualty" list. This was especially true with the Gennas, a family of old-world Sicilians who alternately were allied with or fighting the South Siders, the West Siders, and the North Siders, sometimes on the principle that any enemy of my enemy is my friend. Such a policy worked both ways, of course, until most of them were killed or had fled Chicago. So Landesco's efforts to differentiate among rival bootlegger battles probably were based on fast-breaking news stories, police reports that often were inaccurate or misleading, and some guesswork, but at least they have provided historians with a sense of how confusing things were at the time.

Landesco's recognition of separate and concurrent gang wars reflected the efforts of a scholar to apply scientific method to improve on the journalistic reporting that tried to link the killings chronologically. In his summary, he correctly observed that the election of reform Mayor Dever, who tried to enforce an unpopular law (of which he personally disapproved) as a matter of principle, had the contrary result of displacing an orderly system of corruption with something close to anarchy. Commenting on the failings of the criminal justice system, he wrote:

> ... The gang code of silence and personal vengeance rather than legal redress was so compelling that of the 215 murders of gangsters during four years of armed strife, only a handful of arrests and no convictions were secured by the law enforcing agencies. But the police, forced apparently to resort to shooting it out in running battle, succeeded in killing 160 gangsters during this same period.

Noting that Chicago exceeded all other cities in gangland violence, Landesco decided this could not be explained simply by the failure of the majority of citizens to support the Volstead Act: "In the first place, other cities have not experienced so violent a disorder in the enforcement of Prohibition. In the second place, this defiance of law and order by the gunman and his immunity from punishment by the orderly processes of law are not limited in Chicago to the field of Prohibition," but prevail in every field of criminality as a result of institutionalized collusion between criminals, politicians and to a large extent the police.

The Landesco version of Chicago's Beer Wars begins with the advent of Prohibition, the killing of Jerry O'Connor in 1923, the move to Cicero by Torrio and Capone, and concludes in 1927. This was before Capone moved back to the Lexington Hotel and before the "Pineapple Primary" of 1928, when Capone was secretly called upon by Frank Loesch of the Chicago Crime Commission to suppress gangland violence before the national elections in November of that year. The Landesco text is verbatim; the casualty lists sometimes are abbreviated and/or parenthetically explained.

> **1. Origins.** In the period immediately after Prohibition, the former legitimate owners of breweries sought to dispose of their plants. Gangsters were often the purchasers of these breweries or else "fronted"; i.e., assumed ownership in order to face the rigors of the law, for the legitimate owners of breweries and distilleries which continued to run in disregard of the statute.
>
> On February 23, 1923, it was reported that a gigantic conspiracy to control the sale of beer in Chicago had been uncovered. Torrio had, since 1922, already secured ownership or control of three breweries. At the same time another group of men, headed by Terry Druggan and Frankie Lake, late of the Valley Gang, always lieutenants in charge of armed forces in the Eller elections of the Twentieth Ward, also began to come into ownership of breweries. They first purchased the George Hoffman Brewery—the transfer came through the hands of Richard Phillips, who had been a partner in Colosimo's Café, after the latter's death. Later, Frankie Lake and Terry Druggan were operating five breweries with Joseph Stenson, former co-partner in the Stenson

Brewing Co.: the Gambrinus, the Standard, the Hoffman, the Pfeiffer, and the Stege Brewing Companies. There was no war between Terry Druggan and Frankie Lake and John Torrio.

They received their protection from the same sources under the first two administrations of William Hale Thompson and they controlled the same orderly organization of beer running.

Frankie Lake (left) and Terry Druggan, who bought into breweries and took up "gentlemanly" bootlegging at the start of Prohibition, usually in collaboration with the equally business-minded John Torrio. The two looked and dressed enough alike to be called the Bobbsey Twins.

Then Dever's administration came, with a genuine attack upon bootlegging as well as upon gambling and vice, and the consequent break-up of the feudal city-wide organization of crime and vice and politics. The system of the orderly allotment of territories and protection that had grown up under the Thompson administrations was suddenly destroyed. Even Torrio himself was not powerful enough to ward off arrest in the Sieben Brewery raid. Consequently, "the union of each for the good of all" under the leadership of Torrio was over. It was followed by "The war of each against all," in which the chief lieutenant of Torrio, Al Capone, became the leading contender for the overlordship.

The beer war started when the "Spike" O'Donnells on the South Side tried to invade the territorial rights of Saltis and McErlane established under the Torrio rule.

During the four years prior to October 1926, the years of the greatest activity for the control of the booze and beer business in Cook County, two hundred fifteen gangsters murdered each other. The police during these same four years, in literally running battle, killed one hundred sixty beer feudists and gangsters. Within the city limits of Chicago, forty-two men were slain in the booze war during the ten months subsequent to January 1, 1926. Within Cook County, for the same period, the total reached fifty-four. Neither of the latter figures includes sixty other deaths which were the result of frays with policemen.

2. The South Side Beer War. The campaign of the Saltis-McErlane group was first against the "Spike" O'Donnell brothers; later against the Ralph Sheldon gang, which split from the Saltis-McErlane Gang. The catalogue of the principal casualties in the South Side war follows:[1]

September 7, 1923—Jerry O'Connor, slugger for "South Side" O'Donnells, seeking to encroach on territory allocated by Torrio to Frank McErlane and Polack Joe Saltis, killed by Torrio gunmen in Joseph Klepka's saloon.

September 17, 1923—George Meegan and George Bucher of "South Side" O'Donnells killed for threatening to identify killers of O'Connor. McErlane, Thomas Hoban, and Danny McFall indicted on January 12, 1925; nole prossed, April 9, 1924.

September 18, 1923—Tony Raymond killed; Saltis suspected.

October 30, 1923—McErlane, Thomas Hoban and Danny McFall indicted for the killing of Jerry O'Connor.

December 1, 1923—Thomas "Morrie" Keane killed (first "one-way ride" victim) [see p. 266] and William Egan wounded during McErlane hijacking of their beer truck from Joliet. Indicted: McErlane, Saltis, Hoban, Willie Channel, Ralph Sheldon, and Willie Neymoth.

December 5, 1923—Dominic Armato, Saltis-McErlane Gang member, possibly involved in killing of Morrie Keane.

December 18, 1924—Homer Finch, roadhouse owner, killed by "Spike" O'Donnell gang; possible stickup. On May 4, 1924, occurred the murder of Thaddeus Fancher, for which McErlane was later tried. Frank

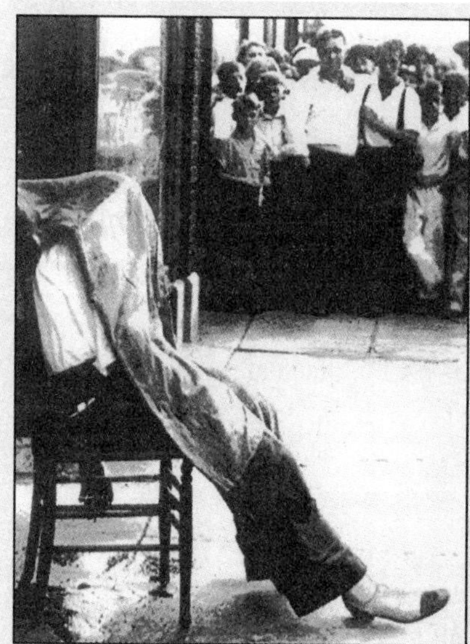

Police (or someone) granted Cicero gangster Tony Marino the small courtesy of partly covering his body, but Dominic Aiello, uncle of Chicago's Aiello brothers, provided block-party amusement for local children who routinely turned out to marvel at fresh gangland killings.

Cochran, the state's main witness, was murdered. After a notable legal contest, McErlane was acquitted. The same year, November 28, in a "hi-jacking" foray in Los Angeles, McErlane was held for a shooting and slugging. These two events are considered extrinsic of the beer war in Chicago.

July 4, 1924—Alfred Deckman, slugged by Walter O'Donnell, dies; O'Donnell charged with murder, released because of "indefinite identification."

December 19, 1924—Leo Gistinson and Jack Rappaport killed in revenge for shooting of John "Mitters" Foley.

April 17, 1925—Walter O'Donnell shot during roadhouse stickup; died May 9.

July 23, 1925—George "Big Bates" Karl, killed by the Saltis-McErlane Gang.[2]

August 1925—William Dickman killed: "Knew too much."

September 26, 1925—Attempt to kill "Spike" O'Donnell by Saltis-McErlane. [This attack on O'Donnell at the corner of Sixty-third Street and Western Avenue was the first use of a Thompson submachine gun in gangland warfare. Three such guns had been purchased by Dean O'Banion in Denver, on his way back to Chicago, a few days before he was killed; and one or more apparently were loaned to the Saltis-McErlane Gang.]

October 4, 1925—Ragen's Colts clubhouse, headquarters of Ralph Sheldon gang, raked by Saltis-McErlane machine-gunners; Charles Kelly killed [first Tommy-gun fatality]; Thomas Hart wounded [dies a few days later].

October 13, 1925—Ed Lattyak, Sheldon gangster, killed by Saltis-McErlane.

October 16, 1925—Attempt to kill O'Donnell by Saltis-McErlane.

October 22, 1925—Pasquale Tolizotte of O'Donnell gang killed by Saltis-McErlane. [October 25, police were seeking Frank McErlane and brother Vincent for murder in connection with robbery of International Harvester Co.]

November 16, 1925—Joe Saltis wounded in gun battle with O'Donnell gang.

December 3, 1925—Dynamite Joe Brooks (peddler of "alky") and County Highway Policeman Edwin Harmening (independent bootlegger) killed by Saltis-McErlane.[3]

February 10, 1926—Sheldon allies William Wilson and John "Mitters" Foley wounded by Saltis-McErlane machine-gunners.

April 15, 1926—Frank DeLaurentis and John Tuccello, Sheldon associates, killed; McErlane sought by police.

July 20, 1926—Attempt to kill Vincent McErlane.

July 23, 1926—Frank Conlon killed,[4] Vincent McErlane narrowly missed; Mitters Foley suspected; Sheldon threatens to kill Saltis if he kills Foley.

July 29, 1926—Attempt to kill Walter Stevens.

August 6, 1926—Foley killed by Saltis. Thomas Foley corroborates revenge motive on part of Saltis; witnesses identify Earl "Big Herb" Herbert, Frank "Lefty" Koncil, and John "Dingbat" Oberta. Saltis and Koncil indicted and captured; witnesses disappear 8/22/26; 11/9/26, Saltis and Koncil acquitted.

September 15, 1926—Vincent McErlane and North Side Gang member Peter

Gusenberg arrested for Grand Trunk train robbery. This is first indication of alliance between McErlanes and North Siders. [Landesco was seemingly unaware of the secret alliance between Saltis-McErlane and O'Banion that shortly predated O'Banion's murder.]

October 11, 1926—Earl "Hymie" Weiss and "Paddy" Murray killed; attorney W. W. O'Brien, Sam Peller, and Benny Jacobs wounded. Machine-gun ambush outside Holy Name Cathedral attributed to Torrio-Capone gang after failure to make peace with North Siders following the November 10, 1924, murder of O'Banion at Schofield's flower shop, across from the Cathedral.

October 19, 1926—Bombing of Joseph Kepka's saloon, 4801 Honore St., attributed to his failure to contribute to Saltis defense fund.

November 11, 1927—Saltis and Koncil found "not guilty."

March 11, 1927—"Lefty" Koncil and Charles "Big Hayes" Hrubec killed by either Sheldon gang or the O'Donnell brothers.

November 3, 1927—McErlane acquitted in Indiana. [This presumably was the occasion when McErlane, while drinking in a tavern, decided to show off his marksmanship by randomly shooting a patron off a barstool. State's witness to the shooting was soon murdered.]

The Saltis-McErlane Gang seem to have been pursued most energetically by Captain John Stege. Upon the election of Thompson, in 1927, Stege was removed from the force by a dubious civil service trial. It is widely believed that Joe Saltis was the chief influence behind this discharge.[5]

3. The West Side Beer War. On the West Side the dispute over territory was between the "Klondike" O'Donnell brothers (the West Side O'Donnells) and Al Capone, the trusted lieutenant of John Torrio, later himself in complete command when Torrio went to jail. The first of a series of murders was involved in the expansion of the west suburban territory and its defense.

The Genna brothers had organized the home industry of distilling in the Taylor Street district (Little Sicily) [This neighborhood was better known as Little Italy on the "Near Southwest Side"; Little Sicily occupied a square mile or so on the "Near Northwest Side," perhaps a mile west of O'Banion's "North Side" that extended over to Lake Michigan.] Their large family was in command of a further intimate group of co-villagers from Marsalla, Sicily, and important politically through their patronage and strength in the Unione Siciliana. In the struggle for supremacy after the retirement of Torrio over the booze-collecting and distributing rights, the Genna brothers of the West Side fought the O'Banion gang on the North Side. Between the Gennas and Capone there were many lasting ties—the Gennas had grown up under the protectorate of the old Torrio overlordship; there were racial affiliations and obligations, though Capone is a Calabrian.

With the murder of Dion O'Banion the West Side beer war began. Later the raising of the defense fund for Scalise and Anselmi, which was a phase of this war, involved the murders of wealthy Italians and the collectors of the fund. It is fair to conjecture that all of these wealthy Italians had profited by the booze trade with the Gennas and were obligated to contribute to the fund.

Al Capone was in command of the armed forces for the Torrio interests in their expansion in the west suburban area, which he later defended against incursions by the "Klondike" O'Donnell brothers. Still later he participated in the war for the booze supremacy between the Genna brothers and the O'Banion gang.

April 1, 1924—Frank Capone killed by Chicago police sent to restore order during violent primary elections in Cicero that marked take-over of western suburbs by Torrio-Capone, following the crackdown by Chicago's reform mayor William E. Dever and disruption of the old order under Mayor Bill Thompson.
May 8, 1924—Joseph Howard killed for "talking out of turn" in Capone affairs regarding Capone killings. [When three witnesses developed sudden amnesia, Landesco may have had qualms about identifying Capone as the murderer.]
November 1924—Eddie Tancl, popular saloon owner, killed for resisting Torrio-Capone expansion into suburbs.
November 10, 1924—Dean O'Banion, North Side Gang chief and former Torrio subordinate killed in his flower shop while preparing floral arrangements for the funeral of Mike Merlo, president of the Unione Siciliana. Mike Genna and two unidentified Sicilians shoot O'Banion six times. [Killers never officially identified, but one presumably was Brooklyn's Frankie Yale, also suspected of killing "Big Jim" Colosimo as a favor to Torrio and Capone in 1920; and the two Sicilians probably were Scalise and Anselmi rather than any of the Gennas.]

Opening of the Genna-O'Banion series of killings.

January 12, 1925—Attempt to kill Capone; chauffeur Sylvester Barton wounded; North Sider reprisal for O'Banion murder.
January 24, 1925—Torrio survives near-fatal wounding by North Siders; serves his sentence from the Sieben Brewery conviction, visits Italy, and returns to New York, leaving his organization to Al Capone.
March 17, 1925—Newspaper editor Arthur St. John beaten and driven out of Cicero by Capone gangsters, now firmly in control of the city.
May 26, 1925—Angelo Genna killed in running gun battle with Capone gangsters.
June 13, 1925—Gun duel involving Genna and O'Banion gangsters leads afterward to chase and shootout between Gennas and police, the killing of Chicago officers Harold Olson and Charles Walsh, and the mortal wounding of Michael Genna.
July 8, 1925—Anthony Genna killed from ambush.
July 10, 1925—Tony Campagna, killed.[6]
July 15, 1925—Sam Lavenuto, killed.[7]

July 15, 1925—James Russo, killed.[8]
January 10, 1926—Henry Spingola, brother-in-law of Angelo Genna, killed, allegedly for refusing to contribute to Anselmi-Scalise defense fund.[9]
January 24, 1926—Augustino and Antonio Moreci killed, allegedly for refusing to make additional contributions to Anselmi-Scalise defense fund.[10]
February 15, 1926—Orazzio "The Scourge" Tropea, supposed collector for Anselmi-Scalise fund, killed almost on the spot where Spingola was murdered.
February 21, 1926—Vito Bascone.[11]
February 23, 1926—Eddie Baldelli killed.[12]
March 7, 1926—Tony Finalli killed.[13]
March 19, 1926—Samuzzo Amatuna killed for attempting to stabilize the chaotic booze production and trade of the embattled Genna organization.
April 27, 1926—Assistant State's Attorney William McSwiggin, and bootleggers James Doherty and Thomas Duffy, members of the "Klondike" (West Side) O'Donnell gang then engaged in warfare with Capone organization, machine-gunned outside Cicero speakeasy.
May 21, 1926—Cremaldi, Italian booze peddler, killed attempting to operate in North Siders' "Gold Coast" territory.
July 17, 1926—Joseph Novello wounded.
August 10, 1926—Gun battle between North Side leader Vincent Drucci (successor to O'Banion) and Capone gangsters in front of the Standard Oil Building on Michigan Avenue. Possibly an attempted stickup; no one hit.[14]
August 20, 1926—Joseph Nerone (aka Spano, "The Cavalier") killed to avenge the death of Anthony Genna, or possibly for invading Capone's Chicago Heights territory.
September 20, 1926—Hawthorne Hotel in Cicero, Capone headquarters since election of Dever, riddled by several carloads of North Siders firing machine guns and shotguns in reprisal for O'Banion killing.
October 11, 1926—"Hymie" Weiss and "Paddy" Murray killed in Capone machine-gun ambush that wounded O'Brien, Peller, and Jacobs. Alliance between North Siders and Saltis-McErlane confirmed by O'Brien's representation of Saltis in the Foley murder and possession by Weiss of a confidential jury list.

[The murder of Weiss led to meetings at the Morrison and Sherman Hotels, and a temporary truce among gang leaders still was holding at the time Landesco completed his report in 1927. However, he continued to record other killings involving persons prominent in criminal circles without ascribing them to specific "wars."]

4. The Truce. The meeting took place at the Morrison Hotel on October 21, 1926, with a complete representation of the leading gangs of Chicago. Vincent Drucci and Big George Moran represented the North Side Gang; Eddy Vogel, Julian "Potatoes" Kaufman, Frank Citro and Peter Gusenberg joined their interests with Drucci and Moran. "Klondike" O'Donnell and his brother Myles, of the West Side, participated in the conference. Capone, representing Torrio interests, had a representative there, perhaps Antonio Lombardo. Ralph Sheldon, enemy of Saltis-McErlane, was present. Maxie Eisen appeared as mutual peacemaker. Drucci and Moran took the responsibility for securing the approval of Saltis and McErlane, then in jail. The conditions of the peace were that each gang was to stay in its own territory.

The North Side Gang, with Drucci as chieftain, controlled the territory from the lake on the east and north to the suburbs, on the south and west from the river to the Wisconsin line; each took the exclusive beer and whiskey rights for both wholesale and retail trade and revenues from small gamblers. [This seems to represent either some geographical or typographical confusion, as the North Siders' territory extended from midtown, between the Chicago River and Lake Michigan, and north along the lakeside suburbs to the Wisconsin line. The Roger Touhy gang on the Northwest Side is not mentioned.]

Joe Saltis and Ralph Sheldon divided the South Side of Chicago, extending south from the river to the Indiana line and from the lake on the east to the townships on the west. Sheldon's position was strengthened by the partisanship of Capone and the fact that Saltis and McErlane were incarcerated.

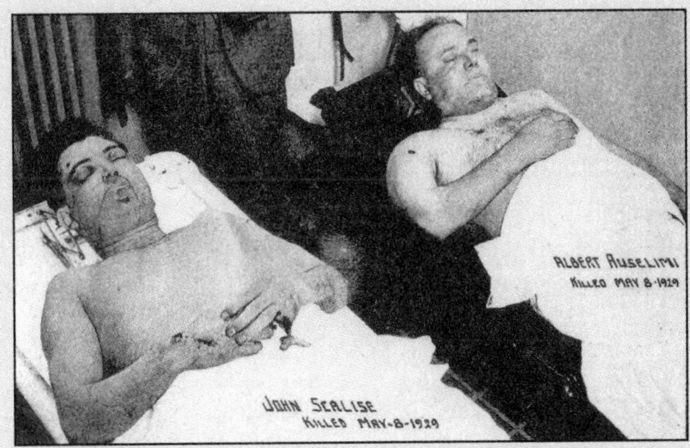

Legend has it that Capone staged a mock celebration at a roadhouse, personally beat John Scalise and Albert Anselmi to bloody pulps (with either a baseball bat or a ten-pin), and dumped their bodies and that of Joe Guinta (left) in a deserted part of northern Indiana, possibly as a courtesy to Chicago's police who would not have to investigate. Morgue photographs, however, suggest only that they were beaten up, shot, and "taken for a ride."

Capone land included the far West Side and the western suburbs.

The truce seems to have held so far as the war of the leaders was concerned, but in the establishment of the exclusive rights in each territory, considerable individual sniping and murder continued through the remainder of the period of the Dever administration and to the present day.

January 16, 1927—Murder of Theodore Anton, "The Greek," manager of Hawthorne Hotel and owner of neighboring Anton Hotel, Capone's first residence upon vacating Chicago: "Wanted to retire."

March 14, 1927—Alphonse Fiori, Genna henchman, killed.
April 4, 1927—Drucci, arrested on Election Day, killed in scuffle with police while being driven to the station for questioning.
May 3, 1927—Police find body of Cicero saloon keeper John Costenaro who tried to operate independent of Capone and had disappeared January 3.
July 27, 1927—Frank Hitchcock, saloon keeper and distiller, killed for competing with Capone in Burnham.
August 10, 1927—Anthony K. Russo and Vincent Spicuzza, small manufacturers of "alky" in Aiello territory, both killed.
September 9, 1927—Bombed: A distillery said to be owned by Anselmi and Scalise, probably one of the Genna interests or possibly an explosion by gas.

The death of Drucci further disorganized the North Side Gang and while "Bugs" (Big Joe) Moran [he meant to call him Big George] has attained leadership, he did not go into action until after the beginning of the gambling war during the present Thompson administration when, allied with the Aiello brothers and Bertsche and Ed Zuta, he carried on the war against the Capone-Lombardo interests.

5. Guerrilla Warfare. At this time there is a period of comparative quiet, but peace in the beer war did not come from extermination in the struggle of "gangster killing gangster," as many predicted. Indeed, the peace arranged by the chieftains, while it seems to have settled the major points of disputes over territory among the gang leaders, did not and probably could not prevent many conflicts arising among their followers and especially with independent operators. Consequently, the present period of peace might be more accurately described as one of guerrilla warfare. Killings still continue, but they are either reprisals against individual intruders into the territory of a syndicate or they represent some shifting of power in underworld organization.[15]

6. Summary. The extraordinary phenomenon of gang war and gang peace in a modern American city shocked not only the people of Chicago and the United States, but the nations of the world. Few persons, even in Chicago, realize the powerful nature of criminal gang organization, the extent of their political alliances, and the enormous amount of profits from beer-running and booze distribution. Our survey of the beer war leads to certain outstanding findings:

1. The solidified and politically protected organization of former vice lords and younger gunmen and gangsters under the leadership of John Torrio for the manufacture and distribution of alcoholic beverages disintegrated under the Prohibition enforcement policy of the Dever administration and the beer war broke out.

2. In the war of rival factions which followed, the gang code of silence and personal vengeance rather than legal redress was so compelling that of the two hundred fifteen murders of gangsters during four

years of armed strife, only a handful of arrests and no convictions were secured by the law enforcing agencies. But the police, forced apparently to resort to shooting it out in running battle, succeeded in killing one hundred sixty gangsters during this same period.

3. While the heavy casualties of the beer war did not lead to the extermination of gangsters, as many law-abiding citizens optimistically expected, they did induce the leading gangsters, for different reasons, to agree to peace terms which defined the territory within which each gang or syndicate might operate without competition and beyond which it should not encroach upon the territory of others.

4. The huge stakes of beer running and whiskey distribution, providing not only enormous profits for gang leaders but a large number of high salaried positions for an army of minor gunmen and gangsters are, in large part, the explanation for the survival and the growth of beer and whiskey syndicates in spite of the heavy mortality risk of this business.

5. The fact remains for the serious consideration of all the friends of law and order, that even under the very adverse conditions with the federal and city authorities united in a strenuous policy of law enforcement, and with a bitter internecine war between rival factions, the underworld groups and syndicates for traffic in liquor maintain operations on a large, if not increasing, scale, in defiance of the laws of the State of Illinois and the Constitution and laws of the United States.

If this condition were an isolated phenomenon limited to the enforcement of the national Prohibition law, it might be explained on the basis of the failure of the Eighteenth Amendment and the Volstead Law to command the support of the majority of citizens in a metropolitan and cosmopolitan city like Chicago. Two facts, however, prevent us from accepting this conclusion. In the first place, other cities have not experienced so violent a disorder in the enforcement of Prohibition. In the second place, this defiance of law and order by the gunman and his immunity from punishment by the orderly processes of law are not limited in Chicago to the field of Prohibition.

NOTES:

1. Interspersed with the actual beer-war killings it has been necessary to bring in the other killings for which McErlane was tried, in order to bring all the episodes into proper perspective.

2. Karl and Dickman were associates of Saltis-McErlane, and it was said that the first was killed for his roll, $12,000, and the second for having knowledge of the murder.

3. It is probable that the split with Sheldon occurred at this time because Brooks was a friend of Sheldon's. No attempts made to kill Sheldon after the break with Saltis-McErlane.

4. On August 19, 1926, Vincent McErlane captured and questioned with regard to the murder of Conlon. On September 15, 1926, Vincent McErlane and Peter Gusenberg, of the O'Banion gang, were arrested for the Grand Trunk train robbery. This is the first indication of an alliance between the O'Banion gang and the McErlane gang. [Landesco apparently was unaware that the Saltis-McErlane Gang had secretly affiliated with the O'Banion gang before his "handshake murder" in November of 1924.]

5. Captain Stege was later reinstated in August 1928, upon the retirement of Commissioner Hughes and the appointment of Commissioner Russell, and was made deputy commissioner in charge of the Detective Bureau.

6–8. Independents who made "alky" in Capone territory.

9–10. The Moreci brothers and the Spingolas were of wealthy Italian families and the best available information yielded a theory that they were killed because of their refusal to contribute to the Scaise-Ansemi defense fund. Other deaths during this period were identified as those of collectors of the fund.

11–13. Collectors for Anselmi-Scalise fund, killed in revenge for killing of Spingola and Morecis.

14. The first attempt at peace occurred immediately after this machine-gun battle. Antonio Lombardo emerged for the first time as a representative of the Capone interests. He attended a meeting in the Morrison Hotel, at which it was said a police official was present, and made overtures to "Hymie" Weiss, who insisted that he wanted the attackers of Vincent Drucci "placed on the spot." [Landesco apparently confuses the meetings and the Morrison and the Sherman Hotels, and it supposedly was at the latter that "Hymie" Weiss wanted Scalise and Anselmi "put on the spot" for the killing of O'Banion, to which Capone answered, through his representative at the meeting, that he "wouldn't do that to a yellow dog."] The refusal of Capone was followed by the masterly plan to establish a machine-gun [nest] next door to the headquarters of the O'Banion gang, which resulted in the casualties on October 11, 1926.

15. One reason why wholesale casualties have not exterminated gangsters may be gained from a description of the present organization and activities of one syndicate in the alcohol traffic as reported in the *Daily News* of March 24, 1928. This article not only indicates the enormous profits of the illegal traffic in alcohol and the large number of gangsters who find employment in it, but it also discloses the situation in which conflicts arise between rival syndicates:

> An alcohol traffic of more than $2 million a year is controlled by the Guilfoyle-Winge-Kolb syndicate on the near Northwest Side.*
>
> The alcohol traffic, the pet project of Martin Guilfoyle, slayer of Peter Gentleman, for net profits, now overshadows the prosperous beer business built up by Al Winge, former police lieutenant, and his ally, Matt Kolb.
>
> The syndicate's sales, supervised generally by Guilfoyle, are in direct charge of Joey Fisher, who has been active in the "alky racket" since the Volstead law went into effect. Sales Manager Fisher has a staff of high-pressure salesmen that rises, when business is good, to more than fifty men.
>
> Fisher's headquarters are at 2009 Division Street, first floor; telephone Brunswick 4943. Daily his salesmen appear at this spot or a distributing point at 3448 Fullerton Avenue, to listen to the current price on alcohol.
>
> When something of importance is to be said, Mr. Guilfoyle calls his henchmen to his personal headquarters in a building on the northeast corner of Kedzie and Chicago avenues.
>
> The quaint expression "Check your gun at the door" is not a matter for joking on visits to the Guilfoyle headquarters. When the peddler, saloon-keeper or other caller appears, he enters the barroom, steps behind the bar and there checks his gun.
>
> They troop out of the bar and up the Kedzie Avenue entrance where Guilfoyle is waiting to receive them. A few "wise cracks" from various hoodlums, then Guilfoyle clears his throat, calls the meeting to order, and the peddlers and saloon-keepers listen respectfully while the "big shot" has his say.
>
> The subject of more than one of these meetings has been the activities of Lewis and Max Summerfield, rival alcohol "racketeers," sole thorn in the syndicate's side.
>
> The Summerfields, old-timers on the Northwest Side, had things pretty much their own way prior to Guilfoyle's advent in the alcohol business. Guilfoyle's organizing ability, Sales Manager Fisher's high-pressure staff, and the Kolb-Winge prestige cut in on the Summerfield's business sadly.
>
> Stubbornly they fought the syndicate and paid for and got such police protection as they could, and they are still operating in a small way. Repeatedly at these meetings Guilfoyle has warned his henchmen to boycott the Summerfields:
>
> "You'll only get into trouble if you play with the Summerfields," Guilfoyle tells his men. "Don't use their stuff. Don't have anything to do with them. We'll run them out of the district yet."
>
> After one of these "pep" meetings a few months ago, pineapple tossers descended on the Summerfield headquarters at 1910 Milwaukee Avenue. An explosion resounded through the district, and the Summerfield headquarters was in need of considerable repair.
>
> The police rushed up, made their customary investigation and announced to a waiting world that they were confronted with another "bombing mystery."

---

*This group was largely absorbed by the Touhy mob in DuPage County, neighboring Chicago's Cook County on the northwest.

GANGSTER FUNERALS

The murder of "Big Jim" Colosimo in 1920 began the tradition of spectacular gangland funerals. His was conducted "without benefit of clergy" (Cardinal Mundelein was put off by "public sinners"), but the Apollo Quartet sang hymns, musicians played "Nearer My God to Thee," and his honorary pallbearers included three judges, eight aldermen, an assistant state's attorney, a congressman, a state representative, members of the Chicago Opera Company, and various gamblers and dive-keepers.

Five thousand mourners included a thousand members of the First Ward Democratic Club headed by "Bathhouse" John Coughlin and Michael "Hinky Dink" Kenna, who led the cortege through the Old Levee vice district. In the procession were an amazing assortment of lesser vice lords, respectable businessmen, crooks, gunmen, and what the newspapers called "painted women."

The sendoff for Unione Siciliana president Mike Merlo in 1924 included not only a vast crowd, but also featured a giant statue of Merlo made of flower blossoms and leaning a bit precariously in the back seat of an open touring car.

Dean O'Banion's funeral in 1924 was even more lavish. He lay in state at the nearby Sbarbaro Undertaking Rooms (operated by Judge Sbarbaro, who was becoming gangland's official mortician) in a $10,000 bronze and silver casket (in 1924 dollars) specially designed in Pennsylvania and shipped to Chicago in its own railroad car. The funeral procession included twenty-four carloads of flowers, 122 funeral cars, and a crowd estimated at five thousand following on foot or watching from the sidewalk and apartment windows. Even this spectacle was surpassed in 1928 by New York's Frankie Yale, who had early insisted that his casket cost more than O'Banion's—which it did, at $15,000.

Thousands turned out for the funeral of one of the Gennas who, in Chicago's Little Italy, were seen as "local boys who made good."

University of Chicago John Landesco observed, first and foremost, that such funerals were estimations of influence, political power, dependability, and personal loyalty that crossed social and cultural bounds. He quoted a *Chicago American* reporter's rhetorical analysis:

> "No matter what he may have been in the past, no matter his faults, Jim was my friend and I am going to his funeral."
>
> These and similar words were heard today from the lips of hundreds of Chicagoans. They were to be heard in the old Twenty-second Street levee district, over which Jim for so many years had held undisputed sway, they dropped from the mouths of gunmen and crooks. . . . They were heard from many a seemingly staid business man in loop skyscrapers and from men famous and near-famous in the world of art and letters, who had all mingled more or less indiscriminately with the other world which walks forth only at night. . . .

Landesco noted that the underworld and the political world were feudalistic in that both rested more on personal relationships than on abstract laws. Gangs and politicians alike were organized upon "loyalties, upon friendships, and, above all, on dependability. That is one reason why politicians and criminal gangs understand one another so well and so frequently enter alliances with each other against the more remote common good." He added that "friendship, which is one of the most amiable and commendable of human characteristics, frequently does undermine the more formal social order."

The diminishing grandeur of gangland funerals he attributed to the increasing role that money played in the rackets. "Political protection for the powerful financial interests of organized crime is coming to rest less and less upon friendship and more and more upon pecuniary considerations."

By the 1930s the pomp and pageantry of gangland funerals quickly diminished, probably for the reasons mentioned by Landesco, but also because some undertakers had figured out a racket of their own. Schultz ally Danny Iamascia's family purchased what was supposed to be a silver casket worth $10,000; it turned out to be silver-plated and worth about $3,000.

One criminal of note who went to his grave uncelebrated was "Mad Dog" Coll, whose bullets had killed one child and wounded others in New York in 1931. He was buried on a bleak, rainy morning, his casket borne by pallbearers across a barren field to his final resting place, their shoes covered in the mud.

John Sbarbaro, an assistant state's attorney and later municipal judge, also owned an undertaking establishment near O'Banion's flower shop and was commonly called upon to refurbish the corpses of dead mobsters from different gangs in the city—in this case, the remains of North Sider Vincent Drucci.

The Wickersham Commission

In May 1929, President Herbert Hoover, moved by the spectacle in Chicago and the *Illinois Crime Survey* with its Landesco report, and the expansion of Chicago-style violence to other cities, established the National Commission on Law Observance and Enforcement, chaired by former Attorney General George W. Wickersham. This was a federal version of the Illinois study and became popularly known as the Wickersham Commission, which went on a nationwide tour like a great circus, holding much-publicized hearings in every major city and systematically describing Prohibition enforcement conditions almost county by county.

The Wickersham Commission toured the country and examined Prohibition in great detail, but it came to no conclusions.

But its final report, issued in 1931, dismayed both "Wets" and "Drys" with its failure to reach conclusions that either side could use to its advantage. Thus it joined other mammoth and costly government studies quickly entombed in the bowels of libraries that traditionally hold old Congressional records, investigations, and hearings, to be immortalized only as footnotes in graduate theses and dissertations.

The Scranton Republican

Wickersham Belittles Proposal for 2.75 Beer

Green Says A. F. L. Recognizes Only One Miners' Union

Boat Passengers Burned to Death As Oil Explodes

Cellmates Say That Gungirl Told of Crime

Labor Chieftan Offers His Aid In Conciliation

"Scarface Al" And Bodyguard Are Released

Holds Beverage Will Not Satisfy "Robust Tastes"

So much for the Wickersham Report, a monument to equivocation that had but one interesting feature. While surveying most states, including New York, in only a few pages, it devoted an entire volume to Illinois, with a separate section concentrating on Chicago, where the action was.

Its local investigator, Bureau of Prohibition agent Guy L. Nichols, described the Chicago situation with the enthusiasm of a cub reporter, taking it upon himself to skulk about the city with car, camera, and bodyguards, sneaking pictures of notorious gangster headquarters, hangouts, and saloons, referring to himself in the third person and describing his adventures with great excitement:

> Leaving the Metropole, a Capone stronghold at 2300 South Michigan Avenue, a block south of the Lexington Hotel, where he headquartered from 1928 to 1932, your investigator, in a large, closed car, accompanied with a bodyguard of three in civilian clothes, stopped in the center of the street and from the middle side car window photographed the Paddock Grill, 2507 South Wabash Avenue. . . . At the time it was snapped a lookout was seen through the window. He immediately stepped aside and Jack Heinan, a former pugilist and a present partner of Ralph Capone, came to the window.
>
> After snapping the picture from inside the car, we sped on to other scenes, but had not proceeded over two blocks when it was discovered that a car had put out through curiosity from the Paddock and was following us. The chase was given up in the maze of traffic.

While touring the valley of the shadow of death, investigator Nichols and his bodyguards penetrated to the heart of the enemy camp in visiting the Anton (later Alton) Hotel in neighboring Cicero, living not only to tell the tale but to draw a ground-floor plan of the place. Since the Anton's restaurant, bar, and gaming rooms were heavily patronized by a public who enjoyed these amusements with no fear of being murdered, it's likely that Investigator Nichols and his men were the most conspicuous party in the place, and possibly a source of amusement.

But his work certainly would not have been complete had he failed to attempt a survey of the gangs and their members. With even less insider knowledge than Landesco, he assembled an impressive list of some "330 alleged gangsters" and their affiliations, using yet a different scheme that again illustrated the difficulty in trying to figure out the structure of Chicago's criminal community. The spellings are Wickersham's:

20TH WARD GROUP

Ben Zion, Benjamin "Buddy" Jacobson (also identified with O'Banion and Weiss), Sam Peller (same as Jacobson),

Sam Kaplan, Louis "Big" Smith, Izzie "Nigger" Goldberg, Jules Portuguese, Sam "The Greener" Jacobson, "Nails" Morton (first to organize in 20th Ward with Hirshie Miller; Morton showed Dean O'Banion and his gang the way), Hirshie Miller, Maxie Miller (brother of Hirshie and later associated with O'Banion; the fact that O'Banion once shot it out with the Millers seems to have been overlooked), Maxie Eisen No. 2 (there were two Maxie Eisens in the rackets), Dave Edelman, William "Sailor" Freedman.

VALLEY GANG: DRUGGAN AND LAKE OUTFIT
20TH WARD

Terrance "Terry" Druggan, Frankie Lake, Eddie Tancl (cabaret owner, later moved to Cicero, Leo Klimas (associated with Tancl), James Sexton, Myles O'Donnell, William "Klondike" O'Donnell, James Doherty, Thomas Duffy (Myles and "Klondike" O'Donnell, Doherty, and Duffy later organized further on the West Side of Chicago and sought to infringe on Capone's Cicero rights; Assistant State's Attorney William McSwiggin was killed in Cicero, in company of Doherty and Duffy, who were also slain), Joseph "Red" Bolton, John Bolton ("Red's" brother), Paddy "The Bear" Ryan Sr., Paddy "The Cub" Ryan Jr., John Touhy, James "Fur" Sammons (identified with O'Donnell-Doherty gang), Harry Madigan (Cicero saloon keeper identified with O'Donnell-Doherty gang), Michael Windle (Wendle; same as Madigan).

GENNA GANG
NEAR WEST SIDE, 20TH AND 25TH WARDS

Anthony "Tony" D'Andrea, Joseph "Diamond Joe" Esposito, succeeded D'Andrea, Mike Genna, Angelo Genna, Tony Genna, Sam Genna, Joseph LaGera, Joseph Montana, Sam "Samoots" Amatuna, Orazia "The Scourge" Tropea, Henry Spingola, John Scalise, Albert Anselmi.

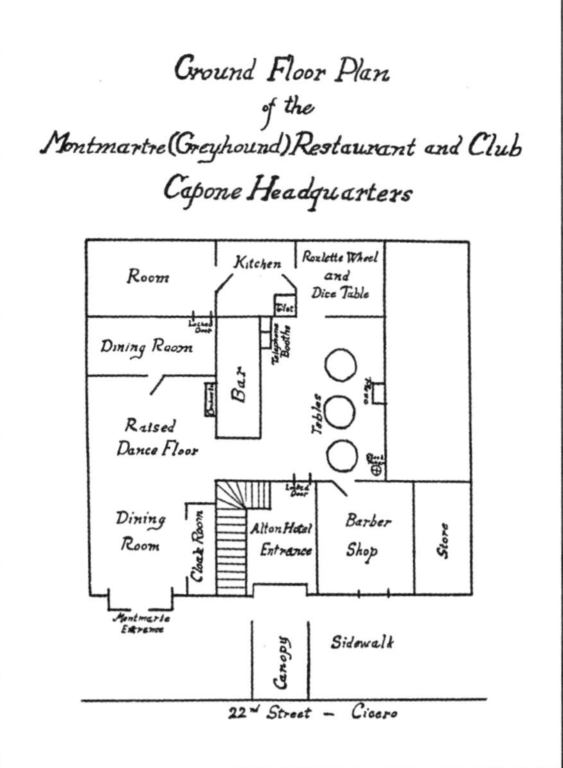

Investigators for the Wickersham Commission carefully photographed, cautiously penetrated, and secretly mapped various hoodlum hangouts, probably to the amusement of regular customers, who had only stray bullets to fear. The sketch above shows part of the Alton (formerly Anton) Hotel complex in Cicero, Illinois.

O'BANION GANG

Near North Side "Gold Coast"

Dean O'Banion, Louis Alterie, Earl "Hymie" Weiss (succeeded O'Banion), Vincent "Schemer" Drucci (succeeded Weiss), George "Bugs" Moran (now leader; succeeded Drucci), Irving "Sonny" Schlig (possibly the first airplane bootlegger), Frank Gusenberg, Peter Gusenberg (brother of Frank), Julian "Potatoes" Kaufman, Frank Citro (same as Frank Foster), Patrick Henry, "Big" Ed Vogel, Edward Newberger, John Carr, John Duffy, Leo Mongoven, Phillip May, Frank Foster, Harry Berman, John May, John Dougherty, Albert R. Weinshank, James Clark, Reinhart Schwimmer, Adam Heyer, George "Big" Karl, John Sheehy.

AIELLO GANG

Near North Side (Little Italy)

Carl Aiello, Joseph Aiello, Tony Aiello, Dominick Aiello, Samuel Aiello, Joseph Mule, Peter Meruea.

SALTIS-McERLANE GANG

South Side, "Back of the Yards"

Joseph "Polack Joe" Saltis, Frank McErlane, John "Dingbat" O'Berta, Frank "Lefty" Koncil, Nick Cramer, William Dickman, William Niemoth, Vincent McErlane, Clarence Barrett, Fred Beiglebeck, Patrick Sullivan, Eddie Fitzgerald, "Big" Earl Herbert, George Hert (alias Darrow, alias Otto Kosteneck), John Conlon, Tom Hoben, Danny McFall, Eddie Kaufman.

RALPH SHELDON GANG

South Side, "Back of the yards"

Ralph Sheldon, Michael McGovern, Hugh "Stubby" McGovern, William "Gunner" McFadden, Hilary Clements, Edward Clements, Dennis Doherty, Denny Stanton, Martin Garrity, Frank Ryan, Frank Kane, William "Rags" McCue, John "Mitters" Foley.

EDWARD "SPIKE" O'DONNELL GANG

South Side, "Back of the Yards"

Edward "Spike" O'Donnell, Charles O'Donnell (brother of "Spike"), Thomas O'Donnell (brother of "Spike"), Steve Donnell (brother of "Spike"), Walter Stevens, Jerry O'Conner, Joe Larson, John Quiqley, George Bucher, William "Sonny" Dunn.

CAPONE GANG

Cicero

Alphonso Capone (alias Al Brown, alias Scarface), Ralph Capone (Al's brother), Antonio "Tony" Lombardo (formerly head of Sicilian Union), Pasquale Lolardo (succeeded Tony Lombardo, Tony "Mops" Volpe (Capone's chief lieutenant, former associate of "Diamond Joe" Esposito), Frank Rio (alias Cline), Frank Perry, Sam Marcus, Joseph Guinta, Louis Barko (alias Valerie), Theodore Anton, Rocco Fanelli, Joseph Moreil (alias Ferraro), Phil D'Andrea, John Torrio, Michael Butero, Nick Mastro, Jack Demore (often spelled De Mora; alias McGurn, alias "Machine-Gun" McGurn, Sam Compagna, F. C. "Denver Blackie" Bursham, Anthony Curlinglone (alias Tom Ross), Sante Cellebron, Robert McCollough, Tony Spano (alias Tom Herone, alias "The Chevalier), Johnny Patton ("Boy Mayor of Burnham"), Harry Guzik, Jack Zuta, Laurance "Dago" Mangano, Frank Yale (alias Uale; New York), James "Jim" Colosimo (started Capone, Torrio, and others on their careers).

CAPONE GANG
CHICAGO HEIGHTS

Phillip Plasso, Frank Camora, Joseph Catenda, Francisco Capello.

INDEPENDENTS OR GANG CONNECTIONS NOT KNOWN

(Gang names in brackets added, based on later information.)

Nick Carone, Vito Ardito, Giovanni Gaspari, Joseph Agnello, Diago Altemorte [Aiello], Lorenzo Alegno [Aiello], Nuncio Junerrico [Aiello], Simson Golieto, Frank Salerno, Casper Alegne, Giolanni Blandine [Aiello], James Reggi, Frank Cremaldi, Tony Geddino, Agostine Ganlili, Salvatore Dori, Philip Mundio, Frank Rubini, John Ogren, Sam Scotti, Vern Harrie, Lazzaro Clemente, James Depola, Otto Fupielo, Joseph Lauer, Sam Volenta, Sam Guzzardo, Charles Howell, Anthony Russo [Aiello], Vincent Spicuzza [Aiello], Frank Hitchcock [Capone], Charles "Muscle Man" Conino, Matt Lombardo, Ben Applequist, Peter Gardina, John Kane, John Thorson, Robert Dregmay, Joseph Salamone, John Shearer, Edward Donovon [Clever Gang armed robber], John Shields, Ed Smith, William "Red" Golden, Peter Procepio, Dominick Culandrico.

Angelo Passerolli, John Dane, Milan Hylick, Jack Gibbons, Salvatore DeGrazio, Ralph "Polack Joe" Breje, George Grapham, Charles Garrao, William Thomas [former police officer], Angela Lamantic, Phillip Leonetti, Ernest Applequist, Tony Capezio [Capone], Toto Cere, Francis "Doc" White, Peter Salvo, James Velleco, William McMahon, Gus Hanson, Louis Schievone, Anthony Cevico, John "Two-gun" Gardino, Martin Costello, Peter Mangles, Tom Tuilt, Jack Drissoll, David DeCoursey, Charles Miller, Robert Jankowski, George Lewis, Frank McKnight, Peter Bensone, James Muzzo, William Reggio, John Elia, John Marsullo, Edward "The Eagle" Baldelli, Eddie Zine, Danny Vallo [O'Banion, later Capone], Albert Coffill, Joe Calebrose, Eddie Toff, Charles "Hurley Red" Wells, James Hickey Benter, Peter Pizzo, Frank Constanza, James Sandellar.

Raymond "Crane-Neck" Nugent [Capone], Peppy Genero, alias Annereno [Capone], Mike Vinci, James Vinci [Vinci], John Oliveri, Ralph J. Murphy, Sam Pulleno, Paul Swain, William "Red" Kinsella, Francis Sexton, James Chotin, Joseph Carville, Daniel McGeogehen [Clever Gang armed robber], John Flannery [Clever Gang armed robber], Virgil Litzinger [Clever Gang armed robber], Eddie "Mack" Maciejewski [armed robber], Willie Doody [armed robber], Charles "Limpy" Cleaver [Clever Gang, robber], Carlos Fontano ["42" gang, then Capone], "Big Dave" Earsman, Dominick Nuccio [Capone], Patsy Tardi ["42" gang], Ralph Orlando, Sam Gleeana, Michael "Rube" Quinlan (also called "Bubs" Quinlan) [North Sider, later Capone], Anthony Kissane, Mike "De Pike" Heitler [Capone], Henry Kimmel, Eugene "Red" McLaughlin [Capone], Danny Hartnett, William "Billy" Skidmore [North Sider], Frisco "Dutch" Schmidt (aka Frisco Dutch" Steinhardt or Robert Schmitt) [often associated with North Siders; later a St. Paul gangster], Sam Settipani, Thomas Abbott, Herman Prince Nowicki.

Both the Landesco and Wickersham investigators confuse Little Italy and Little Sicily, and they overlook the members of the Capone Outfit who one day would follow in the footsteps of "The Big Fellow." Frank Nitti already was in place, if maintaining a low profile. Joey Aiuppa, Paul Ricca, Tony Accardo, and Sam Giancana still were young drivers, advisers, and gunmen who had been toiling in the vineyards of Prohibition, but starting in the 1940s they would become the leaders of the Chicago mob. [See Appendix I on p. 611 for additional information.]

5

DEPRESSION-ERA CRIME

In 1933, the New Deal Justice Department, with a different agenda, declared its nationwide "War on Crime" against bank robbers and kidnappers, some of whom were much less formidable than their predecessors and made relatively easy targets once J. Edgar Hoover's new G-men had learned from their early mistakes. They included "Pretty Boy" Floyd, "Bonnie and Clyde" (actually brought down by a former Texas Ranger), "Machine Gun" Kelly, "Baby Face" Nelson, John Dillinger (for whom no one could think up an appropriately colorful nickname), and "Ma" Barker, wrongly considered the ringleader of the Barker-Karpis Gang. The "war" lasted only from 1933 to 1936 but immortalized the G-men and their "public enemies," as the press called anyone who rated a bureau press release.

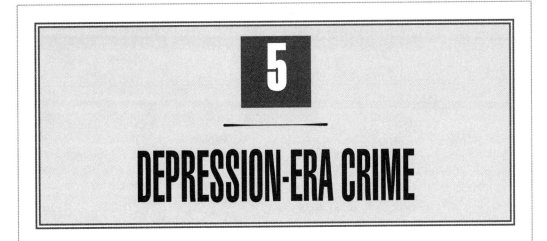

IF HOLDUPS INCREASE.
The Chicago Daily News.
STEPPING OUT TO POST A LETTER
May take the form of an armed sortie.

Holdups became so common during the Great Depression that few "respectable" people ventured out after dark without some kind of weapon. Prohibition actually had reduced street crime, but by the 1930s, cops and criminals alike were "motorized."

The FBI can be credited with revolutionizing police work the way the car had revolutionized crime, and with restoring a measure of confidence in the federal government. It did so by means of new federal anti-crime laws that were long overdue in the age of the interstate fugitive, but which failed to address or even recognize nationally organized crime in the form of racketeering that grew nearly unmolested until the 1950s.

Those criminals who made Depression-era headlines or were targeted as "interstate" robbers and kidnappers during the U.S. Justice Department's "War on Crime" are listed on pages 417-419.

DEPRESSION-ERA CRIME CHRONOLOGY
1930–1940

1930

January 2—Detroit Police Inspector Henry J. Garvin is wounded by gangsters who fire on his car from another vehicle in an assassination attempt. An eleven-year-old girl also is wounded.

January 6—Lester Joseph Gillis (alias George "Baby Face" Nelson) and four accomplices rob Mr. and Mrs. Charles M. Richter of $25,000 worth of jewelry in their Chicago mansion at 1418 Lake Shore Drive.

January 10—Harry Veasey, Queens beer runner formerly associated with Arnold Rothstein, is found shot to death near the Hoboken waterfront. Jack "Legs" Diamond is suspected.

January 15—Eddie Diamond, brother of Jack "Legs" Diamond, dies of tuberculosis at Saranac, New York.

January 22—George "Baby Face" Nelson, the alias of Lester Gillis, and three accomplices rob the Lake Forest, Illinois, home of lawyer Stanley J. Templeton, taking $5,000 worth of jewelry.

February 5—Charles Arthur "Pretty Boy" Floyd and others rob the Farmers & Merchants Bank at Sylvania, Ohio, of $1,720.

— Philip H. Meagher, construction superintendent for H. B. Barnard & Co., is murdered by two gunmen in a black sedan on the University of Chicago campus. H. B. Barnard will appeal the next day to Colonel Robert Isham Randolph, president of the Chicago Association of Commerce, for help.

February 11—The executive committee of the Chicago Association of Commerce offers a $5,000 reward for the arrest and conviction of the murderers of Philip Meagher and authorizes Colonel Robert Isham Randolph to form a "committee of citizens of known courage and action" to make a study of crime and a program for combating it.

February 13—Gangster Carmine Barelli and girlfriend, May Smith, are shot to death by their former friend Vincent Coll and accomplices at 170th Street and Inwood Avenue in New York for betraying Coll's plan to break away from "Dutch" Schultz and form a rival gang.

February 18—Colonel Robert Isham Randolph announces formation of a group of "men of courage" to fight Chicago gangsters. He refuses to name the members of his team, which reporters call the "Secret Six." This group will hire a staff and a mixed bag of undercover cops and other operatives (including Eliot Ness's "Untouchables") who become the "vigilante" arm of the Chicago Crime Commission.

February 25—Chicago gangster Frank McErlane is recovering from a gunshot wound inflicted by his mistress, Elfrieda Rigas (Elfreda or Elfrida were newspaper spellings), in a domestic dispute when two would-be killers invade his room at German Deaconess Hospital, 5421 South Morgan. As they start shooting, he pulls a revolver from under his pillow and drives them off, wounding one.

February 26—Gaetano (Tom) Reina, boss of a New York City Italian crime family, is killed by shotgun fire at 1522 Sheridan Avenue. His murder was ordered by Giuseppe "Joe the Boss" Masseria, self-styled leader of the Italian underworld, who sought to gain control of Reina's profitable ice-distribution monopoly. Masseria appoints Joseph Pinzolo as new boss of the Reina Family.

February 28—Thomas Holden and Francis Keating, convicted mail train robbers, escape from Leavenworth Federal Penitentiary, using forged trusty passes.

March 2—Clyde Barrow is arrested in Waco, Texas, for burglary and car theft.

March 6—Chicago gangster John "Dingbat" Oberta is found shot to death in his car at 103rd

Street and Robert Road. His bodyguard, Sam Malaga, lies in the same condition in a nearby ditch. Killer suspected to be Frank McErlane, in revenge for the recent hospital attack.

March 8—Marvin "Buck" Barrow, brother of Clyde and convicted burglar, escapes from Huntsville, Texas, state prison.

— Patrolman Harland F. Manes is fatally shot in Akron, Ohio, by bank robber James Bradley, alias Bert Walker, an associate of "Pretty Boy" Floyd. Bradley, Bob Amos (alias John King), and Floyd are arrested on suspicion.

March 10—After months as a fugitive on murder charges, Jack "Legs" Diamond surrenders to New York police. He will be discharged by Judge Levine on March 21.

March 11—Clyde Barrow, William Turner, and Emory Abernathy escape from Waco, Texas, jail using a gun smuggled in by Barrow's girlfriend, Bonnie Parker.

March 16—The bound corpse of North Side bootlegger John Rito is found in the Chicago River. Rito was stabbed, beaten, tortured, shot, and had all the skin burned off his hands.

March 17—In Philadelphia, Chicago mob boss Al Capone is paroled from a one-year sentence on gun-carrying charges.

March 18—Clyde Barrow, William Turner, and Emory Abernathy are recaptured in Middleton, Ohio, and are extradited to Texas.

March 19—New York ice racketeer Joseph Riggio is shot to death in his car outside his girlfriend's apartment at 76 Bay Twenty-third Street in Brooklyn.

March 20—Miami police raid Al Capone's Palm Island estate, seize illegal liquor, and arrest Capone's brothers Albert and John, along with "Machine Gun" Jack McGurn, "Diamond Lou" Cowan, and Leo Brothers.

March 23—Alvin Karpis, convicted burglar and Kansas state reformatory escapee, is recaptured in Kansas City, Missouri. Karpis's partner, Lawrence DeVol, is arrested at the same time.

March 24—Al Capone appears on the cover of *Time* magazine.

March 27—Mobster Giuseppe "The Clutching Hand" Piraino is killed by gunmen outside 151 Sackett Street in Brooklyn.

March 31—With accomplices Stanton Randall and Harry Lewis, George "Baby Face" Nelson robs Count and Countess Von Buelow in their home at 5839 Sheridan Road in Chicago, taking $95 in cash and more than $50,000 worth of jewels.

— A temporary federal injunction is granted at Miami, preventing the sheriff from arresting Al Capone.

April 1—Alvin Karpis's partner, Lawrence DeVol, posts a $1,000 bond in Kansas City, is released, and jumps bail.

April 20—Three Capone gangsters, Walter Wakefield, Frank Delre, and Joseph Special, are shot to death by a lone gunman in the "Easter Massacre" in a bar at 2900 South Wells Street in Chicago.

April 21—Clyde Barrow is received at Huntsville, Texas, state prison under a fourteen-year sentence for burglary and car theft.

$5,000 REWARD

For DEAD Bank Robbers

$5,000 cash will be paid for each Bank Robber legally killed while Robbing this bank

THE Texas Bankers Association, a corporation, offers a standing reward of $5,000 for each bank robber legally killed while robbing and holding up a reward subscribing member bank in Texas with firearms during the daytime. Limits of the place and time of such killing are: in the banking house, or as the robbers and holdups leave the bank, while the robbery and holdup and threats are being committed; and as they flee from the bank with the property taken, and are resisting legal pursuit and arrest, within twenty miles of the bank robbed and within six hours after the robbery and holdup. This reward does not apply to night attacks on Texas banks. It is expressly provided that the Texas Bankers Association shall determine whether or not payment of this reward shall be made hereunder, and to whom (if anyone) such payment shall be made, and such determination and judgment shall be final, conclusive and not reviewable.

¶ The Association will not give one cent for live bank robbers. They are rarely identified, more rarely convicted, and most rarely stay in the penitentiary when sent there—all of which operations are troublesome, burdensome and costly to our government.

¶ In order to protect the lives of people in such banks and to protect the property of such banks, the Association is prepared to pay for any number of such robbers and holdups so killed, while they are robbing and holding up its reward subscribing member banks with firearms in the daytime, at $5,000 apiece.

¶ This reward is effective April 1st, 1930, and all other rewards, offers and statements are cancelled and superseded hereby.

TEXAS BANKERS ASSOCIATION

$5,000 in cash will be so paid for the legal killing of any robber and holdup WHILE ROBBING THIS BANK with firearms in the daytime

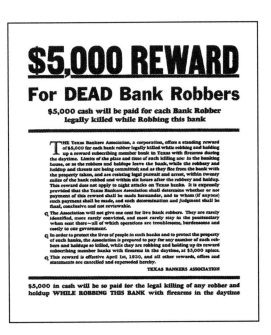

During the Great Depression, the Texas Bankers Association described the difficulty in catching and convicting suspects and declared it would not "give one cent" for "live" bank robbers.

April 24—The Chicago Crime Commission publishes its first list of "public enemies," with Al Capone in the No. 1 position. "Public Enemy No. 1" becomes a popular headline phrase, and other law enforcement agencies will soon adopt their own "public enemy" lists. [Later, newspapers will apply "public enemy" to any major outlaw sought by the FBI.]

April 25—Federal Judge Halsted L. Ritter makes permanent an injunction preventing the Miami sheriff from arresting Al Capone.

April 26—Elderly brothers David and George Smith, wealthy loan brokers from Connecticut, are shot to death in an apparent robbery attempt in Room 817 of the Hotel Severs in Muskogee, Oklahoma. The double homicide is never solved, but prime suspects include four gunmen known to have been in the Muskogee area: Lawrence DeVol, his brother Clarence, Jimmie Creighton (later an associate of Fred Barker), and Pat McDonald.

May 4—Chicago gangster "Orlando Jack" Horton is found shot to death in a strawberry patch at Lafayette, Indiana.

May 8—Al Capone, his brother John and two gang members are arrested by Miami police for investigation.

— Dominick Sciortino is shot dead in the living room of his home at 1233 Carmen Avenue in Chicago by two men "who looked like Italians." Sciortino had received threatening "black-hand" letters and was living alone, having sent his family away to live with a married daughter.

May 9—Al Capone is denied an injunction preventing Miami police from arresting him.

May 13—Al Capone, Nick Circella, and former Chicago Alderman Albert Prignano are arrested by Miami police while attending a prize fight. They will be released on a writ of habeas corpus the next day.

May 15—Anna Urbas, girlfriend of murdered New York gangster Eugene Moran, is strangled and thrown into the East River. "Legs" Diamond mob suspected.

May 19—Al Capone and state politician Albert Prignano are arrested by Miami police while on their way to an American Legion boxing match. They are released on $100 bond.

May 20—"Pretty Boy" Floyd is turned over to Toledo authorities on a bank robbery charge.

May 21—Floyd associate James Bradley, alias Bert Walker, is sentenced to death for murder.

— In Miami, vagrancy charges against Al Capone and Albert Prignano are dismissed by Judge Frank P. Stoneman.

May 25—At Benton, Illinois, former Birger gang member Connie Ritter pleads guilty to the murder of West City Mayor Joe Adams and is sentenced to life in prison.

May 28—As a public relations gesture, Al Capone invites the elite of Miami's business community to an alcohol-free party at his Palm Island estate.

May 29—Four men rob the state bank at Black Earth, Wisconsin, of $31,000 in cash and bonds and escape after locking seven people in the vault. Later, legend will attribute this crime to John Dillinger, who was in prison at the time.

May 31—Detroit mobsters Gaspare Milazzo, also known as Gaspere Scibilia, and Sam Parina are fatally shot by rival gangsters at a fish market at 2739 Vernor Highway.

June 1—Three Capone-affiliated gangsters, Sam Peller, Joseph Bertsche, and Michael Quirk, are machine-gunned to death in the Fox Lake Massacre at Manning's, a popular waterfront resort hotel, 14 North Pistakee Lake Road, Fox Lake, Illinois. George Druggan and Mrs. Vivian McGinnis are wounded. Though the murders are attributed to the Moran-Aiello gang, George "Machine Gun" Kelly will later claim that Verne Miller did the shooting himself for personal reasons—to avenge the murder of his friend, Eugene "Red" McLaughlin.

— Capone gangster Thomas Somnerio is found strangled in a West Side alley.

— Policemen Edward Mayers and Claude Lanstra are killed in a gun battle with rumrunners in the Detroit suburb of Grosse Pointe Park.

June 5—Eugene "Red" McLaughlin's body is found in the Chicago River, bound with baling wire and weighted down with seventy-five pounds of metal.

The Depression-era Desperados

Bandits on horseback had been holding up stages, banks, and trains as the West was being settled, and after the Civil War the discharged soldiers who took up robbery had learned the value of organization and planning. This gave rise to the James Brothers, the Daltons, and other gangs who essentially were civilian versions of military raiding parties.

Horseback outlawry eventually was suppressed by posses of armed citizens and by professional security agencies such as the Pinkertons, whose pursuit of fugitives across state lines made them private-enterprise versions of the future FBI. By the turn of the century, the effectiveness of organized "vigilance" committees and Pinkerton-type "detective" agencies had made commando-style robbery a sufficiently risky proposition that daylight attacks by gangs on horseback were giving way to bank burglaries, which pitted safecrackers against safe makers, who themselves were competing to develop thief-resistant designs.

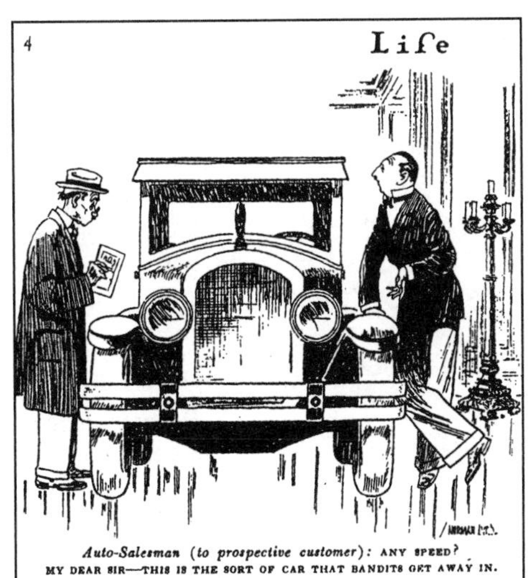

Auto-Salesman (to prospective customer): ANY SPEED? MY DEAR SIR—THIS IS THE SORT OF CAR THAT BANDITS GET AWAY IN.

As historical chance would have it, advances in locks and vault design began to exceed the skills of the average safecracker, or "yegg," about the same time as the transportation industry developed relatively fast and reliable automobiles. The result was a post-World War I revival of daylight armed robbery by James-style gangs at a time when law-enforcement again was mainly in the hands of local police, who found themselves no match for the new "motorized bandits."

Compounding the problem was the advent of Prohibition, which not only ushered in an era of unprecedented graft but also dismantled the principal means used by police to put a lid on crime. In the absence of anything resembling a central criminal records file, district and precinct cops had depended heavily on their network of informants who patronized popular hoodlum hangouts to identify suspects and fugitives. The closing of the established saloons and taverns dispersed the criminal community to speakeasies that came and went like floating crap games, and (thanks to the automobile) to a growing number of roadhouses that ringed every city, catered to local citizens as well as big-spending crooks, and enjoyed police protection—sometimes from other police.

The result was a preoccupation with organized bootleggers who had little to fear from the courts even when prosecuted, and the opportunity for better-equipped armed robbers to regroup as gangs that could resume raiding banks, payroll messengers, and even trains with virtual impunity. Many of the jobs made banner headlines because of the amount of the loot, but identification methods were so primitive and uncoordinated that newspapers could only report that several unidentified men had escaped by car after pulling a "daring daylight robbery."

Another factor in the success of 1920s outlaws was the nation's increasing prosperity. The banks were full of money in the days of Harvey Bailey, Eddie Bentz, the Newton Brothers, and

After raiding the bank in Clinton, Indiana, and having to commandeer three cars, Hermann K. "Baron" Lamm and two accomplices led police on a bloody two-state chase (below) that finally ended at a farm where they died after a lengthy gun battle. At right: the body of "Baron" Lamm.

DIAGRAM AND PHOTO FROM THE LORI HYDE COLLECTION

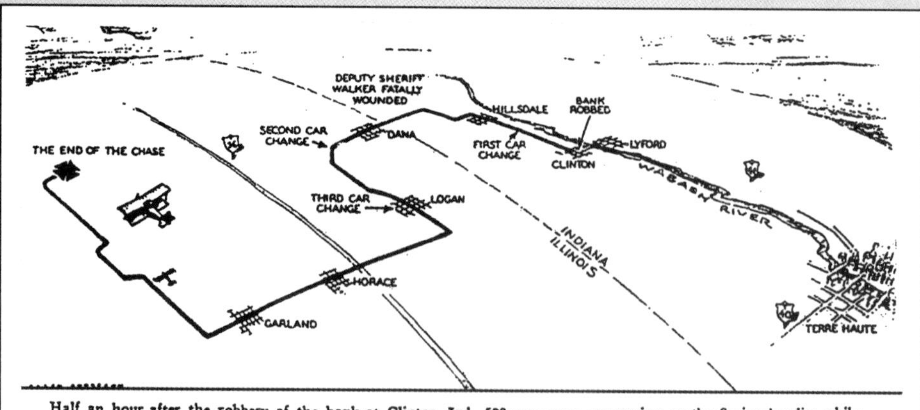

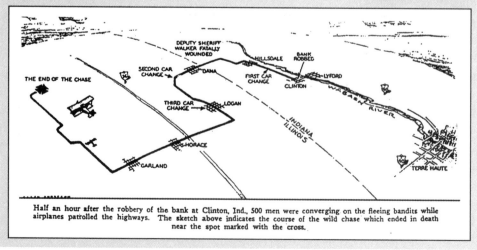

Half an hour after the robbery of the bank at Clinton, Ind., 500 men were converging on the fleeing bandits while airplanes patrolled the highways. The sketch above indicates the course of the wild chase which ended in death near the spot marked with the cross.

"Baron" Lamm,* who plundered the flatlands of the Midwest with its countless farm-to-market roads. The most successful gangs included Jake and Ralph Fleagle, who committed many large robberies while successfully posing in their hometown of Garden City, Kansas, as horse and cattle dealers before a bloody 1928 robbery at Lamar, Colorado, gave them instant notoriety. Ralph and other gang members were sent to the gallows and gave Jake headline status rivaling Fred Burke as "the most wanted man in America."**

Bank robbery had more than doubled from 136 holdups in 1921 to 292 in 1928, and then it nearly doubled again by 1932 (554 holdups) before starting to trend downward. But with Al Capone in prison and Prohibition repealed, lesser outlaws soon would become Depression-era celebrities once they were targeted by the FBI.

Since crime waves are largely a matter of public perception, various robbers, kidnappers and their cohorts were deliberately transformed into symbols of a "national crime problem" by President Roosevelt's attorney general pushing for "federalized crime control," whether or not they constituted gangs in the historic sense. Sometimes all it took was a memorable nickname, supplied either by the press or by the Justice Department, which understood that public support for its "War on Crime" was directly proportional to the notoriety of its criminals.

Other factors were the refinement of wire-service journalism that linked newspapers nationwide and helped forge publishing empires. Crime and scandal were the biggest headline-makers, especially in cities like Chicago, and the larger papers even had their own syndicates that fed the country's appetite for crime news. About the same time, "detective magazines" that began as pulps abandoned crime fiction for crime "fact" in articles about murders, gangsters, robbers, and kidnappers. Some became slick, well-edited, and generous enough to attract good writers whose research was far better than that of the harried newspaper reporter racing to meet a deadline. They became barbershop staples and actually led to the capture of many criminals whose faces became as familiar to readers as to the police.

So it was timing as much as anything that fostered the notoriety of certain criminals who composed "gangs" in the minds of the public, and who went into the history books as such.

For instance there was never a consolidated "Dillinger Gang," but rather a criminal community that included several robbers he worked with when possible and others when necessary, all of whom came and went as luck and the law allowed. Whether they were close confederates or simply filling in on a particular job, some qualified as "members" of the gang only to the extent that any association with Dillinger was their major claim to fame. Early on, Dillinger himself deferred to Harry Pierpont as the gang's leader.

Some outlaws worked with more than one gang, some were involved in only one or two jobs, and some had gang connections that were brief or unknown.

[See p. 417 for a listing of the major gangs that began making headlines during the Depression, when they became identifiable or were targeted by the U.S. Justice Department in its "War on Crime."]

*Better known at the time as Tom Bell, and even his alleged background as a German baron is questionable.

**An "Evil Eye Fleegle" made it into Al Capp's *Li'l Abner*, along with "Fearless Fosdick," a parody of Chester Gould's *Dick Tracy*, whose scientific crime-fighting would make him the comic-strip equivalent of the "G-man."

– Two men rob the Grand Avenue State Bank in Dallas of $10,400 in cash and bonds.

June 7—Three men and one woman rob the Clinton Avenue Branch of the South Side Bank & Trust Co. in Newark of $14,000. "Legs" Diamond mob suspected.

– Willie "The Actor" Sutton and Marcus "Jack" Bassett rob the Woodhaven Branch of the Richmond Hill National Bank in New York of $19,000.

June 9—Mob-affiliated *Chicago Tribune* crime reporter Alfred "Jake" Lingle is murdered by a gunman in a pedestrian underpass at Randolph Street and Michigan Avenue.

June 12—Four gunmen take over the Garfield Arms Hotel at 3256 Maypole Avenue in Chicago for an hour, robbing fifteen guests and the hotel safe before fleeing with an estimated $1,000.

June 14—The state's petition to have Al Capone's Palm Island estate padlocked as a public nuisance is dismissed by Miami Judge Paul D. Barnes. Capone is arrested minutes later for two counts of perjury, allegedly committed in warrants he had issued against S. D. McCreary, director of Public Safety, whom Capone charged with false arrest.

June 16—The body of an unidentified man, riddled with bullets, weighted with iron, and with head, hands, and feet cut off to prevent identification, is churned to the surface of the Chicago River by a passing tugboat.

June 21—Chicago Heights mobster Lorenzo Juliano is found beaten to death in his car at 123rd Street and California Avenue in Blue Island, Illinois.

June 25—Chicago police arrest "Machine Gun" Jack McGurn and Tony "Joe Batters" Accardo on gun carrying charges in a taxi at Dearborn and Harrison streets.

June 26—After stealing a car from an Ottumwa, Iowa, garage, John "Handsome Jack" Klutas is arrested at Washington, Iowa. In the sheriff's office Klutas draws a gun and kills Night Marshal Aaron Bailey and Sheriff Fred Sweet before escaping.

June 30—Cleveland Mafia boss Joe Porrello and bodyguard Sam Tilocco are shot to death at Frank Milano's Venetian Restaurant at Mayfield Road and East 126th Street. Milano eventually will emerge as leader of the Cleveland crime family.

July 3—George Kelly, later known as "Machine Gun" Kelly, is paroled from a three-year sentence at Leavenworth for smuggling liquor onto an Indian reservation.

July 10—Ralph Fleagle, of the Jake Fleagle Gang of bank robbers, is hanged for murder at the Canon City, Colorado, state prison.

July 12—Gangster Salvatore (Sam) Ciluffo is killed by machine-gunners in his car at the corner of Russell and Jefferson streets in Detroit.

July 15—Harvey Bailey, Thomas Holden, George "Machine Gun" Kelly, and others rob the Bank of Willmar at Willmar, Minnesota, of $77,000.

July 16—Purple Gang member David Ovshtein is murdered in an alley near Huber Street in Detroit.

July 19—Herbert Royston and George Abshier, members of the Fleagle Gang, are hanged for murder at the state prison at Canon City, Colorado.

July 23—Radio newscaster Gerald Buckley is assassinated by gangsters in the lobby of Detroit's La Salle Hotel.

August 1—Moran-Aiello gangster Jack Zuta is machine-gunned by Capone mobsters in a resort at Delafield, Wisconsin.

– Al Capone is cleared of a perjury charge in Miami on a directed verdict of acquittal.

August 6—State Supreme Court Justice Joseph Force Crater disappears in New York City and is never seen again.

August 7—A "mad bomber" attempting to rob the Stockyards National Bank in Fort Worth hurls a vial of nitroglycerine, killing himself and bank vice president Fred Pelton and demolishing the lobby. Body parts are reportedly found a block away.

August 13—Sam Silverman, alias Stein, Frank "Weinie" Coleman, and Mike Rusick, suspects in the recent Willmar, Minnesota, bank robbery, are found shot to death near Mahtomedi, Minnesota. (One theory holds they were killed by Verne Miller for double-crossing their friends on loot from the robbery; another is that "Bugs"

Moran blamed them for hijacking a truckload of whiskey.)

August 14—Chicago gangster Danny Vallo is murdered by shotgun killers in Niles Center [now Skokie], Illinois.

August 15—Giuseppe (Peter) Morello, ally of Joe Masseria in his war against Salvatore Maranzano, is killed with Giuseppi Paraino and Gaspar Pollero by gunmen in Morello's New York office at 362 East 116th Street.

August 20—George Kelly, William Naecker, and Abe Shultz rob the Broadway State Bank in Fort Wayne, Indiana, taking $5,912. Contrary to later popular legend, the robber Kelly was not George "Machine Gun" Kelly.

August 22—Catskills bootlegger Harry Western disappears after meeting Jack "Legs" Diamond and attending a party at Haines Falls, New York. Western's bloodstained Buick turns up in a Brooklyn garage, and two members of the Diamond gang are arrested. Western's body is never found.

September—Jack "Legs" Diamond sails to Europe. Denied entry to England, he is arrested at Antwerp, Belgium, and deported to Germany. German authorities again deport him, returning him to the United States aboard the freighter *Hanover.*

September 3—Bill "The Killer" Miller and another man rob the National Bank & Trust Co. at North Kansas City, Missouri, of $14,544.

September 5—In New York, Joseph Pinzolo, Joe Masseria's puppet leader of the Reina crime family, is shot to death in Suite 1007 of the Brokaw Building at 1487 Broadway. The murder was carried out by dissidents in the family who elect Tommaso (Tom) Gagliano as their new boss and join forces with Joe Masseria's enemy, Salvatore Maranzano, head of the Castellammarese faction of the New York Mafia.

September 9—The Harvey Bailey Gang robs the Ottumwa Savings Bank in Ottumwa, Iowa, of $40,000.

September 13—Three men rob the Merchants Trust Co. at South Paterson, New Jersey, of $18,000. Chicago gangsters Fred "Killer" Burke and Gus Winkeler (soon to be spelled Winkler in the press) are identified by witnesses as two of the holdup men. Both also are suspects in the St. Valentine's Day Massacre.

September 14—Angelo Spano, alias Jack Costa, a bodyguard of North Side Chicago gangster Joe Aiello, is murdered in the doorway of Fernwood Apartments, 4056 Sheridan Road, in a barrage of automatic rifle and shotgun fire from a second-floor apartment.

September 16—Judge John H. Lyle signs vagrancy warrants against twenty-six gangsters named by the Chicago Crime Commission as "public enemies."

September 17—Six men rob the Lincoln National Bank & Trust Co. at Lincoln, Nebraska, of more than $2 million in bonds and cash. Thomas O'Connor, Howard "Pop" Lee, and Jack Britt will be wrongly arrested for this crime, and O'Connor and Lee will be convicted of it. This robbery often is attributed to Harvey Bailey, but the FBI in later years named the robbers as Eddie Bentz, Charles J. Fitzgerald, "Big Homer" Wilson, Gus Stone, Avery Simmons (alias Jim Ripley), and Eddie Doll (alias Eddie LaRue).

September 19—Federal Prohibition Agent John J. Finiello is killed in a gun battle with gangsters during a raid on the Rising Sun Brewery in Elizabeth, New Jersey. Nick Delmore and William Weissman are sought as suspects.

– Two men rob the First State Bank at Ripley, Oklahoma, of $2,000.

– Three men rob the Bank of Braidwood at Braidwood, Illinois, of $2,500.

September 22—Arriving in Philadelphia from Hamburg, Germany, Jack "Legs" Diamond is arrested as a "suspicious character."

September 23—A five-man gang robs the Bank of Kaukauna in Kaukauna, Wisconsin, of $35,000 in cash and securities, locking eleven employees and customers in the vault.

September 24—Three gunmen rob the Neches State Bank in Neches, Texas, of $3,500.

September 25—Capone gangsters Harry and Sam Guzik, brothers of Jake, are arrested for income tax evasion.

September 30—Al Capone is arrested in connection with the murder of Jack Zuta.

— Federal agents arrest Jake "Greasy Thumb" Guzik for income tax evasion.

October 2—Peter McTigue and William Boody, members of the St. Louis Cuckoo gang, are killed in a machine-gun attack on a cabin distillery near Valmeyer, Illinois. The raiders were probably members of a dissident gang faction led by Tommy Hayes.

October 3—George "Baby Face" Nelson, Stanton Randall, and Harry Lewis rob the Itasca State Bank at Itasca, Illinois, of $4,600.

October 6—Mary Walker Thompson, wife of Chicago Mayor "Big Bill" Thompson, is robbed by three men outside her apartment on Sheridan Road. Later attributed to George "Baby Face" Nelson.

October 10—Disguised as a Western Union messenger, Willie "The Actor" Sutton attempts to rob the Bay Ridge, Brooklyn, branch of the National City Bank in New York. The attempt was foiled by a watchman.

October 12—Jack "Legs" Diamond is shot and wounded by rival gangsters at the Hotel Monticello in New York City. It is the third known murder attempt on the mobster.

October 14—Gang leader Jake Fleagle is shot by police while boarding a train at Branson, Missouri. He dies the next day at a Springfield hospital.

October 19—Frank "Jelly" Nash, former member of the Al Spencer Gang and convicted murderer and bank and train robber, escapes from Leavenworth, where he has been serving a twenty-five-year sentence for mail robbery.

October 23—Chicago mob boss Joseph Aiello is killed by Capone gangsters using two machine-gun nests outside the apartment building of his henchman Pasquale "Presto" Prestigiocomo at 205 Kolmar Avenue in Chicago.

October 24—John Guida, a member of Chicago's "42" Gang, is found shot to death at 836 North Racine Avenue.

October 28—Gambling boss Solly "Cutcher-Head-Off" Weissman is shot to death at the Turf, a bookie joint at 1211 Baltimore Avenue in Kansas City the

OUT TO PASTURE

"Motorized banditry" didn't spring up overnight, but the first occurrence has eluded historians. Some "cutting edge" outlaw may have fired up a Stanley Steamer to rob a bank (possibly by himself, if all the bank employees and customers were outside marveling at the machine); and after that some would-be robber may have broken his arm trying to crank one of the new internal-combustion engines on a car with the "spark lever" wrongly set. But well before World War I the motor vehicle was overtaking the horse, especially if the roads were dry.

Some bandits used the car and the horse. Outlaws like Henry Starr, Al Spencer, and Ed Lockhart might steal a car to rob a bank, then ditch it outside of town where accomplices were waiting with horses so all could ride "off-road" and into the wilderness. And telephones were rare enough in rural areas that cutting one set of lines might be all it took to disconnect a community.

NAOMI MORGAN

Henry Starr

During the World War I era, which included Pancho Villa's raid on Columbus, New Mexico, in 1916, the U.S. Army put out a call for horses, to chase Villa in the wilds of Mexico and to ready itself for probable battle in Europe. This revived horse thievery in the Southwest by "old" outlaws on horseback who had to ride cross-country with their herds. The Poe-Hart Gang, for instance, started out as horse thieves, then in 1918 took to cars that they used for robbing banks in Oklahoma. And legend has it that Florida's notorious Ashley Gang, in one of their early robberies, reached the edge of a town on horseback, walked to the bank (which they robbed), then stole a car and took along its owner because none of the gang could drive.

By 1919 the getaway horse was being put out to pasture. From December 1920 through early 1922, various "masked men" on horseback still looted a few banks in Arkansas and Oklahoma and also held up a Missouri Pacific mail train, robbing the express car and passengers, but four hooves were fast giving way to four tires. Six years later, however, in far-off Pennsylvania, a lone bandit pulled a robbery in Parkerford on July 18, 1928, and rode off before anyone could locate enough saddle-worthy horses to form a posse. Probably the last such holdup took place in New Mexico on June 1, 1932, when a robber surprised the residents of Hatch by doing a horseback job on their little bank and then galloping out of town.

same day he returned from Minneapolis to face bootlegging charges that were dismissed a few hours before his death. He was killed by Charlie Haughton, described in news accounts as "a white-haired, serene man" who was tired of being "bullied" by Weissman. Haughton was not charged.

— Disguised as a Western Union messenger, Willie "The Actor" Sutton robs M. Rosenthal & Sons jewelry store at 1637 Broadway in New York of $130,000 in gems.

November 3—Gangster John "The Ape" Passelli, while recovering from "falling out of an automobile," is shot to death by two gunmen who invade his private room at Newark General Hospital in Newark, New Jersey.

November 5—Stephen Ferrigno and Alfred Mineo, New York Mafia bosses allied with Joe Masseria, are shotgunned to death by Maranzano gunmen while leaving Ferrigno's apartment at 759 Pelham Parkway South.

November 7—George "Baby Face" Nelson and an accomplice attempt to rob the state bank at Plainfield, Illinois, but are thwarted by cashiers' cages of bulletproof glass. (It is here that George Nelson, the alias of Lester Gillis, acquires his memorable nickname when a witness describes one robber as having a "baby face," probably inspired by a popular song of the day.)

November 9—Frank Smith, alias Frank Ellis; Edward Shannon, alias Sherwood; James "California Eddie" Sargert, Edward Kenney, and Charles Berta, armed with machine guns, rob a Southern Pacific mail train of $56,000 at Nobel, California.

November 10—James Bradley, accomplice of "Pretty Boy" Floyd, is executed for murder at the Columbus, Ohio, state prison.

November 17—Lawrence DeVol, future Barker-Karpis Gang member, murders policeman John Rose in Kirksville, Missouri, after a theater robbery in Hannibal, Missouri.

November 18—Chicago "public enemy" James "Fur" Sammons is convicted of vagrancy, fined $100, and sentenced to six months in the Cook County Jail. Sammons also is charged with the burglary of a Chicago liquor warehouse and is wanted in Baltimore for robbery.

– At 935 South State Street in Chicago, hundreds of jobless citizens line up for free food at a soup kitchen established by Al Capone.

November 20—Capone lieutenant Jake "Greasy Thumb" Guzik is convicted of income tax evasion.

– U.S. Customs officers kill liquor smugglers Frank Barncastle and Jesus Paz near El Paso, Texas.

November 22—George "Baby Face" Nelson, Stanton Randall and Harry Lewis rob the Hillside State Bank in Hillside, Illinois, of $4,000.

– Dewey "The $500 Kid" Goebbels and Lester Barth, members of the rebellious Tommy Hayes faction of the Cuckoos gang, are machine-gunned to death in a parked car in St. Louis by unknown killers. Other Cuckoos are suspected.

November 23—Three women are killed and three more people wounded by eight gunmen in a tavern robbery on Archer Avenue in the Chicago suburb of Summit. Accomplice Stanton Randall will years later name "Baby Face" Nelson as the gang's leader.

November 24—"Pretty Boy" Floyd is convicted of a Sylvania, Ohio, bank robbery and sentenced to twelve to fifteen years at Columbus, Ohio, state prison.

November 25—Willie "The Actor" Sutton is captured at the Childs Restaurant at Seventy-fourth Street and Broadway in New York. His accomplice, Marcus "Jack" Bassett, is captured the next day in Buffalo.

November 26—"Baby Face" Nelson later named as an accomplice in the killing of Edwin Thompson during a Waukegan Road tavern robbery north of Chicago.

December 1—Frank Smith, alias Frank Ellis, wanted for bank, train, and postal robberies from California to Vancouver since 1928, is captured by police at his Oakland, California, home, then killed when he attempts to escape.

December 10—"Pretty Boy" Floyd escapes from a train taking him to prison.

December 11—A Waukegan jury acquits "Bugs" Moran of vagrancy.

December 16—The "Baron" Lamm Gang robs the Citizens State Bank at Clinton, Indiana, of $15,567 and kills Deputy Joe Walker near Mecca, Indiana, but is trapped by a posse at the Leo Moody farm near Fairmount, Illinois. Hermann K. "Baron" Lamm, who has been robbing banks for years, is killed, along with E. H. Hunter. E. W. "Dad" Landy commits suicide, and two other gang members, Walter Detrich and James "Oklahoma Jack" Clark, the latter a suspect in the 1922 Denver Mint robbery, are captured. Detrich and Clark will receive life sentences at the Indiana state prison, where they will teach

Lamm's methods to John Dillinger and his friends. (The first two initials of Hunter and Landy vary in different accounts, and probably their names were aliases.)

– The Farmers State Bank at Plano, Illinois, is robbed of $7,000. Capone mobster Gus Winkeler later will be charged with the robbery.

December 20—Capone lieutenant Frank "The Enforcer" Nitti pleads guilty in Chicago federal court to income tax evasion. He is sentenced to eighteen months in prison and fined $10,000.

1931

January 1—Pasquale "Patsy" Tardi, leader of the notorious "42" Gang, is murdered in Chicago by unknown gunmen.

January 13—Stanton Randall, accomplice of "Baby Face" Nelson, is arrested by police at his apartment at 6236 North Mozart in Chicago. Chicago police also arrest Nelson accomplice Harry Lewis at the Diversey Arms Hotel.

January 15—Lester Gillis, alias George "Baby Face" Nelson, is arrested by Chicago police in his apartment at 6109 West Twenty-fifth Street in Cicero, Illinois.

January 24—Bronx beer baron Arthur "Dutch Schultz" Flegenheimer and Charles "Chink" Sherman, a member of the rival "Waxey" Gordon mob, are wounded in a gun battle at the Club Abbey on West Fifty-fourth Street in New York.

February 2—The bodies of Shelton gangster Joseph Carroll, a former policeman, pawnbroker Theodore Kaminski, and jewelry salesman David Hoffman are found near Granite City, Illinois. All three apparently were machine-gunned to death the night before at Ralph "Wide Open" Smith's gambling house in East St. Louis. Tommy "Mad Dog" Hayes and Carl Shelton are named as suspects.

February 3—Joseph Catania, alias Joe Baker, lieutenant of New York Mafia boss Joe Masseria, is fatally shot by Salvatore Maranzano's gunmen at 647 Crescent Avenue.

February 6—Mobster Chester LaMare is killed by gunmen at his home on Grandville Avenue in Detroit.

February 10—William Goebbels, brother of murdered gangster Dewey Goebbels, is fatally wounded by gunmen in the back room of a Taylor Avenue speakeasy in St. Louis. Killed with Goebbels are two women, Bessie Lynam and Dorothy Evans, both convicted shoplifters.

February 15—Walter Stevens, legendary killer known as the "Dean of Chicago Gunman," dies of pneumonia in Streeter Hospital, 2646 Calumet Avenue, Chicago, at about the age of seventy.

February 18—City plumbing inspector Albert Courchene is murdered by an underworld machine-gunner at 4224 Langley Avenue in Chicago. Labor racketeer Dan McCarthy is sought as a suspect.

February 21—Francis Crowley and two other youths attempt to crash a Washington's Birthday dance at an American Legion post at 290 Bonner Place in the Bronx. When Legionnaires attempt to throw them out, Crowley shoots and wounds two of them, then flees with his companions.

February 25—Chicago police arrest Al Capone for vagrancy.

– Jimmie Creighton, James Thomas, and S. Lawson O'Dell rob the Hastings National Bank in Hastings, Nebraska, of more than $27,000.

February 26—Vice case witness Vivian Gordon is found strangled in Van Cortlandt Park in the Bronx.

March 3—Benita Bischoff, sixteen-year-old daughter of murdered prostitute Vivian Gordon, commits suicide by inhaling gas in Audubon, New Jersey.

March 9—"Pretty Boy" Floyd, Bill "The Killer" Miller, and George Birdwell rob the Bank of Earlsboro at Earlsboro, Oklahoma, of $3,000.

March 13—Francis Crowley avoids arrest in an office building at 369 Lexington Avenue in Manhattan by shooting police detective Ferdinand Schaedel, who is seriously wounded but survives.

March 15—Five men rob the Huguenot Trust Co. at New Rochelle, New York. Francis Crowley later is named as a suspect.

March 16-April 2—St. Louis gangster Leo Brothers is tried in Chicago for the murder of reporter Jake Lingle. Brothers is convicted and sentenced to fourteen years.

March 25—"Pretty Boy" Floyd and Bill "The Killer" Miller murder William Ash and Wallace Ash at Kansas City, Kansas, either for informing to the police or in a dispute over the Ash women.

March 26—Fred "Killer" Burke, notorious bank robber and reputed Capone Syndicate hit man who is wanted for several murders, including the 1929 St. Valentine's Day Massacre, is captured in Green City, Missouri. He will refuse to cooperate with Chicago police but receive a life sentence in Michigan for the murder of St. Joseph policeman Charles Skelly.

March 30—Fred Barker, son of Kate "Ma" Barker and convicted robber and burglar, is paroled from the state prison at Lansing, Kansas.

March 31—The federal grand jury in Chicago

Chicago Tribune *reporter Jake Lingle (right) was assassinated in a Michigan Avenue underpass (below) and given a hero's funeral, complete with marching bands. The* Tribune *trumpeted the capture of Leo Brothers (top right), the city's first gangland gunman convicted and actually sent to prison—on flimsy evidence. Although a hired killer, Brothers, represented by future Dillinger attorney Louis Piquett, received only fourteen years. Lingle fell wearing a belt buckle given by Al Capone to special friends, and soon it would be discovered that he was up to his neck in the rackets. (The belt buckle pictured here belonged to a Miami hotel owner.)*

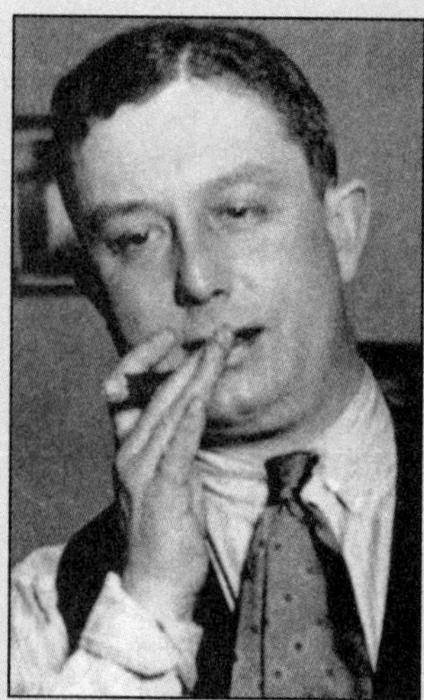

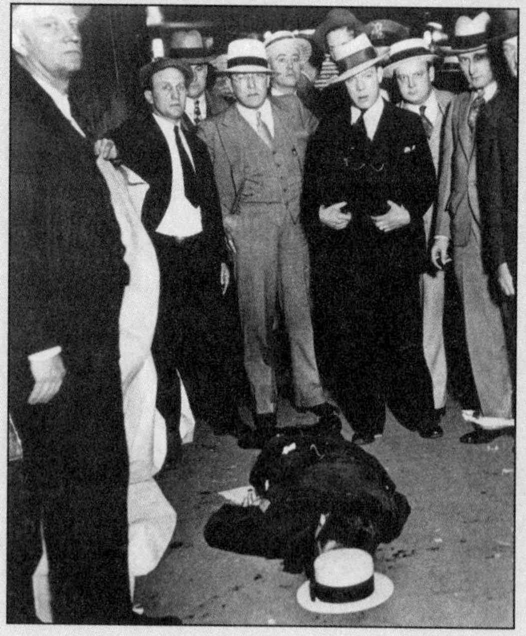

issues a secret indictment of Al Capone for income tax evasion.

April 6—"Pretty Boy" Floyd and Bill "The Killer" Miller rob the Deposit Bank at Mt. Zion, Kentucky, of $2,262.

April 7—Democratic political boss Anton Cermak defeats incumbent Capone favorite "Big Bill" Thompson in the Chicago mayoral election.

April 8—Harvey Bailey, Frank Nash, Verne Miller, "Machine Gun" Kelly, and others rob the Central State Bank at Sherman, Texas, of $40,000.

April 14—"Pretty Boy" Floyd and Bill "The Killer" Miller rob the Whitehouse State Savings Bank at Whitehouse, Ohio, of $1,800.

April 15—Mafia boss Giuseppe "Joe the Boss" Masseria is assassinated in Gerardo Scarpato's Coney Island restaurant at 2715 West Fifteenth Street. His lieutenant, Charles "Lucky" Luciano, ascends to leadership of the former Masseria crime family. Masseria's killers will be named later by informer Abe Reles as Benjamin "Bugsy" Siegel, Joe Adonis, Albert Anastasia, and Vito Genovese, all close associates of Luciano. Masseria's death ends the Castellammarese War between his family and that of rival Salvatore Maranzano for control of the Italian underworld in New York.

– Francis Crowley and two accomplices break into the basement apartment of real estate man Rudolph Adler at 133 West Ninetieth Street in New York. Crowley robs and shoots Adler, who survives five wounds. Crowley and accomplices are driven away by Adler's dog Trixie.

April 16—"Pretty Boy" Floyd murders Patrolman Ralph Castner in a gun battle at Bowling Green, Ohio. Floyd's partner, Bill "The Killer" Miller, also is slain, and the outlaws' "molls," Rose Ash and Beulah Baird, are captured. Floyd escapes.

April 26—John Schrinsher, alias Paul Martin, alleged former member of the "Kimes-Terrill Gang," is captured at a tourist camp near Joinersville, Texas.

April 27—While joyriding in New York with Francis Crowley and Rudolph "Fats" Duringer, dancehall hostess Virginia Brannen resists Duringer's sexual advances. He fatally shoots her, and he and Crowley dump her body at St. Joseph's Seminary on Valentine Street in Yonkers.

– "Legs" Diamond is wounded by gunmen in the Aratoga Inn at Cairo, New York.

April 29—Francis Crowley is spotted driving a green Chrysler sedan on 138th Street in the Bronx, near the Morris Avenue Bridge. Crowley escapes in a running gun battle. Bullets found in the police car match those used in the Virginia Brannen murder and other recent shootings.

April 30—Crowley's green sedan, riddled with bullets and containing bloodstains, is found abandoned at 288 East 155th Street in the Bronx.

– The burned corpse of Chicago vice lord Mike "de Pike" Heitler is found in an icehouse in Barrington, Illinois. Heitler's burned car is found in Itasca, Illinois. Heitler had been informing to police about Al Capone.

May 6—Patrolmen Frederick Hirsch and Peter Yodice discover Francis Crowley and his sixteen-year-old girlfriend, Helen Walsh, parked on Morris Lane in North Merrick, Long Island. Crowley fatally shoots Hirsch and escapes with Helen.

May 7—About 150 New York police, armed with rifles, machine guns, and tear gas, lay siege for two hours to the rooming-house apartment of Francis Crowley, his girlfriend Helen Walsh, and Rudolph "Fats" Duringer, at 303 West Ninetieth Street. A huge crowd gathers to watch. While Helen and Duringer cower, Crowley trades shots with police and tosses back tear gas grenades. He surrenders after being wounded four times, but two pistols are found strapped to his legs, thus earning him the nickname "Two-Gun" Crowley.

May 8—Federal state and local authorities raid a "gangster flat" in East St. Louis, Illinois, and arrest six men, described as "remnants of the Cuckoo and Shelton gangs" and affiliated with the notorious Fred "Killer" Burke. Arrested are Tommy Hayes, Thomas O'Connor, Jack Britt, Howard Lee, E. Hawks, and William McQuillan. Authorities believe the gang has committed more than sixty Midwest bank robberies, including the million-dollar Lincoln robbery, several murders and kidnappings, and possibly the Denver Mint robbery.

"But It's Death to Bonnie and Clyde"

To the extent that Depression-era Texans were at all class-conscious, Clyde Barrow and Bonnie Parker would have been looked upon as "white trash." They distinguished themselves from the state's sizable population of lawbreakers by being impulsive, deadly, and thoroughly unprofessional. They mostly hit filling stations and grocery stores, killing recklessly and provoking John Dillinger to gripe that these were the kind of punks who gave armed robbery a bad name. What earned them a place in criminal history was their elusiveness and the public's fascination with a boy-and-girl bandit team that enjoyed their publicity. They took pictures of each other engaging in horseplay with guns and mailed maudlin poetry to newspapers. Bonnie's main beef with the press was the frequent publishing of a captured photo of her smoking a cigar, which she claimed was taken strictly as a joke.

Clyde Barrow often had to carry Bonnie Parker after her legs were badly burned in a car crash.

Despite their small stature and underage looks, they were armed to the teeth. Clyde favored the heavy Browning Automatic Rifle (the BAR, designed for hefty soldiers), usually stolen from National Guard armories, its stock and barrel sometimes shortened. Their narrow escapes in shootouts became front-page news and taught their pursuers that the Thompson gun would not always penetrate the tough

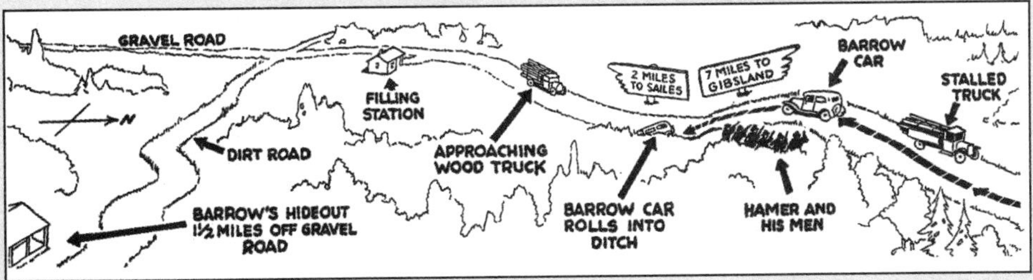

Home Edition
The Topeka State Journal
Today's News TODAY
TOPEKA, KANSAS, WEDNESDAY EVENING, MAY 23, 1934—FOURTEEN PAGES
TWO CENTS

BARROW AND BONNIE SLAIN

CITIES SERVICE WRITE-UP TOLD

Weather

GO INTO SILVER PURCHASE BILL

SOME COMPLAINT AT FIRST

ANOTHER JOB IS DONE

FLY TO OPERATE UPON EXPLORER

DESTROYERS ALSO SENT

WILL ROGERS SAYS:

HIS BODY FOUND

SHOT DOWN AT 85-MILE HOUR PACE

Officers Put End to Crime Career of Southwestern Desperado and Woman Companion Seventeen Miles From Arcadia, La.

GUN ON HER LAP

Bonnie and Clyde kept Texas lawmen in a state of confusion before the gang made their way to Dexfield Park near Dexter, Iowa, where "Buck" Barrow was mortally wounded and Blanche Barrow captured (top right), and Bonnie and Clyde escaped. The man in bib overalls is Virgil Musselman, a member of the posse, often misidentified as "Buck," who was lying on the ground. Bonnie and Clyde were later ambushed by a squad of officers led by former Texas Ranger Frank Hamer.

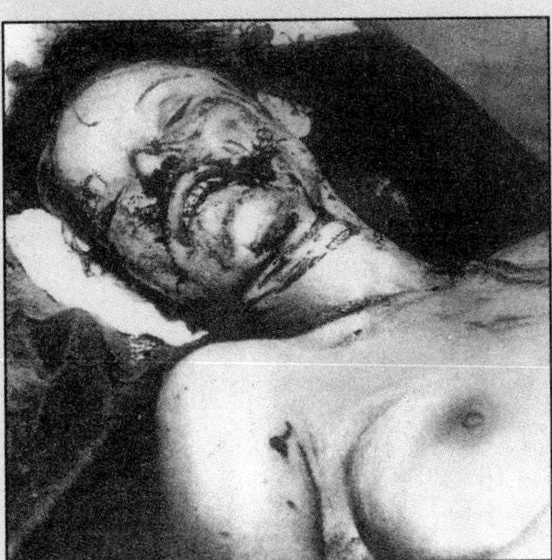

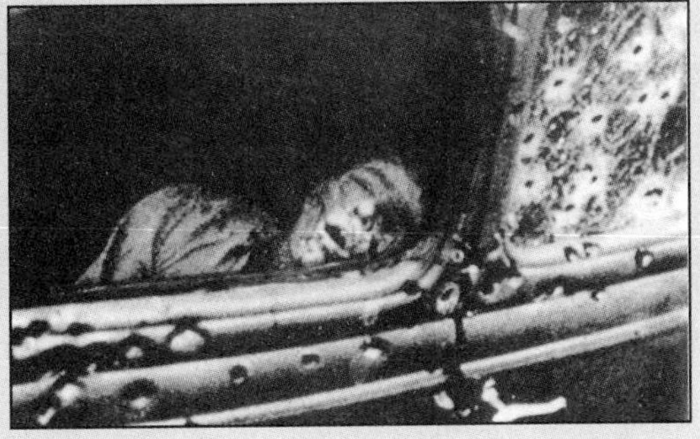

skin of the V-8 Fords that Bonnie and Clyde always tried to use. So when police finally ambushed them in Louisiana with a posse led by Frank Hamer, a legendary former Texas Ranger hired to bring them down, the lawmen literally shredded their car and its two notorious occupants.

Bonnie's and Clyde's deaths made national headlines at the height of the public-enemy era, and the morbidly curious had a field day. The Barrow car was towed to the town of Arcadia with the bodies still inside, and the battered corpses were laid out in gory splendor for the benefit of sightseers, one of whom had to be constrained from cutting off Clyde's trigger finger for a souvenir. Others were content to pose for pictures with the blood-soaked bodies and the bullet-riddled Ford, which has remained a popular tourist attraction wherever displayed.

Despite a minimum of redeeming personal qualities, Bonnie and Clyde still have a large following and have left a legacy of questions still argued in books on their career. Their betrayal is part of the mystery, members of the ambush party later giving conflicting versions. Clyde's sexual character is still debated, largely on the basis of one book; a few will always believe that the authorities covered up Bonnie's pregnancy. Clyde's letter to Henry Ford complimenting his car has now been studied by handwriting experts who question its authenticity (although it may have been written by Bonnie), and a similar letter to Ford from John Dillinger has been flatly declared a forgery.

The two were not buried side by side, as Bonnie had hoped in a poem that concluded, "But it's death to Bonnie and Clyde." However, their respective gravestones bear memorable epitaphs. Bonnie's reads, ironically enough:

AS THE FLOWERS ARE ALL MADE SWEETER
BY THE SUNSHINE AND THE DEW,
SO THIS OLD WORLD IS MADE BRIGHTER
BY THE LIVES OF FOLKS LIKE YOU

Clyde's is a bit more fitting:

GONE BUT NOT FORGOTTEN.

May 10—Alvin Karpis is released on parole from the state prison at Lansing, Kansas. He will later join "Ma" and Fred Barker in Tulsa to form the Barker-Karpis Gang.

May 12—Roy Sloane, known as the "College Boy Bandit," is shot to death by gunmen outside the Mad Dot Boat Club, a speakeasy at 251 Dyckman Street in New York owned by associates of Vincent Coll. Police suspect the "Dutch" Schultz mob, in a case of mistaken identity, because Sloane resembled Coll.

May 14—In a nighttime burglary raid, Alvin Karpis, Fred Barker, and Sam Coker ransack the A. C. Merrill clothing store at Caney, Kansas, of $3,000 in merchandise.

May 16—Jimmie Creighton shoots and kills local man Coyne Hatten for bumping into him on the street outside Morgan's drugstore in Webb City, Missouri, near Joplin. Creighton will be convicted of murder and sentenced to life in the Missouri state prison. Also wanted for a Hastings, Nebraska, bank robbery, Creighton recently had roomed with Fred Barker in Joplin.

May 22—Two men, later believed to be Alvin Karpis and Fred Barker, escape from an apartment house at 6 East Haskell Street in a gun battle with Tulsa police.

May 29—At Mineola, Long Island, Francis "Two-Gun" Crowley is convicted of the murder of Patrolman Frederick Hirsch.

– Harlem racketeers Dominic Bologna and Frank "Big Dick" Amato are shot to death and Joey Rao wounded by gunmen at 164 East 116th Street. All were associates of "Dutch" Schultz and Ciro Terranova. Vincent Coll's gang is suspected.

May 30—Vincent Coll's brother Peter is shot to death by gunmen in another vehicle while driving along St. Nicholas Street near 111th Street in Harlem.

May 31—Gennaro "Chin" Atari, a member of the Schultz mob, is gunned down in a bowling alley at 354 East 149th Street by members of Vincent Coll's gang.

June 1—Francis "Two-Gun" Crowley is sentenced to death. Rudolph "Fats" Duringer is convicted at the Bronx County Courthouse of the murder of Virginia Brannen and also sentenced to death.

June 2—Two carloads of gangsters, members of the rival Schultz and Coll gangs, engage in a running gun battle on 177th Street in Harlem. Coll henchman "Patsy" Del Greco is wounded. The Coll mob later raids a Schultz garage, destroying twenty trucks and 150 slot machines.

June 3—Louis de Rosa, an ally of "Dutch" Schultz, is found shot to death at Rider Avenue and 137th Street in New York, apparently a victim of the Coll mob.

June 5—Al Capone is indicted in Chicago by a federal grand jury on twenty-two counts of income tax evasion for the years 1925 through 1929.

– Willie "The Actor" Sutton enters Sing Sing Prison at Ossining, New York, under a thirty-year sentence for the Rosenthal jewel robbery.

June 8—John Jacapraro, a member of the Schultz mob, is found shot to death in an abandoned Buick at 1347 Stratford Avenue in New York. The Coll gang is suspected.

June 10—Alvin Karpis, Fred Barker, Sam Coker, and Joe Howard are arrested by Tulsa police for burglary. Karpis is held on the burglary charge. Barker is transferred to the jail in Claremore, Oklahoma, and escapes. Coker is returned to Oklahoma state prison to complete a thirty-year sentence for bank robbery. Howard is released on bond and disappears.

June 15—To finance his war against "Dutch" Schultz, Vincent Coll kidnaps George "Big Frenchy" DeMange, henchman of another New York gang leader, Owney "The Killer" Madden, from DeMange's Club Argonaut at West Fiftieth Street and Seventh Avenue. DeMange is released after Owney Madden pays a ransom (reportedly $35,000). Madden and Schultz reportedly each place a $50,000 bounty on Coll's head.

June 16—Abe Rosenberg, a member of the

SETTING OF CAPONE TAX-EVASION TRIAL AS SEEN BY ARTIST

Sketch showing location in federal court of various persons interested in the trial of "Scarface Al" Capone. The numbers indicate: No. 1. Federal Judge James H. Wilkerson, who is presiding over trial. No. 2. "Scarface Al" Capone, the defendant. No. 3. United States District Attorney George E. Q. Johnson, who is directing the prosecution. No. 4. Albert Fink, of counsel for the defense. No. 5. Assistant United States District Attorney Dwight H. Green. No. 6. William J. Froelich, special assistant United States attorney-general. No. 7. Michael Ahern, defense lawyer. No. 8. The jury. No. 9. Adeline Stoll, secretary to Attorney Fink. No. 10. Government agents and spectators. No. 11. Newspaper reporters. No. 12. Joseph O'Sullivan, clerk of the court. [By Vaughn Shoemaker, staff artist of The Daily News.]

The "Confession" of W. D. Jones

In his generally excellent book *The Dillinger Days,* John Toland cited a W. D. Jones statement as the source for his suspicion of Clyde Barrow's bisexuality, but he evidently had not read the document itself. When Jones resurfaced with an "over-the-transom" personal account that surprised the editorial staff of *Playboy,* which published it in November 1968, "W. D." disputed this, and there is nothing to support it in either the statement at the time of his arrest or in the article thirty-five years later. Perhaps Toland misconstrued someone else's use of the word "punk" to refer to a homosexual or bisexual, as used in contemporary prison slang.

W. D. Jones, a sometime member of the Barrow Gang, is often misidentified as "Buck" Barrow.

The "confession" itself was found in old police records by researcher John Neal Phillips and is basically self-serving, downplaying Jones's role in the banditry and killings, emphasizing his desire to "escape" from a psychopathic Clyde (he might have qualified as a volunteer hostage), and blaming auto accidents or woundings for sudden lapses in memory that police must have thought were too convenient; and this would have been a timely opportunity for Jones to mention any sexual peculiarities. That he was drunk when he joined Clyde, drunk at other times, and remarkably obedient does not establish Jones as any kind of mitigating influence on the Barrow Gang. But it may accurately reflect his ambivalence toward violence, animosity toward police, and his rebellious nature in a brutal time. The same might apply to the Barrows and the Parker family, for whom "blood" obligated loyalty above and beyond the law.

THE STATE OF TEXAS

DATE: November 18, 1933
County of Dallas

TO WHOM IT MAY CONCERN:

After I have been duly warned by WINTER R. KING, ASSISTANT DISTRICT ATTORNEY that I do not have to make any statement at all, and that any statement I make may be used in evidence against me on the trial for the offense concerning which this statement is herein made, I wish to make the following voluntary state [sic] to the aforesaid person:

My name is W. D. JONES: I am 17 years old. I was born May 12, 1916, in East Texas, but I do not know the town or county. I have known Clyde Barrow about 11 years, and have known Bonnie Parker, but have only seen her two or three times before I went with them to Temple, Texas. About two days before Christmas, 1932, the exact day I cannot recall, L. C. Barrow, brother of Clyde Barrow, who had been a friend of mine for some time, and myself went riding with Maudine Brennan and another girl, here in Dallas. We started riding around with them about dark that evening. We had a half gallon of whiskey with us and were drinking this freely. We took the girls home about 8:30 in the evening. We were in L. C. Barrow's Ford Coupe, Model A. . . . I was pretty drunk by this time. . . .

Clyde Barrow and Bonnie Parker passed by where we were. They were driving a Ford V–8 Coupe, with two wheels on running board, khaki top. L. C. saw them and suggested that we follow them, which we did. They drove on down a side road to a gravel pit and we drove up behind them and parked there. We talked to them there and Clyde suggested to me that I go with them "down the road," as he put it, but did not say where. I agreed to go and I got in the car [and] we started South of Dallas. We drove on to a point about three miles this side of Temple, Texas, where we turned off the main road and parked on a side road, and remained in the car. I went to sleep. We woke up about eight o'clock and went to a tourist camp out on the highway a short ways from Temple. . . . We stayed in this cabin all that day and all that night without leaving the cabin to go anywhere.

Early the next morning, about eight o'clock, we left the Tourist camp and went into Temple. We went to a grocery store, I don't know the name of the store, but it was a big store right in the edge of Temple, on the side of town nearest the tourist camp we had been staying at. While we were in the Tourist Camp, Clyde Barrow and Bonnie had planned to hold up this grocery store, and had discussed it in detail, but they hadn't said anything about my taking part in it till we got nearly to the store that morning. Then Clyde Barrow handed me an old 45 calibre single-action pistol and told me that "we" were going to hold up the store. I didn't want to do it, but he insisted that I go in with him. He had a 45 calibre pistol, but I do not remember just what kind it was.

We parked around the corner from the store and Clyde Barrow and I got out and went into the store. Bonnie Parker stayed in the car. Clyde Barrow also had a 16-gauge automatic shotgun with a sawed off barrel strapped to his body and concealed under his overcoat when we went in there. When we got into the store, Clyde made some small purchases, and I believe we bought some eggs and some bread, and I was worried and scared about this hold-up, and I shook my head at him to indicate I would not take part in it, and I turned and started out of the store. He followed me and we got back in the car and started driving and Clyde raised hell with me because I hadn't helped him hold up the store. He called me a coward, and Bonnie laughed at me because I was afraid, and I am confident that Clyde was so mad that I barely escaped being killed by him at that time.

We drove around town for awhile. I told Clyde I wanted to go Home. Clyde had been talking about holding up a filling station. We saw a Model A Ford Roadster parked on the street, and Clyde told me to get that car—meaning stealing it. We drove around the corner and parked and Clyde and I got out and went back and walked back by the Ford, and Clyde said if I wanted to go home, to get in that car. I did, and about that time a woman came out of the house and started screaming. I got out and started to run, and Clyde told me to get back in the car and start it. The car was parked the wrong way, so that the left side was next to the curb. Clyde was standing out in the street. I had gotten out on the curb side, but when Clyde told me that I got back in the car, and did not stop in it. I crawled on through the car and got out on the street where Clyde was.

While this was happening, and [sic] old man had come out of the house and started toward the car, but Clyde, standing in the street, had pulled his pistol by this time, and ordered him to stop and the old man stopped. Clyde got in the car, under the steering wheel, and was trying to start the car, and another younger man came out of the house and came up to the car on the side where Clyde was sitting under the steering wheel, and Clyde raised his pistol and fired at this man three times. I did not see the man fall as I started running. Clyde got the car started and drove on down and I jumped on the running board and got in the car and we jumped out of it and ran back and got in the car with Bonnie Parker.

We drove out of Temple and drove nearly to Waco, traveling on small country roads and avoiding the highways. We parked on a little country road most of the day, and then went on at night turning off to the East before reaching Waco, and avoiding towns as much as possible. Late that night we went into a Tourist Camp but I don't know where it was. We stayed there until the next morning.

We went on down in East Texas the next day. Before we got to this Tourist Camp, Clyde Barrow made me get down in the Rutleback [sic] seat and pushed the top of the seat down over me, so no one could see me, and didn't let me out of there until we got into the Tourist Camp so no one saw me, and when we left next morning, he did the same thing.

The next night we stayed at another Tourist Camp somewhere in East Texas. We hid out around East Texas staying in Tourist Camps and avoiding towns from this time, until Friday, January 6th, 1933, when we came back to Dallas.

On Friday, January 6th, 1933, Clyde Barrow, Bonnie Parker and I came back from East Texas, traveling in their Ford V-8 Coupe, which had a khaki top, and in which we had been riding around and hiding out in East Texas, since Christmas Day, 1932, after Clyde Barrow had shot and killed a man at Temple, Texas, in an attempt to steal a Ford Model A car from a street in Temple.

We got back to Dallas a little after dark, and drove out South Lamar Street, to 1214 South Lamar, where Bonnie's mother lived. I went in—to the door—and asked for Mrs. Parker, meaning Bonnie's mother. Some lady had come to the door and she called another girl, whom I learned later was Billie Parker, Bonnie's sister, and she came out to the car with me.

We drove on South on Lamar Street. I was about half drunk and didn't pay any attention to where we went, but we drove out on some country road, and stopped and all got out of the car, and Clyde Barrow, Bonnie and Billie Parker all had quite a conversation which I did not listen to.

We got back in the car and drove back into West Dallas to Lille McBride's home on County Avenue, and Billie got out to ask for some woman, whose name I did not learn. She got no answer and came back and got in the car. This was sometime between 9:30 and 10 o'clock at night, the night Malcom Davis, the Fort Worth Deputy Sheriff, was killed.

We took Billie home and let her out and she told us good-bye. This was at her home on South Lamar.

We came back the same way we had gone . . . [stopping at] the house where Floyd Hamilton, brother of Raymond Hamilton, lived at that time.

Bonnie Parker and I stayed in the car, and Clyde Barrow got out and went around behind the house. He just stayed a few minutes and came back and got in the car. He didn't say who he had talked to there. . . .

We were still driving this same Ford V-8 Coupe . . . and Clyde had a pistol, the same pistol he had used to shoot the man at Temple a few days before. I think it was a 45 calibre revolver.

Bonnie Parker had a 41 calibre pistol. This was the one I had at Temple, and I did not have any pistol. I do not know what kind of rifle it was, but Clyde had the rifle lying up on the back of the seat. There was also a 12-gauge pump shotgun, sawed off, a hammerless gun lying up there on the back of the seat also.

We pulled up and stopped in front of Lille McBride's house, and Clyde told me to get under the wheel. He got out on the left hand side of the car and went around the back of it, and I crawled over Bonnie and got under the wheel. Clyde was trying to get some information about Raymond Hamilton who was in jail at Hillsboro.

Clyde walked around behind the car and on up to Lille McBride's house, carrying his 16-gauge shotgun in his hand. Bonnie and I were still sitting in the car. I don't know whether there was a light in the house or not. I didn't notice. Clyde had gotten up on the porch before the first shot was fired. Then I heard a shotgun fire. I hadn't heard a word spoken up to this time. This was a shot fired by Clyde Barrow. Just about the time the shot was fired I saw two men come around the corner of Lille McBride's house, on the side of the house nearest the Eagle Ford Road. Then the shot rang out and Bonnie Parker told me to start the motor. I saw one of those two men fall, and I began starting the motor. I don't know whether the two men fired or only one of them fired. I was so excited I didn't know how many shots they fired. Bonnie fired her pistol twice or three times, I am not sure which. Clyde fired again also, and I don't know how many other shots were fired. I do not know where Clyde was standing when he fired the second time. He might have come back close to the car by the time he fired this shot. [This was the January 6 gun battle with sheriff's officers, one of whom died.]

Clyde told me to move over, out from under the steering wheel, and I did. Bonnie had moved close to the door of the car while she was firing, and I moved over against her, and Clyde started the car driving very fast. He drove on down County Avenue to Eagle Ford, turning to his right, in a westerly direction. We had a siren in the car and he started it going full blast. We drove on up a block or two on Eagle Road, before turning on lights. We drove on past Mr. Barrow's filling station, where we had stopped before the shooting. We drove on to the first boulevard, and turned to the right. I think this was Westmoreland Road. We turned North on it. It was pouring down rain at this time, and had been raining off and on all that night. We crossed the river and turned to the left on Industrial Boulevard. We went on through the town of Irving. We went on toward Grapevine. We continued in this direction until we came to a short turn and drove on into the ditch. Clyde went up to a farmhouse and got three farmers who came down with a two mule team hitched to a wagon, and pulled the car out of the ditch for him. Clyde paid them for this. I think they got three dollars for it. They unhitched the mules from the wagon, and hitched them onto the back of the Ford and pulled it back up to the road. This was a country road of some kind, not a highway, and we went on sticking to country roads. We went on in a generally northwest direction, and I went to sleep when the car was still going. When I woke up next morning I believe we were in the edge of Oklahoma, because Clyde told me that's where we were. . . .

♔ ♔ ♔

I don't know how much money Clyde had with him, but I didn't have any money at all except what Clyde would give me, a dollar or two at a time.

We rambled around through Oklahoma and Missouri until Buck Barrow got out of the penitentiary about March 22nd, 1933. We only came back to Texas one time during this period, and on that trip we came to Dallas, Texas and Clyde talked to his mother, Mrs. Barrow. This trip was at the time Buck got out and we left word with Mrs. Barrow where Buck was to meet us—at a little town just in the edge of Oklahoma—near Joplin, Missouri. When he met us there we went on to Joplin.

Up to this time, when Buck joined us, we had only pulled one job. That was at Springfield, Mo., where he had stuck up a filling station. I don't recall the date of this job, or how much money it netted.

When Buck Barrow joined us he was driving a Marmon Sedan. Buck's wife, Blanche, was with him at this time. We went on to Joplin, Mo. They rented a house at Joplin, where we stayed about two weeks. All five of us stayed there. We did no jobs while we were there. . . .

I had been trying for weeks to get Clyde to bring us back to Texas, and he finally agreed that he would do so, and Clyde and I started to leave in this Ford Roadster, and Clyde decided it wouldn't make the trip, and we turned back to get another car, and just as we got back to the house the law drove up and the gun battle happened.

I did not have any gun, because I had not been carrying any kind of gun after the man had been killed in Temple, Texas on Christmas Day. But Clyde, Buck and Bonnie had several guns, and I remember that Clyde had the same 16-gauge automatic shotgun with which he had killed the Deputy Sheriff at Dallas on January 6th, and a large pistol not an automatic, but a double action pistol. He also had a 12-gauge shotgun, and Buck had a 16-gauge shotgun.

Three or four days before the gun battle at Joplin, Buck and Clyde brought in some eight or ten more guns, pistols and rifles, and they had a lot of ammunition for all of these guns. They had a big wooden box full. I don't know where they got all these guns. . . .

We drove into the garage and Buck was in there and he closed the door and we got out. . . . They were standing there talking when one of them yelled the law was coming. I think it was Buck who yelled this. I think the laws had the house surrounded by that time. It was still daylight then.

Shots began to ring out from every direction. Clyde and Buck were both shooting. I started to run out the big double door of the garage. And I got shot just as I got to the door. Clyde or Buck one had opened the door, and they were between the two cars. I couldn't see them, but I could hear them talking. When I got shot I went "out," that is I became unconscious. . . . But Blanche Barrow told me I ran back upstairs and fell in the middle of the floor.

I don't know what else happened here, and when I came to next, we were in that Ford V-8 Sedan on a country road. Clyde Barrow, Bonnie Parker, Buck Barrow and Blanche Barrow were all in the car.

It was dark when I came to. Clyde was driving at the time. He was driving very fast. We headed for the Texas Panhandle and drove as fast as we could away from Joplin. I got no medical attention of any kind until Saturday afternoon when Clyde bought some alcohol and mercurochrome at Amarillo, Texas and dressed my wound.

We didn't go back to Joplin any more after this gun battle. But rambled around for several months through a good many states, Texas, Oklahoma, Kansas, Indiana and Louisiana. . . .

♔ ♔ ♔

While we were in Louisiana, and before Clyde and Buck kidnapped the man and woman there, they put me out of the car to steal a Chevrolet automobile for them. I saw this was my chance to escape and I jumped in this car and made my get away and came back to Dallas, Texas. . . .

Late one afternoon—or rather about two o'clock in the afternoon I was out at Bachman's Dam. I was walking along the road intending to go down to the Lake and to go to a dance at the Five Point Dance Hall that night. Bonnie Parker and Clyde Barrow drove up from behind me and stopped. They were in a V-8 Coupe. I hadn't heard from them since I saw them last in Louisiana, and did not know they were back in town until this time.

They spoke to me and told me to get in the car and I got in. They asked me if I wanted to go with them, and I told them I did not, and Clyde said I was going anyway and I did.

We drove on in the direction of Wichita Falls, going mostly on country roads. We stayed that night at the first little tourist camp on this side of Vernon, Texas. We left there early the next morning. He hadn't told me where we were going or anything—just said we were going "up the country."

We drove on all day and into the night. I went to sleep and while I was asleep we had a wreck. A bridge was out and Clyde drove off into the river. I was knocked out. Bonnie was burned on her right leg from the thigh on down. A pretty bad burn.

Bonnie told me afterward that the next thing she remembered was that she came to and we were all in a farmhouse and she didn't know how we got there, and that I brought a rifle in the house, and she told me to take it to Clyde and I went out of the house with it. Bonnie told me I fired a shotgun there which wounded a woman in the hand. I don't know about anything that happened at this farmhouse, because if I did any of these things I was still out of my head from the injuries I had received in the wreck and knew nothing about them.

Bonnie also told me two officers came to the house in a car and we captured them and took their car and the officers with us and started for Oklahoma. I still don't remember this. But I came to while we were in this car. Clyde Barrow was driving and Bonnie Parker and myself and the two captured officers were in the car.

A few minutes after I came to we met Buck Barrow, in the edge of Oklahoma on a bridge. He was driving a Ford V-8 convertible coupe. Blanche Barrow, his wife, was with him. Clyde drove up on one end of the long bridge and blew his horn and stopped, and we set there a few minutes and we heard another horn at the far end of the bridge. Buck stopped his car there and came running up towards us. Clyde got out of the car with the two officers, and told me to drive the Chevrolet down toward Buck's car and put Bonnie in it. I did that, and stayed there until Buck and Clyde came back and I got in the coupe with Buck and Blanche and Bonnie Parker, and Clyde got in the Chevrolet we had taken from the officers.

We headed on north into Oklahoma. On this trip I learned from their conversation that they had held up a bank somewhere and had lots of money. We went on into Arkansas from there. . . .

♔ ♔ ♔

We stayed at a tourist camp in the edge of Fort Smith . . . several days before anything happened. Buck Barrow suggested

Deputy Prentiss Oakley (left) is shown with guns removed from the Bonnie and Clyde death car. An unidentified lawman (above) examines a formidable collection of firearms abandoned after the battle at Dexfield Park.

we go and steal another car. He wanted a sedan in place of the roadster. Buck and I went on this mission. We went to another town. We didn't find a car we liked and started back. We had a wreck on the way back—this was in daytime. He was driving and hit some other car. I was knocked out and don't remember the details clearly. When I came to I was standing in the middle of the road with Buck's 16-gauge shotgun in my hands. It was broken all to pieces and I had lost the plain gold band ring I wear on my little finger. I was frantically looking for this ring. I don't know how it had gotten off my finger but it had and I found it lying in the middle of the road.

While I was doing this I was conscious that shooting was going on around me. Another car had come up, meeting us, and at least one officer was in it—it was his car we got away from there in. I don't know if there were other officers in the car with him or not, but as my head cleared, I saw Buck Barrow in this officer's car, and trying to start it with one hand and shooting his pistol with the other hand, at a house about 200 feet away. Shots were coming from the house toward us, but I did not see who was shooting. I saw a man, evidently the officer whose car we got away in, lying on his back in the ditch by the side of the road, and Buck yelled to me to get his gun which was lying on the ground a few feet from him. I got this pistol, and climbed in the car with Buck, and we drove on, going back the way the car was headed, and in the direction from which we had come.

I did not fire any shots at this time at all.

We circled around and got back on the road we had been going and went back to the tourist camp at Fort Smith, leaving the car before we got there. We didn't drive very far in the officer's car after this shooting when we came to a man and a woman in a car. Buck pulled across the road in front of them, and we made them get out of their car and we took it and went on towards Fort Smith, leaving it out at the edge of the town and going up to the back of the tourist camp on foot. All five of us left this tourist camp in the roadster we had there, and we left right away.

We came back down through Oklahoma again.

We stayed a day or two in Oklahoma and as we had lost most of our guns by that time, and one night while we were in a tourist camp Buck Barrow and Clyde Barrow went off and burglarized an armory and brought back so many guns that it looked like a gun factory. There were some 46 government automatics . . . several rifles and two or three cases of ammunition for the pistols and rifles.

We circled around awhile and went on in to Platte, Missouri. We went to a tourist camp, and . . . the second night we were there the officers trailed us and we had another gun battle. We had two cabins in the camp. Bonnie Parker and Clyde Barrow and I were in one camp and Buck Barrow and Blanche Barrow had the other one. The officers went to Buck's cabin first and asked for a man or some boys. Clyde said "That's the law." I heard Blanche Barrow tell them that boys were over in our cabin. Clyde looked out the door and grabbed his gun out from under the edge of the bed. He told me to get out there and start the car. He started shooting out of doors and windows. I got the key off the dresser and got into the garage. Bonnie had given me the key out of Clyde's pocket to the car, and I started the motor, and shooting was coming from all directions. Clyde told me to open the garage door and I was afraid to do it, and he came and together we opened the door. He made me help him. When we opened the door Buck and Blanche were right in front of the door. Blanche was holding Buck up, holding him under the arms. Clyde told me to go out there and get Buck. I refused to do it, and Clyde went out and got him just about to the door, and handed him to me, and I took hold of him then and while I was putting Buck in the car Clyde was shooting. Buck had been wounded in the head.

I got Buck in the car. Bonnie Parker had managed to get in herself, and Blanche and I got in the back seat with Buck and Bonnie Parker and Clyde got in the front with Clyde driving, and he backed out of the garage and drove off with them shooting at us. Clyde afterward counted 14 or 15 bullet-holes in the car, but none of us was hit. They did hit both the back tires however, and they went flat after we had gone some distance. We ran for a long while on the rim of one of them and ruined it. We patched one of them temporarily but it gave later. We put the spare on one wheel. We made our way to a point close to Dexter, Iowa and hid out in some woods for three or four days. We still had the same car we got away from Platte City, Mo. in after the gun battle there.

Clyde would go into Dexter and get food, and medicine for Buck's wound. Buck's wound was pretty serious, but Buck wasn't out of his head, as I talked with him a lot there. While we stayed there in the woods, Buck and Blanche and Clyde and Bonnie slept in the car, and I slept on a car seat out on the ground and each night they handcuffed me to a tree to prevent my making a getaway, as they feared I knew too much, and they knew I would escape if possible.

While we were there we got a V-8 sedan—we got this at some town about 40 or 50 miles from there. I got the car on this occasion, and we went back to the camp in the woods. Clyde unloaded all the stuff out of the car we had had [during] the battle in Platte City, Mo., and put me to tearing up pasteboard boxes of pistol shells. There were a lot of these and it took me a long time. We went to town to get fresh dressing for Buck's head and to get something for supper. He came back and dressed Buck's head, and we ate supper. I had filled an inner tube with these shells, and he put them back of the seat in the car. We slept there that night. We got up next morning and I had been released, and I was roasting some wieners we had left from supper the night before. Clyde and Bonnie were sitting on the cushion when they saw the officers coming and yelled. Shooting was going on before I could get straightened up. I ran around the other side of the car and then I got shot with buckshot.

One buckshot is still in my hip, one in my right little finger, one in my chest just above right nipple. These buckshot I still have in me. I was shot through the calf of the left leg with a bullet, and a bullet from a machine gun struck me in the chest above the right nipple. I also was shot in left wrist, but don't know what with, and my right thumb was also shot. I was knocked down by the machine-gun bullet that struck me in the chest. But I got to my feet again and went back around the car, and I think it was there that I got the shot in my thumb.

Buck and Blanche were in the back seat of the car, and I don't know whether Buck was doing any shooting or not. Clyde was yelling for me to start the car like he always did when trouble happened, and I got in and tried to start it. Bonnie got in the car too. I don't know whether Bonnie did any shooting there or not. I was so scared I couldn't get it going, and Clyde was shooting all the time, and he came and stood by the door by my side and emptied his rifle standing there. He pulled me out and he got in the car and started it. I crawled up in the back end of the car. Clyde got it started and drove off. We backed off. Then turned around and drove on down a little road, but when he tried to turn around again, he backed the car up on a stump and it hung there and we couldn't get it off, and he made me get out and try to pry it off with a rifle, and we couldn't do it. I took his rifle and told him I was checking out and then Clyde decided to abandon the car, and told me to carry Bonnie, which I did, and we went off through the woods for about a half mile and we stopped and he decided he'd go get us a car to make our getaway in. Bonnie and I waited there, and in a little while he got in another gun battle up on the road and came back. We heard the shooting, and he came back and we went on further on foot. We went about a quarter of a mile, up to a house, and Bonnie and I waited in the cornfield and Clyde went up to the house and put his gun on three men there and took their car, and made them help put Bonnie Parker in the car and he and I got in and he drove off. We rode some distance and wound around through side roads, and country roads for a distance of about 20 or 25 miles, and then we had a flat. In the gun battle back in the woods Clyde was hit several times, one through his right leg, one bullet grazed the side of his head. He had one buckshot in his right shoulder.

When we had this flat we took the tire off and we decided we ought to change cars, so Clyde took in after a Chevrolet and pulled up alongside and ordered the man to stop, which he did, but we were going pretty fast and Clyde couldn't stop our car very quick, running on the wheel, so the man had time to turn around and beat it before we could get back to him. . . . [Soon] we saw a '29 Chevrolet sedan in [a] yard and Clyde handed me a pistol and told me to go get that car. I did and there was a man and a woman in the yard and the woman screamed but the man didn't do anything and I got in the car and backed it out and we all got in it and went on.

We traveled all around in this car, through Nebraska, Minnesota and into Colorado. In Colorado, we saw a newspaper that said they were looking for us there, and we thought they were getting pretty hot on our trail, so Clyde turned back through Kansas and down into Missouri and back into Oklahoma and on across into Mississippi. About 40 miles from Clarksdale, Mississippi, I got away from them again. They let me out to get a car for them. I got it, and Clyde intended to change into this car, but wanted some gas in it first, so he gave me $2.22 to get gas and sent me into a filling station and he was going to stop where he could watch me and told me to come back to him. I bought five gallons, instead of filling it like he told me to, and I drove on up the road and he was supposed to follow me, but I turned off on a little country road. This was at night when I got on that country road, I cut my lights off and he didn't find me. I drove on a piece and got out and left the car and threw away a pistol and a big rifle I had with me, and ran on across the country, and put in most of the night running, and early the next morning, I got a ride on a truck into Clarksdale, Mississippi.

I have never seen Clyde Barrow or Bonnie Parker since that time. I hoboed my way back to Dallas on freight trains. I stayed here a day or two and went down near Sugarland, Texas, to pick cotton.

Then went to Waco from there and picked cotton, my mother and family were with me there and at Sugarland. Then went to Vernon, Texas with them and picked cotton there two weeks and went to Memphis and then back to Vernon, then came back to Dallas. I stayed here about three days then I then went to San Antonio for about three days. Then went to Houston, and was arrested Thursday night about 8:30 at 1519 Franklin Street. This was on November 16, 1933.

About three weeks ago when I was in Dallas the last time, Carl Rushing stopped me in the middle of the street and asked me if I wanted to go places with him that night, and I told him I'd stopped going places, and he asked me if I didn't want to go see Clyde Barrow that night. I told him "Hell, no" and drove off. And I left town right after that.

From what I saw and what Clyde and Buck Barrow have told me, I know that they killed at least six men, and I don't know how many more that I don't know about.

I have examined a copy of the *Joplin Globe* bearing date Saturday Morning, April 15th, 1933, on the front page at the top there are three pictures. One shows two men standing, and this is a picture of Clyde Barrow and me. I am the one on the right. The picture showing a man seated on the bumper of a car with a rifle across his knee is a picture of Clyde Barrow, and the picture of a man and woman is a picture of Clyde Barrow and Bonnie Parker.

(signed) W. D. JONES

Schultz gang, is found beaten and shot to death in Black Swamp Road, Queens. Attributed to Vincent Coll.

June 18—At 1212 Fifth Avenue in Manhattan, Danny Iamascia, bodyguard to "Dutch" Schultz, is killed by police detectives after drawing a gun on them in the mistaken belief they are members of the Coll mob. Schultz is arrested.

June 30—Capone gunman "Machine Gun" Jack McGurn is sentenced to two years in federal prison for conspiracy to violate the Mann Act during trips to Florida with his girlfriend, Louise Rolfe.

July 6—"Legs" Diamond's henchman Charles Entratta is killed by three gunmen in his office at 34 Division Place in Brooklyn.

July 14—Wilbur Underhill, known as the "Tri-State Terror," escapes from the state prison at McAlester, Oklahoma, where he has been serving a life sentence for murder.

July 16—State troopers and New York City police detectives raid a farm in Coxsackie, New York, near the Acra estate of Jack "Legs" Diamond. Eight men and six women, probably members of Vincent Coll's gang, are captured with an arsenal of weapons. Later in the day, the troopers find a dismantled, bloodstained Buick in a Cairo garage. The Diamond and Coll gangs are believed to have joined forces in a war against "Dutch" Schultz.

July 17—Lester Gillis, alias George "Baby Face" Nelson, convicted of armed robbery, is received at the Joliet, Illinois, state prison under a sentence of one year to life.

July 21—"Pretty Boy" Floyd kills Federal Prohibition Agent Curtis C. Burks and a spectator, M. P. Wilson, during a gun battle at the Noto-Lusco Flower Shop in Kansas City, Missouri, and escapes.

July 28—Gunning for Schultz mobster Joey Rao outside the Helmar Social Club at 208 East 107th Street in Harlem, Vincent Coll earns his nickname "Mad Dog" when he misses Rao but hits five children, killing five-year-old Michael Venghalli.

August 1—Wilbur Underhill robs the Fox-Midland theater in Coffeeville, Kansas, of $300.

August 4—"Pretty Boy" Floyd and George Birdwell rob the Citizens Bank at Shamrock, Oklahoma, of $400.

August 6—Gus Winkeler of St. Louis, now a Capone mobster but still wanted as a bank robber and murder suspect, is injured in an auto accident near St. Joseph, Michigan. Taken to a Benton Harbor hospital, Winkeler is wrongly identified by witnesses as a participant in the million-dollar Lincoln bank robbery. Winkeler will be charged with the robbery but freed on $100,000 bond provided by Al Capone.

— Wyandotte County Deputy Sheriff Frank Rohrbach is shot to death while questioning two suspects in a parked car near Kansas City, Kansas. Wilbur Underhill and his nephew, Frank Vance Underhill, later will be named as suspects.

August 9—Vincent "Mad Dog" Coll kidnaps George Immerman, brother of Harlem nightclub owner Connie Immerman, for $25,000 ransom.

August 13—Accompanied by his nephew Frank, Wilbur Underhill robs a Texaco gas station at Ida and Kellogg streets in Wichita, Kansas, of $14.68.

August 14—Wilbur Underhill murders policeman Merle Colver at the Iris Hotel in Wichita. Underhill is wounded and captured by Wichita police the same day in Linwood Park.

August 17—Press reports rumors that Raymond "Crane-Neck" Nugent, wanted killer, bank robber, and St. Valentine's Day Massacre suspect, may have been murdered in Florida.

August 18—Harry "Slim" Morris, suspected participant in the Denver Mint robbery of 1922 and the million-dollar Lincoln bank robbery in 1930, is found shot to death near Red Wing, Minnesota.

August 21—Two gunmen rob the Mendoza Fur Dyeing Co. at 712 East 133rd Street of $4,619, then flee from police in a deadly, gun-blazing pursuit through fifteen miles of New York City streets. They finally are halted by a truck backing from the curb at 154 Dyckman Street, where they die in a hail of gunfire. Two policemen, a taxi driver and a three-year-old girl also are killed in the fray, and ten other people are wounded.

August 29—Philadelphia gang leader Mickey Duffy is murdered by gunmen in his room at the Ambassador Hotel in Atlantic City.

September 4—Wilbur Underhill is received at the state prison in Lansing, Kansas, under a life sentence for murder.

September 8—"Pretty Boy" Floyd and George Birdwell rob the Morris State Bank at Morris, Oklahoma, of $1,743.

September 10—Salvatore Maranzano, self-appointed "boss of bosses" of the Italian crime families in New York, is shot and stabbed to death in his Park Avenue office by killers from the Jewish Bugs & Meyer Mob, employed by "Lucky" Luciano. Luciano shortly will form a national Commission to oversee the interests of Italian crime families (The original members of the Commission allegedly are the five New York bosses: Luciano, Vincent Mangano, Tom Gagliano, Joe Profaci, and Joe Bonanno, plus Al Capone of Chicago and Frank Milano of Cleveland.)

– James LePore, alias Jimmy Marino, a Maranzano follower, is killed by unknown gunmen outside a barbershop at 2400 Arthur Avenue in the Bronx.

– Jacob Kiviat, ousted official of a clothing cutters' union, is shot and killed by two men in a Lower East Side restaurant. New York police attribute the killing to a union quarrel.

September 11—Alvin Karpis pleads guilty to burglary at Henryetta, Oklahoma, and receives a four-year suspended sentence. He rejoins the Barkers at Thayer, Missouri.

September 13—The bodies of Louis Russo and Sam Monaco, with heads bludgeoned and throats cut, are found in Newark Bay. Both were followers of Salvatore Maranzano.

– Italian crime boss Joseph Siragusa is shot to death in his Pittsburgh home. There is no evidence of any connection between this killing and those in New York, and later stories of a massive nationwide Mafia purge (the "Night of the Sicilian Vespers") have proved to be unfounded.

– Pete Carlino, leader of a Calabrian crime family and the so-called "Al Capone of Southern Colorado," is found shot to death near Pueblo. His killing is the result of a bootlegging feud with Denver crime boss Joe "Little Caesar" Roma and is not connected to the East Coast killings.

September 16—Joseph Lebold, Joseph Sutker, and Hymie Paul, members of the Little Jewish Navy gang, are shot to death by rival bootleggers in an apartment at 1740 Collingwood Avenue in Detroit. Three members of the notorious Purple Gang, Harry Keywell, Irving Milberg, and Ray Bernstein, will be convicted of the "Collingwood Massacre" and sentenced to life in the state prison at Marquette, Michigan.

September 21—Patrolman Elisha Haglar is shot, severing his spinal column, while attempting to apprehend four men stealing a Chevrolet from the Hildrith Motor Co. at Monett, Missouri. He will die of his wounds on October 21. Years later, Alvin Karpis will name his friend Fred Barker as Haglar's murderer.

September 24—Bootleg kingpin Leon Gleckman is kidnapped from his home at 2168 Sargent Avenue in St. Paul, probably by a gang working for Gleckman's rival, John P. (Jack) Peifer.

September 29—"Pretty Boy" Floyd and George Birdwell rob the First National Bank at Maud, Oklahoma, of $3,850.

October 2—Members of Vincent "Mad Dog" Coll's gang raid a Schultz "beer drop" at a 151st Street garage in the Bronx; they murder Schultz employee Joe Mullins.

– Francis Keating and Thomas Holden rob First American National Bank messengers at Duluth, Minnesota, of $58,000.

– Bootlegger Leon Gleckman is released by his abductors after paying a reported $5,000 in ransom.

October 3—Frank LePre, one of the alleged kidnappers of Leon Gleckman, is found shot to death on Lake Vadnais Boulevard in St. Paul.

October 7—Alvin Karpis, Fred Barker, and others rob the Peoples Bank at Mountain View, Missouri, of $14,000 in cash and securities.

– Thomas "Kye" Carlile, Robert Trollinger, and Jim Benge rob the First National Bank at Springdale, Arkansas, of $6,000.

October 8—Elfrieda Rigus, mistress of gangster Frank McErlane, and her two dogs are found shot to death in McErlane's car at 8129 Phillips Avenue in Chicago. McErlane is sought as a suspect.

October 12—The bullet-riddled corpse of James "Daffy" Quigley, a member of the "Spike" O'Donnell gang, is found in a Chicago drainage canal.

October 14—"Pretty Boy" Floyd and George Birdwell rob the Bank of Earlsboro at Earlsboro, Oklahoma, for the second time, taking $2,498.

October 15—Los Angeles mobster Joe Ardizzonne disappears and is never seen again.

October 17—Chicago's Al Capone is convicted of income tax evasion and failure to file tax returns.

– Cornelius Vanderbilt Jr.'s interview of Al Capone, entitled "How Al Capone Would Run This Country," is published in *Liberty* magazine.

October 18—Matt Kolb, bootlegging partner of Roger Touhy, is shot to death at his Morton Inn speakeasy in Morton Grove, Illinois. Suspects include Capone gangsters Frank Rio and Claude Maddox.

October 19—Edward Popke, alias "Fats" McCarthy, a member of the Coll mob, kills police detective Guido Passagno in a Manhattan gun battle.

October 20—The Holden-Keating Gang robs the Kraft State Bank at Menomonie, Wisconsin, of $130,000. Two gang members, Charlie Harmon and Frank Weber, and James Kraft, a bank official taken hostage, are killed. Another man, Bob Newborne, will be wrongly tried, convicted, and sentenced to life for this crime.

October 24—Al Capone is sentenced to eleven years in prison and fined $50,000, plus court costs of $30,000.

October 28—Capone bodyguard Phil D'Andrea is sentenced to six months for carrying a gun into federal court during Capone's tax trial.

November 5—"Pretty Boy" Floyd and George Birdwell rob the First National Bank at Conowa, Oklahoma, of $2,500.

November 6—The Citizens State Bank at Strasburg, Ohio, is robbed of $50,000. "Pretty Boy" Floyd is mistakenly suspected.

– Ralph "Bottles" Capone, Al's brother and chief lieutenant, begins serving a three-year sentence for income tax evasion.

November 8—Albert Manley Jackson, Night Marshal of Pocahontas, Arkansas, is shot to death, execution-style, outside town. Two local men, Lige Dame and Earl Decker, will be convicted and imprisoned for this crime, which Alvin Karpis will attribute years later to his friend Fred Barker.

– Vincenzo (James) Genna, one of Chicago's notorious Genna brothers, distinguishes himself by dying naturally of heart disease in Chicago.

November 11—Alexander Jamie, chief investigator for the "Secret Six," an anti-crime group of anonymous businessmen affiliated with the Chicago Crime Commission (and increasingly accused of using vigilante tactics), tells the press that 135 men are working together in a nationwide network of bank robbers. Chicago mobster Gus Winkeler is named as a leader of the group.

– New York police raid the Hotel Franconia, arresting nine Jewish mobsters, including Louis "Lepke" Buchalter, Jacob "Gurrah" Shapiro, and Benjamin "Bugsy" Siegel.

November 23—Special Agent Albert L. Ingle of the U.S. Justice Department's Bureau of Investigation is accidentally killed in Durham, North Carolina, when a pistol falls from his pocket and discharges. Ingle is the third agent of the future FBI to die in the line of duty.

November 30—In New York, Frank Giordano and Dominic "Toughy" Odierno, members of the Coll mob, are convicted of murdering Joe Mullins, a "Dutch" Schultz henchman, and sentenced to death.

December 10—Rudolph "Fats" Duringer is executed in the electric chair at Sing Sing Prison, Ossining, New York.

December 11—Seven federal prisoners, including former members of the Al Spencer Gang, escape from Leavenworth using guns and dynamite smuggled into the prison through the efforts of Frank Nash. William "Boxcar" Green, Grover Durrill, and George "Whitey" Curtis are soon trapped at the nearby farm of E. C. Salisbury and commit suicide to avoid recapture. Tom Underwood, Charles Berta, and Stanley Brown are recaptured the same day.

December 12—Earl Thayer, last of the Leavenworth escapees, is recaptured.

December 16–28—Vincent "Mad Dog" Coll's trial for the Harlem "Baby Massacre" ends in acquittal after his lawyer, Samuel Liebowitz, establishes that the state's star witness, George Brecht, gave perjured testimony.

December 17—After celebrating his acquittal on a kidnapping charge, gangster Jack "Legs" Diamond is shot to death by unknown killers in a rooming house at 67 Dove Street in Albany, New York.

December 18—Store robbery at West Plains, Missouri, by Fred Barker and either Alvin Karpis or "Lapland Willie" Weaver.

December 19—Sheriff C. Roy Kelly is murdered by Fred Barker and either Alvin Karpis or Bill Weaver at West Plains, Missouri. Authorities at West Plains offer a reward totalling $1,200 for information leading to the arrest of Alvin Karpis, Fred Barker, A. W. Dunlop, and "Old Lady Arrie Barker, mother of Fred Barker." The suspects are erroneously described in the reward posters as members of the "Kimes-Inman Gang." (This appears to be the first and perhaps only official notice taken of Mrs. Barker, who generally escaped attention until she was killed with Fred in a Florida gun battle some three years later.) Other gang members flee to St. Paul.

December 23—"Pretty Boy" Floyd and George Birdwell rob the Morris State Bank of Morris, Oklahoma, a second time, taking $1,100.

December 27—Escapee Marvin "Buck" Barrow returns to the state prison at Huntsville, Texas, and surrenders to finish his sentence.

December 29—Six bandits, one armed with a machine gun, abduct the town constable and several citizens in an early-morning raid and ransack a drugstore, hardware store, and the store-owners' homes in Pine River, Minnesota. Possibly an early Barker-Karpis raid.

December 30—The case against Chicago gangster Frank McErlane for the murder of mistress Elfrieda Rigus is nol-prossed.

1932

January 2—Harry and Jennings Young, minor criminals, are surrounded at their mother's farm near Springfield, Missouri, and escape after a spectacular gun battle in which six lawmen are killed. This becomes known as the Young Brothers Massacre, and a surviving officer wrongly identifies Fred Barker as an accomplice. A third brother, Paul Young, and "Pretty Boy" Floyd also were wanted, though they will be exonerated later.

January 5—Harry and Jennings Young allegedly shoot one another to avoid capture after a gun battle with police at a Walker Avenue bungalow in Houston, Texas.

—Alvin Karpis, Fred Barker, and others kidnap Night Marshal Frank Whitney and garage attendant Mark Dunning in a night raid on Cambridge, Minnesota, and ransack the town, looting at least four stores of about $3,000 in merchandise and cash. Authorities note similarity to December 29 raid on Pine River, Minnesota.

—$583,000 in bonds, stolen in the $2 million bank robbery of September 17, 1930, are turned over to officials of the Lincoln National Bank & Trust Co. by Capone gangster Gus Winkeler, not in a secret downtown location as reported in the press, but in the Chicago offices of the "Secret Six." Authorities admit they had little evidence and drop the charges against Winkeler, whom they assumed was not actually involved in the robbery but knew the bandits and could work a deal to recover the loot.

January 14—"Pretty Boy" Floyd, George Birdwell, and an unidentified man rob the Castle State Bank at Castle, Oklahoma, of $2,600. On the same day, three other men rob the First National Bank at Paden, Oklahoma, of $2,500, but Floyd and Birdwell are blamed.

January 21—Francis "Two-Gun" Crowley is executed in the electric chair at Sing Sing Prison, Ossining, New York.

January 22—"Pretty Boy" Floyd and accomplices rob the state bank at Dover, Oklahoma, of $800.

January 27—Raymond Hamilton, in custody for car theft at McKinney, Texas, saws the bars of his cell and escapes.

January 27–28—Local manufacturer Howard Woolverton is kidnapped at South Bend, Indiana, by George "Machine Gun" Kelly and Eddie Doll (alias LaRue). He is released unharmed when unable to pay the demanded $50,000 ransom.

February 1—"Patsy" Del Greco and Fiorio Basile, henchmen of Vincent "Mad Dog" Coll, are machine-gunned to death in a Bronx apartment, along with Mrs. Emily Torrizello. Another man and woman are wounded. Police attribute the killings to the Schultz mob.

February 2—Clyde Barrow is paroled from the state prison at Huntsville, Texas.

February 4—After two trials, Rose Ash and Beulah Baird, Floyd gang "molls," are acquitted of complicity in the Elliston, Kentucky, bank robbery.

February 6—Five bandits, armed with a machine gun and rifles, fight an hour-long battle with residents of Waveland, Indiana, then flee after an unsuccessful attempt to blast the vault of the town bank.

– The Pilot Point National Bank at Denton, Texas, is robbed, probably by George "Machine Gun" Kelly, Albert Bates, and others.

February 7—"Pretty Boy" Floyd and George Birdwell are spotted by police in a car on Admiral Street in Tulsa and escape after a gun battle. Officer W. E. Wilson is wounded.

February 8—Police Detective O. P. Carpenter is killed by bandits attempting to rob the Mercantile Trust Co. in Kansas City, Missouri. "Pretty Boy" Floyd is named as a suspect.

February 9—Vincent "Mad Dog" Coll is machine-gunned to death in a phone booth at the London Chemist drugstore at 314 West Twenty-third Street in Manhattan. Police eventually will attribute the murder to freelance hit men attracted by the large bounties placed on Coll by "Dutch" Schultz and Madden. [Although Leonard Scarnici reportedly confessed to the Coll murder before his later execution for killing a cop, another likely suspect was Tommy Protheroe, who probably worked for Owney Madden and was arrested later with the machine gun used on Coll. He was somehow released and was murdered in 1933.]

February 10—Floyd and Birdwell again are spotted by Tulsa police near Fifth Street and Utica Avenue, but they once more escape in a running gun battle.

February 11—"Pretty Boy" Floyd and George Birdwell battle police and escape from a house at 513 Young Street in Tulsa. Floyd's wife and young son are taken into custody.

– Kansas City criminal Victor Maddi is captured in Houston and charged with the Mercantile Trust robbery in Kansas City.

February 15—"Baby Face" Nelson, already serving a sentence for robbery, is convicted at Wheaton, Illinois, of bank robbery and sentenced to an additional one to twenty years.

February 17—"Baby Face" Nelson acquires a pistol, probably slipped to him by a relative, commandeers the taxi in which he is being returned to the state prison at Joliet, Illinois, and escapes.

March 1—Charles Augustus Lindbergh Jr., infant son of the famed aviator, is kidnapped from his home in Hopewell, New Jersey, spurring a national outcry against the growing epidemic of kidnappings. Federal agents enter the case unofficially even before Congress passes the "Lindbergh Law" three months later. Authorities reject offers of assistance from Al Capone, now in prison, who assures them that the crime was not committed by any organized criminal gang.

March 2—Frank J. Loesch, president of the Chicago Crime Commission, announces his suspicion that the Lindbergh kidnapping was perpetrated by a Midwest gang centered in or near Chicago. Colonel Robert Isham Randolph, the one member of the otherwise "Secret Six" who has acknowledged his membership, disagrees, stating that "no organized gang of kidnappers would ever attempt such a crime" and calls it instead "the act of an insane person."

March 5—Margaret Perry, alias "Indian Rose" Walker, and Marjorie Schwartz, a recent jailmate, are found shot to death in a burning car at Balsam Lake, Wisconsin. Years later, Alvin Karpis will claim that the women were killed by Bernard Phillips, a bank robber and former policeman, on orders from St. Paul crime boss Harry Sawyer, who received the contract from a St. Paul banker. By other accounts, they were murdered on orders of bootlegger Jack Peifer for threatening slot machine king Tom Filben, or the women may have been killed as suspected informers by the Barker-Karpis Gang. Margaret Perry was the mistress of Robert Leon Knapp, alias "Denver Bobby" Walker, one of many suspects in the 1922 Denver Mint robbery.

March 9—Adam "Eddie" Richetti, L. C. "Blackie" Smalley, and Fred Hammer attempt to rob the First National Bank at Mill Creek, Oklahoma. Hammer is killed and Smalley wounded and captured. Richetti is captured later in the day at Sulphur, Oklahoma, and removed to the state prison at McAlester to await trial.

March 10—Four gunmen rob the South Central State Bank at 9 East Seventy-ninth Street in Chicago of $10,000.

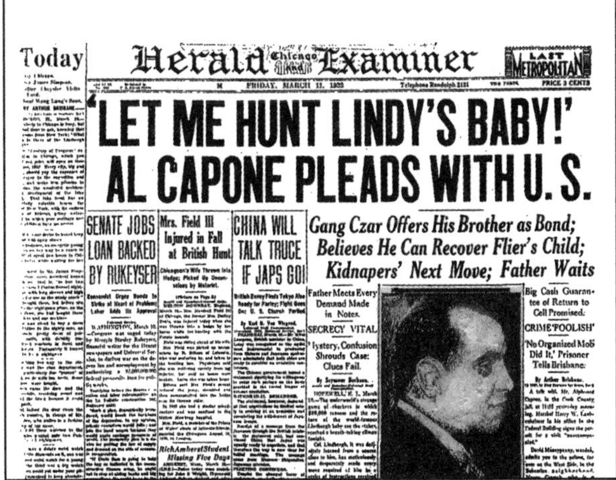
Today

Herald and Examiner

Chicago

LAST METROPOLITAN

FRIDAY, MARCH 11, 1932

PRICE 3 CENTS

'LET ME HUNT LINDY'S BABY!' AL CAPONE PLEADS WITH U. S.

SENATE JOBS LOAN BACKED BY RUKEYSER

Mrs. Field III Injured in Fall at British Hunt

CHINA WILL TALK TRUCE IF JAPS GO!

Gang Czar Offers His Brother as Bond; Believes He Can Recover Flier's Child; Kidnapers' Next Move; Father Waits

Father Meets Every Demand Made in Notes.

SECRECY VITAL

Mystery, Confusion Shrouds Case: Clues Fail.

Big Cash Guarantee of Return to Cell Promised.

CRIME 'FOOLISH'

'No Organized Mob Did It,' Prisoner Tells Brisbane.

The kidnapping of innocent citizens who were held for large ransom demands and sometimes killed anyway—as in the case of the Lindbergh baby—was a form of crime Al Capone found intolerable, and he would have used his intelligence network to rule out the involvement of any organized criminals. When "outlaws" briefly ventured into ransom kidnapping in the 1930s, mobsters not only shunned them for bringing in the "feds," but might even tip off the police.

March 23—"Pretty Boy" Floyd and George Birdwell rob a Meeker, Oklahoma, bank of $500.

March 24—Frank "The Enforcer" Nitti, Al Capone's less flamboyant successor, is released from prison after serving a short term for income tax evasion.

March 25—Clyde Barrow and Raymond Hamilton rob the Sims Oil Co. in Dallas.

March 29—Alvin Karpis, Fred Barker, Thomas Holden, Bernard Phillips, and Lawrence DeVol rob the North American Branch of the Northwestern National Bank in Minneapolis of $266,500 in cash and bonds. First major robbery of the Barker-Karpis Gang.

April 2—Dr. John F. "Jafsie" Condon, intermediary for the Lindbergh family, gives $50,000 in ransom money to a mysterious "John" in St. Raymond's Cemetery in the Bronx. "John," later presumed to be Bruno Richard Hauptmann, says the baby can be found on the boat *Nellie*, near Martha's Vineyard, Massachusetts. There is no such boat.

April 6—"Pretty Boy" Floyd murders state investigator Erv Kelley near Bixby, Oklahoma.

April 8—Capone lieutenant Jake "Greasy Thumb" Guzik begins serving a five-year sentence for income tax evasion.

April 15—Tommy "Mad Dog" Hayes, former member of the St. Louis Cuckoos gang, is found shot to death near Granite City, Illinois. Two Hayes gang members, "Pretty Boy" Lechler and Conrad "Willie G." Wilbert, also are murdered in Madison County. Shelton Brothers gangsters are suspected.

April 19—Chicago police arrest New York mobsters Charles "Lucky" Luciano and Meyer Lansky with Capone gangsters Rocco Fischetti and Paul "The Waiter" Ricca outside the Congress Hotel.

April 20—"Pretty Boy" Floyd and George Birdwell capture deputies at a funeral parlor in Earlsboro, Oklahoma, so they can safely "pay their last respects" to Birdwell's recently deceased father.

April 21—Floyd and Birdwell rob the First State Bank at Stonewall, Oklahoma, of $600.

April 22—Clyde Barrow, Bonnie Parker, and Ralph Fults steal a car at Mabank, Texas, and are pursued by police. Barrow escapes, but Bonnie and Fults are arrested and held in the Kaufman, Texas, jail.

April 24—At Lufkin, Texas, two men rob a Magnolia service station of $26 and a .38-caliber revolver, kidnapping manager K. R. Bivin; they then rob a Gulf service station of $9 and a revolver and also kidnap its manager, Herman Miller. Both men are released unharmed. Clyde Barrow and Frank Clause are suspected.

April 25—Arthur W. Dunlop, "Ma" Barker's former lover, is found shot to death at Lake Fremstadt near Webster, Wisconsin. Police theorize that he was murdered by Alvin Karpis and Fred Barker as a suspected informer.

April 30—Clyde Barrow and Raymond Hamilton are accused of robbing a jewelry store at Hillsboro, Texas, and murdering the owner, John N. Bucher.

May—The College Kidnappers, headed by John "Handsome Jack" Klutas, kidnap Blue Island, Illinois, gambler James Hackett, releasing him after payment of $75,000 ransom.

May 9—The Morris State Bank of Morris, Oklahoma, twice robbed by "Pretty Boy" Floyd, is hit a third time by another gang. One of the bandits, Roscoe "Red" Ernest, is fatally shot and a hostage, Clara Aggas, wounded by a hastily convened posse. The other two robbers escape, but one, Troy Kittrell, will be captured later and convicted of the robbery.

May 12—The decomposed corpse of the Lindbergh baby is found four and a half miles southeast of his home. The coroner reports that the child has been dead about two months, as the result of a blow to the head.

May 19—Searching for "Pretty Boy" Floyd, police raid a Tulsa house, finding only Floyd's wife and son.

May 24—A bandit gang robs the Spring State Bank at Spring, Texas, of $7,380 and escapes despite a barrage of gunfire from cashier H. D. Brown.

June 1—In probably the last "Old West" style robbery, a masked bandit on horseback hits the First National Bank at Hatch, New Mexico, for $2,000 and escapes as several citizens fire at him.

June 7—"Pretty Boy" Floyd and George Birdwell escape a police trap near Ada, Oklahoma. Police theorize the outlaws were wearing bulletproof vests, steel sleeves, and steel skullcaps.

June 10—Violet Sharpe, under investigation as a suspect in the kidnap-murder of the Lindbergh baby, commits suicide by swallowing cyanide at Englewood, New Jersey. Sharpe was a maid in the employ of the baby's grandmother, Mrs. Dwight Morrow.

June 15—Milford Jones, former St. Louis gangster, is shot to death by four gunmen at the bar of the posh Stork Club at 47 Rowens Street in Detroit. Abe Axler and Ed Fletcher of the Purple Gang are questioned as suspects.

June 16—Capone labor racketeer George "Red" Barker is machine-gunned to death in Chicago. The Touhy gang is suspected.

June 17—The Barker-Karpis Gang robs the Citizens National Bank at Fort Scott, Kansas, of $47,000. Frank Sawyer, Jim Clark, and Ed Davis, escaped convicts traveling in a stolen car, are arrested the same day at Rich Hill, Missouri, and wrongly charged with the robbery. All three will be convicted.

June 22—The federal kidnapping statute (the "Lindbergh Law") is passed, making it a federal crime to kidnap and transport a person across state lines for the purpose of ransom.

June 24—Clyde Barrow and Raymond Hamilton are suspected in the theft of four hundred money orders from a post office in Port Sullivan, Texas.

June 27—Bonnie Parker is released from the Kaufman, Texas, jail.

June 29—Sadie "Mother" Ash, Kansas City underworld character whose sons were murdered by "Pretty Boy" Floyd and Bill Miller, dies at her home on Holmes Street.

June 30—Haskell Bohn, son of a refrigerator manufacturer, is kidnapped from his St. Paul home by Verne Sankey and accomplices who leave a note demanding $35,000 in ransom. Bohn is released several days later when the kidnappers settle for only $12,000.

— "Machine Gun" Kelly, Eddie Bentz, and Albert Bates rob the Ponder State Bank of $3,500 at Ponder, Texas. Local legend will later attribute the robbery to the Barrow Gang, and the old bank building will be used to film a holdup scene in the 1967 movie *Bonnie and Clyde*.

July 1—The U.S. Justice Department's Bureau of Investigation, headed by J. Edgar Hoover since 1924, is officially upgraded to the U.S. Bureau of Investigation.

July 1—Dominic Odierno and Frank Giordano, former members of the Coll mob, are executed for murder at Sing Sing Prison in Ossining, New York.

July 7—Thomas Holden, Francis Keating, and Harvey Bailey, members of the Barker-Karpis Gang, are arrested at the Old Mission Golf Course in Kansas City, Missouri, by agents of the U.S. Bureau of Investigation and Kansas City police detectives. Holden and Keating, escaped federal prisoners, will be returned to Leavenworth. Bailey is charged with the Fort Scott bank robbery. Another gang member, Bernard Phillips, an ex-policeman, avoids capture and later is suspected of betraying Holden, Keating, and Bailey. Phillips will disappear later, reportedly murdered in New York by Frank Nash and Verne Miller.

July 11—Edward Popke, alias "Fats" McCarthy, formerly a henchman of "Mad Dog" Coll but suspected of murdering Coll and "Legs" Diamond, is killed by New York state troopers in a hideout near Albany.

July 16—Bookkeeper Roy Evans is kidnapped from his office at the Palestine Ice Co. in Palestine, Texas, then beaten and robbed of $989 by two men he later will identify as Clyde Barrow and Raymond Hamilton.

July 17—Oklahoma Crime Bureau agent Crockett Long and Wylie Lynn fatally shoot one another in a drugstore gun battle in Madill, Oklahoma. Lynn, a former Prohibition agent, was tried and acquitted in 1924 of the killing of legendary lawman Bill Tilghman.

July 21—Former "Bugs" Moran gangster Willie Marks and Teamsters official Patrick Berrill are killed by underworld machine-gunners outside the Lime Kiln Hill Inn near Shawano, Wisconsin.

July 22—Two men with machine guns rob the Farmers & Merchants Bank at Ladonia, Texas, and flee with several hostages who are released unharmed outside town.

July 23—Convicted bank robber Robert "Big Bob" Brady escapes from the state prison at McAlester, Oklahoma.

July 25—The Barker-Karpis Gang robs the Cloud County Bank at Concordia, Kansas, of $250,000 in cash and bonds.

July 27—The First State Bank at Willis, Texas, is robbed of $3,000. Clyde Barrow and Raymond Hamilton are named later as suspects.

July 29—Clyde Barrow and Raymond Hamilton rob the Interurban Railroad Station at Grand Prairie, Texas.

— Notorious bootlegging brothers John, Arthur, and James Volpe are shot to death by unknown gunmen in a Pittsburgh coffee house.

July 31—Robert Sanford, suspected counterfeiter found shot to death with his wife in a New York apartment, is identified through fingerprints as Robert "Bob" Carey, alias Conroy and Robert "Gimpy" Newberry (no relation to Chicago mobster Ted Newberry), former Capone gangster wanted as a suspect in the St. Valentine's Day Massacre and (along with many others) the Lindbergh kidnapping. "Sanford" supposedly had killed his wife and himself in a murder-suicide, but other sources said that Carey was murdered. [About this time "Bugs" Moran, having drinks with an old friend and onetime truck driver, remarked that he had just come back from the coast where he "took care of" a Bob Carey, whose name was unknown to the trucker.]

August 1—Clyde Barrow and Raymond Hamilton rob the Neuhoff Packing Co. in Dallas of several hundred dollars and some diamond rings.

August 3—Former Tulsa policeman H. W. Nave claims to have been robbed of his car and clothing near Blackwell, Oklahoma, by "Pretty Boy" Floyd and George Birdwell. Nave will be arrested for fraud when it is discovered he has sold his mortgaged automobile to a used-car dealer in Oklahoma City.

August 5—Clyde Barrow and Raymond Hamilton kill Deputy Eugene Moore and wound Sheriff C. G. Maxwell outside a dance hall at Stringtown, Oklahoma.

August 8—Pittsburgh mobster John Bazzano is found in a burlap bag on a Brooklyn street after being stabbed and strangled to death.

August 14—Convicted bank robber Aulcie "Aussie" Elliott escapes from the state prison at McAlester, Oklahoma.

— Clyde Barrow, Bonnie Parker, and Raymond Hamilton kidnap Deputy Sheriff Joe Johns near Carlsbad, New Mexico, later releasing him unharmed in San Antonio, Texas.

August 16—J. Earl Smith, the attorney supposedly hired by the Barker-Karpis Gang to defend Harvey Bailey, is found shot to death at the Indian Hills Country Club near Tulsa. Slaying was later attributed to Fred Barker and Alvin Karpis, although the actual killers may have been Harry Campbell, Glen LeRoy Wright, and Jimmie Lawson.

August 17—Harvey Bailey is received at the Lansing, Kansas, state prison under a ten- to fifty-year sentence for bank robbery. This is his first imprisonment in his ten years as a bank robber.

August 18—The Barker-Karpis Gang robs the Second National Bank of Beloit, Wisconsin, taking $50,000.

— Three gunmen rob the First National Bank at Le Sueur, Minnesota, of $5,000.

— Five men rob the Edgewater Trust & Savings Bank in Chicago of $2,000.

August 19—Three or four men rob the Citizens Security Bank at Bixby, Oklahoma, of $1,000. Thomas "Kye" Carlile, Troy Love, Ford Bradshaw, and Eddie "Newt" Clanton are suspected, as is Fred Barker, though probably in error.

August 25—Adam Richetti, awaiting trial for bank robbery, is released from the Oklahoma state prison on $15,000 bond, which he skips.

August 30—Clyde Barrow, Bonnie Parker, and Raymond Hamilton escape a police trap near Wharton, Texas.

August 31—"Machine Gun" Kelly, Albert Bates, and others rob the Security State Bank at Blue Ridge, Texas, of $2,500.

September 1—The Barker-Karpis Gang robs the First National Bank in Flandreau, South Dakota, of $10,000.

September 2—Susie Sharp is killed and her daughter and another woman wounded by several gunmen in a bloody attempted carjacking on Braggs Mountain in Oklahoma's Cookson Hills. The "Cookson Hills Gang" of Thomas "Kye" Carlile, Troy Love, Jim Benge, Ford Bradshaw, and Eddie "Newt" Clanton is suspected.

September 10—Arthur "Doc" [or "Dock"] Barker, son of "Ma" Barker and convicted murderer who has served ten years of a life sentence, is released from the Oklahoma state prison at McAlester on the condition he leave the state. Supposedly the parole was obtained through bribery of state officials by persons connected to the Barker-Karpis Gang. The gang will be unable to obtain a parole for Lloyd "Red" Barker, who is serving 25 years in Leavenworth for mail robbery.

September 11—Gerardo Scarpato, in whose restaurant "Joe the Boss" Masseria was gunned down, is found strangled and stuffed in a burlap bag in a parked car in Prospect Park, Brooklyn.

September 14—Two gunmen rob the First National Bank at Cleveland, Texas, of $10,000.

September 17—Muskogee County Deputy Webster Reece and fellow officer Frank Edwards are mortally wounded in a battle with outlaws near Barber, Oklahoma. Bud McClain, driver of the bandit car, is killed, but "Kye" Carlile, Troy Love, and an unidentified accomplice escape on foot.

September 18—"Kye" Carlile and Troy Love are slain by police in a battle at the Rice Carter farm in eastern Oklahoma. Posseman Andrew McGinnis is killed and Rogers County Deputy Hurt Flippin receives a fatal wound in the same shootout.

Leadership of the "Cookson Hills Gang" passes from Carlile to Ford Bradshaw.

September 21—"Machine Gun" Kelly, Albert Bates, Eddie Bentz, and others rob the First Trust & Savings Bank at Colfax, Washington, of $77,000 in cash and bonds.

September 23—The Barker-Karpis Gang robs the State Bank & Trust Co. at Redwood Falls, Minnesota, of $35,000. Roofing nails spread across the highway flatten the tires of a pursuing sheriff's car, and the gang escapes, despite other pursuit by an airplane. Another gang will be wrongly convicted of this robbery.

September 27—Ford Bradshaw, Tom "Skeet" Bradshaw, Eddie "Newt" Clanton, and Charlie Cotner rob the Bank of Vian, at Vian, Oklahoma, of $6,000.

September 28—Claude Chambers of Sapulpa, Oklahoma, a witness in "Doc" Barker's 1921 murder trial, reports a telephoned death threat from Barker and appeals for police protection. Chambers will later report other threats from Fred Barker and "Pretty Boy" Floyd.

September 29—The Holland State Bank at Holland, Michigan, is robbed.

September 30—Sheriff George Cheek receives a tip that "Pretty Boy" Floyd plans to visit his brother-in-law in Sallisaw, Oklahoma, and sets an ambush. Floyd escapes.

— The Barker-Karpis Gang robs the Citizens National Bank at Wahpeton, North Dakota, of $6,900. The gang originally planned to rob a bank in nearby Breckenridge, Minnesota, on the same day.

October 3—Two fleeing suspects are shot by Deputy Elmer Hutchinson near Enid, Oklahoma. One, never identified, is instantly killed. The other, at first believed to be "Pretty Boy" Floyd, gives his name as "Tom Goggin" before dying in the Enid Hospital.

October 8—Raymond Hamilton robs the state bank at Cedar Hill, Texas, of $1,401. Clyde Barrow also is suspected, but Hamilton will claim later to have committed the robbery alone.

— Chicago mobster Frank McErlane dies of pneumonia at a Beardstown, Illinois, hospital.

October 11—Clyde Barrow is suspected of murdering Howard Hall during a grocery store holdup in Sherman, Texas.

October 16—Bank robber Ford Bradshaw fatally shoots Missouri jail escapee George Martin during an argument in a Muskogee, Oklahoma, speakeasy. Black speakeasy proprietor "Big John" Carter, who witnessed the shooting, will disappear days later, another suspected victim of Bradshaw.

October 18—After $4,400 bank robbery at Amboy, Minnesota, Lawrence DeVol, a Barker-Karpis gangster, will be identified as one of the participants.

November 1—"Pretty Boy" Floyd, George Birdwell and Aulcie "Aussie" Elliott rob the state bank at Sallisaw, Oklahoma, of $2,530.

November 3—Volney Davis, convicted with "Doc" Barker of a 1921 murder in Tulsa, is granted a two-year leave of absence from Oklahoma's state prison and joins the Barker-Karpis Gang in St. Paul. (Apparently Oklahoma granted such "leaves" with some regularity.)

November 7—Ford Bradshaw, Eddie "Newt" Clanton, and Jim Benge rob the American State Bank at Henryetta, Oklahoma, of $11,252. The robbery is blamed on "Pretty Boy" Floyd, George Birdwell, and "Aussie" Elliott.

— Four unidentified machine-gunners rob the State National Bank at Marlow, Oklahoma, of $5,500.

— The Mann Act conspiracy conviction of "Machine Gun" Jack McGurn is reversed by the U.S. Supreme Court after Louise Rolfe's similar conviction is overturned. The Court had ruled that under the wording of the law, a woman could not "debauch" herself, leaving McGurn with no one to have "conspired" with.

November 8—Franklin Delano Roosevelt elected president of the United States.

November 9—Raymond Hamilton and Gene O'Dare rob the Carmine State Bank at LaGrange, Texas, of $1,400.

— While meeting with his associates at the Hard Tack Social Club, 547 Grand Avenue in New York, Benjamin "Bugsy" Siegel is injured when a bomb is lowered down the chimney.

Hoover's "G-men"

J. Edgar Hoover's contempt for the Treasury Department's Prohibition Bureau was based on his antagonism toward a potential rival in Harry Anslinger and on the fact that Anslinger's agents were as corrupt as they were inept. Hoover's appointment as acting director of the Justice Department's Bureau of Investigation in 1924 did not expand his authority to any great extent, but he had kept his pledge to depoliticize the bureau, purge it of rotten apples, and impose a degree of discipline that made him both respected and feared.

The election of President Franklin Delano Roosevelt in 1932 might have cost him his job, however, for the man FDR had intended to appoint as the new U.S. attorney general had personal objections to Hoover and planned a housecleaning of his own. As Hoover's luck would have it, the prospective appointee died en route to the inauguration, and FDR had to quickly find a replacement. The man he chose was Homer Cummings, an obscure party loyalist but an experienced state prosecutor who shared most of Hoover's undeniably progressive ideas about crime control, including the belief that in the age of the automobile and the machine gun, crime had become a

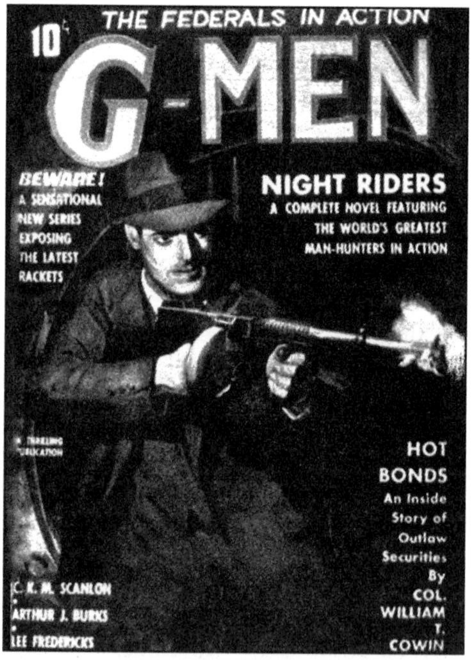

While "Machine Gun" Kelly has been credited with coining the term "G-man"—which actually had been in circulation for at least ten years—J. Edgar Hoover promoted it widely to distinguish his own Justice Department agents from other "government" men once Congress declared a national "War on Crime."

nationwide problem requiring a federal solution. This amounted to a complete reversal of the position taken by the previous Republican administration, which might have recognized the limitations of local law enforcement, but had feared that new federal criminal laws would sooner or later evolve into a national agency serving the federal government—an American secret police.

Aware of strong states'-rights opposition to federalized crime control—especially in the South—and anxious to make his agency look good, Hoover had to discourage Cummings's efforts to create a true national police force—an "American Scotland Yard"—as the New Deal approach to lawlessness. With desperadoes like "Pretty Boy" Floyd, "Machine Gun" Kelly and now Dillinger making national headlines (with a little help from the Justice Department), many Americans were advocating just the sort of federal police others greatly feared; so Cummings and Hoover came off as moderates by proposing new laws that respected the authority of Congress to regulate "interstate commerce," and by extension of that doctrine, only crimes interfering with it. This left plenty of room to maneuver, including the robbery of federally insured banks, but officially it left most crime control the responsibility of local authorities.

Three problems remained to be resolved. Unaware of Hoover's personal agenda, the Roosevelt administration, gearing up for Repeal, took Volstead Act enforcement out of the hands of the Treasury Department and gave it to the Justice Department. This dismayed Hoover, who did not want his accountants and law

trainees confused in the public mind with Treasury's Prohibition agents. The master bureaucrat deftly sidestepped this threat by engineering his own appointment as director of a new Division of Investigation, which would allow him to segregate his BOI agents from the Prohibition agents, keeping them in their respective roles until the Prohibition amendment could be formally repealed.

This was how an obscure Eliot Ness and his so-called Untouchables ended up working for the Justice Department instead of the Treasury Department, and even more closely with Chicago's "Secret Six" crime fighters. They were harassing Capone from the rear while Big Al fought the eleven-year tax-conviction sentence already obtained by the Internal Revenue Service. Ness's attacks on Capone breweries earned him only modest recognition at the time, and he did not achieve fame until he and writer Oscar Fraley teamed up to give Ness a major role in destroying Capone, a considerable exaggeration.*

A second problem confronting Hoover was the announcement by an overeager Cummings that the Justice Department would bring its federal muscle to bear on "racketeering," to which Hoover lent lip service while the issue was hot, but in full awareness that the rackets—from gambling to prostitution to union takeovers—were largely consensual crimes that defied traditional police solutions. Nor did the raft of new federal anti-crime statutes that Cummings rammed through Congress give Hoover laws that would deal effectively with racketeering—to Hoover's considerable relief, since he had persistently denied the existence of nationally organized crime (and to the relief of racketeers, who had learned from the Capone example to maintain the lowest possible profile).

Hoover's token response to racketeering was to create the bureau's Top Hoodlum Program, which supposedly kept track of the more notorious mobsters for the benefit of local authorities, who probably ignored it but still were responsible for crime control within their jurisdictions.

Another challenge Hoover faced was how to differentiate his "feds" from the "feds" of other government agencies that were less fastidious about their men having

*Ness would later battle organized crime in Cleveland, with a measure of success, but his failure to solve a series of mutilation murders combined with his increasing personal problems to conclude his law-enforcement career. After his death in 1957, the year the Fraley book was published, his ashes remained in a family member's garage, ignored until historian/writer Steven Nickel learned of this some forty years later. Nickel arranged a proper burial for a man who had become an American icon, thanks to never-ending reruns of *The Untouchables* television series and to a popular, if typically novelized, movie.

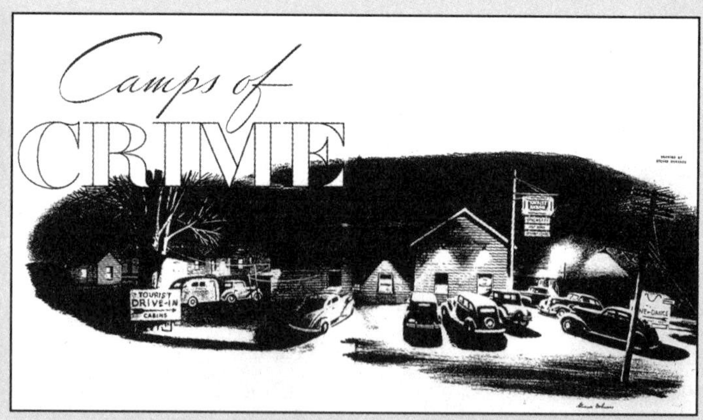

Popular crime writer Courtney Ryley Cooper teamed up with J. Edgar Hoover and worked overtime to virtually invent an image of the "G-man" that would meet Hoover's approval. Their close collaboration on books and magazine articles ended with his suicide in 1940, after he had fallen out of favor with Hoover, possibly because he had taken up with Hoover's archrival, Harry Anslinger.

The country's overnight enthusiasm for the government's "War on Crime" inspired jealousy among state and local police, who regarded federal agents as amateur "briefcase cops."

the sterling qualities demanded by "The Director," as Hoover usually was called. This problem was largely solved by a freelance Kansas City writer named Courtney Ryley Cooper, whose first article captured the essence of the agency that Hoover was trying to fashion out of inexperienced agents whom local authorities tended to sneer at as "briefcase cops." Some early blunders had not enhanced their reputations as streetwise lawmen.

It was Cooper, a hack writer but a popular one, who excelled at the kind of purple prose approved by Hoover in describing the enemies of society, and he was virtually drafted by Hoover as his coach in creating an agency whose image included the best elements of the lone-wolf action detective Americans expected in their fiction. But Hoover's men also understood the need for teamwork (so much for the lone wolf and personal glory), utilized scientific methods of the modern crime lab, and displayed a soldierly obedience to the country's chief crimefighter, Hoover, who was director of what soon would be called the Federal Bureau of Investigation. Attorney General Cummings had made banner headlines by declaring the nation's first "War on Crime" in 1933, but wars are fought by armies led by generals, not politicians; Cummings soon found himself eclipsed by "general" Hoover, whose front-line reports (ghostwritten by Cooper) began appearing in virtually every popular publication of the day.

The formula worked like a charm, especially in combination with the catchy nickname "G-man," to the point where that term came to mean only one thing to the general public—the FBI—as though that agency alone, under Hoover, had invented modern crime control, wiped out America's robbers and kidnappers, established the country's first police training facility, set new standards for police professionalism, recreated (without credit) Col. Goddard's state-of-the-art crime laboratory (established to investigate the St. Valentine's Day Massacre), replaced the International Association of Chiefs of Police as the clearing house for national crime statistics, and so forth.

How this all occurred became a staple of FBI lore promulgated by Cooper, Rex Collier (another Hoover favorite), and other excitable writers—a federal version of the comic-strip detective *Dick Tracy.* Although "Tracy" retained his gadgets and lone-wolf ways, the invincible G-man instantly caught on with the public and the entertainment industry, which had stood accused of glorifying gangsters until the last scenes in the last reel required their spectacular and moralistic demise. Movie makers simply replaced gangsters with the new G-men (James Cagney in *The Public Enemy* followed by James Cagney in *"G" Men*) who at first didn't quite fit the Hoover stereotype as formulated by Cooper, but Cooper soon learned that FBI cooperation was contingent on getting Hoover's message straight.

According to Collier, writing in 1935, the term "G-man" was coined by "Machine Gun" Kelly who had been captured in an apartment in Memphis on September 26, 1935 (by coincidence, the same day that ten men of the future Dillinger Gang broke out of the Indiana state prison). The FBI version of the Kelly capture has never varied to this day and states that when confronted by Hoover's well-armed squad, the fugitive threw up his hands and shouted, "Don't shoot, G-men! Don't shoot!" Supposedly the agents had never heard themselves called G-men before, although the term occasionally crops up in books dating back to the early twenties in reference to government agents in general. In any case, Kelly earned himself a small measure of immortality when his surrender was publicized by Hoover.

This could be fiction, written a year after the fact. Local police described the arrest more prosaically—that a rattled and strung-out Kelly simply grinned sheepishly, dropped his gun and said, "Okay, boys, I've been waiting for you all night."

In the middle thirties, Hoover and Cooper were the Siamese twins of publishing, both authoring books (written by Cooper), to which one or the other would provide the preface; as well as newspaper features and magazine articles by Hoover with Cooper or as told to Cooper. Then something went wrong, possibly something as minor as Cooper padding out an interminable series of FBI articles for *American Magazine* with a couple of pieces done in collaboration with Narcotics Bureau Chief Harry Anslinger (a Hoover nemesis who blamed everything on the Mafia and nationally organized crime, which Hoover insisted did not exist). In

PRIZE-FIGHT FILMS, WHITE SLAVES, AND THE JUSTICE DEPARTMENT

In writing its own history, the FBI (and most other historians, for that matter) usually fails to mention that it sneaked into existence in 1908 after Congress denied the Justice Department the authority to borrow men from other federal agencies to do its "detective work." At the time this amounted to some fraud and bankruptcy cases, policing Indian and government reservations, enforcing the Comstock Act prohibiting the traffic in obscene books and contraceptives, and other relatively boring duties. Then in 1910, "colored" fighter Jack Johnson taunted his way into a world heavyweight championship bout with James Jeffries (an event previously reserved for white contenders), which stretched the Constitution's commerce clause to prohibit the interstate shipment of prize-fight films. Johnson knocked out Jeffries in the fourteenth round, which set off race riots around the country, and in 1912 Congress, in a panic, passed the Sims Act.

Though obviously chagrined that a "Negro" could meet and beat a "White Man" (said one commentator at the time: "Whether he will ever breed brains to match his muscle is yet to be proven"), Congress cited public safety as its excuse for obstructing the distribution of fight films lest they trigger more race riots; a few states banned them entirely. This new application of the interstate commerce clause beyond the importation of dirty books (mainly from France) and the mail-order distribution of birth-control information and condoms (originally the business of postal police), followed the equally racist Mann Act (the White Slave Traffic Act of 1910) aimed at "interstate prostitution" rings that supposedly threatened the voluntary or involuntary "enslavement" of women – mainly white women, from little girls to young ladies to wives and mothers.*

Enforcement of the Mann Act was another duty of the Justice Department's new Bureau of Investigation, and Johnson ran afoul of it, too. In 1920 he surrendered to federal agents on the charge of violating that law by sending his white girlfriend, Belle Schreiber, a railroad ticket to travel from Pittsburgh to Chicago for presumably "immoral purposes." The law, intended to combat commercial prostitution, had thrown in that phrase to cover all bases, and the bureau construed it to include even consensual sex between private individuals. The train ticket was proof enough to earn Johnson a conviction, and he spent a year in Leavenworth before his release in 1921. (The bureau proudly describes its use of the Mann Act to nail a Klansman but neglects to mention that "Machine Gun" Jack McGurn and his "Blond Alibi" [see p. 199] slickly managed to beat it.)

Flamboyant Jack Johnson, the first "Negro" heavyweight contender, ran afoul of the Mann Act passed by Congress in 1910.

The bureau eventually backed off on its enforcement of the Mann Act except in the occasional high-profile case where the defendant was either famous or infamous and another charge wouldn't stick.

And once blacks had turned into the likes of boxer Joe Louis (who nevertheless was warned against gloating, and against having his picture taken with a white woman), the bureau, taken over by J. Edgar Hoover in 1924, ten years later was lobbying a New Deal Congress for federal laws to fight the country's "War on Crime." The Sims Act slipped to lowest priority, but it stayed on the books until 1940 when President Roosevelt signed a law divesting prize-fight films of the threat they posed in "interstate commerce."

---

*The Harrison Narcotics Act of 1914 was passed by a Congress that had largely ignored Chinese opium use until that drug and its derived opiates (long used as medicinal laudanum) were increasingly discovered by whites, and which also felt obliged to remove cocaine from Coca-Cola and cough drops because of its popularity among black musicians.

In 1935 J. Edgar Hoover made the cover of Time *magazine as America's "top cop," but in later years his reputation suffered as the FBI's surveillance practices began spinning out of control.*

any event, the writing team had a falling-out in the late 1930s, and in 1940 Cooper hanged himself in a hotel room, driven to suicide, according to his widow, by some wrong done him by Hoover.

A similar fate supposedly overtook Melvin Purvis, the "ace" G-man whose fame threatened to overshadow Hoover at the height of the public-enemy era. Even with so many agents at the scene of Dillinger's shooting, the bureau had a hard time sorting out events, and under pressure from reporters it finally released an "official" diagram of the ambush that put Sam Cowley close to the action and wrote Purvis out of it entirely. This deletion did not escape the press, which put Purvis back in the picture, though not in the right place.

After Dillinger was killed in July 1934, followed by Floyd in October, Hoover sent Purvis on a series of meaningless missions until he resigned from the bureau in frustration a year later. After that, Hoover always answered Purvis's letters in a manner no longer verging on the flirtatious but still disarmingly cheerful, instructing his staff always to tell a visiting Purvis that he had been called out of town. Meanwhile, he kept track of Purvis, sabotaged his every effort to get back into law enforcement, private security work, or even movie consulting, and had other writers make sarcastic references to "former agents" who had found themselves obliged to endorse commercial products. In 1960, Purvis killed himself at his home in South Carolina—not with the pistol he supposedly carried the night Dillinger died, as the story is often told, but with the nickel-plated .45 automatic formerly owned by Capone gangster Gus Winkeler [see p. 359]. At the time Winkeler was murdered in 1933, he had been cooperating with Purvis, who ended up with his pistol.

Hoover (who had changed Purvis's letter of voluntary resignation into "terminated with prejudice") and virtually every writer have treated Purvis's death as a suicide.

Once Melvin Purvis's prominence threatened to eclipse that of J. Edgar Hoover, he felt obliged to leave the FBI, was unable to find work in law enforcement, and ended up endorsing commercial products.

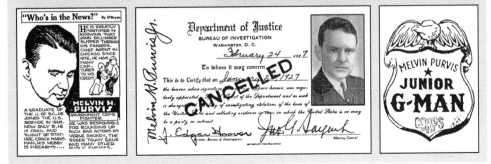

Melvin H. Purvis Jr.

Department of Justice
BUREAU OF INVESTIGATION
WASHINGTON, D. C.
February 24 1927

To whom it may concern

This is to Certify that on January 2, 1927, the bearer, whose signature appear hereon, was regularly appointed of the Department and as such is charged of investigating violations of the laws of the United States and collecting evidence in cases in which the United States is or may be a party in interest.

CANCELLED

J. Edgar Hoover
Director, Bureau of Investigation.

Jno. G. Sargent
Attorney General

However, he left no note, his wife was outside in the garden, the shot went through his neck from a distance that left powder burns on his jaw, and the bullet was a tracer round—hardly the choice for any self-inflicted wound. As his son Alston later described it, he and a friend had taken that gun and two others out of his father's collection, and had not had the opportunity to clean them before Purvis intended to loan the Winkeler pistol to a friend for a display. The cleaning equipment was with the collection, in an attic reached by a pull-down staircase that Purvis was about to ascend. Moreover, Purvis did not like automatics for reasons of safety; and the Winkeler pistol had its next round ready to fire when his wife rushed inside, found her husband shot, and had impulsively picked up the gun.

Refusing even to acknowledge Purvis's death, Hoover later received a terse telegram from his widow:

> WE ARE HONORED THAT YOU IGNORED MELVIN'S DEATH. YOUR JEALOUSY HURT HIM VERY MUCH BUT UNTIL THE END I THINK HE LOVED YOU.

At the bottom of the telegram Hoover scribbled a note: "It was well we didn't write as she would no doubt have distorted it. H."

November 15—Three gunmen rob the First State Bank at Stinnett, Texas, of $5,999.

November 20—Free-lance hit man Tony Fabrizzo is shot to death in New York, supposedly in retribution for the bombing attempt on "Bugsy" Siegel. Fabrizzo and Leonard Scarnici will be accused later of killing Vincent "Mad Dog" Coll.

November 23—George Birdwell, Charles Glass, and C. C. Patterson attempt to rob the Farmers & Merchants Bank at Boley, Oklahoma. Birdwell, Glass, and bank president D. J. Turner are killed in the resulting gun battle, and Patterson is wounded and captured.

November 25—Raymond Hamilton, accompanied by Les Stewart, robs the state bank at Cedar Hill, Texas, for the second time, of $1,900.

November 29—Two men attempt to rob the First National Bank at Cleveland, Texas, but flee when an employee runs out the door to shout for help.

November 30—"Machine Gun" Kelly, Albert Bates, and Eddie Doll rob the Citizens State Bank at Tupelo, Mississippi, of $38,000. Numerous witnesses wrongly identify "Pretty Boy" Floyd as one of the robbers.

— Clyde Barrow, Hollis Hale, and Frank Hardy rob the Farmers & Miners Bank at Oronogo, Missouri, of $115.

December 5—Raymond Hamilton and Gene O'Dare are captured in Bay City, Michigan, and extradited to Texas. Hamilton will be convicted of murder and several robberies and sentenced to 263 years. O'Dare will be convicted of armed robbery and sentenced to 50 years.

— Burglars loot the Farmers State Bank at Pflugerville, Texas, of $4,500.

December 6—In a Chicago Loop mail robbery, five bandits, armed with pistols and shotguns, seize sacks containing $250,000 in bonds and cash.

December 12—Notorious bank robber Willie "The Actor" Sutton escapes from Sing Sing with burglar John Eagen.

— Bank-robbing brothers Ford Bradshaw and Tom "Skeet" Bradshaw are captured by Sheriff John York and deputies near Vinita, Oklahoma. "Skeet" is charged only with carrying a concealed weapon and later released. Ford is transported to Okmulgee to face a bank robbery charge.

December 13—Edna "The Kissing Bandit" Murray, girlfriend of Barker-Karpis outlaw Volney Davis, escapes from the Women's state penitentiary at Jefferson City, Missouri, where she has been serving a twenty-five-year sentence for armed robbery. It is her third prison break. Irene McCann also escapes.

December 16—The Barker-Karpis Gang robs the Third Northwestern Bank in Minneapolis of $22,000 in cash and $92,000 in bonds, killing two policemen and one bystander.

— Willie "The Actor" Sutton, John Eagen, and three other men rob the Bank of Manhattan branch at 169th Street and St. Nicholas Avenue of $15,000.

December 19—A Chicago police detail, headed by Sergeants Harry Lang and Harry Miller, raids a Chicago Syndicate headquarters at 221 North La Salle Street. Capone's successor Frank Nitti is shot, allegedly while resisting arrest, by Lang. Nitti survives. Allegations will arise that Chicago Mayor Anton Cermak and former "Bugs" Moran mobster Ted Newberry (having joined Capone after the 1929 Massacre) had plotted to assassinate Nitti and that Cermak also was urging Des Plaines bootlegger Roger Touhy to make war on the Chicago mob with the assistance of the police department.

December 20—"Big Bob" Brady, notorious bank robber and prison escapee, is captured by police at Des Moines, Iowa. He later will be sent to the state prison at Lansing, Kansas, on a life sentence as a habitual criminal.

— The First State Bank of Willis, Texas, is robbed for the second time in the year.

December 21—Lawrence DeVol, Barker-Karpis Gang member, is captured in St. Paul. He will be convicted of murder and bank robbery and sentenced to life imprisonment in the state prison at Stillwater, Minnesota. He later is transferred to the St. Peter Hospital for the Criminally Insane.

December 25—Clyde Barrow murders Doyle Johnson during an attempted car theft in Temple, Texas.

December 31—Odell Chambless, Les Stewart, and others, suspected to include Clyde Barrow and Bonnie Parker, rob the Home Bank in Grapevine, Texas, of $2,800.

— Convicts Matt and George Kimes, leaders of the Kimes Gang, direct prison guards to the Seminole, Oklahoma, hideout of escapee George Noland. Noland is killed, allegedly by the guards, but the county attorney finds evidence that the Kimes boys were armed and did the actual shooting, possibly in revenge for Noland's shooting of their sister.

1933

January 2—In Seminole, Oklahoma, at an inquest into the death of George Noland, Dr. Dwight B. Shaw testifies that at least one of the fatal bullets did not come from the guns of prison guards. County Attorney O. H. Preston says witnesses saw Matt and George Kimes carrying guns. Nellie and Jackie Kimes, the convicts' sisters who witnessed the killing, deny that Matt and George were armed and swear that Noland was killed by the guards while resisting arrest.

January 3—$74,714 mail robbery at Minneapolis railroad station by "Terrible Tommy" Touhy, John "Killer" Schmidt, Gustave "Gloomy Gus" Schafer and others.

January 5—Three men rob the First National Bank at Cleveland, Texas, of $1,200. "Pretty Boy" Floyd is suspected. It is the third robbery of this bank in one year.

January 6—Clyde Barrow, Bonnie Parker, and W. D. Jones escape a police trap at West Dallas, Texas, home of Lillie McBride (Raymond Hamilton's sister), killing Tarrant County Deputy Malcom Davis.

January 7—Chicago gangster Ted Newberry is found shot to death in northern Indiana, probably on orders from Frank Nitti.

January 11—Three men rob Bank of Ash Grove at Ash Grove, Missouri, of $3,000. "Pretty Boy" Floyd or the Barrow Gang are later suspected.

January 18—Barrow Gang associate Odell Chambless, wanted for bank robbery and suspicion of murder, surrenders to Dallas police. He will be cleared of the murder charge.

January 23—Sheriff John C. Mosely is killed by bandits at Tulia, Texas. Barrow Gang is suspected.

January 25—A federal grand jury in New York indicts Arthur "Dutch Schultz" Flegenheimer for income tax evasion. Schultz becomes a federal fugitive but remains in the city.

January 26—Motorcycle patrolman Thomas Persell is kidnapped by Clyde Barrow, Bonnie Parker, and W. D. Jones near Springfield, Missouri. He is released unharmed at Poundstone Corner, Missouri.

January 28—Earl Doyle, Eddie Green, Thomas "Buck" Woulfe, and "Dago" Howard Lansdon rob Mrs. Dorothy Jolly, messenger for the National Bank & Trust Co. at North Kansas City, Missouri, of $14,500, wounding Marshal Edgar Nall. Woulfe also is wounded. Near Holt, Missouri, the bandits battle a civilian posse, then steal a car from posse members and flee to Iowa.

January 29—The same North Kansas City bandits steal license plates and two more cars and kidnap policemen John Neuman and Bert Conrey at Knoxville, Iowa, escaping back to Missouri. The policemen are released unharmed west of Unionville, Missouri.

February 2—Thomas "Buck" Woulfe, wounded in the January 28 North Kansas City robbery, is captured at the Southeastern Kansas Hospital at Coffeeville, Kansas. Woulfe is transferred to the Clay County Jail at Liberty, Missouri.

February 9—John "Killer" Schmidt, "Gloomy Gus" Schafer, and others rob a U.S. Mail truck of $233,411 at Sacramento, California.

February 12—Denver millionaire Charles Boettcher II is kidnapped by Verne Sankey and accomplices and transported to Sankey's ranch near Chamberlain, South Dakota. Charles Boettcher I agrees to pay a $60,000 ransom, but not until his son is released.

February 15—Chicago Mayor Anton Cermak is fatally shot while meeting President-elect Franklin Delano Roosevelt in Miami's Bayfront Park. The assassin, Giuseppe Zangara, suffering health and probably mental problems, claims to be an anarchist attempting to kill Roosevelt, but some speculate, unconvincingly, that Zangara had made a deal with the Chicago Syndicate and that Cermak was the intended target.

– Two men, one wearing a messenger's uniform, rob the Corn Exchange Bank branch at 28 South Sixtieth Street in Philadelphia. Willie "The Actor" Sutton and John Eagen are suspected.

February 20—Three men rob the Farmers State Bank at Shiro, Texas, of $4,500 in cash and bonds. Later attributed to Clyde Barrow.

– John Eagen, former partner of Willie Sutton, is shot to death with girlfriend Dorothy Miller and bartender Mike "Patsy" Griffin in "Porky" Murray's speakeasy at 267 West Fifty-second Street in New York.

February 24—Thomas "Buck" Woulfe, captured North Kansas City bank robber, is moved from the Clay County Jail to St. Luke's Hospital in Kansas City, Missouri, suffering from a badly infected groin wound that will prove fatal. He is returned to the Clay County Jail the next day.

February 27—Tom "Skeet" Bradshaw and others rob the state bank at Chetopa, Kansas, of $1,300.

March 2—Charles Boettcher II is released unharmed, and Verne Sankey and Gordon Alcorn collect a $60,000 ransom in Denver, as promised by the victim's father.

March 9—In a one-day trial in Florida, Giuseppe Zangara is convicted of the murder of Chicago Mayor Anton Cermak.

March 20—Zangara is executed.

March 22—"Buck" Barrow is released from the state prison at Huntsville, Texas, and with his wife, Blanche, joins Clyde Barrow, Bonnie Parker, and W. D. Jones in Ft. Smith, Arkansas.

March 24—Gangsters in two cars wage a machine-gun battle at Broadway and Eighty-first Street in New York. Attributed to warfare between "Waxey" Gordon and a coalition, including Charles "Lucky" Luciano and Louis "Lepke" Buchalter.

April 3—Three men with machine guns rob the Adkins-Beck Co. in Dallas of $1,500.

April 4—The Barker-Karpis Gang robs the First National Bank at Fairbury, Nebraska, of $151,350. Gang member Earl Christman is mortally wounded and later secretly buried by the gang in a dry creek bed somewhere near Kansas City.

April 11—Bank robber Thomas "Buck" Woulfe dies of his groin infection in the Clay County Jail infirmary at Liberty, Missouri.

April 12—Nineteen-year-old Jerome Factor apparently is kidnapped by gangsters outside a Lunt Street apartment building in Chicago, where he lives with his mother. Jerome's father is John "Jake the Barber" Factor, a former Capone associate and international confidence man wanted in England for a $7 million stock swindle. Jake Factor turns to the Chicago Syndicate for help.

– At the Carteret Hotel in Elizabeth, New Jersey, "Big Maxey" Greenberg and Mandel Gassell, alias Max Hassell, lieutenants of New York's leading bootlegger, Irving Wexler, alias "Waxey" Gordon, are shot to death by rival gangsters. Gordon, under indictment for income tax evasion, escapes death by leaping out the window of an adjoining room. Police attribute the killings to the "Dutch" Schultz mob.

April 13—The Barrow Gang murders Detective Harry McGinnis and Constable J. Wesley Harryman while escaping from a rented house at 3347 Oakridge Drive in Joplin, Missouri.

– Two bandits rob the Union Savings Bank in St. Charles, Missouri.

April 15—Chicago police first learn of Jerome Factor's disappearance. Jake "The Barber" Factor releases a letter, purported to have come from his son's abductors, demanding $50,000 for Jerome's return.

April 19—The Chicago Association of Commerce disbands the Chicago Crime Commission's "Secret Six" anticrime group.

April 21—Jerome Factor is released unexpectedly by his kidnappers, who put him out of a car on West Devon Avenue in Chicago. According to his father, no ransom has been paid.

April 27—H. D. Darby and Sophia Stone are taken hostage and terrorized by the Barrow Gang at Ruston, Louisiana. They are released later unharmed at Magnolia, Arkansas.

April 28—"Killer" Schmidt, "Gloomy Gus" Schafer, and others rob a U.S. Mail car at Salt Lake City, Utah, of $15,500.

– The Barrow Gang is suspected of robbing a gas station at Broken Bow, Oklahoma, stealing only a few dollars but brutally beating the attendant.

May—Union officials Fred Sass and Morris Goldberg, reputed Syndicate gangsters, are apparently kidnapped in Chicago. The Touhy gang is suspected.

– Blue Island, Illinois, gambler James Hackett is kidnapped for the second time by the "Handsome Jack" Klutas Gang and released after payment of $1,500 in ransom.

May 10—John Herbert Dillinger, who has served nine years in Indiana prisons for attempted robbery, is paroled by Governor Paul V. McNutt, but his actual release date is May 22.

May 12—A female bandit wounds two female bystanders with automatic rifle fire in an attempted bank robbery at Lucerne, Indiana. The Barrow Gang is suspected.

– A Paragon, Indiana, bank is robbed. Later many will attribute this crime to John Dillinger, who was still in prison at the time.

May 15—Chicago gangster Rocco "The Crazy Barber" Belcastro [not James "Bomber" Belcastro], once a St. Valentine's Day Massacre suspect, is found shot to death in a parked car on Carroll Street, about a mile from the Loop.

May 19—Two men and two women rob the First State Bank at Okabena, Minnesota, taking $1,400. Floyd Strain, Anthony Strain, and Alice "Stormy" Cosier will be convicted later of this crime, though the actual robbers may have been the Barrow Gang.

May 20—Homer Van Meter, a prison friend of John Dillinger, is paroled from Indiana's state prison at Michigan City.

– The U.S. commissioner at Dallas, Texas, files a federal complaint against Clyde Barrow and Bonnie Parker, charging them with interstate transportation of a stolen car. The Barrow Gang are now federal fugitives under the Dyer Act.

May 21—U.S. marshals arrest "Waxey" Gordon at a hunting lodge in White Plains, New York.

May 22—John Dillinger is released from Indiana state prison and arrives at his home in Mooresville, Indiana, resentful that the delay caused him to miss being with his dying stepmother who had raised him since childhood.

May 25—Four men rob the Lowell National Bank at Lowell, Indiana, of $5,000. Local legend will later wrongly attribute this crime to John Dillinger.

May 27–28—Mary McElroy, daughter of City Manager Henry McElroy, is kidnapped from her home in Kansas City, Missouri, by a gang who demands $60,000 in ransom. They settle for half that amount and release Miss McElroy unharmed.

May 27—Ford Bradshaw is acquitted of the Henryetta, Oklahoma, bank robbery but held for Muskogee County authorities who want him for murder.

May 29—One policeman is killed and another wounded in a $2,000 bank robbery at Rensselaer, New York. The crime is erroneously attributed to "Pretty Boy" Floyd. Later, Leonard Scarnici, a freelance New York hit man, will confess to this murder and thirteen others, including that of Vincent "Mad Dog" Coll, and will be convicted and executed.

May 30—Eleven convicts, including Harvey Bailey, Wilbur Underhill, and "Big Bob" Brady, stage a mass breakout from state prison at Lansing, Kansas, taking hostage the warden and two guards who later are released unharmed. The U.S. Bureau of Investigation suspects that the guns used in the escape were furnished from the outside by Bailey's friend Frank Nash.

May 31—Night policeman Otto L. Durkee is found shot to death at Chetopa, Kansas. Wilbur Underhill is suspected.

—The Bank of Chelsea at Chelsea, Oklahoma, is robbed of $2,800 by six men. Police suspect Eddie "Newt" Clanton and Clarence and Otis Eno of the Bradshaw Gang, though some witnesses identify Wilbur Underhill as one of the robbers.

— H. D. Bradbury and Jim Stribling escape from the state prison at McAlester, Oklahoma.

June 1—Three gunmen battle Police Chief Bob Lafollette at Siloam Springs, Arkansas, after stealing a car and leaving behind another stolen from Lansing, Kansas.

— Miami, Oklahoma, gas station operator Jeff Weatherby is abducted and robbed by four men, one of whom he will later identify as Wilbur Underhill.

— Oklahoma escapees H. D. Bradbury and Jim Stribling are recaptured near Stuart, Oklahoma.

June 2—Walter McGee is captured in Amarillo, Texas, and Clarence Click is captured in Kansas City. McGee, his brother George, Clarence Click and, later, Clarence Stevens, will be convicted under Missouri state law of kidnapping Mary McElroy. Walter McGee will be sentenced to death but the sentence will be commuted. The others will receive long terms in the Missouri state prison at Jefferson City.

— Abe Durst, former chauffeur of mobster "Waxey" Gordon, is found shot to death in a stolen car in the Morris Park section of the Bronx.

June 4—Frank Sawyer, one of the Bailey-Underhill escape party, is recaptured near Chickasha, Oklahoma.

— John Dillinger, William Shaw, and Noble Claycomb rob an Indianapolis supermarket of $100.

— William "Big Bill" Oppenheim, a lieutenant of "Waxey" Gordon, is killed by gunmen at his apartment in Paterson, New Jersey.

June 6—Two bandits rob the First State Bank at Bokchito, Oklahoma, of $1,400.

June 10—John Dillinger and two other men rob the National Bank at New Carlisle, Ohio, of $10,600. Later in the day, with William Shaw and Paul "Lefty" Parker, Dillinger robs Haag's Drugstore and a supermarket in Indianapolis.

— The Barrow Gang wreck their car near Wellington, Texas, and Bonnie Parker is badly burned. The gang takes a farm family hostage, shoot a woman in the hand, and later escape by kidnapping two law officers who are released unharmed at Erick, Oklahoma.

— Two more of the Kansas escapees, Cliff Dopson and Billie Woods, are recaptured near Grand Junction, Texas.

June 12—Three men rob the State Bank of Bussey at Bussey, Iowa, of $8,126. One bandit, Tony Bonacino, wanted for a 1931 Kansas City bank robbery, is slain by a posse five miles west of Bussey, near Marysville, Iowa. Two possemen, Emmet Godfrey of Marysville and Pudd Ballard of Pershing, are wounded. The other two robbers, believed to be Italians, kidnap a coal mine operator about two miles south of Bussey and force him to drive them to the outskirts of Kansas City. Iowa's new police radio network is used for the first time to broadcast descriptions of the Bussey bank robbers.

June 14—The Farmers & Merchants Bank at Mexico, Missouri, is robbed of $1,628 by two men believed to be "Pretty Boy" Floyd and Adam Richetti. On same day Sheriff Roger Wilson and Highway Patrolman Ben Booth are murdered near Columbia, Missouri. The double murder will be wrongly attributed to Floyd and Richetti; Barrow Gang also is wrongly suspected.

June 15–18—St. Paul brewer William A. Hamm Jr., is kidnapped by the Barker-Karpis Gang and held for $100,000 ransom at the Bensenville, Illinois, home of local postmaster Edmund Bartholmey. He is released unharmed upon payment. Police suspect Verne Sankey, the kidnapper of Haskell Bohn and Charles Boettcher II.

June 16—"Pretty Boy" Floyd and Adam Richetti kidnap Sheriff William Killingsworth at Bolivar, Missouri. They abandon his car near Clinton, Missouri, and steal another one driven by Walter Griffith, who also is taken hostage. Both men are released unharmed that night at Lee's Summit, near Kansas City.

– At Hot Springs, Arkansas, agents of the U.S. Bureau of Investigation, accompanied by Chief of Police Orrin "Otto" Reed of McAlester, Oklahoma, arrest notorious bank robber and Leavenworth escapee Frank Nash.

– The Bailey-Underhill Gang robs the First National Bank at Black Rock, Arkansas, of $6,000.

June 17—At the Union Station in Kansas City, Missouri, criminals armed with machine guns attack lawmen in an attempt to free Frank Nash from federal custody. Special Agent Raymond J. Caffrey of the U.S. Bureau of Investigation; Chief Orrin Reed of McAlester, Oklahoma; and Kansas City Police Detectives William J. Grooms and Frank Hermanson are killed, as is Nash himself. Numerous witnesses identify the killers as Verne Miller, Harvey Bailey, Wilbur Underhill, and "Big Bob" Brady. The Bureau of Investigation at first blames the mass murder, known as the Kansas City Massacre, on the Bailey-Underhill Gang but later attributes it to Verne Miller, "Pretty Boy" Floyd, and Adam Richetti.

June 21—On Wheeler Avenue in the Bronx, Lottie Kreisberger Coll and accomplices Joseph Ventre and Alfred Guarino shoot at loanshark Izzy Moroh in an attempted holdup. Moroh escapes, but a young woman named Millie Schwartz is fatally wounded by a stray bullet. Lottie Coll is the widow of Vincent "Mad Dog" Coll and is wanted for several recent holdups.

June 22—Two men, suspected to be Clyde and "Buck" Barrow, rob the Commercial Bank in Alma, Arkansas, of $3,600.

June 23—The Barrow Gang robs a store in Fayetteville, Arkansas, and murders Marshal Henry Humphrey of Alma.

– Lottie Coll, Joseph Ventre, and Alfred Guarino are arrested by New York police at a West Forty-third Street hotel.

June 24—John Dillinger and William Shaw attempt to rob Marshall Field's Thread Mill at Monticello, Indiana. Dillinger wounds manager Fred Fisher. That night they rob a fruit market at Tenth and Belfountain in Indianapolis.

June 27—Lottie Coll and her accomplices are indicted for murder and robbery by a Bronx County grand jury. Authorities speculate Lottie has been trying to raise funds and recruit a gang to avenge the murder of her husband, Vincent "Mad Dog" Coll.

June 29—John Dillinger and William Shaw rob a sandwich shop on East Twenty-eighth Street in Indianapolis.

June 30—Alice Schiffer Diamond, widow of murdered gangster "Legs" Diamond, is found shot to death in the kitchen of her home at 1641 Ocean Avenue in Brooklyn. Alice had reportedly been

The Kansas City Massacre

As the temperature rose steadily on the sunny Saturday morning of June 17,1933, longtime bank bandit and prison escapee Frank Nash was being returned to Leavenworth by several police officers and federal agents after his recapture at Hot Springs, Arkansas. Nash and the others were climbing into two cars in the parking lot of Kansas City's Union Station when two men, possibly three, with submachine guns approached from different directions, one of them shouting "Up! Up! Up!" In the next minute or so, three officers, a federal agent, and Nash himself were dead, and the gunmen—including Verne Miller, a former sheriff turned outlaw—had escaped.

MARCH of EVENTS Herald and Examiner SCREEN and RADIO

CRIME— America's Danger and Disgrace —END IT!

Graphic Illustration By JAMES MONTGOMERY FLAGG From Description By Eye-Witnesses

Kansas City Massacre

A bungled attempt to rescue bank robber Frank Nash led to the Kansas City Massacre of June 17, 1933, the arming of Justice Department agents, and set the stage for the federal government's "War on Crime."

Any number of books and articles have recounted the Kansas City Massacre, which did much to launch J. Edgar Hoover's FBI. The Division of Investigation (as it was called at that time) laboriously and selectively presented the popular account, which largely has been accepted as gospel. The gist of it is that when the news of Nash's arrest reached Miller, he advised John Lazia, an "underboss" for Kansas City's corrupt political leader Tom Pendergast. Lazia declined to put his own hoods at risk in a rescue attempt, and Miller had to recruit Adam Richetti and "Pretty Boy" Floyd, who were passing through town and were conveniently camped at his house. The attackers opened up with submachine guns and killed Nash in the battle that followed.

Chicago Daily Tribune

FINAL

2 CENTS PAY NO MORE!

U.S. AGENTS FIGHT DESPERADO

Verne Miller Flees Trap on Sheridan Road

U. S. QUESTIONS JUDGE'S SON ON SALARY BOOSTS

Woodward Jr. Tells of Law Career.

SELF GOVERNING BUSINESS GROUP URGED FOR U. S.

Swope Offers Plan to Supplant NRA.

NEWS SUMMARY

ILLINOIS HOUSE REJECTS RELIEF BONDS 2D TIME

Seven Votes Short of Requirement.

DON'T TRUST HIM TOO FAR, LADY

That is the official story. Recently uncovered in bits and pieces from thousands of pages of FBI documents, but described most thoroughly by Robert Unger in his book *Union Station Massacre,* is evidence that the FBI's account is based more on speculation, perhaps even perjury (survivors could not initially identify Floyd or Richetti), to give the bureau the excuse it needed to carry firearms and make arrests without local deputization—and to go after Floyd and Richetti.

Miller's body was later found outside Detroit, killed by fellow criminals never definitely identified and for reasons never definitely established, beyond the fact that he was a loose cannon who had managed to antagonize hoodlums in a dozen cities. Floyd and Richetti, soon named as suspects in the massacre, had gone into deep hiding around Buffalo, New York, and managed to elude federal and state authorities for about a year and a half. Economic necessity eventually forced them to seek "work," probably with Dillinger in what would prove to be that gang's last bank holdup, at South Bend, Indiana, and the end of a plan to join Dillinger in a mail-train holdup said to have been arranged by Jimmy Murray (supposedly the same train he had gone to prison for robbing in 1924 [see p. 150].

Dillinger was killed in Chicago on July 22, 1934. Three months later, Floyd and Richetti were spotted by Ohio authorities, who captured Richetti after a gunfight and then called in agents from Chicago. The group was driving around the countryside when they stumbled onto

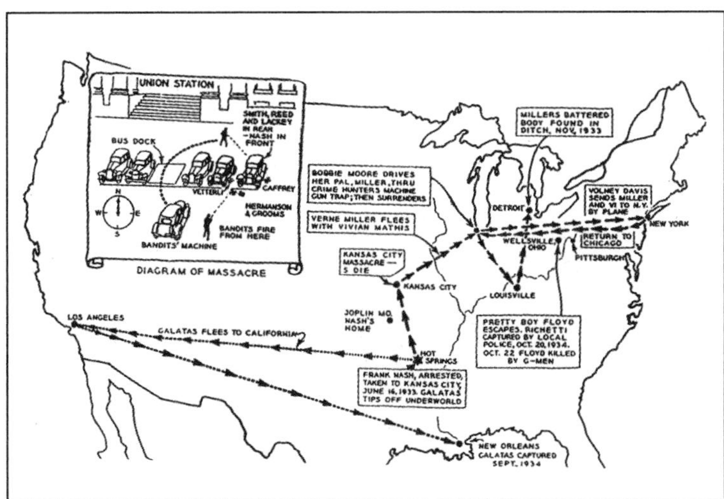

With three officers and one of its agents killed at Kansas City, the Justice Department launched a nationwide manhunt for the machine-gunners, one of whom was Verne Miller, who managed to escape a federal trap in Chicago (above right).

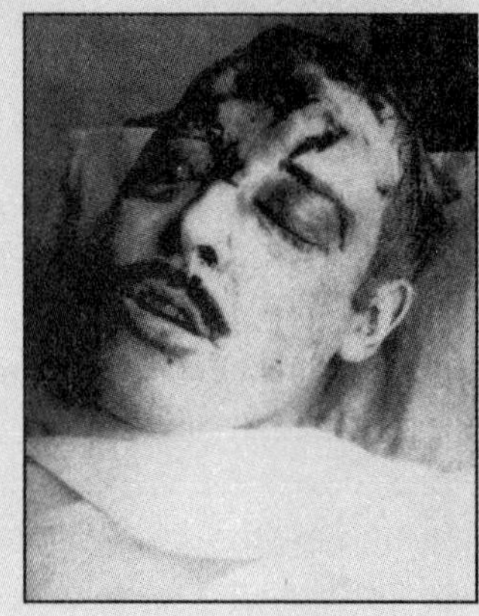

"Pretty Boy" Floyd and Adam Richetti agreed to help Verne Miller rescue bank robber Frank Nash from officers at Kansas City's Union Station in June 1933. Nash (above right) was killed in the shootout, Miller (right) was beaten to death in Detroit by other mobsters the following November, and Floyd (above left) was killed by G-men in Ohio in October 1934. Richetti (above center) claimed he was too hungover to participate in the massacre but still was executed.

and because they believed they could rescue Nash without a fight, not reckoning on the panicky G-man with the quirky Model 1897 Winchester shotgun who may have set off the battle inadvertently. (Some of the ball bearings reportedly were found in the body of his fellow agent, Raymond Caffrey.)

Two other underworld stories circulated, but without much foundation. One was that Miller did not lead the mission to free Nash but to silence him; the other was that Miller, angry that Nash made no effort to escape, shot him, too. Those accounts were circulated second- and third-hand by puzzled underworld characters unaware that Nash may already have been dead from the backseat shotgun, which is largely ignored in available FBI accounts.

The massacre survivors and several witnesses who originally could not identify the attackers became more certain with time, and Richetti was executed in 1938—insisting to the end he was innocent. Technically that may have been true, but through no fault of his own.

Floyd literally by accident and killed him as he fled across a field [see p. 423].

Examined at a mortuary, Floyd's shoulder bore no scars from a wound he supposedly had received in the Kansas City shooting. Worse for the FBI, the captured Nash, as well as one or both of the officers may have been hit by a federal agent sitting behind Nash in the back seat of one of the two cars, firing wildly, and not by the attackers. The agent was trying desperately to work the action of an unfamiliar 16-gauge shotgun loaded with steel ball bearings instead of the customary lead buckshot.

Underworld rumors nevertheless held that one of the shooters was Floyd, who had agreed to join Miller only because Richetti was too hungover from a night of drinking claiming that she knew her husband's killers and also had been target-shooting in her yard with a pistol.

June 30-July 1—Jake "The Barber" Factor, whose son apparently was kidnapped in April, is seized by a carload of gunmen outside The Dells roadhouse on Dempster near the Chicago suburb of Morton Grove, according to his bodyguards. Captain Daniel "Tubbo" Gilbert, chief investigator for the Cook County state's attorney's office and secretly on the Chicago Syndicate's payroll, says the crime is real and blames Des Plaines gangster Roger Touhy. (Touhy is a rival of the Syndicate in bootlegging and labor racketeering and a brother of mail robber "Terrible Tommy" Touhy.) Some attribute the abduction to the College Kidnappers who specialize in "snatching" underworld figures. The British consul and others suggest that the kidnapping is a hoax intended to prevent Factor's extradition to England where he faces a possible twenty-four-year prison sentence for a massive stock fraud.

July 3—The Bailey-Underhill Gang robs the First National Bank at Clinton, Oklahoma, of $3,000.

July 6—Investigating the Kansas City Massacre, Sheriff Thomas Bash, accompanied by deputies and agents of the U.S. Bureau of Investigation, raids the Kansas City home of gangster Frank "Fritz" Mulloy and arrests James "Fur" Sammons of Chicago. Sammons is a Syndicate mobster wanted in Chicago, Philadelphia, and Baltimore for fur and payroll robberies. He later will receive a life sentence in Indiana as an habitual criminal.

July 8—The Barrow Gang robs a National Guard armory in Enid, Oklahoma, stealing forty-six Colt .45-caliber automatics.

July 9—Willie "The Actor" Sutton, Eddie Wilson, and Joe Perlongo rob the Corn Exchange Bank at 100th Street and Broadway in New York of $23,838.

July 12—Jake "The Barber" Factor reappears in LaGrange, Illinois, and claims to have been released by his kidnappers after payment by his wife of $70,000 ransom.

July 14—Two of the Kansas state prison escapees, Kenneth Conn and Alva "Sonny" Payton, attempt to rob the Labette County State Bank at Altamont, Kansas. Conn is killed in a gun battle, and Payton, shot in the eyes and blinded, is captured.

July 15—John Dillinger, Harry Copeland, and William Shaw rob the Bide-a-Wee tavern in Muncie, Indiana.

July 16—William Shaw, Paul "Lefty" Parker, and Noble Claycomb are captured by police at their Muncie apartment. John Dillinger and Harry Copeland escape. Identified by Claycomb as "Dan Dillinger," John attains his first Indiana newspaper notoriety as "Desperate Dan."

July 17—John Dillinger and Harry Copeland rob the Commercial Bank in Daleville, Indiana, of $3,500, with some estimates higher.

July 18—The Barrow Gang robs three gas stations in Fort Dodge, Iowa. One of the stations was also robbed on May 16, allegedly by "Buck" Barrow.

July 19—An attempt by two men to rob the Rockville National Bank at Rockville, Indiana, is disrupted by employee Rolland Crays, who fires on the robbers with a revolver. One robber slugs and disarms Crays, and the two men escape with the gun and about $50. The robbers are subsequently identified as John Dillinger and Harry Copeland.

– The Barrow Gang is surrounded by police at the Red Crown Cabin Camp, at Ferrelview, near Platte City, Missouri, but shoot their way out, wounding three men. "Buck" and Blanche Barrow are also wounded but escape with the others to Iowa.

– Roger Touhy, union official Eddie "Chicken" McFadden, and bodyguards "Gloomy Gus" Schafer and "Wee Willie" Sharkey are involved in a traffic accident at Elkhorn, Wisconsin. Several guns, including a pistol converted to fire full-automatic, are found in their car. The Touhy men are arrested, turned over to Captain Gilbert of the Cook County state's attorney's office, and then to Melvin Purvis of the U.S. Bureau of Investigation, which charges them with the kidnappings of William Hamm and Jake "The Barber" Factor. [Their "full-auto" pistol and others like it probably came from San Antonio gunsmith H. S. Lebman, 111 South Flores, who also supplied such modified guns to "Baby Face" Nelson, a friend of the Touhys.]

July 22—Oklahoma City oilman Charles F. Urschel is kidnapped from the porch of his mansion by "Machine Gun" Kelly and Albert Bates. Urschel is transported to the Paradise, Texas, ranch of Kelly's stepfather-in-law, Robert "Boss" Shannon. A $200,000 ransom is demanded.

July 24—The Barrow Gang is surrounded by a posse at Dexfield Park, north of Dexter, Iowa. "Buck" and Blanche Barrow are captured. Clyde Barrow, Bonnie Parker, and W. D. Jones escape.

— After being arraigned on a bank robbery charge at the Chicago Criminal Courts Building, John Scheck breaks free of his guards and fatally shoots policeman John Sevick. Wounded by a bailiff, Scheck is recaptured and a revolver confiscated. Scheck will later claim the gun was smuggled to him in jail by "Pretty Boy" Floyd.

July 29—"Buck" Barrow dies of a head wound in a Perry, Iowa, hospital.

July 30—E. E. Kirkpatrick, representing the Urschel family, delivers $200,000 to "Machine Gun" Kelly near the La Salle Hotel in Kansas City, Missouri. He later authors a book about the kidnapping titled *Crime's Paradise*.

July 31—Charles F. Urschel is released unharmed at Norman, Oklahoma.

August—Using wiretaps, federal agents overhear conversations between Jake "The Barber" Factor and two other men who threaten to kidnap Factor again unless an additional ransom of $50,000 is paid.

August 4—John Dillinger and Harry Copeland rob the First National Bank at Montpelier, Indiana, of $10,110.

— An attractive blonde woman and two male accomplices rob James Swock's shoe store at 4050 North Avenue in Chicago. Forty-five minutes later, the same trio robs Gustav Hoeh's haberdashery at 5948 West Division, killing Hoeh. One of the gunmen is wounded. Newspapers dub the female bandit "The Blonde Tigress."

August 5—Wounded gunman Leo Minneci, alias Joe Miller, surrenders to Chicago police in front of the Bell Telephone Co. at Madison Street and Homan Boulevard. He confesses to the robberies of the previous day and identifies his accomplices as Eleanor Jarman and her lover, George Dale, alias Kennedy, and blames the murder of Gustav Hoeh on Dale.

— With no cooperative witnesses and little evidence to connect him to murder charges, authorities in Muskogee County, Oklahoma, release Ford Bradshaw on $4,000 bond provided by his father.

August 8—James Kirkland and Maurice Lanham rob the Peoples Bank in Gravel Switch, Kentucky, of $1,200, and later name John Dillinger as their accomplice.

August 9—The Bailey-Underhill Gang robs the Peoples National Bank at Kingfisher, Oklahoma, of $6,024.

— Eleanor Jarman, "The Blonde Tigress," and George Dale are arrested by Chicago police in an apartment at 6323 South Drexel Avenue. Witnesses identify them and Leo Minneci as the perpetrators of at least thirty-seven Chicago robberies. They later confess to forty-eight robberies. Chicago police describe Eleanor Jarman as "the brains of the three" and "a beautiful but vicious animal" who cruelly slugged shopkeepers with a blackjack.

August 10—The Prohibition Bureau is moved from the Treasury Department to the Justice Department where it joins the Bureau of Investigation; the two agencies are renamed the Division of Investigation.

August 10—The district attorney at Elkhorn, Wisconsin, files a complaint against Roger Touhy, Eddie McFadden, Gus Schafer, and Willie Sharkey charging them with unlawful possession of a machine gun "for offensive and aggressive purposes."

August 12—Roger Touhy, Eddie McFadden, Gus Schafer, and Willie Sharkey are indicted in St. Paul for the Hamm kidnapping. Though innocent of this crime, Schafer and Sharkey also are wanted for mail and bank robberies.

— At Paradise, Texas, police and agents of the Division of Investigation, accompanied by Charles

Urschel, raid the Paradise, Texas, ranch of Kathryn Kelly's stepfather, Robert "Boss" Shannon. The Kellys and Albert Bates have fled, but Shannon, his wife Ora, their son Armon and his wife, and bank robber Harvey Bailey all are arrested and charged with the Urschel kidnapping. Bailey, also wanted for the Kansas City Massacre, is innocent of the kidnapping but possesses some ransom money given him by "Machine Gun" Kelly to repay a loan. [Kelly apparently acquires his nickname "Machine Gun" courtesy of J. Edgar Hoover after federal agents trace the Tommygun seized at the ranch to a Fort Worth pawn shop whose owner identifies Kathryn Kelly as its purchaser.]

– Albert Bates, Kelly's partner, is arrested in Denver for passing forged checks.

August 14—John Dillinger, Harry Copeland, and Sam Goldstine [usually but mistakenly spelled Goldstein] rob the Citizens National Bank at Bluffton, Ohio, of $2,100, with some estimates higher.

– Dillinger associates Fred Breman and Clifford "Whitey" Mohler are arrested by Indiana State Police officers at East Chicago.

August 15—Some 300 police and federal agents stake out Mannheim Road near Chicago to trap two men demanding $50,000 in ransom from Jake "The Barber" Factor. The pair, Basil "The Owl" Banghart and Charles "Ice Wagon" Connors, succeed in retrieving a package containing $500 in marked money and escape after a gun battle. Banghart and Connors are alleged members of the Touhy mob.

August 18—Eddie Bentz, "Baby Face" Nelson, and others rob the Peoples Savings Bank at Grand Haven, Michigan, of $30,000. One gang member, Earl Doyle, is captured. John Dillinger is also [but wrongly] suspected of participating in this robbery.

August 22—Dillinger Gang member Sam Goldstine is arrested by Indiana State Police officers in Gary.

August 27—Police invade the Western Open golf tournament at Chicago's Olympia Fields and arrest one of the players, "Machine Gun" Jack McGurn, on a vagrancy warrant, crippling the out-of-work gunman's career as a professional golfer. Heat from the St. Valentine's Day Massacre has rendered McGurn useless to the Chicago Syndicate, now headed by Frank Nitti. Under Nitti, the Outfit is being purged of many Capone loyalists who might present a threat to his leadership.

August 28—"Pretty Boy" Floyd and Adam Richetti are suspected of a $1,000 bank robbery at Galena, Missouri.

August 30—The Barker-Karpis Gang robs Stockyards National Bank messengers of $33,000 at the South St. Paul Post Office, killing one policeman and wounding another.

– William "Whitey" Walker, Irvin "Blackie" Thompson, and Roy Johnson escape from the state prison at McAlester, Oklahoma, when allowed outside to go fishing.

– Eleanor Jarman, George Dale, and Leo Minneci are convicted of murder in Chicago. Dale is sentenced to death, and Jarman and Minneci received 199 years.

September 3—At Platte City, Missouri, Blanche Barrow is sentenced to ten years in prison for assaulting police officers.

September 4—Harvey Bailey escapes from Dallas County Jail at Dallas, Texas. He is recaptured the same day at Ardmore, Oklahoma.

September 6—John Dillinger, Harry Copeland, and Hilton Crouch rob the State Bank of Massachusetts Avenue in Indianapolis of $24,800.

September 11—Eight masked gunmen rob Railway Express Co. employees in St. Paul of two cash boxes containing between $60,000 and $100,000. Suspects include the Touhys and the Barker-Karpis Gang.

September 12—John Dillinger is suspected in a $24,000 bank robbery at Farrell, Pennsylvania.

September 13—Homer Van Meter, Tommy Carroll, Tommy Gannon, and Charles Fisher rob the Union State Bank in Amery, Wisconsin, of $46,000 in cash and securities.

September 15—Joseph "Red" O'Riordan, long sought as the leader of a Detroit kidnapping gang, is captured by police at a South Reno Street apartment house in Los Angeles.

September 20—The Bradshaw Gang robs the First National Bank at York, Nebraska, of $9,000.

September 21—Kansas authorities reveal that Peggy Landon, daughter of Governor Alfred Landon, is under police protection because of a kidnapping plot allegedly hatched against her by Oklahoma outlaws. The kidnapping scheme supposedly is an attempt to force the governor to grant executive clemency to the Harvey Bailey-Wilbur Underhill Gang.

— Four masked machine-gunners rob the Farmers State Bank at Hays, Kansas, and escape after a long and involved flight that included the theft of one stolen car after another and the abductions of twelve people.

September 22—The Barker-Karpis Gang, driving a bulletproof car equipped with smokescreen and oil-slick devices, robs Federal Reserve Bank messengers on Jackson Boulevard in Chicago, wreck their car, and in escaping kill patrolman Miles A. Cunningham. The crime is blamed on "Machine Gun" Kelly, Verne Miller, "Pretty Boy" Floyd, and others who had nothing to do with it. The "take" consists only of cancelled checks.

— John Dillinger is arrested by police at the Dayton apartment of his girlfriend, Mary Longnaker.

— Wilbur Underhill and others rob the Peoples National Bank in Stuttgart, Arkansas, of $1,000.

September 24—After police track the Barker-Karpis car to dealer Joe Bergl in Cicero and learn that his business partner is Chicago mobster Gus Winkeler, both are questioned in connection with the Jackson Boulevard robbery and murder. Police claim that Winkeler, "Machine Gun" Kelly, Verne Miller, Claude Maddox, and James "Fur" Sammons are members of a nationwide robbery and kidnapping syndicate.

September 25—Clyde Barrow and Bonnie Parker rob a grocery store at McKinney, Texas, taking the grocer hostage. He is released unharmed the same day.

— Near Collinsville, Illinois, bootleggers assault Prohibition agents, free a captured confederate, and disable the agents' car with machine-gun fire.

September 26—"Machine Gun" Kelly and his wife, Kathryn, are arrested in Memphis by police and agents of the Division of Investigation.

— Harry Pierpont, Charles Makley, John Hamilton, Russell Clark, Ed Shouse, Walter Detrich, James "Oklahoma Jack" Clark, Joseph Fox, Joseph Burns, and James Jenkins escape from the state prison at Michigan City, Indiana, using guns, smuggled to them by John Dillinger before his arrest in Dayton, Ohio.

September 28—Michigan City escapee James Clark is recaptured in Hammond, Indiana.

— John Dillinger is transferred to the Allen County Jail at Lima, Ohio, and charged with the Bluffton bank robbery.

September 30—Michigan City escapee James Jenkins is killed by vigilantes near Beanblossum, Indiana.

— Harvey Bailey, Albert Bates, and the Shannon family are convicted of participating in the Urschel kidnapping.

— Minneapolis crime bosses Isadore "Kid Cann" Blumenfeld, Sam Kronick, and Sam Kozberg are acquitted of passing the Urschel ransom money, but their lieutenants, Clifford Skelly and Edward "Barney" Berman, are convicted. These are the first convictions obtained under the federal Lindbergh Law.

October 2—Five gunmen rob the Washington Square Branch of the Brookline Trust Co. at Brookline, Massachusetts, of $20,000.

October 3—Harry Pierpont, Charles Makley, John Hamilton, and Russell Clark rob the First National Bank at St. Marys, Ohio, of $14,000.

October 6—"Big Bob" Brady and Jim Clark, former members of the Bailey-Underhill Gang, rob a Frederick, Oklahoma, bank of $5,000 but are captured the same day, near Tucumcari, New Mexico.

— William "Whitey" Walker, Irvin "Blackie" Thompson, and Roy Johnson rob the Buckholts State Bank at Buckholts, Texas, of $3,000.

— Edgar Lebensberger, colleague of Chicago mobster Gus Winkeler and manager of Winkeler's 225 Club, is found shot to death in the bedroom of his home at 1253 Lake Shore Drive. His death is ruled a suicide, but friends believe he was murdered. [Federal prosecutor Dwight Green stated at the time that Lebensberger was right-handed but was shot in the left side of the head and that there were no powder burns.]

October 7—Harvey Bailey, Albert Bates, and Robert and Ora Shannon receive life sentences for the Urschel kidnapping. Armon Shannon receives ten years probation. The money changers, Berman and Skelly, are sentenced to five years apiece.

— Dallas County Deputy Thomas Manion and Grover C. Bevill are convicted of aiding the escape of Harvey Bailey from the Dallas County Jail. Manion is sentenced to two years in Leavenworth and fined $10,000. Bevill is sentenced to fourteen months.

October 9—Chicago's Gus Winkeler, former Syndicate gunman who has acquired increasing respectability as a North Side club owner, is shot to death, probably by Nitti gunmen, outside the Charles H. Weber Distributing Co. at 1414 Roscoe Street. (Verne Miller is initially suspected because Winkeler had been providing information to federal agent Melvin Purvis about Miller and other federal fugitives.)

— Chicago politician John J. "Boss" McLaughlin is charged with complicity in the disposal of $237,000 in stolen bonds from a December 1932 Loop mail robbery.

— Wilbur Underhill and Ed Davis are suspected of robbing the Farmers & Merchants Bank at Tryon, Oklahoma, of $550, but fingerprints found in the bank will disprove this. The American National Bank at Baxter Springs, Kansas, is robbed of $3,000 on the same day, and Underhill later will confess to this crime. Other suspects include Ford Bradshaw.

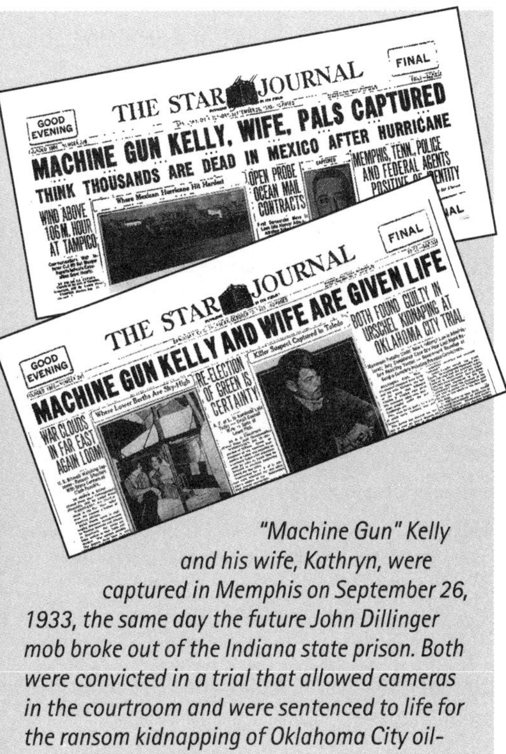

GOOD EVENING

THE STAR JOURNAL

FINAL

MACHINE GUN KELLY, WIFE, PALS CAPTURED

THINK THOUSANDS ARE DEAD IN MEXICO AFTER HURRICANE

WIND ABOVE 106M. HOUR AT TAMPICO

OPEN PROBE OCEAN MAIL CONTRACTS

MEMPHIS, TENN. POLICE AND FEDERAL AGENTS

GOOD EVENING

THE STAR JOURNAL

FINAL

MACHINE GUN KELLY AND WIFE ARE GIVEN LIFE

WAR CLOUDS IN FAR EAST AGAIN LOOM

RE-ELECTION OF GREEN IS CERTAINTY

BOTH FOUND GUILTY IN URSCHEL KIDNAPING AT OKLAHOMA CITY TRIAL

"Machine Gun" Kelly and his wife, Kathryn, were captured in Memphis on September 26, 1933, the same day the future John Dillinger mob broke out of the Indiana state prison. Both were convicted in a trial that allowed cameras in the courtroom and were sentenced to life for the ransom kidnapping of Oklahoma City oilman Charles Urschel.

– Two bandits, armed with a machine gun and a revolver, rob Second National Bank messengers at Warren, Ohio, of $68,000.

October 11—Wilbur Underhill and Ford Bradshaw are suspected in the $1,000 robbery of the International State Bank at Haskell, Oklahoma.

– Two men rob the Normandy State Bank in the St. Louis suburb of Normandy, taking about $7,000.

October 12—Harry Pierpont, Charles Makley, Russell Clark, John Hamilton, Ed Shouse, and Harry Copeland raid the Lima, Ohio, jail, kill Sheriff Jesse Sarber, and free John Dillinger. This group comprises the new Dillinger Gang. Lima authorities request assistance from the U.S. Department of Justice in identifying and apprehending the culprits.

– George and Kathryn Kelly are convicted of the Urschel kidnapping and sentenced to life.

October 13—Texas Senate passes a bill prohibiting the sale, lease, or gift of a machine gun to anyone other than law enforcement officers.

– Maurice Lanham is sentenced to eight years for the August robbery of a Gravel Switch, Kentucky, bank.

October 14—The Dillinger Gang robs a police station in Auburn, Indiana, stealing machine guns, other weapons and bulletproof vests.

– James Kirkland receives a ten- to fourteen-year sentence for his part in robbing of the Gravel Switch, Kentucky bank.

October 15—During his funeral, burglars break into the Lake Shore Drive apartment of murdered Chicago gangster Gus Winkeler and steal ten of his wife's furs, valued at $3,000.

October 17—Will Casey and Cassey Coleman are convicted of harboring "Machine Gun" and Kathryn Kelly. Casey is sentenced to two years in a federal penitentiary, Coleman gets a year and a day.

October 18—Two machine-gunners, identified as Irvin "Blackie" Thompson and William "Whitey" Walker, steal $5,000 from a farmers' community sale at the county fairgrounds in Stillwater, Oklahoma.

October 20—The Dillinger Gang obtains more weapons by robbing the police station in Peru, Indiana.

October 21—John C. Tichenor and Langford Ramsey are convicted in Memphis of harboring the Kellys. Each is sentenced to two and a half years in the federal penitentiary at Atlanta, Georgia.

October 22—Georgette Winkeler, widow of slain mobster Gus Winkeler, attempts to gas herself to death in her apartment at 3300 Lake Shore Drive in Chicago but is saved by her friend Bernice (Bonnie) Burke, the wife of Fred "Killer" Burke.

October 23—The Dillinger Gang robs the Central National Bank in Greencastle, Indiana, of $74,782.

– "Baby Face" Nelson, Homer Van Meter, Tommy Carroll, and others rob the First National Bank at Brainerd, Minnesota, of $32,000.

– Joseph "Red" Carson, "Aussie" Elliott, Eldon Wilson, and two others escape from the Osage County Jail at Pawhuska, Oklahoma.

October 24—The Dillinger Gang is wrongly suspected of a $5,000 bank robbery in South Bend, Indiana. The actual robbers will be apprehended later.

– The Bradshaw-Underhill Gang is suspected in the $6,135 robbery of the Merchants National Bank at Nebraska City, Nebraska.

October 26—Dillinger's daring robberies of banks and police stations prompts Indiana Governor Paul V. McNutt to call out the National Guard. The Dillinger Gang moves to Chicago.

– The "Whitey" Walker-"Blackie" Thompson Gang robs the Robinson State Bank at Palestine, Texas, of $5,500.

October 30—The First National Bank at Galena, Kansas, is robbed of $3,000. The Bradshaw-Underhill Gang is suspected.

November 1—Verne Miller, prime suspect in the Kansas City Massacre, shoots his way out of a trap set by federal agents at the Sherone Apartments, 4423 Sheridan Road, in Chicago's Uptown district.

November 2—Wilbur Underhill, Ford Bradshaw, and others rob the Citizens National Bank in Okmulgee, Oklahoma, of $13,000.

John Dillinger's Wooden-gun Jailbreak

One stunt more than any other made John Dillinger a legendary outlaw—the classic "trickster" of folklore. It resulted in eternal embarrassment for Crown Point, Indiana, especially the keepers of Lake County's supposedly escape-proof jail. In truth, Dillinger's use of a carved wooden pistol to stage one of the most audacious jailbreaks in history was the culmination of a carefully if desperately orchestrated plan hatched by friends in Chicago, which succeeded largely because at least two key individuals at the jail (and probably the warden) were bribed. Collusion was suspected at the time, but even revised accounts include major errors, such as the source of the bribe money and the celebrated "pistol," and what became of it later. This new information was not revealed until 1994, and if it substantially changes the story, it doesn't diminish Dillinger's crowd-pleasing performance.

While the nation's police searched desperately after his Crown Point jailbreak, John Dillinger simply went home to Mooresville, Indiana—the last place he expected anyone to look—and posed outside for pictures with family members and the wooden pistol he had used in making his escape.

The standard version is that the ever-resourceful bank robber used a razor blade to whittle a piece of washboard into something crudely resembling a small automatic, which he used to intimidate

In a rare instance of interstate cooperation, five governors banded together to form a "pact" offering a $15,000 reward for Dillinger with the unsubtle pronouncement: "Get him DEAD or alive."

several guards until he got his hands on the real thing, plus two Thompson submachine guns. Then, with the help of black inmate Herbert Youngblood, arrested for murder, the pair locked up some twenty-six people in different parts of the building, took two hostages, and motored leisurely in the direction of Peotone, Illinois, Dillinger waving his toy, cracking wise, and singing "Git along, li'l dogie, git along." When he dropped off Deputy Ernest Blunk and mechanic Ed Saager at a country crossroads, shook their hands and gave them a few dollars to get home, it was the slickest breakout the public had ever heard of. No shooting or casualties, except the political career of the prosecutor who had posed for pictures with his arm around Dillinger, the reputation of Sheriff Lillian Holley, and the civic image of Crown Point, which became a national laughingstock.

At the time of the escape there was good reason to suspect payoffs, and Blunk and another guard went back on their wooden-gun story only when state authorities brought them up on charges. Both beat the rap for lack of evidence. Later, the FBI, which could now enter the case because Dillinger had driven Sheriff Holley's car across a state line en route to Chicago (his only federal offense up to that point), officially declared the fake gun to have been a real one, though bureau files seem to accept the earlier version.

G. Russell Girardin, friend of Dillinger attorney Louis Piquett in 1935 and coauthor of *Dillinger: The Untold Story*, believed the G-men decided to accept the "smuggled gun" story mainly to embarrass Indiana State Police Chief Matt Leach, who was becoming ever more critical of their work on the case.

According to Girardin, then a young Chicago ad man who had met Piquett and his assistant, Arthur O'Leary, through a mutual friend, the Crown Point escape was a setup from start to finish. O'Leary was Piquett's connection with the East Chicago mob, headed by Sonny Sheetz, who controlled most of northern Indiana and in 1933 had helped Dillinger and his friends get their start. His price was a piece of some prearranged bank robberies, with inflated insurance claims that were shared with the bank officials in on the scheme.

When Dillinger was arrested in Tucson the following January and extradited to Indiana, his own escape plan was anything but subtle. He wanted his friends on the outside to hit the jail like commandos with dynamite, acetylene torches and plenty of machine-gun fire to intimidate the locals. Piquett, via O'Leary and girlfriend Evelyn Frechette, posing as Mrs. Dillinger, managed to convince him that he could as easily take Cuba, what with all the farm-boy National Guardsmen eager to try out their water-cooled machine gun and BARs (Browning Automatic Rifles). That of course, didn't mean a breakout couldn't be arranged, and without a bloodbath, if he could come up with enough money.

Dillinger complained to Piquett that the Tucson cops had seized all his loot as evidence. However, his old prison buddy, Homer Van Meter, was then linked up with the "Baby Face" Nelson Gang, and through Piquett he managed to cut a deal. Dillinger had no use for the cranky, trigger-happy Nelson, but Van Meter and John Hamilton persuaded the Nelson group that Dillinger would give them some badly needed class. The gang advanced Piquett more than $11,000, which eventually would lead to some serious quarreling over who skimmed how much of the bribe money before it reached Crown Point, possibly the jail warden (the FBI later believed), and Dillinger's two ostensible hostages.

Reportedly, $5,000 went to Deputy Ernest Blunk, the chief jailer, and $2,500 to garage man Ed Saager, who maintained the county cars—including Sheriff Lillian Holley's nice V-8 Ford. Dillinger had wanted the money to

. . . just then Nelson and Dillinger emerged from the bank and ran toward the car. As Van Meter turned to join them a storekeeper fired at him and the bullet plowed into the bandit's skull.
MERCHANTS NATIONAL BANK

YOU ALL KNOW ME

Fearless Courageous Cunning Efficient

While many Americans enjoyed the distraction of a national cops-'n'-robbers game, a Wisconsin citizen promoted Dillinger for "Bank Examiner" (left) and an Indiana resident posted an appropriate "Don't Shoot" sign on the back of his truck (below).

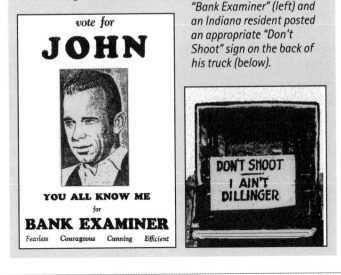

Beryl Hovious (left) divorced Dillinger after he was sent to prison. At right is his more devoted girlfriend, Evelyn "Billie" Frechette.

secure him a real gun, but Blunk rejected that idea from the start. If anything went wrong, he reasoned, he'd be shot first.

O'Leary proposed another plan, or at least took credit for it. As long as Blunk was in on the escape, the gun didn't need to be real, and accordingly he had an elderly German woodworker on Chicago's Northwest Side fashion a crude pistol out of wood and blacken it with shoe polish. The phony pistol had the additional virtue of diverting suspicion from Blunk and others who knew or suspected something. Dillinger would claim he had carved it during the month of February 1934 while pretrial hearings were under way; and to support this he did break up a washboard and whittle a few shavings, which later were found under his bunk.

Even this had proved arduous, and then another problem arose. The wooden-pistol ploy was hatched at the last minute, when Dillinger was fighting transfer to the much more formidable Indiana state prison; and while the woodworker (whom Girardin later met) hurried to complete a credibly crude-looking item, he wasn't clear on the concept. Believing he was doing O'Leary a favor, he bored out the barrel with 3/8-inch bit and inserted the round metal handle of an old safety razor, to give his product a little added realism.

O'Leary took one look and realized that while Dillinger might plausibly claim he had carved the gun in his cell, he certainly didn't have equipment to do the barrel work. O'Leary could not wait for another carving job and had to invent an additional cover story. Had the breakout failed, it would have been obvious the phony gun had been made by some outsider with woodworking tools. The best O'Leary could hope for was that nobody would get a close look at the gun, which Dillinger mostly kept in his pocket; and if worse came to worst, O'Leary and Piquett could speculate that gang member Tommy Carroll had smuggled it to Dillinger by way of Youngblood, who was not under constant observation.

As it turned out, the jailbreak went down perfectly, and the wooden pistol disappeared with Dillinger, who later sent it to his sister in Mooresville along with a letter. "Pulling that off was worth ten years of my life," he wrote. "Don't part with my wooden gun for any price. For when you feel blue all you will have to do is look at the gun and laugh your blues away. Ha! Ha!"

The gun remained stashed with a few other mementos until after Dillinger's death, when financial hardship forced his father to sign on as "curator" of a Dillinger mini-museum at Emil Wanatka's Little Bohemia Lodge in northern Wisconsin, where the gang had been forced to abandon many weapons and personal belongings when nearly trapped there by the FBI in April 1934.

Dillinger was killed in Chicago only three months later, on the Sunday night of July 22, outside the Biograph Theatre on North Lincoln Avenue. He was set up by Anna Sage, a prominent madam with a record, and her boyfriend/partner, Martin Zarkovich, a rogue cop from East Chicago. He had cut a deal with the FBI two days earlier on the condition he could participate in the ambush. Closely linked with the Sheetz mob, presumably his job was to make sure Dillinger didn't survive the trap, learn that he'd been betrayed by friends, and spill his guts. For contrary to the popular accounts, Anna already knew attorney Piquett (probably through his representation of local abortion rings), and had sought his help in avoiding deportation to her native Romania as morally undesirable. Dillinger was staying in her apartment at 2420 North Halsted, recuperating from his plastic surgery some six weeks earlier, no doubt sent there by Piquett. Whether the lawyer was in on the ambush isn't certain. Dillinger was known to be gunning for the lawyer over money matters

THE CRATE WITH THE "X"

In his coauthored *Dillinger: The Untold Story*, the late G. Russell Girardin has a considerably different version of the Indiana state prison escape by future members of the Dillinger Gang on September 26, 1933. The widely accepted version is that one package of guns and ammunition had been thrown over the prison wall, only to be discovered and reported by two other inmates. After that, Dillinger managed to slip pistols and ammo into a crate of thread marked with an X, for delivery to the prison shirt shop where Walter Detrich was working (with variations on that story).

According to Girardin, who presumably got his account from Louis Piquett's investigator Arthur O'Leary, the first package of guns was thrown over the prison wall by Dillinger and successfully retrieved by Detrich, who hid them in a pile of fabric; and it was the second package that the other inmates discovered and reported. He wrote that the package-tossing itself was accomplished after a prisoner (Leslie "Big" Homer) hung a crude arrow out the window of his cell to indicate where the guns were to be thrown or picked up. (Guards either didn't notice the arrow, or assumed it was an inmate amusing himself or playing a game.)

About three months after the breakout, when escapee Walter Detrich was captured and taken back to Indiana, he cooked up the story about the X-marked thread crate and a mob-connected theater owner who had bought it in Chicago, changed the return address to that of the regular thread supplier, and shipped it to the prison shirt shop himself. Both he and Dillinger had been working in the shirt shop, and he did not want to implicate Dillinger, who had been released on parole the previous May.

J. Edgar Hoover, for one, was outraged that Dillinger, captured without a fight in Tucson, Arizona, was treated as a celebrity when extradited to Crown Point, Indiana, where he posed with his prosecutor, Robert Estill. The photo cost Estill re-election.

and had told O'Leary to take his family on vacation until the matter was settled one way or another.

Forewarned, Piquett headed to Platteville, Wisconsin, where he was visiting relatives the night of the shooting. And the nearly two dozen federal agents surrounding the Biograph were so jumpy that when Dillinger walked out with Madam Anna and current girlfriend Polly Hamilton, they simply blew him to immortality, saving "Zark" the effort. (In recent years Zarkovich's .38 revolver was sold at auction for $26,000 as the gun that killed Dillinger.)

A presumably envious police colleague later described the killing in a newspaper series and stated that in the excitement after the shooting, Zarkovich had gone through Dillinger's pockets and taken several thousand dollars in cash before the body reached the Cook County Morgue. Anna later confirmed that Dillinger was carrying his "git" money when they left her apartment, and a perfunctory investigation into the robbing of Dillinger's corpse included at least one report by an FBI agent who said that he had noticed what felt like a large roll of bills in one of Dillinger's pockets.

Melvin Purvis got off with Dillinger's ruby ring and diamond stickpin, but the .380 automatic that ended up in an FBI display of Dillinger's belongings turned out to have been manufactured by Colt's some months after the outlaw's death. A story persists that the gun found at the scene went to J. Edgar Hoover, who gave it as a personal gift to his comedian friend Red Skelton, as it was his practice to curry favors with celebrities in the entertainment industry. The morgue inventory of Dillinger's blood-soaked clothing and seven dollars plus change was accepted by a gullible press simply as evidence that crime did not pay.

The wooden pistol did not come out of hiding until months after Dillinger's death, and by then apparently no one questioned the

Red, have Carroll contact East
Chicago people they will fix it
with B for him to pass gun to
Yungblood Johnnie

Dillinger sent this note to John Hamilton concerning his friends in East Chicago, with "B" obviously standing for jailer Blunk.

bored-and-sleeved barrel. Later it was loaned, along with other Dillinger possessions, to Girardin, to be photographed for a series of articles on which he, Piquett, and O'Leary were collaborating for the Knight Syndicate. Girardin kept it for some months before sending it back to the Dillinger family. However, the wooden gun they received probably was not the one pictured in the family snapshot of Dillinger holding a machine gun and the fake pistol used in the escape.

Girardin knew that O'Leary craved the "real" wooden gun as a souvenir and wanted to make a duplicate. Figuring that the Dillinger family would end up with O'Leary's copy, Girardin held onto the original and eventually gave it to Piquett, who promised to return it to the Dillingers in person. Sometime later they received a wooden pistol, but it probably was not the one used in the escape, and eventually it disappeared, evidently pocketed by a visitor.

The switch went undetected until after O'Leary's death from a heart attack during a trip to Florida about 1960, and his widow decided to sell their house and move there herself. During renovation, a workman named Al Kranz opened an air duct and found, along with papers dating back to O'Leary's collaboration with Girardin, a wooden pistol—almost certainly the "real" one—with a handwritten note from Piquett telling O'Leary to be sure he returned it to the Dillingers. This amounted to a receipt to get Piquett off the hook, and means that O'Leary managed to obtain the original after all.

Kranz sold O'Leary's wooden gun to Joe Pinkston, late owner of a John Dillinger museum in Nashville, Indiana, where it was put on prominent display. Pinkston brought his wooden pistol to Chicago and showed it to Girardin, who believed it was indeed the original loaned to him in 1935 by Dillinger's father (who additionally gave Girardin, as mementos, a decorative pen knife and shaving brush left by his son on visits home, and five pennies he was carrying the night he died), which means there should still be somewhere a second, "phony" wooden pistol—the one from O'Leary which was later lost by the Dillinger family.

As for the other Dillinger wooden pistols: For years the Chicago Historical Society

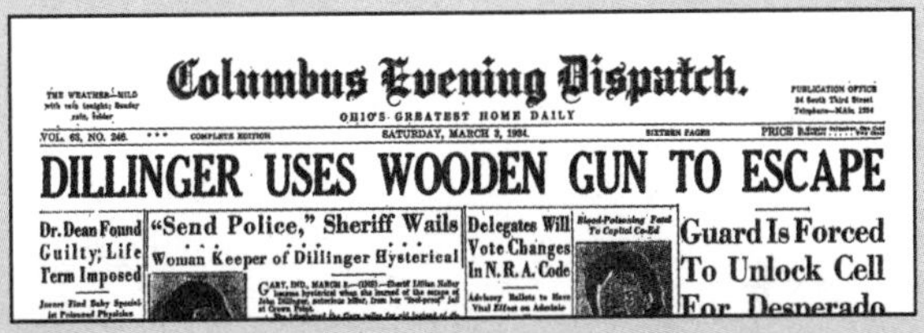

Columbus Evening Dispatch.

OHIO'S GREATEST HOME DAILY

VOL. 63, NO. 246. COMPLETE EDITION SATURDAY, MARCH 3, 1934. SIXTEEN PAGES

DILLINGER USES WOODEN GUN TO ESCAPE

Dr. Dean Found Guilty; Life Term Imposed

"Send Police," Sheriff Wails

Woman Keeper of Dillinger Hysterical

Delegates Will Vote Changes In N.R.A. Code

Guard Is Forced To Unlock Cell For Desperado

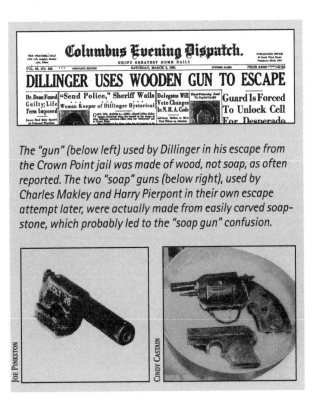

The "gun" (below left) used by Dillinger in his escape from the Crown Point jail was made of wood, not soap, as often reported. The two "soap" guns (below right), used by Charles Makley and Harry Pierpont in their own escape attempt later, were actually made from easily carved soapstone, which probably led to the "soap gun" confusion.

JOE PINKSTON

CINDY CASTAIN

THE CHICAGO DAILY NEWS

GIRL TRICKS DILLINGER

U. S. Agents Slay Gunman at Movie

SPORTS ★★ FINAL

Betrays Outlaw to Get Reward

John Dillinger Dead, but Who Fired Shots Puzzles Coroner's Jury

AMERICAN LEAGUE

NATIONAL LEAGUE

RACE RESULTS

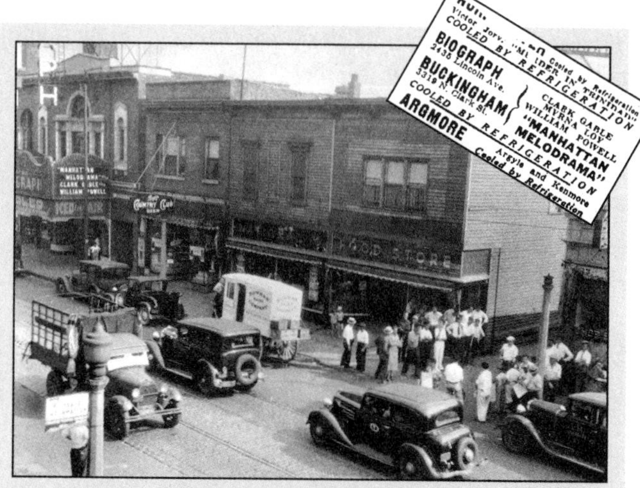

An "official" diagram found in FBI files includes Melvin Purvis and has Agent Cowley "roving," but in a version later released to the press, Purvis is eliminated entirely and the diagram shows Cowley, by name, dashing across the street at Dillinger. Morgue attendants kept having to replace Dillinger's toe tags as reporters were swiping them as souvenirs.

HOW DEATH WAS DEALT TO DEATH-DEALING JOHN DILLINGER

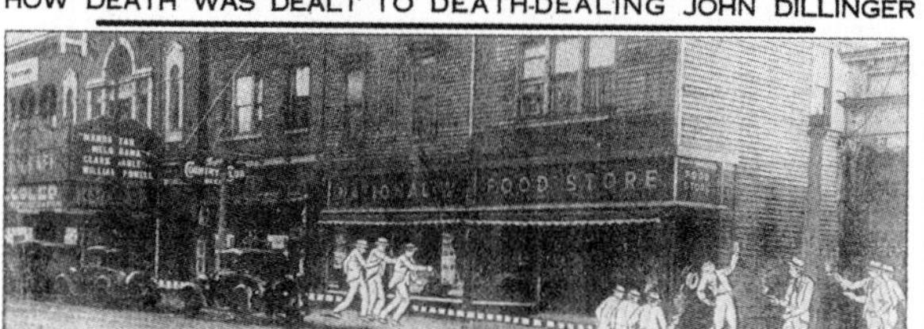

This photo-diagram illustrates how America's most notorious criminal was trapped and shot to death last night. The final act of the Dillinger melodrama began at 10:45 p. m., when the desperado, who had watched—on the screen—the rise and fall of another gangster, stepped from the Biograph Theater at 2433 Lincoln av. Obviously, he did not suspect that he was being watched, that the denouement was near, as he strode south. In the doorway of the tavern two doors south of the theater stood Melvin Purvis. Dillinger passed him. He continued on to the alley. Purvis and two other men followed. Three men closed in from across the street. Two stood on the other side of the alley. Now Dillinger saw the peril. He tried to duck down the alley, tried to pull a gun. The man hunters beat him to it. They fired—a bullet went into the heart; a second found the same vital organ. As Dillinger toppled a third bullet entered his neck. He died a few minutes later.

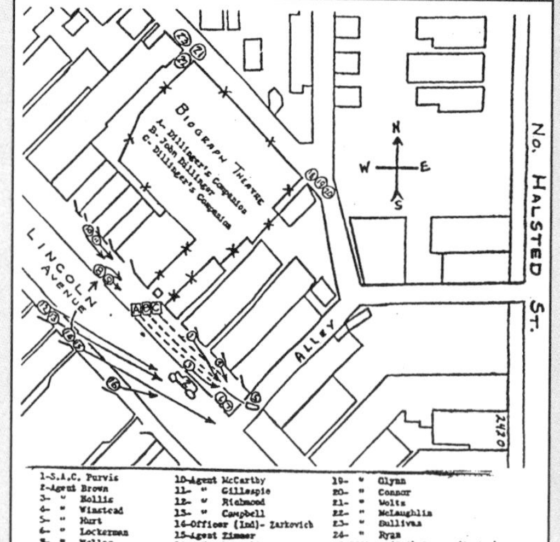

1-S.A.C. Purvis
2-Agent Brown
3- " Hollis
4- " Winstead
5- " Hurt
6- " Lockerman
7- " Weller
8-Officer (Ind) Strech
9- " " Sopsic
10-Agent McCarthy
11- " Gillespie
12- " Richmond
13- " Campbell
14-Officer (Ind)- Zarkovich
15-Agent Zimmer
16- " Metcalfe
17-Officer (Ind) O'Neil
18-Agent Suran
19- " Glynn
20- " Connor
21- " Woltz
22- " McLaughlin
23- " Sullivan
24- " Ryan
25-Officer (Ind) Conroy (Roving)
26-Agent Cowley (Roving)

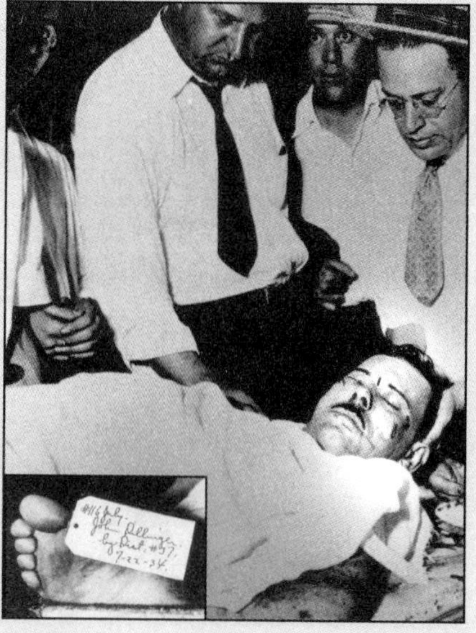

thought it had the real thing, guaranteed original in an apparently perjured affidavit by Deputy Ernest Blunk (which would not be totally out of character for a jailer who evidently accepted $5,000 in Depression-era dollars to help Dillinger escape). Blunk sold it to the owner of the Walgreen's drug chain, who eventually donated it in good faith to the Chicago Historical Society. It shows up in some newsreels of the period, though it obviously was fashioned with a jigsaw and is shaped more like a revolver, with double-edged razor blades tacked on each side to represent the cylinder. One that looks more like an automatic is shown in other films. A British collector bought a "Dillinger" pistol, shaped like a revolver and probably a manufactured toy gun, from the Melvin Purvis estate. Yet another, also shaped like a revolver, came from the Lake County Sheriff's Department and was displayed at the American Police Center and Museum in Chicago.

Since Dillinger's escape made Crown Point unhappily famous, the post office knew exactly where to deliver anything addressed simply to Wooden Gun, Indiana; and it can be assumed that the sheriff's office there received more than a few homemade wooden pistols from people having fun at the expense of the local authorities.

A righteous father (left) shows his pistol-toting son the "wages of sin" (a small irony, added by the cartoonist but missed by many viewers, shows the family library with books on such subjects as pirates and outlaws). The Dillinger Days *author apparently didn't notice that in Emil Wanatka's Little Bohemia postcard (below), John Dillinger's head has been superimposed on someone else's figure.*

Lori Hyde

November 9—The trial of the Touhy gang for the Hamm kidnapping begins in St. Paul.

November 13—Russell Hughes, a member of the "Handsome Jack" Klutas Gang (the College Kidnappers), is killed by police in Peoria, Illinois.

November 15—Police from Indiana join Chicago police in setting a trap for Dillinger outside the office of Dr. Charles Eye at 4175 West Irving Park Boulevard. Dillinger and girlfriend Evelyn "Billie" Frechette escape in a wild car chase. Officers lose Dillinger but manage to shoot out their own windshield, allowing reporters to assume that they had engaged in a dramatic gun battle with the escaping desperado.

– William "Whitey" Walker, his wife, Dolores, and Irvin "Blackie" Thompson rob Jim McMurray's oil refinery in Overton Township, Texas, of approximately $2,500. The crime will be wrongly attributed to Clyde Barrow and Bonnie Parker.

– Basil "The Owl" Banghart, Ike Costner, Ludwig "Dutch" Schmidt, and Charles "Ice Wagon" Connors rob a U.S. Mail truck in Charlotte, North Carolina, of $105,000.

November 16—W. D. Jones, former Barrow Gang member, is arrested in Houston.

November 17—Former Dillinger Gang member Harry Copeland is arrested by Chicago police while having an altercation with his girlfriend in a car parked at North and Harlem avenues, which happens to be the location of Jimmy Murray's Rainbo Barbecue restaurant—a Dillinger hideout.

November 18—Wilbur Underhill brazenly enters the courthouse at Coalgate, Oklahoma, and purchases a license to marry Hazel Jarrett Hudson of Coalgate. Hazel is the sister of the Jarrett brothers, notorious Oklahoma outlaws.

November 20—The Dillinger Gang robs the American Bank & Trust Co. at Racine, Wisconsin, of $27,789.

– Albert Silvers (or Silverman), New York/New Jersey mobster who purchased the car Verne Miller used to flee to Chicago, is found stabbed to death at Somers, Connecticut. Miller, already unpopular with Midwest gangsters because of the "heat" caused by the Kansas City Massacre, apparently also has worn out his welcome in the East Coast underworld.

– New York mobster "Waxey" Gordon goes to trial for income tax evasion. The case is prosecuted by Assistant U.S. Attorney Thomas E. Dewey.

November 22—Clyde Barrow and Bonnie Parker escape a police trap near Sowers, Texas.

November 23—Wilbur Underhill and others rob the State National Bank in Frankfort, Kentucky, of $15,000.

November 24—Dillinger Gang member Leslie Homer is arrested in Chicago. Homer will later be sentenced to 28 years in state prison at Waupun, Wisconsin, for the Racine bank holdup.

November 26—Ed Fletcher and Abe Axler, members of the Detroit Purple Gang, are found murdered near Pontiac, Michigan.

November 28—Roger Touhy, "Gloomy Gus" Schafer, Eddie McFadden, and Willie Sharkey are acquitted of the Hamm kidnapping (to the embarrassment of the U.S. Division of Investigation), but held for Chicago authorities for the alleged kidnapping of Jake "The Barber" Factor.

– Gangster Walter Tylczak is found murdered near Detroit.

November 29—Verne Miller is found murdered at the corner of Harlow Avenue and Cambridge Road in Detroit.

– In Chicago, Vivian Mathis, former mistress of Verne Miller, is sentenced to a year and a day for harboring a federal fugitive.

– In New York, "Waxey" Gordon is convicted of income tax evasion, sentenced to ten years in prison and fined $20,000, plus $60,000 in costs.

November 30—Touhy gangster Willie Sharkey hangs himself in the St. Paul jail.

December 28—Top fugitives on the "public enemy" list for Chicago (impressed by the success of the Chicago Crime Commission's list) include Dillinger and most members of his gang.

December 5—A mail robbery at the Union Station in Washington, D.C., is attributed to the Tri-State Gang, headed by Robert Mais and Walter Legurenza, alias Legenza.

– Prohibition is repealed by ratification of the Twenty-first Amendment, but most bootlegging mobs anticipated this and moved into gambling and labor racketeering.

December 11—Police Detective H. C. Perrow is killed in San Antonio by Tommy Carroll, crime partner of "Baby Face" Nelson, who is in that city acquiring guns from H. S. Lebman.

– Wilbur Underhill, Elmer Inman, and others attempt to burglarize the First National Bank at Harrah, Oklahoma.

December 13—Bandits loot safety deposit boxes at Unity Trust & Savings Bank at 3909 West North Avenue in Chicago. The Dillinger Gang is suspected.

– Wilbur Underhill, Jack "Tom" Lloyd, and Ralph Roe rob the First National Bank at Coalgate, Oklahoma, of $4,000.

December 14—Dillinger outlaw John Hamilton kills Chicago police officer William Shanley in an auto repair shop at 5320 Broadway.

– "Whitey" Walker, "Blackie" Thompson, and Roy Johnson rob John Caldwell's jewelry store in Bryan, Texas, taking about $10,000 in jewelry and cash.

– John "Kaiser Bill" Goodman, Clifford "Kip" Harback and Lillian Tackett rob the state bank at Midland, Arkansas, of $500.

December 16—Chicago Police Captain John Stege organizes a forty-man "Dillinger Squad."

– Cook County State's Attorney Thomas Courtney imaginatively announces a linkup of the Dillinger, Klutas, Touhy, and Harvey Bailey-Verne Miller gangs.

December 17—Arthur "Fish" Johnston (often spelled Johnson), a fence and close Dillinger Gang associate, is arrested at 1742 Humbolt in Chicago.

December 20—Indiana state policeman Eugene Teague is accidentally killed by a fellow officer in the capture of former Dillinger Gang member Ed Shouse at Paris, Illinois.

– The Dillinger Gang moves to Daytona Beach, Florida.

December 22—Acting on a tip that John Dillinger is there, Chicago police raid an apartment at 1428 Farwell in Rogers Park and kill three men—Sam Ginsburg, Lewis Katzewitz, and Charles Tattlebaum. The three were bank robbers but had no known connection with Dillinger.

– Ford Bradshaw and others rob the First National Bank at Syracuse, Nebraska, of $1,500.

December 23—Dillinger associate Hilton Crouch is arrested by Chicago police at 420 Surf Street. He will later be sentenced to twenty years for the Massachusetts Avenue Bank robbery in Indianapolis.

December 27—"Whitey" Walker and "Blackie" Thompson rob the First State Bank at Marlin, Texas, of $44,141 in cash and bonds.

December 30—Wilbur Underhill is fatally wounded by police and Division of Investigation agents at a honeymoon cottage in Shawnee, Oklahoma. Also fatally wounded is Eva Mae Nichols, girlfriend of Underhill henchman Ralph Roe. Roe and Underhill's recent bride, Hazel Hudson, are captured.

– The Ford Bradshaw Gang robs the National Bank at Mansfield, Arkansas, of $1,700.

December 31—Gunmen believed to be the Ford Bradshaw Gang terrorize the town of Vian, Oklahoma, driving through town and peppering a hardware store, a restaurant, and the town jail with bullets. Authorities believe this to be an act of defiant retaliation for the capture of Bradshaw's friend, Wilbur Underhill.

1934

January 1—A gang of machine-gunners robs the Beverly Gardens nightclub in Chicago and shoots two policemen. The crime is blamed on the Dillinger Gang, then vacationing in Florida.

– The former U.S. Army Disciplinary Barracks at Alcatraz Island, in San Francisco Bay, officially becomes a federal penitentiary commonly referred to as "The Rock," intended for the gangsters and outlaws considered the most dangerous and incorrigible. [The imprisonment there of racketeer Al Capone apparently was based mainly on his national notoriety.]

January 4—Joseph "Red" Carson and others rob

the First State Bank at Willow, Oklahoma, of $440.

January 6—Wilbur Underhill dies of wounds at the prison hospital at McAlester, Oklahoma.

— "Handsome Jack" Klutas, Chicago kidnapper, is killed by police at a house in the Chicago suburb of Bellwood. Earl McMahon, wanted for a $50,000 jewel robbery, and former Dillinger associate Walter Detrich are captured in the Klutas hideout. Joseph Aiuppa, alias Joey O'Brien, alleged underworld machine-gun supplier, and several other men also are arrested in the vicinity.

January 7—Oklahoma's Public Enemy No. 1, Elmer Inman, is wounded and captured at Bowlegs, Oklahoma.

January 11-February 2—Roger Touhy, "Gloomy Gus" Schafer, and August John Lamarr, alias Albert "Polly Nose" Kator, are tried for the alleged kidnapping of Jake "The Barber" Factor. First trial ends in a hung jury.

January 13—On Portland Avenue in St. Paul, airline pilot Roy McCord is mistaken for a policeman and machine-gunned by Alvin Karpis and Fred Barker. McCord survives but is crippled for life.

January 15—John Dillinger, John Hamilton, and an unidentified man rob the First National Bank in East Chicago, Indiana, of $20,376, killing Officer William O'Malley. Dillinger is accused of the murder.

— Willie "The Actor" Sutton, Eddie Wilson, and Joe Perlongo rob the Corn Exchange Bank in Philadelphia of $10,980.

January 16—Clyde Barrow, Bonnie Parker, and James Mullen raid the Eastham Prison Farm in Texas, freeing Raymond Hamilton and four other convicts. One guard is killed and another wounded.

January 17-February 7—The Barker-Karpis Gang kidnaps banker Edward George Bremer in St. Paul and transports him to Bensenville, Illinois. Bremer is released unharmed upon payment of $200,000 ransom.

January 19—"Big Bob" Brady, Jim Clark, and five others escape from the Lansing, Kansas, state prison. Brady and Clark, participants in the May 30 breakout from the same prison, split up. Clark and fellow escapee Frank Delmar kidnap teacher Lewis Dresser and steal his car. Dresser is released in Oklahoma, where the escapees meet Clark's girlfriend, Goldie Johnson, waiting in a car with Texas license plates. Dresser subsequently identifies the woman as Bonnie Parker, and the Barrow Gang is erroneously suspected of engineering two prison breaks in three days.

January 20—Four masked gunmen rob the Fort Kearney State Bank at Kearney, Nebraska, of $10,000.

January 22—"Big Bob" Brady is killed by a posse near Paola, Kansas.

January 23—Syndicate gangster William "Three-Fingered Jack" White is shot to death by two men in his apartment at 920 Wesley Avenue in Oak Park, Illinois. White allegedly was an informer for the Justice Department.

— The Barrow Gang robs the First National Bank at Rembrandt, Iowa, of $3,000.

January 25—John Dillinger, Harry Pierpont, Charles Makley, and Russell Clark are captured by police in Tucson, Arizona, when their hotel catches fire. Dillinger will be extradited to Indiana to face charges of murder and bank robbery. The others will be sent to Ohio to be tried for the murder of Sheriff Jesse Sarber.

— The Barrow Gang is suspected of robbing the Central National Bank at Poteau, Oklahoma, of $1,500.

— The Bradshaw Gang robs the Bank of Wellington at Wellington, Kansas, of $4,000.

January 29—"Blackie" Thompson is arrested in Miami, Florida. On the same day, his partners, "Whitey" Walker and Roy Johnson, are wounded by police and captured while attempting to rob the Capital City Bank in Tallahassee.

January 30—On arrival at the Lake County Jail in Crown Point, Indiana, Dillinger scandalizes local authorities by posing for chummy pictures with Sheriff Lillian Holley and prosecutor Robert Estill.

January 31—In a Chicago barber shop, police and Division of Investigation agents arrest kidnapper Verne Sankey. Sankey, charged with the

THE INDIANA INVESTIGATION

Appointed by the governor of Indiana to investigate Dillinger's Crown Point escape on March 3, 1934, Assistant Attorney General Edward C. Barce provided a draft describing his first three days on the case to Philip Lutz Jr., the Indiana attorney general. Some minor typographical errors have been corrected, and lengthy or irrelevant sections have been paraphrased. The more widely circulated official report, authorized by Indiana's Governor McNutt, can be found in the expanded paperback edition of *Dillinger: The Untold Story*.

MARCH 5, 1934 [FIRST DAY OF THE INVESTIGATION]

The following is a report of the developments of the first day of investigation into the Lake County jailbreak at Crown Point, Indiana on March 3rd, 1934.

ONE. At the time of the jail break there were four principal deputies besides the sheriff. The sheriff was in bed and just arising when notified of the escape. The Chief Deputy, Carroll Holley, a nephew of the sheriff, was in bed. The third deputy Jack West was at his home in bed. The fourth deputy was at his home and didn't report until after the escape.

TWO. The jail was in charge of the following persons:

[A list of thirteen persons, including

SANDY JONES

Dillinger, Herbert Youngblood, and their supposed hostages escaped from Crown Point's Lake County Jail through its kitchen door and made it out the back gate before stealing the sheriff's car, which they drove across a state line—Dillinger's first federal offense. Inset at lower right shows the jail shortly before it was closed about 1974.

Sam Cahoon and Warden Baker, four "inexperienced" temporary guards, one jail guard and one National Guardsman in the kitchen, three "special guards" in the residence section, and three trusties. This was more than five weeks after the excitement of Dillinger's arrest in Tucson, and most of his guards had been withdrawn.]

THREE. No regular police officers were on duty.

FOUR: The prison meals were served by trusties who were permitted to go out on the streets to get groceries and other things and permitted to reenter the jail without search.

FIVE: The prosecuting attorney's office and other officials were given the wrong license plate number of the stolen automobile of the sheriff, the number provided being 679-929 Ind. 34, and the correct number being 674-549 Ind. 34.

SIX: Telephone dispatches concerning the break were sent to the following places at the following hours according to the records of the telephone exchange:

[A list of twenty-four cities, most in Indiana, several in Illinois, and one each in Ohio and Missouri. The earliest call was to Gary, Indiana, at 9:35 a.m; Chicago was called at ll:24 a.m.; sixteen were called between early afternoon and late in the evening, concluding with the Crete State Police Barracks at 10:15 p.m.]

SEVEN: Deputies were dispatched in pursuit cars without being provided with any license number.

EIGHT: Experienced police officers and guards were furnished by the various City Police Departments in Lake County for the guarding of Dillinger, but with the exception of two police from the City of East Chicago serving at night, [they] have not been used for the past two or three weeks.

NINTH: The use of the two police tendered and furnished by the City of Hammond Police Department was discontinued some 2 or 3 weeks ago by the Sheriff's office on the ground that their services were no longer needed.

TENTH: The telephone operator at the jail from 7:00 P.M. to 7:00 A.M. is a trusty.

ELEVENTH: The doorkeeper, Arthur Guthmiller with keys to the front and first inner door is a trusty serving a sentence for petit larceny.

TWELFTH: John Kowaliszyn, turnkey, with keys to front door, kitchen and residence is a trusty serving a sentence.

THIRTEENTH: On the morning of the break Sam Cahoon permitted Dillinger and other prisoners to remain in the jail corridor outside their cells when the porters entered with supplies, strictly against the rules of the jail. He admitted this to be the first occasion he had done this in three or four months.

FOURTEENTH: On the morning of the break Sam Cahoon failed to lock the cell gates where Dillinger and others were lodged, which was a violation of the jail rules which he been particularly warned about. He admitted never having done this before.

FIFTEENTH: There is no record at the telephone exchange of any call to the Indiana State Police at Indianapolis, and it will be seen by Item Six that the Tremont State Police Station was not called until 3:37 P.M.

SIXTEENTH: Razor blades were sold to prisoners by Sam Cahoon, and prisoners were permitted to retain same within cells.

SEVENTEENTH: A broom, mop and sink cleaner, all equipped with heavy handles were permitted to remain in the cell room. The handle to the sink cleaner was used by Youngblood as a weapon in escape.

EIGHTEENTH: The following visitors called upon and interviewed Dillinger on the following dates:

Attorney Piquitt of Chicago, February 1;

Attorney Ryan of Indpls. with Dillinger's brother, February 3 or 5; February 13, Piquitt and Ryan; February 15, Piquitt and attorney O'Leary; February 19, Piquitt and Myer Boog; February 26, Piquitt and woman claiming to be Dillinger's wife; at another time Attorneys Conroy and MacAleer of Lake County called.

MARCH 6, 1934 [SECOND DAY OF THE INVESTIGATION]

On February 14, at a time when the removal of Dillinger to the State Prison was strongly under consideration in order to prevent any attempt at escape, the Sheriff's office of Lake County notified the Gary Police that they had sufficient guards to watch the prisoner and that these two guards might be withdrawn. . . . It seems that this published statement [by the Gary police chief, and released to newspapers, had] incensed Mrs. Holley, and the above conversation relative to removal of the guards followed.

[Deputy Sheriff Edward B. Rodgers explains the license-plate mix-up was based on his guess that the plate number was one digit less than the plate on a car undergoing repair, but investigator Barce learned that a third car, a Willis, also owned by the Sheriff's Department, had further confused the matter.]

The following information you will probably desire to keep confidential until later developments appear.

Upon account of the incriminating evidence given by Sam Cahoon and Ernest Blunk, and upon account of many apparent conflicts in their testimony and that of reliable witnesses, and upon account of the fact that Cahoon and Blunk were evidently testifying in collusion, and on account of efforts of Cahoon to keep Blunk from talking, we filed affidavits against each of these persons at one o'clock this afternoon and placed them under arrest. The affidavits were filed in the Criminal Court and charged aiding the escape of a prisoner from jail.

Sam Cahoon is an appointee of the Sheriff and Ernest Blunk an appointee of Judge Murray of the Criminal Court. Judge Murray claims to have made an investigation of the facts in the case and has absolved everyone of everything except carelessness. Now we happen to know that any investigation made by him was extremely limited, and he is anxious to whitewash the whole affair just as if it never happened. This attitude is not only very unfair and unfounded but is fast placing him in disrepute. We have ample evidence for a conviction under the charge which we have filed. However, Judge Murray issued a statement to the newspapers in which he stated that someone had gone off "half-cocked," and when asked if he intended to serve as judge in the cases stated that he did intend to serve. After placing Blunk under arrest and while held by State Police Officer Hire for questioning by Detective Singer of the Hammond Police Department (whom the Hammond Chief of Police assigned to us as his leading investigator), Prosecutor Estill, and myself, Judge Murray's bailiff attempted to talk to him for the purpose, I am convinced, of telling him to shut up, and later during the same examination of Blunk, Judge Murray himself demanded admission to the room in which the examination was being conducted with a bond already made out in the sum of $2,000 dollars for his release, which he caused the prisoner to sign, permitting him to go on his own recognizance without surety.

[Detective Singer requests Judge Murray to keep Blunk and Cahoon from talking to each other, and Judge Murray instructs Sheriff Holley to jail Cahoon when he is

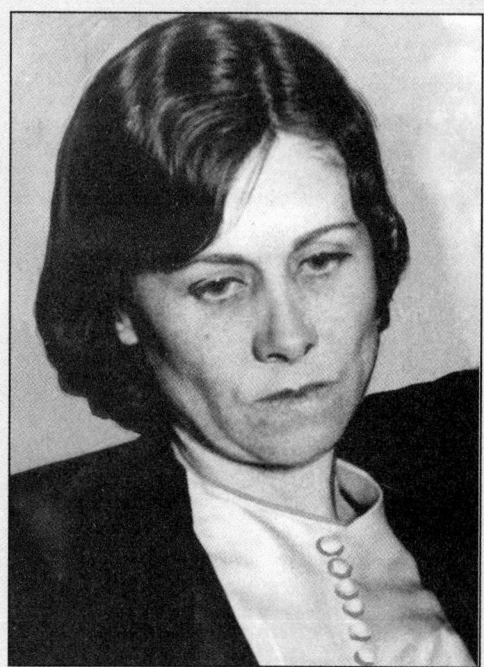

Lake County Sheriff Lillian Holley

returned from questioning in Hammond.]

Upon the return of Cahoon to the jail by state police officer Hire, Hire was very coldly received, and Cahoon informed that he would not be placed in a cell on any account.

It begins to appear as if our main opposition would come from the Judge and the Sheriff's Office....

Tomorrow we will spend the day continuing with the examination of Blunk and Cahoon. Patrick [not identified] called from Chicago this evening after a visit with Captain Stege who assured us of every cooperation and desired Captain Leach to get and keep in touch with him. He assured Herb [not unidentified] that in the event the Chicago Police are able to capture Dillinger either dead or alive, he will be returned to Indiana for trial....

MARCH 7, 1934 [THIRD DAY OF THE INVESTIGATION]

... We worked all forenoon on a couple of blind steers which got us no place.

[Chief Nicholas Mackar of the East Chicago Police Department had urged Prosecutor Estill to have Dillinger transferred to the state prison, and he then called Sheriff Holley, who "did not react favorably to the suggestion, but said that she would sleep over the matter before deciding."]

A short time later Chief Mackar was called on the telephone by Estill and requested to furnish an escort for the delivery of Dillinger to Michigan City state prison. He volunteered to get in touch with the other departments of the county and start an escort to Crown Point at once. He thereupon called the police chiefs of Hammond and Gary and told them he was furnishing two squad cars of men for the escort, and they in turn cheerfully agreed to furnish two squad cars each. These squads were all on their way to Crown Point when a second call was received from Estill telling Chief Mackar that the whole thing was off and that Dillinger was not to be removed. He held a conversation with Estill the next evening in which he was informed by Estill that [Judge Murray] had blocked the move.

Later Chief Mackar interviewed Sheriff Holley and was informed by her that Judge Murray had advised her against moving Dillinger as the same was a bad political move.

[Barce mentions Sheriff Holley's dismissal of the East Chicago guards, two of them on the night before the jailbreak. Then he reports the testimony of Matt Brown, former county commissioner and county treasurer who had been serving as a special guard and was considered a reputable citizen.]

On the morning of March 3rd [Matt Brown] drove to Crown Point in the automobile, bringing with him his wife and a guard Winfield Bryant, the first guard locked in the cell with the two colored porters. Bryant got out at the jail, and he drove his wife to a relative's home in Crown Point. He then proceeded with his car to the garage where he purchased a new tire and left his car and walked to the jail building, arriving there at about nine o'clock.

He rung the doorbell twice before it was answered, and he was admitted by a trusty. Warden Baker was at the desk and informed Brown that he knew he was coming and had already registered him, and that he would place him in a few minutes. (It was the custom for Baker to place the special guards at various posts in the jail.) Brown then moved over to the side of the little walled-in office and assumed a position of waiting whereby he was able to see into the receiving or finger-print room, but not in a position where he could see the entrance to the long corridor running back to the new cell block.

He had no sooner assumed this position when he perceived Blunk approach the door to the main office from the receiving room and said to Baker, "Baker, come on back here." Baker said alright and walked out the side door of the little office informing Brown that he would "come back and place him," and entered through the door, which was unlocked and followed Blunk until they disappeared.

Some two or three minutes later and while Brown was still waiting in the same position he saw Blunk again approach the door between the receiving room and the main office, who called to Brown, "We are ready for you now." Brown of course thinking that Baker was ready to place him, entered through the unlocked door and followed Blunk through the receiving room, into and back through the corridor. Blunk said nothing to him and he said nothing to Blunk. Blunk walked ahead of him. When they reached the end of the corridor they turned to the right, up the steps to the cell section; Blunk opened the gate said "right in here." Brown walked in and the gate was shut after him. He saw all of the people in the cells and then realized for the first time that he had been decoyed into a locked cell.

At no time did he see or hear anything of either Dillinger or Youngblood; no pistol or anything else was jammed into his ribs or back; the first time he saw Dillinger was when he appeared with the machine gun in his left hand, pulled out the wooden pistol, and said, "Here's what I did it with."

I tested his powers of observation, detail and memory and find him above the average in all three particulars.

It will therefore be seen that the things which we found so hard to understand were very simple after all.

There are some things in this case which I hesitate to put in print on account of the persons involved which I will tell you when I get in Saturday.

Will you please show this report to Wayne Coy so that he can communicate with the Governor. In case of material developments I will phone you.

Respectfully yours,

"EDWARD BARCE"

Piquitt should be spelled Piquett, and Myer Boog should be Meyer Bogue who, as it would turn out, was Dillinger's thoroughly crooked acquaintance and his supposed alibi witness who would claim he was in Florida at the time of the First National Bank robbery in East Chicago, during which Officer O'Malley was killed. O'Leary was not an attorney but Louis Piquett's investigator.

kidnapping of Charles Boettcher II, will commit suicide in the Great Falls, South Dakota, prison on February 8.

February 1—Clyde Barrow and Bonnie Parker are identified as participants in the $270 robbery of the State Savings Bank in Knieram, Iowa.

February 2—The Needham Trust Co. in Needham, Massachusetts, is robbed of $14,500, and two policemen are machine-gunned. "Pretty Boy" Floyd is wrongly named as a suspect. The actual killers, Murton and Irving Millen and Abraham Faber, will later be captured, convicted, and executed for this crime.

– Four bandits rob the National Bank & Trust Co. at Pennsgrove, New Jersey, of $130,000. Local authorities will later speculate, incorrectly, that this bank was robbed to finance Dillinger's escape from the Crown Point jail.

– The Barrow Gang is erroneously suspected of robbing the First National Bank at Coleman, Texas.

February 3–4—In a weekend of major violence, eight men are killed in three eastern Oklahoma towns. At Sapulpa, Police Chief Tom Brumley and Patrolman Charles P. Lloyd and bank robbers "Aussie" Elliott, Dubert Carolan, alias Raymond Moore, and Eldon Wilson are slain in a gun battle. At Chelsea, Deputy Sheriff Earl Powell and Ed "Newt" Clanton, a member of the Ford Bradshaw Gang, die in another shootout. At Bokoshe, Oklahoma, Dr. H. T. King is shot to death and his son Howard is wounded. Howard King names his father's slayer as City Marshal Calvin Johnson.

February 4—Ernest Rossi, former Klutas Gang associate wanted for a Holland, Michigan, bank robbery, is shot to death by unknown killers at the Chicago home of his brother-in-law, "Dago" Lawrence Mangano. Rossi is the fifth Chicago mobster slain in recent months for allegedly cooperating with federal authorities. Newspapers speculate that the underworld has a counter-informant working in the Justice Department.

February 5—Willie "The Actor" Sutton is captured by Philadelphia police. He will be sentenced to twenty-five years in Eastern State Penitentiary for bank robbery.

– John Dillinger's trial date is scheduled for March 12. Indiana officials want Dillinger held in the state prison, but Dillinger's lawyer Louis Piquett strongly objects, and Judge William Murray leaves him in Sheriff Lillian Holley's heavily guarded Lake County Jail at Crown Point.

February 9—"Doc" Barker is identified as one of the Bremer kidnappers through a fingerprint found on a gasoline can. Flashlights used by the kidnappers also are found and traced to a St. Paul store. A sales clerk identifies Alvin Karpis from photos as the purchaser.

February 10—At the request of Lee Simmons, head of the Texas Prison System, Frank Hamer, a former Texas Ranger who (newspapers claim) has killed fifty-three criminals in his long career as a peace officer, comes out of retirement to track down Clyde Barrow and Bonnie Parker.

February 12—The Barrow Gang flees into Oklahoma after a running gun battle with officers near Reed Springs, Missouri.

February 13–23—Second trial of the Touhy mob for the Factor kidnapping. Mail robbers Basil "The Owl" Banghart and Ike Costner are captured in Baltimore and rushed to Chicago to testify. Costner swears for the prosecution that he and Banghart participated with Touhy in the kidnapping. Banghart testifies for the defense, stating that he, Costner, and Charles "Ice Wagon" Connors, still at large, were hired by Jake Factor to make the kidnapping look real. The jury believes Costner. Roger Touhy, Gus Schafer, Albert Kator, and Basil Banghart are sentenced to ninety-nine years in the Joliet, Illinois, state prison. Costner later will be convicted with Ludwig "Dutch" Schmidt of the Charlotte, North Carolina, mail robbery and sentenced to 30 years.

February 15—Eddie Doll, alias Eddie LaRue, formerly an associate of Eddie Bentz, is arrested by federal agents in St. Petersburg, Florida. A reputed burglar, bank robber, professional car thief, and freelance hit man, Doll is a suspect in the million-dollar Lincoln bank robbery of 1930 and in the kidnappings of Edward Bremer and

Blue Island, Illinois, gambler James Hackett. He will plead guilty to interstate transportation of a stolen car and receive a sentence of ten years in federal prison.

February 17—Clifford "Kip" Harback, bank robber and murderer, is captured with his mistress and accomplice, Lillian Tackett, after she shoots him in a domestic dispute in Hot Springs, Arkansas.

February 17–18—An army of police and National Guardsmen invade the Cookson Hills of eastern Oklahoma, for decades an outlaw stronghold. Nineteen people are arrested. Eastern newspapers report the event as a dragnet for "Pretty Boy" Floyd and the Barrow Gang, but local lawmen express doubts about their presence and declare that the drive was largely inspired by the activities of Ford Bradshaw and other local bandits.

February 19—The Barrow Gang robs a National Guard armory in Ranger, Texas.

February 24—The First National Bank at Galena, Kansas, is robbed for the second time by a gang, including a woman, that takes $7,100. The Barrow Gang is suspected, but the actual robbers probably were the Ford Bradshaw Gang. The woman may have been Bradshaw's "moll," Stella "Boots" Moody.

– Detroit Chief of Detectives Fred W. Frahm announces that the Purple Gang is no longer in business.

February 26—Alfred Guarino pleads guilty to second degree murder in Bronx County, New York, for the killing of Millie Schwartz and is sentenced to twenty years to life in Sing Sing. Mrs. Vincent (Lottie) Coll and Joseph Ventre plead guilty to manslaughter in the same case. Mrs. Coll is sentenced to six to twelve years in Bedford Reformatory, and Ventre is sentenced to seven to fifteen years in Sing Sing.

February 27—Clyde Barrow and Raymond Hamilton rob the R. P. Henry & Sons Bank at Lancaster, Texas, of a reported $4,138.

February 28—Sebron Edward Davis, former Bailey-Underhill outlaw, is arrested in Los Angeles for robbery and kidnapping. He will be sentenced to life in Folsom Prison.

March 2—The Mais-Legenza Gang (the so-called Tri-State Gang) kills a messenger of the State Planters Bank at Richmond, Virginia, during a $60,000 robbery.

March 3—Using a wooden pistol reportedly smuggled to him by a bribed guard, John Dillinger escapes from the Crown Point jail, along with accused "Negro" murderer Herbert Youngblood. They arm themselves with machine guns and pistols from the sheriff's office, take two hostages who are later released, and flee to Chicago in Sheriff Holley's car. Transporting a stolen car across a state line makes Dillinger at last a federal fugitive and the object of a nationwide manhunt by J. Edgar Hoover's "G-men."

– Bank robber Ford Bradshaw is arrested, handcuffed, then killed while attempting to flee by Deputy William Harper at Ardmore, Oklahoma. Harper is charged with murder, but the charge will be dropped later.

– The Barrow Gang is erroneously suspected of robbing a bank at Mesquite, Texas.

March 4—A carload of men follows salesman Theodore Kidder to his home in the Twin Cities suburb of St. Louis Park; one of the men calls Kidder by name then shoots him dead. Kidder was a salesman for a sporting goods store and may have had dealings with gangsters. The killers' car license later is traced to "Baby Face" Nelson, who purchased it in California under the alias of James Rogers.

March 6—Dillinger joins "Baby Face" Nelson, John Hamilton, Homer Van Meter, Tommy Carroll, and Eddie Green in robbing the Security National Bank at Sioux Falls, South Dakota, of $49,500 and wounding a policeman. Though the group had been assembled by Nelson and Van Meter, who reportedly fronted the bribe money for the Crown Point escape, it immediately is declared the Dillinger Gang, to the annoyance of Nelson. (Most researchers have since made the distinction and call it the "second" Dillinger Gang.)

March 7—Four men rob the Whitesboro National Bank at Whitesboro, Texas, of $13,000, taking three bank employees hostage.

– Bonnie Parker's husband, Roy Thornton, serving a fifty-five-year sentence for robbery, and four others attempt to scale the wall of the Texas state prison at Huntsville. Three of the escapees are wounded by guards and recaptured. Thornton and Robert Hill, convicted of the 1927 "Santa Claus" bank robbery at Cisco, Texas, surrender. Prison authorities attribute leadership of the break to Thornton, citing his continuing love for Bonnie as the motive for the break.

– Syndicate mobster "West Side Frankie" Pope is murdered by gunmen in his Chicago hotel room.

March 8—A federal complaint is filed in Chicago against John Dillinger for interstate transportation of a stolen car, confirming his status as a federal fugitive.

March 10—John Dillinger is suspected in a gun battle with police at Schiller Park, Illinois.

March 10 (approx.)—In a Chicago hideout, Dr. Joseph Moran performs plastic surgery on the faces of Alvin Karpis and Fred Barker and attempts to remove their fingerprints.

March-April—Dr. Moran conspires with Chicago politician John "Boss" McLaughlin Sr., to pass ransom money from the Bremer kidnapping.

March 12—Four men rob the Exchange National and Exchange State Banks, both in the same building, at Atchison, Kansas, of $21,000, taking nine employees hostage, slugging one, and wounding Police Chief Willard Linville with machine-gun fire. To confuse the matter, one robber addresses another as "Dillinger," and this inspires other witnesses (who obviously wanted their banks to be robbed by the best) to identify the other robbers as "Pretty Boy" Floyd and Clyde Barrow. At least one witness named "Barrow" as the man who shot the police chief, and someone else said they had seen a woman smoking a cigar in a nearby hotel lobby, which naturally led to speculation that this was Bonnie Parker. "Dillinger," "Floyd," and "Bonnie and Clyde" all got away and were never seen again—at least in Atchison, Kansas.

March 13—The Dillinger Gang robs the First National Bank at Mason City, Iowa, of $52,344.

March 14—Charles "Ice Wagon" Connors, alleged Touhy gangster wanted for mail robbery and the Factor kidnapping, found murdered near Chicago.

March 15—Six men and two women, including Bremer kidnapping suspects Glen LeRoy Wright and Charles "Cotton" Cotner, are arrested in a dawn raid by federal agents and police on a farmhouse near Mannford, Oklahoma. Cotner is wanted for two murders and the attempted kidnapping of Peggy Landon, daughter of Kansas Governor Alfred Landon.

March 16—Herbert Youngblood, who escaped with Dillinger from the Crown Point jail, kills Deputy Charles Cavanaugh in Port Huron, Michigan, but is mortally wounded by other officers on the scene.

March 19—Raymond and Floyd Hamilton and John Basden rob the state bank at Grand Prairie, Texas, of $1,500.

March 21—Fred Goetz, alias "Shotgun" George Ziegler, former Capone gunman who joined the Barker-Karpis Gang, is shotgunned to death by unknown assailants in Cicero, Illinois. Goetz is believed to have participated in the St. Valentine's Day Massacre of 1929.

March 22—Roy Frisch, witness in a U.S. Mail fraud case against Reno gamblers William Graham and James McKay, disappears, probably murdered by "Baby Face" Nelson and John Paul Chase on a contract from Graham and McKay.

March 24—Dillinger Gang members Harry Pierpont and Charles Makley are sentenced to death for the murder of Sheriff Jesse Sarber at Lima, Ohio; Russell Clark receives life.

March 31—John Dillinger and Homer Van Meter separately shoot it out with Division of Investigation agents and escape from a St. Paul apartment building.

– A special grand jury finds little evidence of political or police corruption in St. Paul and ridicules charges that the city is a haven for outlaws.

– Raymond Hamilton and Mary O'Dare rob the State National Bank at West, Texas, of $1,862.

April 1—The Barrow Gang murders Highway Patrolmen Edward Bryan Wheeler and Holloway Daniel Murphy near Grapevine, Texas. Clyde Barrow is named Texas's Public Enemy No. 1.

April 3—Dillinger Gang member Eddie Green is shot by Division of Investigation agents in St. Paul. His wife, Bessie, is arrested and provides the federal agents with much information about the Dillinger and Barker-Karpis Gangs and the St. Paul underworld.

— Following an anonymous letter with a map showing the body of a "rat," reporter Dick Vaughn of the *Houston Press* discovers the shot and bludgeoned corpse of parolee Wade McNabb, a former trusty at Eastham Prison Farm, in a wooded area near Waskom, Texas. Later rumors indicate that McNabb was kidnapped and murdered by the Barrow Gang as the result of a personal dispute with either Clyde Barrow or Joe Palmer.

April 5—The Tri-State Gang, headed by Robert Mais and Walter Legenza, hijacks a truckload of Camel cigarettes and Prince Albert tobacco, valued at approximately $17,000, near Norlina, North Carolina. The drivers are kidnapped and left handcuffed to trees at Bowling Green, Virginia.

— Cashiers William A. Harlan and Leon Hagan, armed with pistols, reportedly drive away two "machine-gun bandits" in a gunfight at the First State Bank in Bishop, Texas.

April 5–8—John Dillinger, now the country's most hunted criminal, decides no one would expect him to go back home to Mooresville, Indiana, and spends a weekend at his father's farm visiting with relatives and friends. Many of Mooresville's residents will sign a petition asking Governor Paul McNutt to pardon Dillinger if he surrenders.

April 6—The Barrow Gang murders Constable Cal Campbell and wounds and kidnaps Chief of Police Percy Boyd near Commerce, Oklahoma. Boyd is released near Fort Scott, Kansas.

April 9—Division of Investigation agents miss Dillinger but arrest his girlfriend, Evelyn "Billie" Frechette, at Larry Strong's State & Austin Tavern, 416 North State Street.

April 11—Eddie Green dies in a St. Paul hospital after deliriously providing federal agents with the solutions to numerous unsolved crimes.

April 12—William Benjamin "Big Bill" Phillips, a member of the Tri-State Gang, is slain by police at Adams Mill Road and Ontario Place in Washington, D.C.

April 13—John Dillinger and Homer Van Meter rob the police station at Warsaw, Indiana, stealing two revolvers and three bulletproof vests.

April 16—The Barrow Gang robs the First National Bank at Stuart, Iowa, of $1,500.

April 17—News of a federal trap for Dillinger in Louisville is leaked to newspapers, so Dillinger, Hamilton, and girlfriend Pat Cherrington instead visit Hamilton's sister in Sault Ste. Marie, Michigan, which leads to her arrest for harboring.

April 18—John Dillinger is erroneously named as leader of a Montgomery, Louisiana, bank robbery.

April 19—The Dillinger Gang is suspected in a $27,000 robbery of the First National Bank at Pana, Illinois.

— In Chicago, George Dale, accomplice of "Blonde Tigress" Eleanor Jarman, is executed at the Cook County Jail for the murder of Gustav Hoeh. Before walking to the electric chair, Dale reportedly writes a love letter to Jarman, who is serving a 199-year sentence in the women's prison at Dwight, Illinois.

April 20—A lone bandit robs the Iredell State Bank at Iredell, Texas. Clyde Barrow is a suspect.

April 22—The Dillinger Gang shoots its way out of a federal trap at the Little Bohemia Lodge near Rhinelander, Wisconsin. Agents, led by Melvin Purvis, set off the battle by mistakenly shooting three innocent customers, killing one. Later, agent W. Carter Baum is slain and two other lawmen wounded by "Baby Face" Nelson. Three of the gang's women are left behind and captured.

April 23—John Dillinger, John Hamilton, and Homer Van Meter battle deputies near Hastings, Minnesota. Hamilton may be mortally wounded and is taken to the Aurora, Illinois, hideout of Barker-Karpis Gang member Volney Davis and his girlfriend, Edna "The Kissing Bandit" Murray.

April 25—Raymond Hamilton and Ted Brooks rob the First National Bank at Lewisville, Texas, of $2,300 but are captured later in the day near Howe, Texas.

Dillinger's Supposedly Missing Parts

Some credit for the outlaw's enduring popularity must go to a pair of Chicago writers who in 1970 breathed life back into speculation that the man killed outside the Biograph Theatre was not, in fact, John Dillinger. That idea has been around since Dillinger's death in 1934, when people who claimed to have known the outlaw saw his body on the slab in the Cook County Morgue and discovered they could get an inch or two of newspaper coverage by insisting it didn't look like him.

In the late 1930s, a letter ostensibly written by Dillinger reached his family in Indiana and convinced some members that John was still alive. In 1938, an FBI agent, passing through Dillinger's hometown, reported that a substantial number of Mooresville residents still believed that "Johnnie" had somehow pulled a fast one on the feds.

Dillinger: Dead or Alive? attempted to build a conspiracy theory—or theories, since none seemed complete or plausible—on the many discrepancies in official records, and if it had to overlook some convincing evidence of Dillinger's demise, it at least yielded much new information overlooked by other researchers. It also proved that, even if dead and buried, Dillinger still lived in the hearts and minds of many Americans for whom he was the last of the great antiheroes who had become a legend in his own time.

Part of the legend holds that Dillinger's brain was "stolen" during his autopsy, and that belief contains at least some element of truth. The young medical intern and resident, who were buttonholed by police the night of the killing, found themselves performing the postmortem in the absence of the medical examiner (who signed the report for posterity), and they did in fact remove Dillinger's brain and send it to the pathology department. They did so because it seemed like the thing to do, for some in the medical community still expected to discover abnormalities in the features and the brains of arch criminals [see p. 490]. And that was the last they saw of it.

When an undertaker reported the brain was missing and no one claimed to have it, the word "stolen" found its way into newspaper headlines. This led the Dillinger family to threaten a lawsuit against Cook County out of fear it would end up as a carnival attraction (offers for Dillinger's body had been angrily turned down) or that it otherwise would be displayed. In the chaos that prevailed at the morgue that night and all the next day, at least three different parties had bullied or bribed their way past the police and through the crowds to make unauthorized death masks of the infamous Dillinger's face, so the family had reason to believe the worst.

Already criticized for the death-mask making and general treatment of the corpse, Cook County authorities scrambled to solve the mystery of the missing brain without communicating well enough to get their stories straight. Coroner Frank Walsh first denied that the brain was missing, only to learn that Medical Examiner Kearns had acknowledged the removal of an ounce or two of gray matter for scientific testing. Unaware of Kearns's announcement, a coroner's toxicologist contradicted both by declaring that he had half the brain preserved in a jar, and he thought the other half had been put in the corpse's stomach cavity to avoid reopening the skull. Before that information reached Kearns, he suddenly remembered having sent the toxicologist two-thirds of the brain while keeping one-third in his lab.

On August 3, a waggish reporter for the *Chicago Daily Times* totaled up the fractions located in various places and complimented the coroner's office on accounting for more of Dillinger's brain than he had to begin with.

Persuaded that the brain had not been removed for malicious or commercial purposes, the Dillingers dropped their suit, and with what must have been a sigh of relief heard all over Cook County, Walsh advised that whatever portions had been removed were destroyed in various tests, none of which revealed any abnormalities.

Which does not quite end the matter. Years later someone connected with Northwestern University's Medical School is supposed to have discovered Dillinger's brain, more or less intact, hidden in a laboratory

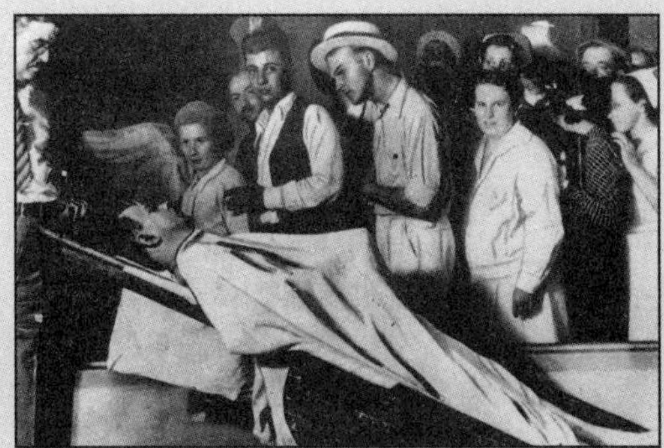

Dillinger's body, with and without his "erection," caused by the position of his arm but flattened by retouchers in most newspapers of the day.

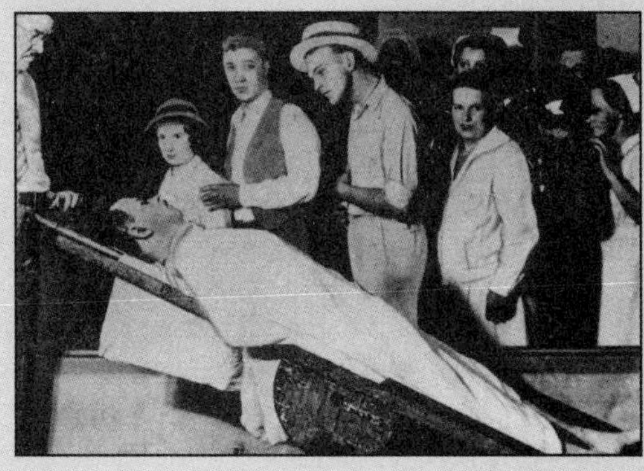

that had undergone remodeling after World War II. Supposedly, one of the professors kept it for a time as a souvenir, then gave it to a physician friend in Kansas, who eventually sold it to a Chicago optometrist named, the story goes, Dr. Brayne.

Which leaves only the matter of Dillinger's sexual endowment. That he easily charmed women with his cryptic smile, romantic style, and display of confidence cannot be questioned. But how that translated into a penis of heroic proportions may forever remain a mystery, since his autopsy revealed an organ of average size. The tendency to endow famous men with great sexual prowess is well known to students of folklore, and in Dillinger's case this may have been enhanced by a front-page photo in the *Chicago Daily News* which appeared to give his sheet-covered body an impressive erection. Most other papers publishing that picture had a retoucher flatten the sheet, whose effect actually was caused by the position of his arm.

But soon after his death the story began to circulate that the size of Dillinger's organ qualified it for display at the Smithsonian Institution, or alternatively at the National Medical Museum long located on the institution's grounds. So widespread was the rumor, at least in certain circles, that both organizations had to print form letters politely and euphemistically denying they have ever possessed, much less displayed, any part of Dillinger's anatomy, that part especially.

Still the story persists. Any number of people have claimed to have seen the specimen, or know someone who has seen it, which has always turned out to be knowing someone else who knows someone who knew someone, etc. In 1968 two California college students, thinking they could trick a response out of J. Edgar Hoover, wrote the FBI that they intended to scotch the penis rumor once and for all and only needed substantiation. Their letter fell into the hands of a subordinate who denounced it as juvenile, disgusting, and not deserving of an answer. At the bottom of the agent's memo Hoover huffed, "I concur."

– Four gunmen rob the First National Bank at Levelland, Texas, of $2,500.

April 26—William Edward Vidler, a bookie, is arrested by federal agents in Chicago for passing Bremer ransom money.

– Elizabeth Fontaine, formerly the "moll" of "Big Bill" Phillips, is shot and seriously wounded by gang leader Robert Mais in an apartment at Upper Darby, Pennsylvania. She survives and provides federal agents with much information on the Tri-State Gang.

April 28—Chicago politician "Boss" McLaughlin is arrested by federal agents for passing Bremer ransom money.

April 30—Federal agents in San Antonio arrest gunsmith H. S. Lebman on suspicion of supplying machine guns and specially modified machine pistols to the Dillinger Gang.

– At the federal court in San Angelo, Texas, Louise Magness is convicted of harboring Kathryn and George "Machine Gun" Kelly and sentenced to a year and a day in the women's federal prison at Alderson, West Virginia.

April 30 (approx.)—John Hamilton supposedly dies at Aurora, Illinois, and is secretly buried near the town of Oswego by Dillinger, Van Meter, and members of the Barker-Karpis Gang [see "The Body Identified as John Hamilton," p. 439].

May 1—Three policemen are slugged and disarmed at Bellwood, Indiana. Dillinger is suspected.

May 3—The Division of Investigation notifies Scottish authorities of a tip that Dillinger is aboard the S.S. *Duchess of York*, bound for Glasgow. Though Dillinger is not on the ship, the tip will lead to the arrest of another fugitive, Trebilsch Lincoln, alias Abbot Chao Kung, German spy during World War I wanted for fomenting rebellion in India.

— The Barrow Gang robs the Farmers Trust Branch Bank in Everly, Iowa, of $700.

May 4—Three men rob the First National Bank at Fostoria, Ohio, of $17,000, shooting five people. Two of the robbers are identified by witnesses as John Dillinger and Homer Van Meter.

— The Federal grand jury at St. Paul returns an indictment charging "Doc" Barker, Alvin Karpis, John J. McLaughlin Sr., John J. McLaughlin Jr., William Edward Vidler, Philip J. Delaney, Frankie Wright, a "Slim," an "Izzy," a "John Doe," and a "Richard Roe" with conspiracy to kidnap Edward George Bremer and transport him from St. Paul, Minnesota, to Illinois.

— A federal complaint is filed at Wilmington, North Carolina, charging Walter Legurenza (alias Legenza), Morris Kauffman, and John Kendrick, members of the Tri-State Gang, with theft from a shipment in interstate commerce.

May 9—Jim Clark, Frank Delmar, Ennis Smiddy, and Aubrey "Red" Unsell rob the Bank of Wetumka in Wetumka, Oklahoma, of $2,000.

May 18—Three men rob the Citizens Commercial Savings Bank at Flint, Michigan, of $25,000. Dillinger is typically suspected.

— Clyde Barrow, Raymond Hamilton, Henry Methvin, and Joe Palmer are indicted by the federal grand jury at Dallas, Texas, for theft of U.S government property—the Army's automatic pistols and BARs.

May 19—The federal grand jury at Madison, Wisconsin, indicts John Dillinger for conspiracy to harbor Tommy Carroll, wanted for post office robbery. Tommy Carroll is indicted for conspiracy to harbor John Dillinger. Homer Van Meter, John Hamilton, and Lester Gillis, alias "Baby Face" Nelson, are indicted for conspiracy to harbor John Dillinger, Tommy Carroll, and each other.

— Billie Jean Mace, Bonnie Parker's sister, is arrested in Gladewater, Texas, on suspicion of murder.

May 20—Barrow Gang associate Jack Nichols is arrested in Longview, Texas.

May 23—Clyde Barrow and Bonnie Parker are killed between Gibsland and Sailes, Louisiana, by Texas and Louisiana peace officers led by Captain Frank Hamer.

— In St. Paul, Evelyn Frechette and Dr. Clayton E. May are convicted of harboring Dillinger. Both are sentenced to two years and fined $10,000.

— Morris Kauffman, member of the Tri-State Gang, is found murdered in Pittsburgh.

May 24—Two policemen are killed near East Chicago, Indiana, probably after investigating a panel truck driven by Homer Van Meter and John Dillinger. Five state governors collectively post a $5,000 reward for Dillinger's capture. *Liberty* magazine offers a $1,000 reward.

May 25—Raymond Hamilton, already serving a 263-year prison sentence, is convicted of another bank robbery and sentenced to an additional ninety-nine years.

May 27—Drs. Wilhelm Loeser and Harold Cassidy begin plastic surgery on the faces and fingerprints of John Dillinger and Homer Van Meter at the Chicago home of ex-bootlegger James Probasco.

May 29—Two gunmen rob the First National Bank at Stafford, Oklahoma, of $500. Adam Richetti and "Shine" Rush are suspected, but Carl Melton and Ray Wilson will be charged later.

May 31—Jim Clark, Frank Delmar, "Red" Unsell, and Ennis Smiddy rob the Peoples National Bank at Kingfisher, Oklahoma, of $3,000. (Clark robbed the same bank in 1933 with Harvey Bailey, Wilbur Underhill, and others.)

May-June—At the urging of U.S. Attorney General Cummings, Congress passes a series of federal anti-crime bills that greatly expand the authority of J. Edgar Hoover's Division of Investigation.

June 2—Dillinger Gang "molls" Opal Long and Patricia Cherrington, sisters, are arrested by federal agents at the Chateau Hotel, 3838 North Broadway, in Chicago. Jean Helen Burke, girlfriend of Dillinger contact Arthur "Fish" Johnston, also is picked up.

— The Tri-State Gang robs a National Guard armory at Hyattsville, Maryland.

June 4—Eddie Bentz and others rob the Caledonia National Bank at Danville, Vermont, of $18,846. Bentz has been a successful bank robber for years and is suspected of participating in the million-dollar bank robbery at Lincoln, Nebraska, in 1930.

— Robert Mais, Walter Legenza, and Marie McKeever, members of the Tri-State Gang, are captured by police after a gun battle near the Fair Grounds in Baltimore, Maryland. Mais and Legenza will be convicted of murder in Virginia and sentenced to death.

June 7—Dillinger outlaw Tommy Carroll is killed by police in Waterloo, Iowa. His mistress, Jean Delaney, is captured. (Jean is the sister of Dolores Delaney, Alvin Karpis's mistress, and of Helen "Babe" Delaney Reilly, wife of Dillinger associate Albert "Pat" Reilly.)

June 8—Dillinger is indicted by the federal grand jury at South Bend, Indiana, for interstate transportation of a car stolen from Sheriff Lillian Holley in the Crown Point jailbreak.

June 13—Raymond Hamilton is sentenced to death for the murder of a prison guard at Huntsville, Texas.

June 14—The Ramsey County grand jury indicts John Dillinger and Homer Van Meter for assault in connection with their March 31 gun battle in St. Paul.

— Former Barrow Gang member Joe Palmer kidnaps a policeman and two other men in Davenport, Iowa. Palmer flees with his hostages to St. Joseph, Missouri, where he will be captured on June 15.

June 20—Jim Clark, Frank Delmar, "Red" Unsell, and Ennis Smiddy rob the Merchants Bank in Crescent, Oklahoma.

June 22—John Dillinger is named the country's "most wanted" (declared the national Public Enemy No. 1 in the press) by U.S. Attorney General Homer S. Cummings, who offers a $10,000 reward for Dillinger and $5,000 for Nelson.

— In Chicago, Dillinger celebrates his thirty-first birthday with new girlfriend Polly Hamilton at the French Casino nightclub, 4812 North Clark Street.

June 23—Dillinger and Polly Hamilton again visit the French Casino to celebrate Polly's birthday.

June 24—Some sixty state and federal officers raid a ranch near Branson, Missouri, on a tip that Dillinger and "Pretty Boy" Floyd are recovering from wounds there.

June 27—Albert "Pat" Reilly is arrested by federal agents in St. Paul on a charge of harboring Dillinger. Reilly claims to have heard that Dillinger is dead.

June 29—Tried for the murder of a Texas prison guard, former Barrow gangster Joe Palmer is sentenced to death. Palmer admits the killing and vainly begs that his accomplice, Raymond Hamilton, be spared from execution.

June 30—John Dillinger, "Baby Face" Nelson, Homer Van Meter and two or three other men rob the Merchants National Bank at South Bend, Indiana, of $29,890, killing Patrolman Howard Wagner. [Contemporary sources indicate some confusion as to whether five or six men took part in the South Bend job. It is now reasonably certain that Jack Perkins, later acquitted of this crime but convicted of harboring Nelson, was present, and evidence from several sources suggests that the other unidentified robber may have been "Pretty Boy" Floyd, which would mark probably the only occasion that Floyd and Dillinger worked together. J. Edgar Hoover later named John Paul Chase as one of the robbers.]

July 6—Patricia Cherrington is convicted at Madison, Wisconsin, of harboring Dillinger and sentenced to two years.

July 10—Mob boss John Lazia, prominent in the Kansas City Massacre case, is machine-gunned by rival gangsters in Kansas City.

— W. H. Ortag and "Buster" Orr rob the First State

Plastic Surgery and Piquett's Plot

Arthur O'Leary, attorney Louis Piquett's investigator, wrote the following statement while he, Dr. Wilhelm Loeser and Dr. Harold Cassidy were awaiting trial in the county jail at Waukegan, Illinois. Toward the end of his account, he mentions that Piquett, confiding to James Probasco, believed his only way out of his increasing troubles with the Justice Department was to put both John Dillinger and O'Leary "on the spot."

In response to the many requests that the true relationship of myself with John Dillinger be known, and in fairness to all concerned, I am writing the facts of my meeting and contacts with him.

My first meeting with John Dillinger took place in the jail at Crown Point, Indiana, where I was introduced by his Lawyer Louis B. Piquett, by whom I was employed as his investigator. My understanding with Mr. Piquett was that I would receive one third of any fee that he would get from this case. Mr. Piquett intended to send me to Florida to see some people that Dillinger had told him could prove that he was in Florida at the time of the East Chicago Bank robbery. My talk with Dillinger was not made because he did not advance the money. I next saw Dillinger several weeks after he escaped from the jail at Crown Point, Indiana.

Late one afternoon a telephone call was transferred to my phone from the switchboard in our office. The party asked if it was possible to get in touch with Mr. Piquett on

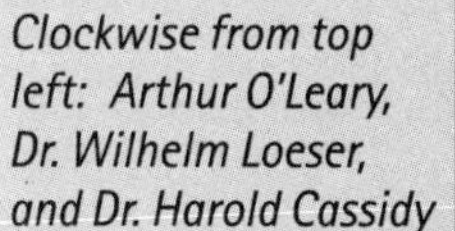

Clockwise from top left: Arthur O'Leary, Dr. Wilhelm Loeser, and Dr. Harold Cassidy

The house of Jimmy Probasco at 2509 North Crawford in Chicago is where Dillinger and Homer Van Meter underwent plastic surgery.

a matter of importance. I stated that Mr. Piquett had gone for the day and could not be reached. I then asked who was calling, and the answer was a client of his. I asked if there was anything I could do, that this was Mr. O'Leary speaking, Mr. Piquett's investigator. The answer was yes, I would appreciate your meeting me at the Wacker Street entrance of your building in about fifteen minutes. I am driving a car, and there is no parking allowed there. I will give you a message for Mr. Piquett. I was standing at this entrance at the time mentioned, when a car pulled up to the curb, and a girl whom I recognized as Evelyn Frechette motioned me to come over. Sitting back of the wheel was John Dillinger.

Dillinger said to Mr. O'Leary, "Billy and I are going to be married just as soon as she can get a divorce from her husband, Ralph Sparks, who is now in the Pen. at Leavenworth, will you ask Mr. Piquett if he would handle this case and hurry her Divorce along. I told him that I would speak to Mr. Piquett in the morning. He said Billy would call in a few days for an answer and drove away.

Several days later Evelyn Frechette (whom he referred to as Billy) called on the phone and asked me to meet her in about an hour at West Madison Street and Homan Ave. I met her there, and she directed me to a car in which Dillinger was sitting. He asked me what the answer was, and I told him that Mr. Piquett was not interested. Dillinger then asked me if I would give him Mr. Piquett's home phone number. I told him that Mr. Piquett had an unlisted number, and that he never permitted it to be given by anyone but himself. He then asked my phone number, and I gave it to him.

The next time I heard from Dillinger, was the nite that Evelyn Frechette was arrested. He phoned my home around eight o'clock and said, Billy was just picked up by the Police or Federal men at the State and Austin restaurant. He asked me to call Mr. Piquett and have him represent her. I informed him that Mr. Piquett was in Washington, D.C., but that I would phone him and find out. Dillinger said I will watch the newspapers.

That nite at twelve o'clock I went down to our office and called Mr. Piquett at the Willard Hotel in Washington. I informed him of what had taken place. He said he was returning to Chicago the following nite. Mr. Piquett on his return appeared before the Court for Evelyn Frechette. An order was given by the Court that she be taken to St. Paul, Minn., for trial. A few days after the Court's decision, Dillinger called our office again and asked if I would meet him in about an hour at the same place as before. I did. He wanted to know if Mr. Piquett would represent Billy in St. Paul, and if not, would he get a Lawyer for her there.

I informed him that this matter had already been discussed, that Mr. Piquett would go to St. Paul and take care of her case. However, it would be necessary for him to advance five hundred dollars. He gave me this amount. At this meeting Dillinger mentioned that he would like to have some plastic surgical work done on his face and requested me to ask Mr. Piquett if he knew a reliable doctor who could do this work and be trusted, also a place where he could stay while this was being done. I told Dillinger I would give Mr. Piquett his message and received one hundred and sixty six dollars. I also delivered Dillinger's message to him. Mr. Piquett said to me, "I will see what can be done."

At this time I asked Mr. Piquett if I was violating any law by making these contacts with Dillinger. He informed me that I, as his investigator, was not subject to any trouble, as the law permitted him as an attorney to contact any of his clients, and that he was not subject to prosecution, and that the same law applied to his investigator, that these contacts were being made at his direction, and that the same law applied here as does between priest and confessor.

Some time later I was called from my office into Mr. Piquett's office, and was introduced by him to a man by the name of Jimmy Probasco. Mr. Piquett said, "I have known Jimmy many years, and he is alright. I have been talking with him about Dillinger staying at his home. He lives on No. Crawford Ave. He is a bachelor, and this would be a good place for Dillinger to stay." Probasco said, "I am in dire need of money, and would welcome the opportunity. It is only a matter of how much he will pay me." Probasco then left. Probasco returned to the office several times after this and wanted to know if Dillinger was going to stay with him, because he was opening a Tavern on Howard Street and needed some money. Mr. Piquett and I told him we did not know, until we hear from Dillinger.

Some days later Mr. Piquett informed me that he had talked to a doctor whom he had known many years, that he could be trusted and that on plastic surgery there was no better. One afternoon later I went with Mr. Piquett to a residence on Wrightwood Ave. and there was introduced by him to Doctor Ralph Robind [an alias usually spelled Robeind] whom I found out later was Dr. Wilhelm Loeser. At this meeting we discussed the nature of the work to be done, the fee to be charged, and how this fee was asked to be divided. Dr. Loeser did not seem to be very anxious. He asked Mr. Piquett whether this plastic work was against the law, whereupon Mr. Piquett assured both Dr. Loeser and myself that this work was entirely within the law. Dr. Loeser then said that if he handled the case the fee would be five thousand dollars. It also was discussed about someone who would act as assistant to Dr. Loeser, and in this capacity the name of Dr. Harold Cassidy was mentioned. It was decided to pay him the sum of six hundred dollars. The balance to be equally divided between Dr. Loeser, Mr. Piquett and myself. This division of the money was made according to the dictum of Mr. Piquett.

Soon after the meeting with Dr. Loeser, perhaps a week or ten days later, Dillinger called the office again and asked me to meet him at Sacramento and Augusta blvds. Dillinger at this meeting discussed the matter of an appeal of the Evelyn Frechette case. I advised that Mr. Piquett thought this should be done, because he thought there were several instances of reversible error in her trial. I also told him the cost would be two thousand five hundred dollars. Dillinger said he would think it over. At this time I spoke to him about Jimmy Probasco and Dr. Loeser, and said to him Mr. Piquett recommends both very highly, and to tell him that he (Piquett) had known both Probasco and Dr. Loeser many years, and that they both were available at any time. Dillinger asked for Probasco's address, and I gave it to him. I also informed him that the doctor's fee would be five thousand dollars. He stated I will let you know shortly.

At another meeting with Dillinger either at the same place or at the home of Jimmy Probasco, he gave me the twenty five hundred dollars, mentioned above, for the appeal of the Evelyn Frechette case. Two thousand dollars of this money was turned over to a St. Paul lawyer, for the appeal of the Evelyn Frechette case. I was paid two hundred and fifty dollars.

On the night of May 27th Dillinger called my home and asked that I have Mr. Piquett meet him at the address I have given him, promptly at ten o'clock. I telephoned Mr. Piquett, and he came over to my apartment. We left my apartment together and drove to Probasco's home at 2509 N. Crawford Ave. We arrived there at the appointed time and met Dillinger. Piquett, Dillinger, and myself entered. Mr. Piquett then introduced Dillinger to Probasco. We then went to the kitchen table, where Dillinger counted out to Mr. Piquett three thousand dollars, saying he would pay the balance after the operation, which he would like to have done the following day. After some further questions by Dillinger regarding Probasco and the doctors, and Mr. Piquett's assurance that they were alright, Dillinger then wanted to know who the woman was that was there. Probasco was called and explained that she was his housekeeper. He told Dillinger that he could rely on her the same as himself, but that if he objected to her being there he would have her stay elsewhere. This seemed to satisfy Dillinger, and he asked if she was a good cook. There was some further discussion about Dr.s Loeser and Cassidy as to their ability, and it was then decided that Dr. Cassidy would remain with Dillinger until he was well. (This matter had been taken up with Dr. Cassidy on several occasions at our office by both Mr. Piquett and myself prior to this meeting.) Probasco and Dillinger then talked about how much money Probasco would receive. This was either twenty-five or thirty-five dollars a day. Mr. Piquett and Dillinger then talked about the Frechette case. Mr. Piquett and I then departed.

When we arrived at my residence Mr. Piquett counted out fourteen hundred dollars to me, directing me to pay Dr. Cassidy six hundred dollars, and to have Dr. Cassidy and Dr. Loeser at Probasco's residence the following day at the appointed time.

The next day I went to see Dr. Cassidy at 1117 No. Dearborn St. and asked him to hire a drive-yourself car and meet me at my residence around seven that evening. When he arrived we drove to Dr. Loeser's home on Wrightwood Ave. I went in and notified Dr. Loeser that we were waiting outside in a car. In a few minutes he came out. Dr. Loeser, Dr. Cassidy and myself proceeded to the Probasco home. Dr. Loeser got out of the car several blocks from Probasco's residence. Dr. Cassidy and I parked the car and then met Dr. Loeser. We entered and I introduced Doctors. Dr. Loeser asked

Dillinger a few questions and then prepared to operate. Dr. Cassidy administered the anesthetic and assisted generally.

Dr. Cassidy gave the ether so profusely to Dillinger so that the latter swallowed his tongue and was blue in the face and was not breathing when Dr. Loeser returned to the room a few moments later. Instantaneously Dr. Loeser used a pair of forceps and pulled Dillinger's tongue out of his mouth, and simultaneously pushed both of Dillinger's elbows into his ribs. This was done automatically and without forethought by Dr. Loeser, evidently as had been done many times previously under similar circumstances, and it brought Dillinger back immediately to normal breathing from a condition which was very close to death by suffocation. Thereafter solely local anesthesia was used. Several hours later Dr. Loeser left. I went home around three o'clock in the morning. Dr. Cassidy remained to take care of Dillinger. Present on this occasion were Probasco, his housekeeper named Peggy, Dr. Cassidy, Dr. Loeser, Dillinger, and myself. Mr. Piquett did not show up.

Law Offices
LOUIS P. PIQUETT
Suite 2110
228 N. LaSalle St.
CHICAGO

Telephones Central 8847
8848

March 7, 1934

Mrs. Eulalia Callender
Galion,
Ohio.

My Dear Mrs Callender,

Yours of March 7th, received and read with great deal of interest. Let me say in behalf of my client I certainly appreciate a very tender feeling reading between the lines of your short message. I can clearly realize the trend of your beautiful heart.

I will undertake seriously to have the message delivered to my client in person. You may rest assured that I am perfectly safe in saying that the party in question will be most appreciative of your very sweet offerings and thought. I, like you, believe that it was the hand of God that enabled this young Christian soul to live on.

From my experience with the party in question, I can safely tell you that he will rob no banks, but it is his firm intention to travel in the path of righteousness. He is a great student of the Bible. The last conversation I had with him he had told me that it was his intention to give the balance of his life in this world to God, and beyond any doubt your sweet prayers have had a great deal to do with this deliverance.

I will be most happy to talk in person with as sweet a mind as I think you have, so if any time in the near future you feel well enough to come to Chicago you may meet me at my office address. I will be more than glad to discuss this matter with you further.

With very deepest appreciation for your very kind and thoughtful message, I beg to remain yours very sincerely and truly,

LPP/MB

Louis P. Piquett

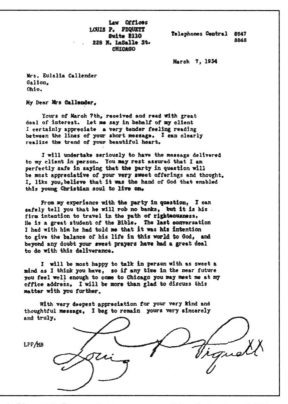

Louis Piquett's flowery letter assures a Mrs. Calender of Ohio that his client has taken up the Bible and will henceforth travel the path of righteousness, not yet aware that Dillinger had already robbed the bank at Sioux Falls, South Dakota, the previous afternoon.

Saturday afternoon of this week Dr. Cassidy departed. This was June 2nd. On this same nite Mr. Piquett and I went over to Probasco's. Dillinger said, "I am going to remain here for another week, because a friend of mine will be here tomorrow nite. He wants the same work done on him, and he will pay the same price. Have both doctors here tomorrow nite." Probasco stated that arrangements had been made for Dillinger's friend to stay with him. At this time the friend's name was not mentioned.

Sunday morning June 3d, Mr. Piquett came to my apartment and asked if I had seen Dr. Cassidy about the appointment that nite. I told him that I had not, but that I would go down stairs and see him. Dr. Cassidy at this time was staying in a room at the same hotel where I was living. I returned in a few minutes and informed Mr. Piquett that Dr. Cassidy was not anxious

"LAWYER TO THE STARS"

John Dillinger's attorney Louis Piquett practiced law the way most Chicago aldermen practiced politics—without fear, favor (except at a price), or anything resembling scruples. He had "read" for his license while working as a bartender and stuffing ballot boxes for Mayor "Big Bill" Thompson. This earned him a job as city prosecutor, which he kept until he had met enough crooks to support him in private practice. He represented local abortion rings and was the designated "fixer" for one or more police districts. When the wife of Russell Gibson (later of the Barker-Karpis Gang) tried to bail out her husband on a jewel-theft charge, the cops told her to keep her money and go see Piquett, who had streamlined the municipal justice system to the point where $500 resolved matters without any burdensome paperwork.

Louis Piquett

Piquett's clients included the renowned con man William Elmer Meade and St. Louis gunman Leo Brothers, whose paid killing of *Chicago Tribune* reporter Jake Lingle in a crowded downtown underpass caused the greatest uproar since the St. Valentine's Day Massacre. Brothers made local history as the first "gangster" convicted of murder since the start of the city's beer wars, but Piquett negotiated a sentence of only fourteen years.

The FBI was not especially surprised when Dillinger, facing an Indiana murder charge, became Piquett's next notorious client, but they never learned the ruse the lawyer and his assistant, Arthur O'Leary, used to accomplish this. Both men knew plenty of Indiana's state prisoners who would have known Dillinger, and Piquett soon had his business card smuggled by O'Leary to the Crown Point jail's celebrity inmate. Written on the back was the message, "Hire no lawyer but this one. Gang raising funds.—Happy."*

That was a name Dillinger apparently knew, and he found in Piquett a legal counselor in some ways less principled than himself. Piquett's services stretched the bounds of attorney-client privilege—from helping engineer Dillinger's wooden-pistol jailbreak (with much help from O'Leary) to providing him and Homer Van Meter with plastic surgeons, an act which ultimately cost him his license and a stretch in prison when a trial established that Van Meter was not legally his client. He ended up financially ruined and avoiding his former friends. The bar Piquett eventually returned to was in a tavern instead of a courthouse.

Piquett was living at 661 West Sheridan Road in Chicago at the time of his death on December 12, 1951, and he is buried in Platteville, Wisconsin, under the family name Piquette.

---

*Probably a former prison inmate; identified in a memo to Indiana State Police Captain Matt Leach as Fred "Happy" Meyers.

to go back. Thereupon Mr. Piquett went to Dr. Cassidy's room and on his return stated that Dr. Cassidy will be there. Mr. Piquett said, "I have already talked with Dr. Loeser, and he will meet you tonight at North Ave. and Clark St. at eight thirty. You and Dr. Loeser take a street car from there, and I will meet you at Probasco's. Sunday nite June 3d, Dr. Loeser and I went over to Probasco's together. Soon after we arrived Mr. Piquett and Dr. Cassidy came in, and we were all introduced to Homer Van Meter. In a bedroom off the living room Dillinger and Van Meter counted out seven thousand dollars and gave it to Mr. Piquett. Mr. Piquett and I remained only a short while as the Doctors were getting ready to operate. There remained at Probasco's residence Probasco, Peggy, Dr. Loeser, Dr. Cassidy, Dillinger and Van Meter.

On our way home Mr. Piquett told me to meet him the following morning at eleven thirty at Dr. Loeser's room, and that he would be there and then divide the money. I arrived at Dr. Loeser's room at noon. The money was laying on a cot, and from this he paid me twenty one hundred dollars. Mr. Piquett informed me that he had already paid Dr. Cassidy. I then departed leaving Mr. Piquett and Dr. Loeser together.

Twice in the evening and once in the afternoon during that week I stopped at Probasco's, and during one of these visits Mr. Piquett was present. I do not know what date Dillinger and Van Meter left the Probasco residence.

On July the first or second Probasco telephoned my home and left a message for me to see him. The following afternoon I went to Probasco's residence and found Van Meter there. Probasco said that he had called Dr. Cassidy at his Hotel and asked him to come over, but that he had not shown up. He pointed to Van Meter's head over which was a small piece of tape and remarked, Van Meter didn't know until now that I also am a doctor. I have stopped an infection from spreading. A few minutes later Dr. Cassidy arrived, looked at Van Meter's head, asked Probasco for some iodine, smeared a little on Van Meter's head, replaced the bandage, and then Dr. Cassidy and I left.

A few days later Dr. Cassidy stopped at my home and asked me to drive him to Hammond, Indiana. He said that he had been going out several times on the train to take care of Van Meter's head, and that he was late for his appointment. I drove Dr. Cassidy to a home in Hammond and remained in my car until he came out. We returned together to Chicago. The following nite I again drove Dr. Cassidy to Hammond, Indiana, and on this occasion Van Meter came out to the car and asked me to have a bottle of beer with him. In the home Van Meter remarked that Dr. Cassidy's bill should come out of the five thousand dollars which he had already paid, but that he would speak to Dillinger about it. Dr. Cassidy and I then returned to Chicago.

The following day Dillinger called me, and asked me to meet him that nite at eight O'Clock at 1400 North on Sacramento Blvd. Dr. Cassidy and I drove over and met Dillinger at that time, and Dillinger paid Dr. Cassidy five hundred dollars, saying this is from Van Meter for your work. Dillinger also gave me one hundred dollars and asked me to give this to Probasco for him. Dillinger had with him a girl whom I had never seen before. We were never introduced.

She remained on the sidewalk while Dillinger, Dr. Cassidy and myself talked in the car. This was the last time I saw John Dillinger. After leaving Dillinger Dr. Cassidy paid me two hundred and fifty dollars, Dr. Cassidy and I drove to a motor sales Co. and he purchased a new Ford car. I believe this was the nite of July 14th. The following nite Dr. Cassidy and I drove out to Hammond Ind. in Dr. Cassidy's new car to see Van Meter. This is the last time I saw Van Meter.

Dr. Cassidy and I drove back to Chicago, and I got out of his car at my home. In my apartment was a message saying "call Jimmy." This message was from Probasco. Instead of telephoning I drove over to see him, because I wanted to deliver the one hundred dollars, also pick up a Radio that he had belonging to Dillinger, which Dillinger said I could have.

Probasco said Dillinger called to find out if the one hundred dollars was satisfactory, and I told that it should be at least two hundred and fifty. Probasco then stated, however, this does not concern you, but I want to tell you something that does, which I have already told Dillinger. I was talking to Piquett about this balance due me, and Piquett asked me if I knew where Dillinger was living. I told him I did not know. Piquett said I am afraid we are going to get in a lot of trouble over this matter. The Department of Justice has been following me, in fact I spoke to one of their men and told him "I am going home from here." Piquett said the only way that he and I (Piquett and Probasco) would be safe was for him to find out where Dillinger was living and put you (O'Leary) and Dillinger on the spot, because if Dillinger was gone the government would cool off, and if you were gone, it would take all the heat off his office. He would see to it that Dr. Loeser left town, and that Dr. Cassidy had to stay under cover, as he was under indictment. Probasco said that he had loaned the Radio to the people upstairs, and asked me to return the following day for it. I thanked Probasco and left. I returned the next afternoon and got the Radio. That same nite I left Chicago with my family for Northern Wisconsin on a fishing trip, where I remained until July 24th.

On my return to Chicago I read in the newspapers, that the Department of Justice were looking for two Doctors and another man in connection with some plastic work that had been done on Dillinger. Thinking that the other man was myself I left Chicago at once.

About two weeks later I returned to Chicago, and suspecting, from what I had read in the newspapers, that Dr. Loeser and others were already in custody, I called Mr. Piquett on the telephone and asked how everything was. Mr. Piquett said everything is alright, come on up to the office. However I did not go to the office, but I did leave Chicago. I returned from St. Louis Mo. on August 25th, when I was taken in custody by the Department of Justice at Evanston Ill.

I am writing this article at the Lake County Jail Waukegan Ill., where Dr. Loeser, Dr. Cassidy and myself are being held awaiting disposition of our case.

12/7/1934

Signed A. O'Leary

Witnessed Dr. Wilhelm Loeser

O'Leary's statement covers some of his contacts with Dillinger but fails to mention that he was closely connected with the East Chicago underworld, that he already was on first-name terms with Martin Zarkovich (calling him "Zark"), probably had engineered Dillinger's Crown Point escape with bribe money supplied by "Baby Face" Nelson and Homer Van Meter, and had obtained the fake pistol from a woodworker in Chicago.

It was O'Leary who originally had gotten Piquett and Dillinger together by having Piquett's business card slipped to Dillinger in the Crown Point jail with the message written on the back, "Hire no attorney but this one. Gang raising funds. Happy." O'Leary, a frequent visitor to the Indiana state prison on behalf of Piquett, and Dillinger apparently knew a former prisoner there named "Happy." (At one time, Captain Matt Leach of the Indiana State Police identified a "Happy" as Fred Meyers, 4147 Irving Avenue, Chicago. And in 1936, the FBI received a letter from a "Hap"—half his name obscured by a notation tag—seeking a reward for delivering John Hamilton, whom the bureau believed was dead. See p. 439.)

After Dillinger's escape from Crown Point [see p. 361], O'Leary acknowledges already knowing Evelyn Frechette but avoids mentioning that the two of them met with Dillinger before the breakout or that Evelyn and Meyer Bogue congregated at Piquett's office listening to news of the jailbreak, afterward throwing a party that left Evelyn passed out on a couch. The following July, while Evelyn is still jailed in St. Paul, O'Leary and Cassidy met with Dillinger and a girl he does not introduce, but who must be Polly Hamilton, the friend of Anna Sage, both of whom were with Dillinger on July 22, the night he was killed.

Despite Piquett's persuasive assurances to everyone, his attorney-client privilege did not extend to O'Leary when the plastic surgery was planned and Van Meter entered the picture. It certainly did not extend to Drs. Loeser and Cassidy, or to Probasco (who fell to his death from a high window in the offices of the FBI, probably because he was being dangled outside to secure a confession in a manner earlier described by Jack Perkins and "Boss" McLaughlin).

Loeser had met Piquett while doing time in Leavenworth on a narcotics conviction. Cassidy was O'Leary's cousin, who had tangled with police over an "illegal operation" (abortion), evidently was the defendant in several malpractice suits, and still was wanted by Ottawa police on a perjury charge.

O'Leary was known to Don Costello of Racine, Wisconsin, when Costello was a boy, and he has contributed a previously unrecorded Dillinger yarn to the expanded paperback edition of *Dillinger: The Untold Story.* O'Leary died December 9, 1970, during a trip to Florida.

For commentary on Piquett, see p. 392; the statement of Anna Sage is on p. 398.

Bank at Allison, Texas, only to be killed by a posse later in the day near Sweetwater, Oklahoma.

July 12—Two men, one elderly, rob the First State Bank at Ketchum, Oklahoma, of a mere $300, taking cashier Luther Gregory hostage and releasing him outside town. Gregory and his father, bank president Ealum Gregory, join in pursuit of the bandits and encounter them shortly near Grove, Oklahoma. The elder Gregory is shot dead by the older bandit, and Luther Gregory kills the outlaws. The dead robbers soon are identified as John "Kaiser Bill" Goodman, a noted outlaw of many years, and Bill Quinton.

July 14—A Dillinger Gang meeting at a schoolyard on Wolf Road near Chicago is interrupted by the arrival of two police officers who are shot and wounded by "Baby Face" Nelson.

July 22—John Dillinger is killed by G-men and policemen from East Chicago, Indiana, led by federal agents Melvin Purvis and Sam Cowley, outside the Biograph Theatre at 2433 North Lincoln Avenue in Chicago, after being set up by Polly Hamilton's friend Anna Sage, the so-called "Lady in Red."

– Using smuggled guns, Raymond Hamilton, Joe Palmer, and Irvin "Blackie" Thompson shoot their way out of the Death House and escape from the Texas state prison at Huntsville. Another member of the gang, "Whitey" Walker, is killed attempting to scale the wall, and two other would-be escapees, Charlie Frazier and Roy Johnson, are wounded and recaptured. Hamilton, Palmer, and Thompson are described in press releases as "embryonic Dillingers."

July 24—Dr. Wilhelm Loeser, who performed the plastic surgery on Dillinger, is arrested by federal agents at 1127 South Harvey in Oak Park, Illinois.

– Billie Mace, sister of Bonnie Parker, and Floyd Hamilton, brother of Raymond Hamilton, are acquitted of the Easter Sunday murders of two highway patrolmen at Grapevine, Texas.

July 25—Salvatore Serpa, a reputed member of the Tri-State Gang, wanted in New Jersey for the killing of Edward "Cowboy" Wallace and "gang molls" Florence Miller and Ethel Greentree, is found murdered in Chicago.

July 26—Four men in overalls, carrying pistols and sawed-off shotguns, rob the Farmers Bank & Trust Co. in Henderson, Kentucky, of $34,237. "Baby Face" Nelson is wrongly named as a suspect.

– Three gunmen rob the Bank of Montreal branch at Keel Street and St. Clair Avenue in Toronto of $25,000.

July 27—James Probasco, owner of the house in which Dillinger underwent plastic surgery, supposedly commits suicide by leaping from a nineteenth-floor window of the Division of Investigation offices in Chicago's Bankers' Building. Rumors circulate that he fell to his death while being held out the window during interrogation.

– Raymond Hamilton and "Blackie" Thompson rob a National Guard armory on Lemmon Avenue in Dallas, stealing two heavy machine guns, five pistols, and 1,000 rounds of ammunition. They abandon their stolen car, containing the machine guns, near Houston after colliding with a mule.

Late July 1934—Dr. Joseph Moran, Barker-Karpis associate, disappears in Toledo. No body is found, but the Division of Investigation will hear later that Moran was murdered by the Barker-Karpis Gang.

August 1—Bank robber and Kansas prison escapee Jim Clark is recaptured in Tulsa.

– "Shine" Rush and Clifford "Jack" Boone rob the First State Bank in Wayne, Oklahoma, of $600.

– "Red" Unsell and others rob the First National Bank at Sentinel, Oklahoma, of $1,500.

August 11—Joe Palmer, Texas prison escapee and former Barrow Gang member, is recaptured in Paducah, Kentucky. Palmer brags that he planned the recent Henderson, Kentucky, bank robbery.

August 21—A United States Trucking Corp. armored car is robbed of $427,950 at the Rubel Ice plant in Brooklyn, New York, by the John Manning Gang. It is Brooklyn's first armored-car robbery. Gang member Benny "The Bum" McMahon accidentally shoots himself during the getaway and later dies of blood poisoning.

August 22—Al Capone and fifty-two other prisoners arrive at Alcatraz, transferred from the federal penitentiary in Atlanta.

– Oliver "Izzy" Berg, former "Bugs" Moran gangster, involved in passing the Bremer ransom, is arrested by federal agents at his sister's home in Chicago.

August 23—Homer Van Meter is killed by Tom Brown and other officers in St. Paul after being set up by Brown, for which he was cut out of his share of the Bremer ransom by the Barker-Karpis Gang. (A federal agent later said that in the morgue he had seen Van Meter's money belt containing several thousand dollars before it disappeared.)

– The Billy Pabst Gang, including Maurice Denning and Tom Limerick, robs a National Guard armory at Windom, Minnesota, stealing Springfield rifles, Colt automatics, and other ordnance.

August 24—Reportedly following signals from accomplices in a circling airplane, three gunmen in two cars force a mail truck to the curb in Butler, Pennsylvania, and steal a $51,000 payroll.

– Machine-gun bandits rob two bank messengers in Rome, Georgia, and escape with a $9,785 payroll.

August 29—"Shine" Rush and Clifford "Jack" Boone rob the state bank at Garber, Oklahoma, of $500.

September 4—James Wilson, nephew of Dr. Joseph Moran and former Barker-Karpis Gang

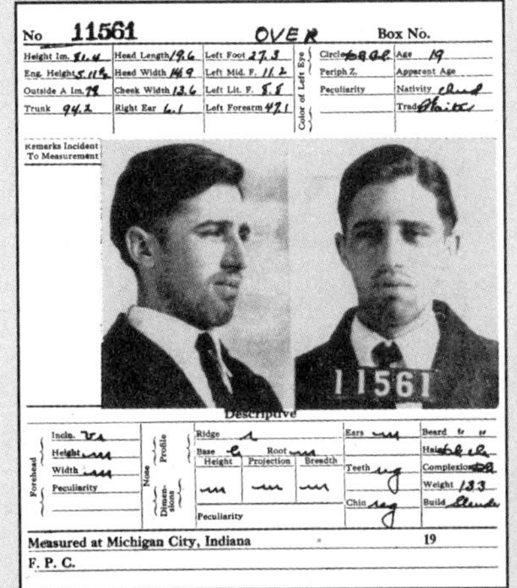

No 11561 OVER Box No.

Height Im. | Head Length 19.6 | Left Foot 27.3 | Color of Left Eye | Circle | Age 19
Eng. Height | Head Width | Left Mid. F. 11.2 | | Periph Z. | Apparent Age
Outside A Im. | Cheek Width 13.6 | Left Lit. F. | | Peculiarity | Nativity
Trunk 94.2 | Right Ear 6.1 | Left Forearm | | | Trade

Remarks Incident To Measurement

Descriptive

Forehead: Incln. / Height / Width / Peculiarity
Nose: Ridge / Base / Root / Profile / Dimensions: Height, Projection, Breadth / Peculiarity
Ears / Teeth / Chin
Beard / Hair / Complexion / Weight 133 / Build

Measured at Michigan City, Indiana 19

F. P. C.

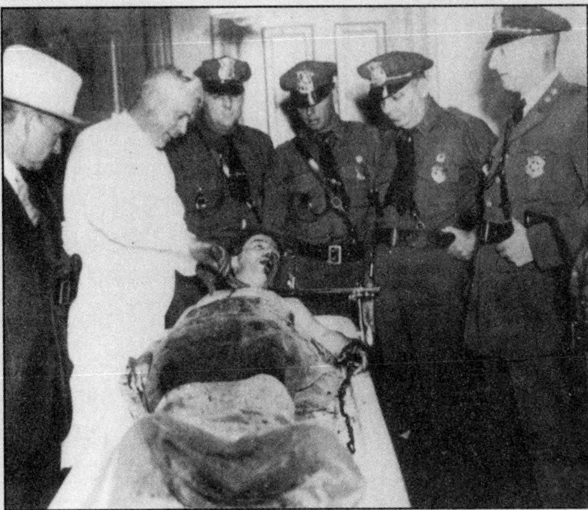

THE SANDUSKY REGISTER

HOMER VAN METER IS SLAIN BY POLICE

10 PERCENT LIMIT MADE FOR WHEAT

Ranks Of Dillinger Gang Again Thinned

MACHINE GUNNER OF DILLINGER MOB SHOT IN ALLEY AT ST. PAUL

TOM BROWN OF QUARTET TELLS ABOUT SLAYING

ROOSEVELT TO CONFER TODAY ON NRA SETUP

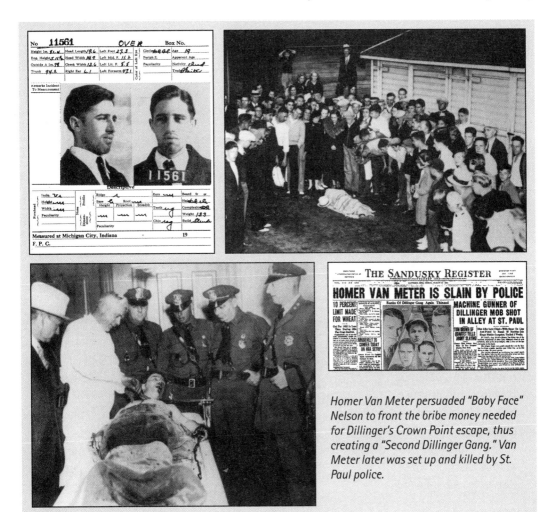

Homer Van Meter persuaded "Baby Face" Nelson to front the bribe money needed for Dillinger's Crown Point escape, thus creating a "Second Dillinger Gang." Van Meter later was set up and killed by St. Paul police.

The Statement of Anna Sage

After John Dillinger's death on July 22, 1934, Anna Sage hurried to her apartment at 2420 North Halsted in Chicago and with her son Steve Chiolak emptied a closet of the outlaw's guns, dumped them in Lake Michigan at Belmont Harbor, and then presented herself to federal agents for the expected questioning and her share of the reward money, which amounted to $5,000. (She also wanted to remind SAC Melvin Purvis of his promise to try to help her avoid deportation to her native Romania on morals charges. When Purvis found J. Edgar Hoover unwilling to intervene, it widened the split that had been developing between them.)

Anna Sage, née Ana Cumpanas, the "Lady in Red"

One of the Chicago agents who had been questioning Anna in Detroit, where she had been taken to avoid the press, recorded some of what she knew and some of what she supposedly had been told by Polly Hamilton; and he put this in a four-page memorandum to Sam Cowley dated July 28. But who knew whom, what, and when remains a mystery. In his book-length manuscript prepared in 1935,* G. Russell Girardin had gotten to know several of the principals, from Arthur O'Leary to Dillinger's father, and he was aware that Polly had worked for Anna at the Kostur House in Gary. As he wrote at the time:

Anna Sage's apartment building at 2420 North Halsted is where Dillinger was staying the night he was killed—less than a five-minute walk to the Biograph Theatre and located by number on the official FBI map.

> Out of the thousands of girls in Chicago, Dillinger happens to meet one whose friend, Anna Sage, has operated "resorts" in Gary and East Chicago, Indiana, where Dillinger has his closest underworld affiliations, and who presently operates a house two blocks from the corner where he has his meets. Moreover, this Anna's long-time associate and paramour happens to be the East Chicago police officer Martin Zarkovich, who knows Dillinger's friends in that city, as well as Arthur O'Leary in Chicago. . . . Whether or not Dillinger knew Anna Sage personally, he was almost certainly sent to her by their mutual friends, and it would have been she who introduced Dillinger to Polly and not the other way around.

O'Leary originally had connected Dillinger with Louis Piquett at Crown Point before Dillinger's escape with a wooden pistol. The fake gun had been fashioned by a German woodworker in Chicago, a friend of O'Leary's, and O'Leary probably was the conduit between the East Chicago underworld (including Zarkovich) and the bribe money advanced by Nelson and Van Meter to facilitate the escape. It was O'Leary's cousin, Dr. Cassidy, who assisted Dr. Loeser, who Piquett had known for years, in Dillinger's plastic surgery.

Had Dillinger survived his capture, he might have taken the betrayal personally and blown the whistle on his supposed friends in Chicago and East Chicago. Presumably this

*Published nearly sixty years later by Indiana University Press as a coauthored book, *Dillinger: The Untold Story*. Girardin has Anna's North Clark Street number as 2862, so she may have operated two houses in the same block.

A picture of Polly Hamilton was found in Dillinger's pocket watch, but she probably knew nothing of the Biograph trap.

was the reason Zarkovich had made the trapping of Dillinger contingent on his participation—to guarantee the outlaw's death. (In 1998, Zarkovich's revolver was sold at auction for $26,000 as "the gun that killed Dillinger," although Hoover privately gave credit to two federal agents.)

In talking to the federal agent in Detroit, Anna had trouble keeping her people and timeline straight—supposedly having met Dillinger through Polly at her place on North Clark Street before moving to Halsted, and both she and Polly apparently knew Dr. Cassidy, one of Dillinger's plastic surgeons, about the time he moved to 4802 North Broadway, renting an office above the Green Mill Gardens (a local mobster hangout, where the Barker-Karpis Gang's Dr. Moran also had an office; and Cassidy previously had worked out of the same Irving Park address as Dr. Eye, where Dillinger was nearly caught in late 1933).

According to Polly, Anna had mentioned that "this same doctor is treating John Hamilton, who is suffering from a badly infected wound,"* and that he had a cousin (obviously O'Leary) working in the office of Piquett. If that didn't red-flag her story, Anna was revealing far too much knowledge about Dillinger's activities in St. Paul, his relationship with Evelyn Frechette, the tips he was getting from someone in Chicago's state's attorney's office, and other details of his bank-robbing career. Most of this did not go into the formal statement Anna gave to Sam Cowley on August 1, which is a tidier version that the FBI has since used in its account of the Dillinger shooting. Whether the bureau failed to "connect the dots," or chose not to, continues to puzzle researchers. Girardin called it a "carefully rehearsed narrative" and wrote, "That the federal government would accept such an explanation defies both reasoning and common sense, but it evidently did."

STATEMENT OF MRS. ANNA SAGE; RESIDENCE 2420 NORTH HALSTED STREET, CHICAGO, ILLINOIS

I, Mrs. Anna Sage, make the following sworn statement to Special Agent S. P. Cowley in the presence of Special Agents J. W. Murphy and T. J. Connor.

. . . I first met John Dillinger about two weeks before moving from 2838 North Clark Street. This was about six weeks ago.

---

*According to Polly, Anna had mentioned that "this same doctor is treating John Hamilton," suggesting that he survived the supposedly fatal injury he had received the previous April after escaping the FBI at Wisconsin's Little Bohemia Lodge [see p. 439]. (The lodge was owned by former Chicagoan Emil Wanatka, who also owned a restaurant in Racine, Wisconsin, and later turned out to be a friend of Piquett.) It was Anna, during her Detroit interrogation, who described Dillinger putting several thousand dollars in various pockets before going to the Biograph Theatre, and it is generally believed, from the statements of others, that Zarkovich made off with the money, leaving only the seven dollars and change reported by newspapers.

DILLINGER "ON THE SPOT"

By the summer of 1934, John Dillinger was the country's hottest commodity, and at least three different groups were conspiring to put him "on the spot."

One was Jimmy Murray and his wife. Murray had harbored Dillinger at his Rainbo Inn until the outlaw started visiting the bar to fraternize with customers and flirt with waitresses. When someone would comment on how much he looked like Dillinger, he'd just laugh and say how everybody thought so. Dillinger left Murray's Rainbo in late May to undergo plastic surgery at the Chicago home of James Probasco.*

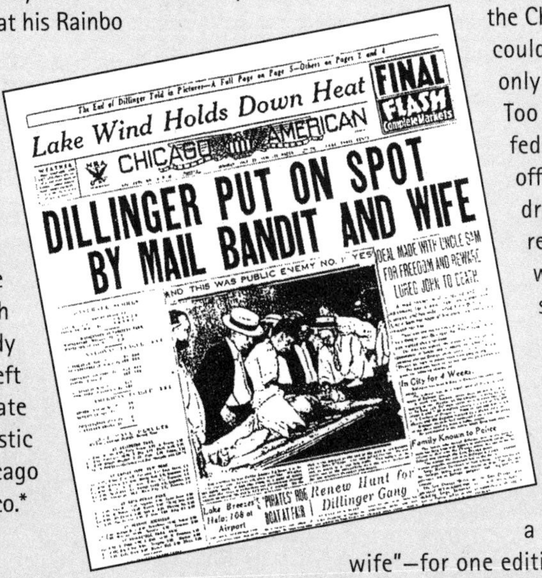

Murray had been arrested some months earlier over stolen bonds he had used to buy Dillinger Gang member Harry Copeland a car in Wisconsin, and through intermediaries he had told the Chicago police that he could finger Dillinger, only to be turned down. Too late, he went to the feds with the same offer: get the bond beef dropped, give the reward money to his wife, and he would set Dillinger up. Word of this somehow reached a reporter, who, the night Dillinger died, mistakenly attributed his entrapment to a "mail bandit and his wife"—for one edition, before the paper learned that the actual betrayers were Anna Sage and Martin Zarkovich. (It's possible that the Justice Department later intervened in Murray's behalf, on the condition he become an informant, for immediately after Dillinger's death he was arrested by Chicago police who evidently did not pursue the stolen-bond case.)

According to the statement of Arthur O'Leary [see p. 387], then jailed at Waukegan, Louis Piquett had been planning the same thing, asking Probasco to locate Dillinger, who had moved in with Anna Sage and Polly Hamilton. Piquett had discovered he was under surveillance by Justice Department agents, and Probasco told

* While at Murray's, Piquett had assigned his investigator Arthur O'Leary to keep Dillinger from "hiding in plain sight," but to little avail. Dillinger dragged O'Leary to Ireland's for frog legs and to local bars where he'd enjoy himself while sipping gin fizzes. His wildest stunt (O'Leary later related to his young friend Don Costello) occurred at Chicago's Riverside Amusement Park. He realized he'd been recognized because a police car showed up, the park closed down, and patrons were asked to leave by one exit, where Dillinger assumed that cops would be waiting. Noticing a lady complaining loudly, he whispered in her ear that the police thought they had Dillinger trapped. While she went ballistic, he and O'Leary jumped into the vacated cop car and roared out on a truck road, yelling at the police posted there that Dillinger was behind one of the rides and they were going for reinforcements.

Martin Zarkovich

O'Leary that Dillinger and O'Leary were going to be sold out to the feds by Piquett in an effort to avoid prosecution for his involvement in the plastic surgery. It may not have been a coincidence that Piquett was visiting his family in Platteville, Wisconsin, the night Dillinger was killed.

Piquett went to prison for two years because he had participated in the plastic surgery also on Homer Van Meter, who was not legally his client.

♔ ♔ ♔

When Dillinger's body was robbed of several thousand dollars—his "git" money, as described by Sage, who had seen him stash it on his person—suspicion fell on Zarkovich. Sage received a $5,000 reward from the Justice Department which, despite efforts of G-man Melvin Purvis, refused to intervene in the immigration service's decision to deport her on morals charges because of her notoriety as a bawdyhouse "madam." And, despite J. Edgar Hoover's private commendation to two federal agents credited with firing the fatal shots, the family friend who had acquired Zarkovich's .38-caliber revolver eventually sold it at auction in 1998 for $26,000 as the "gun that killed Dillinger."

(The gun Dillinger was carrying—a Colt .380 pocket automatic with its serial number ground off—was properly inventoried but then disappeared. It probably went straight to Hoover, who may have privately given it to comedian Red Skelton, putting in the Dillinger display case a similar gun that actually had been made in December 1934 and had been confiscated from Barker-Karpis Gang member Volney Davis.)

More than a few newspapers thought that the feds, after killing Dillinger, had also betrayed Anna Sage.

I met Dillinger through Polly Hamilton. Polly called me up one day and said she had a new boy friend and I asked her to bring him up to the house and she said he didn't want to come. I asked Polly if he was bashful or why couldn't he come, there was nobody here. So one day Polly called me up and said to bake a cake and to make some coffee; that she was bringing her boy friend up, whose name she gave as Jimmy Lawrence. When she rang the bell I went to the door and let them in and she stated his name was Jimmy Lawrence. He kept his head down but I looked at him and got a glimpse of his profile and immediately recognized him as Dillinger.

I asked him then what his name was and he then said Jimmy Lawrence. I then asked him what was wrong with his face and he said he had been in an automobile accident. I told him immediately that his name might be Jimmy Lawrence, but he was John Dillinger. I made the remark in front of Polly and I called Polly out in the bathroom and told her that her boy friend was John Dillinger. She did not admit it. She said that he had told her his name was Jimmy Lawrence and that he was a married man but separated from his wife; that one day while he was waiting outside of the restaurant where she was employed [the S&S Sandwich Shop, 1209 West Wilson], one of the girls in the restaurant remarked to her that Dillinger was outside waiting for her. She did not know whether this girl ever recognized John Dillinger [or was joking]. I told Polly I was going to make that man, meaning Jimmy Lawrence, admit that he was Dillinger or he could leave.

Dillinger told me that he had been [picked up] in Detroit as John Dillinger but was released. I told him then that if he was John Dillinger he would have a gun on him and if he had no gun he was not Dillinger. He did have a gun in his pocket. He also had a coat on at the time.

The next day Polly talked to me and said that if I thought that was John Dillinger, and if it was, that he had been a good many places and nobody else had recognized him. That same night Dillinger told Polly who he was and she said it did not make any difference as she liked him very much. He told her it might cause her lots of trouble but she told him she did not care as it was worth it. . . .

I knew I could trust Martin Zarkovich and about a week after the South Bend, Indiana bank robbery I called Martin Zarkovich and talked to him in a casual conversation and told him I wanted to talk to him about something. . . . About July 19, 1934 Martin called me and said he would come up and see me about three o'clock that afternoon. I was going to tell Martin about Dillinger being there at the house and ask his advice about what to do. I told Polly that Martin was coming to see me and Polly said not to tell John that Martin was coming to see me. Also not to tell John Dillinger that her former husband was a policeman and to tell Martin anything to keep him from coming to the house, and to meet him somewhere else. It was not necessary to do this because about Tuesday or Wednesday of that week, July 17 or 18,

1934, Dillinger went away and did not return until Friday morning. I talked to Martin Zarkovich on Thursday and told him about Dillinger being there. I told him that I would call him on Saturday and let him know definitely if John Dillinger had returned to Chicago and if he hadn't, if Polly had heard from him and knew where he was located. John Dillinger returned to Chicago Friday morning, and came around to my house to see Polly. On Saturday they went to the beach somewhere about the 5800 block North, and I immediately called Martin and told him that I knew plenty and made arrangements to meet him at Fullerton Parkway, where I did meet him, and he introduced me to Mr. Purvis, Special Agent in Charge of the Chicago office of the Division of Investigation [FBI].

John Dillinger never stayed in my house all the time. He did stay at my house while Polly was ill as a result of an automobile wreck about two weeks, and then only stayed there until about daylight, five or six o'clock in the morning. He was with Polly all the time he was at my house until five or six a.m.

I never met or knew Homer Van Meter, John Hamilton, "Baby Face" Nelson, or any other associates of John Dillinger. Neither did I ever learn where Dillinger was residing. The keys Dillinger had on him the night he was killed, July 22, 1934, belonged to Polly Hamilton, and he had taken them away from Polly in the show and put them in his pocket.

I talked to Dillinger about the South Bend, Indiana bank robbery and he said there were five men on the job. He and Van Meter were two of them, but he never told me who the other three were. He said that Van Meter received a scalp wound in the left forehead, but nothing serious. . . .

The two police officers who were killed at East Chicago, Indiana I never knew and one day while talking to John Dillinger while he was at my home, I asked him how come they were killed, and he said they were trying to get a piece of money from somebody. He never told me that he or any member of his gang did the act. Neither did he said who did it. . . .

I do not know whether Dillinger was paying protection to any members of the Police Department of Chicago, Illinois. However, he did not seem to be very much afraid of them as he had stated several times that he had passed squad cars on the street. . . .

I have never been arrested outside of East Chicago, Indiana and Gary, Indiana, although I was picked up one time with the girl Dorothy who stayed in my place while I was residing at 2838 North Clark Street. This was in June, 1934. No charge was placed against me and I was released.

Anna Sage

Mrs. Anna Sage

Subscribed and sworn to before me

this 1st day of August, 1934

Helen Dunkel

Notary Public

associate, fearing for his life, surrenders to federal agents in Denver.

September 5—Paula "Fat-Witted" Harmon, Wynona Burdette, and Gladys Sawyer, Barker-Karpis Gang "molls," are arrested by police after a drunken disturbance at a Cleveland hotel. The Division of Investigation is notified but fails to trap the men of the gang.

September 7—Billy Pabst, Maurice Denning, Earl Keeling, and Francis Harper rob the Cumberland Savings Bank at Cumberland, Iowa, of $900.

September 10—Former Underhill Gang members Ralph Roe and Jack Lloyd rob the First National Bank at Sulphur, Oklahoma, of $3,000.

September 17—Albert W. "Pat" Reilly pleads guilty in the Federal Court at St. Paul to harboring John Dillinger, is sentenced to twenty-one months in the Federal Reformatory at El Reno, Oklahoma, and fined $2,500.

September 18—A ten dollar gold certificate from the Lindbergh ransom is traced through a Bronx gas station attendant to German carpenter Bruno Richard Hauptmann.

September 19—Hauptmann is arrested outside his home at 1279 East 222nd Street in the Bronx, New York City, for the kidnap-murder of the Lindbergh baby.

September 21—At the Federal Court in Madison, Wisconsin, "Pat" Reilly pleads guilty to further charges of harboring John Dillinger and Tommy Carroll and is sentenced to fourteen months on each count, to run concurrently with the previous sentence imposed in St. Paul.

September 22—Former Dillinger outlaws Harry Pierpont and Charles Makley fail in their attempt to escape from the Death House of the state prison at Columbus, Ohio, using fake pistols carved from soapstone (not soap, as commonly reported). Makley is killed, and Pierpont is wounded.

— Richard Tallman (Dick) Galatas, former Hot Springs bookie and conspiracy suspect in the Kansas City Massacre case, is arrested with his wife, Elizabeth, by federal agents in New Orleans.

— Former Barker-Karpis gangster Jess Doyle, with Jack Rich, John Langdon, and Clarence Sparger, rob a U.S. Mail truck at Coffeeville, Kansas.

September 26—Gambler Cassius McDonald is arrested by federal agents in Detroit for passing ransom money from the Bremer kidnapping.

— Bruno Richard Hauptmann is indicted in Bronx County, New York, for extortion.

September 29—Robert Mais and Walter Legenza, Tri-State Gang leaders sentenced to death, shoot their way out of the Richmond, Virginia, jail, killing a policeman.

October 8—Hauptmann is indicted in Hunterdon County, New Jersey, for the murder of Charles Augustus Lindbergh Jr.

October 11—Three men escape after a gun battle with police near Cresco, Iowa. Two are erroneously reported to be "Pretty Boy" Floyd and Adam Richetti.

October 12—Former "Pretty Boy" Floyd associate "Shine" Rush is captured by federal, state, and county officers in a raid on a farm near Norman, Oklahoma.

October 15—Tom Limerick, Maurice Denning, and others rob the First National Bank at Hawarden, Iowa, of $2,113.

October 17—Harry Pierpont is executed for murder in Ohio's state prison.

— Night policemen James Kirlin and Wilbert Clary are wounded in a battle with two gunmen at Missouri Valley, Iowa. The men, suspected to be bank robbers Tom Limerick and Maurice Denning, escape.

— After holding up two other people, Glenn E. Reilly is captured by G-man Robert T. Ross when he attempts to mug the special agent at Magnolia and Leland avenues in Chicago. Ross commandeers a taxi and takes Reilly to the nearest police precinct station. Reilly was unarmed at the time of the robberies but kept his hand in his coat pocket, pretending to have a gun.

October 19—"Pretty Boy" Floyd and Adam Richetti are suspected in a $500 bank robbery at Tiltonsville, Ohio.

October 21—Adam Richetti wounds two and is captured by police near Wellsville, Ohio. "Pretty Boy" Floyd escapes.

October 22—"Pretty Boy" Floyd is killed by police

and federal agents led by Melvin Purvis, near East Liverpool, Ohio.

October 24—A gunman identified as Raymond Hamilton escapes after a battle with highway patrolmen near Buffalo, Missouri.

October 26—The Tri-State Gang kidnaps Philadelphia racketeer William Weiss, demanding $100,000. After much haggling, they agree to settle for $12,000. The kidnapping is not reported to police.

November 1—Three men rob the First State Bank at Temple, Oklahoma, of $1,200. Raymond Hamilton is suspected.

November 5—Albert Mayor, a friend of William Weiss, delivers a package containing $8,000 to a representative of the Tri-State Gang. A second package, containing the remaining $4,000, is apparently overlooked.

November 6—William Weiss is killed by his kidnappers and dumped in Neshominy Creek near Doylestown, Pennsylvania.

November 7—Tom Limerick, Maurice Denning, and others rob the First National Bank at Dell Rapids, South Dakota, of about $10,000 in cash and bonds.

November 8—Raymond Hamilton and two accomplices rob the First National Bank at Okeene, Oklahoma, of $1,100.

November 17—Bank robber Billy Pabst is arrested in a North Side apartment in Chicago by agent Paul Gruber of the Iowa Bureau of Investigation.

November 19—The Philadelphia office of the Division of Investigation receives an underworld tip reporting the Weiss abduction.

November 22—The Limerick-Denning Gang robs the Security National Bank at Superior, Nebraska, of $7,929.

November 26—Matt Kimes, longtime bank robber and convicted murderer of two lawmen, is granted a six-day leave of absence from the state prison at McAlester, Oklahoma, to go quail hunting with his lawyer. He returns.

– Kansas City policeman Myron "Mike" Fanning, despondent over witnessing the Union Station massacre of the previous year, goes on a drunken rampage and fatally shoots fellow officer Grant V. Schroder. Fanning will be convicted of murder and sent to Missouri's state prison.

November 27—"Baby Face" Nelson and John Paul Chase battle federal agents near Barrington, Illinois, killing Inspector Samuel Cowley and Special Agent Herman Hollis. Despite multiple wounds (the commonly reported "seventeen" included exit wounds), Nelson with his wife, Helen, escape in the federal car, Chase driving, but he dies that evening in a hideout at 1627 Walnut in the Chicago suburb of Wilmette.

November 28—Nelson's body is found beside a cemetery in Niles Center [now Skokie], Illinois, and the Justice Department orders its agents to show Helen Gillis "no mercy."

– New York mobster Arthur Flegenheimer, alias "Dutch" Schultz, wanted on federal charges of income tax evasion, turns himself in to the U.S. commissioner at Albany, New York. Schultz will be acquitted after two trials.

November 29—In Chicago, Helen Gillis surrenders to federal agents who conceal this from the press and later insist she was "captured." At least one newspaper interprets the instruction to "show no mercy" as an order to kill, and although she is already in custody, the press proclaims her the first female Public Enemy No. 1.

– "Big Homer" Wilson, called a member of the Barker-Karpis Gang, dies at his Chicago home, apparently of natural causes. Wilson had robbed banks for years without being arrested.

December 1—Denver Police Chief A. T. Clark announces that the "Denver Mint robbery" (actually the $200,000 robbery of a Federal Reserve Bank truck outside the Mint) of December 18, 1922, has finally been solved. The crime supposedly was carried out by five men and two women, the only survivors of the gang being Harvey Bailey and James "Oklahoma Jack" Clark, both serving life sentences for other crimes.

December 4—Joseph Burns, one of the Indiana state prison escapees, is recaptured in Chicago. The search continues for Joseph Fox and for John Hamilton, who is presumed dead.

"RED" RYAN: THE CANADIAN DILLINGER

While John Dillinger was thrilling and chilling Americans, Canadians had "Red" Ryan, a bank robber whose criminal career in some ways paralleled Dillinger's.

Norman John Ryan was born in 1895 and raised in Toronto where he launched his life of crime by stealing chickens and bicycles. That landed him in reform school in 1908. After his release and more stealing, robbing and jailings (which included two dramatic escapes), he moved his operations to the northern U.S. and was captured in 1924—as was Dillinger, upon bungling his first armed robbery.

While Dillinger engaged in such prison mischief as talking in chapel and learning armed robbery, Ryan, serving life, renounced his wicked ways, became the Catholic chaplain's altar boy and lectured other cons on the virtues of clean living. By the early Thirties his multitude of good deeds had kept him in the news as an illustrious model prisoner, and in 1933 one paper gushed that Ryan had become a man who was "kind-hearted, conscientious, loyal, innately honest and big-souled, whose only desire is to do the right thing in a big way if he is permitted."

That was the same year Dillinger was paroled and went into bank robbing. He was killed in July 1934, the year that Canada's Prime Minister visited Ryan in prison and announced, "I was greatly impressed by what he said to me . . . I can only say that his demeanor, his clothes, his sleeping cot, and surroundings were calculated to stimulate him to renewed efforts for usefulness."

If Dillinger bluffed his way out of the Crown Point jail with a wooden pistol, Ryan managed the same thing with his rehabilitation act. When his early-release papers were signed in 1935, he was flooded with job offers and public appearances; and despite an autobiography pronouncing himself "a new man," he mainly renewed his old ways as an armed robber—while still enjoying his celebrity status as a public speaker and car-seller who also took up wrestling.

"Red" Ryan's criminal career in some ways paralleled that of John Dillinger.

On May 25, 1936, police in the town of Sarnia interrupted a liquor store holdup and shot it out with two bandits. An officer was killed and both outlaws were mortally wounded. One robber, behind goggles and bandanna, turned out to be "Red" Ryan, the poster boy for prison rehabilitation, whose double life expired two hours later.

Like Dillinger, he left behind some memorable quotes, including:

"Time, boys, to cut up the melon."

"Knocking them down is the easy part of it, but it is the getaway that counts."

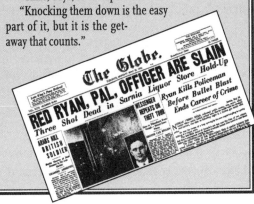

December 6—Irvin "Blackie" Thompson, Huntsville Death House escapee, is slain by police in Amarillo, Texas.

— Raymond Hamilton robs the Continental Oil Co. in Dallas of $182.

December 11—The Tri-State Gang robs a National Guard armory at Morristown, Pennsylvania, taking thirteen pistols, five automatic rifles, and 1,000 rounds of ammunition.

December 13—Philadelphia police raid a North Sixth Street house and arrest Tri-State Gang members Roy Willey, Joseph Darrow, Charles Zeid, Robert Eckert, and Beatrice Wilkerson. Walter Legenza escapes after leaping from an elevated platform at the Wayne Street railroad station. He fractures both feet but eludes capture and flees to New York with Robert Mais and Marie McKeever.

December 17—A federal complaint is filed at Baltimore charging Robert Mais, Walter Legenza, and Marie McKeever with theft of U.S. government property.

December 22—Walter "Irish" O'Malley, Leonard Short, "Dapper Dan" Heady, and others rob two banks in Okemah, Oklahoma, escaping with $19,393 in cash and travelers checks. Raymond Hamilton is named as a suspect.

December 27—John Paul Chase, last of the "second" Dillinger Gang, is captured by police in Mount Shasta, California. [John Hamilton, still missing, is presumed dead.]

1935

January 2—Michael James "Jimmy the Needle" LaCapra, gangster-turned-informer in the Kansas City Massacre case, is released from Sumner County Jail in Wellington, Kansas.

— "Terrible Tommy" Touhy, suffering from palsy and a semi-invalid drug addict, is captured by police at an apartment in Chicago's Logan Square district. He will be convicted of mail robbery and sentenced to twenty-three years in Leavenworth.

January 3-February 13—Bruno Richard Hauptmann is tried and convicted of murdering the Charles Augustus Lindbergh Jr. baby and sentenced to death.

January 4—Richard Galatas, Herbert "Deafy" Farmer, Frank "Fritz" Mulloy, and Louis "Doc" Stacci are convicted of conspiracy to obstruct justice in the Kansas City Massacre case. All are sentenced to two years in a federal penitentiary and fined $10,000.

January 5—Willie Harrison, a Barker-Karpis gangster considered unreliable by the others, is shot to death by "Doc" Barker, thrown into a barn at Ontarioville, Illinois, and burned.

— Tom Limerick, Maurice Denning, and another man rob the First National Bank at Hudson, South Dakota, of $1,363.

January 8—"Doc" Barker and girlfriend Mildred Kuhlman are arrested by Melvin Purvis at 432 Surf Street in Chicago. Other federal agents surround a Barker-Karpis apartment at 3920 North Pine Grove and capture Byron Bolton, Ruth Heidt, and Clara Fisher Gibson. Russell Gibson, alias Roy "Slim" Gray, chooses to fight it out and is killed.

— Chicago attorney Louis Piquett's trial for harboring John Dillinger begins in Chicago. Piquett takes up his own defense when lawyer Edwin T. Peifer suffers a heart attack in the courtroom.

January 15—Louis Piquett is acquitted of conspiring to harbor his former client, John Dillinger.

January 16—"Ma" and Fred Barker are killed by federal agents in a house on Lake Weir at Ocklawaha, Florida, [the FBI and, consequently, most writers misspell the town as Oklawaha] after a four-and-a-half-hour gun battle.

— Elmer Farmer, Barker-Karpis Gang associate, is arrested in Bensenville, Illinois, and admits to participating in the Edward Bremer kidnapping.

— Using guns smuggled into the prison by bank robber Clyde Stevens, four convicts pistol-whip San Quentin Warden James R. Holohan, take four parole-board members hostage, and escape. A short time later, their stolen car is disabled by police bullets at Valley Ford, California. Rudolph "Bad Boy" Straight resists and is killed. The others surrender. Clyde Stevens, outside organizer of the break, and his partner, Albert Kissell, are captured on Sherman Island, California.

— An attempted robbery of the state bank of Leonore, Illinois, results in a three-county pursuit and a series of gun battles in which Marshall County Sheriff Glen Axline, cashier Charles Bundy, and robber Melvin Liest are killed and four people wounded. The other bandits, Arthur Thielen, Fred Gerner, and John H. Hauff, are captured.

– Four men rob the Citizens State Bank at Buffalo, Texas, of $7,011. Raymond Hamilton is wrongly identified as one of the robbers.

January 17—Harold Alderton, former owner of the Bensenville, Illinois, house where Edward Bremer was held by the Barker-Karpis Gang, is arrested by federal agents in Marion, Indiana, and confesses his involvement.

– Federal agents arrest Walter Legenza at a Presbyterian Hospital in New York City. Two other Tri-State Gang members, Martin Farrell and Edwin Cale, are arrested in New York the same day.

January 18—Federal agents and police arrest Robert Mais and Marie McKeever at their Manhattan Avenue apartment in New York City.

January 19—Edward Bremer identifies Harold Alderton's house in Bensenville, Illinois, as the place of his confinement.

– Two gunmen, one identified as Raymond Hamilton, rob the First National Bank at Handley, Texas, of $500.

January 20—Alvin Karpis and Harry Campbell battle police and escape from the Dan-Mor Hotel in Atlantic City. Their girlfriends, Dolores Delaney and Wynona Burdette, are captured.

January 20–21—Alvin Karpis and Harry Campbell take Dr. Horace Hunsicker hostage and commandeer his car near Allentown, Pennsylvania. Hunsicker is left bound and gagged in Ohio, and his car is later found in Monroe, Michigan.

January 22—The federal grand jury at St. Paul returns new Bremer kidnapping indictments, superseding the indictments of May 4, 1934. Arthur "Doc" Barker, Alvin Karpis, Volney Davis, Harry Campbell, Elmer Farmer, Harold Alderton, "Lapland Willie" Weaver, Harry Sawyer, William J. Harrison, Byron Bolton, "John Doe," and "Richard Roe" are indicted for kidnapping Bremer and transporting him from St. Paul, Minnesota, to Bensenville, Illinois. These individuals and Dr. Joseph P. Moran, Oliver A. Berg, John J. McLaughlin, Edna Murray, Myrtle Eaton, James J. Wilson, Jess Doyle, William E. Vidler, Philip J. Delaney, and one "Whitey" also are indicted for conspiring with one another and with deceased conspirators Fred Goetz (alias "Shotgun" George Ziegler), Fred Barker, Russell Gibson and "Ma" Barker to kidnap Bremer.

– The weighted body of William Weiss is recovered from Neshominy Creek, near Doylestown, Pennsylvania.

January 23—Five men armed with pistols and machine guns rob a U.S. Mail truck of $129,000 in Fall River, Massachusetts.

January 30—Volney Davis, Jess Doyle, and John Langan rob the Montgomery County Treasurer's office at Independence, Kansas, of $1,938.

January 31—Joseph "Dutch" Cretzer, Arnold Kyle, and Milton Hartman rob the Union Avenue Branch of the United States National Bank at Portland, Oregon, of $3,396.

February 1—Tom Limerick, Maurice Denning, and Edward Casebeer rob the First National Bank at Smith Center, Kansas, of $2,133.

February 2—Robert Mais and Walter Legenza are executed in the electric chair at Richmond, Virginia.

February 4—Raymond and Floyd Hamilton rob a Carthage, Texas, bank of $1,000. That night they are ambushed by police at their Dallas apartment but manage to escape.

– Chicago labor racketeer Tommy Maloy, head of Local 110 of the Motion Picture Operators Union, is shotgunned to death while driving on Lake Shore Drive by rival gangsters in a passing car. This spares him from prosecution for income tax evasion.

February 6—Barker-Karpis gangster Volney Davis is captured by federal agents in St. Louis.

– In a Philadelphia hospital, Dolores Delaney gives birth to Alvin Karpis's son. The boy, named Raymond Alvin Karpaviecz, is given to Karpis's parents in Chicago.

February 7—Volney Davis escapes federal custody at Yorkville, Illinois.

– Edna "The Kissing Bandit" Murray and Jess

Gang Interconnections

As the Midwest's geographic crossroads and burgeoning trade center, Chicago provided heartland America with gambling and prostitution that became organized and politically protected long before Prohibition gave rise to the Roaring Twenties "gangster." It also was the target of reform movements that came in a steady succession like waves off Lake Michigan, sometimes wetting politicians' feet but leaving the established vice districts high and dry. The police used nightstick law to keep most of the city safe for its permanent residents and for criminals who were politically protected as well as outwardly respectable and who commuted to their workplaces in the red-light and nightlife districts.

St. Paul lacked Chicago's reputation for wide-open wickedness but probably exceeded it in systematic corruption. The police there didn't ignore organized crime; they *were* organized crime, and they employed a law-and-order strategy that bordered on genius. Fugitives from other states could use the city as a sanctuary so long as they tipped the right officials and behaved themselves, which made St. Paul a combination of vacation and convention center for some of the most active felons in the country. This interesting method of local crime control had been formulated at the turn of the century by Police Chief John J. O'Connor, who reigned on and off until his final resignation in 1920. It worked so well that his successors, in and out of the department, carried on the tradition, to the utter frustration of the U.S. Justice Department.

By the time Hoover's G-men were empowered by a New Deal Congress in 1934 to carry guns and catch crooks more dangerous than interstate car thieves (the Dyer Act) and fornicators (the Mann Act), the man supervising the so-called O'Connor system was a saloonkeeper, fence, and racketeer named Harry Sawyer, who served not only as St. Paul's primary fixer but also as underworld banker, and was so well connected he could arrange protection for criminals in other cities. He was a mutual contact of the Dillinger and Barker-Karpis

Gangs, for instance, and some of the ransom money paid in the Edward Bremer kidnapping, which Sawyer had set up for the Barker-Karpis Gang, supposedly was later found at the lodge in northern Wisconsin where the FBI nearly captured Dillinger.

Sawyer's Green Lantern saloon was patronized by a host of celebrity criminals and managed by Albert "Pat" Reilly. Reilly's wife, Helen, had sisters who were the girlfriends of Dillinger Gang member Tommy Carroll and Alvin Karpis. Two other Green Lantern employees once had been housekeepers for bank robber Frank Nash, who had worked with the Barker-Karpis Gang before he was killed in the Kansas City Massacre. The same two were arrested by the FBI while trying to deliver luggage to Dillinger Gang member Eddie Green, a onetime member of the Barker-Karpis Gang.

The FBI discovered that the Barker-Karpis Gang also had close ties with a Reno gambling syndicate connected with San Francisco bootleggers, including a former Chicagoan named Lester Gillis, better known as "Baby Face" Nelson. Nelson had escaped from a guard taking him by train to Joliet state prison after his second bank-robbery conviction, and he was introduced to the West Coast underworld by Chicago mobsters William "Klondike" O'Donnell and William "Three-fingered Jack" White. Later, as a driver-gunman for the Reno mob, he became friends with Alvin Karpis and Fred Barker. He may already have known Karpis, who had grown up in the same part of Chicago, for they had mutual friends in Anthony "Tough Tony" Capezio and Rocco De Grazia, both rising members of the Capone Syndicate and suspects in the St. Valentine's Day Massacre. Two others involved in the Massacre were Byron Bolton and Fred Goetz, who later teamed with the Barker-Karpis Gang in the Bremer and Hamm kidnappings.

As a crime that came under federal jurisdiction in 1932, these kidnappings were the means by which the FBI discovered the extent of St. Paul's police involvement in criminal activities. The bureau would later use the new federal laws to prosecute individuals and local officials. Its investigations not only crippled the so-called O'Connor system, but gradually provided a clearer picture of the criminals who constituted full-fledged gangs, the extent to which they associated or collaborated, and the ties they had with syndicate crime in various other cities.

When finally captured in 1936, Alvin Karpis admitted meeting Bonnie and Clyde, who were peddling guns stolen from a National Guard Armory, and "Pretty Boy" Floyd, who had come out of deep hiding since the Kansas City Massacre looking to join an established gang of bank robbers, preferably Dillinger's. Byron Bolton, who testified against his former associates in the Bremer and Hamm kidnapping cases, named Anthony "Soap" Moreno as a West Coast contact of Alvin Karpis and other members of the Barker-Karpis Gang. Moreno was convicted of harboring "Baby Face" Nelson, as was Frank Cochran of Reno, an air service operator who worked on cars for Nelson and the Barker-Karpis Gang.

Thomas "Tobe" Williams, ex-convict owner of the Vallejo General Hospital in Vallejo, California, also was a mutual contact of "Baby Face" Nelson and the Barker-Karpis Gang and later was convicted of harboring Nelson. Helen Gillis, Nelson's wife, had been treated at Williams's hospital for an illness, and Williams was considered the main West Coast health-care provider for other fugitives.

Another mutual contact of the Dillinger and Barker-Karpis Gangs was Joseph Aiuppa, alias Joey O'Brien, Chicago gambling and nightclub operator who one day would rule the Capone Syndicate. Aiuppa reportedly supplied guns and ammunition to the Dillinger and Barker-Karpis Gangs, who frequented his Chicago nightspots, the Hy-Ho Club (often confused with the Hi-Ho Club) and the Moulin Rouge. Jack Perkins, a close friend of "Baby Face" Nelson, allegedly owned a piece of the Hy-Ho Club and may have provided the bulletproof vests used by the Dillinger Gang in the South Bend robbery.

Aiuppa was one of several people arrested in suburban Bellwood, Illinois, near the house where "Handsome Jack" Klutas, leader of a Chicago kidnapping gang, was slain by police in January 1934. Walter Detrich, a member of the Klutas gang also captured there, was one of the ten convicts who had used guns smuggled in by Dillinger to escape from Indiana state prison the previous September. Klutas had a rumored connection with Dillinger and reportedly had bought the gun found on Detrich at the time of his arrest. Klutas also was a close associate of Fred Goetz, William J. Harrison, "Big Homer" Wilson, and Gus Winkeler, some of whom were connected to the Capone Syndicate and the Barker-Karpis Gang.

Louis Cernocky's notorious roadhouse at Fox River Grove, Illinois, was a popular gathering spot for the Dillinger and Barker-Karpis Gangs, and it was Cernocky who reportedly sent Dillinger and Nelson to Emil Wanatka's Little Bohemia Lodge in northern Wisconsin with a letter of introduction. Wanatka had operated a Little Bohemia restaurant on Chicago's South Side in the early 1920s and had moved to Wisconsin after dodging a murder rap and selling his place to West Side "beer barons" Terry Druggan and Frankie Lake, bootlegging rivals of Capone.

One of Wanatka's attorneys may have been future Dillinger lawyer Louis Piquett, a onetime city prosecutor who also knew Wanatka (as the absentee landlord of another Little Bohemia Restaurant in Racine, Wisconsin, he would invite Piquett up for steaks and drinks whenever he came to town). Piquett represented a Chicago abortion ring, where he probably knew Dr. Joseph P. Moran, who had served time for an "illegal operation," and brothel keeper Anna Sage. As the appointed fixer for a North Side police district, he had once quashed the stolen jewelry charges against Russell Gibson, alias "Slim" Gray, later a member of the Barker-Karpis Gang.

Another gang hangout was the O. P. Inn in Melrose Park, Illinois, operated by Louis "Doc" Stacci, alias Stacey, a Capone gangster convicted of conspiracy to obstruct justice in the Kansas City Massacre case. Those harbored by Stacci included Frank Nash, Verne Miller, Eddie Green, Alvin Karpis, Fred and Doc Barker, and other prominent criminals. Stacci reportedly was a golfing companion of notorious Capone gangster Vincent Gebardi, alias "Machine Gun" Jack McGurn, another suspect in the St. Valentine's Day Massacre and cited in some FBI records as a friend of "Baby Face" Nelson.

The Seafood Inn at Elmhurst, Illinois, was another contact point for the Dillinger and Barker-Karpis Gangs. Dillinger and Homer Van Meter took John Hamilton there to contact Moran after Hamilton was badly wounded by deputies near South St. Paul, Minnesota, following the Little Bohemia battle in April 1934. Moran refused him medical attention, probably on orders of the Chicago Syndicate, which by then was distancing itself from the outlaws who were generating too much heat from police and the FBI.

Hamilton supposedly died at the Aurora, Illinois, apartment of Barker-Karpis gangster Volney Davis, and two years later the FBI found a badly decomposed body in a shallow grave at a gravel pit near the neighboring town of Oswego. The bureau believed the corpse to be Hamilton's, but if a relative is correct [see p. 439], Hamilton, who had been declared dead by his crime partners on more than one occasion) survived and made it back to his native Canada, raising the possibility that the body was that of Moran, reportedly killed by the Barker-Karpis Gang.

Before Nelson and Dillinger teamed up, "Baby Face" had worked with Eddie Bentz, a major 1920s bank robber turned planner and caser, and with Chicago mobster Tommy Touhy of the Roger Touhy mob. Through Bentz, he met San Antonio gunsmith and dealer H. S. Lebman, who had devised a means of converting Colt semiautomatic pistols and Winchester autoloading rifles into fully automatic weapons.

Probably through Nelson, Lebman's customized guns (most with Thompson-style foregrips, compensators, and extra-capacity magazines) made their way to some of the most prominent criminals of the day, including Dillinger, the Touhys, and even "Pretty Boy" Floyd. Lebman supplied Thompsons to some of the same groups. Arrested under a new Texas machine-gun law that predated the National Firearms Act of 1934, he beat the rap on a hung jury, and the continuing efforts of federal authorities to secure a retrial proved fruitless.

After several years, Texas authorities, citing the deaths of most of Lebman's customers and the disappearance of important witnesses, dropped the charges, and Lebman, whose family was locally influential, stayed at the same location another forty years. However, he put most of his efforts into the other side of his business, boot- and saddle-making.

The "Gun Molls"

What constituted a "moll" always has been pretty vague.

The extent to which Bonnie participated in Clyde's crimes remains a matter of disagreement, for while she obviously considered herself his crime partner she probably was less active than generally portrayed. Some killings may have been attributed to her by former accomplices to save their own skins.

"Ma" Barker's role in gang affairs now is known to have been greatly exaggerated by FBI Director J. Edgar Hoover, who felt obliged to instantly demonize her before reporters (who had not yet heard of Mrs. Barker) could find fault with his G-men for killing somebody's mother.

"Machine Gun" Kelly's wife, Kathryn, fostered his criminal career, promoted his reputation, bought him a used machine gun, and even involved her own family by hiding the kidnapped Urschel at their farm, but she took no active part in that crime or in his robberies.

Edna "The Kissing Bandit" Murray (née Stanley) seemed to thrive on the excitement of the chase. She did not participate in bank robberies, but she and her husband, Jack Murray, had been involved in bootlegging, and in Kansas City they robbed a man whom Edna kissed, hence her nickname. Her conviction for this offense led to three prison escapes, between which she had a series of outlaw boyfriends. One was Volney Davis, sent up for murder in Oklahoma in 1924. Then Edna took up with (and supposedly married) a jewel thief and cop killer named Fred "Diamond Joe" Sullivan, who soon after was taken from her by the electric chair in Little Rock, Arkansas.

Then she married Jack Murray, and they both went to prison for highway robbery. Edna's last escape followed Davis's release from McAlester in 1932, and she resumed her relationship with him. Davis and Edna usually were accompanied by Edna's teenage son, Preston Paden, who became a minor criminal himself and later went to prison in Kansas for killing a night marshal during an attempted burglary.

Edna, like Bonnie Parker, originally worked as a waitress. Young and wild, she had been married a couple of times to unexciting farmers before taking up with the likes of Murray, Sullivan and Davis, whom she had first met in a Sapulpa, Oklahoma, café in 1923.

Women as active criminals were rare. Vivian Chase was a noteworthy exception, involving herself in bank robberies, holdups, and kidnappings before she was found murdered in 1935 near St. Luke's Hospital in Kansas City. There were a few other near equivalents of her, Edna Murray, and Bonnie Parker scattered among the southwestern gangs. One was Lillian Tackett, who robbed banks with boyfriend Clifford "Kip" Harback, whom she later shot (not fatally) in Hot Springs. And Lillian really did smoke cigars.

Another was gang leader Ford Bradshaw's girl, Stella "Boots" Moody, who was with him when he was killed and at least showed the spirit of a true "gun moll." Stella had Ford's name tattooed on her arm above a pair of crossed revolvers. Stella sometimes passed herself off as Bonnie Parker. After Ford's death, Stella was involved with other Oklahoma outlaws but eventually settled down as a housewife.

Margaret "Bright-Eyes" Murray was a sixteen-year-old, dime-a-dance girl who took up with gunman Stevie Sweeney and served as the gang's "lookout" on their many holdups in the 1920s. When Frankie Schoenhardt and Harold McCormick tired of taking orders from Stevie and knocked him off, they made the mistake of boasting to Margaret about it. Her testimony would send them to the electric chair.

A lone gunwoman who distinguished herself personally was Sally Scott, called "The Godless Girl" because of her tattoos, one of which displayed the military slogan, "Death Before Dishonor." She borrowed a gun from a girlfriend and in 1930 perpetrated a mini-crime wave in Detroit by robbing two stores in five minutes. Sally's real name turned out to be Dorcas Bancan. Dorcas robbed, she said, because she couldn't make ends meet on the eight dollars a week she earned as a nursemaid and didn't have the

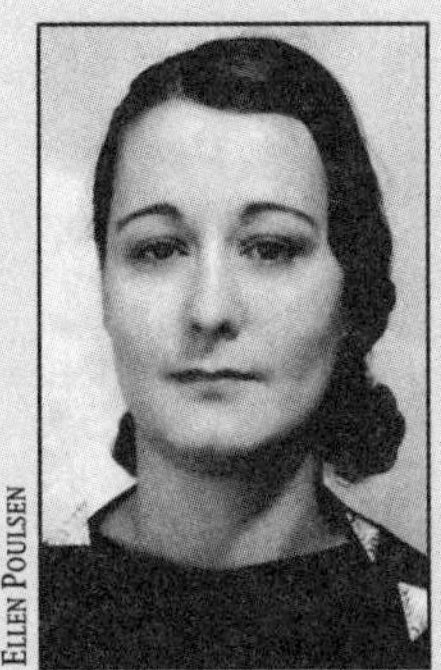

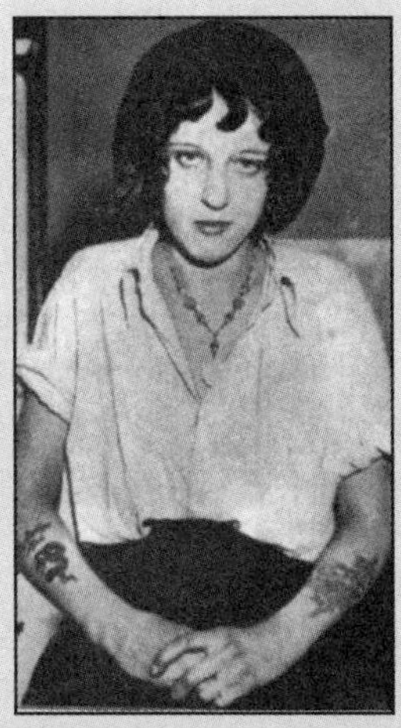

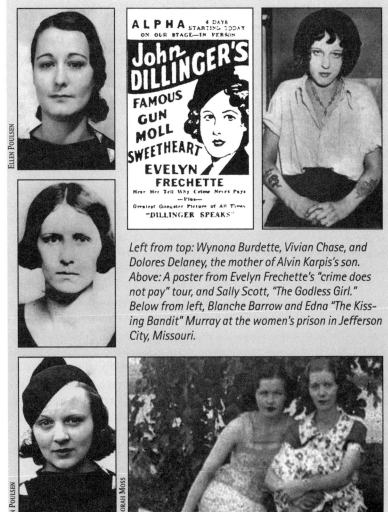

Left from top: Wynona Burdette, Vivian Chase, and Dolores Delaney, the mother of Alvin Karpis's son. Above: A poster from Evelyn Frechette's "crime does not pay" tour, and Sally Scott, "The Godless Girl." Below from left, Blanche Barrow and Edna "The Kissing Bandit" Murray at the women's prison in Jefferson City, Missouri.

education to be a stenographer or bookkeeper. She had borrowed her gun from a girlfriend.

Helen Walsh (the exciting story went) kept reloading weapons for "Two-Gun" Crowley and Rudolph Duringer during their long standoff with police on New York's Upper West Side in 1931. (By other accounts, Helen and Duringer cowered under the bed while Crowley fought alone.) Police supposedly were tipped to their whereabouts by Crowley's jealous ex-"moll," Billie Dunn, who later bragged in newsreels that she and not "that Walsh dame" was "Two-Gun's sweetheart."

Celia Cooney is usually identified as the "Bobbed-Haired Bandit," although this title was popularly applied to other female robbers of the day. With her husband, Ed, Celia (shortened from Cecelia) staged a number of daring robberies in 1921, in Brooklyn and it was Celia who shot Nathan Maze during their robbery of the National Biscuit Co. The two were captured in Florida, where Celia gave birth to a child who died soon afterward. (Police speculated that pregnancy had given Celia a "nervous trigger-finger.")

Both were sentenced to twenty years, and in 1924 Ed lost his left hand in a machine shop accident at Sing Sing. Celia, regarded as a model prisoner at Auburn, was allowed to meet Ed seven years later when he was suing the State of New York over this mishap. She embraced him and wept before returning to prison. Ed won a sizeable settlement, and both were paroled in 1931. Five years later Ed died of tuberculosis that he probably contracted in prison, and Celia faded into obscurity.

Eleanor Jarman, "The Blonde Tigress," reputedly led her boyfriend George Dale and accomplice Leo Minneci in a number of Chicago robberies that culminated in the murder of haberdasher Gustav Hoeh. Police credited the trio with thirty-seven holdups, but they confessed to forty-eight. Dale went to the chair, and Eleanor and Minneci were each sentenced to 199 years, but the story didn't end there. The "Tigress" escaped from the women's prison at Dwight, Illinois, in 1940 and has never been found.

Bank robber Bennie Dickson married teenage Stella Irwin in 1938, and they commenced a brief crime spree in the upper Midwest. Stella proved to be a talented wheelman and displayed her rifle marksmanship by shooting out the tires of pursuing police cars, earning herself the nickname "Sure-Shot Stella." By this time robbery of national banks was a federal crime, and the FBI ran the pair down in April 1939. Bennie was killed by G-men outside a St. Louis hamburger stand, and Stella was arrested the next day in Kansas City. Sentenced to ten years, Stella eventually went straight and died forgotten in 1995.

"Ma" Barker's role as a "criminal mastermind" was invented by J. Edgar Hoover, but a true mother of crime flourished in San Francisco toward the end of the Depression. Juanita "The Dutchess" Spinelli came to the West Coast with her pimp boyfriend Mike Simeone after supposedly working as a "finger woman" for the Purple Gang in Detroit's laundry racket. She earlier had married a bank robber (probably common-law) who reportedly was killed in Mexico, and she had three children, a daughter and two sons. With Simeone, she put together a gang that progressed from rolling drunks to car theft, hijackings, armed robberies, and murders. Eventually caught and doomed by the testimony of a male henchman, Spinelli was sentenced to death, along with Simeone and two other male gang members. A third was pronounced insane. She appealed to no avail and, in 1941, became the first woman to die in San Quentin's gas chamber, protesting to the end that Simeone could clear her name if he was only man enough to do it.

After John Dillinger's death, his first love, Evelyn Frechette, was released from jail, briefly toured with a crime-does-not-pay show, and then returned to Wisconsin where she eventually married an older man named Art Tic. Dillinger's later girlfriend, Polly Hamilton, who had "worked" for Anna Sage, made a rare transition to respectability when she later married a decent businessman named William Black and settled on Chicago's Near North Side, where they annually entertained friends attending the Old Town Art Fair.

"Baby Face" Nelson's wife, Helen Gillis, was intensely devoted, rarely left his side, and was with him during the gun battle that ended his life. She seems to have had no antisocial traits herself and immediately surrendered to the FBI, but not before one newspaper's headline blared, 'Kill Widow of Baby-Face,' U.S. Orders Gang Hunters. (The bureau denied any shoot-to-kill order and admitted that she already was in custody.) After a year in jail, Helen worked at several jobs under the name Gillis, raised her two children, never remarried, and lived her later life in seclusion, probably with some financial assistance from Nelson's boyhood friend, Jack Perkins, who still was active in the Chicago mob.

In any case, reporters of the day made few distinctions between the woman who was a forbearing wife, a thrill-seeking girlfriend, a willing accomplice, or a full-fledged crime partner, and tended to describe any woman associated with a prominent criminal as his "gun moll."

Outlaw Gangs: Members and "Molls"

JOHN DILLINGER GANG

John Dillinger (Mary Longnaker, Evelyn "Billie" Frechette, Rita "Polly" Hamilton Keele)
William Shaw
Noble "Sam" Claycomb
Paul "Lefty" Parker
Hilton Crouch
Harry Copeland
Sam Goldstine [usually spelled Goldstein]
Harry "Pete" Pierpont (Mary "Shorty" Kinder)
Charles "Mac" Makley
John "Red" or "Three-finger" Hamilton (Elaine Dent and Patricia Cherrington, sister of Opal Long)
Russell "Boobie" Clark (Opal Long, alias Bernice Clark)
Edward Shouse
Leslie "Big" Homer
[Frank Whitehouse, James Kirkland, Maurice Lanham, and Dillinger were charged with robbing the bank in Gravel Switch, Kentucky; Fred Bremen, Clifford "Whitey" Mohler, George Whitehouse, John Vinson, Glen "Big Foot" Zoll, and Merrit Longbrake possibly were associated with the gang but never were charged with its robberies.]

("Gun molls" appear in in parentheses)

DILLINGER/NELSON GANG

Lester Joseph Gillis [often listed mistakenly with the middle initial "M" in FBI documents], alias "Baby Face" Nelson, Jimmy Williams, Jimmy Burnett, etc. (Helen Gillis, née Wawrzyniak, sometimes misspelled Warwrzniek)
Homer Van Meter (Marie Comforti [often mistakenly spelled Conforti])
Albert W. "Pat" Reilly (Helen "Babe" Delaney Reilly*)
Eddie Bentz (Verna Bentz)
Thomas Leonard "Tommy" Carroll (Jean Delaney Crompton*)
Harry Eugene "Eddie" Green (Bessie Green, real name Ruth Skinner)
Charles Fisher

*Helen Delaney, Jean Delaney, and Dolores Delaney (a Karpis "moll") were sisters.

Tommy Gannon
Harry Hotson, alias Earl Doyle (wife Hazel)
John Paul Chase (Sally Bachman)
Jack Perkins [later worked for the Chicago Outfit] (wife Grace)
Joseph Raymond "Fatso" Negri

"PRETTY BOY" FLOYD GANG

Charles Arthur "Pretty Boy" Floyd (ex-wife Ruby [or Rubye] and Beulah Baird)
Adam "Eddie" Richetti [shortened from Ricchetti]
George Birdwell
Bill "The Killer" Miller (Rose Baird Ash, sister of Beulah Baird, was also with Richetti; both were widows of two Kansas City brothers killed by Floyd and Miller)
Aulcie "Aussie" Elliott
"Shine" Rush
L. C. "Blackie" Smalley
Coleman Rickerson
Clarence Garatley
Fred Stone
Ed Evans
George Polk
James Bradley, alias Bert Walker
Nathan King, alias Jack Arnold or Jack Atkins
Joe Hlavity [1925 payroll robbery]
Fred Hilderbrand [1925 payroll robbery]
John Moore [an undercover agent for the Burns Detective Agency who infiltrated the gang in 1932 but was jailed for stealing the car used in a robbery]
Verne Miller [participated with Floyd, but possibly not Richetti, in the Kansas City Massacre] (Vivian Mathis)

"MACHINE GUN" KELLY GANG

George Barnes, alias George "Machine Gun" Kelly (Kathryn Kelly)
Albert W. Bates (Clara Feldman)
Robert "Boss" Shannon (Ora Shannon)
Armon "Potatoes" Shannon (Oleta Shannon)
Frank "Jelly" Nash
Francis Keating
Thomas Holden
Eddie Bentz (Verna Bentz)
Edward Doll, alias Eddie LaRue [also worked with Klutas Gang]
Harvey Bailey
Verne Miller (Vivian Mathis)
Bernard Phillips, aka Phil Courtney [occasional partner of Kelly, later with the Barker-Karpis Gang]

BARKER-KARPIS GANG

Arizona Donnie Clark Barker, alias Kate "Ma" Barker (George Barker, Arthur Dunlop, husbands)
Fred Barker (Paula "Fat-Witted" Harmon)
Arthur "Doc" [or "Dock"] Barker (Mildred Kuhlman)
Alvin "Old Creepy" Karpis (Dorothy Slayman Karpis, Delores Delaney, Edith Barry, Jewell LuVerne Grayson, alias Grace Goldstein)
Jimmie Creighton
Joe Howard
William Weaver, alias Bill "Lapland Willie" Weaver; real name Phoenix Donald (Myrtle Eaton)
Jimmie Wilson
Harry Sandlovich, alias Harry "Dutch" Sawyer (Gladys Sawyer)
Thomas James "Tommy" Holden (Lillian Holden)
Francis "Jimmy" Keating (Marjorie Keating)
Lawrence "Larry" DeVol
Bernard Phillips, alias "Big Phil" Courtney (Winnie Williams)
Harvey Bailey
Frank "Jelly" Nash (Frances Nash)
Jesse Doyle (Helen Murray, Doris O'Connor)
Volney "Curley" Davis (Edna "The Kissing Bandit" or "Rabbit," wrongly spelled "Rabbits," Murray; she and Doris O'Conner were sisters)
Earl Christman (Helen Ferguson)
Harry Hull
John P. "Jack" Peifer, with various spellings (Viola Nordquist)
Charles J. Fitzgerald, alias "Old Charley," "Big Fitz" (Isabelle Born)
"Old Gus," alias "Jack," "Schnozzle"; possibly same as Gus Stone or Stevens
Fred Goetz, alias "Shotgun" George Ziegler [often spelled Zeigler; previously a Capone mobster] (Irene Dorsey)
William Bryan Bolton, alias Byron "Monty" Bolton, Monte Carter [briefly a Capone mobster] (Ruth Heidt, widow of William J. Harrison)
Harry Campbell (Wynona Burdette)
Russell "Rusty" Gibson, alias Roy "Slim" Gray (wife Clara Fisher Gibson)
Fred Hunter (Ruth Hamm Robison, alias Connie Morris)

Verne Miller (Vivian Mathis)
"Pinky" Mitchell
Joe Rich
Sam Coker
John Brock
Benson "Soup" Groves, alias Ben Greyson
Eddie Green
[Dr. Joseph Moran, Elmer Farmer, Edmond Bartholmey, Harold Alderton (real name Allderton) and William J. Harrison; Dr. Moran treated outlaws besides the Barker-Karpis Gang, and the others either held kidnap victims or passed ransom money.]

BRADY GANG

Alfred James "Al" Brady (Margaret Larson, Jo Raimondo)
Clarence Lee Shaffer Jr. (Christine Puckett, Minnie Raimondo)
Rhuel James "Jim" Dalhover (Marie "Babe" Meyers, Mary Raimondo)
Charles Geiseking

BARROW GANG

Clyde Barrow (Bonnie Parker Thornton)
Marvin Ivan "Buck" Barrow (wife Blanche Caldwell Barrow)
Raymond Hamilton [brother of Floyd Hamilton] (Mary "The Washerwoman" O'Dare)
Floyd Hamilton
L. C. Barrow
Ralph Fults
Frank Clause
Everett Milligan
Hollis Hale
Frank Hardy
William Daniel Jones, aka W. D. "Deacon" Jones (Billie Parker Mace, sister of Bonnie)
Monroe Routon
Joe Bill Francis
S. J. "Baldy" Whatley
James Mullen
Joe Palmer
Henry "Boodles" Methvin

BAILEY-UNDERHILL GANG

Harvey Bailey, later used his middle name, John, and sometimes was called "Shotgun Tom"
"Mad Dog" Wilbur Underhill (Hazel Jarrett Hudson)
Robert "Big Bob" Brady (Leona Brady)
Jim Clark (Goldie Johnson)
Sebron Edward "Ed" Davis
Frank Sawyer
Jess Littrell
Bill Shipley

KLUTAS GANG
("The College Kidnappers")

Jack "Handsome Jack" [mistakenly called Theodore or Ted] Klutas
Edward Doll, alias Eddie LaRue [also worked with "Machine Gun" Kelly]
Russell Hughes, alias Guy West
Gale Swolley
Frank Souder
Eddie Wagner
Julius "Babe" Jones
Walter Detrich [formerly with "Baron" Lamm, and usually spelled Dietrick]
Earl McMahon
Ernest Rossi

TRI-STATE GANG

Walter Legurenza, alias Legenza
Robert Howard Mais
William Benjamin "Big Bill" Phillips (Marie McKeever)
Morris Kauffman
John Kendrick
Arthur Misanas
Herbert Myers
Martin Farrell
Roy Willey
Robert Eckert
Joseph Coffey
[Anthony Cugino, Salvatore Serpa, John Zukorsky, Edward Wallace, Johnny Horn, and Anthony Zanghi supposedly operated with the Tri-State bandits but may have had their own gang.]

CRETZER-KYLE GANG

Joseph "Dutch" Cretzer (Edna Kyle Cretzer, alias Kay Wallace)
Arnold Kyle, alias "Shorty" McKay (Thelma Cretzer Kyle)
Milton Hartman, alias James Courey
John Oscar Hetzer

As for gang leaders' nicknames, a reporter tried and failed to give the nickname "Snake-eyes" to John Dillinger, whose name already had a proper ring to it (but was correctly pronounced with a hard G). "Pretty Boy" Floyd's nickname supposedly was given to him by Beulah Baird, but researcher Michael Webb discovered that police had much earlier confused him with a petty criminal named "Pretty Boy" Smith and, to his annoyance, the name stuck. "Baby Face" Nelson presumably got his nickname in his early robbery days from a woman bank teller who said he had a "baby face," which probably was in her mind thanks to a popular song of the day ("*You've got the cutest little . . .*"). "Machine Gun" Kelly seems to have acquired his from the FBI after a Fort Worth pawnshop owner identified Kathryn Kelly as the purchaser of a used Tommygun.

Doyle of the Barker-Karpis Gang are captured in Kansas.

February 17—Raymond Hamilton and Ralph Fults steal eight Browning Automatic Rifles from a National Guard armory at Beaumont, Texas.

February 22—Some twenty-three relatives and friends of Clyde Barrow, Bonnie Parker, and Raymond Hamilton are tried at the Federal Court in Dallas for conspiracy to harbor federal fugitives. Hamilton's sister, Lillie McBride, is acquitted, but the others are convicted and sentenced to prison or jail terms of varying lengths.

February 23—Former Capone bodyguard Frank Rio dies of heart disease at his home at 1000 Bellaforte Avenue in suburban Oak Park.

February 25—A clandestine heroin factory explodes at 2919 Seymour Avenue in Brooklyn.

February 28—Alva Dewey Hunt, Hugh Gant, and others rob the state bank at Haines City, Florida, of $4,000.

March 2—The O'Malley-Short Gang robs the First State Bank at Neosho, Missouri, of $17,000.

March 12—In federal court in Kansas, Harry C. Stanley is convicted of harboring his sister, Edna "The Kissing Bandit" Murray. Stanley is sentenced to six months in the Sedgewick County Jail at Wichita and fined $1,000. His wife, Mary, also is convicted and given a five-year suspended sentence.

March 18—John Paul Chase, former associate of "Baby Face" Nelson, becomes the first man to be tried under one of the new federal laws for the murder of a federal agent. He will be convicted and sentenced to life in Alcatraz.

March 19—Raymond Hamilton allegedly kidnaps Houston newspaperman Harry McCormick, dictates his version of his criminal career for publication, then releases him. Years later, the newspaperman will write that he contacted Hamilton and arranged an interview, then concocted the "kidnapping" story to avoid a harboring charge.

March 25—In the federal court at Miami, Florida, Dolores Delaney and Wynona Burdette plead guilty to harboring Alvin Karpis and Harry Campbell. Both are sentenced to five years at the federal women's detention farm in Milan, Michigan.

March 27—The O'Malley-Short Gang robs Goldberg's Jewelry Store in Tulsa, Oklahoma, taking $55,000 in gems.

March 28—Raymond Hamilton and Ralph Fults rob the Bank of Blountville at Prentiss, Mississippi, of $933, then capture fifteen members of a pursuing posse who are later released unharmed.

April 5—In San Francisco, Thomas "Tobe" Williams, Harry "Tex" Hall, Anthony "Soap" Moreno, and Frank Cochran are sentenced to terms in federal prison for harboring "Baby Face" Nelson. Louis "Doc Bones" Tambini and others are acquitted.

— Victor Connellan, wanted in Detroit for counterfeiting, is arrested by police and Secret Service agents in Hoboken, New Jersey. Press accounts proclaim him a survivor of the Purple Gang.

April 6—Raymond Hamilton is captured by Dallas County deputies in Ft. Worth, Texas.

April 10—Four Chicago gunmen are captured in a machine-gun ambush near Albia, Iowa, after stealing a $5,800 payroll of the Smoky Hollow Coal Co. of Hiteman. All will plead guilty two days later and be sentenced to twenty-five years in the State Reformatory at Anamosa.

April 15-May 6—"Doc" Barker and other members of the Barker-Karpis Gang are tried and convicted in St. Paul of kidnapping Edward Bremer. Barker and others are sentenced to life.

April 24—Alvin Karpis, Harry Campbell, and Joe Rich rob a U.S. Mail truck at Warren, Ohio, of $72,000.

May 3—Harry and Gladys Sawyer, Barker-Karpis Gang associates, are arrested by federal agents in Pass Christian, Mississippi.

— Members of the "Irish" O'Malley Gang rob the City National Bank at Fort Smith, Arkansas, of $22,000.

May 10—Raymond Hamilton and Joe Palmer are executed in the electric chair at the Texas state prison in Huntsville.

May 21—Bank robber Dewey Gilmore is captured in Dallas. His subsequent confession will lead to the capture of partners "Irish" O'Malley, "Dapper Dan" Heady, and Leonard Short.

June 1—Volney Davis is recaptured in Chicago by Melvin Purvis.

June 4—Joseph Fox, one of the ten escapees from Indiana's state prison in 1933, is recaptured in Chicago.

June 10—Adam Richetti is tried as a participant in the Kansas City Massacre and sentenced to death.

June 25—Louis Piquett, former attorney of John Dillinger, is sentenced to two years in Leavenworth and fined $10,000 for harboring Homer Van Meter, who was not legally his client.

June 27—Leonard Scarnici, bank robber and confessed slayer of Vincent "Mad Dog" Coll and thirteen others, dies in the Sing Sing electric chair for the 1933 murder of Rensselaer, New York, Police Detective Charles A. Stevens.

July 1—Congress authorizes changing the Justice Department's Division of Investigation to the Federal Bureau of Investigation.

July 18—Leland Varain, alias "Two-Gun" Louie Alterie, one of the last survivors of the "Bugs" Moran gang, is shot to death by unidentified gunmen outside his apartment at 926 Eastwood Terrace in Chicago.

August 1—Alva Dewey Hunt, Hugh Gant, and others rob the state bank at Mulberry, Florida.

August 8—O'Malley gang members Virgil "Red" Melton and Fred Reese are captured at an Arkansas fishing resort.

August 16—FBI Special Agent Nelson B. Klein is mortally wounded in a gun battle with fugitive George W. Barrett at College Corner, Ohio. Barrett is wounded in the legs by return fire from Klein and another agent and captured. A professional car thief and killer who murdered his own mother, Barrett will die in the electric chair in March 1936.

August 21—Michael James "Jimmy the Needle" LaCapra, who testified in the Kansas City Massacre case, is murdered at New Paltz, New York.

August 22—Newark mobster Vincenzo Troia is assassinated by gunmen.

August 28—Acting on information from Volney Davis and Edna Murray, FBI agents recover what they believe is the badly decomposed body of Dillinger Gang member John Hamilton from a shallow grave at a gravel pit outside of Oswego, Illinois [see p. 439].

September 1—"Lapland Willie" Weaver and Myrtle Eaton, former Barker-Karpis Gang members, are captured by the FBI at Allandale, Florida.

September 3—Bank robber Sam Coker is paroled from Oklahoma's state prison, allegedly as the result of bribery by persons connected with Alvin Karpis.

September 8—Philadelphia's Public Enemy No. 1, Anthony "The Stinger" Cugino, is captured in New York City. After fifteen hours of questioning, Cugino confesses to eight murders then hangs himself in his cell. Cugino was believed to be affiliated with the Tri-State Gang.

October 12—Al Brady and Jim Dalhover rob a movie theater in Crothersville, Indiana, of $18.

October 23—Mobster "Dutch" Schultz and three henchmen are fatally shot by rival gangsters at the Palace Chop House in Newark, New Jersey. Police attribute the murders to a rising New York/New Jersey criminal syndicate that has seized control of the Schultz rackets. Leaders of the Syndicate are named as Charles "Lucky" Luciano, Louis "Lepke" Buchalter, Jacob "Gurrah" Shapiro, Frank Costello, Joe Adonis, Benjamin "Bugsy" Siegel, Meyer Lansky, Abner "Longy" Zwillman, and Johnny Torrio. Mob informers will later reveal that the Syndicate murdered Schultz to prevent him from assassinating Manhattan Special Prosecutor Thomas E. Dewey.

October-December—The Brady Gang (Al Brady, Clarence Shaffer, Jim Dalhover, and Charles Geiseking) rob an estimated 150 grocery stores, drugstores and gas stations in Indiana and Ohio.

November 3—Vivian Chase, wanted for bank robbery, jail-breaking and kidnapping, is found shot to death in a parked car outside St. Luke's Hospital in Kansas City, Missouri. Alvin Karpis is mentioned as a suspect.

November 7—Alvin Karpis leads his new gang in robbing a U.S. Mail train of $44,650 in cash and bonds at Garrettsville, Ohio. They make their getaway in an airplane.

November 29—"Dutch" Cretzer, Arnold Kyle and Milton Hartman rob the Ambassador Hotel Branch of the Security National Bank in Los Angeles of $2,765.

November 30—The Brady Gang robs a grocery store at Crawfordsville, Indiana, and wounds two policemen in a gun battle.

December 3—Dewey Gilmore, "Dapper Dan" Heady, Leonard Short, and Russell Cooper, members of the O'Malley Gang, stage a bloody escape from the city jail in Muskogee, Oklahoma, looting the arsenal and killing Chief of Detectives Ben Bolton. Another would-be escapee, John Blackburn, is mortally wounded by Chief of Police Marsh Corgan.

December 5—Russell Cooper is recaptured near Clayton, Oklahoma, by Deputy U.S. Marshal Allen Stanfield and others.

December 6—Deputy Marshal Stanfield, FBI agents, and Muskogee County officers cross an overflowing creek in freezing rain, kill "Dapper Dan" Heady and recapture Dewey Gilmore at an isolated forest cabin on Jackfork Mountain near Weathers, Oklahoma. Leonard Short is found suffering badly from burns when his hideout catches fire and from exposure at a hog shelter where he has taken refuge. He dies on the trip back when a boat capsizes.

December 9—Walter Liggett, muckraking publisher of the *Mid-West American*, is killed in front of his wife and twelve-year-old daughter in a machine-gun assassination outside their apartment at 1825 Second Avenue South in Minneapolis. Mrs. Liggett names local crime boss Isadore "Kid Cann" Blumenfeld as the killer and accuses Minnesota Governor Floyd B. Olson of complicity.

December 19—Capone gangster Joseph "Peppy" Genaro, true name Annorino, is shot to death by unknown killers in a saloon at 1543 East Sixty-third Street in Chicago.

December 29—Albert J. Prignano, state representative and Democratic committeeman in what is now Chicago's "Bloody Twentieth" Ward, is assassinated by gunmen outside his home at 722 Bunker Street. Once a friend of Al Capone, Prignano reportedly defied the order of Capone successor Frank Nitti not to seek re-election as Ward committeeman.

December 30—Former Chicago politician John "Boss" McLaughlin, serving a five-year sentence for passing Bremer ransom money, dies in Leavenworth.

1936

January 6-24—Harry Sawyer, Bill Weaver and Cassius McDonald are tried and convicted in St. Paul for their involvement in the Bremer kidnapping. Sawyer and Weaver are sentenced to life, McDonald to fifteen years.

January 11—Cleveland Safety Director Eliot Ness leads a raid on the Harvard Club, a casino in Newburgh Heights, Ohio, whose owners often have harbored the Barker-Karpis Gang.

January 14—The Hunt-Gant Gang robs the Dixie County State Bank at Cross City, Florida, of $4,000.

January 23—"Dutch" Cretzer, Arnold Kyle, and Milton Hartman rob a branch of the American Trust Co. in Oakland, California, of $6,000.

January 24—Cretzer, Kyle, and Hartman rob the Vineyard and Washington Branch of the Bank of America in Los Angeles of $1,475.

February 15—Capone gunman "Machine Gun" Jack McGurn (an alias of Vincent Gibaldi) is shot to death shortly after midnight by unknown killers in a bowling alley at 805 Milwaukee in Chicago. [Years later, an FBI surveillance tape will suggest that one of the shooters was McGurn's old crime partner, Claude Maddox See p. 200].

March 2—Cretzer, Kyle, and Hartman rob the Melrose and Bronson Branch of the Bank of America in Los Angeles of $6,100.

March 3—The Hunt-Gant Gang robs the Columbia Bank in Ybor City, Florida, of $30,459.

— Anthony DeMora, half-brother of "Machine Gun" Jack McGurn, is murdered by gunmen outside a poolroom in Chicago's Little Italy.

March 4—The Brady Gang steals $8,000 worth of gems from a jewelry store in Greenville, Ohio.

March 13—Edward Wilhelm "Eddie" Bentz,

"Fire Into Him"

The Killing of "Pretty Boy" Floyd

The first of the Depression outlaws to attract national attention was "Pretty Boy" Floyd, whom the *Literary Digest* described as "Oklahoma's Bandit King" for his audacity, cockiness, use of a submachine gun and the fact that his identity was known. Floyd was among the first to acquire personal notoriety, and if his lawbreaking never came close to that of 1920s predecessors like "Baron" H. K. Lamm and the Newton Brothers, he stood accused of committing (or maybe bungling) the spectacular crime the press proclaimed "A Machine-Gun Challenge to a Nation," which helped launch the modern FBI.

CHARLES DEMPSEY FLOYD

"Pretty Boy" Floyd with his wife Ruby (sometimes Rubye) and his son, Charles Dempsey Floyd, commonly called Jack.

Legend as well as fact have turned Floyd into something of a Robin Hood character, thanks partly to the Depression, his absence of gratuitous cruelty (at least in his home state, where he counted on protection), and his admired if self-serving stunt of occasionally destroying bank-loan records, which made farm foreclosures more difficult. Other aspects of his life and death raise questions that do not have the tidy answers found in standard accounts of his career.

The crime that gained Floyd the greatest notoriety was his presumed involvement in the Kansas City Massacre of June 17,

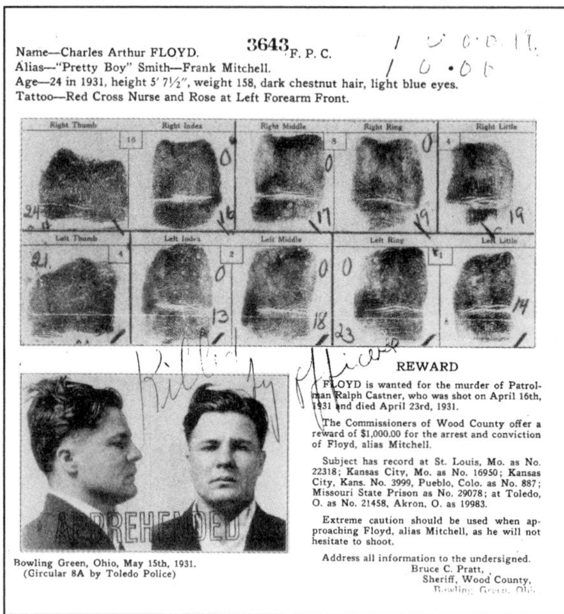

Name—Charles Arthur FLOYD. 3643 F. P. C.
Alias—"Pretty Boy" Smith—Frank Mitchell.
Age—24 in 1931, height 5′ 7½″, weight 158, dark chestnut hair, light blue eyes.
Tattoo—Red Cross Nurse and Rose at Left Forearm Front.

Right Thumb | Right Index | Right Middle | Right Ring | Right Little
Left Thumb | Left Index | Left Middle | Left Ring | Left Little

APPREHENDED

REWARD

FLOYD is wanted for the murder of Patrolman Ralph Castner, who was shot on April 16th, 1931 and died April 23rd, 1931.

The Commissioners of Wood County offer a reward of $1,000.00 for the arrest and conviction of Floyd, alias Mitchell.

Subject has record at St. Louis, Mo. as No. 22318; Kansas City, Mo. as No. 16950; Kansas City, Kans. No. 3999, Pueblo, Colo. as No. 887; Missouri State Prison as No. 29078; at Toledo, O. as No. 21458, Akron, O. as 19983.

Extreme caution should be used when approaching Floyd, alias Mitchell, as he will not hesitate to shoot.

Address all information to the undersigned.
Bruce C. Pratt,
Sheriff, Wood County,
Bowling Green, Ohio.

Bowling Green, Ohio, May 15th, 1931.
(Circular 8A by Toledo Police)

1933, which resulted in the deaths of four lawmen, including federal agent Raymond Caffrey [see p. 352]. A few biographers have found the evidence against Floyd unconvincing, partly because such reckless killing seemed to be out of character. But the FBI made his capture top priority because it involved the death of a federal officer, and he was gunned down on an Ohio farm on October 22, 1934, under circumstances that, by one lawman's account, were a summary execution.

The Kansas City killings made headlines nationwide, and Floyd and Richetti went into hiding around Buffalo, New York. Only when their funds ran low did they venture back to the Midwest in search of a gang to work with. Though more a loner than a joiner, Floyd probably used mutual connections to participate in the Dillinger Gang's last holdup on June 30,1934, when the Merchants National Bank of South Bend, Indiana, lost $30,000, with one policeman killed and four civilians wounded. One of the gunmen was identified as Floyd at the time, though witnesses tended to want their banks robbed only by the famous. But "Fatso" Negri, when later grilled as a pal of gang member "Baby Face" Nelson, said the group did include a notorious but unnamed "guest" robber who somehow had antagonized the hotheaded Nelson to the point where Nelson threatened to kill him. The ever-diplomatic Dillinger told Nelson that killing their new man was a fine idea, if he also was prepared to take on Richetti, whom everyone knew to be Floyd's partner.

Interrogations of other suspects also pointed to Floyd, but Negri best remembered Nelson throwing a minor tantrum when agents killed Floyd in October. Nelson's complaint was that Hoover's meddlesome G-men had deprived him of the pleasure of killing Floyd personally.

Floyd's efforts to find "work" already had led him to contact Clyde Barrow, but Bonnie and Clyde were killed in a Louisiana ambush on May 23, before any jobs could be planned. If he indeed teamed with Dillinger for the South Bend job (Jack Perkins was another suspect, tried and acquitted), Dillinger's death on July 22 ended any further collaboration. Floyd and Richetti were in Ohio when a fight with local authorities led police to call the FBI.

Richetti already had been wounded and

captured when Melvin Purvis, Herman Hollis and several other agents arrived from Chicago to began searching for Floyd in the vicinity of East Liverpool. In fact, the only reason the Ohio lawmen remained involved at all is because the G-men managed to get themselves lost on unmarked country roads and had to call the East Liverpool police for directions. Local officers met the agents at the farm of widow Ellen Conkle, who had unknowingly fed Floyd breakfast that morning, and while showing the federal men the way back to town a policeman in the lead car spotted a suspicious man in a suit dashing behind a corn crib. The FBI's official version of what happened is typically tidy, with no loose ends: Floyd took off running across a field, and the G-men, after ordering him to halt, wounded him mortally with gunfire. He lived only long enough for Purvis to ask him if he was "Pretty Boy" Floyd, involved in the Kansas City Massacre. He supposedly snarled back, "My name is Charles Arthur Floyd," and died.

Forty years later a different version of Floyd's death was described by Chester Smith, the local lawman who had seen Floyd behind the corn crib. According to Smith, he approached the crib and saw Floyd take off running across an open field with a .45 automatic in each hand. When Floyd continued toward a wooded area, Smith fired a shot from his rifle, hitting Floyd in the arm. Or the first shot may have been fired by another officer. In any case, Floyd tried to keep on running and was shot again. Smith picked up both of Floyd's pistols and was starting to talk to him when Purvis ordered the police officer to stand back. Soon, the other federal agents and local lawmen were standing around Floyd as he lay on the ground.

Smith, who made news with his story in the 1970s, says that Purvis exchanged only a few words with Floyd, mainly asking him if he had been involved in the Kansas City Massacre. Floyd supposedly replied, "Fuck you! I wouldn't tell you sonsabitches nothing!" This angered Purvis, who turned to a G-man holding a Thompson and said simply, "Fire into him." The agent fired some single shots from his Thompson, and Purvis left to make a telephone call. Smith assumed that the call was for an ambulance,

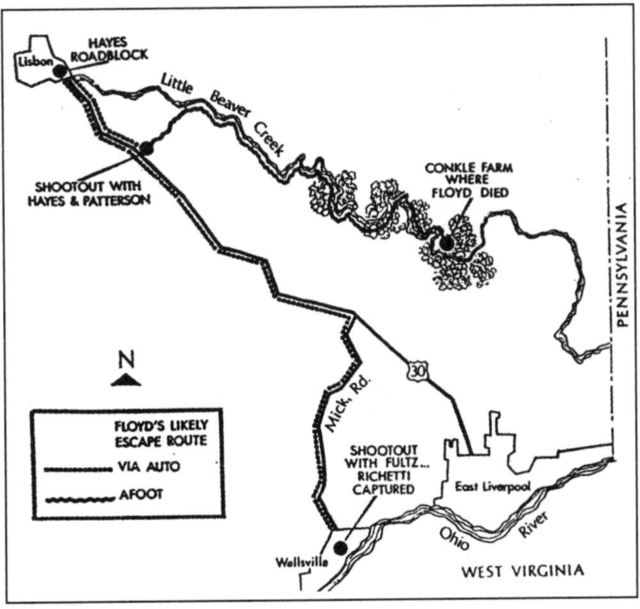

and meanwhile helped carry Floyd's body over to be propped against a tree. (A female neighbor who had heard the shooting said it happened twice, several minutes apart.)

Purvis returned a short time later. He hadn't called an ambulance, but rather J. Edgar Hoover in Washington, D.C., to inform him that, "We've killed Floyd." The officers put the body in the back seat of a car and drove it to an East Liverpool funeral home, where a cursory postmortem examination stated merely that Floyd had died from multiple gunshot wounds while resisting arrest.

Asked why he had waited so many years to tell his story, which had long been rumored, Smith said he had not been asked to file a report and was reluctant to challenge the FBI account. But now that his colleagues were dead and his own health was failing, he felt obliged to reveal what had happened. He also said the shooter was Hollis, who was not at the scene but took over when Hoover ordered Purvis to leave for Chicago immediately and say nothing. (A surviving FBI agent has predictably denied the account.)

Smith, when interviewed by crime researcher Neal Trickel, still had a .45-caliber cupro-nickel slug (the kind of jacketed bullet then used) recovered from Floyd's body by the coroner, and its rifling marks indicated it came from a Thompson, which one of the G-men possessed. He gave it to Trickel, and despite its outwardly clean appearance and the passage of many years in a manila envelope, the bullet has since tested positive for blood, which evidently had dried in the grooves and lead-filled base of the metal-jacketed round.

A subject of continuing curiosity is how "Pretty Boy" got his nickname. The account most widely accepted is that it was bestowed on him by good-natured prostitute Beulah Baird, who liked his fancy clothes and careful grooming. However, Michael Webb, a police chief and researcher in the St. Louis area, has found reason to believe that Floyd acquired it through a simple case of mistaken identity. One of Floyd's early partners in crime was a young hood known as "Pretty Boy" Smith, and police later assumed that Floyd and Smith were the same person. A newspaper account of Floyd's arrest stated simply that the two turned out to be different men, but the name "Pretty Boy" stuck.

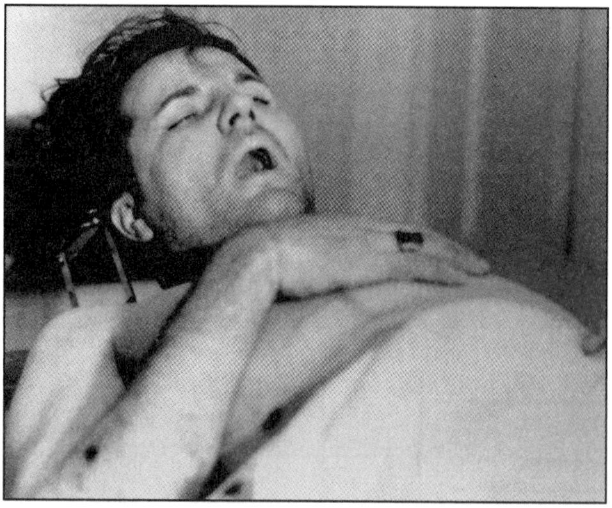

Floyd's body at an East Liverpool, Ohio, funeral parlor of E. R. Sturgis, also the county coroner, who made Floyd death masks.

notorious bank robber, is arrested by the FBI in New York City. He will receive a sentence of twenty years in federal prison for a Danville, Vermont, bank robbery. Bentz boasts of having hidden millions of dollars in stolen bank bonds, which will never be found.

March 19—The Brady Gang steals $6,800 in gems from a jewelry store in Lima, Ohio.

March 26—The FBI nearly captures Alvin Karpis in Hot Springs, Arkansas. It is later alleged that Karpis contributed $6,500 to the mayor's election campaign.

— New York Mafia boss Charles "Lucky" Luciano, under indictment as head of a vice ring, is also living in Hot Springs.

March 30—Preston Paden, son of Edna "The Kissing Bandit" Murray, and other young delinquents murder Night Marshal Ben Wiggins when he catches them attempting to burglarize a safe at the Booker Williamson furniture store in Lyons, Kansas. Paden and the others will be captured, convicted, and sentenced to prison for life.

April 3—Bruno Richard Hauptmann is executed at the Trenton, New Jersey, state prison for the murder of the Lindbergh baby.

April 9—The Brady Gang commits a $27,000 jewelry store robbery in Dayton.

— Charles J. Fitzgerald, former Barker-Karpis outlaw, is arrested by the FBI in Los Angeles and charged with the William Hamm kidnapping.

April 17—Hamm identifies the Bensenville, Illinois, home of Postmaster Edmund Bartholmey as the place he was held in June 1933. Bartholmey is arrested by the FBI and confesses his involvement in the kidnapping.

April 18—St. Paul gangster Jack Peifer is arrested by the FBI for the Hamm kidnapping.

April 22—Alvin Karpis, "Doc" Barker, Charles J. Fitzgerald, Edmund Bartholmey, Byron Bolton, Jack Peifer, and Elmer Farmer are indicted for the kidnapping of William Hamm.

— The U.S. Department of Justice offers a $5,000 reward for the capture of Alvin Karpis or Harry Campbell.

— The Brady Gang murders clerk Edward Linsey in a grocery store holdup in Piqua, Ohio.

April 27—U.S. postal authorities offer a $2,000 reward for the capture of Alvin Karpis.

— The Brady Gang robs the same Lima, Ohio, jewelry store they held up on March 19. Later in the day, they murder police sergeant Richard Rivers in Indianapolis.

April 29—Al Brady is arrested by Chicago police.

May 1—Alvin Karpis, Fred Hunter, and Ruth Hamm Robison, alias Connie Morris, are arrested in New Orleans by FBI agents led by Director J. Edgar Hoover. Karpis later will dispute Hoover's account, claiming he was seized by agents and held at gunpoint while Hoover was summoned to proclaim him arrested.

May 7—Harry Campbell and Sam Coker, Karpis Gang members, are arrested by the FBI in Toledo. J. Edgar Hoover again leads the raiding party. Alvin Karpis is arraigned in St. Paul for the kidnappings of William A. Hamm Jr. and Edward George Bremer and held under $500,000 bond.

May 9—Sam Coker is returned to Oklahoma's state prison to complete a thirty-year sentence for bank robbery.

May 11—Clarence Shaffer of the Brady Gang is arrested at his home near Indianapolis.

— In Manhattan, crime boss Charles "Lucky" Luciano goes to trial on charges of compulsory prostitution. The prosecutor is Thomas E. Dewey.

May 14—Avery Simons, alias Dan or Jim Ripley, wanted for the $2 million bank robbery at Lincoln, Nebraska, in 1930, is arrested by the FBI in Los Angeles while attempting to again flee to South America. Formerly a partner of Eddie Bentz and Eddie Doll, he will shortly rejoin them at Alcatraz under two consecutive twelve-year sentences for bank robbery.

May 15—Brady Gang member Jim Dalhover is arrested in Chicago.

May 19—Mrs. Nicholas Longo in Buffalo, New York, is killed by a bomb probably intended for her brother, Mafia boss Stefano Magaddino, who lived next door.

May 27—Fred Hunter pleads guilty to harboring

Alvin Karpis and is sentenced to two years in federal prison. He later will be convicted of mail robbery.

June 2—The Hunt-Gant Gang robs the Farmers & Merchants Bank at Foley, Alabama, of $7,242.

June 6—Former Barker-Karpis outlaw Lawrence DeVol and fifteen other inmates escape from the St. Peter Hospital for the Criminally Insane in Minnesota.

— In New York, "Lucky" Luciano is convicted under state law of compulsory prostitution.

June 8—John Callahan, former bootlegger, narcotics trafficker, and leading receiver of stolen goods in the Southwest, dies at the age of seventy at his home in Wichita, Kansas. For years Callahan had served as a Fagin figure, training such criminal apprentices as "Pretty Boy" Floyd.

June 18—"Lucky" Luciano is sentenced to thirty to fifty years in Dannamora Prison in New York. His sentence will be commuted in 1945 by his former prosecutor, now Governor Thomas E. Dewey, for using his influence among dock workers to protect against wartime sabotage, and he will be deported to Italy.

June 19—Outlaw Arthur Gooch is hanged at McAlester, Oklahoma, for the kidnapping of two Texas policemen. He is the first man to be executed under the federal "Lindbergh Law."

June 23—At Alcatraz, Texas bank robber James Lucas wounds Al Capone with a pair of scissors.

July 1—"Dutch" Cretzer, Arnold Kyle, and Milton Hartman rob the Wilshire and Vermont Branch of the Seaboard National Bank in Los Angeles of $1,996.

July 5—John Manning, planner of the Rubel Ice plant armored car robbery, is found murdered in Manhattan. Other members of the gang will be imprisoned later for the robbery.

July 8—After robbing a bank at Turon, Kansas, Lawrence DeVol is surrounded by police at the German Village Tavern in Enid, Oklahoma. In the ensuing gun battle, DeVol and Officer Cal Palmer are killed.

July 27—"Dutch" Cretzer, Arnold Kyle, and Milton Hartman rob the Broadway Branch of the First National Bank in Seattle of $14,581.

— Alvin Karpis pleads guilty to the Hamm kidnapping and is sentenced to life imprisonment.

July 31—Charles Fitzgerald is sentenced to life for the Hamm kidnapping. Jack Peifer is sentenced to thirty years for the same crime but commits suicide by chewing poisoned gum in the St. Paul jail. Edmund Bartholmey, in whose house Hamm was held, receives a six-year sentence. Byron Bolton, who testified against the others, is sentenced to three to five years, to be served concurrently with a similar term for the Edward Bremer kidnapping.

August 7—Alvin Karpis enters Alcatraz.

September 12—Brady Gang member Charles Geiseking is arrested in Henderson, Kentucky.

September 25—Ray Terrill, former partner of Herman Barker and supposed leader of the "Kimes-Terrill Gang," is paroled from a twenty-year sentence at the McAlester, Oklahoma, state prison for burglary with explosives. Terrill, whom J. Edgar Hoover later will call a "criminal genius," reportedly reformed and invented a "burglar-proof" lock in prison.

October 11—Al Brady, Clarence Shaffer, and Jim Dalhover escape from the Hancock County Jail at Greenfield, Indiana.

October 13—A complaint is filed before the U.S. commissioner at Cleveland charging Al Brady, Clarence Shaffer, and Jim Dalhover with interstate transportation of stolen property valued in excess of $5,000. The Brady gangsters now are federal fugitives wanted by the FBI.

November 23—The Brady Gang robs a bank at North Madison, Indiana, of $1,630.

November 27—Arnold Kyle and Milton Hartman rob the Greenwood Branch of the First National Bank in Seattle of $8,000.

December 14—FBI agents, led by J. Edgar Hoover, lay siege to an apartment building on West 102nd Street in New York, accidentally setting it afire with a tear gas grenade, and capture bank robber Harry Brunette and his wife.

December 16—The Brady Gang robs a Carthage, Indiana, bank of $2,158.

December 27—Oklahoma outlaw Carl Janaway, mistaken for another fugitive, shoots arresting officer Edward Shulz in the legs on a St. Louis street and attempts to flee. Janaway is struck by a taxi and captured.

1937

January 28—Milton Hartman robs the Sunset and Clark Branch of the Bank of America in Los Angeles of $2,870.

March 29—Arnold Kyle, Milton Hartman, and John Oscar Hetzer rob the Rose City Branch of the First National Bank in Portland of $18,195.

April 6—John Oscar Hetzer is arrested by the FBI at a Los Angeles garage.

April 7—Cornered by the FBI, Milton Hartman commits suicide in his room at the Stuart Hotel in Los Angeles.

April 16—FBI Special Agent Wimberly W. Baker is fatally shot by bank robber Robert Joseph Suhay at a Post Office in Topeka, Kansas, while attempting to arrest Suhay's partner, Glen John Applegate. Suhay and Applegate are captured the same day at Plattsmouth, Nebraska, and later will be executed for murder.

April 27—The Brady Gang robs the Winchester Peoples Loan & Trust Co. branch at Farmland, Indiana, of $1,427.

May 25—The Brady Gang robs the Goodland, Indiana, bank of $2,528. Fifteen miles outside of town they ambush a police car, killing Indiana State Patrolman Paul Minneman and wounding Deputy Elmer Craig.

June 1—Car thief and Oklahoma jail escapee George Guy Osborne kills FBI Special Agent Truett E. Rowe to avoid arrest at his brother's ranch near Gallup, New Mexico. Osborne is captured a few hours later and will receive a life sentence for murder.

June 29—Four gunmen rob the Buckeye Road branch of Cleveland's Central National Bank, taking $13,800.

June 30—At the U.S. District Court in Cleveland, Arthur Hebebrand and John Francis "Sharkey" Gorman plead guilty to harboring Alvin Karpis and Harry Campbell. Hebebrand is sentenced to two years in federal prison and fined $1,000. Gorman is sentenced to three years and fined $1,000.

August 7—The Brady Gang escapes from police after a gun battle in Baltimore, leaving behind an arsenal of weapons and ammunition.

August 23—The Brady Gang robs the Peoples Exchange Bank at Thorp, Wisconsin, of $7,000.

August 31—Edgar Singleton, John Dillinger's first partner in crime in 1924, is killed by a train while sleeping on a railroad track in Morgan County, Indiana.

September 4—Donald Stiver, head of Indiana's Department of Public Safety, requests the resignation of Captain Matt Leach, head of the Indiana State Police, on charges that include criticizing and failing to cooperate with the FBI in the Brady Gang case. Leach and J. Edgar Hoover have been on hostile terms since their rivalry in the pursuit of John Dillinger.

September 16—Matt Leach is fired by the Indiana State Police Board.

September 19—At Folsom Prison in California, a bloody escape attempt results in the deaths of guard H. D. Martin and inmate Clyde Stevens. Warden James Larkin and inmate Ben Kucharski will die several days later. The five surviving participants in the attempted breakout will be sentenced to die in the gas chamber at San Quentin.

September 28—The Brady Gang is suspected in the murder of Highway Patrolman George Conn near Freeport, Ohio.

October 3—Roy Thornton and Austin Avers are killed attempting to escape from the "Little Alcatraz" unit at Eastham Prison Farm in Texas. Thornton had been Bonnie Parker's husband.

October 12—The Brady Gang is surrounded by FBI agents and police at a sporting goods store in Bangor, Maine. Al Brady and Clarence Shaffer are killed, and Jim Dalhover is captured.

December 16—Ralph Roe and Ted Cole become the first inmates to "escape" from Alcatraz and are presumed to have drowned, but their bodies are never recovered. Roe was a former member of the Wilbur Underhill Gang.

The Battle of Barrington

The Death of "Baby Face" Nelson

Of the many headline gun battles that marked the "public enemy" era, the most bizarre and illogical was the machine-gun shootout near Barrington, Illinois, that cost two federal agents their lives and permitted George "Baby Face" Nelson to escape in spite of many wounds. He died a few hours later in the Chicago suburb of Wilmette, attended by a possible FBI informant whom the bureau made no effort to prosecute.

Nelson, born Lester Joseph Gillis, had grown up in a neighborhood on Chicago's Near West Side known as the Patch, had graduated from stealing car parts to robbing banks in the early 1930s, knew several ascending members of the Chicago mob, and escaped from a guard en route to prison. But he had not attracted much attention until Dillinger, using bribe money advanced by Nelson's crew, escaped from the Crown Point jail and joined his fledgling gang. That Nelson suddenly found himself described as a member of the famous Dillinger Gang, instead of the other way around, seriously bruised his ego, leaving Dillinger obliged to flatter "Jimmie Williams," Nelson's favorite alias, and defer to his sense of personal importance. More difficult was keeping peace

Lester Joseph Gillis, aka "Baby Face" Nelson. For some reason, FBI "Wanted" posters, I.O.s (Identification Orders) and nearly all its documents refer to him as Lester M. Gillis.

among the members of this "second" Dillinger Gang because of the irascible Nelson's willingness to shoot police and civilians unnecessarily; he even had threatened to shoot crime partners who easily incurred his wrath. On the other hand, he was cool in a crisis and utterly fearless.

Lake Como Inn, near Lake Geneva, Wisconsin, was operated by Hobart Hermansen who catered to the criminal community. Nelson had intended to rent a separate cottage called the "Doll House" but spotted an FBI trap and was heading for Chicago when he was intercepted by G-men and died after the "Battle of Barrington."

After Dillinger's death in July 1934, Nelson and his wife, Helen, fled to California, leaving their young children, Ronald and Darlene, with relatives. That November the two returned to the Chicago area with a starstruck young bootlegger named John Paul Chase, intending to hole up at Wisconsin's Lake Como Inn (now the French Country Inn) just north of the Illinois state line. The Lake Como was a pleasant, no-questions-asked waterfront resort owned by Hobart Hermansen (not Hermanson, as commonly spelled), a former bootlegger courting the estranged wife of "Bugs" Moran, who had his summer place a little farther down the same dirt road.

From the back seat of Nelson's Ford, John Paul Chase fired several shots from a Monitor (the civilian version of a Browning Automatic Rifle) before an FBI bullet hit the Nelson car's fuel pump (not the water pump, as often reported) and disabled it at the outskirts of Barrington.

Tipped off that the Nelsons intended to winter at the hotel, FBI agents scared Hermansen into loaning them his house but were caught off guard on the day a Ford they mistook for the owner's pulled up in front. Nelson realized he'd driven into an unset trap about the same time that the agents recognized their

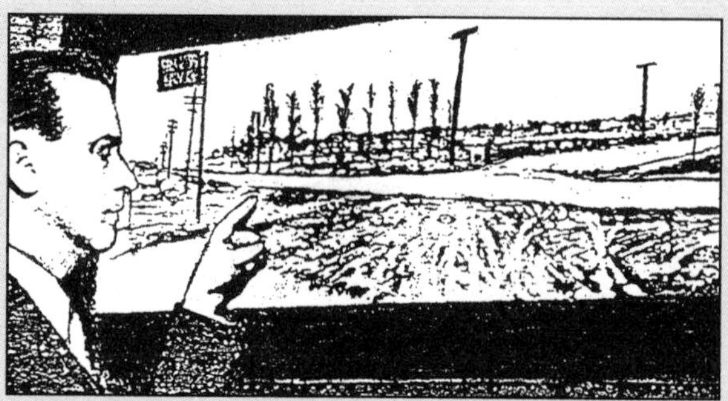

A court official describes the site where two federal agents lost their lives during the Barrington gun battle. The mortally-wounded Nelson (coming from Lake Como rather than Fox Lake) still managed to escape in the government's car and made it as far as Wilmette, where he died in a house belonging to Jimmy Murray.

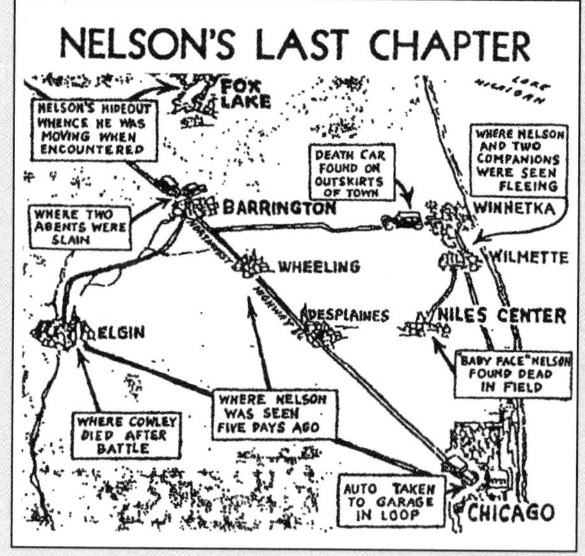

visitor. Nelson, pistol under a newspaper, exchanged a few pleasantries and sped off unhindered, for one agent had driven the FBI car to the nearby town of Lake Geneva to pick up groceries.

A frantic phone call to the Chicago office sent three carloads of federal agents rushing toward Wisconsin in hopes of intercepting Nelson on what still is called the Northwest Highway (then US 12, later US 14). The first team of G-men in a coupe driven by Agent Thomas McDade encountered Nelson's car near the village of Fox River Grove and turned around to give chase, only to discover that Nelson had done the same thing. As the two vehicles passed a second time, Nelson, instead of running, again spun his car around and began pursuing his pursuers. The surprised agents floored their coupe and began firing out the window as Nelson's Ford sedan closed the gap.

With Helen Nelson crouching on the front floorboards, Chase, in the back seat, let go with a burst of fire from a .30–06 Monitor, the commercial version of the military Browning Automatic Rifle. However, a lucky shot from the FBI car had punched through Nelson's radiator and disabled the fuel pump (not the water pump, as often reported), allowing the agents to escape. A mile or so down the road, the bureau car skidded off the road and its two agents prepared an ambush.

Meanwhile, an FBI Hudson, carrying Inspector Sam Cowley and Agent Herman Hollis, had encountered the running gun battle, wondered why it was going in the wrong direction with the wrong car in pursuit, and turned around to catch Nelson from behind. But Nelson's Ford already was conking out, and the agents' Hudson skidded to a stop near where Nelson ditched his car at the dirt road entrance to Barrington's city park. Hollis died with a bullet in his head when he ran for cover behind a telephone pole. Nelson, already hit by a Thompson slug, let out a curse and marched straight into the blasts from Cowley's shotgun, killing the second agent, as well.*

Though mortally wounded, Nelson managed to back the FBI Hudson up to his own disabled car, help load it with guns and ammunition, and with Chase driving made it into the Chicago suburb of Wilmette, where he was turned away by a trusted but now horrified priest, Father Phillip Coughlan. Coughlan agreed to lead them to shelter, but (according to Coughlan) the Nelson car turned off and lost him, going instead to a cottage at 1627 Walnut Avenue—one of several "safe houses" used by former mail-train robber James Murray [see p. 150].

There Nelson died about 7:30 that evening and was found late the next morning, wrapped in a blanket next to St. Paul's cemetery in the neighboring town of Niles Center (now Skokie). Helen Nelson surrendered herself on a downtown street the next day, but the FBI kept this secret long enough for newspapers to declare her a "public enemy" to be killed on sight. That was the lurid interpretation of a "show no mercy" order by the Justice Department, as the bureau quickly tried to explain; but it would still insist that she had been "captured."

Few details of Nelson's death were reported in the usually inquisitive press, nor

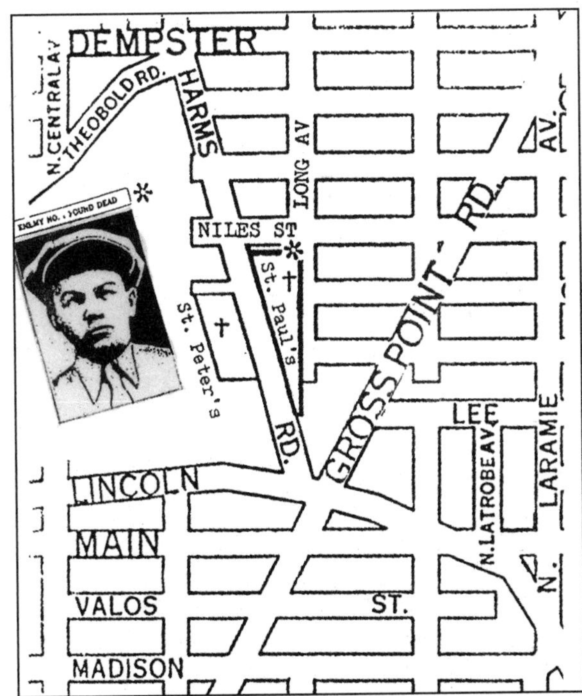

Nelson's body was not "dumped in a ditch," as most newspapers reported, but was wrapped in a blanket and laid in the grass next to St. Paul's Cemetery in the nearby town of Niles Center, now called Skokie.

*Contrary to other accounts, Nelson had emptied his Tommygun and then the Monitor, and when his reloaded Thompson jammed he attacked the agents with such rapid fire from a .351 Winchester rifle that it may have sounded like a machine gun. Cowley's .45 bullet had slipped under the vest Nelson was wearing (now owned by a Chicago woman who had worked for the FBI and rescued it from a scrap bin), and the seventeen hits he reportedly received included several exit wounds.

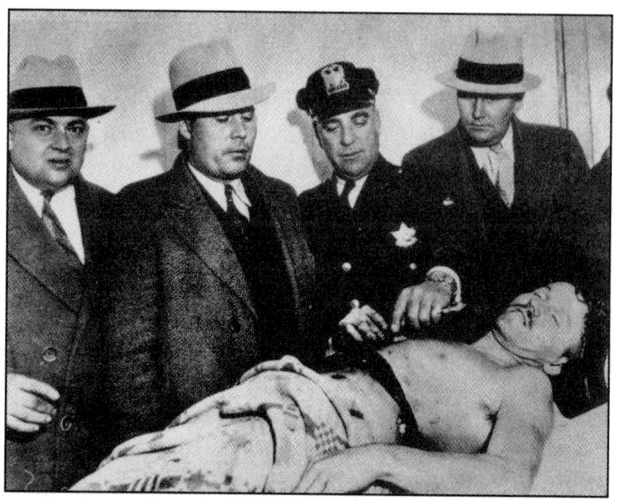

While police officers examine the body of "Baby Face" Nelson at a local funeral parlor (above), the Justice Department found itself in hot water for an ambiguous "show no mercy" statement regarding Helen Nelson that some papers translated into a "shoot to kill" order (below), even though Helen secretly had surrendered to the FBI a day later.

did the FBI reveal where he had died or charge those who had tried to save his life. Although agents placed the Wilmette house under close surveillance, bureau files are strangely silent about the investigation, despite its prosecution of a dozen or more other people whose contact with Nelson was sometimes minimal or even innocent.

The only clue to this decision can be found in a document filed some four years later containing the statement of another Wilmette resident. He told the bureau that a woman, Marie Henderson, still living in the house on Walnut, had dropped by for a visit and was telling him how surprised he'd be if he knew where "Baby Face" Nelson had died. Without specifying that it was at her place, she said that the house belonged to someone connected with the FBI, probably as an informant, who also had been supplying Nelson with inside information concerning the bureau. Nelson, she went on, had decided to go where the G-men would never think to look for him. She added that as far as she knew, Nelson's guns were still somewhere in the city, looking for a buyer.

Despite the limited information, it permits speculation that the bureau, after discovering where Nelson died, decided to let the matter go rather than reveal that the most notorious "public enemy" of the day had spent his last hours in the care of someone the FBI had thought was a useful informant, even if he helped Helen move Nelson's body the night he died.

Ashleys Divorced, Hold Doug Guilty

FINAL MARKETS Closing Prices

CHICAGO AMERICAN

BABY FACE SHOT DEAD!

Body Found in Niles Center Ditch

DUKE WINS IN WEDDING ROW WITH KING

Forces Own List of Guests Upon His Royal Parents

EXTRA

in U. S. War on Crime

Herald and Examiner

2 CENTS SPECIAL SPORTS

'KILL WIDOW OF BABY-FACE!' U. S. ORDERS GANG HUNTERS

Marina Becomes George's Bride in Glittering Pageant

Silver Shoes—Rose Petals

PRESIDENTIAL KNIFE CARVES 'FIRST TURKEY'

Hope Mingles With Thanks

BEARS DEFEAT DETROIT

1938

January 11—Alva Dewey Hunt and Hugh Gant are captured by the FBI in Houston.

January 25—Under the alias of Kay Wallace, Edna May Cretzer is arrested for operating a house of prostitution in Pittsburgh, California, and released on bond. Edna is the wife of fugitive bank robber Joseph "Dutch" Cretzer.

May 2—FBI Special Agent William R. Ramsey and bank robber Joseph Edward Earlywine kill one another in a gun battle at Penfield, Illinois.

– Mobster Joe Tocco is fatally shot by rival gangsters in Detroit.

June 7—Floyd Hamilton and Ted Walters rob a Bradley, Arkansas, bank of $685.

June 23—Ruth Hamm Robison, alias Connie Morris, pleads guilty in federal court at Little Rock, Arkansas, to harboring Alvin Karpis. She is sentenced to a year and a day.

July 21—Three suspected bandits, one identified as Floyd Hamilton, battle highway patrolmen and escape a police trap at Wills Point, Texas.

July 31—Missouri Highway Patrol officers unsuccessfully pursue three bandits, two identified as Floyd Hamilton and Ted Walters.

August 3—Bank robber Bennie Dickson marries fifteen-year-old Stella Mae Irwin at Pipestone, Minnesota.

August 5—Three men rob a messenger of the First National Bank at Wood River, Illinois, of $34,000. Floyd Hamilton and Ted Walters are suspects.

August 8—Two heavily armed men, believed to be Floyd Hamilton and Ted Walters, escape police in a running gun battle near Fort Worth.

August 12—Floyd Hamilton and Ted Walters rob a Coca-Cola bottling plant in Nashville, Arkansas, escaping with only $67.36.

August 21—Floyd Hamilton and Ted Walters are captured in Dallas. Both will be sent to Alcatraz for long terms.

August 25—Bennie and Stella Dickson rob the Corn Exchange Bank at Elkton, South Dakota, of $2,174. It is the eve of Stella's sixteenth birthday.

September 4—S. J. "Baldy" Whatley, a former friend who served a prison term for harboring Clyde Barrow and Bonnie Parker, fires a shotgun at Barrow family members outside Henry Barrow's gas station on Eagle Ford Road in West Dallas, shooting out Cumie Barrow's right eye. The attack was apparently in retaliation for a brass-knuckle beating Whatley received from L. C. Barrow, Clyde's younger brother. The Barrows will have Whatley arrested, resulting in a twelve-year sentence. Friends of Whatley later will make unsuccessful bombing attempts against members of the Barrow family.

October 7—Adam Richetti dies in the gas chamber of the Missouri state prison at Jefferson City.

October 14—James Murray, George Slade, and John Dorsch rob the Peoples National Bank at Clintonville, Pennsylvania, of $85,000 in cash, securities, and jewelry. Murray, a former Chicago politician and bootlegger, already had served time for masterminding the 1924 train robbery at Rondout, Illinois, and later associated with Dillinger and Nelson.

October 29—In a Little Rock, Arkansas, federal court, Jewell LaVerne Grayson, alias Grace Goldstein, former girlfriend of Alvin Karpis, along with Hot Springs Police Chief Joseph Wakelin, Chief of Detectives Herbert "Dutch" Akers, and Lieutenant Cecil Brock, are convicted of harboring Karpis. Each is sentenced to two years in a federal penitentiary. Verdicts of not guilty are directed against other alleged harborers, including Morris Loftis, Mrs. Al C. Dyer, and John Stover, operator of the Hot Springs Municipal Airport.

– Lloyd Barker is paroled from Leavenworth after serving sixteen of a 25-year sentence for mail robbery.

October 31—Bennie and Stella Dickson rob the Brookings, South Dakota, branch of the Northwest Security National Bank of Sioux Falls of $47,233 in cash and bonds.

November 18—Brady Gang member James Dalhover is executed in the electric chair at the Indiana state prison in Michigan City.

November 24—Bennie and Stella Dickson separately escape police at a tourist camp in Topeka, Kansas. Stella spends the night under a bridge.

Bennie drives to South Clinton, Iowa, hijacks another car, and meets Stella again the next day near Topeka. Over the next few days, they will battle police in Michigan, with Stella shooting out the tires of a patrol car, then take three men hostage and steal two more cars in Michigan and Indiana.

November 30—Citing insufficient evidence and his belief that both men are dead, prosecutor Clayton Wright dismisses charges against John Dillinger and Harry Copeland for the 1933 robbery of a Hartford City, Indiana, bank. Copeland, in fact, is in prison at the time.

December 6—Former Hot Springs Chief of Detectives Herbert "Dutch" Akers is convicted of harboring bank robber Thomas Nathan Norris and sentenced to an additional two years.

December 8—Jewell LaVerne Grayson, alias Grace Goldstein, former Hot Springs madam and mistress of Alvin Karpis, is convicted of violating the Mann Act by bringing her teenage niece up from Texas to engage in prostitution. She is sentenced to five years, to be served after her two-year sentence for harboring Karpis. (Besides harboring Karpis, Jewell also was bedding the local chief of police.)

December 16—Albert Kessel, Robert Cannon, Fred Barnes, Wesley Eudy, and Sebron Edward Davis, participants in the attempted breakout from Folsom Prison, are executed at San Quentin.

1939

January 13—Arthur "Doc" Barker is fatally wounded while attempting to escape from Alcatraz.

February 8—Arnold Kyle robs the Kansas State Bank in Wichita of $9,115.

April 5—Jack Miller, former member of the "Irish" O'Malley Gang who testified against other gang members, is found shot to death in a dry creekbed near Chelsea, Oklahoma.

April 6—Bennie Dickson is killed by FBI agents at a hamburger stand in St. Louis. Stella Dickson escapes.

April 7—Stella Dickson, now known as "Sure-Shot Stella," is arrested by the FBI in Kansas City. She will be convicted of bank robbery in South Dakota and sentenced to ten years.

April 8—Elmer Inman, former member of the Barker and Underhill Gangs, is released from the state prison at McAlester, Oklahoma, after serving a sentence for armed robbery.

April 16—FBI agents arrest former Dillinger and Nelson associate James Murray at his Chicago home for a bank robbery at Clintonville, Pennsylvania. Murray, having already served time for the 1924 Rondout train robbery, will be convicted and sentenced to twenty-five years in federal prison.

May 18—Under the alias of Raymond J. Palmer, Arnold Kyle is arrested for drunken driving in Minneapolis and turned over to the FBI.

May 19—Kansas City political boss Tom Pendergast pleads guilty to two counts of income tax evasion. Pendergast is sentenced to three years in prison and fined $10,000 on one count, five years' probation on the second, and ordered to pay $430,000 in back taxes and penalties.

June 7—Arnold Kyle pleads guilty to bank robbery and is sentenced to twenty-five years in the federal penitentiary at McNeil Island, Washington.

July 22—On the fifth anniversary of John Dillinger's death, a prisoner named Sam Goldstein is found hanging in a jail cell in Lima, Ohio, and declared a suicide. Contrary to later published accounts, this was not the same Sam Goldstine who once robbed banks with Dillinger.

August 24—At Fifth Avenue and Twenty-eighth Street in New York, mob boss Louis "Lepke" Buchalter, wanted for murder, narcotics conspiracy, extortion, and antitrust violations, arranges with celebrity newsman Walter Winchell to surrender in person to FBI Director J. Edgar Hoover. Buchalter will be the first prominent mobster sentenced to death by the State of New York when he is executed in 1944.

August 27—"Dutch" Cretzer is arrested by the FBI in Chicago.

October 20—Kansas City mob boss Charles Carrollo begins serving an eight-year prison sentence at Leavenworth for income tax evasion, mail fraud, and perjury.

November 6—Edna Kyle Cretzer pleads guilty to harboring her husband, Joseph "Dutch" Cretzer, and is sentenced to eighty-five days in jail.

November 8—Edward J. O'Hare, dog track owner and informer in the Capone tax case, is shotgunned to death in his car by unidentified killers on Ogden Avenue in Chicago.

November 16—Al Capone, in failing health from untreated syphilis, is released from Alcatraz.

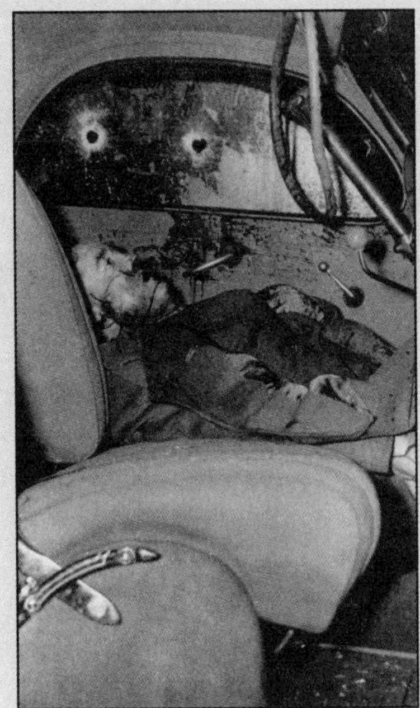

Dog track manager Edward O'Hare, a witness against Al Capone, was killed in 1939 (left) after trying to shake the mob for the sake of his son "Butch" (above), for whom Chicago's O'Hare International Airport would be named after he became a naval aviation hero during World War II.

1940

January 24—Joseph "Dutch" Cretzer pleads guilty to bank robbery charges at the federal court in Los Angeles and is sentenced to twenty-five years in the U.S. penitentiary at McNeil Island, Washington.

April 11—"Dutch" Cretzer and Arnold Kyle escape from the prison but not from McNeil Island. They will be recaptured on April 14.

July 10—Fred "Killer" Burke, serving a life sentence for murder, dies of natural causes in Michigan's state prison at Marquette.

August 8—Eleanor "The Blonde Tigress" Jarman, Depression-era bandit and convicted murderess, escapes from the state women's reformatory at Dwight, Illinois. She is never recaptured.

August 22—Joseph "Dutch" Cretzer and Arnold Kyle are sentenced to five additional years for their attempted escape, and they assault U.S. Marshal A. J. Chitty in the courtroom in another failed escape attempt. Chitty dies of a heart attack. Cretzer and Kyle are sentenced to life at Alcatraz.

REST IN PEACE:

February 28, 1941—George Elias Barker, husband of Kate "Ma" Barker, dies at his home in Webb City, Missouri, near Joplin.

March 25, 1941—Capone lawyer Albert Fink dies in Tucson, Arizona.

October 1, 1941—Benson Groves, alias Ben Grayson, Karpis Gang member wanted since 1935 for a Garrettsville, Ohio, train robbery, is captured during an attempted bank holdup at Carthage, Ohio. The sixty-five-year-old outlaw will plead guilty to mail robbery and be sentenced to twenty-five years in federal prison.

February 22, 1942—Bank robber Irving Charles Chapman is killed by the FBI near Philadelphia, Mississippi.

August 14, 1942—Cumie Barrow, mother of Clyde and "Buck," dies in Dallas. Three of her remaining children are in prison at the time.

October 9, 1942—Roger Touhy, Basil "The Owl" Banghart, Edward Darlak, William Stewart, Martlick Nelson, James O'Connor, and St. Clair McInerney escape from the Joliet, Illinois, prison.

The FBI enters the case on the novel legal point that the escapees have changed addresses without notifying Selective Service, thereby violating the draft law.

December 18, 1942—The Touhy-Banghart gangsters are suspected of a $20,000 truck robbery in Melrose Park, Illinois.

December 28, 1942—James O'Connor and St. Clair McInerney are killed by FBI agents while resisting arrest at 1254 Leland Avenue in Chicago.

December 29, 1942—Roger Touhy, Basil Banghart, and Edward Darlak are captured by FBI agents, led by J. Edgar Hoover, in an apartment at 5116 Kenmore Avenue in Chicago. It is Hoover's last "personal arrest."

March 19, 1943—Frank "The Enforcer" Nitti, Al Capone's successor, commits suicide by shooting himself after being indicted by a federal grand jury in Chicago for conspiring to extort millions of dollars from Hollywood movie studios.

May 5, 1943—Former bootlegger Danny Stanton and henchman Louis Dorman are killed by five men with shotguns in a tavern at 6500 South May in Chicago.

September 22, 1943—Capone lawyer Michael Ahearn dies at his Chicago home at 4536 North Mozart.

November 3, 1943—John Dillinger Sr., dies in Mooresville, Indiana.

March 4, 1944—Louis "Lepke" Buchalter and henchmen Emanuel "Mendy" Weiss and Louis Capone die in Sing Sing's electric chair.

March 19, 1944—Former mayor of Chicago "Big Bill" Thompson dies under an oxygen tent at Chicago's Blackstone Hotel a week after suffering a heart attack.

June 26, 1944—Vivian Gibson Mathis Kennedy, onetime mistress of Verne Miller, dies of tuberculosis in Sioux Falls, South Dakota.

June 29, 1944—"Lapland Willie" Weaver, serving a life sentence for the Bremer kidnapping, dies at Alcatraz.

August 3, 1944—"Dago" Lawrence Mangano is murdered in Chicago.

September 21, 1944—Emma Parker, mother of Bonnie Parker, dies in Dallas.

January 9, 1945—Charles J. Fitzgerald, serving a life sentence for the Hamm kidnapping, dies at Leavenworth.

December 1, 1945—1920s bank robber Matt Kimes, on leave of absence from the McAlester, Oklahoma, state prison and wanted for a recent bank robbery at Morton, Texas, is run over by a poultry truck and fatally injured in North Little Rock, Arkansas.

May 24, 1946—An escape attempt from Alcatraz erupts into a bloody riot as convicts raid the prison arsenal and take guards hostage. U.S. Marines and prison guards lay siege to the convicts' cellblock stronghold. Inmates Bernard Paul Coy, Joseph "Dutch" Cretzer, and Marvin Hubbard, and guards William A. Miller and Harold P. Stites are killed. Several other guards are wounded.

July 30, 1946—Dr. Harold Cassidy, who assisted in Dillinger's plastic surgery, commits suicide at his sister's home in Chicago.

November 20-December 22, 1946—Miran Edgar "Buddy" Thompson, Sam Shockley, and Clarence Carnes, survivors of the Alcatraz riot, are tried and convicted of the murder of guard Miller. Thompson and Shockley are sentenced to death, Carnes to life imprisonment.

January 25, 1947—Al Capone dies at his estate on Palm Island, Florida.

February 10, 1947—Willie "The Actor" Sutton and others escape from Holmesburg Prison in Philadelphia.

April 25, 1947—Anna Sage, the notorious "Lady in Red," dies of liver failure in her native Romania.

June 20, 1947—Benjamin "Bugsy" Siegel is murdered by Syndicate gunmen in his Beverly Hills mansion at 810 North Linden Drive.

August 20, 1947—Former police chief Joseph Wakelin, once convicted of harboring Alvin Karpis, dies in Hot Springs, Arkansas.

October 23, 1947—Carl Shelton, leader of the Shelton Brothers gang still active in southern Illinois rackets, is shot to death in his Jeep while

THE BODY IDENTIFIED AS JOHN HAMILTON

On April 23, 1934, J. Edgar Hoover called a press conference expecting to announce the killing or capture of the entire Dillinger Gang at northern Wisconsin's Little Bohemia Lodge. Instead, dozens of FBI agents would mistakenly shoot three departing customers, killing one and setting off a lopsided gun battle that allowed the gang to escape out the unguarded rear. While the G-men poured more than a thousand bullets and buckshot into the empty floors of the lodge, the robbers stole cars at neighboring farms and resorts and headed in different directions.

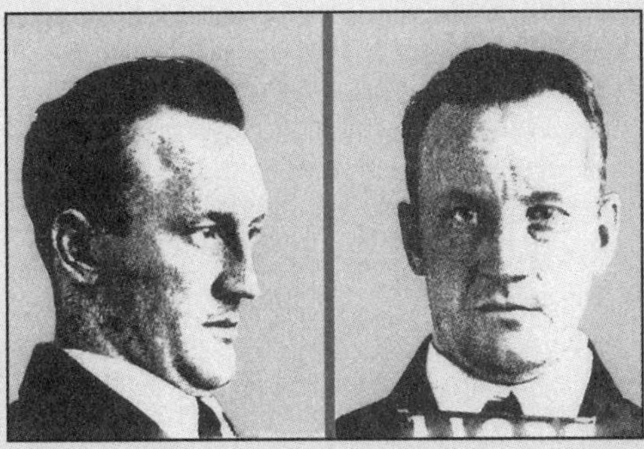

John "Red" Hamilton

"Baby Face" Nelson killed one federal agent and wounded another, as well as a local officer, at a nearby resort. John Dillinger, Homer Van Meter and John Hamilton remained together and commandeered a Ford coupe. Tommy Carroll eluded everyone, and it was the last time Hoover would call a press conference in advance of a raid that might turn into a fiasco.

Later that night, Minnesota police spotted the Dillinger car and began firing at it with rifles. One bullet pierced the trunk and struck Hamilton in the back. The three escaped nevertheless, and Hamilton supposedly died several days later in the Aurora, Illinois, apartment of Volney Davis, one of the Barker-Karpis Gang. Davis's girlfriend, Edna Murray, had been told to scram before Hamilton's arrival and would not have heard of his death and burial until she reunited with Davis later that year. Meanwhile, Dillinger was killed in Chicago on July 22, 1934; Van Meter in St. Paul on August 23; and Nelson the following November 27 after a bloody firefight near Barrington, northwest of Chicago.

Volney Davis

Dr. Joseph Moran

But so far as the FBI knew, and despite the blood in the abandoned coupe, Hamilton's death was still uncertain, based on second- or third-hand accounts of others connected with Dillinger. One rumor had him buried in the sand dunes of northern Indiana. Another had him weighted and dropped into the water flooding an abandoned mine shaft in Wisconsin. Not until Davis himself had been arrested, escaped, and arrested again the following summer did he tell agents of the unsuccessful efforts of Dillinger and Van Meter to get Hamilton medical treatment from Dr. Joseph Moran in Chicago. Moran had refused, probably warned to have no further dealings with outlaws who were bringing too much federal heat on the mob. Dillinger, it now turns out, had persisted. After Dillinger was killed on July 22, Polly Hamilton said that his betrayer, Anna Sage, had told her Hamilton was being treated for a "badly infected wound" by Dr. Harold Cassidy, meaning Hamilton was still alive as of June 1934 or later (see "The Statement of Anna Sage," p. 398.)

Nevertheless, Davis (and others) stuck to the story that Hamilton had died in much agony at his Aurora apartment soon after he was shot, and he provided a general location of the burial site. There were inconsistencies as to the actual time and place of Hamilton's death and the persons involved in his burial, but more than a year later, on August 28, 1935, G-men digging around in an Oswego gravel pit finally found a badly decomposed body.

Before the body was found, the bureau had been receiving reports from police and individuals claiming "Three-Fingers Jack" Hamilton was alive and hiding in northern Indiana. Since he had been reported killed on other occasions, the search continued until the body was discovered, minus a hand and so desiccated from lye poured over the remains that the agents had little to go on besides some strands of hair and a belt size. In fact, the best they could do was pull several molars from the skull and send them to the physician at the Indiana state prison. He compared them to Hamilton's dental chart, which showed some of the fillings, and declared that the agents had indeed found their man. This satisfied Hoover, who proclaimed the belated discovery of the last member of the Dillinger Gang in every daily newspaper in the country. Case closed.

Reports that Hamilton was alive continued coming in to the FBI but apparently were disregarded and possibly not seen by Hoover, who typically scribbled his initials or a comment at the bottom of the memo. Some could be written off as cases of mistaken identity, but one was particularly convincing:

This letter was recorded by the FBI on August 24, 1936—another year after the body was found at Oswego—and there may have been no follow-up. It might have come from a former prisoner called "Happy"* (only "Hap" is visible on a bureau document) who knew some of the gang members, as well as Arthur O'Leary, investigator for Dillinger's attorney Louis Piquett. But by the time the body was found, Hoover had won the national "War on Crime," earned himself the cover of *Time* magazine, and was turning his attention to communism.

That same year, Bruce Hamilton was born to Harriet and Wilton Hamilton, the son of one of several brothers and sisters of John B. Hamilton. Five years later World War II intervened and gasoline rationing postponed any major trips until after 1945. About that time Wilton, John's nephew, began traveling back and forth to northern Wisconsin, supposedly to hunt deer. This struck young Bruce as odd, since there were

August 3rd, 1936.

Mr. J. Edgar Hoover,
Washington, D. C.

Dear Sir:

Will you kindly advise how much you will guarantee in cash secret and confidential information about the movements of John Hamilton.

There are three people who know that he is still living and happen to know the most details concerning him.

If interested please make pffer thru Personal Column of Chicago Tribune as follows, HAP-Will buy ,ooo bushels, meaning of course that many thousand dollars for this information and place ED after the word bushels. If this offer is OK you will be supplied with an amazing detail report on his present physical condition and his movements. Money must be on deposit at your Chicago Office but will not have to be paid until this man is captured or killed or both. This information must be kept strictly confidential between you and I and must be kept out of the newspapers except code transactions between you and I. I am a hard working electrican and took considerable time and money to get this data and do not want to risk my life for the deal. Everything will be handled by correspondence and code in the Chicago Tribune. If your offer is accepted, I will make you proposals which must be guaranteed by you as a strictly gemtlemens agreement.

Yours ve

HA

AUG 24 1936
RECORDED

AUG 20 1936 P. M.

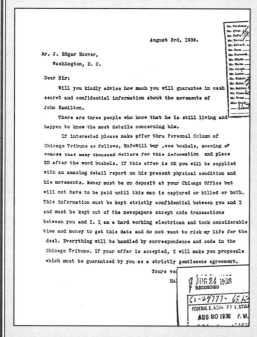

In the summer of 1934, J. Edgar Hoover had been sent a fairly convincing letter asking a reward for fingering John Hamilton, who may have survived the gunshot wound he received after the Little Bohemia gun battle.

*In a memorandum from a Gene Ryan to Captain Matt Leach of the Indiana State Police, a "Happy" is identified as an associate of Dillinger named Fred Meyers, 4147 Irving Avenue, Chicago.

G-men Uncover Body of Hamilton

Body Found.

DILLINGER AID FOUND BURIED BY ROADSIDE

Greatest Manhunt in Nation Ends at Illinois Grave.

John Hamilton Not Dead, Ohio Officer Believes

Voices Opinion After Questioning Former Wife of Dillinger Mobster.

5¢ SUNDAY TIMES FINAL

HAMILTON DEATH IN FLIGHT BARED!

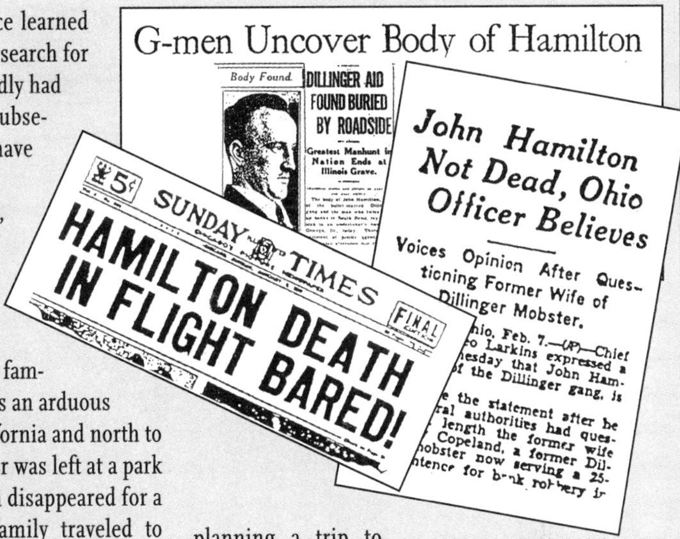

plenty of deer close by. Later Bruce learned that the purpose of the trips was to search for money the Dillinger Gang supposedly had buried somewhere. Judging from subsequent events, this money may have been found in late 1946.

That year (or in early 1947), Wilton Hamilton paid off the mortgage and sold their home in South Bend, Indiana. He purchased a twenty-seven-foot house trailer and headed "out west" in the family's pre-war Chevrolet. The trip was an arduous one that ranged from Texas to California and north to Roseburg, Oregon, where the trailer was left at a park on the Umpqua River while Wilton disappeared for a week. When he returned, the family traveled to Phoenix, Arizona, where a real estate agent whom Wilton had known in South Bend showed him a house for $8,000. At this time Bruce was about eleven and heard his father remark that if he bought the property for cash, he would have $2,000 left.

However, Wilton decided to move back to South Bend, bought a house there in 1948, and two years later purchased a bronze-colored four-door Ford—the family's first new car. Less than a year later he began planning a trip to Sault Ste. Marie on the Canadian border "to see relatives" at the home of John Hamilton's sister, Anna Campbell Steve. The journey was made by Wilton and Harriet Hamilton, older son Douglas, daughter Jane Margaret, and Bruce, who by now was fifteen. While John Hamilton had been the subject of guarded conversation, Bruce formed the impression that his great-uncle John still might be alive. About a dozen family members were present, and it was after a trip to a house in Canada's Sault Ste. Marie that young Bruce met the man he afterward was told was his black-sheep relative, John Hamilton. He and others were told not to discuss the trip.

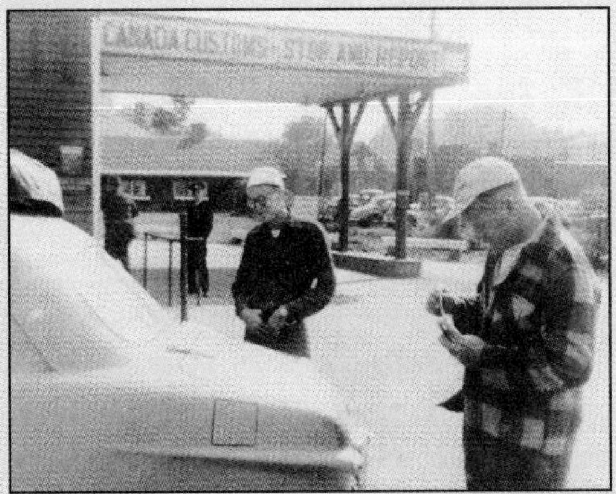

In the late 1940s, Bruce Hamilton remembers his father's "mystery" trips that yielded enough money to buy a new Ford and move the family to New Mexico.

About this time John Hamilton's brother Foye, himself recently released from prison, came into a good deal of money, which he used to build a large machine shop in Rockford, Illinois. He also purchased Turtle Island in the Great Lakes area near Sault Ste. Marie, Canada, as well as boats and a seaplane to provide access. Bruce suspected that the island with its large log cabin became the safe harbor for Canadian-born John Hamilton. His own interest in Hamilton increased with his age and knowledge, and from his father, Wilton, he eventually learned more details.

Apparently the wounded Hamilton, after stopping at Aurora and then Chicago (where the FBI initially

The presumed grave of John Hamilton near Oswego, Illinois, was uncovered by G-men on a tip in 1935. Hoover declared the body to be Hamilton's, but it was too decomposed to be identified except by prison dental records that were not mentioned in a book later written by the same doctor, who discussed the deaths of other members of the Dillinger Gang. Another person, who disappeared about the same time, was mob physician Dr. Joseph Moran, who had refused to treat the badly wounded Hamilton.

believed he had died), obtained treatment from Dr. Cassidy and went into hiding with his brother Sylvester in East Gary, Indiana. Dillinger then returned to Aurora, while Sylvester took John to Bruce Hamilton's grandfather William in South Bend. William helped him to a hideout previously used by the Dillinger Gang, in a place near South Bend called Rum Village Woods. According to a cousin's letter to Bruce, written several years ago, John Hamilton had recuperated sufficiently to work as an electrician at a family-owned bowling alley in South Bend about 1936 or 1937. Her signed and witnessed letter to this effect states that "Ham [as Wilton was known to friends] would run into him occasionally here and there, and Uncle John would look at him and then cover his hand with some fingers missing. But they didn't speak to each other." Bruce Hamilton's father has since died, and other members of the family, including those who had made the trip to Canada, refuse to discuss John Hamilton.

Bruce had put this much of the story together by 2003 when an aunt, about age ninety and living in Florida, supported his account, telling her niece that John Hamilton had successfully faked his death in 1934 and later escaped to Canada. The aunt also claimed to know where Hamilton is buried.

More recently, in the summer of 2006, the niece—John Hamilton's granddaughter—visited the family near Pickford, Michigan, that had raised some of the Hamilton children, and she called Bruce with the news that John Hamilton had indeed survived, made his way to Canada, and occasionally slipped back into the U.S. to see them at their home, about twenty-five miles south of Sault Ste. Marie. He presumably lived on his brother Foye's island until his death sometime in the 1970s.

Which raises the question of whose body—if not Hamilton's—was disinterred at Oswego in 1935. One possibility is that it was that of Dr. Moran, who had refused to treat Hamilton's wound in Chicago and later disappeared. Hoover had continued pursuing Moran for months, and putting no date on the event, later declared in *Persons in Hiding* that the Barker-Karpis Gang had taken him for a one-way boat ride on the Great Lakes, while writer Herbert Corey and Alvin Karpis say only that he was murdered and buried.

Worth noting is the fact that the Michigan City prison doctor, Patrick Weeks, discusses his career in *The Big House of Mystery*, in which he describes the deaths of Dillinger and other gang members in some detail. This book was published in 1938, less than three years after he had assured the FBI that the teeth he examined were John Hamilton's; but his only reference to Hamilton concerns treatment he received years earlier for peritonitis.

driving near his farm outside Fairfield, Illinois.

November 28, 1947—Former Barker-Karpis Gang member Thomas James Holden is paroled from a 25-year sentence for mail train robbery.

December 2, 1947—William Schofield, onetime florist partner of Dean O'Banion, dies in Chicago after a long illness.

December 4, 1947—Benjamin M. "Manny" Gault, one of the officers who killed Bonnie and Clyde, dies of natural causes while serving as Texas Ranger captain in Lubbock, Texas.

January 24, 1948—Herbert "Deafy" Farmer, former Joplin, Missouri, contact of the Barker-Karpis Gang who served a short term as a conspirator in the Kansas City Massacre case, dies of natural causes at his home in Joplin.

April 19, 1948—Former Barrow Gang member Henry Methvin is hit by a train and killed at Sulphur, Louisiana. Rumors persist in the area that Methvin, alleged to have betrayed Bonnie and Clyde in 1934, actually was murdered.

July 2, 1948—1920s outlaw George Kimes, serving a fifty-year sentence for bank robbery, escapes from Oklahoma's state prison.

July 4, 1948—Albert Bates, serving a life sentence for the Urschel kidnapping, dies on Alcatraz.

July 19, 1948—Elmer Irey, who led the successful income tax investigations of Capone and other mobsters, dies in Maryland.

July 26, 1948—Bernie Shelton is fatally shot by an unknown rifleman outside his Parkway Tavern in Peoria, Illinois.

September 14, 1948—Depression bank robber Glen LeRoy Wright, serving a life sentence for robbery, shoots his way out of Oklahoma's state prison with a smuggled pistol.

December 2, 1948—"Buddy" Thompson and Sam Shockley are executed in the San Quentin gas chamber.

March 18, 1949—Lloyd "Red" Barker, last surviving son of "Ma" Barker, is murdered by his wife, Jennie, at their home in Westminister, Colorado, near Denver.

May 3, 1949—Patricia Cherrington, former Dillinger Gang "moll," is found dead, apparently of natural causes, in her room at the Burton Hotel, 1424 North Clark Street, Chicago. She was forty-five.

May 24, 1949—"Big Earl" Shelton is wounded in his Fairfield, Illinois, gambling club by an unknown attacker firing from the roof of a neighboring building.

June 5, 1949—Thomas James Holden escapes police after murdering his wife, Lillian, and her two brothers in a drunken argument at their Chicago apartment.

June 8, 1949—George Kimes, employed at a lumber camp, is recaptured by deputies at Burns, Oregon.

June 17, 1949—Alton Crapo and Albert Gladson, described as former members of the Barker Gang, are killed by police near Howell, Nebraska, after a $75,000 jewel robbery.

December 31, 1949—Julius "Babe" Jones, onetime member of the College Kidnappers who turned informer and brought about the death of "Handsome Jack" Klutas and convictions of other gang members in the 1930s, fatally shoots his wife, Grace, and wounds John Fitzgerald at the Jones apartment, 6248 Harper Avenue, in Chicago. Jones tells police he was "in a trance" from drinking and believed his wife and Fitzgerald were "gunmen seeking vengeance" against him.

March 9, 1950—Willie "The Actor" Sutton leads new gang in robbing the Manufacturers Trust Co. at 4711 Queens Boulevard, Long Island, of $63,942.

March 14, 1950—1930s outlaw Thomas Holden becomes the first fugitive named to the FBI's new "Ten Most Wanted" list. (Newspapers habitually had described the FBI's most notorious fugitive as a "public enemy.")

March 20, 1950—Willie "The Actor" Sutton is named to the FBI's "Ten Most Wanted" list.

March 22, 1950—Glen LeRoy Wright is named to the FBI's "Ten Most Wanted" list.

June 7, 1950—Roy Shelton is shot to death while driving a tractor on his brother's farm near Fairfield, Illinois.

September 26, 1950—Joe Bergl, whose Cicero garage provided specially equipped and armored cars to such criminals as Capone, "Machine Gun" Kelly and the Barker-Karpis Gang, dies at his home in suburban River Forest, Illinois.

December 13, 1950—Glen LeRoy Wright is recaptured by the FBI at Salina, Kansas.

April 11, 1951—Charles "Trigger Happy" Fischetti, cousin of Al Capone, dies of a heart attack in Miami.

May 27, 1951—Leo Brothers, convicted of Jake Lingle's slaying, dies in Murphysboro, Illinois, of an infection from a recent gunshot wound.

June 19, 1951—Capone gangster Hymie "Loud Mouth" Levin dies at Chicago's St. Luke's Hospital.

June 28, 1951—Lula Shelton Pennington and husband Guy are wounded in a machine-gun ambush in Fairfield, Illinois. Lula is a sister of the notorious Shelton Brothers.

July 13, 1951—Capone mobster Willie Heeney dies of throat cancer in Chicago's Mercy Hospital.

June 23, 1951—Thomas Holden is captured by the FBI at Beaverton, Oregon.

December 12, 1951—Louis Piquett, John Dillinger's attorney, dies of a heart attack while living at 661 West Sheridan Road in Chicago.

February 18, 1952—Willie Sutton is recaptured by Brooklyn police on a tip from clothing salesman Arnold Schuster.

March 8, 1952—Arnold Schuster is shot to death near his Brooklyn home.

October 1, 1952—Vincenzo (James) Capone, better known as James "Two-Gun" Hart, dies in Homer, Nebraska; he had worked off and on as a Prohibition and Bureau of Indian Affairs agent, concealing that he was the "white sheep" brother of Chicago's Al Capone.

December 18, 1953—Thomas Holden dies in prison in Illinois while serving a life sentence for murder.

May 7, 1954—Former Cookson Hills outlaw and "Ten Most Wanted" fugitive Glen LeRoy Wright dies at the Oklahoma state reformatory while serving a life sentence for armed robbery.

July 18, 1954—George "Machine Gun" Kelly dies of a heart attack in Leavenworth soon after turning fifty-four.

August 18, 1954—Capone mobster Charles "Cherry Nose" Gioe is murdered in Chicago.

August 21, 1954—Frank Maritote, alias Frank Diamond, is murdered in Chicago.

May 30, 1955—Louis "Little New York" Campagna dies of a heart attack while on a Florida fishing trip.

June 14, 1955—Matt Leach, former chief of the Indiana State Police and author of a book manuscript on the Dillinger case, is killed with his wife in an automobile accident on the Pennsylvania Turnpike while returning from a meeting with his publisher. Leach's manuscript disappears.

June 23, 1955—Harry Sawyer, once the St. Paul connection for the Dillinger and Barker-Karpis Gangs, dies of cancer in Chicago.

July 7, 1955—Anthony "Tough Tony" Capezio dies of a heart attack (not struck by lightning as often reported) while playing golf at the White Pines Country Club in Bensenville, Illinois.

July 10, 1955—Retired Texas Ranger Frank Hamer, who led the ambush of Bonnie and Clyde, dies at his home in Austin.

November 18, 1955—Ted Bentz, brother of notorious bank robber Eddie Bentz, is paroled after serving twenty-one years for the 1933 Grand Haven, Michigan, bank robbery actually committed by his brother and "Baby Face" Nelson.

— Former Barker Gang member Elmer Inman is killed in a traffic accident at Project City, California.

December 8, 1955—Capone-era mobster Alex Louis Greenberg is murdered in Chicago.

February 21, 1956—Jake "Greasy Thumb" Guzik dies of a heart attack at his home at 5492 Everett Avenue in Chicago.

May 13, 1956—Former Chicago chief of detectives John Stege dies of a heart attack in Santa Monica, California.

August 19, 1956—Sam "Golf Bag" Hunt dies in Schnectady, New York.

December 23, 1956—John "Boy Mayor of Burnham" Patton dies in Earl Park, Indiana.

December 25, 1956—Robert "Boss" Shannon, pardoned in 1944 from his life sentence for the Urschel kidnapping, dies in a hospital at Bridgeport, Texas.

February 25, 1957—Former Capone rival George "Bugs" Moran dies of lung cancer in Leavenworth while serving a sentence for bank robbery.

May 16, 1957—Eliot Ness dies of a heart attack in Coudersport, Pennsylvania, before publication of *The Untouchables*, Oscar Fraley's fictionalized version of Ness's Prohibition days in Chicago.

June 19, 1957—Henry Barrow, father of Clyde and "Buck," dies in Dallas.

October 15, 1957—Bienville Parish Sheriff Prentiss Oakley, who took part in the killing of Bonnie and Clyde, dies in Louisiana.

October 25, 1957—Albert Anastasia is shot to death by masked gunmen while being shaved in the barbershop of the Park Sheraton Hotel in New York.

November 14, 1957—A raid by state police on the Apalachin, New York, estate of Joseph Barbera uncovers a "Mafia meeting" of at least sixty-three organized crime figures from across the nation.

June 13, 1958—Henderson Jordan, former sheriff of Bienville Parish and one of the participants in the ambush of Bonnie and Clyde, is killed in an auto accident.

June 21, 1958—Claude Maddox dies in bed at his home at 3536 South Harlem in Riverside, Illinois.

January 8, 1959—Tom Brown, onetime St. Paul police chief, demoted and fired in the 1930s after his underworld ties were exposed, dies in Ely, Minnesota.

January 11, 1959—Jim Benge, former member of the Wilbur Underhill-Ford Bradshaw Gang, is found beaten to death near Haskell, Oklahoma.

June 9, 1959—Kathryn Kelly, convicted of the Urschel kidnapping in 1933, is freed on bond pending appeal. Her mother, Ora Shannon, also is released. They remain free when the FBI lets the case lapse by refusing to release records pertinent to their conviction.

September 14, 1959—Former Dillinger Gang member Ed Shouse dies of a heart attack in Chicago.

November 24, 1959—After serving twenty-five years for the supposed kidnapping of Jake "The Barber" Factor, former bootlegger Roger Touhy is paroled after courts decide the kidnapping was a hoax.

December 16, 1959—Roger Touhy is murdered on the front porch of his sister's home at 125 North Lotus in Chicago.

February 29, 1960—Melvin Purvis dies of a self-inflicted gunshot wound at his home in Florence, South Carolina. Although ruled a suicide owing to health problems, his death may have been accidental.

May 16, 1960—Roger Touhy's brother Tommy dies in Chicago of a liver ailment under the name Thomas Toohey.

June 29, 1961—Basil "The Owl" Banghart is released from Statesville Prison at Joliet, Illinois, after commutation of his ninety-five-year sentence for the supposed kidnapping of Jake "The Barber" Factor.

July 24, 1961—Harvey Bailey, wrongly convicted of the Urschel kidnapping in 1933, is released from the Federal Correctional Institution at Seagoville, Texas, only to be rearrested by Kansas authorities who still want him for his 1933 prison escape.

August 18, 1962—Former judge and Barker Gang attorney Quiliki P. McGhee dies in Oklahoma.

August 20, 1962—Edward "Spike" O'Donnell dies of a heart attack at his home on Chicago's South Side.

December 30, 1962—Carol Hamilton Tankersley, onetime "moll" of Herman Barker, dies in Oklahoma City.

January 20, 1963—Jimmy Murray, planner of the Rondout train robbery and later associated with Dillinger and Nelson, dies in Chicago.

May 13, 1963—Former Dillinger Gang member William Albert "Pat" Reilly dies in St. Paul.

May 15, 1963—The federal penitentiary on Alcatraz is closed.

June 8, 1963—Roy Kimes, career criminal and jail-breaker since the 1930s, is shot and killed by store owner Bill Cason during a burglary in Kiowa, Oklahoma. Kimes was the cousin of 1920s outlaws Matt and George Kimes.

December 7, 1963—Former Dillinger Gang member Harry Copeland is killed in Detroit when he drunkenly walks into the path of a car.

May 23, 1964—Former Dallas County Deputy Bob Alcorn dies thirty years to the day after participating in the ambush of Bonnie and Clyde.

November 24, 1964—Gangster-fighting Judge John H. Lyle, defeated for mayor and later author of *The Dry and Lawless Years*, dies in Chicago after a long illness.

March 31, 1965—Harvey Bailey is released on parole from the state prison at Lansing, Kansas.

May 4, 1965—Edward Bremer, kidnapped by the Barker-Karpis Gang in 1934, dies at Pompano Beach, Florida.

November 23, 1965—Murray "The Camel" Humphreys dies in Chicago.

April 13, 1966—Edna "The Kissing Bandit" Murray dies as Martha Edna Potter.

August 7, 1966—Dr. Horace Hunsicker, kidnapped by Alvin Karpis in 1935, dies in Philadelphia.

October 14, 1966—Harvey Bailey marries Esther Mary Farmer, the widow of his friend Herbert Farmer from Joplin, Missouri. The Baileys use their middle names and live as cabinet-maker John and Mary Bailey at 826 St. Louis Avenue.

October 31, 1966—John Paul Chase, "Baby Face" Nelson's accomplice convicted in 1935 of murdering an FBI agent in the Barrington, Illinois, gun battle, is released on parole from Leavenworth.

January 31, 1967—Matthew "Matt the Mooch" Capone, younger brother of Al, dies.

April 1, 1967—Gladys Sawyer dies in Denver.

May 20, 1967—William A. Rorer, G-man who led the capture of "Machine Gun" Kelly, dies in Albany, Georgia. Rorer also took part in the Little Bohemia battle and served at different times as Special Agent in Charge of thirteen different FBI offices. He reportedly was involved in more 1930s gangster cases than any other FBI agent.

April 6, 1968—Peter Von Frantzius, gangland armorer of the 1920s, dies in Chicago.

August 14, 1968—Former Dillinger Gang member Russell Clark, dying of cancer, is released from the state prison at Columbus, Ohio, after serving thirty-four years of a life sentence for the murder of Sheriff Jesse Sarber.

December 24, 1968—Russell Clark dies in Hazel Park, Michigan.

January 13, 1969—Evelyn Tic, formerly Evelyn "Billie" Frechette, dies at the age of sixty-one at Shawano, Wisconsin.

January 14, 1969—Alvin Karpis is released on parole from the federal prison at McNeil Island, Washington, and deported to Canada. Karpis (with probably the only successfully obliterated fingerprints from his hoodlum days) tells reporters he plans to see the movie *Bonnie and Clyde*.

February 19, 1969—Edythe Black, formerly Rita "Polly" Hamilton Keele, John Dillinger's last girlfriend who has since married and attained respectability, dies in Chicago.

July 31, 1969—Former Dillinger Gang "moll" Opal Long Kosmal dies in Chicago.

September 18, 1969—Kansas Governor Robert Docking pardons Frank Sawyer after receiving an affidavit from Alvin Karpis admitting that he committed the bank robbery for which Sawyer was convicted. Sawyer technically is still wanted in Oklahoma for kidnapping and jailbreaking.

October 30, 1969—Former East Chicago, Indiana, policeman Martin Zarkovich, friend of Anna Sage who claimed to be one of the shooters of John Dillinger, dies at St. Catherine's Hospital in East Chicago, Indiana.

December 9, 1969—Enoch "Nucky" Johnson dies.

December 24, 1969—Willie Sutton is released from Attica Prison in New York.

January 3, 1970—1920s bank robber George Kimes dies in Carmichael, California.

February 17, 1970—The Towne Hotel (formerly the Hawthorne, Al Capone's Cicero headquarters and still operated by the mob) burns down. It has housed the office of Joey Aiuppa, and firemen find secret basement room containing gambling paraphernalia.

July 29, 1970—Ruby Floyd, former wife of "Pretty Boy" Floyd, dies in Broken Arrow, Oklahoma.

August 20, 1970—William A. Hamm Jr., kidnapped by the Barker-Karpis Gang in 1933, dies in Minneapolis.

– E. W. Floyd, brother of "Pretty Boy" Floyd, dies in his twenty-second year as sheriff of Sequoyah County, Oklahoma.

December 9, 1970—Arthur O'Leary dies in Daytona Beach, Florida.

October 14, 1971—Elderly 1930s bank robber "Terrible Ted" Walters, formerly the partner of Floyd Hamilton, is shot to death by Texas Rangers while holding a farm family hostage near Fort Worth.

May 1–2, 1972—J. Edgar Hoover dies in his sleep after forty-eight years as director of the FBI. It is the thirty-sixth anniversary of Hoover's personal capture of Alvin Karpis in New Orleans.

January 13, 1973—Julius "Babe" Jones dies in Chicago.

February 2, 1973—Former Dillinger Gang member Jack Perkins, later with the mob, dies in Chicago.

August 3, 1973—Retired FBI agent Charles B. Winstead, officially credited with killing John Dillinger in 1934, dies at the age of eighty-two in Albuquerque, New Mexico.

October 5, 1973—John Paul Chase dies of cancer at Palo Alto, California.

June 4, 1974—Irene Dorsey Moore, former "moll" of Fred Goetz, dies in Wilmington, Illinois.

August 20, 1974—Former Barrow Gang member W. D. Jones is shot to death in a brawl in Houston.

October 22, 1974—On the fortieth anniversary of "Pretty Boy" Floyd's death, Chester Smith, former East Liverpool, Ohio, police officer and one of the last surviving members of the posse that killed Floyd, claims the wounded outlaw, was in, fact executed by an FBI agent on orders from Melvin Purvis. Smith will repeat the allegation in 1979, with slight variations. The story is denied by the only other survivor of the party, former FBI agent W. E. "Bud" Hopton.

November 20, 1974—Harry Campbell, former Barker-Karpis Gang member, dies in Amarillo, Texas.

November 22, 1974—Ralph "Bottles" Capone, brother of Al, dies in Hurley, Wisconsin.

November 4, 1975—Clarence Hurt, one of the two FBI agents officially credited with shooting Dillinger, dies of cancer in McAlester, Oklahoma.

January 20, 1976—Paul "Lefty" Parker, former Dillinger associate, is killed in a truck accident.

July 11, 1976—Hilton Crouch, former Dillinger Gang member, dies of a brain tumor in Indianapolis. He will be buried at Crown Hill Cemetery, not far from Dillinger's grave.

October 27, 1977—Former Dallas County Deputy Ted Hinton dies, soon after completing his book, *Ambush—The Real Story of Bonnie and Clyde*. Hinton was the last surviving member of the posse that killed Bonnie and Clyde.

December 6, 1977—William Shaw, early crime partner of John Dillinger, dies in Chicago after falling asleep with a lit cigarette.

June 16, 1978—Mamie Floyd, mother of "Pretty Boy" Floyd, dies in Sallisaw, Oklahoma, at the age of ninety-seven.

July 25, 1978—Former Barker-Karpis gangster Francis Keating dies at a St. Louis Park, Minnesota, nursing home.

March 1, 1979—Harvey Bailey dies at the age of ninety-one in Joplin, Missouri.

April 11, 1979—Former Dillinger Gang member Walter Detrich dies in St. Louis.

July 20, 1979—Former Barker-Karpis Gang member Volney Davis dies in Corte Madera, California.

August 26, 1979—Alvin Karpis dies in Torremolinos, Spain, of an overdose of the sleeping pills to which he had become addicted.

October 31, 1979—Eddie Bentz dies in Tacoma, Washington.

May 21, 1980—Ora Shannon dies in Oklahoma.

October 16, 1980—1920s bank robber Ray Terrill dies in Oatman, Arizona.

November 2, 1980—Willie Sutton dies at Spring Hill, Florida.

April 5, 1982—Basil "The Owl" Banghart dies at his home in Los Angeles.

June 25, 1982—Bertha Battles, former wife of Matt Kimes, is fatally injured in a traffic accident in Tahlequah, Oklahoma.

November 11, 1982—Fred Hunter, former accomplice of Alvin Karpis, dies in Hot Springs, Arkansas.

September 17, 1983—The former Bessie Green, wife of Dillinger gangster Eddie Green, dies in Minnesota.

July 24, 1984—Depression-era bank robber Floyd Hamilton dies in Grand Prairie, Texas.

October 23, 1984—Former East Liverpool, Ohio, policeman Chester Smith, involved in the killing of "Pretty Boy" Floyd, dies one day after the fiftieth anniversary of Floyd's death.

April 1985—Dolores Delaney dies in Arizona.

May 28, 1985—Kathryn Kelly dies in Oklahoma.

April 16, 1986—Mae Capone, widow of Al, dies in a Florida nursing home.

November 27, 1986—Helen "Babe" Delaney, former wife of "Pat" Reilly, dies in Seattle.

March 30, 1987—Audrey Hancock, John Dillinger's older sister, dies at age ninety-eight.

July 3, 1987—Helen Gillis, widow of Lester "Baby Face Nelson" Gillis, dies of a cerebral hemorrhage in St. Charles, Illinois.

December 24, 1988—Blanche Caldwell Barrow Frasure dies of cancer in Dallas.

February 20, 1989—Former FBI agent Virgil Peterson dies in Riverside, Illinois. Peterson was Melvin Purvis's assistant in the Thirties and later served as longtime head of the Chicago Crime Commission.

January 1, 1991—Former FBI agent G. C. Campbell, who took part in the ambush of Dillinger, dies of a heart attack at Palo Alto, California.

May 10, 1991—Mary Longnaker dies in Dayton.

May 27, 1992—Tony Accardo dies of congestive heart failure at St. Mary of Nazareth Hospital in Chicago.

March 17, 1993—Ralph Fults, last known survivor of the Barrow Gang, dies in Dallas, Texas.

November 30, 1993—Beryl Hovious, who had divorced John Dillinger during his fifth year in prison, dies in Mooresville, Indiana.

December 10, 1993—Mildred Kuhlmann Auerback, "Doc" Barker's last girlfriend, dies in Sandusky, Ohio.

February 15, 1994—Darlene Gillis, daughter of Lester "Baby Face Nelson" Gillis, dies in Wisconsin.

June 12, 1994—Lillian Holley, sheriff at the time of Dillinger's "wooden gun" jailbreak from the Lake County Jail, dies at her Crown Point, Indiana, home at the age of 103.

March 6, 1996—Retired FBI agent Tom McDade dies. A noted crime bibliographer who befriended Alvin Karpis in his later years, McDade had participated in the FBI's final shootouts with "Baby Face" Nelson and the Barkers.

April 14, 1997—Thomas J. Connor, last surviving member of the FBI group who ambushed Dillinger at the Biograph, dies at home in Southbury, Connecticut.

February 14, 1999—Ronald Gillis, son of Lester "Baby Face Nelson" Gillis, dies near Chicago.

March 23, 1999—Charles (Jack) Dempsey Floyd, son of "Pretty Boy" Floyd, dies in Vacaville, California.

April 30, 2001—Flossie Kimes, former wife of George Kimes, dies in Redmond, Oregon.

October 11, 2001—Raymond Alvin Karpis, son of Alvin Karpis, dies in Chicago.

July 9, 2004—Albert "Sonny" Capone, son of Al Capone, dies in California.

September 18, 2006—Frank Hamer Jr., whose father led the ambush of Bonnie and Clyde, dies in Texas.

September 24, 2006—Former bank robber Willie Radkay dies in Fort Scott, Kansas.

The Rise and Fall of the Last Great Outlaw Gang

Corrupt Cops Meet the New FBI

After 1933, Capone was in prison, and Repeal was ending the Prohibition Era of big-city bootleggers. As Roosevelt's New Deal administration declared a federal "War on Crime" spearheaded by a newly empowered FBI, a seemingly new peril confronted the American public in the form of kidnappers and bandit gangs "terrorizing the Midwest." In fact, the most successful armed robbers had been operating for years with virtual immunity from law enforcement because of their anonymity, mobility, and the uncoordinated efforts of state and local authorities. Newspapers frequently headlined the raids of "daring daylight bank robbers," but in the absence of an effective central criminal records agency the bandits usually went unrecognized, and a fast escape to another state frustrated pursuit. Harvey Bailey, the Newton Brothers, "Baron" Lamm, Eddie Bentz, Jake Fleagle, and Homer Wilson knocked over countless banks, payrolls, and even trains in the 1920s without local police knowing who

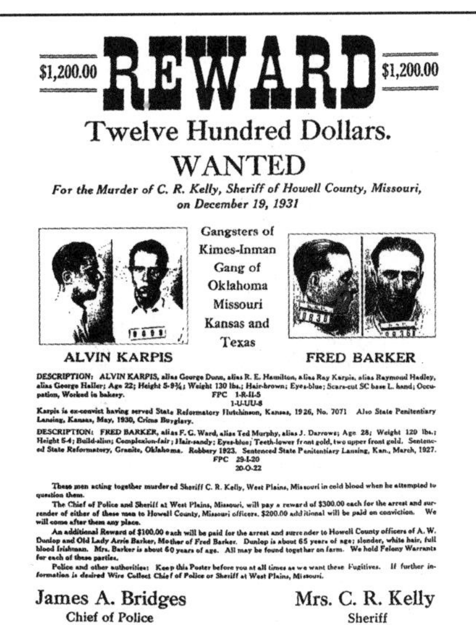

$1,200.00 REWARD $1,200.00

Twelve Hundred Dollars.

WANTED

For the Murder of C. R. Kelly, Sheriff of Howell County, Missouri, on December 19, 1931

Gangsters of Kimes-Inman Gang of Oklahoma Missouri Kansas and Texas

ALVIN KARPIS — FRED BARKER

DESCRIPTION: ALVIN KARPIS, alias George Dunn, alias R. E. Hamilton, alias Ray Karpis, alias Raymond Hadley, alias George Haller; Age 22; Height 5-9¾; Weight 130 lbs.; Hair-brown; Eyes-blue; Scars-cut SC base L. hand; Occupation, Worked in bakery. FPC 1-R-II-5 1-U-UU-8

Karpis is ex-convict having served State Reformatory Hutchinson, Kansas, 1926, No. 7071 Also State Penitentiary Lansing, Kansas, May, 1930, Crime Burglary.

DESCRIPTION: FRED BARKER, alias F. G. Ward, alias Ted Murphy, alias J. Darrows; Age 28; Weight 120 lbs.; Height 5-4; Build-slim; Complexion-fair; Hair-sandy; Eyes-blue; Teeth-lower front gold, two upper front gold. Sentenced State Reformatory, Granite, Oklahoma. Robbery 1923. Sentenced State Penitentiary Lansing, Kan., March, 1927. FPC 29-I-20 20-O-22

These men acting together murdered Sheriff C. R. Kelly, West Plains, Missouri in cold blood when he attempted to question them.

The Chief of Police and Sheriff at West Plains, Missouri, will pay a reward of $300.00 each for the arrest and surrender of either of these men to Howell County, Missouri officers. $200.00 additional will be paid on conviction. We will come after them any place.

An additional Reward of $100.00 each will be paid for the arrest and surrender to Howell County officers of A. W. Dunlop and Old Lady Arrie Barker, Mother of Fred Barker. Dunlop is about 65 years of age; slender, white hair, full blood Irishman. Mrs. Barker is about 60 years of age. All may be found together on farm. We hold Felony Warrants for each of these parties.

Police and other authorities: Keep this Poster before you at all times as we want these Fugitives. If further information is desired Wire Collect Chief of Police or Sheriff at West Plains, Missouri.

James A. Bridges, Chief of Police — Mrs. C. R. Kelly, Sheriff

West Plains, Missouri

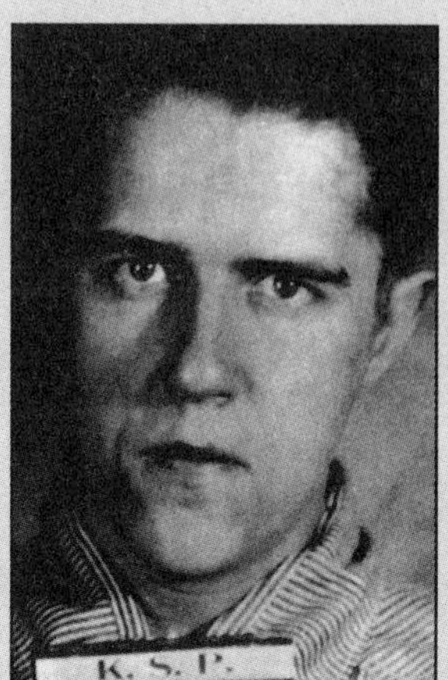

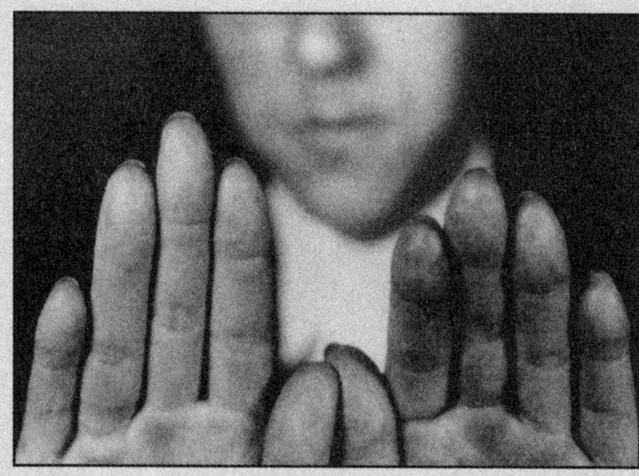

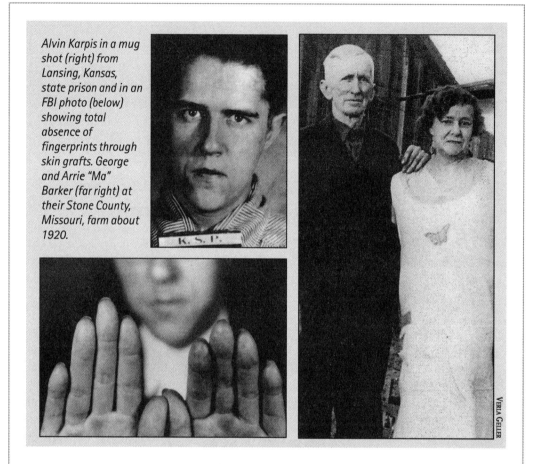

Alvin Karpis in a mug shot (right) from Lansing, Kansas, state prison and in an FBI photo (below) showing total absence of fingerprints through skin grafts. George and Arrie "Ma" Barker (far right) at their Stone County, Missouri, farm about 1920.

they were; and the "snatch racket" that involved criminals kidnapping one another did not greatly concern the public, the police, or the press. Not until the kidnap-murder of the Lindbergh baby in 1932 was that crime made a federal offense, and then it was over the objections of President Herbert Hoover's attorney general.

By that year, only "Pretty Boy" Floyd and Bonnie and Clyde had earned any national publicity, usually because they were locally known or left calling cards in one form or another. But while all had one or more partners in crime, they didn't lead gangs in the usual sense of the word. In 1933, "Machine Gun" Kelly became a household name not because he led a gang (despite newspaper accounts), but because he was involved in the most sensational "civilian" kidnapping since the Lindbergh case and eluded authorities long enough to earn personal notoriety.

The famous outlaw gangs of the Depression were largely the invention of the FBI, with two conspicuous exceptions. The Dillinger Gang, consisting initially of convicts he helped break out of Indiana's state prison (Dillinger actually deferring to Harry

Pierpont as the gang's leader), worked closely as a group, but only from September 1933 until the following January, when most were arrested in Tucson because a fire in their hotel led to their recognition. After Dillinger himself escaped from the Crown Point, Indiana, jail two months later, using bribes and a wooden pistol, he was forced to team with "Baby Face" Nelson, who had put together his own band of robbers and had to grudgingly accept identification of his group as the "Dillinger Gang" by the national press (researchers now refer to Nelson's bandits as the "second Dillinger Gang"). Dillinger's own criminal career lasted only another four months before he was set up by supposed friends and killed by federal agents outside Chicago's Biograph Theatre.

The only group that qualified as a bona fide gang in the traditional sense was the one headed by Alvin Karpis and the Barker brothers, mainly Arthur and Fred, and supposedly captained by the notorious "Ma" Barker. Despite two more civilian kidnappings, many burglaries, several murders, and dozens of bank, train, and payroll holdups since the 1920s, the FBI was not even clear on their existence until the bureau captured a talkative associate of the Dillinger Gang in the spring of 1934. Their depredations spanned the entire "public enemy" era; and while the Barkers and Alvin Karpis were always the principals, they teamed with many criminals from other gangs and also worked with organized crime groups in several cities, especially Chicago.

The headline-making gangs of "Pretty Boy" Floyd, "Machine Gun" Kelly, and Bonnie and Clyde were far more loosely structured than suited headline writers, the general public, or the FBI. But the nucleus of the Barker-Karpis Gang always was the Barker family, who came from a part of the Ozark backwoods that was isolated from the mainstream of American culture and a longtime breeding ground of desperados. "Ma" Barker's role in the gang is a matter of dispute. Legend based largely on FBI publicity has it that she deliberately groomed her sons as lawbreakers and managed their criminal careers. There's no doubt she knew of her sons' crimes, which necessitated constant moving to elude the police. But she never participated in their robberies or kidnappings, and no member of the gang ever named her as their leader.

Alvin Karpis would characterize "Ma" as an ignorant old hillbilly who traveled with her sons because they were "family," and she came in handy as camouflage. A later member of the gang, Harvey Bailey, told author L. L. Edge in *Run the Cat Roads*: "The old woman couldn't plan breakfast. When we'd sit down to plan a bank job, she'd go in the other room and listen to *Amos 'n' Andy* or hillbilly music on the radio." Bailey found laughable the idea that the Barkers, Alvin Karpis, Frank Nash, and other professionals would depend on "Ma" to plan their crimes. The image of "Ma" Barker as a cunning, ruthless gang leader appears to be as exaggerated as the largely mythical exploits of Belle Starr, to whom she has often been compared.

J. Edgar Hoover's characterization of her as "a monument to the evils of parental indulgence" may be a little more accurate than the "Bloody Mama" figure familiar to moviegoers, comic book fans, and devotees of crime literature, factual and otherwise. But the latter image, too, was created by Hoover. "Ma" Barker's troubles seem rooted in a simple-minded devotion to her sons, whom she chose to believe were driven to crime by hard times and constant police persecution. In this respect, she was similar to the mothers of the Jameses, the Youngers, the Daltons, the Barrows, and countless other bandit teams of the rural Southwest. She probably qualified as a fairly dense and nonjudgmental matriarch of a clannish tribe from the Ozarks whose careers just happened to be in crime.

According to an FBI report dated November 18, 1936, "Ma Barker in the formative period of her sons' lives was probably just an average mother of a family which had no aspirations or evidenced no desire to maintain any high plane socially. They were poor and existed through no prolific support from "Ma's" husband, George Barker, who was more or less a shiftless individual. . . . The early religious training of the Barkers . . . was influenced by evangelistic and sporadic revivals. The parents of the Barkers and the other boys with whom they were associated did not reflect any special interest in educational training and as a result their sons were more or less illiterate. . . ."

Years later, J. Edgar Hoover would write that "over the backyard fence 'Ma' boasted to neighbors: 'I got great days ahead of me, when my children grow up. Silk dresses. Fur coats and diamond rings.'" This hardly sounds like someone without aspirations to wealth, but by then the mythmaking was in full swing, and Hoover was its leading propagator.

Had she not died with her son Fred in battle with the FBI, "Ma" Barker might have gotten off with a short jail sentence for harboring her murderous offspring, as did the mothers of Bonnie and Clyde. But once the bureau ended its siege of their hideout in January 1935 and discovered it had killed an old lady who would turn out to be "Ma," she had to be instantly villainized. And if Americans had found something almost romantic in a boy-and-girl bandit team despite their murderous ways, the notion of mother-and-son bandits also appealed to the country's streak of rebellion against duly constituted authority, especially when most police of the day were regarded as only a cut above the crooks they were supposed to catch.

"Ma" was born Arizona Donnie Clark near Ash Grove, Boone Township, northwest of Springfield, Missouri, on October 8, 1873. When she married George Elias Barker, some fourteen years older, at Aurora, Missouri, on September 14, 1892, she listed her name on the marriage license as "Arrie Clark" but at some later point adopted the name Kate. They made their home at different times in Aurora and on backwoods Ozark farms. Her first pregnancy resulted in a miscarriage, according to relatives. Between 1893 and 1903 they had four sons, Herman, Lloyd, Arthur (called "Doc" or "Dock," he used both spellings), and Fred, before moving to Webb City, near Joplin, possibly after 1910. There George reportedly found work in the area's lead and zinc mines and left the child-rearing to "Ma."

In 1935, crime reporter Harrison Moreland interviewed Webb City residents who remembered the Barkers' early years. One of Herman's favorite antics, said Moreland, was riding a pinto pony into the town's saloons in imitation of his hero, Jesse James, who was supposed to have ridden into saloons, shooting. The Barker boys soon went beyond mere rowdiness, however, acquiring reputations as petty thieves. Legend has it that neighbors who complained to George Barker about his sons' activities were shrugged off with: "You'll have to talk to Mother. She handles the boys." "Ma" Barker would then rage at the accusers, call them liars, and send them packing. A widespread impression was that she had an almost paranoid belief that the community had singled out her sons as scapegoats.

On March 5, 1915, Herman Barker was arrested by Joplin police for highway robbery. Popular accounts state that "Ma" got him released and declared that she could no longer abide living in such an intolerant town, and the whole family moved to Tulsa, Oklahoma. In reality, Herman remained in Missouri and was convicted of burglary the following year but escaped from the Springfield jail. He moved on to Billings, Montana, where he adopted the alias of Bert Lavender, was again convicted of burglary, and drew a sentence of six to twelve years in the state prison at Deer Lodge.

At some point between 1915 and 1920, the rest of the family moved to Tulsa, probably because Ma's mother and stepfather (a Tulsa County deputy) were living there. Contrary to most popular accounts the family was not living together in a two-room shack at this time but lived at different residences at different times, sometimes with "Ma's" mother and stepfather. Before 1918 none of the boys except Herman seem to have developed serious criminal records. Strangely, census records show that George and "Ma" were residing in 1920, without the boys, in Stone County,

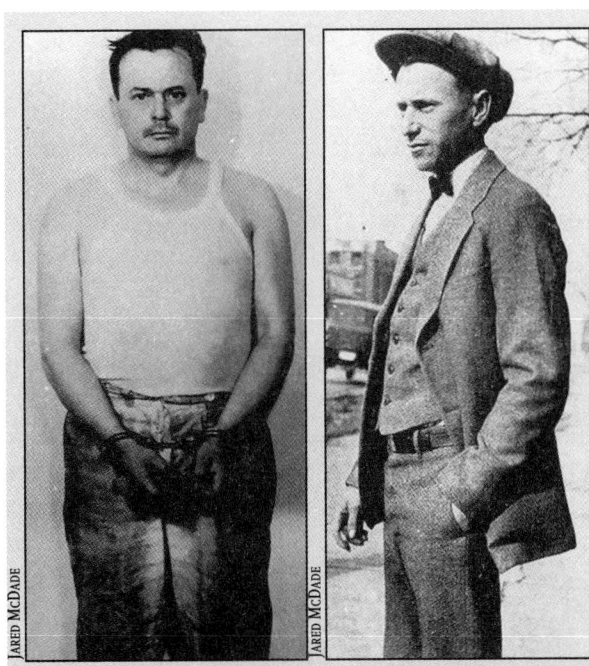

Barker brothers Arthur "Doc" (left) and Fred, pictured in a snapshot found in the Ocklawaha, Florida, house where he and "Ma" Barker were killed.

Missouri. Either the move to Tulsa occurred later than commonly supposed, or George and Kate returned to Missouri for a time, leaving their sons in Oklahoma.

Herman Barker languished in the Montana prison until 1920, then moved on to Minnesota where he was caught in another burglary. Under the alias of Clarence Sharp he received an indeterminate term for grand larceny in the state prison at Stillwater.

The other boys soon ingratiated themselves with other young hellions who hung around Old Lincoln Forsythe School and the Central Park district. The result was an aggregation of delinquents called the "East Side Gang" or "Central Park Gang," which in time numbered more than twenty young thieves and hoodlums. These included Volney "Curley" Davis and Harry Campbell (later important members of the Barker-Karpis Gang), and William "Boxcar" Green. Green would play a leading role in a 1931 mass breakout from Leavenworth and then commit suicide to avoid recapture.

John Karpowicz, father of Alvin Karpis, glares at reporters outside his house at 2420 North Francisco in Chicago.

"Doc" Barker was arrested on the Fourth of July, 1918, for stealing a government-owned car in Tulsa. (His brother Lloyd showed a more conventional streak of patriotism by enlisting in the Army, where he served as a cook and stayed out of civilian mischief until mustered out in February 1919). "Doc" escaped, was recaptured in Joplin in 1920 and returned to Tulsa, then escaped again. On January 15, 1921, as Claud [sic] Dale, "Doc" was arrested for attempted bank burglary in Coweta, Oklahoma, and jailed at Muskogee. Ray Terrill was arrested at the same time, under the alias of G. R. Patton. Both were transferred to McAlester for safekeeping. "Doc" was discharged by court order on June 11, 1921. Terrill later was sentenced to three years for second-degree burglary and released on March 1, 1923. He was subsequently arrested for other crimes but either "beat the rap" or escaped.

On August 26, 1921, night watchman Thomas J. Sherrill was killed by burglars at the construction site of Tulsa's St. John's Hospital. "Doc" was arrested for this murder, tried, and convicted. On February 10, 1922, he was sentenced to life at McAlester. Nearly a year later, Volney Davis, a member of the Barkers' "Central Park Gang," also was sent to prison for life for the Sherrill slaying. Davis escaped from McAlester in January 1925 but was recaptured thirteen days later in Kansas City.

Lloyd "Red" Barker was reportedly picked up by Tulsa police for vagrancy in

1921. On June 17, with Will Green and another man, he robbed a mail truck at Baxter Springs, Kansas, for which he was tried and convicted. On January 16, 1922, as inmate 17243, Lloyd was received at Leavenworth facing a twenty-five-year sentence. This marked the end of Lloyd Barker's criminal career. Paroled in 1938, he went straight, again enlisting in the Army in World War II and working as a cook at a P.O.W. camp at Fort Custer, Michigan. After the war, he received an honorable discharge, married, and became an assistant manager of a bar and grill in Denver. On March 18, 1949, his wife killed him with a shotgun at their home in Westminster, Colorado. She subsequently was placed in an insane asylum.

Herman Barker was released from prison in 1925 and was soon operating with a new gang, burglarizing banks and stores throughout the Southwest. This group, known sometimes as the Terrill-Barker-Inman Gang, at one time or another included Ray Terrill, Elmer Inman, Alvin Sherwood, Joe Howard, Bill Munger, Ralph Scott, Danny Daniels, Charles Stalcup (alias Pale Anderson) and others. Their favorite technique, popularly credited to Terrill, was to back a stolen truck up to a bank, winch out its portable safe, and drive away to crack it at their leisure. For a time, the gang used the Radium Springs Health Resort near Salina, Oklahoma, as a hideout.

Radium Springs was operated by Herman Barker and his (probably common-law) wife, Carol, under the names of Mr. and Mrs. J. H. Hamilton, but the actual owner was Q. P. McGhee, a corrupt former judge from Miami, Oklahoma, who collaborated with and served as the gang's mouthpiece. McGhee always was on hand to bail out captured gang members or fraudulently gain their release with bogus warrants claiming they were wanted elsewhere. The resort was fortified and equipped with a powerful electric light that served as a warning beacon if lawmen came to visit. Safes stolen by the gang were emptied and dumped off a nearby bridge into the Grand River.

From brotherly love or a need for career counseling, or both, Fred Barker soon joined his older brother at the resort. Fred had been arrested for "investigation" at Miami, Oklahoma, September 5, 1922. A month later he was picked up for vagrancy in Tulsa and jailed for thirty days. In June 1923, he was convicted of armed robbery and sentenced to five years in the state reformatory at Granite, Oklahoma. Fred made parole only to be arrested soon afterward for robbing a bank. He was later arrested as a fugitive at Little Rock, Arkansas; for burglary in Ponca City, Oklahoma; and was wounded in a gun battle with Kansas City police. These scrapes with the law yielded no jail time, probably thanks to McGhee, who sometimes was accompanied by a crooked Miami County deputy.

Under the alias of Ted Murphy, Fred was arrested again at Winfield, Kansas, November 8, 1926, for burglary and grand larceny. For this he was convicted and sentenced to five to ten years in the state prison at Lansing, Kansas. Investigators discovered that Herman Barker, who avoided arrest on that occasion, likely had participated in the Winfield burglary. The car Fred was driving at the time of his arrest had been bought by Herman from a Nash agency in Tulsa.

Winfield Police Chief Fred C. Hoover told the FBI (then known as the Justice Department's Bureau of Investigation) that the sheriff of Mayes County, Oklahoma, site of the Radium Springs Health Resort, was a friend of the Barkers. He also believed that Herman Barker and Elmer Inman often frequented Wetump's roadhouse near Ponca City, operated by Fred "Wetump" Tindle. Barker and Inman were wanted for interstate car theft, which made them federal fugitives under a law passed in 1919 (the Dyer Act, a slight stretch of the Constitution's interstate commerce clause) to facilitate the return of cars stolen in one state and recovered in another.

Barker and Inman had driven a Paige coupe, stolen from Henry Ward of Fairfax, Oklahoma, to Fort Scott, Kansas, on or about June 6, 1926. They were arrested the next day and extradited to Oklahoma, where both also were wanted for robbery. McGhee saw that they didn't remain in custody long. Herman Barker, charged with robbing the county attorney at Miami, Oklahoma, of approximately $600 in money and valuables, was released on bond on June 22. Elmer Inman, former son-in-law of Kansas state prison warden J. K. Coddings, was charged with bank and post office robbery at Ketchum, Oklahoma, but also made bond. Inman was arrested again at Ardmore, Oklahoma, with Ray Terrill, for burglary. Together they overpowered a county jailer at Ardmore on September 27, 1926, and escaped.

About this time, Matt and George Kimes began their own crime spree, terrorizing Oklahoma with daring daylight bank holdups and wild shootouts and jailbreaks. George was captured early and sent to prison, but Matt carried on. Somehow the Kimes and Terrill gangs became linked in the public's mind, probably through a 1927 reward poster offered by the Oklahoma Bankers Association for the capture of Matt Kimes and Ray Terrill. There is no evidence that the two groups were ever connected, but the "Kimes-Terrill Gang" often found its way into print. Herman Barker, Ray Terrill, and Elmer Inman were commonly but wrongly implicated in crimes of the Kimes gang.

Inman was recaptured on December 27, 1926, while burglarizing a store in Oklahoma City. For this he was convicted and sentenced to seven years but escaped on March 17, 1927, en route to McAlester, by leaping from a train. On January 10, 1927, Matt Kimes and Ray Terrill were named as members of a gang who had robbed the State Bank at Sapulpa, Oklahoma, of $42,950. They were later blamed for a bank robbery in Pampa, Texas, but it's likely that neither was involved.

On January 17, about 5 a.m., the gang attempted to burglarize the First National Bank at Jasper, Missouri, near Joplin. Arriving in two cars and a truck, they entered the bank by cutting the bars from a rear window, stole the bank's safe, and wheeled it out the back door. A baker spotted them and phoned the night telephone operator, who alerted the town marshal. Police in Joplin and Carthage quickly deputized a posse of citizens to ambush the gang. The burglars had to abandon the safe and their truck, but still managed to escape in two cars.

One car sped west into Kansas. Herman Barker and Ray Terrill were in the other car. They returned to their hideout, a house at 602 East Main in Carterville, Missouri, which Joplin and Webb City police were watching on a tip that it was "the headquarters of an organized band of outlaws." In a gun battle, Barker was wounded, and he and Terrill were taken into custody.

Herman Barker was extradited to Fayetteville, Arkansas, on charges of robbing a Westfork bank. On January 19, Ray Terrill, a McAlester escapee who still owed Oklahoma twenty years on his earlier bank robbery conviction, was returned to that state but again escaped, leaping from a moving car as it neared the prison. On March 30, Herman also escaped, sawing the bars of his cell and taking along a suspected forger named Claude Cooper.

More bank jobs followed. On May 12, bandits stole a safe containing $207,000 in securities and cash from the State Bank at McCune, Kansas. Ray Terrill was named as a suspect. On May 18, two carloads of gunmen, led by Matt Kimes, robbed two banks at Beggs, Oklahoma, and escaped after a another gun battle in which they killed Marshal W. J. McAnally. Soon after these robberies, several members of the Kimes gang were arrested in Texas and Oklahoma. Matt Kimes was captured at the Grand Canyon in Arizona on June 24, but turned out to have no connection with the Barkers beyond operating in the same general territory.

On August 1, 1927, a man appeared at the American National Bank in Cheyenne, Wyoming, using the name R. D. Snodgrass, and cashed three American Express Travelers Cheques. "Snodgrass" then left the bank and entered a blue Chrysler coach with Idaho license plates. A woman with dark hair and a dark complexion also was in the car. The teller quickly identified the checks as having been stolen in a Buffalo, Kansas, bank robbery in December 1926. He chased after "Snodgrass," who simply ignored him and drove away. "Snodgrass" was actually Herman Barker, and the woman was his supposed wife, Carol Antone, known as Carol Hamilton, who was part Indian.

Herman was stopped at Pine Bluffs, about forty miles east of Cheyenne, by Deputy Sheriff Arthur E. Osborn. As the deputy approached the car, his own gun still holstered, Barker drew a .32 automatic and shot him twice, then sped off. A half hour later Osborn was found unconscious and dying near the highway by a Nebraska deputy who just happened along. At first, Osborn's killer was mistakenly identified as Elmer Inman.

On August 29, after robbing an icehouse in Newton, Kansas, Herman Barker and two other men shot it out with police in Wichita. In that gunfight, Herman killed another officer, Patrolman Joseph E. Marshall, but was so badly wounded in the exchange that he shot himself rather than be taken alive. One of his companions, Charles Stalcup, alias Pale Anderson, was taken into custody. The other man, first thought to be Inman, escaped. He actually was another Oklahoma outlaw named Porter Meeks, killed the next day by Wichita policeman Merle Colver, who would himself be slain in 1931 by Wilbur Underhill, soon to be dubbed the "Tri-State Terror."

Ray Terrill and Elmer Inman were captured at Hot Springs, Arkansas, on November 26, 1927. They soon joined the Kimes brothers at the Oklahoma state prison, although Inman would be released in time to later join Wilbur Underhill's gang. Carol Hamilton subsequently pleaded guilty as an accessory to the Osborn murder and admitted it was Herman, not Elmer Inman, who had killed Osborn. She was sentenced to two to four years but, since Wyoming had no separate facility for female prisoners, served her time in the Colorado state prison at Canon City. She was received there on September 29, 1927, and was paroled on October 2, 1929. Soon afterward, she was working as a prostitute out of the Carlton Hotel in Sapulpa, Oklahoma, and briefly became the girlfriend of Alvin Karpis. Karpis would later marry her niece, Dorothy Slayman.

George and Kate Barker buried their oldest son at the Williams Timberhill Cemetery near Welch, Oklahoma, where they and Fred would eventually join him. The family plot was bought by McGhee, who would soon be convicted of aiding and abetting Herman Barker and Elmer Inman. They separated about 1928, apparently because "Ma" and a friend were seeing other men in Tulsa. George moved back to Webb City, Missouri, and spent his remaining years operating a filling station. "Ma" took up with an alcoholic billboard painter named Arthur W. Dunlop who moved in with her at 401 North Cincinnati Avenue in Tulsa. They later moved to another house on Archer Avenue.

Dunlop spent more time drinking than painting; and with Herman dead and the other boys in prison, the family income fell dramatically. "Ma" became dependent on her "daughter-in-law," Carol Hamilton, for groceries. She despised Carol, whom she considered a "hussy," as she did all her sons' women. Throughout her life, "Ma" Barker would vainly attempt to discourage or sabotage her sons' relationships with other women. J. Edgar Hoover would call her a "jealous old battle-ax." According to Alvin Karpis, "Ma didn't like female competition. She wanted to be the only woman who counted with her boys."

Alvin Karpis, born in Montreal in 1908, met Fred Barker at the Kansas state prison in 1930. Received at the State Industrial Reformatory at Hutchinson, Kansas, on February 25, 1926, under a five-to-ten-year sentence for burglary, Karpis became a prison protege of Lawrence DeVol, a safecracker and cop killer. The two escaped from Hutchinson on March 9, 1929, and engaged in a burglary spree. Recaptured in Kansas City on March 23, 1930, Karpis was returned to the reformatory but soon transferred to the penitentiary when officials there found knives in his possession. Still, he earned time off his sentence by working in the coal mine and hiring lifers to mine coal for him—another trick he had learned from DeVol. Karpis and Fred Barker became close friends and agreed to form a criminal partnership.

When Fred was paroled on March 20, 1931, and Karpis the following May 10, they contacted Carol Hamilton and "Ma" Barker in Tulsa. "Ma" sent a telegram to Fred, then living at 701 Byers in Joplin with another ex-convict named Jimmie Creighton, alias Jones, wanted in Hastings, Nebraska, for kidnapping, robbery, and attempted murder. Creighton also was a suspect, with Lawrence DeVol, in the April 1930 murders of two businessman brothers at the Hotel Severs in Muskogee, Oklahoma. Karpis soon joined Fred in Joplin, and they committed a series of small burglaries.

On the night of May 16, 1931, Fred's former roommate, Creighton, shot and killed a local man, Coyne Hatten, outside the Morgan drugstore in Webb City, apparently over Hatten's failure to apologize profusely for bumping into him on the street. Karpis and Barker fled back to Tulsa in Creighton's car, and Creighton was later convicted of murder and sentenced to life imprisonment. Interestingly, one of Creighton's companions at the time of the slaying was Mickey Carey, through whom Karpis would later meet Clyde Barrow and Bonnie Parker at the home of Herb Farmer. Farmer, also from Webb City, was an old friend of the Barkers and now owned a chicken farm south of Joplin. He was a confidence man and pickpocket with a long record of arrests who reputedly harbored many southwestern outlaws, including "Pretty Boy" Floyd.

ELLEN POULSEN

Other members of the Barker–Karpis Gang as collected by the FBI.

Herb Farmer was an especially close friend of Fred. An FBI report would later note that "it is safe to assume that Fred Barker received considerable education in the school of crime from Farmer." Farmer would later serve a term at Alcatraz as one of the Kansas City Massacre conspirators.

On June 10, 1931, Tulsa police arrested Fred Barker, Alvin Karpis, Sam Coker, and Joe Howard. Karpis was transferred to Henryetta, Oklahoma, to face charges of burglarizing a jewelry store. He returned the stolen jewelry, pleaded guilty to burglary on September 11, 1931, and received a sentence of four years, but he was paroled because he made restitution and already had served three months in the county jail. Barker was transferred to Claremore, Oklahoma, on another burglary charge but escaped on

August 16 with other prisoners. Coker was returned to the McAlester prison to complete a thirty-year sentence for bank robbery. Howard was released on bond and disappeared.

Karpis joined Fred and "Ma" Barker and Arthur Dunlop on a rented farm near Thayer, Missouri, close to the Arkansas line. On June 20, 1931, Phoenix Donald, alias Bill "Lapland Willie" Weaver, had been paroled from McAlester after serving six years of a life sentence for murder and bank robbery, and was residing on his sister's farm only two miles away across the state line. On October 7, 1931, Karpis, Fred Barker, Weaver, and one Jimmie Wilson robbed the Peoples Bank at Mountain View, Missouri, of $14,000 in cash and securities. According to the later recollections of Alvin Karpis, Fred Barker also killed two policemen that fall, one in Monett, Missouri, and another in Pocahontas, Arkansas, but this is open to doubt because other men were convicted.

On the night of December 18, McCallon's Clothing Store in West Plains, Missouri, was burglarized. Two strangers in town, driving a 1931 DeSoto, had aroused enough suspicion that some residents noted their license plate numbers. The following day, three men drove a 1931 DeSoto into the Davidson Motor Co. garage in West Plains to get two flat tires repaired. A repairman noticed the tires matched tread marks left by the burglars' car and told his boss. The suspicious garage owner stepped out of the building and called Sheriff C. Roy Kelly and Clarence McCallon, owner of the clothing store. When they arrived, two of the DeSoto's occupants opened fire, killing the sheriff, then fled. The murderers subsequently were identified as Alvin Karpis and Fred Barker. Karpis probably fired the fatal shots with a .45 automatic, putting four bullets into Kelly's chest. Barker, armed with a .38 revolver, shot the sheriff in the right arm. (In his autobiography Karpis claimed Barker's accomplice at West Plains was Bill Weaver, by then long dead, but also wrongly stated that there were no witnesses.)

The third man in the garage was arrested and released. He was J. Richard Gross, a twenty-year-old college student picked up by Karpis and Barker while hitchhiking from Jonesboro, Arkansas, to Springfield.

Area law officers raided the farm near Thayer, only to find it deserted. The house stood on a hill, with a good view in every direction. It was surrounded by barbed wire, the front gate hooked to an electric alarm bell. In the house, officers found photos of the Barkers, Karpis, and Dunlop, as well as letters, including one to "Ma" from Lloyd Barker in Leavenworth thanking her for Christmas gifts, and an interior drawing of the First National Bank of West Plains, Missouri. The farm rented by Bill Weaver also was vacant.

West Plains Police Chief James A. Bridges and Howell County Sheriff Lula Kelly, succeeding her murdered husband, offered a $1,200 reward: $500 each for the arrest and conviction of Alvin Karpis and Fred Barker and $100 each for the arrest of "A. W. Dunlop and Old Lady Arrie Barker, Mother of Fred Barker." This was the first official notice of "Ma" Barker, who would make no further news until she was killed by federal agents three years later. Fred Barker and Karpis were listed on "wanted" posters as "Gangsters of the Kimes-Inman Gang of Oklahoma, Missouri, Kansas, and Texas."

Just after Kelly's murder, a redheaded woman with a "hardboiled appearance" arrived in West Plains on a bus from Chicago, looking for a Raymond Hamilton. She gave her name as Lee Hamilton but turned out to be Dorothy Slayman Karpis (Alvin had been known in the area as R. E. or Ray Hamilton, which may have added to later official confusion of Karpis with Raymond Hamilton, connected with the Barrows). Dorothy was questioned, jailed for a while, and released. She did not see her husband again until 1935, when he visited her in Tulsa, gave her some money, and told her to get a divorce. By this time Dorothy had followed in Aunt Carol's footsteps and become a prostitute.

The Barkers, Karpis, Weaver, and Dunlop had fled to the home of their old friend Herb Farmer, near Joplin. Farmer advised them to go to St. Paul and contact Harry Sawyer. Coincidentally, Karpis's trigger-happy friend, Lawrence DeVol, arrived in St. Paul about the same time. Considered by Karpis a mentor and teacher, DeVol had murdered a policeman in Kirksville, Missouri, in November 1930 and was suspected of several other killings in Muskogee, Oklahoma; Omaha, Nebraska; and Washington, Iowa.

For years, St. Paul had been a "safe town" for criminals. Out-of-town fugitives could harbor there with no interference from the police, so long as they paid a protection fee and committed no crimes within the city limits. In 1928 the manager of this layover system, fixer and bootlegger "Dapper Dan" Hogan, had been killed by a car bomb, and his successor, Harry Sawyer, imposed even fewer restrictions. He no longer enforced the rule forbidding crimes within the city, so long as he shared in the proceeds. The police department was as corrupt as ever, visiting criminals were still safe from arrest, but a city that had been nearly crime-free since the turn of the century was now racking up more and more robberies, gang murders, and even kidnappings.

After checking in with Sawyer, as was the custom, the Barker-Karpis group rented an apartment at 1031 South Robert Street in West St. Paul. Fred and Karpis again busied themselves with small burglaries, holdups, and hijackings. In December 1931 and January 1932 they and some accomplices staged well-planned night raids on the Minnesota towns of Pine River and Cambridge, taking several citizens hostage and systematically looting the major businesses and several private homes. Furthermore, through Harry Sawyer, Barker and Karpis soon made their most important future business connections.

The formation of the Barker-Karpis Gang as such might be dated to December 31, 1931. Karpis and Fred Barker attended a gala New Year's Eve party at Harry Sawyer's Green Lantern saloon, 545½ Wabasha, where they met some of the elite of the Midwest underworld. These included Minneapolis crime boss Isadore "Kid Cann" Blumenfeld, Capone gangster Gus Winkeler (later named as a participant in the St.

Valentine's Day Massacre, see p. 186) and several leading bank robbers, including Harvey Bailey, Tommy Holden and Francis "Jimmy" Keating, "Big Homer" Wilson, and Frank "Jelly" Nash, a former member of the old Al Spencer Gang who may have known the Barkers during their Tulsa days. Nash had escaped from Leavenworth on October 19, 1930.

Holden and Keating also had escaped from Leavenworth. Sentenced to twenty-five years for a $100,000 mail train robbery at Chicago's southern suburb of Evergreen Park, they were sent to Leavenworth in May 1928, soon meeting and befriending Frank Nash and other Spencer Gang veterans. Another new friend was a minor Oklahoma bootlegger named George Kelly, who had been serving a short sentence for smuggling liquor onto an Indian reservation. Kelly, whose real name was George Barnes, would later make headlines as "Machine Gun" Kelly, but at the time he worked in the photographic section of the prison's records room. On February 28, 1930, Holden and Keating walked out of Leavenworth, using trusty passes allegedly forged by Kelly. They fled to Chicago and then St. Paul, where they were joined later that year by Kelly and Nash.

In St. Paul, Holden and Keating teamed up with Harvey Bailey, who had been committing major and minor bank robberies for nearly a decade. A former bootlegger, Bailey had been arrested only once and had served no time in prison, but he was considered the nation's top bank robber by law enforcement agencies that bothered to keep score. He was suspected of participating in the Denver Mint robbery of December 18, 1922, which actually involved the robbing of a Federal Reserve Bank truck parked outside the Mint.

Bailey's regular associates included "Big Homer" Wilson, another longtime bank robber once arrested by Seattle police as a train robbery suspect but otherwise unknown; Charles J. Fitzgerald, a criminal in his sixties who had Chicago mob connections, many aliases and an unusually long arrest record; Verne Miller, a decorated World War I veteran and former South Dakota sheriff turned bootlegger, bank robber, and professional killer, and whose increasing mental instability (possibly aggravated by drug use, advanced syphilis, or both) eventually led to his murder by other underworld characters endangered by his erratic stunts; and Bernard Phillips, alias "Big Phil" Courtney, a onetime Chicago policeman turned bandit. A loose aggregation of criminals, with floating membership, soon developed. Though Bailey seems to have been the real leader, the group became known as the Holden-Keating Gang.

This gang, or members of it, committed a number of spectacular crimes: the $70,000 robbery of a bank in Willmar, Minnesota, on July 15, 1930; the $40,000 robbery of a bank at Ottumwa, Iowa, on September 9, 1930; the record-breaking $2.7 million robbery of the Lincoln National Bank & Trust Co. in Nebraska on September 17, 1930; and the $40,000 robbery of the Central State Bank at Sherman, Texas, on April 8, 1931. On October 2, 1931, Holden and Keating robbed First American National Bank messengers in Duluth of $58,000. On October 20, the same two and others robbed the Kraft State Bank at Menomonie, Wisconsin, of $130,000. Cashier James Kraft, son of the bank's president, was taken hostage and murdered. Two gang members, Charlie Harmon and Frank Weber, were found shot to death, along with Kraft; and one theory holds that other gang members killed them for shooting their hostage. Harmon's widow, Paula, known as "Fat-Witted," later joined Fred Barker.

The deaths of Harmon and Weber left vacancies in the gang. On December 11, 1931, seven federal prisoners escaped from Leavenworth, taking Warden Thomas White hostage. They seized White in his office as he was interviewing inmate Lloyd "Red" Barker. This may have been only a coincidence, as Lloyd didn't join in the escape and may have had no prior knowledge of it, but the escapees included Grover Durrill, George "Whitey" Curtis, and Earl Thayer of the old Spencer Gang, and William "Boxcar" Green, one of Lloyd's mail robbery partners. Durrill, Curtis, and Green were cornered by police in a nearby farmhouse and committed suicide. The others soon were caught, and the warden survived his ordeal. As it turned out, the break had been financed and engineered by Frank Nash, who had smuggled guns and explosives into the prison.

The gang soon acquired new recruits. Alvin Karpis and Fred Barker joined Tommy Holden, Bernard Phillips, and Lawrence DeVol on March 29, 1932, in the well-planned holdup of the North American Branch of the Northwestern National Bank in Minneapolis. No one was killed, and the gang escaped with $266,500 in currency, coins, and bonds, fleeing in a fast Lincoln stolen especially for the job. The car had belonged to an executive of the National Lead Battery Co. of St. Paul.

A few weeks before this robbery, a double homicide occurred, which may have been connected with the gang's activities. Two women were found shot to death in a burning Buick at Balsam Lake, Wisconsin, on March 5, 1932. One was Margaret Perry, alias "Indian Rose" Walker, Margaret Burns, Maggie Shecog, etc., a Chippewa Indian and the former mistress of "Denver Bobby" Walker, a suspect in the Denver Mint robbery. The other was her recent jailmate, a prostitute named Marjorie Schwartz or Sadie Carmacher, with other aliases. The car had been borrowed by Bernard Phillips from Alvin Karpis, who had stolen it from one O. S. Werner on January 5, when the gang ransacked the town of Cambridge, Minnesota. In later years Karpis claimed that Harry Sawyer was offered $50,000 by a St. Paul banker to have the women murdered. By other accounts, the women had threatened to inform on the gang.

Nick Hannegraf, their landlady's son, recognized pictures of Alvin Karpis and Fred Barker in *True Detective Mysteries* and dutifully called the police. St. Paul Police Chief Tom Brown, who was on Harry Sawyer's payroll, advised Hannegraf to report this at the Central Police Station. The desk sergeant there told Hannegraf he would have to come back later and see Inspector James Crumley, another Sawyer flunky. Seven hours after the call to Brown, St. Paul police raided the house on South Robert Street, by which time the Barkers, Karpis, and Arthur Dunlop were long gone.

Dunlop was found dead the next day on the shore of Lake Fremstadt, near Webster, Wisconsin. He had been shot three times at close range. The FBI later would theorize, probably correctly, that Karpis and Fred Barker had killed him as a suspected informer.

Heat from the Dunlop killing caused the gang to temporarily shift its base to Kansas City. The Barkers and Karpis stayed at the Longfellow Apartments in Kansas City from May 12 until July 5, 1932, as "Mrs. A. F. Hunter and sons," then rented an apartment at 414 West Forty-sixth Terrace. Harvey Bailey, Frank Nash, Holden and Keating, Bernard Phillips, and Lawrence DeVol also rented apartments in the area.

On June 17 this group robbed the Citizens National Bank at Fort Scott, Kansas, of $47,000. Jess Doyle was released on parole from the Kansas state prison on the same day, met Fred in Kansas City, and joined the gang. Proceeds from the robbery were spent on a lavish "coming out" party for Doyle at the Barker-Karpis apartment.

On July 7 Kansas City police officers, accompanied by Special Agent Raymond Caffrey of the future FBI, arrested Harvey Bailey, Tommy Holden, and Francis Keating on the Old Mission Golf Course in Kansas City after letting them play a few holes. A fourth gang member, Bernard Phillips, escaped to warn the others. Phillips was later suspected of betraying the trio, particularly after other gang members learned he was a former policeman. Phillips disappeared later in the year on a trip to New York with Frank Nash and Verne Miller; he is believed to have been murdered.

A Liberty Bond from the recent bank robbery was found in Bailey's pocket and turned over to Fort Scott authorities for use as evidence at his trial. Holden and Keating were returned to Leavenworth, and the rest of the gang headed back to Minnesota. The Barkers, Karpis, and Frank Nash rented cottages on White Bear Lake, and FBI files indicate that Fred Barker and Karpis hooked up with a shady Tulsa lawyer named J. Earl Smith, who supposedly was retained by the gang to defend Bailey.

Smith took the money but never showed up in court, and Bailey was defended by a court-appointed lawyer named James G. Shepperd. On August 16, Smith was shot to death at the Indian Hills Country Club near Tulsa, where he had gone in response to a mysterious phone call from an unknown client. The next day, Bailey was sentenced to ten to fifty years in the Lansing, Kansas, state prison.

Most accounts indicate that Smith was murdered by Fred Barker and Alvin Karpis for failing to defend Bailey. Other versions have it that Smith either informed on the gang or cheated them out of their money. Some FBI reports name Smith's actual murderers as Harry Campbell, Jimmie Lawson, and "Jew Eddie" Moss in what likely was also a dispute over money.

Bailey would escape from the Kansas state prison on Memorial Day 1933, along with Wilbur Underhill and nine others, using smuggled guns. Frank Nash and the Barker-Karpis Gang later would be erroneously suspected of arranging the breakout. After a brief bank robbery spree, Bailey was recaptured in the summer of 1933 and accused of involvement in the Kansas City Massacre and the kidnapping of Oklahoma oilman Charles Urschel. No solid evidence linked him to the Kansas City killings, and he apparently had no personal involvement in the Urschel kidnapping. He was unlucky enough to be laying low, and fast asleep, at the farm of "Boss" Shannon when it was raided by federal agents looking for the kidnappers. He was convicted, along with the Shannons, Albert Bates, George and Kathryn Kelly, and their associates.

That left Fred Barker and Karpis running the gang, though Karpis at first deferred to Fred, considering him the real leader. The on-the-job training they had received from Bailey, Holden and Keating had made them big-time but little-known criminals.

On July 25, 1932, Karpis, DeVol, Fred Barker, Jess Doyle, and Earl Christman robbed the Cloud County Bank at Concordia, Kansas, of $250,000 in cash and bonds. On August 18, they probably struck the Second National Bank at Beloit, Wisconsin, for $50,000. The very next day Fred Barker was wrongly identified as one of three or four men who robbed the Citizens Security Bank at Bixby, Oklahoma, of $1,000, which was later more reasonably credited to the Cookson Hills gang of Ford Bradshaw.

Arthur "Doc" Barker was paroled from his life sentence at McAlester on September 10, 1932, on the condition he leave Oklahoma forever. The parole was secured by an agent of the gang named Jack Glynn, a corrupt private detective at Leavenworth, Kansas, who knew whom to bribe. "Doc" visited with his father in Missouri, then joined the gang in St. Paul.

The Barker-Karpis Gang robbed the State Bank & Trust Co. at Redwood Falls, Minnesota, on September 23, 1932, escaping with $35,000. On September 30, they robbed the Citizens National Bank at Wahpeton, North Dakota, of $7,000. They had planned to rob the bank at nearby Breckenridge, Minnesota, on the same day, but decided not to push their luck. On October 18, Lawrence DeVol was identified as a robber of a bank in Amboy, Minnesota, which had lost $4,400 to several gunmen.

"Doc" Barker wanted a parole for his "rap buddy" Volney Davis, still in McAlester for the Sherrill murder. Karpis later claimed in his autobiography that he contacted "a big operator in St. Paul" who said he could arrange an early release for $1,500. However it was accomplished, Davis, convicted murderer and former escapee, was released from the Oklahoma state prison on November 3, 1932, not on parole but on a two-year "leave of absence." Davis was due back at McAlester on July 1, 1934, but instead joined the gang in St. Paul and soon accompanied "Ma" Barker on a trip to California to visit her sister.

Davis's girlfriend, Edna "The Kissing Bandit"* Murray, escaped from the women's state prison at Jefferson City, Missouri, on December 13, 1932. It was her third prison break, which earned her the additional nickname of "Rabbit." Edna had been serving a twenty-five-year sentence for highway robbery, and when Davis learned of her escape

*So called because she kissed a man that her husband Jack Murray and she had held up in Kansas City in 1929.

he returned to the Midwest to join her and her teenage son, Preston Paden.

The Barker-Karpis Gang, now including Bill Weaver and Verne Miller, robbed the Third Northwestern Bank in Minneapolis on December 16, killing two policemen and a bystander. They escaped with $22,000 in cash and $92,000 in bonds, using the same Lincoln they had driven in the bloodless March robbery. After the Minneapolis job, Miller returned to Kansas City, and the rest of the gang, except for DeVol, headed to Reno.

DeVol got drunk, crashed a party at 298 Grand Avenue in St. Paul, and was arrested, still in possession of $17,000 of the bank loot. He was convicted of robbery and murder and sentenced to life in the state prison at Stillwater, Minnesota. (Three years later he was transferred to the St. Peter Hospital for the Criminally Insane and escaped with fifteen other inmates on June 6, 1936. After a series of crimes, he died a month later in a gun battle with police at Enid, Oklahoma, taking an officer with him.)

In 1932 John Dillinger was still an inmate at the Indiana state prison, while the equally unknown Barker-Karpis Gang wintered in Reno and San Francisco, making good contacts through the Reno gambling syndicate headed by Bill Graham and Jim McKay. It was probably there that Karpis met Illinois prison escapee Lester Gillis, who had grown up in the same general part of Chicago and preferred the name Jimmy Williams to his later alias of George "Baby Face" Nelson. Karpis sometimes dined with Gillis, his wife, Helen, and their children, Ronald and Darlene, in their apartment at 126 Caliente Street in Reno. Gillis introduced Karpis to the ex-convict owner of a private hospital in Vallejo, California, also a Williams, named Thomas but better known as "Tobe." His staff performed illegal abortions, treated Gillis's wife, Helen, as a regular patient, and took care of sick or wounded fugitives under any name they chose. Karpis had his tonsils removed there in February 1933, shortly before the gang returned to the Midwest.

Another useful contact was Frank Cochran, a Reno airplane mechanic and garage owner who serviced cars for criminals, putting a siren on Nelson's to facilitate escapes, or because he just liked sirens. In return for favors rendered, Karpis lined up Gillis, aka Nelson, in the summer of 1933 with a gang of experienced bank robbers headquartered in Long Beach, Indiana, near the Michigan City penitentiary from which Dillinger had just been paroled. These included the aristocratic Eddie Bentz, semiretired collector of rare books and coins, and such younger disciples as Tommy Carroll and Homer Van Meter, a prison friend of Dillinger's and also recently released. (It was here that Nelson and Dillinger, who patronized the same Army-Navy store operated by a local underworld character, probably became acquainted.)

The Barker-Karpis Gang returned to St. Paul in February, but a month later moved back to the Chicago area after Harry Sawyer's police informants tipped him that a gang apartment was scheduled to be raided. Needing to replenish their protection money, they planned another robbery.

On April 4, 1933, Alvin Karpis, Fred and

"Doc" Barker, Frank Nash, Volney Davis, Earl Christman, Jess Doyle, and Eddie Green robbed the First National Bank at Fairbury, Nebraska, of $151,350 in cash and bonds. They escaped after a wild gun battle in which a deputy and two citizens were wounded. Earl Christman also was wounded and taken by the gang to Verne Miller's home at 6612 Edgevale Road in Kansas City. Miller called an underworld doctor, but Christman died anyway and was buried by the gang outside the town.

Returning to St. Paul, Karpis and Fred Barker were summoned by bootlegger Jack Peifer (variously spelled in police records) to a meeting at his Hollyhocks nightclub. Peifer introduced them to two friends, Fred Goetz (alias Shotgun George Ziegler, or Zeigler) and Byron "Monty" Bolton (alias Carter). Goetz and Bolton were two of the American Boys who worked for the Capone Syndicate and had participated in the St. Valentine's Day Massacre, Goetz as one of the gunmen and Bolton as a not-too-bright lookout who mistook another gangster for "Bugs" Moran. He also left behind a letter, and possibly a medicine bottle, with his name on it.

Goetz and Bolton occasionally moonlighted as freelance crooks, and now they had a business proposition for the Barker-Karpis Gang. They were hiring help for a Peifer-sponsored kidnapping in St. Paul, and, after much urging, Fred and Karpis agreed. Soon they were joined by "Doc" Barker and Charles Fitzgerald. They abducted William A. Hamm Jr., head of a well-known St. Paul brewery, on June 15, 1933. Hamm was blindfolded and driven all the way to the Chicago suburb of Bensenville, where he was held at the home of Edmund Bartholmey, the town's future (and soon deposed) postmaster, until the family raised a ransom of $100,000. The bills, whose serial numbers had been recorded, were fenced through the Graham-McKay syndicate in Reno.

Chicago beer baron Roger Touhy and members of his mob were arrested on general principles, tried amidst great hoopla, and acquitted for lack of evidence, to the embarrassment of the FBI. (Later, Touhy was convicted of kidnapping local underworld figure Jake "The Barber" Factor in what the courts, after twenty-five years, concluded was a frame-up on the part of competitor Frank Nitti. About the time of his release in 1959, Touhy coauthored his ordeal in *The Stolen Years*, and soon afterward was killed on the front porch of his sister's home by shotgun blasts from a passing car. His famous last words, "The bastards never forget!" were cooked up by a reporter.)

On the same day as the Hamm kidnapping in 1933, Frank Nash was captured by the FBI in Hot Springs, Arkansas. Two days later, as he was being returned to Leavenworth, Nash and his captors were ambushed by gunmen at the Union Station in Kansas City. In a release attempt gone wrong, Nash, a federal agent and three other officers were shot to death in the Kansas City Massacre of June 17, though the battle may have been set off when another federal agent accidentally blasted Nash while trying to operate an unfamiliar shotgun. Before that was confirmed unofficially, Congress quickly authorized federal agents to carry guns and to make arrests without first being "deputized" by local police.

In any case, Verne Miller had led the Kansas City mission, and the FBI would first name Harvey Bailey and Underhill as his accomplices before evidence at Miller's house pointed instead to Adam Richetti and his crime partner, "Pretty Boy" Floyd (later stories claimed that Richetti became too drunk to participate and that Floyd reluctantly filled in). Several underworld figures in Hot Springs, Joplin, Chicago, and Kansas City eventually would be convicted of conspiracy, including Barker's friend Herb Farmer. According to statements to the FBI by Byron Bolton and Edna Murray, a small portion of the Hamm ransom was set aside as a defense fund for Farmer.

Joe Bergl's garage (above), located next door to the Cotton Club, owned by Ralph Capone (below right, in hat), was where cars were "smokescreened" and "bulletproofed." A part-owner was St. Valentine's Day shooter Gus Winkeler (below left), who was questioned when the Barker-Karpis Gang pulled a robbery but crashed their car, which was traced to Bergl.

At the South St. Paul post office on August 30, 1933, the Barker-Karpis Gang robbed Stockyards National Bank payroll messengers of $33,000, killing one policeman and wounding another. On September 22, driving a car equipped with smokescreen and oil-slick devices, they robbed Federal Reserve Bank messengers on Jackson Boulevard in Chicago, killing another policeman and wrecking their car but still managing to escape, only to discover the bags they took contained useless checks.

The car was traced to the shop of one Joe Bergl at 5346 West Cermak Road (formerly Twenty-second Street) in Cicero, next door to Ralph Capone's Cotton Club. Bergl's partner in the business turned out to be Gus Winkeler, and his customers, the FBI would learn, included members of the Capone mob and such visiting outlaws as "Machine Gun" Kelly. Some had steel plates installed in their cars to protect the occupants from gunfire, while the economy versions had their trunks and backseats "bulletproofed" with thick Chicago telephone directories.

(Bergl's competitor on Chicago's Near North Side was Clarence Lieder's Oakley Auto Construction Co., 2300 West Division, who serviced, supplied, and modified cars for "Baby Face" Nelson and his cronies, stored the dirt-track racer Nelson sometimes drove at Chicago's Robey Speedway on the city's South Side, and who also developed a smokescreen device by way of a tube-and-valve arrangement that would squirt motor oil into a car's hot exhaust manifold. The Capone mob had used a such a car, probably from Bergl, in an unsuccessful attempt to kill mobster Jack Zuta in downtown Chicago. This scared Zuta into hiding out at a Wisconsin roadhouse where Capone's men still tracked him down, motioned other customers out of the way, and machine-gunned him on the dance floor.)

After another vacation in Reno, the Barker-Karpis Gang returned to St. Paul, where Harry Sawyer, annoyed at being shortchanged on the Hamm ransom, convinced the gang to pull another kidnapping, this one more profitable for him. The target was Edward G. Bremer, president of the Commercial State Bank of St. Paul, against whom Sawyer held some unknown personal grudge. Bremer was abducted on January 17, 1934, and, like Hamm, transported to Bensenville, Illinois, where he was held for nearly a month at the home of former bootlegger Harold Allderton (usually spelled Alderton) until his family raised $200,000.

Things didn't go as smoothly this time. Gasoline cans used by the kidnappers were found along the route of the ransom drop, and one bore a fingerprint of "Doc" Barker. Flashlights used by the gang to signal the payoff location also were found and traced to a St. Paul store, where a clerk identified Alvin Karpis as the purchaser. "Doc" and Karpis were added to the FBI's wanted list. This money was so hot that the Reno gamblers who had laundered the Hamm ransom refused to touch it. Soon it began turning up in Chicago, and some of the money-changers there, including crooked politician John J. "Boss" McLaughlin, were arrested.

By March 1934 Karpis and Fred Barker (if not the gang as a whole) paid a call on their favorite family physician, Dr. Joseph Moran, Chicago's leading underworld health specialist. Moran had offices at one of the city's underworld hotels, The Irving, on Irving Park Boulevard, near where police had failed to trap Dillinger at another doctor's office the previous November. Once a skilled physician and still competent when sober, Moran had served time for one or more botched abortions. In prison he had met some high-powered felons who helped him find his true calling—drinking and treating wounded gangsters, particularly members of the Capone "Outfit" (a term Capone himself coined).

Moran tried to alter the faces of Karpis and Barker through plastic surgery, without great success, but did manage to remove the fingerprints of Alvin Karpis by the painful use of a scalpel instead of caustic chemicals.

When soused, which was often, Moran tended to brag about his medical accomplishments and unwisely suggested to members of the criminal community that his talents were indispensable. As a result, he was taken for the traditional one-way ride—by boat on Lake Erie, where he was killed and scuttled, dumped in the Chicago River (which seems unlikely), or, according to Karpis and contemporary author Herbert Corey (*Farewell, Mr. Gangster*), by car, to be bumped off and buried. His disappearance makes him at least a possible candidate for the grave in which the FBI later believed it had found the decomposed body of Dillinger gangster John Hamilton. Hamilton's ostensible burial was attended by Dillinger and members of the Barker-Karpis Gang, whose stories did not quite match [see "The Body Identified as John Hamilton," p. 439].

Fred Goetz, who divided his time between the Capone mob and the Barker-Karpis Gang, also was talkative when drunk. Late on March 21, 1934, he was killed by shotgun blasts outside the Minerva Restaurant in Cicero, Illinois, about a block west of the Hawthorne Hotel (which remained the local mob headquarters even after one-term reform Mayor Dever lost to "Big Bill" Thompson, and Capone took over Chicago's mammoth Lexington Hotel south of the Loop, in the city's slightly reformed vice district). The generally accepted theory is that Goetz was losing his marbles and talking about past crimes. It remains uncertain whether his killers were the Barker-Karpis Gang, friends of "Bugs" Moran, or Frank Nitti, who succeeded Al Capone and was purging the Outfit of Capone loyalists. In one pocket police found a thousand-dollar bill, allegedly compensation from the Reno gamblers afraid to handle the Bremer kidnap money.

In April, Dillinger gangster Eddie Green, formerly a member of the Barker-Karpis mob, was shot by FBI agents in St. Paul. He died eight days later in a hospital, after deliriously babbling the details of past crimes while agents took notes. His wife, Bessie, captured at the same time, also provided much information. The Greens gave the FBI its first real knowledge of the Barker-Karpis Gang as a cohesive group. From Bessie Green, the bureau learned that Karpis and the Barker brothers usually traveled in the company of a dowdy old woman who (according to the FBI) "posed" as their mother. Enter "Ma" Barker, so far unimportant and mentioned only in passing by the West Plains police.

By the end of the year, the Barker-Karpis Gang was scattered across the country, dodging the FBI while trying to pass the Bremer ransom. Various gang members were captured, and Bremer money was recovered as far away as Havana, where Karpis lived briefly with his pregnant girlfriend ("paramour" was the bureau's favorite term), Dolores Delaney. Dolores was one of three sisters with similar tastes in men. One was married to Albert "Pat" Reilly, a St. Paul hoodlum employed by Harry Sawyer. Another was the girlfriend of Tommy Carroll, then identified with Dillinger, whose Crown Point escape and worldwide name recognition had robbed Nelson of credit for forming the gang originally.

Dillinger, Floyd, Bonnie and Clyde, and Nelson—the most publicized "public enemies"—were all killed in 1934, leaving only the Barker-Karpis Gang to make J. Edgar Hoover famous. On January 8, 1935, an army of agents raided a courtyard apartment building at 3920 North Pine Grove, without telling the leak-prone Chicago police. They created such a commotion with gas and gunfire that city cops rushed to the scene without knowing what to expect. A G-man waving credentials prevented a general bloodbath, and the cops joined the spectators, who were rooting for both sides after agents had thoroughly terrified residents and lobbed tear-gas shells into the wrong apartment.

Byron Bolton, Clara Fisher Gibson, and Ruth Heidt, widow of a recently murdered gang member, surrendered as soon as they could, but Clara's husband, Russell Gibson, alias Roy "Slim" Gray, chose to fight. He donned a bulletproof vest, armed himself with an automatic rifle and .32- caliber automatic pistol, and tried to escape out the back. Gibson barely made it onto a rear fire escape before an FBI agent with a Winchester rifle sent a slug through his chest. Gibson died a short time later, a bureau report stated, "with a curse on his lips for all law enforcement officers." Gibson, who had joined the gang as a money passer in the aftermath of the Bremer snatch, had been wanted since 1929 for a $75,000 bank messenger robbery in Oklahoma City. He also had been arrested for possession of stolen jewelry, but Chicago police, who had long since streamlined their criminal justice system, told his distraught wife to give her bail-bond cash to Louis Piquett, the district's designated fixer and future Dillinger attorney, who cleared the matter up without any bothersome paperwork.

Earlier the same day as the Pine Grove Avenue battle, which angered the police as well as the newspapers, "Doc" Barker and his girlfriend Mildred Kuhlman were arrested by the FBI outside their apartment at 432 Surf Street. Inside, agents found a Florida map with the Ocala region circled. "Doc" had no comment, but Byron Bolton told his interrogators that "Ma" and Fred Barker, and possibly other gang members, were living on a lake in Florida, where Fred supposedly had been using his submachine gun to hunt a huge alligator called Old Joe by the locals.

Eight days later, on January 16, 1935, a small army of federal agents surrounded a house on Lake Weir at Ocklawaha, Florida, and called on the occupants to surrender. They were answered by machine-gun fire. During a prolonged battle the G-men poured more than 1,500 rounds into the two-story structure. Some forty-five minutes after the return fire had ceased, Inspector E. J. Connelly sent Willie Woodbury, the Barkers' black handyman (whom the Barkers presumably would spare as a noncombatant), into the house to see what was left of any residents. At first Woodbury did not like the idea, but he was unable to resist a few dollars ponied up by some agents, partly in jest.* He found Fred Barker dead in an upstairs bedroom with fourteen bullet

---

*According to Jared McDade, citing the written account of his father, Agent Thomas McDade, who also was in the first of two federal cars that encountered "Baby Face" Nelson outside Barrington, Illinois.

wounds, and "Ma" with three, although some unlikely accounts have her committing suicide, or Fred finishing her off when capture seemed imminent.

According to J. Edgar Hoover, a Thompson was found on the floor between her and Fred. The newspapers, using Hoover's account, embellished this considerably, arming her with a "smoking" submachine gun. Hoover would later declare that her devoted son Fred had given her the Thompson with a hundred-round drum, making do himself with one whose magazine held only fifty cartridges. Agents also found two shotguns, two .45 automatics, a .380 automatic, a Winchester rifle, a large quantity of ammunition, several bulletproof vests, and cash totaling $14,293. The arsenal was carefully arranged on the front steps of the house for the benefit of photographers.

An artist's imaginative depiction of "Ma" and Fred Barker battling G-men before both were killed at the house in Florida.

The bodies of "Ma" and Fred were allowed to mummify in the Ocala morgue until October, when George Barker could afford to bring his son and his estranged wife home for burial. George successfully sued for recovery of the cash seized at Ocklawaha, because the government could not prove any of it was ransom money.

"Doc" Barker and other members of the gang were convicted of the Bremer kidnapping and sentenced to life, partly on the testimony of Byron Bolton, who pleaded guilty to the Hamm and Bremer kidnappings and received concurrent sentences of three to five years. "Doc" was sent to Leavenworth, then Alcatraz. On Friday, January 13, 1939, guards killed him with rifle fire at the beach as he was attempting to escape on a homemade raft. His last words were, "I'm all shot to hell!"

"Doc" was buried at Olivet Memorial Park Cemetery in Colma, California, identified only by his prison number. He remains there today, although there is a marker with his name on it in the family plot at Williams Timberhill Cemetery in Welch, Oklahoma.

George Barker died on February 28, 1941, in his home at 1201 East Seventh Street in Webb City, Missouri. He also was buried at Timberhill. George, Kate, Herman, and Fred Barker now lie in the isolated northwest corner of Williams Timberhill Cemetery. Only Herman's grave has a monument. Lloyd Barker is buried in an unmarked grave in Brighton, Colorado.

After the killing of "Ma" and Fred Barker, Alvin Karpis and Harry Campbell fled north to Atlantic City. Cornered by police at the Dan-Mor Hotel, on January 20, 1935, they shot their way out and escaped. Their girlfriends, Dolores Delaney and Wynona Burdette, were captured and later sentenced to five years for harboring federal fugitives. Dolores gave birth to a son while in prison, named him Raymond Alvin Karpis, and gave him to Karpis's parents in Chicago to raise.

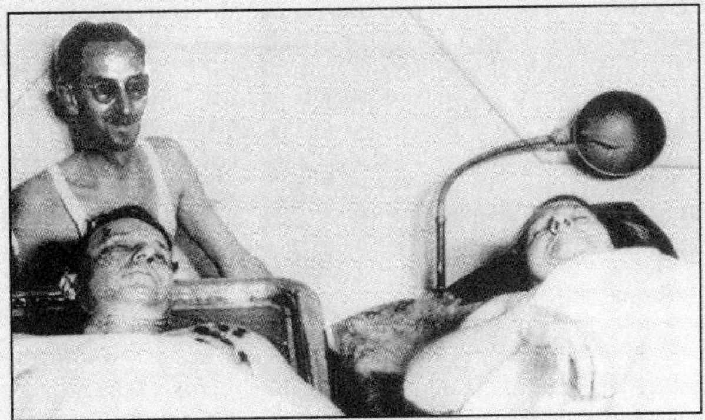

Above: the bodies of Fred and "Ma" Barker (above) at a local funeral parlor. Below: the arsenal found by federal agents in the "death house" at Ocklawaha, Florida.

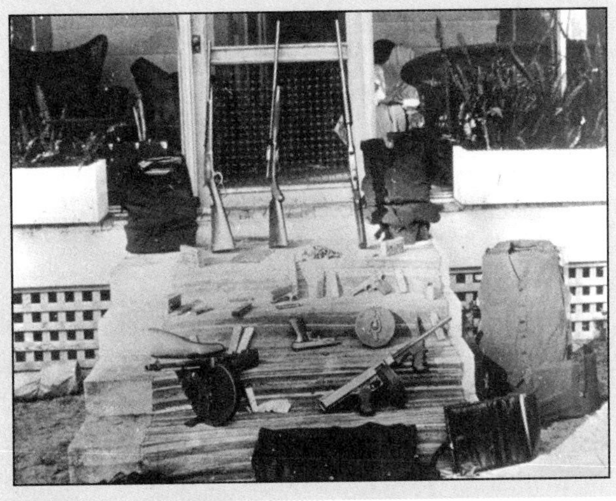

Karpis and Campbell kidnapped a doctor in Pennsylvania and stole his car, releasing him unharmed in Ohio and abandoning the car in Michigan. They later organized a new gang and on April 24, 1935, robbed a Warren, Ohio, mail truck of $72,000. The following November they hit a mail train at Garrettsville, Ohio, for $34,000. One member of the new but unsung gang was the Barkers' old friend Sam Coker, whose parole from the Oklahoma state prison was allegedly bought by Karpis.

After a long pursuit and some embarrassing blunders, the FBI finally tracked Karpis to a rooming house in New Orleans. J. Edgar Hoover, smarting from criticism that he lacked police experience and let his men take all the risks, rushed there by plane and took personal credit for arresting Karpis on May 1, 1936. Karpis later remarked that Hoover had stayed safely out of range until agents were holding him at gunpoint, then took charge for the benefit of the newspapers.

Since no one had remembered to bring handcuffs, Karpis's hands were bound with Agent Clarence Hurt's necktie, and he jokingly offered to give the visiting G-men directions to the federal building, claiming that he'd thought about robbing the post office there. Arrested with him was Fred Hunter, who would be convicted for harboring Karpis and for mail robbery. Five days later, Hoover led another squad of agents in capturing Harry Campbell and Sam Coker in Toledo. Coker's Oklahoma parole was revoked, and Campbell would receive a life sentence for the Bremer kidnapping.

Flown to St. Paul, Karpis pleaded guilty to the Hamm kidnapping and received a life sentence. Altogether he spent some thirty-three years in federal prisons, mostly Alcatraz, before he was paroled in 1969 and deported to Canada, which initially balked at accepting a man with no fingerprints. He later moved to Spain and died there on August 26, 1979, of an overdose of sleeping pills, which some believe was accidental. Karpis's New Orleans capture, stage-managed or not, proved J. Edgar Hoover a man of action after all and marked the end of what most Americans thought of as the "public enemy" era.

In a mere thirteen months and after maybe a dozen bank jobs, Dillinger had made Melvin Purvis a household name, to Hoover's great displeasure and Purvis's regret. Far more deliberately but less successfully, Hoover tried to establish his own crime-fighting reputation by destroying the Barker-Karpis Gang. That group, with countless robberies and killings from the twenties to 1936, was far more formidable than Dillinger's desperados but also far less likable, and hard as he tried, Hoover seemed to understand he could never get the mileage out of Karpis that he had gotten out of "Ma." This required popular crime writer and Hoover's private publicist, Courtney Ryley Cooper, to engage in major exaggeration, but Cooper had no qualms in that regard. In a book (*Ten Thousand Public Enemies*) and one of the dozen or so articles ghostwritten or coauthored by Cooper for *American Magazine*, Hoover portrayed "Ma" in prose both purple and fanciful, as if the two had battled it out nose to nose. Wrote Hoover, with a little help from his friend,

> The eyes of Arizona Clark Barker, by the way, always fascinated me. They were queerly direct, penetrating, hot with some strangely smouldering flame, yet withal as hypnotically cold as the muzzle of a gun.

Cooper later hanged himself, supposedly after a falling out with Hoover. And Hoover, after mopping up a few uncelebrated fugitives in the late 1930s, would concentrate on subversives, spies, and saboteurs, while racketeering evolved into nationally organized crime.

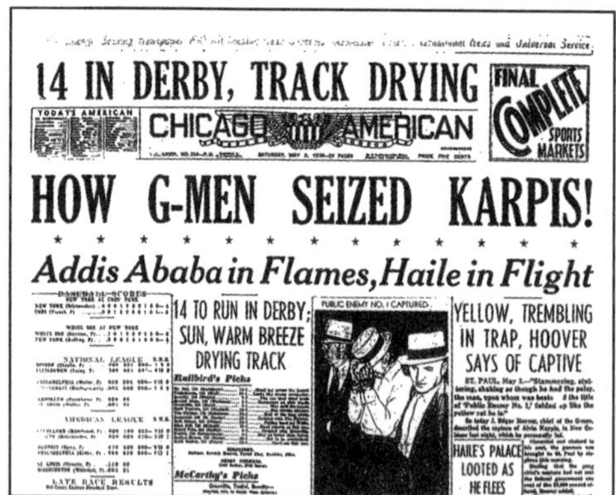

14 IN DERBY, TRACK DRYING

CHICAGO AMERICAN

FINAL COMPLETE SPORTS MARKETS

HOW G-MEN SEIZED KARPIS!

Addis Ababa in Flames, Haile in Flight

14 TO RUN IN DERBY; SUN, WARM BREEZE DRYING TRACK

Railbird's Picks

McCarthy's Picks

PUBLIC ENEMY NO. 1 CAPTURED

YELLOW, TREMBLING IN TRAP, HOOVER SAYS OF CAPTIVE

HAILE'S PALACE LOOTED AS HE FLEES

Alvin Karpis later disputed the story of how FBI Director J. Edgar Hoover captured him "personally" in New Orleans in 1936.

— Rick Mattix, based on research for a book he is coauthoring with R. D. Morgan.

6

CRIME CONTROL

The American legal system had its roots in British common law, but in an underpopulated, rapidly expanding nation that rejected a strong central government, lawmaking and law enforcement were deliberately relegated to state and local authorities who put together an amazing patchwork of statutes reflecting regional conditions and priorities. Thus law enforcement was highly politicized from the start, and crime control largely was a do-it-yourself proposition. Sheriffs, marshals, posses, vigilance committees, and private detective agencies like the Pinkertons were "the law" in the West, where dangerous criminals were jailed, hung, or killed in gun battles. Lesser lawbreaking was handled out of court one way or another, or adjudicated by a justice of the peace with a minimum of legal formalities.

Despite its reputation for lawlessness, in the sparsely settled West citizens felt a moral duty to protect one another, and in most ways the towns were safer than the nation's cities. Even when municipal governments began establishing official police departments in the mid-nineteenth century, in places like Chicago and New York, no sensible person ventured out at night without a

—Cartoon in Brooklyn Eagle.

Is the equipment of our present legal system old-fashioned when it comes to coping with modern crime?

In New York, the "line-up" began as a "show-up," possibly because the abundance of crooks and fences would begin recognizing the relatively few police "detectives," who commonly received a gratuity for returning stolen property to its rightful owner.

sword cane or pocket pistol, and it was not until 1911 that New York City passed the Sullivan Act, which prohibited the unlicensed carrying of guns. Increased demands for police professionalism included departments that, at least in theory, were responsible to the mayor or his personal representative, such as a chief or a superintendent.

Despite civil service formalities and fledgling efforts to institute training, the typical metropolitan police district remained nearly autonomous, ruled by a captain who had more practical authority than his superiors. He was the instrument of his ward boss's own law-enforcement policies and employed politically loyal patrolmen who kept the peace with their nightsticks. Municipal codes were enforced (or ignored) differently from one ethnic neighborhood to another, accommodating the vice operations that paid for protection and were acceptable to local residents. Citizens correctly regarded city police as the private army of whichever party was in power. Justice, at least at the neighborhood level, was commonly dispensed by a ward boss who held his own form of court without legal authority, but sometimes with enough impartiality to gain a reputation for fairness and common-sense decisions that avoided legal wrangling in an often fixed, formal trial.

The Progressive Movement had included public safety among its campaigns for civic reforms, but it was not until the 1920s that such efforts produced substantial changes in law-enforcement organization, strategies, and performance. These occurred largely in response to the dramatic increase in crime that followed World War I and coincided with Prohibition. Previously, holdups by gangs of armed men had been sufficiently rare that such crimes still were called "highway robberies," an expression left over from the days when desperadoes on horseback waylaid stagecoaches. Now the country was confronted with a revival of

What first strikes the stranger
on arriving in New York.

Until newspapers began to complain, beat cops in New York had a common strategy for dealing with strangers or anyone else who came to their attention.

outlawry in the form of "motorized bandits" who had discovered the automobile. They were striking it rich robbing banks, payroll messengers, jewelry stores, and even gambling spots, creating turmoil in cities whose police had limited means of pursuit or communication.

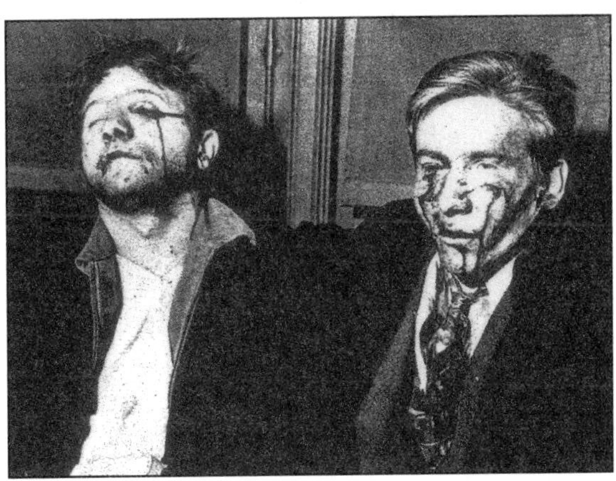

In a 1936 Startling Detective *column called "The Chief's Chair," the caption ignores the trifling issue of brutality and reads: "Showing proof of police determination to take no chances with desperate criminals, Edward Metelski (left) and Paul Semenkewitz, who made a daring escape from the New Brunswick jail, are pictured at Newark immediately after their capture. . . ."*

Many foreign countries were far ahead of the U.S. in every phase of police work, from organization and administration to the forensic sciences. In the U.S., police departments were slower in acquiring automobiles and motorcycles and better weapons, compiling statistics, setting up identification bureaus, and discovering radio and the teletype. Fingerprinting gradually became a long-overdue replacement for the complicated Bertillon system of physical measurements imported thirty years earlier from France, and which stayed on many police identification cards, below the fingerprint boxes, throughout the 1920s. Even ballistics testing did not find wide use or legal acceptance until 1929, when the St. Valentine's Day Massacre inspired some wealthy Chicagoans to personally fund the establishment of this country's first Scientific Crime Detection Laboratory—one more advanced in firearm and bullet comparisons, but otherwise like those used in other countries for many years. The progress of police professionalism in America during this period can be measured crudely by the ongoing debate over use of the "third degree" on criminal suspects and by testimonials promoting the whipping post.

A revolution in crime control and the triumph of professionalism occurred by political happenstance when President Franklin D. Roosevelt all but reversed the country's antiquated law-enforcement philosophy, policies, and practices. In response to a heavily promoted crime wave featuring a new crop of Public Enemies (by now a term applied mainly by the press to describe any headline-making outlaw), Congress reluctantly passed a series of unprecedented federal laws that would ultimately make J. Edgar Hoover the world's most celebrated crime fighter. Hoover used every trick in the book to promote the image of his special agents as a new breed of incorruptible scientific investigator (with a few experienced gunfighters quietly thrown in) and to set an example for the nation's state and municipal police agencies, whether they liked it or not.

Once Justice Department publicity made the G-man a national hero and role model, local departments had to swallow their resentment of FBI grandstanding and join the program, or appear as backward and corrupt as many actually were. Some resisted reform, but they no longer had the luxury of near autonomy and selective enforcement policies that existed well into the "public enemy" era—as perpetuated by newspapers and mistakenly attributed to the FBI.

CRIME CONTROL CHRONOLOGY
1920–1929

Including 1919 as a prologue

Based on the New York Times *Index and various books on crime and Prohibition that do not always agree on exact dates, with the year 1919 listed to include ratification of the national Prohibition amendment and establishment of the Chicago Crime Commission.*

1919

January 16—After war-time prohibition, thirty-six states ratify the Eighteenth Amendment establishing national Prohibition, to be enforced after one year under the Volstead Act.

February 28—New York's police commissioner advances theory that recent crime wave is the work of "demented soldiers."

April 7—Eleven robberies reported in New York in twenty-four hours.

April 12—New York's mayor denies existence of any crime wave.

June 19—Chicago Association of Commerce establishes independently funded Chicago Crime Commission as a watchdog and advisory group of prominent private citizens to improve police department efficiency and administration. This begins a national movement in which nearly every state and many cities establish similar commissions.

July 1—William J. Flynn named director of Justice Department's Bureau of Investigation.

August 21—The Chicago field office of the U.S. Department of Justice's Bureau of Investigation (later FBI) is established, with James P. Rooney as special agent in charge.

September 9—Boston police strike of 1,117 patrolmen protesting long hours and low pay is first to leave a major U.S. city without police protection; mayor calls on the militia to put down crime and rioting that kills two and wounds many more; Governor Calvin Coolidge replaces strikers with new men, including war veterans, and virtually guarantees his later election as U.S. president by declaring, "There is no right to strike against the public safety by anybody, anywhere, any time."

October 27—President vetoes Volstead Act; overridden by House same day and by Senate the next.

November 15—California's Alameda County reveals plan to frighten confessions from suspects by having stunt pilots take them on perilous airplane rides.

1920

January 1—Chicago merchants declare plans to install electric sirens outside their stores and answer calls with shotguns.

January 13—Chicago police announce the roundup of 600 suspects in the previous week.

January 16—National Prohibition (Eighteenth Amendment) banning the manufacture, transportation, and sale of alcoholic beverages, to be enforced under the federal Volstead Act.

January 17—Volstead Act goes into effect at 12:01 a.m.

May 17—Federal agents raid the Sibley Warehouse & Storage Co. warehouse at 325 North Clark Street in Chicago and seize fifteen barrels of whiskey.

June 7—U.S. Supreme Court declares Eighteenth Amendment valid and binding on all legislative bodies, courts, and public officials.

September 13–14—New York Mayor Hylan suggests Police Commissioner Enright employ automobiles to intercept suspicious night gangs. Enright forms special automobile squad.

November 10—New York, the first major city to pass a restrictive firearms law (the Sullivan Act, 1911), discovers justices of the peace selling pistol permits indiscriminately for as little as $2 each.

December 3—New York City appropriates funds for a fleet of police motorcycles for night patrols.

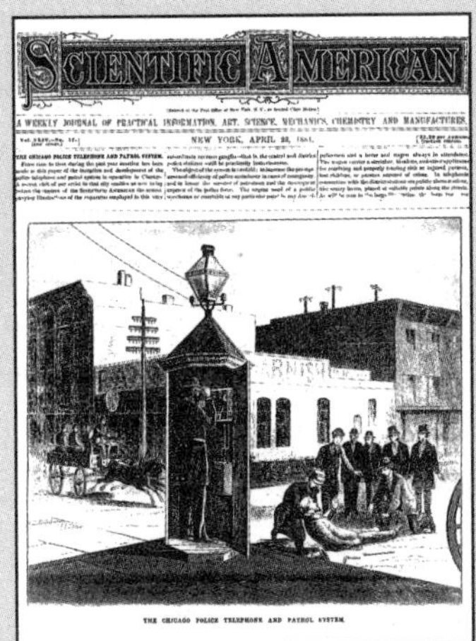

SCIENTIFIC AMERICAN

Scientific American.

THE CHICAGO POLICE TELEPHONE AND PATROL SYSTEM.

SIGNAL TRANSMITTER.

Scientific American *magazine detailed the latest police gadgetry instituted in the latter decades of the nineteenth century.*

December 8—Philadelphia judge approves carrying of revolvers during outbreak of lawlessness.

December 9—Chicago police begin using gas grenades against barricaded criminals.

December 17—New York's Fifth Avenue jewelers' organizations form vigilance committee; fifty detectives are assigned to patrol the city day and night, using automobiles; National Jewelers Board of Trade reports $359,000 in robberies in six weeks; president of Women's Republican Club asks mayor and police commissioner to declare martial law.

– In Baltimore, 100 holdups and burglaries reported in two months; police will be ordered to watch for influx of New York crooks.

December 20—American Legion and Military Order of the World War offers New York 500 to 5,000 ex-servicemen to back up police; police commissioner calls crime wave a little "flurry" but abolishes patrolmen's thirty-minute lunch break and orders them to question citizens on the street at late hours.

December 20–31—Assistant U.S. attorney calls on New Yorkers to form Citizens Protective League to fight crime.

– New York grants and then rejects police commissioner's request for 769 additional patrolmen, but he then adds 700 police reserves, transfers 600 men from desk jobs to patrol duty; assigns twenty hand-picked riflemen and patrol cars to seek out robbers; organizes special squads to guard all entrances to the city; and assigns sidecar motorcycles to patrol the Bronx, Queens and Staten Island. Mayor asks judges whether arrested suspects may pledge loot for bail.

– Chicago police chief denies criticizing New York police.

December 22—A New Jersey bill would subject "highwaymen" to life imprisonment.

– Missouri legislature will consider making robbery punishable by death.

– Chicago aldermen endorse promotion of patrolmen who kill armed robbers; police arrest 100 in twenty-four hours.

December 27—Tulsa, Oklahoma, police commissioner urges stores to employ armed guards.

December 28—Toledo, Ohio, police are ordered to arrest every "suspicious character" and shoot to kill if necessary.

– Citizens of Wappinger Falls, New York, form vigilante group to guard village; Westchester County citizens also will organize patrols.

1921

January 3—After two fatal holdups, Cleveland police receive orders to shoot to kill.

January 4—Chicago police forbid films showing criminals at work.

January 6—New York relents and grants police commissioner money to hire 600 police recruits.

January 8—Press reports that several Long Island towns have organized citizen posses to curtail crime.

January 18—New York City Board of Aldermen resolution calls for life imprisonment for gunmen.

January 22—New York police commissioner proposes life imprisonment for burglars.

January 31—Delaware law passed making robbers subject to forty lashes, twenty years in prison, and $500 fine.

February 1—Arkansas senate passes bill providing death penalty for bank robbery.

February 7—Vigilantes now patrolling highways in Union County, New Jersey.

March 7—National Surety Co. declares that the automobile is responsible for much of the country's crime.

April 12–28—Chicago police experiment with "wireless telephone" communications, new police auto patrol, and "bulletproof" shield.

April 23—Detroit establishes first "one-way" police radio system in standard broadcast band; Federal Radio Commission (predecessor to the Federal Communications Commission) insists station KOP be licensed as "entertainment," mandating the playing of music during broadcasts—an obstacle soon overcome by playing part of "Yankee Doodle" before each police call.

June 10—Roy A. Haynes affirmed as first national Prohibition Commissioner.

July 11—Ships forbidden to bring liquor within three miles of U.S. coast (the "three-mile limit," which later will be extended to twelve miles).

July 28—Detroit Clearing House Association offers $5,000 for each bank robber slain.

August 21—William J. Burns replaces William J. Flynn as director of Justice Department's Bureau of Investigation.

August 25—Brooklyn district attorney begins investigation into organized traffic in pistol permits.

September 7—Chicago banks announce tunnel plan to protect messengers from holdups.

September 28–29—New York's Nassau County sheriff equips deputies and policemen with riot shotguns for use against bandits.

October 14—Cedar Grove, New Jersey, will ring fire bell in case of attacks on women.

October 22—U.S. judges, district attorneys, and state governors propose confiscation of all firearms of less than three feet in length, heavier punishment for robbers, and less prison reform as a means of checking daylight holdups.

November 14—Judge Scanlan calls Chicago the most lawless community in the world.

November 17—A *New York Times* editorial compares current crime wave with that of 1864.

1922

January 1—Bronx announces plan to organize vigilance committee.

January 9—New York magistrate advocates amendment to the Sullivan law making carrying of firearms a felony.

January 12—New York state senator introduces bill requiring ammunition purchasers to have license.

January 13—New York district attorney advocates the branding of criminals.

January 26—Six Chicago policemen suspended for substituting six strangers for suspects being held in a cell.

February 6—New York police commissioner blames crime on too much leniency toward criminals and too much prison reform.

February 8—Rochester, New York, bank employees will be trained to shoot robbers.

February 13—Pennsylvania Bankers Association advocates making bank robbery a capital crime.

March 6—Woodlynne, New Jersey, announces it will tar and feather highway robbers.

March 14—Armed robber interrogated by New York City police states that most criminals purchase their guns from mail-order houses.

March 27–28—New York police will begin patrolling the city with ten Ford motor cars, one assigned to each precinct.

April 6—*New York Times* editorial reports on citizens arming in self-defense.

April 7—New Jersey state law, possibly signed by mistake, will permit vehicle owners to be armed.

April 14—After seven safecrackings, New York police commissioner cancels all vacations and orders captains to sleep in their stations.

May 21—Chicago's city council votes to oppose use of city funds to enforce Prohibition.

– Wealthy Chicagoans are reported hiring private policemen to guard their homes.

July 26—Long Island residents plan vigilance committee.

August 11—American Bar Association advocates banning private ownership of handguns.

October 6—U.S. attorney general holds that national Prohibition law applies even to U.S. vessels on the high seas.

December 15—Crestwood, New York, announces vigilance committee to halt robberies.

December 23—New York police commissioner mobilizes all police forces with extra automobile squad to repel influx of western outlaws.

December 30—Five prisoners flogged in Wilmington, Delaware.

1923

January 2—New York district attorney declares crime wave has been ended by speedy trials.

February 13—President of U.S. Revolver Association supports passage of law regulating sale of firearms.

April 1—Scores of automobiles added to New York police fleet, and entire department, including inspectors, ordered on patrol duty as holdups and burglaries increase.

May 4—Rebelling against the Volstead law, the New York legislature repeals its own Prohibition Enforcement Act; other states begin to do the same.

July 25—Muskegon, Michigan, judge advises he will begin jailing wives in home brew cases.

August 2—Bronx jewelers organize to train in use of firearms.

November 16—New York police commissioner abolishes lunch hour, suspends all vacations and time off, and orders extra duty for every policeman in effort to check crime wave.

1924

January 8–13—New York police commissioner plans drive against "undesirables" coming from Philadelphia; city declared clear of known criminals after arrest of 250 (none, however, from Philadelphia); magistrate denounces spectacular raids that result in few prosecutions.

January 16—New York police commissioner calls for federal ban on pistols similar to his city's Sullivan law.

March 13—New York police commissioner urges Civitan Club to support federal bill to tax handguns out of existence; Boy Scouts will join police in ridding city of gunmen.

March 19—New York Kiwanis Club luncheon told that half of Sing Sing's inmates are younger than twenty-five.

April 20—Responding to crime wave, Chicago's police chief orders all policemen to carry their revolvers in a position for quick use.

April 13–21—Long Island firemen will aid police by blocking roads after holdups; Suffolk and Nassau county firemen will organize as emergency police and carry guns.

May 7—Prudential Life Insurance Co. releases statistics indicating 10,000 murders in U.S. in 1923.

May 10—Attorney General Harlan Fiske Stone promotes J. Edgar Hoover to acting director of the Justice Department's Bureau of Investigation.

July 1—At the urging of the International Association of Chiefs of Police, Congress authorizes the

THE "FIVE-STATE PACT"

The First Experiment in Cooperative Crime Control

Just as the Constitution favored state militias over a strong peacetime army, it also made crime control the responsibility of state and local authorities, and for essentially the same reason: fear that a national police or military force could become an instrument of political tyranny. The Palmer "Red Raids" after World War I and the excesses of federal Prohibition agents in the 1920s were reminders of this possibility. Even when the 1932 kidnap-murder of the Lindbergh baby forced Congress to pass a federal kidnapping law, President Herbert Hoover's attorney general warned an outraged public that "you are never going to end the crime problem in this country by having the federal government step in."

The Roosevelt administration took the opposite position, declaring violent crime to be a national problem requiring a national solution; or one beyond the capabilities of localized law enforcement and requiring, at the very least, federal coordination of local efforts. Mindful of fears over too much centralized authority, President Roosevelt, U.S. Attorney General Homer Cummings, and especially J. Edgar Hoover, director of the Justice Department's Bureau of Investigation, discarded the idea of an "American Scotland Yard" (thoroughly misconstruing the role of Scotland Yard) as too radical and probably unconstitutional, but nevertheless created a modified version of it in what would later become the Federal Bureau of Investigation.

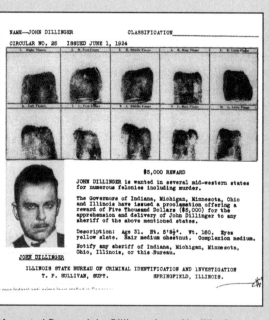

NAME—JOHN DILLINGER CLASSIFICATION________

CIRCULAR NO. 25 ISSUED JUNE 1, 1934

1. Right Thumb	2. R. Fore Finger	3. R. Middle Finger	4. R. Ring Finger	5. R. Little Finger
6. Left Thumb	7. L. Fore Finger	8. L. Middle Finger	9. L. Ring Finger	10. L. Little Finger

$5,000 REWARD

JOHN DILLINGER is wanted in several mid-western states for numerous felonies including murder.

The Governors of Indiana, Michigan, Minnesota, Ohio and Illinois have issued a proclamation offering a reward of Five Thousand Dollars ($5,000) for the apprehension and delivery of John Dillinger to any sheriff of the above mentioned states.

Description: Age 31. Ht. 5'8½". Wt. 160. Eyes yellow slate. Hair medium chestnut. Complexion medium.

Notify any sheriff of Indiana, Michigan, Minnesota, Ohio, Illinois, or this Bureau.

JOHN DILLINGER

ILLINOIS STATE BUREAU OF CRIMINAL IDENTIFICATION AND INVESTIGATION
T. P. SULLIVAN, SUPT. SPRINGFIELD, ILLINOIS.

A wanted flyer on John Dillinger, issued by Illinois, mentions four states but represents the first significant example of interstate police cooperation. The flyers were distributed by the Justice Department, with its bureaus listed on the back.

As part of Roosevelt's New Deal in law enforcement, the Justice Department quickly demonstrated the effectiveness of interstate crime control by cracking the sensational Urschel kidnapping case in about a month with a well-orchestrated investigation that covered some twenty-six states and immortalized George "Machine Gun" Kelly, a bootlegger whose machine gun was a gift from his wife. The hoopla over this success sold most Americans on the idea of a federal police force, but Hoover wisely (and politically) agreed that the role of the Bureau of Investigation should be limited to establishing national fingerprint files, a crime records repository, a state-of-the-art crime lab such as then existed in Chicago, a police training academy, and otherwise helping the state and local authorities coordinate their crime-control efforts. It would be strictly an "investigative agency."

Before Cummings managed to overcome state's-rights opposition to more federal anti-crime laws, Hoover's bureau contented itself with promoting interstate cooperation and offering its services as a central clearinghouse for information on interstate fugitives. This included reprinting and distributing "wanted" posters issued by the individual states, but listing on the reverse side the federal offices that could be contacted by any state that nabbed a fugitive wanted in another state. This was both a calculated courtesy and a nod to the idea of state sovereignty in matters of criminal-law enforcement, for Justice Department agents at the time could neither make arrests nor carry guns unless deputized by state or local authorities.

However, the violent crime that seemed to increase during the Depression (thanks partly to the FBI's inauguration of centralized recordkeeping) led several midwestern states to heed Justice Department admonitions and begin cooperating with one another. Early in 1934 Governors Horner of Illinois and Townsend of Indiana proposed a five-state "pact," inviting Michigan, Ohio, and Minnesota to join them in offering a $5,000 reward for the capture of the country's most notorious criminals, starting with John Dillinger (whose only federal offense to date was interstate car theft after his escape from an Indiana jail). Dillinger's subsequent "rampage" through the Midwest compelled a reluctant Congress to pass a series of national criminal laws that expanded federal police powers just enough to suit J. Edgar Hoover. He could conveniently ignore gangsters and racketeers as "consensual" criminals (in the strict legal sense) who were nearly impossible to convict, and instead would target "interstate" outlaws and kidnappers who stole property and people at gunpoint. But until Cummings obtained his new federal laws in the summer of 1934, the "wanted" posters most widely distributed that spring were eight-by-eight-inch "Identification Orders" resembling those of the states, but distributed nationally by the U.S. Department of Justice with Bureau of Identification offices listed on the back.

The "five-state pact" had became a four-state pact when Minnesota and Ohio opted out and Wisconsin opted in, but it represented the first time regional law enforcement officials relaxed their jurisdictional jealousies and grudgingly began working together, granting each other's police the authority to cross state lines in pursuit of fugitives. The FBI still described itself as a primarily investigative agency and at least technically deferred to local authorities unless a crime was already a federal violation, or if local authorities (usually to satisfy a clamoring public, and often with reluctance) would formally ask for FBI assistance in a particularly sensational or difficult case that usually involved its crime lab.

Postal Telegraph

SYI 1-171 4 EXTRA SPRINGFIELD ILL MAY 7 1105P

GOVERNOR PAUL V MCNUTT=

FRENCHLICK IND=

IN ORDER TO PROVIDE AN ADDITIONAL INCENTIVE THE FOR APPREHENSION OF THE EXCAPED CRIMINAL JOHN DILLINGER WILL YOU JOIN THE STATE OF ILLINOIS IN OFFERING A JOINT REWARD FOR HIS CAPTURE STOP ILLINOIS STANDS READY TO OFFER ONE THOUSAND DOLLARS THE MAXIMUM ALLOWED BY OUR LAW AND IF THE STATES OF INDIANA OHIO WISCONSIN AND MINNESOTA WILL JOIN US A TOTAL OF FIVE THOUSAND DOLLARS WILL BE THE REWARD TO THE PERSON OR PERSONS CAPTURING HIM AND TURNING HIM OVER TO A DESIGNATED OFFICER IN EITHER OF OUR STATES STOP I AM MAKING THE SAME SUGGESTION TO THE GOVERNORS OF THE OTHER STATES STOP IT WILL BE WORTH THIS COMBINED REWARD TO PLACE DILLINGER IN CUSTODY STOP SO LONG AS HE IS AT LARGE THE WELFARE AND PEACE OF OUR CITIZENS ARE MENACED AND THE ENFORECEMENT OF LAW AND ORDER IS THREATENED STOP WHILE THIS JOINT OFFER MAY BE UNUSUAL THE CIRCUMSTANCES JUSTIFY IT STOP I URGE YOUR SERIOUS CONSIDERATION OF THIS PLAN AND YOUR PROMPT REPLY=

HENRY HORNER GOVERNOR.

Before Cummings's "Twelve-Point Program" of federal crime control struggled into law, minus some of its points, the bureau had demonstrated its approval of the "Pact" by issuing the state posters and I.O.s listing the jointly offered reward money. After Cummings's laws were passed, the eight-by-eight-inch I.O.s were redesigned as "Division of Investigation" cards with the familiar block of fingerprints above the mug shots, with federal offices now officially on the reverse.*

*At the time of Dillinger's death, the bureau (since renamed the division) was in the process of moving its headquarters. Thus, the original I.O.s listed the Hurley-Wright Building as the FBI's Washington office. Hoover had since received a privately made death mask of the desperado, which led to an investigation establishing that at least three had been made: by the Dental Reliance Co., which wanted to demonstrate its "moulage" technique to the bureau; by the Worsham College of Embalming Science, whose mask was confiscated by officious police and given to the Goddard crime lab (but not before another was made in the cops' absence and smuggled out, only to disappear); and a crude version by a fast-talking letter-waver, whose mask ended up in the possession of a Chicago collector.

After satisfying himself that no local laws were conspicuously broken, Hoover managed to get additional mileage out of Dillinger by means of the mask sent to him unsolicited by the Reliance people. Many state and local law enforcement officials wanted copies, and Hoover was pleased to supply them, along with the original Dillinger I.O.s from a post-mortem print run, the back of which this time listed the FBI's Washington office as the Justice Department Building.

Some of these evidently were sent to the Chicago office for local promotional purposes and ended up in the hands of Melvin Purvis, who probably also had some originals. In any case, after quitting the bureau, Purvis's 1936 book *American Agent* went through more than one undesignated printing, some of which display the Dillinger I.O. with an obvious dust speck on the face, and some without, just to confound the collecting community.

Many years later—probably starting in the 1960s—the FBI assembled an entire package of reprinted I.O. cards for tourists, with differently screened mug shots and most of them overstamped with a dark-red CANCELLED.

Justice Department to establish an identification division within the BOI as a national fingerprint repository.

July 13—Indianapolis police announce 261 arrests in campaign to check local crime wave.

August 16—U.S. Post Office plans to order 3,000 armored cars to protect against mail robberies.

November 2—*New York Times* publishes a special feature on the U.S., naming it the most lawless nation.

November 14—Chicago's Sears, Roebuck & Co. will discontinue sale of firearms.

November 29—St. Louis police mobilize against new crime wave.

December 10—J. Edgar Hoover named permanent director of Bureau of Investigation.

– In Chicago, Illinois Federation of Women's Voters is told that the city needs to hang criminals to discourage crime.

December 21—Press reports that the U.S. Supreme Court has overturned murder conviction of Chinese student subjected to police "third degree."

1925

January 6—At New York City dinner for Committee of One Thousand for Law Enforcement, Chicago's Mayor Dever declares that strict enforcement of Prohibition has remedied the city's crime wave.

January 8—Chicago and Cook County Bankers Association plan burglar-alarm system and armed motorcycle patrols.

January 10—Chicago Crime Commission cites crime figures for 1924 to support charges of police demoralization.

January 16—Chicago's police chief orders cops to put a stop to crime or quit the force.

January 17—Brooklyn judges blame crime and violence on the evil influence of improper films.

January 19—St. Louis businessman personally offers rewards to policemen who capture or kill robbers.

February 10—New York state senator introduces bill extending maximum armed robbery term from twenty to forty years.

March 2—U.S. Supreme Court affirms "probable

cause" as granting right to search vehicles without warrant.

March 3—Congress passes law permitting seizure of vessels and vehicles used in violation of national Prohibition.

March 10—Vermont restricts police use of "third degree."

March 24—New York police, ordered to arrest all known crooks, jail ninety-eight during first day of roundup.

March 25—Delaware legislature votes to retain whipping post.

April 3—New York, Chicago, and San Francisco experiment with system for wiring criminals' pictures between cities.

April 16—Michigan state senate discusses establishment of whipping posts.

April 28—Illinois senate passes bill providing for hanging armed burglars.

May 10—Illinois senator plans bill to disinherit murderers.

May 27—New York chief magistrate blames crime on pistols, narcotics, and automobiles.

June 15—Chicago police arrest 400 in roundup of suspected gangsters.

June 23—Retired General Smedley Butler, as new public safety director, declares "war to the finish" on crime in Philadelphia.

July 5—Chicago and Cook County Bankers Association offers $2,500 for each bandit killed.

July 27—Chicago Crime Commission Director H. B. Chamberlin declares crime conditions beyond control.

August 5—Chicago's Mayor Dever appeals to residents to correct impression of city's criminality and general lawlessness.

August 12—National Crime Commission is privately organized in New York City to promote police professionalism and crime laboratories, gather uniform crime statistics and study punitive measures in various states; includes future president Franklin D. Roosevelt, Supreme Court Chief Justice Charles Evans Hughes, former Illinois Governor Frank Lowden, and former Secretary of War Newton Baker.

September 13—New York State Supreme Court Justice Smith supports repeal of law that juries may not infer guilt from refusal of defendants to testify.

September 23—Milwaukee Clearing House offers $2,500 reward each for dead bank robbers and $1,000 each for live ones.

October 6—Boston post office fortified in response to citywide crime wave.

October 25—New York City judge urges alarm sirens in stores and arming of employees.

November 4—New York City police commissioner announces new "anti-bandit patrols" using nine radio-dispatched cars specially equipped with Thompson submachine guns, rifles, bombs, and shotguns (a revival of an unsuccessful 1922 "Control of the Road" plan using radio-

In 1925, New York inaugurated its police Emergency Service equipped for both riot control and rescue work.

dispatched motorcycles with sidecar-mounted submachine guns).

November 18—Former U.S. Attorney General George W. Wickersham calls for centralized crime records bureau.

December 4—Kings County grand jury recommends life sentences for burglars.

December 30—New York chief magistrate urges ban on toy pistols.

1926

February 3—New York state assemblyman calls for adoption of whipping posts.

February 5—New Jersey legislature passes bill restricting sale of machine guns; subcommittee of National Crime Commission meets in New York to draft law banning private ownership of machine guns.

February 6—New York's Citizens' Crime Conference adopts plan to wear silver buttons supporting the Marshall Stillman Movement, an organization for rehabilitating criminals, to ward off holdup men.

February 7—New York officials call Marshall Stillman button plan ridiculous and no deterrent to robbers.

March 1—New York fire chief submits plan to mayor for police telegraphic intercommunication system like fire department's.

March 2—Chicago newspapers publish photographs of State's Attorney Robert Crowe and other prominent officials attending banquet for the notorious Genna brothers.

March 4—New York police commissioner urges parole boards be suspended during crime-wave emergencies.

March 18—Police commissioner vetoes New York's annual police parade, declaring policemen need to fight crime.

April 2—Milwaukee sets example for speedy justice by catching, convicting, and sentencing four robbers in one day.

April 6—U.S. authorities report that 35 percent of federal prisoners are drug-law violators.

April 9—Bankers associations of Illinois, Indiana, Wisconsin, Minnesota, and Iowa claim their concerted drive against bandits reduced robberies by 80 percent in 1925.

April 15—Civitan Club Crime Committee declares that comfortable prison life is alluring to criminals.

April 16—Chicago trial judge claims there are 118,000 unpunished murderers at large in the U.S.

April 24—New York state legislature ends session after passing twenty-five bills proposed by the Baumes Legislative Crime Commission to introduce new laws and law-enforcement policies, tighten parole practices, and drastically increase existing criminal penalties, including life prison sentences for fourth offenders who commit even nonviolent crimes.

May 8—President of New York's Holmes Electric Protective Co. suggests crime would be reduced by jailing crime victims who tempt thieves with displays of goods.

May 20—Supreme Court Justice Black proposes death penalty for perjury in murder cases.

June 19—Representative J. E. Miller introduces bill to ban interstate transportation of crime movies on grounds they breed criminality.

Cincinnati police will be equipped with cameras.

July 20—International Secret Service Association condemns police use of "third degree" methods to gain confessions.

July 29—Average age of Sing Sing prisoner drops to twenty-two.

August 29—Newspapers report on "camera gun" that takes a picture of whatever it shoots.

August 31—Governor Ferguson of Texas discovered to have issued 2,333 clemency proclamations in twenty months.

September 1—New York police will require each man on force to carry copy of monthly bulletin to help identify suspects.

September 16—State penitentiary at Trenton, New Jersey, erecting siren to warn city of prison breaks.

October 20—New Jersey official advocates use of machine guns and radio to combat crime wave.

Criminal Identification

From Bertillon Method to Fingerprints

With evidence as arcane as DNA routinely used in present-day trials, it may seem strange that an identification technique as generally simple and as nearly infallible as fingerprints should have taken so long to find acceptance in the American legal community. But well into the 1920s both the police and the public considered crook-catching one of the manly arts, like shooting—more a craft than a science—and the average juror found it hard to accept that something so trifling as the swirls on a fingertip could be enough to identify an entire human being.

Fingerprints had long been used as a kind of signature, though it isn't clear whether the patterns were understood to be unique to an individual or mainly symbolic. In any case, they lacked forensic significance until the middle of the nineteenth century, and then the absence of any system of classification limited their value in police work.

Instead, police and penal authorities made do with the laborious and imperfect Bertillon method, developed in the 1870s by a French anthropologist who sought to identify adult individuals by means of photographs and a dozen or so body measurements. At best, the system served no investigative purpose, but only provided an improvement over name and general physical description for identifying people already in custody.

Even when recognized as individually unique, fingerprints still were employed mainly for identification, and thus made their way into the U.S. legal system first by way of prisons as an improvement over the Bertillon system. The shortcomings of that method had become glaringly apparent in 1903 when officials at Leavenworth refused to believe that a newly arrived inmate named Will West was not a veteran of their pen. Records showed the previous incarceration of a William West, whose photograph

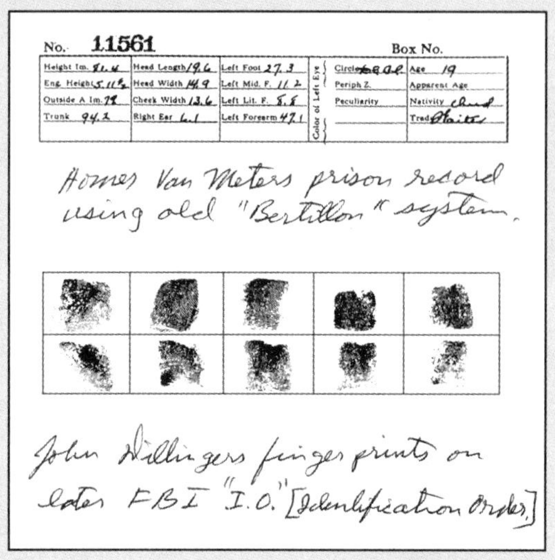

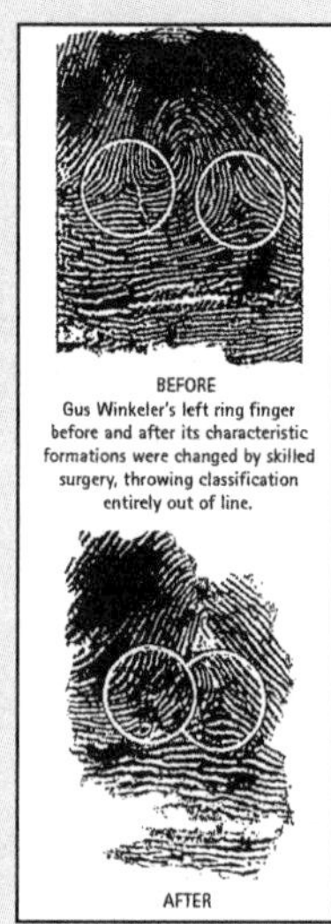

Gus Winkeler's left ring finger before and after its characteristic formations were changed by skilled surgery, throwing classification entirely out of line.

John Dillinger's efforts to obliterate his fingerprints were conspicuously unsuccessful, but mobster Gus Winkeler transformed his with a surgical procedure and Alvin Karpis *[see p. 450]* *had his permanently removed by scalpel and skin replacement that troubled customs authorities when he was eventually released from Alcatraz and deported to Canada.*

and Bertillon measurements seemed to identify him as the same man. When officials bothered to check, they discovered that William West was still in their prison.

The almost impossible coincidence of two criminals being nearly identical in age, appearance, body measurements, and names, but with different fingerprints, blew a hole in the Bertillon system that its defenders could not patch. Only habit and technological inertia had American police departments still measuring culprits with calipers for another quarter century, resisting adoption of a fingerprint classification system devised some years earlier by Britain's Sir Edward Richard Henry, by then commissioner of London's metropolitan police. His was an improvement on even earlier systems developed by criminalists in several countries more scientifically inclined than the U.S. It was not until 1911 that an appellate court in Illinois deemed fingerprints admissible as evidence, leaving the credibility of expert witnesses up to the jury.

When science finally took this country by storm in the 1920s, the Henry system, with refinements, was adopted and promoted by J. Edgar Hoover's Bureau of Investigation, which flogged Congress into authorizing a national fingerprint repository in 1924. By the 1930s, "scientific crime detection" had taken on the proportions of a fad, aided and abetted by Hoover's new G-men, who had "borrowed" the techniques of Chicago's post-Massacre lab of Calvin Goddard, and soon the bureau was fighting the country's first "War on Crime" with microscopes, as well as machine guns. Local authorities, whose virtual autonomy had allowed them to combine a modest amount of crime control with consummate corruption, had no choice but to go along. How much the public's sudden enthusiasm for "crime labs" was influenced by Mark Twain's fictional promotion of fingerprinting and the test-tube performances of Sherlock Holmes is anybody's guess.

The Development of Fingerprinting

Both the Romans and the Chinese used fingerprints for some legal and identification purposes during the first century A.D., but their systematic use seems to have awaited improved methods of magnification. In fourteenth-century Persia, various official papers had fingerprints, and one doctor, a government official, speculated that no two fingerprints were exactly alike.

1684–86—Using the newly developed microscope, University of Bologna anatomy Professor Marcello Malpighi comments on "certain elevated ridges" forming "loops and spirals" on the tips of fingers, but apparently considered these to be of mainly academic interest.

1823—In a treatise published at the University of Breslau, anatomy professor Johannes Purkinje notes the diversity of ridge patterns on fingertips and divides them into nine categories, still without recognizing this as having any practical value.

1858—In his district of Bengal, India, British administrative officer Sir William James Herschel decides that natives should affix their fingerprints, as well as signatures to contracts, mainly as a touch of ceremony to increase their sense of obligation. He further determines that such prints do not change with age and begins their first large-scale use to prevent fraudulent collection of army pay.

1877—Eventually noting that prints appear unique to each individual, Herschel requests permission to fingerprint prisoners as a means of identification. His superiors reject the idea, possibly because Herschel proposes no convenient system of classification.

1880—After taking up the study of "skin-furrows" and while stationed at a hospital in Tokyo, Dr. Henry Faulds comments in the English scientific journal *Nature* on the practical use of fingerprints for identifying prisoners. He recommends a thin film of printers ink for use as a transfer medium and demonstrates fingerprints' crime-solving potential by describing his use of latent prints to identify a culprit who had been nipping from the hospital's stock of ethyl alcohol. He also devises a form of classification, which he sends to the aging Charles Darwin, who explains he can be of no assistance but will forward Faulds's work to his cousin, Sir Francis Galton.

1882—Gilbert Thomas, a U.S. government geologist working in New Mexico, makes the first known use of fingerprints in this country by applying his own to commissary orders as a forgery deterrent.

1883—Mark Twain publishes *Life on the Mississippi,* in which one episode relates the identification of a murderer by his thumbprint. Eleven years later, in his novel *Pudd'nhead Wilson,* Twain will stress the uniqueness of fingerprints and even use them as evidence in a fictional court case.

1891—Argentina will adopt fingerprinting as an official means of criminal identification, using a classification system devised by police official Juan Vucetich (sometimes spelled Vucetitich) and based on the British studies of Charles Darwin's cousin, Sir Francis Galton. The following year, an Argentine court case results in what may be the first murder conviction based on fingerprints left at the scene of a crime.

1892—Galton's extensive studies of what is becoming known as "dactylography" are reported in his landmark book *Finger Prints,* which confirms the uniqueness and permanence of prints and proposes a system of classification.

1901—England and Wales officially adopt fingerprints as a means of criminal identification, and Galton's system is simplified by Sir Edward Richard Henry to make it more useful in police investigations.

1902—Dr. Henry P. DeForest, American fingerprint pioneer and chief medical examiner for the New York Civil Service

Criminal Anthropology

Long after phrenology had lost the support of the scientific community, the belief persisted that there still must be some correlation between criminal behavior and physical abnormality. This seemed obvious to the general public, accustomed to seeing newspaper photographs of thugs captured by police and not looking their best, and cartoon caricatures of hoodlums with low foreheads and big chins.

But if physiologists rejected the original theories of the Italian Cesare Lombroso, who later doubted them himself but still qualifies as criminology's pioneer, they were on the right track in suspecting that some criminal behavior might be associated with brain abnormalities. Thus the brains of John Dillinger and other notorious criminals were sometimes removed for study, without yielding any useful information. The technology of the times was not

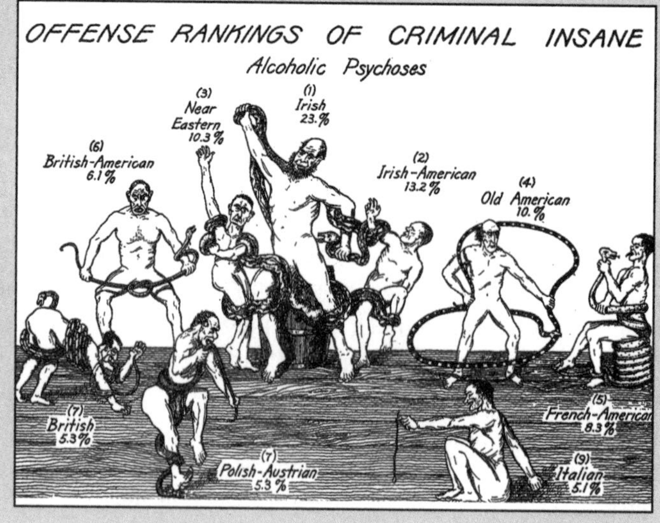

As late as 1938, the prestigious Harvard University Press published a book purporting to categorize criminals according to their facial features and their crimes by nationality and insanity.

Commission, institutes this country's first systematic use of prints to prevent applicants from having more-qualified substitutes take their tests.

1903—The New York State prison system becomes the first criminal-justice institution to adopt fingerprinting for the purpose of inmate identification. Meanwhile, the Bertillon system suffers an eventually mortal blow when Leavenworth authorities discover they have two unrelated but otherwise identical men, Will and William West.

1904—Motivated by the idea of "progress" fostered by the World Exposition in St. Louis and its Scotland Yard display, that city's police department becomes the first U.S. law-enforcement agency to establish a fingerprint bureau. Coincidentally, the federal penitentiary at Leavenworth, Kansas, expands its fingerprint operations to include

sufficiently advanced to detect inconspicuous defects, giving support to the "nurture" school of criminology before researchers developed more sophisticated tests that found many criminals to have brain disorders of one kind or another.

The inability of pathologists to find obvious abnormalities led to a brief revival of Lombrosian theories under the more scientific-sounding nomenclature of "criminal anthropology." A leading proponent of this new version of phrenology was an American anthropologist named E. A. Hooten, who somehow persuaded Harvard University Press to publish his hefty volume titled *Crime and the Man* as late as 1939. Hooten took body measurements of thousands of inmates in prisons around the country and came up with some of the most bizarre findings ever to see print, especially in the academic community.

Concluding flatly that "the primary cause of crime is biological inferiority," he did not stop with obvious physical characteristics but went on to attribute different criminal propensities to different nationalities in what now would be a monument to political incorrectness, especially concerning race. Today the book reads like pseudoscientific gibberish, and its illustrations would cause professorial heart failure, but there probably exists no better reflection of attitudes, prejudices, and preconceptions that were widely accepted by the American public and lawmakers of the times.

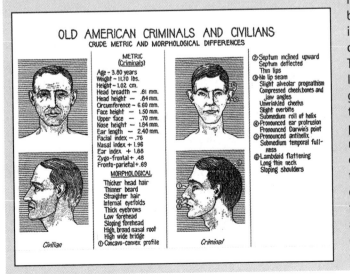

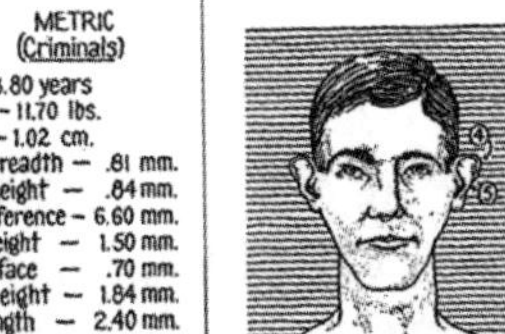
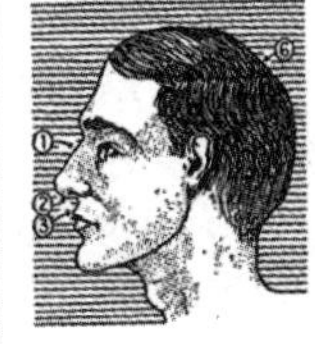

a central file and clearinghouse for the free exchange of prints among state and municipal police forces, some of which are slow to take advantage of the service; and later a National Bureau of Criminal Identification with a similar service is established by the International Association of Chiefs of Police.

1905—The U.S. Army institutes the first military fingerprint program, with the Navy following in 1907 and the Marine Corps in 1908.

1911—New York City reportedly is the first U.S. police department to secure a conviction (that of a burglar) based on fingerprints.

1915—International Association for Criminal Identification founded in Oakland, California.

1918—Edmond Locard declares that twelve points of similarity are enough to establish positive identification, although other countries have not adopted this number and it is now considered arbitrary even in the U.S.

1924—The Leavenworth case of the two Will Wests persuades an increasing number of law-enforcement agencies that fingerprints not only are useful for recording captured crooks but also have much potential for identifying, pursuing, and convicting perpetrators. On July 1 an act of Congress creates an Identification Division within the Justice Department's Bureau of Investigation, which consolidates records from Leavenworth and the International Association of Chiefs of Police into the first nationwide fingerprint repository. Many police departments continue to use the Bertillon system, partly because it incorporates photographs, but since photography also complements fingerprinting, most departments eventually convert to prints and photos.

1928—The robbery of a bank in Lamar, Colorado, on May 23, leads to the identification of Jake Fleagle on the basis of a single fingerprint, according to the federal Division of Investigation (the future FBI).

1932—On March 1, the U.S. joins several other countries in establishing an international fingerprint exchange.

1933—The Bureau of Investigation creates a special Latent Fingerprint Section for the examination of inked prints from the divisions of prisons and police departments and of latent prints obtained from objects and crime scenes. A Civil Identification Section is added on November 10 of that year, and by 1939 the number of fingerprint cards is approaching ten million.

1934—Oskaloosa, Iowa, to foster the new technology, becomes the first U.S. city to invite residents to voluntarily submit to fingerprinting.

1936—After a talk by an FBI official, Watertown, South Dakota, becomes the first U.S. city to institute fingerprinting of its senior high school students.

1946—During World War II, the civil fingerprint records of aliens, military personnel, and defense industry employees greatly exceeds the number of arrest prints, and on January 31, 1946, the Federal Bureau of Investigation (as it is now called) announces, with considerable fanfare, that its grand total has reached 100 million.

October 27—The Post Office announces it will supply the Marine mail guards with 250 Thompsons, making that branch of the armed forces the first to acquire the submachine gun, which it will soon use in Nicaragua against the Sandinista rebels.

November 1—U.S. Supreme Court holds that a violator of the Prohibition law may be tried in federal and state courts for the same offense.

November 2—Former Alabama prison warden charged with murder of inmate who apparently died from being plunged into hot and cold water as punishment.

December 25—Cleveland issues police "shoot to kill" orders to combat new crime wave.

December 27—Chicago police plan to acquire thirty-four Thompson submachine guns.

December 30—Sing Sing officials quoted as claiming judges are reducing felony charges to misdemeanors to circumvent harsh Baumes Laws.

1927

January 5—American Railway Express advises it will cooperate with authorities in stopping firearm shipments to New York City.

February 5—National Crime Commission drafting legislation to stop sale of machine guns to civilians.

February 22—National Crime Commission proposes uniform state law drastically restricting sale of handguns.

April 6—Michigan House of Representatives passes bill favoring whipping post for bank robbers.

May 10—New federal law bars sending firearms through U.S. mail.

May 16—U.S. Supreme Court rules that profits from illicit liquor dealing are not exempt from federal income tax.

August 16–28—Chicago subjects gunmen to sanity tests. "Machine Gun" Jack McGurn among first tested; Frank and Vincent McErlane seek release from psychiatric ward on habeas corpus writs; "Polack Joe" Saltis and "Dingbat" Oberta attempt to avoid tests.

November 19—Though the term "racket" probably originated in New York, Cook County prosecutor credited with coining the word "racketeers" to describe Chicago criminals who prey on businessmen.

1928

January 8—Chicago police plan to take motion pictures of crooks at lineups for identification purposes.

January 13—More than 1,500 out of 2,000 Prohibition agents fail to pass Civil Service examination.

January 31—Increasing criticism of Baumes Laws in recent months leads New York City assemblyman to introduce a bill to modify "fourth felony" section.

March 27—Michigan convict serving life for illegal possession of one pint of gin wins right to appeal his sentence.

March 30—Lake County, Indiana, sheriff acquires airplane for pursuit of bandits.

March 31—Supporters of Chicago's Mayor Thompson protest efforts of federal agents to track down bombers during so-called Pineapple Primary.

April 3—Federal agents ignore Chicago officials and investigate bombings of homes of a senator and a judge.

May 8—New York City Bar Association asks New York State Crime Commission to investigate police brutality in use of "third degree."

May 9—Chicago Bar Association files criminal court petition charging State's Attorney Crowe's faction with murder, kidnapping, assault, bombing, and vote thievery.

July 27—American Bar Association formally opposes Baumes Law "fourth offense" provision.

August 14—Bronx County Jail report reveals majority of prisoners held for violent crimes are between sixteen and twenty-one years old.

August 28–30—Philadelphia grand jury finds

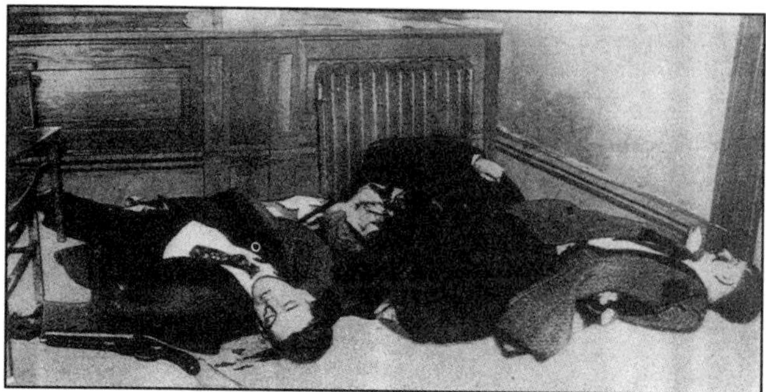

Tipped off in advance, four Chicago cops awaited the arrival of three young gunmen bent on terrorizing some union officials and simply blew them away.

bootleggers deposited $10 million in city banks over past year; district attorney charges alliance between Max "Boo Boo" Hoff and Chicago's Al Capone.

September 4–28—Philadelphia's mayor gives police department twenty-four hours to "clean up" the city, but speakeasies merely suspend business until after raids; district attorney reports bootlegger bribes to police reach $2 million yearly; twenty-three policemen at one station jailed, more arrests predicted.

October 1–31—In Philadelphia, former police captain and two detectives indicted on charges of extorting saloon keepers; more police indicted, 4,800 transferred; entire police force ordered to fill out wealth questionnaires; mayor suspends twenty-one police officials.

October 18—The Special Intelligence Unit of the Internal Revenue Service opens a file on Al Capone for possible violations of income tax laws.

November 3—Chicago grand jury recommends that polling places be guarded by armed volunteers.

November 8—Philadelphia police "bandit division" formed; prevention squad of 200 motorcycle policemen planned.

December 2—After two burglaries, owner of Haverstrow, New York, garage purchases guard bears.

December 5—Twenty-three Sicilian gangsters from around the country are arrested by local police while holding a "grand council" at Cleveland's Statler Hotel to discuss the ongoing war over leadership of Chicago's Unione Siciliana.

December 8—Prohibition Bureau reports 75,307 arrests and 58,813 convictions under the Volstead Act since January 1920.

December 26—New York police commissioner revives "strong-arm" squad and employs vagrancy law to rid city of thugs; courts become jammed.

1929

January 1–3—New York police "strong-arm" squads raid sixty dens with orders to rough up gangsters; criminals reported leaving city for Chicago; Chicago promises to return them "in boxes."

January 5—To discourage influx of New York and Chicago gangsters, Detroit commissioner announces bounty of a $10 gold piece for each criminal killed by his police.

January 6—Federal and state raiding party of 150 seizes control of Chicago Heights and arrests entire city police force for corruption.

January 9—White Plains, New York, directs that bandits be shot on sight.

January 10—Bill introduced in Missouri legislature providing death penalty for bombers.

January 13—Hammonton, New Jersey, begins drive against gangsters; nets thirty-four traffic offenders.

January 17—Indianapolis bill would make gun carrying punishable by whipping.

January 20–21—One hundred Chicago police squads arrest 2,600 in record raid, bringing total to 3,994.

January 21—New York City police commissioner plans to close 996 crime nests by naming owners.

January 30—Michigan state senator drafts bill to curb publication of crime news.

January 31—Memphis police chief issues "shoot to kill" orders to check local crime wave.

February 3—Police commissioner claims New York City gunmen have been dispersed.

February 15—Cook County state's attorney announces $25,000 reward for information leading to the arrest of people responsible for the St. Valentine's Day Massacre.

February 18—Cook County Board of Commissioners disallows state's attorney's $25,000 reward; Chicago authorities make 255 detectives account for their activities at time of St. Valentine's Day Massacre.

February 20—Civic leaders and state officials subscribe funds and persuade Chicago police commissioner to offer Massacre reward money of $100,000.

February 23—New York City resident charged under Sullivan Law after showing pistol he had wrested from would-be robber.

February 24—Chicago police link St. Valentine's Day Massacre to old Egan's Rats gang of St. Louis but fail to pursue leads.

February 25—New York City's police commissioner declares that "strong-arm" methods will keep New York from becoming a second Chicago.

February 26—Major F. D. Silloway transferred from Prohibition Bureau in Chicago after charging that Massacre may have been committed by local police.

February 28—New York plans alarm signals combined with traffic lights.

March 2—New York City's police commissioner asks for legislation enabling police to arrest, fingerprint, and arraign young "loafers" and "potential" criminals.

March 12—Major Silloway dismissed from Prohibition Bureau.

March 25—New York approves $277,000 for new, fast police cars.

Apri1 19—Thief receives life sentence under New York's Baumes Laws for fourth offense of stealing one dollar.

April 24—After suspending days off for police, Philadelphia public safety director issues "shoot to kill" orders to end crime outbreak.

May 1—For the first time in recent years, New York newspapers report no homicides during the week ended April 27.

May 3—Chicago grand jury indicts 124 in one week, including city officials, six police captains and numerous gangsters in connection with slot machine racket said to yield $10 million a year.

May 16—Al Capone, leaving first nationwide "organized crime" conference in Atlantic City, submits to arrest, believed prearranged, on weapons charge in Philadelphia and receives, to Capone's annoyance, the maximum one-year jail sentence.

May 20—President Herbert Hoover creates National Commission on Law Observance and Enforcement under chairmanship of former Attorney General George W. Wickersham. Known as the Wickersham Commission, the group is the first to hold hearings throughout the country and develop voluminous statistics on Prohibition-era crime and corruption. It did not conclude that national Prohibition should be repealed.

June 2—Detroit announces that its new radio-equipped police cars, part of the country's first full-scale police radio system, enabled ninety-six captures during the month of May.

August 17—New York City Pistol License Bureau reports issuing 32,400 gun permits.

September 5—New York City's police commissioner tells New York Governor Franklin Roosevelt that Baumes Laws are too harsh.

September 21—Philadelphia police plan to establish radio station and use machine guns to combat banditry.

September 22—Governor Roosevelt requests change in Baumes Law, which has mandated life terms for fourth offenders.

October 13—Uniform plan for recording crime statistics outlined by National Commission on Law Observance and Enforcement (Wickersham Commission).

Chicago's "Scientific Crime Detection Laboratory"

Calvin Goddard and the Country's First Full-service Crime Lab

The St. Valentine's Day Massacre exceeded any gangland killings before or after February 14, 1929, throwing the city into a frenzy of police activity, awakening the Chicago Crime Commission, and dismaying civic-minded businessmen who were tired of hearing their city called the world's "gangster capital." Coroner Herman Bundesen, wielding more authority than any medical examiner before or since, virtually took charge of the case and immediately selected a "blue-ribbon commission" of leading citizens who became part of a special grand jury that would attend a year's worth of hearings.

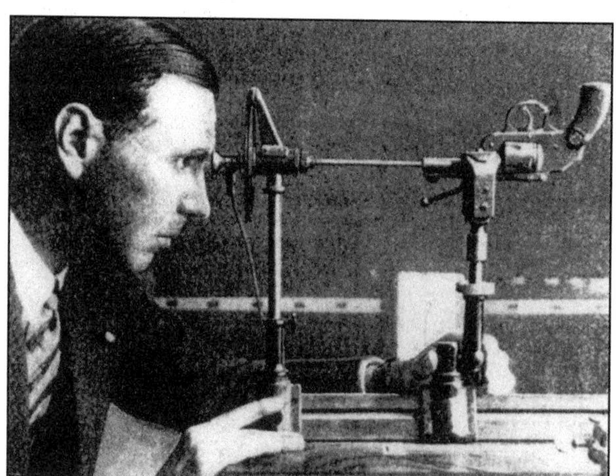

Calvin Goddard uses a "helixometer" to examine the rifling and powder residue of a revolver barrel.

The hearings accomplished as little as the police investigations—except in one respect. Bert Massey, vice president of the Colgate Palmolive Peet Co., had heard of a New York "criminalist" named Calvin Goddard who had tried to introduce the new science of forensic ballistics into the court case of Nicola Sacco and Bartolomeo Vanzetti, the self-described anarchists who were accused of a 1920 payroll robbery in Braintree, Massachusetts, in which a paymaster and a guard were killed. Microscopically examining the smallest striations on the death bullets and bullets fired from the guns of both defendants, he established that the Colt .32 automatic found on Sacco at the time of his arrest, but not Vanzetti's .38 Harrington & Richardson revolver, had fired the fatal shots. Such "ballistics" evidence was too arcane for the court, and the jurors ignored it in favor of their prejudices against "anarchists" poised to destroy America. In 1927, both Sacco and Vanzetti fried.

Two years after that, the City of Chicago was too preoccupied with closing speakeasies and arresting "the usual suspects" to give much thought to science or to spending city funds on it. But Massey had been sufficiently impressed by Goddard's work that he enlisted support from Walter Olson, president of the Olson Rug Co., and they used their own funds to hire Goddard's services.* He immediately left his private laboratory in New York in the hands of two colleagues and began setting up an even more elaborate lab in Chicago to work on the Massacre. At Bundesen's suggestion—because the police themselves were still suspects—a Scientific Crime Detection Laboratory was soon established under the auspices of the Northwestern University Law School, between Chicago's famous Water Tower (a souvenir of the Great Chicago Fire) and the Lakefront.

Goddard's was a full-service laboratory, patterned partly after a lab set up five years earlier by August Vollmer in California and partly after laboratories long-established in several European countries. The Europeans were far ahead of the United States in most areas of forensic science; where they came up short was in ballistics. Their specialists (and Vollmer's, as well) had a basic understanding of the rifling marks on bullets, but for evaluation they still were wrapping slugs in tinfoil and trying to match them by studying the patterns with a magnifying glass. Goddard employed a new split-image comparison microscope developed by Phillip Gravelle, which actually was a pair of

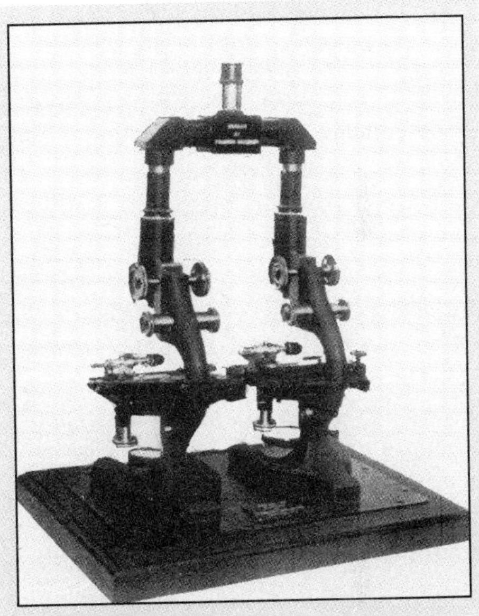

Goddard improved upon the comparison microscope, adapting it to examine bullets. The crime that secured his prominence in forensic ballistics was the Massachusetts case of Sacco and Vanzetti.

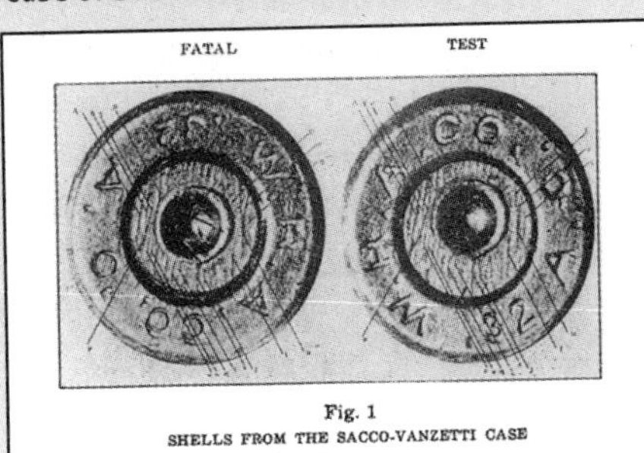

FATAL
TEST
Fig. 1
SHELLS FROM THE SACCO-VANZETTI CASE

*Goddard, trained as a physician who became a major and then a lieutenant colonel in World War I, already had an abiding interest in firearms and joined with Charles E. Waite, Phillip Gravelle, and John Fischer to form the privately owned Central Bureau of Forensic Ballistics in New York in 1922.

microscopes linked to a single eyepiece and had two independently rotating posts instead of a mirror-and-plate arrangement that would normally hold a slide. Bullets mounted with wax on each post could be slowly turned until the nearly invisible striations perfectly matched. Or failed to match, if the bullets came from different guns.

Goddard also used a "helixometer," newly developed by John Fischer based on the medical cytoscope, which could optically examine the interior of a gun barrel for residue, confirm its caliber, and determine the pitch of the rifling. Riflings differed among manufacturers and usually were unique to a particular brand, model, and caliber. Similarly, each gun left marks on the primers and casings of their empty shells that also were unique to a single weapon.

Using slugs taken from the Massacre victims and seventy shell casings picked up off the floor, Goddard first spent many hours explaining the theory and practice of forensic comparison, and then established to the satisfaction of the coroner's jury that two .45-caliber Thompson submachine guns had been used, one with a fifty-round drum and the other with a twenty-round "stick" (or straight) magazine.

Since two of the Massacre killers had worn police uniforms, Goddard obtained and test-fired all the Thompsons belonging to the police departments in Chicago and its suburbs. These were ruled out, and it was not until sheriff's police raided a house near St. Joseph, Michigan, in December 1929 and found an arsenal of ordnance that included two Thompson guns, that these were delivered to Goddard's laboratory for examination. They turned out to be the weapons used in the Massacre, and the man who possessed them—a Frederick Dane, who turned out to be Fred "Killer" Burke—had beat it out of town. The New York police were aware of Goddard's new crime lab and sent bullets taken from the body of local gangster Frankie Yale, which were found to have come from one of the Massacre guns. (A second machine gun used on Yale had been left in the car abandoned in Brooklyn by the killers.)

Besides advancing the science of forensic ballistics, coupled with shooting angles and distances, Goddard's laboratory soon was doing hair and fiber investigations, discovering new chemistries for use in serology (blood), and employing the new "moulage" technique to make rubber-and-plaster casts of footprints and tire tracks. The lab even utilized Leonarde Keeler's new "lie-detector" equipment, which could help police narrow their list of suspects (but which is still not admissible as courtroom evidence).

Additionally, in 1931, the Scientific Crime Detection Laboratory set up monthlong classes to train future criminalists, one of whom turned out to be a G-man who took his knowledge back to Washington, D.C., to help set up a national crime laboratory using the same equipment and technologies some eighteen months later. When FBI Director J. Edgar Hoover chewed out Melvin Purvis for doing business with the Chicago lab, and also refused to give the lab any credit, Goddard was burned up.

After the early financing by Massey and Olson, Northwestern University funded the work of laboratory, which was partly offset by charging for services performed. Even that was not enough to make the laboratory self-supporting, and during Chicago's World Fair of 1933, the lab had to set up an exhibit and sell souvenirs, such as matchbox-size containers enclosing a bullet and shell casing. The inscription read:

> THIS BOX contains a .45 caliber metal-jacketed Bullet and a .45 caliber Shell both fired from a Machine Gun taken from Chicago Gangsters.

In the early 1930s the laboratory outgrew its quarters and was moved from 469 Ohio Street to a nearby Northwestern building at 222 East Superior. Calvin Goddard went back to New York, leaving the lab in the hands of Fred E. Inbau and a well-trained civilian staff. By 1938 the Chicago police had lost its gangster-era stigma, purchased the facility for $25,000, including two chemical laboratories, a photography room and darkroom, its comparison microscopes and related equipment, a chamber outfitted with a "lie detector," a document examiner's room, a library that included some 1,000 books on scientific crime detection, and an exhibits room containing many hundreds of guns and other implements of crime.

Most of the civilian staff was employed to operate the police department's lab, to be located in the police headquarters building at 1121 North State Street, and when the department expressed a desire to replace these men with police personnel, Inbau began training officers who had at least some background in science.

One of the original crime lab's major and lasting contributions was its *American Journal of Police Science*, first published in January-February 1930 by the Northwestern University Press, and which since has been incorporated into the *Journal of Criminal Law and Criminology*, published originally in 1910 by Northwestern as an academic periodical and still widely circulated today.

After the St. Valentine's Day Massacre, members of the coroner's jury (below) congregate around a table with Calvin Goddard (seated at far left), who determined that two Thompson submachine guns had been used. Coroner Herman Bundesen is seated next to Goddard, and Chicago Police Commissioner William F. Russell is holding one of the Thompsons recovered at the house of Fred "Killer" Burke. At left are slugs removed from the victims' bodies and bullet casings linking the Thompsons and Burke to the crime.

November 1—Philadelphia police will make "talking motion pictures" of criminals' confessions.

November 22—Arkansas judge orders destruction of "electric chair" used by sheriff to force confessions.

November 24—Distrust of city's police lead sponsors of Calvin Goddard's new Scientific Crime Detection Laboratory to affiliate it with Chicago's Northwestern University Law School, which will work on criminal cases and offer classes in the forensic sciences.

December 4—Sing Sing Warden Lewis Lawes reports average age of bandits is nineteen.

December 9—Wife of Alabama inmate discloses use of "electric chair" by prison officials to force her husband's murder confession.

1930

January 11—New York and Chicago police departments agree to share ballistics information.

February 9—New York City police launch drive against crime that nets 3,000 arrests in a week, including 1,017 arrested in one night; few are held.

– Pennsylvania authorities report the state's new teletype system has resulted in 234 arrests.

February 15—Detroit police blame upsurge in crime on gangster exodus from Chicago.

February 27—Chicago Association of Commerce, sponsor of the Chicago Crime Commission, announces organization of a secret committee employing its own "detectives" who will seek to end the city's crime problem within six months. Dubbed the "Secret Six" by the press, the group will consist of prominent but anonymous business leaders and their hired guns who will not be known to the Chicago underworld.

March 22—Newark forms "Committee of One Thousand" to fight crime.

April 23—Chicago Crime Commission creates first official "public enemy" list of twenty-eight notorious hoodlums, which generates national publicity; Al Capone declared Public Enemy No. 1. City of Chicago, and other cities and states, will create lists of their own.

May 7—Maxim Co. announces it will discontinue the manufacture of firearm silencers.

May 26—U.S. Supreme Court holds that Volstead Act applies to sellers of beer or liquor but not to those who purchase it.

June 16—Chicago Police Commissioner William F. Russell and Captain John Stege forced by city administration to resign after murder of *Chicago Tribune* crime reporter Jake Lingle, who will turn out to have close ties with the Chicago mob. City Council will investigate police department corruption.

July 23—Michigan governor threatens to call in troops after crusading Detroit radio announcer becomes eleventh murder victim in ten days.

August 9—Chicago police establish one-way police radio communications similar to the system pioneered by Detroit. Initially, police calls will interrupt regular radio programming on station WGN, courtesy of Colonel Robert McCormick, also owner of the *Chicago Tribune*.

August-September—New York gangster "Legs" Diamond attempts to vacation in Europe, only to be constantly denied entry, arrested, driven from one country to another. Finally deported back to U.S. by Germany, he sues German authorities for illegal detention.

October 18—Success of police radio in Detroit and Chicago leads fifty-one cities to plan similar systems.

October 19—Chicago suburb of Evanston encourages arming of citizens to combat anticipated crime wave.

November 3—Al Capone supposedly offers to quit "racketeering" in exchange for a monopoly on supplying beer; his offer is rejected by Chief Justice McGoorty.

November 26—President Herbert Hoover calls for nationwide war on gangsters but opposes extension of federal laws, holding that crime control is the responsibility of the states.

December 26—Philadelphia declares itself rid of "racketeers."

1931

January 19—After two years of study, Wickersham Commission, appointed by President Hoover, recommends revision but not repeal of Prohibition.

February 28—Federal government reports intentions to prosecute gangsters under income tax laws.

March 22—Oklahoma's governor exiles three paroled convicts; three days later he states that use of the whipping post has substantially reduced crime in his state.

April 16—Michigan legislature considers bill to establish whipping posts.

May 8—American Law Institute opposes limitations on the right of the police to kill or wound criminals.

June 27—In Colorado, some thirty individuals file claims for the reward money offered for capture of the Fleagle Gang.

July 30—Recent killing of child and wounding of four others by "Mad Dog" Coll prompts New York's Mayor Jimmy Walker to support police instructions to "shoot to kill" gangsters; Patrolmen's Benevolent Association offers $10,000 reward for child's killers; *New York Daily News* planning offer of $5,000; Coll eventually acquitted.

July 31—Chicago Crime Commission designates an additional twenty-eight as "Public Enemies."

August 4—U.S. Attorney General Mitchell repeats President Hoover's contention that law enforcement is the responsibility of the states, not the federal government.

August 14—American Legion announces plans to "mobilize" 30,000 members on August 24 as a warning to gangsters.

August 22—Boston police superintendent declares a war against crime and instructs his men to "shoot to kill."

August 24—Twenty thousand New Yorkers attend anti-gang rally; radio equipment voted for police cars.

August 29—After major robbery and gun battle in which taxi drivers aided in bandit chase, New York citizen writes to suggest deputizing cabbies.

August 30—Two woodsmen from Maine declare they will come to New York to show police how to track gangsters.

September 11—New York judge proposes whipping post to deal with second offenders.

September 15—Newspapers report that New York Mayor Jimmy Walker, visiting England, tells Londoners that gangsters should be beaten by police.

September 18—Government reports racketeers and hoodlums rushing to pay income taxes after convictions. New York State probation authorities back Wickersham Commission's report condemning police use of "third degree."

October 17—Al Capone convicted of income tax evasion, fined $50,000, and sentenced to eleven years in prison.

October 21—Provision of New York State "public enemy" law, permitting arrest of anyone who associates with persons of "bad repute," faces constitutional challenge. Nine will later be freed on grounds that prosecution failed to prove unlawful intent.

December 20—Chicago Crime Commission optimistically declares that its year's work has resulted in the crushing of organized crime.

December 26—Chicago police report the slaying of seventy "outlaws" during the past year.

1932

March 25—Frank J. Loesch of the Chicago Crime Commission reports earlier secret meeting with Al Capone, who agrees to "police" the city for primary and presidential elections.

April 5—Increasing opposition to the harshness of New York State Baumes Laws leads Governor Franklin Roosevelt to sign bill reducing the mandatory life sentence for fourth offenders to a minimum of fifteen years.

April 9—New York City Boy Scouts declare "war on crime."

April 19—Chicago police arrest "Lucky" Luciano and Meyer Lansky with Capone gangsters Rocco

Fischetti and Paul Ricca in front of Congress Hotel, confirming connection between New York and Chicago mobs.

June 22—Kidnap-murder of the Lindbergh baby compels Congress to pass first federal kidnapping law, despite reservations of President Hoover and his attorney general about involving the federal government in crime control.

July 1—Justice Department's Bureau of Investigation, headed by J. Edgar Hoover since 1924, is officially upgraded to the United States Bureau of Investigation, although its jurisdiction still is limited to a few federal crimes, such as interstate transportation of stolen cars (Dyer Act), of women "for immoral purposes" (Mann Act), of prize-fight films (Sims Act), and now interstate kidnapping.

The kidnap-murder of the Lindbergh baby in 1932 so riled the American public that a federal kidnapping law was passed, paving the way for further expansion of federal police powers once President Franklin Roosevelt took office.

October 10—Members of Philadelphia's Presbyterian Ministers' Social Union call for whipping post as "cure for crime."

November 8—Atlanta organizing vigilante group in response to a series of major crimes.

November 24—After enrolling federal agents in the country's first Scientific Crime Detection Laboratory directed by Calvin Goddard in Chicago, Bureau of Investigation establishes the first national crime lab, using Goddard's techniques.

December 2—Atlantic City follows Chicago's lead in listing sixty "Public Enemies."

December 7—The New Jersey Grange association recommends return of whipping posts.

1933

January 10—Murray "The Camel" Humphreys replaces Al Capone as Chicago's new Public Enemy No. 1.

January 17—Chicago Mayor Anton Cermak orders city policemen to stop working with the Citizens' Committee for the Prevention and Punishment of Crime ("Secret Six"), whose vigilante practices have been increasingly criticized.

February 11—Renewing an earlier position, Texas Bankers Association posts $5,000 reward for "dead" bank robbers on grounds that "live" ones often elude justice.

March 10—North Carolina bill would permit lashing in petty crimes to relieve jail overcrowding.

March 20—Congress legalizes 3.2% beer, to take effect April 7.

April 16—In Kentucky, six self-appointed crime fighters indicted under state law against "night riders."

April 19—The Chicago Association of Commerce, with its Chicago Crime Commission, disbands the "Secret Six" anticrime group, whose working personnel have been accused of mismanagement and vigilantism.

June 10—U.S. Attorney General Homer Cummings, reversing policies of his predecessors,

Bulletproofing Cars

Payroll messengers and unprotected money trucks were easy prey for the new "auto bandits," who found them easier to stop than trains [see p. 150]. The attacks on money messengers gave rise to an armoring industry that borrowed ideas from early military vehicles, and by the 1930s it was building armored cars and trucks specially designed to stand off bandit attacks. Soon big-league gangsters and outlaws also were having their machines "bulletproofed," sometimes adding sirens and smoke-screen devices to facilitate escape from the scene of a shooting or robbery.

After an otherwise well-planned bank-messenger holdup in downtown Chicago netted them only bags full of canceled checks, the Barker-Karpis Gang made their getaway in a professionally armored sedan, only to wreck it a few blocks away. They piled out, guns blazing, and escaped in a car taken from a passing motorist. Police traced the bandit car to Joe Bergl, whose garage just happened to adjoin Ralph Capone's Cotton Club, barely outside Chicago's western city limits on the main boulevard (Twenty-second Street, later Cermak) into Cicero. They deduced that Bergl had provided similar cars for Capone gunmen, including one that escaped from police in downtown Chicago by means of billowing smoke. Bergl also had armored a car for "Machine Gun" Kelly and probably others. The police investigation of

Marines were issued Thompsons and ordered to guard the U.S. Mail after a bloody machine-gun attack on a postal truck in New Jersey in 1926 (left). Soon banks and security firms began armoring their own trucks (right).

THEY WILL
GET THOSE BANDITS!
Because
THEY ARE SAFE BEHIND
INDESTRUCTO
BULLET RESISTING GLASS

Popular
Mechanics
1937
Guard on armored car has clear view in all directions from "conning tower" at rear which has dual ignition switch and brakes for emergency control
Money Car with Gun Turret
Has Bullet-Absorbent Walls

"Motorized bandits" first inspired a police car with ramming capabilities (one was actually built), then bullet-resistant glass, and by 1937 a "Money Car with Gun Turret."

his business discovered that a partner in Bergl Auto Sales was former East St. Louis gunman Gus Winkeler, related to Bergl by marriage and close friend of Fred "Killer" Burke, whose successful hit on New York's Frankie Yale in 1928 readied him, Burke, and Capone's other American Boys to participate in the St. Valentine's Day Massacre.

Bergl's chief competitor in the car-armoring business was Clarence Lieder, owner of the Oakley Auto Construction Co. at Division and Oakley on Chicago's Near Northwest Side. He was a longtime friend of "Baby Face" Nelson and also supplied cars to crooks, adding smoke-screen devices upon request. John Dillinger and Homer Van Meter had used his garage as a hideout in the late spring of 1934, when they were too hot to find a safe haven with anyone they could trust. They spent some weeks living out of a panel truck, driving the back roads around East Chicago, Indiana; and if contact with attorney Louis Piquett or his assistant Arthur O'Leary required a visit to Chicago, they would use Lieder's garage, parking at night in his vehicle elevator, which they would raise to a position between the first and second floors. When Dillinger was killed and Nelson had fled to California, Lieder, figuring the end was near, put a "closed" sign on his shop and disappeared.

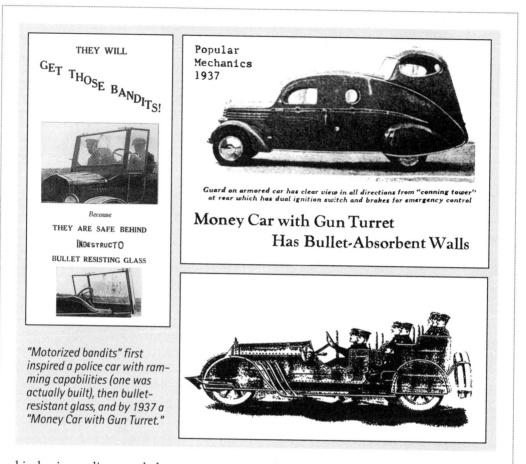

BULLETPROOFING PEOPLE

The willingness of criminals to do battle with the police partly reflected their sense that most cops also were crooked, and if they could be bought they could also be shot. This view was not shared by the police or the public, and paralleling the armored car industry were efforts to develop bullet-resistant glass, shields, and garments.

Around the turn of the century a Chicagoan named Casimir Zeglen, distraught over the assassination of Mayor Carter Harrison in 1893, began a serious effort to develop a new kind of body armor. Around 1890 a German tailor named Dowe also developed a vest made of felt and probably metal (he would not disclose its components) that weighed about ten pounds, but it was stiff and therefore cumbersome.

Zeglen was aware of stage stunts here and in Europe in which performers wearing supposedly bulletproof vests let assistants shoot them with no apparent harm, usually with trick bullets, or real bullets but very light loads. What Zeglen sought was a flexible vest that could be worn unobtrusively by civilians—a forerunner of recent-day Kevlar and later materials that were even more bullet-resistant.

Zeglen was a Catholic brother and sacristan at St. Stanislaw's Church who took care of priestly raiments made of heavy silk that he found was nearly impenetrable. He persuaded his superiors to let him use such silk toward developing a more or less bulletproof vest, which could be worn by dignitaries and sold to armies that presumably had God on their side. After much research he found a silk-based fabric that would stop most bullets of the day, he persuaded the U.S. military to witness a demonstration. The *Brooklyn Eagle* carried an article in its October 9, 1902, edition:

> [Mr.] C. W. Ryder, who exhibiting the armor cloth in Brooklyn, has arranged for a test in the Montauk Theater building next Tuesday a 3:30 p.m. . . . . Dr. Ashley A. Webber, who is known as one of the greatest marksmen in the country, will fire the shots. Mr. Ryder has made an offer of $500 reward if Dr. Webber succeeds in penetrating the fabric. It is expected that the Rev. Mr. Zeglen will be present in person to wear the vest.

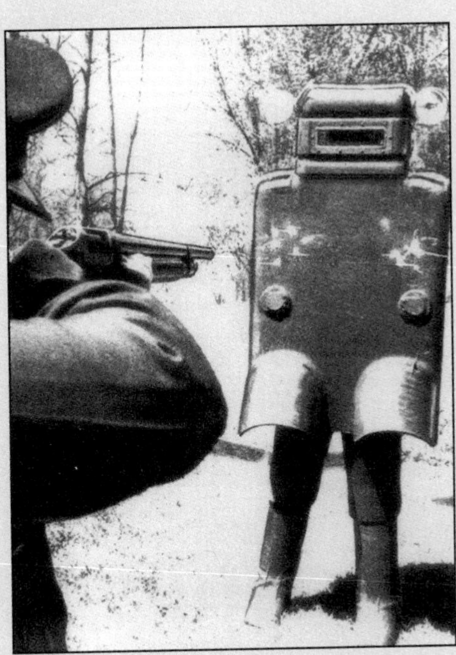

Some efforts to armor-plate police officers reached fairly ridiculous proportions.

In Chicago, Zeglen arranged for similar tests, set up his own company, found a manufacturer able to replicate the vests, and

HERR DOWE SUBMITTING TO THE TEST.

Supposedly bulletproof vests made their first appearance on stages in the nineteenth century, and in most cases they were capable of protecting the "magician" only from lightly loaded rounds.

Al Dunlap, publisher of a police trade magazine called *The Detective*, and Elliot T. Wisbrod, a metallurgist working with gun dealer Peter von Frantzius, both developed "hard" body armor similar enough in design and appearance that each accused the other of patent infringements. To promote their vests, each had police officers constantly staging demonstrations, shooting at the respective inventors or at each other at recklessly close range with pistols and machine guns, while other cops crowded around approvingly, oblivious to ricochets. Similar equipment was marketed by Bovite and Federal Laboratories.

Predictably, gangsters also bought or otherwise acquired the vests, including two of the shooters who carried out the St. Valentine's Day Massacre. An investigation after those murders determined that von Frantzius and Dunlap were selling not only vests but also submachine guns to nearly everyone on any pretext. One of the machine guns used in the Massacre had come from von Frantzius, as had the revolver of victim Frank

managed to sell a substantial number to the Russian Imperial Army. But in the absence of any major wars, no profitable market developed, and his vest proved to be an invention whose time had not yet come.

Nothing comparable emerged from the First World War, probably because smokeless powder and advances in projectile design led to rifle bullets with much greater penetrating power. However, the sharp increase in violence that accompanied Prohibition involved mostly handguns and shotguns and revived interest in bulletproofing people, especially police. It also resulted in fierce competition between other Chicago inventors to develop "hard" body armor—overlapping steel plates sewn into vests tailored to look as much as possible like ordinary clothing.

Toward the end of the nineteenth century, Chicagoan Casimir Zeglen, a Catholic brother, developed a bullet-resistant vest made of vestment silk. He sold some to the Russian army, but it was an idea whose time had not yet come.

Zeglen Bullet Proof Cloth
TESTED
in all countries and proved to resist
ALL Revolver Bullets of Calibres and at Distances
RUSSIA
ordered 4,000 garments made of Zeglen Bullet Proof Cloth for the Manchurian Army. Results of the test held
near Cronstadt were most satisfactory.
The fabric is made of silk; it is thin, light, flexible and absolutely bullet proof. Special rates to police officers, sheriffs and detectives. For particulars write to
Zeglen Bullet Proof Cloth Co.
Dean Building
South Bend, Ind.

82 P. VON FRANTZIUS, 608 Diversey Parkway, Chicago, Illinois

Police Equipment

Bullet Proof Vests

Front Fig. 1 | Back Fig. 2 | Side Fig. 3

These new modern light-weight Bullet Proof Vests are endorsed and used by policemen, sheriffs, detectives, Federal officers, bank messengers, guards, etc., all over the country.

The death list record of men killed by revolver bullets shows that over 90 per cent of these deaths were caused by wounds received in the body between the shoulder and the groin. Statistics further show that an average of 30 citizens are killed daily in the United States by firearms in the hands of desperate gunmen. No doubt the lives of these men could have been saved had they worn a Bullet Proof Vest.

When a bullet strikes the vest, it mushrooms or flattens out and cannot glance off or ricochet and injure anyone. The Vest is flexible, evenly balanced, gives freedom of action to all parts of the body and is equally adaptable for foot, mounted or motorcycle duty. It covers and protects all vital parts of the body and fits and looks like an ordinary vest. It is tailored of good quality blue serge and has a modern cut and appearance, the same as any vest with pockets belonging to a nice suit of clothes. It is made "bullet proof" by a secret processed, light steel armor evenly distributed. The complete vest weighs about as much as a thick winter overcoat.

Description: The Vest may be grouped into three parts. The front (Fig. 1) consists of a series of flexible plates, "A," covering the body from the neck to the thighs. A hinged detachable plate "L" covers the groin. The flexible side plates "C" (Fig. 3) are hinged over the spine and firmly cover the sides of the body. The ends are tied over the chest. The flexible back plates "B" (Fig. 2) are buttoned to the front part of the Vest at the shoulders and are snugly held with elastic straps under the arms and sides, thus covering the spine from the neck to the seat. The Bullet Proof Vest can be put on and taken off very quickly.

Guarantee: The manufacturer guarantees the Bullet Proof Vest to stop—with the resistance of the body—any caliber revolver and pistol bullet, up to and including the .45 cal. Colt's Automatic steel jacketed bullet. Rifle bullets and German Luger and Mauser Pistol Bullets are not included.

Bullet Proof Vests are life savers. No price is too high to save a human life; nevertheless, our prices are unusually low and within the reach of every police department and individual.

The Thompson Automatic Gun

Equipped With Cutts Compensator

The Thompson Automatic Carbine is a new type of firearm combining the portability of a rifle with the effectiveness of a machine gun and was especially designed as an auxiliary to police departments and for the protection of Banks, Payrolls, Plants, Warehouses, Mines, Ranches, Railroads, and business and property of all kinds. Adopted and used by the leading banks of the United States, also police departments, state constabularies, detective agencies and many other businesses.

SPECIFICATIONS: Caliber 45. Weight 9 lbs. 11 ounces. Length, 33 inches.

Peter von Frantzius was an equal-opportunity seller of machine guns and bulletproof vests to Chicago's various gangs. He figured prominently in the hearings that followed the St. Valentine's Day Massacre. (The Thompson advertised in his catalog is a now-rare Model 1927 semi-automatic.)

Gusenberg, found dying on the floor of the garage. Under grand jury questioning von Frantzius admitted that he rarely turned away a potential customer; and that for an additional two dollars his shop would obligingly grind off firearm serial numbers, unaware that the crime lab established since the Massacre usually could restore them with acid. (Removing a gun's serial number later became a federal offense, but it was perfectly legal at the time.)

Outlaws, if they didn't have time to shop around, stole them in raids on police stations. The Dillinger Gang was especially adept at this, and when "Baby Face" Nelson went down in battle in November 1934, his legs were full of buckshot, but his vest had stopped all but one of the .45-caliber machine-gun slugs fired at him by FBI agents. (The one that missed the vest mortally wounded him in the lower stomach.) The next January, the bureau laid siege to a Chicago apartment building occupied by Russell Gibson of the Barker-Karpis Gang, and he died when his vest was penetrated by a metal-jacketed rifle bullet.

Such vests went out of fashion in the late 1930s, and the next revival of protective garments came during World War II, when American and other flyers took to wearing lighter but again-flexible flak jackets that were not intended to stop bullets but protected bomber crews from shrapnel. The development of Kevlar by DuPont in the 1960s renewed an interest in various kinds of "soft" vests that presently can be worn inconspicuously by police, or outside the clothing of kill-worthy criminals.

Eliott Wisbrod designed one of several bulletproof vests and developed a "Duralumin" bullet shield that found little use at the time but was a forerunner of later types of police and military body armor.

declares that the Justice Department will fight racketeering.

July 13—Cummings announces plans for new federal legislation to combat racketeers.

July 27—President Roosevelt confers with Cummings, proposes a "super-police force" to combat interstate crime; will use Justice Department's Bureau of Investigation as nucleus of federal campaign against racketeering, a plan quietly opposed by bureau Director J. Edgar Hoover.

July 29—Increasing interest in police crime laboratories leads New York University and the Bellevue Hospital Medical College to form departments of forensic medicine.

July 15—Bronx police seize three armored gang cars, but their drivers escape.

July 26—Citizen "Minute Men" organizing in Indiana to fight crime and gangsters.

August 6—Federal Bar Association proposes national police force.

August 10—United States Bureau of Investigation officially renamed Division of Investigation, incorporating the Bureau of Prohibition under Hoover's direction. Hoover establishes a separate Bureau of Investigation (soon to be called G-men) to distinguish it from the Prohibition agents, who are notoriously inept and corrupt.

August 13-14—Warden Lewis E. Lawes urges U.S. Senate subcommittee to make all major crimes federal offenses and asks President Roosevelt to declare modified martial law pending adoption of a constitutional amendment eliminating state lines.

August 27-October 25—Senate committee will seek ban on machine guns; New York's governor signs bill making machine-gun possession by civilians a felony; arms industry offers suggestions for keeping machine guns out of criminals' possession; small-arms manufacturers establish code to restrict sale of machine guns and submachine guns to governments, banks, and security firms.

September 10—Four Chicagoans jailed under new municipal law that permits arrests on criminal reputations alone.

September 12—Los Angeles begins anti-crime campaign by requiring the registration of all felons.

September 15—American Society of Composers, Authors, and Publishers opposes the sale of popular song sheets on the streets by youths, declaring this breeds criminals.

September 26—"Machine Gun" Kelly arrested in Memphis by federal agents; according to later FBI lore, he coined the term "G-man," adopted by Hoover to distinguish his Bureau of Investigation agents from those of the Bureau of Prohibition. (Coincidentally, several members of the future Dillinger Gang break out of Indiana's Michigan City state prison.)

September 27—U.S. Justice Department, despite Hoover's concerns, announces that its war on racketeering will include prosecution of lawyers who aid and abet crimes of their clients.

October 1—U.S. Flag Association awards first-place prize in its anti-crime contest to entrant advocating censorship of crime news.

In the same papers covering the trial of a police shooting of Frank Nitti in his downtown Chicago office, other front-page stories describe the September 26, 1933, capture of "Machine Gun" Kelly and the Indiana prison escape of the future Dillinger Gang.

THE CHICAGO DAILY NEWS
FINAL MARKETS
THREE CENTS
COMPLETE WANT ADS
LANG SWEARS CERMAK ORDERED NITTI RAID
TESTIFIES MAYOR FEARED FOR LIFE, SOUGHT GUNMAN
Trace $75,000 Urschel Ransom to Kelly
1,000 Armed Men Hunt Escaped Indiana Felons
BASEBALL
NATIONAL LEAGUE
AMERICAN LEAGUE
RACE RESULTS
BATES OBTAINED LIKE SUM, SAYS U.S. AGENT KEITH
LIFE THREATENED!
TRACING JAIL-BREAK GUNS
SHERIFF STILL MISSING
CASE IS NEAR JURY
Fights Gold Order; First

October 7—Chicago Crime Commission Director Frank Loesch urges U.S. Justice Department to establish a federal "public enemy" list. Proposal is rejected by J. Edgar Hoover, but newspapers persist in identifying "most-wanted" fugitives as "public enemies."

October 19—U.S. Supreme Court voids Michigan's "public enemy" law provision that forbids associating with suspected criminals.

December 5—Utah convention approves Twenty-first Amendment, repealing national Prohibition. (Many states have been repealing their own prohibition enforcement laws since the mid-1920s.)

December 11—Prohibition is formally over, but most bootlegging mobs anticipated this and have moved into gambling and labor racketeering.

December 16—New York City supports plan to require visitors with criminal records to register with police.

December 28—Chicago and Illinois (adopting the campaign started by the Chicago Crime Commission) declare John Dillinger Public Enemy No. 1.

1934

January 1—Fiorello LaGuardia sworn in as mayor of New York City, declares "war" on organized crime, and will seize more than 2,000 slot machines.

January 2—Warden James A. Johnston arrives on Alcatraz.

January 29—New York State Chamber of Commerce issues report suggesting registration of U.S. citizens and aliens and the fingerprinting of all aliens.

February 10—New York County Lawyers Association urges law requiring persons ever convicted of any felony or of certain misdemeanors to register with police and file their fingerprints with the Bureau of Identification.

February 15—New York judge proposes electrically powered whipping post for lashing racketeers.

February 19—Attorney General Homer S. Cummings interprets Constitution's interstate-commerce clause to include his "Twelve-Point Program" of federal crime control.

March 12–13—New York police commissioner proposes system of ostracism; all with criminal records to be banned from cities of the "First Class"; modifies suggestion as applying only to "habitual" criminals.

April 21—Illinois Supreme Court voids law that permitted jailing of individuals on the basis of their criminal reputations.

April 26—Attorney General Cummings says War Department has offered planes for use in anticrime drive.

April 28—Pittsburgh repeals ordinance permitting the arrest of "suspicious" persons.

May 7–11—New York City police department urges "banishment" of 10,000 criminals; 207 arrested as reprisal for cop killings.

May 9—New Jersey governor signs bill defining "gangsters."

May 18—President Roosevelt signs six of Cummings's federal anticrime bills.

June 6—Roosevelt authorizes Justice Department to offer reward money.

June 18—Congress grants Bureau of Investigation agents full arrest powers in federal cases and authorizes their carrying of firearms.

June 22—John Dillinger is named as the country's "most wanted" (declared U.S. Public Enemy No. 1 in the press) by U.S. Attorney General Homer S. Cummings, who offers $10,000 for Dillinger and $5,000 for Nelson.

June 30—Assistant Attorney General J. B. Keenan warns that unless law enforcement improves, police power will be taken over by the federal government.

October 7—Attorney General Cummings calls for a national conference on crime.

November 1—New York State Chamber of Commerce adopts resolution promoting a system for registering all U.S. citizens.

November 5—Grand jury declares Kansas City controlled by criminal gangs and racketeers.

November 27—New York's police commissioner orders his force to "terrorize" known criminals.

November 31—U.S. Justice Department orders

POLICE RADIO

In the early 1920s, police in many cities were hoping that Marconi's newfangled "wireless" apparatus could somehow help them combat the new "motorized bandits" and decrease their response time in urban emergencies. State-of-the-art equipment then consisted of fragile one-tube radio receivers little better than "cat-whisker" crystal sets, with ungainly aerials that looked like kites without their paper, and cars with transmitters that filled the entire back seat and were hooked to smokestack-like towers wrapped with wire, or trucks festooned with a topside antenna array that resembled a maze of clotheslines. Reception in the countryside was intermittent at best, and in the cities it often was blocked by tall buildings. One of the few police departments that did not abandon the idea as completely impractical was Detroit's.

The Detroit police continually experimented as the technology improved, and by the late 1920s it had established a functional "one-way" radio system surpassed only by the commercial broadcasting services of the day. An unforeseen problem was getting its station licensed. The Federal Radio Commission (predecessor to the FCC) viewed land-based radio as purely an entertainment medium and insisted that even police radio, call letters KOP, broadcast music between its official messages. This provoked the police commissioner to ask, "Do we have to play a violin solo before we dispatch the police to catch a criminal?" Detroit's lawmen accommodated that bureaucratic obstacle with what can only be admired for its wit and imagination: They preceded each police call with the opening notes of "Yankee Doodle Dandy."

On February 14, 1929—the morning of the St. Valentine's Day Massacre—several Chicago police officials were in Detroit inspecting that city's marvelous KOP radio operation. When they returned and the story of Detroit's police radio system was widely reported in the *Chicago Tribune*, Publisher Colonel Robert McCormick donated $10,000 to the Chicago police to set up a similar facility. And until that was up and running, McCormick's radio station, WGN (which stood, modestly enough, for

The greatest obstacle to police radio was the size and awkwardness of the equipment.

As early as 1922, New York experimented with—and gave up on—a "Control of the Road" plan that fielded sidecar motorcycles equipped with a Tommygun and a "one-tube, one-way" radio.

"World's Greatest Newspaper"), thrilled the city by interrupting its regular music broadcasts for police calls. The downside to this was that any good gangland killing or spectacular robbery attracted a sizeable crowd of Chicagoans.

Before the Chicago police had their own transmitter operating, it was still in the era of "Calling All Cars," which could easily be tuned in by civilians, especially those who could afford $85 for a nifty five-tube Auto-Craft radio. Such an expense was hardly a problem for Chicago's gangsters. As this was described by Maurice Frank, the company's president in 1932:

> Various important mob figures began coming in for Auto-Craft radios. They rolled century bills off their bankrolls. Hardly a day passed that one of the Capone gang did not appear. I happened to mention this to the foreman of our installation department who said, "Didn't you know our set gets the police calls better than the police cars?" I didn't know and thought we had better do something about it before the police did it for us. We instructed the manufacturing foreman to eliminate the police frequency. Our sales to mobsters continued. Evidently they found someone to change the frequency back.
>
> One day Fred [a new partner in the company] came into my office all excited. He was single and a few years younger than me. I was an old man of twenty-eight and, of course, married. I quote Fred verbatim, "Maurie, I just met the most gorgeous blonde. She's having a radio installed in her white convertible and I made a date with her. She's sitting in my office now. Take a look." I did, and then went back to Fred with these words, "Freddie, for your information, you have a date with 'Machine Gun' Jack McGurn's 'blond alibi.'"

If Fred's date was actually a "date" with Louise Rolfe, he cancelled it.

A demonstration of Chicago's first police-owned radio station had taken place on June 16, 1930, with the kind of hoopla for which the city already was well known. Five police "cruisers"—mostly Cadillac touring cars, each equipped with the latest radio receivers and normally carrying five detectives—roared about the city filled with aldermen and other civic officials, sirens screaming, bells clanging, and headlights flashing alternately, "to determine the efficiency of the system." They returned to headquarters only long enough to discharge one group and pick up another.

The passengers evidently were satisfied, and in less than two years some forty suburbs had installed equipment linking them to the Chicago Police Radio Network. The number of radio-equipped cars also had expanded to include some 180 five-man detective bureau touring cars and smaller, two-man squad cars.

The radio procedure employed the existing emergency number, "Police 1313," with thirteen lines routed through a Bell Telephone switchboard to eight operators who would judge the urgency of the call, record it on the proper form, and forward it to the "radio announcer." After looking at a map displaying the forty-one police districts, he would generally make two calls to two cars to ensure reception, and then hand the complaint form to the supervising squad operator.

One of the system's major problems was the greatly varying distances over which police calls could be heard. Depending on the ionosphere, a dispatcher might be heard twenty miles away or a thousand, which often interfered with police communications in a distant city if both were using the same "police" frequency that manufacturers had started marking on their radio dials, especially if both cities had certain streets with the same names. That problem was solved first in Bayonne, New Jersey, when an amateur radio operator named Frank Gunther, W2ALS, talked the city fathers into installing "two-way" radios in police cars and moving the frequency up to the VHF (Very High Frequency) band to limit their range.

This was bad news for the now-booming car radio industry that already had sold thousands of police units designed for one-way reception. But in March 1933, despite the Depression, Bayonne instituted a two-way VHF communications system that other cities soon began to adopt.

Over the next few years, the police car with a two-way Motorola radio and a long spring-loaded "whip" antenna became the "scourge of the roads" (most gangsters having put their guns away) to speeding motorists ever on the lookout for a long antenna on a car with a chrome-plated siren mounted on the roof, ready to howl and blink an angry red light that meant "pull over." That combination prevailed into the late 1960s, when mechanical sirens gave way to the electronic, the lights went "strobe," and antennas started shrinking to near invisibility.

strict enforcement of laws against harboring criminals.

December 10—National Conference on Crime opens in Washington, D.C.

1935

January 26—New York's Mayor LaGuardia backs police commissioner's order to terrorize criminals.

January 31—Kentucky National Guard called up to combat lawlessness in Clay County.

March 10—New York discovers professional substitutes are appearing in lineups instead of those arrested.

May 19–25—Federal revenue agents list seven major New York gangs; intend to charge principals under income tax laws.

July 1—Justice Department's Division of Investigation renamed Federal Bureau of Investigation; alcohol regulation transferred to different agencies that ultimately become the Treasury Department's Bureau of Alcohol and Tobacco;

— District Attorney Thomas E. Dewey to head a major New York City investigation into gangs and racketeering.

July 3—Birmingham, Alabama, to register all ex-felons.

July 20—Link revealed between underworld and St. Paul police.

August 5—J. Edgar Hoover featured on the cover of *Time.*

October 30—New York City police to revive strong-arm "gangster squad."

November 2—Bandits reported terrorizing northwestern Iowa.

November 25—Chicago Crime Commission's Frank Loesch says New York is now nation's crime capital.

November 26—New York police commissioner says it isn't.

December 24—Delaware and other state assemblies will consider legislation to remove state-line obstacles to law enforcement.

1936

January 5—Minneapolis grand jury calls for war on rackets.

January 7—New York State appeals court voids convictions under state's "public enemy" law.

January 10—Five thousand special deputies will be sworn in to help in New York anti-crime drive.

January 23—New York senator submits bill that would allow police to make arrests across state lines.

February 13—Philadelphia city council will require all criminals to register with police.

February 26—New York's governor signs bill providing additional penalties for crimes committed with weapons.

March 2—New St. Paul law will require residents convicted of felonies in past ten years to register with police.

March 14—Minneapolis mayor orders special police drive against vice and gambling.

May 6—New York legislature passes bill to make "public enemy" law permanent.

June 16—Philadelphia police assemble photos of 10,000 criminals before Democratic National Convention.

July 3—Birmingham, Alabama, will register all ex-felons living in city.

August 19—Authorities report racketeers rushing to pay New York's state income and corporation taxes to avoid Dewey investigation.

October 5—FBI official credits favorable G-men publicity with reducing juvenile delinquency.

1937

January 2—Philadelphia's mayor orders police to drive all known gangsters and racketeers from city.

March 4—Dewey's rackets war continues unabated, earns him a medal from the Hundred Year Association; police helping Dewey will be cited and promoted.

April 22—New York Senate kills bill that would have banned use of "third-degree" methods by police.

June 10—New York prosecutor Dewey credited with sixty-one racketeering convictions without an acquittal.

October 23—FBI announces compilation of file on criminals' nicknames.

December 20—U.S. Supreme Court declares wiretapping violates Federal Communications Act, but U.S. Circuit Court of Appeals will rule intrastate wiretapping legal; decisions debated in Washington.

1938

January 30—Two New York City magistrates criticize police policy of wholesale arrests and discharge most of 600 cases.

February 5—Special grand jury impaneled in Philadelphia to investigate links between gangsters in that city and New York.

June 1—New York's Mayor LaGuardia announces special "rules" for gangsters during the coming World's Fair.

July 13—Chicago police department announces purchase of Northwestern University's Scientific Crime Detection Laboratory, the country's first full-service "crime lab" established in 1929 by Calvin Goddard after the St. Valentine's Day Massacre.

August 17–19—Philadelphia grand jury finds connections between city officials, police, and crime ring, recommends firing eleven policemen. Civil Service Commission will hear charges against forty-one in September.

August 27—*Chicago Tribune* Publisher Colonel Robert McCormick attacks the continuing alliance between politicians and criminals in northern Indiana.

September 3—Delta Theta Phi law fraternity favors denying legal services to habitual criminals.

October 18—Records of 7,200 prisoners discovered stolen from Brooklyn's Bergen Street police station.

October 31–November 3—Dewey condemns conditions in Brooklyn, as well as Tammany Hall's protection of racketeers, citing onetime appointment of "Dutch" Schultz as Bronx deputy sheriff by Democratic leader E. J. Flynn.

1939

March 27—U.S. Supreme Court holds New Jersey's Gangster Act of 1931 unconstitutional.

April 10—Antiquated Bertillon method of criminal identification eliminated by law in New York.

April 19—Philadelphia police receive demonstration of equipment to transmit photos of criminals by radio.

August 5—President Roosevelt signs national bill ending statute of limitations for crimes involving the death penalty.

August 24—After twenty-five months as a federal fugitive on antitrust charges, Lepke Buchalter personally surrenders to J. Edgar Hoover in New York City; tried by local authorities for murder and becomes the only prominent mobster to be executed.

September 3—Federal grand jury finds New York City racketeering dominated by "Bugsy" Siegel and Meyer Lansky crime ring.

November 16—Al Capone, health failing, released early from Alcatraz to undergo treatment for syphilis.

1940

January 3—Attorney General Murphy urges federal registration of firearms.

January 8—Women of Forest Hills and Kew Gardens, in Queens, New York, threaten to form own vigilante committee unless they receive more police protection.

January 27—Dr. Hrdlicka denies the existence of "criminal types."

February 19—American Legion Post asks New York City to send firearms seized under the Sullivan Act to Finland, but Commissioner Valentine says this would violate the law.

March 17—Evidence of murder-for-hire ring emerges during investigation by Brooklyn District Attorney William O'Dwyer; press will dub killers "Murder, Incorporated."

April 8—New York governor signs Merritt bill barring arrest of persons who turn in weapons to police.

May 11—J. Edgar Hoover reports most arrests are occurring among nineteen-year-olds.

June 3—Brooklyn District Attorney O'Dwyer claims fifty-six murders solved by his investigators.

July 31—Vieux Carre Property Owners Association calls mass citizen rally to demand cleanup of crime conditions in New Orleans.

August 29—U.S. War Department announces ban on Army recruiting of persons convicted of crimes.

September 4—National Conference of Commissioners on Uniform State Laws approves new uniform pistol act, then excludes plan for registration of household weapons.

October 14—Court orders two pistols turned over the New York City police to be sent as a gift to Britain.

November 19—Warden F. B. Henderson protests War Department's ban on recruiting of ex-felons.

December 7—Central States Probation and Parole Conference appoints a committee to draft uniform criminal code.

December 30—U.S. District Attorney Cahill reports conviction rate of 99.2 percent in cases handled by him and his staff in Southern District of New York.

Alcatraz, 1868–1963

"The Rock"

New Deal-era Attorney General Homer Cummings needed something more impressive than a package of federal laws to symbolize the country's first "War on Crime," and he found it in the middle of San Francisco Bay.

Alcatraz Island had been a military fortification and then an army prison, but by the 1930s it had little strategic value. Nevertheless, it still was isolated by nearly a mile of cold, rough water and was large enough to serve as a highly and ominously visible monument to the federal government's crackdown on criminals.

With little discussion, the War Department turned the facility over to the Justice Department, which then transformed it into a maximum-security federal penitentiary that amounted to an American Devil's Island. Other federal prisons were probably as secure, but well-publicized policies and practices verging on simple brutality made "The Rock" an incarceration experience to be dreaded as truly the end of the line for incorrigible offenders—or at least criminal celebrities, for which it became a showcase.

On October 12, 1933, the War Department transferred Alcatraz to the Justice

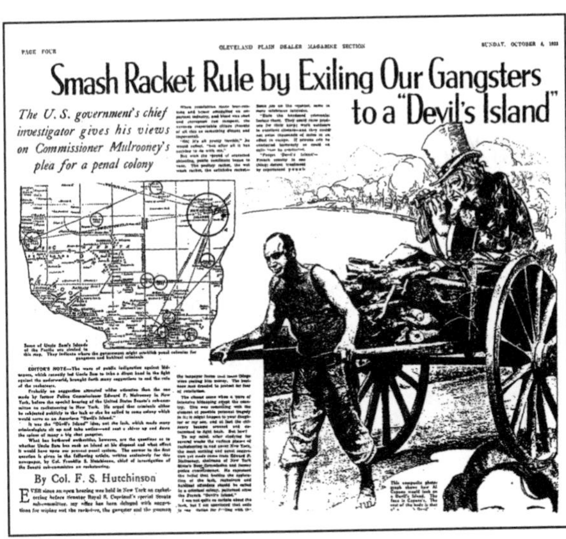

PAGE FOUR

CLEVELAND PLAIN DEALER MAGAZINE SECTION

Smash Racket Rule by Exiling Our Gangsters to a "Devil's Island"

The U.S. government's chief investigator gives his views on Commissioner Mulrooney's plea for a penal colony

By Col. F. S. Hutchinson

With Alcatraz still on the federal prison drawing board, some newspapers proposed a "Devil's Island" solution—this one featuring a composite picture of Al Capone—complete with maps of possible sites.

Department's Bureau of Prisons, and it would be populated by such scoundrels as Al Capone, "Machine Gun" Kelly and Alvin Karpis. On March 21, 1963, after an increasing number of escape attempts, the last twenty-seven prisoners were removed from "The Rock" and sent to other federal prisons. Two months later Alcatraz was officially closed by Attorney General Robert Kennedy. After a tedious cleanup it was reopened in 1973 to the sightseeing public.

HISTORY

November 4, 1854—Lighthouse completed as a navigation aid, with warning beacon tended by lightkeeper Michael Cassin. Military installations become operational; designated Fort Alcatraz.
1868—Converted into an army prison for military personnel.
1933—Transferred from the War Department to the Justice Department for use as a federal penitentiary on October 12.

WARDENS

James A. Johnston: January 2, 1934, to May 2, 1948.

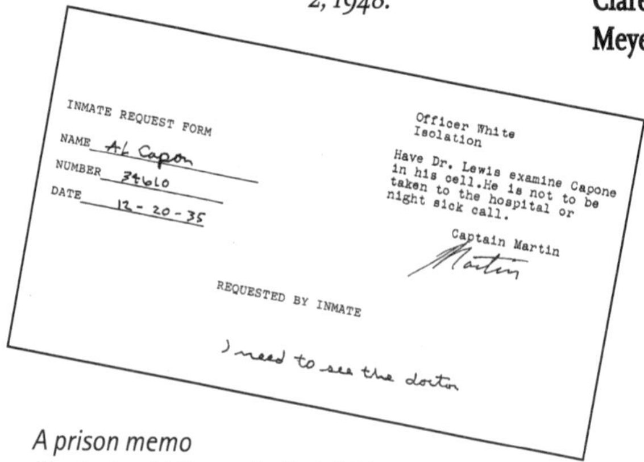
INMATE REQUEST FORM
NAME Al Capon
NUMBER 34610
DATE 12-20-35

Officer White
Isolation

Have Dr. Lewis examine Capone in his cell. He is not to be taken to the hospital or night sick call.

Captain Martin
Martin

REQUESTED BY INMATE

I need to see the doctor

A prison memo illustrates Al Capone's diminishing mental state.

Edwin Swope: May 2, 1948, to January 30, 1955.
Paul J. Madigan: January 30, 1955, to November 26, 1961.
Olin G. Blackwell: November 26, 1961, to May 15, 1963.

NOTORIOUS PRISONERS

Alphonse Capone, 85-AZ
George "Machine Gun" Kelly, 117-AZ
Francis Keating, 130-AZ
Albert Bates, 137-AZ
Thomas Holden, 138-AZ
Harvey Bailey, 139-AZ
John Paul Chase, 238-AZ
Arthur "Doc" Barker, 268-AZ
Volney Davis, 271-AZ
Harry Sawyer, 297-AZ
Edward Bentz, 307-AZ
Alvin "Creepy" Karpis, 325-AZ
Herbert Farmer, 332-AZ
James Murray, 514-AZ
Floyd Hamilton, 523-AZ
Joseph Cretzer, 548-AZ
Robert "The Birdman of Alcatraz" Stroud, 594-AZ
Basil "The Owl" Banghart, 595-AZ
Clarence "The Choctaw Kid" Carnes, 714-AZ
Meyer Harris "Mickey" Cohen, 1518-AZ

ESCAPE ATTEMPTS

April 27, 1936—Joe Bowers, trying to escape, is killed by Officer Chandler.
December 16, 1937—Theodore Cole and Ralph Roe escape from the prison laundry and are never found.
May 23, 1938—Rufus "Whitey" Franklin, Thomas Limerick, and Jimmy Lucas (who had stabbed Al Capone in 1937). Lucas surrenders, Franklin is captured, and Limerick is killed. During the

escape, Officer Royal Cline dies of a fractured skull.

January 13, 1939—Arthur "Doc" Barker, Dale Stamphill, Rufus McCain, Henri Young, and William Martin. McCain, Young, and Martin are captured; Stamphill surrenders; Barker is shot and dies the next day. McCain will be killed by inmate Henri Young on December 3, 1940.

May 21, 1941—Joseph Cretzer, Sam Shockley, Lloyd Barkdoll, and Arnold T. Kyle subdue guards in the prison workshop but surrender after an unsuccessful attempt to cut through bars with a grinding wheel.

September 15, 1941—John Bayless escapes from custody but is recaptured in a hiding place near the launch dock.

April 14, 1943—Harold Brest, Freddie Hunter, James Boarman, and Floyd Hamilton escape over the fence. Brest and Hunter are captured, Boarman is shot and killed, and Hamilton surrenders after two days in a water- and debris-filled shoreline cave.

August 7, 1943—Huron Walters is captured while hiding among rocks on a hillside above the beach.

July 31, 1945—John Giles uses a uniform, patched together while working with military laundry, to disguise himself as an army technical sergeant. He boards the army ship *General Coxe* but is captured by Associate Warden Miller and Lieutenant Bergen while leaving the vessel at Angel Island.

May 2, 1946—Joseph Cretzer, Bernard Coy, Marvin Hubbard, Miran Thompson, Sam Shockley, and Clarence Carnes fight a three-day "Battle of the Rock" in which one guard is killed. Cretzer, Coy, and Hubbard are found dead in a corridor. Thompson and Shockley will be put to death side by side in San Quentin's gas chamber on December 2, 1946. Clarence Carnes survives, eventually is transferred to another prison, and is released in 1970.

July 26, 1956—Floyd P. Wilson captured while still on the prison grounds.

September 20, 1958—Aaron Burgett is recaptured, and Clyde Johnson drowns.

July 11, 1962—Frank Morris, Clarence Anglin, and brother John Anglin plan for months, then place dummy heads in their bunks, break out through air vents, use floats made from raincoats, and disappear.

December 16, 1962—John Paul Scott and Darl Lee Parker escape through a basement window and enter the water on the west side of the island. Parker is soon recaptured on a small cluster of rocks known as "Little Alcatraz." Although authorities always had denied the possibility, Scott apparently swims to the mainland where he is seen by two boys under the Golden Gate Bridge and arrested by local police.

THE CLOSING OF ALCATRAZ

March 21, 1963—The last twenty-seven prisoners are removed from "The Rock" and sent to other federal prisons.

May 15, 1963—Alcatraz is officially closed by Attorney General Robert Kennedy.

November 20, 1969—A Native American group takes control of the island and holds it for several months.

June 1, 1970—Four buildings and the original lighthouse are destroyed by fire.

June 11, 1971—The last fifteen Native Americans occupying the island surrender to twenty federal marshals.

October 27, 1972—A bill establishing the island as the Golden Gate National Recreation Area is signed by President Richard Nixon.

October 27, 1973—Alcatraz opens to the public.

WILLIE RADKAY

Alcatraz Inmate No. 666

Born to Croatian immigrants in the ethnic community known as "Strawberry Hill" in Kansas City, Kansas in 1911, William Isaac Radkay made an early transition from altar boy to holdup man, eventually being branded as "one of the most notorious armed robbers in Kansas City history." The Mother Superior at St. John the Baptist church early on praised Willie for his intelligence and good manners and urged him to study for the priesthood. Later, as news of his criminal escapades spread, she called him the "Incarnation of the Devil."

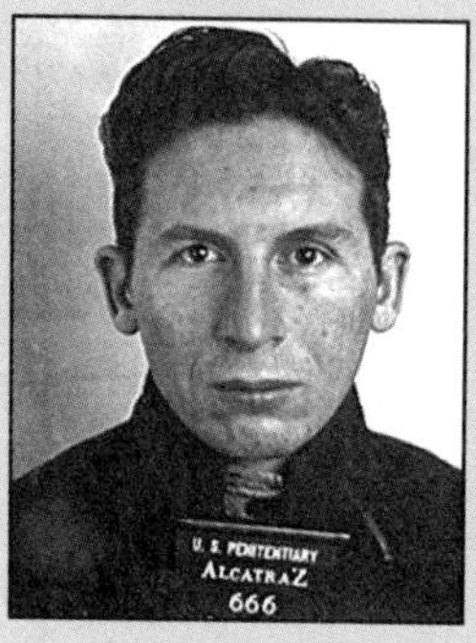

PATTY TERRY

Shot twelve times after a 1935 robbery, Radkay (left, in 1945; right, in 2006) attributed his survival to "tough skin, soft bullets, and they didn't hit anything important."

Willie's father died in 1915 and his mother placed Willie and the other three children in an orphanage till such time as she would be able to support them. She allowed Willie's godparents to adopt him, but their only interest in him was through a life insurance policy on his grandfather that made Willie the beneficiary. As his guardians, they would have control of the money.

Willie gravitated early to crime, first as a delivery boy for area bootleggers then—by age sixteen—to armed robbery. He got his first gun from a prostitute, whose pimp planned to rob him. Willie called himself "Little Al Capone" and led a gang of other young toughs in store robberies. Later they progressed to hijacking liquor and holding up speakeasies. Willie could afford the best legal talent and made the right connections. Sentenced in 1932 to 10 to 21 years in the State Industrial Reformatory at Hutchinson, Kansas, he was paroled after only two years.

He rejoined his old gang, but Kansas City was now hot and they moved on to the wide-open gambling mecca of Covington, Kentucky, to rob casinos, and from there to Buffalo, New York, hitting still more gambling joints.

Radkay and his gang committed robberies throughout the Midwest, including bank holdups. "We used to hijack bootleggers and stick up gambling houses," he told one interviewer in later years. "When Prohibition ended, we lost our victims, so the only thing left to do was rob banks." Somewhere along the way he met "Pretty Boy" Floyd and "Machine Gun" Kelly.

Shot six times while fleeing from Kansas City, Kansas, police on March 5, 1934, Willie was left lying in a jail cell until the coroner suggested to the captain that he move Radkay to a hospital or be held accountable for his death. Taken to a hospital on the Missouri side of the river, Willie remained unattended and still bleeding profusely. Nevertheless, when his police guard briefly left the room, so did Willie, leaping out a first-floor window to freedom and fleeing in his hospital gown. He carried those six slugs in his body the rest of his long life.

Willie received twelve more slugs almost a year later, when he was caught after a $15,000 jewelry store robbery in Kansas City, Missouri. Asked years later by his niece how he survived, Willie replied, "Tough skin, soft bullets, and they didn't hit anything important." He was severely wounded in the arms, back, and upper legs. This time Willie drew a ten-year sentence in the state prison at Jefferson City, Missouri. He was paroled in October 1940.

After a series of bank robberies, Radkay began a twenty-year federal prison sentence in 1943, first at Atlanta but his record as a jailbreaker ensured his transfer to Alcatraz where his inmate number was, ironically, 666-AZ. On "The Rock" he worked in the Industries Office with George "Machine Gun" Kelly and Basil "The Owl" Banghart, and they became a close circle, dubbed by guards as the "Gruesome Threesome." Other close friends included Jimmy Murray and Harvey Bailey, and Radkay renewed his acquaintance with Alvin Karpis, who worked in the prison kitchen as a baker when he wasn't making moonshine. Radkay would later recall that Karpis could bake a great pie as long as he was sober. Later transferred to Leavenworth, Radkay again occupied a cell near his friend Kelly, whose death he witnessed in 1954.

Paroled in 1954, Willie went to Chicago and got a job with a boilermaker's union through his politically connected friend Jimmy Murray [see "Jimmy Murray and the Great Rondout Train Robbery," p. 150] but soon gravitated back to robberies of jewelry stores and banks. Convicted of a Flint, Michigan, bank job, he returned to Leavenworth. There he met the love of his life, Louise Finland, who lived near his mother, cared for her during Willie's periods of incarceration, and accompanied her on prison visits to him.

Louise apparently turned his life around. They were married after his parole in 1969, and she moved him out of the city—away from former associates—to Prescott, Kansas, where he got a job as a school janitor and was eventually promoted to janitorial supervisor for five Linn County high schools. He retired after eleven years, a pillar of his community. Of Louise, who died in 1991, Willie said, "The longer I was with her, the more I knew I would never do anything to lose her."

In 1994, Willie Radkay began attending annual reunions of former prisoners and guards on Alcatraz and soon became a star of the event. This brought renewed media attention and Willie appeared in numerous television documentaries about Alcatraz and was interviewed by various authors, including L. L. Edge and Clark Howard. At one Alcatraz gathering, park ranger John Cantwell introduced Willie as "the most famous 'Rock star' you'll ever meet."

An elderly poster boy for rehabilitation, Willie once said, "I got everything I want: three dogs, four cats, a bright-red Thunderbird, and a suit for every day but Monday."

Radkay spent his final years, wheelchair-bound, in a nursing home in Fort Scott, Kansas. He collaborated with his niece, Patty Terry, on his autobiography, *A Devil Incarnate*, but refused to commit his words to tape. "I might get pinched," he said, as there were still some crimes the cops didn't know about. He was anxious for another "parole," to return home to his beloved dogs, and Patty hoped to use the book profits to hire nurses for him. Willie suggested instead that she buy him a black Cadillac with a gold grille and wheels and get him a tall, large-breasted redhead as a chauffeur.

Perhaps the last surviving Depression outlaw of any stature, Willie Radkay passed away peacefully on September 24, 2006. It was his ninety-fifth birthday.

CHUCK STUCKER

Willie Radkay spent much of his Alcatraz time in the company of such "War on Crime" prisoners as "Machine Gun" Kelly and Harvey Bailey.

Homicide, Gun Control, and "Flaming Youth"

Sales and Possession of Firearms as Consensual Crimes

Just as earlier reformers blamed the saloon and the liquor interests for the country's extravagant drinking, their modern counterparts blame its impressive murder rate on the abundance of firearms and the national gun lobby. The connection seems obvious. The unregulated saloon fostered public drunkenness, indirectly; the drinking itself was voluntary. And most killings are committed with guns, especially handguns; but deciding who should own them is as hard to legislate as temperance. The problems associated with booze and bullets have uncomfortable similarities.

When Sunday closing laws and other legal measures failed to remedy drunkenness, the word "temperance" became a euphemism for prohibition. Today, laws restricting firearm sales seem unrelated to violence, so the expression "gun control" is now understood by the militants on both sides to be a euphemism for gun prohibition. This was a major semantic victory for the anti-gun movement, which can accuse those who fail to support even some totally impractical measure as being "against gun control."

Since most Americans support controls short of prohibition, this fuels the ongoing debate between highly vocal pro-gun and anti-gun minorities for whom it masks quite different life experiences, attitudes, and political agendas.

The fact that there are nearly as many guns as people in the U.S., and that they can be found in half the country's households, can be translated two ways: Americans are dangerously gun happy, armed far beyond the limits of any other modern, Western, industrialized nation (such qualifiers greatly limit the comparisons); or Americans, although armed to the teeth, have proven themselves the safest and most responsible gun owners in the world.

Firearm opponents can proclaim that U.S. deaths by gunfire exceed those in selected foreign countries by ten or 100 to one, and having an inside track to a media largely controlled by the "liberal establishment," their message is widely promulgated. The gun community challenges this idea with valid but tedious research that fails to overcome the gut feelings of those who caricature the National Rifle Association and gun dealers the way prohibitionists once portrayed brewers and bartenders.

Prohibition led to a decline in so-called social drinking, which no doubt saved some individuals from themselves, but at a terrible cost in corruption, crime, and literally thousands killed or maimed by trigger-happy Prohibition agents and poisonous alcohol. It also transformed drunkenness from a working-class vice into a fashionable form of middle-class rebellion that coincided with the proliferation of automobiles, creating yet a new national problem.

In recent times more and more gun laws seemed essential to reduce murder rates that had doubled since the fifties and early sixties, but this modern mayhem only matched the killings in the Roaring Twenties and early 1930s, when the U.S. population was half what is today, and gun laws were practically nonexistent. Nor did the laws in places like New York and Chicago regulate thousands of suburban dealers, pawn shops, and magazine advertisers, from whom firearms could be purchased for cash or ordered by mail with no papers to fill out and no questions asked. Certain periods of the nineteenth century were so murderous

CHICAGO HERALD AND EXAMINER—A PAPER FOR PEOPLE WHO THINK

NATION'S BIGGEST CRIMINAL GROUP—AGED 20!

BANDIT, KILLER, 12—

COP-KILLER, 18—Jennings Young,

BANDIT, KILLER, 12—

COP-KILLER, 15—

ROBBERS, ALL UNDER 20—

KIDNAPER, KILLER, 17—

GIRL ROBBER-GANG LEADER—

MURDERER, 19—

ROBBER-HI-JACKER, 17—

Check Crime Among Our Youths!

"FINISHED" AT 2 OF CRIME—

Youth Predominates in Crime

16 YEARS 15 YEARS 17 YEARS 13 YEARS 21 YEARS 18 YEARS 21 YEARS

ALL CHARGED WITH KILL

Prisons Monuments to Neglected Youth

Auto Theft Burglary Robbery

Newspapers regularly decried the youthfulness of this country's criminals and usually compared—as they still do—American homicide rates to those of other countries. This spread includes Jennings Young, involved in a 1932 "police massacre" near Springfield, Missouri [see p. 533].

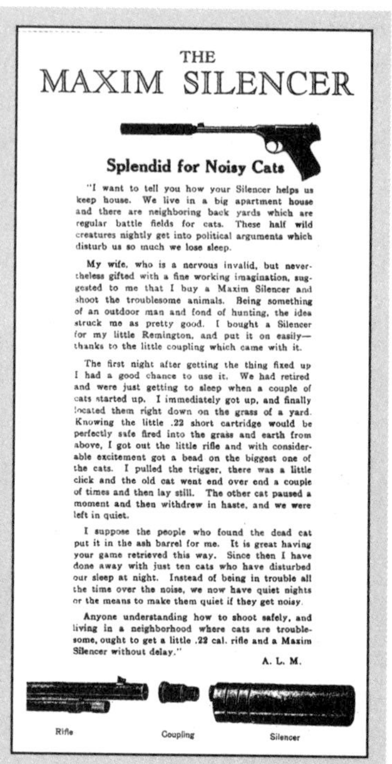

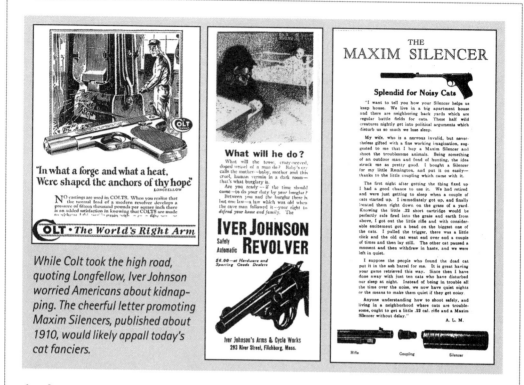

While Colt took the high road, quoting Longfellow, Iver Johnson worried Americans about kidnapping. The cheerful letter promoting Maxim Silencers, published about 1910, would likely appall today's cat fanciers.

that few people went out, especially at night, unarmed or unescorted; and one of the objections municipal police then had to wearing uniforms or even badges was that these invited murderous attacks by neighborhood gangs.

Killing, with or without firearms, reflects a number of social conditions, the most important of which is the population of young people in their crime-prone years. Booze wars and drug wars always aggravate violence, but a study of newspapers from the twenties and thirties finds them filled with alarmist articles on murder "epidemics" and full-page features on the homicidal tendencies of youngsters in their teens.

So it hardly serves the gun-control community to report that the 10,000 or so increasingly restrictive laws it has managed to pass locally and nationally since the twenties have done little more than make it harder to purchase firearms legally. Nor does it serve the pro-gun people to cheerfully remind Americans that people are not killing each other more often today than in the 1920s, despite a vast increase in the national gun population. Gun buffs try to get across the fact that the firearm accident rate actually has plummeted and that the suicide rate has not significantly changed in the past hundred years. But even they recognize this as negative advertising, hardly reassuring to residents of a crime-ravaged city or to the "gun grabbers," as they like to call their adversaries.

Two things make statistics on legal

firearm ownership nearly meaningless when it comes to violent crime. One is that nearly all gun violence involves a tiny fraction of 1 percent of the total gun population, and almost all of these already are in criminal or irresponsible hands, outside the gun-control loop. The second is that while robbing or shooting somebody is definitely a reason to call the cops, unlawful firearm sales and possession are in fact "consensual crimes," like prostitution or drugs, prohibited by laws that are nearly impossible to enforce. A small irony here is that a convicted felon, who cannot legally possess a firearm, also cannot be prosecuted for failing to register one, for that would be self-incrimination under the Fifth Amendment.

A third factor undermines practical efforts at "gun control." Police in cities like New York and Chicago routinely confiscate well over 20,000 guns a year, despite the fact that handgun sales and possession are virtually prohibited (in New York since 1911 and in Chicago since 1982). These guns are taken from people who have done something to attract police attention. A few years ago a Chicago study of gun-law violators found that out of 100 persons charged with UUW (Unlawful Use of a Weapon, the city's catch-all for simply having a gun), only one in ten was convicted, and only one in ten of those received a jail sentence. The police kept the guns, but even those convicted got off with fines then averaging $47. Hence Chicago's ban on guns strikes little fear in the hearts of kids who tangle with cops so often that the district station is like a second home.

Partly in response to the notion that criminals are the last to comply with gun laws, a number of states now are licensing ordinary citizens to carry weapons. Thousands of such licenses now have been issued, but instead of the bloodbath predicted by some, crime rates have generally declined, presumably because second thoughts now cross the minds of predatory criminals who must weigh the possibility that a prospective victim might have a pistol. In this case, the unintended consequence is that the robber may pass up a prosperous-looking businessman in favor of little old ladies cashing their Social Security checks.

Urban geographies, unequal police protection, and the recent concept of "victimology" make personal risk factors hard to establish, especially with the better medical attention shooting victims receive. No doubt with good intentions, the FBI early on defined a "friends, family, and acquaintances" category of murder, as distinct from the felony murder committed during a holdup or some other crime. Such polite terminology implies that these killings are bedroom and barroom crimes of passion that proved fatal mainly because a gun was handy. This remains an article of faith in the anti-gun community, along with the "dead burglar" statistic showing that few professional burglars are killed by armed homeowners.

A closer examination finds that police use this friends-and-family category as a dumping ground for most homicides where the victim was known to his assailant, who might be a rival drug dealer, a street-gang member, or acquaintances who didn't like each other anyway. It often includes victim-precipitated murders, when a threatened individual pulls a gun to avert a beating, and his opponent proclaims that he hasn't got the guts to use it. [Police usually find that one or both parties were influenced by drugs or alcohol, and that one or both had a history of arrests.]

Even so, the murder rate for handguns is about five per 100,000, which puts the peril in perspective—especially when it's understood that the vast majority of U.S. murders occur in a few of our largest cities (many of which prohibit handguns) and in certain high-crime neighborhoods where danger and risk-taking are antidotes to boredom. In these neighborhoods guns circulate as freely as drugs, with no paperwork or waiting periods.

Such social realities have no meaning in the gun-control debate, which represents a clash of cultures, lifestyles, and prejudices, much as did Prohibition. The "gun control" advocates, who tend to be educated and insulated urban professionals, harbor a conviction that in the city most gun people are criminals, and elsewhere they are rednecks who would shoot Bambi's mother; that firearms serve no good purpose in modern society; and that somehow, some way, fewer guns simply have to mean fewer killings.

With equal sincerity and simplicity, their gun-buff adversaries, usually remote from daily urban worries, feel righteously protected by the Second Amendment and consider possession of a means of self-defense to be an Eleventh Commandment—the one thing that still is right with America. These positions are as deeply felt and nonnegotiable as the right to life or the right to choose.

The magnitude of the problem, and the practice of comparing the U.S. murder rate with that in other countries, is a perennial theme in newspaper reporting. Both alarms were woven into a typical article published in the *Chicago Tribune* for April 9, 1931, headlined: "HOMICIDE RATE LEAPS FROM 9.9 TO 10.9 IN YEAR."

The story quoted a reformer who actually was arguing against the death penalty, but the writer found his murder statistics to be more newsworthy than his ideas and used those to deplore the willingness of Americans to kill each other:

> The homicide rate for the country leaped from 9.9 in 1929 to 10.9 last year. It has been higher only twice since 1900—in 1924 it was 11.2, and in 1923 it was 11.3.
>
> The 1929 figure for England and Wales was 0.5 [while] Germany, in 1927, had a rate of only 2.0.

Until the FBI started keeping national crime statistics in the 1930s, newspapers pulled numbers together from insurance companies and the Census Bureau and had to assume that some homicides were never reported or properly recorded, so their figures varied considerably. What was apparent, however, and hard to explain, was absence of any obvious correlation with guns, gun laws, or even the size of the population. The only thing truly predictable was that the U.S. murder rate per 100,000 usually involved firearms and tracked closely with the percentage of Americans in their "crime-prone" years, a relationship that goes up or down depending on other factors like immigration, mandatory public education, and marriage age.

The murder rates below differ from the figures in old almanacs and earlier books on homicide, and are those currently reported by the Bureau of Justice Statistics.

The earlier statistics probably are educated guesswork erring on the low side, reflecting westward migration, war, urbanization, population growth, population ages, and other variables. In recent years professionalized policing has tamed the towns much more than the cities, about a dozen of which presently account for nearly 80 percent of the nation's murders, with homicide rates approaching fifty to ninety per 100,000 in high-crime neighborhoods. So the only thing such figures definitely establish is that violence, as the man said, is as American as apple pie. On the other hand, despite rapid population growth, soaring gun sales, and tighter gun laws (offset by individual and full-time "straw-man" purchases), the murder rate since the early 1990s has dropped by nearly half, back to middle-1960s levels.

A situation puzzling enough to rarely see print is that the proliferation of firearms has had no apparent effect on the suicide rate, which has ranged between ten and fifteen per 100,000 since 1900. And while every child killed accidentally with a

U.S. Murder Rates Per 100,000 Population

1900. . . . .1.2	1921. . . . .8.1	1942. . . . .5.9	1963. . . . .4.9	1984. . . . .8.4
1901. . . . .1.2	1922. . . . .8.0	1943. . . . .5.1	1964. . . . .5.1	1985. . . . .8.4
1902. . . . .1.2	1923. . . . .7.8	1944. . . . .5.0	1965. . . . .5.5	1986. . . . .9.6
1903. . . . .1.3	1924. . . . .8.1	1945. . . . .5.7	1966. . . . .5.9	1987. . . . .8.7
1904. . . . .1.3	1925. . . . .8.3	1946. . . . .6.4	1967. . . . .6.8	1988. . . . .9.0
1905. . . . .2.1	1926. . . . .8.4	1947. . . . .6.1	1968. . . . .7.3	1989. . . . .9.3
1906. . . . .3.9	1927. . . . .8.4	1948. . . . .5.9	1969. . . . .7.7	1990. . . .10.0
1907. . . . .4.9	1928. . . . .8.6	1949. . . . .5.4	1970. . . . .8.3	1991. . . .10.5
1908. . . . .4.8	1929. . . . .8.4	1950. . . . .5.3	1971. . . . .9.1	1992. . . .10.0
1909. . . . .4.2	1930. . . . .8.8	1951. . . . .4.9	1972. . . . .9.4	1993. . . .10.3
1910. . . . .4.6	1931. . . . .9.2	1952. . . . .5.2	1973. . . . .9.7	1994. . . . .9.6
1911. . . . .5.5	1932. . . . .9.0	1953. . . . .4.8	1974. . . .10.1	1995. . . . .8.7
1912. . . . .5.4	1933. . . . .9.7	1954. . . . .4.8	1975. . . . .9.9	1996. . . . .7.9
1913. . . . .6.1	1934. . . . .9.5	1955. . . . .4.5	1976. . . . .9.0	1997. . . . .7.4
1914. . . . .6.2	1935. . . . .8.3	1956. . . . .4.6	1977. . . . .9.1	1998. . . . .6.8
1915. . . . .5.9	1936. . . . .8.0	1957. . . . .4.5	1978. . . . .9.2	1999. . . . .6.2
1916. . . . .6.3	1937. . . . .7.6	1958. . . . .4.5	1979. . . .10.0	2000. . . . .6.1
1917. . . . .6.9	1938. . . . .6.8	1959. . . . .4.6	1980. . . .10.7	
1918. . . . .6.5	1939. . . . .6.4	1960. . . . .4.7	1981. . . .10.3	
1919. . . . .7.2	1940. . . . .6.3	1961. . . . .4.7	1982. . . . .9.6	
1920. . . . .6.8	1941. . . . .6.0	1962. . . . .4.8	1983. . . . .8.6	

gun receives the coverage of an airplane crash, the press also has ignored the 50 percent decline in firearm accidents during the same years. Gun buffs, unwise in the ways of journalism, see this as a conspiracy of silence.

Another journalistic hypocrisy, conscious or otherwise, is the steady diet of reports on the criminality of youth. The most conspicuous difference between teenage violence now and in the "public enemy" era is that the perpetrators then were white, at least as portrayed in newspapers so comfortably racist that they ignored any mayhem that confined itself to the black community. In 1933 the *Chicago Herald and Examiner* devoted a full page to the problem of "THE NATION'S BIGGEST CRIMINAL GROUP—AGED 20!" Two years later, the *Chicago Daily News* published a similar page headlined, "YOUTH PREDOMINATES IN CRIME—60,000 JAILED EACH YEAR."

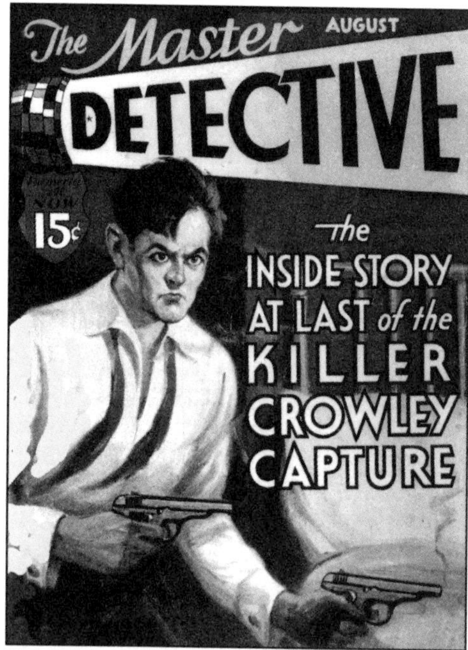

"Two-Gun" Crowley might have attracted little attention had he not barricaded himself in an apartment building on New York's Upper West Side, holding police at bay long enough to become a local tourist attraction.

By then the offenders' average age had started its slow if steady decline but had only reached nineteen, which included Francis "Two-Gun" Crowley, who concluded a short but impressive crime spree in New York by killing a policeman before barricading himself in an Upper West Side apartment building. From there, he and his partner, Rudolph Duringer, with a girlfriend loading their guns (according to the papers), battled more than 200 cops in the street, in other buildings and on rooftops, while countless spectators subwayed to the scene to watch. Crowley made nationwide headlines with his spectacular last stand until he was exhausted, wounded, probably out of ammunition, and captured; his case stayed on the front pages until he was executed at Sing Sing.

The battle involved one quirky incident that illustrated the inability of most people (at least in the days before answering machines) to ignore a ringing telephone. Some enterprising reporter obtained the number of the apartment where Crowley was bunkered and dialed it to see what, if anything, would happen. Despite the fact that the police were shooting the place to pieces, the embattled "Two-Gun" stopped his own firing to answer the phone. When the caller identified himself as a newsman, all Crowley could think of to say was that he was "too busy" to talk to him.

KILLED IN THE LINE OF DUTY

It may be that the policeman's lot is no happier today than it was during many early periods of law enforcement history, though usually for different reasons. The first efforts to organize urban police departments encountered resistance to the use of uniforms, sometimes even to the display of badges, which invited physical attacks by organized and often politically protected street gangs (especially in New York) long accustomed to imposing their own rules in neighborhoods they controlled.

The general public was ambivalent, sometimes heroizing the "men in blue" or "New York's Finest," sometimes regarding them as little more than goons on the city payroll hired to oppress minorities, immigrants, and "radicals," or otherwise do the bidding of the corrupt politicians to whom they owed their jobs. The role of the "detective" often was not the prevention of crime or the arrest of criminals, but negotiating (for a price) the return of stolen property to its rightful owners.

"New York's Finest" were considered fair game until the mid-nineteenth century, when progressive municipal authorities finally turned politically hired thugs into a uniformed police force.

The Boston police strike of 1919 threw a scare into the entire country when a major city found itself unprotected against violent crime and property crime. In the end, order was restored by military forces, the strike fizzled, and citizens and civil authorities had to acknowledge that even a poorly trained or crooked cop was better than no cop at all.

A snail-paced movement toward police professionalism enjoyed increasing public support but suffered a setback under Prohibition. Not many police could resist the bribery of bootleggers and speakeasy operators who didn't blink at weekly cash payoffs that might exceed an officer's annual salary. Paradoxically, such graft, while again diminishing the public's respect for the law and its ostensible enforcers, did not necessarily lessen a policeman's personal commitment to keeping the peace and protecting the general public. Many used their ill-gotten gains to finance their children's college educations that they never could have afforded on a policeman's salary. More than a few bootleggers did the same, using part of their illicit profits to move their families out of the slums where they had grown up and into good neighborhoods, schools and legitimate businesses. How many law and medical degrees were directly financed by Prohibition is anybody's guess, but even sociologists of the day discovered that the Volstead Act served as a kind of G.I. bill for the children of families on both sides of the law.

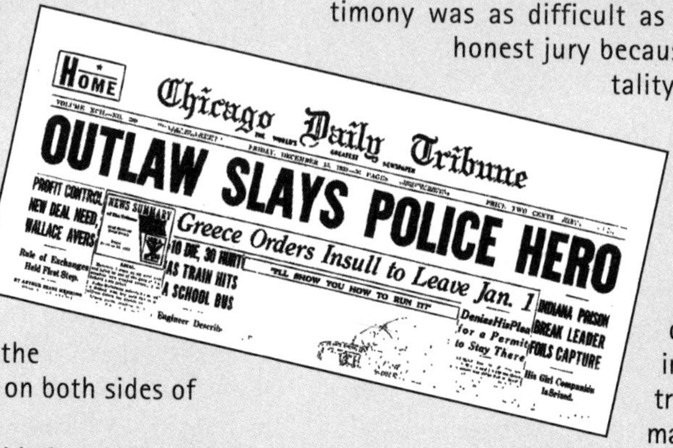

HOME

Chicago Daily Tribune

OUTLAW SLAYS POLICE HERO

PROFIT CONTROL NEW DEAL NEED, WALLACE AVERS

Rule of Exchanges Held First Step.

NEWS SUMMARY

Greece Orders Insull to Leave Jan. 1

10 DIE, 30 HURT AS TRAIN HITS A SCHOOL BUS

Engineer Describ

"I'LL SHOW YOU HOW TO RUN IT"

Denies His Plea for a Permit to Stay There

INDIANA PRISON BREAK LEADER FOILS CAPTURE

His Girl Companion Is Seized.

The downside to this form of social climbing was a renewed contempt for local and federal law enforcers and for officers of the court, whose collusion with hoodlums and crooked politicians did not always stop with "honest graft." The protection purchased by the criminal community had no finely drawn lines, which crippled efforts of the justice system to deal with far more serious crime: It delivered virtually no gangland murder convictions over more than a decade. The guilty verdict returned against Leo Brothers in the killing of Chicago journalist Jake Lingle, himself a mob insider, was hailed as a milestone of justice in a front-page editorial cartoon published by the *Chicago Tribune* (which had been Lingle's employer), but even that was a farce. There persists some doubt whether Brothers was guilty or the fall-guy. For stalking and shooting Lingle execution-style in the back of the head, Brothers, a professional gunman, received only fourteen years, no doubt thanks to his attorney, Louis Piquett, who would one day represent John Dillinger.

Such conditions made crime control in Chicago, New York, and other cities less a campaign of reform than a grudge match between cops and crooks who had crossed each other personally or who tangled in public in ways that made a gun battle mandatory. Even in clear-cut murder cases with plenty of eyewitnesses, securing truthful testimony was as difficult as empaneling an honest jury because of high mortality rates or bribe offers that might be fatal to turn down.

One vivid example of such quirky justice involved three trials and ultimately the acquittal of two of Chicago's most vicious hoodlums. Albert Anselmi and John Scalise, known as the "homicide squad," killed not only two policemen after a high-speed car chase, but also in all likelihood, members of their own Little Italy community who failed to contribute to their defense fund.

After a hung jury necessitated a second trial, their attorney, the dashing Michael J. Ahearn (who specialized in defending top mobsters), got them a verdict of manslaughter on the remarkable grounds that their pursuers lacked probable cause to arrest even such notorious criminals: "If a policeman detains you, even for a moment, against your will, you are not guilty of murder, but only of manslaughter. If the policeman uses force of arms, you may kill him in self-defense and emerge from the law unscathed." During yet a third trial, both simply were acquitted by jurors bombarded by threats on their lives.

Thus death in the line of duty was a far greater occupational hazard for police officers then than now, when killing a cop guarantees relentless pursuit by a far better organized and far less corrupt law enforcement community.

Local and Federal Officers Killed in the Line of Duty 1920–1940

CHICAGO POLICE

William Allison	6/23/25
Theodore J. Anderson	7/23/26
Thomas J. Baggington	1/26/25
James P. Baggott	6/7/25
George T. Barker	3/13/22
Floyd A. Beardsley	10/31/26
Joseph Bender	2/10/27
Frank J. Blazek	4/29/26
Stanley F. Bobosky	7/6/34
David Boitano	9/25/24
Julian A. Bonfield	12/15/26
Oscar E. Brosseau	6/20/33
William F. Bunda	4/7/24
Thomas W. Burke	6/16/21
Thomas Burke	12/21/31
Harry J. Busse	1/17/20
John J. Byrnes	9/30/26
David J. Cairns	2/4/27
Daniel J. Carey	12/15/23
James H. Carroll	11/28/25
James J. Casey	7/1/31
Ernest H. Cassidy	4/3/22
John Chiska	4/5/28
Thomas J. Clark	5/10/22
Edward J. Cleary	11/29/24
Martin J. Collins	1/4/21
John L. Conley	5/31/29
Charles R. Conlon	12/16/20
James Cooley	4/4/27
James S. Corcoran	11/25/30
Patrick J. Costello	4/3/31
John Cronin	6/3/31
Harry J. Crowley	11/8/24
Frank J. Cunningham	7/19/32
Miles Cunningham	9/22/33
Patrick J. Daley	6/27/26
James F. Day	9/19/34
Edward E. Dean	6/11/25
Patrick F. Delaney	10/4/27
Hubert J. Dillon	11/25/30
Patrick H. Doherty	8/10/22
Patrick Durkin	5/2/31
Thomas J. Egan	8/25/21
Arthur F. Esau	4/27/28
James C. Farley	6/23/27
Harry W. Fielder	4/14/31
Edward F. Finnegan	3/27/26
Joseph M. Fitzpatrick	10/25/30
Harry Francois	11/20/39
John J. Freichel	8/23/36
Louis F. Furst	9/22/34
William G. Gagler	6/19/32
Patrick J. Gallagher	4/14/31
William Gallagher	9/25/29
Robert Gibbons	6/26/22
Vincent Gillispie	12/1/27
George F. Giovannoni	10/19/29
Robert H. Granger	4/9/32
Leo Grant	3/12/27
Harry J. Gray	11/2/25
John J. Guiltanane	7/18/30
Hubert N. Hagberg	5/32/29
Edwin Halloran	12/27/26
Lawrence C. Hartnett	10/27/23
Joseph P. Hastings	8/14/23
Thomas J. Healy	8/8/27
William E. Hennessy	8/23/20
James A. Henry	12/1/25
William E. Hoard	9/10/33
William Holmes	12/24/24
Jesse D. Hults	9/26/29
Joseph Isola	11/1/35
Leonard T. Iagla	9/4/28
Thomas J. Johnson	6/22/31
Roscoe C. Johnston	3/21/33
Eugene J. Keegan	2/9/28
Thomas W. Kehoe	6/23/27
Phillip J. Kelly	5/10/39
Raymond C. Kelly	4/3/32
Thomas Kelma	5/31/35
William R. King	5/25/20
Bernard Klinke	2/22/37
Joseph Klocek	10/8/35
Martin Knudson	2/5/32
Joseph Kurtz	6/7/21
Michael T. Langan	12/30/29
Earl K. Leonard	6/9/29
Walter E. Lilly	2/28/28
Thomas Locashio	9/9/30
William D. Lundy	12/9/32
Stanley J. Lutke	4/30/33
Michael J. Lynch	12/8/28
Thomas Lynch	11/23/27
Edward J. Lynn	11/30/38
Terrence Lyons	5/11/22
Patrick Madden	11/20/32
Michael A. Madigan	6/18/26
Maurice Marcusson	1/23/33
Edward W. Marpool	10/26/20
Raymond E. Martin	5/15/29
Edward F. Mashek	4/8/26
William I. McCann	9/16/30
Jerome M. McCauley	5/29/36
Frank C. McGlynn	7/8/24
Patrick J. McGovern	6/22/25
Edward McGuire	2/24/28
Frank J. McGurk	8/3/20
Fred Mudloff	10/6/29
James A. Mulcahy	8/23/20
John Mullen	1/3/21
Edward T. Murphy	2/9/28
Jerry E. Murphy	1/14/30
Thomas Murphy	2/1/34
Michael Murtaugh	10/11/24
Arthur D. Mutter	4/18/23
George R. Neil	7/18/30
James J. O'Brien	9/16/28
Jeremiah E. O'Connell	7/30/28
Timothy O'Connor	12/20/20

William A. O'Connor	6/4/28
Edward M. J. O'Donnell	6/9/31
Patrick E. O'Malley	8/30/38
William J. O'Malley	12/30/22
Patrick J. O'Niell	3/23/21
Michael W. Oakley	12/13/31
John R. Officer	4/13/34
Henry Olsen	2/8/30
John A. Olsen	10/20/38
Harold F. Olson	6/13/25
Elmer R. Ostling	7/22/33
Charles Poldina	1/20/22
William F. Penney	7/24/34
William A. Perrin	11/30/24
Joseph L. Puanowski	11/18/20
Patrick J. Redmond	5/9/34
Walter J. Riley	10/26/26
William A. Roberts	5/14/20
William P. Rumbler	10/12/30
Anthony L. Ruthy	4/30/31
John R. Ryan	1/24/30
Patrick J. Ryan	8/8/33
Frederick M. Schmitz	11/9/25
Paul Schutz	10/16/21
John G. Sevick	7/24/33
William T. Shanley	12/14/33
Emil Shogren	4/18/28
Vincent Skiva	1/7/24
John Skopek	7/22/33
Edward F. Smith	5/30/31
Elmer Smith	11/12/28
Jesse Sneed	4/11/28
Ralph S. Souders	12/19/22
Vincent Spiro	7/9/23
Alfred M. Stokke	1/24/35
William H. Stringfellow	10/3/35
Victor H. Sugg	4/24/34
Arthur J. Sullivan	1/14/37
Lawrence Sullivan	4/14/25
Blanton W. Sutton	6/4/23
Arthur Swanson	5/21/36
John J. Sweeney	7/7/29
Louis C. Szewczyk	1/27/30
George W. Thompson	11/14/25
Thomas E. Torpey	9/22/33
Michael Toth	11/8/36
Arthur Vollmar	2/22/29
John Vondruska	1/1/31
Charles B. Walsh	6/13/25
Dennis Wilson	4/9/20
Kazimar Wistert	6/7/27
Arthur Wittbrodt	1/16/32
Martin Wolski	3/26/38
Anton Zapolsky	7/30/34

NEW YORK CITY POLICE

Hubert Allen	8/5/27
Isador Astel	8/11/37
James R. Baker	3/28/23
Howard Barrows	12/21/30
James A. Barry	8/7/28
Henry C. Behnstedt	11/5/28
David P. Beyer	1/20/36
Harry D. Bloomfield	8/9/30
Morris Borkin	5/17/27
John Bosworth	8/11/37
Joseph Bridgetts	2/17/21
John P. D. Briggs	12/23/39
Jeremiah C. Brosnan	9/13/28
Albert Bruden	1/11/29
Francis J. M. Buckley	1/6/22
Anthony E. Buckner	10/24/39
Joseph P. Burke	6/18/32
James J. Burns	6/4/32
Thomas J. Burns Jr.	12/31/39
Thomas L. Burns	8/6/35
Edward T. Byrns	11/19/26
Benjamin Cantor	6/4/27
Emmett Cassidy	6/6/39
Dominick Caviglia	7/28/30
Edwin V. Churchill	8/21/31
Philip Clarius	3/15/34
Clarence C. Clark	11/23/38
John H. Conk	5/3/21
Timothy J. Connell	7/12/24
Joseph L. Connelly	3/27/21
Harold Conway	1/31/31
Victor C. Cooper	11/23/38
Peter Costa	11/25/33
Richard J. Coughlin	2/24/30
James Cullen	6/11/25
Frank A. Daszkiewicz	1/22/26
William Deans	6/24/22
William H. DeGive	6/28/31
Jerome DeLorenzo	9/18/27
Arthur J. DeMarrais	11/7/37
Francis P. Dolan	3/16/40
John T. Donohue	2/16/23
James Dowling	12/24/35
Albert L. Duffy	8/2/23
John J. Duffy	11/17/29
William J. Duncan	5/17/30
James F. Dursee	8/25/28
William F. Eberhardt	9/15/31
John E. Egan	9/1/23
Patrick Fahey	1/31/28
Charles L. Farrell	9/23/32
Henry J. Farrell	3/4/27
Arthur C. Fash	8/4/28
Angelo E. Favata	7/11/38
Wilson A. Fields	6/26/30
John Fink	10/15/32
James Fisher	6/3/38
John Fitzpatrick	5/21/20
Michael J. Foley	4/10/37
John J. Fraser	9/28/34
Joseph H. Gaffney	1/26/24
Thomas Gaffney	3/2/24
Lawrence Gallagher	7/14/36
James Garvey	4/21/34
George L. Gerhard	12/14/32
John D. Gibbons	10/4/28
William Goddy	8/7/27
Charles L. Godfrey	5/12/25
James B. Goodwin	2/15/32
John H. Grattan	12/9/32
Andrew Grennan	6/28/27
George Grossberger	12/31/29
Bernardino Grottano	5/26/24
Thomas Hackett	5/4/38
Chester A. Hagan	2/14/25
Martin A. Hanke	10/18/38
Maurice F. Harlow	2/22/25
Thomas L. Harnett	4/2/30
Douglas W. Hay	5/18/22

Richard Heneberry	8/6/25
William Higgins	3/18/26
Thomas E. Hill	7/28/30
John P. Hoey	5/4/31
Charles Hoffman	11/12/22
William J. Hogan	9/26/40
John A. Honahan	11/5/24
John J. Hopkins	1/20/35
Floyd Horton	12/16/20
Arthur Howarth	7/9/38
John L. Hubbard	2/28/28
John Hyland	7/26/24
Henry Immen	2/21/20
Joseph T. Jockel	12/28/29
Edward P. Keenan	2/23/30
Thomas F. Kelly	4/17/25
William E. Kelly	1/31/28
Charles Kemmer	12/22/27
John Kennedy	12/3/22
Arthur J. Kenny	4/2/26
William A. Kertin	7/28/29
James J. Killion	1/18/35
David Kilpatrick	1/28/38
John Kranz	1/2/32
Joseph Kussius	12/22/40
Arthur Loewe	7/22/22
Michael J. Lonto	11/24/39
Edward P. Lynch	12/7/37
Joseph J. Lynch	7/4/40
Francis Mace	12/11/22
Thomas Madigan	11/3/31
Henry F. Masterson	2/25/38
James M. Masterson	1/31/27
Joseph P. McBreen	8/11/37
William Joseph McCaffrey	10/3/29
Ernest F. McCarron	1/7/34
Richard J. McCormick	8/26/36
Richard McHale	10/24/35
James F. McMahon	12/23/30
James H. McMail	3/15/22
Stephen McPhillips	12/20/25
Henry E. A. Meyer	9/16/27
Clarence Mihlheiser	8/28/39
George A. Miller	2/12/30
William A. Miller	1/5/22
Joseph Misischia	1/23/34
Patrick Mitchell	6/20/30
Eugene Monahan	2/4/33
John T. Monahan	12/3/34
Nicholas C. Moreno	5/23/39
John J. Moriarty	7/2/22
Michael Morosco	12/8/32
James A. Morrissey	4/15/32
John J. Morrissey	5/15/34
Philip F. Morrissey	12/10/29
Humbert Morruzzi	4/17/38
Otto W. Motz	1/19/22
Philip S. Mundo	7/14/22
Frank Murphy	8/8/26
Walter Murphy	1/7/33
George Nadler	2/1/35
Daniel J. Neville	8/27/21
Maurice D. O'Brien	1/30/30
William O'Connor	5/19/31
Will O'Shaughnessy	6/9/31
Oscar A. Oehlerking	8/6/26
Harry J. Padian	7/7/38
Dioniso P. Pasquarella	3/15/36
Joseph Pellosi	12/11/24
Guido J. Pessagano	10/22/31
Howard L. Peterson	11/1/31
George W. Pierson	11/8/37
Harry L. Pohndorf	5/10/22
Charles D. Potter	7/22/21
Arthur P. Rassmussen	5/4/34
Charles B. Reilly	4/5/26
Joseph P. Reilly	2/16/23
Joseph P. Reiner	12/25/35
Joseph A. Reuchle	9/28/21
Charles J. Reynolds	7/26/23
John Ringhauser	5/7/31
Frank E. Romanella	7/26/23
Edward Roos	1/27/38
Charles Sauer	12/20/29
Chris W. Scheuing	2/19/31
William Schmelter	4/14/29
John Schneider	1/13/24
Joseph F. Scott	3/11/30
Walter Senk	11/22/30
Paul J. Shafer	1/7/30
Leroy J. Sheares	4/20/36
David Sheehan	8/22/25
John Sheridan	2/14/21
Bernard Sherry	5/3/31
John M. Singer	8/11/26
George Smith	2/20/21
James Smith	12/20/36
Ferdinand Socha	7/4/40
Michael J. Speer	12/23/29
William J. Stoeffel	10/8/28
Alexander C. Stutt	6/9/39
Daniel Sullivan	4/6/37
Ale Swider	11/1/23
Frederick Thomas	8/14/24
Anthony V. Tomatore	1/9/38
Alfred A. Van Clieff	12/4/23
William T. Vorden	11/15/30
Thomas J. Wallace	10/9/28
John Walsh	1/21/32
Lawrence A. Ward	5/6/34
Walter J. Webb	8/21/31
Joseph Weckesser	6/16/27
Charles Weidig	11/8/30
Theodore F. Werdann	5/12/32
Frank White	2/10/26
Louis G. Wiendieck	12/13/33
Melvin Williams	5/31/38
John H. A. Wilson	9/23/37
James I. Young	2/12/36
Frank Zaccor	1/15/38

FEDERAL AGENTS

U.S. MARSHALS SERVICE

Will Cross	8/12/22
W. F. Deiter	3/1/32
Raoul Dorsay	11/25/37
Colby S. Farrar	10/7/39
E. F. Flanery	3/28/28
John H. Glenn	7/31/40
Andrew H. Leonard	11/14/22
Samuel Lilly	7/29/24
John Luses	9/8/38
George Meffan	7/31/40

Adrian Metcalf	7/31/29
Herbert Ray	2/2/33
Clyde Rivers	5/16/31
Ed H. Sherman	4/21/30
Robert Sumter	8/9/33
R. G. Warnke	6/20/29
Whit G. Wright	8/2/39

PROHIBITION BUREAU

Charles F. Alexander	1/2/29
Robert G. Anderson	4/16/23
Herman Sutton Barbrey	1/5/34
Stafford E. Beckett	3/22/21
William Franklin Berry	3/18/38
Charles Bintliff	5/13/27
William R. Blandford	5/12/34
James E. Bowdoin	2/16/25
William R. Braden	7/22/35
Jacob P. Brandt	12/9/26
Albert L. Brown	6/9/30
Robert M. Buck	2/1/32
Remus W. Buckner	5/12/26
Curtis C. Burke	7/22/31
Otto P. Butler	12/10/29
William T. Butler	9/28/37
Atha Carter	12/24/22
Theodore H. Chunn	11/19/24
Daniel S. Cleveland	7/10/24
Donald C. Cleveland	11/22/36
E. Guy Cole	12/15/22
William E. Collins	3/6/25
Charles F. Cooley Jr.	7/30/29
Walter T. Creviston	7/30/31
Louis M. Davies	1/14/30
Malcolm M. Day	2/14/25
Norval L. DeArmond	1/1/40
William D. Dorsey	6/13/20
George A. Droz	7/12/29
Robert E. Duff	12/9/22
George W. Dykeman	1/14/27
Harry Elliott	6/22/33
Holmer L. Everett	5/2/31
Raymond L. Ezzell	7/28/31
John Finiello	9/19/30
Howard Henry Fisher	7/22/22
Rosie Lester Flinchum	6/17/30
John T. Foley	10/26/21
John R. Foster	5/14/36
Warren C. Frahm	6/18/28
Kirby Frans	11/20/20
Westley A. Frazer	1/2/28
Gary D. Freeman	7/22/22
Robert D. Freeman	2/8/30
Jacob F. Green	3/1/21
Richard Griffin	12/6/20
William S. Grubb	3/31/33
Parker H. Hall	2/3/34
Oscar C. Hanson	3/28/28
James A. Harney	9/23/32
Major A. Hart	7/16/27
Charles E. Howell	7/17/21
Dano M. Jackley	5/14/29
Eugene Jackson	7/15/32
Richard W. Jackson	12/16/20
Jesse R. Johnson	11/21/21
Ludwig P. Johnson	7/25/28
Dale F. Kearney	7/16/30
Jack E. Kenford	6/14/32
W. T. Lewis	7/15/27
Chester A. Mason	11/12/32
Frank A. Mather	10/15/32
Lawrence A. Mommer	6/27/29
Robert Knox Moncure	1/18/30
Harold V. Mooring	9/21/23
John M. Mulcahy	9/3/25
Murdock E. Murray	10/20/25
George Nantz	7/20/27
John Nicola	10/4/28
John O'Toole	2/17/22
Howard B. Ousler	10/12/32
Joseph B. Owen	9/6/22
Mack C. Parsons	9/20/30
Franklin R. Patterson	1/18/30
Eugene J. Pearce	2/9/32
Glenn Henry Price	9/3/22
Joseph Allen Purvis	3/20/38
Paul A. Read	7/12/33
Carl L. Rehm	10/16/29
J. H. Reynolds	8/26/21
Dallas A. Roberts	1/20/26
J. H. Rose	10/25/20
Charles C. Rouse	6/12/27
Richard J. Sandlands	8/7/29
Willie B. Saylor	2/24/24
Irby U. Scruggs	4/30/21
Roy Shafer	6/30/30
William Paul Spigener	12/9/24
Charles O. Sterner	6/25/22
Horracio M. Stetson	6/29/24
Charles F. Stevens	9/25/29
George H. Stewart	11/11/23
Hunter Riser Stotler	7/26/27
Ray Sutton	8/28/30
Clyde L. Taylor	5/11/29
H. Thorwalderson	12/20/26
Grover C. Todd	9/3/22
Walter R. Tolbert	2/22/28
George V. Traybing	8/19/31
Levi G. Trexler	3/31/33
Ballard W. Turner	9/29/32
Ernest V. Vlasich	10/15/32
Ernest W. Walker	3/5/21
Archie Warnke	6/20/29
Erving S. Washburn	7/13/28
John Watson	5/3/21
Stanton E. Weiss	10/28/20
Leonard A. Welty	4/13/33
George H. Wentworth	11/24/26
John I. Wilson	7/22/31
Lamar Watson York	4/12/30
Leroy J. Youmans	4/3/23
Arthur A. Zimmerman	8/11/29

JUSTICE DEPARTMENT [FBI]

Wimberly W. Baker	4/17/37
W. Carter Baum	4/22/34
Raymond J. Caffrey	6/17/33
Samuel P. Cowley	11/28/34
Herman E. Hollis	11/28/34
Albert L. Ingle	11/24/31
Nelson B. Klein	8/16/35
Paul E. Reynolds	8/9/29
William R. Ramsey	5/3/38
Truett E. Rowe	6/1/37
Edwin C. Shanahan	10/11/25
Rupert V. Surratt	10/8/33

Police Massacre

The murder of six lawmen at a farm near Springfield, Missouri, on January 2, 1932, remains the largest number of police killed during a single raid in what has become known as the Young Brothers Massacre.

Harry, Jennings, and Paul Young and eight other brothers and sisters were children of James David and Willie Florence Young, owners of a hundred-acre farm in Greene County, a few miles southwest of Springfield. By all accounts the family was classically "dysfunctional," the father honest and hardworking but suspicious of all authorities, the mother loathing those authorities and continually defending the three youngest of the boys whose property crimes landed Jennings and Paul in prison at an early age. They were incarcerated at the time of their father's death, and when they were released became the "Young Triumvirate" of petty criminals, who advanced from stealing to burglary, robbery, safecracking, and the unproven murder of a city marshal who had tried to arrest Harry for drunken driving.

By Thanksgiving of 1931 the boys were wanted in several states, and Chief Ed Waddle had reason to believe they both, or all three, had returned to the family home. Not wanting to upstage Sheriff Marcel Hendrix who was out on a call, he deferred to county authorities. Hendrix elected to raid the Young farm

Rescuers found Deputy Crosswhite (1) behind the cellar of the Jennings house. Deputy Mashburn was sitting erect at (2). One of the killers is presumed to have taken route (3) to reach Crosswhite while the other killer fired at him from the dining room window (4). It is thought the killers used the rear door and route (5) to escape.

the next afternoon. When assembled in the vicinity, the raiding party consisted of the sheriff, seven county officers, two police officers, and a civilian who had gone along for the excitement.

Hendrix, who had once lived nearby and thought he knew the Youngs, scoffed at the notion he faced danger. "They wouldn't harm a hair on my head if they knew it was me. I've tried them out before. You know yourself I used to live in this neighborhood before I became sheriff." That quote is from a magazine-size booklet titled *The Young Brothers Massacre*, by John R. Woodward, et al, first published in 1932 and now reprinted by the Greene County Library. It describes the events of the afternoon and early evening, written in the style of that time, including the most grisly details.

The sheriff's and city police had surrounded the house as best they could, given that it had a barn, other outbuildings, and a large cornfield; and they had tried the doors and looked in windows. Noises had been heard, but the absence of anyone in ground floor rooms suggested that any occupants had gone upstairs. Hendrix had a Federal tear-gas gun that probably had never been used, and his decision to fire it may have been a costly mistake. Already alarmed at the number of police outside, the two occupants, Harry and Jennings Young, may have panicked when a large shell crashed through a bedroom window and began flooding the place with gas. A second shot missed, bouncing off the side the house. And those happened to be the only gas cartridges the officers had thought to bring.

At this point Deputy Wiley Mashburn and Hendrix kicked in a door. Then:

> A gun BANGED with an awful roar. A well-aimed charge of bird shot smote the left side of [Mashburn's] face in the region of the eye. Flesh and blood blew backward in a seeming spray. His left eye, facial skin, nose and right eye were peeled from the bone of the skull to drop down in a ghastly flap over his mouth and chin. Sheriff Hendrix hollered, "God, boys, they mean business," and stepped in to the opening left by Mashburn as the latter faltered back.
>
> "BANG," another shot rang out. It struck Sheriff Hendrix full-force in the upper part of the shoulder just below the right collar bone, tearing a ragged hole through the first and second ribs. The charge went downward to the left and backward. He was leaning over, so part of the shot remained at a tangent to the general direction of the wound in the chest muscles near the right arm. The main load ripped on to tear a jagged course through the chest cavity and into the external part of the upper lobe of the right lung, where it embedded itself to sear and sizzle in the blood of the Sheriff who had come as an old-time neighbor to peacefully weave the fetters of the law around errant sons of an honest and upright friend. . . .
>
> Without uttering a single sound Deputy Sheriff Mashburn straightened up . . . and as he faltered back inch by inch he pulled his clinched fists down, down, down in spasmodic, muscled jerks, his hands opened and with his fingers he fumbled in the empty sockets where his eyes had been. . . .

Both men died, and in the next four hours so also did Springfield Police Officer Charlie Houser, Police Detective Sid Meadows, Special Deputy Ollie Crosswhite, and Chief of Police Detectives Tony Oliver. The death of each was described in similarly gruesome detail.

The two Young brothers, both experienced hunters, had become deadly marksmen with a rifle and a shotgun—a Remington .25–20 semi-automatic and a Remington 12-gauge pump repeater with a "full choke" attached to the muzzle to keep the shot from spreading. As the casualties mounted, and the raiding party lost track of one another, the brothers managed to escape—after dark, probably through the cornfield.

Meanwhile, the road to the house was clogged with police cars, ambulances, and spectators, many armed, and getting the ambulances anywhere near the farm took a great deal of shouting and maneuvering. In the general chaos, it took another hour to conclude that the shooters were no longer there. Greene County lawmen and citizens were understandably dismayed and horrified at the carnage, as were the police in adjoining states. They mounted a massive manhunt, but not before the brothers had reached Houston.

Three days later, on Tuesday morning, January 5, a carpenter called Houston's chief of police to report that two young men had rented a room in his house, and from pictures in the morning paper he recognized them as the Young brothers. The police closed in with every kind of weapon, from submachine guns to riot shotguns and gas guns. The brothers tried to escape the gas by retreating to a bathroom, from which they fired three shots that missed the invading officers. A few minutes later one of the boys shouted, "We're dead—come and get us," and they simultaneously fired at one another. As described by the booklet's author: "Trapped like rattlesnakes [they] played the ace to cheat at last society and their God. What they thought cannot be written or told, but what they did is history—Harry and Jennings Young, at bay at last to square accounts, spat their venom into each other and died."

Today a monument commemorates the six slain officers, who have been further memorialized by the public library's reprinting of its rare book that ironically carries several advertisements from Federal Laboratories Inc. of Pittsburgh, including one patterned like a newspaper article that shouts:

> EXTRA!
>
> YOUNG BROTHERS CAPTURED
>
> BY FEDERAL TEAR GAS
>
> This story of the pitiless massacre of six officers might never have been written had the unfortunate victims used plenty of Federal Gas in the proper way. . . .

In an earlier commentary on the Young brothers' father, Woodward lamented, as though he were still alive: "At that time of life when most men expect some surcease from toil, when they hope to be arrayed in a halo of respectability for their own flesh and blood, when they most desire praise from society and compassion from God, James David Young was to bow his head in shame because he had been a weak and forgiving father when he should have been a stern and willful parent. . . ."

7

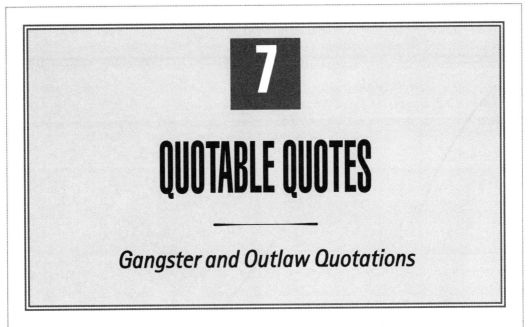

QUOTABLE QUOTES

Gangster and Outlaw Quotations

You can get much farther with a smile, a kind word, and a gun than you can with a smile and a kind word.
— Al Capone

The adage above is probably the most colorful remark attributed to Al Capone, and it has appeared in several "famous quotations" books without source or citation. It probably is also apocryphal, the invention of some writer who decided that if Capone didn't say it, he could have or should have said it.

But during his reign as the country's most notorious gangster, "The Big Fellow" could not resist entertaining reporters with comments and commentary they found highly quotable, and which now seem to reveal a person more complex than the vicious, flamboyant thug usually portrayed in gangster films.

Other criminals were as capable and crafty, but either they lacked Capone's capacity for introspection or they learned from his example that the notoriety he obviously enjoyed only made him the most conspicuous symbol of Prohibition-era crime and thus an ever-larger target for reformers and rivals alike.

At least as well known is the quote attributed to Willie Sutton when asked why he robbed banks. Supposedly he answered, "Because that's where the money is." Sutton later denied he ever said that and credited it to a reporter who simply made it up. Likewise, Roger Touhy allegedly said, "The bastards never forget!" This, too, was some journalist's idea of what he should have said.

"We can't all be saints," is a memorable quip probably made by John Dillinger to a reporter who has so far eluded researchers.

The following quotes are better substantiated:

AL CAPONE

"When I sell liquor, they call it bootlegging. When my patrons serve it on silver trays on Lake Shore Drive, they call it hospitality."

"I'm a businessman. I've made my money supplying a popular demand. If I break the law, my customers are as guilty as I am."

"I've seen gambling houses, too—in my travels, you understand—and I never saw anyone point a gun at a man and make him go in. I've never heard of anyone being forced to go to a place to have some fun."

"I never stuck up a man in my life. Neither did any of my agents ever rob anybody or burglarize any homes while they worked for me. They might have pulled plenty of jobs before they came with me or after they left me, but not while they were in my Outfit."

"Ninety percent of the people of Cook County drink and gamble, and my offense has been to furnish them with those amusements. Whatever else they may say, my booze has been good, and my games have been on the square. Public service has been my motto."

"Graft is a byword in American life today. It is law where no law is obeyed. It is undermining this country. The honest lawmakers of any city can be counted on your fingers. I could count Chicago's on one hand."

"A crook is a crook, and there's something healthy about his frankness in the matter. But the guy who pretends he's enforcing the law and steals on his authority is a swell snake."

"The worst type is the Big Politician who gives about half his time to covering up so that no one will know he's a thief. A hard-working crook can buy these birds by the dozens, but he hates them in his heart."

"Union members look at dues the same way they look at taxes: just something you got to pay the thieves who run things."

"There's always some wiseacre who stands in the wings and criticizes. You've got two choices. You either buy these wiseacres off by giving them jobs . . . or you scare them off. If they don't scare, you take them in the alley. When they get out of the hospital, if they still want to squawk, you get rid of them."

"People who respect nothing dread fear. It is upon fear, therefore, that I have built up my organization. But understand me correctly, please. Those who work with me are afraid of nothing. Those who work for me are kept faithful, not so much because of their pay as because they know what might be done with them if they broke faith."

"Every time a boy falls off a tricycle, every time a black cat has gray kittens, every time someone stubs a toe, every time there's a murder or a fire or the Marines land in Nicaragua, the police and the newspapers holler, 'Get Capone!' I'm sick of it. As soon as I possibly can, I'll clear out of here."

"They've hung everything on me but the Chicago fire."

"Nobody was ever killed except outlaws, and the community is better off without them."

"I have always been opposed to violence, to shootings. I have fought, yes, but fought for peace. And I believe I can take credit for the peace that now exists in the racket game in Chicago. I believe that the people can thank me for the fact that gang killings here are probably a thing of the past."

"I'm tired of gang murders and gang shootings. It's a tough life to lead. You fear death at every moment, and worse than death, you fear the rats of the game who'd run around and tell the police if you don't constantly satisfy them with money and favors."

"Now get me right. I'm not posing as a model for youth. I've had to do a lot of things I don't like to do. But I'm not as black as I'm painted. I'm human. I've got a heart in me."

"Let the worthy citizens of Chicago get their liquor the best way they can. I'm sick of the job. It's a thankless one and full of grief."

"You gotta have a product that everybody needs every day. We don't have it in booze. Except for the lushes, most people only buy a couple of fifths of gin or Scotch when they're having a party. The workingman laps up half a dozen bottles of beer on Saturday night, and that's it for the week. But with milk! Every family every day wants it on the table. The people on Lake Shore Drive want thick cream in their coffee. The big families out back of the yards have to buy a couple of gallons of fresh milk every day for the kids. . . . Do you guys know there's a bigger markup in fresh milk than there is in alcohol? Honest to God, we've been in the wrong racket right along."

The agonizing shrieks of the wounded, the throaty coughs of the dying and the barking guns drowned out the panting and cursing of the hard-working executioners, repeating that left-to-right, right-to-left sweep of destruction as they glutted their murderous appetites upon the feast of blood. Bullets ripped into soft, yielding flesh, some tearing off bits and burying themselves with the ribbons of flesh into the wall ahead. Others tore into the fresh wounds and made gaping holes. A shotgun roared above the din, its charge obliterating a man's face, stenching the air with the acrid smell of powder fumes and loosing the steam of warm flesh and blood. The withering blast kept up until the last man was down. Satisfied with the havoc wrought, the leader ordered a halt. The four right-faced and marched out, two in front with their hands up, the two in uniform behind them, prodding them with their smoking guns.

The St. Valentine's Day Massacre was finished!

— *True Detective Mysteries,* March 1931

"The one island of law and order is St. Louis, whose police are notably well equipped and whose police chief, Colonel Joseph A. Gerk, is outstandingly able and honest."

—*Fortune* magazine

♔ ♔ ♔

If Capone had the morals and mindset of a robber baron, his outlaw counterpart was John Dillinger, a daredevil bandit less articulate but also concerned with his public image. He differed from most other "Public Enemies" in seeming to possess a fairly conventional value system—one that included a basic sense of right and wrong, tempered with a flexibility that was also an American trait. Unlike some contemporaries who displayed a sadistic streak, he viewed himself as a professional bank robber engaged in crimes against property and who faced the same occupational hazards as those paid to kill or capture him. As a fugitive he was less accessible to the press, but when in custody he, like Capone, would banter with reporters.

JOHN DILLINGER

"We can't all be saints."

"I don't smoke much, and I drink very little. I guess my only bad habit is robbing banks."

"Never trust a woman or an automatic pistol."

"I'd like to have enough money to enjoy life; be clear of everything—not worry, take care of my old man, and see a ball game every day."

MARY KINDER

(about Dillinger)

"Johnnie's just an ordinary fellow. Of course he goes out and holds up banks and things, but he's really just like any other fellow, aside from that."

J. EDGAR HOOVER

(about Dillinger)

"He had his weaknesses—women, for one thing, and a flair for the spectacular."

LAKE COUNTY SHERIFF LILLIAN HOLLEY

(about Dillinger, before his escape)

"We do not expect to have any trouble with our newest prisoner. Of course, I warned him the first thing that we would stand for no monkey business."

> The electric chair yawns for its fodder of calloused human beasts whose warped minds prompt evil deeds. The wages of sin is Death! Sooner or later, it will get John Dillinger. That, or the searing death of hot bullets fired from eager guns! . . . CRIME NEVER PAYS!
>
> —Narrator in 1934 movie documentary

♔ ♔ ♔

Most criminals were not particularly inclined to introspection or self-expression, but a few had memorable remarks:

RAYMOND HAMILTON

"I'm Raymond Hamilton, and I don't intend to give you any trouble. I'm just fresh out of ammunition, money, whiskey, and women. Let's go to jail."

JACK "LEGS" DIAMOND

"The bullet hasn't been made that can kill me." (Attributed)

"I'm just a young fellow trying to get ahead."

"BABY FACE" NELSON

"It's getting dark, Helen—say goodbye to mother."

"PRETTY BOY" FLOYD

"They'll get me. Sooner or later I'll go down full of lead. That's how it will end."

CHARLIE BIRGER

"I kill only bad people."

"MACHINE GUN" KELLY

"My people are good people even if I turned out to be an awful heel." (Kelly's most famous quote, *"Don't shoot, G-men!"* may have been a fabrication of the FBI, although the *Chicago American* interviewed Agent Rorer by telephone, and he reported that Kelly's wife, Kathryn, did say, *"Honey, I guess it's all up for us. The 'g' men won't ever give us a break."*)

"MOTHER IS THE BEST BET, AND DON'T LET SATAN DRAW YOU TOO FAST"

The Last Words of "Dutch" Schultz

Arthur Flegenheimer, alias "Dutch" Schultz, was in the men's room of the Palace Chop House in Newark, New Jersey, on October 23, 1935, when gunmen walked in and shot three of his companions seated at the rear of the restaurant (one, photographed face down on the table, is commonly identified as Schultz). Not recognizing any of them as their intended victim, and almost as an afterthought, one gunman entered the men's room and there shot the man they actually had come to kill.

Rushed to a hospital, Schultz lived until 8:35 the next evening with a police stenographer trying to take notes. Toward the end, Schultz's temperature reached 106 degrees, and his fevered ramblings were taken down verbatim, to become a dying mobster's longest "last words" that in some ways were deliriously poetic.

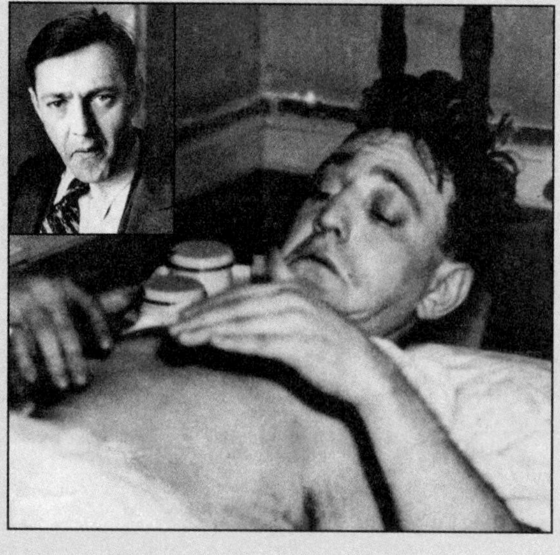

♔ ♔ ♔

George, don't make no bull moves. What have you done with him. Oh, Mama, Mama, Mama. Oh, stop it. Stop it—Oh, oh, oh. Sure, sure, Mama—Now listen, Phil, fun is fun. Aha—Please, papa. What happened to the sixteen? Oh, oh—He done it. Please—please—John, please. Oh, did you buy the hotel? You promised a million—sure. Get out. I wish I knew. Please make it quick, fast, and furious—Please. Fast and furious. Please help me get out. I'm getting my wind back, thank God! Please, please, oh, please. You will have to, please—Tell him, you got no case. You get ahead with the dot and dash system. Didn't I speak that time last night? Whose number is that in your pocketbook, Phil? 13780. Who was it?

Oh—please, please—Reserve decision. Police, police, Henry and Frankie—Oh, oh, dog biscuit, and when he is happy he doesn't get snappy—Please, please to do this. Henry, Henry, Frankie, you didn't meet him, you didn't even meet me. The glove will fit what I say—Oh, kayiyi, kayiyi. Sure, who cares when you are through? How do you know this? Well then—Oh, Cocoa, no—thinks he is a grandpa again, and he is jumping around. No, Hoboe and Poboe I think mean the same thing.

Question by Sergeant Conlon: Who shot you?

Answer: The boss himself.

Q: He did?

A: Yes: I don't know.

Q: What did he shoot you for?

A: I showed him, boss—did you hear him meet me? An appointment. Appeal stuck. All right, mother.

Q: Was it the boss shot you?

A: Who shot me? No one.

Q: Was it bow-legs?

A: Yes, he might have shot me; it wasn't Robeck (?) or the other guy. I will see him. I never forget, and if I do I will be very careful.

Q: Was it bow-legs who shot you?

A: I don't know who shot me, honest to God! Suppose you help me get up now, like a swell fellow.

Q: We will help you.

A: Will you get me up? O.K., I won't be such a big creep. Oh, Mama, I can't go through with it, please. Oh—and then he clips me. Come on—cut that out, we don't owe a nickel. Hold it. Instead, hold it against him. I am a pretty good pretzler—Winifred—Department of Justice. I even got it from the department, sir. Please, stop it. Say, listen, the—last night.

Sergt. Conlon: Now, don't holler.

A: I don't want to holler.

Q: What did they shoot you for?

A: I don't know, sir, honestly I don't. I don't even know who was with me, honestly. I went to the toilet; I was in the toilet and when I reached the—the boy came at me.

Q: The big fellow gave it to you?

A: Yes, he gave it to me.

Q: Do you know who that big fellow was?

A: No.

Schultz: See, George, if we wanted to break the ring. No—Please, I get a month. They did it. Come on. (Name not clear) cut me off and says you are not to be in the beneficiary of this will. Is that right? I will be checked and double-checked and please pull for me.

(One of the detectives): We will pull for you. Schultz? Will you pull? Will you pull?

These native children make this and sell you the joint. How many good ones and how many bad ones? Please, Joe. Please. I had nothing with him. He was a cowboy in one of the—seven days a week fight. No business, no hangout; no friends, nothing. Just what you pick up and what you need.

Sergeant Conlon: Who was it shot you?

Schultz: I don't know.

No. Don't put anyone near this check, the check. You might have—oh, please. Please do it for me. Let me get up, sir, heh? That is Connie's, isn't it? Uh, heh. In the olden days they waited and they waited. Please give me my shot. Please. Oh. Oh. It is from the factory. O.K. Sure, that is a bad—well, oh, go ahead, that happens for crying. I don't want harmony. I want harmony. Oh, Mama, Mama. Who give it to him? Who give it to him? Tony? Let me in the district—fire—factory that he was nowhere was near. It smoldered. No, No! There are only ten of us and there are ten million fighting somewhere in front of you, so get your onions up and we will throw up the truce flag. Oh, please let me up. Leo, Leo. Oh, yeh. No, no. I don't—please. Please shift me.

Police are here. Communistic—strike—baloneys. Please. Honestly it is a habit I get. Sometimes I give it and sometimes I don't. Oh, not. I am all in. Say—that settles it. Are you sure? Please, he eats like a little sausage baloney maker. Please, let me get in and eat. Let him harness himself to you and then bother you. Please don't ask me to go there. I don't want to. I still don't want him in the path. Please, Leo, Leo. I was looking for something. Meet my lady, Mrs. Pickford, and I am sorry I acted that way so soon, already. Sure, it is no use to stage a riot. The sidewalk was in trouble and the bears were in trouble and I broke it up. Please, oh, Mama! No knock to her, she didn't know. Look, that is it. She let her go the opposite. Oh, tell me. Please put me in that room. Please keep him in control.

My gilt-edge stuff, and those dirty rats have tuned in. Please, mother, mother, please, the reaction is so strong. Oh, Mama, Mama, please don't tear, don't rip, that is something that shouldn't be spoke about. That is right. Please get me up, my friends. I know what I speak of. Please, look out, the shooting is a bit wild, and that kind of shooting saved a man's life. Oh, Elmer was. No, everything frightening. Yes, no payrolls, no walls, no coupons. That would be entirely out. Pardon me. Oh, yeh. Oh, I forgot I am plaintiff and not defendant.

Look out, look out for him, please—and he owes me money, he owes everyone money. Why can't he just pull out and give me control. All right, please do. Please, mother. You pick me up now. Please, you know me. Oh, Louie, didn't I give you my door bell? Everything you got, the whole bill. And did you come for your rest in the doctor's office, sir? Yes, I can see that. Your son-in-law, and he isn't liked, is he? Harry, does he behave? No, don't you scare me. My friends think I do a better job. Oh, police are looking for you all over. Please be instrumental in letting us know. That wouldn't be here. They are Englishmen and they are a type I don't know who is best, they or us. Oh, sir, and get the doll a roofing. Please. You can play jacks, and girls do that with a soft ball and do tricks with it. Please. I may take all events into consideration. No, no. And it is no. It is confused and it says no. A boy has never wept, nor dashed a thousand kim.

Did you hear me? Now leave it or take it. No, I might be in the playing for I know. Come on over here, come on over. Oh, Duckie, see we skipped again.

Question by Detective: Who shot you?

A: I don't know.

Q: Was it the big fellow?

A: I don't know.

Q: When you were coming out of the toilet?

A: I don't know. Pick me up. No, no, you have got to do it as I see it. Please take me out of the bed.

Q: The doctor wants you to lie quiet.

A: That is what I want to do. I can't come. Express office was closed. Oh, Mama, Mama. Please, please.

Q: How many shots were fired?

A: I don't know. None.

Q: How many?

A: Two thousand. Come on, get some money in that treasury. We need it. Come on, please get it. I can't tell you to. You are telling the truth, aren't you, Mr. Harris? That is not what you have in the book. Oh, yes I have. Oh, please, warden. Please. What am I going to do for money? How is that, how do you like that? Please put me up on my feet, at once. Thank you, Sam, you are a hard-boiled man. I do it because you ask me to. Did you hear me? I would hear it, the Circuit Court would hear it, and the Supreme Court might hear it. Come on, pull me up, sir. All right, Cam Davis. Oh, please reply. N.R.A. If that ain't the payoff. Please crack down on the Chinaman's friends and Hitler's commander. All right, I am sore and I am going up and I am going to give you honey if I can. Look out. We broke that up. Mother is the best bet, and don't let Satan draw you too fast.

Question by detective: What did the big fellow shoot you for?

A: Him? John? Over a million, five million dollars.

Q: You want to get well, don't you?

A: Yes.

Q: Lie quiet.

A: Yes, I will lie quiet.

Q: John shot you. We will take care of John.

That is what caused the trouble. Look out. All right, Bob. Please get me up. Come on, John, get me up. If you do this you can go on and jump right here in the lake. I know who they are. They are French people—Malone—All right, look out, look out. Mama, Mama—Oh, my memory is gone. A work relief—Police. Who gets it? I don't know and I don't want to know, but look out. It can be traced. That is the one that done it, but who had that one. Oh, oh, Mama, please let me get up—He changed for the worse. Please, look out; my fortunes have changed—and come back and went back since that. It was desperate Ambrose, a little kid. Please. Look out—Look—Mike—Please, I am wobbly. You ain't got nothing on him, but we got it on his helper. Please—

Q (Detective): Control yourself.

A: But I am dying.

Q: No you are not.

A: Move on, Mick and Mama. All right, dear, you have got to get it.

(At this point, the nurses changed the dressing, and at 4:40 p.m. Mrs. Flegenheimer was brought in.)

Mrs. Flegenheimer: This is Frances.

A: Then pull me out. I am half crazy. They won't let me get up. They dyed my shoes. Open those shoes here. Give me something. I am so sick. Give me some water, the only thing that I want. Open this up, break it so I can touch you. Dannie, will you please get me in the car. Now he can't butt in. Please, Nick, stop chiseling.

(Mrs. Flegenheimer leaves the room.)

Question by Detective: Who shot you?

A: I don't know; I didn't even get a look. I don't know. Who can have done it? Anybody. Kindly take my shoes off.

Q: They are off.

A: No, there is a handcuff on them. The Baron does these things.

I know what I am doing here with my collection of papers, for crying out loud. It isn't worth a nickel to two guys like you or me, but to a collector it is worth a fortune. It is priceless. I am going to turn it over to— Turn your back to me, please, Henry. I am so sick now. The police are getting many complaints. Look out. Yey, Jack. Hello, Jack. Jack, Mama. I want that G-note. Look out for Jimmie Valentine, for he is an old pal of mine. Come on, Jim, come on, Jimmie. Oh, thanks. O.K. O.K. I am all through. Can't do another thing.

Hymie, won't you do what I ask you this once? Look out, Mama, Mama. Look out for her. You can't beat him. Police. Mama. Helen. Mother, please take me out. Come on, Rosie. O.K. Hymie would do it. Not him. I will settle—the indictment. Come on, Max, open the soap duckets. Frankie, please come here. Open that door, Dumpey's door. It is so much, Abe, that—with the brewery. Come on. Hey, Jimmie. The chimney sweeps. Take to the sword. Shut up, you got a big mouth. Please help me up, Henry. Max come over here—French Canadian bean soup—I want to pay, let them leave me alone.

♔ ♔ ♔

Added later by writer:

At 6 p.m. Schultz fell into a coma. The stenographer was withdrawn. At 8:20, Dr. Earl Snavely, superintendent of the hospital, gave the word to let Frances Flegenheimer come in. She went to the bed, bent over and whispered, again, "Arthur, this is Frances." There was no response and she withdrew, sobbing. A few minutes later another doctor checked the pupils of Schultz's eyes, put a stethoscope to his chest at 8:35, and said, "It's all over."

Much of the account above is taken from *Kill the Dutchman* (1971) by Paul Sann and is used with the permission of his son Howie and the Sann estate.

CLYDE BARROW

"No man but the undertaker will ever get me. If officers ever cripple me to where I see they will take me alive, I'll take my own life."

(in a letter to a newspaper, possibly from Bonnie)

"Say, boy, can't robbers get away fast these days? I'm glad this country is different from what it was when Jessy James lived here."

BONNIE PARKER

"Tell the public I don't smoke cigars. It's the bunk."

BLANCHE BARROW

(while in prison)

Across the fields of yesterday
She sometimes come to me
A little girl just back from play
The girl I used to be
And yet she smiles so wistfully
Once she has crept within
I wonder if she hopes to see
The woman I might have been—

HARRY PIERPONT

"I'm not like some bank robbers—I didn't get myself elected president of the bank first."

FRANK GUSENBERG

(mortally wounded in the St. Valentine's Day Massacre)

"Nobody shot me."

WILBUR UNDERHILL

(mortally wounded by FBI agents)

"Tell the boys I'm coming home."

"RED" RYAN

The "Canadian Dillinger")

"Time, boys, to cut up the melon."

"Knocking them down is the easy part of it, but it is the getaway that counts."

(last words)

"You've got me, boys. I've had enough."

BUGS MORAN

"I hope, when my time comes, that I die decently in bed. I don't want to be murdered beside the garbage cans in some Chicago alley."

(to Chicago Detective Captain John Stege)

"Why don't you book yourself a room at the Fuckoff Hotel?"

"MACHINE GUN" JACK McGURN

(when questioned by police)

"I don't own a machine gun and never fired one."

JAKE "GREASY THUMB" GUZIK

"You buy a judge by weight, like iron in a junkyard. A justice of the peace or a magistrate can be had for a five-dollar bill. In Municipal Court he will cost you ten. In the Circuit or Superior Courts he wants fifteen. The state Appellate Court or the state Supreme Court is on par with the federal courts. By the time a judge reaches such courts he is middle-aged, thick around the middle, fat between the ears. He's heavy. You can't buy a federal judge for less than a twenty-dollar bill."

EDWARD "SPIKE" O'DONNELL

"I've been shot at and missed so often I've a notion to hire out as a professional target. Life with me is just one bullet after another."

SAM GIANCANA

"What's wrong with the Syndicate? Two or three of us get together on some deal and everybody says it's a bad thing, but those businessmen do it all the time and nobody squawks."

"DAGO" LAWRENCE MANGANO

"Us Public Enemies gotta stick together."

"They were all bum raps. And besides, I had a good lawyer."

BENJAMIN "BUGSY" SIEGEL

(to a contractor)

"There's no chance you'll get killed. We only kill each other."

VINCENT "MAD DOG" COLL

(accused of a shooting in which a baby was killed)

"I'd like nothing better than to lay me hands on the man who did this. I'd tear his throat out."

FRANCIS "TWO-GUN" CROWLEY

"Aw, I know I'm going to burn, and I want to get it over with—right away. What's the use of fooling around with a trial?"

FRANK COSTELLO

"Some people are common gamblers. I am an uncommon gambler."

ARNOLD ROTHSTEIN

"Look out for No. 1. If you don't, no one else will. If a man is dumb, someone is going to get the best of him, so why not you? If you don't, you're as dumb as he is."

LOUIS "LEPKE" BUCHALTER

"I may have done a hundred things wrong, but my conscience is clear."

(on his way to the electric chair)

"The fix is in, you'll see."

"LUCKY" LUCIANO

"Anything I ever did in my life, I felt justified in doing. I never abused anybody in my life. If people abuse me, and I abuse them back—that ain't abuse."

"Taking raps wears you out after awhile."

LOUIS "TUBBY" TOBYMAN

"If you want to do anything for me, get me a good doctor."

ARTHUR "DUTCH SCHULTZ" FLEGENHEIMER

"If I'd stuck to Flegenheimer, I'd never be in trouble like this. Schultz is a short word, and swell for the headlines. You'd-a never stuck Flegenheimer in the headlines, and nobody'd ever heard of me."

"I never did anything to deserve that reputation, unless it was to supply good beer to people who wanted it."

(hallucinating on his death bed)

"Mother is the best bet, and don't let Satan draw you too fast."

JOE VALACHI

(admitting to murders going back to the 1930s)

"You imagine my embarrassment when I killed the wrong guy."

GERALD CHAPMAN

"At least we do not take money from poor people. What we steal hurts nobody. Everything that is sent by mail or express is fully insured, and in the end the sender loses nothing. The man who comes out the winner on Wall Street is respected, and he is envied for his yachts and cars and homes, while we are hunted and despised. I think I am the more honorable of the two."

A killing by a crime partner led to Chapman's capture and to his execution in 1926, but three years earlier, on April 7, 1923, while he was still a fugitive, the usually solemn *New York Times* took note of Chapman's colorful robberies of banks and mail trucks, his daring escapes, his notoriety that inspired fan clubs, and editorialized:

> It is getting to be rather difficult to keep in mind the fact that Gerald Chapman is a thoroughly bad man, whose right place is in jail. The difficulty arises from the fact that in his battle with the law he shows qualities—courage, persistence, ingenuity and skill—which it is impossible not to admire. The result is that unless one is careful one finds one's self hoping that he isn't caught, and, so great are the odds against him, that the struggle seems somehow unfair. . . . That he hates imprisonment is only human, and that he takes desperate risks in his efforts to get out is rather to his credit than his discredit—from every standpoint except the safety of society.

♔ ♔ ♔

CAPTAIN FRANK HAMER

(after the ambush of Bonnie and Clyde)

"I hate to bust a cap on a woman, especially when she's sitting down. . . ."

Finally, a few choice words from two Chicago attorneys representing their clients:

MICHAEL AHERN

(Capone lawyer, to the jury while defending cop-killers Anselmi and Scalise)

"If a policemen detains you, even for a moment against your will, you are not guilty of murder, but only of manslaughter. If the policeman uses force of arms, you may kill him in self defense and emerge from the law unscathed."

LAWRENCE O'TOOLE

(defending armed robbers who had killed a shopkeeper)

"This is a free country. A man can go out and pull a stickup if he can get away with it. No guy has the right to resist. That makes it self-defense for the stickup man."

BIBLIOGRAPHY

of 1920s & '30s Gangsters and Outlaws, Police, Crime Control, and Criminology

A

Abadinski, Howard. *Organized Crime.* Boston: Allyn and Bacon, 1981; Second Edition, Chicago: Nelson-Hall, 1985. [Academically excellent and entertaining study of the origins, rise, and operations of modern organized crime by a true authority on the subject; debunks many popular accounts. Also produced scholarly studies of the Gambino and Genovese crime families (*The Mafia in America,* 1981; *The Criminal Elite,* 1983).]

Adamic, Louis. *Dynamite: The Story of Class Violence in America.* New York: Viking Press, 1931. [Attack on racketeering as a by-product of capitalism comes off as a lively polemic virtually promoting class warfare.]

Adams, Bill. *The Shelton Gang: They Played in Peoria and They Played War in "Bloody Williamson County."* Philadelphia: Xlibris Publishing, 2005. [Good account of the Shelton boys, especially their later days in Peoria, by a Peoria newspaperman. Slightly disorganized in the early chapters but worthwhile.]

Adams, Verdon R. *Tom White, The Life of a Lawman.* El Paso: Texas Western Press, 1972. [White was a Texas Ranger, an FBI agent in the 1920s, and later a warden at Leavenworth. He was taken hostage by former members of the Al Spencer Gang during their 1931 prison break, which was engineered from the outside by Frank Nash. White's father and brothers also were lawmen. One brother was James "Doc" White, an FBI agent who participated in the capture of "Machine Gun" Kelly, the Dillinger investigation, and the killings of "Ma" and Fred Barker and Russell Gibson of the Barker-Karpis Gang. This book goes well with *The Gonif,* the memoirs of White's friend Morris "Red" Rudensky (former burglar and expert jailbreaker), which also includes a good account of the Leavenworth crashout.]

Addy, Ted: *The Dutch Schultz Story.* Derby, CT: Monarch Books, 1961. [Paperback fictionalized "biography," written like a novel but with dates and events, some clearly fictional. Reprinted with photos in 1968 by Tower Books, New York, as part of their "Public Enemies of the 1930s" series.]

Adler, Polly: *A House Is Not a Home.* New York: Rinehart & Co., 1953. [Autobiography of America's most notorious madam of the twenties and thirties, with much material on her gangster friends, especially Arthur "Dutch Schultz" Flegenheimer and Charles "Lucky" Luciano, plus Al Capone, Frank Costello, "Bugsy" Siegel, others.]

Ahearn, Danny: *The Confessions of a Gunman.* London: Routledge, 1930; U.S. edition, *How to Commit Murder.* New York: Ives Washburn, 1930. [Unsubstantiated mobster melodrama.]

Albini, Joseph L. *The American Mafia, Genesis of a Legend.* New York: Appleton-Century-Crofts, 1971. [Sees the name "Mafia" as a "synonym for syndicated crime," rather than an actual organization.]

Alcorn, Robert Hayden: *The Count of Gramercy Park.* London: Hurst & Blackett, 1955. [Biography of Gerald Chapman.]

Alexander, Michael: *Jazz Age Jews.* Princeton, NJ: Princeton University Press, 2003. [Jewish roles in twenties america examined through the lives of Arnold Rothstein, Felix Frankfurter (defender of Sacco and Vanzetti and later Supreme Court Justice), and Al Jolson.]

Alix, Ernest Kahlar: *Ransom Kidnapping in America, 1874-1974: The Creation of a Capital Crime.* Carbondale, IL: Southern Illinois University Press, 1978. [Scholarly work on the history of kidnapping in America. Excellent source on the "Lindbergh Law" and all the legal ramifications of the crime. Good chapter on the gangster era.]

Allen, Edward J. *Merchants of Menace—The Mafia.* Springfield, IL: Charles C. Thomas, 1962. [By a police chief who views the Mafia as highly structured.]

Allen, Eric: *Crossfire in the Cooksons.* Muskogee, OK: Hoffman Publishing, 1974. [80-page book covering the adventures of a Sallisaw-area lawman named Jones and his encounters with mostly drunks and petty criminals in the 1938-1950 period. Slight and largely unsubstantiated material on the Kimes boys but little else on the outlaw legends of the Cookson Hills.]

Allen, Frederick Lewis: *Only Yesterday: An Informal History of the 1920s.* New York: Harper & Row, 1931. [History of 1920s, with good chapter on Capone.];

———. *Since Yesterday: The 1930s in America.* New York: Harper & Row, 1939.

Allen, Oliver E. *The Tiger: The Rise and Fall of Tammany Hall.* New York: Addison-Wesley, 1993.

Allen, Robert S. (editor): *Our Fair City. New York*: Vanguard Press, 1947. [Survey of American cities and their political and police corruption.]

Allen, Troy: *Gang Wars of the Twenties.* Chatsworth, CA: Barclay House, 1974. [Undistinguished paperback containing some photos not commonly seen.]

Allsop, Kenneth: *The Bootleggers and Their Era.* London: Hutchinson Publishing, 1961. [Good history of Chicago bootlegging gangs and booze wars in 1920s. Reprinted in 1968, with new introduction by Allsop, as *The Bootleggers: The Story of Chicago's Prohibition Era,* by Arlington House, New Rochelle, N.Y.]

America: An Illustrated Diary of Its Most Exciting Years. New York: American Family Enterprises, Inc., 1972-73. [21-volume anthology series of American events from the 1920s through '50s, mostly stories from *Liberty* magazine. Volume 1 includes "The Twilight of the Gangster" by Edward Doherty, centering on the downfalls of Capone and "Legs" Diamond, and two other pieces by Will Irwin on Bonnie and Clyde and the death of Dillinger, both taken from the January 1935 *Liberty* series by Irwin, "Our New Civil War." Two other volumes are subtitled *Gangsters* and *Gangbusters* and consist entirely of crime stories, though not all are gangster-related. Does have much on Capone and Prohibition, however, "Why Dillinger's Gang Is Doomed" by Al Dunlap, Richard Reese Whittemore, the disappearance of Judge Crater, Willie Sutton, etc.]

American Heritage (editors): *The American Heritage History of the 1920s & 1930s.* New York: American Heritage Publishing Co., 1970. [Includes biographical profiles of Al Capone and John Dillinger. Reprinted by Bonanza Books, New York, 1987.]

Anbinder, Tyler: *Five Points: The 19th Century New York City Neighborhood That Invented the Tap Dance, Stole Elections, and Became the World's Most Notorious Slum.* New York: Plume Books, 2002. [Spawning grounds of many well-known gangsters.]

Anderson, Frank W. *The Border Bank Bandits.* Surrey, BC and Blaine, WA: Hancock House Publishers, 1990. [88-page paperback booklet covers the Reid and Davis gangs, automotive bank robbers who operated in Montana and Canada in the 1920s. Excellently demonstrates shortcomings of the era's law enforcement.]

Andrews, Wayne: *Battle for Chicago.* New York: Harcourt, Brace, 1946.

Angle, Paul M. *Bloody Williamson.* New York: Alfred A. Knopf, 1952. [Scholarly work on the violent history of Williamson County, Illinois, up to and including the bloody Birger-Shelton gang war of the 1920s that involved military-style battles and culminated in the public hanging of Charlie Birger.]

Anglo, Michael: *Nostalgia Spotlight On the Twenties.* London: Jupiter Books, Ltd., 1976. [Chapter on Al Capone.]

———. *Nostalgia Spotlight On the Thirties.* London: Jupiter Books, Ltd., 1976. [Chapter on John Dillinger.]

Anonymous: *Life and Exploits of S. Glenn Young.* Herrin, IL: Mrs. S. Glenn Young, Publisher, 1925. [S. Glenn

Young was a colorful character in southern Illinois during the 1920s, both as Prohibition agent and as Ku Klux Klan vigilante, who fought the Birger and Shelton Gangs but also lined his pockets by ransacking the homes of honest citizens, as well as bootleggers. He was murdered in 1925, apparently by the Shelton Gang, and his devoted wife, blinded in an assassination attempt, produced this less-than-objective biography. Reprinted in 1989 by Gordon Pruett, aka Crossfire Press, Herrin, Il.]

Anonymous: *The Life Story of Charlie Birger: History of the Crimes of the Birger Gang.* Marion, IL: Illinois Book Company, 1927. [Good early booklet biography of the notorious southern Illinois gang leader, written after Birger's conviction for murder but before his hanging. Available in reprint since 1994 from Williamson County Historical Society, Marion, IL.]

Anonymous: *The Inside Story of Chicago's Master Criminal.* Minneapolis: Graphic Arts Corporation (Fawcett Publications), 1929. [One of the earliest Capone books, in magazine form.]

Anonymous: *X Marks the Spot: Chicago Gang Wars in Pictures.* Chicago: Spot Publishing, 1930. [Quite detailed contemporary account of Prohibition gang wars, published in magazine format. Some time later the author revealed himself to be a Chicago journalist named Hal Andrews, who wrote a brief article in *Real Detective* criticizing the way moralists in Chicago and other cities righteously denounced the booklet for its photos of dead bodies and suppressed its distribution-to go with a full page ad offering it by mail order.]

Anonymous: *The Life of Al Capone in Pictures and Chicago's Gang Wars.* Chicago: Lake Michigan Publishing Company, 1931. [Magazine format biography of Capone, similar to *X Marks the Spot.* Reprinted since 1982 by The Hideout, Inc., Couderay, WS.]

Anonymous: *The Morgue: The Gangster's Final Resting Place.* Chicago (?), 1933. [Magazine format collection of perfectly gruesome morgue photos with short biographies of the better-known Chicago gangsters.]

Anonymous: *Uncle Sam's Gang Smashers.* (no city): Security Publishing, 1937. [Extremely rare magazine-format picture book glorifying Hoover's G-men and their gang-smashing exploits.]

Anonymous: *Alcatraz.* San Francisco: E. Crowell Mensch, 1937.

Anonymous: *I Worked for "Lucky" Luciano.* New York: Avon Publications, 1954. [Allegedly the work of a New York newspaperman. Junk fiction that purports to be a first-person narrative by a former prostitute (actually a composite of several women), according to the actual author, who wisely elected to forgo a byline. Later retitled *I Am A Marked Woman.*]

Anonymous: *I, Mobster.* Greenwich, CT: Fawcett Gold Medal, 1958. [Lurid supposed confessions of a crime czar who dares not reveal his true identity.]

Anonymous: *The Story of Suicide Sal.* Ill-Vis Rules Publications, (?), 1987. [Miniature and amateurish booklet containing one of Bonnie's poems, illustrated with newspaper clippings, drawings and photos of Bonnie and Clyde. Only 400 copies printed, so may be of some remote interest to collectors. "Sal," and Parker's other masterpiece, "The Story of Bonnie and Clyde," have been published many times in books, newspapers, etc. Back-cover illustration is nude morgue photo of Bonnie.]

Anonymous: *Curious Facts About John Dillinger & J. Edgar Hoover.* Fort Wayne, IN: Kekionga Press, 2005. [76-page paperback boasting index, 182 source notes and thirteen point text for easy reading.]

Anslinger, Harry J., with Oursler, Will: *The Murderers: The Story of the Narcotic Gangs.* New York: Farrar, Straus & Cudahy, 1961. [America's war on narcotics traffickers, as told by the longtime head of the Federal Bureau of Narcotics, probably the man most responsible for popularizing the term Mafia in the U.S. and substituting the marijuana menace for the alcohol peril once Repeal left thousands of Prohibition agents looking for work.]

———. *The Protectors.* New York: Farrar, Straus, 1964

———, and Tompkins, William F. *The Traffic in Narcotics.* New York: Funk & Wagnall, 1953.

Arm, Walter. *Pay-Off, The Inside Story of Big City Corruption.* New York: Appleton-Century-Crofts, 1951.

Arnold, Ann. *Gamblers & Gangsters: Ft. Worth's Jacksboro Highway in the 1940s & 1950s.* Austin: Eakin Press, 1998. [Good history of the violent Fort Worth underworld in the 1940s and '50s, including surviving older gangsters, with many photos.]

Asbury, Herbert. *The Gangs of New York: An Informal History of the New York Underworld.* New York: Alfred A. Knopf, 1927. [Deals mainly with such 1800s and early 1900s street gangs as the Bowery Boys, Dead Rabbits Gang, "Big Jack" Zelig, "Gyp the Blood," etc., ironically declaring the "gangster era" to be ending in the 1920s thanks to new and enlightened civic policies that were striking at the roots of urban crime. By the time the book appeared, the old "fighting gangs" were indeed history but had been supplanted by a new style of criminal gang spawned by Prohibition, and the term gangster had been repopularized to describe professional bootleggers and racketeers.]

———. *The Barbary Coast: An Informal History of the San Francisco Underworld.* New York: Alfred A. Knopf, 1933.

———. *All Around the Town.* New York: Alfred A. Knopf, 1934. [More on the early New York City underworld.]

———. *The French Quarter: An Informal History of the New Orleans Underworld.* New York: Alfred A. Knopf, 1936. [Like The Gangs of New York, these books deal mainly with nineteenth Century crime and vice in their respective cities.]

———. *Sucker's Progress: An Informal History of Gambling in America from the Colonies to Canfield.* New York: Dodd, Mead, 1938.

———. *Gem of the Prairie: An Informal History of the Chicago Underworld.* New York: Alfred A. Knopf, 1940. [Asbury catches up with the times and provides a highly entertaining description of the city's crime and vice lords from the eighteenth century through the "gangsters" of the Capone era.]

———. *The Great Illusion: An Informal History of Prohibition.* Garden City, NY: Doubleday, 1950.

Asinof, Eliot. *Eight Men Out.* New York: Holt, Rinehart & Winston, 1963. [Good detailed account of the "Black Sox" scandal, the 1919 World Series fix allegedly masterminded by Arnold Rothstein.]

Askins, Colonel Charles. *Texans, Guns & History.* New York: Bonanza Books, 1970. [Includes an inaccurate chapter on Bonnie and Clyde, which reprints Frank Hamer's account of their ambush (originally published in Walter Prescott Webb's The Texas Rangers).]

Aswell, Thomas E. *The Story of Bonnie and Clyde.* Ruston, LA: H. M. G., Inc., 1968. [Slim but good booklet, from the scene of one of the Barrow Gang's crimes.]

Auble, John. *A History of St. Louis Gangsters.* St. Louis: National Criminal Research Society, Inc., 2000. [Slim paperback strings together newspaper clippings in a less-than-successful attempt to trace the history of organized crime in St. Louis.]

Audett, James Henry "Blackie." *Rap Sheet: My Life Story.* New York: William P. Sloane, 1954. [Widely sold "autobiography" of a thirties bank robber who claimed involvement with nearly every crime and gang from the Kansas City Massacre to John Dillinger. Largely fiction.]

B

Bain, Donald. *War in Illinois.* Englewood Cliffs, NJ: Prentice-Hall, 1978. [Account of Birger-Shelton gang war of 1920s, with good photos and contemporary sketches by Birger gangster Harvey Dungey but in novelized form with fictional dialogue. Reprinted as Charlie and the Shawneetown Dame.]

Bain, George F. *The Barrow Gang: Clyde Barrow and Bonnie Parker, The Real Story.* Privately printed, 1968. [Despite title's claim, is actually a fifty-cent "dime novel" that is obviously fiction, though in places it reads like somebody's confused recollections.]

Ballou, James, et al. *Rock in a Hard Place: The Browning Automatic Rifle.* Toronto: Collector Grade Publications, 2000. [Coffee-table history of the Browning automatic rifle, similar to Tracie Hill's Tommygun compilation. Includes chapter by Rick Cartledge on the Barrow Gang and use of the B.A.R. on both sides of the law in 1930s.]

Balousek, Marv. *Wisconsin Crimes of the Century.* Madison, WI: William C. Robbins/Straus Printing, 1989. [Mostly deals with notorious murderers and crimes of a non-gangster nature but does have an interesting chapter on John Dillinger. Some errors.]

———. *More Wisconsin Crimes of the Century.* Oregon, WI: Badger Books/Waubesa Press, 1993. [Includes bloody 1931 Menomonie bank robbery by the Holden-Keating Gang.]

———. *50 Wisconsin Crimes of the Century.* Oregon, WI: Badger Books/Waubesa Press, 1997.

Balsamo, William, and Carpozi, George Jr. *Always Kill A Brother: The Bloody Saga of the Irish-Italian Gang War That Put the Mafia in Power!* New York: Dell Publishing, 1977. [1920s gang war between Frankie Yale's (Francesco Uale's) Brooklyn Mafia group and the Irish "White Hand" gang, headed by "Peg Leg" Lonergan, who allegedly was killed by Al Capone. No documentation, but author Balsamo declares kinship to a "key participant."]

———. *Under the Clock: The Inside Story of the Mafia's First Hundred Years.* Far Hills, NJ: New Horizon Press,

1988. [History of the Mafia, according to Balsamo and Carpozi. Incorporates their earlier book. Reprinted in 1991 as Crime Incorporated.]

Barbican, James. *The Confessions of a Rum-Runner.* New York: Ives Washburn, 1928. [Highly personalized and dramatized, but thoroughly undocumented and largely undetailed, account of a self-described rumrunner, apparently an Englishman using a pseudonym, who blundered into the business somewhere along the upper East Coast.]

Barnes, Bruce. *Machine Gun Kelly: To Right A Wrong.* Perris, CA: Tipper Publications, 1991. [Life story of George Barnes, alias George "Machine Gun" Kelly, at least as he related it to his son Bruce. Bruce Barnes also corresponded extensively with his stepmother, Kathryn Kelly, for a time. Less than detailed and somewhat overblown, but corrects many common errors about Kelly's family background and personal history. First book to give Kelly's correct birthplace and birthdate and his full true name.]

Barnes, Harry Elmer. *Battling the Crime Wave: Applying Sense and Science to the Repression of Crime.* Boston: Stratford, 1931. [Prominent prison reform advocate's excursion into contemporary crime control, treating it as a quasi-military campaign with crooks as the enemy.]

———. *The Repression of Crime: Studies in Historical Penology.* 1926. Reprint, Montclair, NJ: Patterson Smith, 1969.

Barrett, Paul W., and Barrett, Mary H. *Young Brothers Massacre.* Columbia, MO: University of Missouri Press, 1988. [Well documented account of the killing of six law officers by Harry and Jennings Young at their mother's farm near Springfield, Missouri, in January 1932. Speculation that Fred Barker might have been involved, and some new material on "Pretty Boy" Floyd, who apparently knew the Youngs and was also, but erroneously, suspected.]

Barrow, Blanche Caldwell (edited by John Neal Phillips). *My Life With Bonnie and Clyde.* Norman, OK: University of Oklahoma Press, 2004. [Long-lost manuscript written by Blanche Barrow during her term in the Missouri state prison, giving an inside account of the Barrow Gang. Discovered ten years after her death by Blanche's friend and estate executor Lorraine Weiser and authenticated by Phillips and fellow Barrow historian Ken Holmes. Much new information.]

Barzini, Luigi. *The Italians.* New York: Atheneum, 1964. [Insightful and highly readable study of the manners and morals of late twentieth-century Italy by a noted Italian sociologist. Includes a chapter on "Sicily and the Mafia" which examines the criminal brotherhood's hold on western Sicily and its tenuous ties to Italian-American crime families in the U.S.]

———. *From Caesar to the Mafia.* New York: Library Press, 1971. [Popular sequel to The Italians, again with a chapter on the Mafia.]

Baxter, John. *The Gangster Film.* New York: A. S. Barnes, 1970. [Though primarily about gangster movies, contains inaccurate biographical sketches of Capone, Dillinger, Bonnie and Clyde, the Barkers, and other real-life gangsters. Author refers to Chicago as "Capital of the state of Illinois."]

Beacher, Milton Daniel, M.D., and Perfit, Dianne Beacher (editor). *Alcatraz Island: Memoirs of a Rock Doc.* Lebanon, NJ: Pelican Island Publishing, 2001. [Interesting journal of an Alcatraz doctor in the late thirties, including his recollections of and conversations with many of the inmates. Edited into a book by Dr. Beacher's daughter, who added her father's correspondence and photos.]

Beeley, Arthur L. *The Bail System in Chicago.* Chicago: University of Chicago Press, 1927.

Behr, Edward. *Prohibition: Thirteen Years That Changed America.* New York: Arcade Publishing, 1997. [Social history of Prohibition with much on George Remus, Ohio's "King of the Bootleggers."]

Benjamin, Stan, with Rozema, Terry. *Tucson Police Department: 1874-2004.* Tucson, AZ: privately printed, 2005. [Good book compiled by Tucson police on their departmental history, including the 1934 capture of the Dillinger Gang.]

Bennett, James O'Donnell. *Chicago Gangland.* Chicago: Tribune Publishing, 1929, paperback. [Good contemporary illustrated account of Chicago gangsters and gang wars, based on his series of articles published in the *Chicago Tribune.* Similar to *X Marks the Spot,* but smaller format.]

Berger, Meyer. *The Eight Million.* New York: Simon & Schuster, 1942. [New York journalist's view of the city's dark underbelly in the Thirties, whose juicy content includes "Lepke" and "Murder, Inc.," Harlem marijuana dives, etc.]

Bergreen, Laurence. *Capone: The Man and the Era.* New York: Simon & Schuster, 1994. [Overblown and less-than-definitive biography of Al Capone, covering for its lack of detail on the Prohibition beer wars with revisionist nonsense picturing Capone as both a pawn of the Chicago Heights mob and a cocaine addict (based on the flimsy evidence of his prison records that reveal a "deviated septum," more likely the result of Capone's syphilis). Other "revisions" are simply old news about Eliot Ness and Capone's older brother James, the supposed white sheep of a black-sheep family. Another diversion from the real story of Al Capone is a brief, inaccurate recounting of the careers of Dillinger and the other Depression outlaws. Far inferior to the Capone biographies by Kobler, Pasley, and Schonberg.]

Berliner, Louise. *Texas Guinan: Queen of the Night Clubs.* Austin, TX: University of Texas Press, 1993. [Biography of the legendary speakeasy hostess, whose life provided the basis for the movies *The Roaring Twenties* and *Incendiary Blonde.* See also *Hello Sucker!* by Glenn Shirley.]

Berman, Susan. *Easy Street.* New York: Dial Press, 1981. [Memoirs of a gangster's daughter. Dave Berman's career extended from Midwest bank robberies in the twenties to operating mob-controlled hotel-casinos in Las Vegas in the fifties. Author has since been murdered. For more on this see *Murder of a Mafia Daughter: The Life and Tragic Death of Susan Berman* by Cathy Scott (New York: Barricade Books, 2002).]

Best, Harry. *Crime and the Criminal Law in the United States.* New York: Macmillan, 1931. [Exhaustive and exhausting (615 pages) study of law enforcement and the criminal justice system.]

Betz, N. T. (Tom). *The Fleagle Gang: Betrayed By a Fingerprint.* Bloomington, IN: AuthorHouse, 2005. [Jake and Ralph Fleagle were two of the nation's most successful and anonymous bank robbers until Jake left a fingerprint behind in the aftermath of the bloody Lamar, Colorado, bank robbery. Largely forgotten today, Jake Fleagle rivaled Fred Burke in 1930 headlines that proclaimed him one of the most wanted men in America. Available in book form and cheaply downloadable from the publisher's Web site.]

Biffle, Kent. *A Month of Sundays.* Denton, TX: University of North Texas Press, 1993. [Collection of columns from Biffle's *Dallas Morning News* column on Texas history. Long section on "Texas Outlaws" naturally includes Bonnie and Clyde (also interesting chapters on Bonnie's husband, Roy Thornton, and Raymond Hamilton), the Newton brothers who took part in the famous $2 million train robbery at Rondout, Illinois, in 1924; the 1927 "Santa Claus bank robbery" in Cisco, Texas; and "Machine Gun" Kelly and Harvey Bailey. Also a section on Bailey's biographer, Jay Evetts Haley.]

Bilbo, Jack (pseudonym of Hugo C. K. Baruch. *Carrying A Gun For Al Capone.* New York: G. P. Putnam's Sons, 1932. [Completely fraudulent "autobiography" written by an English artist claiming to be a former Capone bodyguard. Also published in England and Germany during the thirties and forties, illustrating mainly the worldwide popularity of anything concerning Capone.]

Binder, John J. *The Chicago Outfit.* Chicago: Arcadia Publishing, 2003. [Slim, well-written photo history of the Chicago mob, from the Colosimo era to the present, with many rare photos. Part of the Images of America series.]

Blanche, Tony, and Schreiber, Brad. *Death in Paradise: An Illustrated History of the Los Angeles County Department of Coroner.* Los Angeles: General Publishing Group, 1998. [Includes deaths of "Bugsy" Siegel, Thelma Todd, Mob mouthpiece Sam Rummel, and others. Probably the only coroner's office in the U.S. with a gift shop and mail-order catalog.]

Block, Alan. *East Side—West Side: Organizing Crime in New York, 1930-1950.* Cardiff, U.K. University of Cardiff Press, 1980. [Excellent and revisionist account (with many mug shots) of the interconnection between gangland violence and political life during a twenty-year period in New York City. Includes what is probably the best critical account of "Murder, Incorporated"]

Block, Lawrence (editor). *Gangsters, Swindlers, Killers & Thieves: Lives and Crimes of Fifty American Villains.* New York: Oxford University Press, 2004. [Anthology of stories on various American criminals from Colonial times to the present, including Capone, Dillinger, "Dutch" Schultz, "Machine Gun" Kelly, and others.]

Blumenthal, Ralph. *Miracle at Sing Sing: How One Man Transformed the Lives of America's Most Dangerous Prisoners.* New York: St. Martin's Press, 2004. [Life and career of Sing Sing's famous and progressive warden, Lewis E. Lawes.]

Boar, Roger, and Blundell, Nigel. *The World's Most Infamous Crimes and Criminals.* London: Octopus Books, 1987. [More than 700 pages on murderers, murderesses, tyrants, war criminals, swindlers, and lawbreakers of all sorts. Most of the gangster material is in a chapter called "Thieves and Villains," which includes

Bonnie and Clyde, the Mafia, Lansky, Luciano and Genovese, Al Capone, "Bugsy" Siegel, "Legs" Diamond, and "Dutch" Schultz. Strangely missing is John Dillinger. Reprinted by Dorset Press, New York, 1991, as *Crooks, Crime, and Corruption.*]

Boardman, Barrington. *From Harding to Hiroshima.* New York: Dembner Books, 1988. Reprinted by Harper & Row as Flappers, Bootleggers, "Typhoid Mary" & The Bomb: An Anecdotal History of the United States from 1923-1945.

Boettiger, John. *Jake Lingle, or Chicago on the Spot.* New York: E. P. Dutton & Co., 1931. [Detailed account of local crime conditions and the murder of *Chicago Tribune* reporter Jake Lingle, regarded as a martyr to investigative journalism until a closer look revealed his apparent involvement in the rackets. *Tribune* writer Boettiger soft-pedals Lingle's mob connections and appears to believe the killer was, in fact, a minor hoodlum named Leo Brothers, who distinguished himself mainly as Chicago gangland's only convicted murderer during the Prohibition era. Represented by future Dillinger attorney Louis Piquett, Brothers was found guilty despite somewhat dubious evidence, and his relatively light sentence of 14 years may have been part of an underworld "deal."]

Bonanno, Joseph, with Lalli, Sergio. *A Man of Honor: The Autobiography of the Boss of Bosses.* New York: Simon & Schuster, 1983. [Interesting and informative insider's view of life within Italian crime families in the United States. Bonanno considers what outsiders call "Mafia" to be a "Sicilian tradition" rather than an actual organization, once represented by "Men of Honor" (as he considers himself) but gradually corrupted by young "Americanized" gangsters and such non-Sicilians as Al Capone (whose last name, says Bonanno, means "castrated male chicken"). Valachi made "Joe Bananas" a celebrity in the sixties, but Bonanno had headed a Brooklyn crime family since 1931. Has much on Castellammarese War in New York, and Luciano, Capone and Aiello, etc. This book supposedly landed Bonanno his first jail sentence, when he refused to testify in the "Mafia Commission" trial. Bonanno also sued his publisher for a cover illustration he thought made him look like a "cheap gangster."]

Bonanno, (Salvatore) Bill. *Bound By Honor: A Mafioso's Story.* New York: St. Martin's Press, 1999. [In the 1960s, Bill Bonanno, to his father's disdain, collaborated with Gay Talese on *Honor Thy Father.* Thirty years later Bill followed in his father's footsteps with a book of his own. Slightly more controversial, especially in his allegations of mob involvement in the JFK assassination. How much is true is anyone's guess. Bill's wife, Rosalie, added her bit to the Bonanno saga with the 1990 book *Mafia Marriage.*]

Booker, Anton S. *Wildcats in Petticoats: A Garland of Female Desperadoes—Lizzie Merton, Zoe Wilkins, Flora Quick Mundis, Bonnie Parker, Katie Bender and Belle Starr.* Girard, KS: Haldeman-Julius, 1945. [Trivial but collectible 24-page booklet.]

Boynton, Captain Tom. *The Gang Wars of Chicago and the Rise of the Super Chiefs.* Chicago (?): Prohibition Research Association, 1930. [Magazine format booklet similar to *X Marks the Spot,* more chronological and biographical, but less professionally written.]

Brashler, William. *The Don: The Life and Death of Sam Giancana.* New York: Harper & Row, 1977. [Excellent biography of the notorious Chicago mobster, whose career began in the Capone era.]

Brearley, H. C. *Homicide in the United States.* Chapel Hill, NC: University of North Carolina Press, 1932. Reprint, Montclair, NJ: Patterson Smith, 1969. [One of several academic efforts to examine Americans' penchant for killing each other; includes some good data and insights but sometimes misses the obvious.]

Brennan, Bill. *The Frank Costello Story.* Derby, CT: Monarch Books, 1962. [Avoid any of the several "gangster biographies" from Monarch Books.]

Breuer, William B. J. *Edgar Hoover and His G-Men.* Westport, CT: Praeger, 1995. [Attempts to pay homage to the FBI's gang-busting thirties exploits, but details often are wildly inaccurate.]

Brian, Denis. *Sing Sing: The Inside Story of a Notorious Prison.* Amherst, NY: Prometheus Books, 2005.

Brown, Mark Douglas. *Capone: Life Behind Bars at Alcatraz.* San Francisco: Golden Gate National Parks Conservancy, 2004. [70-page booklet sold at Alcatraz with brief biography of Capone and details of his life on "The Rock." Reproduces many fascinating reports from Capone's prison record and also includes rare photos of Al in and out of prison.]

Browning, Frank, and Gerassi, John. *The American Way of Crime: From Salem to Watergate, A Stunning New Perspective on American History.* New York: G. P. Putnam's Sons, 1980.

Bruns, Roger A. *The Bandit Kings: From Jesse James to*

Pretty Boy Floyd. New York: Crown, 1995. [Superficial treatment of all the big-name outlaws from the frontier period through the Public-Enemy era, interesting mainly for its design, superior production, and good collection of photos.]

Buckland, Gail, and Evans, Harold. *Shots in the Dark: True Crime Pictures.* New York: Bullfinch Press, 2001. [Gruesome collection of historic crime photos, published as a companion piece to a Court TV documentary of the same name.]

Bukowski, Douglas. *Big Bill Thompson, Chicago, and the Politics of Image.* Chicago: University of Illinois Press, 1998. [Excellent academic account of Chicago's wildly corrupt mayor in the twenties.]

Burns, Walter Noble. *The One-Way Ride.* Garden City, NY: Doubleday, Doran, 1931. [An exciting and melodramatic, if historically dubious, account of the Capone era in Chicago. Burns is perhaps better known for *The Saga of Billy the Kid,* a work of lurid fiction posing as history.]

Burrough, Bryan. *Public Enemies: America's Greatest Crime Wave and the Birth of the FBI, 1933-34.* New York: Penguin Press, 2004. [Bestselling history of the Depression crime wave from the Kansas City Massacre on. Perhaps contains too much dialogue, much of it apparently deriving from late author Bill Trent's interviews with Alvin Karpis, and many errors occur throughout. Still perhaps the best detailed account of the FBI's baptism of fire in the first national "war on crime" and the rise and fall of "Pretty Boy" Floyd, the Barker-Karpis Gang, Bonnie and Clyde, "Machine Gun" Kelly, Dillinger, and "Baby Face" Nelson since John Toland's *The Dillinger Days.* Also gives due credit to many of the "G-men" active in the gangster cases rather than just Melvin Purvis and Sam Cowley.]

Burroughs, William S. *The Last Words of Dutch Schultz.* New York: Viking Press, 1975. [Written as a play, but contains many photos and the poetically delirious deathbed ramblings of the mortally wounded Schultz.]

Busch, Francis X. *Enemies of the State.* New York/Indianapolis: Bobbs-Merrill, 1954. [Contains a fairly good chapter on Al Capone, marred by a few errors.]

Butts, Edward. *Outlaws of the Lakes: Bootlegging and Smuggling From Colonial Times to Prohibition.* Toronto: Lynch Images, and Holt, MI: Thunder Bay Press, 2004. [Prohibition material includes Chicago and Detroit gangsters, Rocco Perri, and Wisconsin "Bootleg Queen" Jenny Justo.]

C

Calderone, Carmen. *The Genealogy of American Organized Crime.* Charleston, SC: BookSurge, 2002. [Extensive list of the twentieth century lines of succession of leadership in Italian crime families and also various Jewish, Irish, and other "independent" mobs in cities throughout the United States. Contains many famous and obscure names but also some erroneous dates.]

Calhoun, Frederick S. *The Lawmen: United States Marshals and Their Deputies, 1789-1989.* Washington, DC, and London: Smithsonian Institution Press, 1989. [200-year history of the U.S. Marshals Service includes chapter on Prohibition describing how Deputy U.S. marshals arrested bootleggers based on evidence gathered by Prohibition agents, and how the Treasury agents who arrested Capone for tax evasion were acting as U.S. marshals specially deputized for that purpose by the Justice Department. Touches briefly on the marshals service's rivalry with the FBI.]

Callahan, Clyde C., and Jones, Byron B. *Heritage of An Outlaw—The Story of Frank Nash.* Hobart, OK: Schoonmaker Publishers, 1979. [Biography of Frank "Jelly" Nash, killed in the Kansas City Massacre of 1933. Contains gangster genealogy similar to that in Paul Wellman's A Dynasty of Western Outlaws. Published in Nash's hometown.]

Callahan, Jack. *Man's Grim Justice: My Life Outside the Law.* New York: J. H. Sears & Co., 1928. [Melodramatic supposed autobiography of a gangster.]

Campbell, Rodney. *The Luciano Project.* New York: McGraw-Hill, 1977. [Details "Lucky" Luciano's contribution to the war effort in World War II. From a New York prison cell, Luciano apparently collaborated with Naval Intelligence in suppressing espionage and sabotage on the New York waterfront and later worked with the OSS (forerunner of the CIA) in setting up a Mafia resistance movement to aid the Allied invasion of Sicily. Well researched and appears to be "on the level," as Luciano probably would say.]

Cantor, George. *Bad Guys in American History.* Dallas: Taylor Publishing, 1999. [Paperback coffee-table book provides superficial coverage of "bad guys" from the colonial era to the twentieth century. Includes chapters on Al Capone, Dillinger, Bonnie and Clyde, and "Bugsy" Siegel.]

Capeci, Jerry. *The Complete Idiot's Guide to the Mafia.* New York: Alpha Books, 2001. [A nice "beginner's guide" for the fledgling Mafia expert, despite its "idiotic" title, from a noted organized crime reporter.]

———. *Wiseguys Say the Darndest Things: The Quotable Mafia.* New York: Alpha Books, 2004. [Collection of mobster quotes.]

Caren, Eric C. (collected by). *Crime Extra: 300 Years of Crime in North America.* Edison, NJ: Castle Books, 2001. [Collection of newspaper stories from across the nation of famous crimes and criminals.]

Carey, Arthur A., with McLellan, Howard. *On the Track of Murder.* London: Jarrolds, 1930. [Adventures and recollections of longtime New York Homicide Bureau deputy inspector, with extensive coverage of local hoodlums before and during Prohibition. Reprinted in U.S. in abbreviated form as Memoirs of a Murder Man. Garden City, NY: Doubleday, Doran & Co., 1930.]

Carney, Gene. *Burying the Black Sox: How Baseball's Cover-up of the 1919 World Series Fix Almost Succeeded.* Dulles, VA: Potomac Books, 2006.

Carpozi, George Jr. *Gangland Killers of the '30s.* New York: Whitestone Publications, 1968. [One-shot magazine consisting of articles by Carpozi on the St. Valentine's Day Massacre, "Legs" Diamond, Raymond Hamilton, Bonnie and Clyde, Al Capone, "Dutch" Schultz, "Pretty Boy" Floyd, and the Kansas City Massacre, "Mad Dog" Coll, the Barker-Karpis Gang, "Baby Face" Nelson, "Machine Gun" Kelly, and John Dillinger. Grossly inaccurate and fictionalized.]

———. *Bugsy: The High-Rolling, Bullet-Riddled Story of Benjamin "Bugsy" Siegel.* New York: Pinnacle Books, 1973. [Slim paperback "biography" compares poorly with Dean Jennings's *We Only Kill Each Other.* Reprinted in 1992, by Shapolsky, New York, with new introduction contrasting the real Siegel to Warren Beatty's character in the movie *Bugsy* and retitled *Bugsy: The Bloodthirsty, Lusty Life of Bugsy Siegel.*]

———. *Gangland Killers.* New York: Manor Books, 1979. [Paperback reprint of Carpozi's 1968 magazine, minus the photos and Bonnie and Clyde chapter but still including Raymond Hamilton.]

Carr, Jesse. *The Second-Oldest Profession: An Informal History of Moonshining.* Englewood Cliffs, NJ: Prentice-Hall, 1972.

Carse, Robert. *Rum Row.* New York: Holt, Rinehart & Winston, 1959.

Carter, Lauren. *The Most Evil Mobsters in History.* London: Michael O'Mara Books, 2004. [Superficial and not always accurate biographical chapters on various gangsters from Al Capone to John Gotti.]

Casey, Robert J., and Douglas, W. A. S. *The Midwesterner.* Chicago: Wilcox & Follett, 1948. [A cryptically titled but well-written biography of Illinois' slightly quirky Governor Dwight Green that includes an absorbing account of Chicago's underworld warfare, the fall of Capone, and battles with other colorful scoundrels of the period.]

Cashman, Sean Dennis. *Prohibition: The Lie of the Land.* New York: Free Press, 1981.

Cawelti, John G. (editor). *Focus on Bonnie and Clyde.* Englewood Cliffs, NJ: Prentice-Hall, 1973. [Historical and movie material on Bonnie Parker and Clyde Barrow, including excerpts from Fugitives by Emma Parker and Nell Barrow Cowan.]

Chamberlain, John. *Farewell to Reform.* New York: Liveright, 1932.

Chambers, Walter. *Samuel Seabury: A Challenge.* New York: Century, 1932. [Contemporary work on Judge Samuel Seabury's probe of vice and corruption that drove New York's Mayor Jimmy Walker out of office.]

Chandler, David Leon. *Brothers in Blood: The Rise of the Criminal Brotherhoods.* New York: E. P. Dutton & Co., 1975. [Interesting but mostly undocumented genealogy of Mediterranean criminal brotherhoods (the Spanish Garduna, the Camorra, Mafia, "Cosa Nostra," and Unione Corse) and history of their transplantation to North America and Australia. Among other things, accepts the widely discredited myth of the 1931 Mafia purge, or "Night of the Sicilian Vespers," and asserts that a machine gun was not used in the Frankie Yale murder.]

Charbonneau, Jean-Paul. *The Canadian Connection.* Montreal: Optimum, 1976. [Biography of Rocco Perri, the Canadian Capone. See also Dubro and Rowland, *King of the Mob.*]

Charyn, Jerome. *Gangsters and Gold Diggers: Old New York, the Jazz Age, and the Birth of Broadway.* New York: Four Walls Eight Windows, 2003.

Cherrington, Earnest H. *The Evolution of Prohibition in the United States of America.* Westerville, OH: American Issue Press, 1920. Reprint, Montclair, NJ: Patterson Smith, 1969. [Thoroughly biased but still useful, mainly for its extensive and detailed description of America's Prohibition movement going back to the colonial period.]

Chiocca, Olindo Romeo. *Mobsters and Thugs: Quotes from the Underworld.* Toronto: Guernica Editions, 2000. [Slim book of gangster quotes with superficial commentary. All are from previously published sources, some spurious and some misattributed.]

Chipman, Art. *"Tunnel 13": The Story of the DeAutremont Brothers and the West's Last Great Train Holdup.* Medford, OR: Pine Cone Publishers, 1977. [Good account of one of the twenties' most spectacular and disastrous crimes, the bloody attempted train robbery near Siskiyou, Oregon, led to the long international pursuit of the DeAutremont boys. See also Sturholm and Howard, *All for Nothing.*]

Christianson, Scott. *Condemned: Inside the Sing Sing Death House.* New York: New York University Press, 2000. [Collection of photos and documents on many Sing Sing executions, including the "Murder, Inc." killers.]

Churchill, Allen. *A Pictorial History of American Crime.* New York: Holt, Rinehart & Winston, 1964. [Oversize and superficial, featuring the most widely published crime photos.]

Churney, Dan. *Capone's Cornfields: The Mob in the Illinois Valley.* Charleston, SC: BookSurge, 2004. [Vignettes of Chicago mob spillovers into the Illinois hinterlands.]

Cipes, Robert M. *The Crime War: The Manufactured Crusade.* New York: New American Library, 1968. [Includes published material from other sources, tending to discredit the "war on crime" campaigns as more political than practical.]

Cirules, Enrique. *The Mafia in Havana: A Caribbean Mob Story.* New York: Ocean Press, 2003. [History of mob gambling in Cuba.]

Citizens Police Committee. *Chicago Police Problems.* Chicago: University of Chicago Press, 1931. Reprint, Montclair, NJ: Patterson Smith, 1969. [A critical examination of how police administrative and organizational policies were crippling law enforcement in most large cities where policing efforts were fragmented, poorly coordinated, and sometimes competitive due to district political influence.]

Claitor, Diana. *Outlaws, Mobsters and Murderers.* New York: M&M Books, 1991. [Nicely produced and profusely illustrated coffee-table book covering nearly all the famous gangsters and outlaws, serial killers, spectacular crimes, etc. Nothing new but fairly accurate.]

Clarahan, Donald. *The Great Rondout Train Robbery.* Bloomington, IL: Norfolk-Hall, 1980. [Slim, terribly inaccurate, and fictionalized account of America's greatest train robbery, carried out in 1924 by the Newton boys and others and masterminded by Jimmy Murray.]

Clarens, Carlos. *Crime Movies: From Griffiths to The Godfather and Beyond.* New York: W. W. Norton & Co., 1980. [Probably the definitive work on gangster movies.]

Clarke, Donald Henderson. *In the Reign of Rothstein.* New York: Vanguard Press, 1929. [Probably the first biography of Arnold Rothstein, published just after his murder.]

Clayton, Merle. *Union Station Massacre: The Shootout That Started the FBI's War on Crime.* New York/Indianapolis: Bobbs-Merrill, 1975. Story of "Pretty Boy" Floyd and the Kansas City Massacre. Derived mainly from newspaper clippings, although the writer apparently had access to FBI files. Fairly accurate.]

Coates, Tim (editor). *The St. Valentine's Day Massacre, 1929: FBI Files Relating to the Murder of Seven Members of the "Bugs" Moran gang on 14 February 1929.* London: The Stationary Office, 2002. [Slim paperback compilation of FBI files from the FBI's Freedom of Information Reading Room. From a series entitled uncovered editions of previously unpublished documents. Nice collector's piece, but the whole series of reports is now downloadable from the FBI's Web site free; for seventy cents, plus postage, one can buy the entire Massacre file from the bureau.]

Cocker, Andrew, and Leith, David Dean (photographer). *NYPD: An Illustrated History.* New York: Odyssey, 2000. [Slim photo history of New York Police Department with great Tommygun photo on cover. Highlights include sections on Joe Petrosino and Frankie Yale.]

Coffee, Thomas M. *The Long Thirst, Prohibition in America: 1920-1933.* New York: W. W. Norton & Co., 1975. [Social history of Prohibition.]

Cohen, Daniel. *The Encyclopedia of Unsolved Crimes.* New York: Dorset Press, 1988. [Gangster material includes the murders of Arnold Rothstein, Abe "Kid Twist" Reles, and Roger Touhy, possible mob involvement in the disappearance of Judge Crater and the death of Thelma Todd, the escape of "Terrible Tommy" O'Connor and Jay Robert Nash's conspiracy theory of Dillinger's survival, which Cohen considers and quickly dismisses.]

Cohen, Mickey, with Nugent, John Peer. *Mickey Cohen: In My Own Words.* Englewood Cliffs, NJ: Prentice-Hall, 1975. [Cohen worked for Al Capone and "Bugsy" Siegel, was a Los Angeles bookmaking boss, survived Mafia assassination attempts, and spent time in Alcatraz with Alvin Karpis, but his "own words" make for dull reading. Brags that he "never killed a guy who didn't deserve it," but offers little original information.]

Cohen, Rich. *Tough Jews: Fathers, Sons and Gangster Dreams.* New York: Simon & Schuster, 1998. [Stylishly written but less carefully researched account of New York's Jewish gangsters.]

Cohen, Sam D. *100 True Crime Stories.* Cleveland/New York: World Publishing, 1946. [Short accounts of miscellaneous and unmemorable murders and robberies, mostly in the U.S., mostly from the 1930s.]

Cohn, Art. *The Joker Is Wild: The Story of Joe E. Lewis.* New York: Random House, 1955. [Overdone biography of comedian Joe E. Lewis, who survived a throat-slashing after quitting his job at a Capone nightclub, The Green Mill (still in operation, but under new management). Much on Capone, "Machine Gun" Jack McGurn, other Chicago gangsters, plus a chapter on "Dutch" Schultz.]

Colby, Robert. *The California Crime Book.* New York: Pyramid Books, 1971. [Routine paperback collection of California crime stories. Includes chapters on the murders of "Bugsy" Siegel and Chicago hood Nick DeJohn.]

Collins, Frederick Lewis. *The FBI in Peace and War.* New York: G. P. Putnam's Sons, New York, 1943. [Like other FBI-approved books, this one has an introduction by J. Edgar Hoover, lauds the bureau war on crime and saboteurs, and has much on Depression outlaws, who were then recent history.]

Condon, John F. *Jafsie Tells All!* New York: Jonathan Lee, 1936. [Dr. John "Jafsie" Condon was the payoff man in the Lindbergh kidnapping, but also once was school principal to the young Arthur Flegenheimer, later known as "Dutch" Schultz.]

Conway, John. *Dutch Schultz and His Lost Catskills' Treasure.* Fleischmanns, NY: Purple Mountain Press, 2000. [40-page booklet detailing the legend of a $7 million hoard allegedly buried by Schultz before his death.]

Cook, Fred J. *A Two Dollar Bet Means Murder.* New York: Dial Press, 1961. [Some superficial history, but mostly argues that gambling is the steadiest source of income for the modern day mob.]

———. *The FBI Nobody Knows.* New York: Macmillan, 1964. [Cook, aided by a former agent, critical of the FBI, covers Dillinger, Urschel kidnapping, Kansas City Massacre, and Barker-Karpis Gang, with mentions of Bonnie and Clyde, Capone, and Louis "Lepke" Buchalter. Historical errors throughout.]

———. *The Secret Rulers: Criminal Syndicates and How They Control the U.S. Underworld.* New York: Duell, Sloan & Pierce, 1966

———. *Mafia.* Greenwich, CT: Fawcett Publications, 1973.

Cooney, John. *The Annenbergs: The Salvaging of a Tainted Dynasty.* New York: Simon & Schuster, 1982. [Former Chicago gangster and race-wire magnate Moe Annenberg took the whole rap himself in the nation's biggest tax evasion case, allowing his son Walter to gain respectability as a publishing magnate and eventual ambassador to Britain under Nixon (a post also once held by former bootlegger Joe Kennedy).]

Cooper, Courtney Ryley. *Ten Thousand Public Enemies.* Boston: Little, Brown & Co., 1935. [Mainly about Depression outlaws, including Dillinger, Floyd, Nelson, Barker-Karpis Gang, "Machine Gun" Kelly, the Barrows, Wilbur Underhill, Jake Fleagle, Tri-State Gang, and many other lesser-known criminals, with some references to Capone, partly derived from Cooper's own series of articles in *American Magazine.* Much glorification of J. Edgar Hoover and the FBI (then called the Division of Investigation) in the purple prose of the day. Great literary license taken, but as Hoover's favorite writer and personal crony he enjoyed full FBI cooperation and thus provides much valuable information from the bureau's confidential files. Flowery forward by Hoover, who is said to have followed Cooper's advice in popularizing the term "G-man" and fostering the bureau's image as a dedicated team of selfless, incorruptible, invincible scientific crime-fighters. Cooper later committed suicide, supposedly after falling into disfavor with Hoover.]

———. *Here's To Crime.* Boston: Little, Brown & Co., 1937. [Largely rehash of *Ten Thousand Public Enemies,* with added material on rackets, miscellaneous crime, police, prisons, courts, other federal investigative agencies, etc. In 1939 authored a lurid study of prostitution, *Designs in Scarlet.*]

Cordry, Dee. *Oklahoma Outlaw and Lawman Map, 1865-1935.* Oklahoma City: Oklahoma Heritage Association,

1990. [Compiled by an agent of Oklahoma's State Crime Bureau, this map includes dozens of sites connected with southwestern outlaws of the twenties and thirties, including Al Spencer, Frank Nash, the Kimes and Terrill gangs, the Barkers, "Pretty Boy" Floyd, Bonnie and Clyde, "Machine Gun" Kelly, Harvey Bailey, and Wilbur Underhill, as well as earlier criminals from the horseback era. Photos and text on Oklahoma's outlaw and lawman history. Extremely well researched.]

———. *Alive if Possible . . . Dead if Necessary.* Mustang, OK: Tate Publishing, 2005. [Early history of the Oklahoma Crime Bureau, founded in the twenties to fight the growing epidemic of bank robberies. More outlaw gangs flourished in Oklahoma than any other state, from the territorial days through the Depression. Examines the Osage Indian murders, Al Spencer, the Kimes and Terrill gangs, and the career and assassination of Luther Bishop, exemplary lawman prominently involved in these cases.]

Corey, Herbert. *Farewell, Mr. Gangster!* New York: D. Appleton-Century Co., 1936. [Another complimentary, detailed, and apparently factual account (far less lurid than Cooper's) of the FBI's extermination of the Depression outlaw gangs. Foreword by Hoover indicates Corey also had access to FBI files.]

Corrina, Joe. *Mobsters: A Who's Who of America's Most Notorious Criminals.* North Dighton, MA: JG Press, 2003.

Courtney, Thomas J., Crowley, Wilbert F., and Kearney, Marshall B. Statement in Opposition to the Release of Banghart: "The Factor Kidnapping Was Not a Hoax, Touhy Was Not Framed." Chicago: Champlin-Shealey Co., circa 1960.

Cox, Bill G., et al. *Crimes of the 20th Century.* New York: Crescent Books, 1991. [Contributors include Bill G. Cox, Bill Francis, William J. Helmer, Gary C. King, Julie Malear, Darrell Moore, David Nemec, Samuel Roen, and Billie Francis Taylor. Some personal reports, but mostly from published sources, some accurate, some not.]

Cox, Roger A. *The Thompson Submachine Gun.* Athens, GA: Law Enforcement Ordnance Co., 1982. [Includes chapters on gangster and police use of the Thompson. Many good photos, though the caption labeling one Tommygun as belonging to "Ma" Barker is pure lore. Introduction by William J. Helmer, *The Gun That Made the Twenties Roar,* regarded as the most comprehensive story of the Thompson gun.]

Craig, Jonathan, and Posner, Richard. *The New York Crime Book.* New York: Pyramid Books, 1972. [Undistinguished paperback.]

Crain, Milton (editor). *Sins of New York.* New York: Boni & Gaer, 1947. [Anthology of New York underworld stories, including accounts of the tong wars by Herbert Asbury and "Murder, Inc." by Meyer Berger.]

Cressey, Donald R. *Theft of the Nation: The Structure and Operations of Organized Crime in America.* New York: Harper & Row, 1969. [Academic study of the Italian crime families known as the Mafia or La Cosa Nostra, mostly in the sixties, mainly inspired by the Senate revelations of mob turncoat Joe Valachi. Some historical background on the twenties and thirties.]

Cressey, Paul G. *The Taxi-Dance Hall: A Sociological Study of Commercial Recreation in City Life.* Chicago: University of Chicago Press, 1932.

Cromie, Robert, and Pinkston, Joseph. *Dillinger: A Short and Violent Life.* New York: McGraw-Hill, 1962. [The first carefully researched and heavily detailed Dillinger biography. The late Joe Pinkston was the country's leading Dillinger authority and for years operated the John Dillinger Historical Museum at Nashville, Indiana. Reprinted in 1990 in paperback by The Chicago Historical Bookworks, Evanston, Ill. See also Matera, *John Dillinger: The Life and Death of America's First Celebrity Criminal.*]

Crouse, Russell. *Murder Won't Out.* Garden City, NY: Doubleday, Doran, 1932. [Accounts of various unsolved New York City murders.]

Crowe, Richard T., with Mercado, Carol. *Chicago's Street Guide to the Supernatural.* Oak Park, IL: Carolando Press, 2000. [Guide to alleged haunted sites in Chicago by noted ghost hunter Crowe includes gangster sites such as the Biograph Theatre and alley where Dillinger died and the vacant lot that once housed the S.M.C. Cartage Company, site of the St. Valentine's Day Massacre.]

Crump, Irving, and Newton, John W. *Our G-Men.* New York: Dodd, Mead, 1937. [Contemporary juvenile work on the gangbusting "G-men."]

Culver, Dorothy Campbell (compiler): Bibliography of Crime and Criminal Justice, 1927-1931. New York: H. W. Wilson, 1934. Reprint, Montclair, NJ: Patterson Smith, 1969.

———. *Bibliography of Crime and Criminal Justice, 1932-1937.* (1939).

Cummings, Homer S. *Selected Papers.* New York: Charles Scribner's Sons, 1939. [A collection of Cummings's crime-fighting ideas that were considered progressive, even revolutionary, at the time.]

———. *We Can Prevent Crime.* Privately published, 1930s. [Slender and elegantly self-published (bound in red leather with gold lettering) 34-page collection of four articles from *Liberty* magazine by the first U.S. attorney general under President Roosevelt, brimming with New Deal optimism and naivete.]

———, and McFarland, Carl. *Federal Justice: Chapters in the History of Justice in the Federal Executive.* New York: Macmillan, 1937. [Appointed attorney general by President Roosevelt in 1933, Cummings launched the national "war on crime" that unleashed J. Edgar Hoover and the FBI and used celebrity fugitives like Dillinger to obtain passage of unprecedented federal anti-crime laws. Reprinted by Da Capo, New York, 1970.]

Currotto, William F. (editor). *Newspaper Accounts of Machine Gun Kelly and the House at 1408 Rayner.* Memphis, TN: Patchwork Books, 1995. [Kelly's capture as described in local news accounts.]

Curzon, Sam. *Legs Diamond.* Derby, CT: Monarch Books, 1961. [Slightly better than average for Monarch, but still mainly of interest to collectors of obscure crime paperbacks. Some good trivia about 1920s gangsters and Prohibition, but also much fiction. Reprinted with photos by Tower Books, 1969.]

D

D'Amato, Grace Anselmo. *Chance of a Lifetime: Nucky Johnson, Skinny D'Amato, And How Atlantic City Became the Naughty Queen of Resorts.* Harvey Cedars, NJ: Down the Shore Publishing, 2001. [Atlantic City's wild past as recounted by the sister-in-law of Paul "Skinny" D'Amato.]

Danforth, Harold, with Horan, James D. *The D.A.'s Man.* New York: Crown Publishers, 1957. [Harold Danforth was an investigator for the New York District Attorney's office under Thomas E. Dewey and Frank Hogan and worked on the Dutch Schultz, Luciano, and Jimmy Hines cases.]

Davis, Bruce. *We're Dead, Come on in.* Gretna, LA: Pelican Publishing, 2005. [Account of the 1932 "Young Brothers Massacre" at Springfield, Missouri, in which six law officers died.]

Davis, John H. *Mafia Dynasty: The Rise and Fall of the Gambino Crime Family.* New York: HarperCollins, 1993. [Traces history of Gambino family from the "Castellammarese War" of 1931 to the fall of John Gotti in 1992.]

Davis, Robert E. *A History of a Clyde Barrow Shotgun and Related Artifacts.* Waco, TX: Texian Press, 2001. [Thirty-two page booklet authenticating details of a Barrow shotgun and items recovered with it.]

———, and Davis, Mary Ann. *Blanche Barrow—The Last Victim of Bonnie & Clyde: Prison Letters from 1933 to 1936.* Waco, TX: Texian Press, 2001. [Sixty-four-page booklet provides family background and rare insights into the most neglected member of the Barrow Gang. See also *My Life With Bonnie and Clyde* by Blanche Caldwell Barrow.]

Day, James M. *Captain Clint Peoples, Texas Ranger: Fifty Years A Lawman.* Waco, TX: Texian Press, 1980. [Among the miscreants pursued by Captain Peoples were Bonnie and Clyde.]

deFord, Miriam Allen. *The Real Bonnie & Clyde.* New York: Ace Books, 1968. [DeFord's sources consisted of the 1934 book *Fugitives* by Bonnie's mother and Clyde's sister, Toland's *The Dillinger Days,* and a few newspaper stories. Nothing new here. Slim paperback cash-in on the movie *Bonnie and Clyde.*]

———. *The Real Ma Barker.* New York: Ace Books, 1970. [Worse yet. Terribly inaccurate account of Barker-Karpis Gang takes up only half the book. All from published sources, including Alan Hynd's mostly fictional *We Are the Public Enemies.* Filler material is equally inaccurate biographies of other gangsters of the period, both bank robbers and racketeers. Quick cash-in on the movie *Bloody Mama.*]

Deitche, Scott. *Cigar City Mafia: A Complete History of the Tampa Underworld.* Fort Lee, NJ: Barricade Books, 2004.

Delap, Breandan. *Mad Dog Coll: An Irish Gangster.* Dublin: Mercier Press, 1999. [Excellent long-overdue biography of one of the most notorious New York gangsters of the Prohibition era. Well-researched and one of the more intelligent gangster biographies. Like author Delap, "Mad Dog" Coll was born in Ireland and has apparently grown to legendary proportions in his homeland.]

De Leeuw, Hendrik *Underworld Story: The Rise of Organized Crime and Vice-Rackets in the U.S.A.* London:

Neville Spearman/Arco, 1955. [One of several spin-offs of De Leeuw's principal book, *Sinful Cities of the Western World*, dealing more with vice, brothels, and sleaze than gangsters.]

Demaris, Ovid. *The Lucky Luciano Story*. Derby, CT: Monarch Books, 1960. [Another novelized "biography." Reprinted with photos in 1969 by Tower Books, New York, as part of their "Public Enemies of the 1930s" series, and again in 1973, by Belmont Tower, as *The Lucky Luciano Story: The Mafioso and the Violent '30s*, as part of their "Godfather" series.]

———. *The Dillinger Story*. Derby, CT: Monarch Books, 1961. [More low-grade Monarch. Reprinted by Tower in 1968 and by Belmont Tower, as *Dillinger*, in 1973.]

———. *Captive City: Chicago in Chains*. Secaucus, NJ: Lyle Stuart, 1969. [Good account of organized crime and political corruption in Chicago, especially considering Demaris' paperback work. Focus is on modern Syndicate activities and personalities, but has much on Capone era.]

———. *America the Violent*. New York: Cowles, 1970. [Routine history of American crime.]

———. *The Director: An Oral Biography of J. Edgar Hoover*. New York: Harper & Row, 1975. [Slight gangster material (mostly on Dillinger) but interesting views of a tarnished American legend.]

———. *The Last Mafioso: The Treacherous World of Jimmy Fratianno*. New York: Times Books, 1981. Stool pigeon Jimmy Fratianno's criminal career began in the 1940s, and his early associates included the likes of "Bugsy" Siegel, Frankie Carbo, Mickey Cohen, Jack Dragna, John Rosselli, and even "Baby Face" Nelson's Reno friends Bill Graham and Jim McKay.]

———. *The Boardwalk Jungle*. New York: Bantam, 1986. [Study of mob involvement in Atlantic City gambling includes historical background on 1920s criminal/political boss Enoch "Nucky" Johnson.]

DeNeal, Gary. *A Knight of Another Sort: Prohibition Days and Charlie Birger*. Danville, IL: Interstate Printers & Publishers, 1981; revised and updated version published in 1998 by Southern Illinois University Press with new information and a foreword by Jim Ballowe. [Excellent biography of Birger, with good collection of photos. Well-researched and probably the most detailed account yet of the Birger and Shelton gangs.]

DeNevi, Don. *Western Train Robberies*. Millbrae, CA: Celestial Arts, 1976. [Includes chapters on train robberies in the 1920s.]

———, and Bergen, Philip. *Alcatraz '46: The Anatomy of a Classic Prison Tragedy*. San Rafael, CA: Leswing Press, 1974. [Well-researched account of the 1946 Alcatraz riot-escape attempt. Interesting to compare to Clark Howard's *Six Against the Rock*, dealing with the same subject.]

DeRamus, Troy. *Days of Bonnie and Clyde*. Boyce, LA: privately published. [Collection of Bonnie and Clyde and Depression anecdotes from northern Louisiana collected by a local historian.]

Des Moines Police Department. *Behind the Badge: Stories and Pictures From the DMPD*. Peglow Art & Design Publishing/Des Moines Police Burial Association, 1999. [Excellent history of the Des Moines Police Department. Includes chapters on the old "red light" district, illegal gambling, the Barrow Gang shootout at Dexter, Iowa, and the Capone mob's move into Des Moines, spearheaded by Charles "Cherry Nose" Gioe. Mentions but tends to downplay the later criminal activities of Gioe's successor, Luigi "Lew Farrell" Fratto.]

DeSimone, Donald. *"I Rob Banks: That's Where the Money Is!": The Story of Bank Robber Willie "The Actor" Sutton and the Killing of Arnold Schuster*. New York: Shapolsky Publishers, Inc., 1991. [Purports to tell the true story of the Schuster killing. Uses fictional dialogue and reveals little new about Willie Sutton.]

DeSola, Ralph. *Crime Dictionary*. New York: Facts on File, 1982.

De Stefano, George. *An Offer We Can't Refuse: The Mafia in the Mind of America*. New York: Faber & Faber, 2006.

de Toledano, Ralph. *J. Edgar Hoover, The Man in His Time*. New Rochelle, NY: Arlington House, 1973. [Tribute to Hoover, written soon after his death. Gangster cases covered include Dillinger, "Machine Gun" Kelly, Barker-Karpis Gang, Bonnie and Clyde, "Lepke" Buchalter. Many errors.]

Dewey, Thomas E. *Twenty Against the Underworld*. Garden City, NY: Doubleday & Co., 1974. [Tom Dewey's activities as a "racket-busting" prosecutor were the foundation of his political career. Among others, he convicted "Waxey" Gordon and "Lucky" Luciano (whom he later paroled). He didn't get Dutch Schultz, but Schultz nearly got him. Edited by Rodney Campbell, author of *The Luciano Project*.]

Dickie, John. *Cosa Nostra: A History of the Sicilian Mafia*. London: Hodder & Stoughton, 2004. New York: Palgrave Macmillan, 2004. [History of the Sicilian Mafia, with long chapter on the establishment of Sicilian crime families in the U.S.]

Dillon, Richard H. *The Hatchet Men.* New York: Coward-McCann, 1962. [History of the tong wars of San Francisco's Chinatown. Mainly nineteenth century, but last chapter includes 1920s and mentions probably the first use of a machine gun in gang warfare (a .30-caliber water-cooled Browning mounted on an automobile in 1914).]

Dingler, Jerry (compiler). *Historical Collector Edition: Bonnie and Clyde Ambush.* Privately printed, Arcadia, LA, 1984. [Fiftieth-anniversary commemorative newspaper includes contemporary articles on the famous ambush, which occurred near Arcadia.]

Dinneen, Joseph F. *Underworld U.S.A.* New York: Farrar, Straus & Cudahay, 1955.

Dobyns, Fletcher. *The Underworld of American Politics.* New York: self-published, 1932. [Good contemporary account of underworld political influence in the Prohibition era.]

Dorigo, Joe. *Mafia: A Chilling Illustrated History of the Underworld.* Secaucus, NJ: Chartwell Books, 1992. [Slim, poorly researched coffee-table book of interest chiefly for its good photos.]

Dorman, Michael. *Pay-off.* New York: David McKay Company, 1972. [Organized crime and political corruption across the nation. Chapter entitled "The Big Fix" details rise to prominence of Jack Halfen, a minor Southwestern bandit of the thirties who later became a big-time gambling boss and organized-crime bagman in Texas. Includes interesting anecdotes on his alleged early associations with "Pretty Boy" Floyd, Clyde Barrow, and Bonnie Parker.]

Dornfeld, A.A. *Behind the Front Page: The Story of the City News Bureau of Chicago.* Chicago: Academy, 1983. Reprinted in softcover as *Hello, Sweetheart, Get Me Rewrite!,* Chicago: Academy, 1988. [Illuminates some interesting features of the "Chicago school of journalism" and includes anecdotal material on press coverage of such historic crimes as the St. Valentine's Day Massacre.]

Downey, Patrick. *Gangster City: The History of the New York Underworld, 1900-1935.* New York: Barricade Books, 2004. [Comprehensive volume on New York City gangsters. Much on Schultz-Coll war, Owney Madden, Frankie Yale, early gangsters such as "Kid Dropper" and Johnny Spanish, Chinatown tong wars, the Morello-Terranova Family, Irish "White Hand," and others. Much focus on obscure but important figures of the twenties and thirties, including the likes of the Amberg and Shapiro Brothers, "Chink" Sherman, and Irv Bitz and Salvatore Spitale.]

Draper, W. R. *On the Trail of "Pretty Boy" Floyd.* Girard, KS: Haldeman-Julius, 1946. [Pamphlet consisting mainly of articles Draper wrote for a Kansas City newspaper in 1934. Fairly accurate account of Floyd's career, with minor errors. Includes chronology of Floyd's crimes and interviews with his wife and mother.]

———, and Draper, Mabel. *The Blood-Soaked Career of Bonnie Parker: How Bandit Clyde Barrow and His Cigar-Smoking Moll Fought It Out With the Law.* Girard, KS: Haldeman-Julius, 1945. [A twenty-four-page pamphlet in the "dime novel" style.]

Dubro, James, and Rowland, Robin F. *King of the Mob: Rocco Perri and the Women Who Ran His Rackets.* Markham, Ontario: Penguin, 1988. [Perri was Canada's equivalent of Chicago's Al Capone, without the national publicity. See also Charbonneau, *The Canadian Connection.*]

Duncombe Stephen, and Mattson, Andrew *The Bobbed Hair Bandit: A True Story of Crime and Celebrity in 1920s New York.* New York: New York University Press, 2006. [Biography of Cecelia Cooney, celebrated "fun girl" of the Twenties.]

E

Edge, L.L. *Run the Cat Roads: A True Story of Bank Robbers in the '30s.* New York: Dembner Books, 1981. [Mainly about the Memorial Day 1933 escape of eleven convicts, led by Harvey Bailey and Wilbur Underhill, from the Lansing, Kansas, state penitentiary; the crimes and recapture of the Bailey-Underhill Gang; and related events, such as the Urschel kidnapping and the Kansas City Massacre. Edge apparently interviewed some surviving participants in these events, including Harvey Bailey, but seems to have drawn heavily on J. Evetts Haley's *Robbing Banks Was My Business,* an earlier and fairly obscure biography of Bailey. He also makes some drastic errors when discussing other outlaws, especially Dillinger and Barker-Karpis gangs.]

Edmonds, Andy. *Hot Toddy: The True Story of Hollywood's Most Sensational Murder.* New York: William Morrow, 1989. [Contends that film star Thelma Todd was murdered on orders from "Lucky" Luciano. Biographical sketches of Luciano and Al Capone are highly inaccurate.]

———. *Bugsy's Baby: The Secret Life of Mob Queen Virginia Hill.* New York: Birch Lane Press, 1993. [Repeats the errors of *Hot Toddy* but otherwise a fairly good biography of Hill. Ed Reid's *The Mistress and the Mafia* and Dean Jennings' *We Only Kill Each Other* are much better, but Edmonds' book contains an especially interesting account of the alleged murder of Hill.]

Edwards, Peter, and Auger, Michel. *The Encyclopedia of Canadian Organized Crime: From Captain Kidd to Mom Boucher.* Toronto: McClelland & Stewart, 2004. [While giving attention to more rigidly structured groups, the authors also include pirates and outlaws from Colonial times to the present, based on recent Canadian "anti-gang laws" defining groups of three or more professional criminals as "criminal organizations."]

Eghigian, Mars, Jr. *After Capone: The Real Untold Life and World of Chicago Mob Boss Frank "The Enforcer" Nitti.* Nashville, TN: Cumberland House, 2006. [Wonderfully definitive biography of Frank Nitto, famously called Nitti, who succeeded Capone as boss of the Chicago "Outfit" and virtually rebuilt it during the lean Depression years. Reveals Nitto's true origins and the confusion surrounding his name and activities. Expertly debunks the myth of a Mob-directed hit on Mayor Cermak.]

Einstein, Izzy. *Prohibition Agent No. 1.* New York: Frederick A. Stokes Company, 1932. [Izzy Einstein and Moe Smith, with their comical disguises and subterfuges, were practically the Abbott and Costello of Prohibition agents. A lot more fun than Eliot Ness. They arrested more than 4,000 New York bootleggers in the twenties and confiscated an estimated 5 million bottles of booze before their notoriety got them sidelined. Another writer who gives no source says Izzy's memoirs sold only 575 copies.]

Eisenberg, Dennis, Dan, Uri, and Landau, Eli. *Meyer Lansky: Mogul of the Mob.* New York: Paddington Press, 1979. [Meyer Lansky's version of his life story, as presented by the Israeli journalists who interviewed him. Supplemented by FBI and Narcotics Bureau files. Tends to corroborate some aspects of the controversial Luciano memoirs (Gosch and Hammer) but might also have borrowed from them.]

Elliott, Neal. *My Years With Capone: Jack Woodford-Al Capone, 1924-1932.* Seattle: Woodford Memorial Editions, Inc., 1985. [Allegedly a long interview with thirties pornographer Woodford. The subject actually was not Woodford but a Chicago lawyer named Luis Kutner, who didn't want to be named. How much is true is anyone's guess.]

Elliott, Paul. *Brotherhoods of Fear: A History of Violent Organizations.* U.K.: Cassell/Blandford, 1998. [History of various political, religious, and just plain criminal terrorist organizations. Crimes for profit chapter includes coverage of the Mafia in Sicily and the U.S., along with other organized crime groups.]

Ellis, George. *A Man Named Jones.* New York: Signet Books, 1963. [Biography of Gus Jones, FBI agent who led the investigations of the Kansas City Massacre and the Urschel kidnapping investigations.]

Ellis, John. *The Social History of the Machine Gun.* New York: Random House, 1975. [Includes analytical coverage on the use of machine guns by real and movie gangsters.]

Elman, Robert. *Fired in Anger: The Personal Handguns of American Heroes and Villains.* Garden City, NY: Doubleday & Co., 1968. [Has chapters on Dillinger and "Baby Face" Nelson, "Pretty Boy" Floyd. Inaccurate on their criminal careers but has interesting details about reputed gangster guns.]

Emery, Richard. *Sam Cowley: Legendary Lawman.* Springville, Utah: Cedar Fort Books, 2004. [Slim (ninety-six-page) paperback tribute to FBI Inspector Sam Cowley, sent by J. Edgar Hoover to oversee Melvin Purvis in the Dillinger case. Cowley and Herman Hollis died in "Baby Face" Nelson's last stand at Barrington, Illinois.]

Engelman, Larry. *Intemperance: The Lost War Against Liquor.* New York: Free Press, 1979. [Includes a good account of the Purple Gang.]

English, T. J. *Paddy Whacked: The Untold Story of the Irish-American Gangster.* New York: Regan Books, 2005. [Generally good account of Irish gangsters across the nation from nineteenth century street gangs through the "Westies" and "Whitey" Bulger. Exhaustive study of gangsters and political bosses, including such marginal figures as the Pendergasts and Joe Kennedy, but marred by a few major flaws. "Bugs" Moran actually was not Irish (see Rose Keefe, *The Man Who Got Away*). English also suggests that the supposed coalition of "Legs" Diamond and "Mad Dog" Coll was to form an

Irish opposition to the Italian-Jewish combine of Luciano and Lansky, which ignores the fact that most of Coll's gang were Italians and the Diamond mob was ethnically mixed, as well.]

Enright, Laura L. *Chicago's Most Wanted: The Top Ten Lists of Murderous Mobsters, Midway Monsters and Windy City Oddities.* Dulles, VA: Potomac Books, 2005. [Minor compendium of "top ten" lists of Chicago's history and culture with obligatory nods to the city's gangsters.]

Enright, Richard T. *Al Capone on the Spot.* Minneapolis: Graphic Arts Corporation, 1931. Reprinted in 1987 by Northstar Maschek Books, Lakeville, MN, with introduction and some supplementary materials by Ray R. Cowdery.]

———, and Cowdery, Ray R. *Capone's Chicago.* [See above, *Al Capone on the Spot.*]

Eshelman, Byron E., with Riley, Frank. *Death Row Chaplain.* Englewood Cliffs, NJ: Prentice-Hall, 1962. [Rev. Eshelman's career as prison chaplain included tours of duty at the Federal Detention Headquarters in New York, Alcatraz, and San Quentin. Includes reminiscences on Louis "Lepke" Buchalter, George "Machine Gun" Kelly, and Alvin "Old Creepy" Karpis.]

Esslinger, Michael. *Alcatraz: A Definitive History of the Penitentiary Years.* Carmel, CA: Ocean View Publishing, 2003. [This is the first complete history of Alcatraz, from its early years as a fortress and military prison, through the penitentiary years to its closing in 1963 and beyond to the "Indian Occupation" and the island's present incarnation as a national park. Based largely on interviews with former inmates and guards and Bureau of Prison records, this is as definitive an account as it gets. Hundreds of new photos, detailed accounts of the escape attempts, and a complete listing of Alcatraz inmates.]

Ettinger, Clayton J. *The Problem of Crime.* New York: Long & Smith, 1932. [Weighty examination (538 pages) of nearly every aspect of criminality, criminology, penology, and the criminal justice system.]

F

Faber, Elmer (editor). *Behind the Law: True Stories Compiled from the Archives of the Pennsylvania State Police.* Greenberg, PA: Charles H. Henry Printing, 1933. [Reflects Justice Department support of greater police professionalism.]

Falcon, William D. *Deskbook on Organized Crime.* Washington, DC: Chamber of Commerce/U.S. Government Printing Office, 1969. [Pamphlet provided by Chamber of Commerce to businesses warning of possible dangers of infiltration by organized crime. Includes historical background on the Mob.]

Farr, Finis. *Chicago: A Personal History of America's Most American City.* New Rochelle, NY: Arlington House, 1973.

Fedder, Joshua B. *Gangsters: Portraits in Crime.* New York: Mallard Press, 1992.

Feder, Sid, and Joesten, Joachim. *The Luciano Story.* New York: David McKay Company, 1954. [One of the first biographies of Charles "Lucky" Luciano, written while the mob boss was living in exile in Naples. One of the better Mafia books of the 1950s, considering how little was known about the Mafia at that time. A revised and updated version was published in paperback by Award Books, New York, in 1972. Sid Feder also was co-author of *Murder, Incorporated*]

Federal Bureau of Investigation. *Uniform Crime Reports.* Washington, D.C.: U.S. Government Printing Office. [National crime statistics, published annually from 1930.]

———. *Law Enforcement Bulletins.* Washington, D.C.: Federal Bureau of Investigation, [Published monthly after September 1932. Includes articles and bibliographies on crime and criminology, listings of wanted fugitives and of those recently apprehended.]

———. *Digested History of the FBI.* Washington, DC: Federal Bureau of Investigation, Office of Congressional and Public Affairs, 1940.

———. *The Mafia Monograph.* Washington, D.C.: Federal Bureau of Investigation, Research and Analysis Section, July 9, 1958. [Unpublished book-size study of the Mafia in both Sicily and the U.S., now declassified and available from FBI's FOIPA Section.]

———. *The Story of the Federal Bureau of Investigation.* Washington, D.C.: U.S. Government Printing Office, n.d. [Before the Freedom of Information Act, the FBI used to send this small pamphlet to people requesting information on FBI cases. Not the most unbiased source, nor very revealing.]

———. *FOIPA Preprocessed List.* Washington, D.C.: Federal Bureau of Investigation, FOIPA Unit, updated annually from 1970s. [List of FBI files declassified and available for inspection and duplication at FOIPA

(Freedom of Information-Privacy Acts) office at FBI Headquarters. Gangster files listed include Al Capone, the St. Valentine's Day Massacre, John Dillinger, Dillinger Gang, "Pretty Boy" Floyd, "Baby Face" Nelson, Barker-Karpis Gang, Alvin Karpis, "Ma" Barker and sons, Bonnie and Clyde, "Bugsy" Siegel, Abner "Longy" Zwillman, "Lucky" Luciano, "Machine Gun" Kelly, Purple Gang, "Bugs" Moran, Frank Nitti, Roger Touhy, Arthur "Dutch Schultz" Flegenheimer, Louis "Lepke" Buchalter, "Owney" Madden and others and the "Mafia Monograph," a 285 page, two-volume report compiled by the Bureau's Research and Analysis Section under William Sullivan in 1958 which got Director Hoover to reluctantly admit, if only in a margin scrawl, that "the Mafia does exist in the United States"; also files on Melvin Purvis, leader of G-men who killed Dillinger and Floyd, and Eliot Ness. Much of this material is now also available on CD-ROM.]

———. *FBI Special Agents Who Have Given Their Lives in the Performance of Duty.* Washington, D.C.: Federal Bureau of Investigation, Office of Congressional and Public Affairs, n.d. [Lists all FBI agents killed in the line of duty. Includes W. Carter Baum, Samuel P. Cowley and Herman E. Hollis, all slain by "Baby Face" Nelson, and Raymond J. Caffrey, a victim of the Kansas City Massacre.]

———. *Abridged History of the Federal Bureau of Investigation.* Washington, D.C.: Federal Bureau of Investigation, Office of Congressional and Public Affairs, 1983.

———. *Fingerprint Identification: The Identification Division of the FBI.* Washington, D.C.: U.S. Government Printing Office, n.d. [Chronology entries to 1985];

———. *Chronological History of La Cosa Nostra in the United States: January 1920-August 1987.* Washington, D.C.: FBI Criminal Investigative Division, Organized Crime Intelligence and Analysis Unit, 1987. [Mafia chronology compiled by the FBI for President Reagan's Commission on Organized Crime. Goes to amusing lengths to somehow tie everything that ever happened in organized crime to Valachi's story.]

———. *FBI: Facts and History.* Washington, D.C.: U.S. Government Printing Office, n.d. [Revised pamphlet of FBI history. Nice summary of the gangster era with some good photos.]

Ferber, Nat. *I Found Out!: A Confidential Chronicle of the Twenties.* New York: Dial Press, 1939. [Entertaining but regrettably rare memoirs of what today would be called an investigative reporter who worked for several New York papers and hassled name-brand hoodlums and politicians with journalistic exposes.]

Ferrier, J. Kenneth. *Crooks and Crime.* Philadelphia: J.B. Lippincott, 1927.

Fiaschetti, Michael, with Burinelli, Prosper. *You Gotta Be Rough: The Adventures of Detective Fiaschetti of the Italian Squad.* New York: Doubleday, 1930. [Personal experiences of an old-school New York cop with a flamboyant streak, who became a minor celebrity during Prohibition. British edition same year titled *The Man They Couldn't Escape.*]

Fido, Martin. *The Chronicle of Crime: The Infamous Felons of Modern History and Their Hideous Crimes.* New York: Carroll & Graf Publishers, Inc., 1993. [Attempts to cover the world's headline crimes and criminals from 1800 to 1993 in 320 pages (including index). Many photos but no real comprehensive coverage and also many errors (places the famous Boston Brink's robbery of 1950 in Chicago). Fido, who also authored *Murder Guide to London* and *The Crimes, Detection and Death of Jack the Ripper,* may be on firmer ground with British crime.]

Finnamore, Allison. *Big Jim Colosimo: Chicago's Flashiest Gangster.* Canmore, Alberta, Canada: Altitude Publishing, 2006. [Typically forgettable entry in Altitude's slim paperback *Amazing Stories* series.]

First National Bank of Cisco, Texas. *The Santa Claus Bank Robbery.* Cisco, TX: Longhorn Press, 1958. [Commemorative booklet put out by the Cisco, Texas, bank that was the site of the notorious, and bloody, "Santa Claus bank robbery" of December 23, 1927. Well-researched and with good collection of contemporary photos. Introduction by bank president James P. McCracken. Cover painting by Randy Steffin, described as a "well known Western artist, who formerly lived in Cisco."]

Fischer, Steve. *When the Mob Ran Vegas: Stories of Murder, Mayhem and Money.* Boys Town, NE: Berkline Press, 2005.

Fish, Donald E. *The Dillinger Connection: What Part Did John Dillinger Play in the Brainerd Bank Robbery?* St. Paul: Bywords Printing, 1986. [Booklet speculating on Dillinger's possible involvement in the Brainerd, Minnesota, bank robbery actually committed by "Baby Face" Nelson's gang. Dillinger was robbing the Greencastle, Indiana, bank on the same day.]

Fisher, Jim. *The Lindbergh Case.* New Brunswick, NJ: Rutgers University Press, 1987. [The all-time definitive account of the Lindbergh crime. Witten by a former FBI agent.]

———. *The Ghosts of Hopewell: Setting the Record Straight on the Lindbergh Case.* Carbondale, IL: Southern Illinois University Press, 1999. [Fisher skillfully demolishes the various crackpot theories suggested over the years by Hauptmann apologists and Lindbergh baby impersonators. Presents the conclusive evidence of Hauptmann's guilt, plus analytical coverage of all the Lindbergh kidnapping literature.]

Florio-Khalaf, Jenny, and Savaglio, Cynthia. *Mount Carmel and Queen of Heaven Cemeteries.* Chicago: Arcadia Publishing, 2006. [History of two famous suburban Chicago cemeteries with a chapter on the many well-known gangsters reposing there.]

Flynn, William J. *The Barrel Mystery.* New York: McCann, 1919. [One of the earliest books on the Mafia in America by a former Secret Service chief, now dismissed by some scholars as largely fictional].

Fosdick, Raymond B. *American Police Systems.* New York: Century, 1920. [Early effort to promote greater professionalism in police work.]

Fowler, Gene. *The Great Mouthpiece: A Life Story of William J. Fallon.* New York: Blue Ribbon, 1931. [New York criminal lawyer (emphasis on criminal) rivaled only by Dixie Davis in his talent for outwitting the system on behalf of leading mobsters.]

———. *Beau James: The Life and Times of Jimmy Walker.* New York: Viking Press, 1949. [New York's playboy mayor, whose boodling and colorful antics equalled those of Chicago's "Big Bill" Thompson.]

Fox, Stephen. *Blood and Power: Organized Crime in Twentieth Century America.* New York: William Morrow, 1989. [Excellent, well-documented history of organized crime, covering all aspects and then some, such as the theory that the mob assassinated John F. Kennedy.]

Fraley, Oscar. *Four Against the Mob.* New York: Popular Library, 1961. [Basically a sequel to *The Untouchables.* After leaving the Prohibition Bureau, Eliot Ness became Cleveland's Safety Director, battled Moe Dalitz and the Cleveland mob, and unsuccessfully pursued a serial killer called "the Mad Butcher."]

———, with Robsky, Paul. *The Last of the Untouchables.* New York: Universal, 1962. Paperback reprint, New York: Award, 1976. ["Personal" sequel to *The Untouchables* about another aging Untouchable.]

Frank, Martin M. *Diary of a D.A.* New York: Holt, Rinehart & Winston, 1960. [Memoirs of a former Bronx County district attorney. Has a good chapter on Vincent "Mad Dog" Coll.]

Frasca, Dom. *King of Crime: The Story of Vito Genovese, Mafia Czar.* New York: Crown Publishers, 1959. [Little documentation, and the usual effort to overstate the subject's importance.]

Fredericks, Dean. *John Dillinger.* New York: Pyramid Books, 1963. [Novelized nonsense, similar to the Monarch gangster series.]

Fried, Albert. *The Rise and Fall of the Jewish Gangster in America.* New York: Holt, Rinehart & Winston, 1980. [Well-researched history of Jewish organized crime, from early street gangs through the Syndicate and eventual displacement of Jewish gang leaders by Italians. Chapters or passages on Irving "Waxey Gordon" Wexler and Dutch Schultz, Louis "Lepke" Buchalter, and Meyer Lansky.]

Friedman, Lawrence M. *Crime and Punishment in American History.* New York: Basic Books, 1993. [Major effort to touch every base results in more scope than depth.]

G

Gage, Nicholas. *The Mafia Is Not An Equal Opportunity Employer.* New York: McGraw-Hill, 1971. [One of a rash of Mafia books that followed the success of Mario Puzo's *The Godfather* and the much-publicized Gallo-Colombo gang war in New York. Includes a biographical chapter on Meyer Lansky and much other historical information.]

——— (editor). *Mafia, U.S.A.* Chicago: Playboy Press, 1972. [Collection of Mafia stories from various books and other publications.]

Gallagher, Basil. *The Life Story of John Dillinger and the Exploits of the "Terror Mob."* Indianapolis: Stephens Publications, 1934. [One of the earliest Dillinger books, in magazine form.]

Galligan, George, and Wilkinson, Jack. *In Bloody Williamson.* Privately printed, 1927. Reprinted by Williamson County (IL) Historical Society, 1985. [Galligan was sheriff of Williamson County, and Wilkinson was his deputy in the 1920s. Deals mainly with battles against S. Glenn Young and the Ku Klux Klan but mentions the Birger and Shelton gangs, who briefly were allied with Galligan against the Klan. Includes brief section on the later feud between Charlie Birger and the Shelton brothers.]

Gambino, Richard. *Vendetta: A True Story of the Worst Lynching in America, the Mass Murder of Italian-Americans in New Orleans in 1891, the Vicious Motivations Behind It, and the Tragic Repercussions That Linger to This Day.* Garden City, NY: Doubleday, 1977. [Seeks to demolish the popular legend of Mafia involvement in the 1890 assassination of New Orleans Police Chief David Hennessy.]

Gardner, Arthur R. L. *The Art of Crime.* London: Philip Allan, 1931. [British writer's somewhat genteel view of criminal enterprise in general.]

Gatewood, Jim. *Decker: A Biography of Sheriff Bill Decker of Dallas County 1898-1970.* Garland, TX: Mullaney Corporation, 1999. [Includes material on Bonnie and Clyde, Raymond Hamilton, and gambling boss Lester "Benny" Binion.]

———. *Benny Binion: The Legend of Benny Binion, Dallas Gambler and Mob Boss.* Garland, TX: Mullaney Corporation, 2002. [Biography of the Dallas and Las Vegas gambling figure.]

———. *Captain Will Fritz and the Dallas Mafia.* Garland, TX: Mullaney Corporation, 2004. [Dallas policeman's crusade against the underworld. Covers Bonnie and Clyde, Hollis de Lois Green, Benny Binion, the Chicago Mob's invasion of Texas, and Jack Ruby's Syndicate connections with possibility of Mob involvement in the Kennedy assassination.]

Gaute, J. H. H., and Odell, Robin. *The Murderers' Who's Who.* Montreal: Optimum Publishing Co.; and London: Harrap, 1979. [An encyclopedia of notorious murderers and murder cases from around the world. Mostly serial killers and such, but also entries on the Barkers, Bonnie and Clyde, and Louis "Lepke" Buchalter. Gangster material comes mainly from Nash's *Bloodletters and Badmen* and has some errors. Subject titles indexed to bibliography titles. Also has list of addresses for booksellers specializing in true crime. Revised and updated version, *The New Murderers' Who's Who,* published in 1989 by Dorset Press, New York.]

Gelman, B., and Lackmann, R. *The Bonnie and Clyde Scrapbook.* New York: Nostalgia Press, n.d. (circa 1970). [Large paperback picture book, with slight text largely culled from *Fugitives,* by Parker and Cowan. Good collection of Barrow Gang photos, news clippings, etc., with brief references to other gangs; section of stills from the movie *Bonnie and Clyde.*]

Gentile, Nicola. *Vita di Capomafia.* Rome: Editori Riuniti, 1963. ["Life of a Mafia Boss." Reputedly a high-ranking Mafioso who spent thirty years as a traveling peacemaker among the families of various cities, Gentile jumped bail on a narcotics smuggling charge in New Orleans in the Thirties and returned to Sicily, spilling his life story in old age to Italian journalists. While melodramatic and self-glorying, Gentile's account of events such as the "Castellammarese War" confirm much of the Valachi testimony and sometimes is claimed to have finally convinced J. Edgar Hoover of the reality of an American Mafia.]

Gentry, Curt. *J. Edgar Hoover: The Man and the Secrets.* New York: W. W. Norton, 1991. [Massive and seemingly well-documented negative biography of J. Edgar Hoover's political blackmailing. Much gangster material, including previously unpublished photos of "Ma" and Fred Barker dead in the house at Ocklawaha, Florida, after their shootout with FBI.]

Gervais, G. H. *The Rumrunners: A Prohibition Era Scrapbook.* Scarborough, Ontario: Firefly Books, Ltd., 1980.

Giancana, Antoinette, with Renner, Thomas C. *Mafia Princess: Growing Up in Sam Giancana's Family.* New York: William Morrow & Co., 1984. [Life of, and with, Chicago mobster Sam Giancana, as told by his daughter. Antoinette has since coauthored, with John R. Hughes and Thomas H. Jobe, *JFK and Sam,* published by Cumberland House in 2005, about the alleged connections between her father's murder and the JFK assassination.]

Giancana, Sam, and Giancana, Chuck. *Doublecross: The Explosive, Inside Story of the Mobster Who Controlled America.* New York: Warner, 1992. [Generally dismissed as unsubstantiated yarns, by the original Sam's nephew and brother.]

Gibson, Walter B. (editor). *The Fine Art of Robbery.* New York: Grosset & Dunlap, 1966. [Includes reprinted accounts of the Rondout train robbery and Brooklyn armored car holdup.]

Gilfoyle, Timothy. *City of Eros: New York City, Prostitution, and the Commercialization of Sex, 1790-1920.* New York: W. W. Norton, 1994.

Girardin, G. Russell, with Helmer, William J. *Dillinger: The Untold Story.* Bloomington, IN: Indiana University Press, 1994. [Based on an unpublished manuscript written about 1935 by Girardin in collaboration with Dillinger's lawyer Louis Piquett and his assistant Arthur O'Leary; revised by Girardin just before his death in 1990 to reveal previously concealed information on Dillinger Gang, wooden-pistol escape, etc.; edited and expanded by Helmer with new introductory material and copious endnotes elaborating on Girardin's story. Expanded edition published in 2005 with much new information by Helmer and Rick Mattix with help from their expanding network of researcher friends.]

Gish, Anthony. *American Bandits.* Girard, KS: Haldemann-Julius, 1938. [Long pamphlet containing brief biographical sketches of outlaws from the Colonial period through the 1930s. Gish cited J. Edgar Hoover as the source of information on modern bandits. Includes Al Spencer, Frank Nash, Verne Miller, the Barkers, Alvin Karpis, "Machine Gun" Kelly, Jake and Ralph Fleagle, Wilbur Underhill, "Pretty Boy" Floyd, Eddie Bentz, Harvey Bailey, Fred "Killer" Burke, John Dillinger, "Baby Face" Nelson, Bonnie and Clyde, and others, including some who still were fugitives at the time of publication. Many errors.]

Godwin, John. *Alcatraz: 1868-1963.* Garden City, NY: Doubleday & Co., 1963. [Many errors, including some serious ones (mistakenly claims Karpis and John Paul Chase died in prison).]

———. *Murder U.S.A.* New York: Ballantine Books, 1978. [Godwin improves his gangster information but adds nothing new.]

Goldin, Hyman E., O'Leary, Frank, and Lipsius, Morris (editors). *Dictionary of American Underworld Lingo.* New York: Twayne Publishers, Inc., 1950. [E.g., "Dillinger. Any brazen act of banditry or prison escape by combined bluff and force, in the manner of the once notorious John Dillinger. ('To pull a Dillinger'—to operate recklessly"). O'Leary and Lipsius were Sing Sing inmates, and Lipsius gained personal notoriety as the stool pigeon who set up "Waxey" Gordon's narcotics bust.]

Gollomb, Joseph. *Crimes of the Year.* New York: Horace Liveright, Inc., 1931. [Includes chapters on Capone and Birger and Shelton gangs.]

Gong, Eng Ying (Eddie), with Grant, Bruce. *Tong War!* New York: Nicholas L. Brown, 1930. [Then leader of the Hip Sing Tong gives his version of the early years of Chinese organized crime in America. Gong's stories are accepted by many popular crime writers but sometimes debunked in the more accurate accounts, such as Dillon's *The Hatchet Men.*]

Goodman, Avery. *Why Gun Girls?* Minneapolis: Fairway, circa 1932. [A "noted sociologist" ostensibly studies gang molls and female felons in a heavily illustrated, interestingly written but unfortunately rare magazine-format booklet similar to *The Morgue* and *X Marks the Spot,* with plenty of gangland stiffs included as photographic fodder.]

Goodman, Jonathan (editor). *Masterpieces of Murder.* New York: Carroll & Graf, 1992.

Gosch, Martin A., and Hammer, Richard. *The Last Testament of Lucky Luciano.* Boston: Little, Brown & Co., 1975. [Allegedly based on taped interviews of Luciano by Martin Gosch. The authenticity of this memoir has been seriously questioned by Luciano buffs.]

Gosnell, Harold F. *Machine Politics, Chicago Model.* Chicago: University of Chicago Press, 1937; reprint 1968.

Gottfried, Alex. *Boss Cermak of Chicago: A Study of Political Leadership.* Seattle: University of Washington Press, 1962. [Conventionally crooked but crafty mayor killed during a Miami political tour by an assassin's bullet fired at Franklin Roosevelt; rumors persist that Cermak was the intended target of a demented anarchist paid by Chicago mobsters.]

Goulart, Ron. *Lineup Tough Guys.* Los Angeles: Sherbourne Press, 1966. [Has biographical chapters on Capone, Dutch Schultz, Owney Madden, "Legs" Diamond, other Chicago and New York mobsters; also John Dillinger, Alvin Karpis, and "Machine Gun" Kelly. All from published sources but fairly accurate on most. Repeats Godwin's error of Karpis dying in prison. Brief commentary on gangster movies, comics, etc.]

Gouth, George. *Booze, Boats & Bad Times: Recalling Wyandotte's Dark Days of Prohibition.* Wyandotte, MI: Wyandotte Historical Society, 2004.

Graham, Hugh Davis, and Gurr, Ted Robert (editors). *Violence in America: Historical and Comparative Perspectives, A Report to the National Commission on the Causes and Prevention of Violence.* Washington, DC: U.S. Government Printing Office, 1969. Reprint, New York: New York Times/Bantam Books, 1969.

Grams, Martin, Jr. *Gang Busters: The Crime Fighters of American Broadcasting.* Churchville, MD: OTR Publishing, 2004. [700-page history of the *Gang Busters* radio program, which produced dramatizations of criminal cases and also spotlighted fugitives, often leading to their apprehension. Includes case histories of criminals whose stories were featured, such as former Barker-Karpis outlaw Lawrence DeVol, and Martin Durkin, first murderer of an FBI agent, who tried to block airing of his case. Also biographies of the show's creator, Philip H. Lord, and the lawmen who sometimes hosted the show, H. Norman Schwartzkopf (of Lindbergh case fame) and former New York police commissioner Lewis J. Valentine. Plus synopses of all 1,000-plus episodes of the series.]

Granlund, Nils T., with Feder, Sid. *Blondes, Brunettes and Bullets.* New York: David McKay Company, 1957. [A New York radio celebrity in the twenties, Granlund knew such mobsters as Dutch Schultz, Jack "Legs" Diamond, Larry Fay, Arnold Rothstein, Nicky Arnstein, "Lucky" Luciano, and Anthony Carfano, alias "Little Augie" Pisano.]

Grant, Bruce. *Fight for a City: The Story of the Union League of Chicago and Its Times, 1880-1955.* Chicago: Rand McNally, 1955. [Includes less-than-thrilling discussion of a civic group's battle against corruption.]

Green, Jonathon. *The Directory of Infamy.* London: Mills & Boon, 1980. [Biographical sketches of more than 600 criminals from around the world, including most of the major twenties and thirties mobsters and outlaws. Many errors. Green's sources, all published material, include Demaris' *The Dillinger Story* and Nash's *Bloodletters and Badmen.* Reprinted by Stein & Day, New York, 1982, as *The Greatest Criminals of All Time.*]

Green, Valerie. *The Purple Gang.* Canmore, Alberta, Canada: Altitude Publishing, 2006.

———. *St. Valentine's Day Massacre.* Canmore, Alberta, Canada: Altitude Publishing, 2006. [Part of Altitude's *Amazing Stories* series.]

Greene, A.C. *The Santa Claus Bank Robbery.* New York: Alfred A. Knopf, 1972. [Bloody bank robbery at Cisco, Texas, in December 1927, committed by a gang whose leader wore a Santa Claus suit. Novelized style detracts from the author's otherwise good research.]

Gregg, Leah. *Scarface Al: The Story of "Scarface Al" Capone, Profession Gangster. His Ruthless Machine-Gun Massacres Shocked the Nation.* Girard, KS: Haldeman-Julius "Little Blue Books," circa 1930s. [Miniature booklet, recounting Capone's career in dime-novel fashion but fairly accurate.]

Grieveson, Lee, Sonnet, Esther, and Stanfield, Peter. *Mob Culture: Hidden Histories of the American Gangster Film.* New Brunswick, NJ: Rutgers University Press, 2005. [Anthology of analytical treatises on the changing social, moral, political, ethnic, and gender issues of the gangster movie, from the earliest silent films to the present. Cover many obscure "race" films, portrayals of early street gangs, white slavery, the "Black Hand" and Chinese tongs, the legend of "Ma" Barker, and the Kefauver Committee's impact on crime films of the fifties. Emphasis is on lesser-known films.]

Grisham, Violet. *Sheriffs of Williamson County & the Bloody Crimes of Their Times.* Marion, IL: Williamson County Historical Society, 2002. [Volume by local historian on sheriffs of "Bloody Williamson" and the county's long and violent history. Includes much on the Birger and Shelton gangs.]

——— (editor). *The Shelton Gang: News Articles of the Infamous Shelton Gang.* Marion, IL: Williamson County Historical Society, n.d. [Collection of newspaper and magazine articles on the Sheltons.]

Gruber, Frank. *The Dillinger Book.* Mt. Morris, IL: R.C. Remington, 1934. [Early Dillinger book (published before his death), allegedly suppressed in its first printing by FBI. Cover printed in red ink. Extremely rare, with many rare photos. Second printing (1934) slightly smaller page size with new cover as *The Life and Exploits of John Dillinger.*]

Guerin, Eddie. *The Autobiography of a Crook.* London: Murray, 1928. [Reprinted as *I Was a Bandit.* New York: Doubleday, 1929.]

Guns & Ammo, editors of. *Guns & Ammo Guide to Guns of the Gunfighters.* Los Angeles: Petersen Publishing, 1975. [Chapters (originally articles from *Guns & Ammo*) on various outlaws, lawmen, soldiers, and other "gunfighters" of nineteenth and twentieth Centuries and the guns they used. Includes Dillinger, Bonnie and Clyde, Melvin Purvis, Thompson submachine gun, and other 1920s-'30s gangster guns. Reprinted by Bonanza Books, New York, 1982, as *Guns and the Gunfighters.*]

H

Hack, Richard. *Puppetmaster: The Secret Life of J. Edgar Hoover.* New York: New Millennium, 2004. [Fair biography with little new information and marred by novelistic flourishes and unsourced dialogue. Hack denies allegations of Hoover's alleged homosexuality and suggests the director's true sexual outlet was in smut collected in the bureau's "Obscene Materials" files.]

Hagerty, James E. *Twentieth Century Crime: Eighteenth Century Methods of Control.* Boston: Stratford, 1934. [The failure of traditional, localized law enforcement agencies to combat lawlessness in the age of the automobile, machine guns, and interstate crime.]

Haley, Jay Evetts, and Bailey, John Harvey. *Robbing Banks Was My Business: The Story of John Harvey Bailey, America's Most Successful Bank Robber.* Canyon, TX: Palo Duro Press, 1973. [Biography of 1920s-'30s bank robber Harvey Bailey, who was interviewed extensively by Haley. Seemingly well detailed, though Bailey's recollections seem hazy at times, and his stories often are at variance with other accounts.]

Hall, Angus (editor). *The Gangsters.* New York: Paradise Press, 1975. [Magazine-style book consisting of articles originally published in the twenty-volume set *Crimes and Punishment.* Includes Capone, Dillinger, Bonnie and Clyde, the 1934 Rubel Ice Company robbery (Brooklyn's first armored car job), along with the Brinks robbery and various English and European gangsters.]

Hallwas, John E. *The Bootlegger: A Story of Small-Town America.* Champaign, IL: University of Illinois Press, 1999. [The rise, fall, and violent end of bootlegger Kelly Wagle in the small mining community of Colchester, Illinois. Like the Birger and Shelton gangs, this proves it didn't all happen in the cities.]

Halper, Albert (editor). *This Is Chicago: An Anthology.* New York: Henry Holt, 1952.

——— (editor). *The Chicago Crime Book.* New York: World Publishing Company, 1967. [Collection of stories from various publications on Chicago crime. First section of book deals with Chicago gangsters of the twenties and thirties. Includes much on Al Capone and Prohibition gang wars, St. Valentine's Day Massacre, Roger Touhy case, Lingle murder, Toland's account of the death of Dillinger.]

Hamilton, Charles. *Men of the Underworld.* New York: Macmillan, 1952. [Routine chapters on Capone and other well-known gangsters with little original information.]

Hamilton, Floyd. *Public Enemy No. 1.* Dallas: Acclaimed Books/International Prison Ministry, 1978. [Former bank robber and Alcatraz inmate Floyd Hamilton was a friend of Clyde Barrow and Bonnie Parker. His brother Raymond was a member of the Barrow Gang and was executed in the Texas state penitentiary in 1935.]

———, with Chaplain Ray (Raymond Hoekstra). *Floyd Hamilton Public Enemy No. 1 and Other True Stories.* Dallas: Acclaimed Books/International Prison Ministry, 1983 (?). [Magazine-format book contains transcript of radio interview with Floyd Hamilton, "last of the Bonnie and Clyde gang," by Chaplain Ray, prison evangelist, followed by other stories of Christianized convicts.]

Hamilton, Stanley. *Machine Gun Kelly's Last Stand.* Lawrence, KS: University Press of Kansas, 2003. [Good updated account of the Urschel kidnapping, slightly revisionist.]

Hamilton, Sue L. *Public Enemy Number One* (series). Minneapolis: Abdo & Daughters/Rock Bottom Press, 1989. [*Public Enemy Number One* series of children's books (*Baby Face Nelson, The Barkers, Bonnie and Clyde, John H. Dillinger, Machine Gun Kelly,* and *Pretty Boy Floyd*) by Sue Hamilton may be avoided by the serious researcher. Each is thirty-two pages long, in large print. The Pretty Boy Floyd book has no photos of Floyd but reprints one photo of Adam Richetti three times, each erroneously captioned as Floyd.]

Hammer, Richard. *Playboy's Illustrated History of Organized Crime.* Playboy Press, Chicago, 1975. [Just what the title says. Originally serialized in *Playboy* and edited by William J. Helmer. Reissued by Playboy Press in 1975 in two paperback volumes: *Gangland U.S.A.: The Making of the Mob* and *Hoodlum Empire: The Survival of the Syndicate.*]

Hanna, David. *Bugsy Siegel: The Man Who Invented Murder, Inc.* New York: Belmont Tower, 1974.

———. *Carlo Gambino: King of the Mafia.* New York: Belmont Tower, 1974.

———. *Frank Costello: The Gangster of A Thousand Faces.* New York: Belmont Tower, 1974.

———. *The Killers of Murder, Inc.* New York: Nordon Publications, 1974.

———. *Vito Genovese.* New York: Belmont Tower, 1974.

———. *The Lucky Luciano Inheritance.* New York: Belmont Tower, 1975.

———. *Virginia Hill: Queen of the Underworld.* New York: Belmont Tower, 1975.

———. *The Mafia: Two Hundred Years of Terror.* New York: Manor Books, 1979.

[David Hanna's series of paperbacks is of interest only to collectors of the rare and worthless.]

Hannigan, William (editor). *New York Noir: Crime Photos From the Daily News Archive.* New York: Rizzoli

International Publications, Inc., 1999. [Perfectly grisly collection of New York City crime photos, 1920s-'50s. With an introduction by Luc Sante.]

Harland, Robert O. *The Vice Bondage of a Great City: Or, The Wickedest City in the World; The Reign of Vice, Graft and Political Corruption.* Chicago: Young People's Civic League, 1912. [Expose of Chicago's "monstrous Vice Trust" in the same vein as the earlier William Stead classic, *If Christ Came to Chicago!*]

Harris, Louis. *The Story of Crime.* Boston: Stratford, 1929.

Heckethorne, Charles William. *The Secret Societies of All Ages and Countries.* London: George Redway, 1897. [One of the earliest English language books to cover the Mafia (in Sicily and New Orleans) and the Camorra, as well as other criminal organizations. Attributes Mafia's founding to Italian revolutionary Giuseppe Mazzini.]

Heimel, Paul W. *Eliot Ness: The Real Story.* Condersport, PA: Knox Books, 1997. [Little known but far superior version of *The Untouchables,* tracking Ness' sometimes rocky career in Chicago and Cleveland.]

Heise, Kenan. *Alphonse: A One Man Play Based on the Words of Al Capone.* Evanston, IL: Chicago Historical Bookworks, 1989. [See also LeVell and Helmer, *The Quotable Al Capone.*]

Helmer, William J. *The Gun That Made the Twenties Roar.* New York: Macmillan, 1969. [Technical, social, criminal, military, and business history of the Thompson submachine gun and General Thompson's Auto-Ordnance Corporation, based partly on correspondence and interviews with the men who once worked for the company and actually designed the gun. Reprinted by Gun Room Press, Highland Park, N.J. See also Hill, Tracie L., *Thompson, the American Legend.*]

———, and Bilek, Arthur J. *The St. Valentine's Day Massacre: The Untold Story of the Gangland Bloodbath That Brought Down Al Capone.* Nashville, TN: Cumberland House, 2004. [The definitive revisionist account of the Massacre. Probably as close as we'll ever get to the truth. Co-author Bilek is working on a biography of "Big Jim" Colosimo.]

———, with Mattix, Rick. *Public Enemies: America's Criminal Past, 1919-1940.* New York: Facts on File/Checkmark Books, 1998. [Predecessor of the present volume.]

Hendley, Nate. *Al Capone.* Canmore, Alberta, Canada: Altitude Publishing, 2005.

———. *Dutch Schultz: The Brazen Beer Baron of New York.* Canmore, Alberta, Canada: Altitude Publishing, 2005. [Hendley's books on Capone and Schultz are part of Altitude's *Amazing Stories* series.]

Herigstad, Gordon: *Colt Thompson Serial Numbers: Numerical Listing, Index, History.* Burbank, CA: privately published, 1999. [Includes much on gangster guns, especially Dillinger's.]

Herzog, Asa S., and Erickson, A. J. *Camera, Take the Stand!* New York: Prentice-Hall, 1940. [Contemporary study of forensic photography in 1930s-'40s criminal cases. Includes photos of fingerprint cards of John Dillinger and Jake Fleagle.]

Hibbert, Christopher. *The Roots of Evil: A Social History of Crime and Punishment.* Boston: Little, Brown, 1963 (also published by Weidenfeld and Nicholson, London). [Short encyclopedia-style entries on crime and criminals, U.S. and foreign, sometimes factual, sometimes analytical; includes passages on Capone, Dutch Schultz, and others.]

Hill, E. Bishop. *Complete History of the Southern Illinois Gang War.* Harrisburg, IL: Hill Publishing, 1927. [One of the earliest books on the Birger and Shelton gangs.]

Hill, Tracie L., et. al. *Thompson, the American Legend: The First Submachine Gun.* Cobourg, Ontario: Collector Grade Publications, 1996. [Well-illustrated coffee-table epic on all aspects of the Tommygun. Various contributors, including authors of the present volume.]

Hinton, Ted, with Grove, Larry. *Ambush: The Real Story of Bonnie and Clyde.* Bryan, TX: Shoal Creek Publishers, 1979. [Ted Hinton was one of the six officers who ambushed and killed Bonnie and Clyde, but his personal friendship with Barrow and Parker families gives this book a uniquely personal viewpoint rarely found among lawmen. Still, Hinton's memory of some events is faulty. The account of the Stringtown, Oklahoma, shooting has Bonnie Parker present (she wasn't) and, moreover, is taken almost word for word from the Drapers' 1945 dime novel, *The Blood-Soaked Career of Bonnie Parker,* the chapter on Harvey Bailey and "Machine Gun" Kelly is badly flawed; and even his version of the final ambush is questionable.]

Hirsch, Phil (editor). *The Racketeers.* New York: Pyramid Books, 1970. [Collection of gangster stories by various writers dealing mostly with modern organized crime, but also covers Al Capone, "Hymie Weiss," "Pretty Boy" Floyd, and the wipeout of the Shelton gang by Frank

"Buster" Wortman. Also published by Pyramid as *The Mafia*. Reprinted in magazine format by Peacock Press, Franklin Park, IL, as *The Underworld*, in early 1970s.]

Hoekstra, Raymond (as Chaplain Ray). *God's Prison Gang*. Dallas: Acclaimed Books/ International Prison Ministry, 1977. [Life stories of Christianized convicts, including former Bonnie and Clyde gangster Floyd Hamilton and George Meyer, alleged Capone mob wheelman (see also Hamilton's *Public Enemy No. 1* and Meyer's *Al Capone's Devil Driver*). Available free upon request or donation to International Prison Ministry. There also is a video version featuring prison sermons by the boys.]

Hoff, Syd. *Scarface Al and His Uncle Sam*. New York: Coward, McCann & Geoghegan, 1980. [Children's book.]

Hoffman, Dennis E. *Business Vs. Organized Crime: Chicago's Private War on Al Capone*. Chicago: Chicago Crime Commission, 1989. [Booklet describing the the downfall of Capone through the combined efforts of the Chicago Crime Commission, the "Secret Six" and the IRS. Gently discredits Eliot Ness, who had nothing to do with sending Capone to prison, contrary to popular belief.]

———. *Scarface Al and the Crime Crusaders: Chicago's Private War Against Al Capone*. Carbondale, IL: Southern Illinois University Press, 1993. [Hoffman's earlier work, elaborated into a hardcover book. Extremely well-researched and documented.]

Hollatz, Tom. *Gangster Holidays: The Lore and Legends of the Bad Guys*. St. Cloud, MN: North Star Press, 1989. [Large-size paperback picture book covers gangsters who vacationed in Wisconsin: Al and Ralph Capone, "Polack Joe" Saltis, Roger Touhy, other Chicago mobsters, but also John Dillinger and "Baby Face" Nelson and the Little Bohemia gun battle.]

Holmes, L. W. *An Englishman Among Gangsters*. London: Herbert Jenkins, Ltd., 1933. [Written by a former detective of the William J. Burns agency, this book includes chapters on Al Capone, Owney Madden, other gangsters and gun molls. Should be used with caution as pseudonyms are used without notice.]

Homer, Frederic D. *Guns and Garlic: Myths and Realities of Organized Crime*. West Lafayette, IN: Purdue University Press, 1974. [A persuasive reappraisal of the history and nature of organized crime that debunks the popular concepts with a carefully reasoned approach comparable to Abadinski's.]

Hooten, Ernest Albert. *Crime and the Man*. Cambridge: Harvard University Press, 1939. [Last-gasp, almost comical effort to salvage notions of pioneer criminologist Cesare Lombroso that criminals are anthropologically inferior and physically distinguishable from ordinary citizens. Combines immigrant stereotypes and predictable criminal traits to make this about the most politically incorrect book ever issued by an academic press, reputable or otherwise. Incredible illustrations.]

Hoover, J. Edgar. *Persons in Hiding*. Boston: Little, Brown & Co., 1938. [Hoover's revenge for Melvin Purvis' *American Agent*, an otherwise flattering history of the FBI that refers to Hoover rarely and then only as "the Director," reflecting Purvis' bitterness at his treatment by Hoover. Ghostwritten in purple prose by Hoover's "kept" writer, Courtney Ryley Cooper, this version of the outlaw era minimizes cases involving Purvis—who is never mentioned by name—and credits the killing of Dillinger almost entirely to Sam Cowley in an account that differs noticeably from other reports. Includes chapters on less-familiar criminals such as Eddie Bentz and Eddie Doll, and otherwise concentrates on the molls, associates, and harborers of the more notorious public enemies.]

Hopkins, Ernest Jerome. *Our Lawless Police*. New York: Viking Press, 1931.

Horan, James D. *The Mob's Man*. New York: Crown Publishers, 1959.

———. *The Desperate Years: A Pictorial History of the Thirties*. New York: Crown Publishers, 1962. [Includes the Depression gangsters.]

Hornung, Rick. *Al Capone*. New York: Park Lane, 1998. [Companion to the A&E *Biography* episode on Capone.]

Horwood, Harold, and Butts, Ed. *Bandits and Privateers: Canada in the Age of Gunpowder*. Toronto: Doubleday of Canada, 1987. [History of Canadian outlaws, with a Depression era chapter including Alvin Karpis and "Red" Ryan.]

Hostetter, Gordon L., and Beesley, Thomas Quinn. *It's A Racket!*. Chicago: Les Quin Books, Inc., 1929. [Declares Chicago the birthplace of modern rackets and racketeering, defined as the systematic take over or exploitation of legitimate businesses and unions by professional criminals; good contemporary account of the problem in Chicago, with a list of 157 bombings between October 1927 and January 1929 and a glossary of hoodlum lingo.]

Hounschell, Jim. *Lawmen and Outlaws: 116 Years in Joplin's History.* Joplin, MO: Walsworth Publishing and Fraternal Order of Police Lodge #27, 1989. [Interesting history of Joplin Police Department, written by a Joplin policeman. Has chapters on Bonnie and Clyde, the Kansas City Massacre, the Barkers, and "Machine Gun" Kelly. Some new information and many photos. Strangely overlooks Wilbur Underhill, a Joplin native who's buried there.]

Howard, Clark. *Six Against the Rock.* New York: Dial Press, 1977. [Account of the bloody Alcatraz prison riot and escape attempt in 1946, with biographical sketches of Karpis, Kelly, other notorious Alcatraz prisoners. Research and writing leave much to be desired.]

Hughes, Rupert. *Attorney for the People: The Story of Thomas E. Dewey.* Boston: Houghton Mifflin, 1940. [Contemporary look at Tom Dewey in his days of gang-busting glory.]

Hunt, C.W. *Booze, Boats and Billions: Smuggling Liquid Gold.* Ontario: McClelland & Stewart, 1988.

Hyde, Montgomery H. *United in Crime.* New York: Roy, 1959 (U.S. edition). [By British lawyer and member of Parliament who generalizes about crime, detection, and punishment in England and other countries with interesting commentary and case histories, providing international perspective on the subject but only a brief discussion of conditions in the U.S.]

Hynd, Alan. *The Giant Killers.* New York: Robert M. McBride, 1945. [Income tax prosecutions of gangsters and political bosses by Elmer Irey and his "T-men" colleagues.]

———. *We Are the Public Enemies.* New York: Gold Medal, 1949. [Error-filled and fictionalized paperback, with chapters on Dillinger, Floyd, Barrows, and Barker-Karpis Gang (Lloyd Barker is called "Floyd"), of interest only to collectors.]

———. *Murder, Mayhem and Mystery.* New York: A.S. Barnes, 1958. [Includes chapter on the Urschel kidnapping.]

———. *Defenders of the Damned.* New York: A.S. Barnes, 1960. [Slim bios of famed criminal lawyers Clarence Darrow, William J. Fallon, and Earl Rogers.]

———. *Brutes, Beasts and Human Fiends.* New York: Paperback Library, 1964. [Includes a chapter on 1930s New York gangster Louis "Pretty" Amberg.]

———. *In Pursuit: The Cases of William J. Burns.* Camden, NJ: Thomas Nelson, 1968. [William J. Burns preceded J. Edgar Hoover as director of the Bureau of Investigation and founded his own world-famous detective agency.]

———. *Great True Detective Mysteries.* New York: Grosset & Dunlap, 1969. [Includes fair chapter on the Urschel kidnapping.]

I

Ianni, Francis A. J., with Reuss-Ianni, Elizabeth. *A Family Business: Kinship and Social Control in Organized Crime.* New York: Russell Sage Foundation, 1972. [Based on a study of the "Lupollo Family" (a pseudonym), Ianni sees an informal network of interrelated Italian crime families rather than an organized Mafia or Cosa Nostra. Includes historical background from 1920s. Ianni also authored *Black Mafia* (New York: Simon & Schuster, 1974), which espoused the case for ethnic succession in organized crime, suggesting that Black and Hispanic mobsters would displace Italians in the underworld.]

——— (editors). *The Crime Society: Organized Crime and Corruption in America.* New York: New American Library, 1976.

Illinois Association for Criminal Justice. *The Illinois Crime Survey.* Chicago: 1929. Reprint, Montclair, NJ: Patterson Smith, 1968. [Part III consists of John Landesco's justly famous *"Organized Crime in Chicago"* (See Landesco, John).]

Illman, Harry R. *Unholy Toledo: The True Story of Detroit's Purple-Licavoli Gang's Take-Over of An Ohio City.* San Francisco: Polemic Press Publications, 1985. [Cover blurb reads: "An Informal History of A Typical American City Which Was Not Muckraked By Lincoln Steffins Because of His Friendship With Two of the City's Outstanding Mayors." No bibliography but heavily footnoted. A few photos.]

Inbau, Fred E., and Reid, John E. *Lie Detection and Criminal Investigation.* Baltimore: Williams & Wilkins, 1942. [Includes origins and development of the polygraph.]

Inciardi, James A. *Careers in Crime.* Chicago: Rand McNally College Publishing, 1975.

———. *Reflections on Crime: An Introduction to Criminology and Criminal Justice.* New York: Holt, Rinehart & Winston, 1978.

———, and Pottieger, Ann E. (editors). *Violent Crime: Historical and Contemporary Issues.* Beverly Hills, CA: Sage Publications, 1978. [Little history, except for a stiffly academic chapter disputing traditional views of frontier crime and law enforcement.]

Iorizzo, Luciano. *Al Capone: A Biography.* Westport, CT: Greenwood Publishing, 2004. [Pretty fair Capone biography for the beginner, with good sociological and historical insights.]

Irey, Elmer L., as told to Slocum, William J. *The Tax Dodgers: The Inside Story of the T-Men's War With America's Political and Underworld Hoodlums.* Garden City, NY: Garden City Publishing, 1948. [One of the government officials—not Eliot Ness—who actually got Capone tells the story. Also, chapters on Johnny Torrio, Murray "The Camel" Humphreys, "Waxey" Gordon, Moe Annenberg, Tom Pendergast, Enoch "Nucky" Johnson, and other victims of the IRS.]

J

Jacobs, James B. *Mobsters, Unions, and Feds: The Mafia and the American Labor Movements.* New York: New York University Press, 2006.

Jacobs, Timothy. *The Gangsters.* New York: Mallard Press, 1990. [Attractive coffee-table book with lots of pictures. Classic photo on front side of dust jacket of Birger gang posed with their arsenal. Flip side shows old police photo of Vito Genovese. Chapters on Capone, Luciano, Dillinger, Floyd, Nelson, Barkers, Kelly, and Bonnie and Clyde. Errors throughout, however, such as confusing southern Illinois' Shelton gang with Ralph Sheldon gang of Chicago.]

Jeffers, H. Paul. *Gentleman Gerald: The Crimes and Times of Gerald Chapman, America's First "Public Enemy No. 1."* New York: St. Martin's Press, 1993. [Author admits to creating "scenes, actions, and dialogues" in this "biography" of million-dollar mail bandit Gerald Chapman. Also, the "Public Enemy Number One" title was created by the Chicago Crime Commission several years after Chapman was hung.]

Jenkins, John H., and Frost, H. Gordon. *I'm Frank Hamer: The Life of a Texas Peace Officer.* Austin: Pemberton Press, 1968. [Biography of the ex-Texas Ranger who led the ambush of Bonnie and Clyde; his version varies from others on several significant points.]

Jennings, Dean. *We Only Kill Each Other: The Life and Bad Times of Bugsy Siegel.* Englewood Cliffs, NJ: Prentice-Hall, 1968. [The best biography of Siegel.]

Johnson, Curt, with Sautter, R. Craig. *Wicked City: Chicago, From Kenna to Capone.* Highland Park, IL: December Press, 1994. [Entertaining trade paperback along the lines of *Gem of the Prairie*, but rounds up additional information from many sources and contains much original material on "Diamond Joe" Esposito.]

Johnson, David R. *American Law Enforcement: A History.* Arlington Heights, IL: Forum Press, 1981. [Good description of the evolution of U.S. police work.]

Johnson, Lester Douglas. *The Devil's Front Porch.* Lawrence, KS: University Press of Kansas, 1970. [History of the state prison at Lansing, Kansas, written by a former inmate, who was there in the twenties and thirties. Johnson knew Alvin Karpis as a boy in Topeka, served time with him and Fred Barker later in Lansing and also with Harvey Bailey, Wilbur Underhill, and other gangsters; witnessed the Memorial Day escape of the Bailey-Underhill Gang in 1933. Johnson's memory is questionable at times, but there's much information here. Also includes brief histories of other Kansas gangs, including those of Jake Fleagle and Ray Majors.]

Johnson, Malcom. *Crime On the Labor Front.* New York: G. P. Putnam's Sons, 1950. [Includes material on Capone, George Scalise, Willie Bioff, and others.]

Johnson, Nelson. *The Birth, High Times, and Corruption of Atlantic City.* Medford, NJ: Plexus Publishing, 2002.

Johnston, James A. *Alcatraz Island Prison.* New York: Charles Scribner's Sons, 1949. [Johnston was the first warden of Alcatraz, when Capone, Kelly, Karpis, Arthur "Doc" Barker, and other notorious gangsters were imprisoned there.]

Jones, Ken. *The FBI in Action.* New York: New American Library, 1957. [Includes J. Edgar Hoover's account of the capture of Karpis, who says he already was being held at gunpoint when Hoover was summoned to perform the arrest.]

Jones, Peter D'A., and Holli, Melvin G. *Ethnic Chicago.* Grand Rapids, MI: William B. Eerdmans, 1981. [Indirectly assesses criminality associated with immigrant communities.]

Jonnes, Jill. *Hep-Cats, Narcs, and Pipe Dreams: A History of America's Romance With Illegal Drugs.* Baltimore and London: John Hopkins University Press, 1999. [Academic study of the drug culture in American history with good material on Arnold Rothstein's organization of drug trafficking routes in the twenties, succeeded by Luciano and others, and on gangster involvement with jazz musicians and others in the drug culture. Also details the shocking extent of corruption in the old Federal Bureau of Narcotics, whose long-time director, Harry J. Anslinger, was largely responsible for both the "Reefer Madness" campaign of the thirties and for popularizing an American Mafia. Illustrates well illustrates that criminalization of drugs, like alcohol Prohibition, created more problems than it solved, but author does not advocate legalization.]

Joselit, Jenna W. *Our Gang: Jewish Crime and the New York Jewish Community, 1900-1940*. Bloomington, IN: Indiana University Press, 1983. [Academic study of Jewish organized crime, comparable to Fried's *The Rise and Fall of the Jewish Gangster in America*.]

K

Kaplan, George. *Big-Time Criminals Speak!* New York: Maximum Exposure Advertising, Inc., 1980. [Hardly a serious source of information. Commentary by Kaplan is bad and highly inaccurate. Chapters are illustrated with stills from movies about the featured subjects. Gangster material includes Capone, Dillinger, Bonnie and Clyde, "Ma" Barker, "Mad Dog" Coll, the Mafia, and Prohibition. Includes Mary McElroy's account of her kidnapping and snatches of Cornelius Vanderbilt's *Liberty* interview with Capone. "Bonus Section," entitled "Sick Chicks," seems to be mainly devoted to plugging Mimsy Farmer, a film actress who has played a number of psychotic roles and to whom the book is dedicated. Interesting mainly as a curiosity.]

Karpis, Alvin, with Trent, Bill. *The Alvin Karpis Story*. New York: Coward-McCann & Geoghegan, 1971. [Karpis' version of his life of crime, from taped interviews. Karpis' memory is sometimes faulty, or his coauthor was careless filling in gaps. Mentions Dillinger being killed on Chicago's North Clark Street (site of the St. Valentine's Day Massacre), his taking his girl to see *Manhattan Melodrama*, the movie attended by Dillinger, the same night; and Homer Van Meter being killed days after Dillinger in St. Paul. Karpis understandably puts himself elsewhere whenever a murder was committed. Still, many interesting anecdotes on the Barker-Karpis Gang and other gangsters, much of which can be corroborated in FBI files and elsewhere. Karpis scoffs at Hoover's account of his arrest and claims that "Ma" Barker was merely used as a cover by him and her sons. Also published in Canada by McClelland and Stewart, Ltd., Toronto, as *Public Enemy Number One: The Alvin Karpis Story*.]

———, with Livesay, Robert. *On the Rock*. Don Mills, Ontario: Musson/General, 1980. [Karpis' account of life on Alcatraz, published after his death. Surprisingly candid. Karpis often is claimed to have spent more time on Alcatraz than any other prisoner, but John Paul Chase actually was there longer.]

Katcher, Leo. *The Big Bankroll: The Life and Times of Arnold Rothstein*. New York: Harper & Bros., 1959. [The best biography of Rothstein.]

Katz, Helena. *Gang Wars: Blood and Guts on the Streets of Early New York*. Canmore, Alberta, Canada: Altitude Publishing, 2005.

Katz, Leonard. *Uncle Frank: The Biography of Frank Costello*. New York: Drake Publishers, 1973. [Mostly Costello anecdotes and trivia that make the Mafia boss sound like a jolly good fellow.]

Kavanagh, Marcus. *The Criminal and His Allies*. Indianapolis: Bobbs-Merrill, 1928. [Criminals and corruption denounced by a hanging judge of the times.]

———. *You Be the Judge*, Chicago: Reilly & Lee, 1929.

Kavieff, Paul R. *The Purple Gang: Organized Crime in Detroit, 1910-1945*. New York: Barricade Books, 2000. [Otherwise good history of Detroit's premier gangsters of the Prohibition era is marred by typos and the absence of many dates.]

———. *The Violent Years: Prohibition and the Detroit Mobs*. New York: Barricade Books, 2001. [Companion follow-up to *The Purple Gang* and a far superior book to its predecessor. A well-researched study of Detroit's other Prohibition-era mobs, especially the Italian bootlegging gangs but also including bank robbers and kidnappers.]

———. *The Life and Times of Lepke Buchalter: America's Most Ruthless Labor Racketeer*. New York: Barricade Books, 2005. [Excellent and highly readable biography of America's premier labor racketeer. Well documented.]

Keating, H. R. F. *Great Crimes*. London: Weidenfeld and Nicholson, Ltd., 1982. [Gangster chapter includes sketchy biographies of Capone, Dillinger, and Bonnie and Clyde. Accepts Nash's bizarre theory that Dillinger wasn't killed at the Biograph. Coffee-table book reprinted by Harmony Books, New York, and General Publishing Company, Ltd., Canada.]

Keating, William, with Carter, Richard. *The Man Who Rocked the Boat*. New York: Harper, 1956. [Keating was an assistant district attorney who prosecuted waterfront crimes and other rackets in New York in the O'Dwyer years.]

Keefe, Rose. *Guns and Roses: The Untold Story of Dean O'Banion, Chicago's Big Shot Before Al Capone.* Nashville, TN: Cumberland House, 2003. [First major biography of O'Banion, probably the definitive version, written by an excellent researcher with scrupulous regard for accuracy.]

———. *The Man Who Got Away: The Bugs Moran Story.* Nashville, TN: Cumberland House, 2005. [Rose Keefe's excellent research into the North Side Gang strips away the myths and reveals for the first time the true background and long-obscured life history of George "Bugs" Moran who missed being massacred on Valentine's Day and outlived rival Al Capone. An important and indispensible volume on one of the Prohibition era's most colorful and neglected mobsters. With foreword by Rick Mattix.]

Keeler, Eloise. *Lie Detector Man: The Career and Cases of Leonarde Keeler.* Telshare Publishing, no city, 1984. [Development of polygraph testing and Keeler's work at the Goddard Crime Laboratory in Chicago, with mentions of the Jake Lingle case and the giving of one of the St. Valentine's Day Massacre machine guns to the president of Zenith Radio Corporation.]

Kefauver, Estes. *Crime in America.* Garden City, NY: Doubleday & Co., 1951. [Organized crime in America, reported by the senator who made "Mafia" a household word and a TV star of Frank Costello's hands.]

Kefauver Committee. *Senator Kefauver's Crime Committee Report.* New York: Arco, 1951. [See U.S., Special Committee to Investigate Organized Crime in Interstate Commerce: *Interim Reports.*]

Kelly, Bill. *Treasure Trails and Buried Bandit Booty.* Westport, CT: Stagecoach Publishing/PPC Books, 1993. [Though it may be primarily of interest to "Old West" buffs, much of this book deals with alleged buried treasures of the likes of Dillinger, "Machine Gun" Kelly, Jake Fleagle, Alvin Karpis, Sam "Samoots" Amatuna, California train robber Frank Ellis, and others of the gangster era. Kelly has also written numerous gangster articles for detective magazines.]

Kelly, George "Machine Gun" (pseudonym of John H. Webb), as told to Jim Dobkins and Ben Jordan. *Machine Gun Man: The True Story of My Incredible Survival Into the 1970's.* Phoenix: UCS Press, 1988. [Author claiming to be "George 'Machine Gun' Kelly" was actually an old fraud named John H. Webb, who apparently was a criminal. Almost entirely fiction. In same category as Audett and Bilbo.]

Kelly, Robert J. *Encyclopedia of Organized Crime in the United States: From Capone to the New Urban Underworld.* Westport, CT: Greenwood Press, 2000.

Kennedy, Robert F. *The Enemy Within.* New York: Harper & Bros., 1960. [As chief counsel to Senator McClellan's labor rackets committee, Kennedy came face-to-face with many of America's top mobsters, most of whom were survivors of the old Prohibition mobs.]

Kenney, Dennis J., and Finckenaur, James O. *Organized Crime in America.* Belmont, CA: Wadsworth Publishing, 1994.

Kessler, Ronald. *The Bureau: The Secret History of the FBI.* New York: St. Martin's Press, 2002.

Keylan, Arleen, and DeMirjian, Arto, Jr. (editors). *Crime As Reported by The New York Times.* New York: Arno Press, 1976. [Full page reprints, story continuations and follow-up articles on famous crime stories from 1870s to 1970s, from *The New York Times.* Includes murders of Arnold Rothstein, "Legs" Diamond and Dutch Schultz, St. Valentine's Day Massacre, killings of Bonnie and Clyde, John Dillinger, "Pretty Boy" Floyd, and "Ma" and Fred Barker, and capture of Alvin Karpis.]

King, David C. *Al Capone and the Roaring Twenties.* Woodbridge, CT: Blackbirch Marketing, 1998. [Capone book intended for the juvenile set.]

King, Hoyt. *Citizen Cole of Chicago.* Chicago: Horder's, 1931. [Battles against crime, vice and corruption by a Chicago reformer, who was marginally effective but largely forgotten.]

King, Jeffery S. *The Life and Death of Pretty Boy Floyd.* Kent, OH: Kent State University Press, 1998. [King finds plenty of circumstantial evidence that Floyd was involved in the Kansas City Massacre. His research covers Floyd's criminal career in general and has him joining up with the Dillinger Gang in their last robbery at South Bend. More objective and probably more accurate than Michael Wallis' "sweeping" 1992 life and times epic, but King relies primarily on documentary evidence and Wallis on personal interviews. While both are good, neither constitutes the last word on Floyd, and Robert Unger's *The Union Station Massacre* presents compelling evidence for a remarkably revisionist scenario of that crime.]

———. *The Rise and Fall of the Dillinger Gang.*

Nashville, TN: Cumberland House, 2005. [First detailed book on the backgrounds of all the major members of the Dillinger Gang.]

Kirchner, L. R. (Larry). *Triple Cross Fire! J. Edgar Hoover & the Kansas City Union Station Massacre.* Kansas City, MO: Janlar Books, 1995. [Extensively researched, well-illustrated (other than including a photo of a World War II vintage Tommygun), but highly speculative softcover effort to pin the Kansas City Massacre not only on Verne Miller but also on William Weissman, Harvey Bailey, Wilber Underhill, Bob Brady, and Ed Davis, while exonerating "Pretty Boy" Floyd as a patsy put on the spot by J. Edgar Hoover for reasons of publicity and pursuit. Kirchner draws upon FBI files for his conclusions but also upon the discredited testimony of "Blackie" Audett, who claimed to have witnessed the massacre but actually was in prison at the time.]

———. *Robbing Banks: An American History, 1831-1999.* Rockville Centre, NY: Sarpedon, 2000. [Terribly inaccurate history of American bank robbers. Major errors abound, and the book is entirely untrustworthy.]

Kirkpatrick, E. E. *Crimes' Paradise: The Authentic Inside-story of the Urschel Kidnapping.* San Antonio: The Naylor Company, 1934. [Kirkpatrick was the Urschel family friend who delivered the ransom money to "Machine Gun" Kelly.]

———. *Voices From Alcatraz.* San Antonio: The Naylor Company, 1947. [Reprint of Crimes' Paradise, with additional chapter on "Machine Gun" Kelly and Urschel kidnappers on Alcatraz.]

Klein, Henry H. *Sacrificed: The Story of Police Lieutenant Charles Becker.* New York: Isaac Goldmann Company, 1927. [Early examination of Becker-Rosenthal case, which rocked the New York Police Department and Tammany Hall and sent allegedly crooked cop Becker and four East Side gangsters to the chair. Suggests Becker was framed.]

Klerks, Cat. *Lucky Luciano: The Father of Organized Crime.* Canmore, Alberta, Canada: Altitude Publishing, 2005.

———. *Johnny Torrio.* Canmore, Alberta, Canada, 2005. [Part of the *Amazing Stories* series.]

Klockars, Carl B. *The Professional Fence.* New York: Free Press, 1974.

———. *The Idea of Police.* Newbury Park, CA: Sage Publications, 1985. [Describes the gradual and sometimes grudging acceptance of legally constituted law enforcers in place of defensive measures and do-it-yourself crime control.].

——— (editor). *Thinking About Police.* New York: McGraw-Hill, 1983. [An investigation of popular attitudes drawn from factual and fictional sources.]

Knight, James R., with Davis, Jonathan. *Bonnie and Clyde: A 21st Century Update.* Austin: Eakin Press, 2003. [Legends are dispelled, and all available facts correlated in what may be the definitive work on Texas' favorite boy-girl bandit team.]

Kobler, John. *Capone: The Life and World of Al Capone.* New York: G. P. Putnam's Sons, 1971. [The first and so far most successful effort at a definitive Capone biography.].

———. *Ardent Spirits: The Rise and Fall of Prohibition.* New York: G.P. Putnam's Sons, 1973. [Good social history of Prohibition.]

Koch, Michael. *The Kimes Gang.* Bloomington, IN: AuthorHouse, 2005. [First book-length study of the Kimes boys, available in paperback and as an Internet "e-book."]

Kohn, George C. *Dictionary of Culprits and Criminals.* Metuchen, NJ: The Scarecrow Press, Inc., 1986. [Less than impressive in writing style and production quality but otherwise fairly comprehensive and well-researched biographies of gangsters, outlaws, murderers, and other criminals up to modern times.]

Kooistra, Paul. *Criminals As Heroes: Structure, Power and Identity.* Bowling Green, OH: Bowling Green State University Popular Press, 1989. [Scholarly study of American "social bandits," including Capone, Dillinger, "Pretty Boy" Floyd, Bonnie and Clyde, as well as earlier criminals.]

Krippene, Ken. *Buried Treasure.* New York: Garden City Publishing, 1950. [Popularized the myth that Dillinger buried a fortune in stolen bank loot at Little Bohemia.]

Kuhlman, Augustus Frederick. *A Guide to Material on Crime and Criminal Justice.* New York: Wilson, 1929. Reprint, Montclair, NJ: Patterson Smith, 1969. [A boat anchor of a bibliography more for the professional than the public; includes a vast number articles and books on crime and crime control published through 1927, some reflecting contemporary views of anti-social behavior that now seem naive and uncomprehending if not totally bizarre.]

Kunkin, Art, and Miller, Marvin (compiler). *Organized Crime Behind Nixon! (Volume 3 of The Breaking of a*

President 1974). City of Industry, CA: Therapy Productions, Inc./Collectors Publications, 1974. [Magazine-style volume resulting from the Watergate scandal. Much historical background on organized crime and political corruption, including Tammany Hall, the Tweed Ring, Capone, and Prohibition gang wars, and the birth of the Syndicate. The Nixon-Mob connections outlined, while not overly relevant to the present work, are sometimes shocking but usually fairly tenuous and overblown. The entire series was later published in hardcover as *The Breaking of a President 1974*.]

L

Lacey, Robert. *Little Man: Meyer Lansky and the Gangster Life*. Boston: Little, Brown & Co., 1991. [Contains a wealth of new information on Lansky, including his probable actual birthdate. Disputes Meyer's alleged wealth in later years and contends that the only gangsters who actually died wealthy were those who went straight. Well documented.]

Lageson, Ernest B., Jr. *Battle at Alcatraz: A Desperate Attempt to Escape the Rock*. Omaha: Addicus Books, 1999. [Personal recollection of the bloody 1946 Alcatraz battle by the son of one of the hostage guards who was shot.]

Lait, Jack. *Put On the Spot*. New York: Grossett & Dunlap, 1930.

———, and Mortimer, Lee. *New York Confidential*. Chicago: Ziff-Davis Publishing, 1948.

———. *Chicago Confidential*. New York: Crown Publishers, 1950.

———. *Washington Confidential*. New York: Crown Publishers, 1951.

———. *U.S.A. Confidential*. New York: Crown Publishers, 1952. [The Lait-Mortimer *Confidential* series is sensational, sometimes amusing and otherwise nearly worthless but its view of the "Mafia" as an all-powerful worldwide conspiracy swayed many in the naivete of the Fifties.]

Landesco, John. *Organized Crime in Chicago: Part III of the Illinois Crime Survey*. Chicago: Illinois Association for Criminal Justice, 1929. [Scholarly and fascinating contemporary view of Capone's Chicago. Essential. Reprinted by University of Chicago Press, with new introduction by Mark H. Haller, 1968, and in print from Patterson Smith Books, Montclair, New Jersey.]

Langum, David J. *Crossing the Line: Legislating Morality and the Mann Act*. Chicago: University of Chicago Press, 1994. [Academic account of the Mann Act, forbidding interstate transportation of women for "immoral purposes." Intended to combat the "white slave" prostitution syndicates alleged to flourish in the early 1900s, this law was long used, or misused, for the prosecution of targeted individuals such as boxing champ Jack Johnson and gangster "Machine Gun" Jack McGurn, and along the way claimed as victims many mere mortals who just happened to take their girlfriends across state lines.]

Lardner, James, and Reppetto, Thomas. *NYPD: A City and Its Police*. New York: Henry Holt, 2001.

Larsen, Lawrence H., and Hulston, Nancy J. *Pendergast!*. Columbia, MO: University of Missouri Press, 1997. [Biography of Tom Pendergast, whose Democratic machine long dominated both politics and crime in Kansas City.]

Laurence, John. *A History of Capital Punishment: With Special Reference to Capital Punishment in Great Britain*. London: Samson, Lowe, Marston, n.d. (biblio through 1931).

Lavine, Emmanuel H. *The Third Degree: A Detailed and Appalling Expose of Police Brutality*. New York: Vanguard Press, 1930.

———. *Gimme*. New York: Vanguard Press, 1931. [Contains an account of the shooting of "Legs" Diamond at the Hotel Monticello in New York in 1930.]

———. *Cheese It—The Cops!* New York: Vanguard Press, 1936. [Contemporary expose of police corruption. Includes a chapter on the Dutch Schultz murder. FBI chapter includes a disguised version of the Dillinger shooting. Reprinted in 1937 by Garden City Publishing, Garden City, NY, as *Secrets of the Metropolitan Police*.]

Lawes, Lewis E. *20,000 Years in Sing Sing*. New York: Ray Long & Richard Smith, 1932. [Lawes' account of his first twelve years as warden of Sing Sing.]

Letts, Mary. *Al Capone*. London: Wayland Publishers, 1974. [Skimpy ninety-five-page biography, heavily illustrated.]

Levell, Mark, and Helmer, Bill (William J.). *The Quotable Al Capone*. Crestwood, IL: Chicago Typewriter Co. & Mad Dog Press, 1990. [Nifty quotes from Big Al on nearly everything, plus commentary and lists of gang members provided by Chicago police to FBI in 1936.]

Levine, Gary. *Anatomy of A Gangster: Jack "Legs" Diamond*. Cranbury, NJ: A. S. Barnes, 1979; revised edition published in 1996 by Purple Mountain Press, Fleischmanns, NY. [First serious biography of Diamond. Well-researched, with many rare photos.]

Lewis, Jerry D. (editor). *Crusade Against Crime*. New York: Bernard Geis, 1962. [Collection of crime stories from various authors, including Dillinger, "Murder Incorporated," Lindbergh kidnapping, etc.]

Lewis, Lloyd, and Smith, Henry Justin. *Chicago, The History of Its Reputation*. New York: Harcourt, Brace, 1929. [Contemporary view of Chicago's image problem at its worst.]

Lewis, Norman. *The Honored Society*. New York: G. P. Putnam's Sons, 1964. [History of the Sicilian Mafia. Includes Luciano's alleged contributions to the Allied war effort in World War II.]

Liggett, William, Sr. *My Seventy-Five Years Along the Mexican Border*. New York: Exposition Press, New York, 1964. [Recollections of an old Arizonan. Chapter on "Arizona Lawmen" includes Dillinger material.]

Lindberg, Richard C. *Chicago Ragtime: Another Look at Chicago, 1880-1920*. South Bend, IN: Icarus, 1985. Well-researched and entertaining, with astute observations on Chicago's culture, crime, cops, and politics, which combined to gain the city worldwide notoriety during the Roaring Twenties. Reprinted by Academy Chicago as *Chicago By Gaslight: A History of Chicago's Netherworld, 1880-1920*.]

———. *To Serve and Collect: Chicago Politics and Police Corruption From the Lager Beer Riot to the Summerdale Scandal: 1885-1960*. New York: Praeger Press, 1991. [Exceptionally detailed, brilliantly written, regrettably scarce, but reprint planned by Southern Illinois University Press.]

———. *Return to the Scene of the Crime: A Guide to Infamous Places in Chicago*. Nashville, TN: Cumberland House, 1999.

———. *Return Again to the Scene of the Crime: A Guide to Even More Infamous Places in Chicago*. Nashville, TN: Cumberland House, 2001.

Linn, James Webber. *James Keeley, Newspaperman*. New York: Bobbs-Merrill, 1937. [The interesting and often dark side of Chicago, and of newspaper journalism generally, told through the biography of an equally interesting reporter and editor who deserves more recognition.]

Liston, Robert. *Great Detectives*. New York: Platt & Munk, 1966. [Children's book. Chapters on Elmer Irey and J. Edgar Hoover, which focus on Al Capone and the Barker-Karpis Gang.]

Logan, Andy. *Against the Evidence: The Becker-Rosenthal Affair*. New York: McCall Publishing, 1970. [Thoughtful examination of the Becker-Rosenthal murder case of 1912 that rocked Tammany Hall, sent police Lieutenant Charles Becker and four Lower East Side gangsters to the electric chair and may have brought about the murder of gang leader "Big Jack" Zelig, a contemporary of Arnold Rothstein and immediate predecessor of Jewish mobsters of the Twenties. Suggests a possible frame-up of Becker.]

Longstreet, Stephen. *Chicago: 1860-1919*. New York: David McKay, 1973. [Setting the stage for Chicago's Roaring Twenties.].

———. *Win or Lose: A Social History of Gambling in America*. New York/Indianapolis: Bobbs-Merrill, 1977.

Look, editors of. *The Story of the FBI: The Official Picture History of the Federal Bureau of Investigation*. New York: E. P. Dutton, 1947. [Introduction by J. Edgar Hoover.]

Loth, David. *Public Plunder: A History of Graft in America*. New York: Carrick & Evans, 1938.

Louderback, Lew. *The Bad Ones: Gangsters of the '30s and Their Molls*. Greenwich, CT: Fawcett Publications, 1968. Fairly thorough picture history of Depression outlaws. Many good photos and some new information, but also many errors and possibly some fiction. Accepts "Blackie" Audett's imaginary version of the Kansas City Massacre. Has chapters on "Ma" Barker, "Machine Gun" Kelly, Bonnie and Clyde, "Pretty Boy" Floyd, John Dillinger, "Baby Face" Nelson, and Alvin Karpis.]

Lovegrove, Richard, and Orwig, Tom. *The FBI*. New York: Exeter Books, 1989. [Coffee-table history of the bureau, updating Whitehead's *The FBI Story* but with a more balanced view. Excellent text and many photos. Much on gangster era, including gangster movies.]

Lowenthal, Max. *The Federal Bureau of Investigation*. New York: William Sloane, 1950. [The first anti-FBI book, and Lowenthal is guilty of distortions by taking quotes out of context. As biased in its way as the countless books glorifying the FBI. Only slight gangster material, dealing with the apprehensions of John Dillinger, Alvin Karpis, and Louis "Lepke" Buchalter. Reprinted in 1970s by Harcourt Brace Jovanovich, Inc., New York.]

Luisi, Gerard, and Samuels, Charles. *How to Catch 5000 Thieves*. New York: Macmillan, 1962. [The well-told adventures of a New York insurance investigator who liked police work in and out of state and managed to involve himself in general crime fighting against some notable hoods of the twenties and thirties.]

Lundberg, Ferdinand. *The Rich and the Super-Rich: A Study in the Power of Money Today.* New York: Lyle Stuart, 1968. [Chapter on "Crime and Wealth" disputes the popular image of organized crime as amassing countless billions in illegal wealth and mentions most of the prominent New York and Chicago gangsters of the Twenties and Thirties.]

Lustgarten, Edgar. *The Illustrated Story of Crime.* Chicago: Follett Publishing Company, 1976. [Broad subject typically condensed by British author. American gangster material includes Al Capone, Frank Costello, Joe Adonis.]

Lyle, Judge John H. *The Dry and Lawless Years.* Englewood Cliffs, NJ: Prentice-Hall, 1960. [Story of Al Capone and the Prohibition gang wars, as told by a judge who himself became a celebrity for harassing gangsters with vagrancy laws, high bonds, and any legal dirty tricks he could come up with.]

Lynch, Denis Tilden. *Criminals and Politicians.* New York: Macmillan, 1932. [Similar to Fletcher Dobyns' *The Underworld of American Politics,* blaming ineffectuality of police on political corruption. Lynch also wrote *Boss Tweed: The Story of a Grim Generation* (1927).]

M

Maas, Peter. *The Valachi Papers.* New York: G. P. Putnam's Sons, 1968. [Street-level view of the history of organized crime, 1920s-'60s, as seen by New York Mafia defector Joe Valachi.]

Maccabee, Paul. *John Dillinger Slept Here: A Crook's Tour of Crime and Corruption in St. Paul, 1920-1936.* St. Paul: Minnesota Historical Society Press, 1995. [Excellent in all respects, including photos, addresses, maps, and chronologies.]

MacDonald, Alan, and Reeve, Philip (illustrator). *Al Capone and His Gang.* New York: Scholastic Paperbacks, 2000. [Children's book from the series *Famous Dead People.*]

MacKaye, Milton. *Dramatic Crimes of 1927: A Study in Mystery and Detection.* Garden City, NY: Crime Club, 1928. [Good chapters with new twists on the Birger-Shelton gang war in southern Illinois and on the first armored car bombing in Pennsylvania.]

MacKenzie, Frederick. *Twentieth Century Crimes.* Boston: Little, Brown & Co., 1927.

MacKenzie, Norman (editor). *Secret Societies.* New York: Crescent Books, 1967. [Mafia chapter by David Annan has superficial coverage of Italian crime families in U.S. Chapter by Barbara Ward on Chinese secret societies briefly touches on the old tong wars in American Chinatowns.]

Maddox, Web. *The Black Sheep.* Quannah, TX: Nortex Press, 1975. [Book on notorious Texas outlaws, mostly from the "Old West," but includes long chapter on Bonnie and Clyde with some uncommon details.]

Mark, Norman. *Mayors, Madams and Madmen.* Chicago: Chicago Review Press, 1979. [Entertaining, anecdotal, and touches all the bases.]

Marston, William Moulton. *The Lie Detector Test.* New York: Richard R. Smith, 1938. [Origins of a new crime control tool, before the doubts set in. Little-known trivia: Polygraph pioneer Marston, under the pseudonym "Charles Moulton," created the comic-book heroine Wonder Woman.]

Martin, Brian G. *The Shanghai Green Gang: Politics and Organized Crime, 1919-1937.* Berkeley, CA: University of California Press, 1996. [Shanghai was a prime source for U.S.-bound opium, morphine, and heroin in the twenties and thirties, and the Ching Pang, or "Green Gang," mentioned in Courtney Ryley Cooper's *Here's to Crime,* controlled the narcotics trade there under the benevolent protection of Chiang Kai Shek, who probably was a member of this criminal organization and used them for his dirty work. This included the mass murder of Communist trade unionists in 1927. This is a scholarly account, well-researched but hard to read if one is unfamiliar with the modern spellings the author employs for Chinese names; i.e., Jiang Jieshi for Chiang Kai Shek.]

Martin, John Bartlow. *Butcher's Dozen and Other Murders.* Harper & Bros., New York, 1945 (revised, 1950). [Revised 1950 edition includes a substantial and interesting reprint of a magazine article on the Shelton and Birger gangs.]

Marx, Samuel. *Texas Guinan, the ace of (night) clubs.* Girard, KS: Haldeman-Julius, 1929. [Thirty-page "Little Blue Book" on the famous speakeasy hostess.]

———. *Broadway Gangsters and Their Rackets.* Girard, KS: Haldeman-Julius, 1929. [Thirty-two-page "Little Blue Book."]

Mason, Philip P. *Rumrunning and the Roaring Twenties: Prohibition on the Michigan-Ontario Waterway.* Detroit: Wayne State University Press, 1995.

Matera, Dary. *FBI's Ten Mosted Wanted.* New York: HarperCollins, 2003. [History of the "Ten Most Wanted" list, with a chapter on Thomas Holden.]

———. *John Dillinger: The Life and Death of America's First Celebrity Criminal.* New York: Carroll & Graf, 2004. [Based on the research of the late Joe Pinkston and Tom Smusyn, two of the nation's foremost Dillinger historians, and condensed and rewritten from an 1,800-page manuscript of theirs. Matera obviously lacks their expertise, errors creep in, and some might quibble with his flippant writing style, but the original research still shows, and a fantastic amount of new information is unveiled, along with rare photos. One also has to wonder about the subtitle. Wasn't Jesse James our "first celebrity criminal"? As close as we're likely to see of Pinkston's own monumental work, though, and worth reading.]

May, Allan. *Mob Stories.* Hauppauge, NY: Nova Science Publishers/Kroska Books, 2001. [Compilation of historical Mob stories by a noted organized crime columnist.]

Mayo, Katherine. *Standard-bearers: True Stories of Law and Order.* New York: Houghton, 1930.

McCarthy, Pat. *America's Bad Men (Stories of Famous Outlaws).* Middletown, CT: Xerox Corporation, Middletown, 1974. [Children's book, illustrated by Harry Wallengren and with photos. Has chapters on Dillinger, "Machine Gun" Kelly and Bonnie and Clyde.]

McClellan, John L. *Crime without Punishment.* New York: Duell, Sloan & Pierce, 1962. [Senator McClellan chaired two Senate committees investigating organized crime.]

McConal, Patrick M. *Over the Wall: The Men Behind the 1934 Death House Escape.* Austin: Eakin Press, 2000. [Great account of the Huntsville Death House escape which might have turned Raymond Hamilton and "Blackie" Thompson into living legends had not Dillinger been killed the same day. The careers of Thompson and his friend "Whitey" Walker were overshadowed by Bonnie and Clyde, who were blamed for some of their crimes, but McConal amply demonstrates that the Walker gang deserves closer scrutiny.]

McConaughy, John. *From Cain to Capone, or Racketeering Down Through the Ages.* New York: Brentano's, 1931. [Early effort to view crime as "organized," from biblical times to Prohibition.]

McCormick, Harry, as told to Carey, Mary. *Bank Robbers Wrote My Diary.* Austin: Eakin Press, 1985. [In 1935, Houston newspaperman McCormick was conveniently kidnapped by bank robber Raymond Hamilton, former member of the Barrow Gang who had managed to escape from the Texas state prison's death house and wanted his own version of events to reach the public.]

McCoy, Alfred W., with Read, Cathleen B., and Adams, Leonard P., II. *The Politics of Heroin in Southeast Asia.* New York: Harper & Row, 1972. [While this may seem an unlikely choice for inclusion in a bibliography of Twenties and Thirties crime, much historical background on drug use, drug trafficking, and U.S. organized crime is included in this scholarly work. Contends that narcotics syndicates and international drug routes were disrupted and largely destroyed by vigorous law enforcement efforts and the coming of World War II but were revived in the Cold War as drug traffickers were recruited by the CIA to fight Communism. Since updated with expanded international scope as *The Politics of Heroin: CIA Complicity in the Global Drug Trade.*]

McIllwain, Jeffery Scott. *Organizing Crime in Chinatown: Race and Racketeering in New York City, 1890-1910.* Jefferson, NC: McFarland Publishing, 2004. [Traces growth of Chinese organized crime through wars between the rival Hip Sing and On Leong tongs. Academic study patterned after Alan Block's *East Side, West Side.*]

McLean, Don. *Pictorial History of the Mafia.* New York: Pyramid Books, 1974. [Usually found as a thick, heavily illustrated paperback chronology of organized crime that includes hundreds of photos, information and interesting trivia, but unfortunately the research and writing leave much to be desired; exists also in hardcover published the same year by Galahad Books, New York City].

McNicoll, Susan. *Sam Giancana.* Canmore, Alberta, Canada: Altitude Publishing, 2006;

———. *Mobster Molls.* Canmore, Alberta, Canada, 2006. [Part of the *Amazing Stories* series.]

McPhaul, John J. *Deadlines and Monkeyshines.* Englewood Cliffs, NJ: Prentice-Hall, 1962. [Newspapering and crime reporting in Chicago in the Roaring Twenties, reprinted in paperback in 1969, as *Chicago: City of Sin,* by Book Company of America, Beverly Hills, Ca.];

——— (as Jack McPhaul). *Johnny Torrio: First of the*

Gang Lords. New Rochelle, NY: Arlington House, 1970. [Purports to be a detailed biography of Torrio, whom McPhaul regards as the inventor of organized crime, but relies too heavily on the writer's imagination: Has Torrio grief stricken over the suicide of Abner "Longy" Zwillman, though this occurred two years after Torrio's death. Good photo collection, however, and useful chronology at the end.]

McRae, Bennie, Jr. *Attempted Bank Robbery in Boley, Oklahoma.* Trotwood, OH: LWF Publications, 1997. [Pamphlet on the ill-fated 1932 raid on a bank in the black community of Boley which resulted in the death of "Pretty Boy" Floyd's pal George Birdwell.]

McSherry, Peter. *The Big Red Fox: The Incredible Saga of Norman "Red" Ryan, Canada's Most Notorious Criminal.* Toronto: Dundurn Press, 1999. [The "Canadian Jesse James" robbed many banks in Canada and the U.S. in the Twenties.]

McWilliams, John C. *The Protectors: Harry J. Anslinger and the Federal Bureau of Narcotics, 1930-1962.* Newark, DE: University of Delaware Press, 1990.

Mencken, August. *By the Neck: A Book of Hangings.* New York: Hastings House, 1942. [Case histories of two centuries of hangings, including Gerald Chapman.]

Merriner, James L. *Grafters and Goo Goos: Corruption and Reform in Chicago, 1833-2003.* Carbondale, IL: Southern Illinois University Press, 2004.

Meskil, Paul. *Don Carlo: Boss of Bosses.* New York: Popular Library, 1973. [Paperback biography of Carlo Gambino, written before his death.]

Messick, Hank. *The Silent Syndicate.* New York: Macmillan, 1967. [Cleveland Syndicate, Jewish allies of Meyer Lansky.]

———. *Syndicate in the Sun.* New York: Macmillan, 1968. [Miami as a Mob playground.]

———. *Syndicate Wife.* New York: Macmillan, 1968. [Biography of Ann Drahmann Coppola, wife of "Trigger Mike" Coppola, with some historical background.]

———. *Secret File.* New York: G. P. Putnam's Sons, 1969. [IRS prosecutions of gangsters and political bosses.]

———. *Lansky.* New York: G. P. Putnam's Sons, 1971. Revised and updated, 1973.

———. *John Edgar Hoover.* New York: David McKay Company, 1972. [Highly critical biography.]

———. *The Beauties and the Beasts: The Mob in Show Business.* New York: David McKay Company, 1973. [Messick's books generally contain much good information but little documentation, many errors, and too much invented dialogue.]

———, with Nellis, Joseph L. *The Private Lives of Public Enemies.* New York: Peter H. Wyden, Inc., 1973. [Collaborator Nellis served on the legal staff of the Kefauver Committee. This book and Messick's picture book collaborations with Burt Goldblatt are somewhat superior to Messick's solo work.]

———, and Goldblatt, Burt. *The Mobs and the Mafia: The Illustrated History of Organized Crime.* New York: Thomas Y. Crowell, 1972. [Pictorial history of organized crime, similar to *Playboy*'s but much slimmer. Some rare photos, including one of Capone with "Legs" Diamond. Reprinted in 1973 in paperback by Ballentine Books.]

———. *Gangs and Gangsters: The Illustrated History of Gangs from Jesse James to Murph the Surf.* New York: Ballentine Books, 1974. [Includes chapters on Dean O'Banion, John Dillinger, and Alvin Karpis. Also, pre-1900 New Orleans Mafia and San Francisco tong wars. Includes baby picture of "Baby Face" Nelson.]

———. *Kidnapping: The Illustrated History.* New York: Dial Press, 1974. [Includes underworld help in Lindbergh case, "Mad Dog" Coll, the Urschel, Hamm, and Bremer kidnappings, and Roger Touhy and Jake "The Barber" Factor.]

———. *The Only Game in Town: An Illustrated History of Gambling.* New York: Thomas Y. Crowell, 1976.

Meyer, George H., as told to Chaplain Ray (Raymond Hoekstra) and Max Call. *They Called Me Devil.* Dallas: Acclaimed Books/International Prison Ministry, 1979. [Reprinted as *Al Capone's Devil Driver*, probably just to work Capone's name into the title. Both printings say first edition. "Alleged wheelman...St. Valentine's Day Massacre" reads the blurb on the cover. Memoirs of this "born again" reformed gangster probably are imaginary.]

Mezzrow, Milton "Mezz," with Wolfe, Bernard. *Really the Blues.* New York: Random House, 1946. [Anecdotal material on Mob control of nightclubs and performers during Prohibition.]

Miers, Earl Schenck. *The Story of the F.B.I.* New York: Grosset & Dunlap, 1965. [FBI-approved children's book. Basically an expanded version of the FBI's own pamphlet, *The Story of the Federal Bureau of Investigation.* Slightly longer gangster section, with before-and-after photos of Dillinger's fingerprints.]

Milligan, Maurice M. *Missouri Waltz: The Inside Story of the Pendergast Machine by the Man Who Smashed It.* New York: Charles Scribner's Sons, 1948. [Early account of the Pendergast machine by the federal prosecutor who fought them.]

Mills, Eric. *Chesapeake Rumrunners of the Roaring Twenties.* Centreville, MD: Tidewater Publishers, 2000.

Mills, George. *Rogues and Heroes From Iowa's Amazing Past.* Ames, IA: Iowa State University Press, 1972. [Collection of stories about famous and infamous people associated with various Iowa cities. Has much gangster material, including Dillinger Gang's Mason City bank robbery, 1943 embezzlement trial at Cedar Rapids of Jake "The Barber" Factor, biographical sketches of George E. Q. Johnson, federal prosecutor who sent Al Capone to prison, and Tom Runyon, 1930s bank robber and murderer who became an Associated Press correspondent and author while serving a life sentence in Iowa state penitentiary; also a million-dollar 1920 train robbery at Council Bluffs. Drawings by Frank Miller and photos.]

———. *Looking in Windows: Surprising Stories of Old Des Moines.* Ames, IA: Iowa State University Press, 1985. [Includes accounts of Des Moines gangsters such as Charles "Cherry Nose" Gioe and Luigi "Lew Farrell" Fratto.]

———. *One-Armed Bandits and Other Stories of Iowa's Past and Present.* Ames, IA: Focus Books, 1997. [Includes chapters on the Bonnie and Clyde shootout at Dexter and on the gambling industry in Iowa, from the days of illegal casinos and slot machines down to the present legal state lottery.]

Millspaugh, Arthur. *Crime Control by the National Government.* Washington, DC: The Brookings Institution, 1937. [Examines the issue of the country's new federalized law enforcement, still resisted by many states' rights advocates opposed to a "national police," and feared by many state and local officials as a threat to their corruption.]

Milner, E. R. *The Lives and Times of Bonnie & Clyde.* Carbondale, IL: Southern Illinois University Press, 1996. [Utilizing primary sources and good documentation, Milner provides detailed coverage of even some of the Barrow Gang's minor crimes, including gas station holdups and car thefts. The effect is marred, however, by factual errors and typos that occur throughout.]

Mitgang, Herbert *The Man Who Rode the Tiger: The Life and Times of Judge Samuel Seabury.* Philadelphia: J.B. Lippincott, 1963.

———. *Once Upon a Time in New York: Jimmy Walker, Franklin Roosevelt, and the Last Great Battle of the Jazz Age.* New York: Free Press, 2000.

Mockridge, Norton, and Prall, Robert H. *The Big Boss.* New York: Henry Holt, 1954. [Mayor O'Dwyer and Prosecutor Dewey still battling post-Depression graft and corruption in New York City.]

Mollenhoff, Clark R. *Strike Force: Organized Crime and the Government.* Englewood Cliffs, NJ: Prentice-Hall, 1972. [Recounts past failures of the federal government in suppressing organized crime with the successes of the modern Justice Department "Strike Forces" in cities across the U.S. One chapter deals with the FBI investigation of Kansas City vote frauds in 1936, a rare early case in which the bureau confronted the Mob. Another is Mollenhoff's personal recollections, as a young Des Moines police reporter in the thirties, of Luigi "Lew Farrell" Fratto, longtime manager of the Chicago mob's Iowa branch. Mollenhoff has authored other works of investigative journalism, including *Tentacles of Power: The Story of Jimmy Hoffa.*]

Monaco, Richard, and Bascom, Lionel. *Rubouts: Mob Murders in America.* New York: Avon Books, 1991. [Chapters on celebrated gang murders, 1929-1990. Nothing new here; a few good photos with the usual errors and some fictional dialogue. Despite its '29 starting point, only briefly mentions the St. Valentine's Day Massacre.]

Montague, Art. *Canada's Rumrunners: Incredible Adventures in Canada's Illicit Liquor Trade.* Canmore, Alberta, Canada: Altitude Publishing, 2004.

———. *Crime Boss Killings: The Castellammarese War.* Canmore, Alberta, Canada: Altitude Publishing, 2005.

———. *Meyer Lansky: The Shadowy Exploits of New York's Master Manipulator.* Canmore, Alberta, Canada, 2005.

———. *Gang Wars of Early Chicago.* Canmore, Alberta, Canada, 2005. [These books comprise part of Altitude's *Amazing Stories* series.]

Mooney, Martin. *Crime, Incorporated.* New York: Whittlesey House, 1935. [One of the earliest books on syndicated crime. Speaks of a vague national network called "Crime Incorporated" controlling "sixteen sinister rackets" across the nation and hinting that the FBI soon would take appropriate action. Book opens with a letter of approval from J. Edgar Hoover, but few great revelations follow. Mooney also authored *Crime Unincorporated.*]

Moore, Gerald E. *Outlaw's End.* [From thirties or forties, but publisher and date not listed. [Strange book. Biography of old outlaw Henry Wells, as told by Wells to a fictional character (his "long-lost son") to illustrate why young men should steer clear of crime. Little is known of the real Henry Wells, other than that he served a term in the Oklahoma state penitentiary for bank robbery in about 1915. He claimed, though, to have later been involved in bank robberies with Henry Starr, Al Spencer, and Frank Nash, to have given "Pretty Boy" Floyd his start as an outlaw, and to have thwarted a Floyd plot to kidnap millionaire oilman Frank Phillips in 1933. Probably less fact than fiction.]

Moore, William Howard. *The Kefauver Committee and the Politics of Crime.* Columbia, MO: University of Missouri Press, 1974.

Moore, William T. *Dateline Chicago: A Veteran Newsman Recalls Its Heyday.* New York: Taplinger, 1973. [Interesting recollections of the newshounds from glory days of Chicago journalism, when crime stories were front-page news.]

Morgan, John. *Prince of Crime.* New York: Stein & Day, 1985. [Slim but useful biography of Capone gangster Murray "The Camel" Humphreys. Also published in U.K. as *No Gangster More Bold.*]

Morgan, R.D. *The Bad Boys of the Cookson Hills.* Stillwater, OK: New Forums Press, 2002. [Well-researched, detailed, and thrilling paperback account of the crimes and pursuit of Oklahoma's Cookson Hills bandits Thomas "Kye" Carlisle, Ford Bradshaw, Wilbur Underhill, and others. There were plenty of "bad boys" in the hills besides "Pretty Boy" Floyd. For sheer meanness the "Cookson Hills Gang," who killed in drunken revelry and whose victims included women, children, and other innocent bystanders, are hard to top.]

———. *Desperadoes: The Rise and Fall of the Poe-Hart Gang.* Haskell, OK: EZ Lane Publishing, 2002; revised and reprinted in 2003 by New Forums Press, Stillwater, OK. [World War I-era gang of Oklahoma horse thieves who became pioneers in automotive bank robbery. A few gang members made it into the twenties. New Forums edition is re-edited and considerably cleaned up, with much clearer photos, as well.]

———. *The Bandit Kings of the Cookson Hills.* Stillwater, OK: New Forums Press, 2003. [Excellent "prelude" to his previous work, *The Bad Boys of the Cookson Hills*, tracing the history of the original horse-to-auto bad boys of the 1920s, remnants of Henry Starr's gang such as Ed Lockhart and John "Kaiser Bill" Goodman, the "Fagin of the Hills." Some of these boys were still robbing banks in the thirties. With Foreword by Rick Mattix.]

———. *The Tri-State Terror: The Life and Crimes of Wilbur Underhill.* Stillwater, OK: New Forums Press, 2005. [Long overdue and classic biography of "Tri-State Terror" Wilbur Underhill. With foreword by Rick Mattix.]

———, with Koch, Mike: *Armed & Dangerous: Tales of Crime and Punishment in Old Oklahoma.* Haskell, OK: EZ Lane Publishing, 2002. [Quaintly produced but factual and entertaining collection of crime cases from the twenties and thirties, with much on "Pretty Boy" Floyd, Matt Kimes, and other outlaws but also emphasizing the deeds of respected law officers, such as Homer Spaulding, Mark Lairmore, Perry Chuculate, and Erv Kelley. Articles evoke the feeling of thirties detective mags.]

Morello, Celeste A. *Before Bruno: The History of the Philadelphia Mafia (Book 1, 1880-1931).* Philadelphia: Jefferies & Manz, 2000. [Somewhat revisionist academic work by a criminologist who claims descent from Sicilian Mafiosi and has incited the ire of some organized crime experts by disparaging the work of noted journalists in the field. First of three volumes.]

———. *Before Bruno: The History of the Philadelphia Mafia (Book 2, 1931-1946).* Philadelphia: Jefferies & Manz, 2001.

Mori, Cesare. *The Last Struggle with the Mafia.* New York: G. P. Putnam, 1933. [Memoirs of Mussolini's Prefect of Police, whose suppression of the Sicilian Mafia drove many Italian criminals to the United States in the 1920s. Translated from Italian, this probably was the first widely read English-language book with "Mafia" in the title, according to crime book authority Patterson Smith.]

Morley, Jackson, et al (editors). *Crimes and Punishment: A Pictorial Encyclopedia of Aberrant Behavior.* Phoebus Publishing/BPC Publishing, U.S. & U.K., 1973-74. [20-volume set covering all aspects of crime, illustrated by famous cases, also an A-Z listing for the leftovers. Gangster coverage includes Capone, Dillinger, "Ma"

Barker, Luciano, the Mafia, Bonnie and Clyde, the Birger and Shelton gangs, Louis "Lepke" Buchalter, the Rubel Ice robbery, Willie "The Actor" Sutton, etc.]

Morris, Newbold. *Let the Chips Fall: My Battles Against Corruption.* New York: Appleton-Century-Crofts, 1955. [New York City political reformer's review of political corruption in the U.S., especially New York City, with anecdotal material on mobsters.]

Morris, Ronald L. *Wait Until Dark: Jazz and the Underworld, 1880-1940.* Bowling Green, OH: Bowling Green University Popular Press, 1980.

Morton, James. *Gangland International: The Mafia and Other Mobs.* New York: Time-Warner, 1999.

Mullady, Detective Frank, and Kofoed, William H.. *Meet the Mob.* New York: Belmont Books, 1961. [Co-authored by a cop, with a preface by former Kings County, N.Y., district attorney Leo Healy, this slim paperback still is about the same quality as the low-rent Monarch books. Includes chapters on Al Capone and Jake Guzik, the Genna brothers, "Lepke," Anastasia and the "Murder, Incorporated" boys, Dutch Schultz, and "Mad Dog" Coll. Good collection of photos, including "Bugs" Moran in his casket.]

Munn, Michael. *The Hollywood Murder Case Book.* New York: St. Martin's Press, 1987. [Includes Thelma Todd and "Bugsy" Siegel.]

———. *The Hollywood Connection: The True Story of Organized Crime in Hollywood.* London: Robson Books, 1996. [Posits rival attempts by Capone and Luciano to control the Hollywood movie industry, continuing after their imprisonments through Chicago Mob flunkies Willie Bioff and George Browne and Luciano agent "Bugsy" Siegel.]

Murray, George. *The Legacy of Al Capone: Portraits and Annals of Chicago's Public Enemies.* New York: G. P. Putnam's Sons, 1975. [Biography in which Murray attempts to evaluate Capone's lasting impact on Chicago life and politics.]

N

Napoli, Antonio. *The Mob's Guys.* College Station, TX: Virtualbookworm.com, 2004. [Poorly written but informative work on Chicago Mob and labor racketeering.]

Nash, Jay Robert. *Citizen Hoover: A critical study of the life and times of J. Edgar Hoover and his FBI.* Chicago: Nelson-Hall, 1972. [Hatchet job on Hoover by the man who says Dillinger got away.];

———. *Bloodletters and Badmen: A Narrative Encyclopedia of American Criminals From the Pilgrims to the Present.* New York: M. Evans & Co., 1973. [Nash's mini-magnum opus, vast in scope, with less-than-carefully researched biographical entries on all the better known criminals and gangsters. Many errors, large and small.]

———. *Murder America: Homicide in the United States from the Revolution to the Present.* New York: Simon & Schuster, 1980.

———. *Almanac of World Crime.* New York: Anchor Press, 1981.

———. *Look For the Woman: A Narrative Encyclopedia of Female Poisoners, Kidnappers, Thieves, Extortionists, Terrorists, Swindlers and Spies from Elizabethan Times to the Present.* New York: M. Evans & Co., 1981. [Little gangster material, including inaccurate entries on "Ma" Barker, Bonnie Parker, and Kathryn Kelly.].

———. *The True Crime Quiz Book.* New York: M. Evans & Co., 1981.

———. *The Dillinger Dossier.* Highland Park, IL: December Press, 1983. [Recycled version of *Dillinger: Dead or Alive?* Nash presents more "evidence" of Dillinger's survival in the form of interviews with notorious liar "Blackie" Audett, who earlier authored a book of tall tales entitled *Rap Sheet.* Original printing of *The Dillinger Dossier* included an advertisement offering cassette tapes for sale of Nash's interviews with Audett, but these must be exceedingly rare.]

———. *Jay Robert Nash's Crime Chronology.* New York: Facts On File, Inc., 1984.

———. *The Encyclopedia of World Crime* (6 vols.) Wilmette, IL: Crime Books, Inc., 1990. [This enormous work, covering all crime in all times, carefully retains every error found in the prolific Nash's previous books.]

———. *World Encyclopedia of Organized Crime.* New York: Paragon House, 1993. [Extracted from Nash's earlier *Encyclopedia of World Crime* set.]

———. *The Great Pictorial History of World Crime.* Lanham, MD: Scarecrow Press, 2004.

———, and Offen, Ron. *Dillinger: Dead or Alive?* Chicago: Henry Regnery Co., 1970. [Convoluted theory, based on usual discrepancies in documents and records, that the FBI shot the wrong man outside the Biograph and that John Dillinger possibly was still alive, hiding in California. Only contribution, besides generating interest in Dillinger, is its wealth of research minutia agonizingly construed (or conveniently ignored) to support a variety of sometimes conflicting conspiracy scenarios, none of which made sense.]

Nathan, Daniel A. *Saying It Ain't So: A Cultural History of the Black Sox Scandal.* Chicago: University of Illinois Press, 2003.

National Troopers Coalition. *State Trooper: America's State Troopers and Highway Patrolmen.* Paducah, KY: Turner Publishing, 2001. [Histories of State Police and Highway Patrol organizations across the United States, including comprehensive state-by-state listings of officers killed in the line of duty.]

Nee, Victor G., and Nee, Brett de Bary. *Longtime Californ': A Documentary Study of an American Chinatown.* Stanford, CA: Stanford University Press, 1972. [Interesting study of San Francisco's Chinatown, emphasizing the waning influence of the tongs, who were about to be revitalized by the new influx of Chinese immigrants. Interviews with longtime residents provide much historical background.]

Nelli, Humbert S. *The Business of Crime: Italians and Syndicate Crime in the United States.* New York: Oxford University Press, 1976. [Debunks the widely believed myth of the "Night of the Sicilian Vespers," the alleged mass purge of the old "Mustache Pete's" in 1931 that supposedly "Americanized" the Mafia under Luciano, and the new generation of Italian-surnamed mobsters.]

Nelson, Derek. *Moonshiners, Bootleggers & Rumrunners.* Osceola, WI: Motorbooks International, 1995. [Paperback coffee-table book on bootlegging throughout the U.S., before, during, and after Prohibition, with many photos and surprisingly detailed and impressive text.]

Ness, Eliot, with Fraley, Oscar. *The Untouchables.* New York: Julian Messner, 1957. [The book that made a legend of Eliot Ness. Probably as much fiction as fact, creating the mistaken impression that it was Ness and his men who destroyed Capone.]

Newman, Peter C. *King of the Castle: The Making of a Dynasty—Seagram's and the Bronfman Empire.* New York: Athenium, 1979. [Many sidelights on the often questionable, sometimes illegal, activities of some major booze kings, most of whom eluded U.S. Prohibition authorities and gangland heat to prosper as businessmen and politicians.]

Newton, Michael. *The Encyclopedia of Robberies, Heists, and Capers.* New York: Facts on File, 2002.

———. *The Encyclopedia of Kidnappings.* New York: Facts on File, 2002.

———, and Newton, Judy Ann. *The FBI Most Wanted: An Encyclopedia.* New York: Garland Publishing, 1989. [Listing of all fugitives who have made the FBI's "Ten Most Wanted List" since its inception in 1950. Mainly of interest here for its inclusion of some 1930s bank robbers, notably Thomas James Holden and Glen LeRoy Wright (former Barker-Karpis Gang associates), John Allen Kendrick (a veteran of the Tri-State Gang), and, of course, Willie "The Actor" Sutton.]

Newton, Willis and Joe, as told to Claude Stanush and David Middleton. *The Newton Boys: Portrait of an Outlaw Gang.* Austin, TX: State House Press, 1994. [Entertaining and long-overdue autobiography of the Newton brothers–Willis, Joe, Jess, and Doc–who looted dozens of banks and trains from Texas to Canada before going to jail for the "greatest of all mail robberies" (more than $2 million) at Rondout, Illinois, in 1924.]

Nicaso, Antonio. *Rocco Perri: The Story of Canada's Most Notorious Bootlegger.* Mississauga, Ontario, Canada: John Wiley & Sons, 2004. [Originally written in Italian and poorly translated but with impressive new photos.]

Nicholas, Margaret. *The World's Wickedest Women.* London: Octopus Books, Ltd., 1984. [Includes chapter on Bonnie Parker, with the usual previously published inaccuracies. Reprinted in paperback by Berkeley Publishing, New York, 1988, with famous cigar-smoking Bonnie photo on cover.]

Nickel, Steven. *Torso: The Story of Eliot Ness and the Search for a Psychopathic Killer.* Winston-Salem, NC: John F. Blair, 1989. [Far more interesting, if less publicized, than his "Untouchable" career in Chicago was Ness' stint as Cleveland's Safety Director in the mid-thirties, highlighted by his manhunt for an uncaught serial killer.]

———, with Helmer, William J. *Baby Face Nelson: Portrait of a Public Enemy.* Nashville, TN: Cumberland House, 2002. [Finally, a full-length biography of Lester Gillis, aka "Baby Face" Nelson, and probably the definitive one. Written off in the past as a "mad dog punk" or "trigger-nervous runt of the Dillinger Gang," Nelson emerges at last as a three-dimensional, historical, and very human, personage, rather than the cardboard stereotype created by J. Edgar Hoover. A nice revisionist companion to Girardin's and Helmer's *Dillinger: The Untold Story.*]

Northrop, William B., and Northrop, John B. *The Insolence of Office: The Story of the Seabury Investigations.* New York: G. P. Putnam's, 1932.

Nown, Graham. *The English Godfather.* London: Ward Lock Limited, 1987. [Otherwise good biography of English-born New York gangster Owney "The Killer" Madden is marred by a slight lapse into delirious literary license when J. Edgar Hoover stares at Dillinger's death mask months before Dillinger's death.]

O

O'Connor, Dick. *Headline Hunter: Behind America's News Sheets.* London: John Long, 1938. [Includes pieces and illustrations on Capone, Dillinger, Karpis, Barkers, others.]

———. *G-Men At Work: The Story of America's Fight Against Crime and Corruption.* London: John Long,1939.

O'Connor, John James. *Broadway Racketeers.* New York: Liveright, 1928. [Despite its title focus is actually more on con men than gangsters.]

O'Connor, Len. *Clout: Mayor Daley and His City.* Chicago: Henry Regnery, 1975.

O'Connor, Richard. *Hell's Kitchen: The Roaring Days of New York's Wild West Side.* Philadelphia: Lippincott, 1958. [Wild history of New York's West Side and its gangs.]

O'Kane, James M. *The Crooked Ladder: Gangsters, Ethnicity, and the American Dream.* New Brunswick, NJ: Transaction, 1992. [Scholarly examination of ethnic succession in organized crime and of gangsterism as a vehicle for upward mobility in American society.]

O'Sullivan, Frank Dalton. *Crime Detection.* Chicago: O'Sullivan Publishing House, 1928. Curious, large (667 pages), wide-ranging work on virtually all aspects of crime, criminality, and the new scientific crime detection, including contributions by prominent police officials and a section on outstanding crooks of the day.]

———. *Enemies of Industry: Gang Invasion of Business and Industry.* Chicago: O'Sullivan Publishing House, 1932. [Contemporary look at racketeering.]

Ogden, Christopher. *Legacy: A Biography of Moses and Walter Annenberg.* Boston: Little, Brown, 1999.

Olsen, Marilyn. *Gangsters, Gunfire & Political Intrigue: The Story of the Indiana State Police.* Indianapolis: .38 Special Press, 2001. [Includes chapters on the Dillinger and Brady gangs and good material on Captain Matt Leach, the Indiana lawman largely responsible for promoting Dillinger's legend.]

Ottenberg, Miriam. *The Federal Investigators.* Englewood Cliffs, NJ: Prentice-Hall, 1962. [Brief histories of the FBI, IRS, Secret Service, Postal Inspectors, Immigration Service, other federal investigative agencies. Briefly mentions Dillinger and other Depression outlaws but has much material on organized crime figures, including Al Capone, Paul "The Waiter" Ricca, Joe Adonis, and others.]

Overstreet, Harry and Overstreet, Bonaro. *The FBI in Our Open Society.* New York: W. W. Norton, 1969. [A pro-FBI book, written mainly to answer published criticisms of the Bureau, particularly those of Max Lowenthal and Fred J. Cook. As biased in its way as the anti-FBI books, full of nitpicking, but also makes some very valid criticisms of Lowenthal in particular. Little gangster material but does include a listing of the 1934 anti-crime laws that enabled the FBI to wage war on the Depression gangs.]

Owen, Collinson. *King Crime: An English Study of America's Greatest Problem.* New York: H. Holt & Co., 1932. [Britishers seem perpetually fascinated by American gangsters, who make their own hoods look tame.]

Owen, Richard, and Owen, James. *Gangsters and Outlaws of the 1930s: Landmarks of the Public Enemy Era.* Shippensburg, PA: White Mane Publishing, 2003. [Slim but useful tour guide of Midwestern and Southwestern crime sites associated with all the major Depression outlaws, with photos of many of the sites as they appear today. Not all, unfortunately, are photographed in the exact location. Includes chronologies of the major gangs and lists of lawmen killed.]

Owens, Ron. *Oklahoma Justice: The Oklahoma City Police, A Century of Gunfighters, Gangsters and Terrorists.* Paducah, KY: Turner Publishing, 1995. [Good history of Oklahoma City Police Department, including the gangster era.]

———. *Oklahoma Heroes: A Tribute to Fallen Law Enforcement Officers.* Paducah, KY: Turner Publishing, 2000. [Histories of the 560 fallen law enforcement officers honored in the Oklahoma State Police Officers Memorial.]

———. *Jelly Bryce: Legendary Lawman.* Paducah, KY: Turner Publishing, 2003. [Renowned for his lightning-fast draw, Bryce killed several criminals in face-to-face shootouts with the Oklahoma City Police Department in the early thirties and joined the future FBI in 1934 as one of Hoover's "hired gunslingers" upon the recommendation of his close friend and former Oklahoma City colleague Clarence Hurt. Before joining the bureau, both participated in the shooting of Wilbur Underhill, and Hurt was one of the agents who later killed Dillinger.]

P

Pantaleone, Michele. *The Mafia in Politics: The Definitive History of the Mafia.* New York: Coward-McCann, 1966. [Good account of Mafia corruption in Sicily, with details of Luciano's collaboration with the OSS in the invasion of Sicily.]

Park, Robert E., Burgess, Ernest W., and McKenzie, Roderick D. *The City.* Chicago: University of Chicago Press, 1925. [One of the early efforts of the "Chicago School of Sociology" to cover many social, cultural, and even journalistic aspects of Chicago when Mayor Dever's reform efforts upset the relatively peaceful corruption under Mayor "Big Bill" Thompson and helped trigger a five-year period of underworld warfare.]

Parker, Emma, and Cowan, Nell Barrow, with Fortune, Jan. *Fugitives: The Story of Clyde Barrow and Bonnie Parker.* Dallas: The Ranger Press, 1934. [Bonnie's and Clyde's side of the story, as told by their relatives. Thoroughly biased, of course, but a useful source of "inside" information. Collectors should note that there apparently are two "first" editions, the more valuable (and probably the actual first) of which contains photos. Reprinted in paperback in 1968, by Signet, New York, as *The True Story of Bonnie and Clyde*, with a poetic, rambling, but interesting foreword by Nelson Algren that has little to do with the book.]

Parr, Amanda J. *The True and Complete Story of "Machine Gun" Jack McGurn.* Leicester, UK: Troubador Publishing, 2005. [The only full-length biography to date of Capone's No. 1 hit man unfortunately contains so many ludicrous errors that is embarrassing and untrustworthy.]

Partridge, Eric. *A Dictionary of the Underworld.* London: Routledge & Kegan Paul, 1950. [Lingo from British and American underworlds, from eighteenth century onward.]

Pasley, Fred D. *Al Capone, The Biography of a Self-Made Man.* New York: Ives Washburn, 1930. [The first serious Capone biography, written while Al was still in power and supposedly with his tacit approval, judging from its considerable "inside" information on the Chicago underworld. Pasley was about the only crime writer of the era to write dispassionately and with intelligence, and it's this book and Kobler's *Capone* that most writers use as their main sources of information.]

———. *Muscling In.* New York: Ives Washburn, 1931. [Pasley on racketeering.]

Patterson, Richard. *Train Robbery: The Birth, Flowering, and Decline of a Notorious Western Enterprise.* Boulder, CO: Johnson Books, 1981. [History of train robbery in the West, from 1866 to 1937. Last chapter focuses on the gangster era, though Patterson's later *Train Robbery Era* is more detailed.]

———. *The Train Robbery Era: An Encyclopedic History.* Boulder, CO: Pruett Publishing, 1991. [Accurate and comprehensive volume of train robbers and robberies in the U.S. in nineteenth and twentieth centuries. Mainly of interest to Western buffs but does have material on the gangster era, including Al Spencer, the Newton brothers, and the 1924 Rondout, Illinois, train robbery, possibly the largest in American history. Karpis buffs likely will be disappointed, though, by the omission of the Garrettsville, Ohio, job.]

Pensoneau, Taylor. *Brothers Notorious: The Sheltons, Southern Illinois' Legendary Gangsters.* New Berlin, IL: Downstate Publications, 2002. [Excellent and long-overdue biography of the Sheltons makes a nice companion to Gary DeNeal's biography of Charlie Birger.]

Petacco, Arrigo (translated by Charles Lam Markmann). *Joe Petrosino.* New York: Macmillan, 1974. [Originally published in Italy. New York policeman Petrosino was assassinated by the Mafia in Sicily in 1909.]

Peterson, Virgil W. *Barbarians in Our Midst.* Boston: Little, Brown & Co., 1952. [Well-informed history of organized crime in Chicago by a former FBI agent who later headed the Chicago Crime Commission. Peterson had been Melvin Purvis' assistant in the thirties, so there's much good material also on the Depression outlaws, especially the Dillinger and Barker-Karpis gangs and their Chicago Mob contacts.]

———. *The Mob: 200 Years of Organized Crime in New York.* Ottawa, IL: Green Hill Publishers, Inc., 1983. [Barbarians in New York. Peterson scores heavily in debunking much of the Valachi testimony.]

Phillips, Charles, and Axlerod, Alan, with Kemper, Kurt.

Cops, Crooks, and Criminologists: An International Biographical Dictionary of Law Enforcement. New York: Facts on File, 1996. [Some notable criminals are included, but emphasis is on lawmakers, lawmen, and criminologists, from ancient times to the present, based more on their achievements and overall impact than on notoriety. Included are the likes of ballistics pioneer Calvin Goddard, lie detector man Leonarde Keeler, Joliet prison warden Joseph Edward Ragen, and sociologist Walter Reckless (author of *Vice in Chicago*).]

Phillips, John Neal. *Running With Bonnie and Clyde: The Ten Fast Years of Ralph Fults.* Norman, OK: University of Oklahoma Press, 1996. [One of the better Bonnie and Clyde books, based largely on interviews with the last surviving witnesses, all of whom now are dead. Still, with much of the information coming from kin of the outlaws it appears somewhat biased in their favor. Credibility would be more enhanced if Phillips had left out Ralph Fults' tale of a $33,000 bank robbery that the author in his endnotes admits to be wholly undocumented.]

——— (editor). *My Life With Bonnie and Clyde.* Norman, OK: University of Oklahoma Press, 2004 [see Barrow, Blanche Caldwell].

Pierce, Theresa. *The Bloody Demise of Bonnie and Clyde.* Buffalo, MN: Pierce and Associates, n.d., circa 1995. [Slim booklet on the death of Bonnie and Clyde. Some good photos but little substance.]

Pietrusza, David. *Rothstein: The Life, Times and Murder of the Criminal Genius Who Fixed the 1919 World Series.* New York: Carroll & Graf, 2004. [Good recent biography of Rothstein but few new revelations.]

Pitkin, Thomas Monroe, with Cordasco, Francesco. *The Black Hand: A Chapter in Ethnic Crime.* Totawa, NJ: Rowman & Littlefield, 1977. [Scholarly account of Black Hand extortion in the Italian community, mostly pre-Prohibition.]

Plate, Thomas, and *New York Magazine*, editors of. *Mafia At War.* New York: New York Magazine Press, 1972. [One-shot magazine detailing Mafia gang wars, mostly in New York, 1915-72. An apparent attempt to capitalize on the Gallo-Colombo feud that was making news. Also includes material from Kobler's *Capone* on Prohibition wars in Chicago. Combines original material with excerpts from several books, including Maas' *The Valachi Papers* and Tyler's *Organized Crime in America.* Has paintings of famous gang murders (from "Big Jim" Colosimo to Joe Gallo but including the fictional 1931 Mafia purge) and a chart showing genealogy of New York Mafia.]

Ploscowe, Morris (editor). *Organized Crime and Law Enforcement.* New York: Grosby Press, 1952.

Porrello, Rick. *The Rise and Fall of the Cleveland Mafia: Corn Sugar and Blood.* New York: Barricade Books, 1995. [Good history of the Cleveland Mafia, written by a Cleveland policeman whose grandfather and uncles were Prohibition-era Mafiosi. Porrello has since authored other good books on modern organized crime, *To Kill the Irishman* and *Superthief.*]

Potter, Claire Bond. *War on Crime: Bandits, G-Men, and the Politics of Mass Culture.* New Brunswick, NJ: Rutgers University Press, 1998. [Scholarly examination of the New Deal Justice Department's "war on crime," suggesting that politics may have played a hand in J. Edgar Hoover's avoidance of organized crime. Only briefly, and inaccurately, mentions the Kansas City Massacre, which provided Hoover with the political ammunition he needed to turn his agents into gun-toting "G-men." Otherwise good book is somewhat frustrating in that many names are omitted from the index.]

Poulsen, Ellen. *Don't Call Us Molls: Women of the John Dillinger Gang.* New York: Clinton Cook Publishing, 2002. [Excellently researched and written volume on the surprisingly fascinating lives of the Dillinger Gang's women. A wonderful slant on the Dillinger story, crammed with new information gleaned from FBI files and other primary sources. The best Dillinger book since Girardin's. Foreword by William J. Helmer. Poulsen is writing a book on the Luciano vice trial.]

Powell, Hickman. *Ninety Times Guilty.* New York: Harcourt Brace, 1939. [Reprinted in 1975 by Citadel Press, New York, as *Lucky Luciano (His Amazing Trial and Wild Witnesses).*]

Powers, Richard Gid. *G-Men: Hoover's FBI in American Popular Culture.* Carbondale, IL: Southern Illinois University Press, 1983. [Excellent study of the rise of the myths, carefully orchestrated, and realities of the FBI.]

———. *Secrecy and Power: The Life of J. Edgar Hoover.* New York: Free Press, 1987. [Thorough and relatively balanced biography of J. Edgar Hoover.]

Prall, Robert H., and Mockridge, Norton. *This Is Costello.* New York: Gold Medal, 1951. [Biography of Frank Costello, then star of Kefauver Senate crime hearings.]

Prassel, Frank Richard. *The Western Peace Officer: A*

Legacy of Law and Order. Norman, OK: University of Oklahoma Press, 1972. [Good account of the development of modern law enforcement in the American West in the nineteenth and twentieth Centuries.]

———. *The Great American Outlaw: A Legacy of Fact and Fiction*. Norman, OK: University of Oklahoma Press, 1993. [Scholarly study of outlaws and gangsters in history, literature, films, and folklore, from Robin Hood to Capone and Dillinger.]

President's Commission on Law Enforcement and Administration of Justice. *The Challenge of Crime in a Free Society*. Washington, D.C.: U.S. Government Printing Office, 1967. Reprint, New York: Avon Books, 1968. [Organized crime chapter provides historical background, largely drawn from the testimony of Joe Valachi.]

Proveda, Tony G. *Lawlessness and Reform: The FBI in Transition*. Pacific Grove, CA: Brooks/Cole, 1990. [Useful as an original and balanced examination of the changes in the FBI: its early glory days as proponent of scientific crime fighting and law enforcement professionalism, its decline into the private army of an aging and increasingly eccentric director, and post-Hoover efforts at self-reform.]

Pryor, Alton. *Outlaws & Gunslingers: Tales of the West's Most Notorious Outlaws*. Westport, CT: Stagecoach Publishing, 2001. [Includes chapters on Dillinger, the Barkers, "Pretty Boy" Floyd, Wilbur Underhill, "Big Bob" Brady, "Bugsy" Siegel, and quick-draw FBI agent "Jelly" Bryce, along with various legendary "Old West" gunmen.]

Purvis, Alston, with Tresinowski, Alex. *The Vendetta: FBI Hero Melvin Purvis's War Against Crime and J. Edgar Hoover's War Against Him*. New York: PublicAffairs, 2005. [Purvis's son gives excellent account of how Hoover's jealous rage and lifelong vindictiveness drove the "ace G-man" out of the bureau and sought to purge him from FBI history.]

Purvis, Melvin. *American Agent*. Garden City, NY: Doubleday, Doran, 1936. [Purvis' version of his FBI career, including Dillinger, "Pretty Boy" Floyd, Barker-Karpis Gang, Roger Touhy case, and others. Very approving of the bureau itself but conspicuously avoids mentioning Hoover by name, referring only to "the Director." Occasional lapses into political incorrectness of the time, especially with regard to "darkies," but an indispensible first-hand account of the public enemy era.]

———. *The Violent Years*. New York: Hillman Books, 1960. [Paperback "uncensored abridgement" of *American Agent*, published soon after Purvis' death.]

Q

Quimby, Myron J. *The Devil's Emissaries*. Cranbury, NJ: A.S. Barnes, 1969. [Interesting book on Depression outlaws, with individual chapters on "Machine Gun" Kelly, "Pretty Boy" Floyd, "Ma" Barker and sons, Alvin Karpis, Bonnie and Clyde, Dillinger, and "Baby Face" Nelson. Based largely on newspaper reporting that provides more detail than most other accounts, but also many errors. Some are embarrassing, such as giving John Herbert Dillinger's middle name as "Herman."]

R

Raab, Selwyn. *Five Families: The Rise, Decline, and Resurgence of America's Most Powerful Mafia Empires*. New York: Thomas Dunne Books, 2005. [Mostly rehashed history of the rise and fall of New York's once powerful crime families. Speculates that the government's new attention to the "War on Terror" may divert enough attention from the Mafia to lead to its "resurgence" but offers no evidence to support this dubious notion.]

Radkay, William, with Terry, Patty. *A Devil Incarnate: From Altar Boy to Alcatraz, The Autobiography of William Radkay #666AZ*. Leawood, KS: Leathers Publishing, 2005. [Autobiography, as told to his niece, of a Depression-era bandit and Alcatraz inmate whose prison friends included "Machine Gun" Kelly, Harvey Bailey, and Basil "The Owl" Banghart. Also includes recollections of Karpis, "Doc" Barker, Eddie Bentz, Jimmy Murray, and others. Some other details may be a little fuzzy, but Willie's account of his own criminal career and years of imprisonment is fascinating.]

Ramsey, Winston (editor). *On the Trail of Bonnie & Clyde, Then and Now*. London: After the Battle, 2003. [An impressive, detailed and accurate history of the Barrow Gang and an excellent tour guide to their crime trail throughout the Southwest and Midwest, with many photos including the sites "then and now." 304 pages and more than 800 photos, but the detailed text, including contemporary news accounts and interviews with participants and witnesses, make this far above and beyond a picture book. From an English publisher normally specializing in military history.]

Rappleye, Charles, and Becker, Ed. *All American Mafioso: The Johnny Roselli Story.* New York: Barricade Books, 1991. [Roselli (aka Rosselli, true name Filippo Sacco) began his career as a Capone henchman, later became a West Coast representative of the Chicago Mob, ingratiating himself with Hollywood and even helping produce some movies before being sent to prison in the 1940s movie extortion plot. Later active in Las Vegas, his downfall began when he and Sam Giancana cooperated with the CIA in unsuccessful assassination plots against Castro. A fascinating double life in the underworld and upperworld eventually led to this mobster's gruesome demise.]

Reader's Digest, editors of. *Great True Stories of Crime, Mystery & Detection.* Pleasantville, NY: The Reader's Digest Association, 1965. [Includes a chapter on "Doc" Barker by J. Edgar Hoover, Treasury Agent Frank Wilson's story of the Capone tax case, other stories on the 1934 Rubel Ice Company robbery in Brooklyn, mail robber Gerald Chapman, and Paul "The Waiter" Ricca.]

Reckless, Walter. *Vice in Chicago.* Chicago: University of Chicago Press, 1933. Reprint, Montclair, NJ: Patterson Smith, 1969. [Much statistical data on organized and unorganized prostitution. Predictably dry, but provides a good sense of Mob involvement in the city's nightlife during Prohibition, spiced up with pseudonymous interviews.]

Reddig, William M. *Kansas City and the Pendergast Legend.* Philadelphia: J.B. Lippincott, 1947.

Reed, Lear B. *Human Wolves: Seventeen Years of War on Crime.* Kansas City, MO: Brown-White-Lowell Press, 1941. [Author was a former FBI agent and Kansas City's chief of police from 1939 to 1941.]

Reeve, Arthur B. *The Golden Age of Crime.* New York: Mohawk Press, 1931. [A popular mystery writer of the day examines the newly identified business crime called racketeering.]

Reid, Ed. *Mafia.* New York: Random House, 1952. [Early fifties Mafia book demonstrates how little was really known about the subject around the time of the Kefauver hearings.]

———. *The Shame of New York: The Inside Story of the Secret Crime Kingdom Which Reaches from City Hall to the Farthest Suburbs.* New York: Random House, 1953.

———. *The Grim Reapers: The Anatomy of Organized Crime in America, City by City.* Chicago: Henry Regnery Co.,1969. [Update on *Mafia* and considerably improved. Focus is on modern Mob but has much historical material.]

———. *The Mistress and the Mafia: The Virginia Hill Story.* New York: Bantam Books, 1972. [Was Virginia just a "dumb broad" mistress to the likes of Joe Adonis and "Bugsy" Siegel? Or a cunning bagwoman and dope trafficker who manipulated the hoods around her? Reid takes the latter view, quoting government documents as a source. Another source frequently cited, though, is Lee Mortimer, co-author of the worthless "Confidential" series.]

———. *Mickey Cohen, Mobster.* New York: Pinnacle Books, 1973. [Slim paperback biography of "Bugsy" Siegel's right-hand man and successor. Only slightly more informative than Cohen's own uninspired book. Opens with a chapter on the 1916 gang war between the Mafia and Camorra in Brooklyn, which has precious little to do with Cohen.]

———, and Demaris, Ovid. *The Green Felt Jungle.* New York: Trident Press, 1963. [Organized crime in Las Vegas, with emphasis naturally on gambling. Includes murder of "Bugsy" Siegel, much on Capone Syndicate, Moe Dalitz and Cleveland Mob, Detroit Mafia and Purple Gang, others.]

Reith, Charles. *A New Study of Police History.* Edinburgh/London: Oliver and Boyd, 1956. [Gradual development in professionalism in law enforcement, from a British point of view.]

Rendell, Kenneth W. *Forging History: The Detection of Fake Letters and Documents.* Norman, OK: University of Oklahoma Press, 1994. [Author helped expose fraudulent diaries of Hitler, Mussolini and Jack the Ripper. Includes coverage of a forged Bonnie and Clyde letter.]

Reppetto, Thomas. *The Blue Parade.* New York: Free Press, 1978. [Development of American police work from Colonial times onward. Authored by a former cop and president of the New York City Citizens Crime Commission.]

———. *American Mafia: A History of Its Rise to Power.* New York: Henry Holt, 2004. [Standard history of Italian crime families in the U.S., with the emphasis as usual on New York. Reppetto also coauthored *NYPD: A City and its Police* with James Lardner.]

Reynolds, Marylee. *From Gangs to Gangsters: How Amer-*

ican Sociology Organized Crime, 1918-1994. Albany, NY: Harrow & Heston, 1995. [Acknowledges the pioneer effort of John Landesco's *Organized Crime in Chicago* while tracing the reluctance of Chicago sociologists to recognize the emergence of sophisticated criminal networks.]

Reynolds, Quentin. *Courtroom*. New York: Farrar, Straus & Giroux, 1950. [Biography of legendary lawyer and judge Samuel Liebowitz. Has material on Al Capone, who turned down Liebowitz' legal advice, and Vincent "Mad Dog" Coll, acquitted through Liebowitz' legal talents.]

———. *Smooth and Deadly*. New York: Farrar, Straus & Giroux, 1953. [Autobiography of bank robber Willie "The Actor" Sutton, as told to Quentin Reynolds. Reprinted by Paperback Library, New York, 1970, as *I, Willie Sutton* (with a nice color photo on cover of Willie in blue pinstripes).]

———. *The FBI*. New York: Random House, 1954. [Children's book, with emphasis on gangster era.]

———. *Headquarters*. New York: Harper & Bros., 1955. [New York police cases, as seen through the eyes of veteran Detective Frank Phillips. Includes Dutch Schultz, "Mad Dog" Coll, Willie Sutton, "Legs" Diamond, Francis "Two Gun" Crowley, and Rubel Ice Company robbery.]

Rhodes, Henry T. F. *Alphonse Bertillon: Father of Scientific Detection*. New York: Abelard-Schuman, 1956. [Like Cesare Lombroso, a pioneer criminologist whose main contribution was to sell police on the usefulness of science.]

Roberts, Joseph B. (editor). *The Armed Citizen*. Washington, D.C.: National Rifle Association, 1989. [Clippings from NRA's *American Rifleman* magazine from five decades, intended to illustrate the usefulness of privately owned guns in combating crime. Long section entitled "GUNS vs. BANDITS—1932-1939" has much gangster material. Criminals aren't mentioned by name, but some of the incidents will be recognized by gangster buffs.]

Robin, Martin. *The Saga of Red Ryan and Other Tales From Canada's Past*. Saskatoon, Saskatchewan, Canada: Western Producer Prairie Books, 1982.

Robinson, Henry Morton. *Science Catches the Criminal*. New York: Bobbs-Merrill, 1935. [Excitement over new crime-fighting technology.]

Rockaway, Robert A. *But—He Was Good to His Mother: The Lives and Crimes of Jewish Gangsters*. Jerusalem: Gefen, 1993. [The first edition was great, but an extensively rewritten, revised version, with corrections and a wealth of new information, was published by Gefen in 2000.]

Roemer, William F. *Man Against the Mob: The Inside Story of How the FBI Cracked the Chicago Mob by the Agent Who Led the Attack*. New York: Donald I. Fine, 1989. [Book that made the late Bill Roemer a local if not national celebrity, even if his law enforcement colleagues would say his accomplishments (largely through electronic surveillance) were not as single-handed as the story implies. Roemer always maintained, with some credibility based on the bugs and taps, that onetime driver for Jack McGurn and eventual mob boss Tony Accardo played a role in the St. Valentine's Day Massacre.]

———. *Accardo: The Genuine Godfather*. New York: Donald I. Fine, 1995. [Fair biography of a mobster Roemer seems to have truly respected and possibly the last real successor to Al Capone. Roemer's speculations about Accardo's participation in the St. Valentine's Day Massacre and several other early incidents are highly doubtful, and his knowledge of the Capone era clearly doesn't match up with his expertise on the "Outfit" in the sixties. Roemer also authored *The Enforcer*, a biography of latter-day Chicago and Las Vegas hood Anthony Spilotro, and *War of the Godfathers*, a novel about a fictional gang war for control of Las Vegas between the Chicago Mob and the Bonanno Family. Regrettably, some writers have carelessly accepted the latter book as a factual work.]

Rogers, W. Lane. *Crimes & Misdeeds: Headlines from Arizona's Past*. Flagstaff, AZ: Northland Publishing, 1995. [Paperback collection of Arizona crime stories, including 1934 roundup of the Dillinger Gang. John Dillinger's Tucson mug shot graces the cover.]

Rollier, Christopher. *House of Shadows: The Mistress of Al Capone*. Frederick, MD: PublishAmerica, 2005. [House allegedly bought by Al Capone for his mistress, who supposedly continues to haunt it. Author admits his inability to prove Capone bought the house.]

Root, Jonathan. *One Night in July: The True Story of the Rosenthal-Becker Murder Case*. New York: Coward-McCann, 1961.

Rorabaugh, W. J. *The Alcoholic Republic: An American Tradition*. New York: Oxford University Press, 1979. [Well-researched study of national drinking habits that always were excessive and that set the stage for national Prohibition, when the saloon came to symbolize drunkenness, especially among working-class immigrants.]

Rosen, Ruth. *The Lost Sisterhood: Prostitution in America, 1900-1918*. Baltimore: John Hopkins University Press, 1982. [Academic work contains a chapter debating the myth or reality of white slavery.]

Rosen, Victor. *A Gun in His Hand*. New York: Gold Medal, 1951. [Slim paperback biography of Francis "Two-Gun" Crowley, and probably more than he deserves.]

Ross, Robert. *The Trial of Al Capone*. Chicago: privately published, 1933. [Rare paperback account of Capone's tax trial.]

Ross, Ron. *Bummy Davis Vs. Murder, Inc.: The Rise and Fall of the Jewish Mafia and an Ill-Fated Prizefighter*. New York: St. Martin's Press, 2003.

Roth, Andrew. *Infamous Manhattan: A Colorful Walking Tour of New York's Most Notorious Crime Sites*. Secaucus, NJ: Carol Publishing, 1996.

Rothstein, Carolyn. *Now I'll Tell*. New York: Vanguard Press, 1934. [Less-than-candid memoirs by the widow of murdered New York gangster Arnold Rothstein.]

Royko, Mike. *I Could Be Wrong, But I Doubt It*. Chicago: Henry Regnery Co., 1968. [A collection of Royko's newspaper columns. Has an interesting Bonnie and Clyde chapter consisting of interviews with the sons of Barrow Gang victims, telling of their disrupted lives.]

———. *Boss: Richard J. Daley of Chicago*. New York: E. P. Dutton, 1971. [Rise of the Richard J. Daley Democratic machine with commentary on its more spectacularly corrupt Republican predecessors. One of the few books to mention Gus Winkeler as one of the St. Valentine's Day Massacre gunmen.]

Rudensky, Morris "Red," with Riley, Don. *The Gonif*. Blue Earth, MN: Piper Co., 1970. [Autobiography of a former safecracker, robber, hijacker, expert jailbreaker. Also a sometime employee of Al Capone and the Purple Gang and later a fellow inmate of Capone and "Machine Gun" Kelly.]

Runyon, Damon. *Trials & Other Tribulations*. Philadelphia: J. B. Lippincott, 1947. Reprint, New York: Dorset, 1991. [Runyon-style reportage on famous crimes of his times, with entertaining chapters on the murder of Rothstein and the tax trial of Capone.]

Runyon, Tom. *In for Life*. New York: W. W. Norton, 1953. [Autobiography of a Depression outlaw, written in the Iowa state penitentiary at Fort Madison. Runyon, a convicted murderer and bank robber, one-time escapee, became a best-selling author and Associated Press correspondent in prison. Erle Stanley Gardner and others campaigned for his parole, but Runyon died in prison in 1957.]

Russo, Gus. *The Outfit: The Role of Chicago's Underworld in the Shaping of Modern America*. New York and London: Bloomsbury, 2001. [Detailed history of the Chicago Mob from the post-Capone era of expansion into legitimate business, national politics, and the entertainment industry, to its decline in the 1980s and '90s. Focuses on Tony Accardo, Paul "The Waiter" Ricca, Murray "The Camel" Humphreys, John Rosselli, and Sam Giancana as the most prominent inheritors of the Capone-Nitti regime. Partly drawn from interviews with Murray Humphreys' widow and may overstate his importance somewhat. The extensive bibliography also includes some possibly questionable Internet sources, but this is the most comprehensive and up-to-date work on the "Outfit" and an essential for anyone's crime library.]

Ruth, David E. *Inventing the Public Enemy: The Gangster in American Culture, 1918-1934*. Chicago: University of Chicago Press, 1996. [Excellent study of the evolution of the concept of the modern-day gangster.]

S

Sabbag, Robert. *Too Tough to Die: Down and Dangerous with the U.S. Marshals*. New York: Simon & Schuster, 1992. [Another book on the U.S. Marshals' Service. Similar to Calhoun's *The Lawmen* but focuses on present-day activity. Brief mention of Capone and other Prohibition gangsters. Also covers rivalry of Marshals' Service and FBI.]

Sabljak, Mark, and Greenberg, Martin H. *Most Wanted: A History of the FBI's Ten Most Wanted List*. New York: Bonanza Books, 1990. [Similar to the Newtons' *FBI Most Wanted: An Encyclopedia*, but also has a chapter on public enemies of the 1930s.]

———. *A Bloody Legacy: Chronicles of American Murder*. New York/Avenel, NJ: Gramercy Books, 1992. [Routine rerun on the St. Valentine's Day Massacre, Bonnie and Clyde, "Legs" Diamond, Louis "Lepke" Buchalter, and Albert Anastasia.]

Salerno, Ralph, and Tompkins, John S. *The Crime Confederation: Cosa Nostra and Allied Operations in Organized Crime*. Garden City, NY: Doubleday, 1969. [Structure, organization and operations of modern organized crime, with much historical perspective on the twenties and thirties. Draws heavily on Joe Valachi's testimony but emphasizes that organized crime—the "Confederation" as the authors call it—is a coalition including many non-Italian gangsters. Author Salerno was a long-time organized crime investigator with the New York Police Department.]

Sanborn, Debra. *The Barrows Gang's Visit to Dexter.* Dexter, IA: Bob Weesner, 1976. [Bonnie and Clyde pamphlet printed and sold locally in Dexter, Iowa, site of the 1933 shootout in which "Buck" and Blanche Barrow were captured.]

Sann, Paul. *The Lawless Decade.* New York: Crown Publishers, 1957. [Photo history of 1920s. Much on Prohibition gang wars (especially Chicago), St. Valentine's Day Massacre, chapters on Al Capone, Johnny Torrio, "Big Jim" Colosimo, biographical sketches of Dutch Schultz, Owney Madden, "Legs" Diamond, "Mad Dog" Coll, Louis "Lepke" Buchalter and Jacob "Gurrah" Shapiro, "Lucky" Luciano, and Frank Costello. A revised and updated version was printed by Fawcett Publications, Greenwich, CT. 1971.]

———. *Kill the Dutchman! (The Story of Dutch Schultz).* New Rochelle, NY: Arlington House, 1971. [Good biography of Schultz, with many photos and the Dutchman's complete deathbed statement.]

Sante, Luc. *Low Life: Lures and Snares of Old New York.* New York: Farrar, Straus & Giroux, 1991. [Exploration of vice, gambling, opium dens, and accompanying crime of the Manhattan tenement scene from 1840 to 1919.]

Scaduto, Tony. *Lucky Luciano: The Man Who Modernized the Mafia.* U.K.: Sphere Books, Ltd., 1976.

Schatzberg, Rufus. *Black Organized Crime in Harlem, 1920-1930.* New York: Garland Publishing, 1993. [Views the takeover by politically-protected, violent white mobsters of African-American Harlem policy racket as a form of racism.]

———, and Kelly, Robert J. *African-American Organized Crime: A Social History.* New Brunswick, NJ: Rutgers University Press, 1997. [Traces black gangsterism from 1920s numbers running through modern urban street gangs.]

Schiavo, Giovanni. *The Truth About the Mafia and Organized Crime in America.* El Paso, TX: Vigo Press, 1962. [Italian-American sociologist argues that American view of the Mafia reveals misunderstanding of Italian history and culture.]

Schlosser, Alexander L. *The Gentle Art of Murder 1934.* New York: Vanguard Press, 1934. [Contains various contemporary crime stories, including "Society Teaches John Dillinger A Lesson."]

Schmidt, John R. *"The Mayor Who Cleaned Up Chicago": A Political Biography of William E. Dever.* DeKalb, IL: Northern Illinois University Press, 1989. [Reform efforts of the well-meaning Dever actually caused Capone to take over neighboring Cicero and threw the underworld into a state of disarray that made Chicago more violent and notorious than before.]

Schoenberg, Robert J. *Mr. Capone: The Real—and Complete—Story of Al Capone.* New York: William Morrow & Company, 1992. [Some new information, slightly revisionist, but a worthy expansion of Kobler with greater emphasis on the business side of crime. Author received significant help from Chicago Capone expert Mark LeVell (Levell). Vastly superior to Bergreen's book, though.]

Schur, Edward M. *Our Criminal Society: The Social and Legal Sources of Crime in America.* Englewood Cliffs, NJ: Prentice-Hall, 1969. [Examines crime patterns historically and questions conventional crime control policies.]

Schwartzman, Paul, and Polner, Rob. *New York Notorious: A Borough-By-Borough Tour of the City's Most Infamous Crime Scenes.* New York: Crown Publishers, Inc., 1992. [Amazingly dull descriptions of New York's notable crimes; includes some gangster material, such as the murder sites of Arnold Rothstein and "Mad Dog" Coll.]

Schwartz, Daniel R. *Broadway Boogie Woogie: Damon Runyon and the Making of New York City Culture.* New York: Palgrave Macmillan, 2003.

Sciacca, Tony. *Luciano: The Man Who Modernized the American Mafia.* New York: Pinnacle Books, 1973. [Scaduto and Sciacca books appear to be U.S. and U.K. versions of the same, published under different names. Both dedicated to Ernie "The Hawk" Rupolo, a Mafia informer whose luck finally ran out. *The Last Testament of Lucky Luciano* yet repeats the myth of the "Night of the Sicilian Vespers."]

Scott, Sir Harold (editor). *Concise Encyclopedia of Crime and Criminals.* New York: Hawthorne, 1961. [Unfortunately scarce, but unusually comprehensive and authoritative, with customary emphasis on American law and lawbreakers.]

Seagrave, Sterling. *The Soong Dynasty*. New York: Harper & Row, 1985. [Heavily conspiratorial and sensationalist account of Chiang Kai Shek's involvement in drug trafficking and organized crime.]

Seidman, Harold. *Labor Czars, A History of Labor Racketeering*. New York: Liveright Publishing Corp., 1938. [Early history of labor rackets.]

Selvaggi, Giuseppe (translated and edited by William A. Packer). *The Rise of the Mafia in New York*. New York/Indianapolis: Bobbs-Merrill, 1978. [As told by an Italian journalist, based on interviews with deported gangsters. Original Italian language version was *La Mia Tomba E New York*. May have lost much in translation.]

Servadio, Gaia. *Mafioso. A History of the Mafia from Its Origins to the Present*. New York: Stein & Day, 1976; London: Secker & Warburg, 1976.

Sharpe, May Churchill. *Chicago May: Her Story*. New York: Gold Label, 1928. [More collectible than informational, but an entertaining autobiography of a colorful female scoundrel's international life of crime.]

Shirley, Glenn. *Henry Starr, Last of the Real Badmen*. New York: David McKay Company, Inc., 1965. [Definitive biography of Starr, one of the last of the legendary "Old West" outlaws and also one of the first automotive bank robbers. Well-documented, as one might expect from the late Glenn Shirley, a conscientious researcher and the foremost authority on Southwestern outlaws of the late nineteenth and early twentieth centuries.]

———. *"Hello, Sucker!" The Story of Texas Guinan*. Austin: Eakin Press, 1989. [Good biography of the legendary speakeasy hostess.]

———. *Purple Sage: The Exploits, Adventures and Writings of Patrick Sylvester McGeeney*. Stillwater, OK: Barbed Wire Press, 1989. [Biography of Western adventurer, deputy U.S. Marshal, filmmaker, and writer Patrick McGeeney, whose pen name was "Purple Sage." In his youth, McGeeney thwarted a train robbery by Henry Starr, whom he came to know well in later years and worked with on Western movies, before Starr reverted to crime. Some good information on Starr's later criminal career, including his unfulfilled scheme to use an airplane as a getaway vehicle.]

Shoemaker, Arthur. *The Road to Marble Halls: The Henry Grammer Saga*. BWB Company, no city, 2000. [Slim paperback biography of Henry Grammer, who went from renowned rodeo star to reputed "Bootleg King of the Osage Hills" and figured in several shootings before dying in a mysterious car wreck in the twenties. Often linked to the likes of Bill Hale (of the Osage Indian murders), Al Spencer, and even Wilbur Underhill, Grammer probably was the only bootlegger to ever be inducted (posthumously) into the National Cowboy Hall of Fame.]

Short, Martin. *Crime Inc.: The Story of Organized Crime*. London: Thames Methuen, 1984. [Good, if conventional, history of organized crime, from the BBC TV documentary series.]

Sifakis, Carl. *The Mafia Encyclopedia*. New York: Facts On File, 1974.

———. *A Catalogue of Crime*. New York: New American Library, 1979. [Slim paperback, crammed with historical crime trivia.]

———. *The Encyclopedia of American Crime*. New York: Facts On File, 1984 and 1992. [Similar to Nash's *Bloodletters and Badmen*, but far superior in content, intelligence, writing, accuracy, and production.]

Silberman, Charles E. *Criminal Violence, Criminal Justice*. New York: Random House, 1978.

Simmons, Lee. *Assignment Huntsville: Memoirs of a Texas Prison Officer*. Austin: University of Texas Press, 1957. [Lee Simmons brought former Texas Ranger Frank Hamer out of retirement to track down Bonnie and Clyde. Simmons' memory is faulty (gives wrong month for Barrow-Parker ambush), but he also furnishes notes of his 1935 interviews with Barrow gangster Joe Palmer, made shortly before Palmer's execution. Some material on Matt Kimes and other outlaws.]

Singer, Kurt (compiler). *My Strangest Case*. London: W. H. Allen, 1957. [Recollections of police notables, including the J. Edgar Hoover version of "Ma" Barker and the Barker-Karpis Gang, entitled "Matriarch With a Machine-Gun."]

Sinese, Jerry. *Black Gold and Red Lights*. Austin: Eakin Press, 1982. [Vice, corruption, and violence in the oil-boom town of Borger, Texas, a haven in the twenties for such outlaws as Matt Kimes and Ray Terrill.]

Siragusa, Charles, with Wiedrich, Robert. *The Trail of the Poppy: Behind the Mask of the Mafia*. Englewood Cliffs, NJ: Prentice-Hall, 1966. [Longtime agent of the Federal Bureau of Narcotics recounts his crusade against Mafia drug traffickers.]

Slate, John, and Steinberg, R.U. *Lawmen, Crimebusters and Champions of Justice*. New York: M&M Books,

1991. [Nice companion volume to Donna Claitor's *Outlaws Mobsters and Murderers.*]

Smith, Alson J. *Syndicate City.* Chicago: Henry Regnery Co., 1954. [Lesser known but interesting and somewhat revisionist history of Chicago organized crime. Like other fifties gangster books, this one does go somewhat off the deep end, however, on the subject of "Mafia."]

Smith, Brad. *Lawman to Outlaw: Verne Miller and the Kansas City Massacre.* Bedford, IN: JoNa Books, 2002. [Excellent and well-researched biography of one of the Public-Enemy era's most interesting figures: the sheriff-turned-gangster who orchestrated the Union Station massacre, accompanied by "Pretty Boy" Floyd.]

Smith, Dwight C. *The Mafia Mystique.* New York: Basic Books, 1975. [Another unsuccessful attempt to demolish the myth of the Mafia but still a fine study of the legend's growth and a valuable and scholarly contribution to the literature.]

Smith, Richard Norton. *Thomas E. Dewey and His Times: The First Full-Scale Biography of the Maker of the Modern Republican Party.* New York: Simon & Schuster, 1982. [Covers Dewey's collaboration with reform Mayor Fiorello LaGuardia to clean up a city long ruled by gangs under the likes of playboy Mayor Jimmy Walker, forced out of office by the state-supported Seabury investigation.]

Smith, Sir Sidney. *Mostly Murder.* New York: David McKay, 1959. [Wonders of scientific crime detection told autobiographically by a leading British forensic pathologist.]

Soderman, Harry, and O'Connell, Chief Inspector John J. *Modern Criminal Investigation.* New York: Funk & Wagnalls 1935. [Major effort to sell backward, local police agencies on the latest breakthroughs in scientific crime detection.]

Sondern, Frederic, Jr. *Brotherhood of Evil: The Mafia.* New York: Farrar, Straus & Giroux, 1959. [Another 1950s Mafia book, displaying that period's ignorance of that organization. Includes chapters on Al Capone and "Lucky" Luciano. Capone chapter verges on the hilarious.]

Spencer, James. *Limey: An Englishman Joins the Gangs.* London/New York: Longman's/Green, 1933. [An Englishman's memoirs of his excursions into the American underworld.]

Spiering, Frank. *The Man Who Got Capone.* New York/Indianapolis: Bobbs-Merrill, 1976. [Story of Treasury agent Frank Wilson and his crucial role in putting Capone behind bars. Spiering also has authored books on Jack the Ripper and Lizzie Borden.]

Starr, Henry. *Thrilling Events. Life of Henry Starr by Himself.* Tulsa, OK: R. D. Gordon, 1914. Reprinted by Creative Publishing, College Station, TX, 1982. [Technically outside the scope of this bibliography, as it deals with Starr's pre-twenties crime career but listed for the benefit of readers interested in this transitionary badman of the World War I-to-Prohibition era. Written in the Colorado state penitentiary and originally sold for fifty cents, original editions of this are exceedingly rare.]

Stead, William T. *If Christ Came to Chicago!* Chicago: Laird & Lee, 1894. Reprint, Evanston, IL: Chicago Historical Bookworks, 1990. [Classic expose of Chicago's crime, vice, corruption, and opulent depravity that was in full flower long before Prohibition gave rise to the Roaring Twenties "gangster." British muckraker Stead, a pioneer in tabloid journalism, went down with the *Titanic* in 1912.]

Steele, Phillip W., with Scoma, Marie Barrow. *The Family Story of Bonnie and Clyde.* Gretna, LA: Pelican Publishing, 2000. [Not long on accuracy, despite the participation of Clyde Barrow's sister, who died just before to publication. Has some good rare photos, though.]

Steffens, Lincoln. *Shame of the Cities.* New York: McClure, Phillips, 1903. Numerous later reprints. [Probably the most influential "muckraking" expose of corruption, squalor, and depravity, city by city, that became a combination bible and guidebook for urban activists during the age of reform. A rich source of material for journalistic attacks on entrenched politicians. In the same vein as Stead's *If Christ Came to Chicago*, but national in scope.]

Steiger, Brad. *Bizarre Crime.* New York: Penguin Books, 1992. [Shoddy paperback with gangster section that includes chapters on "Big Jim" Colosimo's supposedly missing gems, the mythical $200,000 treasure Dillinger buried at Little Bohemia and the widely discredited legend of "Ma" Barker.]

Stein, Max. *"The March of Crime" U.S. WAR ON CRIME "BRING 'EM BACK" ALIVE OR DEAD.* Chicago: Stein Publishing House, 1939. [Series of flimsy pamphlets, described as "Instructive Discussions" and subtitled "DESPERATE BATTLES and SCIENTIFIC DETECTION of BOOTLEGGERS, GANGLAND PUBLIC ENEMIES."

Includes Evelyn Frechette's story of her life with Dillinger, accounts of the Dillinger Gang, Bonnie and Clyde, St. Valentine's Day Massacre, etc.]

Steinberg, Alfred. *The Bosses.* New York: Macmillan, 1972. [Substantial biographies of Frank Hague, Ed Crump, James Curley, Huey Long, Gene Talmadge, and Tom Pendergast, the "ruthless men who forged the American political machines that dominated the twenties and thirties."]

Steinke, Gord. *Crossing the Line: Mobsters and Rumrunners.* Alberta, Canada: Folklore Publishing, 2004.

Sterling, William Warren. *Trails and Trials of a Texas Ranger.* Austin: Privately printed, 1959. ["General Bill" Sterling rose through the ranks to become commander of the Texas Rangers in the 1930s. Includes chapters on former Rangers Frank Hamer, who led the ambush of Bonnie and Clyde, and Gus Jones, who joined the FBI and headed the Kansas City Massacre and Urschel kidnapping investigations, plus a few pages on 1920s outlaws Matt Kimes and Ray Terrill. Reprinted by University of Oklahoma Press, Norman, OK, 1968.]

Stern, Michael. *The White Ticket: Commercialized Vice in the Machine Age.* New York: National Library Press, 1936. [Examines organized prostitution in New York at the time of the Luciano trial.]

———. *No Innocence Abroad.* New York: Random House, 1953. [Overseas misdeeds of various luminaries of crime and scandal. Includes chapters on "Lucky" Luciano, "Bugsy" Siegel's former girlfriends Virginia Hill Hauser and Countess Dorothy di Frasso, Sicilian bandit Salvatore Giuliano, and others.]

Stevens, Steve, and Lockwood, Craig. *The King of Sunset Strip: Hangin' With Mickey Cohen and the Hollywood Mob.* Nashville, TN: Cumberland House, 2006.

Stewart, Tony. *Dillinger: The Hidden Truth, A Tribute to Gangsters and G-Men of the Great Depression Era.* Philadelphia: Xlibris Publishing, 2002. [Somewhat amateurish, repetitive, and poorly written and edited, but well-meaning attempt to tell John Dillinger's side of the story. Contains (despite its subtitle) vitriolic attacks on J. Edgar Hoover and the FBI and some previously unknown family information, by virtue of author's interview of his great aunt Beryl Hovious, the former wife of Dillinger.]

Still, Charles E. *Styles in Crime.* New York: J. B. Lippincott, 1938. [Potpourri of famous criminal cases, crime fighters, police history, punishment, and whatever else struck the author as illustrative, colorful, or bizarre.]

Stockdale, Tom. *The Life and Times of Al Capone.* Broomall, PA: Chelsea House, 1997.

Stolberg, Mary M. *Fighting Organized Crime: Politics, Justice, and the Legacy of Thomas E. Dewey.* Boston: Northeastern University Press, 1995. [Scholarly study of the political motivations behind Republican prosecutor Dewey's "war on crime."]

Strickland, Ron. *Texans: Oral Histories from the Lone Star State.* New York: Paragon House, 1991. [Includes a chapter of recollections from Joe Newton of the outlaw Newton brothers who took part in the $2 million Rondout, Illinois, train robbery in 1924.]

Stuart, Hix C. *The Notorious Ashley Gang: A Saga of the King and Queen of the Everglades.* Stuart, FL: St. Lucie Publishing, 1928. [John Ashley and his gang were notorious bank robbers, hijackers, and bootleggers who terrorized Florida in the early 1920s. Includes photos and a statement of his criminal career, allegedly made to the author by Ashley. Possibly the first book on the era's new "motorized bandits," but somewhat fictionalized.]

Stuart, Mark A. *Gangster #2: Longy Zwillman, The Man Who Invented Organized Crime.* Secaucus, NJ: Lyle Stuart, 1985. [Biography of New Jersey gangster Abner "Longy" Zwillman, marred by fictional dialogue. Stuart also falls into the usual gangster biographer's syndrome (as evidenced by title) of exaggerating the importance of his subject.]

Sturholm, Larry, and Howard, John. *All For Nothing: The True Story of the Last Great American Train Robbery.* Portland, OR: BLS Publishing, 1976. [Story of the DeAutremont brothers, as related to the authors by Ray DeAutremont.]

Sullivan, Edward Dean. *Rattling the Cup on Chicago Crime.* New York: Vanguard Press, 1929. Reprinted in U.S. and U.K. as *Look At Chicago.*

———. *Chicago Surrenders.* New York: Vanguard Press, 1930.

———. *The Snatch Racket.* New York: Vanguard Press, 1932. [Sullivan was a classic Chicago crime writer who produced two of the earliest books on Capone and Chicago gangs. *The Snatch Racket* superficially describes the gangland practice of holding rivals for ransom and seems to have been a rush job to capitalize on the kidnap-murder of the Lindbergh baby. Blames the increase in abductions largely on Prohibition.]

———. *This Labor Union Racket.* New York: Hillman L. Curl, 1936. [Dramatic contemporary expose of racketeer and Communist influence in Depression-era union activity.]

Sullivan, Robert (editor). *Mobsters and Gangsters: Organized Crime in America from Al Capone to Tony Soprano.* New York: Time, Inc., 2002. [Coffee-table history of American gangsters, from Jesse James to John Gotti, produced by the editors of *Life.* Typical Time-Life production, with superficial text but many good photos. One photo of the James Gang is bogus.]

Sullivan, William, with Brown, Bill. *The Bureau: My Thirty Years in Hoover's FBI.* New York: W. W. Norton, 1979. [Important critical book on Hoover and the bureau, written by a former assistant director of the FBI. Mainly of interest to gangster buffs for its chapters on Charles Winstead, the G-man who shot Dillinger. In his early years with the bureau, Sullivan worked closely with Winstead, who also claimed to have shot "Ma" Barker.]

Summers, Anthony. *Official and Confidential: The Secret Life of J. Edgar Hoover.* New York: G. P. Putnam's Sons, 1993. [Maintains, largely on the basis of uncorroborated gossip and hearsay, that Hoover was a homosexual blackmailed by certain mobsters into ignoring and even disputing the existence of organized crime. Provides evidence of some truly bizarre aspects of Hoover, including his alleged hots for Melvin Purvis, but any writer who gives credence to the Dillinger survival theory cannot be taken too seriously, and Summers' attempt to personalize Hoover by referring to him throughout as "Edgar" is both unprofessional and annoying.]

Sutherland, Edwin H. *The Professional Thief.* Chicago: University of Chicago Press, 1937. [Emphasis on white-collar crime.]

Sutton, Willie, with Linn, Edward. *Where the Money Was.* New York: Viking Press, 1976. [Autobiography of New York bank robber, burglar, escape artist, master of disguise, known in the underworld as "Slick Willie" and "Willie the Actor." His career as a big-time bank robber, interspersed with prison terms, spanned the 1920s to early '50s, when he made the "Ten Most Wanted List." Includes material on Dutch Schultz and other New York mobsters.]

Swierczynski, Duane. *This Here's a Stick-Up: The Big Bad Book of American Bank Robbery.* New York: Alpha Books, 2002. [Large-size paperback coffee-table book offering superficial and not always accurate coverage of American bank robberies. Still vastly superior to Kirchner's *Robbing Banks.*]

———. *The FBI's Ten Most Wanted List: 1950 to Present.* New York: Facts on File/Checkmark Books, 2004.

Symons, Julian. *A Pictorial History of Crime: 1840 to the Present.* New York: Crown Publishers, New York, 1966. [Extensive if superficial photo history of famous crimes and criminals from around the world. Gangster section includes biographical sketches of Arnold Rothstein, Johnny Torrio, Al Capone, John Dillinger, and Depression outlaws, the Mafia, labor rackets, and birth of the Syndicate. Also published by Studio Vista, London, 1966, as *Crime and Detection: An Illustrated History From 1840.* Reprinted in U.S. by Bonanza Books, New York, in the 1970s.]

T

Taggert, Ed. *Bootlegger: Max Hassel, The Millionaire Newsboy.* Lincoln, NE: Writer's Showcase Press, 2003. [Biography of a "Waxey" Gordon lieutenant.]

Tallant, Robert. *Ready to Hang: Seven Famous New Orleans Murders.* New York: Harper, 1952. [Not particularly relevant, except for its chapter describing a much-reported killing and lynching incident in 1907 and promoting the largely discredited notion that the Mafia had entered the U.S. by way of New Orleans.]

Talese, Gay. *Honor Thy Father.* New York: World Publishing Co., 1971. [Bestselling but boring account of the Bonanno Family, which endeavors to show what boring lives Mafia men led. Based largely on interviews with Bill Bonanno, much to his father's annoyance. See also Joe Bonanno's fascinating, if self-promoting, autobiography, *A Man of Honor,* and Bill's somewhat overblown sequel, *Bound by Honor.*]

Tashjian, Leon. *Al Capone, The Hawk, Prohibition.* New York: Vantage Press, 1989. [Quaint recollections of deputy marshal known as "The Hawk" on Prohibition and relating dubious anecdotes on various criminals including Capone, Dillinger, "Dago" Lawrence Mangano, and Joseph "Yellow Kid" Weil.]

Taylor, Merlin Moore. *The Inside Story of Dillinger* (cover title) or *Dillinger's Sensational Story (Inside Dope on Public Enemy No. 1).* Garden City, NY: Doubleday, Doran, August 1934. [Long, detailed account of Dillinger's life and career up through the battle at Little

Bohemia, published by Doubleday in thick *Star Novels Magazine*. Unusually accurate period piece, especially interesting in that it was written while Dillinger was alive. Other stories are fiction.]

Terrett, Courtenay. *Only Saps Work: A Ballyhoo for Racketeering*. New York: Vanguard Press, 1930. [An informative early look at the expansion of bootlegging gangs into business rackets. Title reflects increasing pre-Depression cynicism toward honest jobs and politicians.]

Tejaratchi, Sean (editor), and Dunn, Katherine (text). *Death Scenes: A Homicide Detective's Scrapbook*. Los Angeles: Feral House, 1996. [Gruesome photo collection from the scrapbook of Jack Huddleston, a Los Angeles Police Department homicide detective whose career spanned the twenties to fifties.]

Theoharis, Athan G. *J. Edgar Hoover, Sex, and Crime*. Chicago: Ivan R. Dee, 1995. [Scholarly debunking of the rumor that Hoover was a compromised homosexual blackmailed by the Mob, as popularized by Anthony Summers' shoddy expose *Official and Confidential*. Theoharis' status as a prominent anti-Hoover writer enhances his credibility, and his scholarship easily outdistances Summers' gossipy tabloid style.]

———, and Cox, John Stuart. *The Boss: J. Edgar Hoover and the Great American Inquisition*. Philadelphia: Temple University Press, 1988. [An anti-Hoover book. Gangster chapter ("Crusade Against Crime") is largely inaccurate. Theoharis also authored *From the Secret Files of J. Edgar Hoover* (Ivan R. Dee, Chicago, 1991), which is devoid of gangster material.]

Thompson, Craig, and Raymond, Allen. *Gang Rule in New York*. New York: Dial Press, 1940. [Good early book on New York gangs of the twenties and thirties.]

Thompson, Nathan. *Kings: The True Story of Chicago's Policy Kings and Numbers Runners*. Chicago: Bronzeville Press, 2003. [History of black "policy kings" who ruled the numbers racket until it was taken over by white mobsters, who were themselves later succeeded by the state-operated legal lotteries of today.]

Thorwald, Jurgen. *Century of the Detective*. New York: Harcourt, Brace & World, 1964.

———. *Crime and Science: The New Frontier in Criminology*. New York: Harcourt, Brace & World, 1966. [Historical background to modern forensics.]

Thrasher, Frederic. *The Gang: A Study of 1,313 Gangs in Chicago*. Chicago: University of Chicago Press, 1927. [Important scholarly study of the street gang phenomenon, but one which failed to appreciate how the enormous profit potential of Prohibition would transform existing gangs into wealthy and powerful underworld organizations.]

Thurman, Steve (pseudonym of Frank Castle). *"Baby Face" Nelson*. Derby, CT: Monarch Books, 1961. [Another Monarch "novelized biography."]

Tiffany, Ernest L., M.D. *War With the Underworld*. Butler, IN: The Higley Press, 1946.

Time-Life Books, editors of. *This Fabulous Century: 1920-1930*. Alexandria, VA: Time-Life Books, 1969. [One of a series of volumes of hardcover photo histories of American life, decade by decade, through the 1960s. Includes Al Capone and Prohibition. The entire series was later condensed into a boxed set of paperback volumes.]

———. *This Fabulous Century: 1930-1940*. Alexandria, VA: Time-Life Books, 1969. Includes brief photo section on Dillinger, Floyd, Nelson, the Kellys, the Barkers, and Bonnie and Clyde, followed by a glorifying chapter on J. Edgar Hoover.]

———. *True Crime: Mafia*. Alexandria, VA: Time-Life Books, 1999. [Coffee-table book with many good photos.]

Tofel, Richard J. *Vanishing Point: The Disappearance of Judge Crater and the New York He Left Behind*. Chicago: Ivan R. Dee, 2004. [Sees Crater's disappearance as leading directly to the decline of Tammany Hall. Considers the suspicion of murder, eventually settling on the notion that the judge died naturally in a bout with one of Polly Adler's whores, and Polly called on friend Dutch Schultz to dispose of the body.]

Toland, John. *The Dillinger Days*. New York: Random House, 1963. [Comparable to Cromie's and Pinkston's *Dillinger: A Short and Violent Life*, but treats Dillinger in much less detail for covering all the other major gangs of the period.]

Tosches, Nick. *King of the Jews*. New York: HarperCollins/Ecco, 2005. [Somewhat offbeat "biography" of Arnold Rothstein, who seems to be presented as kind of a "Messiah" figure and is absent through much of the book as the author offers his rambling opinions on misinterpretations of the Bible, Jewish history, and history in general.]

Touhy, Roger, with Brennan, Ray. *The Stolen Years*. Cleveland: Pennington Press, 1959. [Touhy, convicted of kidnapping Jake "The Barber" Factor, finally convinced the courts that the crime was a hoax perpetrated by Capone to put him out of business. Finally released in 1959 and murdered only a few days later. Includes an amusing reference to the St. Valentine's Day Massacre being carried out by Capone's men disguised as priests instead of cops.]

Train, Arthur. *Courts, Criminals, and the Camorra.* New York: Scribner's, 1912. [Attempt by a former assistant district attorney for New York County to sort out criminal organization within the city's Italian-American community. The term "Mafia" had not yet come into popular usage in this country, and "Black Hand" seems to have been temporarily displaced as a result of international publicity given to a mass trial of Camorra leaders in Naples in 1911.]

Trautman, Jim. *Murder Inc.: New York's Infamous Gangsters for Hire.* Canmore, Alberta, Canada: Altitude Publishing, 2005.

Treherne, John. *The Strange History of Bonnie and Clyde.* New York: Stein & Day, 1984. [Fair account of Bonnie and Clyde, but British author dwells more on psychology, folklore, and movies than do more conventional biographers. Less detailed than most accounts but provides some information missing from earlier books and different photos than usual. Phillips' *Running With Bonnie and Clyde*, Underwood's *Depression Desperado,* and Knight's and Davis' *Bonnie and Clyde: A 21st Century Update* are recent works far superior to Treherne's.]

Trekell, Ronald L. *History of the Tulsa Police Department, 1882-1990.* Tulsa: Tulsa Police Children's Scholarship Fund, 1990. [Good history of police department but inaccurate chapter on Tulsa-area gangsters, including "Ma" Barker and sons, Alvin Karpis, "Pretty Boy" Floyd, Wilbur Underhill, and Matt and George Kimes.]

Trespacz, Karen L. *The Trial of Gangster Al Capone: A Headline Court Case.* Springfield, NJ: Enslow Publishers, 2001. [For juvenile readers.]

Trott, Lloyd. *Mafia.* Cambridge: University of Cambridge Press, 1977. [Bibliography of works on the Mafia.]

Trovillion, Hal W. *Persuading God Back to Herrin.* Herrin, IL: Herrin News, 1925. [Obscure contemporary account of crime and labor violence in Illinois' "Bloody Williamson" County.]

Tucker, Kenneth. *Eliot Ness and the Untouchables: The Historical Reality and the Film and Television Depictions.* Jefferson, NC: McFarland & Co., 2000.

Tully, Andrew. *Treasury Agent: The Inside Story.* New York: Simon & Schuster, 1958. [Glorifying look at Treasury Department investigative agencies, with case studies from the IRS, Federal Bureau of Narcotics, Customs Bureau, and Secret Service. Includes chapters on Al Capone, "Lepke" Buchalter, "Waxey" Gordon, Mickey Cohen, Frank Costello, "Lucky" Luciano, and the Mafia. Foreword by then-Secretary of the Treasury Robert B. Anderson.]

———. *The FBI's Most Famous Cases.* New York: William Morrow, 1965. [Introduction and commentary by J. Edgar Hoover adds it to the long list of books glorifying the bureau.]

Tuohy, John W. *When Capone's Mob Murdered Roger Touhy: The Strange Case of Touhy, Jake the Barber and the Kidnapping That Never Happened.* New York: Barricade Books, 2001. [Interesting if sometimes questionable account of the Touhy-Factor case.]

Turkus, Burton, and Feder, Sid. *Murder, Inc.: The Story of the Syndicate.* New York: Farrar, Straus & Young, 1951. [Turkus was the assistant district attorney who prosecuted the "Murder, Incorporated" gangsters in New York.]

Turner, William W. *Hoover's FBI.* Los Angeles: Sherbourne Press, 1970. [Anti-FBI book written by a former FBI agent (fired after ten years in the bureau). Much good information but also many errors. Most interesting for its inclusion of filched FBI files tending to minimize Kathryn Kelly's role in the Urschel kidnapping.]

Tyler, Gus (editor). *Organized Crime in America.* Ann Arbor: University of Michigan Press, 1962. [Anthology of organized crime with chapters from various books from the twenties to early sixties. Introduction by Estes Kefauver.]

U

Underwood, Sid. *Depression Desperado: The Chronicle of Raymond Hamilton.* Austin: Eakin Press, 1995. [Overshadowed in history by his partners, Bonnie and Clyde, Hamilton is finally rescued from relative obscurity—and frequent confusion with his brother Floyd—in an excellent account of his character and career that set him above and apart from his criminal contemporaries. His blazing escape from the Texas state prison only delayed his execution but should have earned him a more enduring place in the annals of American outlawry (see also McConal, *Over the Wall.*]

Ungar, Sanford J. *FBI: An Uncensored Look Behind the*

Walls. Boston/Toronto: Little, Brown & Co., 1976. [Mainly deals with post-Hoover bureau but some historical material, including the gangster era.]

Unger, Robert. *The Union Station Massacre: The Original Sin of Hoover's FBI.* Kansas City, MO: Andrews, McNeel, 1997. [Unger considers "Pretty Boy" Floyd and Adam Richetti unlikely suspects in the Kansas City Massacre, and his excellent research damages the case that Hoover's FBI was trying to build against them, discussing the turf war between Hoover and a local ballistics expert and Hoover's willingness to suppress evidence that would have been favorable to the defense. Also builds a strong case that much of the carnage at Union Station actually was inflicted by an agent attempting to work an unfamiliar shotgun. His suggestion of a frame-up is less impressive, especially the far-fetched notion that the 1934 FBI was technically capable of planting false fingerprints.]

U.S. Senate, Special Committee to Investigate Organized Crime in Interstate Commerce. *Interim Reports of the Special Committee to Investigate Organized Crime in Interstate Commerce Pursuant To S. Res. 202 (81st Congress) A RESOLUTION TO INVESTIGATE GAMBLING AND RACKETEERING ACTIVITIES.* Washington, D.C.: U.S. Government Printing Office, 1951. [Report of the Kefauver Committee confirmed existence of nationally organized crime and popularized the term Mafia as the catch-all phrase for all forms of racketeering, revealing that the old twenties mobsters (Costello, Lansky, Guzik, Adonis, et. al) had been using the country's preoccupation with outlaws to quietly establish the criminal empires that have prospered ever since. Self-wrappered government report became a nationwide bestseller; later reprinted in hardcover by Arco (leaving out seven pages) and Didier (complete).]

U.S. Senate, Permanent Subcommittee on Investigations of the Committee on Government Operations. *Hearings (Organized Crime and Illicit Traffic in Narcotics).* Washington, DC: U.S. Government Printing Office, 1964. [The televised "Cosa Nostra" hearings that made a star of Joe Valachi.]

U.S. Senate, Permanent Subcommittee on Investigations of the Committee on Governmental Affairs. *Organized Crime: Twenty-five Years After Valachi.* Washington, D.C.: U.S. Government Printing Office, 1988. [Includes the FBI report *Chronological History of La Cosa Nostra in the United States: January 1920-August 1987.*]

V

Valentine, Douglas. *The Strength of the Wolf: The Secret History of America's War on Drugs.* New York and London: Verso, 2004. [History of the Federal Bureau of Narcotics from the thirties to the sixties, based partly on interviews with former agents. Includes the bureau's war against organized crime, its often less-than-harmonious relations with the FBI and CIA, and the many flaws of drug prohibition and often-conflicting priorities of U.S. political and intelligence interests in the drug trade.]

Valentine, Lewis J. *Night Stick: The Autobiography of Lewis J. Valentine.* New York: Dial Press, 1947. [Valentine was New York police commissioner in the twenties and thirties. Includes material on Arnold Rothstein, "Legs" Diamond, Dutch Schultz, "Mad Dog" Coll, Willie Sutton, the Whittemore Gang, Luciano, etc. Introduction by former Mayor Fiorello H. LaGuardia.]

Van Cise, Philip S. *Fighting the Underworld.* Boston: Houghton Mifflin, 1936. [Prosecutor's account of smashing Denver's Lou Blonger Gang in the early twenties.]

Van Devander, Charles W. *The Big Bosses.* New York: Howell, Soskin, 1944. [Jacket blurb: "The story of State and City political machines in New York, Massachusetts, Illinois, Pennsylvania, New York, California and the South." Includes the fall of Chicago's "Big Bill" Thompson Republicans, along with Al Capone, and the post-Prohibition rise of the modern Kelly-Nash Democratic machine that at least drew a broader line between "honest graft" and unconcealed corruption.]

Van Every, Edward. *Sins of New York: as "exposed" by the Police Gazette.* New York: Frederick A. Stokes, 1930.

Van Meter, Jonathan. *The Last Good Time: Skinny D'Amato, the Notorious 500 Club, and the Rise and Fall of Atlantic City.* New York: Three Rivers Press, 2004.

Villard, Oswald Garrison. *Some Newspapers and Newspaper-men.* New York: Alfred A. Knopf, 1923. [Commentary on the different papers, reporters, and publishers who battled for readership and to promote their personal visions and political agendas.]

Vizzini, Sal, with Fraley, Oscar, and Smith, Marshall. *Vizzini: The Story of America's No. 1 Undercover Narcotics Agent.* New York: Arbor House, 1972. [Posing as an Air Force major, Vizzini, of the Federal Bureau of Narcotics, became the trusted confidant of "Lucky" Luciano in Naples in the 1950s (though he was never able to make a case against the Mob boss). Includes Luciano's recollections, according to Vizzini, of Capone, Dutch Schultz, and "Legs" Diamond.]

Vollmer, August, and Parker, Alfred E. *Crime, Crooks and Cops.* New York: Funk & Wagnall, 1937. [Routine anti-crime polemic, disappointing in that its primary author was considered a foremost authority on law enforcement tactics and policies.]

W

Waldrop, Frank C. *McCormick of Chicago: An Unconventional Portrait of a Controversial Figure.* Englewood Cliffs, NJ: Prentice-Hall, 1966. [Biography of the *Chicago Tribune*'s powerful and eccentric publisher in the glory days of yellow journalism.]

Walker, Clifford James. *One Eye Closed the Other Red: The California Bootlegging Years.* Barstow, CA: Backdoor Publishing, 1999. [Largely anecdotal account of California's Prohibition bootlegging gangs. Much on "Baby Face" Nelson's West Coast days.]

Walker, Stanley. *The Night Club Era.* New York: Frederick A. Stokes Co., 1933. [Contemporary history of the gangster-speakeasy scene during Prohibition. Also includes a chapter on freelance crime, including the Urschel kidnapping (which Walker attributes to "Harvey Bailey and his gang"). Indexed, unlike most early gangster books.]

Wallace, Stone. *Dustbowl Desperadoes: Gangsters of the Dirty '30s.* Alberta, Canada: Folklore Publishing, 2003. [Slim volume with chapters on all the major Depression outlaws. All from published sources and showing no evidence of original research. Circulates the same old legends and usual misinformation and gives credence to J.R. Nash's largely discredited theory of Dillinger's survival. Photos are few and common.]

Waller, George. *Kidnap: The Shocking Story of the Lindbergh Case.* New York: Dial Press, 1961. [Good account of the Lindbergh kidnapping.]

Waller, Irle. *Chicago Uncensored: Firsthand Stories About the Al Capone Era.* New York: Exposition Press, 1965.

Waller, Leslie. *The Mob: The Story of Organized Crime in America.* New York: Delacorte Press, 1973.

Wallis, Michael. *Oilman: The Story of Frank Phillips and the Birth of Phillips Petroleum.* Garden City, NY: Doubleday & Co., 1988. [Biography of legendary Oklahoma oilman Frank Phillips, whose many friends included celebrities from both sides of the law. One was bank robber Henry Wells, and Wallis here repeats Wells' fable of how he foiled a kidnap plot against Phillips by "Pretty Boy" Floyd (see *Outlaw's End* by Gerald E. Moore). Wallis regrets having included this, as his subsequent research (see below) has convinced him that Floyd was not one to stoop to kidnapping for ransom. Also some material on other Oklahoma outlaws (Henry Starr, Al Spencer, Frank Nash) and on the Shelton Gang, who were briefly employed by Philips as strikebreakers in East St. Louis.]

———. *Pretty Boy: The Life and Times of Charles Arthur Floyd.* New York: St. Martin's, 1992. [Sweeping, "life and times" biography of the Southwest's leading bandit of the 1930s. Well researched but largely through interviews with sources close to Floyd and perhaps somewhat lacking in objectivity. Wallis would like to think that "Pretty Boy" was not involved in the Kansas City Massacre and unfortunately bolsters this contention by placing some credence on the discredited testimony of "Blackie" Audett. Presents both versions of Floyd's death but leans heavily toward the execution scenario presented by former policeman Chester Smith in 1974.]

Walsh, George. *Gentleman Jimmy Walker: Mayor of the Jazz Age.* New York: Praeger, 1974.

———. *Public Enemies: The Mayor, The Mob and the Crime That Was.* New York: W. W. Norton, 1980. [New York Mayor William O'Dwyer and Frank Costello.]

Wannall, Ray. *The Real J. Edgar Hoover: For the Record.* Paducah, KY: Turner Publishing, 2000.

Ward, Bernie. *Families Who Kill.* New York: Pinnacle Books, 1993. [Contains a completely inaccurate account of the Barkers, largely culled from the error-ridden works of Jay Robert Nash and the fertile imagination of Nash's goofy friend, "Blackie" Audett.]

Warden, Rob, and Groves, Martha (editors). *Murder Most Foul (And Other Great Crime Stories From the World Press).* Athens, OH: Ohio University Press, 1980. [Includes conventional accounts of St. Valentine's Day Massacre and killing of Dillinger, but also the murder of "Two-Gun" Louie Alterie.]

Warren, George. *Gang Wars of the '30s.* Chatsworth, CA: Barclay House, 1974. [Slim paperback with no new information but some rare photos. Chapters alternate between organized crime and Depression outlaws. Includes birth of the Syndicate, murder of Dutch Schultz, "Murder, Inc.," "Ma" Barker, "Pretty Boy"

Floyd, Bonnie and Clyde, Dillinger, and "Baby Face" Nelson. Contains excerpts of an interesting *True* magazine interview with Bonnie and Clyde slayer Ted Hinton, published long before Hinton's book, *Ambush*. Very critical of FBI.]

Washburn, Charles. *Come into My Parlor: A Biography of the Aristocratic Everleigh Sisters of Chicago*. New York: Knickerbocker, 1934. Successes, trials, and tribulations of two famous madams whose flamboyant operations in Chicago's red-light district inspired reforms welcomed by the city's criminal community, which could then take over prostitution.]

Waters, Robert A., and Waters, John T. *Outgunned! True Stories of Citizens Who Stood Up to Outlaws—And Won*. Nashville, TN: Cumberland House, 2004. [Along with "Old West" material, includes chapters on the "Santa Claus" robbery at Cisco, Texas, ill-fated robbery attempts in Boley and Mill Creek, Oklahoma, by "Pretty Boy" Floyd accomplices George Birdwell and Adam Richetti, and the bloody Holden-Keating Gang robbery at Menomonie, Wisconsin.]

Watson, Frederic. *A Century of Gunmen*. London: Ivor Nicholson & Watson, 1931. [British book devoted mainly to Old West gunmen but could not resist including a chapter on Al Capone.]

Watson, William P. *Union, Justice and Bonnie & Clyde: A Louisiana Legacy!* Bossier City, LA: The Everett Companies, 1989. [Strange work purports to be true story of ambush of Bonnie and Clyde, but told in the form of a book-length stage play presenting posthumous trials. Author interviewed Bossier Parish residents, including relatives of Henry Methvin, alleged betrayer of the Barrows, but still has many errors. Includes FBI wanted poster on Clyde Barrow and coroner's reports on Clyde and Bonnie. Some revisions (taped inserts over the original words!) since original printing, either to improve accuracy or avoid disputes.]

Watters, Pat, and Gillers, Stephen (editors). *Investigating the FBI: A Tough, Fair Look at the Powerful Bureau, Its Present and Its Future*. Garden City, NY: Doubleday & Co., 1973. [Proceedings of an essentially anti-FBI conference at Princeton University in 1971. Some gangster material, including Dillinger.]

Webb, Walter Prescott. *The Texas Rangers: A Century of Frontier Defense*. Boston: Houghton Mifflin, 1935. [Includes Frank Hamer's account of the killing of Bonnie and Clyde. Reprinted in 1965 by University Press of Texas, Austin, with foreword by Lyndon B Johnson.]

Weeks, Patrick H., M.D. *The Big House of Mystery: A Physician-Psychiatrist Looks At Ten Thousand Crimes and Criminals*. Philadelphia: Dorrance & Co., 1938. [Written by a doctor of the state prison at Michigan City, Indiana, this book includes an interesting chapter on John Dillinger and his gang. Reveals that Dillinger did indeed suffer from heart disease, as his autopsy later showed, refuting author Jay Robert Nash's contention—in support of his wrong-man-shot theory—that a rheumatic heart would have prevented Dillinger from leading the stressful life of a bank robber. For what it's worth, Alvin Karpis, who outlasted Dillinger in the same profession, survived 33 years in prison, mostly on Alcatraz, and died of a drug overdose ten years after his parole, had a defective heart, as mentioned in *The Alvin Karpis Story* and also Quimby's *The Devil's Emissaries*.]

Weir, William. *Written With Lead: Legendary American Gunfights & Gunfighters*. Hamden, CT: Archon Books, 1992. [Includes everything from the American Revolution to the Brinks' robbery (this is a gunfight?). Twenties and thirties gangster material includes chapters on the St. Valentine's Day Massacre, Bonnie and Clyde, the death of Dillinger, and the murder of Dutch Schultz. Weir refutes some common errors but makes a number of his own and places too much credence on Jay Robert Nash's theory of Dillinger's survival. Apparently unfamiliar with Paul Sann's *Kill the Dutchman!*, he states that no book-length biographies of Dutch Schultz have been written.]

Wellman, Paul I.. *A Dynasty of Western Outlaws*. Garden City, NY: Doubleday & Co., 1961. [Traces connections of outlaw gangs in Missouri, Oklahoma, and Kansas from the Civil War to the Depression. Includes map of outlaw sites, genealogical chart, and chronology of Southwestern outlaws. Has chapters on 1920s gangs (Al Spencer and Eddie Adams) and "Pretty Boy" Floyd. Well written but many errors. Wellman was a police reporter in Wichita in the twenties, though, and knew some of the gangsters and law officers of the period. Wellman also authored *Spawn of Evil*, covering bandits and river pirates of the post-Revolutionary/Early National period.]

Wendt, Lloyd, and Kogan, Herman. *Lords of the Levee: The Story of Bathhouse John and Hinky Dink*. New York: Bobbs-Merrill, 1943. Later editions include softcover reprint retitled *Bosses in Lusty Chicago*

(Bloomington, IN: Indiana University Press, 1971.) [Lively account of Chicago's institutionalized vice and shameless corruption, which easily weathered sporadic reform movements during much of the city's history.]

———. *Big Bill of Chicago*. New York: Bobbs-Merrill, 1953. [Thoroughly entertaining biography of Chicago's clown mayor in cahoots with the city's underworld.]

Werner, M.R. *Tammany Hall*. Garden City, NY: Doubleday, Doran & Co., 1928.

West, C. W. "Dub". *Outlaws and Peace Officers of Indian Territory*. Muskogee, OK: Muskogee Publishing, 1987. ["Indian Territory" in the title refers to eastern Oklahoma, not to the territorial period alone. Book actually is a collection of newspaper clippings, from old Muskogee papers, about various Oklahoma outlaws and lawmen through 1930s. Includes chapters on "Pretty Boy" Floyd, Alvin Karpis, Matt and George Kimes, others.]

Weston, Paul B. *Muscle on Broadway*. Evanston, IL: Regency, 1962. [From outward appearances, an unillustrated, thoroughly ignorable, 50-cent paperback from an obscure Chicago-area publisher, which purports to describe Mob rule in New York during the twenties and thirties, carrying the byline of a retired deputy chief inspector of police, but told mostly in first person by an anonymous informant and survivor of the Dutch Schultz gang calling himself "Max." Where Max's story is complemented by the author's commentary is left to the reader to puzzle out, yet the combined effort provides a remarkably interesting insider/outsider collaboration heavy with details (including the murder of Schultz) and an apparent familiarity with the subject, presented from both sides of the legal fence. Outwardly lurid, oddly presented, cheaply produced.]

Wetzel, Donald. *Pacifist: Or, My War and Louis Lepke*. New York: Permanent Press, 1986. [Memoirs of a conscientious objector who spent World War II in prison. Written largely as a justification of his political beliefs and of interest mainly for recollections of his brief prison friendship with Louis "Lepke" Buchalter. Ludicrously stretches his beliefs with comparisons of war to organized crime and Hiroshima to Buchalter's death in the electric chair.]

Wharton, Charles S. *The House of Whispering Hate*. Chicago: Madelaine Mendelsohn, 1932. [Prison memoirs, based on a journal he kept in Leavenworth, of Charles "Limpy" Cleaver's attorney, in whose home the loot from the Evergreen Park train robbery was divided, which earned Wharton a two-year prison term. Wharton was a former Illinois Congressman (Republican, though a onetime crony of Democratic Tammany boss "Big Tim" Sullivan of New York), and a former assistant prosecutor under Cook County's Robert Crowe, and his other legal clients included millionaire murderer Harry K. Thaw. A rare book containing brief anecdotes of other well-known Leavenworth inmates of the time, including Thomas Holden and Francis Keating, Frank Nash, Oklahoma train robber Jeff Duree, and "Birdman" Robert Stroud. Author's credit reads: "by Charles S. Wharton, Ex-Congressman, Ex-Lawyer, Ex-Convict," and editor Harry Read's foreword blames Wharton's misfortune on Prohibition.]

Whipple, Sidney B. *The Lindbergh Crime*. New York: Blue Ribbon, 1935.

——— (editor). *The Trial of Bruno Richard Hauptmann: Edited with a History of the Case*. Garden City, NY: Doubleday, Doran & Co., 1937 [Good contemporary accounts of the Lindbergh case.]

Whitehead, Don. *The FBI Story: A Report to the People*. New York: Random House, 1956. ["Authorized biography" of FBI, with forward by J. Edgar Hoover. Has material on Al Capone, John Dillinger, the Barker-Karpis Gang, Union Station (Kansas City) Massacre, Urschel kidnapping, Jake Fleagle and capture of Louis "Lepke" Buchalter. Probably inspired by Max Lowenthal's unprecedented attack on the FBI a few years before. An abridged version was published for younger readers.]

Whyte, William Foote. *Street Corner Society: The Social Structure of An Italian Slum*. Chicago: University of Chicago Press, 1943. [Scholarly investigation of the ghetto society that produces gangsters. Reprinted by University of Chicago Press often from 1955.]

Wickersham Commission. *Reports*. 1931. Reprint, Montclair, NJ: Patterson Smith, 1969. [With Mooney-Billings Report. 15 reports in 14 volumes.]

Willemse, Cornelius W. *A Cop Remembers*. New York: E.P. Dutton, 1933.

———, with Lenner, George J., and Kofoed, Jack. *Behind the Green Lights*. New York: Alfred A. Knopf, 1931. [Scarce, thoroughly engrossing, autobiographical adventures of a New York detective who tangled with some of the city's best-known hoods during his forty-year career as a gangbuster.]

Williams, Nathan Glenn. *From Alcatraz to the White House.* Seattle: Wiljoy Publishing, 1991. [Autobiography of a former bank robber and prison friend of Alvin Karpis. Some good Alcatraz stories. Cover shows author shaking hands with Reagan.]

Williams, Roger M. (editor). *The Super Crooks.* Chicago: Playboy Press, 1973. [Anthology of previously published material by various authors. Includes chapters on Dillinger and Willie Sutton, from *The Dillinger Days* by John Toland and *Smooth and Deadly* by Quentin Reynolds.]

Willis, Clint (editor). *Mob: Stories of Death and Betrayal from Organized Crime.* New York: Thunder's Mouth Press, 2001.

——— (editor). *NYPD: Stories of Survival from the World's Toughest Beat.* New York: Thunder's Mouth Press, 2002.

——— (editor). *Crimes of New York: Stories of Crooks, Killers, and Corruption from the World's Toughest City.* New York: Thunder's Mouth Press, 2003. [Routine anthologies of New York crime and police stories, fact and fiction.]

Willoughby, Malcom F. *Rum War At Sea.* Washington, DC: U.S. Government Printing Office, 1964. [Official, thorough, and very boring account of Treasury Department and Coast Guard efforts to combat rum-running.]

Wilson, Colin, Schott, Ian, Shedd, Ed, Wilson, Damon, and Wilson, Rowland (editors). *Colin Wilson's World Famous Crimes: The World's Worst Gangsters, Crooks, Conmen and Scandals.* New York: Carroll & Graf, 1995. [Consolidation of material from previous books by the popular British crime writer, including chapters on his American favorites, from Capone to Bonnie and Clyde, with some elaborating sidebars.]

Wilson, Frank J., with Day, Beth. *Special Agent.* New York: Holt, Rinehart & Winston, 1965. [Treasury agent Wilson was active in the Capone income tax investigation.]

Wiltz, Christine. *The Last Madam: A Life in the New Orleans Underworld.* New York: Faber and Faber, 2000. [Life of New Orleans brothel madam Norma Wallace, active from the 1920s to the '60s, partially based on interviews recorded before her death. Credit Norma with giving the tip that led to the capture of Alvin Karpis.]

Winter, Robert. *Mean Men: The Sons of Ma Barker.* Danbury, CT: Rutledge Books, 2000. [The first detailed history of the early careers of the Barkers, ending with the formation of the Barker-Karpis Gang in 1931. Well-researched paperback, marred by typos.]

Wolf, George, with DiMona, Joseph. *Frank Costello, Prime Minister of the Underworld.* New York: William Morrow, 1974. [George Wolf was Costello's attorney, as well as Luciano's.]

Wolf, Marvin J., and Mader, Katherine. *Fallen Angels: Chronicles of L.A. Crime and Mystery.* New York: Facts On File, 1986. [Includes Tony Cornero, murder of "Bugsy" Siegel, and speculation of organized crime's involvement in death of Thelma Todd.]

Woodbury, Marda Liggett. *Stopping the Presses: The Murder of Walter W. Liggett.* Minneapolis: University of Minnesota Press, 1998. [Crusading Minneapolis newspaperman's assassination by Minneapolis "Kid Cann" mob, as told by his daughter, who witnessed the murder as a child.]

Woodiwiss, Michael. *Crime, Crusades, and Corruption.* New York: Rowman & Littlefield, 1988. [Study of historical prohibitions of gambling, vice, booze, drugs, etc. sees "organized crime" as as a political camouflage for the unenforcibility of these laws.]

———. *Gangster Capitalism: The United States and the Globalization of Organized Crime.* New York: Carroll & Graf, 2005. [Equates capitalism with organized crime and argues that big business and government have traditionally surpassed common gangsters in their own game.]

———. *Organized Crime and American Power: A History.* Toronto: University of Toronto Press, 2002. [Argues that overemphasis of the Mafia as an "alien conspiracy" distracts from the true governmental and societal causes of organized crime.]

Woodside, John R., et. al. *The Young Brothers Massacre.* Springfield, MO: Springfield Publishing Co., 1932. [Wonderfully florid but accurate contemporary account of the slaughter of six lawmen near Springfield by minor outlaws Harry and Jennings Young. "Written and Illustrated Especially for Law Enforcement Officers" and containing marvelous Federal Laboratories advertisements for tear gas and police paraphernalia. Available in reprint and indexed by Terry M. Tyndall from the Greene County Archives and Records Center in Springfield, Missouri.]

Woog, Adam. *Gangsters.* San Diego: Lucent Books, 2000. [Children's book from the *History Makers* series.]

Wright, Richard O. (editor). *Whose FBI?* Chicago: Open Court Publishers, 1974. [Pro-FBI book, written in answer to Princeton University conference (see Watters and Gillers, *Investigating the FBI*).]

Y

Yancey, Diane. *Desperadoes & Dynamite: Train Robbery in the United States.* Danbury, CT: Franklin Watts, Inc., 1991. [Slim (sixty-three-page) children's book covering U.S. train robberies, 1866-1937.]

———. *Al Capone.* San Diego: Lucent Books, 2002. [Children's book from the *Heroes and Villains* series.]

———. *Life During the Roaring Twenties.* San Diego: Lucent Books, 2002. [Children's book.]

———. *Al Capone's Chicago (Travel Guide to).* San Diego: Lucent Books, 2003. [Slim children's book serves as not-too-accurate tour guide to 1929 Chicago.]

Z

Zeiger, Henry A. *Frank Costello.* New York: Berkeley Publishing, 1974.

———. *The Hit Parade.* New York: Berkeley Publishing, 1976. [Routine rehash of major gang murders and wars, 1920s-'70s.]

Zion, Sidney. *Loyalty and Betrayal: The Story of the American Mob.* San Francisco: CollinsPublishers, 1994. [Photo history of organized crime. Published as companion to Fox TV special of the same name.]

Zorbaugh, Harvey W. *The Gold Coast and the Slum: A Sociological Study of Chicago's Near North Side.* Chicago: University of Chicago Press, 1929. [For today's Chicagoans, a lucid and lurid picture of the North Michigan Avenue when it included the rich, the wretched, the radicals, bootleggers, and the remnants of the city's literary/bohemian community, before wealthy merchants transformed it into the "Magnificent Mile" for the credit-card class.]

APPENDIXES

Appendix I

FBI GANG MEMBERSHIP LIST

The following gang-membership list comes from the FBI, presumably part of its "Top Hoodlums" program that the bureau had started assembling about the time Attorney General Cummings announced that the Justice Department would wage war against racketeering, a form of "nonviolent" crime that the bureau's director much preferred to leave to local law-enforcement authorities.

Chicago, Illinois

July 28, 1936

MEMORANDUM FOR THE FILE:

On July 22, 1936, the following list was obtained from Lieutenant J. C. Wilamowsky [correct spelling Wilamovsky], firearms identification expert for Cook County Coroner. The list includes the names of all members of former and present Chicago gangs and indicates an asterisk those now dead.

This current data was compiled by Lieutenant Wilamowsky with the assistance of "Jiggs" Donahue, Chicago policeman attached to the coroner's office and asserted to be more conversant with Chicago gangs and gangsters than any other one person in Chicago.

It might be noted that Hymie Levine is alleged to be the present leader of the Capone gang in the absence of Frank Nitti.

CAPONE GANG South Side)

*Jack McGurn
Nick Perry
Louis "Little New York" Campagna
Frank Diamond
"Mops" Volpe
*Frank Rio
*Albert Anselmi
*John Scalise
*Louis "Diamond Louie" Cowan
Ralph "Bottles" Capone
Tony Accardo, alias Joe Batters
Danny Stanton
Charles Blakely
*Danny Vallo
Claude Maddox
*Tony Belcastro
Louis Clemente
*Joseph Guinta
Johnny Torrio
*Tony Lombardo
Joe Lolordo
*Pasqualino Lolordo
Harry Guzik
Jake Guzik
Hymie Levine
Frank Nitti
Johnny Patton
Frankie Kelly
Mike Kelly
Charles Fischetti
*John Genaro
"Dago" Lawrence Mangano
Carlos Fontana
Ernest Fontana
Martin O'Leary
Mike Corrozzo
Sam Guzik
Jack Heinan

SALTIS GANG (Southwest Side)

Joe "Polack Joe" Saltis
Paddy Sullivan
*John "Dingbat" Oberta
Willie Neimoth
*Frank "Lefty" Koncil
Steve Saltis
Jack Geis
"Big Earl" Herbert
*Frank McErlane
*George Kostenek, alias Geo. Darrow
*Charles "Big Hayes" Hubacek
*George "Big" Karl
*William Dickman
*Sam Melaga

MORAN GANG North Side)

George "Bugs" Moran
*Willie Marks
William Skidmore
Frankie Foster
Leo Mongoven
*Joe Aiello
Tony Aiello
*Jack Zuta
*Frank Gusenberg
*Peter Gusenberg
*Rinehart Schwimmer
*John May
*James Clark
*Albert Weinshenk
*Adam Heyer
Anthony "Red" Kissane
*Ted Newberry
*Dean O'Banion
*Earl "Hymie" Weiss
*Vincent "Schemer" Drucci
*"Red" McLaughlin
*Louie Alterie
Maxie Eisen
Henry Finkelstein

O'DONNELL GANG (West Side)

"Klondyke" O'Donnell
*Miles O'Donnell
Bernard O'Donnell
*George "Red" Barker
*William "Three-Fingered" White
*James Doherty
*Thomas "Red" Duffy
*William "Rags" McCue
Harry Madigan
"Mickey" Wendel
*"Mickey" Quirk

GHETTO GANG (West Side)

Sammy Kaplan
Johnny Armondo
James Balcastro
Abe "Humpy" Klass
*Jules Portuguese
Ben "Buddy" Jacobson
*Harry Portuguese

*Teddy Stein
*Louis "Big" Smith
Sam "Sammy the Greener" Jacobson
*Sam "Samoots" Amatuna
*Sam Peller
Rocco Fanelli
Alex Portuguese

VINCI GANG (South Side)

Sam Vinci
*Jimmy Vinci
*Mike Vinci
Joe Annoreno
*John Minatti
*Peppy" Genero
Johnnie Genero
*Joe "Machine Gun Joe" Granata

VALLEY GANG (West Side)

Terry Druggan
Frankie Lake
*Frank "Red" Krueger
John "Paddy the Cub" Ryan
*"Paddy the Bear" Ryan
*"Bummy" Goldstein
*Walter Quinlan
*Harry "The Schoolmaster" Schneider
*"Big Steve" Weisnewski

RAGEN COLTS GANG (South Side)

Ralph Sheldon
*Hugh "Stubby" McGovern
*William "Gunner" McPadden

*George Maloney
*Michael "Bubs" Quinlan
Danny Stanton
*Charles Kelly
Danny McFall

CIRCUS GANG (Northwest Side)

Claude Maddox
Tony "Tough Tony" Capezio

"RED" BOLTON GANG (West Side)

"Red" Bolton

*"Dinky" Quan
*Frank Wilson
*Ryan

NORTHWEST SIDE GANG

Marty Guilfoyle
*Matt Kolb
Al Winge
Jimmy Barry
Leonard Boltz
Sam Thompson
Christ Madsen
Louis Stryker

Respectfully submitted,

JEROME DOYLE
Special Agent

Purple Gang Members, March 1932

From list furnished to the U.S. Bureau of Investigation by the Deroit police.

Harry Keywell, #31293, was arrested in Detroit in September, 1931, on charges of murder and has been in jail continuously ever since. In January, 1932, he received a life sentence in connection with this charge since which time he has been confined in the Michigan State Penitentiary at Marquette.

Phillip Keywell, #27946, was sentenced sometime in 1930 to life imprisonment in the Michigan State Penitentiary on charges of murder.

Irving Millberg, #28547, has likewise been in jail since September, 1931, in connection with the same murder for which Harry Keywell was sentenced to life imprisonment. Millberg is likewise confined in the Michigan State Penitentiary.

Raymond Burnstein, #28545, is the third member of the Purple Gang doing a life sentence in connection with the murder involving Millberg and Keywell. Burnstein has likewise been confined in jail continuously since September, 1931.

Abe Burnstein, #14861; Joe Burnstein, #14498; Charles Leiter, #32564; Abe Axler, #29655; Sam Axler, #29766; Joe Miller, #29767; Henry Fletcher, #28544; Henry Fleisher, #16151 at present wanted by Michigan authorities.

All of the above are listed as known ringleaders of the Purple Gang.

In addition to the above persons the so-called Purple Gang in Detroit comprises the following men:

Frank Klayman	#17355	Sam Davis	#27718
Fred Smith	#24775	Sam Goldforb	#24243
Zizzie Selbin (killed 10-26-29)	#32548	Henry Shoor	#10278
		Ben Marcus	#4780
Henry Miller	#29277	Louis Gellerman	#25710
George Harris	#——	Alfred Russell	#24687
Arthur Kelley	#——	Louis Orthman	#32562
Harry Wein	#——	Jack Redfern	#32560
Chas. Stein	#——	John Wolf	#32561
Jack Cohen	#——	James Powell	#——
Joles Joffe	#29663	Louis Rapport	#32613
George Cordell	#18602	Sam Potasink	#——
Abe Miller	#30750	Jack Levites	#32563
Abie Zussman	#24031	Maurice Raider	#10320
Abe Kaminski	#26157	Joe Lieberoff	#33780
Issie Kaminski	#29286	Joe Sascer	#33771
Erwin Shapiro	#24151	Zigie Selbin	#33770
Sam Bernstein	#28205	Sam Purple	#11663
Issie Bernstein	#31571	Jacob Willman	#29505
Louis Fleischer	#27717	Hymie Altman	#28453
Jack Stein	#30083	Abe Olenick	#41273
Willie Laks	#31946	Edw. Shaw	#30452

Appendix II

CAPONE GANG DEATH DATES

Anthony "Joe Batters" Accardo—Died of natural causes, Chicago, May 27, 1992.

Joseph Aiuppa, alias Joey O'Brien—Died of cancer, Chicago, February 22, 1997.

John Annerino, alias Genero—Murdered in Chicago, March 21, 1931.

Joseph "Peppy" Annereno, alias Genero—Murdered in Chicago, December 19, 1935.

Albert Anselmi—Found murdered near Hammond, Indiana, May 9, 1929.

Theodore "The Greek" Anton—Murdered in Cicero, Illinois, November 28, 1926.

Dominick Armato—Murdered in Chicago, December 6, 1923.

George "Red" Barker—Murdered in Chicago, June 16, 1932.

James "King of the Bombers" Belcastro—Died of heart attack, Chicago, August 23, 1945.

Rocco "The Crazy Barber" Belcastro—Murdered in Chicago, May 15, 1933.

William (Willie) Bioff—Murdered in Phoenix, Arizona, November 4, 1955.

William Bryan Bolton, alias Byron "Monty" Bolton—Died in Los Angeles, March 1977.

Leo Brothers—Died in Murphysboro, Illinois, May 27, 1951.

Fred "Killer" Burke—Died of natural causes, Marquette, Michigan, state prison, June 10, 1940.

Louis "Little New York" Campagna—Died of heart attack on Florida fishing trip, May 30, 1955.

Anthony "Tough Tony" Capezio—Died of heart attack, July 1955, while playing golf (often wrongly reported to have been struck by lightning).

Albert Capone, alias Albert Rayola, Bert Novak—Died of natural causes, June 1980.

Alphonse (Al) Capone—Died of natural causes, Palm Island, Florida, January 25, 1947.

Ermino John "Mimi" Capone, alias John Martin (?)—Was living in early 1980s).*

Matthew "Matt the Mooch" Capone—Died of natural causes, January 31, 1967.*

Ralph "Bottles" Capone—Died of natural causes, Hurley, Wisconsin, November 22, 1974.*

Salvatore (Frank) Capone—Killed by police, Cicero, Illinois, April 1, 1924.*

Bob Carey, alias Bob "Gimpy" Newberry, Robert Sanborn—Alleged suicide by gun, New York City, July 29, 1932.

Nick Circella, alias Nick Dean (?)—Was living in Mexico in 1950s.

Tommy Cuirigione, alias Tommy Ross—Murdered in Chicago, August 3, 1926.

Philip D'Andrea—Died of natural causes, Chicago, September 18, 1952.

Rocco "Rocky" DeGrazia—Died of natural causes, Melrose Park, Illinois, December 17, 1978.

Paul DeLucia, alias Paul "The Waiter" Ricca—Died of natural causes, Chicago, October 11, 1972.

Anthony DeMora, alias DeMory—Murdered in Chicago, March 2, 1936.

Terry Druggan—Died of natural causes, May 4, 1954.

Joseph "Diamond Joe" Esposito—Murdered in Chicago, March 21, 1928.

Charles "Trigger Happy" Fischetti—Died of natural causes, Miami, April 11, 1951.**

Rocco Fischetti—Died of natural causes, Massapequau, New York, July 5, 1964.**

Joseph Fusco—Died of natural causes, December 5, 1976.

Angelo "Bloody Angelo" Genna—Murdered in Chicago, May 25, 1925.

Antonio "Tony the Gentleman" Genna—Murdered in Chicago, July 8, 1925.

***Brothers of Al Capone**
****Cousins of Al Capone**

Mike "The Devil" Genna—Killed by police, Chicago, June 13, 1925.

Peter Genna—Died of natural causes in Chicago, May 13, 1948.

Sam Genna—Died of heart attack at Blue Island, Illinois, December 20, 1951.

Vincenzo (Jim) Genna—Died of natural causes, Chicago, November 8, 1931.

Vincent Gibaldi, alias "Machine Gun" Jack McGurn—Murdered in Chicago, February 15, 1936.

Charles "Cherry Nose" Gioe—Murdered in Chicago, August 18, 1954.

Fred Goetz, alias "Shotgun" George Zeigler—Murdered in Cicero, Illinois, March 21, 1934.

Alex Louis Greenberg—Murdered in Chicago, December 8, 1955.

Joseph "Hop Toad" Guinta—Found murdered near Hammond, Indiana, May 9, 1929.

Jake "Greasy Thumb" Guzik—Died of natural causes, Chicago, February 21, 1956.

Willie Heeney—Died of throat cancer, September 13, 1951.

Mike "de Pike" Heitler—Found murdered in Barrington, Illinois, April 30, 1931.

Murray "The Camel" Humphreys—Died of natural causes, Chicago, November 23, 1965.

Sam "Golf Bag" Hunt—Died of natural causes in Schenectady, New York, August 19, 1956.

Frank Lake—Died of natural causes, January 11, 1947.

Frank LaPorte—Died of natural causes, Chicago Heights, Illinois, October 30, 1972.

Hymie "Loud Mouth" Levin—Died of natural causes, Chicago, June 19, 1951.

Pasqualino "Patsy" Lolordo—Murdered in Chicago, January 8, 1929.

Antonio (Tony) Lombardo—Murdered in Chicago, September 7, 1928.

Claude Maddox, alias Johnny "Screwy" Moore—Died of natural causes, Chicago, June 21, 1958.

"Dago" Lawrence Mangano—Murdered in Chicago, August 3, 1944.

Frank Maritote, alias Frank Diamond—Murdered in Chicago, August 21, 1954.

Robert "Big Bob" McCullough—Died of natural causes, Florida (?), January 24, 1989.

Edward (Ted) Newberry—Found murdered near Chesterton, Indiana, January 7, 1933.

Francesco Nitto, alias Frank "The Enforcer" Nitti—Committed suicide, Riverside, Illinois, March 19, 1943.

Raymond "Crane-Neck" Nugent—Reportedly murdered, circa 1932; body never found.

Edward (Eddie) O'Hare—Murdered in Chicago, November 16, 1939.

William "Klondike" O'Donnell—Died in Chicago area, December 1976.

John Patton—Died of natural causes, Earl Park, Indiana, December 23, 1956.

Ralph Pierce—Died of natural causes in Chicago, July 1976.

"West Side" Frankie Pope—Murdered in Chicago, March 7, 1934.

Mike "The Greek" Potson—Died in Greece, September 27, 1955.

Frank Rio—Died of heart attack at home, Oak Park, Illinois, February 23, 1935.

John Rosselli—Murdered in Florida, August 1976.

Ernest Rossi—Murdered in Chicago, February 4, 1934.

James Sammon, alias James "Fur" Sammons—Died May 20, 1960.

John Scalise—Found murdered near Hammond, Indiana, May 9, 1929.

Danny Stanton—Murdered in Chicago, May 5, 1943.

Walter Stevens—Died of pneumonia in Chicago, February 15, 1931.

John (Johnny) Torrio—Died of natural causes, New York City, April 16, 1957.

Daniel (Danny) Vallo—Murdered in Niles Center, Illinois, August 14, 1930.

Eddie "Dutch" Vogel—Died of leukemia, Palm Springs, California (?), June 12, 1977.

Anthony "Mops" Volpe—Died of heart attack, Cicero, Illinois, January 1965.

William "Three-Fingered Jack" White—Murdered in Oak Park, Illinois, January 23, 1934.

Gus Winkeler—Murdered in Chicago, October 9, 1933.

Appendix III

HOOVER AND THE LCN

Why the nation's premier lawman, J. Edgar Hoover, so long denied the existence of a "Mafia" or even nationally organized crime mystified his friends and enemies alike. Even though New York racket-buster Thomas Dewey had taken on Murder, Incorporated, in the late thirties and exposed the operations of powerful criminal associations with affiliates around the country, Hoover continued to regard racketeering as a local phenomenon to be prosecuted by local authorities, if they availed themselves of FBI training, identification, and crime-laboratory services.

The bureau reluctantly had collected data on local mobsters by way of its "Top Hoodlums" program, but the fall of Al Capone and the repeal of Prohibition ended popular concern over modern organized crime before it was recognized as such and before the FBI had acquired much authority to deal with it. The New Deal Justice Department's "war" against interstate banditry was being so successfully conducted by the bureau's new breed of scientific detectives that Hoover could declare victory over America's criminal gangs with the capture of Alvin Karpis in 1936, leaving only a few stragglers to be mopped up.

However, the criminals vanquished by the FBI were fugitive outlaws, not racketeers. The powerful urban criminal organizations spawned by Prohibition had only sighed with relief when the flamboyant Al Capone, the Chicago Crime Commission's first Public Enemy No. 1, tripped over the federal tax laws and could be ceremoniously locked up in the new maximum-security fortress of Alcatraz, as though it had been built especially for him. Repeal spelled the end of organized crime as the average citizen understood it.

With the election of President Roosevelt at the height of the Depression, the Justice Department's new attorney general had reversed course completely—or at least partly, after initial threats against racketeers whom Hoover preferred to ignore, arguing that their crimes were not sufficiently "interstate." For public attention had shifted to bank robbers and kidnappers instead of out-of-work bootleggers, providing an exciting national game of cops 'n' robbers. Meanwhile, the Frank Nittis and Jake Guziks and "Lucky" Lucianos quietly transformed their racketeering into a cartel that soon qualified as nationally organized crime.

The systematic takeovers of unions and shakedowns of industries were dismissed by Hoover's FBI in favor of sexier targets like Communism, Nazi saboteurs, and then postwar Communists again. But by 1950 enough "organized" criminal activity could be observed in action that the U.S. Senate launched the first of several investigations into racketeering. The Kefauver Committee held hearings in fourteen cities, heard testimony from more than 600 witnesses, and announced proof of the existence of the "Mafia." This was just what Hoover's nemesis, Harry Anslinger of the Narcotics Bureau, had been harping about for years—a sinister, nationwide criminal conspiracy, transplanted and transformed from its origins in Sicily to become the glue that bound the country's racketeers together as a national syndicate. After the "Americanization" of the Mafia under Luciano in the 1930s, the mob still was dominated by foreign-sounding names, but as a practical matter it had become an equal-opportunity employer that included men like Meyer Lansky, "Bugsy" Siegel and Moe Dalitz.

The Kefauver Committee largely reflected the beliefs already held by local crime commissions, the Bureau of Narcotics, and journalists, and it perpetuated every misconception, exaggeration, and myth voiced by law-enforcers and law-breakers alike. More significantly, it did so through the exciting new medium of television, which kept millions of Americans riveted to their black-and-white sets, and the resulting Mafia madness inspired countless books containing some of the most naive and crackpot descriptions of organized crime ever to thrill and chill a nation.

Probably the commission's greatest contribution was to give names to the mobsters who had managed to infiltrate the American labor movement and business community at nearly every level while Hoover's G-men were ridding the land of bank robbers. It seemed not to have occurred to the media that the Costellos, Anastasias, Genoveses, Lanskys, Siegels, Giancanas, and Accardos, who now stood exposed as the leaders of organized crime, were no longer the colorful young gangsters of the Prohibition era, but middle-aged or even elderly mob bosses who had been growing wealthy in the rackets all their adult lives with welcome anonymity. The Kefauver investigations segued into others that took similar delight in parading mobsters great and small before the TV cameras, much to the aggravation of Hoover, who still maintained that a large agglomeration of hoodlums did not a Mafia make.

The first major event to shake Hoover's convictions was the discovery in November 1957 of a mobster summit meeting near Apalachin, New York. A nosy state trooper (according to legend) observed a large number of expensive cars with out-of-state plates congregating at the rural estate of Joseph M. Barbara, and a police raid sent nearly a hundred hoodlum chiefs fleeing in all directions. The sixty or so who were arrested had Italian names that dispelled any remaining public doubt of a nationwide Mafia, providing much fodder for the journalistic community and the McClellan Committee, which already had decided to investigate mob control of the Teamsters Union.

If the Kefauver Committee witnesses had confirmed the existence of organized crime merely by "taking the Fifth" in response to nearly every question, the McClellan Committee struck gold in one Joseph Valachi, a low-ranking member of the Genovese crime family serving time on a narcotics conviction who believed he was marked for death anyway. When put on the stand in 1963, he enthralled the senators and the nation with graphic descriptions of life (and death) in an organized-crime family, confirming every suspicion, myth, and rumor about the Mafia. Much of his testimony was hearsay, shoptalk and legend, but it painted a thrilling picture of capos, capo regimes, and capo de tutti capis, as well as secret ceremonies with daggers and blood oaths of what one author called *The Brotherhood of Evil.* What Valachi called it was not the Mafia, however, but "La Cosa Nostra."

La Cosa Nostra translated as "our thing," or "this thing of ours," and did not suggest a single monolithic organization. Although it still was dominated by Italian-Americans, a better, if hardly catchy, term might have been "crime families," which usually mediated their differences and usually respected one another's territories and rackets (a glaring exception being the "Banana Wars" of the 1960s). And giving it that new name, right out of Valachi, spared Hoover the embarrassment of admitting he had been fooled.

One questionable explanation for Hoover's denials held that he had a tacit agreement to lay off organized crime because he was personally corrupt and accepted favors from racketeers (especially their hospitality and their willingness to write off his gambling losses). Another was that Hoover had no wish to turn over rocks that might reveal ties between organized crime and U.S. senators or congressmen, especially any who might hold the bureau's purse strings. A more ominous explanation to surface later contended that Hoover was an active but homophobic homosexual, living in sin with his faithful Clyde Tolson, and that the Mafia had photographic or other incriminating evidence it was holding over his head.

But there were several practical reasons the FBI had seemed to ignore organized crime, or OC as it was now becoming known, and Hoover's refusal to acknowledge it may have been more a personal idiosyncrasy and public relations consideration than a bureau blind spot. While the New Deal Justice Department's "war on crime" supposedly included racketeers, the fact was that Attorney General Homer Cummings's celebrated Twelve-Point Program of federalized crime control did not include laws that gave the FBI effective jurisdiction over some of the new and increasingly sophisticated forms of crime emerging in the post-outlaw era. Moreover, Hoover primarily was an advocate of police professionalism who honestly wanted to depoliticize law enforcement, offer advanced training at an academy staffed by experts, provide centralized record-keeping and criminal-identification facilities, and maintain a state-of-the-art crime laboratory that could serve the scientific needs of law enforcers from the largest metropolitan police agencies down to one-man departments in the smallest towns.

That was Hoover's personal mission, but he also was a master publicist who had honed his agency into a highly independent, squeaky-clean parody of itself. He did not relish a campaign against anything as amorphous as organized crime, which would require collaboration with other state and federal agencies, weaken his voice in policy matters, and loosen his control of his own men, who still tended to lord it over the locals by not reciprocating with bureau information. When Repeal was pending before 1933 and Prohibition enforcement was transferred to the Justice Department, Hoover had barely avoided contaminating his new Division of Investigation with an army of notoriously inept and corrupt Prohibition Bureau agents from the Treasury Department. He created an enforcement agency, which included Eliot Ness, but persuaded Cummings to keep it separate from his G-men, who had won the public's hearts and minds and soon would be members of the Federal Bureau of Investigation.

Also, Hoover's bureau had created for itself an image of invincibility based on tidy statistics of ever-greater numbers of fugitives captured and convicted. This was no great feat given the bureau's selection of targets and increasingly effective investigative tools, but the success of the FBI in the eyes of the public probably did more than anything else to restore faith in the national government, whose other reforms were less tangible and certainly less interesting.

Another consideration was the rivalry between Hoover and Harry Anslinger, director of the Bureau of Narcotics, whose "reefer madness" mentality had been trying to make the Mafia a bogeyman since the 1930s. Indeed, Hoover's counterparts in other federal agencies conspired to embarrass him at every opportunity, partly out of resentment of Hoover's self-promotion and partly out of plain jealousy, making inter-agency cooperation all but impossible.

So while the bureau could have gotten into the game by way of several federal laws that might have inconvenienced organized mobsters, these were riddled with loopholes that made serious prosecution efforts difficult. Then the marching orders issued by Attorney General Robert Kennedy put Hoover on the spot. He had no choice but to acknowledge that his Top Hoodlums had a closer working relationship than previously realized, and that this now looked like a job for the FBI.

At the same time, Congress armed the Justice Department with new wiretap authority and a new law specifically tailored to deal with the problem—the Interstate Transportation in Aid of Racketeering Act. Probably for reasons of ego, Hoover still shunned the word "Mafia" and went instead with the term used by Valachi, La Cosa Nostra, which was not inconsistent with Hoover's Top Hoodlum program. So the FBI's version of the Mafia became the LCN, the top hoodlums of which had been tracked by the bureau for years, he could say, as a service to local authorities.

Once the bureau was in the business, its investigations increased steadily from 131 in 1965 to 813 in 1972, the year of Hoover's death. Two years previously, Congress had passed a new piece of legislation that, when its important provisions survived the usual Supreme Court challenges and when a newly motivated bureau learned the tricks of using it, struck fear into the hearts of organized crime families. After 1970, confronted by the Racketeer-Influenced and Corrupt Organizations Act, the RICO law, combined with some successful prosecutions and a general disintegration of gang discipline, the underworld machinery that had operated smoothly for more than twenty years began showing its age. Even before the federal organized-crime task forces demonstrated the full power of RICO, the bureau could point to some prosecutions that had symbolic importance, if not much jail time. Most were young gangsters in the late twenties and thirties who had risen from gunman or driver to "middle management" and finally to mob leadership at the time of their convictions:

June 1, 1965—Chicago's Sam Giancana, contempt of court

November 10, 1967—Johnny Dioguardi, federal bankruptcy fraud

March 8, 1968—New England's Ray Patriarca, racketeering

March 21, 1968—New Jersey's Sam DeCavalcante, extortion

August 8, 1968—Buffalo's Stefano Magaddino, interstate gambling

July 9, 1969—Los Angeles' Nicolo Licata, jailed for contempt

May 9, 1970—Chicago's John Cerone, interstate gambling

April 26, 1972—St. Louis's Anthony Giordano, interstate gambling

Perhaps the best explanation for Hoover's slow response to organized crime was that he had become less a crook-catcher than an image maker and an empire builder. After his death, a top-ranking bureau official revealed that when the Apalachin meeting left the FBI open to criticism and embarrassment, Hoover called on him with naive questions about the Mafia and accepted his offer to conduct a major study of organized crime. His impression was that Hoover truly didn't understand the nature or extent of the problem. Others attempting to discuss policy issues found Hoover frozen in time, still stalking the ghosts of Dillinger and Nelson and "Machine Gun" Kelly; and in his dotage he would exhaust the patience of guests by revisiting those glory days with accounts of the bureau's triumphs over the outlaws who had made the G-men famous, and vice versa.

With Hoover finally in his grave, the FBI waged full-scale war on organized crime, even creating a chronology, or perhaps a genealogy, in 1987 of the rise and fall of America's top crime bosses since 1920. It still did not use the term Mafia, except in an introductory reference, and steadfastly referred to the crime families of the U.S. as the LCN. Its introduction provides interesting insight into the bureau's conception of the history and structure of organized crime, including its misconceptions. Whether the 1890 murder of New Orleans Police Chief Hennessy was a "Mafia" crime, as the chronology asserts, is open to debate, but LCN remained in vogue until the awareness of Jewish and other non-Italian or Sicilian gangsters brought OC—Organized Crime—into vogue. The chronology still buys the Valachi account of the1931 purge known as the Night of the Sicilian Vespers, as memorialized in the movie The Godfather, despite the discovery by some nit-picking historians that it never happened.

The following is the FBI's somewhat belated, and not entirely accurate, account of the supposed origins of the American LCN and historical guide that runs from 1920 to 1986 but here includes only events of the twenties and thirties.

CHRONOLOGICAL HISTORY OF LA COSA NOSTRA IN THE UNITED STATES

On October 15, 1890, David Hennessy, Superintendent of Police of New Orleans, was ambushed by assassins. In the aftermath of his assassination, a large number of immigrants from Italy and Sicily were indiscriminately arrested, some for no more reason than that they did not speak English well.

On November 20 of that year indictments were returned against 19 prisoners. On February 16, 1891, a trial of some of the defendants began. The trial lasted until the middle of March and was covered extensively by the press. The jury went out on March 12, 1891. The following afternoon the jury declared itself deadlocked as to three defendants, and it found the others not guilty. Since additional charges were pending, those found not guilty, as well as the others, were remanded to the Parish Prison.

On March 14, 1891, a mob marched to Orleans Parish Prison, where the warden, realizing the futility of resistance, released the 19 prisoners, so that they might have a chance to hide. This tactic saved the lives of eight of them, but the remaining 11 were shot or hanged or both. Of the 11 who were lynched. Three had been acquitted, three had been declared subjects of a mistrial, and five had not been tried at all.

The Hennessy killing and the subsequent murders created perhaps the first significant public awareness of the La Cosa Nostra (LCN). Newspapers nationwide reported the killings, and relations between. Italy and the United

States were strained for a time. The New Orleans grand jury investigating the incident reported that "our research has developed the existence of the secret organization styled 'Mafia'. . . . Officers of the Mafia and many of its members were not known. Among them are men born in this city of Italian origin. . . . The larger number of the society is composed of Italians and Sicilians. . . ." (we know today that the LCN is strictly a North American phenomenon and distinctly different from its cousin organizations in Europe).

Because of the rapidly changing face of the LCN in the United States (changing from the rough characters of the early years to the sophisticated influential members of today), an easy reference guide was needed. This guide was deemed necessary in that it will assist all personnel assigned to the Organized Crime Program in developing a working background of the LCN. . . .

1920–1929

January 16, 1920—The Eighteenth Amendment to the Constitution became effective, making Prohibition a national law. The following day, the Volstead (or Prohibition Enforcement) Act became effective. Although organized crime had existed in the United States prior to this time, it was the bonanza of Prohibition which enabled the small, but powerful, LCN to capitalize upon its international contacts, its reputation for ruthlessness, and—above all—its rigidly disciplined structure of cooperating gangs to establish the position of unrivaled eminence it holds in the American underworld today. [1]

May 11, 1920—James (Big Jim) Colosimo, Chicago Camorra head, was shot and killed in his restaurant. He was succeeded by Johnny Torrio. [2]

February 6, 1921—Vito Guardalabene, boss of the Milwaukee LCN Family, died of natural causes. He was succeeded by his son, Peter Guardalabene.

May 12, 1921—Anthony D'Andrea, boss of the Chicago LCN Family, was shot to death during the early morning hours while returning from a card game. He was succeeded by Mike Merlo. [3]

May 6, 1922—Pelligrino Scaglia, member of the Colorado LCN Family, was shot to death, precipitating such a crisis in the Colorado and Kansas City Families that a "general assembly" of LCN leaders had to be called in New York to resolve the dispute. [4]

July 9, 1922—Joseph Peter DiCarlo, boss of the Buffalo Family, died of natural causes. He was succeeded by Stefano (Steve) Magaddino. [5]

August 11, 1922—Umberto Valenti, alleged former "right arm" of New York City LCN boss Salvatore D'Aquila, was shot to death on the running board of an automobile after his friends had conducted an intensive campaign to get D'Aquila to cancel the "contract" he had issued for Valenti's murder.

November 8, 1924—Mike Merlo, boss of the Chicago Family, died of natural causes. He was succeeded by Antonio Lombardo. [6]

November 10, 1924—Dean O'Banion, Chicago gang leader, was shot to death in his flower shop while preparing the floral arrangements for Mike Merlo's funeral. Since he had been head of one of the major independent mobs then competing with the LCN in the power struggle known as the Prohibition "beer wars," O'Banion's death marked an important milestone in the LCN's march to eventual domination of the American underworld. Indicative of the bloodiness of this struggle is the fact that more than 700 gangland slayings occurred in the Chicago area alone between 1920 and 1933, with 76 being recorded in the year 1926 and 72 in 1928. [7]

January 24, 1925—Chicago Camorra head Johnny Torrio was shot and seriously wounded. He subsequently resigned his position and was succeeded by Alphonse (Scarface Al) Capone. [8]

March 28, 1927—Joseph Amato, boss of the Milwaukee Family (having succeeded Peter Guardalabene in approximately 1924), died of natural causes. He was succeeded by Joseph Vallone.

October 13, 1927—Joseph Lonardo, boss of the Cleveland Family, was shot and killed—along with his brother John—in a local barbershop. He was succeeded by Salvatore Todaro. [9]

July 1, 1928—New York mobster Frankie Yale (true name: Uale) was shot to death while taking a Sunday afternoon drive in Brooklyn, New York. [10]

September 7, 1928—Antonio Lombardo, boss of the Chicago Family, was shot and killed on a downtown sidewalk. The importance of Lombardo's death is that it is said to have sealed the merger of the LCN and the Camorra in the Chicago area. Reportedly, Al Capone, head of the Chicago branch of the Camorra, was offered membership and a ranking position in the LCN if he would have Lombardo murdered. [11]

October 10, 1928—Salvatore (Toto) D'Aquila, head of what is now the Carlo Gambino Family and allegedly "boss of all bosses," was shot and killed while standing beside his automobile in New York City. He was succeeded as Family head by Frank Scalise.

November 4, 1928—New York City gambling figure Arnold Rothstein was shot at the Park Central Hotel and died two days later. [12]

December 5, 1928—More than 20 LCN leaders were arrested in the early morning hours at a Cleveland hotel. Two, Joe Profaci and Joe Magliocco, were among those later in attendance at the 1957 Apalachin, New York, meeting. [13]

February 14, 1929—Six followers of George "Bugs" Moran and a visiting optometrist were murdered in a Chicago garage (reportedly by members of the Capone mob) in what has come to be known as the "St. Valentine's Day Massacre." [14]

May 16, 1929—Al Capone, boss of the Chicago Family, was arrested by the Philadelphia Police Department on a charge of carrying concealed weapons shortly after leaving what he described as a 3-day "peace conference" of leading mobsters in an Atlantic City, New Jersey, hotel. [15]

June 11, 1929—Salvatore (Black Sam) Todaro, boss of the Cleveland Family, was shot to death while approaching a parked car. He was succeeded by Joe Porrello.

August 6, 1929—Steve Monastero, boss of the Pittsburgh Family, was shot to death at the entrance to Allegheny General Hospital. He was succeeded by Joseph Siragusa.

1930–1939

February 20, 1930—Carlo T. Piranio, leader of the old Dallas, Texas, Family, died of natural causes. He was succeeded by his brother, Joseph T. Piranio.

February 26, 1930—Gaetano (Tommy) Reina, boss of what later became the Thomas Lucchese Family, was shot and killed leaving a building in New York City. He was succeeded by Joseph Pinzolo. The murders of D'Aquila and Reina (allegedly by followers of Giuseppe Masseria) are said to have been two of the main causes of the bloody Castellammarese gangland war that raged throughout much of 1930 and 1931. [16]

May 31, 1930—Gaspare Milazzo, boss of the Detroit Family, was shot to death in a fish market. His successor is not known. [17]

July 5, 1930—Joe Porrello, boss of the Cleveland Family, was shot to death—along with his bodyguard—in Frank Milano's restaurant. He was succeeded by Milano. [18]

September 5, 1930—Joseph Pinzolo, boss of the former Reina Family in New York City, was shot to death in a Manhattan office building. He was succeeded by Thomas Gagliano and, later, by Thomas Lucchese. Lucchese was arrested for Pinzolo's murder, but the grand jury failed to indict him. [19]

October 23, 1930—Joseph Aiello, former underboss of the Chicago Family, was shot and killed leaving a friend's apartment house. [20]

November 5, 1930—Stephen Ferrigno and Manfredi Mineo, top aides to Giuseppe Masseria, were shot to death in New York City by followers of rival gang leader Salvatore Maranzano. [21]

April 15, 1930—Giuseppe Masseria, "boss of all bosses," was shot to death in a Coney Island, New York, restaurant. [22] He was succeeded as Family head by Salvatore "Lucky" Lucania [23] and as "boss of all bosses" by Salvatore Maranzano. After Masseria's murder, there were significant changes in the LCN's structure. Individual groups became known as families and the fathers became "bosses." Regional designations were dropped and the families took the names of their original leaders. More important were organizational shakeups during 1931. Lucania took over the Masseria (Napolitana) Family, with Frank Costello as underboss; Vito Genovese was a trusted associate, and later became the boss and the organization was known as the Genovese family. Joseph Profaci retained control of the Villabate group that now bore his name and later became the Joseph Colombo Family. Philip Mangano assumed control of the Mineo (Palermitana) Family, which later became the Carlo Gambino Family. Gaetano Gagliano became boss of the Reina (Siciliani) Family, later identified as the Thomas Lucchese Family. Joseph Bonanno became underboss in the Maranzano (Castellammare) Family which eventually bore his name. [24]

September 10, 1931—Salvatore Maranzano, successor to Masseria, was shot and stabbed to death in his Manhattan office building by four members of Meyer Lansky's Jewish mob posing as police officers. [25] This assistance rendered to one of the warring factions in the Castellammarese War consolidated Lansky's alliance with the victorious segment and accounts for much of the respect he enjoyed in the underworld. A second, and still more important, result of Maranzano's death was the abolition of the old title "boss of all bosses" and the establishment of the Commission system to assign territories, adjudicate disputes, and exercise internal discipline. Members included: Salvatore Lucania (known variously throughout the underworld as "Charley Lucky" and "Lucky Luciano"); Joe Profaci; Thomas Gagliano; Joseph Bonanno; Vincent Mangano (who had deposed Frank Scalise as head of the old D'Aquila Family); Frank Milano, of Cleveland; and Al Capone, of Chicago. [26]

September 13, 1931—Joseph Siragusa, boss of the Pittsburgh Family, was shot to death in his home. He was succeeded by John Bazzano.

October 15, 1931—Joe Ardizzonne, boss of the Los Angeles Family, disappeared and is presumed to have been murdered. He was succeeded by Jack Dragna. Following the death of Salvatore Maranzano, a wave of gangland killings, known as the "Sicilian Vespers," swept the country, allegedly including both Ardizzonne and the previously mentioned Siragusa. [27]

October 17, 1931—Al Capone, boss of the Chicago Family, was convicted on Federal charges of income tax evasion. He was fined $50,000 and sentenced to 11 years in prison.

December 18, 1931—Jack (Legs) Diamond, New York City hoodlum, was shot to death in an Albany, New York, boardinghouse after reportedly refusing to take sides in the Castellammarese gangland war. His murder is said to have been committed by an unidentified member of the Vito Genovese faction. [28]

February 8, 1932—Vincent (Mad Dog) Coll, New York City hoodlum, was shot to death in a Manhattan telephone booth, reportedly at the instructions of LCN boss Salvatore Lucania. [29]

July 29, 1932—John, Arthur and James Volpe—notorious underworld figures and bootleggers—were shot to death in a Pittsburgh coffee shop, allegedly at the orders of John Bazzano, boss of the Pittsburgh Family.

August 8, 1932—The body of John Bazzano, boss of the Pittsburgh Family, was found in the middle of a Brooklyn, New York, street—strangled and stabbed to death and sewn into a burlap sack. Bazzano was reportedly murdered when, called to New York City to explain the slayings of the three Volpe brothers, he replied that what he did in Pittsburgh was no concern to anyone else in the organization. Bazzano was succeeded by Vincenzo Capizzi as head of the family.

June 17, 1933—FBI Agent Raymond J. Caffrey, 3 police officers, and hoodlum Frank Nash were killed in the Union Station parking lot during the infamous Kansas City Massacre. Reportedly the Kansas City LCN Family declined a request that it participate in the operation. One of the gunmen (Vernon C. Miller, an associate of New York City mobster Louis "Lepke" Buchalter) was found murdered in Detroit on November 29, 1933, allegedly killed by followers of New Jersey gang leader Abner Zwillman. [30]

December 5, 1933—The Twenty-first Amendment to the Constitution became law, repealing Prohibition. The resulting end of their bonanza caught mob leaders with large hoards of wealth, vast fleets of trucks, and whole armies of trained gunmen at their disposal. Most branched out into other fields of criminal endeavor (such as gambling, loan sharking, narcotics, labor racketeering, etc.), whereas quite a few added to their flow of illicit wealth by investing their funds in a succession of legitimate investments, ranging from real estate and manufacturing plants to hospitals and theatrical agencies. It also was at this time that many racket leaders tried to play down their past histories and adopt an air of pseudorespectability in their local communities.

January 1, 1934—Fiorello H. LaGuardia was sworn in as mayor of New York City and immediately declared war on organized crime. Between February and May, more than 2,000 slot machines controlled by LCN member Frank Costello and his partner, "Dandy Phil" Kastel, were seized by local police, with LaGuardia serving as committing magistrate. Costello and Kastel decided to move the center of their slot machine operations and, in August 1935, founded the Bayou Novelty Company in New Orleans. [31]

July 10, 1934—John Lazia, boss of the Kansas City Family, was fatally shot in front of his residence during the early morning hours. He died later that afternoon and was succeeded by Charles V. Carrollo. [32]

September 19, 1934—Ferdinand (The Shadow) Boccia was shot to death in Brooklyn, New York. Subsequently developed as a prime suspect in the slaying, Vito Genovese fled to Italy and did not return until after World War II.

January 30, 1935—Frank Milano, former boss of the Cleveland Family, entered Mexico. He was granted a permanent immigration visa on April 13, 1942. He was succeeded as boss by Alfred (Big Al) Polizzi. [33]

August 22, 1935—Vincenzo Troia, formerly a close associate of "boss of all bosses" Salvatore Maranzano and himself a nominee for the position following the death of Giuseppe Masseria in 1931, was shot to death for allegedly plotting to seize control of the Newark, New Jersey, Family.

October 23, 1935—Arthur "Dutch Schultz" Flegenheimer, a participant in the Castellammarese gangland war of the early 1930s, was fatally shot in a Newark restaurant after an "open contract" had been issued by LCN officials for his murder. He died the following evening. [34]

February 15, 1936—Vincent Gebardi, better known as "Machine Gun" Jack McGurn, was shot to death at a Chicago bowling alley. [35]

May 19, 1936—Mrs. Nicholas Longo, sister and next-door neighbor of Buffalo Commission member Steve Magaddino, was killed by an early morning bomb blast intended for her brother.

June 7, 1936—Salvatore Lucania ("Lucky" Luciano) and 8 associates were convicted on 62 counts each of compulsory prostitution charges. Luciano was sentenced to a prison term of 30–50 years. Succeeded by Frank Costello, Luciano served more than 9 years before New York Governor Thomas Dewey recommended clemency. He noted that Luciano had cooperated with the Armed Forces during World War II when the Navy, fearing sabotage, had asked his help in gathering intelligence and controlling the docks. Luciano was paroled and immediately deported. [36]

August 17, 1936—"Big Nose" John Avena (also known as John Nazzone), boss of the Philadelphia Family, was shot to death while talking to a friend on a Philadelphia street corner. He was succeeded by Joseph Bruno.

January 8, 1937—The Cuban Cabinet approved plans to place certain gambling operations under control of the army, headed by Colonel (later President) Fulgencio Batista. Shortly thereafter, New York City gambling czar Meyer Lansky led a vanguard of American hoodlums imported to help operate the major Cuban casinos. Although World War II and Batista's removal from office during the latter part of the 1940s drove Lansky to seek greener pastures (such as those beginning to blossom in the Nevada desert), Batista returned to power in March 1952, and soon asked Lansky to come back and "add a touch of class" to the Cuban operations.

June 14, 1937—Francesco Lanza, boss of the San Francisco Family and father of the future boss,

James Lanza, died in San Francisco of natural causes. He was succeeded by Anthony J. Lima. [37]

October 5, 1937—Nicolo Gentile, formerly a high-ranking member of families in Kansas City, Pittsburgh, and New York City, was arrested at New Orleans in a nationwide narcotics raid involving more than 80 subjects. Gentile later jumped bond and fled back to Sicily to avoid standing trial. [38]

May 2, 1938—Detroit gang leader Joe Tocco was fatally shot in the back and died the following day. Reportedly, his death was one of the major factors leading to the ultimate consolidation of power in the Detroit area by LCN Commission member Joe Zerilli.

August 24, 1939—New York City hoodlum Louis "Lepke" Buchalter, after 25 months as a fugitive on Federal Antitrust charges, surrendered to FBI Director J. Edgar Hoover in New York City. Buchalter was subsequently turned over to local authorities and executed for murder. [39]

October 20, 1939—Charles V. Carrollo, boss of the Kansas City Family, was incarcerated in the United States Penitentiary at Leavenworth, Kansas, for violating Federal tax laws. Reportedly, he was succeeded by Charles Binaggio. [40]

November 16, 1939—Al Capone was released from Federal custody and committed to a hospital for treatment of paresis. [41]

[Either the "LCN" suspended operations for the next two years, or the FBI had its hands full scrutinizing Communists and the German-American Bund. The next entry in the chronology is for November 12, 1941, when Abe Reles, a prime witness in New York's investigation of "Murder, Incorporated," fell or was pushed to his death from a guarded hotel room in Coney Island, New York.]

NOTES

[1] Informer Joe Valachi told the FBI in 1962 that the national network of Italian-American crime families, commonly called "the Mafia" by the public, was known to its members as Cosa Nostra, an Italian expression meaning "Our Thing." This may be only a generic phrase used mainly by members of the New York families. In Buffalo and Boston, the Italian crime families were called, respectively, "the Arm" and "the Office." No one had ever heard the words "Cosa Nostra" in Chicago, whose racketeers referred to their organization, the former Al Capone mob, as "the Syndicate" or "the Outfit." When Valachi testified publicly about the organization's existence, on the orders of Attorney General Robert F. Kennedy, the name became a convenient hook for FBI Director J. Edgar Hoover, who always had denied the existence of the Mafia but now was being forced into the battle against organized crime. The FBI added a "La" to the name and began publicizing the crime families as La Cosa Nostra, which they abbreviated in official communications to "LCN."

Since Valachi, law enforcement agencies, reporters, and writers frequently have used the name Cosa Nostra to differentiate between the Italian-American crime families and the original Mafia of Sicily. The issue became more confused in the 1980s when informers such as Tommaso Buscetta revealed that Sicilian Mafiosi had become more structured because of the expanding drug trade and also were calling their organization Cosa Nostra, possibly learning that from American crime figures who were being deported.

The rise of organized crime to prominence during Prohibition owes much to its international connections, especially with the Sicilian Mafia. Italian-American crime families gained a large boost in membership in the 1920s owing to Mussolini's persecution of the Mafia in Sicily. Another advantage Italian mobsters enjoyed was many otherwise honest Italian-Americans had home stills and wine-making apparatus in their homes before Prohibition. The Italians thus had a head start in bootlegging over other ethnic groups.

Considering the prominence and power of the Chinese Triads, the modern-day Colombian drug cartels, the Yakuza gangs of Japan, the Hell's Angels and other motorcycle gangs, the Mafia of Sicily, and the Russian and Mexican "Mafias" in the United States and other countries, the "unrivaled eminence" of La Cosa Nostra is now questionable.

[2] The Camorra is or was a criminal organization in southern Italy, largely based in Naples. By various accounts it was founded in the Naples prison system in the nineteenth century, though some authorities trace its ancestry to the Garduna, a criminal society founded in Seville, Spain, in 1417 and later transplanted to Italy as hired assassins for the Bourbons. Some Camorra families were active in New York in the early 1900s and warred with Sicilian (Mafia) families before the groups finally made peace and merged about the time of World War I. There is no evidence that the Camorra existed in Chicago, or that Colosimo or his successors, Torrio and Capone, were ever members of that organization. Colosimo was a native of Calabria, not Naples, and was known at the time as a South Side vice lord. Many members of his organization were not even Italian, much less Camorra members. Colosimo was murdered in the vestibule of his restaurant, the famous Colosimo's restaurant and nightclub at 2126 South Wabash in Chicago. The motive for Colosimo's slaying is believed to have been his unwillingness to enter the profitable field of bootlegging. Torrio's killer probably was Frankie Yale, a Brooklyn gangster for whom Torrio and Capone had once worked. Yale, true name Francesco Ioele, often spelled Uale, was in Chicago at the time of Colosimo's murder and was questioned but released. Upon assuming control of Colosimo's gang, Torrio made Al Capone his partner.

[3] D'Andrea was shot to death outside his home at 902 South Ashland. He was supported by the South Side Genna brothers' gang and recently had campaigned for election as alderman of the "Bloody Nineteenth" Ward, losing to John "Johnny de Pow" Powers, who had the support of rival gangsters. D'Andrea probably was

killed by supporters of Powers. D'Andrea and his successor, Mike Merlo, may never have heard of "Cosa Nostra," but both were leaders of the local branch of the Unione Siciliana, a legally chartered fraternal organization for the betterment of Sicilian immigrants that had been founded in Chicago in 1895. This organization, which changed its name to the Italo-American National Union in 1926, had been taken over by Italian gangsters in some cities. In Chicago, which had 40,000 dues-paying members, gangsters often fought for control of the Unione, whose national leader was considered to be Brooklyn mobster Frankie Yale.

[4] By the early 1930s, Denver's Italian underworld was under the control of Joe "Little Caesar" Roma, whose rule was challenged by the Carlino brothers of Pueblo. Sam Carlino and a henchman named James Colletti were shot to death on May 8, 1931. On September 13, Pete Carlino, known as the "Al Capone of Southern Colorado," was found shot dead outside Pueblo. Both these criminal "families" were Calabrian, not Sicilian. Joe Roma nearly survived Prohibition but was murdered on February 18, 1933. The Smaldone brothers, Eugene, Clyde, and Clarence, eventually emerged as Denver's leading crime bosses.

[5] Magaddino, a cousin of Joseph Bonanno, would rule the Buffalo Family until his death by natural causes in 1974, the longest reign of any Cosa Nostra boss.

[6] Merlo was president of the Chicago chapter of the Unione Siciliana. He may not have been boss of an actual crime family, but he was influential in the underworld, long keeping the peace between the Torrio-Capone mob and the North Side mob led by Dean O'Banion, an uneasy truce that collapsed altogether after Merlo's death by cancer. Merlo's immediate successor as Unione president was Angelo Genna, a Torrio-Capone ally who would be shotgunned to death by the O'Banion gang on May 26, 1925.

[7] "Dion" was the baptismal name of Dean Charles O'Banion. O'Banion was shaking hands with a supposed friend who gripped his gun hand while two companions shot him to death. The murder occurred in O'Banion's flower shop at 738 North State Street. Brooklyn gangster Frankie Yale was once more in Chicago (ostensibly to attend Mike Merlo's funeral) and was a suspect in the O'Banion slaying. Five years of gang wars followed. Earl "Hymie" Weiss, O'Banion's successor, attacked both Torrio and Capone before he himself was killed on October 11, 1926. Vincent "The Schemer" Drucci was killed by a Chicago policeman on April 4, 1927, and his North Side successor, George "Bugs" Moran, would flee Chicago after the 1929 St. Valentine's Day Massacre.

[8] Torrio was born in Naples in 1882. Al Capone was born in Brooklyn, New York in 1899, the son of immigrants from Naples. Despite their Neapolitan backgrounds, however, there is no evidence that either Torrio or Capone was a member of the Camorra, or that a Chicago branch of that organization even existed. Many members of their mob were not Italian, and Torrio and Capone probably were leaders of an independent crime syndicate, though they certainly had connections with other Italian mobsters. Joe Valachi, the son of Neapolitan immigrants, claimed to have met a New York Camorra boss in Sing Sing Prison in the 1920s, Allessandro Vollero, who offered to send him to a former Brooklyn Neapolitan who had moved to Chicago—Al Capone.

After his abdication from the Chicago rackets, Johnny Torrio served a brief jail term in the northern suburb of Waukegan for Prohibition violations, vacationed in Europe, then resumed a career in organized crime in New York, becoming a close associate of "Lucky" Luciano and "Dutch" Schultz. Convicted of income tax evasion in 1939, Torrio served a brief prison sentence and then apparently retired from the rackets. He died of a heart attack in Brooklyn on April 16, 1957.

[9] Joseph "Big Joe" Lonardo and his brother John were shot to death on October 13, 1927, at the Porrello brothers' barbershop on Woodland Avenue in Cleveland. Joe Porrello would succeed "Big Joe" Lonardo and Salvatore Todaro as boss of the Cleveland Family, only to be murdered himself on July 5, 1930.

[10] Yale was shot with two Thompson submachine guns. It was New York's first machine-gun murder, leading to immediate suspicion that Chicago's Al Capone, a former ally of Yale, was responsible. Moreover, a Thompson found in an abandoned getaway car was traced to Chicago gun shop owner Peter von Frantzius, and slugs from Yale's body would turn out to match some taken from St. Valentine's Day Massacre victims when an arsenal was found later at the home of Fred Burke. Yale had been interfering with liquor shipments to Chicago, had designs on Capone's dog tracks, and supported Capone's rival, Joseph Aiello.

[11] Antonio (Tony) Lombardo was the Capone-backed head of the Chicago Unione Siciliana. Capone warred with Sicilian gang leader Joseph Aiello for control of the Unione Siciliana, and it was probably Aiello, not Capone, who ordered Lombardo's murder. If there was a Cosa Nostra family in Chicago, Aiello probably was its leader and was unlikely to have offered "membership and a ranking position" to his enemy. Aiello joined forces with another Capone enemy, George "Bugs" Moran, and also ordered the murder of Tony Lombardo's successor, Pasqualino (Patsy) Lolordo, on January 8, 1929. Again, there is no evidence that the Capone was a member of the Camorra or any other secret society.

[12] More than a mere "gambling figure," Arnold Rothstein was the "Big Bankroll" of the New York underworld. Alleged mastermind of the 1919 World Series fix, Rothstein also controlled the Democratic political machine at Tammany Hall, financed the first international rumrunning shipments, and was a major narcotics trafficker and loan shark. Many of New York's leading underworld figures, including Jack "Legs" Diamond, Irving "Waxey Gordon" Wexler, Arthur "Dutch Schultz" Flegenheimer, and Charles "Lucky" Luciano, got their start working for Rothstein. He was far more important than any Italian gangster in New York at that time, something the FBI seems to have overlooked in its efforts to tie everything in U.S. organized crime to the testimony of Joe Valachi.

[13] Twenty-two Sicilian gangsters were arrested on December 5, 1928, at the Hotel Statler in Cleveland. Some were local men, and the others came from New York, Chicago, Buffalo, Tampa, Newark, Detroit, and St. Louis. Newspaper accounts would later describe this as a meeting of the "Grand Council of the Mafia."

[14] The St. Valentine's Day Massacre occurred at the S.M.C. Cartage Company garage at 2122 North Clark Street in Chicago and was the result of four years of off-and-on warfare between the

Capone Syndicate and the North Side mob formerly headed by Dean O'Banion. The victims were Albert Weinshank, Adam Heyer, James Clark, John May, and Frank and Peter Gusenberg of the North Side Gang, plus a visiting optometrist friend, Dr. Reinhart Schwimmer. The garage was a liquor depot for the gang. Some of the killers, believed to have been members of the Capone mob, wore police uniforms, and the victims apparently allowed themselves to be disarmed in the mistaken belief it was a police raid. They then were torn apart by machine-gun fire. The major intended victim, gang leader George "Bugs" Moran, was running late and thus survived, but he was nevertheless finished as a gangland power. No one was ever convicted of the St. Valentine's Day Massacre, but the two Thompson submachine guns used in the slaughter were later recovered from the Michigan hideout of Fred "Killer" Burke, a sometime bank robber and Capone torpedo. Ballistic tests proved these were the massacre guns and that one also had been used in the 1928 murder of Frankie Yale, but Burke was never tried for the massacre. He was later convicted of the murder of a policeman and sentenced to life in the Michigan state prison, where he died in 1940.

[15] On May 13–15, 1929, mobsters from New York, Chicago, Kansas City, Detroit, Cleveland, Newark, Boston, and Philadelphia met at the President Hotel in Atlantic City to arrange for the peaceful resolution of disputes and reconsolidate bootlegging and racketeering. Many historians regard this meeting as the beginning of the national crime syndicate. Besides Capone, delegates to the conference included Frank Nitti, Jake Guzik, and "Polack Joe" Saltis of Chicago and New York gangsters Johnny Torrio, Charles "Lucky" Luciano, Frank Costello, Joe Adonis, Arthur "Dutch Schultz" Flegenheimer, Meyer Lansky, Benjamin "Bugsy" Siegel, and Larry Fay. The meeting almost certainly was called in response to the intense heat resulting from such gangland violence as the St. Valentine's Day Massacre. After the meeting, Capone and his bodyguard, Frank Rio, took a train to Philadelphia where they were met by detectives and arrested for carrying guns. Both pleaded guilty and were given a year in prison. The speedy trial and long sentence were applauded by Chicagoans dismayed by the massacre, although many thought the arrests were prearranged (the detectives had been guests at Capone's estate in Florida) as a reprimand or for his protection, as Capone continued to conduct business from a separate and luxuriously furnished cell.

[16] Reina was killed by shotgun fire at 1522 Sheridan Avenue, allegedly on the order of his supposed ally, Giuseppe "Joe the Boss" Masseria. Masseria wanted control of Reina's near monopoly of New York City ice distribution, a profitable racket in the days before electric refrigeration. Masseria appointed his own man, Joseph Pinzolo, as boss of Reina's family. Reina's daughter later married Joe Valachi.

[17] Gaspare Milazzo and his bodyguard, Sam "Sasha" Parina, were shot to death at the Vernor Fish Market on May 31, 1930. Some crime historians believe the murders were the result of a feud between Milazzo and rival bootlegger Chester "Big Chet" LeMare, who was himself gunned down on February 6, 1931.

Milazzo's eventual successor was Joseph Zerilli, who continued as boss of the Detroit Family until his death by natural causes in 1977. Peter Licavoli and his brother, Thomas "Yonnie" Licavoli, who extended the gang's operations to Toledo, were much better known in the 1930s than Zerilli. It also has been alleged that the Detroit family was long governed by a "ruling council" consisting of Zerilli, Peter Licavoli, William "Black Bill" Tocco, John "Papa John" Priziola, and Angelo Meli. Many of the Detroit Family originally came from St. Louis and are believed to have been "imported" as gunmen by the Jewish Purple Gang. The Purple Gang largely disintegrated in the early 1930s from internal strife, the murder convictions of several prominent members, and encroachment by the Italians, who controlled the Purples' old territory after Prohibition was repealed.

[18] Joe Porrello and bodyguard Sam Tilocco were shot to death at Frank Milano's Venetian Restaurant at Mayfield Road and East 126th Street in Cleveland on July 5, 1930. Milano was closely allied to the Cleveland Syndicate, a powerful Jewish mob headed by Morris "Moe" Dalitz, Louis Rothkopf, Morris Kleinman, and Samuel Tucker.

[19] Joseph Pinzolo was shot to death in the offices of Thomas "Three-Finger Brown" Lucchese's California Dry Fruit Importers, Suite 1007 of the Brokaw Building at 1487 Broadway. Pinzolo had been appointed boss of the former Reina Family by Giuseppe "Joe the Boss" Masseria, self-styled "boss of bosses" of the New York Cosa Nostra. The family lieutenants, including Tommaso (Tom) Gagliano, Thomas Lucchese, and Dominick "The Gap" Petrilli, rebelled against outside leadership, according to the later testimony of Joe Valachi, and murdered Pinzolo. They then joined forces with Masseria's enemy Salvatore Maranzano.

[20] If Capone was boss of the Chicago Family, as the FBI alleges, then Aiello could not have been the underboss, as they were enemies. Aiello, with his brothers, headed a Sicilian gang that may have qualified as a Cosa Nostra family, had allied himself with "Bugs" Moran's North Siders, and was Capone's rival for control of the Unione Siciliana (by now called the Italo-American National Union). At any rate, Aiello walked out of the apartment of his henchman, Pasquale "Presto" Prestigiocomo at 205 Kolmar Avenue, and into a spray of machine-gun bullets coming from an apartment across the street at 202 Kolmar Avenue. Aiello then fled into the line of fire of a second machine-gun nest at 4518 West End Avenue and died with fifty-nine slugs in his body. Capone and Aiello had been at war for three years and besides their local disputes were interested in the outcome of the so-called Castellammarese War. Capone supported Masseria, and Aiello supported Maranzano, according to Joe Valachi and Joe Bonanno.

[21] Stephen Ferrigno, alias Samuel Ferraro, and Alfred Mineo, alias Manfredi, bosses of families allied to Masseria, were shotgunned to death while leaving Ferrigno's apartment at 759 Pelham Parkway South. The killers fired from an apartment at 760 Pelham Parkway South. Some thirty years later Joe Valachi testified that he had rented the latter apartment and that the other members of the hit squad were Girolamo "Bobby Doyle" Santucci, Nick "The Thief" Capuzzi, and a former Capone gangster whom he knew only as "Buster from Chicago." "Buster" has never been firmly identified, although Valachi claimed he was killed in a craps game dispute in 1931. Joe Bonanno remembered a former Chicago gangster in Maranzano's employ named Bastiano "Buster" Domingo but said that he did not resemble Valachi's "Buster." (Valachi diminished his own credibility by recalling that "Buster" carried a

machine gun in a violin case. This is a staple of gangster fiction and cartoons, but a Thompson submachine gun will not fit in a violin case.) Some organized-crime experts believe that Valachi may have invented "Buster" to cover murders he himself had committed.

[22] Giuseppe "Joe the Boss" Masseria was fatally shot in the back and head while dining at Gerardo Scarpato's Nuova Villa Tammaro restaurant at 2715 West Fifteenth Street in Coney Island. His underboss, Charles "Lucky" Luciano is believed to have ordered the killing of Masseria to arrange a truce with Salvatore Maranzano and end the Castellammarese War. According to Valachi, Vito Genovese, Ciro Terranova, Frank Livorsi, and Joseph "Joe Stretch" Stracci also were present at Masseria's murder. An earlier informant, Abe "Kid Twist" Reles, named Masseria's killers as Vito Genovese, Benjamin "Bugsy" Siegel, Joe Adonis and Albert Anastasia. Siegel, with Meyer Lansky, led the Jewish Bugs & Meyer Mob, allied with Luciano.

[23] Charles "Lucky" Luciano's real name was Salvatore Lucania. Legend has it that his nickname derived from his surviving a "one-way ride" in which he was kidnapped and tortured by rival gangsters and left for dead on Staten Island. The incident occurred on the night of October 16, 1929, but was only a beating, not an attempted murder. Years later, Luciano told Sal Vizzini, an undercover agent of the Federal Bureau of Narcotics, that his attackers were not rival gangsters but detectives searching for his then-friend Jack "Legs" Diamond, wanted at that time for murdering two other hoodlums in his Hotsy Totsy Club. Luciano actually had been known as "Lucky" for years. By some accounts he got the name as a teenager after a large winning in a craps game. By other versions, he simply liked people to think of him as a "lucky guy," or it was simply a contraction of his last name.

[24] According to Joseph Bonanno, Frank Scalise replaced Mineo as family boss but later stepped down and was replaced by Vincent Mangano. Philip Mangano was Vincent's brother.

The organizational structure of a "classic" Cosa Nostra family is as follows: Head of the family (borgata) is the boss (capo); below the boss is the underboss (sottocapo), the second in command, who may or may not succeed the boss, depending on his popularity within the family and at the discretion of the national Commission (which can, when necessary, veto or appoint a boss). On the same level as the underboss is the consigliere, or counselor, who advises the boss but has no powers of command. Below the underboss are the caporegima—lieutenants or captains—sometimes called capos, each of whom leads a "regime" or "crew" of "soldiers." Some families are further broken down into units of ten men, each commanded by a capo-decina (literally "head of ten"). Soldiers are the bottom-level members of the family but also may lead crews of prospective family members or nonmember associates.

[25] Salvatore Maranzano was killed by four unknown men posing as federal agents at 2:30 p.m. on September 10, 1931, in his office at the Eagle Building, 230 Park Avenue. Cause of death was four gunshot wounds and six stab wounds. The killers are believed to have been members of the Bugs & Meyer Mob, headed by Luciano's allies Meyer Lansky and "Bugsy" Siegel. According to Joe Valachi, the hit squad was led by Sam "Red" Levine, a member of the Bugs & Meyer Mob. An earlier informant, J. Richard "Dixie" Davis, named Abe "Bo" Weinberg, a henchman of "Dutch" Schultz, as another of the gunmen. Davis was "Dutch" Schultz's attorney, and Schultz was another of Luciano's Jewish allies at the time. Valachi also claimed that Maranzano had hired "Mad Dog" Coll to kill Genovese and Luciano, and since Luciano was Schultz's friend and Coll his enemy, "Dutch" may have been involved in the murder of Maranzano.

[26] Al Capone's tenure as a member of the Commission lasted only a month, until October, when he was convicted of income tax evasion.

[27] Underworld rumors, repeated by informants "Dixie" Davis and Abe Reles and exaggerated over the years by various crime writers, told of a great purging of the Mafia or Cosa Nostra, in which dozens of Salvatore Maranzano's supporters were murdered across the country in a two- or three-day period after their leader's demise. The supposed number of victims has been reported as anywhere from forty to ninety men. This bloodletting was cited for years in the *Guinness Book of World Records* as the "greatest Mafia killing," and sensationalist writers have dubbed it the "Night of the Sicilian Vespers" (a name deriving from an historical thirteenth-century uprising in which Sicilian rebels slaughtered their French Angevin rulers). In truth, no such massacre occurred, as Humbert Nelli and other researchers have established by a thorough search of contemporary newspapers across the country. There were no more than five murders that could be linked in any way to Maranzano's death. On September 10, 1931, James LePore, alias Jimmy Marino, was shot to death in front of a barbershop at 2400 Arthur Avenue in the Bronx. On September 13, the bodies of Samuel Monaco and Louis Russo, with throats cut and heads crushed, washed up in Newark Bay. According to Joe Valachi, these three were Maranzano followers and the only ones he knew of who were killed. Joseph Siragusa, boss of the Pittsburgh Family, was shot to death on the same day in a killing that may or may not have been connected with events in New York. Colorado mobster Pete Carlino also was found shot to death, near Pueblo, on September 13. This was most likely the result of local gang war that happened only to coincide with the New York killings. Gerardo Scarpato, owner of the Coney Island restaurant where Masseria was slain, often is wrongly reported to have died in the alleged mass purge. But Scarpato was murdered a year later, on September 11, 1932. Despite the flimsy evidence, the FBI apparently accepts this prolonged massacre as historical fact.

[28] The murder of Jack "Legs" Diamond, at 67 Dove Street in Albany, is usually attributed to his most notorious adversary, "Dutch" Schultz. Schultz's attorney, "Dixie" Davis, blamed Schultz for the Diamond murder and stated that "Bo" Weinberg was the actual killer. Owing to Diamond's untrustworthy nature, his frequent hijackings and encroachments, and his recent alliance with the "outlawed" Vincent Coll, he had more enemies than friends in the New York underworld. Luciano, Lansky, and Siegel, "Owney" Madden, "Waxey" Gordon, or any number of other gangsters are as likely as Schultz to have arranged Diamond's killing. "Legs" was in fact popularly known as the "Clay Pigeon of the Underworld," having survived at least three previous murder attempts. Police at the time suspected that two of Diamond's former henchmen, Irving Bitz and Salvatore Spitale, who had broken away to form their own mob (and who later would gain notoriety as "underworld detec-

tives" in the Lindbergh kidnapping case), were probably the responsible parties, but even Diamond's widow, Alice, who had put up with years of infidelity, was a suspect. In any case, Alice Diamond was shot to death by unknown persons in the kitchen of her home at 1641 Ocean Avenue in Brooklyn on June 30, 1933, supposedly after boasting that she knew her husband's killers and planned to go after them.

[29] "Mad Dog" Coll was machine-gunned to death in a telephone booth at the London Chemist drugstore, 314 West Twenty-third Street, in Manhattan. His killing is unsolved but, like his former partner "Legs" Diamond, Coll was hated and feared by most of the New York underworld. gang leaders "Dutch" Schultz and Owney Madden reportedly had each offered a bounty of $50,000 for his demise. Schultz's attorney, "Dixie" Davis, later claimed that "Bo" Weinberg had driven the getaway car for the killers. A former member of the Coll mob, Edward "Fats McCarthy" Popke, was suspected of both the Diamond and Coll hits. "Fats," also wanted for the murder of a New York policeman, was killed by New York State Police at his Albany hideout on July 11, 1932. Leonard Scarnici, bank robber and freelance hit man, reportedly confessed to the Coll slaying and others before his execution at Sing Sing on June 27, 1935, for the murder of a policeman. Scarnici's alleged partner in the Coll slaying was Anthony Fabrizzo, who was shot to death in New York City on November 20, 1932, supposedly in retaliation for a bombing attempt on the life of "Bugsy" Siegel. Or Coll's killer may have been Tommy Protheroe, a West Side gunman working for Owney Madden, who was arrested in the Tommygun slaying of one Francis Smith on October 18, 1933, in which the same gun was used. Protheroe himself was killed outside a Queens apartment building on May 16, 1935.

[30] In addition to Special Agent Caffrey and prisoner Frank "Jelly" Nash, victims of the Union Station Massacre (as it was also called) included police detectives William Grooms and Frank Hermanson, and Otto Reed, chief of police of McAlester, Oklahoma. The killings resulted from an abortive attempt to free Nash from police custody. Verne Miller, who planned and led the attack, was a friend and sometime bank-robbing partner of Nash, but he also was a freelance hit man said to have worked for Louis "Lepke" Buchalter and other top mobsters. Miller supposedly asked Kansas City mob boss John Lazia for two gunmen to aid in the delivery attempt but was turned down. According to the FBI, Miller then recruited Charles "Pretty Boy" Floyd and Adam Richetti, Oklahoma bank robbers who had drifted into town and were needing a place to stay. After the massacre, Lazia provided Miller, Floyd, and Richetti with a car and safe escort out of town. Miller himself went to New York City and was harbored by "Lepke" Buchalter until the FBI learned of his presence there. He then moved to New Jersey and briefly found refuge with Abner "Longy" Zwillman's mob, but was again forced to flee when the FBI moved in. Miller was found murdered in Detroit on November 29, 1933. The killing is unsolved, as Miller had many enemies and created much "heat" with the Kansas City Massacre (which was billed as the "machine-gun challenge to the nation"; and the FBI contends that he most likely was murdered by the Zwillman mob. Richetti was captured by Wellsville, Ohio, police on October 21, 1934, and "Pretty Boy" Floyd was killed by FBI agents the next day on a farm near Wellsville, Ohio. Richetti was convicted of the massacre and died in the gas chamber of Missouri's state prison at Jefferson City on October 7, 1938.

[31] Frank Costello and "Dandy Phil" Kastel moved their slot machine operation to Louisiana at the invitation of Governor Huey Long, who received a sizeable cut of the take.

[32] John Lazia was gunned down in the driveway of the Park Central Hotel where he lived. Lazia's wife and Charles Carrollo, their driver and bodyguard, survived. Ballistics tests established that the Tommygun used to kill Lazia also had been used in the Kansas City Massacre. Carrolla, along with Charles "Mad Dog" Gargotta, Gaetano (Tano) Lacoco, Tony Gizzo, Sam Scola, and Gus Fascone, were allegedly the men who escorted "Pretty Boy" Floyd and Adam Richetti out of Kansas City after the massacre.

[33] In his book *The Rise and Fall of the Cleveland Mafia*, Rick Porrello writes that Dr. Joseph Romano, who led a secret double life as mobster and wealthy and respected surgeon, actually succeeded Milano as boss of the Cleveland Family. Dr. Romano was murdered on June 11, 1936, after which Al Polizzi became boss. Porrello was a Cleveland police officer whose grandfather and three uncles were prominent members of the Cleveland Family in the twenties and thirties.

[34] Schultz was fatally shot, along with three of his men (Bernard "Lulu" Rosencrantz, Abe "The Misfit" Landau, and Otto "Abbadabba" Berman) in the Palace Chop House on East Park Street in Newark. The order for Schultz's death allegedly came from "Lucky" Luciano, to prevent Schultz from trying to murder Special Prosecutor Thomas E. Dewey. Louis "Lepke" Buchalter provided the gunmen, named as Emmanuel "Mendy" Weiss and Charles "The Bug" Workman. An unidentified third man, known only as "Piggy," said to have been a member of Willie Moretti's New Jersey gang, drove the getaway car. Weiss later was convicted with Buchalter of another murder and executed in Sing Sing in 1944. Workman was convicted of the Schultz killing and sentenced to life imprisonment in 1941. He was paroled from New Jersey state prison in 1964.

[35] "Machine Gun" Jack McGurn (true name: Vincent Gebaldi, aka Gerbardi or James Vincenzo DeMora) was shot to death by unknown killers in a bowling alley at 805 Milwaukee Avenue in Chicago, just after midnight on February 15, 1936. This was a few minutes past the seventh anniversary of the St. Valentine's Day Massacre, for which McGurn was a prime suspect; and a comic valentine card was left poking fun at his current financial straits. McGurn probably was killed on the orders of Frank Nitti, who was eliminating Capone loyalists. McGurn's half-brother, Anthony DeMora, was murdered outside a poolroom in Chicago's Little Italy two weeks later, on March 3, to preempt any plan to retaliate.

[36] Special Prosecutor Thomas Dewey convicted "Lucky" Luciano of compulsory prostitution in 1936, a few months after Luciano may have saved Dewey's life by ordering the murder of "Dutch" Schultz. Some believe the conviction was a frame-up. Polly Adler, New York City's leading madam in the 1930s, said she had never heard of his involvement in prostitution. Joe Valachi, a member of the Luciano Family, stated, "Charley Lucky wasn't no pimp. He was a boss."

Dewey was elected governor of New York largely on his fame as a racket-busting prosecutor. In another ironic twist, Dewey pardoned Luciano in 1945 on the grounds that Luciano had cooperated with the armed forces in World War II. At the request of Naval Intelligence, Luciano had instructed his underworld associates, who controlled the New York waterfront, to guard against enemy sabotage. Later, Luciano provided the Army's OSS with a list of contacts in the Sicilian Mafia who were opposed to Mussolini and would be willing to provide support and intelligence for the invasion of Sicily. Luciano was deported to Italy upon his release.

[37] Francesco Lanza is regarded as the founder and first boss of the San Francisco Family, but other Italian gang leaders briefly flourished in the area during the twenties and thirties, and most died violently. One of San Francisco's leading bootleggers, Jerry Feri, was shot to death on April 28, 1928, supposedly by his rival, Alfredo Scariso, who was murdered on December 19, 1928. Mario Filippi was gunned down on December 23, 1928, and Frank Boca was killed on July 30, 1929. Both were suspects in the Scariso murder. Genaro Broccolo, known as the "Al Capone of the West," was shot dead on October 30, 1932.

Another San Francisco gang leader was narcotics trafficker Antonio "Black Tony" Parmagini, whose dope operation extended to Seattle, San Diego, and Denver. His control was absolute, and the price of morphine, heroin, and cocaine reportedly tripled in the Western states for a year or so after Parmagini's narcotics conviction in 1929. "Black Tony" was sentenced to seventeen years and died of intestinal cancer in Leavenworth in 1936. Ironically, his treatment for the cancer turned Parmagini into a morphine addict.

One San Francisco gang briefly attracted the attention of the FBI in the early thirties. Joseph Parente, in partnership with Hans Strittmatter, ran a bootlegging operation that included Frank "Nippi" Constantine, Anthony "Soap" Marino, Louis "Doc Bones" Tambini, Ralph "Scabootch" Rizzo, William Schivo, "Red" Kennedy, and Joseph Raymond "Fatso" Negri. The reason for FBI interest was Lester Joseph Gillis, an Illinois bank robber who joined the Parente mob for a short time after his escape from Joliet's state prison in 1932. Gillis would later become notorious as "Baby Face" Nelson, member of the Dillinger Gang and murderer of three FBI agents, two of whom died in Nelson's final shootout with G-men on November 27, 1934. The Parente mob also was connected to the legal gambling operation in Reno, Nevada, headed by Bill Graham and Jim McKay, for whom Nelson allegedly murdered a witness in a mail fraud case in 1934.

[38] In exile, Nicolo Gentile became probably the first Mafia member to author an autobiography, *Vita di capomafia*, published in Rome in 1963.

[39] Convicted of the murder of Joseph Rosen, Louis "Lepke" Buchalter died in the electric chair at Sing Sing Prison in Ossining, New York, on March 4, 1944, the only Syndicate boss to be legally executed. Two of his henchmen, Emanuel "Mendy" Weiss and Louis Capone (no relation to Al), also were executed on that date.

[40] Charles Binaggio was shot to death in Kansas City on April 6, 1950, along with associate Charles "Mad Dog" Gargotta.

[41] Eight days before Capone's release from prison, Edward J. O'Hare, a dogtrack owner who had been an informant in Capone's tax case, was shot to death in his car by unknown killers on Ogden Avenue in Chicago. O'Hare Airport would later be named after his son, also named Edward, a Naval aviator who died a hero's death in the Pacific during World War II.

Appendix IV

THE 'MAFIA' MENACE

Few subjects in the history of crime inspire more controversy and confusion than the Mafia. As a criminal organization—or a network of affiliated organizations, or of competing organizations—in western Sicily, the name long has been popularly applied also to the network of Italian-American crime families in the United States. Many regard the Mafia as the backbone of American organized crime while overlooking the presence of non-Sicilians in the families, the absence of Italian gangsters in many cities or regions, and the prominence in some areas of non-Italian mobsters. And some see the "American Mafia" or "La Cosa Nostra" as a myth fostered by imaginative writers and anti-Italian prejudice, especially if they were members of mobster Joe Colombo's Italian-American Anti-Defamation League.

Many criminologists now regard "the Mafia" as a dying cultural phenomenon and see it as far less structured than the rigid military-style organization pictured by police (complete with candles, knives, and blood rituals) and the FBI. Law enforcement agencies have presented considerable evidence of a highly organized network of Italian crime families in the United States, whatever state of decline they may be in, and if it needs a name, "Mafia" probably is as good as any and likely is here to stay anyway.

Linguists and etymologists have long debated the origin of the word. It has been variously recorded as a Sicilian slang term for beauty, nobility, or manliness; a Piedmontese word for gang; or, just as often, as Arabic for "place of refuge" as applied to the mountainous and wilderness strongholds of Sicilian bandits. This reflects Sicily's heritage as the military key to the Mediterranean and as an island occupied many times over the centuries by foreign invaders (Romans, Greeks, Carthaginians, Moors, Norsemen, French, Germans, Americans, and no doubt even Italians, in the view of some Sicilians), and many believe the Mafia to have originated as simply an underground movement opposed to foreign oppression.

One of the more ridiculous explanations of the term derives from the historical "Sicilian Vespers" in March 1282, in which Sicilians rose in revolt and slaughtered the island garrisons of French Angevin soldiers. In the realm of folklore, the uprising supposedly began with the attempted rape of a Sicilian bride-to-be on her wedding day by a drunken French soldier. The girl struck her head on a church wall, died, and the maddened groom pounced on her attacker, crying, "Morte alla Francia!" ("Death to France!"). The Sicilian underground then expanded this into a battle cry, "Morte all Francia Italia anela!" ("Death to France Italy Cries!"), whose initial letters formed the acronym "MAFIA." There are obvious historical flaws. The nation of Italy did not exist before 1860, and it's doubtful many thirteenth-century Sicilians would have considered themselves part of it anyway. This story doesn't seem to have appeared in print before the 1890s but has since turned up in many Mafia books and even enjoys some popularity among alleged Mafiosi, who are fond of repeating it. In his book A Man of Honor, Joe Bonanno offered a variant account in which the bride's mother screamed, "Ma fia! Ma fia!" ("My daughter! My daughter!") The original slaughter is doubtlessly the inspiration for this country's "Night of the Sicilian Vespers," the orgy of bloodletting in the 1930s that, thanks to the Mafia books, has become a durable urban myth.

Mafia also is an acronym in one of the first English language books to mention the organization. Charles W. Heckethorne, in his 1897 work *The Secret Societies of All Ages and Countries*, attributed the society's founding to Giuseppe Mazzini, an Italian patriot and ally of Garibaldi in 1860. Mazzini was noted for forming secret societies and engaging in terrorism for political and monetary gain, according to Heckethorne, and in the cause of Italy's unification he supposedly allied himself with criminal organizations such as the Camorra. Heckethorne claimed that "MAFIA" stood for "Mazzini Autorizza Furti, Incendi, Avvelenamenti!" ("Mazzini authorizes thefts, arsons, poisoning!") The Mazzini theory is undocumented and appears to have been picked up by Heckethorne from a book published in Rome in 1880, La Mafia by A. Vizzini. David Leon Chandler, in his equally undocumented 1977 book Brothers in Blood, accepts the Mazzini theory. Few crime historians buy this, but they do join Heckethorne and Chandler in rejecting ancient or medieval origins for the Mafia.

The prevailing view nowadays is that the Mafia originated in the turmoil of post-Napoleonic times from armed bands employed by absentee (often foreign) landowners to guard their estates. This may have been a factor, but the brutal poverty of southern Italy produced many criminal gangs and organizations in the nineteenth century, notably the Camorra of Naples and the N'drangeheta (or "Honored Society") in the Calabrian boot. The Camorra sometimes is considered an offshoot of the Garduna, a Spanish society supposedly dating to fifteenth-century Seville and long employed by wealthy clients to commit crimes for hire. Among their employers were the Bourbon rulers of the Kingdom of Two Sicilies and clerics of the Spanish Inquisition. The Garduna, mentioned in novels by Cervantes, was broken up in Spain in the 1820s, and its leaders, who kept written records of their crimes dating back two centuries, were hung. A more prosaic explanation has it that the Camorra originated as a convict gang in the Naples prison system about 1830. The proliferation of criminal bands in southern Italy, Sicily, Sardinia, and Corsica attracted much attention, especially after Italy's unification, and drew unflattering comments from foreigners and the industrial north alike on the character of southern Italians.

The Camorra gained great power in the city and province of Naples, for a short time even serving as tax collectors until they took too big a cut and attracted the king's ire and military suppression, but attention soon focused on the Sicilian "Mafia." An 1863 play by Giuseppe Rizzotto, about a gang (Il Mafiusi) operating in the Palermo jail of La Vicaria drew attention to the criminal bands (or cosche) of Sicily and the name "Mafia" (sometimes rendered as "Maffia" or "La Mafia") entered the popular vocabulary. Members were known as Mafiosi or Mafiusi. Whether these gangs had any real central organization at this time or any formal name is unknown but doubtful. Many simply were rural bandits, engaged in theft and cattle rustling, while others operated in the cities and levied extortion on merchants and industries. Some were outlaws, while others collaborated with corrupt officials and infiltrated local government. Informers were killed, sometimes after speaking of stylized initiation rites similar to those of the Camorra. Beginning in the 1870s, the Italian Army launched the first of many unsuccessful but internationally publicized campaigns against the Mafia.

Some fugitive criminals followed the waves of Italian immigrants (mainly southern Italians) to the U.S., and Sicilian, Neapolitan, and Calabrian crime families eventually formed in the Italian ghettos of many cities. Some derived from the traditions of the Italian criminal brotherhoods while others began as ethnic street gangs, possibly as a measure of protection against the marauding gangs of Irish, Jewish, and other criminals from neighboring slums. The publicity given the Sicilian Mafia gradually took hold. As early as 1878 a gang of Sicilian robbers in San Francisco was publicized as members of "La Mafia."

In October 1890, Police Chief David Hennessy was killed by gunmen in the wildly corrupt and wide-open New Orleans. A controversial figure with many political enemies (Hennessy himself had shot one of his own predecessors), his murder remains unsolved. Hennessy had sided with one Italian faction, the Provenzano brothers, against another, the Matrangas, in a feud over control of stevedores unloading fruit in what seems like typical waterfront racketeering. Hennessy labeled the Matrangas as "Mafia" and defended the Provenzanos as upright businessmen, although both groups clearly engaged in shooting and operated outside the law. Whether these groups actually were "Mafia" or not is open to doubt, as both appealed to the police at one time or another during their "War of the Oranges." And Hennessy's partiality in their feud may or may not have led to his death, but it brought him an undeserved martyrdom as an incorruptible lawman. It also whipped up a Mafia frenzy and strong anti-Italian sentiments among the city's resident vigilantes. A New Orleans grand jury, acting on flimsy and questionable evidence, concluded that the Mafia had been in operation in New Orleans for years and was responsible for more than ninety murders. Many of the listed crimes were conventional killings whose victims happened to have Italian (or Italian-sounding) names.

Nineteen Italians or Italian-Americans were indicted for the murder of Hennessy. Most, if not all, probably were innocent. One was a fourteen-year-old boy. Another was Joseph Macheca, a New Orleans-born shipping magnate who probably knew nothing about Sicily or the Mafia but whose parentage and success were enough to earn him the enmity of the Anglo community. A mistrial resulted for three of the defendants, and the others were acquitted but held in "protective custody" long enough for an angry mob to storm the parish prison. Eleven of the defendants were lynched, and much of the nation applauded. The "Mafia Incident" brought condemnation from Italy and talk of war until President Benjamin Harrison agreed to pay reparations to the victims' families.

There is no evidence for the popular supposition that the "American Mafia" was founded in New Orleans or that members of the New Orleans family quickly established chapters in other cities. Whether the Mafia even existed in New Orleans in 1890 may be doubted, although an Italian crime family certainly flourished there in later years.

Elsewhere, before World War I, Sicilian and Neapolitan crime families battled one another for control of gambling and rackets in New York's Little Italy in what has been called a "Mafia-Camorra war." Several of the Neapolitan gang members were convicted of murder in 1917 and went to prison or the electric chair, and the remnants of Brooklyn's "Camorra" were integrated with the Sicilians in what might be called the first "Americanized Mafia." The families would become further Americanized by the Castellammarese War in 1930–31.

During Prohibition, Italian and less-publicized Jewish mobsters rose to dominance, largely replacing the Irish, German, and Polish gangs, and the name Mafia again came into vogue. Harry J. Anslinger (today best known as proponent of the "Reefer Madness" scare of the thirties that led to the ongoing and equally unsuccessful prohibition of marijuana) was appointed commissioner of the new Federal Bureau of Narcotics in 1930. He saw the obvious network of Italian mobsters as proof of an American Mafia. The FBN over the years compiled a list of eight hundred alleged Mafia members and saw them as an international organization of narcotics smugglers, possibly directed from Palermo. The longstanding rivalry between Anslinger, of the Treasury Department, and J. Edgar Hoover, in a Justice Department obsessed with bank robbers, may explain Hoover's refusal to acknowledge the existence of national racketeering and the FBI's long record of inactivity against organized crime.

In the late forties and fifties, sensationalist writers exploited Anslinger's notions of the Mafia, often adding their own creative touches. Chief among these were Jack Lait and Lee Mortimer, whose lurid works (beginning with *New York Confidential* and moving on to Chicago and other cities) painted a wildly exaggerated picture of the Mafia as a worldwide crime syndicate directed from Sicily and controlling virtually all organized crime. These farcical books sold millions and may even have influenced the Kefauver Committee hearings in 1951. The Kefauver Committee probed deeply into organized crime and concluded that in most American cities it was controlled by a "shadowy nationwide organization" called the Mafia "with international ramifications." Despite many revelations of prosperous ex-bootleggers still thriving in crime and in legitimate business, the televised hearings produced no real proof of a "Mafia"—only a lot of testimony from narcotics agents that there was such a thing and a lot of Italian mobsters pleading the Fifth when asked if they were members. The Kefauver hearings resulted in yet another spate of nail-biting books, such as Ed Reid's *Mafia*.

On November 14, 1957, New York State Police broke up a meeting of at least sixty-three Italian mobsters from around the country at the Apalachin estate of Joseph Barbara, to the embarrassment of J. Edgar Hoover, who still publicly maintained there was no American Mafia. This was followed by publication of Frederic Sondern Jr.'s popular book *Brotherhood of Evil: The Mafia*. While more balanced than earlier Mafia books, it still contains many errors and reiterates popular misconceptions of the period.

In 1962 at the federal penitentiary in Atlanta, Joe Valachi killed a fellow prisoner after mistaking him for a hit man sent by his boss, Vito Genovese. A convicted narcotics trafficker, Valachi was marked for death as a suspected stool pigeon. Questioned first by the Federal Bureau of Narcotics and later by the FBI, Valachi, a member of a New York crime family since 1930, related the history of what he called "Cosa Nostra." An Italian phrase meaning "Our Thing" (or "our affair," "our group," "our mob,"), it may or may not be a proper name for the organization. The words had been picked up already by FBI agents in illegally bugged conversations of mobsters and may have been fed to Valachi by his interrogators. Little of what Valachi told was really new, and none of it resulted in convictions, but it was the first insider's confirmation that any sort of American Mafia existed. Over the protestations of J. Edgar Hoover, Attorney General Robert F. Kennedy placed Valachi on national television the next year to tell his story before the McLellan Committee and the American public. It gave Kennedy the leverage to bring the FBI actively into the fight against organized crime, and Hoover, still averse to a Mafia, was able to claim discovery of "La Cosa Nostra," or "LCN," as the FBI likes to abbreviate it.

The bureau's formal abbreviation of LCN came at the height of the James Bond craze, in which the fictional secret agent was pitted against organizations like SMERSH and SPECTRE, and one of the hit TV shows was "The Man from UNCLE," but the new name didn't really catch on. The FBI still uses it but leans nowadays more toward "OC" for "Organized Crime," to better reflect the involvement of other ethnic groups. Of course the public and press still prefer "Mafia," whether accurate or not. In reality, the organization may not have a formal name.

Cosa Nostra now appears to be a generic phrase, used by mobsters who sometimes speak in Italian to confuse eavesdroppers or throw it around just to worry them. Even at that, it's rarely heard in this country outside the eastern families, primarily those in the New York/New Jersey/Philadelphia area. Members of the Italian mob in Buffalo refer to themselves as "the Arm." In Boston it's "the Office." The Chicago Mob, which includes non-Italians, is known locally as the "Syndicate" or the Outfit (a term coined by its founder Al Capone). Law enforcement officers since the sixties have used Cosa Nostra to distinguish the American crime families from the Mafia of Sicily, although the Sicilian Mafia seems now to have developed a more rigid hierarchy, including a Commission—something it may owe to the influence of American mobsters who have been deported, and to the mutual involvement of U.S. and Italian crime organizations in narcotics and money laundering. It's possible that the phrase "Cosa Nostra" may have been exported from the U.S. to Italy, rather than the other way around.

Perhaps the closest thing to a formal name for any of these crime families (although it may annoy the Quakers) is another generic phrase commonly used by Italian mobsters on both sides of the Atlantic: societa degli amici ("society of friends"). But it will never replace "Mafia."

INDEX

I

J

N